Hospital and Healthcare Security

Hospital and Healthcare Security

Sixth Edition

Tony W. York

Don MacAlister

AMSTERDAM • BOSTON • HEIDELBERG • LONDON
NEW YORK • OXFORD • PARIS • SAN DIEGO
SAN FRANCISCO • SINGAPORE • SYDNEY • TOKYO

Butterworth-Heinemann is an imprint of Elsevier

Acquiring Editor: Tom Stover
Editorial Project Manager: Hilary Carr
Project Manager: Priya Kumaraguruparan
Designer: Mark Rogers

Butterworth-Heinemann is an imprint of Elsevier
The Boulevard, Langford Lane, Kidlington, Oxford OX5 1GB, UK
225 Wyman Street, Waltham, MA 02451, USA

First Edition: 1976 published by Security World Pub. Co.

ISBN: 978-0-12-420048-7

British Library Cataloguing in Publication Data
A catalogue record for this book is available from the British Library

Library of Congress Cataloging-in-Publication Data
A catalog record for this book is available from the Library of Congress

For Information on all Butterworth-Heinemann publications
visit our website at http://store.elsevier.com

Contents

About the Authors

Tony W. York, CPP, CHPA, has over 20 years' experience administering healthcare security programs and is chief operating officer for HSS Inc., a specialized security firm based in Denver. York, who is board certified in security management, holds the Certified Protection Professional (CPP) designation and the Certified Healthcare Protection Administrator (CHPA) designation. A past president and board chair of the International Association for Healthcare Security & Safety (IAHSS), York chairs the Council on Guidelines. This council produces the Healthcare Security Industry Guidelines and Healthcare Security Design Guidelines. A regular contributor to the advancement of the healthcare security field, York is recognized internationally as an industry expert and is a frequent lecturer and author on healthcare security and leadership. A native of North Carolina, he earned a B.S. degree in Criminal Justice from Appalachian State University, an M.S. in Loss Prevention & Safety from Eastern Kentucky University, and an MBA from the University of Denver.

Don MacAlister, CHPA, is the Chief Operating Officer for Paladin Security Group, a privately owned full service security company and the largest provider of healthcare security in Canada. He has more than 35 years of experience in the security industry, learning the fundamentals while working in the federal prison system early in his career, before moving on to university security as a precursor to his nearly quarter century spent in healthcare, in both the public and private sectors. As the Executive Director of Integrated Protection Services, he oversaw security and parking for 27 hospitals and more than 300 community sites in the Vancouver-area, before moving to Paladin in 2011. Don is a past member of the IAHSS Board of Directors and has been a member of the Association's Council on Guidelines since 2008. Don was named Canada's Security Director of the Year in 2010. Originally from Scotland, he grew up on Canada's west coast, where he earned a B.A. degree in Criminal Justice from the University of the Fraser Valley.

Foreword

Few texts have had an impact on their professions as much as *Hospital and Healthcare Security*. Impact is something all of us hope for in life. Impact is the ability to influence the lives of others in a positive way, and over the years this text has most certainly influenced and enhanced security and safety in healthcare facilities around the world.

Hospital and Healthcare Security has most definitely positively impacted my life. As a young security manager on the first day of the job in January 1981, I was handed the first edition, then titled *Hospital Security*. The outgoing security manager handed it to me and said, "This is the bible of healthcare security. Read it, study it, and refer to it often. You will learn about the hospital security discipline. It will help as you look for ways of addressing new and old problems related to securing this hospital."

This was good advice in 1981, and I wholeheartedly recommend and endorse it in 2015. I love books and as a professional librarian's son, I read a lot! While reading, I often write on, highlight, fold over, and comment on the pages with my personal reflections and information I may need to refer to later. Each of my personal editions of *Hospital Security* and *Hospital and Healthcare Security* are dog-eared, highlighted, written on and worn. They are all a mess! If I had to categorize their condition for resale on Amazon, they would definitely not sell. Each edition has had significant impact on me as a security professional, on each facility where I have worked, and now at each of my clients in my consulting business. Each edition has also continued to advance security and safety in healthcare facilities. Mr. Russell L. Colling wrote the first four editions and provided foundation for each successive edition. He and Mr. Tony York wrote the fifth edition together; this edition placed great emphasis on the IAHSS Guidelines. Mr. Colling and Mr. York both chaired the IAHSS Guidelines Council, providing guidance and perspective as these increasingly important works have gained acceptance and utilization.

This edition is cowritten by Mr. York and Mr. Donald MacAlister and continues to emphasize the IAHSS Guidelines. Don has an international perspective that has been previously missing from the text and he also has added depth of knowledge and importance to this text due to his corporate and private security experience in British Columbia.

It has been my privilege to know and work with Russ, Tony and Don for many years through our work with the IAHSS. I can personally attest to the depth of knowledge, expertise, professionalism and dedication they have infused into this work. I advise anyone reading this book to do so with a pen in hand or, I should say, their digital recording device, so you can extract every available nugget of wisdom from it. I hope that you may feel it impacts you as much as it has me in my career. **"Read it, study it, and refer to it often. You will learn about the hospital security discipline. It will help as you look for ways of addressing new and old problems related to securing your healthcare facilities."**

Tom Smith
President
Healthcare Security Consultants, Inc.

Acknowledgements

The authors are extremely appreciative of all the support and encouragement received by the International Association for Healthcare Security and Safety, not to mention it being the catalyst that brought the two of us together a little over a decade ago. The contributions of the Association and so many of its voluntary leaders are truly making a difference in making healthcare safer. Our profound thanks go to all of you who give so tirelessly to create a safe environment where healing can occur.

We specifically would like to acknowledge our colleagues on the IAHSS Council on Guidelines with whom we have had the privilege to work side by side to promulgate healthcare security industry standards and enhance the professionalism of healthcare security worldwide. We have learned so much from Tom Smith, Kevin Tuohey, Mike Cummings, Jack Connelly, Tim Portale, Darren Morgan, Lisa Pryce-Terry—each of you have continuously challenged our thinking about how best to safeguard the healthcare environment. Your advice, support, and friendship are irreplaceable.

We would also like to thank Dr. Tracy Buchman, who helped us write a new chapter on emergency management. Tracy is a leading EM authority and the significant improvements made to this chapter are evidence of her expertise.

We would also like to thank Wayne Schell, CEO of HSS Inc., and Ashley Cooper, CEO of Paladin Security Group, for their encouragement and unrelenting support to update this classic text. Without this support, coupled with that received from our collective teams at HSS and Paladin, we would never have been able to tackle such a demanding project.

Above all, we want to thank our loving wives, Cara and Heather—without their sacrifice and support, this text would never have been possible. Tony would like to say a special "thank you" to Leah and Gareth, who supported and encouraged him in spite of all the time it took him away from them.

Special Acknowledgement of Russell Colling

I would like to take the opportunity to express my profound gratitude and deep regard for Russell Colling and the tireless commitment he has made to enhance the professionalism of hospital security – no one has had more influence on the safety and security of healthcare.

Russ has long been revered as the patriarch of hospital security and for good reason; he wrote the first four editions of *Hospital and Healthcare Security* asking only for my involvement on the fifth edition to make certain the tradition of the book would be carried forward. He stressed how important it was for those new to the industry and the old hands alike to understand and apply the fundamental principles of security and protection while always looking for new and innovative ways to create a safe environment for hospital staff and the patients they care for.

Most healthcare security professionals can remember their first introduction to *Hospital and Healthcare Security*. I received my first copy, the third edition, from George Jacobs during my internship at North Carolina Baptist Hospital. George required me to read it from cover to cover. It was inspirational for me and the reason why I chose hospital security as my profession. The text sold me on how a quality security program could make a positive difference to patient care.

As a personal friend and professional mentor, Russ epitomizes what it means to make a difference to an industry. The tradition of *Hospital and Healthcare Security* still carries much of Russ's original philosophy and thinking. Words cannot describe how honored Don and I are to continue his legacy. Russ's vision and foresight for our industry are second to none; he truly has helped raise the bar of professionalism in the healthcare security industry.

Tony York

CHAPTER

THE HEALTHCARE ENVIRONMENT 1

The only constants in today's healthcare environment are the dynamic challenges continuously facing healthcare administrators and posing daily tests for security leaders charged with protecting these healing environments. The delivery of healthcare changes rapidly and is vastly different from what it was just a few years ago. Hospitals are no longer an isolated group of freestanding buildings. They are critical infrastructures forming complex medical centers, serving diverse patient populations, with visitors travelling great distances to seek care and receive specialized medical treatment. It is not uncommon for medical centers and hospitals alike to find themselves as parts of a large healthcare system, or delivering care in the community in a model reflecting the full continuum of care. These healthcare systems often have dozens of facilities serving communities near the main facility, or they may be part of a system with facilities many states removed. The competitive nature of healthcare has challenged administrators and security professionals alike to present a safe and secure environment that is coupled with a warm and open feel.

The current security landscape affects all types of organizations and all aspects of the healthcare industry. Heightened safety concerns following the 9/11 terrorist attacks have compelled government agencies, the healthcare industry, and commercial establishments worldwide to employ sophisticated security services. Alarmed by the vulnerability of their legacy systems, many organizations are upgrading to state-of-the-art security programs and systems, which include monitoring surveillance services and well-trained security ambassadors. This trend is likely to continue as healthcare institutions, and various other establishments, seek greater security due to growing workplace and patient-generated violence and changing patient populations (due to reduction of mental health reimbursement). As well, looming challenges of staff (physician and nurses) shortages, employee thefts, continuing downward pressure on Medicare reimbursements and the changing structure of the medical care model are all contributing to the increased focus on security. The growth of electronic health records, and associated data security breaches and patient privacy concerns, medical insurance fraud, the threat of terrorism, and the need for better preparation and response to man-made and natural disasters must also be viewed as cogent factors.

The need for increased security has provided an unprecedented challenge in the methods and philosophies regarding protection of our healthcare organizations. Their safeguarding cannot be completely dependent on the security department. Many aspects of protecting healthcare organizations reach far beyond the control of the commonly accepted elements of a healthcare security department. Today, in order to achieve a high level of security, managers, top executives, and boards of directors must be more involved, through appropriate funding levels, with managing and supporting security and other risk management issues. These leaders must accept a greater responsibility and ownership for security and risk mitigation, in their day-to-day management obligations.

Practically everyone uses healthcare, or has a close connection to someone who uses healthcare, in any given year. In 2012, the U.S.'s healthcare bill climbed to about $3 trillion.[1] On the average, healthcare consumes over $8,500 per person per year—approximately one-sixth of the average American income and growing much faster than the rest of the economy, with healthcare spending projected to nearly double in the next decade.[2] It's not all private spending; U.S. taxpayer funding provides close to 50% of this amount.

The Canadian Institute for Health Information data supports the U.S. trend in rapidly rising healthcare costs in Canada, projecting healthcare spending to grow to $211 billion in 2013, consuming 11.2% of Canada's gross domestic product (GDP).[3] The delivery of healthcare is primarily a provincial responsibility in Canada, with healthcare now consuming 40%, or more, of provincial budgets.[4] UK and New Zealand spending on healthcare is also in the vicinity of 10% of GDP, while Australia is slightly lower at 8.7%. These countries spend about half of the U.S. amount on a cost-per-person basis, somewhere between $3000 and $4000 per person, with all of these countries dwarfing the $4 per person expenditure committed to healthcare in Myanmar (Burma).[5] However, the trend is clear—countries are spending more and more on healthcare, and the rising trend continues.

For more than two decades, the cost of healthcare has exceeded the general rate of inflation (or the rate of growth of the economy),[6] and is rising faster than wages. Many of these costs are incurred by the sickest patients. It is estimated half of the U.S. population accounts for only 3% of all healthcare expenditures, while about 10% of the population accounts for more than 60% of healthcare costs. The top 5% of the population accounts for nearly half of U.S. healthcare spending, while the top 1% accounts for 20%.[7] Despite private, freestanding ambulatory care centers, declining patient days, long-term care facilities, wellness programs, and advances in outpatient and home care, the hospital remains the primary source of healthcare in terms of dollars expended.

The increased costs of providing healthcare are at least partly the result of the success of our healthcare delivery system—with larger numbers of people living to an older age, and needing increasing amounts of care. There continues to be an explosive growth in the numbers of individuals with chronic conditions, a seemingly insatiable demand for emergency care services and intensive care, progressive expansion of applications for minimally invasive surgery and other procedures, and heightened concerns about inefficiency, access to care, and medical errors across the healthcare delivery system. A 2008 analysis by PricewaterhouseCoopers concluded that more than $1.2 trillion dollars in the U.S. healthcare system are wasted. Medical errors, inefficient use of information technology and poorly managed chronic diseases, related to obesity and being overweight, were all cited as factors. Dwarfing these reasons is a phenomenon in which doctors order tests to avoid the threat of a malpractice lawsuit—otherwise known as "defensive medicine." At $210 billion annually, defensive medicine is one of the largest contributors to waste. A 2005 survey in the *Journal of the American Medical Association* found that 93% of doctors reported practicing defensive medicine[8] and there is no indication this trend has changed.

CATEGORIES OF HEALTHCARE

Direct clinical care of patients is being delivered in all kinds of organizations and in all types of settings. In the U.S., this diversity is generally the result of a particular entity wanting greater patient market share, and creating environments with low overhead to maintain cost control. A basic concept is to bring the delivery of care geographically closer to the patient. Lower unit costs are also intended to provide greater patient accessibility to quality care. This geographical spread of organizational facilities is based on the great number of outpatient procedures, once done only in the hospital. Healthcare can be viewed on a continuum from assisted living (low acuity) to acute care (high acuity). This progression follows these basic steps:

- **Assisted Living –** provides some help with day-to-day living activities, often including transportation services to healthcare delivery sites, some limited medical care presence in the living facility, and general staff watchfulness.
- **Home Care –** healthcare staff generally visit and provide care in the home with a coordinated plan of treatment and services.
- **Outpatient Services –** include surgery, clinic visits, physical therapy, psychological counseling, speech therapy, and dental care.
- **Intermediate Care –** provides 24-hour oversight, and is often tied closely to geriatric care.
- **Skilled Care –** requires intervention skills by caregivers as opposed to caretakers.
- **Short-Term Acute Care –** is generally medically complex and includes postsurgical intensive rehabilitation, respirator care, and intensive oversight.
- **Acute Care –** occurs when a patient is medically unstable and includes extensive use of invasive procedures, high level of staff skills, close monitoring, and complex care plans.

TYPES OF HOSPITALS

Hospitals in the United States are owned by a wide variety of groups and are even occasionally owned by individuals. Most hospitals are community hospitals, providing general acute care for a wide variety of diseases. In terms of ownership, three major types of facilities exist:

- *Government hospitals* are owned by federal, state, or local governments. Federal and state institutions tend to have special purposes such as the care of special groups (military, mentally ill) or education (hospitals attached to state universities). Local government includes not only cities and counties, but also in several states, hospital authorities have been created from smaller political units. Local government hospitals in large cities are principally for the care of the poor (also referred to as Safety-Net Facilities), but many in smaller cities and towns are indistinguishable from not-for-profit institutions. Unfortunately, there are 350 fewer public hospitals today than 20 years ago, with Safety-Net hospitals having closed in Los Angeles, Chicago, New York, Washington, D.C., St. Louis and Milwaukee as well as others in Georgia, Florida and Pennsylvania in recent years.[9] In 2011, state or local government hospitals represented 21% of all hospitals in the U.S.[10]
- *Not-for-profit hospitals* are owned by corporations established by private (nongovernmental) groups for the common good, rather than individual gain. As a result, they are granted broad federal, state, and local tax exemptions. Although they are frequently operated by organizations that have religious ties, secular (or nonreligious) not-for-profit hospitals constitute the largest single group of community hospitals, both in number and in total volume of care, exceeding religious not-for-profit, government, and for-profit hospitals by a wide margin. In 2011, nonprofit owned facilities represent just over 58% of all U.S. hospitals.[10]
- *For-profit hospitals* are owned by private corporations, which are allowed to declare dividends or otherwise distribute profits to individuals. They pay taxes like private corporations. These

hospitals are also called investor owned. They are usually community hospitals, although there has been rapid growth in private specialty hospitals. Historically, the owners were doctors and other individuals, but large-scale publicly held corporations now own most for-profit hospitals. These facilities have had different periods of growth and now account for more than 20% of all hospitals.[10] Except for having the obvious right to distribute dividends and the obligation to pay taxes, for-profit owners function similarly to not-for-profit owners.

In countries like the UK, New Zealand, Australia and Canada, the healthcare delivery systems remain primarily part of the public healthcare system through the universal healthcare model. While the private sector is increasingly involved as an alternative in some aspects of the health system in these countries, health services are primarily delivered through the publicly funded model. In these countries there has been a clear move toward grouping hospitals, and indeed other aspects of the health service delivery continuum, into health systems, authorities, regions, trusts and networks, with these structures responsible for oversight of health services in their jurisdictions.[11] The province of Alberta, in Canada, as an example has one health entity, Alberta Health Services, vested with responsibility through the Ministry of Health, for health services in the entire province. In the UK this model is taken a step further, with the National Health Service responsible for all health services for an entire country, the United Kingdom.

Most of the U.S. hospitals are small but larger hospitals provide the majority of the services. The number of hospitals in health systems has also grown over the last decade, from just over 2,500 in the year 2000 to almost 3,000 in 2010.[12] In the wake of the enactment of the Affordable Care Act, this growth trend is expected to continue. The merger of hospitals has reduced the number of beds in the U.S. to just under a million in 1990 to just over 800,000 in 2010[12] as healthcare delivery shifts away from the expense of acute care, delivering care in the community and in patient homes, where possible.

In addition to the ownership of hospitals, the type of medical specialty is another way to differentiate facilities. Basic medical specialties include pediatric, medical/surgical, rehabilitative, long-term care, and psychiatric facilities. The teaching hospital generally has elements of these specialties, in addition to research, education and clinic activities. Each of these specialty care facilities present unique security and safety challenges, which will be explored throughout this text.

The critical access hospital program, created by U.S. federal law in 1997, was designed to slow the closing of small rural hospitals. To be awarded the designation as a critical access hospital, the organization must have no more than 25 beds, and must be the sole healthcare facility within a 35-mile drive. Critical access hospitals enjoy a financial advantage over other hospitals, in that they are reimbursed by Medicare on a cost-plus basis instead of at a flat fee by procedure. This financial advantage has allowed many small rural hospitals to remain open and viable.

NONHOSPITAL SIDE OF HEALTHCARE

The traditional healthcare campus has expanded its service boundaries. Physician offices, outpatient surgical centers, home healthcare, and outpatient mental health clinics expand the horizon of healthcare and the role of the security department, on and off campus. These include clinics and community health centers, long-term care and assisted care facilities, pharmacies, dental clinics, skilled nursing and specialty-care facilities, home care programs, hearing centers, hospices, and durable medical equipment suppliers. Many of these are affiliated with general hospitals and clinics, but may also operate as independent entities.

These care organizations have become important industries themselves, while remaining a relatively small part of the total expenditure for healthcare.

The recent expansion and success of these programs can be attributed to the changes in the delivery of healthcare services and patient care patterns, which have stemmed from managed care organizations. With managed care, there is increasing need for case management, which can result in the earlier discharge of patients. Today, it is common for an emergency department to assess and triage a patient and determine they are not "sick enough" for hospital admittance and refer them to a home health agency. Bed utilization consultations occur every morning in many organizations, as healthcare professionals look to match patients in acute care with available treatment settings in the community, as part of an ongoing process of relieving pressure on the acute care hospitals. Ever increasingly, healthcare professionals are traveling into the community to provide services to their customers in the home environment.

DIVERSE STAKEHOLDERS

The stakeholders in the healthcare environment are numerous and display a vast variety of characteristics. The patient can be a newborn infant, a teenager, a middle ager, or be of advanced age—each with unique security concerns and needs. Patients' medical conditions and treatment regimens often render them less able to take responsibility for their own safety and security. The healthcare provider organizations must understand they have a moral and legal duty to provide a safe and secure healing environment for all patients. This duty is heightened when the patient is less able to provide basic elements of self-protection due to age, dementia and other mental health issues, mobility and administered medicines.

The healthcare staff ranges from the highly educated physician and technical caregiver to the support staff in nutrition services, facilities management and biomedical equipment repair. A high percentage of caregivers are female, which presents certain protection concerns relative to working late night shifts, often in remote locations.

STAFFING THE MEDICAL CARE FACILITY

The delivery of medical care is very labor-intensive, and utilizes a wide range of professional and service staff. The staff-to-patient ratio is traditionally high in the pediatric specialty facility and is much lower in long-term care facilities. The diversity of technical positions continues to evolve as new equipment and care procedures develop, yet the need for nurses continues to increase, driving an extraordinary labor demand. Job growth is expected to continue for the healthcare sector well into the future. The industry saw 25% employment growth between 2000 and 2010, while total U.S. employment dropped by over 2% during the same period. The Center for Health Workforce Studies projects that, between 2010 and 2020, jobs in the healthcare sector will grow by 30%, more than twice as fast as the general growth.[13] As a result, the search for qualified workers is becoming increasingly competitive with the shortage of registered nurses, home health aides, nursing aides and attendants, physical and respiratory therapists, radiology technicians, pharmacists and pharmacy technicians, as well as physicians and physician assistants. The need to replace workers, due to retirement and high job turnover, is also a factor creating the increased labor demand.

The technical specialization of patient care is expected to create a nurse shortage of epidemic proportions, as nursing schools cannot keep up with demand. The median age of registered nurses is 46, with more than 50% of the nursing workforce close to retirement. Recent reforms in healthcare will give millions of people access to the American healthcare system, placing a need for more nurses and health professionals.[14] Coupled with the issue, America—and indeed most other countries—is seeing vast increases in the number of people over 65. The strain this age group will put on its health system has resulted in an imbalance between the supply of, and the demand for, qualified nursing staff.

The shortage of registered nurses is already having ill effects on the U.S. healthcare delivery system: 90% of long-term care organizations lack sufficient nurse staffing to provide even the most basic of care; home healthcare agencies are being forced to refuse new admissions; and there are 126,000 nursing positions currently unfilled in hospitals across the country. As news of the shortage has reached the American public, 81% are aware that there is a shortage, 93% believe that the shortage threatens the quality of care, and 65% view the shortage as a major problem.[15] Further, the current nurse staffing shortage is burgeoning at a time when patient acuity is higher, care more complex, and demand for services often exceeds capacity. Given the anticipated additional demand for healthcare services, it is estimated that by 2020, there will be at least 400,000 fewer nurses available to provide care than will be needed. The nursing shortage is not confined to the U.S., as many countries grapple with this challenge and seek creative solutions.

The healthcare industry includes establishments ranging from small-town private practices of physicians, who employ only one medical assistant, to busy inner-city hospitals that provide thousands of diverse jobs, including labs, nursing, various therapies, behavioral/mental health, and so forth. Supported by increasing demand and historic profit margins, the healthcare industry is the largest and the fastest growing industry in the U.S.

Healthcare firms employ large numbers of workers in professional and service occupations. Together, these two occupational groups account for three out of four jobs in the industry. The role of outsourcing in healthcare depends on the mix of workers needed and varies, depending on the size, geographic location, goals, philosophy, funding, organization, and management style of the institution.

The healthcare industry has begun to focus a great deal of attention on eliminating waste and unproductive work, in turn placing emphasis on implementing best practices and resource efficiency. This has given rise to interest not only in Six Sigma, but its close cousin, Lean Process Thinking, which focuses on eliminating waste and other "non-value-added" activity.

Cost containment also is shaping the healthcare industry, as shown by the growing emphasis on providing services on an outpatient, ambulatory basis; limiting unnecessary or low-priority services; and stressing wellness and preventive care, which reduces the potential cost of undiagnosed, untreated medical conditions. Enrollment in managed care programs continues to grow. These prepaid plans provide comprehensive coverage to members and control health insurance costs by emphasizing preventive care. Cost effectiveness also is improved with the increased use of integrated delivery systems, which combine two or more segments of the industry to increase efficiency through the streamlining of functions, primarily financial and managerial. These changes will continue to reshape not only the nature of the healthcare workforce, but also the manner in which healthcare is provided.

THE HEALTHCARE SECURITY ADMINISTRATOR

Today's healthcare protection professional is facing continuous strain on security resources and leadership challenges. Changes in the delivery of healthcare services, multiple campus environments, free-standing emergency departments, homecare, hospice, and clinics are driving care deeper into the community, and off the traditional campus. The closing of mental health facilities (stand-alone and internal hospital departments) has required emergency departments, and other areas within the hospital, to manage a significant influx of patients with acute and chronic mental healthcare problems. This, coupled with restrictions promulgated by the Centers for Medicare and Medicaid Services (CMS) requiring that the least restrictive alternative and method for restraint and seclusion be used, has direct bearing on the soaring amounts of patient-generated violence against medical staff and security personnel.

Evolving accreditation standards from The Joint Commission (TJC), the threat of terrorist attacks, correctional care responsibilities, emergency preparedness and the ability to manage patient surge in the event of a disaster, an increase in weapons being brought into healthcare facilities, possible occurrences of infant abductions, and data security requirements of the Health Insurance Portability and Accountability Act (HIPAA) all mean more scrutiny of the effectiveness of healthcare security programs.

The healthcare industry continues to face financial pressures requiring greater security program justification (that is, performance measurements, return on investments, and development of 3–5-year security master plans). Operating budgets and capital budget requests are under greater scrutiny, and require a business-minded security administrator who can think strategically and act tactically. The industry remains people intensive—over two-thirds (73%) of healthcare security budgets are dedicated to staff resources.[16] This requires individuals who can effectively lead others while leading themselves and the change necessary to increase the levels of protection in the industry.

THE JOINT COMMISSION

The Joint Commission, through its standards and Elements of Performance (EP), has had the most significant impact of any single element in the improvement of safety and security in America's healthcare facilities over the last 20 years.

The Joint Commission was founded in 1951 as the Joint Commission on Accreditation of Hospitals (JCAH), until 1987, when it adopted the name Joint Commission on Accreditation of Healthcare Organizations (JCAHO). In 2007, it introduced a new brand identity with a shortened name—The Joint Commission.

The Joint Commission is governed by a Board of Commissioners comprising 29 individual members and corporate members that include: the American College of Physicians, the American College of Surgeons, the American Hospital Association, the American Medical Association and the American Dental Association. It should be noted that the Canadian Medical Association was a corporate member when The Joint Commission was formed in 1951 and withdrew in 1959 to form their own accrediting organization, now called Accreditation Canada.

Table 1-1 TJC Healthcare Industry Manuals and Standards

Joint Commission Standards Manuals	
• Ambulatory Health Care • Behavioral Health Care • Critical Access Hospital • Home Care • Hospital	• Laboratory Services • Nursing Care Center • Office-Based Surgery • Primary Care Medical Home Certification

The Joint Commission accredits and certifies more than 4,500 hospitals and a total of more than 20,000 other healthcare organizations that provide home care, long-term care, behavioral healthcare, laboratory, and ambulatory care services. An independent, not-for-profit organization, it is the U.S.'s oldest and largest standards-setting and accrediting body in healthcare. More recently, they have introduced Joint Commission International (JCI) to develop international consultation, accreditation, publications and education. Together with their affiliate organizations, JCI and Joint Commission Resources (JCR), they offer a wide range of products and services to help improve patient safety and quality, in healthcare worldwide.

The stated mission of The Joint Commission is "to continuously improve the safety and quality of care provided to the public, through the provisions of health care accreditation and related services that support performance improvement in health care organizations." Table 1-1 lists all of the specific healthcare industries in which The Joint Commission has manuals and standards.

The security standards and elements of performance are found in the *Hospital Accreditation Standards Manual*, which is a subscription series with quarterly updates. The subject of security is specifically addressed in the chapter titled "Management of the Environment of Care (EC)." There are various standards relating directly and indirectly to the security function in other chapters of the *Hospital Accreditation Standards Manual* as well.

DESIGN AND IMPLEMENTATION

The format of the standards is broken into two categories, referred to as *Design* and *Implementation*. The first category is concerned with the organization plan for compliance. The plan is developed through the assessment process and the application of organizational (or outsourced) resources. The second category is putting the plan into action to achieve the compliance goal. Immediately upon implementation, the plan and performance objectives are measured as an ongoing activity in a cycle, to constantly improve (or maintain) performance. This cycle, demonstrated in Figure 1-1, can be referred to as the EC management process.

ORGANIZATION SURVEYS

The Joint Commission's approach to accreditation is patient-centered and data-driven. The on-site accreditation process is centered on the Tracer Methodology, where surveyors follow the actual experiences of a sample of patients as they interact with their healthcare team, and evaluate the actual provision of care provided to these patients. This review is designed to look at how the individual components of an organization interact to provide safe, high quality patient care.

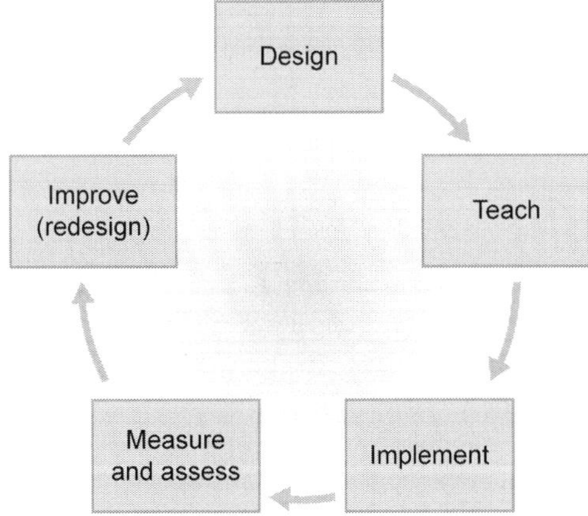

FIGURE 1-1

Environment of care management process.

An organization seeking accreditation is generally surveyed on a 3-year cycle, with visits by Joint Commission surveyors a minimum of once every 39 months (2 years for laboratories), to evaluate standards compliance. All regular Joint Commission accreditation surveys are unannounced. Joint Commission surveyors are doctors, nurses, hospital administrators, laboratory medical technologists, and other healthcare professionals.

Joint Commission accreditation does not begin and end with the on-site survey. It is a continuous process. Random surveys, surveys for cause, and sentinel events can result in a limited review survey. Every year, organizations evaluate their ongoing standards compliance through a periodic performance review. The Periodic Performance Review (PPR) is a tool designed and used for self-evaluation of an organization's compliance with The Joint Commission standards. Organizations have the option of asking Joint Commission staff to review the PPR and associated action plans. TJC staff can make suggestions to help the organization improve the quality of care it provides.

In 2007, the Joint Commission began conducting on-site validation surveys of a sample of those organizations that are required to submit Evidence of Standards Compliance (ESC). Designed to replace the original random unannounced surveys of all accredited organizations, the Joint Commission shared in 2014 that 2% of accredited organizations will be selected for unannounced on-site ESC evaluations, down from its previous goal of 5%.[17]

When a new standard with an annual reporting or measurement requirement is implemented midyear, it is expected the requirement be met no later than 1 year from the implementation dates; e.g., for an effective date 7/1/XX, the associated annual requirement would be due by every 6/30/XX.

Denial of accreditation, conditional accreditation, or provisional accreditation can result in various remedial and follow-up actions by the accrediting body.

Accrediting bodies in other countries

There are various accreditation bodies and processes in place in other countries, for example Accreditation Canada referenced earlier in this section, although there are no security standards in the Canadian accrediting process. In the UK, the equivalent accrediting body is The Care Quality Committee,[18] and in 2013, the Australian Commission on Safety and Quality in Healthcare introduced a new national health services standards and accreditation "scheme" to that country.[19] In most countries there exists some form of independent review or accreditation body with a mission similar to The Joint Commission, constructed around continuous improvement in the quality of care provided by an organization.

SCORING OF STANDARDS

In 2004, The Joint Commission changed its scoring and accreditation decision process from a score-base system that encouraged organizations to "ramp up" to do well on a survey to achieve a high score, to its current accreditation decision process, based on the criticality of the standards and other requirements regarding their relationship to the quality and safety of patient care.[20]

Compliance with the standards is scored by determining compliance with Elements of Performance (EP), which are specific performance expectations that must be in place. EPs are scored on a three-point scale:

0 = insufficient compliance
1 = partial compliance
2 = satisfactory compliance

All partially compliant or insufficiently compliant EPs must be addressed via the ESC submission process. The time line for completing the ESC submission depends on the "criticality" of findings and immediacy of risk, and is due either within 45 or 60 days.[20]

Each standard has one or more EP. Each EP is labeled in the accreditation manual and all have the same weight. EPs are divided into three scoring categories:

- **"A" Elements of Performance** – usually relate to structural requirements (for example, policies or plans that either exist or do not exist, such as infant abduction response).
- **"B" Elements of Performance** – relates to the presence or absence of requirements and usually answered yes or no. If the organization does not meet the requirements, the EP is scored 0. If there is concern about the quality or comprehensiveness of the effort but the principles of good process design were met, the EP is scored 1. If applicable principles are met, the EP is scored 2.
- **"C" Elements of Performance** – are frequency-based EPs and are scored based on the number of times an organization does not meet a particular EP.

THE ENVIRONMENT OF CARE COMMITTEE

The "environment of care" (EOC) is made up of three basic components—building(s), equipment, and people—with responsibility for monitoring seven programs and their impact on the health and safety of the environment:

1. Fire Safety
2. Utility Systems
3. Medical Equipment
4. Safety
5. Security

6. Hazardous Materials
7. Emergency Management

A variety of key elements and issues can contribute to creating the way the space feels and works for residents, families, staff and others experiencing the healthcare delivery system. For this purpose, a multidisciplinary group within the hospital comes together to form the EOC Committee, to address all seven elements of the environment of care. This should include the most senior security protection administrator at the facility, and involve other security department leaders as determined by the Committee.

The Committee advises hospital staff and reviews changes to the EC standards and intents. New standards, or clarification of standards, are discussed in this committee and may be forwarded on to other committees such as the Executive Council for discussion and feedback. Joint Commission surveyors closely review group communications and dynamics—surveyors are often found analyzing how well this group collaborates and cooperates together on issues facing the environment in which care is provided. In particular, objectives for this committee should involve:

- Reducing and controlling environmental hazards and risks.
- Preventing accidents and injuries.
- Maintaining safe conditions for residents, staff, and others coming to the organization's facilities.
- Maintaining an environment that is sensitive to resident needs for comfort, social interaction, and positive distraction.
- Maintaining an environment that minimizes unnecessary environmental stresses for residents, staff, and others coming to the organization's facilities.

In Canada, the Accreditation Canada process has begun to move away from the Environment of Care model and the associated committee usually formed for the accreditation process, as many of the EOC standards have moved to other sections, including Leadership. This is largely in response to more organizational/system-wide standards, moving away from the pure hospital-based structures, with a focus on a continuum of care for the patient experience.

THE SENTINEL EVENT

Patient safety is at the core of TJC's standards and policies related to sentinel events (any unexpected occurrences involving death or serious physical or psychological injury, or risk thereof). The term "sentinel event" is a very broad term utilized by TJC in relation to their accreditation process. TJC's Sentinel Event Policy calls for every accredited organization to identify, voluntarily report, evaluate and evoke sentinel event prevention strategies. The policy requires organizations to investigate the root causes of adverse events, implement appropriate strategies to prevent reoccurrence, monitor the effectiveness of these strategies, and advise the affected patients and families of errors or unexpected outcomes and the steps taken to correct them.

The sentinel event not only relates to protection, but to a wide array of adverse patient outcomes. Such events are called "sentinel" because they signal the need for immediate investigation and response.[21]

There are four primary goals for the Joint Commission sentinel event policy:

1) To have a positive impact in the improvement of patient care.
2) To focus organization attention on the event to provide an understanding of the underlying cause, and to make changes in systems and procedures to reduce the probability of such an event in the future.

3) To increase the general knowledge about sentinel events, their causes, and preventive strategies.
4) To maintain the confidence of the public in the commission accreditation process.

There are two basic categories of the sentinel event relative to the investigation and reporting of such incidents. The first is the event referred to as "reviewable" by The Joint Commission. The second is an event that is handled internally within the organization. In the latter event, the organization is required to have a policy regarding a review process that meets The Joint Commission criteria, but the event does not need to be reported.

The subsets of sentinel events that are subject to Joint Commission review at the time of occurrence and that are security-related consist of: (1) an event resulting in an unanticipated death or major permanent loss of function, not related to the natural course of the patients' illness or underlying condition, or (2) the event is one specified by The Joint Commission and the outcome is not death or major permanent loss of function. This second category specifically includes security incidents of infant abduction or discharge to the wrong family, or rape.

The Joint Commission is not very clear regarding its definition of an infant or the distinction of an abduction (stranger to stranger versus domestic custody). There is a vast difference in these two categories of infant abduction incidents.

The rape of a patient is a reviewable sentinel event. The determination of rape is to be based on the organization's definition, consistent with applicable law and regulation. An allegation of rape is not reviewable under Joint Commission policy. Applicability of the policy is established when a determination is made that a rape has actually occurred.

Reported sentinel events are compiled into a database, which currently contains over 9,980 cases reviewed by The Joint Commission from 1995 through June of 2013.[22] As noted in Figure 1-2, the number of sentinel events has increased dramatically since 1995. This vast knowledge base of adverse outcomes helps inform and improve The Joint Commission's standards and policies, and provides "lessons learned" information to healthcare organizations to support their safety improvement efforts.

The terms "sentinel event" and "medical error" are not synonymous; events are called "sentinel" because they signal the need for immediate investigation and response. For the healthcare security administrator, examples of reviewable and nonreviewable sentinel events under The Joint Commission's Sentinel Event Policy include:

1. Suicide of any patient receiving care, treatment and services
2. Abduction of any patient receiving care, treatment, and services
3. Discharge of an infant to the wrong family
4. Any elopement, that is, unauthorized departure, of a patient from an around-the-clock care setting resulting in a temporally related death (suicide, accidental death, or homicide) or major permanent loss of function
5. Rape, assault (to include sexual abuse), or homicide of any patient receiving care, treatment, and services
6. Rape, assault (to include sexual abuse), or homicide of a staff member, licensed independent practitioner, visitor, or vendor while on site at the healthcare organization.[24]

Figure 1-3 shows the number of reported assaults, rape and homicide by year since 1995. Figure 1-4 shows the number of reviewed elopement-related events resulting in death or permanent loss of function.

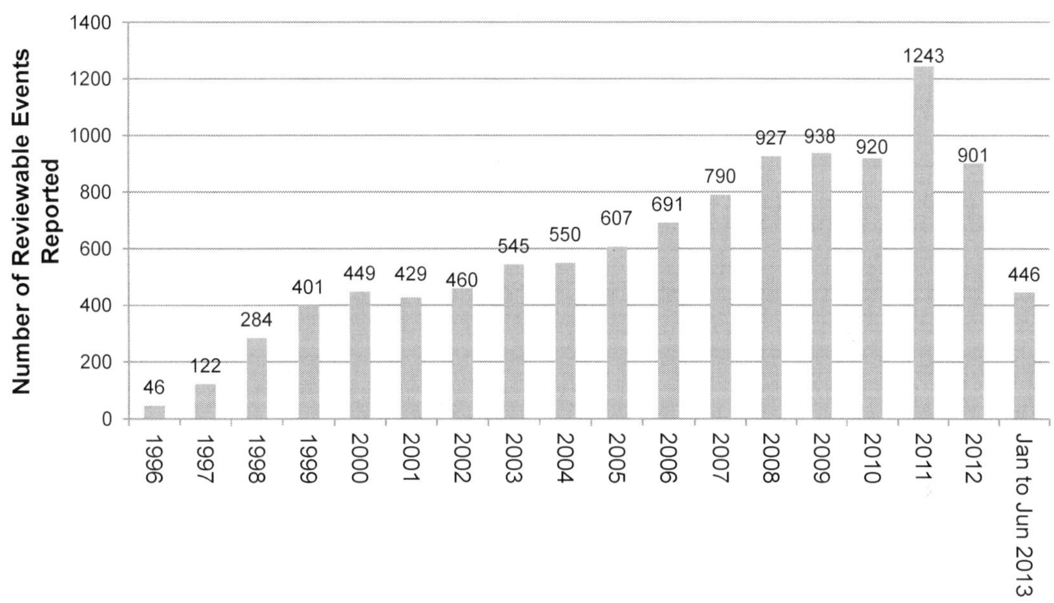

FIGURE 1-2

Total sentinel events reviewed by year.[23]

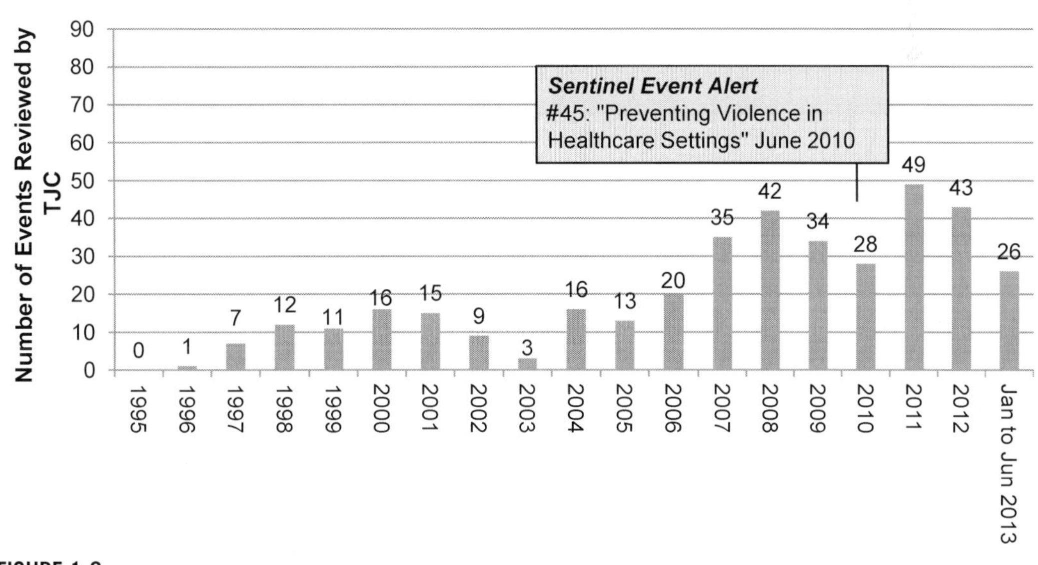

FIGURE 1-3

Sentinel events by year: Assault, rape, homicide.[23]

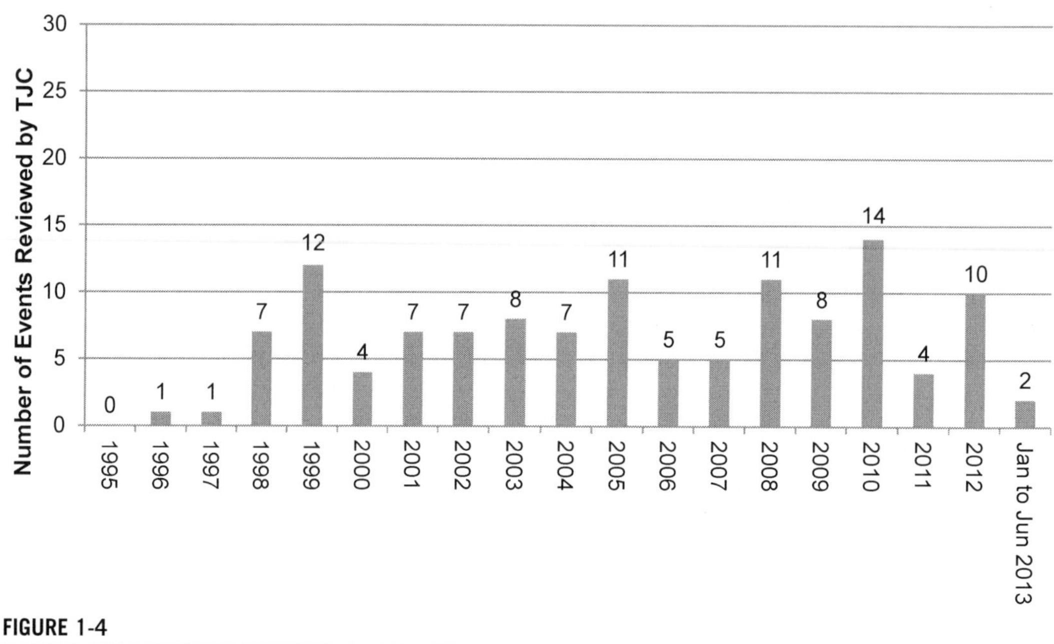

FIGURE 1-4

Sentinel events by year: Elopement-related events resulting in death or permanent loss of function.[23]

The Joint Commission encourages accredited organizations to report all reviewable sentinel events. It should be noted the reporting of most sentinel events is voluntary and The Joint Commission believes it represents only a small proportion of actual events. The Joint Commission may also become aware of a reviewable sentinel event through patient contact, family, media, or a staff member. Regardless of how the accrediting body is made aware of the event, the organization is expected to prepare a root cause analysis report and action plan within 45 calendar days of the event or of becoming aware of the event. The analysis and action plans are to then be forwarded to The Joint Commission. Upon receipt of the information, they will determine the acceptability of the analysis and action plan.

An organization that does not submit an acceptable analysis or action plan within the 45-day period may be put on Accreditation Watch. This designation is considered to be public information. The Accreditation Watch is not an accreditation status; rather, it is an attribute of the organization's official accreditation.

The removal of an Accreditation Watch is a determination of The Joint Commission's Accreditation Committee. The decision to remove this accreditation attribute generates an Official Accreditation Decision Report. This report will assign an appropriate follow-up activity for the facility, typically a written progress report or follow-up visit to be conducted within a specified period of time.

Accreditation Canada does not fulfill the sentinel event reporting mandate described for The Joint Commission. While sentinel events of course do occur in all countries (sometimes called adverse events), responsibility for follow-up and investigation usually rests with the organization in which the event occurred. Oversight for this process is usually provided by the government entity with responsibility for the health organization—usually the Ministry of Health in Canada's provinces.

THE CENTERS FOR MEDICARE AND MEDICAID SERVICES

The Medicare and Medicaid programs were signed into law in 1965. There have been various changes in the law since that time, when the basic Centers for Medicare and Medicaid Services (CMS) programs were part of Social Security. CMS was known previously as the Health Care Financing Administration. CMS is responsible for administering Medicare, Medicaid, and Child Health Insurance Programs.

The stated mission of CMS is to ensure effective, up-to-date healthcare coverage and to promote quality care for beneficiaries. A principal element of the CMS provider reimbursement program for rendering medical care is to "approve" the provider. Upon this approval the provider must formally agree to the CMS Conditions of Participation (CoP) to be eligible for payment of services rendered.

In relation to hospitals, CMS relies on several accreditation programs to inspect (survey) patient care practices in terms of meeting quality control standards. Currently there are three CMS approved accreditation programs, which are:

- The Joint Commission (TJC)
- American Osteopathic Association (AOA)
- Det Norske Veritas Healthcare, Inc. (DNV)

DNV

The DNV program is called the National Integrated Accreditation for Healthcare Organization (NIAHO). Its program integrates with the International Organization for Standards' ISO-9001 quality management system standards with the Medicare conditions of participation. When CMS granted deeming status to DNV in 2008, it was the first accreditation service approved since the inception of Medicare. DNV surveys are yearly, due to the ISO requirements, and accreditation decisions also differ from The Joint Commission with three types of survey findings:

1. NC (Nonconformity) Category 1 – Condition Level: the most egregious level where the hospital is found "completely or substantially out of compliance."
2. NC Category 1: applied when "objective evidence exists that a requirement has not been addressed (*intent*), a practice differs from the defined system (*implementation*), or the system is not effective (*effectiveness*). It could also mean the absence of one or more required system elements, or a situation that raises significant doubt that services will meet specified requirements. NC 1 is used for significant findings that need to be addressed."
3. NC Category 2: the least onerous level, applied with a finding of "a lapse of either discipline or control, during the implementation of system/procedural requirements, which does not indicate a system breakdown or raise doubt that services will meet requirements. Overall system requirement is defined, implemented and effective."

Despite 25% to 30% annual growth, DNV is not ready to dethrone The Joint Commission. DNV has accredited about 300 hospitals with another 80 or so awaiting accreditation. In comparison, The Joint Commission has accredited about 4,200 hospitals and another 380 critical access hospitals.[25]

In addition to making healthcare payments to providers and the states on behalf of beneficiaries, CMS provides Survey and Certification programs to ensure that providers and suppliers comply with federal health, safety, and program standards. These are administered per agreements with state survey agencies to conduct onsite facility inspections. The Joint Commission is recognized by the CMS as an equivalent substitute for its own inspections, but a facility is not immune to a CMS inspection in the days or weeks following a Joint Commission survey.

CMS utilizes regulation and enforcement activities to help meet its vision of "the right care for every person every time," that affects all aspects of the U.S. healthcare delivery system—hospitals, nursing homes, laboratories, and home care. Applicable standards are set that affect the healthcare security administrator in the area of security's involvement in patient care—elopement (prevention and response), restraint and seclusion, and use of defensive equipment that may be carried by security staff. The reduction in the use of physical restraints has been one of CMS's major quality initiatives, which is discussed in great detail in Chapter 13, "Patient Care Involvement and Intervention." The CMS conditions of participation, and corresponding surveyor interpretations, have blurred the issue of what is or is not related to patient care, and what can or should be viewed as law enforcement events. We will delve deeper into the issue of defensive equipment and considerations surrounding their use in the healthcare environment in Chapter 9, "The Security Uniform and Defensive Equipment."

Once again, in Canada at least, there is no process that would see an agency come to a hospital or healthcare organization unannounced, to inspect or audit any aspect of the security or emergency preparedness program or related processes. However, some progressive security/protection programs have moved toward a position of compliance with U.S. standards in these areas, as they strive for best practices for their organizations.

HEALTH INSURANCE PORTABILITY AND ACCOUNTABILITY ACT

The U.S. Health Insurance Portability and Accountability Act (HIPAA) was enacted as federal law in 1996 under the direction and control of the Department of Health and Human Services (HHS). The law applies to health information, often referred to as Personal Health Information (PHI), created or maintained by healthcare providers who engage in certain electronic transactions, health plans, and healthcare clearinghouses. The Office of Civil Rights (OCR) is the departmental component responsible for implementing and enforcing the privacy regulation. The agency issued a final Privacy Rule that became effective in April 2001 and became enforceable for most covered entities in April 2005. Regulations are designed to safeguard Personal Health Information (PHI) maintained or transmitted in electronic form. Personal computers, external portable hard drives (including iPods and similar devices), magnetic tape, removable storage devices such as USB memory sticks, CDs, DVDs and other digital memory cards, PDAs and smartphones, the Internet and extranets are examples of electronic media that may contain PHI.

There is a distinction between the HIPAA terms *Privacy Rule* (PR) and *Security Rule* (SR). The Privacy Rule basically defines what data must be protected, regardless of format, and how it can and cannot be utilized by the organization maintaining and responsible for controlling the data. The Security Rule provides requirements for protecting the defined PHI and defines physical safeguards as "*physical measures, policies, and procedures to protect a covered entity's electronic information systems and related buildings and equipment, from natural and environmental hazards, and unauthorized intrusion.*"[26]

The Physical Safeguards section, titled Facility Access Control, requires healthcare facilities to implement policies and procedures to limit physical access to its electronic information systems, and the facility (or facilities) in which they are housed, while establishing that properly authorized access is allowed. This includes implementation of procedures to control and validate a person's access based on role (or function), including visitor control, and control of access to software programs.

The Facility Security Plan section requires defining and documenting the safeguards used to protect the healthcare facility. It is a "reasonable and appropriate" expectation that requires implementation of policies and procedures to safeguard the facility, and the equipment housed within it, from unauthorized physical access, tampering and theft. This includes documenting repairs and modifications of physical security equipment and safeguards on a regular basis, including changing locks, making routine maintenance checks and installing new security devices.

The Facility Security Plan should establish basic expectations for the physical attributes of the building proper, and those surrounding a specific workstation, or class of workstation, which can access electronic protected health information. Workstation security safeguards at their heart should be designed to restrict those who access PHI to only authorized users.

The device and media controls of the security plan are expected to govern the receipt and removal of hardware and electronic media that contain PHI, into and out of the facility, as well as the movement of these items within the facility. Disposal of electronic media containing PHI should make certain devices are unusable and/or inaccessible. This may include degaussing or physically damaging the device beyond repair.

It is obvious from the Security Rule requirements that HIPAA compliance in the healthcare environment involves several disciplines which include security, risk management, and information technology. It requires a multiple disciplinary management approach for implementing compliance policy and procedures.

With regard to HIPAA enforcement activities (nonprivacy), the CMS continues to operate based on a complaint-driven process, addressing complaints filed against covered entities by requesting and reviewing documentation of their compliance status and/or corrective actions.

Historically, the OCR's approach to Privacy Rule violations has been passive; however, this started to change in 2011 when the OCR fined Cignet Health in Maryland $4.3 million for its violation of the Privacy Rule. The OCR found Cignet had violated the rights of 41 patients by denying them access to their medical records.[27] In the same time period, OCR reported a $1 million settlement with Massachusetts General Hospital for losing 192 patient records.

The American Recovery and Reinvestment Act of 2009 (ARRA) established a tiered civil penalty structure for HIPAA violations noted in Table 1-2. The Department of Health and Human Services still has discretion in determining the amount of the penalty, based on the nature and extent of the violation, but is prohibited from imposing civil penalties (except in cases of willful neglect) if the violation is corrected within 30 days.

The term "convergence," meaning an organized and coordinated effort of security and information technology, is truly at play in managing HIPAA requirements in addition to other major areas of managing security risks. The security function of the healthcare organization will be charged with, and responsible for, the physical protection of the data and in the area of law enforcement disclosures.

It is not uncommon to receive requests for information from law enforcement officials who are unaware their requests violate either HIPAA, other laws, or confidentiality protocols. An example of such a situation occurred in Wisconsin where a nurse was prosecuted for refusing to release

Table 1-2 HIPAA Violations and Enforcement[28]

HIPAA Violation	Minimum Penalty	Maximum Penalty
Individual did not know (and by exercising reasonable diligence would not have known) that he/she violated HIPAA	$100 per violation, with an annual maximum of $25,000 for repeat violations (Note: maximum that can be imposed by State Attorneys General regardless of the type of violation)	$50,000 per violation, with an annual maximum of $1.5 million
HIPAA violation due to reasonable cause and not due to willful neglect	$1,000 per violation, with an annual maximum of $100,000 for repeat violations	$50,000 per violation, with an annual maximum of $1.5 million
HIPAA violation due to willful neglect but violation is corrected within the required time period	$10,000 per violation, with an annual maximum of $250,000 for repeat violations	$50,000 per violation, with an annual maximum of $1.5 million
HIPAA violation is due to willful neglect and is not corrected	$50,000 per violation, with an annual maximum of $1.5 million	$50,000 per violation, with an annual maximum of $1.5 million

information to law enforcement, citing the rules of HIPAA. The nurse was charged with obstructing an officer and contempt of court for refusing to allow an officer to serve a patient with a restraining order.[29] It would appear there was no request by law enforcement for PHI and that simply acknowledging the patient was in the facility at a specific location would not have violated the HIPAA Security Rule.

REFERENCES

1. Munro Dan. U.S. healthcare hits $3 trillion. *Forbes* 2013, January 19. Retrieved January 4, 2014, from http://www.forbes.com/sites/danmunro/2012/01/19/u-s-healthcare-hits-3-trillion/.
2. Hall Katy, Diehm Jan. Why U.S. health care is obscenely expensive, in 12 charts. *Huffington Post* 2013, November 11. Retrieved January 4, 2014, from http://www.huffingtonpost.com/2013/10/03/health-care-costs-_n_3998425.html.
3. Canadian Institute for Health Information. *Health spending data*. 2013. Retrieved January 14, 2014 from http://www.cihi.ca/CIHI-ext-portal/internet/EN/SubTheme/spending+and+health+workforce/spending/cihi015954.
4. Canadian Institute for Health Information. *Canada's health care spending slows*. 2012. Retrieved January 14, 2014, from http://www.cihi.ca/CIHI-ext-portal/internet/EN/document/spending+and+health+workforce/spending/release_30oct12.
5. Rogers Simon. Healthcare spending around the world; country by country. *The Guardian* 2012, June 30. Retrieved January 14, 2014, from http://www.theguardian.com/news/datablog/2012/jun/30/healthcare-spending-world-country.
6. U.S. Department of Health and Human Services. *CMS financial report (fiscal year 2012)*. 2012. Retrieved January 4, 2014, from http://www.cms.gov/Research-Statistics-Data-and-Systems/Statistics-Trends-and-Reports/CFOReport/Downloads/2012_CMS_Financial_Report.pdf.
7. National Institute for Health Care Management. Understanding U.S. health care spending. *NIHCM Foundation Data Brief* 2011, July. Retrieved January 2, 2012, from http://nihcm.org/images/stories/NIHCM-CostBrief-Email.pdf.

8. Pho K. Wasted medical dollars. *USA Today* 2008, April 23. Retrieved June 13, 2009, from http://blogs.usatoday.com/oped/2008/04/wasted-medical.html.
9. Johnson Carla. *Caring for poor, hospitals reach brink of closure*. 2011, May 9. NBCNews.com. Retrieved January 4, 2014, from http://www.nbcnews.com/id/42961431/ns/health-health_care/#.Ush9np3n9D8.
10. Kaiser Family Foundation. *Hospitals by Ownership Type*. 2011. Retrieved on January 4, 2014, from http://kff.org/other/state-indicator/hospitals-by-ownership/.
11. Commonwealth of Australia. *A National Health and Hospitals Network for Australia's Future*. 2010. Retrieved January 14, 2014, from http://www.yourhealth.gov.au/internet/yourhealth/publishing.nsf/Content/nhhn-report-toc/$FILE/NHHN%20-%20Full%20report.pdf.
12. American Hospital Association. *2012 Chartbook: Trends affecting hospitals and health systems*. 2012. Retrieved December 9, 2013, from http://www.aha.org/research/reports/tw/chartbook/2012chartbook.shtml
13. The Center for Health Workforce Studies. *Health Care Employment Projections: An analysis of Bureau of Labor Statistics occupational projections, 2010–2020*. 2012, March. Retrieved January 5, 2014, from http://www.healthit.gov/sites/default/files/chws_bls_report_2012.pdf.
14. American Nurses Association. *Nursing shortage*. 2014. NursingWorld.org (website). Retrieved January 4, 2014, from http://www.nursingworld.org/nursingshortage.
15. The Joint Commission. *Health care at the crossroads: Strategies for addressing the evolving nursing crisis*. 2009, June 29. Retrieved July 8, 2009, from http://www.jointcommission.org/NR/rdonlyres/5C138711-ED76-4D6F-909F-B06E0309F36D/0/health_care_at_the_crossroads.pdf.
16. Weonik R. *Securing our hospitals: GE Security and IAHSS healthcare benchmarking study*. Presented at International Association for Healthcare Security and Safety Mid-Winter Meeting and Seminar; 2008, January 21.
17. The Joint Commission. *Summary of changes: 2014 Comprehensive Accreditation Manual for Hospitals*. 2014, January. Retrieved January 5, 2014, from https://store.jcrinc.com/assets/1/14/CAH14_Sample_Pages.pdf.
18. UK Treatment. *Hospital Accreditation*. 2013. Retrieved January 14, 2014, from http://www.uktreatment.com/why-the-uk/hospital-accreditation/.
19. Australian Commission on Safety and Quality in Health Care. *Health Services Standards and Accreditation*. 2011. Retrieved January 14, 2014, from http://www.safetyandquality.gov.au/our-work/accreditation/.
20. The Joint Commission. *Facts about scoring and accreditation decisions for 2014*. 2014. Retrieved January 4, 2014, from http://www.jointcommission.org/assets/1/18/Scoring_and_Accreditation_Decisions_for_2014_8_22_13.pdf.
21. Special Report on Sentinel Events. *Perspectives*. Oakbrook Terrace, Illinois: Joint Commission Resources; November/December 1998. p. 19–42.
22. The Joint Commission. *Summary data of sentinel events reviewed by The Joint Commission*. 2013. Retrieved on January 4, 2014, from http://www.jointcommission.org/assets/1/18/2004_to_2Q_2013_SE_Stats_-_Summary.pdf.
23. The Joint Commission. *Sentinel event data: Event type by year 1995–June 2013*. 2013, January. Retrieved December 31, 2013, from http://www.jointcommission.org/assets/1/18/Event_Type_by_Year_1995-2Q2013.pdf.
24. The Joint Commission. *Sentinel event. Comprehensive Accreditation Manual for Hospitals*. 2013. Retrieved December 31, 2013, from http://www.jointcommission.org/assets/1/6/CAMH_2012_Update2_24_SE.pdf.
25. American Society of Healthcare Engineers. DNV attracts attention from health care organizations. *Health Facilities Management* 2013:6–7 (September).
26. Centers for Medicare & Medicaid Services. *HIPAA Security Series 3, Security Standards: Physical Safeguards*. 2007, March. Retrieved January 10, 2014, from http://www.hhs.gov/ocr/privacy/hipaa/administrative/securityrule/physsafeguards.pdf.

27. Campus Safety Staff. *Trend Alert: Dept. of Health more aggressively enforcing HIPAA*. 2011, March 10. Campussafetymagazine.com. Retrieved March 10, 2011, from http://www.campussafetymagazine.com/Channel/Hospital-Security/News/2011/03/10/Trend-Dept-of-Health-Increases-HIPAA-Enforcement.aspx?ref=HospitalSecurityUpdate-20110310.
28. American Medical Association. *HIPAA violations and enforcement*. 2014. Retrieved January 10, 2014, from http://www.ama-assn.org//ama/pub/physician-resources/solutions-managing-your-practice/coding-billing-insurance/hipaahealth-insurance-portability-accountability-act/hipaa-violations-enforcement.page.
29. Tomes JP. Prescription for data protection. *Security Management* 2005;**78** (April).

CHAPTER

PROTECTING A HEALING ENVIRONMENT

2

The healing environment presents a host of different and unique settings where patient care is the primary mission. These traditional environments include hospitals, clinics, physician and dental offices, stand-alone emergency departments, neighborhood urgent care centers, home care rehabilitation, long term or residential care, and free-standing surgery centers—each presenting unique needs for protection of patients, staff, visitors, contractors, and property.

There are also healing environments that often function outside the more conventional patient care environments, such as veterinary hospitals, clinical trials, clinics, outpatient diagnostic centers and blood banks.

DEFINING HEALTHCARE SECURITY

The terms *security* or *protection for healthcare facilities* can often be vague and elusive. These are in fact relatively ill-defined concepts that can and do take on different connotations in different settings. In the context of protecting healthcare facilities, security can be generally defined as a system of safeguards designed to protect the physical property and to achieve relative safety for all people interacting within the organization and its environment.

This definition, of course, leaves the problem of defining *relative safety*. What is safe today may not be safe tomorrow. It is a difficult task to evaluate the environment of a particular facility to determine if relative safety has in fact been achieved and such evaluations are somewhat subjective in nature. The realistic goal of protection, or security, is intended to reduce the probability of detrimental incidents and mitigate incident damage, not to necessarily eliminate all such risks. Security, then, is not static but dynamic, and can be viewed as a state or condition that fluctuates within a continuum. As environmental and human conditions change, so does the status or level of protection. It is this phenomenon that requires organizations to constantly evaluate and reevaluate their system of protection on a continuous basis.

In some cases, healthcare security practitioners tend to view security too strictly or too definitively. The organization being served is the entity that provides the ultimate definition of the security system; after all, the organization provides the funding. This is not to say that the protection program and the philosophy and objectives of the principal security administrator do not have a strong influence on molding the organizational definition. However, truly effective healthcare security programs reflect an alignment with the mission, vision and strategic objectives of the organization they serve.

A common error for healthcare organizations is to view security as being closely aligned with the law enforcement function. Although some common ground may exist between security and law enforcement, at least 90 percent of their respective activities are different. Security of the healthcare organization must be viewed as a business function specific to that organization, while law enforcement

Table 2-1 Comparing Basic Characteristics of Law Enforcement and Security

Security	Law Enforcement
Prevention of Incidents	Apprehension of Offenders
Protecting an Organization	Protecting a Society
Administrative Remedies	Legal Remedies
Organization Defined	Statute Defined
Private and Tax Funding	Tax Supported
Return on Investment	Public Opinion

NOTE: Some law enforcement agencies are supported by quasi-private funding such as the Public Safety Department of various colleges and universities.

may be viewed as external protection that attempts to uphold the law for all of society. Having said that, law enforcement, and even the military, has the overall goal of providing a "state of security." Table 2-1 portrays the general differences between law enforcement and security.

An extremely important concept guiding the healthcare security system is that of "administrative remedy" vs. "law enforcement remedy." The goal of the administrative remedy is to resolve a situation in the best interests of the organization, possibly negating the need for a law enforcement approach when facts and circumstances indicate there may be a better organization-based resolution. These circumstances might include petty theft where restitution and disciplinary action or a substance abuse issue may best be resolved through employee/physician assistance programs. The administrative remedy concept does not in any way imply that criminal information should not be reported to the police. Law enforcement agencies and prosecution in virtually all jurisdictions must set priorities consistent with resources available. The result is that minor crimes can often be ignored or lost in the process. Once an organization has "handed off" a situation to law enforcement, it is often more difficult to then attempt to effect an organizational remedy.

BASIC RATIONALE OF HEALTHCARE SECURITY

There are a multitude of reasons behind the provision of the proper level of security and safety for the healthcare environment. These reasons include a moral responsibility, legal concerns, complying with accreditation/regulatory requirements, contributing to the provision of quality patient care, maintaining the economic/business foundation of the organization, and maintaining sound public, community and staff relations.

In terms of moral responsibility, the organization has an obligation to manage its environment for "the good" that minimizes the possibility of injury or death to all persons on its premises. This moral responsibility extends to reasonable steps to preclude the destruction, misuse, or theft of property. A second justification for providing protection services is a legal responsibility. The healthcare organization has a duty to exercise care and skill in the day-to-day management of corporate affairs. The healthcare organization's obligation to its patients is contractual in that the organization assumes certain responsibilities toward them.

The issue of liability in the management of patient medical services and care facilities has become more acute in recent years, particularly in the U.S. An organization may be held liable for the negligence of an individual employee under the doctrine of *respondeat superior* or for corporate negligence. In terms of employee negligence, two general factors are requisite for imposing liability on the corporation: an employer–employee relationship must exist, and the employee's act or failure to act must occur within the scope of her or her employment. Corporate negligence occurs when the organization maintains its building and grounds in a negligent fashion, furnishes defective supplies or equipment, hires incompetent employees, or in some other manner fails to meet accepted standards, and such failure results in harm or injury to a person to whom the organization owes a duty.

One aspect of the legal rationale is the growing element of punitive damages. Jury awards that punish organizations for not taking appropriate security measures continue to increase in frequency and in higher awards. In many jurisdictions punitive damage awards are not covered by insurance and must be paid from the organization's funds.

A third important reason for maintaining a safe and secure environment is the responsibility of complying with accreditation and licensing, as well as federal, state, and local regulatory agencies. Failure to meet such compliance requirements can seriously undermine the success and viability of the organization.

A fourth rationale for providing a protection system is to maintain a sound economic foundation for the organization. In this regard, healthcare has faced mounting criticism, especially in regard to the rapidly escalating costs of delivering quality medical care. Critics often cite the lack of cost-containment measures that, in part, relate to preventing theft and the waste of supplies and equipment. It is estimated that between 3% and 10% of hospital expenditures could be saved if proper security controls were implemented. In countries such as Canada, Australia, New Zealand, the United Kingdom and others, this responsibility is also to the taxpayer, as their hospitals are largely publicly funded. Yet in most cases, the entire protection budget for healthcare facilities is generally less than 1% of the total operating budget, with the vast majority of the security budget directed to personal safety issues.

Finally, a safe and secure environment is required to maintain good public, patient and employee relations. Although this reason does not appear to be as important as the others, it has probably been responsible for providing more funds for the security budget than the other four justifications combined. Healthcare administrators who face bad media coverage relative to a security problem or restless employees threatening to walk out over a security incident somehow find new funds to make positive adjustments in the protection program. In the U.S., passage of the Affordable Care Act in 2010 dramatically increased the importance of patient care surveys with Hospital Consumer Assessment of Healthcare Providers and Systems (HCAHPS) survey scores now being used by the Centers for Medicare & Medicaid Services (CMS) to determine 1% of a hospital's reimbursement payment. In the seven areas patients are asked to evaluate, four can definitely be impacted by the performance of security: communication, responsiveness, cleanliness, and quietness at night.

EVOLUTION OF HEALTHCARE SECURITY

The evolution of *healthcare* security is based on *hospital* security. A large part of hospital security's heritage can be found in the history of Great Britain. History reveals that one of the first traces of an organized hospital in the United Kingdom was the St. Bartholomew Hospital at Smithfield in London, founded in 1123. The hospital was granted a Royal Charter by King Henry VIII in 1546. In 1552 the

House of Governors authorized the implementation of "the Order of the Hospital," what are now known as position or job descriptions. The Office of the Porter was responsible for the beadles, or the stationed guards. This marks the beginning of healthcare security as we know it today.

Until 1948, hospitals in the United Kingdom operated under boards of governors. In 1948, the Department of Health and Social Security was created, and the Social Services Act went into effect. At this time hospitals in major cities employed a security officer known as a *house detective*. In the late 1950s and early 1960s the position title was changed to *security advisor*.

During the early 1970s, hospitals made a concerted effort to create a more efficient protection system and now have very good protection programs in place. The authors gratefully acknowledge John E. Nichols, former District Security Officer of the British Health Service and author of *Guide to Hospital Security* (Gower Publishing Co. Ltd., Aldeshot, Hampshire, England, 1983), for this information.

PROGRESSION OF HOSPITAL SECURITY IN THE UNITED STATES

To understand better the current status of healthcare security, a review of how hospital security has evolved over the last 100 plus years in the United States will provide a basic perspective. For purposes of discussion, this history has been divided into six periods, each of which reflects a somewhat different philosophy or overall approach to the concept of hospital security.

1900–1950

During this time period little mention was made of the term *security* in relation to protecting the hospital. Initially, the basic protection activities were performed entirely by maintenance workers as they completed their physical plan duties. As facilities grew in size, some hospitals hired a guard to conduct facility rounds to relieve the maintenance person of this task. The primary emphasis of the guard's rounds was the fire watch. Maintaining the physical plant, including the fire watch, was the primary responsibility of the engineering/maintenance function.

1950–1960

Around 1950 protection was expanded to include various aspects of law enforcement. The fire watch continued to be an important protection function; however, the fire watch and law enforcement operated independently of each other. During this time there was an abundance of police officers in many of the larger police departments; however, criminal activities were beginning to be noticed in and around hospitals. It became fairly common for larger police departments to station a police officer at a hospital or at least to use a hospital as the hub of the neighborhood beat. The police presence at hospitals came at taxpayer's expense, but at this time the nation's hospitals were viewed as public and community institutions. As the need for more protection became apparent, hospitals naturally hired off-duty policemen to provide additional security. The shift from the beat officer to vehicle patrols basically eliminated city-funded coverage for most hospitals.

1960–1975

Beginning around 1960 hospitals became aware that protection of the organization was not limited to just fire hazards and criminal activities. Security was perceived as a specialized management service touching all departments and functions of the healthcare organization. The idea of security as a management service created the need to review the organizational reporting level of the protection function.

The result was the creation of a security department that reported to an administrative-level position. In many cases the security department reporting level was to the Director of Maintenance and Engineering. The use of off-duty police officers declined during this period and security departments began staffing with in-house personnel as a general rule.

1975–1990

The management services concept continued to prevail during this period, but the definition and day-to-day functions of security continued to expand. The most noticeable activity in this regard was in the area of safety. Many security departments became so involved in safety that they were renamed *Security and Safety*. The department director became more involved as a member of the top management team. During this period the mission of the security department changed from being primarily a reactive function to a proactive (prevention) type of program. During this period the use of off-duty police officers continued to decline while the utilization of contract security officers began to increase.

1990–2000

In the early 1990s rapid change began to take place. The concept of risk management, introduced in the 1980s, was now maturing and bringing a new appreciation for the protection effort. Security departments were expanding their service roles while at the same time facing severe budget constraints. They were being asked to do more with less. There also developed a great diversity of security programs with a general trend to break away from security, resulting in two complementary but separate programs. On one hand, some security departments were downsizing in terms of staffing, function, and budget, while other programs were growing. The growing programs simply had a broader view of security and the interrelationship of other hospital functions to the protection program. In these programs the security department often took up the slack of providing a broader range of services due to the downsizing of other hospital support programs or the elimination of patient support positions such as orderlies. A good example of the movement is the merging of security and hospital telecommunications into a single department. Another area of consolidation can be found in the merging of transportation services and security into a new and expanded department. Also, moving into the new century, outsourced services continued to replace proprietary security departments, along with the outsourcing of other hospital support departments such as food and nutrition services, environmental services, biomedical engineering and laundry services.

2000–2014

The introduction of new and expanded electronic security technology had a very positive impact on protection programs. At the same time, it introduced a host of new and changing security risks and the need for security master planning. The integration of physical security elements of protection and the concept of convergence reshaped the working interrelationship of security and information technology. Convergence led to the concept of enterprise risk management, which continues to develop and will continue to be a major linkage in protecting the healthcare environment.

The mission and goals of security and those of safety became more distinct and separate as both disciplines continued to grow and mature. This distinction of roles and the growing importance of each have apparently escaped the comprehension of TJC. In 2009, TJC combined safety and security standards into a single element of the Environment of Care.

The working relationship and the need for greater coordination and support between security and emergency management became quite clear in this 10-year time period. The events of 9/11 and Hurricane

Table 2-2 Summary of Changing Characteristics of U.S. Healthcare Security by Time Period

Period	Basic Changes/Characteristics of Healthcare Security
1900–1950	Primary duty was a fire watch as a function of maintenance and engineering.
1950–1960	A general law enforcement approach evolved.
1960–1975	The development of in-house security departments with expanded duties and responsibilities.
1975–1990	The security function was viewed as an integral part of management and the function became a valued component of the patient core team. Outsourcing of security increased.
1990–2000	Security continued to expand services while at the same time safety was generally separated into its own department. As risk management developed, security took on a greater role in prevention of incidents and improving emergency response capabilities. Somewhat in response to reduced police resources/response.
2000–2014	Increased patient-generated violence, terrorism concerns and organization demand for increased security services prevailed. New technology both aided security and created new and often complicated security risks. Increased violence and lack of mental healthcare resources created increased security support of patient care issues, downgrading overall protection levels.

Katrina each demonstrated important lessons for hospitals about organizational response and overall preparation for mass casualty events and the associated security risks. These coordinated efforts will continue to expand in the years ahead and the role of emergency management will continue to be a major component of the overall facility protection program.

During this period there has also been a growing challenge and concern with managing patient-generated violence. There has been unprecedented utilization of security staff resources, along with a need to offer hospital staff training programs focused on the management of aggressive behavior. This utilization occurs primarily in the emergency department due in large part to the reduction of funding and subsequent lack of medical care resources for the treatment of mental health patients.

This period has seen a significant reduction of armed security officers inside healthcare with an influx of Tasers® introduced in the environment as a force continuum tool that is more risk appropriate for the healthcare environment. Table 2-2 provides a summary of the changing characteristics of U.S. healthcare security by time period.

Outside the U.S., the history of the healthcare security profession is not as well documented. In Canada, the functions developed in much the same manner as has been described in this section for the U.S. The evolution from night watchman, to fire warden, to front-line management of aggressive behavior occurred a decade or more after the U.S. experiences in most jurisdictions, but occurred nonetheless. In the last decade the move in most provinces to multifacility and multiprogram health systems, many of them enormous entities, has created a requirement for corporate security business leaders who can function effectively in these complex environments.

SECURITY, RISK MANAGEMENT, SAFETY

The security program is not a single stand-alone function that provides total protection for the healthcare organization. Virtually all departments and functions within the organization are expected, and do, contribute to the overall level of facility safety and security. The safety function and the risk management function are two primary contributors to the protection system. Security must interact with these functions on a day-to-day basis, providing a coordinated and supportive approach to the common goal of maintaining a safe environment.

SAFETY SERVICES

The equipment, processes, and procedures used to cure illness and treat injuries combine to create an environment requiring a high level of safety programming. There is an interrelationship between security and safety in that the goal of each is to prevent human suffering and avoid costs to the organization. Safety deals primarily with acts and conditions where there is generally no conscious rationale to do harm. On the other hand, the primary business of security deals with acts where there is a conscious decision or rationale to do harm. An example is fire. Safety is basically concerned with accidental fires, while security would be more directly concerned with the arson aspects of fires. Both security and safety play an important role in the prevention of fire, regardless of the cause. Security is expected to directly support the safety effort through accident investigations, hazard reporting, and the correction and/or reporting of unsafe acts.

The prevention of accidents is a primary objective of the safety efforts that requires identifying safety risks. While inspections are intended to identify risks, a good accident reporting system will supplement the inspection process.

Patient accident reporting is generally the responsibility of the caregiver as it clearly falls into the realm of patient care. Only in rare circumstances would security be called upon to conduct an investigation or to file a report in these cases. Examples of the need for security involvement could, however, include a suicide, attempted suicide, disappearance of a patient, a fire and when a patient accident occurs in a public area of a facility.

The investigation and reporting of staff accidents are generally the responsibility of department supervision. Security would become involved if the accident was severe and emergency response was required.

The reporting and investigation of visitor accidents is frequently neglected, despite the fact that the visitors are the source of many litigation proceedings against healthcare facilities. The basic problem appears to be that the responsibility for reporting visitor incidents is not as clearly defined as staff and patient accident reporting policies and procedures. Because it is everyone's responsibility, sometimes it is not accomplished. The investigation of all visitor accidents should be a security function responsibility.

In most healthcare organizations today, the safety functions are usually separated into staff safety, through an Occupational/Workplace Health program often embedded in human resources, and a Patient Safety function that may be situated in a medical administration portfolio.

RISK MANAGEMENT

The term *risk management* is relatively new compared with the term *security*, at least in the healthcare environment. Healthcare risk managers are a group of staff support personnel for healthcare provider organizations. Their role developed approximately 30 years ago as medical malpractice claims and patient safety became major concerns. The goal of risk management in the healthcare setting is to prevent patient injury and prevent or limit financial loss to the healthcare organization. Risk managers often spend a great deal of time dealing with contracts, equipment technology,

1 Security
2 Employee Health
3 Patient Safety
4 Employee Safety
5 Patient Representative
6 Infection Control
7 Disaster Program
8 Bio-Medical Instrumentation Testing
9 Insurance/Claims Management
10 Incident Reporting/ Review/Action
11 Environmental Safety (Including Fire)
12 Product Evaluation
13 Medical Audits
14 Contracts Evaluation

FIGURE 2-1

Typical components of risk management.

insurance administration, and problems involving potential or actual liability. It is thus not surprising to find that many risk managers have a background in law and/or clinical experience.

Components of risk management

Although it varies from organization to organization, a written statement of function, authority, and responsibility is absolutely essential to the effective functioning of a risk management program. The security effort should be considered an element of total organization risk management. Until recently, security rarely reported to risk management. However, many organizations have transitioned this reporting relationship with good success and outcomes. As shown in Figure 2-1, numerous elements can be integrated into a coordinated program.

DEVELOPING THE SECURITY SYSTEM

A healthcare security system is developed by applying security safeguards to manage the security vulnerability and risks identified by the organization. A safeguard is simply an element or component of the protection system. Safeguards can be viewed in two basic categories: physical safeguards and psychological safeguards.

Although one can differentiate between psychological and physical control, most physical controls also provide an element of psychological protection. A good example is night lighting. Just because a parking lot is well lit does not mean that it is more difficult for a crime to be committed there than in a poorly lit lot. The lighting itself is a physical control, and also functions as a psychological deterrent. The security camera or monitor cannot reach out to stop an incident or to catch a wrongdoer. It serves as a psychological deterrent, however, since wrongdoers, or potential wrongdoers, probably do not know the extent of the system. They might wonder who may be watching, what resources may be deployed, and whether a recording is translating the images into evidence. Table 2-3 lists some of the more common security safeguards.

Table 2-3 Common Physical and Psychological Security Safeguards

Psychological	Physical
Signage / Video Display Monitors	Security Officers
Visitor Badging / Sign-In Logs	Alarms
Marking / Labeling	Video Surveillance
Aggressive Incident Investigation	Glazing
Policy of Prosecution	Barriers
Conditions of Employment	Lighting
Enforced Disciplinary System	Safe / Containers
Greetings / Staff Acknowledgement	Access Controls
Way Finding & Guidance	Identification Badges
Landscape Design / Architecture	Emergency Communication Devices

PSYCHOLOGICAL DETERRENTS

Realizing that physical controls cannot protect all things in all places, professionals also use psychological deterrents, which are directed at the decision-making process of the individual. For the purposes of security planning a psychological deterrent is defined as an individual's interpretation of a situation in which the potential positive or negative aspects of behavior serve to prevent or preclude the expression of that behavior.

The fundamentals of Crime Prevention through Environmental Design (CPTED) follow these principles as they include using the physical environment and other aspects of design to manage behavior. The proper design and effective use of the built environment can lead to reduction in the incidence of and fear of crime, as well as affect the behavior of people by providing physiological and psychological deterrents.

SECURITY SAFEGUARDS RELATING TO THE INDIVIDUAL DECISION-MAKING PROCESS

Conditions of employment

In many organizations an applicant must sign a form titled "Security Conditions of Employment." These conditions are generally aspects of security policy that are highlighted to establish an understanding between the applicant and the organization. Examples of these conditions include the organization's policies on employee identification badges, parking, locker inspections, package inspections, the use of personnel entrances, and others.

In the same programs these security rules and regulations are included in the employee handbook with other general personnel policies. Regardless of the method used to inform employees of an organization's policy, all employees should be required to complete a form that states that they have read and understand what is expected of them during their employment. This form becomes a permanent part of the employee's personnel record.

New employee orientation

The security portion of an orientation for new employees serves several purposes, one of which is to psychologically create an image of protection. New employees who begin their jobs with the understanding that the organization takes its protection responsibility seriously will be less inclined to become involved in undesirable activity.

The security orientation should be presented in a positive fashion, stressing that the security system is provided for the welfare of the organization and the employees. It is also recommended that the presentation indicate the organization's clear position when staff or physicians become involved in security situations. This position should include the organization's policy on criminal prosecution and reflect a strict enforcement of the disciplinary system. The new employee orientation sets the stage for further security education, which must be carried out on a continuing basis.

SECURITY PATROLS

One of the primary purposes of security officer patrol is to prevent security incidents, both by physically preventing the act and by creating the image that the organization is properly protected. No part of a complex is too remote or too unimportant to receive unannounced patrols by security. Employees who are performing their assigned job, patients and legitimate visitors view the patrolling officers as a support service and derive a perception of added safety. Dishonest employees and illegitimate visitors will view the officer as an important reason to refrain from negative behavior. It is well recognized that as visible security patrols increase, the number of adverse incidents decrease.

Signs and notices have significant value as psychological deterrents. Almost everyone has seen and reacted to such community signs as "Beware of Dog" and "Radar Patrolled." Many security companies use a sign or decal to advertise their presence with the intent of deterring criminal activity. "Premises under Video Monitoring" and "Firearms Prohibited" are examples of signage utilized to deter wrongdoing. Many healthcare organizations have hung video display monitors at specific entrances and select waiting areas in lieu of signage. Most security administrators believe this tactic is a more effective psychological deterrent than signage, as people consciously look at camera monitors whereas they do not consciously read posted signage.

Employee lockers are sometimes receptacles for such items as stolen property, gambling equipment and data, drug abuse paraphernalia and contraband such as liquor or weapons. A conspicuous sign that indicates locker inspections are conducted, or one that offers a reward for information leading to the arrest and conviction of people responsible for theft or malicious destruction of property, is good advertising. This type of signage reinforces the protection image and can result in receiving good information from concerned staff.

FALSE SECURITY EXPECTATIONS

In applying psychological security deterrents there is a difference between inhibiting negative behavior and creating a false sense of security. In the former, the target is the potential perpetrator, and in the latter the focus is on the potential victims. Creating a false sense of security has legal ramifications. A false sense of security can be created in several different ways but generally involves physical security, signage, or written material that either is false or exaggerates the level of protection provided. Examples of false security are "dummy" video surveillance cameras and signs that claim there is a security patrol or electronic surveillance, when there is not. A false sense of security can occur when security safeguards are compromised or not implemented during a malfunction or temporary absence of a normal safeguard. An example of the latter is a parking lot that is normally protected by a chain link fence. If a section has been removed for construction, an additional safeguard must be implemented to equate with the protection normally in place and mitigate the risk caused by the absence of the safeguard.

Investigations

Incident investigation is a very real, tangible security activity that also has certain psychological deterrent ramifications. In some programs the investigation responsibility is taken lightly, with little or no follow-up, especially in the area of property losses. In some facilities a nurse or department supervisor prepares the loss report, which is forwarded to the administration, often with no further action. If the loss is due to an employee, the perpetrator sees no activity resulting from the crime. The organization conveys the message that it does not care, which makes it easier for the criminal to repeat the crime without inhibition and with little fear of the consequences. Also, in this ineffective system the nurse or supervisor may find it relatively easy to neglect to file a report of the incident because of the perception that nothing will be done.

All protection programs must provide an immediate field response to security incidents. In larger programs a security officer responds to the incident location; in smaller programs an administrative aide, maintenance worker, or nursing supervisor may respond. That someone in authority is concerned and asking questions about the incident is important. A follow-up inquiry is also important in many cases to bring the matter to a successful conclusion.

The objective of any incident investigation is to record the facts properly and to attempt to resolve the problem. One should not infer that making a show or going through the motions is the objective. Rather, the demonstration of security is a by-product of proper investigation, and it has positive effects on preventing incidents.

Each malefactor different

There is no question that each malefactor or wrongdoer is different. The system of physical security and psychological deterrence in the healthcare setting is intended to prevent as many negative acts as possible. The security fence cannot be built high enough to exclude or deter all those who wish to prey on healthcare organizations. How high to build the "fence" in a particular organization is a management decision based largely on the value or importance that the organization places on security and its risk tolerance.

BASIC SECURITY PROGRAM OBJECTIVES

Basic objectives of the healthcare security program can be viewed as:

- Contributing to the overall mission of the healthcare organization in the provision of excellent medical care services.
- Preventing security-related incidents through a proactive system of security safeguards.
- Responding to security incidents in such a manner that property damage or injury to persons is prevented or at least mitigated through competent timely actions.
- Creating a sense of confidence in the minds of staff, visitors and persons being served that they are in a reasonably safe and secure environment.
- Providing services and activities in a positive and effective manner that supports the goals and culture of the organization being served.

The planning and implementation of program elements to achieve these basic objectives are influenced by both internal and external forces.

INTERNAL FORCES

The internal forces of the healthcare organization will be the primary elements of the type, style, and ultimate effectiveness of the operating security system. The four major internal forces are the (1) organizational philosophy/culture, (2) leadership, (3) funding, and (4) corporate policy, each interacting with the others to shape the program.

Organization philosophy/culture

The philosophy and culture of the healthcare organization greatly influence the development and functioning of the security programs. Tradition, cultural factors related to the population being served, type of treatment programs offered, and open versus closed facilities are drivers linked to produce a somewhat unique environment for each individual healthcare organization. While virtually all healthcare treatment facilities strive to achieve market share and/or organizational reputation through an open, welcoming, and patient-centered environment, there is a trade-off in also providing a reasonable level of security and safety. An extremely open environment, which allows the public free and uncontrolled access to the facility, unduly endangers patients, staff and visitors.

Planetree, Inc. is a nonprofit membership organization founded in 1978 that facilitates the creation of patient-centered care in healing environments. The Planetree model has a patient-centered focus as opposed to a provider focus. This model recognizes, in part, facility architecture and design factors that are barrier free and encourage family participation in patient care and treatment. In principal, most would agree that the model makes good sense until the aspects of barrier free and inadequate control of public access become significant dangers. This danger can create an environment that falls below the standard of care in providing a reasonable and prudent level of safety and security for the healthcare environment stakeholders.

Leadership responsibility

The leadership of the healthcare organization from the board of directors downward through the chain of command ultimately determines the level and type of security program protecting the organization. The well-versed and professional director or manager of security can, however, greatly influence top leadership's perception of and commitment to an effective and productive security system. Conversely, the ill-informed, ill-prepared, and unqualified security administrator can greatly reduce top management's support through lack of credibility. In the same vein, the security administrator who may have sound and progressive ideas/plans must be able to effectively communicate with top management regarding the appropriateness of their recommendations in order to move forward. Sound rationale and a plan of implementation generally precede acceptance and program funding. The professional healthcare administrator will constantly strive to improve on business management skills as well as keep abreast of challenges and industry best practices in the field of healthcare security.

In a 2008 national survey relative to hospital security less than 20% of the respondents indicated that security was a top priority of upper management.[1] In many respects this extremely low percentage rating can be traced back to both insufficient development (education and training) of healthcare administrators in protection and a general lack of sufficient exposure of the healthcare administrator to the benefits afforded by a sophisticated security program. Whatever the reason, this lack of priority by healthcare organizations is not shared by patients, staff, or visitors who are counting on being safe and secure in "the healing environment."

Funding

There never seem to be sufficient budgeted funds to implement the healthcare security administrator's desired protection plan. Security budgets compete with clinical care budget requests which, from the onset, places security budget requests behind the curve. In most cases the budgeting process involves various elements of a return on investment (ROI) philosophy. The term ROI is quite often viewed in dollars and cents. Dollars often predominate over the less tangible ROI aspects of preventing incidents, mitigating damages when events occur, the quality and scope of services rendered, and the enhancement of community/staff reputation and good will. Security budgets should always be based on a valid justification of need and organizational risk tolerances.

Corporate Policy

Many hospitals have shifted from being a single, stand-alone type of organization to being an entity of a larger healthcare system. This change has been brought on by mergers, partnerships, government-driven initiatives and the sale of healthcare organizations. As a result of the changing governance of the individual healthcare organization the direction and philosophy of the security program is subject to degrees of change ranging from minor reorganization to complete transformation. While these changes are intended to have a positive effect on the security program of each single entity, that is not always the case. Too often a corporate policy or practice is formulated that works well for a member facility with certain characteristics but is ineffective, inefficient, and possibly a burden on a facility with different characteristics. Included in these different attributes would be type of health services being provided, population being served, size and location of the facility, crime demographics, and the level of public safety agency support.

Corporate direction and involvement with the individual facility security program will vary according to the management model put into place. These variations can range from minimal impact to a strong central control of policies, procedures, and philosophical approaches. Numerous corporate healthcare security system models are more fully discussed in Chapter 6, "Security Department Organization and Staffing." Box 2-1 outlines many of the external entities that influence the healthcare security program.

EXTERNAL FORCES

The internal forces influencing healthcare security programs previously discussed must be integrated into a host of external forces or entities such as those shown in Box 2-1. These entities are a mix of trade associations, regulatory agencies, accreditation bodies, and allied healthcare organizations, often with conflicting and inconsistent approaches and regulations relative to the security of healthcare organizations.

THE JOINT COMMISSION

The primary Joint Commission security standards are contained within the functional chapter entitled "Management of the Environment of Care" in the Security/Safety Management section.

As part of its Emergency Operations Plan requirements for hospitals, internal safety and security standards during an emergency are also found in the Emergency Management (EM) section. These

BOX 2-1 ORGANIZATIONS INFLUENCING HEALTHCARE SECURITY

External Entities that Influence the Healthcare Security Program

- The Joint Commission (TJC) / Joint Commission Resources
- National Center for Missing and Exploited Children (NCMEC)
- Occupational Safety and Health Administration (OSHA)
- Center for Medicaid and Medicare Services (CMS)
- International Association for Healthcare Security and Safety (IAHSS)
- ASIS International
- Emergency Nurses Association (ENA)
- Facility Guidelines Institute (FGI) – Guidelines for Design and Construction of Hospitals and Outpatient Facilities
- National Fire Protection Association (NFPA)
- State Health Departments
- Federal, State and Local legislation/ordinances
- National Health Service (United Kingdom)
- Accreditation Canada
- Australian Commission on Safety and Quality in Healthcare

include making advanced preparations, identifying the role of community security agencies (police, sheriff, National Guard) and coordinating their security activities during an emergency. The controlled entrance into and out of the facility, the movements of individuals within the facility, and the control of vehicles accessing the facility during an emergency are also addressed.

In addition, there are other standards that have a direct bearing on security in terms of action and compliance requirements. These standards are considered "whole house," applicable to all hospital staff, and are principally found in the chapters on Human Resources (HR), Leadership (LD), Improving Organization Performance Standards (PI), and Management of Information (IM). The healthcare security administrator must coordinate with other departments and functions to determine specific action items and compliance oversight regarding security standards.

In the area of security, this impact is, however, beginning to erode as The Joint Commission in 2009 combined the safety and security standards within the Management of the Environment of Care. This has not improved safety and security but served only to dilute the protection measures used to make our healing environments safe. The disciplines of safety and security should be separate to promote a safer and more secure environment. As the body of knowledge continues to evolve for each of these disciplines, the educational offerings available will remain separate. There are very few higher education institutions that combine these two disciplines in the same degree program.

In 2010, Sentinel Event Alert issue #45 (SEA 45) was issued on preventing violence in the healthcare setting. It specifically addresses assault, rape or homicide of patients and visitors as perpetrated by staff, visitors, other patients and intruders to the institution. The majority of SEA 45 is focused on traditional workplace violence scenarios and offers important foundational recommendations for healthcare facilities. However, the majority of violence to which healthcare is exposed today is patient-to-staff generated violence. We must protect our patients and SEA 45 has laid out a solid baseline for that. But what TJC apparently does not fully comprehend is the violence being perpetrated by patients against our care providers, security officers, and others who work in and around the emergency department.

Since the issuance of SEA 45, surveyors are placing greater emphasis on the issue of violence in healthcare, specifically the security risk assessment for determining the potential for violence and the response plan through the use of focused "violence" tracers.

The Joint Commission Resources (JCR) is the official publisher and educator of TJC. They work with healthcare organizations, ministries of health and governmental bodies around the world providing accreditation preparation and advocating for patient safety strategies in the areas of infection prevention, medication safety, and the environment of care.

References to the various TJC security standards will be made in the subsequent discussion on specific elements of the healthcare security program. Figure 2-2 provides an overview of how TJC Environment of Care standards have evolved since 1990.

NATIONAL CENTER FOR MISSING AND EXPLOITED CHILDREN

The National Center for Missing and Exploited Children (NCMEC) has been a resource for law enforcement and the healthcare industry on the topic of infant abductions since 1989. As the nation's clearinghouse on missing and exploited children, NCMEC maintains statistics regarding the number and location of infant abductions and provides technical assistance and training to healthcare and security personnel in an effort to prevent infant abductions from occurring in their facilities.[2]

The number of nonfamily infant (birth to 6 months) abductions from hospitals and birthing centers continues a downward trend. This reduction is due, in large part, to the efforts of the NCMEC. The work of John Rabun (former vice president and chief operating officer) and Cathy Nahirny (administrative manager of the Jimmy Rice Law Enforcement Training Center), along with staff of the NCMEC, has provided the tools and support to prevent and respond to infant abductions. It was not until the NCMEC started to study the problem of infant abductions, specifically from hospitals, that the extent of these incidents was known. Their study data began in 1983 and their research and tracking continues as an ongoing NCMEC program.

The NCMEC does not just study the problem but provides ongoing training and education about the prevention of and response to infant abductions, as well as being an instantly available resource to healthcare facilities and law enforcement agencies during and after an incident. The work of the NCMEC goes far beyond hospital abductions; however, for the purposes of this text, the focus is on nonfamily abductions within the healthcare delivery system. The delivery system involves some four million plus births each year in approximately 3,500 U.S. birthing facilities, with care continuing to a limited degree after discharge to the home environment. Hospital operated, or independent, home and public healthcare agencies frequently provide aftercare to mother and baby in the home. The healthcare security administrator must also be aware that there can be a certain degree of organizational responsibility for infant safety in the home after discharge from the hospital. In the event information, actions, or inactions on the part of the healthcare organization caused or contributed to a criminal act in the home, there could be certain legal ramifications.

OCCUPATIONAL SAFETY AND HEALTH ADMINISTRATION

Worker safety is the primary focus of the Occupational Safety and Health Administration (OSHA), in contrast to patient safety which is the focus of The Joint Commission. Under the Occupational Safety and Health Act of 1970, employers are responsible for providing a safe and healthy work place for their

The Joint Commission Environment of Care Time Line

1990–1992
Plant Technology and Safety Management, and Statement of Construction in existence

1993
Standards revised and reformatted
Plant Technology and Safety Management retitled as "Management of the Environment of Care," which includes:

- EC.1: Design
- EC.2: Teach/implement
- EC.3: Measure/assess
- EC.4: Other environmental considerations
- EC.5: Smoking

Statement of Construction retitled "Statement of Conditions"
Random unannounced surveys initiated

1996
Sentinel Event policy released

1999
Building Maintenance Program becomes available

Performance Standards become "Performance Monitoring"
Expanded testing of features of fire protection with National Fire Protection Association references

2001
Standards reformatted to include:

- EC.1: Planning
- EC.2: Implement/teach
- EC.3: Other environmental considerations
- EC.4: Monitor/improve

Worker safety reconfigured as separate standard
Smoking moved under safety standard
Environmental Protection Agency and Occupational Safety and Health Administration cited as examples of applicable law and regulation

Emergency Preparedness becomes "Emergency Management" and includes:

- Incident command
- Hazard vulnerability analysis
- Community integration

Airborne contaminants and waterborne pathogens added to utilities standard

Training issues consolidated to one standard

"Accreditation with Commendation" eliminated
Patient safety standards announced

2002
Emergency Management "clarifications" issued in response to 9/11

2003
Communitywide emergency drill added
Preconstruction Infection Control Risk Assessment added
First National Patient Safety Goals issued

2004
Complete revision and reorganization of standards, organized as:

- Planning and implementation
- Measuring and improving

New scoring system issued
Measures of success added
"Shared Visions-New Pathways" survey process introduced, including:

- Triennial survey and periodic performance review
- Tracer methodology
- Environment of Care Interview replaces Environment of Care Document Review
- Construction issued added to EC Interview
- Corrective action plan required in 90 days
- Requirements for improvement cutoffs added for accreditation decisions

Risk assessment emphasized
Workplace violence and infant abduction requirements added
Department of Transportation requirements added as applicable law and regulation footnote
Involvement of leadership and medical staff required in emergency management
2000 Life Safety Code adopted

2005
45 days for corrective action plan initiated
Scoring modifications issued
Addition of Life Safety Code Specialists to survey
Addition of competency requirements for person completing Statement of Conditions
Medical equipment maintenance based on life support and non-life support
Utilities maintenance based on life support, infection control support and non-life support

2006
All surveys unannounced
Emergency Management Observation added to survey
Identified observer added for emergency exercises
Changes to emergency exercise critique requirements

2007
Addition of validation surveys

2008
All hospitals surveyed by Life Safety Code Specialist

Hospitals over 750,000 square feet surveyed by Life Safety Code Specialist for two days

Total rewrite of emergency management requirements, including:

- Inventory issues
- Stand-alone capability
- Security issues
- Communications

2009
Total rewrite of all standards with emergency management and Life Safety Code compliance as separate chapters in accreditation manual
Combination of Safety and Security into one standard

FIGURE 2-2

TJC Environment of Care standards time line.

(Reprinted with permission from Health Facilities Management Magazine.*)*

employees. Although OSHA is a federal regulatory agency, individual states may create a state OSHA agency which, in general, must equal or exceed federal requirements. OSHA's stated role is to promote the safety and health of America's work force by setting and enforcing standards; providing training, outreach, and education; establishing partnerships; and encouraging continued process improvement in workplace safety and health. The vast resources of OSHA and its state partners include approximately 2,100 inspectors, plus discrimination complaint investigators, engineers, physicians, educators, standards writers and other technical and support personnel in over 200 offices.

The major impact of OSHA relative to security relates to workplace violence as it affects staff. An initial and primary document produced by OSHA is *Guidelines for Preventing Work Place Violence for Health Care and Social Service Workers* (OSHA 3148, 1996). The National Institute for Occupational Safety and Health (NIOSH) has published *Violence: Occupational Hazards in Hospitals*, April 2002, which is also a significant reference for the security practitioner.

There is a formal joint working relationship between OSHA and TJC. This relationship is defined in the OSHA and The Joint Commission/Joint Commission Resources Alliance.

CENTERS FOR MEDICARE AND MEDICAID SERVICES

The Centers for Medicare and Medicaid Services (CMS) impact on healthcare security more often than not is in relation to a major security event occurring in an approved provider facility. The ensuing investigation by CMS contracted staff (i.e., State Health Departments) in many cases results in surveyor interpretation/preference of the CMS standards/rules, which can have the effect of actually decreasing the overall protection level being provided for patient, visitor, and staff by the provider organization. Two examples bring this issue to the forefront. One example is found in the state of Pennsylvania, where state surveyors have strongly suggested that the use of Tasers and handcuffs by healthcare security personnel be forbidden. This demarcation by CMS surveyors does not even distinguish "appropriate" use or the use of such tools in nonpatient care settings. The second example is even more concerning, when a CMS inspector attempted to hold a Northfield (MN) City Hospital responsible for violating patient rights for the deployment of a Taser by the local police. The Minnesota Department of Health said the hospital failed to protect the patient. The Minnesota Hospital Association and other industry observers say that Northfield did nothing wrong. However, regulators say that the hospital should have been better prepared to deal with the violent patient. The authors agree with David Feinwachs from the Minnesota Hospital Association who questioned the logic of such absurdity: "To suggest somehow seeking the intervention of law enforcement is an impropriety on the part of a healthcare provider seems to be illogical. In case of bizarre circumstances, throw yourself in harm's way before you call the police."[3]

INTERNATIONAL ASSOCIATION FOR HEALTHCARE SECURITY AND SAFETY

The International Association for Healthcare Security and Safety (IAHSS) is the primary resource that shapes, designs, and affects the scope of practice in healthcare security. The Association was formed in 1968 as the International Association for Hospital Security and in 1990 changed to the International Association for Healthcare Security and Safety. It was incorporated in the State of Illinois in 1968 as a private, not-for-profit organization.

The first annual meeting of the Association was held in June 1968 at the New York Hilton. In addition to the business meeting there was a panel/attendee discussion on what security functions and

BOX 2-2 HOSPITAL SECURITY FUNCTIONS AS IDENTIFIED BY IAHSS IN 1968

Hospital Security Functions and Responsibilities in 1968

1) Uniformed patrols
2) Elevator operators
3) Information desk
4) Lost and found
5) Key control
6) Identification
7) Fingerprinting
8) Education of employees in safety and fire protection
9) Accident reports on hospital grounds
10) Manual of procedures
11) Disaster procedures
12) Training security officers
13) Alarm systems
14) Maintaining good relations with official police
15) Transportation
16) Decreased patient property

responsibilities were appropriate to a hospital security department. There was a consensus of those present that these responsibilities included those shown in Box 2-2, Hospital Security Functions and Responsibilities in 1968.[4]

This bit of history indicates how the field of healthcare security has changed over time, eliminating certain functions and maintaining certain functions, while adding new areas of responsibility.

The IAHSS has evolved into a major association with a sharply defined focus, which recognizes that the healthcare environment has unique security risks and vulnerabilities. There are currently over 2,000 members of the association working together to improve the management of healthcare security programs. While the accomplishments of IAHSS are many, the association is especially strong in its security officer training programs, the credentialing of management level personnel, and the development of Healthcare Security Guidelines and the more recently published Healthcare Security Design Guidelines.

In 2007, the Association introduced a new organizational structure to better align resources, including their strong voluntary leadership. Much of the original structure remains and includes a Council on Education; the Commission on Certification; a Council on Membership and Regional Leadership; and the Council on Guidelines.

The development of basic guidelines is the responsibility of an established association Council on Guidelines. This Council is comprised of members from various settings of the healthcare environment to include representation of large, small and university affiliated facilities, contract providers, and consultants. This Council also has international representation to ensure the broadest possible range of applicability for the work they produce.

The IAHSS Healthcare Security Guidelines are especially important to the forward movement of healthcare security. They provide a consensus approach to the basic fabric and direction of the structure of this emerging discipline, a discipline that is an essential element in the provision of excellence in patient care, regardless of facility size, geographic location, or patient demographics served.

The Preamble to the security guidelines provides an explanation of the purpose and detail regarding the application of the guidelines. The Association publishes an annual booklet containing the guidelines; however, as these guidelines are subject to continuous review and changes, the Association website contains the most current and up-to-date information.[5]

PREAMBLE

Healthcare Security: Basic Industry Guidelines

Healthcare Facilities (HCFs) and Healthcare Organizations (HCOs) are responsible for providing a safe and therapeutic environment while respecting the rights and privacy of those entrusted to their care. These guidelines are intended to assist healthcare administrators in fulfilling their obligation to provide a safe, secure and welcoming environment, while carrying out the mission of their healthcare organization.

Healthcare facility (HCF), for purposes of these guidelines, shall mean any facility used in providing healthcare service or treatment simultaneously to four or more patients;

- who may be primarily incapable of self-preservation due to physical or mental limitation; or
- who are undergoing treatment or testing which may temporarily render a patient incapable of taking effective action under emergency conditions without assistance from others.*

The statements and intents of these guidelines are designed to be applicable to all HCFs. It is recognized, however, that the actual implementation of these guidelines will vary from facility to facility—dependent upon, among other considerations, the nature, size and location of the facility; and the reasonably foreseeable risks to be protected against.

These guidelines support the need to comply with all national, state/provincial, county and local requirements and are intended to be in harmony with all regulatory, accreditation, and other healthcare professional association requirements and guidelines.

These guidelines are periodically reviewed by the IAHSS Guidelines Council. Changes, modifications and new guidelines are posted on the International Association for Healthcare Security and Safety (IAHSS) website, upon being approved by the IAHSS Board of Directors.

Comments and suggestions are encouraged and may be directed to the IAHSS Guidelines Task Force, P.O. Box 5038, Glendale Heights, IL 60139.

*National Fire Protection Association [NFPA] #730 – guide to Premises Security.

The IAHSS Healthcare Security Design Guidelines were developed by a Task Group from the Guidelines Council, along with industry design and system engineers and architects, and were completed in 2012. These guidelines, in contrast to the operationally focused Healthcare Security Guidelines, were created to assist security leaders, design professionals and planning staff build security into each new construction and renovation project.

ASIS INTERNATIONAL

ASIS International (formerly the American Society for Industrial Security), founded in 1955, is the world's largest organization for security professionals, with more than 38,000 members worldwide. This organization embraces virtually all aspects and environments of security through 29 professional interest councils. One of these councils is the Healthcare Security Council. The stated purpose of this

Council is to provide "credible resources and information on healthcare best practices and providing a forum for the exchange of information and expertise in all areas of healthcare security."[6]

Although not specific to healthcare security, ASIS International has developed a number of guidelines and standards that serve as a resource for the healthcare security practitioner. ASIS International is an accredited Standards Developing Organization conferred by the American National Standards Institute (ANSI). As such, ASIS International actively participates in international standard initiatives as a member of the International Organization for Standardization (ISO).

Security standards and guidelines that are currently available or pending committee action are:[7]

- Business Continuity Management Standard
- Chief Security Officer (CSO) Organizational Standard
- Conformity Assessment and Auditing Management Systems for Quality of Private Security Company Operations
- Management System for Quality of Private Security Company Operations – Requirements with Guidance
- Maturity Model for the Phased Implementation of a Quality Assurance Management System for Private Security Service Providers
- Maturity Model for the Phased Implementation of the Organizational Resilience Management System
- Organizational Resilience: Security, Preparedness and Continuity Management Systems – Requirements with Guidance for Use Standard
- Quality Assurance and Security Management for Private Security Companies Operating at Sea – Guidance
- Security Management Standard: Physical Asset Protection
- Workplace Violence Prevention and Intervention Standard

Although the standards and guidelines are not specific to healthcare security, they serve as a valuable information resource, at least in part, for adaptation to the healthcare sector.

NATIONAL FIRE PROTECTION ASSOCIATION

The National Fire Protection Association (NFPA) is an international, not-for-profit organization established in 1896 for the purpose of reducing the burden of fire and other hazards on the quality of life by providing and advocating consensus codes, standards, research, training and education as a trade association. Organizational membership totals more than 70,000 individuals around the world and more than 80 national trade and professional organizations. It is the world's leading advocate of fire prevention and an authoritative source on public safety. Their codes and standards are regularly adopted by licensing/regulatory/accreditation and public safety agencies that become the legal enforcement entity for such standards.

In terms of healthcare security, one of the most utilized NFPA codes is the Life Safety Code 101. It is this code adopted by most fire Authorities Having Jurisdiction (AHJ), Joint Commission, CMS, and licensing authorities that significantly impacts security systems, design, and operations.

In 2007, the Federal Emergency Management Agency (FEMA) and the Department of Homeland Security (DHS) issued a National Incident Management System (NIMS) alert that recommended private sector entities adopt the NFPA 1600 and NFPA 1561 standards as a means of complying with NIMS. With this in mind, the healthcare security administrator may be confused as to why NIMS is needed. It is important because, when a disaster or emergency strikes a healthcare facility, the responsible personnel must know how the incident command system works. NFPA 1561 defines the structure(s) and responsibilities of the organizational incident command.

The NFPA has published NFPA 730, Guide for Premises Security, 2011 edition. In this document Chapter 12 is titled "Health Care Facilities." The information contained in the two pages devoted to healthcare in this 82-page document is very general and in some cases not always practical. As an example, Section 12.4.4.5(E) states, "Burglar alarms, fire alarms, and video surveillance systems should be monitored at a central station console that is constantly manned." This standard would not only be impractical but cost prohibitive, and virtually impossible for a small healthcare facility that does not even maintain a security force.

FACILITY GUIDELINES INSTITUTE

The Facility Guidelines Institute (FGI) Guidelines for Design and Construction of Health Care Facilities began as General Standards published in the *Federal Register* on February 14, 1947. Updated periodically, the document only covered the design and construction of hospitals until nursing homes were added in the 1980s. FGI was founded in 1998 to formalize the revision process and ensure the Guidelines are reviewed and revised on a regular cycle with a consensus process carried out by a multidisciplinary group of experts. Beginning with the 2014 edition of the *Guidelines for Design and Construction of Health Care Facilities*, FGI will publish two standards: one for hospital and outpatient facilities and one for residential health, care, and related support facilities. The Joint Commission, many federal agencies, and authorities in 42 states use the Guidelines either as a code or a reference standard when reviewing, approving and financing plans; surveying, licensing, certifying, or accrediting newly constructed facilities; or developing their own codes.[8]

The 2014 edition marks the first time security standards have been included in the Guidelines. FGI has accepted the IAHSS Healthcare Security Design Guidelines and incorporated them into the Guidelines for hospitals. Additionally, two healthcare security experts have been invited by the FGI to join the Healthcare Guidelines Revision Committee—Kevin Tuohey from Boston University Medical Center and Tom Smith from the University of North Carolina Hospitals. These two accomplishments are important to the healthcare security industry as they provide a greater voice in the decisions that are shaping the future of healthcare.

The Association of Healthcare Research and Quality (AHRQ) is promoting the FGI Guidelines with the creation of an online Safety Risk Assessment (SRA) toolkit to support the facility design process. The SRA will be available in early 2015. A specific security workgroup has been established to develop white papers and guidelines to support the use of the SRA and to detail the process for implementing it across the facility life cycle as well as create an educational platform to promulgate successful SRA activities.

STATE HEALTH DEPARTMENTS/LEGISLATION/ORDINANCES

Virtually all states in the U.S. and most other countries' political/government subdivisions have entities that license or oversee healthcare services. A role of state health departments that bears directly on healthcare security is that of licensing and contracting with CMS for certain services. These services include follow-up inspections and investigatory activity. As with any regulatory or quasi-regulatory authority, new and changing license requirements can emanate from crisis situations or incidents.

Directed changes in license requirements, often with short turnaround times, are a result of this reactionary investigative activity.

California hospitals are required to meet additional security requirements to improve security in emergency rooms, as revisions to Assembly Bill (AB) 1083 were enacted by the state legislature beginning July 1, 2010. Under the terms of the revised law, hospitals in the state are required to annually review and update their security and safety assessment plans to help ensure patients and workers do not become victims of acts of aggression and violence while inside the healthcare facility. Additional changes require updates to the training of security personnel, greater cooperation with local law enforcement and consultation with employees and their unions. Further, AB1083 requires that security personnel receive eight hours of hospital-specific training prior to assignment at the facility.

The passage of the federal law Patient Safety and Quality Improvement Act of 2005 has resulted in numerous healthcare reporting systems at both state and federal levels mandating the reporting of healthcare errors relating to patient safety.

The National Quality Forum (NQF) has been a leader in establishing a list of the types of healthcare errors that need to be reported and evaluated since 2002. The NQF publication "Serious Reportable Events in Healthcare—2011 Update: A Consensus Report,"[9] identifies 28 adverse events that are serious, largely preventable, and of concern to healthcare providers, consumers, and all stakeholders, and 12 new events are being considered. Events are grouped into six categories. The two categories of direct interest and general involvement of security are:

Patient Protection Events

1) Discharge or release of a patient/resident of any age, who is unable to make decisions, to other than an authorized person; i.e., infant discharged to wrong person.
2) Patient death or serious disability associated with patient elopement (disappearance).
3) Patient suicide, or attempted suicide, or self-harm that results in serious injury, while being cared for in a healthcare facility.

Potential Criminal Events

1) Any instance of care ordered, or ordered by, someone impersonating a physician, nurse, pharmacist, or other licensed healthcare provider.
2) Abduction of a patient/resident of any age.
3) Sexual abuse/assault on a patient or staff member within or on the grounds of a healthcare facility.
4) Death or serious injury of a patient or staff member resulting from a physical assault (i.e., battery) that occurs within or on the grounds of a healthcare facility.

In addition to being knowledgeable of federal and state legislation affecting healthcare security, the security practitioner must consider any local laws or ordinances. As an example, some municipalities have enacted ordinances relative to the provision of security in parking facilities.

In summary, it is the responsibility of the healthcare security administrator/practitioner to diligently research such laws and ordinances that may affect the provision of security services for the healthcare organization.

EXTERNAL INFLUENCING AGENCIES (NON-U.S.)

Outside of the United States, there are legislative provisions, accrediting organizations, and licensing entities that influence healthcare security in their respective countries, such as in the United Kingdom, Canada and Australia.

United kingdom

In 2003, the National Health Service (NHS) in the United Kingdom, now called NHS Protect created the Security Management Service and provided them with legislated authority over all healthcare security issues across the NHS in England—the first time a dedicated organization has had such a charge. This includes:

1) Protecting NHS staff from violence and abuse.
2) Taking appropriate action against those who abuse, or attempt to abuse, NHS staff.
3) Helping to ensure the security of property, facilities, equipment and other resources such as drugs.
4) Defining operational structure for security management.

The remit of the NHS Security Management Service extends to the protection of all NHS resources—which include staff, facilities, equipment, drugs and even items such as the radioactive materials used in some operations.

The Care Quality Commission was established by the Department of Health of the United Kingdom to promote and drive improvement in the quality of healthcare and public health in England and Wales. Independent of the NHS, the Care Quality Commission is an independent regulator of health and social care in England.

Canada

If The Joint Commission is viewed as perhaps the key external influence on healthcare security in the United States and the Security Management Service conceded as the centralized national authority in this area in the United Kingdom, it is important to view Canadian healthcare security through a different lens, one where there are a number of local, provincial and federal bodies influencing policy and practice.

Like most countries, Canada has regulatory requirements around many professional and specialized fields in healthcare that can impact on the healthcare security profession—narcotic control measures and protection of radioactive materials as relevant examples. Canada is not unique in that building and fire codes exert significant regulatory influence over designing healthcare facilities for security and in healthcare staff training in preventing and responding to emergency events such as fire alarms.

However, if we look for standards and regulation around healthcare security in the Canadian milieu we discover a patchwork of provincial and local health jurisdiction initiatives, both formal and informal, that serve to loosely govern and influence the healing environment. With respect to established standards for training security personnel in Canada, including healthcare security personnel, a growing trend is found, from province to province, toward training and licensing requirements that can be viewed as an inexorable march toward professionalizing the industry. However, these standards differ from province to province and are managed and monitored by provincial bodies in each jurisdiction. It is often left to healthcare organizations and/or private security companies to build on these baseline standards to manage the complexities that confront security personnel in healthcare.

Accreditation Canada, the healthcare accreditation body for the Canadian healthcare industry, is relatively silent in the application of standards for healthcare security. Unlike The Joint Commission, which applies rigorous standards in a defined review process, there are no Canadian requirements for Security Management Plans, as an example, and security programs are not evaluated on their own but rather as a component of a broader review such as patient/client safety or emergency response capacity. While the fire safety and emergency management disciplines have well-defined standards to address through the Accreditation Canada process, the security function does not. However, just as there is a clear Canadian trend toward mandatory training and licensing requirements for security personnel, there is also a movement within some Canadian healthcare entities to ensure the development of a professional program that would meet Joint Commission-like standards should the Canadian process evolve in that direction. The IAHSS Healthcare Security Guidelines are a good example of a tool available to Canadian healthcare security program leaders to support a move in this direction.

According to Jeffery Young, Executive Director of Integrated Protection Services for four health entities and 27 hospitals and more than 300 community sites in the Vancouver area of British Columbia, there are indeed regulatory and nonregulatory bodies that yield significant influence on the Canadian healthcare security industry. The Worker's Compensation Boards of Canada influence the risk assessment processes and the ability of an organization to respond to aggression in healthcare, as an example. This, in turn will impact areas such as security design, training and even security staffing levels in some cases. It can be argued that healthcare unions—and in particular nurses unions in Canada—play a significant role in shaping safety and security measures and, by extension, the healthcare security programs in many jurisdictions. The unions have been successful, in some provinces, in negotiating provisions in their collective agreements that influence healthcare security policy and practice. This involvement can include the development of policy and protocol around "flagging" potentially violent persons, on the practice of police laying charges against those who assault staff and even exerting influence on the design of secure environments in Canadian hospitals. In British Columbia this has resulted in the development, and in 2012 the implementation, of a joint provincial comprehensive violence prevention curriculum, developed by healthcare employer and union representatives along with industry experts.

So, while there is no single influencing body in Canada as there is in the US and the UK, it should be clear there are a number of governmental and nongovernmental agencies that yield considerable influence over the healthcare security industry in Canada.

Australia

The Australian Commission on Safety and Quality in Healthcare was established on January 1, 2006 by Australian Health Ministers to develop a national strategic framework to improve safety and quality across the healthcare system in Australia. The Commission's role is to lead, coordinate, and monitor improvements in the safety and quality of patient care. The Commission takes on educational and standards setting role as it disseminates knowledge and advocates for safety and quality. Like the TJC, the Commission has specific standards and reports on sentinel events occurring in Australian hospitals.

BODY OF KNOWLEDGE

All disciplines, including healthcare security, develop a "body of knowledge" over time. One of the basic criteria for a defined profession is a body of knowledge that is generally accepted by the majority of persons operating within a specific discipline. There is a difference between the term profession and the term professional. While the healthcare security discipline may not yet have all the ingredients of a true profession, it should be the practitioner's goal to act in a professional manner. In this respect the healthcare security practitioner must maintain a current "working knowledge" of the general principles of healthcare security. A display of professional conduct by practitioners is a precursor to achieving a professional discipline that is accepted as such by the general population.

DEVELOPING "THE KNOWLEDGE"

The development of the vast body of knowledge in healthcare security has gradually taken place on both a formal and informal basis. This development of information defines and shapes the accepted concepts of today's successful security program. Commonly accepted principles evolve which become generally accepted by persons both within and outside the discipline. The healthcare security discipline has been building a body of knowledge for several centuries, with its roots well established in England. This healthcare body of knowledge has changed dramatically during its life and occasionally makes strange twists and turns.

An example of a dramatic change for healthcare security occurred in about the middle of the last century. At that point in time healthcare security was primarily viewed as a law enforcement function operating somewhat outside the sphere of the healthcare delivery system. Over a short period of time, in the mid-to-late 1960s, healthcare security became integrated into the healthcare delivery system, becoming an important stakeholder within the "healthcare team." Today security, in virtually all disciplines, is viewed as an important function and is only generally associated with the criminal justice aspects of years gone by.[10]

ACCESSING "THE KNOWLEDGE"

Where does one find this body of knowledge? It is found in the literature, in the classroom, at seminars and workshops, in litigation proceedings, in accreditation/regulatory requirements, in healthcare security departments, and in the minds of healthcare security practitioners. All this accumulated knowledge is subjected to interpretation and evaluation leading to a general consensus within the discipline. This knowledge is then loosely translated into basic elements. These elements are then transformed, and more precisely viewed, as ***industry standard practices***, ***best practices***, and a ***standard of care***. These three terms are distinct, and different, yet have a linkage or relationship to each other. Their definitions and meanings help us in "organizing" our healthcare security body of knowledge.

Industry standard practice

An *industry standard practice* (ISP) is an operational plan or activity that is common to healthcare security operations as a basic concept or premise. As such the implementation of the ISP may vary in detail unique to an individual facility or organization but will generally produce, or is intended to yield, a common outcome. An example of a healthcare industry standard practice is to provide designated security officer coverage in the hospital setting. This practice is applicable to most hospitals; however, it should be noted that some very small facilities located in rural areas, or in very low crime areas, may not need the services of designated security officer coverage. They do, however, need to have a plan for security and especially a plan for response to security critical incidents. Another ISP is the training and education of all facility staff. Staff must be trained in the basics of organizational security and their individual responsibility in support of the overall security program.

Industry security practices may emanate from outside sources such as accreditation/regulatory organizations (i.e., CMS, OSHA, TJC, State Health Departments) and resource organizations that have developed information with relevancy to healthcare security (i.e., NCMEC, NFPA, ASIS, IAHSS). The NCMEC efforts in regard to infant abductions is a good example of how an outside resource can shape an industry standard practice and even relate directly to a standard of care. Their publication, *For Healthcare Professionals: Guidelines on Prevention of and Response to Infant Abduction*, ninth edition, 2009, in effect sets a nationally recognized healthcare security standard.[11] The support of the "guidelines" by various organizations, as shown on the cover of this document, provides a strong consensus of agreement in this very important area of healthcare security. It is perhaps one of the most "prescriptive" of our industry standard practices which has *de facto* transitioned into a basic standard of care involving hospital infant security.

Best practice

A *security best practice* is an act, procedure, or operational activity that tends to validate its worth (merit, value, useful) with demonstrated repetition. A best practice is often associated with a practice that is utilized in the majority of protection programs; however, in fact, this should not be the sole evaluative criterion. The term "benchmarking" should not be viewed as having the same meaning as "best practice." In many instances benchmarking merely means a comparison of statistics which produce interesting data but does not correlate to a best practice. On the other hand, an example of a healthcare security best practice is the manner in which security officers are attired. It is generally accepted that a standard security/police uniform (uniform vs. soft clothes) is an industry best practice. In this case the majority of healthcare security officers are uniformed in traditional military style attire in over 90% of our nation's healthcare security programs. This practice has met the test of value and usefulness over time.

Another example of a security best practice is the picture identification type of badge to be worn by healthcare staff. It is a healthcare standard (both security and clinical care provider requirement) that staff be properly identified. In complying with this standard a color photograph of the person, position, and proper display of an identification badge has become a security and business best practice.

There is a direct linkage between the security industry standard practice and organizational best practice. Not all best security industry practices involve just security personnel alone. They can, and will, often involve other organizational staff. The eloped (missing) patient provides a clear illustration of this point. One of the standards of care in terms of a missing patient is to conduct a timely and thorough search. An industry standard practice is to involve general staff as well as security personnel. The best practice is to have assigned areas of search. A basic practice is to have security and/or maintenance personnel begin their search of the perimeter of the facility and work inward while clinical and other staff conduct the internal search moving outward.

WHAT ARE STANDARDS?

Standards are voluntary, or legally mandated, guidelines and best practices that improve the quality and consistency of goods and services. They provide predictable action and reactions as well as provide direction and control of security operations in managing both manmade and natural security risks and vulnerabilities. Standards are essential in advancing the discipline of "healthcare security" toward the goal of stakeholder understanding and participative support in the long road to a professionally established status.

National standard of care

The term *standard of care*, in relation to security, refers to the protection level in place under the conditions of the specific security risk at any given point in time. The security standard of care is a level of protection in place in terms of being reasonable and prudent in view of all circumstances. The term *standard of care* is often referred to when an event has taken place; however, its meaning and application are not limited to an event. As we are aware, the level of protection provided by the healthcare organization is dynamic in that it flexes between meeting the standard of care for the referenced risk and falling below the standard of care. There are endless examples that illustrate this flex concept: for example, locking hospital nursery doors at all times and equipping with self-closing (latching) devices to meet the security standard of care. For sake of discussion, let us assume that one morning it was discovered that the self-closing device was not functioning properly (this is often referred to as an "engineering failure" by some). At this point in time the security standard of care is breached and the level of protection does not meet the acceptable standard of care. Short of immediate repair of the device, the meeting of the standard of care could be restored by implementing a new (generally temporary) security safeguard that provides protection that meets or exceeds that of the failed safeguard. In this illustration a person, unit staff or security officer, could be assigned to monitor door activity until equipment repair is accomplished to maintain an acceptable standard of care.

Standard of care—organization specific

In addition to the national security standard of care, a healthcare facility (or system) will often develop a protection system that, in part, exceeds that of the national standard. This situation develops as we often ascribe to the adage that "more security is better." In all probability it does however; raise "the bar" in terms of the security standard of care for a specific organization.

Common goals

It is not uncommon that regulatory, legislative or local fire department edicts conflict with established security standards of care. These situations must be addressed with all parties to find a workable solution to these conflicts of interpretation. An example of such a conflict was experienced by a hospital in a Chicago suburb. The Village Board enacted an ordinance mandating that interior stairwell doors be unlocked in buildings taller than four stories. The hospital (nine stories) could not comply with the ordinance and still meet the security standard of care regarding such areas as labor and delivery, pediatrics, and a closed psychiatric unit. The ordinance was passed as a "knee-jerk" reaction to a fire in another community. Later the Village Board enacted an ordinance that allowed specific stairwell doors of the hospital to be locked but stipulated that in the event of a fire alarm activation, the doors would be electrically unlocked. While these conflicts do occur with a certain frequency, both security and safety entities must have the common goal to prevent property loss, injury and deaths with good faith problem resolution which can result in meeting the security standard of care.

REFERENCES

1. Weonik R. *Securing our hospitals: GE security and IAHSS healthcare benchmarking study*. Presented at International Association for Healthcare Security and Safety Mid-Winter Meeting and Seminar; 2008, January 21.
2. Infant abductions. *National Center for Missing and Exploited Children website*. 2013. Retrieved November 2, 2013, from http://www.missingkids.com/InfantAbduction.
3. Butler Alan B, York Tony W. *Emergency Department Violence: Healthcare's Everyday Threat*. Webcast presentation; 2010, November 10. HCPro.
4. Annual meeting held in New York. *International Association for Hospital Security Newsletter* 1968, September;**1**(1):1.

5. International Association for Healthcare Security and Safety (2014). Website available at https://www.IAHSS.org.
6. ASIS International. *Healthcare Security Council*. 2013. Retrieved November 3, 2013. https://www.asisonline.org/Membership/Member-Center/Councils/hcs/Pages/default.aspx.
7. ASIS International. *Standards & Guidelines*. 2013. Retrieved November 3, 2013. https://www.asisonline.org/Standards-Guidelines/Pages/default.aspx.
8. Facility Guidelines Institute. *Guidelines for Design and Construction of Health Care Facilities*. 2013. Available from http://www.fgiguidelines.org/. Retrieved November 3, 2013.
9. National Quality Forum. *Serious reportable events in healthcare 2011*. 2007, March. Available from http://www.qualityforum.org/Publications/2011/12/Serious_Reportable_Events_in_Healthcare_2011.aspx. Retrieved November 3, 2013.
10. James R. Higher education and security management. *Security Products* 2004, January;**8**.
11. National Center for Missing and Exploited Children. *For healthcare professionals: Guidelines on prevention of and response to infant abduction*. 9th ed. 2009. Retrieved June 13, 2009 from. http://www.missingkids.com/en_US/publications/NC05.pdf.

CHAPTER

HEALTHCARE SECURITY RISKS AND VULNERABILITIES 3

The foundation of a healthcare organization protection system is the identification and assessment of the types of threats and the degree (impact) of damage if the threat becomes an actual occurrence. Damage includes the impairment of the usefulness of property and the interruption to the business of delivering care, including destruction, loss and personal injury including death. Threats may be natural disasters or manmade actions such as accidental incidents or criminal actions. When a threat progresses to an actual event, the organization's viability is diminished in varying degrees, depending on the magnitude and seriousness of the resulting damage.

The terms *threat*, *risk*, and *vulnerability*, in the context of healthcare security, are often used somewhat interchangeably, just as the terms *policy* and *procedure* are more often than not treated as being the same. On close examination, however, each term has a specific and different definition. The important fact is that threats, risks, and vulnerabilities need to be identified and measured in terms of degree of probability and the degree of impact on the organization. Appropriate security safeguards must be developed to manage (prevent or mitigate) damage to the organization's property and establish an acceptable level of personal safety of the stakeholders.

The term *hazard vulnerability analysis* (HVA) is frequently referred to in the management of healthcare organizations. This term includes security vulnerabilities as a subsection of the broader, more inclusive, "all-hazards" approach considered a part of the risk management or emergency management responsibility. The healthcare organization utilizes the HVA as a basis for defining the preparedness and mitigation activities that will mobilize and manage essential resources. For the purposes of this text, the term *risk* will be utilized to describe the type of risks, which are typically event driven, such as theft, assault, abduction, vandalism, fire, flood and other natural disasters. The latter events are sometimes more appropriately evaluated and managed under the emergency management function while the potential manmade events or criminal acts are more directly the responsibility of the security program. In this chapter the focus will be on the criminal or security type of event.

Once the types of security risk are identified, they must be evaluated in terms of the probability of their occurrence. The probability of occurrence of a specific security risk may vary significantly when viewed in terms of facility location. As an example a food and nutrition cashier in the cafeteria, during a high-traffic lunch period, would be less likely to be assaulted than a female laboratory technician working alone at night in a remote location, or the surgical nurse going to a vehicle after an exhaustively long surgery in the middle of the night. Security risks should not only be evaluated in terms of probability but also in terms of the consequences or the degree of damage that may result from such an occurrence.

A properly conducted security assessment of the organization is essential in identifying security exposures in a methodical manner. The security system must be based on a valid analysis rather than be event-driven or a response to a singular security event. Security incidents do, however, provide important "lessons learned" and are helpful in determining the need for modifying the protection system.

BASIC HEALTHCARE SECURITY RISKS/VULNERABILITIES

All healthcare facilities, regardless of size, are exposed to basic security risks. These risks have been grouped into some 21 major categories for the purposes of this text. The magnitude of each risk category, which varies to a considerable degree from facility to facility, determines the threat to the organization. The risks identified in Figure 3-1 must be individually assessed by each facility. These risks can be viewed as primary security risks while acknowledging that there are also safety risks involved with the security program.

PRIMARY SECURITY RISKS

Healthcare organizations have their own set of security risks inherent in securing a patient care facility. The following defined risks are found in most healthcare facilities. The risk levels will, however, vary according to the unique operating environment of the organization.

ASSAULTS

An assault is the unlawful intentional inflicting, or attempted or threatened inflicting, of injury upon another.

All healthcare facilities face the multifaceted and extremely acute problem of assaults to patients, staff and visitors. The risk of assault for purposes of this category can be viewed in terms of simple assault or aggravated assault which includes sexual assaults. The simple assault involves the threatening of injury to another while the term aggravated assault refers to the actual striking or touching of another with the intent to inflict serious injury or harm. Assaults can take place inside facilities and on the grounds. Incidents range from simple threats to rape. Serious assaults get immediate attention by organizational leadership and can account for a large number of security-related lawsuits against healthcare facilities.

Patients are particularly at risk to attack due to their physical and mental condition as well as their level of accessibility. A person would never check into a hotel and go to sleep at night with the room door open, yet hospital patients do it every day. Aggravating this risk is the added challenge that many patients are sick or injured and less able to protect themselves. The patient is at risk of assault by another patient, a visitor, or even the legitimate caregiver charged with rendering care to the patient. The caregiver is responsible for the majority of assaults against hospital in-patients, particularly in the area of sexual assault. These incidents run the gamut of fondling of a patient in the dentist chair to the reported rapes of patients in a recovery room by a recovery room nurse. Nursing home patients are also at risk relative to rough handling (assaults) and sexual assaults. In 2012, a Toronto nursing-home worker was convicted of sexually assaulting a 71-year-old female resident who was suffering from severe dementia.[1]

A 17-year-old was charged in 2011 with sexual assault after a patient at the University of Michigan's C.S. Mott Children's Hospital reported that she was attacked. The victim had been hospitalized with multiple traumatic injuries but was coherent during the assault.[2]

Assaults are not limited to high-risk, high-crime communities and hospitals. A Salina, Kansas man was arrested and charged with the rape of an elderly patient at Salina Regional Health Center.

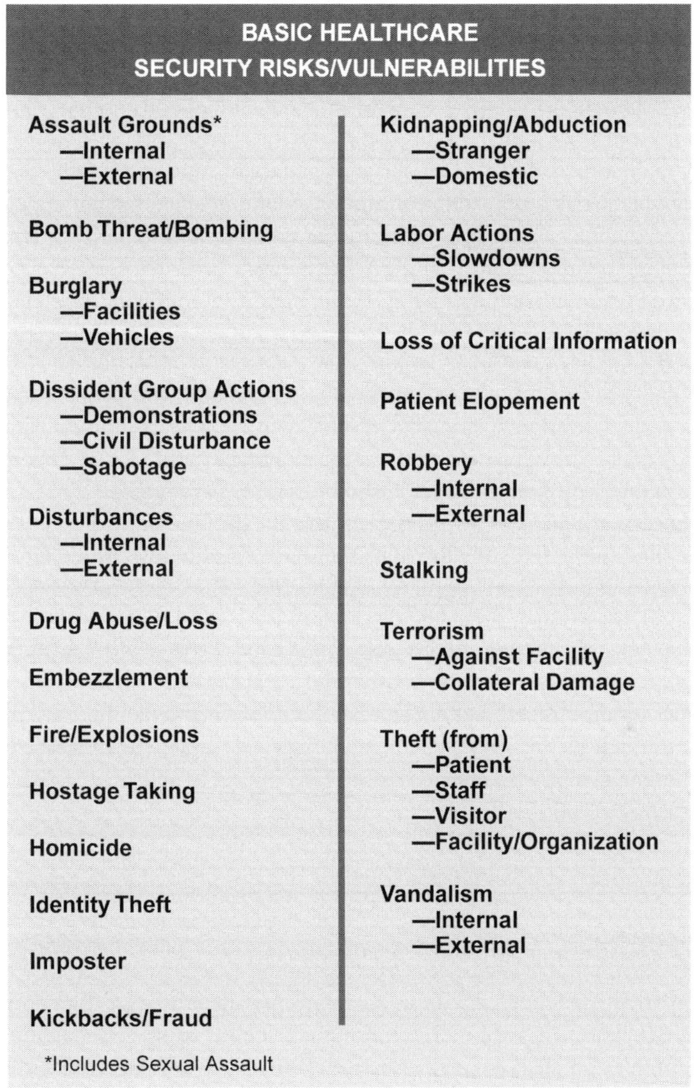

FIGURE 3-1

Basic healthcare security risks and vulnerabilities.

A nurse found the man, who came off of the street, in the room when she was checking on patients. The nurse and other hospital employees were able to subdue the perpetrator and held him until police arrived.[3]

It is not always the patient who is the victim of assault. Healthcare staff and visitors are also at risk. Examples include a nurse who was pulled from a stairwell in a construction area and raped, and a visitor sexually assaulted in a parking structure.

Although sexual assaults command the most attention, other assaults occur. These include assaults between patients and staff, between staff and visitors, and among family members.

Hospital emergency departments, intensive care units and behavioral health treatment areas are frequently the scenes of assaults to staff. Within the hospital, nurses and ancillary staff often work alone at night in remote areas or have a need to travel through these types of areas. Some nursing units may have only two staff members on duty. When one staff member is absent from the unit on an errand or a break, the other may be at risk. In a south Florida hospital a hospice patient appeared at the nursing station and beat the two nurses on duty so severely that both required lengthy in-patient medical treatment. Patient-generated assaults against care providers are a growing concern and are addressed in detail in Chapter 20, "Preventing and Managing Healthcare Aggression and Violence."

The assault problem is also evident outside the facility. The facility grounds, parking facilities, and streets surrounding the facility may offer opportunities for assaults to occur. Healthcare organizations can experience difficulty in recruiting staff for the evening and night shifts because of the security risk to staff. It is not uncommon for organizations to provide patrols on nearby streets, and many offer escort services to bus stops and nearby residential areas for employees and visitors. Escorts walk people to their destination or in many programs a vehicle shuttle service is provided.

The home healthcare provider is also at risk of assault. In most cases home healthcare providers work alone and can find themselves in situations that have resulted in serious injury and even death. Such was the case when Waneta Boatwright, a home healthcare nurse, went to a rural Kansas home to provide care for an elderly woman. What she discovered were two bodies on the floor. She dialed 911 but the call was disconnected. Arriving authorities found the 23-year-old son in the house. The two deceased victims were on the floor and the visiting nurse care provider had also been shot and killed. The son pulled a gun on the officers but was arrested without incident.[4] In 2009 the National Health Service in the UK, through its Security Management Service, implemented a program to protect lone workers, including home health workers, across the UK, in part to address the risk of assault to home caregivers.

BOMB THREATS

The use of an explosive or incendiary device with willful disregard for the risk to persons or property.

Bomb threats involving healthcare facilities are not as prevalent today as they were in the late 1960s and 1970s. The risk, however, is very real, requiring constant readiness in dealing with this security problem area. The motives for such threats range from revenge, to the excitement of causing trouble, to labor unrest and disgruntled employees. An escaped inmate in Alabama, as an example, caused the evacuation of three medical facilities in that state in 2013 when he called in a bomb threat and authorities believed he might have terrorist links.

Despite the number of bomb threat calls, seldom are two calls exactly alike. Each call must be treated as though it were genuine. Action to be taken as the result of a bomb threat must be based on preplanning and the nature of the information received, as occurred at the Baldwin Area Medical Center in Wisconsin. The hospital administrator received a bomb threat on his direct telephone line. The caller said "bomb 20 minutes." All nonessential personnel were evacuated from the facility; however, patients were kept in the hospital as well as necessary staff to care for them.[6] What made this threat somewhat unique was the specified time frame.

While most bomb threats are received by telephone, that is not always the case. In November 2008 the Sudbury Regional Hospital in Sudbury, Ontario, Canada received a written bomb threat and decided to go public with the information for the first time, although this was not the first time the hospital had received a bomb threat. Security officers were deployed to greet visitors with a prepared written script explaining the threat and that security had been heightened. All patients, staff, physicians and volunteers were also advised of the situation. This allowed for various appointments and routines to be changed if necessary; however, the hospital continued to conduct business as usual.[7]

In a stark example of how universal the bomb threat phenomenon is in healthcare, a June, 2013 bomb threat in Poland was deemed so credible by authorities that 21 hospitals were among the government buildings evacuated.[8]

Bomb threats often are just that, a threat, but there can also be real bombs, as San Francisco General Hospital learned firsthand. In May 2007, a pipe bomb was found on the hospital's loading dock. Then just two weeks later two more devices (wired and ready to detonate) were found on the perimeter of a campus building. Police and explosive experts were able to render this second round of devices inert without further incident.[9] In November 2008, Memorial Hospital of Union County in Marysville, Ohio had to evacuate after a smoke bomb was thrown inside an entrance door. A second device was placed in a trash container near another entrance but with no damage.[10]

BURGLARY

The unlawful entry of a structure, with or without force, with the intent to commit a felony or larceny.

The loss of assets does not always occur through theft and robbery. Burglary, too, is common in healthcare facilities. Although one might suspect that the hospital pharmacy would be a primary target, the advent of 24-hour pharmacies has been instrumental in reducing the number of such burglaries. As well, the application of security technology in pharmacies offers after-hours protection to these settings. However, there are numerous other targets for burglary in a hospital. The operating room narcotics and anesthesia supply is a primary target. The operating room is generally isolated and is usually closed at night, contributing to its vulnerability. Cash storage locations, regardless of amounts, are at higher risk for a hospital burglary along with storerooms, work areas, and offices.

The physician's office, dental practice, and medical office buildings in general are also common burglary targets. Since very few drugs are kept in these areas, the burglar is usually after money and computer equipment. In some cases expensive medical equipment is also taken. Optical shops have a high risk for burglary with eyeglass frames being the primary target.

Medical specific equipment and supplies found in healthcare facilities are not the only targets for burglaries. In late 2008, copper thieves struck Ben Taub Hospital in Houston, turning off the water to the toilets in a number of restrooms and stealing copper flush valves.[11] Not all burglaries occur late at night or involve closed facilities. In Toronto, Canada in 2013, three suspects stole a baby grand piano from the fourth floor of a hospital, telling staff who questioned them as they loaded it on a dolly that they were removing it for "musical servicing."[12]

Hospital parking areas are another frequent source of burglaries or which deserve a high level of preventive security safeguards. Many healthcare facilities have seen a significant increase in the volume of auto thefts. A large health system in Phoenix, AZ shared that auto theft and auto break-ins were their greatest security risks as they were creating a high volume of employee turnover and negatively impacting employee engagement and patient satisfaction scores.

DISSIDENT GROUP ACTIONS

Person, or persons, who differ in opinions or feeling with general refusal to conform to authority, sentiment, or policies of a majority.

Major healthcare facilities have not experienced a great deal of disruption or damage related to demonstrations, civil disturbances or sabotage in recent years. The abortion and animal rights issues are perhaps the current hot spots in this regard. A large hospital in Halifax, Canada, as an example, has experienced a group of anti-abortion protestors who spend forty consecutive days each year, for the past several years, situated on the periphery of the hospital property.

The numerous civil disturbances of the late 1960s and more recent Los Angeles riots are a reminder that healthcare facilities are not immune from incurring damage to facilities and injury to staff. Experience has shown that victims of dissident group actions are generally a mix of rioters, prisoners, bystanders, and public safety type personnel. This mix of "players" creates a major challenge for the healthcare security administrator.

The list of security concerns to be managed during a civil disturbance varies, depending to a large extent on whether the hospital is located within the disturbance area or outside of it. Problems common to both situations include:

- The separation of rioters and riot control personnel while they are being treated.
- Strict visitor control, as injured rioters often are accompanied to the facility by friends or relatives who may wish to continue confrontational actions.
- An area-wide curfew, which can affect the reporting and releasing from duty of employees.
- The housing of personnel who cannot return home and people from the community who may seek refuge within the facility.

In addition to these common factors, a facility that is the target of civil disturbances or located within the area of the disturbance must deal with the following:

- Employees seeking access to a police controlled area when attempting to report for work.
- Safety of arriving and discharged patients.
- Safety of personnel traveling within the controlled area.
- Sniper fire at or around the facility.
- Fires set within the facility.
- Fire bombs thrown into the facility or onto low roofs.
- Sabotage of the physical plant.
- The acquisition of additional supplies and equipment, and the general need for increased housing.

Planning for civil disturbance activities can generally be viewed as an extension of the management of the security risks of the facilities identified in emergency management planning.

DISTURBANCES

The actions of a person, or persons, to interfere with the normal tranquility and order of an environment.

A continuing security risk is the disturbance or disorderly conduct incident. This type of incident can occur virtually anywhere within or outside the facility, including parking lots, employee locker rooms, lobbies, work areas, and patient rooms. Disturbances can involve patients, visitors, or staff. Many incidents of disturbance simply involve verbal arguments of varying degrees; however, these verbal arguments frequently lead to assault and the destruction of property. The number of disturbances taking place can often be correlated directly to the size, location, and type of facility. The type of patient, which relates to the type of visitor to some degree, must also be factored into the security plan for preventing and managing disturbances.

A common area for disturbances is the emergency department. Large urban hospitals with busy emergency rooms can experience incidents on almost a daily basis. Many such facilities have found it necessary to station security personnel in the emergency area on a 24-hour basis. Patients who become combative in an emergency room will usually be intoxicated, drug-impaired, mentally impaired, head injured or forensic (police custody) patients.

The patient is not the only source of disturbances. Persons accompanying the patients are often involved. Many such incidents are precipitated by long waits for medical treatment, lack of information, or alleged improper treatment. Minor disagreements can end up in physical confrontation and property destruction. Increasingly, hospitals are recognizing the importance of good communication with those awaiting treatment as a means of mitigating volatile behaviors.

A particularly dangerous source of trouble is the person who comes to the healthcare facility with the intention of engaging in a domestic confrontation with a spouse, boyfriend, girlfriend, or significant other. These incidents can lead to serious injuries, and the security officer can easily become injured in attempting to control this type of confrontation.

Another fairly common occurrence involves a visitor who is intoxicated, or under the influence of drugs, and demands to visit a patient. These persons can usually be talked down or escorted from the property before causing a disturbance. This type of incident often requires a show of force and must be handled very quickly to control an escalation of the problem.

DRUG ABUSE

The use of drugs to one's physical, emotional and/or social detriment without being clinically addicted.

A security risk that appears to be prevalent in recent years is that of drug abuse among healthcare employees. Although drug abuse is not unique to employees in the healthcare field, it is of great concern because patients may be placed in danger. Despite increased security measures, namely electronic dispensing systems such as Pyxis machines, and other unit dose systems, the theft of drugs from healthcare facilities continues to occur at extremely high levels. Healthcare facilities simply do not aggressively address this problem. A typical scenario can be found in the arrest of a surgical nurse at a Boulder, Colorado hospital. According to reports, as many as 350 patients who underwent surgery within one 30-day period could have been denied the full amount of the painkiller drug Fentanyl.

The nurse accessed the pain medication as often as 25 times in one day, replacing the drug with a saline solution by removing the vial's flip-top seal. It is of course no surprise that a hospital spokesman, following the arrest of the nurse, stated that the hospital's pharmacy had upgraded its system for monitoring drugs to flag any suspicious patterns.[13] In Australia the level of drug loss and theft at public hospitals rose nearly 20% in 2010.[14]

Theft of anesthesia type drugs is so prevalent that several major teaching hospitals have a program of random drug testing of anesthesiologists. Both Massachusetts General Hospital and the Cleveland Clinic Foundation conduct random urine drug testing in their anesthesia residency teaching programs. The Cleveland Clinic conducted a survey, in 2005, of anesthesiology residency programs and found that 80% of such programs reported problems with drug substance abuse, with 19% of these programs reporting a death resulting from overdoses.[15]

It is well known among healthcare security administrators that a large number of employees in healthcare facilities have purposely selected the facility with the intent of diverting drugs. Narcotics addiction among doctors and nurses is a much more serious problem than is generally recognized. The ease with which various caregivers can obtain narcotics contributes significantly to the problem.

EMBEZZLEMENT

> The misappropriation, misapplication, or illegal disposal of entrusted property with the intent to defraud the owner or beneficiary.

The healthcare setting presents an environment with a host of opportunities for the crime of embezzlement to occur. The proliferation of electronic transfer of funds by individuals and third-party payers has reduced the opportunity for large-scale funds loss due to embezzlement. Nevertheless, there remains ample opportunity to commit this type of crime. Money changes hands in cafeterias, gift shops, cashiers, and registration areas, and petty cash accounts are handled throughout daily operations in our healthcare facilities.

Recent cases in 2013 range from a hospital administrator sentenced to 8 years for embezzling in excess of $1 million from a Kansas hospital, [16] to health inspectors in Vietnam finding a public hospital using unauthorized drug and equipment suppliers, and doctors there embezzling hospital assets and overcharging.[17]

FIRE/EXPLOSION

> The ignition of combustible materials.

Arson is a security risk that can have grave consequences not only in property damage but in human suffering as well. Incidents involving arson do occur in healthcare facilities. The disgruntled employee, or ex-employee, is often responsible for these acts. Labor disputes sometimes spawn this type of act and organizations should be especially aware during these times. Areas that require close attention are storerooms, employee locker rooms, lounge areas, equipment rooms, linen storage areas, loading docks and especially employee and public washrooms.

HOSTAGE TAKING

A person held by a party as security that specified terms (demands) will be met by the opposing party.

Healthcare organizations have experienced a relatively high number of hostage taking incidents. These incidents have been most prevalent in the emergency department setting; however, physician offices, administrative offices, clinics, and pharmacies have not been immune to such events. While hospital staff members have been the primary victims of healthcare hostage incidents, visitors and patients can also be victims. At Scott and White Memorial Hospital in Temple, Texas in 2012, police shot and killed a man who had taken two nurses and a security officer hostage in the emergency department. The police officer fired on the suspect after one of the hostages tried to wrestle a gun away from the perpetrator.[18]

Other major hostage events have taken place within healthcare facilities throughout the U.S. and internationally.

HOMICIDE

Killing of one person by another.

Healthcare organizations experience frequent incidents of homicide. These incidents involve practically all the different categories of stakeholders in the medical care environment as both victims and perpetrators.

The motives for homicide incidents involve intimate personal relationships, angered patients, disgruntled staff and visitors, prisoner patient escape attempts, as well as mercy killings by staff and loved ones. Of particular note relative to homicides in the healthcare environment is that the motive is quite frequently an issue over alleged poor medical treatment. In this regard, there can be a rather long time period between the alleged care and the actual act of retaliation.

In Baltimore, Maryland at the world-famous Johns Hopkins Medical Center in 2010 a man, distraught while being briefed on his mother's medical condition by a surgeon, pulled a gun and shot the doctor, then killed himself and his mother in her hospital room. The surgeon survived.[19]

In 2006, Derrick McFarland, a security officer at Montgomery Regional Hospital in Blacksburg, VA, was killed by a prisoner as he escaped from custody while being treated at the healthcare facility. The prisoner, William Morva, overpowered a sheriff's deputy assigned to watch over him and was able to obtain the deputy's gun. Once in the hallway, he came across Officer McFarland and shot him, and escaped by shooting through a glass doorway. Morva had been an inmate for over a year and was not considered an out-of-the ordinary security risk.[20]

A gunman opened fire at a Monroe County, North Carolina nursing home and killed eight people, including seven elderly residents and a nurse, and wounded three others. The motive of the gunman is unclear, but authorities believe Robert Stewart was attempting to kill his estranged wife, who worked at the nursing home. She was not among those killed.[21]

In Australia in 2011 Roger Dean, a nurse at the Quakers Hill Nursing Home, deliberately set two fires to cover his theft of painkillers, and killed 11 elderly residents of the home in the horrific blaze.[22]

Mercy killings of patients in the hospital are often carried out by a spouse or "loved one." Multiple killings have also been committed by caregivers throughout the course of history of medical care giving. A case in point is one Charles Cullen, a nurse, who has been charged with murder after confessing to killing 30 to 40 patients in Pennsylvania and New Jersey between 1987 and 2003, by injecting them with drugs. During this time, Cullen worked in some ten different medical care facilities.[23]

Gangland-style homicides have also been experienced in medical care facilities. In Mexico City in 2012, two gunmen dressed as medical personnel killed an alleged gang leader in a hospital where he was recovering from gunshot wounds.[24] In 2013 in Kingston, Jamaica, two armed men entered May Pen hospital, tied up a security officer and shot a patient four times as he slept.[25]

IDENTITY THEFT

Identity theft occurs when someone else uses another person identifying information (e.g., name, Social Security number, credit card number, etc.) without permission, to commit fraud or other crimes.

It is estimated, from the 2010 U.S. Bureau of Justice statistics, that as many as 8.6 million Americans have their identity stolen each year, affecting at least one person in 7% of U.S. households. While some identity theft victims can resolve their problems quickly, others are required to spend large sums of money and time repairing the damage to their name and credit record. Victims may lose out on job opportunities, be denied loans, and in some cases may even be arrested for crimes they did not commit.

Healthcare sites can be a lucrative setting for the identity thief. The public access to offices, clinics, treatment areas, cafeterias, and patient rooms can be good "hunting grounds" for the purse, wallet, laptop, or tablet left unprotected. The use of credit cards and records maintained during the normal course of providing patient care can also lead to identity theft by staff.

The three stages of identity theft are: *acquisition* of identity information, *use* of the information, and *discovery* of loss. The longer it takes to discover the theft, the greater the loss incurred and diminished chances for a successful prosecution. Older persons and those that are receiving inpatient or outpatient medical treatment are at high risk of being an identity theft victim.

This growing problem is due, in part, to the shift by providers of healthcare to greater utilization of electronic records. Medical identity theft victims are at risk of being denied medical care and have few options in restoring their medical records, especially given the privacy restrictions of recent government regulations. In 2013, two thieves stole two laptops from an administration building of a California-based medical group, potentially compromising sensitive personal information of more than 729,000 patients.[26]

IMPOSTERS

One who engages in deception under an assumed name or identity.

The imposter represents another security vulnerability that occurs with a high degree of frequency. The certified nursing assistant (CNA) or licensed practical nurse (LPN) who has fraudulent identification indicating the status of a registered nurse (RN) appears in all segments of the healthcare industry. There have been numerous accounts of people who claimed to be physicians, visited patients, gave care, and interacted in their assumed role for considerable lengths of time before their false identity was discovered.

In California, a woman in a Santa Cruz hospital in 2013 posed as a doctor in order to gain access to secured areas and steal credit cards from staff.[27] In India this phenomenon saw thieves pose as doctors twice in a ten-day period in 2013 at the Bokaro General Hospital to steal valuables from patients.[28]

In the two-week period from February 26, 2005 to March 3, 2005, there were three reported cases of imposters entering hospitals in Los Angeles, Boston, and Detroit. There were similarities in these three incidents including physical descriptions of the persons, posing as TJC surveyors, questions asked, and time frames. The Joint Commission officials verified that no surveys of those hospitals had been scheduled at those times.[29] In a Florida hospital in 2011, in circumstances reminiscent of the movie *Catch Me if You Can*, 18-year-old Matthew Scheidt impersonated a physician assistant and dressed wounds, examined disrobed patients and even performed CPR.[30]

KICKBACKS/FRAUD

Kickback – Money or something of value given to an employee of an organization by a vendor or contractor in exchange for a consideration.

Fraud – An element of an offense consisting of deceit or intentional misrepresentation with the objective of illegally depriving an entity of the owner's property or legal rights.

As organizations grow, the risk of kickbacks to well-placed staff members also grows. As the dollar amount of contracts, purchases, and construction grows, so does the potential for kickbacks. Proving that a person is guilty of accepting a kickback can sometimes be difficult to accomplish. In many of the kickback scenarios there are only two persons with knowledge of the crime and both parties have realized a financial gain. The size, complexity, number of financial transactions, and big dollar expenditures make healthcare organizations at high risk for kickback situations to occur.

Healthcare organizations are at high risk for vendor fraud perpetrated by employees due to the high number of miscellaneous supplies ordered. A typical method of vendor fraud is for an employee to create a small shell company. The employee then forges a billing to the employer and approves paying organizational funds to the shell company. Signs that should alert organizations to vendor fraud include a Post Office box address especially in a nearby zip code, an email address from a for-fee internet provider and missing information in any vendor-data records.[31]

The cost of fraud to individual healthcare provider organizations is insignificant, however, when contrasted to Medicare/Medicaid losses, which are multibillions of dollars a year. The extent of this fraud is so extensive that any meaningful projections are difficult to impossible to calculate.

KIDNAPPING/ABDUCTION

A kidnapping or abduction takes place when a person is detained or taken away by using threatening or physical force.

Virtually all healthcare provider organizations, and the general public, are aware of the risk of infant abductions from hospitals and other birthing centers. The risk of infant/pediatric abductions can be viewed as either an abduction by a nonfamily member (stranger) or an abduction by a family member (domestic). It is the stranger-to-stranger abduction that is the most problematic for the healthcare organization.

The National Center for Missing and Exploited Children, in partnership with Mead Johnson Nutrition, has produced an educational program titled "Safeguard Their Tomorrows." This program is directed primarily to healthcare professionals involved with birthing and pediatric care. It has been presented to over 64,000 healthcare and public safety personnel in the U.S. and Canada since its inception over 20 years ago. The program, updated several times, is credited to a large extent with reducing a significant number of nonfamily abductions. The prevention of and response to infant and pediatric abductions from healthcare facilities is treated more fully in Chapter 21, "Areas of Higher Risk."

LABOR ACTIONS

A labor action, in the context of security, is an activity that is designed to interrupt or cause a financial burden on an organization by a labor organization.

In 1974 healthcare employees came under the jurisdiction of the National Labor Relations Act. The Act gives employees the right to collective bargaining representation. In order to preclude interference with patient care during the process of unionization, the National Labor Board defines what groups are eligible for bargaining representation. It should be noted that the law generally provides that an employer is not obligated to recognize a union for security personnel at a specific healthcare facility if the proposed union represents any other employee group at the facility (commonly referred to as a "mixed guard" unit).

Labor disputes can create a myriad of protection problems including threats, harassment, destruction and damage to property, intimidation, sabotage, and injury to both the innocent person and the person who is either represented by a union, seeks representation, or is simply sympathetic to the organized labor cause.

Protection problems encountered during a strike are somewhat similar to those to be managed during a civil disturbance. These problems include the following:

- The disruption of services from within;
- The disruption of external services, such as deliveries and trash removal;
- Malicious destruction of facility-owned property and the personal property of employees, such as parked vehicles;
- Intimidation and assault of pro-management employees;
- Harassment in general, such as illegal secondary boycotts;
- Altercations between pro-union and anti-union persons;
- Potential compromise of sensitive organizational information.

LOSS OF INFORMATION

The loss of information critical to the mission of the organization or information of others entrusted to the organization.

The theft and or misuse of confidential information, or privileged information, are security risks that are often overlooked in medical clinics and hospitals. Of primary importance are the medical records of the patient. These records often contain valuable information concerning lawsuits and other legal action. The methods of stealing information have changed radically over the years with the advent of electronic health records. A whole new industry regarding the protection of critical information has evolved. Loss of information can occur as the result of theft of computer hardware, unauthorized access, unsecured networks, and inadequate security for database files. The growing use of the telehealth/telemedicine systems by healthcare providers has created a whole new opportunity for the compromise of information. Other types of proprietary data that must be properly safeguarded include incident reports, bid specifications, certain financial records, and legal documents.

ROBBERY

The unlawful taking or attempted taking of property that is in the immediate possession of another by force or threat of force.

Armed robbery within healthcare facilities and on the grounds is a continuing security problem. A main threat to a medical center involves the pharmacy, which routinely stocks large quantities of desired narcotics and other dangerous drugs. While neighborhood pharmacies face the threat of an armed robbery, it is generally the result of seeking cash as opposed to drugs. Although most drug-related armed robberies in the medical center involve the pharmacy, there have also been reports of robberies occurring in the emergency room and even at nursing stations. A nurse leaving for a smoke break at a southern Colorado hospital was brusquely met at gunpoint at the emergency exit and forced to reenter the facility and access the narcotic dispensary, where the armed assailant took a large amount of narcotics and left the facility without further incident.

In addition to drugs, another target of armed robbery is cash. The main cashier is a likely target, but robberies of cafeterias, gift shops, outpatient cashiers, parking lot cashiers, and other areas where cash is handled or stored have occurred. The robber's timing, however, is not always right. In one case two armed people held up a cafeteria cashier at 3:30 p.m. and escaped with less than $20. Just minutes before, the breakfast and lunch cashier had cashed out the register drawer for the afternoon cashier to take over.

Robbery is also of major concern on medical center grounds. Victims are often visitors, which can lead to negative public relations for the organization. The hospital inpatient can become very upset, especially if the victim is a spouse who was on the way home from visiting the patient. Other patients quickly learn of the incident, and word spreads to relatives and friends. Thus, the healthcare organization becomes a secondary victim to the robbery resulting in collateral damage.

STALKING

Stalking is to pursue by tracking stealthily.

The healthcare environment provides many opportunities for the stalker to operate. A stalker is one who tracks his victim and generally attempts to make unwanted personal contact. While the contacts are usually in person, the stalker will sometimes pursue his victim through telephone calls, faxes, letters, or electronic mail. Stalking can be a precursor to escalating threats and physical confrontation. The high number of female staff and the openness of medical center campuses results in a high number of stalking incidents. Most stalking problems are based on a previous relationship of the two persons.

However, there are cases of a stranger-to-stranger situation. In the case of the latter, the victim is often a well-known personality in the community. As with bomb threats each reported stalking incident must be taken seriously and it is an area where considerable proactive preventive steps can be taken. A common proactive step is the obtaining of a restraining order; however, in a survey it was reported that 80% of these decrees were violated.

TERRORISM

The calculated use of violence or threat of violence to inculcate fear; intended to coerce or to intimidate governments.

The terrorist act is a risk that is actually a combination of other risks: fire, bomb, bomb threats, destruction of property, and kidnapping (hostage taking). It is, however, considered a separate risk due to the distinct motive that precipitates the act. As in strikes and civil disturbances, the primary safeguards to be applied are the expansion of the everyday protection elements in place—e.g., increased security personnel, greater facility restricted access, increased staff awareness and attention to good everyday security practices. Serious debate continues among healthcare security practitioners as to the level of risk to healthcare facilities by terrorist action. In general the consensus of opinion is that healthcare facilities are at relative low risk; however, a terrorist act in the geographical area of a healthcare facility can produce a high level of collateral damage.

A familiar tool for domestic and international terrorists, bombs have been used to execute some of the world's most devious and radical acts of terrorism, such as the Madrid, Spain train station bombings in 2005. The Boston Marathon bombings served to accentuate this in 2013 when local area hospitals, despite being overwhelmed by mass casualties from the bombings, ensured that all 264 victims who arrived at a hospital alive and were treated survived. As critical infrastructures serving important community roles, hospitals specifically must take the risk of terrorism with great seriousness and not underestimate the potential for harm and significant organizational disruption.

THEFT

Theft is the act of larceny, often referred to as stealing.

The pilferage or theft of supplies, equipment, and personal property is a reality for all healthcare organizations. There are as many estimates of the extent of theft in hospitals as there are estimators. A generally accepted estimate of loss for U.S. hospitals by industry experts is between $7,000 and $8,000 per bed per year. In terms of losses for all healthcare organizations, a conservative estimate projects a cost exceeding $50 billion on an annual basis.

It is virtually impossible to calculate the specific losses of any single facility. Like an iceberg, only a small part of the problem actually surfaces and it is often difficult to properly attribute the loss to theft, waste, or loss of accountability. In the opinion of knowledgeable administrators, however, loss is a substantial item in the cost of operating any medical care facility, regardless of size or location. Because more than 3,000 items purchased by healthcare facilities are usable in the home, the list of items being taken from hospitals is quite lengthy. Items that top the list are drugs, linens, food supplies, medical equipment, and maintenance parts and materials.

A pathologist and three other people were charged with the illegal sale of human organs, tissues, and fluids, which were in the custody of a Veterans Administration hospital in California. These parts of the body, removed during autopsies, were sold to biomedical companies. Biomedical firms use human organs and fluids to do research and develop diagnostic tests.

Equipment thefts from U.S. hospitals are unfortunately all too common and reflect how large amounts of expensive medical equipment can be stolen in a short time. In Wales in the UK, beds, baths and even x-ray machines were reported stolen from hospitals in 2012[32] while mad cow disease testing equipment was stolen from a Florida hospital also in 2012.[33] These are but two examples of a phenomenon that has significant fiscal impact on every healthcare organization.

A disturbing trend is the theft of sharp containers. Often used for the wasting of Fentanyl patches and syringes used for narcotic dispensing to patients, thieves have targeted these boxes, ripping them off the wall. Not as common is the theft of pain pumps (drug administering machines for chronic patients), but two hospitals in metropolitan Denver, Colorado have had drug-seekers steal the device and the schedule II narcotics they were dispensing directly from the patient room while in use.

EMPLOYEE THEFT

Security practitioners agree that the majority of healthcare organization losses from theft can be attributed to employees. The employee thief works every day, creating a constant drain on resources, as opposed to people from outside the organization who generally do not have recurring opportunities to steal. Numerous ingenious employee theft schemes have been revealed; however, the biggest loss comes from the magnitude of employees who simply dip into supplies with only a slight chance of being caught.

Although the data was collected more than 30 years ago, the most in-depth research into employee theft in hospitals was conducted by the Sociology Department at the University of Minnesota under a Law Enforcement Assistance Administration grant.[34] In this study, 37% of hospital employees who responded to the survey indicated they had been involved in taking hospital supplies; 11% of those employees admitted engaging in the theft of supplies on a monthly or more frequent basis.

Factors in employee theft

An objective of the Minnesota study was to determine the circumstances under which employee theft was most likely to occur. Although the study did not focus on counterproductive behavior, its incidence appears to have a direct correlation to theft. The employees who reported above-average theft levels were also quite prone to above-average counterproductive behavior, such as taking extra-long lunch and coffee breaks, working slowly or poorly, using drugs or alcohol at work, and abusing sick leave.

The study concluded that the younger and never-married employees have a high level of theft involvement. An explanation for this is that they are less vulnerable to management sanctions, including dismissal, because they have no dependents and generally a low seniority status.

Job dissatisfaction also leads to higher theft involvement, especially in the younger work force. The most consistent source of employee dissatisfaction was found to be in the employee–supervisor relationship. The study also concluded that employees who frequently got together with co-workers after hours were involved in a higher level of theft activity.

The most consistent predictor of theft involvement found by the study was the employee's perceived chance of being caught and the potential of being fired or arrested. When there was a visible and strong opposition to theft on the part of management and co-workers, the amount of theft decreased. It is of interest that the inferred sanctions imposed by co-workers appear to have had a much stronger influence in shaping antitheft behavior than did the more formal action of management.

Effects of controls on employee theft

Another important goal of the Minnesota study was to determine how effective certain actions or controls imposed by the organization were on reducing the amount of employee theft. The controls reviewed were the security department, management policy, inventory, financial procedures, and pre-employment screening.

The study indicated that the level of sophistication of a security department has little effect on theft reduction. This is not surprising, as the major thrust of the majority of security operations reviewed addressed the problem of patient-generated violence, grounds safety, employee safety, and other non-employee theft-related activities.

As one would expect, clearly defined theft policies, inventory programs geared to detecting losses, and effective pre-employment screening of job applicants all tend to lower the level of theft in an organization.

Reporting healthcare facility property losses

It is extremely difficult to develop a program of theft control unless the extent of the problem can be measured. One method of measurement is a good reporting system that requires all employees to promptly report missing property. It is in this area, however, that the healthcare organizations have failed miserably. It is estimated that the healthcare security departments receive reports on facility property losses in only 1% or 2% of cases. The chief reason for poor reporting is that the supply lines are so open that stocks are quickly replenished as ordered. In addition, employees do not want to get involved, especially when facility management does not seem to care. Property losses can also be viewed as supervisory failures, and thus staff at all levels tend to ignore the problem.

Patient property losses

Theft and loss of patient property is a continual concern for all healthcare provider organizations. Although the value of missing patient property is minimal when compared to the loss of facility property, most organizations place more emphasis and more effort on protecting patient property and investigating patient losses then they do on protecting their own assets. Missing patient property can seriously affect public relations, and the patient can interpret this problem as an indication that the medical care may also be inferior. In some instances patients become so upset over a theft of their property that their medical condition is adversely affected.

The healthcare employee is not always responsible for patient property losses. In one case a patient in a nursing home could not locate his false teeth. Investigators solved the case when the teeth were discovered in the mouth of another patient.

One of the serious questions facing an organization when a loss is reported is whether the matter is one of accountability or actual loss. Many patient belongings are reported stolen when in actuality the property has been misplaced, accidentally discarded, or taken home by a family member or friend.

In such cases where property has unknowingly been taken home, the claim of theft is usually made in good faith, and most patients let the hospital know if the item is found. Some patients, however, rationalize that, since the hospital thinks something was stolen, it might reimburse them for the loss.

It is not uncommon for these patients to feel that they deserve anything the hospital pays them because they are paying extremely high hospital charges. Other patients may be embarrassed that they caused trouble over nothing and thus hesitate to inform the hospital that the lost item has been found as opposed to being stolen.

The question of responsibility or liability is usually raised in the investigation of a loss that is not successfully recovered. Laws vary, of course, but the healthcare organization generally cannot be held responsible for all property brought into the facility by a patient or visitor. The organization must take every reasonable precaution to see that the patient's property is safeguarded so that losses do not occur, but it is generally accepted that any loss is the responsibility of the patient and that the organizations should not automatically reimburse patients for losses.

An exception exists where the facility has a valuables protection system. In such a system, where the patient has actually been given a receipt for the property and the property is subsequently controlled by the facility, the organization would, of course, be liable for any loss.

A complicating factor concerning patient property is that the property in the custody of the patient is not constant. Patients rarely go home with the same property they had when they are admitted into the care facility. Visitors often bring gifts, and the patient often requests that additional items be brought to the facility by relatives or friends. Thus, the property belonging to, and in control of the patient, is in a constant state of change.

Employee property losses

The loss of employee property is another problem that confronts virtually all hospitals, clinics, and long-term care facilities. This risk can generally be correlated to the size of the organization. In a large facility, the anonymity factor and the erosion of interpersonal relationships combine to create an environment that tends to increase the theft of employee property. This does not imply that larger organizations necessarily have more theft. The application of security safeguards can effectively manage this risk, resulting in a good record of theft prevention for any facility if administration is seriously concerned with the proper management of this risk.

The most common loss among employees is the purse or wallet left on an open shelf at a nursing station or under an office desk. Other commonly stolen items are articles of clothing and electronic media.

Like patient property, the actual fiscal value of employee property loss is relatively low when compared to organizational losses. Regardless of monetary value, however, employee property loss is often a key factor in employee relations. No one wants to work in a facility where losses, distrust, and suspicion are ongoing problems.

SECURITY-RELATED RISKS

There are risks facing healthcare organizations that often receive attention as security issues but are not directly related to the security program. These security-related issues are actually more clinical in nature and should be managed and controlled within the operating department. The security function may play a supporting role; however, the ownership of the risk does not reside with security. Two good examples of these security-related risks would be in the misuse of medical record information and the infrequent, but serious, problem of infant switching or discharge to the wrong family. Healthcare providers have a responsibility to guard protected health information from loss, misuse, and the compromising of confidentiality. This responsibility rests with the functional department in possession of the information, as well as with the information systems department. The growing use of electronic health records (EHR) systems mandates that the physical and information security of these systems be addressed.

The baby switching or wrongful discharge problem is one of providing proper clinical management within the specific medical care unit. The protocols, including infant identification, staff and mother education, and compliance with established policy and procedure, rest squarely with the operating unit. Though these occurrences are conceded to be relatively rare, it remains a risk that security administrators must consider.

SAFETY-RELATED RISKS

Among the safety-related risks that affect the protection level of the organization and relate directly to the security program are accidents, fires, and disasters.

Accidents

All facilities must be concerned with employee, visitor, and patient safety. Safety in this regard refers principally to preventing injury caused by unsafe physical conditions or the inadvertent act of the victim or another person.

It is somewhat paradoxical that the safety records of some healthcare facilities are inferior to those of the major industries that send accident victims to them for care. Because they treat a wide variety of accident cases, hospitals should have a special awareness of the need to maintain an adequate safety program. Many of the accidents involving healthcare employees are similar in nature to those occurring in industry, although the major problem of "needle sticks" is somewhat unique to the healthcare working environment.

The courts have consistently ruled that all medical care facilities are required to maintain safe premises and patient safety is a major focus of The Joint Commission and international accrediting bodies outside the U.S. The costs of medical care, loss of services, malpractice and public insurance liability, loss of materials and equipment, human suffering, and damage to public reputation are just some of the reasons why medical care facilities must constantly guard against accidents.

Fires (Accidental)

Fires in medical care facilities can contribute to a high loss of life and property. The number of accidental fires and explosions in healthcare facilities has been reduced over the past years. This reduction in the number of fires, and certainly in their severity, has been due to, in large part, the TJC standards, advancements in Building and Fire Code requirements and local fire department fire prevention efforts. The issue of accidental fires and explosions clearly falls within the safety function with a good deal of support from security. Fires caused by smoking have been significantly reduced through increasingly more stringent smoking restrictions in healthcare facilities.

Internal and external emergencies (Disasters)

Security responsibilities during an external disaster often center on controlling visitors, safekeeping patient valuables, controlling external traffic of pedestrians and vehicles, providing extra security support to the treatment areas, and securing a designated area for the dissemination of information concerning the injured. Increasingly, the function of security is built into the healthcare Emergency Operations Center structure, ensuring a prominent place in the organizational response to disaster. As emergencies strike, new and often unanticipated factors present themselves to challenge even the most comprehensive and well-developed disaster plans. The major responsibility for managing the emergency management/disaster risk rests with the organization's emergency management function.

FACILITY SECURITY RISK ASSESSMENT

The identification of specific risks generally begins with a facility security review process. The identification of the magnitude of security threats or risks, along with their potential impact on the healthcare organization, is but an initial step in protecting the organization. The objective of the security assessment/analysis is to identify organizational security exposures so a comprehensive, effective, and cost-justified protection plan can be developed and implemented. Analysis and evaluation of the risks provides supporting rationale for making sure security measures (safeguards) are implemented appropriately, based on protecting critical resources, while accepting a calculated degree of risk. It is understood an asset cannot be protected completely without substantial cost or unduly inhibiting the primary mission of providing efficient and quality patient care. The goal of implementing countermeasures for security risks is to make it difficult for a security breach to occur—to harden the facility as target. The level of target hardening to be implemented depends on the value of the asset and the organization's tolerance for risk.

When embarking on the process of a security risk assessment it is important to keep in mind the subtle differences between a risk assessment, security survey, security program review, and a security audit:

1. The assessment is conducted to identify and evaluate security risk by the level of protective measures (safeguards) in place to manage an acceptable level of risk.
2. A survey is a more random evaluation of the overall program to determine the completeness, acceptance, strengths, and weaknesses in the program.
3. The review is much the same as the survey; however, it will often focus on a specific area of security such as the emergency department, mother–infant unit, or change in space design.
4. The audit is rather narrow in focus to determine the validity and operational aspects of a specific element of the security program. The audit is to determine if a defined element of the security system is operating in the manner intended and producing the anticipated outcome.

In security we most often refer to the term *audit*, relative to a review of a procedure, to determine the degree of compliance with the procedure process. From this a need to make appropriate changes for identifying the requirement for training can emerge. Rarely does security become involved in financial types of audits except in connection with an investigation.

WHO SHOULD DO A FACILITY SECURITY RISK ASSESSMENT?

A basic question that must be answered is: Who should conduct the assessment? As one might expect, there are several approaches. The first approach is to delegate this task to the person who is responsible for the day-to-day security program. An advantage of this approach is the individual already possesses knowledge of the environment, including past problems, community assessment in terms of criminal activity, organizational philosophy, and the organizational structure. This person has access to department heads and supervisors, all of whom may be more candid in their discussion of operational procedures and problems than they would be with someone from outside the organization. The main concern with the in-house approach pertains to the qualifications of the individual. The mere fact of being in a position does not in itself qualify a person to conduct a valid security risk assessment.

A qualified person conducting a healthcare security risk assessment should possess a certain level of education and experience often validated by various professional association credentials. The person should possess the designation of a Certified Healthcare Protection Administrator (CHPA) conferred by the International Association for Hospital Security and Safety or that of a Certified Protection Professional (CPP) conferred by the Professional Certification Board of ASIS International. Lacking one or both of these credentials can be compensated for by involving a person with these credentials as part of the assessment process. Experience in security, safety, or risk management in more than one healthcare provider organization is also a general requirement.

The second approach for conducting the security assessment is to use an outside consultant. The major advantage of this approach is that the consultant can be more objective. The consultant can generally perform the assessment task in much less time than the internal person, and can bring a broad range of varied operational experience to the assessment process. In other words, the consultant does not need to identify solutions from scratch and will not have personality conflicts with the facility staff or preconceived opinions regarding the organization. Internal politics and staff personalities can be avoided or at least mitigated through the consultant approach. The primary downside is the cost of the consultant.

Regardless of who completes the assessment, employees often view the process as an investigation rather than being a nonthreatening business management review. The healthcare administrator must use every avenue available to communicate to stakeholders the objective of the review process. The objective is to assist departments in the performance of their specific function, contributing in a positive manner to the overall mission and security of the organization.

HOW DETAILED SHOULD THE ASSESSMENT BE?

There are a great many methodologies and formats utilized to assess security risks and to measure the severity of those risks. There are two basic principles to keep in mind regarding security risk assessments. The methodology should not be overly complicated, and the fact is that risk level conclusions are largely subjective in nature in terms of probability. The second principle is that a formal security risk assessment, conducted on a periodic basis, is simply a baseline that can and should be modified on an ongoing basis. Virtually every security event provides an opportunity for lessons learned which may affect the assessment. Changing neighborhood and patient dynamics and renovation and construction projects are also among activities that may have a bearing on the security risk analysis. Additionally, new and modified patient care programs, including changing space allocations, are important to consider.

The tendency to group all security assessments into a single category should be avoided. Not all assessments are intended to examine every aspect of the entire healthcare facility. Many security risk assessments are conducted for a specific department or function as circumstances dictate.

A security risk assessment must be viewed in terms of the depth of the review process. A security risk assessment can consist of a general review or an in-depth, department-by-department and function-by-function process.

The International Association for Security and Safety has developed a Healthcare Security Guideline relative to healthcare security risk assessments. The association also has a "Risk Assessment Toolkit" available which describes an in-depth approach to this important aspect of security risk management. The IAHSS Healthcare Security Design Guidelines can provide a foundation for any physical security review of a healthcare facility.

WHAT THE SECURITY RISK ASSESSMENT SHOULD INCLUDE

A general security risk assessment of a healthcare facility need not be overly structured. There are no ready-made checklists that fit every organizational risk. Keep in mind every facility is unique. Checklists and guidelines are only resources that may assist in the review process. Just as there are no set guidelines on what should be reviewed, there is no exact starting point. The assessment should review the physical facilities, major functions, and high-risk processes of the organization. Figure 3-2 is a sample mental health facility security review checklist. The full checklist can be found in Appendix I.

A good place to begin is with the physical facilities on the extreme perimeters of the property. Security can be referred to as *layers of protection*. In this concept the application of security safeguards becomes more strict or stringent as one advances to the interior. A simplified example of this concept is the protection of a hospital's main narcotic supply. The grounds may be fenced; there may be limited traffic control, well-trimmed shrubs, and night lighting. Next is the building in which the pharmacy is located. This perimeter will be protected by walls, doors and locks, window protection, limited access control, and various security measures. Next is the pharmacy area, which will again be protected by walls, doors and locks, window protection if required, as well as good department access control

MENTAL HEALTH PHYSICAL SECURITY REVIEW CHECKLIST

SITE: DATE OF REVIEW:

UNIT:

UNIT DESCRIPTION							
Item #	Category/Area	Questions /Criteria	*Rationale/Assessment Methods*	Met	Partially Met	Not Met	Comments
1	Site/Building Perimeter	1 a. Does the site in which the MH unit is situated have CCTV coverage of the perimeter of the site? 1 b. Does the building in which the MH unit is located have CCTV coverage of the perimeter of the building? 1 c. Are the CCTV images recorded and capable of being retrieved quickly?	*Recovery – Can assist in the rapid recovery of an eloped patient by having the patient identity confirmed and departure from building and/or site and potential direction of travel identified through CCTV*				

FIGURE 3-2

Sample mental health facility security review checklist (courtesy of Paladin Security Group, Vancouver, BC).

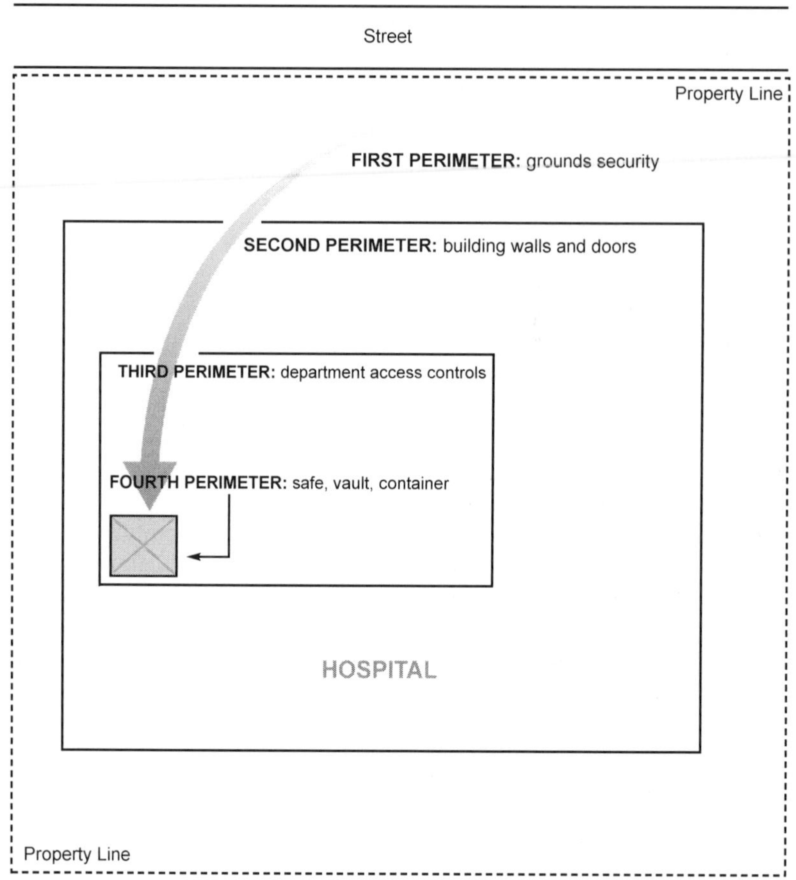

FIGURE 3-3

Layers of protection.

including alarm systems and video surveillance. The final perimeter may be the safe, vault, or electronic dispensing system within the pharmacy itself. Figure 3-3 provides a visual depiction of this concept of using concentric rings of control and protection. The General Guideline section of the IAHSS Security Design Guidelines also models this process.

ASSESSING RISK

Each of the security risks identified must be assessed in terms of the degree of threat (real, perceived, and potential) to the organization. In rendering this assessment basic sources of information should be utilized. These information sources are shown in Figure 3-4.

Analyzing risk in terms of real or perceived threat is more easily addressed than in terms of potential threat. Environmental criminology is the study of the spatial patterns of wrongdoing, perceptions and space awareness of the criminal, criminal mobility patterns, target selection, and the decision to commit

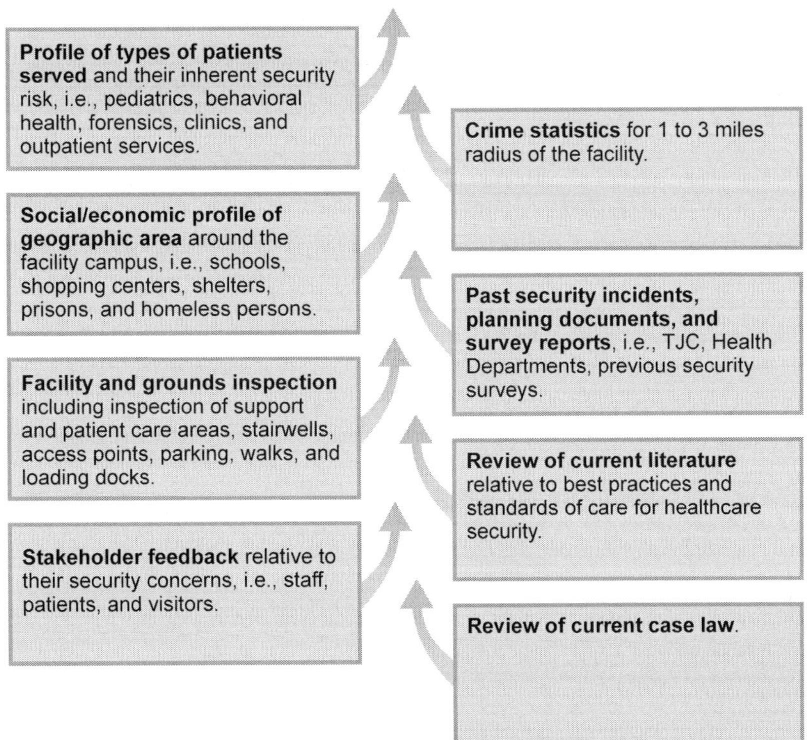

FIGURE 3-4

Security risk assessment information/data.

a crime. Although these factors pertain more directly to crime outside the organization, they do relate to varying degrees of internal crime and other negative acts.[35]

In addition to the foregoing, the legal implications of *foreseeability* must be taken into consideration. The courts consistently take the position of "totality of circumstances," as proposed to the strict view of whether a similar incident previously occurred that would put the organization on notice. Such notice can go far beyond the organization's property, to include situations or incidents occurring down the street or across the nation. The best example of being on "national notice" is the vulnerability of infant kidnapping from hospitals. It would be very difficult for any hospital to defend itself using the premise that it did not know that this type of event could occur.

The whole area of a foreseeable criminal act relates directly to the probability of crime. Predicting the probability of crime for any given address, principally in the U.S. and Canada, is the business of CAP Index headquarters in Eaton, PA. The CAP Index Company produces a variety of reports that are widely accepted by security professionals as part of the risk assessment process. The basic CAP Index report/map utilize some 84 demographic variables, which are weighted, from updated census track data, to predict crime probability for a specific address. The report/map produces a numerical score of crime probability for the address and compares the score to the national, state and county averages. Also provided in the report are comparison scores, a past time period, current date, and a projected date. The CAP index report can be ordered for a given date in the past and is frequently utilized in premises liability litigation.

The assessment of each security risk can be expressed in a number of ways, such as low, medium, or high or a scale of one to ten. The higher the risk, the greater the effort required to implement safeguards that will provide an adequate level of protection. Figure 3-5 is an example of a matrix used to list the security risks and address the degree, or level, of risk for specified areas or functions.

Risk levels should be expressed, in terms of addressing the threat, by considering the safeguards already in place, not the prevalence of the risk. For example, the risk of fire is well known; however, a well-trained staff, fire control construction, fire-safe practices, and physical fire detection and control equipment may relate to fire being a very low risk for the organization.

ANNUAL SECURITY RISK ASSESSMENT

0								00-01-1900		
AGGRAVATION▸	Probability	Potential for Personal Harm	Potential for Unaccompanied Minor or Infant	Potential for Hazardous Materials	Potential for Property Crime	Presence of Confidential Information	Environmental Concerns	Security Incident History	MITIGATION	RISK 0 = Low, 100 = High
▼SECURITY SENSITIVE PROCESSES▼	0 = N/A, 1 = Low, 2 = Moderate, 3 = High									
Emergency Patient Care							0		0.0	0%
Behavioral Health Patient Care							0		0.0	0%
Infant Patient Care							0		0.0	0%
Pediatric Patient Care							0		0.0	0%
Forensic Patient Care							0		0.0	0%
Sensitive Research							0		0.0	0%
Health Information							0		0.0	0%
Information Technology Systems							0		0.0	0%
Cash Handling Areas							0		0.0	0%
External Environment							0		0.0	0%
Controlled Access to Facility							0		0.0	0%
Narcotics Storage and Distribution							0		0.0	0%
Additional Process 1							0		0.0	0%
Additional Process 2							0		0.0	0%
Additional Process 3							0		0.0	0%
AVERAGE▸	#DIV/0!	#DIV/0!	#DIV/0!	#DIV/0!	#DIV/0!	#DIV/0!	0.0	#DIV/0!	0.0	

FIGURE 3-5

Example of a Security Risk Assessment worksheet.

MATCHING SAFEGUARDS TO RISK

After the risk assessment is completed, and the degree of risk calculated, each risk is viewed in relation to the safeguards currently in place and additional safeguards that may be needed to maintain an acceptable risk level. In some cases the safeguards are the direct responsibility of the security function, and in others a specific operating department may be responsible. Seldom is the application of all safeguards the responsibility of one particular department; rather, responsibility is usually a combination of security and the operating department. In the US, the management of security risks is often the function of the hospital's Environment of Care committee. Further, a given safeguard applied to a specific risk will, in many cases, also impact other vulnerabilities. For example, the security officer is a safeguard utilized to help manage a substantial percentage of all known risks.

In assessing risk and applying safeguards, the security professional is concerned not only with existing risks, evidenced in part by incidents, but also with potential risk, as prevention is a key concept. In practical terms, it is difficult to obtain resources and gain organizational support for preventive safeguards. Unfortunately, many safeguards currently in place are due to past events, and were put in place as a reactive measure, without sound planning and rational justification.

Security program safeguards should have some relation to the level of threat. Figure 3-6 depicts a concept of an identified threat level to risk categories and the corresponding safeguards. The basic

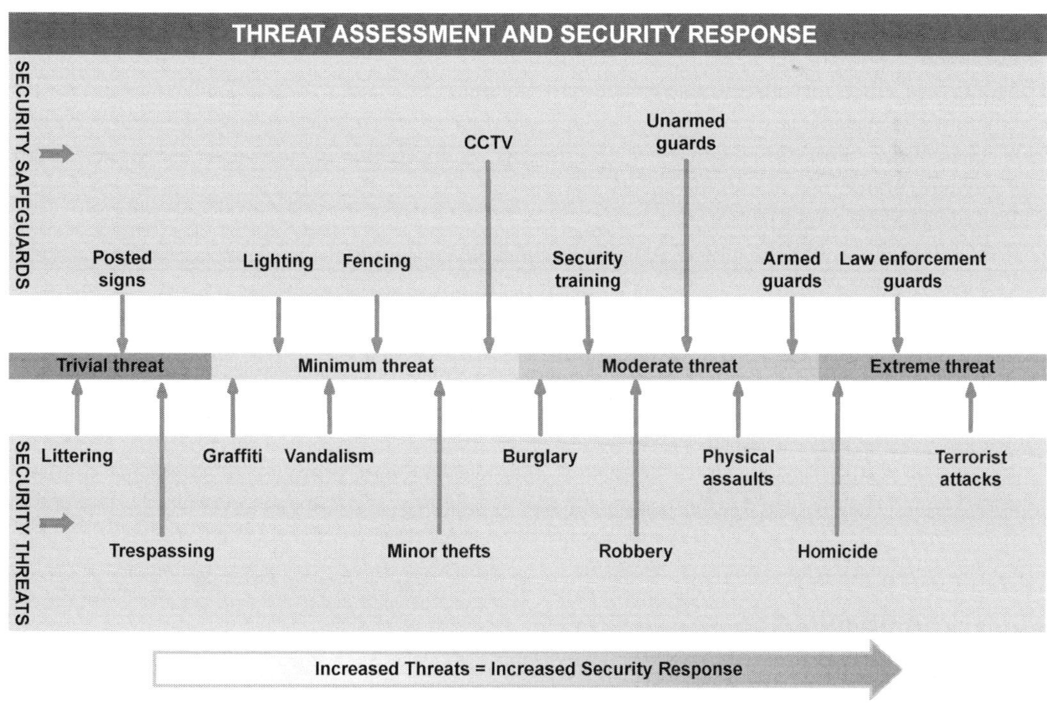

FIGURE 3-6

Security threat assessment and physical security safeguards.

thought is simply applying safeguards commensurate with the level of risk to avoid unnecessary cost and operational inconvenience. In terms of cost the healthcare security administrator will be frequently tasked with addressing the return on investment (ROI) of various components or elements of the current protection system and in terms of requesting additional security staffing or upgrading security technology/equipment.

In this section of the text the main focus has been on identifying and assessing security risks rather than on reviewing the specific safeguards and their applications. The following example, however, will help the reader to understand the conceptual model of matching safeguards and multidepartment responsibilities in managing a specific risk. In this example, the stated risk is protecting people in various facility parking lots.

Risk identified: personal safety in parking areas

Safeguards Implemented:

1. Security Force:
   - Patrol parking areas
   - Fixed post assignments during specific shift changes
   - Escort people on request
   - Provide various departmental in-service education programs
   - Follow up and investigate incidents
2. Install emergency communication devices in strategic and highly visible locations that are connected directly to the security dispatch center.
3. Monitor by video surveillance designated parking areas.
4. Operating Departments:
   - Standardize work shifts with other departments when possible
   - Advise employees of security escort service
5. Provide adequate night lighting.
6. Check trees and shrubs for proper placement and keep well pruned.
7. Personnel Department:
   - Provide parking lot safety and security services information to new employees
   - Address parking lot safety and security services in the employee handbook
8. Nursing/Admissions:
   - Inform visitors and patients of security escort services and means of requesting this service.

As one can readily see, the above safeguards and defined responsibilities are somewhat similar to those that would be considered in addressing the risk of break-ins and damage to vehicles in the parking areas.

A CONTINUOUS PROCESS

Once the process of risk assessment has been completed, an abatement plan has been devised, and safeguards have been blended into a security program, this process begins again. The identification of security vulnerabilities and risks is ongoing. Risks previously identified may no longer exist, and new risks may appear as the dynamics of a healthcare environment continually change.

The following IAHSS guideline refers:

01.04 SECURITY RISK ASSESSMENTS

Statement

Security Risk Assessments will be conducted on a regular and ongoing basis. The objective of the Security Risk Assessment is to identify assets of the Healthcare Facilities (HCF) primary mission and operations, threats to and vulnerabilities of those assets, and develop reasonable risk mitigation strategies to protect assets.

Intent

a. Security risk assessment should be conducted by a qualified professional who has training and experience in healthcare security.

b. Identify assets of the HCF:

  1) People assets may include direct care providers and patients along with other persons such as visitors, family, and support personnel

  2) Property assets include not only buildings but tangible assets used to provide patient care (such as medical gases, medical equipment, utilities, and supply lines), intangible assets, such as the organization's reputation, and information assets

c. Inventory current security measures in place to protect critical assets including policies and procedures, physical/electronic security equipment and systems, and security personnel.

d. The inventory process should include a review of all available security documentation such as security plans, security officer deployment, training, and post orders.

e. The inventory may be accomplished using:

  1) An outside-in approach (begin at the perimeter and work toward the identified critical assets through each line of defense)

  2) An inside-out approach (begin at each critical asset and work out to the perimeter)

f. Threats should be identified, assessed and trended quantitatively and qualitatively related to the prioritized list of the HCFs identified assets. Data should be gathered from several sources, including:

  1) Internal data from security incidents, facility statistics, and staff interviews

  2) Local police crime statistics

  3) Exchange of information with similar organizations

  4) Other law enforcement sources

  5) Industry publications and news clipping sources

g. Consider improvements of the organization's protection of assets in light of the threats to and vulnerabilities identified to determine security enhancements needed to mitigate risks. A cost-benefit analysis of options may be needed to select appropriate measures that reduce risk to an acceptable level and comply with applicable healthcare industry standards, guidelines, and regulatory agency requirements.

h. Results of formal risk assessments should be documented for on-going review and forwarded to appropriate leadership.

References/General Information

Colling, Russell L. and York, Tony W. (2010). Hospital and Healthcare Security. 5th Ed. Woburn: Butterworth-Heinemann.

Vellani, Karim H. (2006). Strategic Security Management: A Risk Assessment Guide to Decision Makers. Woburn: Butterworth-Heinemann.

Risk Assessment Toolkit CD (October 2008), IAHSS

Approved: April 2009

Last Revised: October 2011

REFERENCES

1. Welsh Moira. Nursing home worker jailed 12 months for sex assault. *Toronto Star* 2012, October 17. Retrieved November 7, 2013 from http://www.thestar.com/news/canada/2012/10/17/nursinghome_worker_jailed_12_months_for_sex_assault.html.
2. Battaglia Tammy S. *17-year-old charged in sexual assault at C.S. Mott Children's Hospital.* Detroit Free Press; 2011, October 1. Retrieved February 10, 2011, from http://www.freep.com/article/20111001/NEWS05-/110010452/17-year-old-charged-sexual-assault-C-S-Mott-Children-s-Hospital.
3. Man accused of raping hospital patient. *Salina Journal* 2010, February 23. Retrieved on March 03, 2010 http://www.saljournal.com/news/story/alleged-rape-at-hospital-22210.
4. Milburn J. Three fatally shot in Girard. *Topeka Capital-Journal* 2008, February 8. Retrieved from http://www.cjonline.com/stories/020800/kan_girard.shtml.
5. 3 Alabama hospitals evacuated after bomb threat. *Montgomery Advertiser*. 2013, April 22. Retrieved November 10, 2013, from http://www.montgomeryadvertiser.com/article/20130422/NEWS/130422004.
6. In brief, bomb threat. *Hospital Security and Safety Management* 2002, April;**22**(12).
7. CS Staff. *Bomb threat causes Canadian hospital to increase security.* Campus Safety Magazine; 2007, November 30. November/December 2008. Retrieved June 14, 2009, from http://www.campussafetymagazine.com/article/bomb-threat-causes-canadian-hospital-to-increase-security/podcasts.
8. Polish hospitals, offices, evacuated after fake bomb threats. 2013, June 25. Retrieved November 10, 2013, from http://www.reuters.com/us-poland-evacuation-idUSBRE95O01620130625.
9. Two bomb scares offer this hospital a chance to upgrade its planning. *Briefings on Hospital Safety* 2007, September;**15**(9):1.
10. Zachariah H. *Smoke bomb tossed into Memorial Hospital.* The Columbus Dispatch; 2008, November 2. Retrieved from http://www.dispatch.com/live/content/local_news/stories/2008/11/02/hosp03.html.
11. Thieves steal copper from hospital restrooms. *Healthcare Security Weekly* 2007, December 10. Retrieved June 14, 2009, from http://www.hcpro.com/HOM-201801-1423/Thieves-steal-copper-from-hospital-restrooms.html.
12. Baby grand piano stolen from Toronto hospital in brazen daytime heist. *Toronto Star* 2013, July 22. Retrieved November 8, 2013, from http://www.thestar.com/news/crime/2013/07/22.
13. Pankratz H. *Nurse arrested in drug thefts.* Denver Post; 2008, November 20. Retrieved from http://www.denverpost.com/search/ci_11026752.
14. Jensen E. *Rise in drug thefts at hospitals by employees.* The Sydney Morning Herald; 2012, January 24. Retrieved November 9, 2013, from http://www.smh.com.au/national/health/rise-in-drug-thefts-at-hospitals-by-employees-20120123-1qe44.html.
15. *Two major hospitals implement random drug testing for anesthesiologists.* Campus Safety Magazine; 2008, November 13. Retrieved June 14, 2009, from http://www.campussafetymagazine.com/News/?NewsID=2346.
16. *Kansas hospital worker gets 8 years for embezzlement.* Associated Press; 2013, September 25. Retrieved November 8, 2013 from. http://www.cjonline.com/news/2013-09-25/kansas-hospital-worker-gets-8-years-embezzlement.
17. Inspectors uncover embezzlement, gouging at Vietnam public hospital. 2013, October 18. Retrieved November 8, 2013, from http://www.thanhniennews.com/society/inspectors-uncover-embezzlement-gouging-at-vietnam-public-hospital-939.html.
18. Shocked neighbors of Temple gunman say he was a nice guy. 2012, June 17. Retrieved November 9, 2013, from http://www.kxxv.com/story/18810015/man-killed-after-taking-hostages-at-hospital.
19. Dominguez A. *Doctor expected to survive after Johns Hopkins murder-suicide.* 2010, September 16. Retrieved November 9, 2013, from http://www.chron.com/news/nation-world/article/Doctor-expected-to-survive-after-johns-hopkins-1705025.php.

20. Smith TA. *Patient prisoner security—A call to action*. 2007/2008. Retrieved March 28, 2009, from www.ihf-fih.org/content/download/170/1095/.../59-61%20%20Smith.pdf.
21. Foreman Jr Tom, Maurer Kevin. *7 residents, 1 nurse die in N.C. nursing home shooting*. Charlotte Observer; 2009, March 29. Retrieved March 30, 2009, from http://www.starnewsonline.com/article/20090329/ARTICLES/903299980.
22. *Australian nurse who killed 11 in nursing home fire sentenced to life in prison*. The Telegraph; 2013, August 1. Retrieved November 10, 2013, from http://www.telegraph.co.uk/news/worldnews/australiaandthepacific/australia/10215414/Australian-nurse-who-killed-11-in-nursing-home-fire-sentenced-to-life-in-prison.html.
23. *Ex-nurse says he killed patients*. Denver Post; 2003, December 16. 2A.
24. Gunmen kill patient inside Mexico City hospital 2012, December 19. Retrieved November 10, 2013, from http://www.hindustantimes.com/world-news/gunmen-kill-patient-inside-mexico-city-hospital/article1-974786.aspx.
25. Doctors condemn execution-style murder at Jamaica hospital 2013, January 16. Retrieved November 10, 2013, from http://www.caribbean360.com/index.php/news/jamaica_news/655835.html#axzz2kI9sDqBZ.
26. *Laptop thefts compromise 729,000 patient files*. Los Angeles Times; 2013, October 21. Retrieved November 7, 2013, from http://articles.latimes.com/2013/oct/21/local/la-me-hospital-theft-20131022.
27. Baxter S. *Woman posing as doctor steals nurses' credit cards at Dominican Hospital*. Santa Cruz Sentinel; 2013, January 3. Retrieved November 8, 2013, from http://www.santacruzsentinel.com/ci_22304647/woman-posing-doctor-steals-nurses-credit-cards-at.
28. *Imposters at Bokaro hospital put patients on alert*. The Times of India; 2013, October 23. Retrieved November 9, 2013, from http://articles.timesofindia.indiatimes.com/2013-10-23/ranchi/43324428_1_hospital-staff-bokaro-general-hospital-gold-jewellery.
29. Virginia Fusion Center. *Intelligence Bulletin #05-11*. Virginia: Department of Virginia State Police; 2005, March 18.
30. *Matthew Scheidt sentenced for impersonating physician assistant*. Huffington Post; 2012, October 15. Retrieved November 8, 2013, from http://www.huffingtonpost.com/2012/11/15/matthew-scheidt-impersonates-physicians-assistant_n_2137948.html.
31. *Ask the auditor: Guarding against employee fraud and theft in healthcare organizations*. ASIS Security Management Daily; 2007, May 15. 3.
32. Williams B. *X-ray machines and beds stolen from hospitals in Wales*. 2013, April 12. Retrieved November 9, 2013, from http://www.bbc.co.uk/news/uk-wales-22109590.
33. Jameson M. *Thieves nab discarded equipment used to test patient with mad-cow-like disease*. Orlando Sentinel; 2012, May 17. Retrieved November 10, 2013, from http://articles.orlandosentinel.com/2012-05-17/health/os-mad-cow-equipment-20120516_1_mad-cow-disease-classic-cjd-dairy-cow.
34. Clark JP, Hollinger RC. *Theft by employees*. Security Management; 1980, September.
35. Kennedy DB. *Case your space*. Security Management; 1989, April. 47.

CHAPTER

SECURITY MANAGEMENT PLANNING

4

Security management planning involves the formulation of two basic interrelated but separate types of plans. The first is a **security management plan** (SMP) that relates directly to the day-to-day protection program of the organization. This plan should be considered a short-term plan, focusing on the present, which requires a formal review, evaluation, and modification on an annual basis. It is also a living document that can, and should, change as circumstances and situations develop. The second plan is the **security strategic plan** (also referred to as a security master plan), which relates more toward long-term goals, objectives, philosophy, and program direction and is aligned with the strategic plan of the healthcare organization. The strategic plan can be defined as a "road map" (or master plan), enabling the organization to move forward toward its destination (goals), in an orderly, defined, and efficient pathway. The strategic plan should reflect the mission, vision and values of the security program, as well as those of the healthcare organization.

SECURITY MANAGEMENT PLAN

A security management plan is a description of the protection program, developed by and for the security program, after evaluating security risks and threats to the organization. There are various schools of thought on how general or all-inclusive such a plan should be. A security management plan, however, is a necessary element of managing any healthcare organization. IAHSS has developed a guideline that outlines the basic aspects of such a plan.

There is no set format for a plan for security management, and the plan can vary in length from a few pages to many. The plan should be just that—a plan—and should not generally include policy and procedure in any great detail. It is an operational plan and should address all major components of the security program. In a sense, it equates to a brief business plan, without the financial aspects of a typical business plan.

In addition to the intents of the IAHSS guideline, other areas that may be included in the security management plan are:

- A listing of physical security safeguards as elements of the program
- A listing of the department operating policies and procedures including preparation and review protocols
- Organization staff and others as applicable (i.e., patients, vendors, visitors, neighborhood)
- Program performance standards
- Measurement and improvement strategies

01.01 SECURITY MANAGEMENT PLAN

Statement

Healthcare Facilities (HCFs) will develop a Security Management Plan (SMP). The plan should include preventive, protective, and response measures designed to provide a safe and secure environment.

Intent

a. The plan should be based on the security risk assessment and needs of the HCF.

b. The plan should include, but not be limited to:

1. Security program mission statement
2. Statement of program authority (e.g., a facility organization chart depicting reporting levels)
3. Identification of security sensitive areas
4. An overview of security program duties and activities
5. The documentation system in place (i.e., records and reports)
6. Training program for the security staff and all other staff
7. Planned liaison activity with local public safety agencies and other HCFs as appropriate
8. Security organizational chart
9. A copy of the most recent SMP annual program evaluation report and plan for improvement

c. The plan should be evaluated annually, as well as modified as required as an ongoing activity. Annual reviews should be evidenced by affixing the evaluation date to the plan.

References/General Information

Security Issues for Today's Health Care Organization, (2002), Joint Commission on Accreditation of Healthcare Organizations, Oakbrook Terrace, IL.

Approved: January 2006

Last Revised: October 2011

SECURITY MISSION STATEMENT

The security mission statement is the foundation of the security program and essentially states the reason or purpose of the program—its goal of providing a reasonably safe and secure environment for patients, visitors, employees, volunteers, medical staff, and vendors. The security mission must relate to, and support, the overall mission, vision, and core values of the organization. Figure 4-1 provides an example of a healthcare security mission statement provided by Ken Close, Manager of Security and Parking for the Trillium Health Partners, a Toronto area healthcare organization.

Our Mission

Committed, educated and compassionate professionals dedicated to providing a secure, safe and accessible environment through world class customer services to support a healthier community.

- Customer / patient service focused
- Promoting smart commute initiatives
- Participating in environmental clean-up initiatives

FIGURE 4-1

Example of a healthcare security mission statement.

PROGRAM AUTHORITY

The authority and responsibility for the day-to-day operation of a security program must be assigned to a specific position within the organization. Many routine security tasks may be delegated to others; however, the responsibility for getting the job done rests with the specific position designated by organization leadership. In most cases this position will be displayed in an organization chart. In some instances an organization chart may only portray the function rather than a specific position. In this situation, the security management plan should contain a written directive from the chief executive officer, or the chief operating officer, delegating authority to a specific position to manage the security program. In larger organizations, this authority would generally be conferred upon the director or manager of security. In small organizations it may be a director of facilities, risk management, human resources or another high-level administrative position. IAHSS guideline 01.03 outlines the basic aspects of authority and responsibility of this leadership position.

This is an important component across the delivery of healthcare, regardless of country or government involvement. The National Health Service (NHS) in the United Kingdom requires each Health Trust to have a Security Management Director, a member of the Executive, designated with administrative responsibility for security. Each Trust is also required to identify a Local Security Management Specialist (LSMS), who has responsibility for the day-to-day operation of the protection program, and is trained and credentialed by the Security Management Service of the NHS. In 2011 a new NHS security organization was formed, NHS Protect, to assume the responsibilities previously provided by the SMS. The LSMS can be a stand-alone security administrator or someone who has multiple functional responsibility, for example Health and Safety or Facilities. In Canada, the requirement is not as prescriptive, and Accreditation Canada, unlike The Joint Commission, is largely silent on the designation of a leadership position to be charged with oversight of the security function. The Canadian regulations are

01.03 SECURITY ADMINISTRATOR

Statement

Security Administrators play a critical leadership role in a Healthcare Facility's (HCF) security management program.

Intent

a. Each HCF should identify an individual, designated by leadership, to be charged with primary responsibility for the security program.

b. The designated Security Administrator should be responsible for providing or engaging security expertise and possess policy-making authority in keeping with the review and approval process of the HCF.

c. The designated Security Administrator should be actively involved in:

   1) Developing HCF security strategy involving personnel, deployment, training, equipment, policies and regulatory requirements.

   2) HCF Risk Assessment and Reporting

   3) Planning, design, building, and operational phases of all construction and renovation work.

d. The designated Security Administrator should possess the authority to immediately and independently address any imminent threat that may result in serious injury, death, or significant loss of property. This authority should include standing authorization to deploy and implement timely interim measures.

e. Provision should be made for continued professional development of the designated Security Administrator. Membership in at least one professional security organization, participation in security educational programs and obtaining a Certified Healthcare Protection Administrator credential is strongly encouraged.

Approved: January 2006

Last Revised: November 2013

relatively clear, in most provinces, in requiring a designated lead in health organizations to lead a program for the prevention and management of aggressive behavior against staff—largely through workplace safety legislation. However, the requirement for overall security leadership is not in place.

When the organization chart is included in the security management plan, it must portray at least the next highest hierarchical position, or reporting level, above that of the security administrator position. In most cases the organization chart will show reporting levels at least to the chief operating officer level. An organization chart may also show how the security department or program is organized. The department organization chart may be organized to show program functions, positions, or a combination of both position and function. A program organization chart can be quite helpful in conveying an understanding of the overall picture or concept of the security program. Figure 4-2 is an example of a security program organization chart showing a combination of positions as well as functions.

RISK ASSESSMENT EVALUATION

In this section of the security management plan, it is important the methodology and conclusions of the organizational security risk assessment be addressed. It is recognized that the organizational security risk assessment is a living, day-to-day, continuous process. In this respect, each year there should be a formal review of the risk status of the various threats, but not necessarily as in-depth as the baseline (initial) assessment, which may be several years old. The conclusions of this annual security risk assessment review may be included, with goals for the coming year, in the annual review of the security management plan. It is common practice to use the calendar year (i.e., January–December) for the purpose of review and goal setting. This practice renders the reporting periods to be compared in a clear

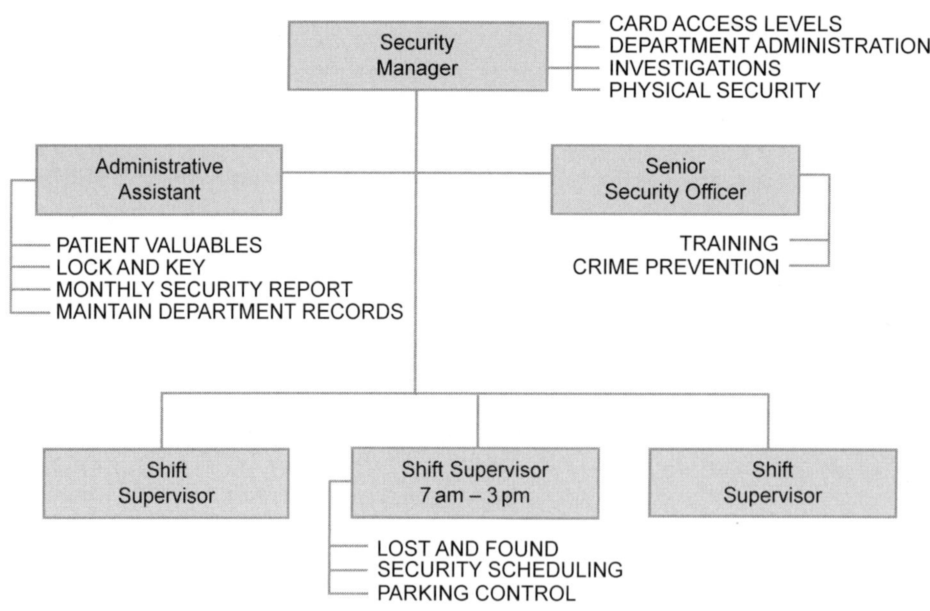

FIGURE 4-2

Security program organization chart depicting positions and functions.

and consistent manner. In some jurisdictions the organizational fiscal year is used as a comparator, often for ease of alignment with financial reporting.

Identification of security sensitive areas

Each healthcare organization must identify those areas that they consider the most security sensitive. This evaluation would be part of the objective of the overall risk assessment process. There is no really clear definition (criteria) of what is, or is not, a security sensitive area for a specific organization. Security sensitive areas should not be necessarily confused with areas of high concern. As an example, safety and security of persons utilizing a parking structure may be of high concern, but would not normally be considered a security sensitive area. The rationale would be that security breaches in the parking area would not severely impact the mission of the organization, as would security breaches in the emergency department relative to the safe and secure delivery of patient care. Chapter 21, "Areas of Higher Risk," covers this subject in much greater detail, as does IAHSS guideline #07.01 – Security Sensitive Areas, which is referenced in that chapter.

SECURITY STAFF POSITION DESCRIPTIONS

The security management plan should contain a brief description of the activities performed by each job position of the security department. An option for this section of the plan could be to include the complete position descriptions in an appendix or attachment to the plan, and simply refer the reader to that document. In utilizing this option it may be useful to include an appendix for other areas of the plan, such as defining skill and competency levels of various positions, a listing of general activities/duties, and a listing or table of contents of security policies and procedures.

This section of the plan is also a good place to include the number of authorized full-time equivalent (FTE) staff for each position. In place of the number of staff for each position, an alternative could be the number of weekly hours required to staff and operate the program. Table 4-1 is an example of portraying staff requirements as an FTE count and the number of deployment hours.

SECURITY PROGRAM OVERVIEW (DUTIES AND ACTIVITIES)

This section of the security management plan is intended to provide the reader with an understanding of what the program does (operations) on a day-to-day basis. This overview bridges the gap between

Table 4-1 Security Department Authorized Staffing Level

Position	FTE	Hours/Week
Security Manager*	1.0	40
Investigator/Trainer*	1.0	40
Shift Supervisor	4.0	160
Security Officer I	11.4	456
Security Officer II	10.6	424
Totals	**26.0**	**1040**

**salaried positions*

mission statement, organization charts, and position descriptions as to the activities performed or accomplished by the security program. This section is important to clearly delineate the role of the security program, which can differ markedly from organization to organization.

SECURITY PHYSICAL SAFEGUARDS

All security programs utilize physical security safeguards to some degree. In this section of the plan each safeguard should be listed, with a general description of how the security program utilizes the safeguard, to include safeguard objectives, responsibility for systems operation, and maintenance. Figure 4-3 is an example of how a physical safeguard might appear in the security management plan.

PHYSICAL SECURITY

SYSTEM DESCRIPTION/PROTOCOL

TYPE: Closed Circuit Television (CCTV)
LOCATION: 4 North Newborn Nursery and Post Partum (Mother/Infant)
OBJECTIVE: General Surveillance/Recorded Movement

GENERAL DESCRIPTION: This CCTV system utilizes four color cameras, a quad (4 screen) monitor, and a recording system. The recording system tapes images from all four cameras, and a ten-day library of recorded images is maintained. The system monitor is located at the 4 North nursing station. It is intended that there will be live monitoring of the cameras only when staff randomly look at monitors or when there is a specific situation requiring attention.

CAMERA LOCATION/PURPOSE: Camera #1 is mounted in the ceiling of the main corridor entry to the mother/infant unit. The purpose of the camera is to record all persons entering the unit.

Camera #2 is mounted in the ceiling of the main corridor entry to the unit back-to-back of Camera #1. The purpose of this camera is to record all persons exiting the unit via this unit corridor.

Camera #3 is mounted in the ceiling of the unit's back corridor (W-E). This corridor cannot be visualized from the nursing station. There is a door at the end of this corridor, leading to a main facility corridor. This door is locked from the main corridor side. The camera is positioned to record all exiting persons and to provide staff at the nursing station a view of this unit's corridor when desired.

Camera #4 is mounted in stairwell #8 facing the stairwell exit door of the mother/infant unit. The purpose of this camera is to view any person exiting into the stairwell. The door is equipped with a 15-second delayed exit device and locked from the ingress side. An alarm is sounded at the nursing station immediately when pressure is exerted on the exit release bar on the door. Staff will immediately respond to the exit door when the alarm is activated.

FIGURE 4-3

A security management plan description of an organization's utilization of video surveillance.

SECURITY STAFF TRAINING

In this section of the plan there will be a review of the various elements of the training provided to security personnel. This training will vary considerably between organizations, but will always relate directly to the job description and skill levels required of each position. Since skill levels, training, and competency all tie together, this section would be a good place to include competency procedures. Competency essentially means verifying skill levels and/or determining the training needs of each staff person, to achieve the desired level of identified skills necessary to satisfactorily perform in the assigned position.

DEPARTMENT POLICIES AND PROCEDURES

A simple listing of security operational policies and procedures is appropriate for this section. This information is often referred to as post (or facility) orders or security protocols. In some instances these could include corporate or organizational guidance noted in policies that have application beyond the security program itself—security of patient valuables and use of security cameras in patient care areas are two such examples. A brief explanation of the process of how these policies and procedures are prepared, approvals required, and how and where they are maintained in a current status help the reader understand the mechanics of this element of the security system. The policy and procedure listing referred to in this section does not include personnel policies, covering staff conduct, disciplinary actions, pay, or benefits. Figure 4-4 is an example of a commonly utilized security policies and procedures.

SECURITY EDUCATION (SECURITY AWARENESS)

A comprehensive security program includes a process of education, training, and motivating persons to be security aware. Being security aware and adhering to good security practices can prevent and reduce security events. While much of this educational effort is directed to staff, it should be clear in this section of the plan who is responsible for providing the various educational activities. For example, the security department may be responsible for new employee security training, or it may be the human resources department or safety officer. Another example is the requirement for staff training relative to security in designated security sensitive areas. Is this training the responsibility of the area supervisor or is it accomplished by the security department? Who develops training material? Where and how are the training records maintained?

The typical security program will involve a variety of departments to accomplish employee security training. The security department should provide the coordination, education and consulting to blend all these efforts into the overall unified security training program. Many medical centers include security-related information in material provided to staff, such as:

- Identification badges
- Security services phone number
- Reportable incidents (disturbances, patient, visitor, employee lost/stolen property, suspicious people/items, smoking on campus)
- Organizational position statement on weapons, including Active Shooter response
- Prisoners as patients and staff responsibilities

COMMON HEALTHCARE SECURITY
POLICIES AND PROCEDURES

Security Staffing and Deployment

Functional Relationship of Security Department Positions

General Security Officer Duties and Activities

Utilization of Security Equipment and Vehicles

Reporting for Duty

Security Assistance/Support
- Patients
- Staff
- Visitors
- Vehicle
- Departments/Programs

Critical Incident and Alarm Response

Outside Agency Interaction/Response

Legal Actions and Guidelines

Investigative Procedures

Report Preparation

Facility Access Control

Enforcing Organization Rules

Safety Services/Response

Parking Control

Facility Property Control/Removal

Patient Property Control

Lost and Found

Security Officer Training
- Helicopter Landings
- Bomb Threats
- No Smoking Enforcement
- Forensic Patients
- Searching for Contraband
- Emergency Management Response
- Use of Force
- Missing Patients

FIGURE 4-4

A list of common healthcare security policies and procedures.

- Access control (keys, cards, codes, business hours versus after-hours, parking, visitor management, assistance alarms)
- Securing personal items
- Infant abduction prevention and response
- Department-specific security information.
- Targeted violence/domestic threat processes/bullying position statement
- Working alone, personal safety, including escorts to parking areas

Chapter 15, "Employee Involvement and Security Awareness," covers the subject of engaging employees in the healthcare protection program in greater detail.

PUBLIC SAFETY AGENCY LIAISON

In this section of the security management plan, only a brief discussion of the relationship and coordination with the various public safety agencies is required. Information included should identify the law enforcement organizations with jurisdiction and the emergency service agencies responsible for providing emergency services to the facility. Operational and protocol procedures with these agencies is generally not referred to in the security management plan.

SECURITY RECORDS AND REPORTS

The security management plan should outline basic security records and reports prepared and utilized in the security program. This outline should provide a brief explanation of the objective of each document, who is responsible for preparation of the document, distribution protocols, how and where each document is available for review, guidelines for follow-up/improvement activities, and the assigned document retention time period. Figure 4-5 is a sample format for how each document (form) in the security program is prepared and utilized.

PERFORMANCE STANDARDS AND PERFORMANCE IMPROVEMENT MEASURES

Program performance standards must be in place to determine if program goals and objectives are accomplished. All successful healthcare security programs measure actual activity to determine the level of service provided. A common goal is to develop an action plan to improve activities or areas not meeting standards. Look for opportunities to set higher standards where possible. When an adverse change is identified in performance metrics, the leaders assess the relative severity of the change and determine an appropriate response. Table 4-2 identifies sample performance measures for event elements within the protection program. Many organizations will also monitor program and activity elements to address preventive and compliance activities.

A key management responsibility is to ensure that standards are set at a realistic level. If standards are too low the program stagnates with little incentive to improve. On the other hand, standards must be realistically achievable. IAHSS guideline #06.01 outlines the basic aspects of standards and improving performance.

SECURITY DOCUMENTATION

SYSTEM DESCRIPTION/PROTOCOL

TYPE: Security Incident Report
LOCATION: All Campus Facilities
OBJETIVE: The completion of an accurate and timely report of all security incidents occurring on facility property, or affecting the organization from a protection perspective. The report will clearly set forth facts and include all actions taken by personnel in relation to the incident.

GENERAL DESCRIPTION

Security Incident Reports (SIR), form SD-104, will be completed by the assigned security officer responding to the incident or by off-site personnel as directed by a member of the security department. The SIR will be completed as soon after the initial management of the incident has been accomplished. The completed report will be reviewed by the security shift supervisor and be placed in the investigator's "in box" located in the central security control station.

REPORT UTILIZATION

The security shift supervisor, or the assigned investigator, will effect any emergency or routine notification of other appropriate parties relative to a security incident.

The assigned investigator will determine the need for any follow-up investigation of the incident and if so will coordinate this follow-up activity. The investigator will enter summary incident information into the computer log file after verifying the appropriate incident report classification. The computer log file will be utilized to generate the monthly, quarterly, and annual security incident report utilized by security administration and reporting to the facility safety committee.

REPORT STORAGE/RETENTION

The completed SIR, with attached supplemental reports if appropriate, will be filed chronologically as the master file. These reports will be maintained for a 5-year period except for a report where there is a perceived need for the report to be maintained in excess of 5 years. Retention of these reports will be determined on an individual basis by the Director of Security.

FIGURE 4-5

A sample format for explaining the security incident report in the security management plan.

THE JOINT COMMISSION STANDARDS

The Security Management Plan should address how each Joint Commission accredited, or nonaccredited, U.S. healthcare organization complies with each specific Element of Performance (EP) of the standards pertaining to security. The plan should not, however, be limited to just The Joint Commission requirements. Simply addressing their standards and elements alone will not provide a complete and comprehensive protection plan for the organization.

There were two major changes affecting security in The Joint Commission Standards in 2009 that are still in place today. The first was the combining of security and safety into a single standard. The second change was to remove the Emergency Management (EM) standard from the Environment of Care (EC) chapter. The Emergency Management standard thus became a new stand-alone chapter.

Table 4-2 Security Department Sample Performance Measures

Performance Measures—Security Event Elements				
Measure Description	**Period**	**Trigger Value**	**Actual Value**	**Action(s) taken when Actual Value exceeds Trigger Value**
The average number of Patient Assistance-ER events, in a quarter, do not exceed the 2013 average	Q1 = 121 Q2 = 202 Q3 = 198 Q4 = 255	±5%	211 255 249 303	
The average amount of time spent on Patient Assistance-ER events, in a quarter, does not exceed by 5% the 2013 average	Q1 = 2:15 Q2 = 2:49 Q3 = 3:18 Q4 = 3:02	±5%	3:02 3:45 4:13 2:58	
The average number of "crime related" events (Assault, Burglary, Missing Property–Stolen or –Whole Vehicle, Murder, Robbery, Suicide, Vandalism), in a quarter, do not exceed 2013 average	Q1 = 4 Q2 = 0 Q3 = 1 Q4 = 5	anything> avg.	2 2 0 3	
The average number of "open door/ window" conditions, in a quarter, do not exceed the 2013 average	Q1 = 77 Q2 = 44 Q3 = 31 Q4 = 54	±5%	64 45 25 60	

The Safety and Security Standard EC.02.01.01 contains the following Elements of Performance specific to security:

- "The hospital identifies safety and security risks associated with the environment of care. Risks are identified from internal sources such as ongoing monitoring of the environment, results of root cause analysis, results of annual proactive risk assessment of high-risk processes, and from credible external sources such as Sentinel Event Alerts."
- "The hospital takes action to minimize or eliminate identified safety and security risks in the physical environment."
- "The hospital identifies individuals entering its facilities." Note: "The hospital determines which of those individuals requires identification and how to do so."
- "The hospital controls access to and from areas it identifies as security sensitive."

IAHSS – HEALTHCARE BASIC SECURITY GUIDELINE #06.01

Program Measurement/Improvement

Statement

Healthcare Facilities (HCF) will formally evaluate the effectiveness of their security system on a regularly scheduled basis and will identify areas in which program improvement is appropriate. Goals, process for improvement, and elements for measuring progress will be identified in the Security Management Plan or in a security improvement performance plan.

Intent

a. It is essential that performance measurement(s) be in place to evaluate the security program.
b. Security performance improvement goals should be consistent with the HCF organizational goals.
c. The improvement of security performance and achievement of improvement goals should be approached as an ongoing and continuous process.
d. Performance measurement should be goal driven. If a goal is to reduce a certain activity, or increase a perception of security, the measurement should reflect a starting and ending point. If the goal is to mitigate risks associated with potential emergencies, the measurement should reflect the implementation of the identified mitigation.
e. An annual assessment may reveal the need to reprioritize the program goals. The annual assessment may include a hazard vulnerability assessment to assist in prioritizing specific training drills and emergency plans.
f. The tools to gain information should be reliable and consistently used from one measuring time to the next. Charts, graphs, heat maps and other visual enhancements may be useful in presenting the data in a concise and clear manner.
g. Trending of performance improvement data is a common methodology for benchmarking security performance or analyzing elements of activity and incidents. A security program should track security incidents and a statistical summary of those incidents, by category, should be maintained on a monthly basis. This summary should reflect the number of incidents and should compare the current and previous months and allow for comparison of specific months within the current and previous years for more in-depth incident trend analysis.

Approved: October 2008
Last Revised: July 2013

- "The hospital has written procedures to follow in the event of a security incident, including an infant or pediatric abduction."
- "When a security incident occurs, the hospital follows its identified procedures."[1]

Another important safety and security standard, EC 04.01.010, contains the following:

- "The hospital established a process(es) for continually monitoring, internally reporting, and investigating security incidents involving patients, staff, or others within its facilities."
- "Every 12 months, the hospital evaluates each environment of care management plan, including a review of the plan's objectives, scope, performance, and effectiveness."[2]

The specific components required as part of the annual Joint Commission security plan review should address the following elements:

Objective – Review the goal of the security management plan and the overall mission of the security department. Do these facilitate a healing environment? Do they help the facility meet its stated mission, vision, and core values? If the objective (or mission) of the department changes, identify the new statement in the evaluation. If the objective of the plan does not change, state the current objective and mission will continue for the next plan year.

Scope – Review the scope of the plan to include verifying all locations covered by the Security Management Plan including all off-site locations, new construction or acquisition of new locations during the past year or planned for the upcoming plan year. Specifically review each declared security sensitive area and determine if the department will continue to be so declared in the upcoming plan year and identify, by name, departments added or subtracted from this declaration and why.

Performance **–** In this section, recap the performance measures/indicators or performance improvement initiatives undertaken for security. Provide the results of each performance standard with an appropriate year-end analysis that includes a specific comment on how effective the measure was to improving the overall security posture at the facility.

Provide year-end statistics for the security incident activity tracked for the past year and if possible, provide a 3–5 year comparison of this data. Denote significant increases/decreases that have occurred, identifying the reasons and any action taken as a response. This same process can be used for the reporting of facility security condition reports.

Program Effectiveness – Denote if the plan was effective in meeting its objectives of minimizing physical hazards and managing staff activities to reduce the risk of injury or loss/damage of property. Use this opportunity to discuss the accomplishments of the security department during the past year to include:

- Changes made to the Security Management Plan and reasons why
- Installation/upgrade of physical security measures or electronic security technology to include security cameras or recording devices, duress or intrusion alarms, emergency communication devices or radio systems, access control devices or lock and key systems
- Newly written/revised security-specific policy and procedures or security-specific drills conducted to include infant abduction, prisoner as a patient, active shooter/hostage, VIP or other
- Security-specific education and training programs offered to the hospital staff to include the security section of new employee orientation, aggression management/de-escalation, Security Fairs, personal safety or other departmental or staff presentations offered
- Changes (increases/decreases) made to the security-staffing plan or alterations to the deployment/responsibilities of security staff to include assuming responsibility for fire-alarm testing, well-being checks, morgue transports, patient valuables, lost and found, etc.

There are countless accomplishments made by security each year. This section should be used to comprehensively denote each, and the opportunity taken to express the value and benefit of security to the facility served. This is a frequently absent component of many reviews and should be used by the security program to share the many successful undertakings of the department.

Recommendation for Plan Improvement – Most departments denote a level of success for the security program during the course of the annual review and, although The Joint Commission does not explicitly require it, a good practice is to indicate where opportunities for program improvement exist, and state the goals for the department for the upcoming year. Not to be misconstrued with performance indicators or performance improvement initiatives, these goals should identify the strategic initiatives set forth to improve the overall security posture for the upcoming plan year. These recommendations also create an excellent benchmark for determining program effectiveness at the end of the next plan year.

The Emergency Management (EM) chapter contains a variety of elements with a direct impact on security operations during an emergency. Standard EM.02.02.05, Elements of Performance, requires an Operations Plan describing the following security involvement:

- "The hospital's arrangements for internal security and safety."
- "How the hospital will coordinate security activities with community security agencies (for example, police, sheriff and National Guard)."

- "How the hospital will control entrance into and out of the health care facility during an emergency."
- "How the hospital will control the movement of individuals within the health care facility during an emergency."
- "The hospital's arrangements for controlling vehicles that access the health care facility during an emergency."[3]

There are, of course, many other aspects of the Emergency Management Plan that require input, coordination, and support from the security program.

The Human Resources (HR) chapter contains a number of standards that bear directly on the administrative and operational aspects of the security program. Included is the responsibility to establish and verify staff qualifications, orientation of staff, and the implementation of effective staff training. While Joint Commission standards generally task human resources to provide for on-the-job assessment of staff competence and performance, the actual methodology and effort in this regard is the responsibility of the security program administrator.

Of particular note for the security administrator is the TJC Standard HR.01.04.01 Element of Performance Number 7, which states, "The hospital orients external law enforcement and security personnel on the following:

- How to interact with patients
- Procedures for responding to unusual clinical events and incidents
- The hospital's channels of clinical, security, and administrative communication
- Distinctions between administrative and clinical seclusion and restraint."[4]

An additional information source relative to forensic staff includes the IAHSS Healthcare Security Guideline "Prisoner Patient Security," (02.03), which is further discussed in Chapter 13, "Patient Care Involvement and Intervention."

Standards and Elements of Performance, as published, should always be reviewed on a periodic basis to determine any additions, deletions or changes, relative to the accreditation process and specific EP requirements. Subscriptions to *Environment of Care News*, a publication of Joint Commission Resources, and *Environment of Care Leader* are smart investments to help the security administrator stay on top of the variety of changes issued by The Joint Commission and interpretations of how those changes may affect a hospital protection program.

SECURITY MANAGEMENT CYCLE

There really is no endpoint in security management planning and operations. The protection program must be viewed as a cyclical process. It is a dynamic process, geared to react to new issues and concerns, as well as eliminating ineffective or obsolete practices as an ongoing process. The starting point is, of course, identifying and quantifying security risks as identified in Chapter 3, "Healthcare Security Risks and Vulnerabilities." This starting point is repeated day in and day out as the management cycle continues to provide new information. Figure 4-6 graphically reveals the security management process/cycle.

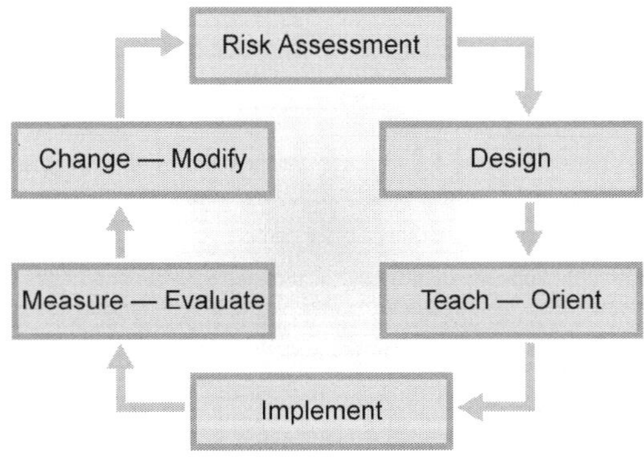

FIGURE 4-6

Security management process/cycle.

SECURITY STRATEGIC PLAN

The security strategic plan is the second major plan required of the healthcare organization. As opposed to the day-to-day security management plan previously discussed, this plan sets the philosophy and direction of the protection program for a longer term (3–5 years), and should include elements of financial planning, the integration of technology and incorporating recognized industry best practices over time. The major components of this plan are organization-wide security coordination and control, neighborhood stability and security/crime prevention involvement, public safety agency coordination, criminal justice system interface, a philosophy regarding the type and extent of physical security safeguards to be utilized, the degree of employee/staff involvement in the protection program (i.e., centralization vs. decentralization), and building configuration and design considerations. Figure 4-7 illustrates the components of the healthcare organization security strategic plan.

There are various methodologies, approaches and processes in strategic planning; however, they typically involve the following three-step process to some degree:

1) Situation – evaluate the current situation and how it came about.
2) Target – define goals and/or objectives that are sometimes referred to as the ideal state.
3) Path – map a route to obtain the agreed-upon goals and/or objectives.

A major intent of the security strategic plan is to provide the mechanisms and philosophy of achieving the overall direction of the protection system agreed upon by the stakeholders. It should be reflective of guiding beliefs and align these with daily practices in the protection program. The strategic plan should be sensitive to the overall demographics of the healthcare organization, and explore opportunities for building synergies with other departments and outside agencies.

ORGANIZATION-WIDE SECURITY COORDINATION

Basic organizational policy must create a clear understanding of the authority and responsibility of the various layers of management, in regard to the protection program. In this respect the security department

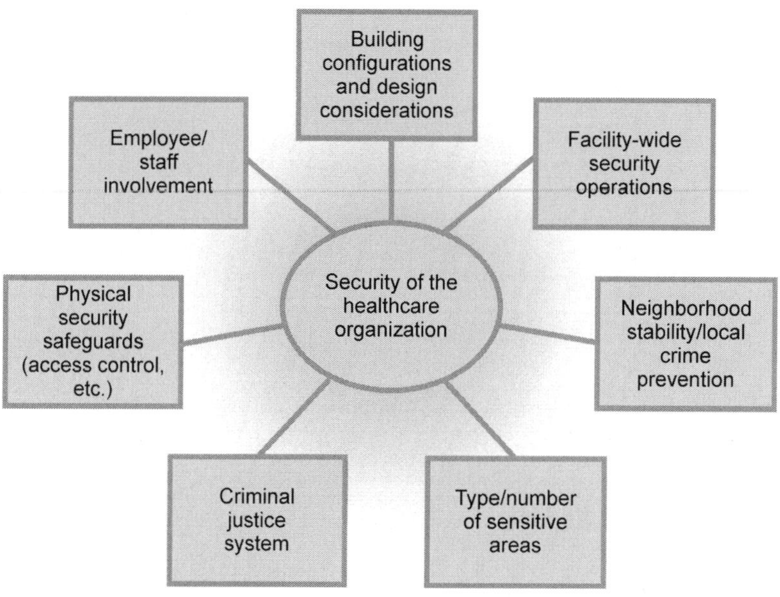

FIGURE 4-7

Components of the healthcare organization security strategic plan.

is seldom responsible for all the components of the protection program. What security responsibilities are and what security decisions can be made, within an operating department, versus those reserved totally for the security department, must be clearly articulated. This question involves the philosophy of security centralization versus decentralization. The same questions attach to a multilocation organization, which may have two or three campuses and a dozen or more freestanding patient facilities many miles removed from each other. Does security provide all the direct services as a mandate to the freestanding facility, or does management at the facility make independent decisions regarding reporting of events, key control, alarm systems, etc.? In a totally decentralized approach the Director of Security on the main campus may serve only as a consultant, upon the request of the autonomously operating freestanding facility.

Even within the main facility, various departments may be performing security-related functions almost totally removed from the security department. Background checks, including criminal histories, are a significant element of the protection program but may be almost exclusively the responsibility of the human resources department—not only in performing the activity, but making the decision relative to the depth and methodology of such background investigations.

A small example of the types of questions that should be answered with the preparation of corresponding protocols is:

- Who has the authority, and under what circumstances can the police be called to effect an arrest on behalf of the organization?
- Who has the authority to make decisions in reference to locks and keys? Can any employee order a lock installed, removed, or changed? Who approves the issuance of keys? Who assigns security access levels in a card or biometric access security system?

- Can departments order and install a security alarm or camera in their department without security approval?
- What about physical security safeguard funding? What types of security equipment and supplies are purchased with security department allocated funds, versus operating department funds?
- Does the nurse decide if missing property will be reported? If reported, does the unit nurse or security representative prepare the missing property report? If the nurse completes the report is it mandated that a copy be sent to security, nursing administration, or risk management?
- Who decides restitution questions regarding property loss or damage relative to patients, staff, and visitor property?
- When security is called to a patient treatment area due to the inappropriate behavior of patient or visitor, who is in charge relative to the required actions to be taken?
- What formal decisions must be made to determine the use of force tools carried by security staff or written guidelines on when or under what circumstances the devices should be used in the healthcare setting or used on a patient? This includes the incident review process after deployment of defensive equipment.

These questions and many more require clear direction and are instrumental in shaping the type of security program that evolves for the protection of the healthcare organization.

NEIGHBORHOOD STABILITY AND SECURITY/CRIME PREVENTION ACTIVITIES

A healthcare security protection program goes beyond the physical property lines of the campus. Community involvement should take place, to some extent, in all protection programs. The environment surrounding the campus severely impacts the security risks to the organization, and all persons coming to and from the facilities. Visitors and staff being assaulted on or off the property may mean little, except in litigation, in terms of creating and maintaining an area where people feel safe. In many cases an event occurring a block or more from a facility will be reported as being "at the medical center." Some security departments work at community involvement and others tend to withdraw from this activity. Examples of security community outreach are:

- Security patrols of the neighborhood by organization security departments. These patrols may be funded totally by the healthcare organization, contracted by businesses, or neighborhood associations, or a cost-sharing arrangement.
- Active involvement in neighborhood watch and community associations. The healthcare organization may provide funding, meeting places, and sometimes allow use of equipment, and attend appropriate community meetings.
- Block parties are a popular event, blending the medical area campus into the surrounding neighborhood. These events provide tours, food, entertainment, and fun activities for old and young alike. The concept is to be a good corporate neighbor and an integral part of the community.
- Alarm monitoring and response is another element of community involvement. Alarms generally pertain to businesses; however, a really involved healthcare organization outreach program could provide this service for private homes in their neighborhood as well.

PUBLIC SAFETY COORDINATION

The primary public safety agencies that the security program must work with would be homeland security, law enforcement agencies, fire, disaster preparedness and response, and possibly a governmental city-wide ambulance service. The law enforcement coordination presents many additional issues and opportunities. This topic is generally covered in a separate section of the healthcare security strategic plan. In these cases the master plan should include a reference to these important agencies which refers the reader to appropriate documents or departments.

CRIMINAL JUSTICE INTERFACE

This section of the plan requires specific policy to define appropriate staff interactions with law enforcement agencies at all levels: prosecutors, probation, parole, and correctional personnel. A major issue is what will be reported to law enforcement and who will make these decisions as situations occur. On the surface this appears to be quite simplistic but as the subsets to these questions develop, it becomes more complex. There are confidentiality issues, as well as philosophical differences, especially between security and the human resources department or privacy officer, who often view the relationship with law enforcement from a different perspective.

The police, on the other hand, often insist all crime be immediately reported to them but then, politely or otherwise, expound on their overload of work and desire not to be bothered with minor crime. In some jurisdictions the police will not even respond to the scene of certain crimes, unless there is a suspect being detained. In this respect, does the organization report the loss of one dollar from the bedside of a patient, five dollars, twenty, fifty, or one hundred? Or does the organization leave all reporting of missing personal property to the victim? Does the police agency permit, or foster, reporting certain crimes directly to a specialized investigative unit, or must all reporting be accomplished through a police dispatcher or mail-in report? An example is missing narcotics. In many jurisdictions, it is appropriate to report directly to the police narcotics unit and, in others, this direct reporting is prohibited. It is often difficult to define some of these relationships, as law enforcement agencies often give out conflicting information, not to mention changes in philosophies when new police administrators are anointed. These problems have been minimized in some jurisdictions, where a specific municipal or county police liaison person has been specifically assigned to work with the healthcare organization (i.e., community policing). There tend to be fewer liaison problems at state and federal levels, as contacts are less frequent and issues are more situational, with specific decision makers readily available.

UTILIZATION OF PHYSICAL SECURITY SAFEGUARDS

Virtually all healthcare organizations utilize physical security (hardware) as a component of their protection system. This utilization may include locks, lighting, barriers and state-of-the- art electronics. Unfortunately, many of our nation's healthcare organizations have ended up with a high-cost, uncoordinated "conglomeration" of ineffective equipment. Security staffing and physical security safeguards are intended to complement each other, in forming a balanced blend of staffing resources and equipment.

There should be an objective or purpose for every component of physical security in how it fits into the overall protection plan. Physical security safeguards are usually purchased in relatively small amounts over a number of years, due to budget considerations. To best coordinate, there should be a road map (plan) to establish how each purchase fits the technical aspects of being compatible with current equipment, product standardization from a cost maintenance and replacement viewpoint, and user buy-in and acceptance. The philosophy of the organization should also be factored into the direction of the program, i.e., restrictions regarding signage, and use of covert security cameras, as well as the broader issue of restricted vs. uninhibited access into the facility or department.

Video surveillance is used in almost every security program and provides a good example of how strategic planning should be used to help shape system implementation and use. A series of questions can help shape the plan.

- Will the system be centrally monitored or departmentally monitored, or will it be monitored via "dark screen"? Indeed will it be monitored at all, or simply available for after-the-fact investigative purposes?
- Will it be used to monitor patient activity? How will those images be monitored? How will the images be stored?
- Will the system be centrally recorded or departmentally recorded? Will the system operate on the available hospital IT infrastructure or stand-alone?
- What is the policy or plan regarding the use of fixed cameras versus movement (pan, tilt, zoom) cameras?
- What is the policy or plan regarding covert versus overt camera placement?
- Will the camera system be integrated with other electronic physical security components, fire systems and/or building management systems?
- What is the policy or plan on utilizing "legacy" equipment and, moving forward, the plan to migrate to an IP platform with the flexibility to adapt to technological change?
- What other departments inside the healthcare facility will be part of the design and evaluation process?
- Who can determine camera placement and utilization?
- Who is authorized to purchase equipment?
- Who is authorized to release archived images?
- Will equipment be standardized as to manufacturer and/or technical specifications?
- Will equipment be maintained by an in-house or vendor arrangement?
- What is the maintenance and equipment replacement schedule?
- What is the optimum size of the system in relation to the total security program?

There should be a business plan approach to the utilization of physical security safeguards. This plan should address the current year and project plans, objectives, and funding for a minimum of five years. It is common to divide the plan into short-term and long-term sections. The physical security and technology plan should be developed in conjunction with stakeholders from the Facilities and Information Services programs, to ensure alignment with their strategies for the organization and give security early access to the planning and design process.

EMPLOYEE/STAFF INVOLVEMENT IN THE PROTECTION PROGRAM

It is universally agreed that healthcare staff must take ownership and directly contribute to the protection of the organization. However, there are issues beyond practicing good security. One such issue is the authority and responsibility for intervention with aggressive behavior. When security is called to a nursing unit because a patient or visitor is out of control, who is responsible for directing actions—security or nursing? The answer is either one may be appropriate; however, this role should be clear in the strategic plan and reflected in the resultant policy/procedure. When there are drugs missing from the pharmacy, is this a pharmacy problem with support from security, or a security problem to be resolved by security, with support from the pharmacy? When a laptop computer belonging to the organization is stolen, can the employee simply order another one, or does it require a report to security, before the purchasing unit will order or otherwise provide a new one? These are the types of questions that must be answered from a strategic context to provide the proper operating fabric and coordinated direction of the protection effort.

BUILDING CONFIGURATION AND DESIGN

The most cost-effective security is designed and planned during renovation or new construction. Traffic patterns can be planned and new security hardware installed at far less cost than a retrofit situation—some security professionals and design engineers estimate savings to be a third of the overall costs. Funding is often more easily obtained when it is included in the total construction package. New construction will often present the opportunity to begin a phased approach for introducing a new system for the whole campus. The best example is the introduction of an electronic card access system. An enterprise access system for a large campus may cost in excess of a million dollars or more at build-out. This large expenditure is typically spread over several years. The first phase may be a physician office building with proper strategic planning that includes the basic hardware and software to accommodate the entire campus, and all off-site facilities. The strategic plan should stipulate that no construction or installation of security hardware can be purchased or installed without the review, and approval if necessary, of the director of security or the designated person responsible for total organization protection.

STRATEGIC PLAN UNIQUE TO ORGANIZATION

The security strategic plan will be unique to each specific organization as to form, format, and subject area. This plan, however, is necessary for all organizations to provide clear program direction. Without the framework of strategic security policy and infrastructure, a program simply becomes one of day-to-day reaction, which typically results in higher costs and less fruitful outcomes.

The strategic plan, in its final format, affords additional protection as it helps document "the why" behind what is being done in the protection program. In the event of an adverse situation, the protection afforded by this alone is significant. It demonstrates the importance of security to the organization and comprehensively documents all that has been done. It shows how important security is taken within the organization and helps obtain buy-in from the highest levels of organizational leadership.

ALIGNMENT WITH OVERALL ORGANIZATION STRATEGIC PLAN

As healthcare organizations have become more business-focused, healthcare security leaders have evolved their planning processes to strengthen and profile their alignment with organizational priorities. In some healthcare security programs, this has resulted in a tiered, or layered, series of plans that begins with a security strategic plan, clearly connected to the strategic plan of the healthcare organization it serves.

In this model, demonstrated in Figure 4-8, the security strategic plan is linked to the healthcare organizational strategic plan, with the security management plan (including annual goals and

ALIGNMENT OF SECURITY PROGRAM PLANS			
HEALTHCARE ORGANIZATION STRATEGIC PLAN	SECURITY PROGRAM STRATEGIC PLAN	SECURITY MANAGEMENT PLAN Includes Annual Goals and Objectives	INDIVIDUAL PERFORMANCE PLANS Linked to goals and objectives

FIGURE 4-8

Alignment of security program plans.

objectives) feeding into the security strategic plan, The next layer would see individual performance plans for each of the security program team members feed into the security management plan and, more specifically, to annual goals and objectives for the security program.

Virtually every hospital or healthcare organization will have a strategic plan, usually prominently featured in short form on their website and visible within the healthcare facilities. As an example, in Australia we can look at Melbourne Health and find a 28-page Strategic Plan for 2010–2015, that contains not only their mission, vision and values but also their Strategic Goals for 2010–2015.[5]

As with most organizations, Melbourne Health has both a long and short form of these strategic goals. The short form is intended to be easily understood by staff and the community alike and serves to create and reinforce the culture of the organization. The Melbourne Health Strategic Goals for 2010–2015 are delineated as:

- Develop our workforce
- Improve the quality and safety of our services
- Develop and encourage strategic relationships
- Foster a culture of research and innovation
- Build a sustainable organization

Many of these, and like themes, can be found in healthcare organizations across the world— they are all in the business of caring for patients after all.

In this Security Planning model, however, it is imperative that the security administrator be able to demonstrate a connectivity between the security strategic plan and the organizational strategic plan, to embed the purpose and the work of the security program within the organizational mission and culture. This connectivity should be achieved at the expense of the key elements of strategic planning described elsewhere in this chapter.

If we use the Melbourne Health Strategic Goals and envision ourselves as the security administrator there, we may be drawn immediately to words like "safety" and the notion of "workforce development" as areas where security strategies could readily emerge. But with a little effort we can see how one or two security strategies could be drawn from each of the five Melbourne Strategic Goals. For example, workforce development: we can talk about a skilled security workforce and all that entails. Additionally, another pillar may be enhancing leadership competencies and capacity in the security program. Quality and safety have no bounds in the security world, but a focus on developing a culture of patient-centric service in the department may be an important strategic initiative. Strategic relationships may lead into the realm of the public safety liaison role and department stakeholder involvement in the security program. The culture of research and innovation may involve innovative practices in security training as an example, which could also fit in strategic relationships if it involved the engagement of clinical or other internal stakeholders. Finally building a sustainable organization could encompass managing financial resources while another strategy could speak to integrated security systems as contributing to as sustainable organization.

From a leadership perspective, the visionary security administrator is able to connect her or his team with the organizational strategies, the purpose of security in the unique environment that is healthcare. At the same time the security strategic plan will resonate with healthcare organization executives and the rest of the organization, as important and relevant in support of the mission of the organization.

Once the strategic plan is developed, the Security Management Plan brings it to life and adds substance to how it will be achieved in a given year, and the annual goals and objectives serve as the measurements for how the strategic goals over the 3 to 5 year period (may also be considered mileposts). The annual development of individual performance plans for the Security Administrator and members of the security team allow for the goals and objectives to be met as a team and individual.

Properly developed, the process outlined allows individual plans to weave together to meet annual goals and objectives in the Security Management Plan, which serves, on an annual basis, to move the program closer to completing its strategic goals—and always in concert with the organizational strategic plan. In some jurisdictions, this model is taken one step further by aligning the organizational strategic plan with the state or provincial health strategic plan. What must be reinforced is the cyclical nature of this process; it is in constant motion and with continuous improvement being sought. The strategic plans must be reviewed annually, and revised and refreshed when required, both by the healthcare organization and, by extension, the security program.

REFERENCES

1. Joint Commission Accreditation Healthcare. *2014 hospital accreditation standards*. Oakbrook Terrace, IL: Joint Commission Resources; 2014. p. 29–30.
2. Joint Commission Accreditation Healthcare. *2014 hospital accreditation standards*. Oakbrook Terrace, IL: Joint Commission Resources; 2014. p. 44–45.
3. Joint Commission Accreditation Healthcare. *2014 hospital accreditation standards*. Oakbrook Terrace, IL: Joint Commission Resources; 2014. p. 57.
4. Joint Commission Accreditation Healthcare. *2014 hospital accreditation standards*. Oakbrook Terrace, IL: Joint Commission Resources; 2014. p. 74.
5. *Melbourne Health Strategic Plan 2010-2015*. 2010. Retrieved February 11, 2014, from http://www.mh.org.au/publications/w1/i1001231/#StrategicPlans.

CHAPTER

MANAGING THE BASIC ELEMENTS OF HEALTHCARE SECURITY

5

The function of a healthcare security program goes far beyond simply addressing security risk and vulnerabilities. The program must provide a whole host of services. In this chapter we will review the basics of healthcare security—the fundamentals that healthcare security administrators can never afford to lose sight of.

Various functions of the healthcare security program must work together to reduce security risks and provide tangible benefits in support of the organizational mission. Each organization must determine how the functional security program elements will be implemented and managed. They may be assigned to different individuals and departments, or they may be brought together under a specific department or division. In this respect not all elements of a protection system are performed by one department. An example of this concept is the background investigation of applicants seeking employment. The background investigation is an element of the protection system but is generally performed by the human resources department rather than by security.

Security programs must be structured to protect the organization within the restrictive factors of organizational mission, vision, and core values; physical design; patient and community demographics; employee and public relations; budget and resource availability; and the operational requirements of the facility. It is essential that the healthcare security program mirror and support the culture of the organization.

The security function should not be applied in such a manner that it is unduly confining in terms of the operational efficiency of providing quality patient care. The healthcare security function must be viewed as an element of management that supports the creation of an environment in which healing can occur. This support will involve numerous systems and subsystems of protective services.

The security function cannot be static; rather, it must continuously evolve to meet the changing needs of society. It must remain flexible to cope with the constant changes in security risks and vulnerabilities that occur in a changing patient-care environment and the community as a whole. It must also be continuously evaluated to ensure that the protection function is fulfilling the organization's objectives and needs.

The security function has a different focus, however slight, in each and every facility. Despite this, security practitioners and healthcare administrators agree on one point: the security function must always be rooted in a service orientation and not based solely on a law enforcement focus. The law enforcement function is designed to provide protective services from an external or environmental standpoint, and it cannot provide the internal safeguards that comprise up to 90% of an organization's security system—prevention, education, and public relations. Investigations and policy enforcement are important roles of a sophisticated protection program but should not drive the structure and organizational mission of the security department.

Security programs still tend to be constructed and developed in a manner that reflects the strengths, weaknesses and philosophy of the person responsible for the program, rather than organizational needs. For example, if the responsible person has a background as a firefighter, the protection program will often be structured toward a strong fire prevention and control system. A person with a strong background in investigation will use investigation as the backbone of the program, and the other elements that support this emphasis.

It cannot be stated strongly enough that the organization—not the individual responsible for security—defines the security function. This does not mean that the security administrator cannot craft the security master plan or provide directional input. However, the underlying security philosophies put into place by the facility should not be developed in a vacuum. The process should include key constituents of the organization to include leadership representatives from clinical leadership, including the emergency department, IT, human resources, facilities, and risk management. However, in the end, administrative leadership of the organization must support and give approval—designating the responsibility, providing authority and allocating the resources necessary to implement the security program.

Protection safeguards for smaller healthcare organizations will vary significantly as to who is assigned responsibility. In a critical access hospital, protection responsibilities could include the nursing supervisor, plant operations staff, risk manager, the facility administrator, or any combination. In the case of medical clinics and nursing homes, the entire responsibility often rests with the business manager. Less formalized than in larger organizations, the assignment of responsibility is often unwritten and vague. One of the inherent challenges in smaller healthcare organizations is that employees often have responsibilities for disciplines outside of their experience or educational specialty. No one can be completely knowledgeable in all fields. When one individual must perform many varied tasks, the protection system is often given a lower priority.

This trend was demonstrated in a stinging report issued in 2008 when investigators for the inspector general for the U.S. Department of Health and Human Services (DHHS) said that the vast majority of nursing homes have been cited for violations of federal safety and health standards. The DHHS report alluded to the absence of effective security processes and procedures and inadequate security investments as issues affecting patient/resident safety.[1] Since the writing of the last edition, there has been an increase in interest and investment in electronic security solutions, aggression management training, emergency management planning and other physical security safeguards by rural hospitals, long-term care facilities, urgent care centers and other smaller healthcare facilities. Although available funding resources are limited in most of these facilities, their investment in security-related safeguards continues to increase.

A security operation cannot be superimposed, like an umbrella, on a healthcare organization with any degree of effectiveness. Rather it must be integrated into the routine operations of the organization and cannot successfully function from a position outside the patient-centric environment. To produce the maximum return on the investment, security must be a service-oriented entity.

When security officers culturally assimilate to the service philosophy, they become a viable and important part of the healthcare delivery system. The officers themselves develop a better understanding of how protection efforts help the organization meet its mission of providing quality patient care. When officers understand how their services contribute to an organization, three very important things can occur. First, they find greater job satisfaction. Second, the officer's status is generally elevated in the eyes of the entire organization. Third, as a person or function becomes more valuable to a system,

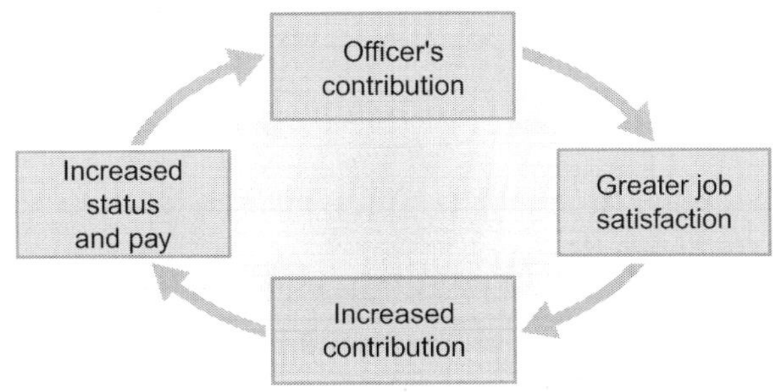

FIGURE 5-1

Relationship of security officers' effort to job status.

the payment for services is generally increased. All organizations review their program in terms of worth, or return on investment. The complementary interrelationship of these factors is illustrated in Figure 5-1.

In general, although security officers perform many customer service oriented services, they also provide a visible deterrent to crime and are available for emergencies if needed. Moreover, in the course of providing services, the officer's interaction with other employees, patients, and visitors is often instrumental in collecting information concerning the protection of the organization that would never have been reported or would not be available elsewhere. In other words, conversations and observations that occur in the course of providing services often yield valuable security information.

A case in point concerned the theft of a considerable amount of money from a medical clinic. As the security officer escorted a receptionist to her vehicle, he remembered that she had previously told him she was afraid her car might be repossessed because she was behind in her payments. Several weeks later, the receptionist told the security officer that she was now current with her payments. An inquiry revealed that the receptionist had in fact made four payments the day after the theft. Subsequent investigation resulted in her confession.

Security administrators do not need much imagination to find ways to be of service to the organization, either in a general way or by specifically supporting a single department. The concept of service can, of course, be carried too far; and one must constantly keep in mind that the security department's primary responsibility is protection. An example of this is the delivery of lab specimens to off-site locations after hours, pulling the only patrolling security officer off-campus, effectively rendering them unavailable for service. However, the program that carries the concept of service too far is rare.

The basic functions of a healthcare security program are: customer service, maintaining an orderly environment, preventative patrol, incident reporting and investigation, response to requests for service, security communications, parking and traffic control, accident reporting and investigation, security education and training, applicant background investigation, response to internal and external emergencies, enforcement of rules and regulations, access control, liaison with law enforcement and other government agencies, internal and external audits, physical and electronic security, and a host of supportive services. Figure 5-2 is a listing of the variety of services provided by the Loss Prevention and

LOSS PREVENTION SERVICES - OFFERED SERVICES	
Access control programming (access cards, door / event control)	Key Production (remote - Hospitals, Clinics and Pharmacies)
Accident Investigations	Key System design and implementation (hospitals and clinics)
Air Quality testing	Law Enforcement liaison
Alarm Monitoring and Response (remote sites)	License Plate Checks
Alert and Event notification (system-wide)	Lost and Found
Audio-Visual Equipment Setup	Maintenance functions as needed (salting, etc.)
Auto service (jump starts, auto relocations, etc.)	Medical records pickup and transport
Breathalyzer Tests	Medication and vaccine refrigeration monitoring
Caregiver escorts	MSDS collection
Cash escorts and deposits (Officer or vehicle and bank runs)	Notary Public
Clinic Security (access control and Officer staffing)	Parking Control
Clinical supplies pickup and transport	Patient Lifting / Restraint / Transport
Communication / Command Center	Patient Standbys (ER & Behavioral Health - Suicidal, homicidal, etc.)
Court appearances representation	Patrols (Officer on foot or vehicle)
Dietary pickup and transport	Pharmacy security (inpatient and retail)
Door Locking/Unlocking	Property Pickups/Returns
Employee Interventions	Remote alarm security (clinics and pharmacies)
Escort liaison (Visiting Nurses Association)	Safety / Security Education and Briefing
Executive Travel and Protection monitoring	Security systems design and maintenance
Fire Alarm Monitoring	Sexual assault evidence pickup / inventory and release to LE
Fire Drills and education	Slip and Fall investigations
First Reponse	Special Events management and staffing
Flight for Life Security	Termination Processing for Human Resources
Identity Theft / Fraud Investigations	Termination Standbys (exiting Caregivers)
Infant Abduction Drills and System Testing	Threat Assessments
Interim life safety measure implementation	Training and Professional Development (MOAB and DAAT)
Investigations	Valuable Pickups/Returns
Key Pinning & Production (Hospital based sites)	Visitor Control

FIGURE 5-2

Listing of functions, activities, and services of a large security program.

(Courtesy of Mike Cummings, CPP, CHPA, Senior Vice President, Aurora Healthcare, Milwaukee, Wisconsin.)

Security Department within Aurora Healthcare that serves 15 hospitals and a large number of clinics and other facilities in Milwaukee and throughout southeastern Wisconsin.

CUSTOMER SERVICE

The successful healthcare security program incorporates the principles of good customer service. The historical perspective of security and customer service being polar opposites is no longer acceptable. Today's healthcare environment is heavily influenced by the hospitality industry.

Competition is found not only for physicians and patients (customers and consumers) but also internal resources and the talent needed to provide quality patient care (nurses and other allied healthcare professionals).

Often, security officers are among the first people patients and visitors see. They need to create positive feelings about the healthcare facility while enhancing the perception of personal safety for everyone on campus. A simple yet effective approach is the greeting of all persons a security officer comes into contact with. Eye contact and acknowledgement of others is a proven technique for deterring unwanted behavior and activities. The late Sam Walton introduced the concept of greeting all customers at the front entrance of all of his stores and found that the reduction in shoplifting alone more than offset the expense of the position. However, store customers view the greeting as great customer service, not a security procedure. The application of this concept in healthcare is widely used with great success by security and department staff alike.

Long-term security program success evolves from a customer-service focused department. More than just security, staff members are ambassadors for the organization they serve, practicing the rules of customer first and courteous enforcement. Their image, actions, and interactions with patients, visitors, and staff should leave a positive impression of the hospital and the security program. This will include being available to answer questions, providing directions and escort service and serving the general purpose of being a "walking around" information desk. In general, the uniform presence is symbolic of a person of authority and someone who is knowledgeable. Great customer service and security service blend together for the collective good when helping others find their way. When guests and patients are provided good way-finding and direction, a feeling of goodwill is formed. Persons are able to get to where they are going without confusion and anxiety. From a security perspective, they are not allowed to wander around the facility aimlessly and encounter opportunities for criminal activity that are present in every healthcare facility.

MAINTAINING AN ORDERLY ENVIRONMENT

Wherever there are crowds of people, there will be manifestations of disorderly conduct, including destructive and disruptive acts that must be controlled. There is often a fine line between settling a minor incident by handling it internally and having to call for police assistance. A challenging but common example of this is found in the waiting areas for intensive care units (ICUs). Families of patients in the ICU are often in the area for extended periods, distraught because of the condition of their loved one and highly emotional. Their expressions are frequently frenzied and unrestrained. Security staff must assist in controlling the environment so that other patients and visitors are not overly disturbed by this type of outburst. In some instances, outside assistance may be needed due to the size of the family and their lack of cooperation with security directives. The underlying issue here is that not all acting-out situations occurring in the healthcare environment have a criminal intent. The very nature and purpose of the healthcare organization can elicit many emotions and strong reactions in patients and visitors that are unlike any other environment—a basic element for every security staff member to know and understand.

The function of maintaining an orderly environment relates directly to the other roles of providing patrol and supportive services. The main objective is to prevent incidents entirely or to handle problems effectively when they occur, with a minimum of disruption, harm to persons, or adverse publicity.

PREVENTATIVE PATROL

A fundamental security role is the patrol or surveillance of an area to determine that conditions are normal and to serve as a deterrent to negative behavior. This element of protection is not always just the responsibility of the on-site security officer. It can be performed by a variety of different people or processes within and outside the organization. Medical clinics, for example, may rely on virtual security patrols to randomly check the exterior of the premises after normal business hours and periodically during the night. Smaller hospitals may perform this function by assigning the task to employees: for example, maintenance personnel in the normal course of their duties, nursing supervisors conducting their rounds, and of course, the security officer on patrol. Increasingly, healthcare facilities are supplementing physical patrol by virtually monitoring images captured through their video surveillance system. Conducting virtual patrols through a central command station on a periodic, scheduled basis or as emergent events dictate is an effective method to determine that conditions are normal.

INCIDENT REPORTING AND INVESTIGATION

No security program can be effective without proper reporting of security incidents and investigative follow-up of these incidents. An important factor in reporting incidents is to maintain a simple and easy-to-access procedure. One telephone call should be all that is required of an employee, visitor, or patient to report a security incident. Trending collected data is important to measure changes in the security environment over time. Analyze the data monthly and review how reported security incidents trend by day of the week and hour of day. Compare month over month statistics, year over year data and seasonal tendencies that affect the safeguarding of a healthcare organization. Use the reports to identify changes in workloads, which may require staffing or deployment adjustments and as part of the overall annual review of the Security Management Plan per The Joint Commission requirements. A few sample security department reports are included in Appendix I.

The industry has not produced a recommended list of incident or activity classifications; however, the list in Figure 5-3 for Security Incident Classification and Figure 5-4, Security Activity Classifications are utilized by HSS Inc. and integrated into the security program at many hospitals in the U.S.

A major element of protection is investigation, required regardless of the size of the healthcare organization. In this frame of reference, the term "investigation" takes on a rather broad meaning and is not limited to the initial response or follow-up of a criminal incident. It refers to the collection and preservation of data or materials and the proper analysis of collected materials to manage criminal or civil actions, business situations, and as a basis for protective services programming.

Investigation is necessary for such general purposes as the following:

- To discover the facts and to determine the cause of an incident that may have resulted in loss or possible injury to staff, visitors, or patients
- To determine adequate procedures and safeguards to manage the various organizational protection vulnerabilities (for example, to analyze the system of handling patient valuables to ensure safekeeping or to determine whether such handling is designed to minimize the risk of various malefactions)
- To successfully resolve a crime

CATEGORY	SUB CATEGORY	TYPE	SUBTYPE
Alarm-Environment	Actual, Drill, Malfunction		
Alarm-Fire	Drill, Malfunction, User Error, Arson		
Alarm-Security	Actual, Drill, Malfunction, User Error	To Patient, Staff, Visitor, Vehicle	
Assault	Aggravated, Rape, Sexual, Simple	To Patient, Staff, Visitor	
Auto Accident	Personal Injury, Property Damage		
Burglary	To Building, Vending Machine, Vehicle		
Chemical Event	Internal, External	Actual	Contained, Not Contained
Code Assistance	Internal, External	Actual	Blizzard
Code Assistance	Internal, External	Actual	Bomb Threat
Code Assistance	Internal, External	Actual	Cardiac Arrest/Medical Emergency
Code Assistance	Internal, External	Actual	Cash Escort
Code Assistance	Internal, External	Actual	Chemical Exposure
Code Assistance	Internal, External	Actual	Civil Disturbance
Code Assistance	Internal, External	Actual	Combative Person
Code Assistance	Internal, External	Actual	Communications Failure
Code Assistance	Internal, External	Actual	Dam Inundation
Code Assistance	Internal, External	Actual	Drought
Code Assistance	Internal, External	Actual	Earthquake
Code Assistance	Internal, External	Actual	Electrical Failure
Code Assistance	Internal, External	Actual	Epidemic
Code Assistance	Internal, External	Actual	External Disaster
Code Assistance	Internal, External	Actual	Fire Alarm Failure
Code Assistance	Internal, External	Actual	Flood, External
Code Assistance	Internal, External	Actual	Forensic Admission
Code Assistance	Internal, External	Actual	Fuel Shortage
Code Assistance	Internal, External	Actual	Generator Failure
Code Assistance	Internal, External	Actual	Hazmat Exposure
Code Assistance	Internal, External	Actual	Hostage Situation/Active Shooter
Code Assistance	Internal, External	Actual	Hurricane
Code Assistance	Internal, External	Actual	HVAC Failure
Code Assistance	Internal, External	Actual	Ice Storm
Code Assistance	Internal, External	Actual	Infant/Pediatric Abduction
Code Assistance	Internal, External	Actual	Information Systems Failure
Code Assistance	Internal, External	Actual	Internal Disaster
Code Assistance	Internal, External	Actual	Labor Action
Code Assistance	Internal, External	Actual	Landslide
Code Assistance	Internal, External	Actual	Large Internal Spill
Code Assistance	Internal, External	Actual	Lift Assistance/Manpower
Code Assistance	Internal, External	Actual	Lockdown/Restricted Access
Code Assistance	Internal, External	Actual	Mass Casualty Hazmat Incident

FIGURE 5-3

Security incident classifications.

CATEGORY	SUB CATEGORY	TYPE	SUBTYPE
Code Assistance	Internal, External	Actual	Mass Casualty Hazmat Incident
Code Assistance	Internal, External	Actual	Mass Casualty Incident
Code Assistance	Internal, External	Actual	Medical Gas Failure
Code Assistance	Internal, External	Actual	Medical Vacuum Failure
Code Assistance	Internal, External	Actual	Missing Patient
Code Assistance	Internal, External	Actual	Natural Gas Failure
Code Assistance	Internal, External	Actual	OB Hemorrhage
Code Assistance	Internal, External	Actual	Radiologic Exposure, External
Code Assistance	Internal, External	Actual	Severe Thunderstorm
Code Assistance	Internal, External	Actual	Sewer Failure
Code Assistance	Internal, External	Actual	Small Casualty Hazmat Incident
Code Assistance	Internal, External	Actual	Small Casualty Hazmat Incident
Code Assistance	Internal, External	Actual	Small-Medium Sized Spill
Code Assistance	Internal, External	Actual	Steam Failure
Code Assistance	Internal, External	Actual	Steam Failure
Code Assistance	Internal, External	Actual	Structural Damage
Code Assistance	Internal, External	Actual	Supply Shortage
Code Assistance	Internal, External	Actual	Temperature Extremes
Code Assistance	Internal, External	Actual	Terrorism, Biological
Code Assistance	Internal, External	Actual	Terrorism, Chemical
Code Assistance	Internal, External	Actual	Terrorism, Radiologic
Code Assistance	Internal, External	Actual	Tidal Wave
Code Assistance	Internal, External	Actual	Tornado
Code Assistance	Internal, External	Actual	Tornado
Code Assistance	Internal, External	Actual	Transportation Failure
Code Assistance	Internal, External	Actual	Transportation Failure
Code Assistance	Internal, External	Actual	VIP Situation
Code Assistance	Internal, External	Actual	Volcano
Code Assistance	Internal, External	Actual	Water Failure
Code Assistance	Internal, External	Actual	Wild Fire
Drug Abuse	By Employee, Patient, Student, Visitor		
Elevator Entrapment			
Escort Assist	Contractor Specials, Vendor, Other		
Found Property			
Information Only			
Inspections	Employee, Vehicle, Vendor, Random, Other		
Medical Emergency	Standby, Render First Aid/CPR		
Missing Property	Lost, Stolen, Unknown	Facility, Personal, Whole Property	
Murder	Of Employee, Patient, Visitor		
Patient Assistance	Behavior Health, ER, Other	Medical, Psychiatric	

FIGURE 5-3 Continued

CATEGORY	SUB CATEGORY	TYPE	SUBTYPE
Robbery	Armed, Unarmed		
Security Event	Incident, Breach, Suspicious Package		
Special Assignment	Electrical Shut Down		
Slip or Fall	Of Employee, Patient, Visitor		
Suicide	Of Employee, Patient, Visitor		
Suspicious Person	Contacted, Not Contacted		
Traffic Control	Construction, Vehicle Exterior		
Threat	Bomb, Phone, Physical, Terrorist, Verbal		
Trespassing			
Vandalism	Facility, Personal, Vehicle		
Weather Conditions	Low Visibility, Snow, Tornado		
Violations			

FIGURE 5-3 Continued

- To determine if in fact a crime has been committed
- To determine the facts and causes of employee work accidents
- To obtain additional information for law enforcement agencies in cases in which the organization may have an interest
- To determine the truthfulness of an improper conduct allegation against an employee

The follow-up that stems from investigations serves many purposes. These include the physical and psychological deterrence to employees, reflecting how important the previously listed issues are viewed to be within the organization. The prevention of future crimes is an important component of the investigative effort, as investigative follow-up allows for immediate identification of procedural changes that may need to be altered. An example is the Ambulatory Surgery Center office manager who reports a theft of surgical instruments from an unsecured storage area. The investigator can quickly identify steps to take to secure the area and help facilitate the process quickly to prevent a future reoccurrence.

RESPONSE TO REQUESTS FOR SERVICE

The response to requests for assistance is a major facet of a healthcare security program. There is some disparity among security professionals around the type of requests that are appropriate for security interaction. In most programs, security responds to almost any situation when called on, even though at times it is necessary to refer action to another department or outside agency. Successful security departments have learned that requests for service must be encouraged and handled with efficiency regardless of the validity of some requests. It is much better to receive some requests that are inappropriate than to receive no requests from the customers who could access the services being offered.

A common performance measurement for hospital security departments is the ability to respond to routine calls for service in five minutes from the time of the original call. In emergencies, many healthcare organizations strive to respond within two minutes or less. These measures are not always practical, based on other activities that may be currently undertaken and the security staffing levels. However,

LEVEL 1 CATEGORY	LEVEL 2 SUB CATEGORY	LEVEL 3 TYPE
911 Medical Calls		
Alarm-Environment	Drill, Malfunction, User Error	
Alarm-Fire	Drill, Malfunction, User Error	
Alarm-Security	Drill, Malfunction, User Error	
Animal Bite	Cat, Dog, Other	
Animal Call	Internal, External	Domestic, Wild
Audio Visual Request Set Up/Return	Meeting Room	
Bomb Threat	Internal, External	Drill
Building Maintenance		
Building Miscellaneous		
Building Unlock Request		
Cardiac or Pulmonary Arrest	Internal, External	Actual, Drill
Cash Escort		
Charts Pulled		
Condition Report	Internal, External	
Contacted Smoker	Staff, Visitor, Contractor	
Customer Service Assist	Airline, City Line Management, Contractor Escort, Public, Facility, Medical, Crowd Assist, Handicap Assist	
Defective Equipment		
Disturbance		
ED Lockdown		
Elevator Entrapment	Stand By	Elevator Repair, Fire, Paramedics, Police Responding
Emergency Staff Assist	Internal, External	Actual, Drill
Escort	Employee, Patient, Visitor	On/Off Property, AMA
Escort Assist	Employee, Patient, Visitor, Vendor, Contractor Specials	
Exterior Lighting Survey	Monthly	
Extinguisher Checks	Weekly, Monthly, Quarterly	
Faulty Lights		
Fire Watch		
Forensic Patient	Internal	
Found Property	Unclassified	
Funds Assist	N/A	
General Assistance	N/A	
Hazardous Material Release	Internal, External	Actual, Drill
Helicopter Assist		
Hover Jack Lift		
Information Only	Unclassified	
Lift Assist		

FIGURE 5-4

Security activity classifications.

LEVEL 1 CATEGORY	LEVEL 2 SUB CATEGORY	LEVEL 3 TYPE
Lights Left On, Out or Off		
Lock Cut Off		
Lost & Found		
Maintenance Issues		
Malfunction Door	Door, Lock, Key, Other	
Mass Casualty Event, Code is Activated	Internal, External	Actual, Drill
Mass Casualty Event, Event is Confirmed	Internal, External	Actual, Drill
Mass Casualty Event, Facility Evacuation	Internal, External	Actual, Drill
Mass Casualty Event, Unit/Dept Evacuation	Internal, External	Actual, Drill
Medication Delivery		
Missing Person	Unknown	Actual, False Alarm
Missing Property	Lost, Stolen, Unknown	Facility Property, Personal Property, Whole Vehicle
Morgue Assist		
Neighborhood Patrol		
Open Window or Door		
Open/Unsecured Areas		
Parking Violations	Infractions, Violations	
Patient Assistance	Behavior Health, ER, Other	Medical, Psychiatric
Patient Left AMA		
Patient Valuables	In, Out	
Pharmacy Transport		
Security Violations		
Severe Weather Code Activated	Internal, External	Actual, Drill
Severe Weather Code Confirmed	Internal, External	Actual, Drill
Severe Weather Facility Evacuation	Internal, External	Actual, Drill
Severe Weather Unit/Dept. Evacuation	Internal, External	Actual, Drill
Smoking Contact	Patient, Staff, Contractor	
Snow Removal	External	
Special Assignment		
Special Directed Patrol		
Stroke Alert		
Suspicious Package	Internal, External	Actual, False Alarm
Suspicious Person	Contacted, Not Contacted	
Traffic Control		
Transport	Patient, Staff, Contractor	
Trauma Team	Activation	
Unlock Doors		
Unlock Request		
Unsafe Conditions	Exterior / Interior Lighting, Other	

FIGURE 5-4 Continued

LEVEL 1 CATEGORY	LEVEL 2 SUB CATEGORY	LEVEL 3 TYPE
Valuables	In/Lock, Out/Unlock	
Vehicle Assist	Patient, Staff, Visitor	
Violations		
Violent Intruder	Internal, External	
Volunteer Patients		
Weather Condition	Other	
Wheelchair / Wagon Assist		

FIGURE 5-4 Continued

the healthcare facility that cannot consistently meet these goals should closely review their on-site security staffing complement for appropriateness to their environment.

SECURITY COMMUNICATIONS

The successful security function will engage the eyes and ears of all employees in the protection program. To capitalize on employee involvement requires an ability to easily communicate with security staff. Ideally, the healthcare worker is provided with a single number to dial for all security-related calls. Exempla Health, a three-hospital system based in Denver uses an easy to remember acronym to contact Security: "SAFE" or the number 7233 (Figure 5-5).

Answered by a knowledgeable operator who can obtain the name of the person calling, a call back number, and the basic purpose (need) of the call, the operator should have direct communication with the security staff. In larger security departments, this could be a trained security dispatcher, or in some smaller hospitals, the responsibility could fall with the PBX operators. A growing option has been to outsource the function.

In Alberta, Canada, where the Alberta Health Services (AHS) Protective Services department provides security to all of the Province's healthcare facilities, one off-site centralized operations center in Edmonton receives all calls for security service for all sites. This Provincial Security Control Centre (PSCC) dispatches security at AHS sites in response to alarms and calls for service.

Ideally, direct radio communication is used in each option. However, less sophisticated approaches such as cell phones, pagers and overhead announcements can be used in the security program. In each, it is critical that the caller receives acknowledgement of every call made for security services.

FIGURE 5-5

Security number.

(Courtesy of Eric Smith, CPP, Director of Security, Exempla Health, Denver, CO.)

PARKING AND TRAFFIC CONTROL

Parking and the control of traffic are basic services required by most healthcare organizations. The degree to which security is involved in parking depends on program development and enforcement needs. In some cases the control of parking is delegated to a special unit of security, an outside provider of parking management service or even to the maintenance and grounds department.

The volume of vehicle traffic entering and leaving the grounds each day produces a significant problem for most medical care facilities. It is the rare healthcare facility that has built enough parking to meet its high volume needs. In general, lack of available parking is a trend that transcends the healthcare industry as a whole, no matter the location.

The need to keep fire lanes open, assist in minor accidents, ensure orderly parking, and protect parked vehicles is a multifaceted task that requires many resources. In emergencies, The Joint Commission explicitly requires that healthcare organizations control access in and around the facility, specifically the emergency department.

Many organizations will use patrolling security officers to periodically survey vehicles to determine if the owner has left items of value in open view, windows left open or partially down, doors unlocked and even keys left in the ignition. The pending results have proven very successful in soliciting greater employee involvement in the hospital's security awareness and theft prevention programs.

In systems where special parking areas are designated, parking decals are a popular means of control. The vehicle decals, which provide ready identification of the owner or driver of the vehicle, is useful in notifying drivers of lights left on, flat tires, damage, or the need to move the vehicle.

Many organizations use security officers to enforce parking rules and regulations and write safe parking reminders for staff as demonstrated in Figure 5-6. In some larger facilities, this can include obtaining special police powers and writing tickets on city streets. Due to the confusing nature of many

SAFE PARKING INFRACTION

Parking in the prescribed manner is an act of consideration for others.
Your vehicle is parked in violation of facility regulations.
Vehicles are subject to being towed at Security Officer's discretion.

- ☐ Not in authorized space
- ☐ Occupying reserved space
- ☐ Loading zone
- ☐ Prohibitive sign posted
- ☐ Handicap zone
- ☐ Occupying more than one space
- ☐ Sidewalk blocked
- ☐ Driveway blocked
- ☐ Fire zone
- ☐ Other ____________

Vehicle Description	License # and State	Permit # (if Employee)	Location

Issued by	Date/Time	Facility

FIGURE 5-6

Safe parking reminder.

parking areas, some healthcare facilities will use a mobile patrol officer to help visitors and patients locate their vehicle.

ACCIDENT REPORTING AND INVESTIGATION

Properly recording the facts concerning injury to employees, visitors, and vendors is an essential security function. Employee accident reporting should be the responsibility assigned to the employee's direct supervisor, in conjunction with the employee themselves. However, when their efforts are combined with security, a more comprehensive investigation is conducted. The integrity of the investigation is maintained and it helps eliminate false claims. Further, the consistency of having security's involvement in each provides for better data collection that assists with future loss prevention efforts. The employees' supervisor maintains involvement in the reporting procedure and typically has responsibility for any follow-up action that may be required.

The security officer should also be responsible for investigating and recording visitor or vendor accidents. Many unnecessary claims have been paid because an accident report was not filled out or because of an incomplete investigative report. Organizations sometimes fail to assign this responsibility specifically. When it is everyone's responsibility, it often ends up being no one's. Without proper records it can be extremely difficult to defend a case in which the plaintiff has all the facts and the organization has no facts or incomplete facts.

It should be noted that security may be much less involved outside the U.S. in accident investigations, as the organizations operate in much less litigious environments.

SECURITY EDUCATION AND TRAINING

A major element of a successful security program is to stimulate, educate, and motivate employees to be conscious of protection needs and to practice good security awareness. Personnel must be trained in the proper response to managing aggression, infant abduction, active shooter, evacuation procedures, workplace violence and taking ownership of their security responsibilities. In small medical clinics, this function is rather informal and spontaneous; in larger facilities, a more formal approach, using many different communication mechanisms, is necessary.

Presentations, handouts, events, and training (classroom and computer-based) will raise staff awareness of security issues. Not only will this add eyes and ears to your security efforts, but it also will be noted by accreditation surveyors, who are increasingly looking for employee involvement in security. Using input from staff, physicians, visitors, and patients, the security awareness offering should be tailored to the facility, and include such activities as:

- Department-specific training on topics such as infant security, aggression management, and emergency department security.
- Brown Bag Workshops on crime prevention and personal safety.
- Security fairs.
- Security brochures. These can be custom creations by the facility or generic purchases from the National Crime Prevention Council or other outlets.

Organizations are taking on the broader task of helping employees to be safe and secure outside the workplace. Classes on self-defense, identity theft prevention, home safety, and other topics are offered as an employee benefit on the premise that security awareness must constantly be reinforced.

Promoting security awareness among patients and visitors is also an element of security. Visitors and patients often are victims of various crimes, many of which could be prevented through safer practices. Using signage and other subtle reminders is a good security practice. A few examples are signs in parking areas reminding patients and visitors to secure their personal belongings in their vehicle, or admissions staff encouraging patients to send their valuables home with loved ones.

APPLICANT BACKGROUND INVESTIGATION

Investigating prospective employees is generally the responsibility of the human resources department or, in small organizations, the person who actually hires the employee. Verifications usually entail criminal record searches, citizenship requirements, employment verification, Social Security number confirmation, and required education and license validation. Some organizations often rely on security assistance when considering an applicant for a sensitive position, such as cashier, pharmacist, child-care services, or home health worker. Typical services often include conducting a worker's compensation claim review, multiple state criminal history review, sex offender registry, Department of Motor Vehicle history report, or simply contacting the Drug Enforcement Agency (DEA) to ascertain knowledge of past incidents. These services are rarely part of a security program responsibility outside the U.S., however.

Laws are constantly changing to meet society's evolving needs and expectations, but so do technology and the wrongdoers' capability to produce false credentials and diplomas. Almost every healthcare organization has been faced with this issue and must take it seriously. Consistency in the process of background investigations is needed as the theory of negligent hiring is litigated often and with substantial awards in the U.S. Hiring an individual without investigating the person's background or improperly placing an individual in a position that requires higher levels of expertise than the applicant possesses are often cited as reasons for verdicts against an organization.

The courts have ruled that employees who have contact with members of the public (i.e., healthcare workers) are held to even higher standards of reasonable care in terms of hiring. This requirement is imposed because it is reasonably foreseeable that such an employee could cause an unreasonable risk of injury to the public.

REACTION TO INTERNAL AND EXTERNAL EMERGENCIES

One of the most fundamental concerns within a healthcare facility is the ability to manage serious emergencies properly and swiftly. This requires the ability to react to the unexpected and to minimize the negative impact caused by noncriminal emergency situations. Frequently, this requires the ability to manage access into the facility. The speed in which access to the facility can be restricted is a key indicator for facility readiness to many internal and external disasters.

The emergency lock-down procedure (or restricted-access protocol) should be tested regularly to evaluate system capability and organization readiness. System testing should occur at three in the morning, in addition to three in the afternoon when facility staffing is at its peak. Testing should assess the time it takes when security is engaged with other activities such as a fire response or patient surge.

Other types of internal or external emergencies that concern security are fire and explosions; flooding or severe weather that causes property damage or injury; chemical spills and other hazardous situations; loss of power, water, or communication; and isolation from the rest of the community in a disaster situation.

ENFORCEMENT OF RULES AND REGULATIONS

The enforcement of organizational rules and regulations is generally considered a security function. This role, however, should not be isolated from the line authority and program responsibility throughout the organization. In facilities with an established security force, the operating department's supervisory responsibility is often deemphasized; as a result, security is looked to for enforcement. This is a mistake. It forces security personnel into a potential adversarial relationship with other employees and visitors. A good example is the policy prohibiting smoking on campus. Even though the security force acts to ensure compliance on campus, the job should not rest solely with security. It requires the support of and enforcement by every supervisor and position of leadership within the organization.

ACCESS CONTROL

Access control, arguably the most critical aspect of healthcare security, requires blending facilities management, mechanical and electronic technology with good security practices. It is the central role of security to combine these elements to form a cohesive security system.

While many crime statistics point to a rather dire state of society, the hope for better healthcare workers' protection often begins with how the healthcare facility designs and controls its various access points. Many older healthcare designs have a large number of uncontrolled entries and allow too much accessibility to walk-in guests without any kind of record or accountability. In a 2013 Hospital Vendor and Visitor Access Control survey conducted by *Health Facilities Management* magazine, only 27% of the U.S. hospitals had a formal check-in process for nonvendor visitors before they could enter patient floors.[2] Most, however, do control access after normal business hours with a single point of entry where visitors must sign-in and show photo identification. Controlled through one or more designated entrances, the process must channel visitors so that their presence is acknowledged and a visitor's badge issued. During the process, time should be taken to call the unit to be visited and inform staff who is coming. A common unpleasant experience for hospital staff working at night is coming across a stranger walking around the department and having no idea who they are or why they are there.

The proper channeling of visitors and patients into and about the healthcare facility is good security and creates a better experience for patients, visitors and staff alike. Today's technological advancements in access control enable higher degrees of security without compromising aesthetics, customer service, user-friendliness or overall hospitality. Access control can protect critical areas such as pharmacies, surgical rooms, infant treatment rooms, information technology closets/storage rooms and other areas that require separation from the public.

The management of this risk is further challenged by many operating philosophies prevalent in healthcare such as those promulgated by Planetree and other like management philosophies. Offering this open and inviting environment does not eliminate the responsibility to protect patients, staff and visitors; on the contrary, it only changes the dynamics of how this is accomplished.

ACCESS TO LOCKED AREAS

All protection systems use locked doors to preserve the integrity of a given office or work area. Likewise, all efficient organizations must provide a system to grant access to the areas under special circumstances. The term "special circumstances" underscores the need to control special areas and to provide services to people who require legitimate access but do not have a key, access card, code, or other lock-release device.

The security officer is frequently called on to grant special access to areas that require a high degree of control, such as storerooms, medical records areas, libraries, equipment rooms, and other places where a record of entry is required. Access can also be achieved by holding keys in a central area to which those who desire entry must report to check out the required key. Many facilities are incorporating secured key closets that provide a specific electronic audit trail. Thus, keys are distributed only to predetermined authorized personnel who use a unique personal identification number to access a specific key. This works especially well in organizations that are challenged with their key control program for designated high-risk areas.

Efficiently granting access to authorized individuals is a service that improves the overall efficiency of the organization. People lock themselves out, mislay, lose and forget keys frequently. The security department should provide quick response, so that the necessary work of the organization can progress without undue delay. If these requests appear too frequently, the problem should be handled administratively, not through a delay of service.

LIAISON WITH LAW ENFORCEMENT AND OTHER GOVERNMENT AGENCIES

All organizations, regardless of the sophistication of their security program, eventually need to call on local law enforcement and other government agencies. The medical facility must be able to work effectively with many different agencies. It could be the Drug Enforcement Agency when an issue of drug diversion or theft occurs; local law enforcement for coordination of emergency response plans for natural or manmade disasters; the Secret Service if the President or other political dignitaries visit the region; the local fire department for evacuation planning and life safety code compliance; and the list can go on and on.

Establishing public private partnerships is more important today than ever before. Chief Harry Dolan of the Raleigh, North Carolina Police Department commented at the International Association for Healthcare Security and Safety's 2009 Midwinter Seminar that building relationships with local law enforcement and other governmental entities is critical to the success of the healthcare protection program. Chief Dolan shared with the audience that hospitals and complex medical centers are often quite foreign to these agencies. Arranging for tours, getting their involvement in policy and procedure development, and general networking were keys to establishing successful relationships—which he called critical to liaison efforts.

Outreach efforts are often best handled by the leader of the security department with emphasis placed on coordinating frequent information exchanges. At the Anschutz Medical Campus in Aurora, Colorado, the security leadership at Children's Hospital Colorado, University of Colorado Hospital, and University of Colorado Health Sciences Center meet every other month with the local police department and fire department as part of the campus-wide Security Council. Many items are discussed, to include security incident trends and challenges, future large-scale events on campus, new high-risk services, emergency preparedness and exercise planning, and campus-wide policy creation. There are numerous formal programs around the country that function to combine police and security information and activities for the good of the community. Most of these programs are at the local law enforcement level; however, there have been some limited state and federal programs aimed at cooperative law enforcement and security endeavors.

In places like Kingston, Ontario and Surrey, British Columbia we can find good examples of close relationships between federal correctional agencies and the security management responsible for hospitals in these areas. Both of these jurisdictions have numerous federal prisons with offenders frequently in their hospitals and regular meetings, agreed-upon protocols and incident follow-up ensure strong measures are in place to mitigate the risk associated with offender hospital visits.

All parties have a better understanding of their role on campus and have fostered an excellent relationship in the process which can pay great dividends in a time of need.

The role of security should never be to supplant the police or other criminal justice agency, but rather to supplement and assist them. As the criminal mind becomes more sophisticated in its approach to wrong the public and specifically the healthcare industry, protection efforts require a coordinated approach with local law enforcement. The successful security program cannot operate in a vacuum.

A greater demand continues to be placed on security services as traditional law enforcement response becomes less able to answer requests for a physical response. The high cost of law enforcement officers is forcing most communities to alter the method used to respond to requests for nonessential police services. Professional security programs must respond to scarce law enforcement resources in different ways, including limiting calls for police service to the extent possible.

General policy should prohibit healthcare staff from calling for police service as a representative of the organization. In organizations with a full-time security effort, a security representative should make the call for required police service. In organizations without full-time security service, the policy should designate an administrator who will not only approve the call for routine police service, but also generally initiate the call. In times of extreme emergency, the general policy will by necessity be bypassed. The reasoning behind this general policy is basically good business practice. An organization cannot tolerate employees calling the police for organizational problems without administration or security being aware of the problem and determining whether police service is actually required.

The police frequently need to obtain information from patients. If there are no visiting restrictions for the patient, the police will generally present themselves like any other visitor. The request by a law enforcement officer to question a patient must always be referred to the nursing supervisor, who will determine whether the patient is well enough to be interviewed. The police do not always come to medical care facilities to contact patients. Employees may also be the subject of a police interview or arrest. Most police jurisdictions recognize that interviewing people at their place of employment may not always be welcomed by the employer or the employee. In some instances, however, time may be an important factor or the police may not be able to make contact elsewhere. The proper procedure is for the police representative to contact the hospital security representative or human resources department, who should produce the employee without delay.

The emergency room is usually the scene of considerable police activity. Hospitals are required to report cases of persons seeking treatment concerning gunshot wounds, knifings, rape, etc., as specified by law. This should be the responsibility of the emergency room staff and not the security department. However, the security department should be notified if trouble is expected with a person being treated within the facility. The need for security service may involve patients or persons who have accompanied them to the facility. Hospitals that render a large volume of emergency medical service, including police-related cases, generally provide accommodations to help the police complete their work, including a room for interviews that is equipped with a telephone. If the security department maintains an office in the emergency treatment area, the police should be permitted to use or share the space. This combination of use not only conserves space but also, if coordinated properly, can promote good relations between the police and the security department.

Related to security's involvement with patients and law enforcement is the telephone or radio request from law enforcement to detain a patient. Neither private security officers nor medical personnel can legally detain patients against their will. The law enforcement agency that requests that a patient be detained should be made aware that patients cannot be legally held. At the same time, stalling tactics are certainly in the best interests of all concerned, particularly if police personnel are enroute to the facility. Often if the police do not request that a patient be detained, they may request that security ask the patient to wait for the police. If the patient does leave, information such as type of vehicle, license number and direction of travel can be obtained to assist the police.

All requests by law enforcement agencies for information about patients being treated should be referred to the security department, or to medical records for information regarding discharged patients. With the introduction of the Health Information Privacy and Accountability Act (HIPAA) of 1996, and Protected Health Information, which is the acts' privacy rule taking effect in 2005, there has been endless confusion and so many interpretations that the playing field is still less than absolutely clear. Key considerations for information release that the security administrator must be aware of are:

- The law enforcement agency must obtain its evidence in a legal manner or it will not be admissible in court, so they must follow certain guidelines.
- It is desirable, and in the best interest of all concerned, including those under investigation, to ensure fairness and to protect the integrity of the investigation, to keep the information within the investigating agency.
- If the information requested by law enforcement agencies can be supplied voluntarily within the law by hospitals, it will be unnecessary for the law enforcement agencies to obtain search warrants or subpoenas. It should be noted that once a search warrant is filed for or a subpoena requested, the case becomes public information.
- If there is disagreement between the law enforcement agency and the hospital as to the information to be released, it is recommended that the hospital contact the local district attorney's office that is involved and attempt to resolve the problem.
- It should be understood by law enforcement agencies that there may be some instances in which the hospital would prefer that a search warrant or subpoena be obtained prior to release of the information. This request should not be viewed by law enforcement as the hospital being uncooperative.

- Police investigation files are confidential; therefore, release of information to a law enforcement agency is not a release to the public. Also, if the information is information to which the law enforcement agency can compel access through the courts, there would seem to be no basis for liability against the hospital just because it made the information available voluntarily.

These considerations are general guidelines; of course there are distinctions between releasing information pertaining to staff or physicians, via personnel records, as well. There will also be differences between jurisdictions and countries. The security leader can play a key role in working with information and privacy experts from their own organization and with local police representatives to develop clear policy that meets regulated, organizational and law enforcement requirements.

INTERNAL AND EXTERNAL AUDITS

Another important function of any protection effort, and one that is often neglected, is to test the procedures designed to protect the organization against such malefactions as internal theft or fraud. Many fraudulent schemes have been discovered by spot checks and internal audits.

There are basically three kinds of internal audit. The first is an unannounced inspection of a procedure. An example would be to check the patient personal property envelopes that are being held for safekeeping to determine that all are accounted for in accordance with the system in place (that is, serial numbers properly listed, inventories as required, double signatures for deposits).

The second type of control involves spot-checking incoming or outgoing goods to determine whether the records match the actual commodity. One example would be to randomly compare food delivery requisitions with what is actually delivered. Another would be to measure the fuel oil delivery before it is transferred to facility storage tanks.

The third type of check involves the use of an undercover operative to monitor a service to determine whether correct procedures are being followed. An example would be to determine whether a parking booth cashier rings up the proper amount, especially after a customer pays the exact amount due. Security operations are also subject to audit and should receive the same review and scrutiny as other areas of the organization.

EXTERNAL AUDITS (INSPECTIONS)

Many systems are used to keep our healthcare facilities safe. But one of the common missing components is the routine testing of these systems. An external audit is a survey that is concerned mainly with the hardware of the protection system.

At periodic intervals, locks should be inspected, external and stairwell lights checked, video surveillance verified that the correct image is being captured, emergency communications validated to be working, and alarm systems activated to ensure that they are operating correctly. Systems or components found to be ineffective, not working as originally intended, and/or not meeting current needs create undue risk for the healthcare facility. Many electronic security technologies provide automatic system checking to ensure systems are operating properly. There is a need, however, for visual inspection of security elements such as doors, windows, external lighting, fencing and shrubbery control (maintaining sight lines).

This documentation and testing may be considered small and routine. However, its importance is found in the liability protection afforded to the facility and, more prominently, the positive perception of security and the department.

A strategy that works particularly well is to assign someone on staff who, at least on a monthly basis, takes an inventory of all equipment in use, verifying its operational status. If equipment is found missing or not operating as originally intended, document those issues and place them on the internal work order plan to correct the deficiency. When followed, this close-the-loop system ensures systems are working and ready when needed.

The external audit should also include management of the perception of the security program. A negative opinion of security is created when system components have wires dangling or dust buildup. This can include the negative image associated with damage on a security patrol car. The protection program must be cognizant of the symbolic message the ongoing maintenance of security equipment signals to employees, staff, patients, and visitors. Not only will this convey how seriously their protection is taken but it will also have the added deterrent effect on the potential "bad guy" as related to security readiness and the organization's capability to provide protection services.

LOCKS AND KEYS

This protective function is perhaps the most neglected security safeguard, even though it is one that most facilities rely on quite heavily. It is not uncommon for a new lock-and-key system to be out of control within days or weeks of the installation. The control of locks can effectively compel strict adherence to the program. Today, electronic access systems have replaced many locked access points; however, healthcare organizations will always have the need for keys. The issuance of keys at all facilities must be closely tracked and carefully controlled to prevent system breaches.

OTHER SUPPORT SERVICES

In addition to specific responsibilities, security must also provide support to the various departments and sections of the healthcare organization. Chief among these supportive activities is customer service—giving directions and helping people, especially patients utilizing the facility. Other examples can include accepting and properly storing shipments when the receiving department is closed, monitoring blood bank refrigeration temperatures, and escorting cashiers. The list can be exhaustive; however, the important point is that security should provide as many supportive services as possible as long as they do not interfere with security's primary protection responsibility. Security is a service organization, and service is a prime consideration when calculating security cost-effectiveness.

LOST AND FOUND

Lost and found activity is usually a component of the protection system. The lost and found service benefits the entire organization and is of specific value to the security program. Although lost and found is operated as a service, it can contribute directly to resolving reports of stolen property. An efficient system of handling found property can clear up many instances of property loss reported as theft. Whenever property is missing in a busy medical facility, there is always the question of whether the item was lost, accidentally discarded, inadvertently taken by another person, or taken with the intent to deprive the rightful owner.

Careful review and investigation into each reported loss may result, for example, in finding dentures and eyeglasses in dietary waste containers as they are frequently left on food trays. Instituting a specific property retention policy, typically 30–90 days, helps manage the volume and storage of found items. Many healthcare facilities turn over items of value to the local auxiliary for their fundraising and goodwill efforts.

The public and employee relations fostered by an efficient lost and found system are of tremendous value to all healthcare organizations.

CONSERVATION

Helping to conserve resources is a security function that goes hand in hand with support services and preventative patrols. Utility costs have made saving energy everyone's job in the medical care facility. Security officers on patrol can shut off and turn on lights at specific times, switch off coffee pots or other small appliances unintentionally left on, close windows left inadvertently open, report water leaks, manage temperature settings for meeting rooms, and report equipment that is not functioning properly.

DECEASED PATIENTS

Security involvement in handling deceased patients and their property can be found in numerous hospitals and long-term care facilities. This involvement may include safekeeping property, assisting in transporting bodies to the facility morgue, granting undertakers access to the facility, and releasing bodies to the mortuary. Although such tasks are generally considered unpleasant for the security officer, one or all of the assignments are appropriate security program responsibilities. Specific protocols should be established providing guidance on credential verification and proper release procedures. When assigned this responsibility, the security officer must verify the correct identification of the deceased before releasing the remains. This can prevent an embarrassing and potentially libelous situation for the hospital. For example, a southern California hospital settled a claim to the estate of a deceased patient who was released to the wrong mortuary after the body had been harvested for tissues and organs against the patient's stated desire.

The loss of deceased patients' property is a problem familiar to most security administrators. The question often arises whether the disappearance of property occurred before or after death. In some cases, relatives or visitors have removed property from patients as they lay helpless. The blame for the missing property is easily shifted to the facility by the family. Of course, one cannot always place the blame for missing property on the relatives or friends of the patient; many cases have been resolved by ascertaining that a hospital employee was responsible.

Although it is common practice, it cannot be stressed enough that a complete inventory of all of the deceased's personal property should be made by two persons as soon as possible after the death. In some programs, this inventory is completed by the security department with a nursing staff witness, and the property is removed for appropriate storage until it can be properly released.

PATIENT VALUABLES AND BELONGINGS

Most healthcare facilities have a policy in place that addresses patient valuables and clothing that includes an inventory list to catalog patient's belongings. A common element is to have admissions staff encourage all patients coming to the facility for scheduled appointments or treatment to leave their valuables at home. However, there are many instances when this is not feasible—unscheduled treatments or visits (e.g., visits to the emergency department) or patient refusal to cooperate with the request. In these instances, the security department is often involved in collecting, inventorying, and storing patient valuables. Many organizations, however, are distinguishing between patient valuables and patient belongings. Belongings are no longer being accounted for and the hospital is not taking responsibility for those items unless the patient is unable to manage their own belongings, such as in the case of trauma, dementia, confusion, sedation, etc. Most organizations will have the patient sign a waiver if the hospital takes possession of their valuables, to at least partially mitigate the risk associated with this responsibility.

This patient involvement activity requires the healthcare security program to have processes in place to obtain a complete description of all items collected and the creation of a secured storage process that cannot be accessed without two people (double lock and key system). A good security practice is to attach the patient's bar code label on the tamper-proof storage container and insert the inventory contents page inside to prevent unwanted tampering and unneeded awareness of content value. A sample patient valuables inventory form is noted in Figure 5-7.

Security officers are often asked to return stored items to the patient. Verifying the contents with the patient against the original inventory prevents future disagreements and confusion. This should be done every time valuables are accessed by the patient. A tamper-proof storage bag should never be reused even in instances where valuables are accessed for a specific item and returned to the facility for safekeeping.

A relatively new phenomenon is the installation of in-room safes to provide the patient with complete control over their valuables. Found most commonly in trauma and other designated emergency department rooms, in-room safes are also growing in popularity in general medical-surgical units throughout the healthcare facility.

CASH REGISTERS

The handling of cash is a problem for most organizations. According to the accounting firm Ernst and Young, of all cash fraud techniques, cash taken by the failure to record sales accounts for about 30% of all losses.[3]

The security department can lend support to the accounting departments in several ways. First, cash registers should be read and cleared by a person other than the person handling the transactions. This poses a problem for many accounting departments because a number of registers must be cleared at various night hours and on weekends. In many cases, the security department is already responsible for providing escorts when the money is transported to the main vault or cash-holding areas. It is a relatively simple matter for security to provide the additional service of clearing the register and forwarding the tapes directly to internal auditing or another previously designated department.

UMC

UNIVERSITY MEDICAL CENTER

1 7 5 4

MEDICAL RECORD#

DOB

NAME

VISIT#

PATIENT VALUABLES FORM

To be used with Patient Valuables Collection Bag Bag #: ________________

* Required to be filled in

* Storage Location: ☐ Cashier's Office Safe ☐ ED Trauma Safe ☐ ED Rm. 1406 Safe

* Items Collected: (Check item and Include number of each item collected)

☐ Watch _____ ☐ Ring(s) _____ ☐ Necklace(s)_____ ☐ Bracelet(s) _____

☐ Anklet(s)_____ ☐ Earrings _____ ☐ Cards _____ ☐ Cell Phone ☐ Keys

☐ Wallet: description ______________________ ☐ Cash: Amount:____________

☐ Other: (please specify) ____

*Date:____________ *Time: __________ (military)

*Patient Signature: ______________________________ ☐ Patient unable to sign

or

Patient Representative: ________________Relationship to Patient: ______________ ☐ ID verified

*Witness Signature/Title 1:__________________________ Printed Name: _______________

*Witness Signature/Title 2:__________________________ Printed Name: _______________

Valuables Returned: *Date: ____________ *Time: __________ (military)

*Patient Signature: ______________________________ ☐ Patient unable to sign

or

Patient Representative: ________________Relationship to Patient: ______________ ☐ ID verified

*Witness Signature/Title __________________________ Printed Name: _______________

MR-1754 (07/11) WHITE - Medical Record Yellow - Inside Valuables Bag PINK - Patient

FIGURE 5-7

Sample patient valuables inventory form.

Without such a system in place, a large medical center in Dallas, TX experienced all of their parking attendant cashiers working in collusion and circumventing the internal controls in place, costing the hospital over $1 million in lost receipts in a four-year period.

A word of caution concerning cash escorts: the security officer should be just that—an escort. The officer should not be the sole transport unless proper tamper-proof controls have been instituted. The route from the cash collection point to the holding area should be varied just as patrol patterns should be varied.

EMERGENCY SHIPMENTS

A valuable support service is the receiving, signing for, and proper disposition of equipment and supplies that arrive at the facility after normal business hours. It is sometimes impossible for a critical shipment to arrive before the regular receiving area closes. In this case, the security department can provide valuable support to the materials management department and to the hospital.

Clear guidance must be established concerning this support service. Otherwise, outside delivery personnel may not make the effort to deliver on time because they know that security will accept the late shipment. They will deliver first to organizations that do not have after-hours receiving. It is thus important to perform this service on a prearranged request from the materials management department. It should be recognized, however, that flexibility must prevail because it is important that a critical delivery not be refused due to a breakdown in the prearrangement procedure.

Specific handling instructions should be recorded in the system used to pass on information so that all security personnel will be aware of the proper handling of the goods received. At the time the delivery is actually accepted, an entry should be made in the daily activity record indicating the time the delivery was received and where the property was taken for storage.

PACKAGE CHECK

It may be desirable to maintain a checking service for employee property brought into the facility. Not only does this service discourage organization-owned property from being added to the employee's personal property, but it also provides better protection for employee property than storage in a department. In addition to the security aspects, the environmental services function is enhanced when personal suitcases, packages, boxes, and so on that do not pertain to the departmental responsibilities are stored elsewhere.

This system is quite common in department stores, where packages held by security are released as the employee leaves the building. Already practiced in some healthcare facilities, this procedure requires a firm, consistent policy prohibiting the employee from taking certain personal property to his or her work area. This practice can be very difficult to implement in a heavily unionized environment.

MISCELLANEOUS SERVICES

The number and range of security services is almost endless. Services should be implemented only if they fit into the system without jeopardizing the basic protection function. Some miscellaneous services other than those previously listed may be found in specific programs. One of these is turning equipment on or off. This may be a routine service, such as turning on kitchen equipment before food service employees arrive, or the specific environmental control of a researcher's experimental project. Controlling valet parking areas and interacting in facility transport systems is also a frequent role for security departments. In one hospital, the security officer records the number of people using hospital-controlled buses to provide important operational planning data. Another service frequently requested of security officers is helping with patients, in various forms.

Services are limited only by the needs of the organization and the imagination of those in charge. Security administrators who continually object to requests because "that isn't a security function" may only be reflecting their narrow view. One must always remember that security is part of the healthcare team, and patient needs are paramount. Figure 5-8 presents a diagram of the various healthcare security service activities and their functional organization impact.

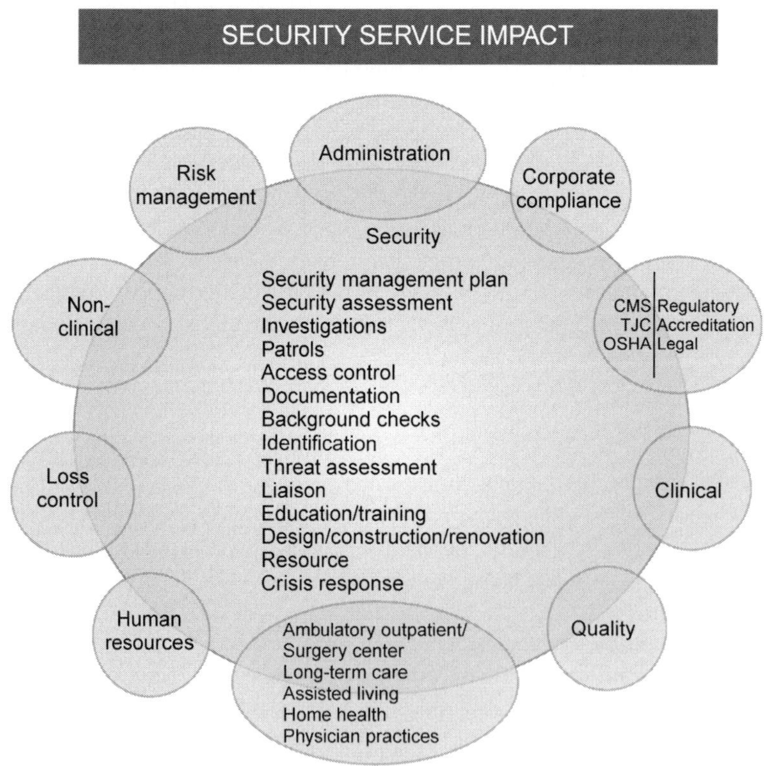

FIGURE 5-8

Basic healthcare security service activities and functional organization impact.

(Adapted from Safety and Security Solutions, L.L.C., Richmond, VA.)

PUBLIC/EMPLOYEE/COMMUNITY RELATIONS

The security effort is created to serve the healthcare organization. The organization is people—all sorts of people, including visitors, employees, patients, physicians, vendors, delivery people, repair technicians, researchers, and students. The overall security program must be accepted and understood by the organization it serves. Security personnel must exhibit a helpful and friendly customer service attitude toward everyone they meet. In many instances, the security officer is often the first and last person that a patient or visitor to a healthcare facility comes in contact with. The image projected by the officer can set the tone for the person's feelings toward the organization. Security cannot operate in a vacuum and must function as part of the team in providing quality patient care.

REFERENCES

1. Solutions by market special publication—Healthcare. *SDM Magazine and Security Magazine* 2008, November.
2. Vesely Rebecca, Hoppszallern Suzanna. Managing points of access: Hospitals assert tighter control over vendor and visitor access to improve safety. *Health Facilities Management* 2013, October: 38–46. Available at http://www.hfmmagazine.com/display/HFM-news-article.dhtml?dcrPath=/templatedata/HF_Common/NewsArticle/data/HFM/Magazine/2013/Oct/1013HFM_FEA_Securitysurvey.
3. Gerboth DL, Hoenecke JB, Briganti R. *White collar crime: Loss prevention through internal control*. Chubb Group of Insurance Companies; 1989. 8.

CHAPTER

SECURITY DEPARTMENT ORGANIZATION AND STAFFING

6

A well-trained and properly supported security force is the basic component of the healthcare protection system. Although the security staff is the backbone of this effort, it is perhaps only 20% to 25% of a well-rounded security and productive security system. A successful security program must also rely on positive security contributions of facility staff, full support of administration, including financial resources, and effective physical security safeguards. In fact, in some small facilities, there are successful security programs in which there are no security personnel; however, there must be a 24/7 designated security function response capability. In these cases it may be the maintenance staff (or other organization personnel) who assume certain security duties and responsibilities. Regardless of facility size, or the size of the security force, it's essential to have an integrated approach with the other organizational resources that contribute to a successful, cost-effective protection program. The creation and ongoing management of this integration is the direct responsibility of the security program administrator.

SECURITY FUNCTION REPORTING LEVEL AND SUPPORT

The security function serves, supports, and is interrelated to all aspects of the healthcare organization. As such, security is considered an element of administration. A required component of the Security Management Plan is to clearly specify the position has the responsibility for the security of the organization, with a clearly defined reporting level for this position. The reporting level of security in the organization reflects the importance administration places on the security function, and their own responsibility to protect persons and property.

It has been argued by some security practitioners that the security function must report only to the chief executive officer (CEO) or the chief operating officer (COO). This may sound good in theory, but it is generally neither practical nor a satisfactory situation. The basic problem is accessibility. Both the CEO and the COO are performing functions that, by necessity, do not generally involve day-to-day nonclinical department operations.

On the other hand, the security function must not report at a level that negatively affects its productiveness. The security function, like many other functions in healthcare, has been a victim of organizational "flattening out." The various management levels in healthcare organizations that once existed are gone. As a result, security has often been pushed lower in the organizational hierarchy. The important aspect of the security reporting level is that it must provide the organizational authority necessary to properly carry out its mission. Practically speaking, security should report to an individual who has both the time for, and interest in, the security function. In short, there must be proper administrative support for a program to be effective and productive. This reporting level must have sufficient stature to carry the ball when a decision is outside his or her realm of direct authority, or when information of a sensitive nature must be communicated to others at higher levels within the organization.

A common reporting level for security is the vice president (or director) of facilities or the risk management administrator who, as a generality, seems to fit the foundation criteria for a successful program. Likewise, other highly successful programs report to the vice presidents of finance, human resources, and administration. In Canada, a common model sees security reporting to a VP or director of support services. Regardless of the reporting level, the professional security administrator must be cognizant of the organizational support level cycle. The concept of the cycle is that, at critical times, security is a top priority of the organization, resulting in a high level of support in terms of funding and philosophy relative to security policy and procedures. At other times, support may be maintained in a routine operating level, where there is minimal day-to-day support. Dennis Dalton, in his book *The Art of Successful Security Management*, suggests the support cycle consists of three phases: strong organization support, confusion, and a lack of support.[1] In Dalton's support cycle, the confusion stage is one that can challenge the security administrator. This confusion cycle can occur when the program is running smoothly and there is little or no perceived security threat. It is a time when management and staff feel safe and may be totally focused on other management and patient care issues.

There are various signs and clues to alert the security administrator that the program has entered, or is entering, this confusion stage of the support cycle. Chief among these signs are:

- A general indifference toward the program by top management, and a lack of understanding of the duties and activities of security that contribute to the healthcare mission
- Advertent or inadvertent exclusions from meetings where issues clearly entered into the area of protection
- Planning of activities or events with protection implications without security involvement
- Department heads and supervisors make assumptions about the security program without seeking clarifications or confirmation of program components
- Decreasing ability to influence or have a voice in sanctions relative to internal misconduct situations
- Increased staff disregard for compliance with security safeguards, policy and procedure.

In the third stage of the support cycle there is outright rejection of plans and programs, top management avoids security input or discussion, and staff show little support for the security function. This is a critical time for the security program and the security administrator, who must do all possible to end this final stage of the cycle and return to the full support phase. Failing to accomplish this objective likely indicates it is time for a change in security leadership.

THE FUNCTIONAL ORGANIZATION CHART

In essence the administrative plan for the entire organization is recapped in the functional organization chart, which defines the relationship of the components of the organization. This chart further establishes the chain of command. However, the chart specifies only formal authority relationships; it omits the many significant informal relationships. Further, it does not generally indicate the degree (limits) of authority that exists at any point in the organizational structure.

The organization of a security department is limited only by the imagination and aspirations of the person responsible for the protection system. Organizational charts range from simple to complex. Each facility or organization has its own format, style, and procedure for preparing the department organization chart. The charts in Figures 6-1 and 6-2 are offered as examples of actual working charts

FIGURE 6-1

Example of a small security department organization chart.

in a single stand-alone facility. They are not intended to be used as models, as each protection program is unique in scope, function, reporting level, and budgetary realities.

As shown in Figure 6-1, there is an allocation of 0.5 FTE for Investigations and Training and 0.5 FTE for an Administrative Clerk. There are several ways these two positions of 20 hours per week each could be staffed. A part-time administrative clerk who works a six-hour shift three days per week (M-W-F) would be ideal. This staffing arrangement would allow flexibility in utilizing the additional four hours per pay period (2 weeks) where most needed.

The investigations and training officer could be staffed by a senior security officer working as such two eight-hour shifts per week and filling in a regular officer duty shift three times per week. A limited amount of investigative and training activity could also be accomplished during regular duty shift time. In short, the deployment plan is left to the creativity of security leadership, balanced with the specific protection needs of the healthcare organization.

HEALTHCARE SYSTEMS

The organizational chart and the delivery of security services in large healthcare systems created by mergers, buyouts and affiliations may look quite different from the stand-alone facility. The various facilities in a system are often located many miles apart, in the same service area or even in multistate locations. These healthcare systems develop their own specific management operating philosophies, and these philosophies range from centralization to quasi-centralization to decentralization, with variations of form in between.

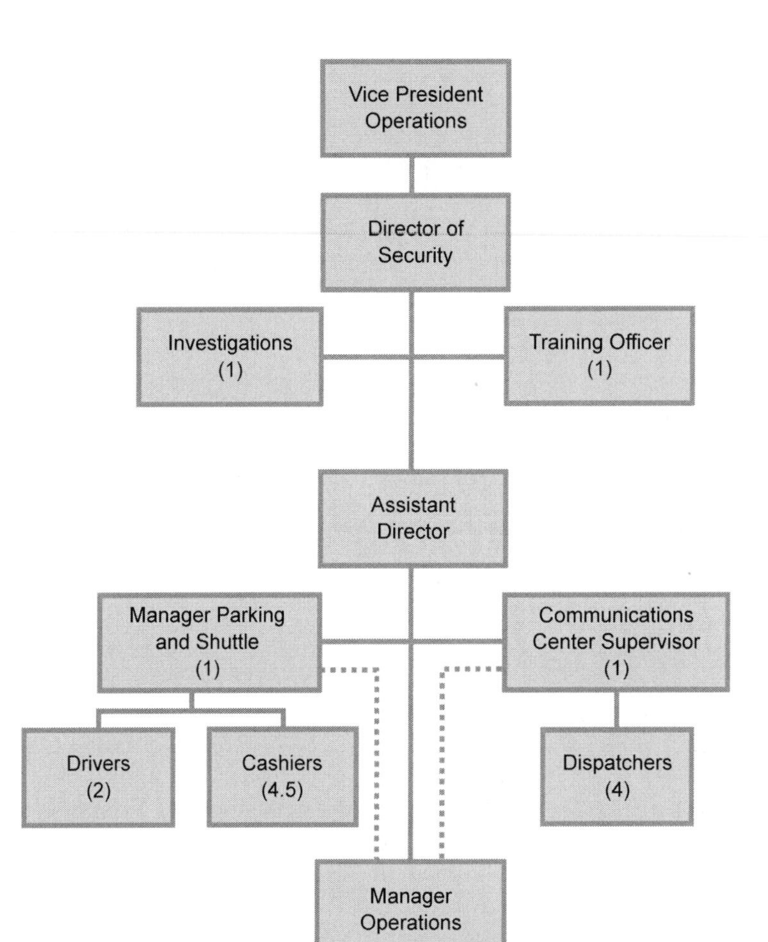

FIGURE 6-2

Example of a large security department organization chart.

SYSTEMS (MULTIFACILITY) SECURITY MANAGEMENT CONTROL

There are various levels of systems management that can be used to achieve standardization of protection services, increase the quality of performance, and provide a favorable impact on budgets. These levels range from an informal working group of security managers from each facility, to a full corporate system administrative and operational control responsibility. The benefits can be optimized by a total centralized system management approach; however, it is the most difficult to achieve, due to many factors, including individual facility philosophies, turf control issues, staff personal prejudices/biases and organized labor issues. The ability of individual facilities to fund their share of the program, and the reality of geographical distances also challenge this model.

In the pure centralized philosophy approach there is one budget, with full line authority to operate a consolidated systems program. There may be some internal cost accounting allocations of facilities being served, but from an operations standpoint each facility would receive security services as a one-campus approach, even though facilities, or sites, may be miles apart. It is only recently has the total centralized security system model been used when facilities are located in multistate locations, and it is not used anywhere in Canada as a multiprovince model.

The quasi-centralization philosophy, which is the most popular, generally operates within a given metropolitan area via a central corporate budget and facility-specific budget for security. In this approach, the central office may provide support functions such as training, investigations, consultation, and documentation. This may include Joint Commission/accreditation compliance, strategic planning, equipment standardization (including maintenance contracts), and a central security operations/communications center. In some programs the central office provides for a common external grounds patrol and/or a consolidated patrol/field supervision approach. In this methodology the patrol field supervisor will often represent the authority of the facility security manager, during evenings, nights, or weekends. Also in this approach security staff for individual facilities are generally hired by the individual facility manager, and usually paid as an employee of the individual facility. The facility manager would report to the central (corporate) director and be paid through corporate funding. This presents a contract management concept for the facility; however, this corporate facility security supervisor would work very closely with the facility administrative person responsible for the security program. In other cases, the facility security supervisor may be an employee of the facility and have a "soft" reporting relationship to the corporate security hierarchy.

In the completely decentralized approach, each facility maintains complete control of their security effort, with no line authority outside of the specific facility. In this approach there may be a centralized corporate security support function; however, this function would generally only be advisory in nature.

Figure 6-3 represents an example of a healthcare system corporate security organization chart that incorporates a centralization of security support services while maintaining a certain management autonomy and program functions at the facility level.

Numerous models are used to provide security services through a multifacility healthcare systems approach. Figure 6-4 portrays seven such approaches on a continuum from the least beneficial to the most beneficial.

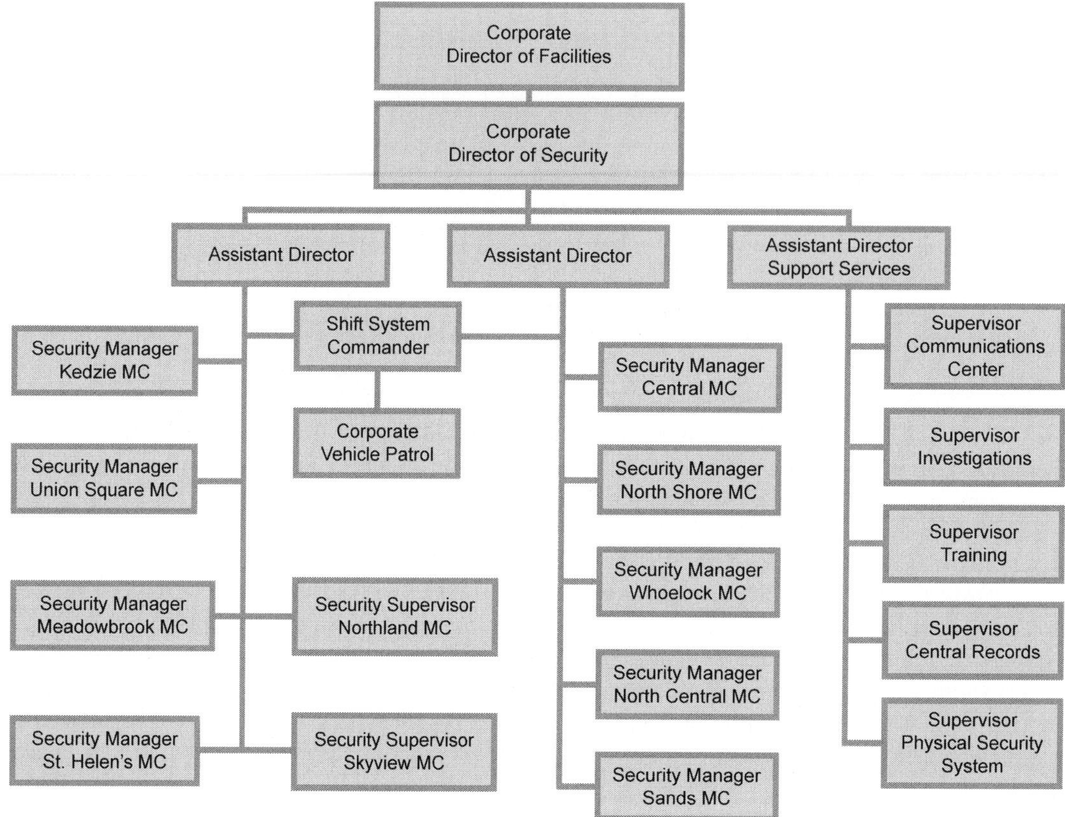

FIGURE 6-3

Example of a healthcare system security department chart.

TYPES OF SECURITY STAFF

Several options are available to healthcare administrators in selecting the type of security force to serve their facility. Each of the different models of staffing has its own advantages and disadvantages. The five basic types of security staffing are:

- Proprietary (in-house) staff
- Outsourced staff (contract service)
- Proprietary security manager or supervisory staff with outsourced security officers
- Outsourced security manager or supervisory staff with in-house security officers
- Off-duty law enforcement personnel (typically used only in the U.S.).

There are also unique individual hybrid staffing models that utilize proprietary, outsourced, and off-duty law enforcement personnel in various combinations.

SYSTEMS MANAGEMENT
for
SECURITY SERVICES

Continuum Legend

1. Informal discussion group of facility security managers
2. A formal discussion/work group of facility security managers with defined leadership, goals, and objectives
3. A paid system staff Director of Security serving in a consultant role
4. System Director of Security, Investigator, Crime Prevention/Training Administrator with defined line authority
5. Same staff as in 4 with central dispatching/alarm monitoring
6. Same staff as in 4 and 5 with a mobile command/task force unit
7. A systems security department that employs, and deploys, all security personnel serving system facilities

FIGURE 6-4

Comparing models in a corporate (multiple facility) security system.

The security program is affected differently, depending on the general character/profile elements of the particular staffing model. Figure 6-5 provides a summary comparison of the value of the different staffing models in relation to various security program components.

There is a significant trend toward the use of outsourcing as a model for security staffing of healthcare security programs. One reason the proprietary model has dropped so drastically (approximately 50% in the last 20 years), with a corresponding rise in the combination model, is that many healthcare organizations froze new hires, but would allow vacancy replacements to be contract service employees. Outside of the U.S. the trend is similar, as healthcare organizations struggle to ensure they fund direct patient care, challenging healthcare security leaders who have traditionally operated more expensive in-house models. A 2013 initiative in Brisbane, Australia serves to illustrate this cost-driven movement from proprietary to contracted security.[2]

It should be noted the GE Security & IAHSS Healthcare Benchmarking Study[3] reports 77% of the 582 hospitals responding stated their facilities utilized a proprietary security staffing model. This high percentage is in sharp contrast to the 34% as shown in Table 6-1. There may be several reasons for this difference. The IAHSS/GE survey report states the survey returns were approximately 10% of the 7,461 surveys sent (381 returns completed the survey fully and 275 returns were partially completed), and the returns skewed to larger hospitals versus the national population. It is a reasonable assumption larger hospitals tend toward proprietary security programs and larger hospitals tend to respond to

	Security program components	Staffing Model			
		Proprietary	Outsource	Combination Out/Propr.	Off Duty
BUDGET	Cost	Fair/Poor	Very Good	Good	Very Poor
	Cost Control	Good/Fair	Very Good	Good	Poor
	Cost Effectiveness	Good	Very Good	Good	Poor
ORGANIZATION	Clear Chain of Command	Very Good	Good	Fair	Poor
	Organizational Control	Very Good	Very Good	Very Good	Fair
	Effective Training	Very Good	Good/Fair	Good	Poor
	Effective Supervision	Good	Good	Good/Fair	Very Poor
	Healthcare Expertise	Very Good	Fair	Good	Very Poor
	Effecting Program Change	Good	Good	Good	Poor
	Integration into Organization	Very Good	Fair	Good/Fair	Poor
	Loyalty to Organization	Very Good	Fair	Good	Poor
	Lack of Tunover	Good	Fair/Poor	Fair	Fair
PROGRAM	Upward Mobility	Fair	Good	Fair	N/A
	Completing Good Documentation	Very Good	Fair	Good	Poor
	Quality of Investigation Activity	Very Good	Good	Very Good	Fair/Poor
	Crime Prevention Efforts	Very Good	Good/Fair	Good	Fair
	Officer Image	Very Good	Good	Good	Fair/Poor
RATING	Overall Effectiveness	Very Good	Good	Good	Poor

FIGURE 6-5

Comparing basic security staffing models.

surveys in greater numbers, partially because they are almost certain to have a security-specific leadership position, unlike many smaller institutions.

PROPRIETARY STAFF (IN HOUSE)

Proprietary staff simply means the security department personnel are employees of the organization. The proprietary security officer may, or may not, be commissioned police officers in the U.S. In Canada, commissioned police officers are not employed in healthcare security programs. The vast majority, over 90%, of proprietary officers are not commissioned. The proprietary commissioned officer is generally

Table 6-1 Comparing the Use of Healthcare Security Staffing Models over 10-Year Periods

Staffing Model	1980	1990	2000	2010
Outsourced/Contract	24%	30%	52%	55%
In-House/Proprietary	64%	60%	34%	31%
Combination of Proprietary and Contract Staff	8%	7%	13%	13%
Proprietary Management and Supervision with Contact Staff/ Off-Duty Police	3%	2%	1%	1%
Off-Duty Law Enforcement	1%	1%	0*	0*

**Less than 1%*

serving a healthcare facility that is part of a university setting, or a large hospital located in a state that allows certain organizations to maintain a fully commissioned private police agency. In North Carolina, the state has a unique law allowing for "Company Police" with authority bestowed by the state attorney general's office.

The main advantage of the in-house staffing model is control. The organization can control the recruitment, selection, supervision, and training and compensation of security personnel.

The proprietary staffing system is virtually always the most expensive in terms of labor costs, despite the fact some expenses may be absorbed by other departments such as administration, accounting, purchasing, employee health, and human resources. Employee fringe benefits for an in-house staff generally range between 30 to 35% of the base salary of the employee plus employer required taxes. The utilization of a contingent of part-time staff will reduce fringe benefit costs; however, increased uniforms and equipment and training time generally increase costs.

Some organizations ignore fringe benefits when computing program costs for periodic budget responsibility reports. The cost of fringe benefits can be controlled to some extent in larger forces, by simply running a duty shift one or two employees short during holiday, vacation, or sick leave absences. This cost-saving method is usually not available in other staffing models. However, if the protection system can operate without a given position, the question of general overstaffing could certainly be an issue. The true hourly cost for proprietary staff can be significantly higher than for an outsourced staff. This higher cost is generally denounced by in-house budget staff, who ignore certain cost items (such as overtime costs and other nonproductive payroll expenses) in order to achieve lower stated cost projections. In Canada organizations save somewhere between 30 and 45% with an outsourced service when compared to the proprietary model, compared to 15 to 20% in the U.S.

A main disadvantage of the proprietary system, in addition to higher cost, is the tendency for a program and its security staff to become stagnant. The routine of security services can easily produce lethargy among employees. It becomes increasingly difficult to stimulate and motivate officers in direct relation to their age and length of employment. The cliché "You can't see the forest for the trees" becomes a real problem as a security officer becomes "one of the well-settled staff." This does not imply all in-house programs deteriorate to an unacceptable level. The implementation of good management techniques can successfully counter this negative trend. As a general rule, proprietary security staff programs should not be considered for programs with a staff of less than 18 to 22 full-time employees. An in-house staff of less than this number of employees may also be mandated in the absence of qualified outsourcing service providers.

OUTSOURCING (CONTRACT STAFF)

In addition to lower cost, organizations contract with an outside agency to be relieved of the burdensome administrative duties of operating an in-house security force. An additional incentive is that costs are fixed, and thus the organization can more accurately forecast budget expenditures. According to the magazine *Security*, the use of contract security officers grows by 12% annually. About 10% of in-house programs in the U.S. convert to contract services each year. However, the net increase of contract services in healthcare security is closer to 2% and is expected to grow in the wake of the passage of the Affordable Care Act in the U.S. There are some cases where a healthcare organization will convert to a proprietary staff from the contract supplied model; however, this has been rare in the last ten years.

Many other advantages of contracting for security services are espoused in articles usually written by members of contract agencies. Many of these arguments could be valid; however, too few contract companies live up to their claims in actual field performance. When one security company bids against another for business, the lowest bid most probably excludes something. Usually, what is missing is quality. A number of the world's largest contract agencies have formed a special healthcare services division or hired a healthcare security practitioner to emphasize their expertise in healthcare security. This is a claim that should be examined closely.

The commonly propounded advantages and disadvantages of contract services, with countering or supporting comments, include the following:

1. *A contract service usually means lower payroll costs.* Unfortunately, lower cost security is almost always achieved by paying contract personnel a low wage, and using a substantial number of part-time employees. The contract agency's full-time officers must generally work more than 40 hours per week to earn a sufficient salary. In some cases the wages are so low that overtime rates for contract security officers are lower than the straight-time wages of proprietary staffs. Excessively long working hours can be detrimental to the security effort, as coverage is not necessarily synonymous with good security. Having too many part-time employees, and a high labor turnover rate, can reduce the continuity of service essential to a high-quality program. These deficiencies can be controlled to a large extent by including specifications in the contract agreement that prescribes wages and benefits to be paid to the security staff.
2. *A contract service relieves the organization of administrative burdens.* This may sound like welcome relief for facility managers who do not want to concern themselves with managing the security function. The downside is the facility can lose an important element of insight and control in achieving organization goals and objectives. Facility management must be involved with these so-called burdens, along with the contract service, to maintain an efficient and viable program. Facility management and contract security management must act as "business partners" to achieve an optimum protection system. In a unionized proprietary model, labor relations demands may

consume a disproportionate amount of security management time, leaving less time for their corporate security management responsibilities expected by the organization.

3. *Contract services can provide additional security officers as needed.* Employing extra officers on short notice or for a short duration of time may, however, require premium hourly payments. At best, additional security personnel who have never been trained at the facility may be of limited value. Further, when one client needs additional security officers due to a flood, civil disturbance, strike, or any other area-wide emergency event, other clients may also need additional security coverage. All contract agencies have limits on the number of additional personnel they can provide, and providing additional coverage may require an extended period of time before they are actually deployed on the client's property.
4. *Healthcare security personnel should be well versed in the specialized area of healthcare security services.* Contract agencies generally provide security services to many different types of organizations and settings. Thus, it becomes virtually impossible for a viable contract security company to serve solely hospitals, airports, hotels, department stores, etc. There simply must be deployment of security personnel among the various types of accounts for a variety of reasons, including promotions, disciplinary problems, personality conflicts, officers' geographical residence in relation to the work site, and others. Even though a regular core of security officers may be assigned to a given account, it is common to temporarily assign a fill-in officer to cover for an unexpected absence. These fill-in officers are often nonproductive and their actions, or lack of action, may be contraindicated.
5. *Unproductive or undesirable contract officers can be handled by advising the contract agency a particular officer is no longer acceptable for duty.* Contract agencies generally shift the officer to another client, who thus ends up with the first client's reject. Of course, it works two ways. An exceptionally good officer can be reassigned by the contractor to another facility without notice. The mobility and flexibility of such reassignments can create such a continuous change of personnel that continuity of service is jeopardized. Indeed, turnover is one of the most frequently cited reasons for avoiding the contract model.
6. *Fraternization is a problem in all security forces.* Contract security officers are less apt to develop friendships that result in their overlooking problems they should correct or report. They are often considered outsiders (this can be positive or negative), and with their sometimes high turnover rate, they have little time to develop close ties. Consequently, contract security officers can be more objective in discharging their duties. On the other hand, they do not always possess the same loyalty as regular employees and are not always as dependent on doing their best to ensure continued employment.

In competing for a contract security service, the lowest bidder usually provides only a warm body to fill a position. The low-bidder provided program is the most expensive system in terms of cost/benefit relationships. The cost of a security service should not be considered only in terms of labor cost, but also in terms of the total annual expenses and the quality of protection services provided. In many cases, labor coverage can be reduced by using better-quality personnel, and annual costs can be maintained or even lowered despite a higher labor unit cost. A competent security consultant can be useful in analyzing security officer deployment schedules and objectively recommending the proper coverage plan.

A major deficiency in the contract security system can be traced to the client, not the contract agency. This deficiency is a lack of involvement in the day-to-day protection needs of their facility.

Management cannot abdicate its role in the security of the facility, by simply delegating the responsibility of protection to a third party. A third party, no matter how competent, cannot by itself provide the protection required.

COMBINATION OF PROPRIETARY AND CONTRACT SECURITY OFFICERS

A staffing system using both proprietary and contract security officers is a methodology utilized in a number of facilities. The basic driver of this approach is to address the control and supervision problems that can occur when the facility staffs with all contract security personnel. Proponents of this hybrid system suggest the in-house supervisor can develop a more in-depth program and make better use of security personnel. The in-house supervisor, an employee of the organization being served, presumably has direct lines of communication within the facility organizational structure. A very serious pitfall of this system can result when an employee of one organization acts in a supervisory capacity over the employee of another organization. In-house supervisors tend to be overly critical of the quality of the contract personnel furnished, and they are less motivated to work with the security officer in dealing with deficiencies, than if the supervisors had made the hiring decision themselves. In-house management may tend to become less realistic and concerned in terms of line staff issues. This potential apathy can seriously affect the quality of day-to-day security operations.

A newer trend is the outsourcing of management of the security program while the facility continues to employ in-house security staff. Following a model that has been used successfully in the delivery of healthcare environmental services and nutrition services, the security manager and supervisory staff hire, train and lead the security team, manage compliance-related activities, oversee the evaluation and deployment of security technology and, frequently, emergency management and preparedness, and all staff engagement activities in the security function.

OFF-DUTY LAW ENFORCEMENT PERSONNEL

The employment of off-duty police personnel has lost favor for the vast majority of U.S. healthcare facilities and is not used in Canada as a rule. This system for securing a facility, even in part, is the least desirable of all staffing systems. High costs, virtually no organized system, little or no healthcare security-specific training, and lack of continuity are all basic reasons supporting this conclusion. Moreover, moonlighters of all types can be accused of just putting in their time, as a second job provides supplementary income rather than being the primary means of support.

Police authority often has appeal to organizations not well versed in their protection needs. The power to arrest is often cited as a primary advantage of the law enforcement officer staffing model. Most professional security administrators, however, view this authority as a disadvantage in terms of public relations, as it often promotes outcomes out of proportion to the seriousness of a situation. Further, progressive police administrators prefer their officers not work in off-duty jobs requiring them to wear the police uniform. The potential for misconduct, which brings adverse publicity to the police agency, and the possibility of the agency finding itself as a defendant in a legal action is a situation to be avoided.

Another disadvantage of using law enforcement officers is availability. A facility may have no coverage at a time of critical need because of overtime required on the officer's regular police assignments (strikes, fires, civil disturbance, training, etc.), court time, and federal assistance programs that fund police operations through the payment of overtime work. Police operations require the routine scheduling of police officers to meet changing conditions and emergency situations. Some of these emergency situations may be the same event(s) that directly affect the healthcare organization, requiring elevated manpower needs.

In some Canadian jurisdictions, healthcare organizations have worked with provincial agencies to designate their proprietary security staff as "special constables." This designation, achieved through a screening and training program approved by the province, allows healthcare special constables particular powers, including powers of arrest, under specific circumstances related to the environment they serve. Mental health, trespass, tobacco enforcement and parking enforcement are the most commonly sought areas for special constable status. It is important to note these individuals are not police but rather security officers who have been given enhanced legal authority in delineated areas. While this model is in place in several Canadian jurisdictions, most notably in the province of Alberta, it is not a common model in Canada.

COMMISSIONED POLICE OFFICERS

There are a few limited programs, such as the Baylor Health Care System, Dallas, TX, Cleveland Clinic, Cleveland, OH, and several more in North Carolina including the University of North Carolina Hospitals, Chapel Hill, Wake Med in Raleigh and New Hanover Regional in Wilmington which operate a security program as a full police agency under the authority of state legislation. These types of programs are often referred to as Departments of Public Safety or Special Police. This model is not generally seen outside of the U.S.

There are significant advantages associated with this model including arrest powers and a perceived higher level of training associated with hiring police officers. However, there are also disadvantages with this approach. In one NC department specifically, there was above average turnover within its special police rank as officers were leaving to pursue higher paying law enforcement opportunities or became disenchanted with the "quasi police" department approach. It was expressed that the hospital was a good starting point for a law enforcement career but the challenges of the healthcare environment and lack of activity was frequently cited as not fulfilling the basic law enforcement desire. Additionally, many patient-first, service-focused behaviors found in a typical hospital security operation can be absent in the attitudes and behaviors in many police officers working in the healthcare environment.

SHARED SERVICES APPROACH

During the last 15 years, the true shared service approach in providing security services has been somewhat changed and altered by healthcare organization mergers, affiliations, and the growth of proprietary hospital organizations. These new healthcare systems simply combine facilities through an organizational structure, as opposed to a shared service membership of separate individually governed facilities. The advantages and disadvantages of the shared approach to security must now be applied to a healthcare systems approach, rather than individual hospitals that had equal status in the governance of the shared services organization.

Although changed, the shared services security approach continues to flourish and is operating a significant number of highly successful hospital security programs. The major roadblocks to the shared systems approach to security in the separate organizations being served as a combined security system continue to be politics, turf, and self-interests.

There is another quasi-shared service approach operating to a limited degree. This approach is purchased services, or sold services, in which one healthcare organization markets a program to one or more other healthcare organizations. The organizational structure for this type of plan is relatively uncomplicated. A healthcare organization that has effective management and a specialized talent in security can generate additional revenue to offset costs, while providing a quality, cost-effective service to other independent organizations. The provider organization must maintain acceptable services within a price structure, and the consumer organization has limited responsibility except when extensive capital investments are required. In the case of capital investments a long-term contract may be required to protect the provider organization. This approach is generally limited to, and is fostered, when organizations are in a very close geographical proximity to each other. This type of a shared security program has had little growth due to the often silent factor related to being a competitive organization.

CORPORATE (SYSTEMS) APPROACH

The systems approach, like the shared service approach, is as much an organizational structure as it is a staffing model. Security services provided to facilities through the systems approach can produce a high level of service within an extremely cost-effective framework. Protection service lends itself particularly to a systems concept.

Security problems that occur in one facility will very likely be transferred to other facilities in that geographical area. When thieves find out how easy it may be to steal computer equipment in one medical care facility, they are quick to "case" other like facilities. Forged prescriptions, short-change operators, and "professional patients" provide examples of problems that tend to travel the healthcare facility circuit. Healthcare workers who are terminated due to involvement in security-type problems invariably turn up in other healthcare facilities. Where else does a registered nurse find ready employment? Even housekeeping employees, food service workers, and maintenance people tend to seek employment in other healthcare facilities once they have been employed in the healthcare field.

In a health system centralized approach, cost containment is achieved through several factors. One is supervision. A combined supervising effort can reduce the total number of supervisors from that required by individual programs.

Another area of cost containment is the purchasing of supplies and equipment—otherwise known as economy of scale. Supplies such as forms and uniforms are less expensive when standardized and purchased in large quantities.

Although important, cost reduction is not the primary reason to develop a centralized systems approach to security. The primary reason is to improve services. Improvement can occur in many areas, most notably in supervision, the training and quality of personnel, the investigative effort, and the efficient deployment of personnel, especially when the facilities are located within close proximity to each other.

Most facilities, except the very largest, may find it difficult to justify the high cost of hiring and retaining a top-quality security director or manager. On the other hand, several facilities within a system (each sharing only a part of the cost) can easily afford a competent security administrator and in turn reap the benefits of a quality protection program for their respective facilities.

The lack of direct supervision is a deficiency found in many healthcare security programs. Generally only the larger security programs can efficiently and effectively provide 24-hour supervision. In many facilities there may be only one or two security officers on duty on a given shift. It is not practical to staff a supervisor to provide supervision for one other officer. Some programs attempt to resolve this deficiency with a lead officer or senior officer when two are on duty at a time; however, this arrangement seldom provides true quality supervision outcomes. The systems supervisor concept is practical, efficient, and simple. When each facility is funding only a fraction of a wage, it is possible to pay a higher wage, thus attracting and retaining a better qualified supervisor. The number of personnel and the size of the geographical area that a supervisor can effectively cover are determined by individual philosophy, workload, level of officer training, and other factors.

A systems security program generally attracts a higher quality applicant than either contract agencies or single facility in-house programs. The main attraction for candidates is the career ladder that larger organizations can offer to individuals who strive to move up to supervisory positions. The training and challenge provided through gaining experience in multiple facilities also contribute to attracting and retaining quality personnel.

Perhaps one of the most important and extremely cost-effective benefits of the systems arrangement is in investigation. Just as law enforcement problems move from city to city, security problems move from facility to facility. The consolidation of records and reports enables system participants to resolve incidents and problems that they would be unable to solve individually. In addition, the system organizations have an opportunity to preclude problem staff members from moving from one facility to another in the system. This is "preventive action" of the highest level, and preventive and mitigation action is the primary objective of any protection program.

The central reporting of incidents leads to another advantage, which is the exchange of information. Matters of common interest can be researched with results and/or conclusions distributed efficiently to the various facilities in the system, eliminating costly, time-consuming duplication of effort. The amount of time and money spent by each facility in sending a representative to security and safety meetings can be drastically reduced. A designated security representative from the system can attend representing all facilities. Information, ideas, and techniques can then be shared within the system.

The systems approach also allows basic facility security policies and procedures to be standardized to some degree. Standardized procedures such as package inspection, accident reporting, fire codes, incident reporting, and the like greatly benefit organizations as general staff and security staff transfer or rotate from facility to facility. A degree of standardization also facilitates more meaningful "benchmarking" when comparing certain data facility by facility.

In Canada, a model has evolved in Vancouver, British Columbia that combines the shared services and corporate services model. One health authority has developed a corporate security services model, with the attributes described above, that allows them to deliver standardized security services to three other healthcare organizations. This program, Lower Mainland Integrated Protection Services, serves 27 hospitals and more than 300 community sites in these four health "systems." Standardized training, reporting, response capacity and investigative functions, along with robust quality measures, are strongly featured in this model.

In short, the systems approach allows security administrators and planners many opportunities to use dollars, labor, and equipment in new and innovative patterns not possible in individual stand-alone facility programs.

HOW LARGE A STAFF IS NEEDED?

When a CEO or COO asks how much security staff is needed, it generally means, "What is the least amount of security needed to get by within an acceptable tolerance of risk?" The number and types of security personnel required for an efficient security program is a fundamental question for every facility. It is not as easy as applying a simple formula using the square feet of buildings, campus acreage size, number of beds, number of employees, comparisons to "like" facilities, or any other profile data. It is indeed an individual facility question, since the numerous factors that must be considered vary in depth and scope from organization to organization. To arrive at the required number of security personnel, it is necessary first to analyze and understand the security mission, determine the level of the organization's security risks and vulnerabilities to be managed, review physical safeguards in place, and to identify the various services to be rendered. The next step is to design a program that supports the mission, properly manage risks, and implement the intended services. Only then can the number of staff required to operate the program be determined.

The IAHSS guideline below refers:

#02.01 SECURITY STAFFING AND DEPLOYMENT

Statement

Several factors affect the staffing model required to provide reasonable protection for Healthcare Facilities (HCF), and its patients, visitors and staff. NO single formula determines an appropriate staffing level for a given HCF. Staffing must provide for inspection, response and service capabilities.

Intent

a. Staffing levels are best determined after conducting a security risk assessment by a competent security professional or security administrator

b. The HCF's philosophy may emphasize a responsive (after-the-fact) posture or more strongly toward a preventative posture. A consideration of the factors listed below can lead to a reasonable and appropriate staffing configuration.

1. Philosophy of the Organization – The level of protection provided and the services rendered by the security department are based on the individual facility's philosophy and identified priorities to meet their unique needs.
2. Staffing Models – The most used staffing models include proprietary, contract, off-duty law enforcement, and various combinations of same. Smaller facilities, without dedicated security staff, will likely assign responsibility to other departments such as Facility Services. Regardless of the model selected, effective training must be provided.
3. Crime Analysis – Consider the type and volume of criminal activity occurring in and around the HCF. Also consider potential untoward circumstances in the event the HCF may provide services to crime victims (i.e., being a Level I Trauma Center).
4. Incident Activity – The severity and frequency of past on-site and nearby incidents will help determine staffing levels.
5. Duties and Expectations of the Security Staff
   - Emergency and Service Response Time – In cooperation with senior administration, develop acceptable average security response times for both emergency response and routine service requests. Track, trend and monitor these response times:
     - Priority I – Emergency situations such as crimes in progress, fire, and other emergency codes
     - Priority II – Urgent calls such as patient assists and responding to incidents
     - Priority III – Routine calls such as unlocking an office, patient valuables, patient transport, motorist assists, unlocking or locking perimeter doors
     - Priority IV – Scheduled tasks such as opening or closing gates, preventative patrols, opening conference rooms, wheelchair recovery
   - Patrol Frequency – Establish a desired frequency of routine day to day patrol. In planning patrol areas and frequency it is helpful to divide areas up into the following general areas:
     - Security Sensitive Areas (See Security Sensitive Areas Guideline 09.01)
     - Parking Areas
     - In-Patient Bed Areas

#02.01 SECURITY STAFFING AND DEPLOYMENT—cont'd

- Clinic Areas
- Public Areas
- Ancillary Patient Care Areas (Radiology, Labs, Physical Therapy)
- Support Areas such as Food Services, Medical Records, Maintenance and Engineering, Administrative Space
- Medical Office Buildings / Satellite / Off campus Facilities

- Fixed Post Assignments – Unnecessary fixed post assignments may reduce the ability to provide for proactive patrol and effect response times if resources are limited.
- Scheduled Routine Functions – Evaluate the number of scheduled functions such as cash escorts, pharmacy escorts, locking and unlocking areas, deliveries, equipment checks, or other similar duties separate and apart from routine patrol.
- Scheduled Special Functions – Based on the crime analysis of the location and within the guidelines of the HCF, provide for crime prevention activities such as personal safety talks, security assessments and security consultations designed as a proactive service of the security department.
- Nonscheduled Activities – Evaluate nonscheduled activities that are routinely performed by security personnel such as:
  - Investigative activities
  - Problem resolution
  - Lost and found
  - Unscheduled locking or unlocking
  - Patient assistance including mental health watches
  - Processing court documents
  - Acting as a witness or preparing incident reports
  - Special assignments – Evaluate special events and celebrations which may dictate the use of significant staffing allocations.

6. Physical and electronic security measures deployed
7. Response Capabilities of Police and Fire Services – The availability and timing of law enforcement and fire responses may affect the staffing model. A lengthy or unpredictable response by outside agencies will usually require additional HCF based staffing and capabilities.
8. Fringe Benefits – Examine fringe benefits including paid time away from work for vacation, sick time, etc. In certain models this may affect the staffing and deployment model, which may determine the need for overtime utilization or part-time or per diem personnel to maintain consistent staffing levels.
9. Training Time – A calculation of the amount of training required for the HCF is also helpful in determining amount of hours required for staffing.
10. Total Campus Area – The total area of the HCF (square footage/acreage) is but one factor related to security staffing and deployment and should not be used as an exclusive factor in determining staffing levels.
11. Patient Volume, Mix & Acuity Level – Patient related factors based upon time of day, day of week or seasonal factors can have an impact on security staffing in the areas of fixed posts, scheduled and nonscheduled activities and must be considered.
12. HCF General Staffing Levels – Reductions in other HCF staff due to reduced patient days or other factors may result in the need for additional security personnel to provide increased patrols of unprotected areas.

References

Colling, Russell L. and York, Tony W., Hospital and Healthcare Security, (2010). Woburn, MA: Butterworth-Heinemann

See Also

- IAHSS Guideline 05.02, Security Role in Patient Management
- IAHSS Guideline 07.01, Security Sensitive Areas
- IAHSS Guideline 07.05, Parking General

Approved: February 2009
Last Revised: October 2011

STAFF AND LINE POSITIONS

Staffing is generally viewed in two categories: staff positions (support) and line positions (field operations). The staff positions may include training coordinator, investigator, crime prevention coordinator, security system specialist, and documentation/communications supervisor. More recently, in larger organizations, staff positions such as analyst and process excellence/quality lead have emerged in some security programs. The line positions for field operations often include fixed post, patrol/response positions, and working shift supervisory personnel. Security systems monitors and/or dispatchers may be considered either support or field operations personnel.

In some healthcare security programs the organizational structure includes a hybrid mix of staff and line positions. An example of this mix is to assign a senior security officer, sometimes referred to as a Security Technician, additional responsibility for a functional segment of security operations. These additional functional areas of responsibility may include administrative and line activities for such areas as lost and found, key and lock control, general staff orientation and training (i.e., new employee security presentation and operating department in service security training), new security officer training and orientation, and periodic physical security safeguard field inspections.

STAFFING LEVEL CONSIDERATIONS

It may be helpful to organize the calculation of the right amount of security staff for a given healthcare organization into categories. These categories are: hard data goals/information; soft data analysis/projections; and subjective considerations/projections. Figure 6-6 provides a summary of security staffing considerations.

Hard data goals/information

This category of staffing considerations is quantitative, and thus can be measured in terms of real number data sets and goals.

- *Emergency Response Time.* It is absolutely critical, for excellence in patient care and the safety of staff and visitors, that the healthcare organization provide the resources to effectively respond to critical incidents. These incidents may be criminal in nature, exposure to hazardous materials, weather related, fires, or accidents. Staff response time can be the major difference between life and death or other damage control. The healthcare facility must maintain a capability to respond to critical incidents in a timely manner and such response should provide a competent skill level of action. The response time goal should be within 3 to 5 minutes of notification. Patient care areas, both inpatient and outpatient, should receive the shortest response time with support areas (i.e., warehousing, maintenance shops, food preparation, etc.) only a minute or two later. When the security department is considered the first responder to critical security incidents, it needs to be staffed and trained accordingly to meet the planned response time.
- *Service Call Response Time.* Service calls are sometimes referred to as nonscheduled duties. It has long been accepted that the security function includes the provision of all kinds of services requested by stakeholders. The security department's image, and often its return on investment (ROI), is sometimes judged more on the services provided than on a preventive or emergency

SECURITY STAFFING CONSIDERATIONS

HARD DATA GOALS/INFORMATION

- Emergency Response Time
- Service Call Response Time
- Scheduled Routine Functions/Activities
- Established Patrol Frequency by Area
- Area Crime Data
- Public Safety Response Time
- Past Security Incidents
- Planned Fixed Post Assignments

SOFT DATA ANALYSIS/PROJECTIONS

- Training Time (Pre-Service/Turnover Rate)
- Fringe Benefits Time Off
- Organization Philosophy/Importance of Security Mission
- Impact of Physical Security Safeguards
- Stakeholder's Perception of Their Safety and Security

SUBJECTIVE CONSIDERATIONS/PROJECTIONS

- Patient Types/Volumes
- Facility General Staffing Levels
- Building Design/Square Feet/Size of Grounds
- Parking Areas
- Temporary Security Risk/Conditions

FIGURE 6-6

Summary of security staffing considerations.

response capability. While response time is not generally critical in providing services, it is important in building stakeholder satisfaction and a positive security department image. The quicker a request for service is accomplished, the more favorable the security image.

- *Scheduled Routine Functions and Activities.* Operational planning for staff deployment often has the goal of limiting scheduled duties due to the flexibility that must be maintained to respond to the unexpected. Nevertheless, there will always be scheduled duties for security, such as cash escorts, lock-ups, unlocks, raising/lowering flags, etc. These duties have a way of requiring time management somewhat out of proportion to the time it actually takes to perform the duty. In some facilities, security assistance with patients who may present risk have become part of a routine or even scheduled function for security. A security presence at mealtime in a behavioral/mental health unit or in the ED during psychiatric rounds may be examples.
- *Established Patrol Frequency by Area.* When establishing security patrols there must be a defined expectation of the frequency of such patrols. Frequency in this regard does not mean an established time; rather, it means an expectation of how often an area will receive a patrol inspection.

Frequency of patrol expectations is different for different areas, time of day, and day of the week. The security staffing requirement is dependent on a mathematical approach to developing time requirements in meeting frequency goals.

- *Area Crime Data.* An important element in determining the number of security officers needed to staff the department is the question, "How safe is the area from a crime perspective?" The answer to this question will impact the size of the security staff differently for different facilities. An inner city hospital that virtually has no external grounds and does not have numerous fragmented parking lots is basically factoring out the need for an extensive external patrol. Many such facilities that fit this profile have property lines that are sidewalk or street sides of their buildings. This situation does not mean the facility ignores or is not concerned with neighborhood crime—it simply means the organization cannot take on the role of city policing. The security program itself will work with law enforcement agencies to develop strategies to create a safer neighborhood.
- *Public Safety Response Time.* The response time of the public safety agencies serving the facility will impact the security staffing level. Just as The Joint Commission requires hospitals to be "sustainable" for a given period of time when disaster strikes (emergency management), so must the facility be prepared to be "security sustainable" until help arrives. Small or medium size towns and municipalities may be able to provide 4- or 5-minute 911 response, while some critical access hospitals located in rural communities may routinely experience 20–30 minutes or even more due to the limited resources available and geographic range of the service area.
- *Past Security Incidents.* It has been said that a predictor of future security incidents can be found in the review of past security incidents. It is hoped this bit of advice is only partially true, as a properly managed security program will take corrective actions to avoid the repeat of a serious incident. It is true, however, past incidents, especially recent serious incidents, serve as powerful motivation for the organization's leadership to take a serious look at security staffing needs—security is too often incident driven.
- *Planned Fixed Post Assignments.* The number of, and the location of, security fixed posts will influence the requirements for frequency of patrol and security emergency response times. A fixed post, especially an access control post, is providing several elements of security at basically the same time. Through proper access control screening procedures there may be an impact of a less frequent need of internal patrols. While controlling access, the security officer's presence is important in promoting a "we are protected" image and deterring negative actions. This presence is also beneficial in establishing the "feeling" of safety and security as perceived by the stakeholders.

Soft data analysis/projections

This category of staffing considerations is basically a combination of subjective and hard data, and is based on projected assumptions of security operations.

- *Training Time (Preservice/Turnover Rate).* The impact of training time relative to security staffing needs will vary from facility to facility. This variance is due in part to the type of security staff (i.e., proprietary, contract, etc.), size of staff, quality of officer training, and staff turnover rate. In organizations that utilize a contract staffing approach, the training time does not appreciably impact the number of deployed security officers, as the training time has been factored into the contract. In this respect, everyday post assignments (field deployment) are fixed and filling all posts is the responsibility of the contractor along with associated costs. Preservice training of new security staff members is also generally the responsibility (cost) of the contractor.

- A serious operational flaw in proprietary staffing systems is the ability to "run short" shifts. In other words, to fluctuate staffing of shifts depending on the number of officers reporting for a duty or to maintain a full staffing schedule through use of call-in part-time staff or the use of overtime. Since overtime money is not unlimited, and generally not looked upon favorably by administration, too many programs follow the practice of "short staffing." This practice results in reducing the level of facility security that in essence falls below the standard of care set by the organization. An opportune time for "Murphy's Law" to come into play, short shifting can also occur when staff terminates. It is not uncommon to find it takes 6–8 weeks, or more, to fill a vacated officer position in the healthcare organization. The sourcing and hiring processes of many healthcare organizations inhibit replacing terminated officer positions through various roadblocks. These roadblocks include: not authorizing a replacement hire until the terminating employee is actually off the payroll and often well beyond this point; mandatory job posting within the organization; delay in recruitment processes; delay in applicant background checks; delay in the starting date. Unfortunately, this delayed process more often than not results in excessive overtime cost or short shifting.
- *Fringe Benefits Time Off.* This consideration for calculating the number of security officers required is fairly easy to determine with defined vacation and sick day benefits. As employees build longevity, the amount of paid time-off work increases. The unknown is the amount of time-off work for such things as medical leave beyond paid sick leave, leaves of absence for a variety of reasons, including military service and family emergencies.
- *Organization Philosophy/Importance of Security Mission.* There are simply some healthcare organizations that give a high priority to patient, staff, and visitor safety, and there are those where safety is espoused but sufficient resources are not provided. It is difficult to determine whether this lack of "understanding the need" is due to lack of knowledge, lack of real concern, or extreme pressure to manage margin pressures or other macroeconomic issues. Security is a "risk tolerance" and is something that can be gambled with if an administrator is so inclined.
- *Impact of Physical and Electronic Security Safeguards.* Most physical security safeguards do not replace or reduce security manpower requirements—they basically increase the effectiveness of the security officer. Certain physical security safeguards may increase the number of security personnel (not necessarily security officers). It is not only the safeguard but also the manner in which it is utilized. As an example, a camera system (or video surveillance) may be installed that is real-time monitored or the system simply records images with no live monitoring. On the other hand, a video surveillance system, along with audio and lock release capability, could be installed to control access points previously staffed by fixed post security officers. Another example is locking of a care unit, such as Pediatrics, with no impact on number of staff, but which does increase the level of security for the unit. Each physical security safeguard must be examined to determine the amount of security staffing required to support the safeguard objectives.
- *Stakeholders Perception of Their Safety.* A major "driver" of security program development is how the staff perceives their personal safety and to a lesser degree the perception of patients and visitors. Patients generally presume they are safe and secure within the walls of the facility. Visitors are generally more concerned with their safety as they come and go, especially at odd hours. The visitor also has a general perception of safety in the specific neighborhood. There is nothing quite as reassuring as the presence of a well-groomed, easily identified, competent and helpful security officer. Well-trimmed shrubbery, good night lighting, parking areas close to the facility and well-controlled facility access enhance the perception of security and safety.

Subjective considerations/projections

This category of staffing considerations is based on projections of patient profiles, general staffing levels, anticipated renovations or additional space allocation, and emergency reactions to the need for increased short-term security.

- *Patient Types/Volumes.* The types of patients and the number of such patients being treated (inpatients and outpatients) require a subjective conclusion regarding security staffing requirements. The facility with a level-one trauma center treating 75,000 to 80,000 patients a year, a large population of forensic patients, both open and secured mental health units, will naturally require more security than the small urban general medical/surgical treatment facility.
- *Visitor Mix.* The visitor mix is somewhat related to the patient mix. Trauma, mental health, and forensic patients tend to bring a different set of visitors than the small neighborhood treatment facility.
- *Facility General Staffing Levels.* Facility staff provides a primary element of facility security. Staff can observe persons in their work area and in general know who belongs and who should be queried concerning their presence. When general staffing is at a proper level, there are more eyes and ears "watching the store." When staffing is substandard, these eyes and ears are not only reduced in number, but staff is stressed to meet minimum patient care standards. They are more narrowly focused on performing their primary tasks. When staffing is low, there tend to be more floats, per diem, and registry staff that by nature do not provide the element of security awareness or concern that regular staff provides.
- *Building Design/Square Feet/Size of Grounds.* Building design of main facility treatment and support areas is a major factor when calculating security staffing requirements. The size of the campus grounds and placement of separate buildings and parking areas is also important. What is of little significance is the number of occupied square footage—it's all in design. It is acknowledged that with higher square footage of occupied space, there will generally be more patients, more staff, and a greater demand for security services. The security staffing impact of square footage in regard to these factors is calculated in the other various considerations, i.e., response times, patrol frequency, calls for service, routine activities, etc., which does to some degree relate to size. Relating the size of the security force to square footage is somewhat akin to the long abandoned law enforcement approach to advocating the number of police officers required to population census numbers. Neither approach has any validity.
- *Parking Areas.* Parking areas have a tendency to heighten concerns of security and safety for most people. These concerns are intensified when parking areas are dark, devoid of other parkers, and remote from the ultimate destination. Parking areas can be protected to some degree through the use of appropriate physical security safeguards; however, the presence of a uniformed security officer is reassuring to most people. Providing this presence at the appropriate times can be labor intensive, especially when a large number of small parking venues are fragmented in various remote campus locations. The consideration of a high level of security officer presence in these parking areas will certainly test administrative leadership's philosophy of safety and budgeting support.
- *Temporary Security Risks/Conditions.* In all but the smallest of security departments, there will be constant requests (often demands) to provide "extra" security officer coverage for special situations. It is common for security administrators to shift coverage assignments almost on a daily basis. Some of this shifting is planned in advance (i.e., special events) and some shifting of officer deployment is at a moment's notice due to the development of increased security risk (i.e., patient assist/watch,

threat of targeted violence, extended period of security incident scene protection, missing patient search, termination standby, community event, fundraiser, etc.). It is generally not feasible or practical to schedule extra officer(s) for such needs; however, when officers are shifted from their normal deployment, there are certain security voids that are created. How large is this void and the organization risks incurred? It is a security management challenge that relates to establishing the level of security officers needed for the specific organization being served and protected.

A 2012 study, that involved a survey of IAHSS members, concluded there were four primary drivers of security staffing levels in the hospital setting:

1) Total security calls
2) Total hospital beds
3) Presence of a Level 1 trauma center
4) Presence of a mental/behavioral health unit[4].

In short, determining the "right size" security force takes a great deal of time, effort, and in-depth evaluation. Healthcare organizations commonly make the mistake of hiring a complement of security officers and then determining what activities they will perform. In a similar vein, some security planners answer every security problem by suggesting the hiring of additional personnel. More people are not always the answer, and in fact, numerous security programs have been upgraded by reducing personnel through improved management, specialized training, and the application of new preventive security concepts. Unfortunately, sound planning and valid program justification often yield to emotions and easy solutions. In reality, more security personnel have been added to existing programs due to traumatic incidents than to sound planning.

Staffing the small facility

The very small facility may not employ any specifically designated security personnel. In these cases required security activity is performed by maintenance, environmental services, or other facility personnel. A small facility located in a relatively low crime area should provide, at a minimum, security officer patrol and called-for security response capability on a 24-hour basis if the facility has 75 or more inpatient beds, regardless of its location or perceived security risks.

Seldom does an organization suddenly decide to employ security personnel around the clock if it has never had an organized security system. As the facility grows, or faces increasing security issues, the facility will at some point in time face the need for security personnel. The first step in a security officer deployment plan generally involves coverage during the night hours. A coverage plan of 6:00 p.m. to 6:00 a.m. is a good first step. In organizations that are not required to pay overtime after 8 hours, it is a consideration for an officer to work the entire 12-hour shift. This deployment plan allows for two officers to each work 3½ days each week, splitting the middle day, working 42 hours each week. The advantage of this deployment is that two officers cover the entire week, providing good continuity and consistency of program application. Some may argue that 12 hours is too long for one individual; however, it depends on the individual. In the case of this 84 hour per week schedule, one on call, or part-time officer, would be required to cover scheduled or unscheduled time off of regular officers.

For the facility that currently provides night coverage, the next step in increasing personnel should be during the weekend. Although weekend days may on the surface seem peaceful enough, this is the time that general facility supervision is minimal, neighborhood street activity increases, and facilities are especially vulnerable to internal and external theft. The creative healthcare security administrator can find many nontraditional security duties that can be performed while still providing weekend day coverage.

All too often facilities attain night and weekend coverage and then have a tendency to stagnate; 24-hour coverage increases the security posture of the organization two- or threefold. Instead of being forced to report property losses to security only during certain hours, for example, the organization can call on security officers at any time. When facilities assign another department or administrative person to pick up the security responsibility, when security officers are not on duty, the protection may fall well below an acceptable level of the standard of care.

When a program advances to providing one officer on duty around the clock a program begins to take shape and becomes much more productive and effective. Security officer deployment during the day is geared to different activity than at night and on weekends. The day officer is usually the facility security supervisor. This officer takes part in committee meetings, works with various departments on planning and administration, as well as responding to calls for service. The day officer is the glue that solidifies all shifts of security into a unified program.

To staff an in-house program with 24-hour coverage for one position 7 days a week requires approximately five full-time equivalent (FTE) employees. This number varies to some extent depending on the facility vacation, holiday, and sick time benefit. In the outsourced staffing model the required number of FTEs required is approximately 4.2 as the outsourced security provider is responsible for all nonproductive paid time.

Staffing problems occur when the schedule goes awry due to sickness, accident, no show, or termination. Untrained managers or supervisors often overlook this costly area of program administration during planning processes. Although this problem is rather straightforward, it is often not considered fully when an organization analyzes the financial implications of maintaining its own security force or contracting with an outside agency.

In programs deploying one officer around the clock a staff of three full-time and three part-time officers works well. Part-time officers who are available to work additional hours to remedy planned or unplanned absences are valuable. Availability is an important criterion when determining an appropriate schedule.

REFERENCES

1. Dalton D. *The Art of Successful Security Management.* Woburn, MA: Butterworth-Heinemann; 1998.
2. Vonow B. *Security guards at hospitals in Brisbane's south likely to face redundancy after jobs outsourced.* The Courier-Mail; 2013, November 20. Retrieved January 29, 2014 from http://www.couriermail.com.au/news/queensland/security-guards-at-hospitals-in-brisbanes-south-likely-to-face-redundancy-after-jobs-outsourced/story-fnihsrf2-1226765034759.
3. Weonik R. *Securing our hospitals: GE security and IAHSS healthcare benchmarking study.* Presented at International Association for Healthcare Security and Safety Midwinter Meeting and Seminar; 2008, January 21.
4. Vellani K, Emery RJ, Parker N. Staffing benchmarks: A model for determining how many security officers are enough. *Journal of Healthcare Protection Management* 2012;**28**(2):1–11.

CHAPTER

LEADERSHIP AND PROFESSIONAL DEVELOPMENT

7

Leadership and professional development activities cannot be lost in the healthcare security program. The success of the security program is largely the responsibility of the security leadership team and a direct reflection of their experience, leadership, responsiveness, and commitment to protection and customer service. If these qualities are not found at the top, they will likely be absent in the security staff.

Helping security leaders at various levels develop the skills and knowledge they need to succeed in their leadership positions can make the organization a better place to work and help the protection program retain its most critical asset—their employees. Many healthcare organizations have seen that investment in the development of its security leaders has a measurable return on investment (ROI), as it helps improve employee engagement and patient satisfaction scores, and reduces the cost of security staff turnover, employment practices liability and inadequate security liability.

DEFINING LEADERSHIP

What is leadership and what does leadership mean to the healthcare protection program? Leadership is defined as the ability to motivate a group of people to perform above their perceived capabilities to achieve a shared goal or vision. When analyzed closely, it can be determined that:

1. **Leaders must have the ability to motivate others.** Not to be misconstrued as charismatic, healthcare security leaders must be able to get security staff excited about performing their job and its importance to the organization. In short, leaders must have the ability to influence the directions, goals, and efforts of others through means that include, but go beyond, the simple exercise of authority.
2. **Leadership is a group activity; it is not about being an individual contributor.** The whole team must perform highly, not just the security leader. Healthcare security leaders must be able to transfer strength to everyone in the security department and in the healthcare organization in general. In short, leadership is achieving results through others.
3. **Leaders must get their team to perform above their perceived capabilities.** When challenged and engaged, healthcare security leaders can elevate security staff members to accomplish goals and objectives they did not think they could otherwise achieve.
4. **Leaders must have a shared goal or vision.** Security leaders have to take the time to gain a sense of ownership in their team. It begins by establishing a vision of what the protection program could be in the future. Providing a clear yet simple vision of what could be achieved if everything went right, one that people can understand and that is tied into emotion, will drive high performance.

LEADERSHIP COMPETENCIES

There are many leadership qualities (competencies) critical to the success of a healthcare security leader. There must be a technical understanding of the discipline of healthcare security and basic business principles that form the foundation for every leader, no matter what industry is involved. The Security Executive Council identified nine practices that the most successful security leaders have in common:[1]

1. The creation of a robust internal awareness program for the security department, including formal marketing communication initiatives
2. Ensuring that senior management is made aware of what security is and does
3. Regularly talking to senior leaders about their issues and how security can help
4. Conversing in business risk terminology, not "security"
5. Understanding the corporate culture and adapting to it
6. Winning respect by refusing to exploit fear, uncertainty and doubt
7. Basing the security program goals on the company's business goals
8. Having top-level support from day one
9. Portraying security as a bridging facilitator or coordinator across all functions.

Today's healthcare security leader must be emotionally and socially intelligent, with strong personal and interpersonal leadership skills. Without fail, the most successful healthcare security leaders have the ability to execute and get things done. Underpinning each of these traits is a values-based foundation that provides meaning and acknowledgement to the team being provided leadership.

Healthcare administrators continue to rank the ability to build relationships (internally and externally), openness to change and growth, courage to make the "right" decision, ability to motivate and inspire others, and the level of self-confidence, as the traits and characteristics most highly coveted in their leadership team. Knowledge about the technical aspects of law enforcement or general protection is less desired. Thus, healthcare security leaders must continue to develop their business acumen, their personal and interpersonal leadership skills, and their ability to execute, to help the healthcare organization achieve the performance and results desired. The security leadership traits and characteristics listed in Table 7-1 are most highly sought after by healthcare administrators.

THE SECURITY LEADERSHIP ROLE

The vice president, director, manager, or coordinator of the healthcare protection program is the single most important person in terms of determining protection program outcomes. This statement does not infer that the person charged with the responsibility to manage the program can do the job alone. There must be administrative support, as well as buy-in from other organizational leaders, line supervisors, and the security personnel themselves.

Historically, healthcare organizations have been rather vague in terms of defining the expectations and objectives of their security program. This systemic deficiency has in turn led to many organizations hiring ill-prepared persons as security administrators to lead this very important function inside the healthcare delivery system. A person who simply has a police or fire safety background, or has experience with a state or federal law enforcement agency (regardless of specialty), may understand criminal

Table 7-1 Leadership Success Traits and Characteristics

Business/Technical Knowledge	Personal & Interpersonal Leadership Skills	Ability to Execute	Values & Ethical Foundation
• Healthcare Security Management • Security Systems • Emergency Management • Talent Management • Performance Management • Project Management • Information Technology • Strategic Management • Business Continuity Planning • Finance / Budgeting	• Emotionally Intelligent • Good Communicator • Self-Awareness • Self-Management of Emotions • Social Intelligence & Awareness • Relationship Management • Ability to lead self • Ability to lead others • Positive Outlook	• Set Priorities • Set Expectations • Hold People Accountable • Problem Solving • Decision Making • People Development • Change Management • Succession Planning	• Sense of Integrity • Inspire Trust & Hope • Build Self-Confidence in Others • Lead by example rather than power, manipulation, or coercion • Authentic • Respect for others • Empathy

investigations, fire prevention, or other isolated elements of the security program. However, these individuals typically do not have the background in security, or understanding of how protection principles and safeguards apply to healthcare. Similarly, the security supervisor who has worked in the protection department for many years, even as the number two person in charge, may not have sufficient leadership experience, skill level or background to properly lead the staff.

Today, the security field is extremely competitive, and to reach the top requires a high level of understanding of the industry, which can only be gained through experience and higher learning. Organizations today seek individuals who are academically prepared, and who have relevant experience and the requisite skills to direct their security programs. Relevant experience will, of course, vary depending on the organization's specialty or service.

SELECTING MANAGEMENT

Healthcare organizations are learning that spending the necessary time, energy and resources upfront, to develop a comprehensive security department mission statement to align the security program with organizational expectations, is well worth the effort. This process should happen prior to recruiting or hiring the security administrator. The result is organizational clarity with the overall expectations of security, demonstrating how important the protection program is regarded from the highest level. It is essential that the design of the security program mirrors and supports the culture of the organization. Otherwise, organizational frustration in the protection program will, in all likelihood, be high. It is important for the organizational leadership to establish clear expectations of the security program, along with customer service goals for the department that are measured and reported to the senior leadership team.

It does not matter if the healthcare security management model is proprietary or out-sourced; the leader selected to administer the security program must align with the leadership philosophy of the organization and be a cultural "fit." If, for example, the organization follows the Planetree model of customer service, as discussed in earlier chapters, senior leaders are going to want a building with an open and welcoming atmosphere. They are not going to want to create a highly visible "security feel" when patients and visitors first walk into the building. If the security administrator comes with a bias for metal screening and armed security officers, the likelihood of organizational fit will be very low.

Business/technical knowledge

The healthcare security administrator must be technically competent and knowledgeable about security management and security systems, but must also have a basic understanding of how to solve problems, set expectations, and hold people accountable. As a recognized leader in the healthcare organization, the security administrator should have a considerable understanding of the principles of finance/budgeting, human resources, and strategic management. In general, the healthcare security administrator must understand the healthcare organization's mission, core values, and how its margin is established.

Ethical leadership

Leadership is an obligation to the organization and employees to do what is right. Integrity and ethics are the most important attributes of leadership. Security leaders are the heart and soul of the protection department because they "set the stage" to create an environment and culture in which security supervisors and officers work, and patients and visitors interact, with security staff. Effective leaders help others to create the vision and understand the organization's purpose. They provide the insight and the framework for making ethical decisions. By acting with integrity, leaders promote fairness and consistency. Leadership, therefore, is a "social" responsibility, a duty, and a trust—to manage the values of an organization.

When selecting security leadership positions, healthcare organizations must insist on the following values and ethical foundation:

- Sense of integrity
- Inspire trust and confidence in others
- Lead by example rather than power, manipulation, or coercion
- Respect for others.

A person who acts on their ethics is a person with integrity. Integrity means to do what is right, even when no one else is looking. The bottom line for life and business is ultimately people. "Business ethics" and "ethical/moral leadership" are inseparable components in the life of every healthcare organization. Ethical standards are basic to how patients, visitors and employees are treated. Obstacles to ethical behavior and integrity are self-interest, self-protection, self-deception, and self-righteousness.

No healthcare security leader can do everything alone; they must learn to trust others—not just to succeed but for the organization to maintain continued existence. It takes courage to trust, to empower employees with responsibility and entrust them with the authority to carry out that responsibility. Trust grows out of trust and, like respect, it must be earned.

Managing a healthcare protection program is not about personal identity, prestige, or status. Self-centered leadership will always end in failure. The impact of such leadership on an organization can be devastating. People become prisoners of the system and eventually focus on themselves to survive. The result for employees is a "me-first" attitude, self-interest before others, and unethical behavior. Control becomes imperative to the self-centered supervisor in order to maintain the status quo. Trust and teamwork are no longer possible. "Psychological beatings" will tear down self-esteem and group cohesion.

Personal or organizational transformations are no longer an option. The loss of respect in leadership and growing negative feelings about the security department become the root for unethical behavior.

To get respect one must first give respect. It is fundamental to establishing, building, and managing relationships with others. Security professionals must be leaders with integrity and treat all people, regardless of their position or status, with dignity and respect, no matter what the situation. In short, the security leader's job is to support the success of others.

SUCCESSION PLANNING

Most people in the healthcare security field have not followed a defined career path—they have either worked their way up through their department or come from another industry. But attracting early careerists to the field has become increasingly important as many senior security leaders prepare to retire. A 2012 survey by Health Facilities Management and the American Society for Healthcare Engineers (ASHE) found that 40% of (security) managers were older than 55—an increase from 35% in the 2009 survey. As this aging workforce enters retirement, there will be a greater need for developing succession plans.[2]

Developing the next generation of healthcare security professionals is a complex task that involves a wide range of activities, such as exposing young people to the field, ensuring that college students receive the knowledge and experience they need to succeed, furthering the career of current security professionals and helping hospitals prepare succession plans that will leave them well-situated when experienced leaders leave.

For those who want a degree, several colleges and universities have begun offering programs related to security and safety. A few select degree programs include:

- *Eastern Kentucky University* – offers undergraduate and graduate degrees through its school of Safety, Security and Emergency Management
- *Michigan State University* – offers a specialization in security management through its school of criminal justice. This program is frequently heralded as the first institution to offer private security curriculum
- *University of Denver* – offers security management graduate degrees in three concentrations: Emergency Planning and Response, Information Security, and Organizational Security
- *John Jay College of Criminal Justice* (City University of New York) – offers an undergraduate major in Security Management concentrating on the analysis of security vulnerabilities and security program administration
- *Appalachian State University* – offers a private security concentration through its criminal justice major
- *San Diego State* – offers a graduate degree in Homeland Security
- *George Washington University* – offers a security and safety leadership degree through its Master of Professional Studies program.

In Canada, while two-year diploma programs related to security have been in place for some time, it is only in recent years that full degree programs in the field have begun to emerge. The Justice Institute of British Columbia, as an example, now offers a 4-year degree program in Emergency and Security Management. In the UK, the University of Leicester offers a degree in Security and Risk Management. Outside of the U.S. many of the security-related programs are aligned with police or criminal justice studies, or with information security programs.

Attracting young people to healthcare security management is an important part of succession planning. But it is also critical to help advance the careers of those already working in the field, so they are prepared to take on new roles as senior leaders retire. Finding a mentor to assist this process is important. Those who desire to grow must understand the requirements needed to advance, and get assistance to develop the plan to gain those experiences, and create a timeline to help turn those goals into reality.

Mentorship programs are often associated with larger security programs, and a number of associations have launched industry-specific programs that help place mentees in a wide range of organizations. Several ASIS chapters have developed mentoring programs that best match the mentor to the protégé with an informal contract establishing goals and logistics. David Gibbs, a security professional in California who help developed the ASIS program, shared that interest has extended well beyond young professionals. Almost half the people applying are seeking a second career as a security professional, and are coming from government or law enforcement.

Creating a robust succession plan keeps a hospital humming even when senior security leaders leave. A succession plan should follow a few simple rules:

1. Obtain buy-in from the C-suite
2. Look at future healthcare trends
3. Develop a formal succession planning program
4. Attract, recruit, retain and mentor the next generation
5. Develop upward mobility for the best of the best in the organization.

The Security Executive Council has worked with top-tier security leaders to develop research, track industry trends and solve problems. The Council found the skills most often lacking in potential security leaders being groomed for higher levels was the lack of strategic thinking and planning skills.[3]

LEADERSHIP DEVELOPMENT

Investing in the development of its security leaders should be a strategic focus for every healthcare organization. In an industry firmly rooted in a "promotion from within" philosophy, this is an excellent way to sustain core values for the healthcare organization and enhance the perception of personal safety and security to all of its constituents.

The people fulfilling the security leadership roles are fundamental to the success of every healthcare protection program. They are the fabric of the security department. Even in the worst and most challenging of times, they will drive security program success. But who is encouraging their development? This is a question every healthcare organization must address. All healthcare security leaders must build, and continually enhance, their personal healthcare security knowledge and build their managerial abilities and leadership prowess. Indeed, it could be argued the successful healthcare security leader must develop a depth of knowledge of healthcare itself, including the clinical programs, to allow them to fully utilize their security expertise in the appropriate organizational context.

There is no "one size fits all" model for leadership effectiveness. Leadership capabilities are developed over a person's career, but unlike in sports, where there is more time practicing than playing, the role of being a security leader provides very few "practice fields" for leadership to be developed. Healthcare security leaders must strive to raise the bar of professionalism in the security industry, and make a conscious decision to rise above the status quo of our industry. The focus of the leadership training and professional development program should be to stimulate learning and improve the overall effectiveness of each security leader, through individual personal development, communication, and specific job training.

Bain Farris, CEO at Exempla Health's Saint Joseph Hospital located in downtown Denver, addressed the Colorado Chapter of IAHSS in a 2012 presentation titled "What the CEO Wants from Security." During his address, Mr. Farris offered the following suggestions to healthcare security leaders:[4]

1. **Get to know your CEO's top priorities.** Understand how security can contribute to the CEO's initiatives and priorities.
2. **Patient care and the safety and security of employees and staff.** Understand how security can impact and positively affect the safety and well-being of patients, staff and visitors.
3. **Expand the perspective of security.** Do not be just the cops of the hospital, be "ambassadors." See the role as broader than just security in order to have the greatest impact. Stress the influence of community policing by connecting and interfacing with the neighborhoods around hospitals.
4. **Develop the "security five-minute story."** Be prepared to highlight the successes of the security department as well as the challenges and opportunities faced.

CONTINUOUS DEVELOPMENT

Even the most senior and experienced security professional must continually seek further training, education, and self-development. There are at least six distinct activities that top-level security administrators must participate in as a professional, covered in the following paragraphs.

1. **Literature review**. Healthcare security administrators must seek out pertinent healthcare security publications and electronic media as it becomes available. Although it is impossible to subscribe to every periodical or newsletter, buy every book, or attain all the information available, security administrators should make it a priority to keep up to date on current literature. Required reading should include material published by the International Association for Healthcare Security and Safety (IAHSS), Joint Commission or other accreditation resources on the topic of security or emergency preparedness, or specific healthcare security-related councils of the American Society for Healthcare Engineering (ASHE) – Council on Safety, Security, and Emergency Preparedness, and ASIS International – Healthcare Security Council. These organizations have dedicated specific resources to advance the healthcare security profession and industry knowledge. They share their insights through various monthly publications, media, and formal presentations.
   While most administrators maintain a personal library, healthcare and public libraries also are sources for this information. Tom Smith, CHPA, CPP, director of police and transportation at the University of North Carolina hospitals, and a past president of IAHSS, uses a simple yet effective tool to stay abreast of current industry events and occurrences – free on-line alerts. Smith created several accounts with a major internet search engine that provides daily e-mails with links to articles written worldwide with the words "hospital security" or "healthcare security." Any words or combination of words can be chosen and used.
2. **Networking with peers**. The road of trial and error is often bumpy and no one should feel obligated to reinvent the wheel. Chances are someone has the information you need or has faced a similar situation. Interactions with peers are also beneficial in detecting possible problems or

circumstances that can lead to proactive programming. One healthcare security administrator makes prearranged visits to healthcare organizations when he is in another city on business—or even on pleasure—in order to meet another peer and see another security operation firsthand.

Membership in the IAHSS is one of the most common platforms used for networking with peers. The Association provides discussion forums that allow members to get together and privately discuss issues or topics of interest to them. This dialogue lets members share healthcare security industry-related information with their industry peers on a wide range of subjects. Many local chapters of IAHSS, such as the Great Lakes Chapter in Michigan, use group lists that distribute e-mails to members in the region on specific security-sensitive topics, policy and procedure development, or to elicit comments on new products, services, or ideas that help the healthcare security administrators improve the overall posture of security at their facility.

Networking should not be limited only to other industry professionals. Efforts should be made to better understand the roles, responsibilities and expectations of key department stakeholders within the healthcare organization, such as the emergency department, ICU, or behavioral health. Working with and understanding the challenges of key constituents within the environment will only help the security administrator develop better protection plans and procedures.

3. **Credentialing programs**. It is important for the security administrator to gain recognition for specialized knowledge. There are two primary credentialing programs for the professional security administrator. The first, and specific to healthcare, is the Certified Healthcare Protection Administrator (CHPA). The second is the Certified Protection Professional (CPP). These certification programs require candidates to meet a basic experience qualification and then demonstrate the requisite knowledge to pass an extensive examination. Classes are not required—only knowledge to pass the certification test. Most candidates go through an extensive study period to prepare, and are required to follow a periodic recertification process to maintain the credential.

Certified healthcare protection administrator

Through IAHSS, healthcare security leaders can achieve the highly coveted Certified Healthcare Protection Administrator (CHPA) designation. Not only does this signify a high level of competence, it also demonstrates the individual's commitment to excellence and continuing study. The CHPA exam is administered by the IAHSS Commission on Certification, to those individuals successfully qualifying to write the exam. The program consists of progressive credentialing levels, with qualified candidates accepted into the credentialing program at the graduate level. Once this level is achieved, each candidate has eighteen (18) months in which to become a Certified Healthcare Protection Administrator (CHPA). Each CHPA is required to recertify every three years by submitting documentation of continuing self-development, training, and education and other contributions to the field.

Although not a credentialing program, the IAHSS Program of Distinction is the first level of the association's overall department accreditation program. Initiated in 2006, the Program of Distinction recognizes healthcare security and safety departments within healthcare facilities that have achieved and maintained a minimum of 80% IAHSS certified security personnel.

Individual certification of officers and directors is granted to those who have successfully passed one of several certification examinations offered by IAHSS. Certified personnel must maintain active certification either through renewal of their IAHSS certifications at their current level, or progress to the next level. Directors must maintain an active CHPA status through the IAHSS.

Certified protection professional

The CPP exam, administered by the Professional Certification Board of ASIS International, is not industry specific. It consists of 200 multiple-choice questions covering tasks, knowledge, and skills in eight broad subjects identified by CPPs as the major areas involved in security management. ANSI accredited, the value of this credential is found in the mastery/competency demonstrated against a defensible set of standards, and shows the aspects, tasks, and knowledge that comprise a security professional's job. As with any course of study, the process of obtaining the CPP provides security industry exposure, and the results of these studies ensure the candidate understands, and is certified in, the role of a security management professional.

ASIS has also introduced the Professional Certified Investigator (PCI) and Physical Security Professional (PCP) credentials for those that specialize in investigations and physical security.

4. **Seminars and educational programs**. The opportunity to attend healthcare-specific security and safety programs is limited only by time and funds. These programs are offered by IAHSS, ASIS International, Joint Commission Resources, state and local healthcare organizations, ASHE, and a whole host of other trade associations and educational organizations. Healthcare security professionals should have little trouble finding such programs in their general geographical area or on a national or international level.

A minimum of one such seminar should be attended on an annual basis, and such attendance can generally be utilized as a credit in the recertification for CHPA and/or CPP.

Basic elements of healthcare security management

One such program that should be considered mandatory for all new healthcare security leaders is the *Basic Elements of Healthcare Security Management.* This is a half-day pre-conference workshop offered by the IAHSS at their Annual General Membership (AGM) meeting and seminar each year. The workshop is an excellent introduction to the fundamental elements of managing a healthcare security program, and provides an overview of what the new security leader must get right. The basic objective of this 4-hour workshop is to bring together individuals who may not be as seasoned as the "old hands" of the field of healthcare security, with a focus on the "what" and the "how" as it relates to implementing a healthcare security program. The workshop is specifically designed for the relatively new healthcare security manager and supervisor, or facilities manager who has a responsibility in the security arena. This "nuts and bolts" program includes a syllabus and extensive workbook, and shares a wide array of sample security policies, procedures, forms, tools, and training materials, which can be readily adapted to individual healthcare security programs. Table 7-2 provides an outline of the curriculum offered by IAHSS.

Table 7-2 IAHSS Curriculum for New Healthcare Security Managers

Basic Elements of Healthcare Security Management Training	
1 – The Mission of the Security Program	6 – Hospital Staff Training / Security Awareness
2 – Security Program Documentation	7 – Physical & Electronic Security Applications
3 – Conducting the Security Risk Assessment	8 – Infant & Pediatric Security
4 – Security Officer Deployment	9 – Managing Violence in Healthcare
5 – Security Officer Training	10 – The Importance of Being a Leader

In 2012, the IAHSS added a second pre-conference seminar at the AGM that works in tandem with the Basic Element program: a 1-hour healthcare emergency management program that covers the basics for the security professional. The program, originally developed and frequently facilitated by Dr. Tracy Buchman, national director of healthcare emergency management for HSS Inc., offers an explanation of the basics of emergency management, and identifies the typical security role in terms of mitigating, preparing, responding and recovering from emergencies that threaten the healthcare organization. The program also helps the new security leader recognize the similarities to first responder concepts and anomalies found within the healthcare arena, while presenting specific information on how to successfully integrate into the hospital's emergency planning team.

5. **Contributing to the body of knowledge**. An essential element of self-development and keeping current is that of completing pertinent research. Research in this context simply means the searching out of information in the study of a specific aspect of security, for either general information or data analysis, to indicate a course of action.

This research may be of benefit to others in the field, and the true professional will seek opportunities to share this information with industry colleagues and students. The *Journal of Healthcare Protection Management* is but one of many trade publications that can be used as a platform to share. IAHSS, ASIS International and other professional organizations also provide numerous opportunities to speak to industry peers about best practices and research conducted. As the old axiom goes, "the teacher learns twice as much as the student."

6. **Active membership participation**. Belonging to and being active in an organization such as IAHSS is a rich and fulfilling way to give back to the emerging field of healthcare security. Active membership is important to the individual as well as leveraging the collective strength and influence of everyone involved in the healthcare protection industry—setting the standards for the future. By combining individual talents and skills with a diverse membership, innovative approaches to complex problems can often be achieved where an individual might feel at a complete loss.

Being a member of a professional security organization can be the platform or catalyst for reviewing literature, networking with peers, and contributing to the body of knowledge through information sharing.

Although not as prevalent, there are also programs aimed at the most senior and experienced security professionals. Most of these are full-fledged high-level MBA programs, but at least one, offered by The Wharton School of Business at the University of Pennsylvania, is a two-week course geared toward top-tier security administrators and others in high-level security management positions. Taught in Philadelphia in two separate week-long segments, the curriculum covers the core business concepts to enhance each participant's strategic perspective and sharpen business instincts. Modules include strategic thinking, managing people, negotiation, finance, and marketing. Emphasis is also placed on communicating effectively with other corporate leaders, especially when tackling the bottom-line implications of security decisions.[5]

As healthcare organizations become larger and more complex, there is an onus on the healthcare security leader to ensure their education and credentialing has prepared them for the business of healthcare. Increasingly we can see senior healthcare security professionals completing graduate degrees outside of the security field itself—in Healthcare Administration or in Leadership, as examples. This serves to augment the technical knowledge, experience and credentialing obtained by the healthcare security professional during their career "journey," by further immersing them in the actual business of healthcare.

Continuous learning and development is not an option for today's healthcare security administrator. Whether it's done on-line or in a classroom, through certification or mentoring, successful security professionals must continue to learn more about the core competency of security and protection and how to successfully operate as a business leader in the healthcare industry.

THE HEALTHCARE SECURITY SUPERVISOR

The security supervisor is typically the person in the middle—a conduit that represents security administration to the security officers, and represents the security officers to administration. The job of first-line security supervisors has become increasingly complex. They are held to a higher standard of integrity, conduct, appearance, and performance than a nonsupervisor.

With the move away from the authority-obedience style of supervision, the application of many varied leadership factors must be applied.

To be a successful supervisor, one must acknowledge and put into practice basic leadership principles that include:

- Setting a good example – Establishing the standard for attendance, attitude, and performance.
- Knowing their employees and looking out for their well-being – Caring develops cohesion and team spirit.
- Keeping people informed – Using the communication tools at their disposal to keep people up to date on information pertinent to their jobs.
- Developing a sense of responsibility in their subordinates – Delegating where appropriate, making sure the task is understood and follow-up occurs.
- Training as a team – Helping all team members understand their roles without exception.
- Making sound and timely decisions – Having courage to make objective and even unpopular decisions.
- Seeking responsibility and taking responsibility for their actions – Using initiative to complete tasks without being told and taking credit for what they do: good and bad.
- Being technically proficient – Fulfilling the role of a resource to their staff and understanding the resources available to them.
- Knowing themselves and their limitations – Seeking to continuously improve their own abilities.

In short, accepting ownership of the responsibility as a supervisor is a must. A successful supervisor is characterized by being caring, committed, courageous, detail oriented, disciplined, forthright, honest, interested, and professional. Thus, supervisory responsibility is not for everyone.

Much has been written about what makes a good supervisor. The quality of leadership is the one factor that stands out. Basic management traits are intertwined with the practices of effective leadership. Basic operational indicators reveal how well a supervisor has developed the traits and practiced the principles. These signs are evident in the proficiency of the operation, the state of morale, and the discipline of the security personnel.

Successful supervisors analyze their strengths and limitations and work to strengthen the positive, and never allow their limitations to become a liability. They resist the desire to be popular—a tendency that an officer promoted from the ranks must overcome. Supervisors must maintain a professional business relationship, getting results by developing trust, confidence, and respect in those they supervise.

SELECTING SUPERVISORS

Filling a supervisory position requires a decision of the highest magnitude. No matter how well-planned a security program may be, its implementation is accomplished by people. How well these people are supervised is a key to the effectiveness of the program.

There are two basic sources of supervisors: they may be recruited from outside the organization or promoted from within. Each source has certain advantages. The advantage of one can often be the disadvantage of the other.

Supervisors selected from outside the organization often assume their role with a high degree of objectivity. They have no pre-established friendships or animosities that must be negated, and they can bring valuable new ideas and techniques to the security operation. Moreover, they can be selected on the basis of demonstrated ability. They must, however, accept the fact that they must learn new organizational goals and objectives, as a first step in becoming a successful leader.

However, most organizations prefer to promote from within to create a career ladder. Promotion from within provides motivation and incentive for security officers who desire to advance in the organization. It provides an avenue and a healthy perception that hard work, job knowledge, and good performance can result in promotion. The dead-end job has little appeal for the types of people who should be filling the ranks of healthcare security officers. Further, there is a direct relationship between turnover and correlation of job satisfaction with the opportunity for job promotion.

A problem often encountered is relatively few front-line security personnel are qualified to be supervisors. It is a mistake to assume a good security officer will be a good supervisor, because the tasks and functions of an officer and a supervisor simply are different. For this reason, a strong training and education program is essential to develop potential supervisors. Unfortunately, only a relatively small percentage of healthcare protection programs are meeting this development need. The importance of such programs is further highlighted as the population continues to age, and with it growing challenges associated with the scarcity of talent available to fill leadership positions. The growing propensity to change jobs among younger generations is also a significant factor.

It is imperative that security administrators structure job promotion within a framework of objectivity. Position requirements and the method of selection must be established to ensure personalities and prejudices are minimized to the fullest extent possible. The promotional structure should be fully understood by the rank and file, to eliminate any possible misunderstandings and to allow officers to prepare themselves to participate in the selection process.

SHIFT SUPERVISION

The need to maintain desirable levels of staff performance is not unique to healthcare security organizations. The very nature of protecting a healing environment, however, does present some unique factors that shape supervisory activities. The quasi-military structure of most security operations generally dictates a high degree of direct personal observation and interaction.

One of the major problems in supervising the work of field security personnel is the lack of clear and concise criteria for measuring the performance of everyday activities. In addition, factors such as time (24-hours-per-day coverage) and area (large complexes) generally require a high proportion of supervisors to the number of line security personnel. In general, if there are three security staff members on duty during a given shift, one of the three should be a supervisor. Not to be misconstrued as a recommended three-to-one ratio for supervisors to security officers, this practice suggests a security supervisor should be on-site if there are three or more security staff members' on duty at any given time.

Supervision is the process by which problems and vulnerabilities are identified, solutions planned, and programs implemented. Shift supervision essentially consists of three broad tasks:

1. Communication: e.g., inspecting and documenting security incidents;
2. Training and supervising employees;
3. Monitoring of performance: e.g., conducting evaluations, enforcing rules and regulations.

Only in the smallest of security organizations can all this be accomplished by one person.

COMMUNICATION

Few management activities are more important in dealing with personnel than effective communications, both upwards and downwards in the organizational hierarchy. It has been said the essence of leadership is communications. George Jacobs, former associate director of security and safety at Wake Forest University Baptist Medical Center in North Carolina, has frequently been quoted as saying, "99% of all problems are a breakdown in communication."

Hospital security officers must communicate with the people they serve each day, and there must be good communications between security officers and supervisors. Security officers, like most employees, want input into decisions that affect them. Supervisors must listen to employees; failure to be responsive to officer needs, or deliver deserved recognition, will result in team members disengaging and not performing to their capabilities.

Like most employees, security officers resist change "done to them" and accept change "made by them." The resistance to change is a protective mechanism of employees who may perceive the change as a threat to habits, job security, or relationships. Resistance can take many forms, such as lack of cooperation, slowdowns, wild rumors, and individual or group behavior aimed at discrediting the change. Recognizing change will meet some form of resistance allows supervisors to plan ways to communicate that will minimize this resistance. Perhaps the key element in this respect is to communicate the reason for the change, if possible. The rationalization for all directives cannot—and out of practicality need not—be explained to all individuals, including supervisors. Security officers and supervisors must maintain confidence in the management of the security system, and accept day-to-day directives, without expecting detailed explanations for each and every change.

TRAINING

Security officers must be prepared to subdue a mentally disturbed patient, apprehend a thief, comfort a distraught mother, escort a lost visitor, and perform any number of other tasks at anytime, anywhere in the facility. The supervisor must help prepare security officers for this demanding job, properly training them to make certain the officer is capable of carrying out the task. Training develops confidence—priming the self-confidence of employees is one of the most fundamental responsibilities of a supervisor. Investing in the development of security staff creates a feeling that the organization, through the supervisor, cares about their personal and professional success, and in turn engages employees to perform at higher levels.

Training cannot be a one-time event. From the time they are hired and throughout their careers, security staff must continue training to learn, improve, and further develop their professional skills. This includes the supervisor being able to detect mistakes that may occur as the employee performs their responsibility. A system of controls must be available to prevent action that would seriously jeopardize the protection system, if the subordinate is unable to carry out the task. In short, the supervisor must be able to verify the competency of their security staff in all required tasks.

The specific aspects of a comprehensive healthcare security training program will be further discussed in Chapter 10, "Training and Development."

MONITORING OF PERFORMANCE

The security supervisor not only has line authority over personnel, but must also audit their ability to perform the many functions and tasks of the position. The monitoring of performance typically requires three primary areas for the supervisor to examine: attendance, performance, and attitude.

Attendance

A basic tenet for every security officer is the consistent ability to show up to work on time when scheduled. The nature of most security officer schedules requires a strict adherence to punctuality that is unlike most traditional work environments. Failure can result in a lapse of required security coverage, exposing the healthcare organization to unnecessary risk for failure to provide adequate protection. If department policy requires security staff to remain on-site until properly relieved, the failure to do so can create inconvenience and dissension with fellow team members, not to mention the increased overtime expense usually undertaken when this occurs. A vital responsibility of a supervisor is to provide all the tools and resources necessary to support employees in their delivery of security service. Therefore, the supervisor must assure everyone is at their position on time and ready to work.

Performance

Supervisors should evaluate performance based on the sole premise of whether an employee can carry out the tasks required for the position. This evaluation requires finesse, may vary by individual, and is often situationally specific. In all instances, it requires direct observation of the employee's performance, appearance, customer service, etc.

Several techniques for monitoring performance do not involve direct observation or contact with subordinates. One of these techniques is the random interviewing of people having contact with, or served by, the officer. These people—who may be complainants, victims, witnesses, administrators, or nursing supervisors—can be a source of information relative to the security officer's attitude and how they handled a specific situation.

Another means of monitoring performance is the officer's written report. The completeness and timeliness of reports is an important indicator of officer performance, in addition to how well organized or well written the report is.

Another useful technique is to conduct a review of an area that has been patrolled by an officer. An officer, of course, cannot be expected to observe everything, but much can be learned by supervisors who perform this type of inspection. A field inspection can help determine whether there are hazards or conditions that have not been corrected or reported by the patrol officer—it also benefits supervisors by helping them maintain knowledge of the specific physical area of the facility.

Attitude

Monitoring the attitude of security staff is the most subjective factor when evaluating performance. Supervisors should look at specific instances of positive or negative behavior instead of a general feeling of good or bad. Supervisors should maintain a running history on each employee's attitude that is maintained by chronological entry. This will help the supervisor and the employee remember the instances used to determine the evaluation. Box 7-1 demonstrates a sample supervisor log of individual employee performance.

The morale of employees is a frequent topic of concern for top management, and often centers on negative attitudes. The supervisor plays a major role in maintaining the morale of subordinates. Obtaining desired performance cannot be accomplished solely by power, prestige, and authority. A supervisor's real power is achieved through a network of satisfactory relationships with subordinates and upper management.

Negativity is contagious. A negative attitude of one officer can quickly spread and infect anyone exposed to it. But because an attitude is difficult to define and explain, we will focus on negative behavior. Negative behavior cannot be ignored, and the sooner a corrective strategy is undertaken, the better.

The beginning of a cure for negativity is professionalism and zero tolerance. The supervisor must be professional and demand professionalism from their team. Supervisors must keep negativity in mind and not allow it to become visible in actions or words. This is the first step. Next, the supervisor must have open and honest discussions with employees (in private) regarding perceived grievances or issues. Involvement by the employee in the solution agreed upon is important to the success of that solution. Sometimes there is no possible solution. In these cases, the supervisor must hold to the standards for employee attitudes, and employees must understand what is expected of them and the consequences if they fail to perform.

BOX 7-1 SAMPLE SUPERVISOR LOG OF INDIVIDUAL OFFICER PERFORMANCE

Supervisor Log
Officer Smith received a positive comment from ED staff for his successful de-escalation of an unruly on 3/17/14.
Officer Cummings reported late for duty twice in one week (1) 10 minutes on 7/21/14 and 15 minutes on 7/23/14.
Officer Greene spotted a trip hazard near the Main Entrance, marked it with a safety cone, and notified Facilities on 8/4/14.
I had to return Officer Browne's reports because they contained many misspellings in the month of April 2014.

RELATIONSHIP WITH OFFICERS

Supervisors must maintain a professional, business relationship with those they supervise. This does not mean a supervisor is cold and impersonal. A supervisor can be friendly and open while still being a leader. It is important a supervisor makes sure security officers understand the relationship and then do nothing to violate the rules of the arrangement. Supervisors are expected to maintain a professional image and bearing at all times—setting the standard for appearance, attitude and performance. It is up to the supervisor to make the most of the time spent with each officer and to give compliments or make corrections.

MOTIVATION

One of the basic responsibilities of supervisors is to instill self-confidence into their subordinates and motivate security officers to do their best. Motivation is very personal, and everyone will not respond to the same stimuli. Motivation also cannot be forced on an individual; thus the supervisor can only establish a climate in which employees can become motivated.

In general, staff want to do a good job and, if they are provided the proper environment, they will do so. Motivating security staff requires supervisors be aware of, and practice, certain basic principles. One of the greatest motivational acts a supervisor can perform is to listen to their staff—carefully and nonjudgmentally. Most people listen at about a 25% efficiency. In other words, we ignore, forget, distort, or misunderstand 75% of everything we hear. To improve, the supervisor must control external and internal distractions, providing a safe place for good communication to occur. The supervisor must be actively involved in the conversation, avoiding the tendency to interrupt. Asking clarifying questions and checking understanding before the end of the conversation, summarizing what has been heard, and asking if that is what he/she meant, will foster a culture of positive motivation.

Psychological studies indicate recognition is one of the most significant factors in motivation, more important than responsibility, salary, advancement, or the work itself. A motivated staff does not need to be paid excessively, but do need to be paid excess attention. To motivate subordinates, supervisors must themselves be motivated and demonstrate a positive attitude. They must believe in the system and support all decisions handed down.

PERFORMANCE MANAGEMENT

All supervisors should understand leadership perfection is not achievable—mistakes will occur when leading others. The very nature of a supervisor's responsibility requires them to correct employees' actions, provide specific direction in the midst of a security incident, or introduce a new policy and procedure. There are no leadership styles or rules and regulations universally accepted by all staff. The supervisor who manages hoping to get consensus from all staff on all decisions will struggle with getting things done, and in the pursuit of trying to please everyone, will please no one. In either situation, staff complaints will arise in the course of duty, and the supervisor must be prepared to handle these situations.

Supervisors should start by putting their employee hat on. Look at what an employee wants from their supervisor/employer. It is quite simplistic. Employees want:

1. To ***See clear***, understandable and publicized rules or policies;
2. To ***Hear*** performance expectations;
3. To ***Receive*** frank feedback on performance and conduct;
4. To ***Be Treated*** uniformly in the application of company standards and work rules;
5. To ***Receive*** a thorough investigation of allegations of misconduct;
6. To ***Tell*** their side of the story;
7. To ***Be Apprised*** of the investigation outcome;
8. To ***Receive*** warning before discharge;
9. To ***Use*** a process of review by management other than their direct supervisor.[6]

PERFORMANCE DOCUMENTATION

It is essential for supervisors and managers to document incidents of both greater and lesser significance, even if it is hard to see how the documentation might be used one day. When employees think of documentation, it is often associated with a negative feeling. Employees often recall a negative experience associated with some corrective action they have received in the past. However, performance documentation must be impartial. Simply put (from the perspective of an employer/employee relationship), performance documentation is a written account of an employee's actions captured at a specific moment in time. Actions are measurable and quantifiable actions of a human being, from a leader's point of view. These actions may be favorable or unfavorable. However, it is important to come to an understanding that good performance documentation records behaviors that are actions.

There are many reasons for a supervisor to document an employee's actions. Table 7-3 includes a list of many of the reasons why a supervisor should document an employee's actions.

Documentation is often important for reasons no one could have foreseen. That is why it is essential for supervisors and managers to document incidents of both greater and lesser significance, even if it is hard to see how the documentation might be used one day. In a legal dispute, good documentation of the events leading up to or surrounding the discipline/discharge can be a crucial part of the employer's proof the decision was proper and reasonable.

Good documentation is the employer's proof the employer acted reasonably, the employee was treated fairly, and the employee was not disciplined/discharged for an illegal reason. The fact of the matter is managers that do not, or cannot, properly document employee performance make themselves vulnerable to litigation, and increase their own difficulty in managing employee behavior in a fair way.

Table 7-3 Reasons for Supervisor Documentation

Reasons for Supervisor Documentation	
• Create a History • Identify Patterns or Changes in Behaviors • Cause Behavior Modification of Negative Behaviors • Prove an Employer's Case in a Trial, Arbitration, or Investigation	• Aid Memory • Encourage the Continuation of Positive Behavior • Add to the Credibility of the Manager's Version of Events

For these reasons, and many more, the ability to properly document employee performance is essential to the success of any supervisor. So what actions should be documented?

Supervisors must remember to document all actions, good and bad, great and small. Avoid ambiguous terms such as "insubordinate," "attitude," and "disrespectful," as they are vague. However, documenting actions in such a way that leads the reader to conclude an employee was insubordinate is invaluable. For example, writing, "S/O Jones was giving me an attitude" is not as effective as writing, "S/O Jones called me an 'idiot' while pointing his finger at me in front of patients and visitors in the ER waiting room."

Supervisors should document attendance, safety violations, violations of organizational policy, job performance, and on the job behaviors. Supervisors should not document gossip or rumors, off-duty activities, opinions or subjective impressions, personal characteristics, or hostile feelings towards a subordinate.

The overall purpose of good documentation and discipline is to bring about a change in behavior or an improvement in employee performance. The purpose is never to punish, humiliate, or otherwise embarrass the employee. Document positive actions, not just those behaviors not wanted to see repeated. Documenting positive actions is a surefire way to improve job performance, not only the actions of the specific employee, but also the actions of their peers as well.

So where and how performance documentation should be delivered is a question many supervisors face. Obviously, positive documentation should be given in front of a group, while performance documentation of a negative action should be conducted in private.

A manager's advantage when issuing corrective action is they have the choice as to when, where, and what the circumstances of the environment will be. This allows managers to plan out what they wish to communicate to the employee, and under what conditions the communication will be delivered. When corrective action is given, the manager should have a clear and concise plan of how the interaction will proceed.

Things supervisors should consider before documenting

Leaders and subordinates are first and foremost human beings. This can prove to be a problematic situation because all human beings make mistakes. This is why a leader cannot manage behavior in a vacuum, separated from their subordinates' lives. An employee's life outside of work can impact their job performance.

In order to be fair, it is recommended a supervisor should answer the questions listed in the following section before giving an employee a corrective action.

HANDLING PROBLEM EMPLOYEES

The following checklist developed by Dr. Leslie M. Slote can help supervisors handle problem employees.[7]

1. What is the employee's past record? Always start any inquiry by assembling the facts to identify the problem. Has the employee committed this type of offense before? When? If punished now, should the employee receive a more severe penalty than a first offender?
2. Has the employee had a fair chance to improve? Review the employee's personnel record. Has the employee been given help in the past? Does the employee fully understand what is expected? Did he or she possess this understanding at the time of the offense?

3. When was the employee first given a fair warning of the seriousness of his or her behavior? Is there a record of this warning? If so, who gave the warning?
4. What action was taken in similar cases? Review similar incidents that have occurred in the department.
5. What will be the effect of disciplinary action on the group? Is disciplinary action fully justified? What will be its effect on others?
6. Are you going to handle this by yourself? Will you need to clear your action with someone else? Will you need assistance? What about the timing?
7. What other possible actions are there? What is in the best interest of the organization? The employee? Is another warning appropriate? Suspension? Termination?

REFERENCES

1. Hayes Bob, Kotwica Kathleen. *The Nine Practices of the Successful Security Leader*. Security Executive Council; 2011. Retrieved from https://www.securityexecutivecouncil.com/knowledge/index.html?mlc=513 on 12/23/11.
2. Martin Deanna. The next generation: Succession planning helps teams to build for the future. *Healthcare Facilities Management* 2013, November. p. 35.
3. Hayes Bob, Kotwica Kathleen. Eleven areas for improvement. *Security* 2011, October 1. Retrieved from http://www.securitymagazine.com/articles/82389-eleven-areas-for-improvement. on 10/18/11.
4. Puttkammer Jeff. What the CEO Wants from Security. *IAHSS Region 5 Newsletter* 2012, January;**3**(1).
5. Hertig Chris. *Educational opportunities: For those in the security field who wish to advance their careers, there are many ways to get on the knowledge train*. Security Management; 2013. November. p. 73–74.
6. York TW. Civil liability and the supervisor. In: *Supervisor training manual for healthcare security personnel*. 3rd ed. Chicago: International Association for Healthcare Security and Safety; 2007.
7. Costello JK, Leibfried C. Employee relations and employee appraisals. In: *Supervisor training manual for healthcare security personnel*. 2nd ed. Chicago: International Association for Healthcare Security and Safety; 2004.

CHAPTER

THE HEALTHCARE SECURITY OFFICER

8

THE SECURITY OFFICER

The security officer is the point of contact for the majority of security services and activities, functioning at the "coal face" of security operations for a facility. A clear understanding of officer authority is a basic foundation of the security program and its operations. The recruitment, selection, training, diversity of staff, compensation, motivation and officer discipline all interact to form an effective security force. Today's security officer must understand the higher purpose of healthcare and be able to function successfully in the dynamic and demanding healthcare environment. Security officers must have a desire to serve and must understand that, after ensuring safety, their key responsibility is customer service. Success stems from creating a safe environment, where care can be delivered, as perceived by highly educated and trained healthcare professionals. Security staff members set the stage and are relied upon by all stakeholders—employees, staff, patients and visitors—to create and maintain a safe and secure environment.

SECURITY OFFICER AUTHORITY

Most healthcare security officers operate with no more authority than the ordinary citizen. Defined by state, or other governing statute, this authority is generally the "right" to prevent or stop the commission of a criminal act in their presence. Security officers act as agents of the organization they have been engaged to protect, and thus their jurisdiction is derived from the organization. Jurisdiction, in this regard, is the legal power to exercise authority. The authority of officers to act on behalf of the organization should be clearly delineated in organizational policy.

What can happen when a security officer does not act properly? In addition to organizational discipline, the officer may be held criminally responsible or liable for civil actions. Criminal charges may include assault, negligent homicide, and battery. A wide variety of civil actions (torts) exists; malicious prosecution, defamation, false imprisonment, and slander are among commonly alleged actions. Not only is the individual officer subject to legal sanctions, but the employer might also be vulnerable. Employers may believe they are protected if the employee acts outside the scope of his employment. It should be noted, however, that the scope of employment may extend further than expected. The case of Rivas v. Nationwide Personal Security Corp.[1] is one example. A security officer became involved in an argument with a store manager and began choking the manager. Rivas, a store employee, witnessed the incident and screamed for help. The officer struck her in the face in an attempt to silence her. Rivas sued the security officer and his employer. The court held that the employer was liable and that the assault on Rivas was within the scope of employment because the incident arose out of an argument concerning the service the officer was performing.

Security officers are often challenged by actions that may fall into grey areas of their legal authority, many of them occurring on a daily basis. A patient in the hospital emergency department (ED) awaiting a mental health assessment tries to leave, as an example. Can the security officer use reasonable force to detain them if they have not yet been assessed by a psychiatrist? As with most of the work of security interfacing with patients, the answer lies in the direction received from clinical staff. This reinforces the concept that the legal authority of the security officer to act derives from the organization they serve. Similarly, many jurisdictions do not have formal trespass laws, making it difficult for security to comply with clinician direction to remove a discharged patient who does not want to leave, or to evict an unruly visitor. In these situations the security officer must rely on their training and communication skills to effect an appropriate outcome—failure to do so would result in an inordinate number of calls to police for support in these situations.

The issue of patient detention was illustrated in a 2010 Maryland case where a patient sued the hospital and the security officers who were involved, for detaining him against his will and for alleged assault and battery (the force used to detain him) as well as false imprisonment.[2] Security staff must be trained to understand the legal implications of their actions and work in concert with the clinicians responsible for the care of the patient.

There are, of course, valid defenses for the actions of security officers, but officers should bear in mind they may be held to a higher standard for their actions than ordinary citizens. Citizens may be excused for their actions or inaction by reason of best intentions, and lack of knowledge of a particular law. Security officers are expected to more fully understand the various provisions of the law. Security officers, by virtue of their training, experience, and responsibility, may be held to a higher legal standard than ordinary citizens. Thus security officers must understand their extent of authority and be well-versed in the legal implications of this authority.

SPECIAL POLICE COMMISSION/SPECIAL CONSTABLE

In many jurisdictions, a special police commission may be conferred on healthcare security officers. These commissions are frequently used to help with street traffic control and ticketing and seldom provide additional authority beyond that of ordinary citizens. In Canada these may be referred to as Special Constables and can sometimes extend the powers and authority of healthcare security officers in the areas of mental health, trespass, or even public health, in the latter instance for the purpose of enforcing smoking regulations.

It must be stated that commissions giving security personnel the same legal power as regular police officers will result in increased exposure to civil litigation. The actions of security officers with these special commissions are judged on the same level as those of regular police officers. The primary difference between special commissions granting full police, or special constable authority, to the security officer is that of time and location. These commissions often restrict police-like authority to the property of the employer and to the actual time the officer is scheduled for duty, as well as to the functions for which the special status is granted. In the U.S., some very large medical complexes, frequently with a university affiliation, utilize security officers with full police authority. These departments are often referred to as Departments of Public Safety.

Security officers can often perform more efficiently without police powers in many ways. The advantage lies in their ability to interview and otherwise interact with organizational employees and visitors within the scope of the employer/employee relationship. Security officers have much more latitude than law enforcement officers. For example, courts have consistently held that private security officers are not held to the provisions of the landmark Miranda case and need not advise the accused of their rights.

As a general rule, whenever a private citizen, including a private security officer, acts as an agent of the police, all constitutional limitations against the police apply. At times, police and security activities are quite similar, and joint activities may raise certain concerns. It is sometimes difficult to determine the point at which private security actions cease, and public law enforcement takes over. Some lawsuits have been predicated on a conspiracy between police and security to violate the constitutional rights of others. Security officers should thus have a basic working knowledge of the Fourth, Fifth, Sixth, Eighth, and Fourteenth Amendments to the U.S. Constitution and similar laws of other countries, such as the Canadian Charter of Rights and Freedoms, which concerns the basic rights of the individual.

The exclusionary rule, which all states and many international jurisdictions basically follow, is of particular interest to security officers. The exclusionary rule was intended to regulate illicit government conduct. In application, the rule excludes the introduction at trial of evidence that a law enforcement agent has obtained illegally. On the other hand, when a private citizen seizes evidence, the evidence cannot be excluded from the trial, no matter the circumstances related to the seizure. However, though the evidence will not be excluded, the citizen who seized the evidence illegally may not be free from criminal or civil actions. When security officers work in concert with a law enforcement agency, the exclusionary rule may well apply to any evidence seized.

LICENSING

Licensing for security personnel should not be confused with police powers. Licensing refers to the regulation and control of persons performing certain types of security services. A common aspect of many licensing statutes, and some special police commissions, is that of generating revenue (taxes) while doing little to actually regulate the quality, training or delivery of security services.

Thirty-seven states have licensing laws governing private security and several that do not, such as Colorado, are giving strong consideration to the enacting of such legislation. A number of U.S. cities have local statutes relative to security licensing in states that do not have licensing laws. In Canada, the licensing of security is a provincial responsibility, with many jurisdictions now governed by licensing requirements. Many of these statutes appear to be directed at regulating the dress requirements of security personnel and the manner in which security vehicles are identified. These statutes, frequently drafted by law enforcement agencies, are often intended to allow the public to readily distinguish security personnel from law enforcement officers. This type of regulation is of course necessary; however, security administrators should make certain that security officers are not easily mistaken for police officers, regardless of the regulations.

Some licensing statutes border on the absurd, and would probably not stand up under a test of constitutionality. One statute in a fairly large western city actually prohibits the use of the word "officer" in "any advertising or upon the premises within the limits of the City…or on any of its vehicles or equipment." In Canada it is not uncommon for licensing requirements to specify the use of the word "guard" when referring to security personnel, while prohibiting the use of the term "officer." The administration of some security licensing laws can pose great difficulty in sourcing and selecting quality security professionals. There is an acknowledged need for private security to be regulated, with basic training standards established and criminal history searches conducted. However, those recruiting for security staff should be aware that many licensing requirements can add significant time to the hiring of new staff. The California Bureau of Security and Investigative Services (BSIS) require a mandatory electronic fingerprint submission for all security applicants, before granting a license to work as a private security officer. This is also common practice in Canada. Mandated for both contract and proprietary security officers, the delay in obtaining the results of the criminal history check, coupled with limited processing availability, makes it extremely difficult to hire new officers and to put someone new to the security industry to work. The delay can be up to six weeks or more in some jurisdictions. The delay may be based on the number of locations an applicant has lived, on the ability of the licensing agency to manage fluctuating applicant volumes, or myriad other challenges. As with the state of Arizona and a growing number of other states, the lack of a temporary license issuance program has severely limited the pool of available security applicants and hindered those who seek the profession as a career path.

To upgrade and regulate the security function, good licensing laws are required. Professional security administrators can and should contribute to the creation of new statutes and ordinances that will eliminate the existing weak or misdirected laws, which are actually a detriment to safe environments. Properly structured and managed, regulated security personnel licensing is an essential element of a professional security industry. State and provincial licensing is to be commended and fostered, and municipal licensing should be actively discouraged. Meanwhile, there have been various attempts in the U.S, through proposed legislation, to regulate security from the federal level of government.

SELECTING SECURITY PERSONNEL

The security force is often viewed as the quality linchpin in a healthcare facility's security program. Often, security officers are among the first people patients and visitors see and the first point of contact with a healthcare organization. The officer should create positive feelings about the facility and enhance the perception of safety within the organization served. In short, the protection program needs a reliable and professional security team, where the security employees are truly ambassadors for the organization and the customers they serve. In order to provide professional security officers, not just security guards, healthcare protection programs must have comprehensive, effective processes for recruiting, selecting, training and retaining high-quality individuals.

Security work is not for everyone. Professional security managers review candidates from many different perspectives, but with one purpose in mind: to select an individual who is right for the job, and to assign him or her to a position appropriate for their skill set. In order to obtain this cultural fit, it is necessary to hire employees who can not only reduce the potential for a negative event, but who also act responsibly if and when an event occurs. Most security administrators agree there are three primary skills needed to be successful as a security officer in the healthcare environment: excellent communication skills, aptitude to learn, and a customer service attitude. A tremendous strategy for identifying these specific characteristics is to develop a competency set that are key indicators for successful performance. Keeping in mind that each environment is unique, the development of multiple competency sets may be necessary.

Healthcare security work can be boring, routine, and monotonous at times, but within seconds can turn into a situation that challenges the mind and body to the limit. Perhaps no other position, within the vast array of jobs found in the healthcare industry or general security industry, has such wide-ranging demands placed upon it. The expectations for a security officer differ widely among staff members and specific departments. Emergency department personnel want a security officer with a strong physical presence, but who can also de-escalate a verbally abusive patient with care and compassion. The night nursing supervisor may prefer someone who will diligently check and recheck the exterior doors. The behavioral/mental health program wants someone who can be empathetic and apply sound psychological and social intelligence to control a situation, while of course having the same strong physical presence the ED requires. The risk manager seeks individuals with good investigative skills, coupled with good report-writing abilities. The healthcare security officer, to be truly effective, brings this diverse skill set to the healthcare setting each day.

Employees also see security officers in many different roles, some of which are created by security officers themselves. One day a security administrator received a call from a night nursing service employee, who complained that the new officer assigned to the parking lot was not doing his job, and certainly did not compare with the previous officer. Upon investigation it was found that the source of dissatisfaction centered around frost on the vehicle windows. The previous officer had taken it upon himself to scrape the windshields of departing staff, but the new officer did not perform this service.

RECRUITMENT

There must be conscious effort to actively source security officer candidates. Viable applicants must be proactively recruited when a vacancy exists. Recruiting strategies must be continuously reviewed and continuously improved, to ensure all appropriate sources are considered for the caliber of person sought. In short, a security officer recruitment program should be an ongoing activity that is well-structured and efficient. By developing a candidate facing process that is simple and inviting, you can greatly increase the number of applicants for each open position that you can consider.

A very serious flaw of many in-house security departments is the time lag between the occurrence of a vacancy, and the actual date the replacement officer is trained and ready for general duty. This delay is usually a result of the regulatory constraints and demands placed on companies by state and federal employment protection organizations and their requirements for tracking and reporting. This process can involve approvals required for replacement, posting of the position in-house, time delays in advertising schedules, preliminary screening, etc. This drawn-out process can often result in security shifts running short of staff, and/or require an excessive use of overtime to fill the master schedule. For these reasons, the recruiting strategy employed must be well aligned with operational needs so these delays can be mitigated as much as possible.

Recruitment efforts will vary to some degree, depending on the geographical unemployment rates, available talent within a market and competing demand for those individuals. Various methods and activities can be used to attract security officer applicants:

- **Employee referral program.** One of the most successful recruiting strategies, the word of mouth advertising generated from an organization's own employees, consistently provides most healthcare security programs with the highest quality personnel and staff. These programs typically offer some type of reward for a successful referral. These rewards may range from simple recognition, to monetary employee rewards. Figure 8-1 provides a sample of employee referral program advertising.
- **Recruitment brochure.** This brochure is distributed in a variety of ways, from organized job fairs, school placement programs, and retirement groups, to current officers being encouraged

EMPLOYEE REFERRAL
PROGRAM TIPS

Do you know someone who would make a good addition to the HSS security team? Introduce them to HSS. You could make a real difference in their career–and in your wallet. Referrals who successfully complete 90 days of employment with HSS make you eligible for an HSS Reward of $50 to $1,000, depending on their position. Here are a few things to keep in mind when making referrals.

Does this person you're referring share the same values as HSS?

- Always make things right for our customer.
- Desire to be a ambassador for each customer.
- Work with the highest levels of honesty and integrity.

Share with your referral a day in the life of an HSS security officer. This will inspire them and better prepare them for the job.

You want to refer people with a strong work ethic, someone you would want on your team.

Who to refer:

- People you have worked with in the past.
- An acquaintance who is looking to change careers.
- A relative (keep in mind they may not be posted at the same site).
- Someone you met who provided you with an amazing customer experience

You know this position better than anyone else, ask yourself are they qualified?

Be sure your recruiting pays off! Make sure when they apply, your name is mentioned.

STEPS

1. Email the names of your referrals to referrals@hss-us.com
2. Your referrals successfully complete at least 90 days of work.
3. You will be credited $50, or another amount, in your HSS Rewards account.

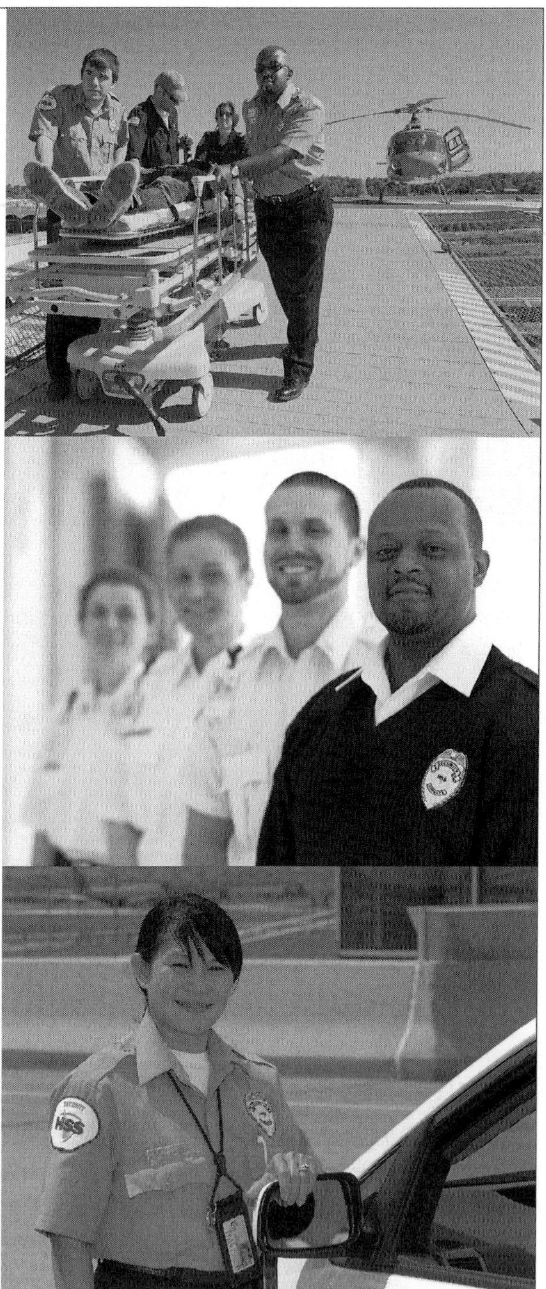

FIGURE 8-1

Sample employee referral program advertising.

to pass them on to others and sharing them with employment centers and training partners. One program reports their recruitment brochure is handed out to all applicants regardless of whether the applicant is hired. Their philosophy is even the rejected applicant may know of another person seeking employment, who may be a more suitable candidate for employment.

- **Signing bonus.** This recruiting incentive is also tied to a short-term retention objective. The basic concept is to pay a sum of money upon hire and then to pay an additional amount at some point of employment longevity. A 90-day period is common; however, many options are available within this concept.
- **Staff recruitment monetary award.** This type of recruitment pays a current staff member a sum of money for referring an applicant who is subsequently employed. As with the signing bonus, there is generally at least one payment at a later time, provided that the referred employee is still employed by the organization.
- **Newspaper and newsletter advertising.** The newspaper advertisement remains the basic component for recruitment of healthcare security staff. Today's newspapers also offer online ad packages which helps to ensure your opportunity reaches as many potential candidates as possible. Some organizations have also reported success by advertising in local business newsletters such as homeowner's associations and church bulletins.
- **Internet resources.** Job boards such as CareerBuilder or, indeed, Craigslist and other industry-specific organization internet sites can produce a consistent flow of candidates, reaching a diverse and computer literate workforce.
- **Social media.** Increasingly social media tools and sites such as Twitter, LinkedIn and Facebook have been found to be effective recruitment mechanisms, for a generation living in "real-time" communication. These sites can also be utilized as a mechanism to draw in additional talent and can be incorporated into many of the other methods and activities listed here.
- **Open house and job fairs.** A well-advertised open house can attract a sizable number of applicants. This method of recruitment is more appropriate to larger organizations with multiple positions. Attracting too many applicants in a tight labor market can be counter-productive. Interested persons who are not hired, or who do not get an interview, are sometimes reluctant to return at a later time. You can mitigate this risk with the development of a solid tracking and contact system to keep these prospects engaged.
- **Military.** Working closely with the military through transition programs, hiring events and other advertising can consistently produce quality personnel, who understand the importance of protecting critical infrastructures such as hospitals and healthcare organizations.
- **Colleges and universities.** Proactively seeking out criminal justice/private security/homeland security students provides a career path for these future leaders through internships, fast-track supervisory programs, and a "promote from within" philosophy. Once well-established, an organization has the potential to influence curriculum and standards through informational sessions and the education of instructional staff which provides greater access to top students and promotes your brand more broadly.
- **Law enforcement agencies and retirement organizations.** Security as a second career is commonplace in a workforce that commonly retires at an age where their maturity and experience can benefit the healthcare security industry.
- **IAHSS.** Members and healthcare organizations can post their leadership positions and other security-based opportunities, providing a national and international recruitment exposure.

SELECTION CRITERIA

Previous security experience is not of paramount importance in the overall selection process. In fact, the amount of retraining required of experienced individuals is often a significant obstacle and cost. Even applicants with previous healthcare security experience generally need to learn new methods and procedures to function in a different system in a new organization. On the other hand, applicants with previous security experience usually realize that duties, even in a good security system, are often routine, requiring diligence and self-motivation. Another advantage of the experienced candidate is that the applicant generally understands that security is a 24-hour, seven-day-a-week operation. Applicants who have not been subjected to this around-the-clock schedule often state they are willing to work nights and weekends, but later discover the new shift hours do not fit their particular lifestyle.

Communication skills are an important factor in selection. The security officer must be able to communicate effectively in both oral and written forms. Written skills can be developed and upgraded; however, improving oral communication skills requires considerably more time and money. The security department as a whole is often judged on the basis of security reports. Not all reports stay within the security section. The incident report, for example, is often used by the facility administrator, risk manager, insurance company, and law enforcement and other government agencies.

Image is another factor of extreme importance, as it directly relates to the *presence* an officer will create. Image is comprised of many elements, and a person either does or does not present a good image. Physical appearance and presence are obvious items involved in applicant evaluation. Another characteristic of image often overlooked is the tendency to talk too much. Many times one is impressed with a person until he or she begins to speak. It is not always what is said, but how much is said and how it is said. Security officers who present a good image have learned good listening skills.

Attitude, image, and a care factor all fit together and should be a major consideration in any selection process in addition to the interpersonal and behavioral competencies needs for the position. A positive attitude toward the job and the employer is a necessary first step in transforming a new officer into a seasoned security professional.

People are what healthcare is all about. Security officers must understand their job entails a great deal of personal contact, and they must enjoy this aspect of the job or their performance will generally suffer. Good public and employee relations are an essential part of an efficient and effective security program. The one word that best describes a good security officer in the healthcare setting is "caring." Officers must care about people, about their position and how it fits into the higher purpose of healthcare, and about themselves.

Figure 8-2 demonstrates the basic traits and characteristics necessary for a security officer to be successful in the healthcare environment. No one candidate is going to flawlessly possess all of these skills; however, the security administrator or other hiring authority should develop an inventory of what skills are most important for the assignment in their particular organization. In developing this list, the security administrator can be sure to identify the strengths and weaknesses of their team and identify skill gaps. New employee selection can be made to fill in these gaps and round out the team capabilities.

Increasingly, organizations are turning to screening tools to help them identify suitable candidates for healthcare security positions. Once mastered, these tools can be excellent predictors of what traits or characteristics can be linked to good performance in the healthcare security field. Human resource professionals or security administrators can then look for these identifiers in applicant responses to the questions in the screening tool, and ensure these individuals receive additional focus during subsequent stages of the intake process.

Assertiveness – A security officer must be direct and persuasive when dealing with others, have the ability to exert influence or direct a self-desired outcome

Empathy – In general, an officer demonstrating empathy will be open-minded and flexible and should have the ability to identify, understand, and relate to the needs and reactions of otherpeople.

Confidence – Successful security officers should have the capability to rebound from negative feedback or criticism and have the ability to approach and respond to situations in a self-assured and consistent manner.

Sociability – The activities and tasks of a healthcare security officer provides ample opportunity to interact with other people. Security staff should be friendly, outgoing, and possesses the ability to initiate contact with others.

Helpfulness – Accommodating, service minded, and team spirited, the healthcare security officer should be internally motivated to help others and work as part of a team.

Thoroughness – Conscientious, with careful attention to detail, to protect a healing environment requires those individuals who take a personal sense of responsibility for the quality of their work.

Problem Solving – Dealing with problems and issues that are complex and unique is a frequent requirement of the security officer. They need to understand and possess the ability to resolve routine problems.

FIGURE 8-2

Characteristics and traits of a successful security officer.

Physical qualifications are controlled to some degree by government regulation. In the U.S., federal legislation makes it unlawful for any person or agency to discriminate against any individual on the basis of race, color, religion, sex, national origin, or age—most countries have some form of similar legislation in place. In some jurisdictions, this protection extends to sexual orientation. In setting physical standards, an employer must be able to prove that certain physical qualifications are required for the job. In a landmark Ohio case, a court ruled on such aspects as physical strength and fitness, physical agility, height and arm's reach, ability to drive a car, and ability to impress others with psychological advantage of height. In each instance the court ruled against the defendants. It was unable to find rational support for the height and weight requirements. Although this litigation involved police officers, the implications concerning the hiring of security officers are apparent.

There are an increasing number of female security officers being added to the ranks of healthcare security forces. Not only have security administrators realized that women can do the job, as they do in police, corrections and other related criminal justice services, but they also recognize that women contribute an additional dimension to the protection effort. Specifically, there have been a number of studies finding women, on average, can often more effectively de-escalate aggressive behavior than their male counterparts. Because the security effort in the typical healthcare setting must deal with many emotions and manage aggressive behavior, it stands to reason that female officers should not only be welcomed on staff, healthcare organizations should be actively trying to recruit female security staff to strengthen their programs. Female security staff can be used effectively in surveillance, checking women-only areas, searching female prisoners, transporting women in vehicles, and other such functions that may be inappropriate for the male officer.

Just as with gender diversity, cultural diversity is an important aspect of a well-rounded security staff. A medical care facility serving a community of diverse ethnic cultures requires a security staff mix that represents these cultures. Security staff members who are available to speak different languages and interpret basic customs of different ethnic groups can offer great assistance in the mission of the healthcare organization. In general, the security staff should be balanced and reflective of the community served.

Managers often hire the best-qualified person, but if the candidate is overqualified, job satisfaction can suffer and with it individual and security department performance. Careful consideration should be given to offering employment to individuals who do not have a career commitment to protection or the healthcare industry.

THE SELECTION PROCESS

In order to ensure excellence in security services, it is necessary to hire security officers who not only reduce the potential for a negative event, but who also act responsibly when it occurs. To this end, every healthcare security program must develop a rigorous employee selection process that, at a minimum, requires compliance with the following basic requirements:

- Have, at minimum, a high school diploma or GED.
- Possess excellent communication skills.
- Have the ability to read, write legibly, and speak English fluently.
- Have a customer service attitude.
- Have an aptitude to learn.
- Pass an employment background check to include previous employment and education verification, criminal history record check, in the U.S., a drug screen and security threat assessment.
- Meet all local and state/provincial licensing requirements for security personnel.
- Have no secondary employment that could be construed as a conflict of interest with the facility.
- Agree to and provide availability to work the hours of the open position being filled.

It takes a great deal of experience to effectively interview security candidates, and even the best interviewers can be misled by applicants. The application and/or resume are the basic selection documents and are used extensively in conducting the interview. During the interview process, the interviewer must find out as much as possible about the candidate, within legal limitations, in a relatively short time to make a well-informed and objective decision as to their suitability for the need.

The interview is quite possibly the single most important step of the selection process and must be well structured and performed effectively to best evaluate the applicant. Setting an interview environment that is welcoming and conversational allows the applicant to best represent and convey their true self. In many cases the interview is simply an effort toward gaining as much knowledge about the applicant as possible. Thus the interviewer should ask specific performance questions that can be used to predict future behavior, and assess the motivational fit of the candidate in effort to identify the best applicant. Scenario-based questions from healthcare settings may also assist the interviewer in gaining insight into the candidate's problem-solving capacity.

A common screening tool is the requirement for healthcare protection applicants to read a predetermined security incident scenario and write an incident report based on the facts provided. Much information is uncovered in this process, to include the applicant's ability to read and interpret the English language as well as demonstrate their writing and critical thinking skills.

Because a group of applicants rarely yields the one individual who possesses all the qualities required for the ideal security officer, especially in a time of low unemployment, the selection process often results in comparing one candidate against another and making your selection based on the highest potential for success.

Not to be forgotten as part of the selection process is the background investigation of the applicant. The first step is to verify as much information as possible concerning what the applicant has written on the application form and has stated during the interview. Is the applicant the person they purport to be? Are there any conflicts of interest that exist? Is the applicant engaged in secondary employment with any enterprise doing business at the facility?

The most common and economical approach is through letters of confirmation, telephone calls, and personal contact. The best single predictor of what a person will do is what he or she has done. A criminal history record check, social security number verification, sex offender registry validation and drug testing are each important aspects of the hiring process. The depth and methodology of the background check will differ between countries. A more detailed process of applicant-checking is contained in another section of this text.

Federal legislation in 1988 in the U.S. prohibited most private employers from requiring polygraph examinations of employees or prospective candidates. Some companies have replaced the polygraph test with psychological exam/integrity tests and now use these to screen applicants. Used to assess varying degrees of aggression, impulse control, suspiciousness, over-controlled anger, and other psychopathology, there is considerable controversy surrounding the value and the possible negative impact of these types of screening tools. The results of most studies fail to produce any clear results on the credibility of these tests.[3]

The passage of the Americans with Disabilities Act of 1990 (ADA) has affected the security officer hiring process. In simple terms, an employer may not exclude hiring a person with a disability when it is not related to requirements of the position, and where the employer can make reasonable accommodations to fit the disabled individual into the work environment. As with most legislation, the law is rather straightforward; however, regulatory interpretations can be rather inconsistent in how this impacts the hiring of security officers.

Security officers must be in good physical health and condition, capable of performing normal or emergency duties requiring moderate to arduous physical exertion. Recently, many healthcare organizations have introduced human performance evaluations (HPEs) to test the physical capability of a security officer to perform the required functions of the position. Conducted only after a conditional

Table 8-1 Sample Human Performance Evaluation Measurements

Task	Required
CARRY Distance 150′	Security Officer must transfer fire extinguisher from wall cabinet to area of need. Must be able to: **Carry 25 lbs. for 150 feet, hold 25 lbs. for 30 seconds**
LIFT / CARRY Vertical Ht. 2″– 36″	Security Officer must transfer with assistance patient from floor to bed. **100 lbs., 1 X in 5 minutes**
PUSH / PULL	Security Officer must drag combative patient when trying to restrain the same **85 lbs., 1 X in 5 minutes**
WALK 1	Security Officer must complete assigned foot patrols; must access all areas of hospital grounds, both inside and out, must respond to calls **Walk 300 yards with twists and turns X 1 in under 3 minutes**

offer of employment has been made, introducing this level of testing can help measure physical fitness and reduce costly worker's compensation expense due to preexisting conditions, or the inability to perform basic functions and tasks required of the healthcare security officer. The essential requirement is that the physical requirements of the position must directly link to the security officer position description. Table 8-1 provides sample HPE measurements.

FULL-TIME VERSUS PART-TIME SECURITY OFFICERS

A security system cannot be effectively or efficiently operated with an overabundance of part-time security officers, nor can the program be operated with only full-time personnel. The appropriate number of part-time personnel depends on several factors. A highly structured system, with strong supervision and training, can successfully operate with a higher percentage of part-time personnel than can a program operating on a more informal basis. It is a generally accepted rule of thumb that a healthcare security staff consists of no more than 20 to 25% part-time officers. An exception to this guideline would be officers who are regularly scheduled to work 32 hours per week. In some cases, an officer working 30 or more hours per week would be classified as a full-time employee.

A workforce consisting of only part-time officers cannot provide the continuity required of successful systems. Moreover, keeping the security staff informed requires constant attention, and full-time employees can generally keep more connected through frequent exposure to the work environment and processes. Officers who work 36 to 40 hours per week are generally better informed than officers who work 12 to 16 hours per week.

Ironically, although part-time officers often possess higher qualifications in terms of experience and education, they are generally less productive. This situation can in large part be traced to the fact that part-time employees usually do not depend on the part-time job for their main source of income. This does not imply that part-timers are consciously not doing their best, but they often lack availability for training and have less flexibility in scheduling. The part-timer must generally schedule training and working hours around another job or other interests. One can only work so many hours in a day or a week without sacrifice to individual performance.

Part-time officers do fulfill an important need in most security departments, however, and should be viewed as a management tool. Just as overtime is an effective management tool, the part-time officer, when correctly used, can fill a void, especially in terms of cost containment. An important aspect of the part-time officer is flexibility. The ultimate goal is to employ part-time officers who are not only competent, but who can readily extend the number of hours they can work in the week. Even better is the part-timer who can switch days or shifts on short notice.

The result of using only full-time personnel is almost always that of overstaffing. Rarely does the right staffing plan turn out to be divisible by 40 hours, or in other words, an even number of full-time equivalents. Thus, an extra officer is often added on a shift to provide the officer with a 40-hour week. Work always can be found for the officer, but it serves only to rationalize the schedule. Further, a staff of only full-time officers offers the department supervisor little choice but to operate short staffed, or to use excessive amounts of overtime, to fill shifts for absences due to vacations, holidays, sickness, and other absences. As a rule of thumb, the average number of absences for each full-time employee is 33 days per year, or 264 hours. Subtracting 264 hours from 2,080 hours (full-time equivalent) leaves 1,816 hours of productive service. Utilizing this formula, it would require 4.7 full-time equivalent (FTE) staff to deploy a schedule of one officer on duty around the clock 7 days per week, not including training time. Staffing schedules become even more complicated as much of the projected 264 hours of nonproductive time is not predictable in terms of when it will be utilized.

A large suburban hospital in southeastern Wisconsin, faced with cost-containment pressures, misguidedly used all part-time security officers in their department staffing and deployment plan in an effort to reduce their costs. Operating under the belief that if the department did not have to pay health, dental, retirement and other hospital benefits to the security staff, they could meet the administrative mandate to cut 10% out of the department's operating costs, without reducing the number of weekly hours of security coverage. The organization quickly found the increased training costs and uniform expense associated with the increase in staff substantially reduced the projected savings. Employee morale declined badly, patient satisfaction scores plummeted, and the overall perception of safety on campus fell, causing the hospital to turn over valuable healthcare professionals. All combined, the hospital actually increased their overall operating costs, and had to enter into a service recovery mode to restore the level of confidence the hospital had with the previous security department staffing model.

Thus, a proper balance of full- and part-time employees must be achieved. A program that requires one officer on duty 24 hours a day can be staffed with three full-time officers and three part-time officers. This system gives each part-timer 16 hours per week and provides a resource to cover additional hours as required. It is generally not productive to hire a part-time officer for less than 16 hours per week. It is also poor practice to employ only part-time staff on the weekends. As discussed, compared to the full-time officer, the part-timer may be less trained, motivated, and informed. Proper deployment of part-time staff is to intersperse their schedule with full-time officers.

WAGE COMPENSATION

Determination of an equitable wage and salary structure is one of the most important phases of the relationship with security officers. For good employee relations, each security officer should:

1. Receive sufficient wages to sustain himself and his dependents.
2. Feel satisfied with a relationship between his wages and wages of other people performing the same type of work in a like organization.

The wage compensation received by security personnel is often determined by a complex method of evaluating the nature of the job, the present worth of security services to the organization, and the effectiveness with which the officer performs the job. Working within the organizations wage and salary program, the basic rationale is to compensate fairly all employees in relation to their contribution to the organization's objectives. In a simple example, if the security officer contributed the same value as a radiological technician, the two wage rates would be the same.

Wage surveys in a common geographical area are often helpful in establishing the average compensation paid for protection services. Because cost of living differences and supply and demand produce wide salary fluctuations, comparing the wage rates of different geographical areas yields little valid information. In reviewing wage rates, one must be constantly aware that security functions differ with organizations, and job titles alone can mean very little when making direct comparisons.

A growing trend in healthcare security is to structure salary scales to training levels. This concept has been fostered in part by the progressive certification standards of the IAHSS. This can also be helpful in producing tiered or levels of wages for security within a given function. In this manner security officers can move through various compensation levels, with the move to the next level determined by performance and training achieved within a given time frame.

RETENTION

Recruiting and hiring good security officers is not enough in an industry notorious for high employee turnover. The key is to retain staff. The successful healthcare security program works to reduce their turnover rates by implementing programs that support open communication and feedback, concern for the individual, competitive compensation, performance rewards and recognition, career advancement, and a positive work environment.

Keeping good security officers and supervisors should be a high-priority objective of every healthcare security leader. The cost of recruiting, selecting, processing, and training new security officers is significant. Estimates range as low as $1,400 to as high as $25,000.

Retention of security staff begins by creating a culture of continuous learning and offering career advancement opportunities. The challenge of protecting the healthcare environment is a great retention motivator. When coupled with a customer service orientation, the ability to collaborate with co-workers and feel a part of the healthcare delivery team, being provided the resources to get the job done, and a sincere interest from senior management in their job, the protection program can overcome the plaguing issue of turnover that has negatively affected so many security programs. Of course, a competitive base pay and overall satisfaction with benefits needed in day-to-day life must lay at the foundation, for retention efforts to be realized.

However, retaining the wrong people can be counterproductive. A principle deficiency found in one healthcare security department program review was too little turnover. In this department of 14 officers, the average longevity was 17 years, with the newest officer being hired 6 years prior to the review. Complacency and negativity had settled into the department. Security administrators must focus on developing a healthy turnover rate, annually weeding or placing on development plans the lowest ten percent, to keep a motivated and engaged workforce.

PERFORMANCE EXPECTATIONS

Maintaining a strong degree of discipline is a high priority for security administrators who operate successful protection programs. Corrective action must be exercised to develop a security force amiable to direction and control. Security officers must set an example for the entire organization. Security officers are often deployed at the point of entry for patients and visitors and thus create a first and often lasting impression. The organization must insist security officers follow rigid regulations to maintain an impeccable image. Some security departments have shown such a professional approach by developing a code of ethics for security personnel or adopting the IAHSS Code of Ethics identified in Figure 8-3.

A security force with poor discipline exhibits the following general characteristics:

- Low morale
- Lack of direction, objectives, and goals
- Inattention to duties
- Careless attitude toward the job, supervisors, and organization
- Common disregard for rules and regulations
- Inability to connect their role with the higher purpose of healthcare and the delivery of care to patients

IAHSS Code of Ethics

Preamble
"Recognizing that the overall quality of healthcare delivery is directly related to the professional services rendered by the International Association for Healthcare Security & Safety, the following Code of Ethics is hereby mandated as a consideration for membership."

As a healthcare security professional, I pledge to dedicate myself to providing a safe and secure environment to the people and institution(s) I serve by:

- Supporting patient care and awareness within my healthcare facility
- Recognizing that my principal responsibilities are security and/or safety services to the healthcare community I serve:
    - to protect life and property and reduce crime through the implementation of recognized crime prevention and investigative techniques, and
    - to provide a safe environment of care in support of the mission of the healthcare facility
- Respecting the moral and constitutional rights of all persons while performing my duties without prejudice,
- Ensuring that confidential and privileged information is protected at all times,
- Maintaining open communication with other professionals with whom I conduct business,
- Striving to further my education, both academically and technically, while encouraging professional development and/or advancement of other security/safety personnel,
- Promoting and exemplifying the highest standards of integrity to those whom I serve while dedicating myself to my chosen profession.

FIGURE 8-3

IAHSS Code of Ethics.

Effecting a high degree of discipline in the security force begins by establishing clear standards and expectations for officer performance and behavior. This establishes a foundation for communication, hiring, training, promotion, and decision-making, and serves as the basis for accountability in the department. Once a department has clarity in its mission and goals, it creates unity in all that needs to be achieved.

Holding security staff members accountable helps create department discipline. The security administrator must remember that security staff are people and people do what is *inspected*, not just what is *expected*. Having high expectations is good, but they must reflect outcomes to be achieved and not be prescriptive "how to" lists. So the security administrator or supervisor should ask themselves four simple questions when defining expectations:

1. Have you clearly communicated your expectations?
2. Do all team members fully understand their roles and responsibilities?
3. Are there current organizational environment conditions that hinder their performance?
4. Are there clear consequences for performance?

The consequences can be both positive and negative, depending on performance. The positive consequences reward the individual to do the right thing, while the negative consequences restrain the individual from repeating the wrong thing. Thus, disciplinary action, when taken, is intended to correct a deficiency and should not necessarily be regarded as a punishment. Regrettably, most disciplinary action is negative in nature; however, both positive and negative practices are valuable in the development of a security officer.

Figure 8-4 illustrates a method of recording positive and negative data, attendance, and general information concerning a specific officer. This record is intended to be a work history summary and is

SECURITY DEPARTMENT				
SERVICE PERFORMANCE RECORD				
NAME:		POSITION:		
Date	Entry Description	Absent	Late	Source
04/01/09	Completed 90-day evaluation with satisfactory performance rating			Lt. James
05/22/09		EU		Sgt. York
07/28/09	Remedial training on panic alarm response			
09/17/09	Officer commended for outstanding customer service by patient (see letter of appreciation in file)			Lt. James
11/08/09			L	Sgt. York
12/07/09		PTO		
12/24/09	Officer counseled on uniform appearance re: wearing white socks			Sgt. York
01/01/10	Officer awarded 1 year anniversary pin			Lt. James

Legend

Absent
- Paid Time Off (PTO)
- Excused Unpaid (EU)
- Called Unexcused (CU)
- No Call/No Show (NS)

Late
- More than 15 minutes (M)
- Less than 15 minutes (L)

FIGURE 8-4

Example security officer chronological history.

a useful tool in evaluating the performance of an officer. It can also serve as a primary document in any unemployment cases or violation of equal opportunity cases that may arise.

POSITIVE REINFORCEMENT

Employee recognition programs are a particularly effective way to hold security officers accountable for delivering exceptional security service—and reward them for achieving it. Many organizations have introduced employee recognition programs to acknowledge and reward employees for their contributions made to the department, and the healthcare organization as a whole. Whereas most disciplinary action is designed to prevent a re-occurrence of a behavior or action, effective security programs will make a significant effort to acknowledge positive contributions to the department mission and vision. This encouragement sends a subtle but powerful reminder for the employee to repeat the behavior.

No formal reward and recognition systems can take the place of personalized recognition. If recognition is not personalized it can be demotivating and hurt individual performance. Paying attention to performance, and celebrating success together, reinforces department values and builds a powerful spirit of cooperation and teamwork.

RULES AND REGULATIONS

Rules and regulations concerning the conduct of security personnel must be in written form so officers are apprised of the ground rules that apply. Unwritten policy is not an equitable method of operating a security program. The guidelines identified in Figure 8-5 are fundamental healthcare security principles that apply for all hospitals and healthcare organizations regardless of size, geographic location, or operating philosophy.

The following prohibitions are generally included in most policies, along with prohibitions peculiar to specific organizations:

1. Security officers will not become involved in discussions of religion or politics while on duty or on the premises of the organization.
2. Security officers will not engage in lengthy social conversations with other employees. This is extremely important for the proper functioning of the organization and the security department.
3. Security officers will not criticize any employee or regulation except to the proper supervisor.
4. Security officers will abide by the organization's tobacco-free campus policy and will not smoke or use any tobacco products on patrol.
5. Except during break time, there will be no eating and no reading of material other than material applicable to the job unless it is specifically authorized by a security supervisor.
6. No radios or TV will be allowed on any post.
7. Security officers will not leave a security assignment until properly relieved.
8. The loaning or borrowing of money among employees is prohibited.
9. No member of the security department will solicit contributions for any purpose, except by permission of the security department head.
10. Security officers will not write notes or letters to employees or visitors concerning security problems, nor will they write personal notes to such persons.

Fundamental

Healthcare Security Principles

BE PROFESSIONAL
CONDUCT YOURSELF IN A MANNER WHICH REFLECTS POSITIVELY ON YOU AND THE ORGANIZATION YOU REPRESENT

MAINTAIN CONFIDENTIALITY
DON'T OPEN YOURSELF UP TO PROBLEMS BY DISCUSSING CONFIDENTIAL PATIENT OR SECURITY INFORMATION

DO YOUR PART
DOUBLING UP AND OVER-SOCIALIZATION TAKE YOU AWAY FROM BEING AN IMPORTANT PART OF THE SECURITY TEAM

SET THE EXAMPLE
DRINK, EAT, AND SMOKE IN DESIGNATED AREAS ONLY; FOLLOW ALL HOSPITAL RULES & REGULATIONS THAT YOU ENFORCE

KEEP THE TEAM INFORMED
NOTIFY YOUR SECURITY SUPERVISOR REGARDING ALL MAJOR INCIDENTS; USE PASS-ON LOG TO ADVISE FELLOW OFFICERS ON SECURITY ISSUES

BE DECISIVE
DISPLAY CONFIDENCE BUT KNOW WHEN TO USE THE CHAIN OF COMMAND

COMMUNICATE
SUBMIT ALL REPORTS BEFORE THE END OF THE SHIFT TO ENHANCE ACCURACY AND THE FLOW OF INFORMATION

PRESENT A POSITIVE IMAGE
FIRST AND LAST IMPRESSIONS ARE OFTEN THE MOST IMPORTANT AND LASTING ONES

BE TRUSTWORTHY
EQUIPMENT AND SUPPLIES ARE FOR BUSINESS USE ONLY

FOLLOW DIRECTION
WHEN PATIENTS ARE INVOLVED PROCEED UNDER THE DIRECTION OF A MEDICAL CARE PROVIDER

LOOK SHARP
WEAR AND MAINTAIN YOUR UNIFORM AND EQUIPMENT PROPERLY

BE RESPONSIBLE
REPORT FOR DUTY ON TIME AND BE READY TO WORK; REMAIN IN YOUR ASSIGNED AREA UNTIL PROPERLY RELIEVED

STAY SAFE
THE PURSUIT OF PATIENT OR SUSPECT BEYOND SET LIMITS IS DANGEROUS AND DISCOURAGED

LOOK TO ASSIST
CUSTOMER RELATIONS THROUGH SERVICE IS THE MOST IMPORTANT FUNCTION YOU CAN PROVIDE

PROTECT YOURSELF
WHEN NECESSARY, WEAR THE PERSONAL PROTECTIVE EQUIPMENT AVAILABLE

FIGURE 8-5

Fundamental security principles.

11. Personal phones and other electronic devices will not be used while the security officer is on shift.
12. Security officers will maintain strict confidentiality of information relative to all persons and organizations obtained during the performance of their duty.

The last item on this list is such an important issue that it is not uncommon for organizations to have security department staff sign a confidentiality statement as a condition of employment. This requirement extends to the need for the security officer to maintain awareness of patient confidentiality during conversations on duty.

DISCIPLINARY ACTION

In addition to general prohibitions, a listing of offenses for which the security officer may also be disciplined should be prepared. These offenses normally include the following:

1. Absence without proper notification.
2. Accepting any gift or bribe in the line of duty.
3. Conduct unbecoming a security officer or prejudicial to discipline of the security department either on or off duty.
4. Consuming alcohol or illegal drugs, being under their influence on duty, or reporting for duty in an impaired condition.
5. Bringing contraband or unauthorized weapons/defensive equipment to the workplace.
6. Enabling any person to secure stolen property.
7. False reporting.
8. Ignorance of rules and regulations after being duly informed.
9. Sleeping on duty or neglect of duty.
10. Excessive force or the improper display or use of a weapon.
11. Unnecessary harshness, violence, or profane language.
12. Willful disobedience of orders of a superior.
13. Failure to report any security incident either observed by the officer or brought to his or her attention by another person.

Written disciplinary policy should delineate the specific types of action that may be taken against an officer and the specific supervisors who may take that action. For example, the policy might include the following degrees of disciplinary action, all of which become part of the officer's personnel record:

- **Employee counseling.** This action may be imposed by any security supervisor and is not normally considered a formal reprimand. However, it is intended to make the officer aware of performance or behavior that, unless corrected, can lead to future disciplinary action.
- **Verbal warning.** With a verbal warning, the supervisor discusses the problem with the employee and the employee is advised what must be done to correct the problem. The verbal warning is typically documented on a disciplinary action form; a signature received acknowledging the conversation and stored in the employee's personnel record.
- **Written warning.** This action is more serious than a verbal warning or is a recurrence of a violation. It is a generally accepted practice the written warning outlines the problem, the required corrective action, a timeline for improvement, and the consequences if the employee fails to

CONFIDENTIALITY AGREEMENT

I understand that in the course of my employment, I may have access to and become acquainted with information of a confidential, proprietary or secret nature which is or may be either applicable or related to the present or future business of the company, its research and development, or the business of its customers. It is my responsibility to in no way reveal or divulge any such information unless it is necessary to do so in the performance of my duties. Access to confidential information should be on a "need to-know" basis and must be authorized by my supervisor.

I agree that I will not disclose any of the above mentioned trade secrets, directly, or indirectly or use them in anyway, whether during the term of my employment or at any time thereafter except as required in the course of my employment with the company.

____________________________ ________________

Applicant's Signature Date

FIGURE 8-6

Sample confidentiality statement.

correct the problem. The security officer's signature indicates he or she is aware of the contents of the warning but does not imply that he or she is in agreement with the reprimand. This form of disciplinary action may be taken by any departmental supervisor.

- **Probation status.** This action lasts for a specific period of time, but typically does not exceed 60 days, during which the officer is evaluated to determine fitness for retention of employment. An officer on probation should not be eligible for overtime assignment, and the officer's merit review date advanced by the length of the probationary period. Probation status typically is imposed only by the department head.
- **Suspension with or without pay.** This action lasts for a specific period of time, usually not to exceed five working days. It is normally imposed only by the department head and should include a follow-up meeting with the employee prior to returning to duty. An officer may also be suspended for a period of time by the department head, pending a review of alleged misconduct.

  Note that an officer may be suspended for the remainder of the shift for any infraction of departmental rules and regulations, when, in the evaluation of any security supervisor, the continued duty of the officer may be prejudicial to the best interests of the organization. This suspension from duty should not be confused with the disciplinary action of suspension as a form of punishment.
- **Dismissal.** Employees do not always improve their behaviors or performance following disciplinary action. Additionally, employees may do something so severe that the only appropriate administrative response is to terminate them. This action may be imposed only by the department head or higher authority Figure 8-6.

REFERENCES

1. *The Spain Report: Rivas v. Nationwide Personal Security Corporation* 559 So. 2nd 668 (Fla. App. 3 Dist. 1990). 1991. p. G1–21.
2. Sorrell AL. *Detaining patients against wishes carries legal risks*. 2010, November 8. Amednews.com. Retrieved April 18, 2014, from http://www.amednews.com/article/20101108/profession/311089941/5/.
3. Office of Technology Assessment Staff. Summary of findings: Use of integrity tests for pre-employment screening. *Security Journal* 1991;**2**(1):44.

CHAPTER

THE SECURITY UNIFORM AND DEFENSIVE EQUIPMENT

9

The attire worn by healthcare security staff, and equipment that may be carried by the security officer, establishes the image of the protection program and very often generates a positive perception of personal safety for those who work on campus or visit the healthcare facility. The assigned responsibilities of and type of attire worn by security officers determine how the security officer will be equipped.

UNIFORMS

There are a wide variety of options available to the healthcare security program as it relates to how the security officer is dressed. A continuous debate is whether security officers should wear a traditional uniform or a blazer and slacks. The security "polo style" shirt and matching uniform pants have also emerged in some organizations as the preferred look for their security staff. The consensus of healthcare security administrators is that security officers should not be outfitted in plainclothes.

The true plainclothes approach, identifying security only by the facility name badge, is practically nonexistent in the healthcare field today. Management, training, or investigative staff often wear business attire due to the nature of their individual roles and functions. However, not to equip security officers with a uniform, regardless of the style chosen, creates a mixed message about the importance of security to the healthcare organization. The lack of visibility and loss of customer service opportunities should steer security programs away from the nonuniform option.

DETERMINING UNIFORM STYLE

The determination of which style of uniform should be worn by security staff is based largely on two specific factors: (1) organizational philosophy and (2) the primary function of the security staff. The healthcare security administrator must be sensitive to each when making the determination of the security staff uniform style for a particular organization, site, or even assigned area or function within a hospital.

Organizational philosophy

The type of healthcare organization, its customer service philosophy, and administrative preference are often the primary drivers of what will be worn by the security staff. For example, will the healthcare organization take its cultural cue from Disney? After investing significant capital expenditure to renovate the hospital lobby to make it a welcoming and comfortable setting for patients and their families, seldom will the organization want a stern "security feel" when patients and visitors first walk into the building. In these instances, the perception and image created by the security officer uniform to patients and visitors is an important criterion in determining which style is worn.

Administrative preference may also take precedence over the style of uniform worn. Several years ago, a hospital administrator in a high-crime area in a downtown metropolitan hospital directed the security staff to move from a traditional military style uniform to the softer, blazer style uniform. When asked about the need for the change, the rationale was based solely on individual preference and previous experience. The administrator had come from a healthcare organization where the security staff wore the blazer style uniform and he "preferred it." Neither the negative perception of personal safety expressed by hospital staff nor the advice of healthcare security experts deterred the decision. Fortunately, the administrator was transferred to a different position before the change could be carried out. Although this was an extreme example, the healthcare protection professional must engage hospital administration in a discussion of the advantages and disadvantage of each uniform style to facilitate a best decision for the organization. Table 9-1 provides a brief overview of the advantages and disadvantages of each uniform style.

Even within these categories, however, there are distinctions. For example, at the Halifax Infirmary in Nova Scotia, Canada, the uniform style worn by the security officers was altered dramatically with the change in security service provider in 2011. After two decades of a traditional military-style uniform worn by security, the facility suddenly found their security officers dressed in bright yellow polo/golf shirts. The color of the shirts and the stark difference from the previous style and color made them stand out; their visibility increased markedly. Hospital staff expressed sentiment about feeling more secure in the setting and commented about having more security staff on campus, when in fact the staffing levels had not changed but rather their visibility and presence improved with a uniform change.

Function of the security staff

What primary function the security department as a whole is tasked with, or more specifically, the role the security officer is fulfilling, should be the greatest influencing factor in determining the uniform to be worn by security staff. The officer with primary foot patrol responsibilities, who the organization wants to be highly visible, will often wear a different uniform option than the officer whose primary function is greeting patients and visitor management. There are many uniform options for the healthcare organization to choose from, with compelling arguments for each. The preferred uniform style is outlined in Table 9-2 by the security function performed.

Table 9-1 Advantages and Disadvantages of Security Uniform Styles

	Uniform Style		
	Traditional Military	**Blazer**	**Polo**
Visibility	Very Good	Fair/Poor	Good
Customer Friendly	Good/Fair	Very Good	Good
Professional Image	Good	Very Good	Fair/Poor
Comfort	Fair/Poor	Good/Fair	Very Good
Commanding Presence	Very Good	Fair	Good/Fair
Reassuring Presence	Good/Fair	Good	Fair
Inclement Weather	Very Good	Fair/Poor	Very Good
Armed	Very Good	Poor	Good

Table 9-2 Preferred Security Uniform Style by Function

Function	Preferred Style	Rationale
Foot Patrol	Traditional military	Visibility/deterrence/respect
Bike Patrol	Polo	Functionality/visibility
Greeter/Security Ambassador	Blazer	Customer service/access control
Metal Detector Post	Traditional military	Command presence
Behavioral/Mental Health	Blazer/Polo	Reassuring presence
Specialized Sitter	Polo	Patient care involvement
Security Dispatcher	Polo or Business Casual	Comfort/image

Traditional military uniform style

The vast majority of healthcare security officers are traditionally uniformed in a military or police style uniform. Wearing this style of uniform readily identifies security staff and commands control when necessary, to regulate behavior and provide a deterrent to criminal activity. The uniform is versatile—it can be worn indoors and outdoors in all climates. This style of uniform is preferred for officers who encounter many confrontational situations or primarily perform foot patrol. Figure 9-1 is a picture of a sample traditional style uniform.

A traditional uniform can be softened in terms of color and style. For example, the visor cap, which strongly suggests a military and authoritarian role, is not part of many uniforms in a healthcare setting.

FIGURE 9-1

Sample traditional style uniform.

Many programs prohibit hats within the facility, and some even prohibit hats outside the facility—in Canada, hats are rarely seen worn by security staff in the healthcare milieu, though the famous Canadian "toque" can be found worn in colder climes. Another example is the use of the "commando-style" sweater. Frequently used in cooler climates, these sweaters can provide additional comfort to the security officer as well as soften their authoritative look without sacrifice of visibility. Many organizations have also introduced cloth badge patches, moving away from the more traditional metal badge. The cloth badge softens the look of the traditional uniform while enhancing officer safety and reducing uniform cost. In some healthcare protection programs, clip-on ties have been added to increase the professional image of this style of uniform and to mitigate the risk presented by traditional ties that could present a choking risk to security staff. At Wheaton Franciscan Healthcare–All Saints in Racine, Wisconsin, the addition of the tie to the standard uniform issuance improved the overall image and significantly improved the perception of the security department by both patients and employees.

Name plates, badges, organizational issued identification, merchant guard licenses, supervisor insignia and recognition pins are commonly found on the security officer uniform. Each serve an important purpose, and can often be a source of pride for the officer. Care should be given to avoid cluttering the uniform shirt with too much paraphernalia, presenting an unprofessional image. To distinguish supervisors from officers, many healthcare facilities have the two wear different color shirts—white for supervisors, blue for officers, as an example.

The style, color, and type of uniform are often controlled by local or state/provincial regulations. With or without regulation, the uniform should not be designed to replicate the uniform of any law enforcement agency. To prevent security officers from looking like law enforcement, the state of Arizona has forbidden the color blue to be prominent anywhere on the uniform. In Texas, a hospital was accused by two legal aid groups of designing its security uniforms to look like the uniforms of U.S. Border Patrol agents. A representative of the Texas Rural Legal Aid claimed that the hospital used the uniforms to discourage Hispanics from seeking medical care and thereby avoiding any violation of the Medicare antidumping law.[1]

The task of distinguishing the security officer from other law enforcement or medical personnel in a healthcare facility can often require the security administrator to be creative in order to accomplish this important distinction. In a busy emergency department, it is common to find police, corrections personnel and paramedics working side by side with the hospital security team. It is important for patients, hospital staff and the public alike to readily distinguish these groups from one another—an often challenging task!

Blazer (Ambassador) uniform style

The blazer style uniform with contrasting slacks (gray slacks and blue blazer) can be a very professional look, and works best for officers who work mainly inside the facility and function primarily in a public relations mode. Many behavioral healthcare facilities prefer security officers working in these environments to work in the blazer style uniform, or employ a polo/golf shirt style, to prevent the uniform from unnecessarily antagonizing, or even frightening, patients or visitors. Figure 9-2 is a picture of a sample blazer style uniform.

If blazers are worn, they should be designed so security officers are readily identifiable. Without readily visible identification, poor public relations and unnecessary confrontations may result. Though not a recommended practice, if the blazer is removed during the course of duty, specific guidance should be given on how the officer is to be identified to the public.

FIGURE 9-2

Sample blazer style uniform.

The blazer style uniform does not offer the same flexibility as the traditional military style uniform. This style of uniform makes working outdoors in weather extremes difficult. Many licensing agencies prohibit security personnel from wearing this style of uniform and working in an armed capacity in the U.S. Even in states where concealed carry weapons (CCW) permits are issued, security officers wearing a blazer style uniform should never carry a concealed firearm. The carrying of a concealed firearm should be strictly prohibited by the healthcare facility and apply to security managers, directors and other leadership roles in the healthcare security program, regardless of their background in law enforcement, military or personal desire.

Polo style uniform

The high visibility polo, or golf, shirt has become a fast-growing nontraditional uniform option for an increasing number of healthcare security programs. Worn with slacks, battle dress uniform (BDU) style pants/shorts, or line uniform trousers, the polo shirt is typically identified with "SECURITY" on the back. This uniform option is frequently used for security officers who perform bike patrol functions. The expanded functionality of this uniform provides the officer with greater freedom of movement required by the bicycle function, and withstands more wear and tear than the traditional uniform for an external patrol officer. These uniforms can also be used for armed security personnel. Figure 9-3 is a picture of a healthcare security officer wearing a polo style uniform.

This style of uniform is also worn by a growing profession in the healthcare protection industry, the *specialized sitter*. These staff members are frequently used to stand by and watch at-risk patients in a one-on-one situation for often extended periods of time. The polo style uniform is the most comfortable and allows these employees to be a visible component of the protection program without provoking the patient. This also has the effect of minimizing the "in custody" feeling that may be projected to a patient and their family in these situations. Additionally, this style of uniform does not have the many

FIGURE 9-3

Polo style uniform.

accoutrements normally found on the traditional military style uniform. This reduces the potential harm to employees or the patient in the event verbal de-escalation attempts are unsuccessful, and a hands-on approach to patient management is required.

The security dispatcher is often located outside of the public view. Outfitting dispatchers in this softer uniform style is usually done for the sole purpose of comfort in the work environment. A recent trend for many healthcare organizations employing security dispatchers is to allow these employees to wear professional attire similar to other nonuniformed employees in the organization. This practice is not recommended for organizations that have dispatchers located in public view, or share patrol functions or other duties with uniformed security staff.

Organizations may elect to adopt all three uniform styles in their protection programs: the regular security officers may wear traditional military style uniforms; bike patrol officers and specialized sitters may wear the polo style uniform, while supervisory personnel may wear blazers. Some job responsibilities may best be fulfilled by a traditionally uniformed officer, while for others, the blazer is preferred. For example, patrol and response officers might wear traditional uniforms, while fixed-post officers, who perform an access control/greeting function, might wear blazers.

SUPPLYING AND MAINTAINING THE UNIFORM

Because the uniform is such an important element in the operation of a security force, the organization should provide and, if possible, maintain the uniform. Ideally, officers should be required to report for duty in personal clothing and change into their uniform. In this system, the organization dry cleans or launders the uniform, and prohibits officers from wearing the uniform off duty. This system is, of course, quite costly and is therefore not a widely utilized practice.

The U.S. courts have interpreted the Fair Labor Standards Act (FLSA) hourly wage regulations to mean that the officers must be paid for their time, if required to change into their uniform on-site, and

UNIFORM DEDUCTION AUTHORIZATION

In connection with your employment, you are required to wear a uniform that has been purchased for your use. Uniforms are of substantial value and will remain the property of ____________. It is your responsibility to keep this uniform clean and in good repair.

Please sign below to indicate that you agree to have $50.00 deducted from your 2nd, 3rd, 4th and 5th paychecks ($200.00 total) as a **security deposit** for the uniform. This deposit will be returned to you in full, provided the entire uniform is returned in good condition within seven days of the conclusion of your employment. A $25.00 cleaning fee will be assessed if the returned uniform has not been dry-cleaned.

Upon resignation/termination, if you do not return all the uniform pieces, as listed on the Uniform Issue Form, in good condition or fail to return the uniform, you acknowledge that __________ will keep the deposit and can deduct from your paycheck or bill you later for the value of any damages, up to and including the full value of the uniform.

______________________	______________________	__________
Print Name	Employee's Signature	Date

FIGURE 9-4

Sample uniform deduction authorization language.

not allowed to change at home. In Lee v. Am-Pro Protective Agency, Inc., 860 F.Supp. 2d 325, 326 (E.D.Va.1994), the courts ruled that security officers are entitled to compensation for changing into uniforms on-site, where they were not allowed to change at home.

Organizations that provide uniforms for security personnel have more control over the quantity and quality of the uniforms. All too often, newly hired officers who must provide their own uniforms find the initial cost outlay a burden. As a result, they sometimes do not purchase enough individual uniform items to maintain a proper appearance.

There are alternatives to having the organization supply the complete uniform. As a condition of employment, some security departments require a uniform deduction to be withheld to offset the cost of uniforms, if the officer resigns or is terminated within a specified time, usually three months. Other organizations hold a deposit until after separation of employment. Some state statutes do not allow either of these practices, so proper legal advice should be sought before implementing this practice. It is recommended that interest be paid on money held as a uniform and equipment deposit; in fact, interest may even be legally required. If money is withheld from an employee's paycheck to cover a deposit, the organization is limited in the amount that can be withheld from any given paycheck. The employee must be paid at least the minimum wage for the hours worked before a deduction can be made. Figure 9-4 provides an example of a standard employee authorization form used by many healthcare organizations that deduct uniform expenses from their employee's paycheck.

Another method of cost control is to require security officers to purchase their original uniform, while replacements are paid for by the organization. This procedure is effective in eliminating applicants who are seeking only temporary employment. One hospital reports it has been able to contain costs by not purchasing an outside jacket for each officer. The facility maintains a supply of jackets in various sizes. Officers select their jackets from the supply at the beginning of the shift when they draw their weapons and other equipment. This practice may help contain costs, but can also significantly reduce employee morale and may even present health hazards. The healthcare security administrator should recognize the attire of security officers also influences their own attitude; a uniform that suggests an air of dignity and action tends to produce officers with those traits.

Larger security forces can reduce uniform costs by making use of existing uniforms. Regardless of the size of the force, returned uniforms represent dollars, and the supply should not be allowed to build up excessively. It is much more economical to expend money on alterations than to order new uniforms. Uniform rental firms also provide an alternative to hospital-owned and officer-owned uniforms. Uniforms should be clean when returned upon termination, and professionally dry-cleaned when appropriate. The failure to return hospital owned uniforms in the appropriate condition should result in a predetermined deduction from the officer's final wages.

Facilities in areas with wide temperature swings often elect to provide both summer and winter uniforms for their staff.

USE OF FIREARMS

This section should begin with the understanding that when we talk of equipping healthcare security staff with firearms, we are focused primarily on the U.S. The notion of arming healthcare security personnel in Canada and the UK, as an example, is completely foreign, the practice unheard of and, in most jurisdictions, prohibited by law. Whether security officers should be equipped with firearms requires constant evaluation and reexamination. The answer is found in individual program needs, and the question cannot be answered with a simple yes or no. For program effectiveness and deterrent value, the preponderance of evidence related to the U.S. supports armed security officers. However, armed officers may prove a detriment in various situations or functions rather than an asset.

Proponents of providing firearms for healthcare security officers argue that if an organization gives officers the responsibility of protecting life and property, it should provide them with the tools to do their job. Officers who can meet force with force can more efficiently carry out their responsibilities, this argument contends. Those against providing firearms often cite the liability involved, and almost always stress a case in which a firearm was used inappropriately. Some opponents argue security officers guard property and need not use deadly force. The firearm does nothing more than allow officers to protect themselves and others while they protect property. The value of property is significant only to the extent it invites intruders. If security officers are expected to confront strangers, their personal safety must be paramount, regardless of property value. The question of how healthcare security officers in some countries perform this function without consideration for arming them extends well beyond the scope of this book, and is a question likely best discussed by criminologists and sociologists, who continue to research, analyze and debate the firearm phenomenon and its impact on societies.

In 2007, when a survey on this issue was conducted, approximately 12% of U.S. healthcare security officers were armed.[2] When an earlier edition of this book was published in 2001, about 15–20% had firearms, down from 30% in 1992. The trend appeared to continue toward unarmed security officers. However, a 2012 survey conducted by ASHE (American Society of Healthcare Engineers) is the first study that has seen this trend starting to reverse. The ASHE survey looked at the percentage of hospital security officers armed with a firearm and found:

- 16% of hospitals had only specific security staff members licensed to be armed
- 4% of hospitals had only off-duty police officers working for the hospital armed
- 6% of hospitals were currently unarmed but were evaluating the introduction of armed security in their environment
- 74% of hospitals were unarmed and had no plans to use firearms.[3]

There are many reasons promulgated for why this trend has changed in the last five years. Most believe it is the sheer volume of active shooter events that have happened in healthcare and in other industries in general, such as the Aurora Theatre Shooting in 2013 and school shootings that have placed some of our most vulnerable members of society at risk. These events have drawn significant media attention and are starting to change the court of public opinion and, with it, the attention of hospital administrators on what their overall security posture should be as it relates to armed security.

The armed versus unarmed debate has no right or wrong answer; it is simply a choice that security leaders and hospital administrators collectively must make. The correct decision is risk-based and should be made for the particular circumstances facing the organization, and must not simply be following a trend.

CONSIDERATIONS IN ARMING OFFICERS

The correct decision on whether to arm security officers for a given organization requires consideration of many different factors. Among these considerations are, first and foremost, the law and any related regulations, personal safety, vulnerability, liability, deterrent value, environmental profile (status of the neighborhood, geographical setting, degree of crime in and around the facility), and quality of personnel.

Personal safety

Personal safety is, of course, the central issue in whether to arm officers. The people at risk are the officers themselves, and the principals (employees, patients, visitors) they are protecting. Armed security officers feel safer as their ability to protect themselves increases. No amount of training, physical response techniques, or other alternatives can match an opponent with a firearm. Conversely, officers are sometimes safer without a weapon. If a security officer is obviously not armed, a foe need not use deadly force to accomplish his objective. The persons the security officer protects have a greater feeling of security when the officer is armed, according to some views. Thus firearms may provide both officers, and those they protect, with a sense of security, regardless of the real need for firearms.

Vulnerability

The degree of vulnerability the officer and the organization face is also an important consideration. In larger acute-care hospitals, the quantities of drugs and money on hand, and the number of serious assaults that occur, differentiate these settings from small suburban or rural facilities. The degree of vulnerability also varies in relation to the environmental setting. For the individual officer, vulnerabilities also vary considerably. A security officer patrolling warehouses and parking lots at 3:00 a.m. is in a different position than an officer assigned to an access control point within the facility. Generally, fewer security staff are armed in programs that are primarily internally focused and worried mostly with the patients and visitors who are invited in, than in programs that must deal with concerning issues internally and externally on campus and many environmental risks, or so-called street problems.

Liability

Potential for legal liability actions is greatest with armed officers. Officers who misuse their weapons can create a liability, of course as can a nurse who misuses a syringe when injecting a patient. However, an unarmed officer who cannot effectively prevent injury to a patient, visitor, or employee might create a liability of a different nature. The problem is one cannot know whether the firearm helped avert an incident that might have led to a liability claim.

There is one approach to providing firearms protection to the healthcare center without arming any of the regular security staff, and that is to hire off-duty law enforcement officers. Although this is an expensive approach, the healthcare center can avoid the training issue and a certain degree of liability by employing this model. What may be problematic with this approach, however, is training and liability may not be avoided at all, as the selection of the specific officer working the off-duty post is often outside of the control of the organization.

An example of what can go wrong when off-duty police officers work at healthcare facilities can be found in the case of Melendez v. City of Los Angeles. In this case, two off-duty police officers working at the facility were involved in an altercation in which a person was shot. The healthcare facility that had hired the off-duty officers avoided a court decision by settling out of court for $550,000. However, a jury found the city liable for $10,212,500, in part because it felt the city was guilty of negligent retention of one of the officers, who had allegedly been involved in other incidents in which excessive force was used. In addition, the jury found that the police officers were acting within the scope of their employment as law enforcement officers at the time of the shooting, despite the fact they were "off duty." This particular case is not unique. The issue of off-duty police officers, working for private organizations, deserves serious attention by private organizations and law enforcement agencies alike.

Deterrent value

One of the strongest arguments in favor of arming security staff is the preventative value of having security officers armed with firearms. One can only assume most serious crimes are planned to some degree, and part of that planning is to select a target in which armed security officers will not be encountered.

Environmental profile

The type of neighborhood, together with the associated level and type of crime, must be analyzed in determining the need for armed security personnel. A quiet residential setting, with an older population, presents far different issues than a derelict commercial or transient community. In reviewing the crime status of the area, the number of crimes as well as the seriousness of the crimes is important. In this respect, a high number of minor crimes can suggest more serious crime is foreseeable, providing there is a linkage. An example is a person stealing car parts in a parking lot who is interrupted, and violence results during an attempted escape. An escalating level of minor crimes is often the forerunner of increasing violence and crimes against persons.

In addition to police crime statistics, CAP Index CRIMECAST® reports should be used to identify the risk potential of criminal activity on campus and the surrounding neighborhood. The model builds upon the strong relationship between a neighborhood's "social disorder" and the amount of crime perpetrated there. By combining surrounding social characteristics, survey information and other databases with known indicators of crime, the CRIMECAST model is able to provide precise scores indicating a site's risk of crime in comparison to national, state and county averages. Figure 9-5 illustrates a sample CRIMECAST Site Data and Map.

Generally, when a healthcare organization makes a decision to go with armed security personnel, they do so because of the aforementioned neighborhood demographics information, but also take into consideration the degree of crime in and around the facility and police response time.

If available, the healthcare facility should ascertain the local police department statistics on crime for the hospital, as well as the crime reporting area, and grid or zone in which it is located. In most cases, these statistics are tabulated monthly, and can be obtained at no charge or for a nominal fee. In many cities now, police crime statistics are available online, usually from a website hosted by the police agency. Often crimes reported from the hospital actually occur elsewhere; they are simply called in to 911 by the victim or medical personnel, usually from the emergency department. This is why it is essential to correlate police crime statistics with hospital incident reports, to determine if a crime actually occurred on campus.[4]

Reviewing the statistics with the local community resource officer can also serve as an invaluable exercise. Often, these representatives of the agency having jurisdiction can help identify changes in the

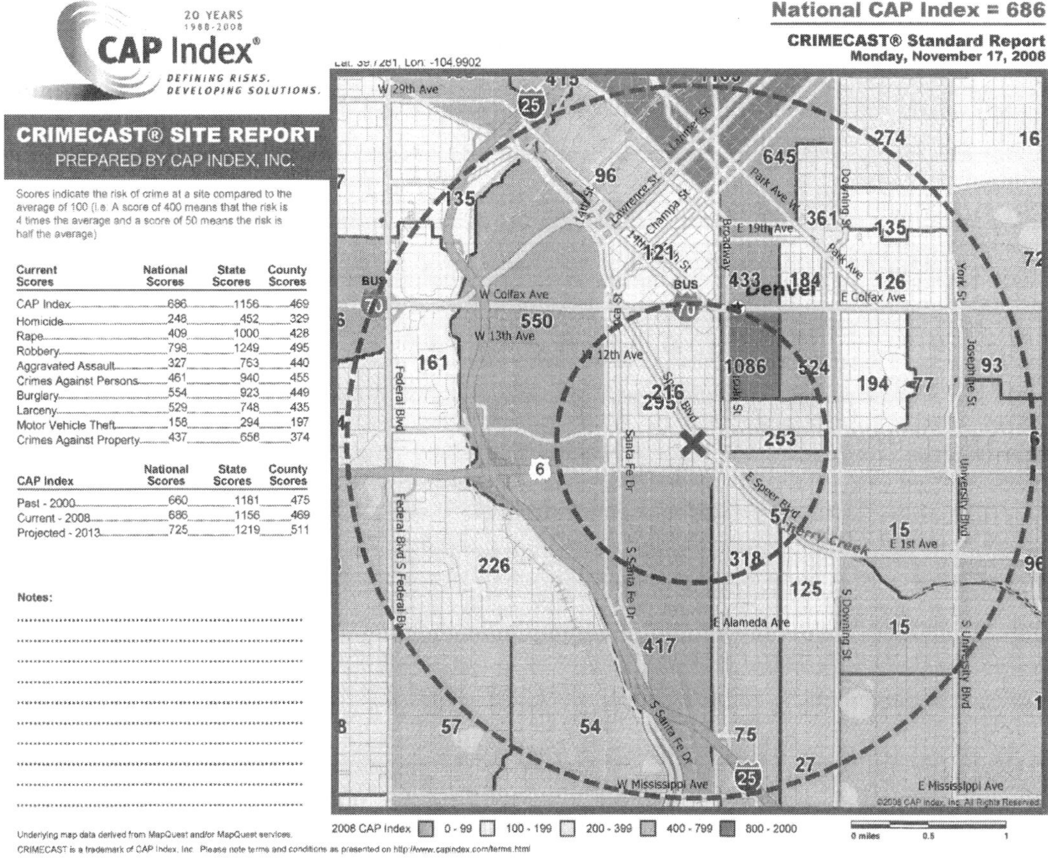
20 YEARS 1988-2008

CAP Index®

DEFINING RISKS. DEVELOPING SOLUTIONS.

CRIMECAST® SITE REPORT

PREPARED BY CAP INDEX, INC.

Scores indicate the risk of crime at a site compared to the average of 100 (i.e. A score of 400 means that the risk is 4 times the average and a score of 50 means the risk is half the average)

Current Scores	National Scores	State Scores	County Scores
CAP Index	686	1156	469
Homicide	248	452	329
Rape	409	1000	428
Robbery	798	1249	495
Aggravated Assault	327	763	440
Crimes Against Persons	461	940	455
Burglary	554	923	449
Larceny	529	748	435
Motor Vehicle Theft	158	294	197
Crimes Against Property	437	658	374

CAP Index	National Scores	State Scores	County Scores
Past - 2000	660	1181	475
Current - 2008	686	1156	469
Projected - 2013	725	1219	511

Notes:

National CAP Index = 686

CRIMECAST® Standard Report
Monday, November 17, 2008

Underlying map data derived from MapQuest and/or MapQuest services.
CRIMECAST is a trademark of CAP Index, Inc. Please note terms and conditions as presented on http://www.capindex.com/terms.html

FIGURE 9-5

Example of a CRIMECAST map and site date.

(Courtesy of CAP Index, King of Prussia, PA)

US Current CAP Index = 686

CRIMECAST® SITE REPORT
PREPARED BY CAP INDEX, INC.

Method Used: CRIMECAST® Standard Report Date Prepared: 11/17/2008
Site ID: 504445
Site Name:
Site Address:
Lat: 39.7281 Lon: -104.9902

Current Scores (2008)	National Scores	State Scores	County Scores
CAP Index	686	1156	469
Homicide	248	452	329
Rape	409	1000	428
Robbery	798	1249	495
Aggravated Assault	327	763	440
Crimes Against Persons	461	940	455
Burglary	554	923	449
Larceny	529	748	435
Motor Vehicle Theft	158	294	197
Crimes Against Property	437	658	374

Scores indicate the risk of crime at a site compared to the average of 100. (i.e. A score of 400 means that the risk is 4 times the average and a score of 50 means the risk is half the average).

Past Scores (2000)	National Scores	State Scores	County Scores
CAP Index	660	1181	475
Homicide	196	397	281
Rape	310	829	364
Robbery	807	1332	522
Aggravated Assault	280	723	400
Crimes Against Persons	404	895	421
Burglary	474	845	403
Larceny	597	850	468
Motor Vehicle Theft	157	304	194
Crimes Against Property	474	730	396

Future Scores (2013)	National Scores	State Scores	County Scores
CAP Index	725	1219	511
Homicide	260	463	350
Rape	469	1135	478
Robbery	805	1259	520
Aggravated Assault	379	840	515
Crimes Against Persons	510	1010	514
Burglary	609	1000	504
Larceny	500	704	425
Motor Vehicle Theft	152	281	202
Crimes Against Property	470	704	415

Please note terms and conditions as presented on http://www.capindex.com/terms.html

FIGURE 9-5—Continued

community, provide a broader understanding of trends in the neighborhood, and provide an understanding of how much police presence the department provides to the medical center.

The objective nature of healthcare security and police crime statistics, coupled with a CAP Index report, provide evidenced-based considerations when evaluating the decision on the need for armed security officers in the healthcare environment.

Past experience with weapons

The presence of illegal weapons on campus is an important indicator in determining the need of armed security personnel. The healthcare organization should ask a few essential risk-based questions when evaluating the need for an armed security presence, or disarming current staff. This should include a comprehensive review of past experience on campus related to:

- Discovery of weapons brought into the facility?
- Discovery of weapons found on campus?
- Incidents where security officers used weapons in the course of duty?
- Incidents where weapons may have been needed?

Weapons are often found when metal detectors are used to screen persons entering emergency departments.[4] A four-year study at Henry Ford Medical Center, Detroit, Michigan reported that 4% of people arriving at their emergency department carried weapons to some points in the hospital.[5] A three-month examination of three Level I trauma centers in Denver, Colorado, employing magnetometers in their emergency department protection efforts, found an unexpected quantity of commandeered items. During the period, one facility confiscated 434 banned items, including three guns. Another took possession of 558 banned items, while a third confiscated over 1200 prohibited objects, with an average of 25 to 30 illegal knives each month. For these three facilities, the volume of illegal weapons confiscated (both firearms and edged weapons) was a significant factor in determining the need for armed security.

Community standard

Another important consideration when evaluating the use of armed personnel is the community standard. The assessment should include a detailed understanding of the use of armed security at other healthcare facilities within the health system and in the region. Identification of this "tipping point issue" is an important consideration before making a change.

For 20 years, trends indicate a large volume of healthcare organizations have transitioned to an unarmed security model. Some criminology researchers would assert the reduction in the crime rate, including violent crime, across the western world in the last decade may reflect a reduction in risk in the surrounding communities, leading to this disarming trend.

If a healthcare facility in the region has recently disarmed their security staff, effort should be made to glean information relative to the decision. Did they have a significant event, or close call, that brought the issue of armed staff to the surface, or was there merely an administrative change in preference or a recognition of shifting crime demographics in the surrounding community as a whole?

Gaining knowledge of the rationale at other healthcare facilities for using an armed (or unarmed) security model can provide significant insight into the decision matrix. The community and patient demographics differ by facility; no two healthcare environments are exactly alike. However, physicians often have privileges at multiple hospitals, and healthcare has a large transient workforce who frequently "job hop," in search of better schedules, shorter commutes, and safer work environments. The knowledge of the model of security in place at other healthcare facilities can help stem negative perceptions of the protection efforts on campus. All too often, the rationale received is that security staff "have been armed since I have been here," and no one has ever questioned that rationale. Unfortunately, many healthcare organizations never review the issue unless a significant event occurs, because "it's just the way it's always been done."

Circumstances for officers to disarm

Many organizations also have protocols on the circumstances for when armed personnel must disarm while performing certain duties. Security and law enforcement have been prohibited from carrying their firearms onto most behavioral/mental health units for years. There may be indications the now almost quarter-century trend of reduced behavioral healthcare funding in the U.S., and indeed across the western world, could be changing. However, as illustrated by the closing of many primary mental healthcare facilities and inpatient units, or at least a dramatic reduction in funded beds, the emergency departments have been flooded with a growing number of mental health patients. Often, the patients present to the emergency department with an even greater level of acuity. As a result, a number of emergency departments have given great consideration to requiring their security officers—and even gone so far as requesting law enforcement—to disarm before entering the medical treatment area of the emergency department.

In Canada, this situation is further complicated in the case of prisoners as patients, under escort from federal prisons (holding those serving sentences of two years or greater). As a result of a union agreement with federal correctional officers, in the case of federal prisoners under escort from a maximum security prison, or a medium prison in particular circumstances, the escort team members must be armed. This too has the potential to create increased risk of armed personnel in the emergency departments of Canadian hospitals, as well as in other areas of the facility, where the prisoner may travel or receive treatment.

The simple act of disarming creates a litany of issues, ranging from gun locker storage location, to additional training requirements to prevent accidental discharges when the firearm is handled in the public arena. The preferences and specific risks must be taken into consideration when evaluating the use of armed security personnel.

Quality of personnel

Many times the problem is not whether a security officer should be armed; it is the availability of competent, well-trained security officers to carry firearms. No amount of pre-service or in-service training can compensate for security officers who do not possess the aptitude to put into practice the training provided.

Regardless of what kind of prior training a security officer has been provided historically—e.g., POST certified or previous company training—every organization should require the security officer to complete its NRA-certified training program. This training should preclude any security officer from carrying a gun on duty unless he/she has fulfilled the competency training standard and firing range proficiency. The quality of the program, and the authority of the instructor to eliminate those officers who should not carry firearms, is paramount.

Type of weapon, holster, and ammunition

The decision to use firearms in a security program mandates additional management responsibility and adds to costs. A major decision that must be made concerns the type of weapon, holster, and ammunition to be used. These decisions are sometimes determined by licensing laws.

Some organizations furnish the weapon, and prefer weapons be checked in and out for each tour of duty. Where economics and other operational factors preclude the organization from owning the weapons, basic standards must be established for officer-furnished weapons and ammunition.

The type of holster to be used is another important consideration. Security personnel should only be allowed to carry a Levels I, II and III safety holster. It must ride close against the body and it must be difficult for another person to remove the weapon from the officer. Too many security officers have been shot with their own weapons, after losing them to an assailant.

Healthcare security officers should never be allowed to carry concealed weapons (even with a concealed weapon permit) while performing hospital services. Not only is this practice evidence of a poor management decision, it can also have serious consequences in terms of public relations and liability issues.

TRENDS IN ARMING SECURITY PERSONNEL

To reduce liability while providing the security system with a limited weapon capability, some programs arm only the supervisory staff. This approach is predicated on the reduced exposure of weapons, and the fact that supervisory personnel are generally better trained and more capable of properly handling weapons.

Another approach is to arm those officers who are assigned to external patrol or a metal detector, and to eliminate firearms for those personnel assigned to the emergency department, behavioral health or other departments commonly found with high-risk patient populations.

Whether to arm security officers or not is a very serious decision that must be made with deliberation. There is always a risk, and the decision must be made on the basis of this question: Does the weapon provide benefits sufficient to offset the liability and cost involved?

MANAGING THE FIREARMS PROGRAM

Where firearms are used by security, a firearms policy is mandatory. The policy must be clear, concise, and understood by every officer. A firearms weapon affidavit should be completed by all officers who carry firearms. Figure 9-6 is an example of such a firearms affidavit. The affidavit could be further expanded to serve as the administrative policy.

It is often claimed that a weapon should not be taken from a holster unless it will be used, and one should never fire a weapon in the air. However, a drawn weapon might be appropriate in some instances, for example when answering an intrusion alarm in a closed pharmacy, or when interrupting a crime in progress and ordering suspects to raise their hands. Firing in the air, or firing warning shots, is considered to be inappropriate in this most fragile of settings.

Firearms training is an essential ingredient in properly managing an armed security program. This training must be an ongoing program of classroom instruction and firing range experience. All armed officers should fire on the range at least twice each year, preferably more frequently.

Training instructors should be carefully selected for two reasons. First, the highest level of instruction possible should be provided. Second, the qualifications of the instructor, and the quality of the instruction, can be of prime importance in any litigation alleging misuse of a firearm by a security officer. The instructor should be qualified by the National Rifle Association (NRA) to teach the police and security program. The minimum requirement for the firearms instructor should be attendance, and successful completion of, the NRA 44-hour tactical handgun course, which entitles the instructor to conduct courses for both police and security personnel.

WEAPON USE AND SAFETY AFFIDAVIT

1. The weapon you carry in the performance of your duty is for the protection of life. Deadly physical force may be used only as a last resort if the Security Officer reasonably believes a lesser degree of force is inadequate, and; the Security Officer has reasonable grounds to believe, and does believe, that he or another person is in imminent danger of being killed or of receiving great bodily harm.

2. All weapons are dangerous, it is mandatory that the Security Officer treat his weapon with care, respect, and remembering that at all times handling the weapon safely is the most important requirement.

3. The person with a firearm in his possession has a full-time job. You cannot guess—you cannot forget. You must know how to use, handle, and store your firearm safely. Do not use any firearm without a complete understanding of its particular characteristics and safe use. There is no such thing as a foolproof gun.

4. From the time you pick up a gun you become part of a system over which you have complete control. You are the only part of the system that can make a gun safe or unsafe.

5. Firearms will not be removed from the holster or otherwise drawn unless there is an immediate threat of death to the officer or other persons present. The firearm will not be removed from the holster for show or display or at the request of other security personnel. Security Supervisors are entitled to inspect the gun to determine the cleanliness of the weapon and whether you are carrying appropriate ammunition.

6. Warning shots will not be fired under any circumstances.

7. I will never leave a loaded firearm where someone else may handle it. When not on my person, my weapon will be secured. This includes at work, traveling to and from work, and at home.

8. The officer must carry the firearm and ammunition that was approved by the local law enforcement agency. Carrying a weapon or ammunition other than that approved is forbidden and could result in termination.

9. The weapon must be cleaned after each shooting session; failure to do so could result in a malfunction of the weapon.

10. Alcohol, drugs, and guns don't mix. Do not handle firearms if you have been using alcohol or are under a doctor's medication containing narcotic derivatives.

11. Do not shoot at or from a moving vehicle. If you disable a driver you have now created a 3,000 pound missile capable of inflicting serious injury or death to an innocent party.

12. I understand that the license issued to me prohibits my wearing the uniform and/or weapon while off duty except to travel directly to and from home. The weapon must be secured in the trunk or placed in a container out of public view.

13. Don't be timid when it comes to gun safety; if you observe anyone violating any safety precautions, you have an obligation to suggest safer handling practices.

14. Any time you pick up a weapon my must adhere to the following practices:

15. Point the gun in a safe direction.
    a. Visually inspect the gun to be certain that the gun is loaded or not loaded. Count the cartridges.
    b. When not in actual use, firearms must be unloaded.
    c. Never touch the trigger on a firearm until you actually intend to shoot.
    d. You must be able to identify your target and what's beyond it.

16. All security personnel shall strictly adhere to this order. Violations of policies set forth herein will result in disciplinary action. This policy shall be effective at all times regardless of location.

PRINT NAME________________________ SIGNATURE____________________ DATE_________

WITNESS______________________ DATE_________________

FIGURE 9-6

Example of a security officer firearms affidavit training.

(Courtesy of HSS Inc., Denver, Colorado)

OTHER SECURITY AND DEFENSIVE EQUIPMENT CONSIDERATIONS

There is a limit on how much equipment a security officer can carry, and the security administrator must decide which defensive equipment is most necessary for a particular system. Officers so loaded down with equipment that they have difficulty moving freely exhibit a poor image. The needs of each program will vary. The following equipment list is offered only as a guide:

- Notebook and pen
- Handheld electronic devices for incident and patrol data capture
- Communication devices
- Handcuffs
- Flashlight
- Personal Protective Equipment (PPE)
- Tasers (Electronic Control Devices)
- Chemical agents (irritants)
- Batons
- Protective vests
- The duty belt

Although not categorized as equipment, a nameplate or other identification consistent with the facility's overall employee identification plan should be worn by all officers.

NOTEPAD AND PEN

Often overlooked, a security officer should never be allowed on a post or patrol without a notebook and writing instrument. It can be a healthcare security officer's most-used equipment. Small enough to fit into the security officer's pocket, the notepad can be used to capture investigative notes and contain needed information such as emergency codes for the facility and radio codes for the department. Some departments even provide their security staff with foldout maps of the facility grounds and security incident report drafts that can help with key questions to ask during simple and complex investigative activity.

As written communication has moved away from paper and pen tools and increasingly toward laptops, tablets and handheld devices, so too can we see this trend for healthcare security. Handheld devices are regularly being used by security officers to document incidents and verify patrols in real time in the field. Some organizations are using customized software and tablets to audit service and performance, also in real time, that allows electronic sign-off by supervisors or those vested with responsibility for program oversight. Care should be given when these systems are introduced to give an appearance that the officer is using the equipment for official purposes and not just texting or using the equipment for other personal communication.

COMMUNICATION DEVICES

The most important piece of equipment a security officer can carry is the two-way radio, which is part of the overall security communications system. A one-way pager is simply unacceptable. Not only does the radio provide an element of personal safety for the officer, but it is essential in achieving an effective security system. However, many facilities expend thousands of dollars for security personnel, yet fail to spend a small amount to achieve a 50% to 100% increase in effectiveness through improved communications. Archived reports attest to the success of radio communications in saving lives, preventing total-loss fires, and apprehending criminals of all types. Radios create a deterrent value when used by a lone security officer confronting a hostile individual(s). A call for assistance alerts the perpetrators that help is on the way.

Radio equipment is available in all shapes and sizes and with varying states of sophistication. Many large and well-funded departments use wide area radio networks or repeater systems for officers to communicate with one another, and to hear broadcasts from the central station. This traditional two-way radio communication is still preferred by most healthcare protection professionals. Advanced two-way radios have multiple channels, one or more of which can be used for supervisory personnel. This allows security leaders to have private conversations so they can discuss sensitive subjects. The text messaging feature available on many radios can also keep communication confidential.

Advanced communications systems available from suppliers such as Sprint have grown in popularity. Providing the ability for officers in the field to link with three independent forms of communication—cell phones, radio, and text messaging—this technology application provides significant redundancy in critical communication for security staff. Preferred for multiple campus locations and smaller departments, signal strength can be amplified inside the healthcare organization for a fraction of the cost of a wide-area radio network.

Some radios have *call alert* and *selective call* features that can page a specific person or group during an emergency, such as an evacuation, power failure or patient emergency. Call alert, or selective call, allows these situations to be managed by appropriate personnel, without disturbing other users who are not involved. The GPS option available on many of the newer radios enables the security officer to communicate due to an accident or assault, or for management to locate that individual to render assistance. The location of each security officer can be displayed on the dispatcher's computer screen for officer safety and asset management.[6]

Good communications equipment is expensive; however, the cost has come down in recent years. Considering the life of today's equipment, the cost, depreciated over the number of usable years, is the best investment of security dollars that an organization can make.

Limited two-way radio codes in security operations can be useful in reducing valuable airtime. The 10 codes that were once popular have generally been found to be of limited value and have sometimes caused more problems than no codes at all. Most law enforcement agencies and security departments have eliminated the 10 codes except for a few basic codes.

Several problems are inherent in any code system; chief among them is the training required. With turnover of personnel, the training issue becomes a major challenge. Another problem is the codes cannot cover the diversified and sometimes specific information that must be communicated. Field analysis has shown departments using extensive code systems do not necessarily use less airtime than do departments that have eliminated their codes. The main items of concern in radio transmission are minimal airtime and clarity (understanding) of the message being transmitted. Both of these goals can be adequately achieved by simply stating the message in concise, everyday language.

Many healthcare security programs are incorporating lapel microphones with their two-way radios. Hospitals are finding improved security communications and officer safety with the microphone as internal communications are not broadcast as with a traditional radio system. An additional tangible benefit is the quieter approach found by using the microphones can contribute positively to the hospital's healing mission and help the organization meet important HCAHPS initiatives in the U.S. The microphones eliminate radio noise in hospital corridors, which in turn helps create a more quiet and restful environment for patients.

HANDCUFFS

Handcuffs are an important piece of equipment carried by many healthcare security officers. Security officers may need to use handcuffs for maintaining custody and control of persons arrested, as well as for detaining persons who exhibit behavior that may be harmful to themselves or others.

In restraining out-of-control patients, regular medical restraint devices will generally be utilized. Historically there have been occasions when the security officer's handcuffs may have been used, as the most expedient means of temporarily maintaining patient control. However, the Centers for Medicare and Medicaid Services (CMS) in the U.S. does not consider the use of handcuffs or other restrictive devices in the application of restraint or seclusion as a safe, appropriate health care intervention.[7]

Handcuffs and flex cuffs can be very useful tools, but their use should be documented and governed by the hospital's patient restraint policy. CMS is very specific about the use of handcuffs in the patient restraint process, and although they do not outlaw their use, they do outline a specific response that includes immediate notification of law enforcement personnel. In short, CMS does not want to see handcuffs used in the patient restraint process unless an arrest is imminent. As a result, many healthcare organizations have reevaluated handcuffs and flex cuffs for their usefulness and application in the hospital setting. An increasing number of hospitals have forbidden security officers to carry handcuffs, to prevent inappropriate use.

The healthcare organization and security administrator should carefully consider the use of handcuffs, as the security officer will frequently use them when responding to major disturbances and other out-of-control situations. In one such situation, officers were called to a medical center parking lot on reports of a man kicking and screaming inside a parked vehicle. As the security officer approached the vehicle, the man exited it and charged the officer. A struggle ensued, and with the help of a second officer, the man was controlled with handcuffs. The man quit struggling as soon as the handcuffs were applied, and one of the officers discovered that the man had quit breathing. Medical assistance was immediately summoned and CPR was initiated. Unfortunately, in this case the man died and the police began an investigation.

In the initial stages of the investigation, a little-known phenomenon called Sudden In Custody Death Syndrome (SICDS) was found. The majority of SICDS cases involve respiratory difficulties brought on by a variety of factors that lead to asphyxia. Asphyxia refers to either reduced oxygen, or elevated levels of carbon dioxide, that leads to the body tissue not getting sufficient oxygen.[8] Persons who are on drugs, abuse alcohol, have a mental illness, or are obese are at greater risk for asphyxia in stressful situations. In physically restraining persons, officers should not leave them on their stomach any longer than necessary, or apply weight to their back or chest (compressing the rib cage). In addition, officers should be cognizant that a person's resistance to physical control may be a struggle for oxygen, as opposed to continued resistance to the restraint. In a review of 21 cases where patients died unexpectedly while being physically restrained, the prone position was associated with each case.[9]

Quality handcuffs are a necessity. In some embarrassing instances, handcuffs had to be cut off a person due to a malfunctioning lock. All handcuffs carried by security officers should operate with the same type of key. Because handcuffs reinforce the police image, they should be completely enclosed within a leather case rather than carried exposed. The line inspection discussed in Chapter 7, "Leadership and Professional Development," should include a physical examination of the officer's handcuffs on a routine basis.

FLASHLIGHT

A flashlight should be carried by all security officers, regardless if working during the day or at night. It is the piece of equipment most often found lacking when reviewing officers in the field. The reluctance to carry a flashlight may be due in part to its size and weight. The newer LED flashlights are more compact than the older two or three-cell C battery flashlights commonly carried by security staff (and often the source of reluctance for carrying). Today's lights have a tactical level output that is also far superior to the older styles. Larger flashlights or lantern-type lights can be stored for special use.

PERSONAL PROTECTIVE EQUIPMENT

The use of gloves in the healthcare setting has escalated in the past 15 years for all staff working in patient care delivery systems. One organization alone, the Mayo Clinic in Rochester, Minnesota, reports using an estimated 10 million pairs of gloves per year. The advent of AIDS and mandates by the Occupational Safety and Health Administration (OSHA) have made gloves a major supply item in the healthcare environment. Gloves offer protection against the transmission of disease and have, thus, become a primary item to be carried by the healthcare security officer. In some settings, security obtains the protective gloves in the nursing unit where their assistance is required, thus obviating the need to carry multiple pairs.

Gloves are the most common type of personal protective equipment (PPE) used in healthcare settings. However, it is reported that as many as 17% of healthcare workers have latex allergies—some so severe they have been forced out of their careers. In addition, powdered gloves create a source of airborne allergen that circulates freely through the air. The use of nonpowdered gloves, gloves with a low latex level, or nonlatex gloves should be considered in equipping security personnel.[10]

Gloves should fit the user's hand comfortably—they should not be too loose or too tight. They also should not tear or damage easily. Gloves are sometimes worn for several hours and need to stand up to the task.

OSHA standards for healthcare workers on blood borne pathogens and tuberculosis provides specific guidance to assist the healthcare security administrator in knowing what other PPE should be provided to security staff. Examples beyond gloves are:

- Goggles to protect the eyes
- Face shields to protect the entire face
- Gowns/aprons to protect skin and/or clothing
- Masks and respirators to protect mouth/nose and the respiratory tract from airborne infectious agents

Under OSHA's General Duty Clause, the healthcare security administrator should recognize that PPE is required for any potential infectious disease exposure. When selecting PPE, there are three key things that should be considered:[11]

1. **The type of anticipated exposure.** This is determined by the type of anticipated exposure, such as touch, splashes, or sprays, or large volumes of blood or body fluids that might penetrate clothing. PPE selection, in particular the combination of PPE, also is determined by the category of isolation precautions a patient is on.
2. **Durability and appropriateness of the PPE for the task.** This will affect, for example, whether a gown or apron is selected for PPE, or, if a gown is selected, whether it needs to be fluid resistant, fluid proof, or neither.
3. **Fit.** How many times have you seen someone trying to work in PPE that is too small or large? PPE must fit the individual user, and it is up to the healthcare organization to ensure that all PPE are available in sizes appropriate for the workforce that must be protected.

Security staff must learn to use PPE when a disaster strikes. The Public Health Security and Bioterrorism Preparedness and Response Act of 2002 recognizes emergency room workers as major responders to the problem of terrorism, and it promotes a national curriculum of training to respond to biological agents. Security staff falls under this guidance and needs personal protection and training so they do not become victims themselves. As first receivers treat victims, security officers will likely maintain order and control traffic and access by victims who may be in a state of panic and need to be decontaminated and quarantined. Security staff must understand the PPE available to them and be properly trained on how to safely don and remove it if such circumstances should arise.

A close working relationship between clinical staff and security can contribute to the most appropriate use of PPE by security. Clinicians with knowledge of the patient's medical condition can, in most circumstances, guide security to wear the correct PPE in a given situation. Universal precautions, designed to protect workers from diseases spread by blood and certain body fluids, are taught and practiced in most healthcare environments.

CONDUCTED ELECTRICAL WEAPONS (TASERS)

While firearms can save the life of a healthcare security officer, they can also be dangerous to the person using them for protection, such as getting into the hands of the opponent. Many medical facilities face a higher risk surrounding the high-risk patient population served, including the homeless, the mentally challenged, and incarcerated patients. For this reason, many healthcare security programs have turned to alternative means of protecting security staff, including the use of conducted electrical weapons such as the Taser.

The Taser is a less-than-lethal device and the most popular conducted electrical weapon (CEW) used in medical facilities today. Tasers are protective weapons designed to incapacitate a person from a safe distance while reducing the likelihood of serious injuries or death.[12] Different from other less-than-lethal weapons such as chemical agents, Tasers do not solely rely on pain compliance. They affect the sensory and motor functions of the nervous system to achieve incapacitation.[12]

The weapon can be used from distances greater than those needed to use an aerosol spray, allowing the deploying officer not to have to go hands on with the opponent. In addition to looking similar and handling like a gun, the Taser can be controlled by the officer. Unlike other use of force options, the effect ends at the moment the Taser 5-second cycle is completed.

Safety is an important factor in the use of Tasers in the healthcare setting. When deployed, the use of spotters is highly recommended to prevent the assailant from falling, a more common cause of injury than deployment of the Taser. However, getting in close enough proximity is not always possible.

While the number of hospitals that use Taser electronic control devices pales in comparison to those that do not, use continues to increase, with many more healthcare facilities now considering the weapons. The October 2012 ASHE survey of U.S. hospitals illustrates that 13% of hospital security departments equip their security officers with Tasers and another 5% do not use but are testing electronic control devices.[3] Hennepin County Medical Center in Minneapolis engaged a team of doctors, led by Jeff Ho, MD, its security leaders and other stakeholders who spent a year studying the viability of introducing Tasers and other technologies that might improve officer and hospital staff safety. Before approving the use of Tasers, they reviewed safety and security best practices within healthcare security and gathered information on past incidents, conducted interviews and studied other hospital security programs. The team also considered a variety of other supplemental security devices and options. Before final implementation, the team had to convince many physicians and staff members who were against the use of Tasers on philosophical grounds, including the strong belief by some doctors and nurses that no use of force should ever be employed on a patient.[13]

Tasers are commonly used by law enforcement agencies within the United States as a complement to their firearms. In contrast, many healthcare security programs have displaced the firearm with the Taser. The device is considered a more suitable, less-than-lethal option, if an escalated use of force tool is warranted.

Most healthcare protection professionals agree that the less-lethal use of force option provided by the Taser is a better tool than the firearm, to combat most escalated situations confronting the healthcare security officer. Many healthcare emergency departments have requested the Taser to be carried by hospital security departments, as the mere presence of the weapon on the side of a security officer has been found to de-escalate physically acting out patients, who have not succumbed to more traditional de-escalation techniques. However, this practice is closely scrutinized by CMS and must be carefully monitored. CMS Interpretive Guidelines §482.13(e) states:

> The term "weapon" includes, but is not limited to, pepper spray, mace, nightsticks, Tasers, cattle prods, stun guns, and pistols. Security staff may carry weapons as allowed by hospital policy, and State and Federal law. However, the use of weapons by security staff is considered a law enforcement action, not a health care intervention. CMS does not support the use of weapons by any hospital staff as a means of subduing a patient in order to place that patient in restraint or seclusion. If a weapon is used by security or law enforcement personnel on a person in a hospital (patient, staff, or visitor) to protect people or hospital property from harm, we would expect the situation to be handled as a criminal activity and the perpetrator be placed in the custody of local law enforcement.

St. John's Hospital in Springfield, Missouri discontinued having their safety and security officers carry Tasers after the hospital examined the CMS regulations.[14] CMS has threatened to pull funding from a number of hospitals for improper use of Tasers. CMS officials found that psychiatric patients at Martin Luther King Jr./Drew Medical Center in Los Angeles were in "immediate jeopardy" of harm, because police officers assigned to the facility were using Tasers and leather restraints to control them. A federal report released details of eight cases where Tasers were used at the hospital.[15]

The use of Tasers is not without critics. The Canadian Medical Association published an editorial in its May 20, 2008 *Journal* calling for healthcare professionals to exclude themselves from using Tasers—calling for randomized testing of Taser guns and subjecting the devices to more objective, rigorous, and independent scientific testing standards and research.[16]

The death of Polish immigrant Robert Dziekanski, after he was stunned several times with a Taser by the RCMP at Vancouver International Airport in October, 2007, has led to more intense scrutiny on the use of Tasers in Canada. Dziekanski, who did not speak English, became agitated after spending more than 9 hours wandering in the airport arrivals area, and was confronted by four RCMP members. He was "tazed" after failing to comply with police instructions, and subsequently died of a heart attack. In 2013 a British Columbia coroner ruled his death a homicide. Taser use by police in British Columbia has fallen 87% since Dziekanski's death.[17]

Emergency medical service providers are seeing more patients who have been subjected to the application of a Taser. An independent study assessing 1,201 patients who had been injured from Tasers found serious injury occurred in only 3 patients. No cardiac dysrhythmias associated with the Taser were documented.[18] Data shared in a study of 75 cases of Taser-related deaths found that sudden deaths can and do occur after Taser use. A common factor in these deaths is extreme agitation, often in the setting of stimulant drug use and/or preexisting heart disease. However, no conclusive direct link to fatal injury has been made.[19] A U.S. Department of Justice-funded study found that (Tasers) are not risk-free; 99.5% of study subjects did not experience significant injuries following a Taser deployment.

The cornerstone of a Taser program is having proper policies, training and oversight in place. Every use of force by security staff involves some liability and litigation risk. For the healthcare organization, they should take responsibility for developing a specific use of force policy and training related to the use of Tasers. Procedural guidelines must be in place to include specific deployment and post-deployment policies and procedures. Taser International does not provide specific policy recommendations to law enforcement agencies; hospital administrators must provide their own guidelines. Many hospitals who have deployed Tasers are willing to share their policies, address common concerns and training procedures and share general insights, and should be consulted.

Deployment of the Taser must be legally justifiable and in accordance with applicable laws and the federal, state/provincial and local level as well as comply with CMS, Joint Commission and other legal requirements.[20] Use of force policies must meet hospital guidelines and be based on community standards and the varying levels of the types of responses available to the security program. Security leaders must work with hospital administrators to ensure new policies meet guidelines set forth by governing standards and hospital or health system leadership. Policy on the use of force should incorporate restrictions outlined in Figure 9-7, Taser Affidavit of Use, and reference the CMS interpretive guideline noted above.

Many security programs supplement their officer's skill sets with aggression management/crisis intervention training. This follows closely with the research conducted by the American College of Emergency Physicians (ACEP) whose Research Forum Abstract, titled "Evaluation of the Use of the Taser and the Elevated Force to Control Workplace Violence in the Health Care Environment," recommends that hospitals include "staff education for early identification of potentially violent persons and initial approaches but allows for the use of Taser in select situations." Thus, training should be specific to the healthcare environment based upon the guidelines that security leaders, hospital administrators and the Taser instructor have issued as part of their protocols.

Oregon Health & Science University (OHSU) has a panel comprised of representatives from its legal, clinical and administrative departments that review every incident in which an officer removes his or her Taser from its holster, even in cases where the device is not used. This is, and should be, considered a deployment.[20]

TASER USE AND SAFETY AFFIDAVIT

Security personnel who have been trained to carry the X26 Taser **MUST** adhere to the following Policies and Procedures.

1. Before going on duty the X26 Taser and the holster must be carefully inspected to ensure that the device is fully charged and operational according to specifications, and the holster is in such condition as to provide for the security of the device.

2. The security of the X26 Taser is the responsibility of the officer to whom the device was assigned. Under no circumstances shall the officer leave the device unsecured. The X26 Taser, in the wrong hands, could represent a serious threat to innocent persons in a healthcare setting.

3. If the X26 Taser is damaged during the officer's shift, a Security Incident Report must be written documenting the nature of the damage and how the damage occurred. This information must be given to the shift supervisor before the end of the shift or the security supervisor at the earliest practical time.

4. Officers must carry the X26 Taser with the safety slide in the SAFE position.

5. The X26 Taser is a device of last resort. T.E.A.M. (Techniques for Effective Aggression Management) should be employed whenever appropriate, unless the subject becomes physically aggressive and represents a threat of injury to persons present. If it becomes apparent to the officer that the subject's behavior is escalating, always call for assistance. A show of force is often the best way to restrain aggressive behavior. The X26 Taser may be used when physical force is legally justified to prevent the reasonable foreseeable threat or actual attempted assault, battery, and/or injury to officers, other persons, and/or the subject. When practicable, avoid prolonged or continuous exposure(s) to the Taser device electrical discharge. The stress and exertion of extensive repeated, prolonged, or continuous application(s) of the Taser device may contribute to cumulative exhaustion, stress, and associated medical risk(s). Severe exhaustion and/or overexertion from physical struggle, drug intoxication, use of restraint devices, etc. may result in serious injury or death. The Taser device causes strong muscle contractions, usually rendering a subject temporarily unable to control his or her movements. Under certain circumstances, these contractions may impair a subject's ability to breathe. If a person's system is already compromised by overexertion, drug intoxication, stress, pre-existing medical or psychological condition(s), etc. any physical exertion, including the use of a Taser device, may have an additive effect in contribution to cumulative exhaustion, stress, cardiovascular conditions, and associated medical risk(s). To minimize the risk of injury, consider the following:
   a. Begin restraint procedures as soon as it is reasonably safe to do so in order to minimize the total duration of exertion and stress experienced by the subject. Avoid touching the probes and wires and the areas between the probes during Taser electrical discharge.
   b. If a Taser device application is ineffective in achieving the desired effect, consider reloading and redeploying or using other force option(s).
   c. If a subject is exhibiting signs or behaviors that are associated with Sudden In-Custody Death Syndrome, consider combining use of a Taser Device with immediate physical restraint techniques and medical assistance.

   Great justification must be provided when the X26 Taser is used against a pregnant female, children, seniors, restrained subjects, and passive individuals who are being arrested. Only when these subjects represent a serious threat of injury to the officers or others should the use of the X26 Taser be considered. The X26 Taser may also be used if the subject represents a serious threat to him/herself.

FIGURE 9-7

Example of security officer Taser affidavit training.

(Courtesy of HSS Inc., Denver, Colorado)

6. ECD (Electronic Control Device) use:
    a. "ECD Displayed:" The ECD is withdrawn from the holster and visible to the subject. The subject complies without further use of the ECD.
    b. "ECD Laser Painted:" The ECD's laser is activated and pointed in the direction of the subject and in response to the Laser printing, the subject complies without further use of the ECD.
    c. "ECD Demonstrated:" The ECD is withdrawn from the holster, the air cartridge removed and the electrical arcing is demonstrated to the subject to attempt to gain voluntary compliance.
    d. "ECD Deploys:" The ECD probes contact the subject's body or clothing and/or a touch stun is used to attempt to gain compliance.

7. Centers for Medicaid & Medicare Services (CMS) does not approve of the use of weapons by any hospital staff as a means of subduing a patient to place that patient in restraint/seclusion. If a weapon is used by security or law enforcement personnel on a person in a hospital (patient, staff, visitor) to protect people or hospital property from harm, we would expect the situation to be handled as a criminal activity and the perpetrator to be turned over local law enforcement. Again, CMS does not consider the use of weapons as safe appropriate "health care" interventions and their use is not appropriate in the application of patient restraint or initiation of seclusion.

8. Never use the X26 Taser near flammable liquids, fumes, or explosive environments.

9. Keep hands away from the front of the unit at all times unless the safety slide is in the SAFE position and the X26 Taser is deactivated.

10. DO NOT fire the X26 Taser near flammable liquids, fumes, or explosive environments.

11. No officer will playfully, maliciously, or intentionally misuse the X26 Taser in a display of power against an individual, except to counter an imminent threat. Violation of this policy will result in disciplinary action.

12. Probes – Biohazard:
    a. Probes that have been deployed and strike the subject will be treated as biohazard sharps. They may be placed point down into the expended cartridge bores and secured (e.g., with latex glove(s), tape, etc.
    b. Where ECD probe deployment is not a reasonably foreseeable issue, and where there is no indication of serious injury, probes and expended cartridges need not be routinely maintained as evidence. They shall be properly disposed of.
    c. If the incident is non-routine, or if serious injury is alleged, then the probes and the expended cartridge(s) shall be maintained as evidence appropriately secured and marked as biohazard.

13. Anytime an officer discharges the X26 Taser, even if the discharge was accidental, a Security Incident Report must be written detailing the nature and reason for the discharge and the supervisor must be immediately notified.

14. When the X26 Taser is used against a person, the person must be evaluated by trained healthcare professionals and monitored for the individual's safety.

PRINT NAME________________________ SIGNATURE___________________ DATE________

WITNESS______________________ DATE_________________

FIGURE 9-7 Continued

It is important to note that ACEP's abstract reports that "when systematic approaches to violent persons do not work, (security) officers require additional means of elevated force to control dangerous behavior. The use of the Taser offers an option that is more effective than baton but less lethal than a firearm." In other words, Taser can be an appropriate response in a hospital setting. They can reduce liability exposure while protecting patients and staff. As with all considerations of force, the proper steps must be taken to ensure successful outcomes for all parties.

CHEMICAL AGENTS

Chemical agents are quite popular in security work; it is estimated that approximately 10–20% of hospital security departments employ chemical agents, with mace and pepper spray being the most commonly carried agents. The use of such defensive equipment has decreased quite substantially over the last ten years, mostly due to the increased utilization of the Taser in the healthcare environment. There are other distinct types of gases: CN gas, CS gas, and oleoresin capsicum (OC spray), a pepper spray commonly used by law enforcement agents and security officers in Australia and the U.S. In Canada and the U.K., it would be rare to find an organization where healthcare security officers carry chemical agents.

Each of these chemical irritants are nonlethal alternatives that can only be used when a security officer is in close proximity to an assailant. Emitting a liquid mix of chemicals, or peppers in the case of capsicum, the intention is to momentarily blind a person and cause temporary pain and discomfort when sprayed in an assailant's face. The use of these canister-type sprays is legal in most states and countries.

Research indicates the effectiveness of chemical agents is somewhat limited by the need for direct eye impact to achieve a rapid reaction. Studies also show severe skin pain starts within 3 seconds and lasts for about 5 to 6 minutes. In addition, there is some question as to the effects of chemical irritants on different types of people. In some cases, no chemical agent will be effective on people under the influence of alcohol or drugs, emotionally disturbed or on focused, combative individuals. People must be able to feel or react to pain for the chemical agent to be effective.

Due to the fear of contaminating inpatient units, many hospitals prohibit the use of chemical agents in their use of force continuum. The concern is if the chemical agent gets into the heating, ventilation, and air conditioning (HVAC) system, the hospital may be forced to evacuate the patient care area. The risk of contamination has been lowered by using pepper foam, which also carries health risks for people who have medical conditions such as asthma or emphysema.[21] This potential risk is worsened if an individual or area is not properly decontaminated after a deployment of the chemical agent.

As pointed out with Tasers, CMS has underscored in its interpretive guidelines specific regulations regarding patient rights, and in particular the use of weapons by any hospital staff as a means of subduing a patient, in order to place that patient in restraint or seclusion: "it is not considered a safe appropriate healthcare intervention."[7] Chemical agents and specifically pepper spray are noted as weapons.

If the healthcare organization elects to allow chemical agents to be carried by security staff, their continued use should be based on consistent training related to when and how the agent is carried and under what circumstances it should be used.

BATONS

The nightstick, or baton, is considered by some to be an attractive alternative to firearms. As security equipment, it is not widely used. This weapon is often associated with brutality and has a more negative connotation for the public than firearms do. Those who favor the baton argue it is a discriminating weapon that copes with the problem at hand, and makes contact only with the intended person. It is difficult, however, to avoid head strikes in many cases. Paralysis or death may occur even days later as a result of subdural or bilateral hematoma.

The collapsible baton has gained considerable favor and can be carried on the duty belt without the same negative perception. The small compact size of this baton eliminates many of the arguments against the use of the regular nightstick or baton. However, its use can still be perceived as undue force. For this reason, most healthcare security programs prohibit their use.

PROTECTIVE VESTS

The advent of soft-bodied armor vests used by many law enforcement agencies has spawned some interest for the healthcare security industry. Today's protective vests are thin enough to be concealed under a uniform shirt. Alternatively, few healthcare security programs wear protective vests on top of their clothing. Whether they choose to conceal the protective vest depends on what type of image the healthcare security program wants to provide to the public.

A survey of 79 hospitals, all in large U.S. cities, indicates very limited use of these protective vests. The hospitals surveyed averaged 318 beds; no hospital with fewer than 200 beds was included in the survey. Results of the survey indicated that 10% had formulated a policy on the use of protective vests. In most cases where vests are utilized, the policy provides that security officers buy their vest and use is optional.[22] Healthcare organizations with employees who are authorized to carry a firearm should strongly encourage their employees to wear protective vests.

Protective vests are not just for firearm combat situations; they can also be worn to shield security officers from the harm of other weapons. In Ireland, security staff at Mercy University Hospital, a city center hospital in Cork, have taken to wearing stab-resistant vests to protect themselves against stabbings. The hospital is believed to be the first in Ireland to wear the protective vests in response to two doctors injured in a stabbing incident involving a psychiatric patient.[23] This follows a trend in the United Kingdom and New Zealand, where hospital security staff are frequently equipped with stab-proof vests, shields, and helmets to protect them against violent patients and relatives. The protective vests have improved security staff morale and contained workers compensation costs. The UK National Health Service estimates that violence costs their hospitals around £100,000 a year in security, time off for affected staff, and legal costs.[24]

Interestingly, the use of protective vests by healthcare security officers in Canada is much more prevalent than the carrying of batons or chemical agents.

Security staff must remember that protective vests only provide partial protection, not absolute protection. A significant residual risk remains even if vests are worn.

BODY CAMERAS

In hopes to deter antisocial behavior and provide evidence for prosecution against violent offenders, hospital security programs have begun to introduce body cameras for security officers. Three hospitals of the NHS Foundation Trust in the UK have invested in this camera technology to help act as a deterrent to events of violence, aggression and acts of antisocial behavior. According to Jug Johal, the trust's head of security, the body cameras support the police and NHS prosecutions against those who commit crimes against trust staff, property, patients and visitors.[25]

There are many wearable, rugged video camera options on the market today. The technology is widely used by law enforcement and the military although it is not widely used in healthcare security programs in Canada or the U.S. today. The benefit of having the security officer actions captured both visually and by sound has been proven to help defuse many situations without further escalation. Advancements in digital camera technology and the video evidence collected when coupled with a more economic price point leads to the anticipation of wider adoption by healthcare security programs throughout the world.

THE DUTY BELT

One of the most important parts of the security officer's uniform is the duty belt, on which security officers carry the equipment that must be with them at all times. At minimum, the healthcare security officer duty belt should consist of a tactical flashlight and holder, a radio and holster and include a key keeper. If organizationally permitted, it could also include a handgun and/or Taser and holster, handcuffs, baton, or chemical spray. Some will also carry their own small notebooks and ink pen, and may also carry a cell phone or other electronic device. All of the equipment carried by the security officer on the duty belt must be evenly distributed across the belt so it is less likely to shift or cause back strain.

Many of the items listed are not lightweight items, but heavy duty, high performance equipment. With few exceptions, the gear that is carried is decided by the healthcare organization, not individual judgment. Hospital security staff are advised to be prepared for any situation, but if the duty belt weighs so much that it fatigues the officer, shifts around while on patrol or responding to a critical event, or does not allow free movement, it can be more of a hindrance than a help. A strict policy of authorized equipment should be prepared that includes standards for how the duty belt is to be worn and what equipment can or is required to be carried.

The traditional use of leather duty belts has given ground to the use of nylon. Nylon has certain advantages over leather:

- It is fairly easy to decontaminate.
- It is durable and therefore lasts a long time.
- It is lightweight.
- It is scratch-resistant and won't stretch.
- It is cost-competitive with leather.

A subject that ties directly to the equipment used by healthcare security officers is the escalating use of force policy that every healthcare security program should have in place. In the context of force, the security officer must be aware of how the equipment operates, possess a clear understanding of when it should be used, and the limitations that may exist with using equipment to facilitate a patient outcome.

USE OF FORCE

The use of force by healthcare security officers is sometimes necessary to maintain order and safeguard staff, patients and visitors in a healthcare environment. The security officer must occasionally use a certain amount of force, from mere presence and verbal persuasion to physical intervention, in order to overcome resistance and ensure compliance with hospital policy and medical care plans.

As outlined in this chapter, there are various tools and mandated limitations on the use of force in the healthcare setting. In Garcia v. Bronx Lebanon Hospital, 2001 WL 128893 N.E. 2d-NY, the appellate courts ruled:

> "even assuming the (security officers) were justified in using force to subdue the patient because of his own inappropriate conduct; the court found an issue remained as to whether the degree of force used was reasonable under the circumstances. Even if the use of force was justified, the security (officers) could lawfully use only that amount of force necessary to control the patient, no more!"[26]

Every healthcare facility should develop a use of force policy that includes the identification of situations, both clinical and nonclinical, in which security officers are permitted to use force. IAHSS has developed two guidelines that outline the basic aspects of such a plan and speak to the use of defensive equipment and use of force techniques.

02.02.05 USE OF FORCE

Statement

Healthcare Facilities (HCFs) will develop policies and procedures that include the identification of situations, both clinical and nonclinical, in which security is permitted to use force. The amount of force to be used will be that which is objectively reasonable and takes into account the totality of the circumstances.

Intent

a) Use of force is defined as any force beyond a guiding touch. Applicable government requirements, accreditation and regulatory guidelines should be consulted in the development of this policy.

b) The policy should contain a use of force educational element such as a matrix or a continuum. This element would provide guidance to security detailing appropriate response to the level of resistance being encountered.

c) The HCF will determine if weapons are to be carried by security personnel. This decision should be based on a security assessment of the individual facility, local crime statistics and other factors as deemed necessary and will help determine what specific weapons, if any, are authorized.

d) The HCF will determine what physical restraints, if any, will be carried by security personnel and under what circumstances they may be used (written in accordance with IAHSS Guideline 02.04 – Security Role in Patient Management). Also, as part of the security assessment this decision would be based on a calculated need as indicated by past experience and current environment.

e) Terms such as "least amount of force" or "only necessary force" should be avoided. The recommended terms "objectively reasonable", the "totality of the circumstances" and "reasonably appears necessary" have been court tested and are preferred.

f) The HCF will provide initial and ongoing training of policies and procedures to include the physical skills training necessary to demonstrate competency in the use of force. This training will be documented and maintained as part of security's training records (written in accordance with IAHSS Guideline 03.01 – Security Officer Training).

g) All incidents involving the use of force by security will be documented. A special use of force form may be maintained as part of the original report of the incident.

References

- Graham v. Conner 490 U.S. 386 104 L. Ed. 2d 443, 190 S. Ct. 1865 (1989)
- International Association of Chiefs of Police National Law Enforcement Policy Center USE OF FORCE Model Policy, August 2001
- Journal of Healthcare Protection Management, IAHSS 2007 Volume 22, No. 2, Page 15, Use of Force in Private Security: A Primer.

Approved: November 2007
Last Revised: October 2012

02. PROGRAM MANAGEMENT

05. Security Officer Use of Force

01. Defensive Equipment and Use of Force Techniques

Statement

How to use, when to use and who can use force must be addressed by all Healthcare Facilities (HCFs). The consideration, selection, and implementation of use of force techniques and defensive equipment are the responsibility of the HCF.

05. Security Officer Use of Force

01. Defensive Equipment and Use of Force Techniques

Intent

a. The HCF should develop a use of force policy that identifies the guiding principles as to when and how the use of force is authorized. The HCF should consider implementing a use of force continuum that complies with applicable laws and regulations and addresses the level in which defensive equipment and techniques are used to protect or meet resistance.

b. A security assessment should be conducted to determine risks to the specific HCF environment. The selection of defensive equipment and use of force should be based on identified risks, aligned with approved de-escalation techniques and be a multidisciplinary leadership team decision. Only HCF approved defensive equipment and use of force should be deployed and utilized.

c. Develop a written procedure for the deployment and use of each type of defensive equipment utilized by the HCF which may include a service baton, shields, incapacitating agents, handcuffs, Taser, or firearm.

d. Develop a plan to authorize and train selected staff members in the use of each type of approved defensive equipment and use of force technique. Training should address competency before initial deployment. Ongoing training should be provided as needed or in compliance with required applicable laws and regulatory agencies.

e. Develop a procedure for the rendering of medical treatment, if necessary, to any injured party following the use of defensive equipment or use of force.

f. A defined incident review process should be in place to evaluate the appropriateness of the deployment of defensive equipment and use of force.

See also

- IAHSS Basic Industry Guideline 02.05 Security Officer Use of Physical Force

Approved: July 2012

TRAINING

Deciding on the proper equipment to be used by security officers is an important first step, but it does not end there. The proper use of each item is essential. Initial officer training must be supplemented with periodic retraining. Equipping the officer with nonessential items needlessly increases the training time and the resulting program cost.

SECURITY OPERATIONS MANUAL

The security operations manual brings together the security policy, standards, and general procedures. This manual should not be confused with the employee handbook, which basically contains the personnel policies of the organization. It is intended to furnish security officers with the information needed to perform their job effectively. The content of this manual varies from organization to organization. The typical manual includes the following general information:

1. Purpose and scope of the healthcare organization.
   - Table of organization
   - Key personnel (possibly with pictures)
   - Plot plans
2. Purpose and scope of the security program
   - Organizational chart
   - Position descriptions (brief narratives)
   - General and special orders
   - Training program
3. Security records and reports.
   - Types
   - Intended utilization
   - Distribution
4. General security information.
   - Use and care of equipment
   - Fire and safety information

The style, format, and content of the security manual are determined by individual program preference. A loose-leaf notebook is one style that permits the easy insertion of revised information or additional material. A powerful new piece of technology is to store the security manual electronically and make it available to the security officer via personal digital assistant (PDA). Carried on the duty belt, and typically small enough to fit in the palm of the hand, these pocket PCs have proven to be invaluable time savers. Communications can be automated and provide security officers with updated checklists and instructions for their day-to-day activities and patrol. Also used for real-time incident notification, this technology can be a valuable resource to security officers who need to view a CCTV image or refer to their specific response during a hospital disaster.

REFERENCES

1. Lutz S. Border hospital's guard garb ripped. *Modern Healthcare* 1990, December 17;**8**.
2. Weonik R. *Securing our hospitals: GE security and IAHSS healthcare benchmarking study*. Presented at International Association for Healthcare Security and Safety Mid-Winter Meeting and Seminar; 2008, January 21.
3. Burmahl Beth, Hoppszallern Suzanna. Converging Worlds – 2012 Hospital Security Survey. *Health Facilities Management* 2012, October:24. Available from www.hfmmagazine.com.
4. Potter AN. *Considerations when arming hospital security officers*. Dissertion to Board of Directors, International Healthcare Security and Safety Foundation; 2006. p. 8. Retrieved March 31, 2009 from http://www.iahss.org/Ref-Materials/Potter-Paper/Contents.htm.
5. Thompson B. *Hospital security and personnel safety concerns*. Presented at Henry Ford Medical Center; 2005, March 3.
6. 6 requirements your radios should address. *Campus Safety*. 2009, April 8. Retrieved April 9, 2009, from http://www.campussafetymagazine.com/MotoEpromo.

7. Department of Health and Human Services. *Hospital conditions of participation: Patient rights*. 2006, December 8. Retrieved June 16, 2008, from http://www.cms.hhs.gov/CFCsAndCoPs/downloads/finalpatientrightsrule.pdf. §482.13(e).
8. McCauley D. Gasping for breath. *Police* 1996, July:56–8.
9. Roberts JR. *The acutely agitated patient: Fatalities and physiology*. Emergency Medicine News; 2007, September. Retrieved April 4, 2009, from http://www.em-news.com/pt/re/emmednews/fulltext.00132981-200709000-00029.htm.
10. Confronting and dealing with problems of latex-based products. *Hospital Security and Safety Management* 1997, March;**17**(11):5–7.
11. Centers for Disease Control. Guidance for the selection and use of personal protective equipment (PPE) in healthcare settings. Retrieved April 4, 2009, from http://www.cdc.gov/ncidod/dhqp/pdf/ppe/PPEslides6-29-04.pdf.
12. Taser International. *Instructor certification course, version 14.2*. 2008, September 9. p. 13. Retrieved June 17, 2009, from http://www.taser.com/training/Documents/Training%20Bulletin%2014.2-01.pdf.
13. Security Management Staff. *How to develop a Taser program*. Security Management. ASIS International; 2013, July. p. 48–52.
14. *St. John's officers to stop carrying Tasers*. Springfield News-Leader; 2008, September 9. Retrieved September 9, 2008, from http://www.news-leader.com/article/20090405/NEWS01/904051542/1007/NEWS01.
15. Hospitals debate stun gun use in security departments. *Environment of Care Leader* 2004, July 26;**9**(14):7.
16. Stanbrook MB. Tasers in medicine: An irreverent call for proposals. *Canadian Medical Association Journal* 2008, May 20;**178**(11). Retrieved April 3, 2009, from http://www.cmaj.ca/content/vol178/issue11/#EDITORIAL.
17. *Dziekanski death at hands of RCMP a homicide, BC coroner rules*. CBC News; 2013, April 8. Retrieved April 30, 2014, from http://www.cbc.ca/news/canada/british-columbia/dziekanski-death-at-hands-of-rcmp-a-homicide-b-c-coroner-rules-1.1411262.
18. Bozeman WP, Hauda WE, Heck JJ, Graham Jr DD, Martin BP, Winslow JE. Safety and injury profile of conducted electrical weapons used by law enforcement officers against criminal suspects. *Annals of Emergency Medicine* 2009, April;**53**(4):480–9.
19. Strote J, Hutson HR. Taser use in restraint-related deaths. *Prehospital Emergency Care* 2006, December;**10**(4): 447–50.
20. Tuttle Steve. *Deploying stun guns in healthcare facilities*. Campus Safety Magazine.com; 2010, May 3. Retrieved May 13, 2010, from http://www.campussafetymagazine.com/Channel/Hospital-Security/Articles/2010/05/Deploying-Stun-Guns-in-Healthcare-Facilities.aspx.
21. Stefan S. *Emergency department treatment of the psychiatric patient: Policy issues and legal requirements*. New York: Oxford University Press; 2006. 37.
22. Bakos B. *Utilization of bullet-resistant vests in healthcare facilities*. Unpublished research study; 1993, July. 1–11.
23. O'Regan E. *Security staff don stab vests as hospital knife crime risks rise*. 2008, September 10. Independent.ie. Retrieved June 18, 2009, from http://www.independent.ie/national-news/security-staff–don-stab-vests-as-hospital-knife-crime-risks-rise-1472815.html.
24. *Hospital staff to wear stab-proof vests as violent patients on the increase*. Evening Standard; 2007, June 3. Retrieved June 18, 2009, from http://www.thisislondon.co.uk/news/article-23387896-details/Hospital+staff+to+wear+stab-proof+vests+as+violent+patients+on+the+increase/article.do.
25. BBC News Staff. *Body cameras for hospital guards*. BBC News, 2010, February 2. Retrieved February 2, 2010, from http://news.bbc.co.uk/2/hi/uk_news/england/humber/8492681.stm.
26. Tammelleo AD. *NY: Hospital security guards subdue patient: Was more than minimum necessary force used? Hospital Law's Regan Report*, 2001, October 1. Retrieved April 10, 2009, from http://www.allbusiness.com/professional-scientific-technical-services/legal-services/823589-1.html.

CHAPTER 10

TRAINING AND DEVELOPMENT

Security officers are the first line of defense for patients and staff, underscoring the need for a well-trained security force. The need for adequate training of security personnel is vigorously espoused by management and front-line personnel alike. It is a subject that receives constant attention at security meetings and seminars, is probed during security reviews and audits, gets considerable space in magazines, newsletters, and journals, is sanctioned by consumers and providers, and is the basis of many lawsuits. However, this almost insatiable quest for proper training appears to break down at the design and implementation stage in many healthcare security programs.

One of the most critical challenges—and one of the most basic responsibilities—of the healthcare facility and the security administrator, is to provide the means for each person in the security department to achieve the competency level required to perform the function as stated in the job description. A good security officer training program requires a master plan that addresses everything from identifying needs for the newly hired security officer, to ongoing education and development activities established for seasoned security staff and security leadership positions. It cannot be overstated how important it is to have clearly identified learning outcomes and a method to verify that the training received resulted in an accepted level of competency for those learning outcomes. The quality of security staff training is critical to the overall success of the security program and a direct reflection on the healthcare facility philosophy of patient care and commitment to employee safety.

Currently, there are no federal guidelines governing mandatory training or a universal training standard for security officers. In many instances, the only training requirements that exist are those promulgated at the state or provincial level governing basic security licensing requirements. However, there are certain basic elements or steps in the training and development process that must be addressed and customized to be relevant to the individual healthcare organization. There should be a combination of universal healthcare security training with training specific to the organization. An example of this blending is that of report preparation. The basics of how to collect information and prepare a report are similar for most healthcare organizations. However, the types of reports and methods utilized to accomplish the completion of a report are specific to each organization. For example, the International Association for Healthcare Security and Safety (IAHSS) basic training manual for healthcare security officers provides a generic approach to healthcare security officer training as a foundation to be supplemented by training relative to specific facility security program tasks. Other important points to remember include:

- Job descriptions should provide the basic source of job task analysis to pinpoint specific skill levels required. Policies and procedures of the entire organization, not just security post orders and traditional practices, should be used to further define capability and skill level needs.
- Determine performance objectives, which in turn will be utilized to develop the knowledge required of the security officer to competently complete the tasks identified. The objective is what the trainee must know. Without clearly stated objectives, there can be no competency-based training.

- Develop clearly identified learning outcomes and measurement standards in order to determine whether the performance objectives of the training endeavor have been accomplished. The objective is to establish that everyone understands what is expected of them and what constitutes below average, average, and excellent performance.[1]
- Verify whether there was a sufficient transfer of information from instruction to actual situation performance. The method to verify if the training received resulted in an acceptable level of competency will depend on the circumstances.
- Develop dynamic (up-to-date) curriculum and select training methods and materials.

Litigation, particularly in the U.S., has been a powerful driving force in the evolution of healthcare security officer training. Claims that healthcare organizations have failed to provide necessary training are used with much success in lawsuits, especially those involving use of physical force, defensive equipment, false arrests, or situations resulting in the elopement or injury to a patient. A well-rounded security training program can help mitigate legal actions but, unfortunately, too many healthcare facilities learn the importance of having an adequate level of security staff training only after such negative experiences. In countries such as Australia and Canada, healthcare unions have been vocal in their efforts to ensure well-trained security personnel in their various healthcare settings.

Are there ever enough security officers to really get the job done? We too often think "more is better," but forget about the "force multiplier" of training. Most security professionals will attest that a trained security officer can be at least twice as productive as a well-intentioned but untrained officer. Ironically, it is usually easier to get resources allocated for an extra position than obtain funding for additional training. Determining the number of security personnel required to establish and maintain a secured environment should take into consideration the training required of and provided for the position. A well-trained officer is an asset to the hospital whose value only appreciates over time as he or she continues to gain valuable experience. Effective training enables the officer to put that experience into proper perspective.[2]

In healthcare facilities, extensive training is apparent in almost all departments. The medical care arena focuses on training and continuous in-service education at almost every level. Dietitians, medical technicians, health information management clerks, nursing assistants, registered nurses, and environmental services personnel undergo training in one form or another. Our demand for the highest quality healthcare requires ongoing education for healthcare providers of every description. Security should be no exception.

One of the primary obstacles that can influence training programs is security officer turnover. An organized security officer training program can reduce turnover as it improves morale and offers an avenue for personal growth. Well-trained officers who know they are competent exhibit a higher level of job interest and job satisfaction than others do. In short, the well-trained officer has a higher level of self-confidence in the duties they are expected to perform, providing for an improved perception of safety in the healthcare facility.

TRAINING CONCEPTS

The term "training" includes pre-assignment training and, more importantly, continuous training throughout the career of the security staff member. Security officers are often classified as "trained" or "not trained." This characterization should yield to the concept of level of training.

Training must be relevant. As simple and basic as this consideration seems, some training is delivered merely to fill the allotted time or because an instructor is available. An often-neglected area of training is the operational aspect of the healthcare delivery system itself. Security officers should learn how various departments and sections of the healthcare system operate to understand better what they are protecting and their role in the mission and delivery of quality patient care. The better officers understand the operations, the formal and informal hierarchy, and the history, objectives, and goals of the organization, the better equipped they will be to carry out their responsibilities. Linking security staff to the business of delivering care to patients, through education and training in this area, will strengthen the alignment of the security function with the primary purpose of the organization.

The Peace Officer Standards and Training (POST) provided to those seeking a law enforcement personnel career does not replace the need for a quality, healthcare-focused training initiative. Although some healthcare organizations have incorporated this requirement into their development program, it is suggested this, and other policing-focused training, be used to supplement the healthcare security specific training program and not replace it. Organizations relying too heavily on this type of training can find themselves at risk of being disconnected from the mission of healthcare and patient-focused goals established by the organization. An example is found in a special hospital police department at a regional hospital in the coastal mid-Atlantic region of the United States. The police training provided by the department was developed to meet the needs of the state attorney general's office, which provided the "authority" for the department. However, the training provided to newly hired officers offered no healthcare-specific understanding or context for providing such a service inside of healthcare. Ongoing development provided to supervisors and officers was solely focused on their law enforcement role, the same as if they were a community agency. This resulted in role conflict for the officers, in grasping and carrying out their primary purpose of helping provide a safe environment of care, and a high level of dissatisfaction in department performance by hospital leaders and care providers alike. The reactionary and law enforcement approach in the department placed it at odds with nursing and physicians on how to best manage acting-out patient behavior. This example is one of many in which the right balance of training of healthcare security staff was not found, causing great friction with those stakeholders who rely so heavily on the services the healthcare security industry provides.

03.01 SECURITY OFFICER TRAINING

Statement

The quality of security officer training is critical to the overall success of the Healthcare Facility (HCF) security program. Individuals performing security services should be appropriately trained to meet any legally required training standards and healthcare security industry best practices.

Intent

- **a.** Security training programs should include healthcare industry best practices and information specific to the HCF and the environment being protected.
- **b.** Job descriptions should identify specific skill levels required. HCF policies and procedures as well as those specific to the security department should be used to define capability and skill-level needs.
- **c.** Training should be relevant to the healthcare security officer and include defined performance objectives and a method to verify that the training received resulted in an acceptable level of competency.
- **d.** An HCF security training program should have clearly identified learning outcomes.
- **e.** New security officer training should provide a foundation of knowledge in the areas of protection, customer service, public relations, response to calls for service and proper documentation of security-related events.

Continued

03.01 SECURITY OFFICER TRAINING—Cont'd

f. The training of security personnel should be designed to establish a standard of performance within a suggested time allocation.

g. Training should guide security staff response and behavior in a manner that reflects the HCF's philosophy of patient care and employee safety. Such training should include:
   1) Verbal de-escalation and voluntary compliance training. The program should be designed to instruct security personnel to successfully manage aggression and the verbal or physical/disruptive behavior of others.
   2) HCF use of force policy and related training providing specific instruction on each item of equipment carried ensuring competency is demonstrated with all equipment before initial deployment.

h. Initial training in predetermined critical tasks with demonstrated competency should be provided prior to a security officer's unsupervised assignment.

i. Training is not a one-time event. Security staff should receive ongoing training to address changes in the environment, to learn, improve and further develop their professional skills. Reinforced or refresher training in critical functions such as use of force; defensive equipment; prevention and management of aggressive behavior should be conducted to established standards.

j. Training records for each individual should be maintained by the HCF according to the HCF record retention policy.

k. Training records should include the subject matter, time, date, duration of training, instructor's name and affiliation, and competency verification.

l. Security staff members should be encouraged to achieve and maintain progressive certification levels developed by IAHSS.

m. If a local authority having jurisdiction prescribes mandatory training for contract officers, but not proprietary officers, the HCF should provide an equivalent level of training for proprietary officers.

n. Off duty law enforcement providing a security function for the HCF should receive an equivalent level of training. This is particularly important in areas of use of force.

General Information

- IAHSS Guideline 02.05. Defensive Equipment and Use of Force Techniques
- IAHSS Progressive Certification Training Programs; www.iahss.org/certification

Approved: January 2006
Last Revised: May 2013

TYPES OF TRAINING

Considerable dialogue and printed materials are available relative to the type and content of training appropriate for healthcare security officers. There are fundamental types of training to which the healthcare security program must give significant consideration: (1) new security officer training, (2) IAHSS Progressive Certification, (3) specialized program training, (4) elective training and (5) security leadership development activities. The focus of this latter point of emphasis is discussed in greater detail in Chapter 7, "Leadership and Professional Development."

The new security officer training is the basic security training, applicable to virtually every healthcare security officer within the department, which provides a foundation of knowledge. Beyond the healthcare facility orientation program for all new employees, new security officers should be exposed to a mixture of instructor-led training, available computer-based training and task specific on-the-job training.

The IAHSS Progressive Certification training programs described in this text are considered basic areas of training which, when supplemented by specialized training, can significantly enhance security officer performance. Specialized training takes into consideration the function and responsibility of the officer in a specific organizational setting. Like the new security officer training, both IAHSS certification and specialized training should be considered a fundamental part of the organization-mandated officer training.

Elective training involves training or education that is generally not mandatory. It is usually taken by the officer who has a personal interest or personal objective for participating in specific self-improvement activities. These training activities are generally pursued on the individual's own time.

NEW SECURITY OFFICER TRAINING

Professional security officer training is a combination of protection, customer service, and public relations. The security officer reflects the customer service attitude and security posture of the healthcare facility. Proper training of newly hired security officers can produce a return on investment in terms of attaining the highest level of security and safety. Each new security employee should receive a series of training modules designed to provide security-specific education and healthcare-specific training in an efficient and verifiable manner. The training of new security personnel should be to a standard of performance within a suggested time allocation.

The amount and quality of preservice training for the new security officer is critical to the success of the officer and to the delivery of high quality services. Unfortunately, much preservice training consists of on-the-job instruction of a new officer by another officer. The disadvantages of this method are obvious. New officers become only as proficient as their teachers, and they often learn the wrong way from the beginning. On the other hand, when a new officer is hired at Barnes-Jewish Hospital in St. Louis, they are put through a 28-day (224 hour) in-house basic academy in addition to a forty (40) hour Pressure Point Control Tactics (PPCT) course. According to their security leadership, blocks of time consist of review of policies and procedures, core tasks, post orders, and response plans, as well as basic officer safety. This type of instructor-led course is cost-prohibitive for many healthcare security programs and illustrates the difficulty of outlining a preservice training program where there are many variables, such as the size of the security force and the availability of resources. The approach for a security force of three or four members must inevitably differ from that of a security department of 30 or more officers.

ON-THE-JOB TRAINING

Although on-the-job training (OJT) has its shortcomings, it is necessary for providing officers with hands-on experience. There is no substitute for demonstrating the tasks that must be completed. A failing of many OJT programs is the lack of a formal structure. The OJT trainer should use a predetermined checklist when providing instruction. Figure 10-1 is an example of an OJT preservice training checklist used at Memorial Hermann Health System in The Woodlands, Texas. Both the OJT trainer and the trainee sign the checklist after the instruction is completed, and this checklist becomes part of the officer's permanent training record. This preservice training should be followed up by some form of competency testing.

CRITICAL TASK FOCUSED TRAINING

Training to a time period versus an established standard, coupled with the absence of a competency verification philosophy and defined post orders, creates risk of liability for inadequate training, supervision, and significantly increases training-related expenses.

Time to train is mostly irrelevant. There are a number of state statutes that mandate how many contact hours should be provided for security staff training. Most healthcare security professionals agree

Memorial Hermann Healthcare System
Integrated Protective Services
On the Job Training

ON THE JOB TRAINING CHECKLIST	TRAINEE INITIAL	TRAINER INITIAL	COMPLETION DATE
1. Introduction			
Site Location			
MHHS IPS and Hospital Organizational Chart			
Hospital Department Locations			
Hospital Floor Plans			
2. Security Officer Job Description			
Security Officer Job Description Signed Copy to file			
Security Officer Job Performance Standard			
3. Security Department Policies & Procedures			
Leadership Structure			
IPS Policies, Procedures, Accountabilities			
Attendance & Scheduling / Leave Request			
Uniform Appearance & Grooming Standards			
4. Security Post Procedures			
Security Dispatch Center			
Posts			
Foot Patrol			
Shift Change			
Daily Activity & Incident Reports (Perspective)			
Specific Duties & Responsibilities			
5. Access Control			
Identification Badges			
Card Access System			
Security Sensitive Areas Policy			
Shipping & Receiving			
Visitation Policy Regular and After Hours			
Removal of Hospital Property & Equipment			
Delayed Egress			
Emergency Lockdown			
6. Patrolling and Procedures			
Patrol (locations and specifics)			
Use of Hospital Vehicles			
Response to Off-Site Facilities-Alarms/ Assignments (if applicable)			
Parking Policy & Issuing Parking Notices			
Perimeter Checks of Buildings			
7. Emergency Response Procedures			
During and After Business Hours			
Code Red			
Code Pink			
Code Green and Code Green Active Shooter			
Code Gray			
Code Black			
Code Silver			
Code Orange			
Maintenance Related Problems			

FIGURE 10-1

A sample of an on-the-job training checklist for a healthcare security officer. Courtesy of Memorial Hermann Health System, The Woodlands, Texas.

Memorial Hermann Healthcare System
Integrated Protective Services
On the Job Training – Cont'd

ON THE JOB TRAINING CHECKLIST	TRAINEE INITIAL	TRAINER INITIAL	COMPLETION DATE
Maintenance Related Problems			
Inclement Weather			
Criminal Activity			
Media Relations			
Interim Security Measures Policy			
Emergency Management Plan			
Team "A " Assignment			
8. Miscellaneous Procedures			
Key Control Policy			
Lost & Found Policy			
Patient Valuables			
Infant Abandonment			
Restraint Policy			
Traffic Control			
Radio Etiquette			
Employee Escort			
Vehicle Assistance			
Telephone Usage – Cell Phone			
Personal Protection Equipment (PPE)			
9. Video Training			
Give'em the Pickle (customer service)			
Flash Point for Healthcare			
Shots Fired for Healthcare			
10. Required Training			
TEAM			
Basic Life Support / EAD			
IAHSS Basic Certification			
Perspective (report writing)			
Radio / Computer			
CAD911			
Emergency Response Team Awareness Training			
Decon & Seclusion Rooms Awareness Training			
Hazmat Awareness			
Wheelchair Safety & Operations			
Driver Training and Inspections			
Emergency Blue Light Call Boxes			
Fire Extinguishers P.A.S.S.			

FIGURE 10-1—Continued

Memorial Hermann Healthcare System
Integrated Protective Services
On the Job Training – Cont'd

ON THE JOB TRAINING CHECKLIST	TRAINEE INITIAL	TRAINER INITIAL	COMPLETION DATE
11. Testing of System			
Infant Abduction system			
Blue Light Call Boxes			
Panic Alarms – In House & Off Site			

ON THE JOB TRAINING RECORD

Trainee Name ____________________ Trainee Signature ____________________

Hire Date ____________________ On The Job Training Completion Date ____________________

I, ______________________, the trainer for this officer attest to the satisfactory completion of all On the Job Training items by direct supervision and observation.

Trainer Signature ____________________ Date ____________________

Comments:

Revised 02/12

FIGURE 10-1—Continued

competency, or the ability to describe or demonstrate knowledge of a given task, is a better indicator of future success. Many healthcare protection programs have determined that there should be a suggested amount of time allocated to training, provided it not be used as a sole gauge of an individual security officer's aptitude to perform the function of protecting a healing environment—their demonstrated competency is a preferred indicator.

Competency-based training has become a buzzword coming from The Joint Commission and the comments made during their on-site surveys. TJC surveyors are no longer solely interested in the documented "check the box" training. The surveyors are asking security officers to demonstrate, or at minimum, describe, their responsibility (competency). An example of this trend is found at a northern California hospital. Two hospital security officers who had been on the job for 6 months were asked detailed questions by a TJC administrative surveyor regarding their specific role and responsibilities in a community-wide mass casualty disaster. Questions asked ranged from traffic control to their individual role in the decontamination process. After the exchange, each security officer was commended by the TJC surveyor for their knowledge and understanding of their role in the disaster. The personnel jacket of each security officer was reviewed later, but specific training documentation was never requested. This example is one of hundreds where TJC surveyors have transitioned their focused questioning from just a basic exposure to that of competency. Similarly, in Canada, Accreditation Canada surveyors have also moved away from paper-based assessments to a more competency-based demonstrable knowledge model, engaging front line staff.

Competency verification

Competency verification starts with security leadership. Security leaders, field training officers or anyone with the responsibility for training security staff must answer a simple question: "How do I know that my staff is competent?" The process begins by identifying those tasks most critical to the healthcare security officer. A training plan is then developed for each task by creating a job list that provides systematic instructions for how each "task" is accomplished. Figure 10-2 demonstrates a sample competency format used for a basic task carried out by a healthcare security officer.

The underlying purpose of this system of learning is identifying information and skills needed by security staff to meet job performance requirements. A security officer who can demonstrate, explain, and define their role and responsibility can perform the following:

- Demonstrate: How the Task is completed
- Explain: Why the Task is completed
- Define: The importance of the Task

Task training should present information in a goal and learning objective concept, so information can be absorbed and retained. Task training information, when presented in a prioritized sequence, provides a systematic approach to identify learning weaknesses and measure learning goals. Some healthcare security programs break down the task list into two sections: (1) the mission-essential competencies that must be known prior to donning a uniform, and (2) those that must be known within a predefined period of time, typically 60–90 days.

The foundation of the competency inventory is developed from security program documents such as the department post orders, policy and procedures, and other protocols, in addition to the Hospital Policy manual, and Hospital Emergency Preparedness manuals. A sample of how a healthcare organization can sequence the learning of a security officer task inventory is shown in Figure 10-3.

Children's Hospital, Colorado
OJT Competency Task

FACILITY: Children's Hospital, Colorado	OFFICER:
EVALUATION CYCLE: OJT	
SUPERVISOR:	EVALUATION DATE:

INSTRUCTIONS: Complete the top portion of this form, cross through the Tasks not considered during this evaluation cycle, circle whether the officer is competent on the remaining Tasks, and return with the other evaluation paperwork.

LEARN SEQ	TASK	COMP
01	Facility Locations	Yes No
02	Communications	Yes No
03	Security Keys	Yes No
04	Security Alarm Locations	Yes No
05	Security Alarm Response	Yes No
06	Discovered Fire Response	Yes No
07	Announced/Observed Fire Alarm Response	Yes No
08	Morgue Escorts	Yes No
09	Helicopter Landings	Yes No
10	Patient Assistance	Yes No
11	Patient Restraint	Yes No
12	Patient Take Down	Yes No
13	Missing Patient/Possible Abduction	Yes No
14	Medical Emergency	Yes No
15	ED Access Control	Yes No
16	Victim of Violence ED	Yes No
17	MRI Safety	Yes No
18	Code Black	Yes No
19	Contaminated Patient Management	Yes No
20	Epidemic Bio Terrorism	Yes No
21	Evacuation	Yes No
22	Patient Evacuation	Yes No
23	Flooding	Yes No
24	Influx of Patients – Mass Casualty	Yes No
25	Security Event (Restricted Access)	Yes No
26	Severe Winter Weather	Yes No
27	Tornado	Yes No
28	Code Silver	Yes No
This Officer is competent in 28 out of 28 Tasks.		Yes No

RE-EVALUATION DATE IF NEEDED:		
Officer Printed Name	Signature	Date
Supervisor/Evaluator Printed Name	Signature	Date
Program Manager Printed Name	Signature	Date

FIGURE 10-2

A sample competency format used for a basic task performed by a healthcare security officer. Courtesy of Brian Sallee, CHPA and Children's Hospital of Colorado.

Children's Hospital, Colorado
OJT Competency Task – Cont'd

FACILITY: Children's Hospital, Colorado		**SUPERVISOR:**	
TASK: Morgue Escort		**LEARN SEQ:** 08	**DATE:**
GOAL: Officer can properly escort staff member, Coroner or Funeral Home Representative to and from the morgue, from inpatient unit to morgue or out of facility.			
OFFICER:	**TRAINER:**		**DATE:**

ELEM	ELEMENT DESCRIPTION	COMP
1	Meet the person at the designated location. Identify the person as an employee, coroner or funeral home employee. Any person picking up a body MUST present two forms of identification. One form must be a valid driver's license. 1. Valid Driver's License 2. Professional ID / Badge. (MUST contain their photo and full name)	Yes No
2	Copy both forms of ID and place the copy in the appropriate file folder in the morgue.	Yes No
3	After confirming that the individual has two appropriate forms of ID, escort the person to the Pathology Suite (Morgue).	Yes No
4	If the person cannot present two forms of identification advise them that the hospital's policy states that they must present two forms of identification described above.	Yes No
5	Work with the person and to secure proof of identification.	Yes No
	Health Information Management is located at the Village Pavilion.	
	FROM CHC UNIT TO MORGUE (Patient Expires at CHC)	
1	All escorts from inpatient units will go by way of patient transport / critical care elevators. You will not allow visitors on the elevators with the escort. Check with the unit to see if they require the morgue cart that is located in the lower level morgue.	Yes No
2	Respond to the unit. Escort the staff member and patient to the morgue. Assist in placing the patient in the cooler. Use personal protective equipment as necessary.	Yes No
3	Remind staff to ensure that the patient's medical chart / documentation are placed in the appropriate file folder in the morgue. Assist staff as necessary with location of folder.	Yes No
4	The staff member will sign the patient into the morgue log. Security will then initial the log after staff completes the sign in.	Yes No
5	Document the escort on an SCR with the name of the employee, unit, room number, and patient number. Enter a report in perspective on the computer. Leave all three copies of the SCR in the Security Office.	Yes No

FIGURE 10-2—Continued

Children's Hospital, Colorado
OJT Competency Task – Cont'd

FROM TO MORGUE TO VEHICLE (Patient expired at CHC, is in the morgue and will be picked up by Funeral Home or Mortuary)		
1	Meet the person at the designated location. Identify the person as an employee, coroner or funeral home employee. Any person picking up a body MUST present two forms of identification. One form must be a valid driver's license. 3. Valid Driver's License 4. Professional ID / Badge. (MUST contain their photo and full name)	Yes No
2	Copy both forms of ID and place the copy in the appropriate file folder in the morgue.	Yes No
3	After confirming that the individual has two appropriate forms of ID, escort the person to the Pathology Suite (Morgue).	Yes No
4	If the person cannot present two forms of identification advise them that the hospital's policy states that they must present two forms of identification described above.	Yes No
5	Work with the person and to secure proof of identification if needed.	Yes No
	Health Information Management is located at the Village Pavilion.	
6	Sign the patient out of the morgue on the morgue log book.	Yes No
7	Obtain the death certificate from the appropriate file folder. The transporting party will take the take certificate with the patient. Only the death certificate should leave with the patient. The medical records / documents will be picked up by CHC HIM.	Yes No
8	Document the escort on an SCR with the name of the employee, unit, room number, and patient number. Enter a report in perspective on the computer. Leave all three copies of the SCR in the Security Office.	Yes No
FROM CHC UNIT TO VEHICLE (Patient expired at CHC, will not be placed in morgue)		
1	When a funeral home, corner, or mortuary picks the patient up directly off the unit. The unit staff should contact security and advise of the direct pick up from the unit.	Yes No
2	Ask the unit if the morgue cart is needed. If so obtain the morgue cart and respond to the unit. For all units expect for the ED; transport will park in the loading dock.	Yes No
3	Escort the individual through the lower level to the patient transport / critical care elevators and to the appropriate unit.	Yes No
4	After obtaining the remains and ensuring all of the appropriate paperwork is complete escort them back down the patient transport / critical care elevators to their vehicle at the loading dock.	Yes No
5	Any patient charts / documentation will be picked up by the transporting party at the unit.	Yes No

FIGURE 10-2—Continued

Children's Hospital, Colorado
OJT Competency Task – Cont'd

6	Respond to the morgue. Sign the patient into the morgue as if they had been placed in the cooler. Sign the patient out of the morgue as if they had been picked up from the morgue. This will generate a record of the patient leaving.	Yes No
7	Document the escort on an SCR with the name of the employee, unit, room number, and patient number. Enter a report in perspective on the computer. Leave all three copies of the SCR in the Security Office.	Yes No
FROM VEHICLE TO THE MORGUE (Patient expired outside of CHC is arriving for autopsy)		
1	An outside transport entity will arrive at CHC to deliver a patient for autopsy. The transport should be directed to park in the loading dock.	Yes No
2	Meet the person at the loading dock. Any person delivering a body MUST present two forms of identification. One form must be a valid driver's license. 1. Valid Driver's License 2. Professional ID / Badge. (MUST contact their photo and full name)	Yes No
3	Copy both forms of ID and place the copy in the appropriate file folder in the morgue.	Yes No
4	Escort the transporting party and patient to the morgue and place the patient in the cooler. Sign the morgue log book indicating that the patient has arrived in the morgue.	Yes No
5	Contact the following individuals and advise that a patient has arrived for autopsy. • On Call Pathologist – 76175 • House Supervisor - 72576	Yes No
6	Document the escort on an SCR with the name of the employee, unit, room number, and patient number. Enter a report in perspective on the computer. Leave all three copies of the SCR in the Security Office.	Yes No
7	***NOTE: After completion of autopsy when patient is picked up there will not be a death certificate or other medical documentation / charts.***	Yes No

FIGURE 10-2—Continued

Children's Hospital, Colorado
OJT Competency Task – Cont'd

FACILITY: Children's Hospital, Colorado		SUPERVISOR:	
TASK: Helicopter Landings		LEARN SEQ: 09	DATE:
GOAL: Officer can properly respond to a helicopter landing			
OFFICER:	TRAINER:	DATE:	

ELEM	ELEMENT DESCRIPTION	COMP
		Yes No
1	Proceed to the helipad within 15 minutes prior to the ETA given, if less than 15 minutes proceed immediately to the pad. Use the patient transport / critical care elevators. There are only two (2) elevators within the patient transport / critical care bank that go to the 10th floor. These elevators are marked by a helicopter sticker in the top left corner. Standby on the helipad for a visual sighting of the helicopter if time permits.	Yes No
2	Use the ERT code blue badge to lock out the elevator on the 10th floor. This will prohibit anyone else from calling the elevator. One officer should standby with the locked out elevator to ensure no one except helicopter staff takes it. The other officer will assist with patient unloading.	Yes No
3	Ensure the landing lights are on. The landing and flood lights are located on the wall by the fire suppression pull station. The landing lights must remain on at all times. The flood lights should only be turned on after the helicopter's rotors have stopped.	Yes No
4	Check the helipad for debris if time permits.	Yes No
5	Do not allow any staff to be present on the landing pad when a helicopter is approaching and landing. All staff should remain behind or just inside the double doors leading on the pad. Ensure that you are positioned in such a way that you can see when the helicopter's rotors stop.	Yes No
6	When the helicopter crew is ready for security and staff to approach the helicopter they will signal by waving you over. Assist staff and crew as necessary. **Never approach a helicopter form the rear.**	Yes No
7	Escort the flight crew/staff/patient to the necessary department. After all staff are in the elevator you must press the floor that they crew is going to and hold the close door button. Once you arrive on the floor swipe the ERT card inside of the elevator to release the elevator for normal operations. If you fail to do this the elevator will not move to another floor when called.	Yes No
8	Stay with the flight crew until they are ready to depart. If you should need to leave you will notify them and have them call when they are ready or come back as soon as you can to escort them back to the pad.	Yes No
9	Escort the crew back to the helipad.	Yes No
10	Document the helicopter assist in Perspective.	Yes No
	During night time hours you will need to turn on the ramp lights as follows:	
11	Locate switch #2 by door 6N01 and turn it on.	Yes No

FIGURE 10-2—Continued

Children's Hospital, Colorado
OJT Competency Task – Cont'd

During nighttime hours and only when the helicopter has landed you will need to turn on the flood lights to the pad as follows:		
12	Locate switch on the near the fire suppression pull station.	Yes No
13	During night time hours when helicopter is ready to take-off you will turn off the flood lights, when the crew boards the helicopter and prepares for take-off.	Yes No
14	Complete a report in Perspective or e-report on the computer or hand held device.	
TASK	The officer can perform 100% of the elements	Yes No

FIGURE 10-2—Continued

A key component for the critical task focused training program is the verification of knowledge by a supervisor or training officer. Officers must confirm their knowledge by demonstrating and/or describing their comprehension of each critical task to a person in a responsible charge position. Separating the responsibility of who trains the security officer and who verifies competency is ideal.

KEY TRAINING TOPICS FOR THE NEW SECURITY OFFICER

Professional security officers must be prepared to subdue a mentally disturbed patient, apprehend a thief, comfort a distraught mother, escort a lost visitor, and perform any number of other tasks at any time and anywhere in the facilities they serve. To prepare security officers for this demanding job, the healthcare organization must invest in the development of a comprehensive, industry-specific, multistep training program focused on protection, public relations, and customer service. Training is not a one-time event. From the time hired and throughout their careers, security officers must continue training to learn, improve, and further develop their professional skills. For many healthcare security programs, regardless of country, stagnancy in training security staff has a long-term negative impact on performance.

Security role in patient care/Aggression management

A primary role of security staff in the healthcare environment is to assist care providers in managing at-risk patient behavior. Healthcare security officers can expect to be called upon to de-escalate and manage aggressive or violent behavior. Every healthcare security program should have a training offering to guide officer response and behavior in a manner that reflects the healthcare facility's philosophy of patient care. Focusing on verbal de-escalation and voluntary compliance, the program should be designed to teach security staff members to successfully control aggression and other verbal or physically inappropriate actions of others in a medical care environment.

Sensitivity training is also important and often combined with the de-escalation-type training. Sensitivity training gives security officers alternatives to the use of force when dealing with people. It takes a humanistic—or sympathetic—approach to solving people's problems and tries to provide insight into why people behave the way they do.

New Employee Training Program
Critical Task Learning Prioritization/Learning Sequence

OFFICER ____________________ **Hire Date** ____________________

PHASE	TASK #	TASK	COMP	PHASE	TASK #	TASK	COMP
ORIENTATION FIRST WEEK	O – 1	Security Documentation	Y N	PHASE I FIRST 2 WEEKS	PH I –1	Patient Searches	Y N
	O – 2	Radio Communications	Y N		PH I –2	Patient Restraint Application	Y N
	O – 3	Courteous Enforcement	Y N		PH I –3	Patient Elopement/Response	Y N
	O – 4	Facility Locations	Y N		PH I –4	Patient Valuables Process	Y N
	O – 5	Codes	Y N		PH I –5	Missing Patient	Y N
	O – 6	Patient Assistance	Y N		PH I –6	Defensive Driving	Y N
	O – 7	Security/Fire Alarm Response	Y N		PH I –7	Security Patrol Vehicle Use	Y N
	O – 8	PPE	Y N		PH I –8	Facility Patrols	Y N
	O – 9	Aggression Management	Y N		PH I –9	Security Alarm Locations	Y N
	O – 10	Security Key Ring/Control	Y N		PH I–10	Report Writing	Y N
	O – 11	Use of Force	Y N		PH I–11	Trauma/Core 0 Team	Y N
	Internal	Hosp. New Emp. Orientation	Y N		PH I–12	After Hours Access Control	Y N
	New Officers must complete Orientation Phase and have Security Manager approval to begin Phase I				New Officers must complete Phase I and have Security Manager approval to begin Phase II		
Security Manager ____________ Date ________				Security Manager ____________ Date ________			

PHASE	TASK #	TASK	COMP	PHASE	TASK #	TASK	COMP
PHASE II FIRST 30 DAYS	PHII–1	Missing/Found Property	Y N	PHASE III FIRST 60 DAYS	PHIII–1	Internal Disaster Response	Y N
	PHII–2	Forensic Patient	Y N		PHIII–2	External Disaster Response	Y N
	PHII–3	Helicopter Assist	Y N		PHIII–3	Bomb Threat Response	Y N
	PHII–4	Morgue Duties	Y N		PHIII–4	Serious Incident Notification	Y N
	PHII–5	Discovered Fire Response	Y N		PHIII–5	Hostage Situation	Y N
	PHII–6	Injured Person Assist	Y N		PHIII–6	CCTV Locations	Y N
	PHII–7	Civil Disturbance	Y N		PHIII–7	Very Important Patient	Y N
	PHII–8	Vehicle Battery Jump	Y N		PHIII–8	Snow Removal	Y N
	PHII–9	Vehicle Tire Change	Y N		PHIII–9	DECON Suit Training	Y N
	PHII–10	Infant/Pediatric Abduction	Y N		PHIII–10	Visitor Management	Y N
	PHII–11	Detox Transport	Y N		PHIII–11	Package Inspection	Y N
	PHII–12	Door Unlock Requests	Y N		PHIII–12	Non-Solicitation Policy	Y N
	PHII–13	Personal Escort	Y N		PHIII–13	Arrest, Search & Seizure	Y N
	New Officers must complete Phase II and have Security Manager approval to begin Phase III				New Officers must complete Phase III and have Security Manager approval to begin Phase IV		
Program Security Manager ____________ Date ________				Security Manager ____________ Date ________			

FIGURE 10-3

A sample sequenced and prioritized critical task list for a healthcare security program.

Some healthcare programs develop and provide their own training programs to deal with disruptive behavior, while others utilize an outside source for this training. Table 10-1 identifies specialized organizations that provide aggression management training for security and healthcare staff.

In Vancouver, Canada a joint effort of healthcare unions, health authorities (systems), provincial regulatory agencies and healthcare security managers, resulted in the 2011 release of a Provincial Violence Prevention Curriculum for healthcare workers across British Columbia. Comprised of eight (8) online and five (5) classroom modules, this training program has become standard for all healthcare workers in the province across a range of healthcare settings. Healthcare security staff must also successfully complete this training which, in addition to providing the obvious benefit of standardized training for all workers who may be involved in aggression management, has the added advantage of being developed by all interested constituents. In the United Kingdom, The National Health Service (NHS) has gone one step further with a national strategy on healthcare violence prevention that includes worker training.

Every security officer should complete this training and demonstrate competence in identified physical maneuvers early in their career—preferably before ever donning a uniform. Ideally, the healthcare protection program offers and requires annual refresher training and periodically audits individual officer ability to perform both the physical control and escape maneuvers.

Use of force

As identified in Chapter 9, "The Security Uniform and Defensive Equipment," every healthcare facility should develop a use-of-force policy that includes the identification of situations, both clinical and nonclinical, in which security officers are permitted to use force. The new officer must be trained on the use-of-force policy upon hire, and be provided specific training on each item of equipment they carry.

Each item of equipment should be provided its own segment of training. The student should be required to demonstrate competency of classroom material presented and a high level of proficiency with the equipment. For example, an officer who carries handcuffs should be required to demonstrate proficiency handling and applying the device, in addition to having a clear understanding of when this tool may be used in their healthcare environment and under what circumstances. This approach should be used with all equipment carried that falls within the healthcare organization's use-of-force continuum: zip ties, chemical agents, batons, electronic control devices, and firearms. The training should meet all applicable state-mandated and industry-recognized standards and include periodic refreshers. While this equipment is utilized much less extensively by healthcare organizations outside of the U.S., the principles delineated in this section will certainly apply where such equipment is used.

Table 10-1 Aggression Management Training Programs for Security and Healthcare Staff

Available Aggression Management Training Programs	
Techniques for Effective Aggression Management (TEAM)	www.hss-us.com
Crisis Prevention Institute (CPI)	www.crisisprevention.com
Management of Aggressive Behavior (MOAB)	www.personalprotectiontraining.com
The Mandt System	www.mandtsystem.com
Verbal Judo Institute	www.verbaljudo.com

Restraint training

CMS has reversed their position on security staff being able to apply medical restraints on a patient. Gone are the days of "observe and report" with the security officer's primary responsibility to stand by while clinical staff apply restraints. Today, security staff are permitted to apply restraints and are often critical team members in this patient care process. CMS recognizes that security staff involvement can cause less harm and often less pain to the patient. The basic requirement is that if a security officer is involved in the application of restraints, they have to be trained and demonstrate competency in the safe application and use of restraints.[3]

The frequency with which restraint training is offered by the healthcare facility can often reduce the ability of the security department to render this basic function. The application of a restraint is a clinical procedure, and training is typically provided by clinical staff. Many healthcare organizations schedule the training in 6-month increments and attrition does not occur that routinely. As a result, the security officer is either not trained to hospital and CMS standards before applying restraints or is not an available resource when a situation arises that calls for medical restraints to be applied. Neither situation is desirable. To overcome this challenge, many healthcare security administrators have coordinated with the resident restraint educator to train an internal security department employee as a trainer for this critical task.

The new security officer must be provided specific training and patient-centered guidelines for this specific technique for managing at-risk behavior. A "least restrictive alternative"[4] approach must be used. By clearly defining individual staff responsibilities and promoting patient and staff safety, these practices can reduce related workers' compensation expense and liability exposure for the healthcare facility.

Report writing

A hospital security officer in the course of his or her duties will encounter numerous events or incidents that require the passing of factual information to others. Of all the security officer's duties, the ability to write an accurate, clear, concise and impartial security incident report is one of the most vital.

Security personnel must receive training in effective report writing early in their career. This training should include how to interview and obtain data, how to record information properly, as well as the rationale for this process.

New security officer training should focus on how to write a security incident report. Many organizations require the completion of sample reports based on the facts gathered on actual events. Training can also cover how the written security incident report is an official document and a reflection of the officer, the security department and the healthcare organization as a whole. It is important for the new officer to understand that the report is frequently reviewed by others such as facility administration, insurance companies, law enforcement, and the courts. Further discussion on the filing and completion of a security incident report is covered in Chapter 11, "Deployment and Patrol Activities" and Chapter 12, "Program Documentation and Performance Measures."

Customer service and security

Customer service is defined as "identifying a customer need and providing a service that meets or exceeds that need." An important responsibility of a healthcare security officer is to establish a safe and secure environment. Healthcare security officers who perform their job correctly spend more than 50% of their time providing general services. This is a key element of a successful security program.

As ambassadors for the organization and the constituents served, the security officer must understand the rules of courteous enforcement and public relations. The long-term success of every healthcare security program is rooted in its evolution as a customer-service focused protection department.

Knapp Medical Center in Waslaco, Texas trained all of their security staff to become customer service representatives. An example of the type of training provided is found in the frequent need for security to calm a visitor who is experiencing a long wait in the emergency department waiting area. The training provided more emphasis on informing patients of the reasons for the back-ups that may be causing the long waits instead of focusing on communicating the ramifications of not complying with the officer's request to calm down; i.e., "we are going to call the cops." The result has been a significant reduction in the number of security incidents stemming from the waiting area. The hospital has also incorporated a "no finger" rule in which all patients and family members in need of directions are escorted to where they desire to go within the hospital.[5]

Many healthcare organizations have incorporated the RATER model to improve and deliver customer service. Invented by Leonard Berry, this model identifies five quality customer service dimensions found to be relevant for the healthcare protection program and its ability to deliver "above and beyond" customer service. In examining the customer service training provided to new security officers, the healthcare protection professional should review:

- ***Reliability*** – Ability of the security officers to perform their service dependably and accurately
- ***Assurance*** – Knowledge and courtesy of the security officers and their ability to inspire trust and confidence in others
- ***Tangibility*** – Appearance and image of the security officers; how they care for equipment and their ability to communicate verbally and in writing
- ***Empathy*** – Building the security officers' understanding of the nature of the healthcare environment and delivery system coupled with a caring attitude
- ***Responsiveness*** – Willingness of the security officers to help customers, provide prompt service and solve problems

More than just security, security staff members are also ambassadors for the organization they serve. Their image, actions, and interactions with patients, visitors, and staff should leave a positive feeling about the hospital and the security program. For many patients and visitors their "first touch" with the healthcare organization is an interaction with security. The initial training provided to new security officers must reinforce this message.

Why is customer service important in healthcare?

Organizations are continually trying to improve their Hospital Consumer Assessment of Health Providers and Systems Survey (HCAHPS) results. The security officer has a direct contribution to those results by providing positive customer experiences through patient satisfaction. Patient satisfaction measures how well we meet patients' expectations or "how satisfied" they are as a result of their visit/stay—how well the outcomes they expected were delivered. Patient satisfaction is an important understanding for all involved in patient care and the opportunity to contribute to a positive patient experience should always be sought. Patient perceptions are often formed by the experience of being in the hospital and the consistency with which we met their expectations. Performance-based perceptions are directly influenced by the person, therefore each encounter is critical. One of the ways healthcare security officers are assessed is by how often and how consistently they interact with customers (patients, medical staff, etc.).

Alan Butler, CHPA, Vice President of Healthcare Security for HSS, Inc., suggests that customer service focused training consider using the same communication model some hospitals are using to help patients understand their care, reduce anxiety, and improve outcomes—the Studer Group's Five Fundamentals of Communication, or AIDET^{SM}:

- Acknowledge – the patient, preferably by their preferred name.
- Introduce – yourself and your role within the organization.
- Duration – how long you are going to take to do whatever you came to do.
- Explanation – explain what you came to do and what you need.
- Thank You – thank them; it is a common courtesy and should be part of every patient interaction.[6]

Cascading a customer service based philosophy used to be considered a good security practice. Today, it is essential to the performance of the healthcare security program and its stewardship of the healthcare facility.

Patrol techniques

The security patrol is the most common activity performed by the healthcare security officer. Patrolling officers have a unique opportunity to provide a positive service to the staff, visitors, and patients of the organization. But more than just "walking around," the security officer must be trained to be "systematically unsystematic" to routinely change their patrol coverage. The new officers must learn that, while on patrol, they are looking for people in need of assistance or dangerous situations and how to use their senses (sight, hearing, smell, touch, and taste) in protecting the healthcare environment.

A properly trained, confident patrol officer can also deter potential illicit activities by projecting vigilance and energy while patrolling. Making eye contact, being observed by others to be interested and curious, and reflecting in body language and walk that patrol is an important function to the security officer can have a positive effect on the perception of security.

The contacting of suspicious persons and the investigation of suspicious situations are some of the most important areas of the patrol function. Officer safety is an important discussion early in the career of the new security officer so they can effectively carry out these functions or respond to a critical incident. Patrolling is also one of the best public relations tools at the security program's disposal. When the officer is seen on patrol, they are helping patients, staff or visitors feel safer and more secure while on campus and in the hospital. This is an important component of the overall patient, visitor and employee experience.

OSHA compliance

Hazard communications, bloodborne pathogen exposure prevention, tuberculosis, universal precautions and other OSHA-required training is mandatory for U.S. healthcare facilities and in many international jurisdictions, prior to the security officer working. The healthcare protection administrator must become familiar with each of these safety and health requirements and specifically address how initial and annual training will occur.

IAHSS PROGRESSIVE CERTIFICATION PROGRAM

The Progressive Certification program of IAHSS is a three-tier training and certification program that helps security officers prepare for and address the special protection needs of healthcare institutions. Providing a foundational understanding of healthcare security, the Basic Training level is the first phase in the IAHSS Progressive Certification program. The Advanced and Supervisory Training levels expand on the Basic Training program and allow security officers to continue their education after becoming certified at the Basic Training Level. The programs are designed for the healthcare security officer who desires to achieve higher levels of responsibility in the organization. The following certifications, administered by the IAHSS Commission on Certification, are available:

- Basic Training certification for the healthcare security officer
- Advanced Training certification for the healthcare security officer
- Supervisory Training certification for the healthcare security professional

Each certification is valid for three years. Before the certification expires, the individual has the choice of being recertified at the same level or progressing to the next level. Information appropriate to certification for each of these levels is meticulously developed and regularly updated by professionals in healthcare security and safety in the IAHSS training manual developed for that specific level:

- Basic Training Manual for Healthcare Security Officers
- Advanced Training Manual for Healthcare Security Personnel
- Supervisory Training Manual for Healthcare Security Personnel

Many healthcare protection departments are firm believers in promoting from within, and offer compensation increases and advancement opportunities to security officers who complete, and maintain, one, two, or all three levels of IAHSS certification. Healthcare organizations are discouraged from making IAHSS certification a mandatory requirement for their security staff, as not all competent security officers are good test-takers.

IAHSS BASIC SECURITY OFFICER TRAINING

The IAHSS initially developed a 40-hour basic training program for security officers in the mid-1970s. The program, which is actually a standard, has stood the test of time. It has been revised from its previous focus on unit hours to its current certification basis and reflects the changes and evolution of the healthcare security profession. With its fifth edition released in 2010, the *Basic Training Manual for Healthcare Security Officers* continues to represent a consensus of what healthcare security administrators consider a basic training curriculum. The curriculum centers on understanding the healthcare environment and its relationship to security. Table 10-2 presents the sections and subject areas covered in the basic security officer training. The Association has also created a Canadian version of its Basic Training Manual and Exam which has been recently revised and updated to reflect input from Canadian healthcare security management professionals.

The successful completion of this training program leads to Basic Training certification by the IAHSS. Certification is granted after the officer passes a closed-book examination consisting of 100 multiple choice questions. The test can be taken on paper or electronically. One need not be employed

Table 10-2 IAHSS Curriculum for Basic Security Officer Training

IAHSS Basic Security Officer Training	
Section One – Introduction to Healthcare Security	
1 – The Healthcare Organization 2 – Security Services in the Healthcare Organization 3 – Customer Relations: Public, Employee, and Labor Relations	4 – Customer Service 5 – Teamwork and Team Building
Section Two – Fundamental Security Skills	
6 – Patrol Procedures and Techniques 7 – Security Interactions in Various Situations 8 – Risk Reduction: Restraints, Self-protection, and Defense 9 – Professional Conduct and Self-development 10 – Crisis Intervention	11 – Interview and Investigation 12 – Report Preparation and Writing 13 – Report Value and Liability 14 – Judicial Process, Courtroom Procedures, and Testimony 15 – Parking and Crowd Control
Section Three – The Role of Security in Healthcare Organizations	
16 – Patient Care Units 17 – Business Office and Financial Services 18 – Pharmacy: Physical Security, Narcotics, and Dangerous Drugs 19 – Emergency and Mental Health Units	20 – Infant and Pediatric Units 21 – Medical Records and HIPPA 22 – Support Units and Ancillary Services
Section Four – Protective Measures	
23 – Vulnerabilities and Risks in Healthcare Settings 24 – Integration and Use of Physical Security and Access Control Systems	25 – Equipment Use and Maintenance 26 – Identity Theft
Section Five – Healthcare Safety and Emergency Management	
27 – Overview of the Incident Command System 28 – Basic Safety Protection for the Officer 29 – Fire Prevention, Control, and Response 30 – Terrorism	31 – Bomb Threat Response Planning 32 – Emergency Management and Response 33 – Civil Disturbances 34 – Violence Issues: Domestic, Workplace, and Hostage Situation
Section Six – Security and the Law	
35 – Criminal and Civil Law 36 – Statutes and Standards Affecting Security Actions	37 – Regulatory Agencies 38 – Public Safety Interaction and Liaison

as a healthcare security officer to become certified; the Association has certified well over 40,000 protection professionals.

Several formats are currently used to prepare the student for the certification examination. One of the most popular is an IAHSS chapter project. This approach ensures a maximum number of students and

The
International Association for
Healthcare Security and Safety

Basic Training Certification

Awarded to

for successful completion of the Basic Healthcare Security Officer examination

CHPA, CPP
President

Date

FIGURE 10-4

Layout and design of the current IAHSS Basic Security Officer Certification certificate.

uses chapter members as instructors and discussion leaders. A high level of training is ensured, costs are shared, and each organization need not devise a unique program. Another format is training through a local university or vocational college. Some colleges offer a regular credit course structured around the standard; others offer an institute-type course that may or may not award credit hours. The college assumes certain standards, which gives the instruction a certain amount of credibility. The student must still successfully pass the IAHSS certification examination. In-house and contractor training formats vary from formal classes, to facilitated study groups, to supervised self-study or a combination of these approaches.

Figure 10-4 shows the layout and design of the current basic security officer certification certificate.

IAHSS ADVANCED SECURITY OFFICER TRAINING

The Advanced Training level is the second phase in the IAHSS Progressive Certification program. Now in its fourth edition, the 2012 released *Advanced Training Manual for Healthcare Security Personnel* program curriculum builds on the knowledge and skills developed from the IAHSS Basic Training certification. It is encouraged, but not required, that the student complete the basic certification

Table 10-3 IAHSS Curriculum for Advanced Security Officer Training

IAHSS Advanced Security Officer Training	
1 – Security Awareness and Crime Prevention	8 – Patient Risk Groups
2 – Enhanced Customer Service	9 – Interacting with Patients
3 – Premise Liability	10 – Special Security Concerns
4 – Methods of Patrol	11 – Security in Sensitive Areas
5 – Investigative Techniques, Reports, and Procedures	12 – Electronic Security Technologies
6 – Off-campus Security and Safety	13 – Critical Incident Response
7 – Workplace Violence	14 – Advancing Professionalism

Table 10-4 IAHSS Curriculum for Supervisory Training

IAHSS Supervisory Training	
1 – Introduction to Supervision	10 – Effective Crime Prevention Programs
2 – Self-Improvement	11 – Authority and Control
3 – Supervisor Responsibilities	12 – Budgeting and Cost Control
4 – Civil Liability and the Supervisor	13 – Leadership
5 – Employee Relations and Employee Appraisals	14 – Principles of Customer Service
6 – Safety and the Supervisor's Responsibilities	15 – Handling Complaints and Grievances
7 – Planning for Emergency Management and Response	16 – Professionalism and Ethics
8 – Developing Training Plans and Programs	17 – Communication Skills in Supervision
9 – Supervisor Development	18 – Security Operations

program as a prerequisite to participating in the advanced training program. This program is separated into 14 different subject areas, as shown in Table 10-3.

The successful completion of this training program leads to Advanced Training certification by the IAHSS. Certification is granted after the officer passes the 50 question, multiple choice Advanced Healthcare Security exam. The test can be taken on paper or electronically. Once certification is issued, the student is recognized as a Certified Advanced Healthcare Security Officer (CAHSO).

IAHSS SUPERVISORY TRAINING

The Supervisory Training level is the third phase in the IAHSS Progressive Certification program. Now in its third edition, the 2007 released *Supervisory Training Manual for Healthcare Security Personnel* curriculum is intended for persons who are in current supervisory positions or persons who want to prepare themselves for supervision. It has been reported that security staff have also completed this program so that they better understand the supervisory process. It is encouraged, but not required, that the student complete the basic and advanced certification program as a prerequisite to participating in the supervisory training program. This program is separated into 18 different subject areas, as shown in Table 10-4.

The successful completion of this training program leads to Supervisor Training certification by the IAHSS. Certification is granted after the candidate passes the 50 question, multiple choice Supervisor

Healthcare Security exam. The test can be taken on paper or electronically. Once certification is issued, the student is recognized as a Certified Healthcare Security Supervisor (CHSS).

The IAHSS has developed a PowerPoint CD designed to specifically help the instructor to present accurate information that will assist students in successfully completing each of the IAHSS Progressive Certification Examinations.

Many healthcare protection departments require the completion of all three levels of IAHSS Progressive Certification for their security supervisory and management staff.

SPECIALIZED OR SUPPLEMENTAL TRAINING

The specialized training developed by the organization is intended to be specific to the needs, philosophy, and concerns of that organization. For example, weapons training would pertain to the use of force tools utilized in the security program. Specialized training may also build on areas of basic training provided during pre-assignment training or in the IAHSS progressive certification training series. For example, the IAHSS basic training includes general crisis intervention; however, a specific organization may want to supplement training in this area by using a nationally recognized program or an in-house developed program.

CONTEMPORARY ISSUES IN HEALTHCARE SECURITY TRAINING

The commitment to the on-going development of security personnel is paramount to the successful healthcare security program. To develop the highest potential in each employee, an organization must offer refresher training throughout the calendar year. This training should update the staff about security protocols and consists of a review of modified Post Orders and contemporary security topics such as gang activity, infant abduction prevention, emergency preparedness, and terrorism.

Gangs

Gangs, gang activity and the results of such activities, can have a negative impact on healthcare organizations, their employees, and others in the healthcare community. In their article "*Gang Culture from the Streets to the Emergency Department*", Bonnie Michelman and George Patak quote the National Alliance of Gang Investigators Association:

> "Once found principally in large cities, violent street gangs now affect public safety, community image, and quality of life in urban, suburban, and rural areas. No region of the United States is untouched by gangs. Gangs affect society at all levels, causing heightened fears for safety, violence, and economic costs."[7]

No single community is immune to gang activity. The issue of gang activity and gang violence is not isolated to just hospital emergency departments, hospital workers throughout the delivery system all have some level of risk and are frequently placed in vulnerable situations when treating gang members and their associates.

Today's gangs are sophisticated, diverse and educated. They cross cultural and socioeconomic boundaries. Gang's members may be males or females. A recent University of Chicago study found gangs are adopting a middle-class appearance, while duplicating techniques used by organized crime. According to a 2008 Department of Justice survey, there are approximately a million gang members in the US alone. And this issue is not limited to the US, gang activity is popping up throughout Canada,

Europe and the Pacific Rim, resulting, in Canada as an example, in a significant increase in facility lockdown or restricted access protocols being activated in the aftermath of gang-related shootings.

Security staff members in all aspects of healthcare must be trained to identify gang affiliations or behavior and other gang identifiers to include graffiti and hand signs. Further, the training should expand on specific protocol and expectations to be followed on what to do if the security officer encounters a gang member while on patrol or as a patient or visitor to the facility. It is a common occurrence for gang members to impersonate friends or family of a patient or gain knowledge or access to the patient when in fact they may be an opposing gang who is interested in doing harm to the patient or "finishing the job" if the patient is in the hospital due to an attack by the gang.[8] The training provided the security staff should provide clear guidance on their authority to restrict visitation to a patient, checking all belongings for weapons, placement of the patient under an assumed identification or introduce extra security precautions if they think a patient or visitor creates an undue risk to the healthcare system.

Weapons of mass destruction/pandemic flu

In order to effectively manage disasters, healthcare security officers need to learn the ABCs of diagnosing exposure models, spotting exposed persons, and donning appropriate contaminate-controlling attire to limit potential exposure. The healthcare security program should establish a Weapons of Mass Destruction (WMD) training program to enhance the organization's capability of helping contain WMD exposures before they adversely impact the institutional setting.[9] All security officers need to be taught the basic symptoms associated with WMDs and learn to identify the symptoms of exposure—from the most common biological, chemical, and radiological agents, to recognizing the warning signs associated with flu symptoms' emanating from these contaminates. Table 10-5 identifies a basic

Table 10-5 Weapons of Mass Destruction Exposures / Agents Guide

WMD Exposures / Agents			
Biological	**Viral**	**Hazardous Chemical**	**Radiological**
Anthrax – a spore that can create an acute infection of the skin, lungs or gastrointestinal system	**Ebola** – the most dangerous virus known to science; requires direct contact with the blood or secretions of bodily fluids. **Smallpox** – an infection which occurs from contact with blood, secretions of bodily fluids or via inhalation from infected persons. **Ricin** – a toxin made from the leftover mash of the castor bean, which is processed for the production of castor oil. Easily accessible and easy to produce. It kills body cells on contact. There is no cure for this toxin.	**Cyanide** – poisons victims through inhalation of gas. The longer the exposure or the higher the concentration of cyanide the quicker a victim will be contaminated **Mustard Gas** – a blistering agent; it is an oily liquid that is heavier than water. The vapors and/or liquid are the danger. **Sarin Gas** – a nerve gas; it disrupts the mechanism by which nerves communicate with the organs causing over stimulation of the organs	**Radiation Poisoning** – is caused by exposure to irradiated uranium that gives off "Alpha" and "Gamma" rays.

Concept developed from work created by Anthony J. Luizo, Ph.D and Ben Scaglione, CPP[10]

guideline for WMD exposures/agents for which security officers need to learn to identify the symptoms of exposure. All security officers need to become familiar with the decontamination and treatment processes associated with mass casualty or pandemic flu victim incidences.

Forensic (Prisoner) patients

Patient-prisoners pose unique safety and security challenges for healthcare organizations. The Joint Commission standard HR.2.10 EP10 requires the organization to "orient and educate forensic staff to include how to interact with patients; procedures for responding to unusual clinical events and incidents; the hospital's channels of clinical, security, and administrative communication; and distinctions between administrative and clinical seclusion and restraint." This function is often performed by the healthcare organization's security staff, and tracked meticulously.

Clear direction and guidance helps keep everyone safe during the delivery of forensic healthcare. With the safety of patients and personnel as a priority, defining the security officer role in the treatment of inmates and arrestees is especially important, but is all too often missing in the security officer training plan. If security staff are summoned for assistance, what can be provided? Does the organization allow for security staff to provide bathroom breaks or spell law enforcement officials in their duty to watch the patient? CMS differentiates in the use of handcuffs or other restrictive devices applied by law enforcement officials.[11] If security staff are expected to render assistance to law enforcement officials, are there modifications to the use-of-force continuum that the officer must be trained on?

A challenging issue for security staff is a clear understanding of what patient information can or cannot be disclosed. All too often, law enforcement officials practice a "drop and run" technique. The patient, known to have broken the law, is not arrested or formally charged. The law enforcement officer leaves the healthcare facility with a mandate for the security officer to notify them prior to discharge. This issue is the subject of many heated discussions in the healthcare community. Can the security officer legally notify the authorities? The answer is that it depends on the healthcare organization's policy and their interpretation of HIPPA.

Some healthcare organizations release this information freely to law enforcement, interpreting that the police officer has "a need to know," while other organizations view the discharge of a patient as confidential medical information that cannot be readily shared. This is a precarious situation for the security officer who needs specialized training on HIPPA rules and regulations and how to maintain collegial relationships and liaison efforts with law enforcement.

Internationally, while the term "forensic" is not universally used to describe prisoners as patients, the same challenges exist for healthcare organizations and the need for security training and their engagement in the prisoner management process cannot be disputed.

More detailed information about the interrelationship of security with forensic patients is discussed in Chapter 13, "Patient Care Involvement and Intervention."

Emergency preparedness/FEMA on-line incident command courses

In the U.S., the Emergency Management Institute of the Federal Emergency Management Agency (FEMA) has developed Incident Command System (ICS) training that is available and specifically designed for the healthcare industry. The *Introduction to ICS (IS-100)* is a free on-line training program that is 2½ hours long and provides foundational understanding of an incident command system for hospitals.[12] Many healthcare facilities require the completion of ICS 100 for all security officers and include the training as part of their mandatory training program.

The follow-up ICS program, *Applying ICS to Healthcare Organizations (IS-200)*, is a 3-hour on-line program that provides additional training on and resources for supervisory personnel who are likely to have a role in the healthcare facilities emergency operations center.[13] A large number of healthcare organizations require completion of both ICS 100 and 200 for the security supervisor positions and above. ICS is also utilized outside of the US with many countries developing training and educational content specific to healthcare emergency management.

Other important training considerations

The very nature of protecting a healing environment requires the healthcare security training program to cover a wide variety of subjects and procedures. The level of intensity and amount of focused training time dedicated will vary according to the nature of the healthcare organization served and the security risks identified. Other specialized type of training offered by healthcare protection programs might be:

- Active Shooter
- Infant Abduction and the Security Officer
- Drug Theft and Diversion Investigation
- Media Relations
- Very Important Patients
- Critical Incident Response/Scene Management
- Terrorism Awareness in the Healthcare Environment
- Laws of Arrest, Search, and Seizure
- Patient Privacy
- Being in a Position of Trust
- Targeted Violence

The list of topics can be exhaustive and, unfortunately, the level of depth any one healthcare security program may go into is directly dependent on the resources available and allocated for education and training. The resourceful security administrator will take advantage of every opportunity for training and development to occur on a daily basis, whether through formal educational classes or shared insights from fellow security staff.

There are many resources the protection administrator can utilize. Articles in security specific and healthcare focused publications and trade journals are excellent developmental resources and do not always require formal instructor-led training. A few industry specific related resources include:

- *Campus Safety*, a monthly magazine and on-line resource center that focuses on the healthcare, college campus and school settings
- *Security Management*, a monthly magazine addressing the issues facing the security industry in general
- *Directions*, IAHSS periodic newsletter that includes articles, industry trends and other topical information for those charged with securing the healthcare environment.
- *Journal for Healthcare Protection Management,* a twice per year publication from the IAHSS that focuses on timely protection related issues
- *Healthcare Security Guidelines* and *Healthcare Security Design Guidelines* produced by the IAHSS. Hard copy booklets are available directly from the IAHSS or individual guidelines can be downloaded from the association website www.IAHSS.org. An example of this resource is found in the role security staff may play in media relations, outlined in their guideline 01.11 Media Relations.

- *Center for Personal Protection & Safety (CPPS)* has produced a number of self-directed learning videos specific to the healthcare environment. Their training video, *Shots Fired*, was thought so highly of by the Colorado Hospital Association that they provided a complimentary copy to every hospital in the state.
- *Canadian Security Magazine* is published 9 times a year and offered in a digital version as well and is the leading publication for security in Canada.

IAHSS – HEALTHCARE BASIC SECURITY GUIDELINE, #01.11

Media Relations

Statement

Healthcare Facilities (HCFs) should establish policies and procedures that define appropriate response to media requests for access or information. HCF responses should consider maintaining a patient's right to privacy, the HCF's image and reputation, and requests for information.

Intent

a) HCF personnel and primary security personnel should be aware of their responsibility to advise those with responsibility for approving the on-site presence of media personnel of any unscheduled or unapproved visits. Implemented procedures may include coordination of a Media/Public Relations staff escort as well as providing services such as door openings, crowd control and trespass removal.

b) The HCF should clearly define the permissions and restrictions on media representatives and the use of recording devices. Restrictions should include the definition of internal and external institutional property and social media release of information by HCF staff and employees.

c) The HCF should identify its representative(s) having authority to permit or restrict media activities or recording devices.

d) Procedures should be established to connect the individuals with responsibility for approving the on-site presence of media personnel, determining appropriate gathering locations and contact with:

  1) Unit(s) or department(s) authorized to visit;
  2) Personnel authorized to interview;
  3) Time restrictions of visit/interview, if appropriate; and
  4) Confirmation of patient approval, if involved

e) HCF personnel including those providing security services should be familiar with patient privacy requirements and be able to either verbally articulate or provide written guidelines to requests for information from the media and others.

f) Specific attention should be paid to restricting access to sensitive areas or operations of historical interest to media representatives or others seeking information. Such areas may include trauma departments, research laboratories or perceived controversial operations such as women's health or animal research.

g) HCF areas housing patient health information should be restricted from unauthorized media access.

h) The HCF should address the presence of media during both the crisis and consequence management phases of emergencies. Media gathering area(s) should be identified as part of the emergency operations plan. Considerations should include:

  1) Location – away from patient care, family or staff gathering areas designated in emergency operations plan or other places that may disrupt the delivery of service
  2) Space – adequate to accommodate multiple media relations representatives and room for authorized HCF personnel to provide regular updates, press releases and other information. Separate location for coordination with information officers from responding agencies.
  3) Basic services – vending, restroom, electricity, internet access, voice and data systems
  4) Access control – plans for extended period of restricted access into the facility, visitor management and security escorts.

See Also

- IAHSS Healthcare Security Guideline 09. 01. Security Sensitive Areas
- IAHSS Healthcare Security Guideline 02.02.01. Targeted Violence
- IAHSS Healthcare Security Design Guidelines 02 Buildings and the Internal Environment

Approved: May 2012

ELECTIVE TRAINING

Elective training is generally considered to be for individual self-improvement, but may have some relevance to the employee's job. Healthcare organizations may offer classes such as general computer training or CPR/First Aid, neither of which may be required of the security officer's position. There are also numerous one- and two-day workshops and seminars offered in communities in which the individual may wish to participate.

TRAINING RESOURCES AND RECORDS REQUIREMENTS

Training does not just happen—it requires considerable planning. The planning begins with identifying the curriculum and the resources available for training. Instructors, lesson plans, training material, methods of presentation, evaluation, competency measurements, and documentation are primary elements of the training program.

INSTRUCTORS/FACILITATORS

As continuing education is prevalent in almost all aspects of the healthcare delivery system, an excellent source of security instructors/facilitators can be found in the organization's staff. Staff are generally quite willing to assist other departments in training, and no one is better able to relate to a specific area's security problems than the person responsible for that area or particular function. Generally, an hour is sufficient to accomplish an acceptable level of general training for a specific operating department or function. One-third of this time might be devoted to explaining how the department interacts as a part of the healthcare team; one-third to the department as it relates to security (vulnerabilities, expectations, policy); and the final third to questions by security personnel. This allows security officers to question certain practices and to suggest ways to improve the security posture of the facility. Often, a questionable practice in the eyes of a security officer can be explained by the departmental supervisor, giving security officers better insight into the rationale behind the practice.

The use of in-house staff as instructors has several important benefits. Staff instructors are forced to give some attention to their own work as it relates to security. It may be the first real look they have given to their security vulnerabilities. In addition, rapport often develops between the staff member and the security department and its officers as security staff learn more about the core business of care. Finally, staff instructors may come to appreciate the security program more as they relate to the professional approach of a trained security force.

Instructors/facilitators from the community are also available to assist in the training program. Likely sources for instructors include insurance carriers, the Red Cross organization, the Occupational Safety and Health Administration, law enforcement officials, state safety agencies, fire prevention bureaus, community relations agencies, healthcare attorneys, and Offices of Emergency Preparedness, to name a few.

TRAINING MATERIALS

Most people can listen at 600 words per minute but talk only at 100 to 150 words per minute, and are easily distracted. According to Richard Cook, president of Kottcamp & Young, Inc., a management consulting firm, all knowledge is gained through the five senses. Sight accounts for nearly 85% of learning; hearing, approximately 10%; smell, about 5%; feel and taste, negligible amounts. Thus, in training, one should not rely solely on lectures.

Technology has brought significant innovation to traditional security content development and delivery methods. Computer-based training via hosted e-Learning modules, simulated videos, and self-directed touch screen learning modules have all been combined with traditional instructor-led learning to provide more options to train personnel than ever before. The technology advancement for the training world is only expected to improve while reducing the overall cost of this technology. Increasingly, young social-media, technically savvy employees are embracing multifaceted training delivery mechanisms that can stimulate their senses. Security is no exception to this phenomenon.

Security trainers who want a customized training program can effectively create and use authoring tools that are relatively inexpensive to build and manage. Another option is to use internally produced video presentations. With each of these mediums, one can tailor the information to individual healthcare environments. Healthcare organizations typically have a range of sophisticated video equipment readily available. Interactive video technology, which combines these three tools, is also currently used for a variety of training applications. In addition, many off-the-shelf training videos are available that cover a wide range of healthcare security topics. A subscription training service is available from many e-Learning organizations.

However, e-Learning and computer-based training is not suited for all types of security training, such as demonstrating competency in physically restraining a patient or demonstrating proficiency with the firearm on the firing range. In addition, there is no opportunity for a trainee to ask questions or benefit from group interaction. There will always be a need for instructor-led training, but much of the basic information a security officer needs can be provided through these mediums. They are less costly and can be excellent resources for remedial or point of need training.

A popular method of training is to include training topics in a periodic "training bulletin" that supports training and development with up-to-the-minute information to security personnel on a number of related security topics. This method can be used advantageously when security personnel are assigned to different facilities, as in a multifacility security system. Figure 10-5 provides an example of training bulletins. Training bulletins can be created in-house by security department staff or purchased through a subscription service.

The training program should incorporate the use of role play. The application of a medical restraint, the use of a fire extinguisher, the management of aggressive behavior, all have a classroom component, as well as a need to be actually conducted via a role play exercise.

RECORDS

No matter how simple or sophisticated a training program is, proper training records must be maintained. A record outlining the training accomplished by each officer should be mandatory. A sample training record is shown in Figure 10-6.

Training records can be entered into the computer and only printed on demand for a specific purpose. In one program the officers' training record is brought up on the screen during the officer's periodic formal evaluation. In another program, each officer's training record is sent to the officer on an annual basis asking for the officers to review its completeness.

Many healthcare organizations and contract security companies have invested in learning management software (LMS) that ties the performance management process directly to individual security officer training plans. Thus, e-Learning and instructor-led training can be based on each security employee's job role and their current skill set, assigning them exactly the courses and learning activities they need.

MAY 2013

SECURITY

Training BULLETIN

HSS

BE SMART ◆ BE AWARE ◆ BE SAFE

Patient Surge within a Hospital

In the twelve years since the 9/11 terror attacks America has experienced many horrific incidents of violence and pandemics that have overrun hospital emergency rooms. Security operations, such as security management and visitor and traffic control management can drastically impact healthcare facilities during a patient surge. Security planning and training are a major part of a successful hospital disaster plan.

What is a Patient Surge?

Patient Surge can be identified as a result of an identifiable incident which may occur all at once or over a period of time. A patient surge event associated with a mass casualty incident (MCI), with an influx of patients, can impact the hospital's immediate resources such as adequate staff, supplies and equipment.

What history has taught us

Before 9/11 hospitals faced challenges with structured disaster plans and struggled to prepare properly to respond to large-scale events. For example, it was difficult for hospitals to handle the surge of patients after a mass casualty event. Large mass casualty events, such as the events of 9/11 and more recent events, such as the Boston bombings, continue to emphasize the importance of hospitals in disaster response plan. In the past twelve years we have seen many disasters that have had a significant impact on our healthcare system. In every event security played a major role in the success of the hospital to deal with the patient surge.

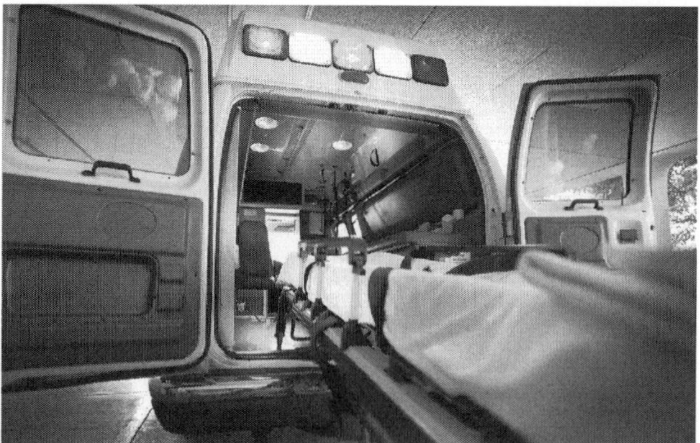

CONTINUED ON OTHER SIDE

FIGURE 10-5

Examples of a healthcare security training bulletin. Courtesy of HSS, Inc.

Our challenge

Every security officer must be knowledgeable of their hospital's disaster procedures and be ready to respond. At HSS we embrace and are integrated into our customers' culture by understanding their needs and maintaining a reputation for service excellence. Beyond the initial surge of patients we must also be mindful of the relationship between the consumption of resources during an MCI event, and the need to effectively manage our security resources, to include staffing and work within the Hospital Incident Command System (HICS).

Types of incidents that create surges

There are many different types of incidents and disasters, both man made and those caused by nature. The most recent events of the Boston bombings in Massachusetts and the Aurora, Colorado theater shooting teach us that our communities are open to terrorism and violence at any time. Hurricanes and tornadoes cause both a patient surge and possible damage to the hospital structure itself. Illnesses like flu outbreaks are unpredictable and strike during many months of the year.

What can I do as a security officer?

During a patient surge at your hospital you may be asked to perform many functions that are different from your normal duties and you may need to work additional hours. Be sure you are aware of, and understand the facility patient surge plans and how security fits into the Hospital Incident Command System (HICS) organizational structure. You should have a personal family plan developed in case you are called in to work and cannot be at home to care for family members. It is extremely important to pre-arrange with other family members, friends or daycare providers to be "on-call" to care for others in case you have to respond to work. **Be familiar with your hospital procedures and HSS policy.** Make sure that any change in information like telephone numbers and/or home address are submitted to HSS as soon as possible.

Patient Surge

Competency Review

HSS

Employee Name: Date: ______________________

1. Patient Surge can be identified as a result of an identifiable incident which may occur all at once or over a period of time.

   True False

2. An outbreak of flu symptoms that send many patients to a hospital in a short period of time could been considered a patient surge.

   True False

3. You should have a personal family plan developed in case you are called in to work and cannot be at home to care for family members.

   True False

4. Every security officer should be familiar with their hospital procedures and HSS policy.

   True False

FIGURE 10-5—Continued

UNITED MEMORIAL HOSPITAL: SECURITY TRAINING RECORD				
Name:		Employee:		Position:
Date	**Subject**	**Duration**	**Instructor & Affiliation**	**Competency Measurement**
07/16/09	New Security Officer Orientation Class	4 hours	Smith, T., Security Trainer	Passed Section I Competency = 88% Passed Section II Competency = 95% Passed Section III Competency = 99% Passed Section IV Competency = 86%
07/17/2009	Aggression Management	8 hours	Smith, T., Security Trainer	Passed De-Escalation Competency = 96% Passed Physical Maneuvers Competency = 100%
07/13-15/2009	OJT Checklist	24 hours	Jones, R., Training Officer	Competencies
07/20/2009	Orientation Competencies	n/a	Bailey, E., Shift Supervisor	Passed Orientation Competencies = 94%
08/03/2009	Phase I Competencies	n/a	Sandoval, E., Shift Supervisor	Passed Phase I Competencies = 98%
08/17/09	Phase II Competencies	n/a	Bailey, E., Shift Supervisor	Passed Phase II Competencies = 97%
08/24-25/09	UMH New Employee Orientation	16 hours	Various	Passed Employee Health and Safety Competencies
09/20/09	Phase III Competencies	n/a	Bailey, E., Shift Supervisor	Passed Phase III Competencies = 95%
10/15/09	Taser Certification	8 hours	Smith, T., Security Trainer	Passed Taser Competency = 91%

FIGURE 10-6

Sample healthcare security officer training record.

A basic industry standard of the IAHSS is that the healthcare organization maintains an individual training record. This record is to be provided to the officer upon termination of employment. Legal situations will often focus on the training provided individual officers. Complete and accurate records become very important in these situations.

REFERENCES

1. Slotnick JA. The future of security training. *Journal of Healthcare Protection Management* 2008;**24**(1):101.
2. Potter Anthony, Woodruff Craig. Public safety training as a force multiplier. *Journal of Healthcare Protection Management* 2012;**28**(1):17–8.
3. Department of Health and Human Services. *Hospital conditions of participation: Patient rights*. 2006, December 8. Retrieved June 16, 2008, from http://www.cms.hhs.gov/CFCsAndCoPs/downloads/finalpatientrightsrule.pdf. §482.13(f), 115.
4. Department of Health and Human Services. *Hospital conditions of participation: Patient rights*. 2006, December 8. Retrieved June 16, 2008, from http://www.cms.hhs.gov/CFCsAndCoPs/downloads/finalpatientrightsrule.pdf. §482.13(f), 96.
5. Bolinger Roxanne. *Security guards' customer rep training reduces ER incidents*. Environment of Care Leader; 2009, October 5. 6–7.
6. Butler Alan. Four ways your security team can impact HCAHPS scores. *Journal of Healthcare Protection Management* 2013;**29**(2):88–92.

7. Michelman B, Patak G. Gang culture from the streets to the emergency department. *Journal of Healthcare Protection Management* 2008;**24**(1):23.
8. Michelman B, Patak G. Gang culture from the streets to the emergency department. *Journal of Healthcare Protection Management* 2008;**24**(1):29.
9. Luizzo AJ, Scaglione BJ. Training security officers to recognize the perils of weapons of mass destruction and pandemic flu contaminates. *Journal of Healthcare Protection Management* 2007;**23**(2):1.
10. Luizzo AJ, Scaglione BJ. Training security officers to recognize the perils of weapons of mass destruction and pandemic flu contaminates. *Journal of Healthcare Protection Management* 2007;**23**(2):2–4.
11. Luizzo AJ, Scaglione BJ. Training security officers to recognize the perils of weapons of mass destruction and pandemic flu contaminates. *Journal of Healthcare Protection Management* 2007;**23**(2):1.
12. Federal Emergency Management Administration. *IS-100.HC Introduction to the incident command system for healthcare/hospitals*. 2007, May 24. Retrieved July 21, 2008, from http://training.fema.gov/EMIWeb/IS/is100HC.asp.
13. Federal Emergency Management Administration. *IS-200.HC Applying ICS to healthcare organizations*. 2013, October 31. Retrieved July 21, 2008, from http://training.fema.gov/EMIWeb/IS/is200HC.asp.

CHAPTER

DEPLOYMENT AND PATROL ACTIVITIES

11

Security operations are primarily concerned with security force deployment, which may include interior and exterior patrols, fixed-post assignments in the emergency department or other high-risk department, visitor managements, and response to requests for routine service and critical events. Operations also involve providing general services such as way-finding and guidance and other customer service needs that make for a better patient and visitor experience. These areas often overlap, with considerable public interaction—the interrelationship of the various security office roles is the basis for creating a viable security staff deployment pattern.

How well the security department carries out its assigned responsibility will depend in large part on planning, controlling, evaluating, and modifying personnel in the field. Security operations require changes in operation, however slight, almost daily. The proper deployment of personnel is a key element of an effective protection program. The cost of security staffing mandates efficient utilization.

Several factors affect the healthcare security staffing model and many healthcare security programs believe they are understaffed. The improper deployment of security personnel is a major deficiency in many protection systems. Despite the professional growth of healthcare security—with the availability of healthcare security industry guidelines, written materials, multimedia information, seminars, and consultants—many programs still operate with excessive cost, causing concern for hospital administrators.

The objective method of determining how many security personnel are deployed is first to determine the functions and the activity to be accomplished. Reference to the number of personnel required is a rather inexact measurement—security staffing requirements are better expressed in terms of full-time equivalents (FTEs) or hours of service. There is no single formula to determine the number of security employees needed to fulfill a master schedule. It is best determined by providing for inspection, response and service capabilities, and including a ratio that considers the amount of unproductive time allotted each security staff member: i.e., required training, absences due to vacation or sick time, etc.

Security staff should ideally be deployed on the basis of objective criteria; however, this is not always the case. A sudden rash of security events, or a major incident, can pressure healthcare leaders to respond quickly. The reaction is often the addition of security personnel. It is generally the quickest thing to do. A short reaction time and visible action can be most important under many circumstances.

Public, staff, and patients expect a safe environment and a responsible reaction to a serious event. The decision to add or discontinue the use of additional security staff, or other protection elements, must be made based on the current security risks and vulnerabilities. A formal review and evaluation should be completed to determine the ongoing need for any additional elements of protection. The review should be well documented and include the rationale for decisions made.

The number of security personnel required is often affected by physical and electronic security applications and organizational policies. For example, the facility that secures its perimeter, designates public entry/exit points, and electronically monitors access usually needs fewer security personnel than does the facility operating in a more open environment. The culture and philosophy of an organization will generally dictate an open or a more closed environment for a facility.

A factor that should not be left out of the equation in determining the number of officers required is the skill level and degree of productivity of each security officer. A well-trained security officer who looks the part, knows and understands the role and consistently performs at a high level is often thought to be more productive than a "guard" who is not properly trained, supervised or engaged in their protection responsibilities. Many healthcare protection administrators agree—one professional security officer can accomplish more than two security guards. A competitive compensation strategy, coupled with a professional security officer training and development program, are key strategies for attaining a high level of engagement and consistent performance. The issue of security officer staffing levels is also discussed in Chapter 6 of this text, "Security Department Organization and Staffing."

DEPLOYMENT OBJECTIVES

The objective of deployment is to provide the right number of security staff at the right time and in the right place. In simplified terms, an officer should not be assigned to check the elevator penthouse when visiting hours are closing or shifts are changing. The four primary goals in deployment are to:

1. Assign officers to times and areas of high risk,
2. Provide rapid response to critical events,
3. Cover peak workload times, and
4. Provide high visibility.

Past incident report records and risk analysis data provide the information required to determine areas and times of high-risk potential. Computer-generated maps have all but replaced the pin map in graphically displaying the types and locations of reported incidents. However, maps, plot plans, and building configuration documents are still useful in portraying certain information. The engineering or planning and facilities departments usually have these types of documents already prepared. Security events should be recorded by time period and type. The properly compiled statistical data can be useful for deployment planning, and for patrolling officers, who can obtain at a glance a picture of the problems in a particular patrol area. This process has been most effective with healthcare facilities that have experienced auto-related thefts and break-ins. Trending the exact location, the make, the model of the vehicle, and the time of day of these troubling incidents has helped many healthcare security programs deploy external security resources to discover the perpetrators, help educate employees on what they can do to help prevent future losses, and identify seasonal trends.

The expectations of security staff with patient assistance in the emergency department can also have a significant impact on the security staffing plan. It is estimated that approximately 80% of hospital security incidents are emergency department generated. A growing number of trauma-designated hospitals, with a high volume of behavioral health patients, report their security staff engage with 5%–10% of their emergency care patients or persons accompanying patients. For these hospitals, their volume of patient- and visitor-generated security interventions is high and growing significantly. The primary cause is the continued reduction of behavioral healthcare funding in the U.S.—the Colorado Department of Human Services reported that the number of psychiatric beds in the state has decreased by 60% between 1990 and 2009. Many other states report similar declines and this phenomenon has also been experienced in Canada. This has created another concerning trend with the growing amount of time security officers spend with high-risk patients in the emergency department, and other areas throughout the healthcare facility. What was historically a 20-minute or less patient intervention today can consume more than 7 hours per reported intervention. The compounded effect of increased volume, and increased time consumed, can result in a very significant proportion of the total security complement devoted to the management of this patient care function.

Healthcare facilities differ in opinion on the use of security staff for patient intervention or prolonged patient watches. Since the business of healthcare exists to deliver care to patients, it could be argued that few security functions could be more important than supporting the safe delivery of care, through these interventions and watches. However, if security officers are used in this manner, their total aggregate amount of time spent with patient intervention activities must be accounted for in the security staffing plan.

A short response time relative to critical incidents is an indicator of success for the security program. The entire complex must be patrolled in a manner that provides an acceptable response time to critical events from all areas of the facility. As response time is shortened, the probability of successfully managing adverse events is greatly enhanced. Monitoring and minimizing response time is perhaps the most important factor a security force can use to build confidence, and a positive perception, in the security system. Security and law enforcement alike are often judged more on how long it took them to arrive than on their actual handling of a disruptive event.

A common missing component is the routine testing of the time it takes for security officers to respond to critical incidents and routine calls for service. A strategy that works particularly well is to make the random test a Joint Commission performance measurement (or improvement initiative) for the security program. With monthly control tests, the security administrator can quantify and measure response time, which can frequently help justify the need for additional security resources.

In Vancouver, Canada the Lower Mainland Integrated Protection Services (IPS) program has established response time to calls, both urgent and nonurgent, as part of their Key Performance Indicators (KPI) with their vendor partner. The Security Operations Center receives all calls for security service for more than 30 healthcare facilities, dispatches the response and electronically tracks the time to respond to the scene for both urgent and nonurgent calls. The response times are monitored and the results for thousands of calls are examined each quarter, to assess performance and take any corrective action necessary.

Covering peak periods of requested and scheduled services is an important goal of deployment. This information is obtained from the facility's previous experience and depends on the functions performed in the protection program. The number of calls for service is an important factor in determining how the organization feels about the security service. A large number of calls for service indicate a high level of acceptance of and confidence in the security department. Response time to provide routine requested services is also important. This response will not be as immediate as that for emergencies; however, a good security force will provide service as soon as possible for even the most routine of services.

Another goal of deployment is high visibility of the security force. This practice provides a maximum protection image and a feeling of security and safety for employees, patients, and visitors alike. The importance of this factor cannot be overemphasized.

FLEXING THE SECURITY STAFFING PLAN

"Flexing" security staffing due to absences and/or vacancies can create undue risk for a healthcare facility in the event of an adverse security incident. It also creates unnecessary payroll expense for the facility when the "*minimum*" staff deployment is exceeded. The security staffing plan should not be viewed as a total FTE count allocated to the department, but rather the complement of staff stated to be on duty at any given time per the master schedule.

Fairly common in the healthcare industry is for the security staffing plan to have two staffing plans: a normal complement of a staff in which the master security plan is based, and a minimum staffing plan. For example, the security staffing plan calls for a complement of three security officers around the clock, but its staffing minimum is two. Unfortunately, in lawsuits for inadequate security (for example, a visitor assaulted in the parking garage), the risk associated with the minimum staffing model is a plaintiff's attorney claiming: "If there were three security officers as designed, there is significant propensity that the deployment of that officer could have prevented this crime from occurring." This argument gives credence to the dispute of inadequate security and often results in a higher negotiated settlement if the case is not taken to court.

In short, the protection program should refrain from flexing security staffing for temporary convenience or budgetary constraints. Absences and vacancies must always be filled unless uncontrollable circumstances exist. Minimum staffing levels should not be stated differently than the master security schedule. Security resources are typically prioritized related to business risk and the impact on quality patient care. Expenses associated with security staffing levels must be managed and balanced against the constant pressures of cost containment. The goal is to obtain commitment on the security staffing levels for the healthcare facility, and maintain a consistent level of security service.

An exception is the use of per diem, also referred to as on-call security staff or in some organizations, specialized security sitters, to help with patient intervention activities. If the security team is actively involved in managing high-risk patient behavior, using an on-demand approach has proven beneficial for many healthcare security programs to contain costs and maintain protection levels. If this approach is used, minimum expectations for response should be established and monitored on an on-going basis. Thus, the right amount of staff can be applied to this fluctuating demand on security services.

SCHEDULING THE SECURITY STAFF

A major administrative function is the scheduling of security personnel into work shifts. Scheduling of security staff does not mean merely putting down names to fill in the open spaces on a schedule. Scheduling and post assignment have somewhat the same basic objective of deploying the most appropriate officer to cover a post assignment. Scheduling comes first and generally refers to shifts and days of the week. Post assignment is the utilization of officers who are scheduled for a particular shift. Thus, appropriate staff must be scheduled for a shift before a post assignment can be effected in the proper manner. Scheduling and post assignment are obviously synonymous when there is only one officer scheduled for a particular shift.

In both scheduling and post assignment, administrative factors include skill level; post specific training; appropriate image; security presence desired (commanding, reassuring, customer service); culture; language spoken; physical ability; and being properly licensed for the assignment if required. All these factors must be taken into consideration, without violating discrimination laws, to assign the best person for the specific assignment.

There are generally two types of schedules: the *master schedule*, which covers a specific time period in advance, and the *working schedule*, which is a day-to-day document that reflects the actual officer who filled the specific shift. The master schedule, when properly constructed, can be modified each day to reflect any changes in actual shift and/or post assignment. This record of persons actually filling an assignment, as opposed to the projected persons, becomes the official document of coverage and should be maintained for historical purposes. Compensation records become a backup record to prove validity of the schedule, if such verification becomes necessary.

A common mistake found in many security schedules is amending the master security schedule to address the personal needs of an individual security officer. The schedule should always take into consideration a reasonableness factor, as it relates to an employee being able to fulfill the shift hours and needs. However, changes made for personal convenience of an individual almost always result in a less than optimum staffing plan, frequently creating vacant positions that are very difficult to fill or creating unnecessary overtime expense.

For many larger departments, labor management software is used quite successfully for maintaining scheduling assignments and post qualifications, and for tracking individual security officer training, certifications and licensing. The programs can, among other functions, search for open shifts, double assignments for a given officer, and assist in identifying officers available in the event of a vacancy. Off-the-shelf programs designed specifically for the security industry are available. Frequently, these add-on modules are available through the healthcare organization's human resource information system (HRIS).

The basic reason most healthcare security personnel are uniformed is to provide visibility to persons being protected and a visible deterrent to the malefactor. Those who are being protected develop a sense of well-being when they can see the security effort in action.

Employees expect to see the security officer at certain times when arriving or leaving the workplace. A problem develops when an officer is called away from normal deployment to perform another activity, such as answering a call for service. Employees may then complain that security personnel are not where they are supposed to be and are thus neglecting their job—or worse yet a serious incident might occur. There are seldom sufficient security personnel to assure consistent preventive deployment patterns.

An example of employee expectations not being met occurred at a hospital where a female employee was sexually assaulted at the medical center as she arrived at work. In the testimony heard by a jury, the employee stated she had grown accustomed to seeing security every night outside, and thus did not overly concern herself with her would-be attacker, who she admitted to seeing prior to leaving her car. The external patrol security officer had been asked to stand-by to watch an at-risk patient in the emergency care center. Although the jury did not believe the security officer was derelict in his duty to protect the healthcare facility, they determined that if the officer had been performing his normal activities, there is reason to believe the officer could have prevented the employee from being a victim of crime. As a result, the jury found in favor of the employee and levied a very high award against the medical center.

DEPLOYMENT PATTERNS AND CONCEPTS

Although the security vulnerabilities, the use of physical and electronic security safeguards, the layout, size, patient demographics and location of the facility and its philosophies are factors that can alter security officer coverage plans, some basic deployment patterns can be applied.

In extremely small hospitals that use only 8 hours of security officer coverage per day, the hours from 6:00 p.m. to 2:00 a.m. generally provide the best coverage plan. In this coverage plan, the security officer reports for duty at about the time managers and supervisors are leaving for the day. The officer is present to cover the period that sees traditionally the highest patient/visitor load (7:00 p.m. to 9:00 p.m.), and after the majority of visitors are gone, the facility access points can be secured. The officer is then available to assist in evening and night shift changes. The movement of personnel and the requests for services generally settle down shortly after 12:30 or 1:00 a.m., allowing the officer to conduct a thorough facility check before going off duty.

To cover a facility from 6:00 p.m. to 2:00 a.m. seven days per week, 56 labor hours are required. By extending this coverage by 32 hours per week, the facility can maintain continuous security coverage from 6:00 p.m. Friday to 2:00 a.m. Monday, along with 6:00 p.m. to 2:00 a.m., Monday through Thursday. Of course, this coverage pattern does not fit all facilities, and the available labor hours must be scheduled for the greatest benefit. If problems develop or new vulnerabilities present themselves, coverage must always be adjusted to meet these needs.

One should not think only in terms of 8-hour blocks. A 10-hour shift from 6:00 p.m. to 4:00 a.m. or 5:00 p.m. to 3:00 a.m. would improve coverage significantly over the above-described 6:00 p.m. to 2:00 a.m. plan. The most advantageous deployment plan may require 4-, 6-, 10-, or 12-hour shifts. In each, the schedule must consider how reasonable it is the position can be staffed. Many security administrators have created creative security plans only to find that they cannot keep consistent staff, sometimes due to the unavailability of transit after hours that can be used by security personnel.

Ten-hour shifts have become popular alternatives to the traditional 8-hour shift for several reasons. Employees put a high premium on time off. The 10-hour shift allows a 4-day workweek, which in effect yields a 3-day weekend. A 4-day workweek also benefits employees financially by reducing work expenses, such as meals and commuting costs. The 10-hour shift allows organizations to work an officer 50 hours per week if necessary and still give the officer two days off. The challenging aspect of 10-hour shifts is found in the 168 hours of coverage in the 24-hour/7-day-a-week schedule—it is not evenly divided by 10. Thus, a variation in the plan must be created. To offset, many organizations use a mixture of 8- and 10-hour shifts in their master schedule.

POST ASSIGNMENTS

Security officer deployment plans normally consist of a combination of post assignments. The variety of post assignments can be separated into four distinct categories:

1. Fixed post
2. Modified fixed post
3. Sectored or zone patrol
4. Unrestricted patrol.

The latter two assignments are often referred to as roving patrols. Each of these post assignments has specific objectives and purposes; however, all are intended to provide a degree of activity accountability. The most accountable assignment is the fixed post.

The fixed post is a stationary post located at a specific location for a specific time period. A true fixed post requires the assigned officer to be relieved for any absence whatsoever. The fixed post is expensive and is generally used to provide a certain function, such as an after-hours access control point, staffing of a walk-through magnetometer, visitor management, and dispatch operations. It may also be used to provide a presence, or visibility. Officers in fixed-post assignments are typically not available to respond to calls for service. If fixed-post officers respond to calls, they are not performing the assignment as originally intended, which can lead to complaints and even legal problems should an adverse event occur while the officer is absent. Employees depend on this protection being in place, but on the other hand they have difficulty understanding why officers cannot leave the post to render routine assistance. For example, an employee who has locked his keys in a car must wait for a patrol officer to be dispatched to render assistance.

A modified fixed post is used in a number of healthcare security programs. The post is left unoccupied at times to conduct patrol rounds or to answer a call for service. A good example is a modified fixed post located in an emergency department. The security officer may be responsible for the general area, including the parking lots outside the emergency area. The officer may at certain times leave the post to conduct a short security patrol or to assist patients or visitors within the general emergency department area.

Another variation of the modified fixed post is the random rotation to two or more fixed-post locations. For example, three areas of the facility—the main lobby, the patient care tower, and the loading and receiving dock—may be designated as rotating posts. Security officers assigned to this type of post divide their time between the three areas on a nonpatterned schedule. They are not asked to patrol other areas of the facility—only one of the three designated areas.

Sectored (zone) patrol and unrestricted patrol are basic methods of deployment, but are still considered to be post assignments. The purpose of these roving patrols is to achieve protection objectives through security officers who round within prescribed areas. Their actions can be divided into four primary categories: response to critical events, inspection services, routine preventive patrol, and response to provide courtesy or routine services. Sectored patrols, in which the patrol area is strictly defined, are used in larger programs when a patrol officer is assigned to a given area for a specific period of time. In unrestricted patrols, officers are free to patrol the entire complex. During any given shift, a single officer may be assigned to a variety of different post assignments.

A frequent challenge in today's healthcare environment is how to handle calls for extra staffing. In healthcare organizations providing patient assistance, there is a need for the department to preplan how multiple patient assists are managed. If additional security staff are pulled from the existing complement, arrangements must be made to offset the reduction in force in other areas. In such circumstances, a team lead or security shift supervisor plays an important role in determining how precious resources are to be redeployed, based on risk and activity in "real time." How temporary department coverage requests are managed will vary by organization. Some organizations empower their security staff to call in extra security support to include specialized sitters or off-duty officers, while other facilities make prearrangements for the external patrol officer to cover both internal and external patrol duties. The important component is that extra security needs occur in every facility from time to time and the security staff should have a clear understanding of the organization's expectation of how it should be managed.

BASIC PATROL DEPLOYMENT PLANS

Security officers who perform patrol duties should be assigned to specifically defined areas. The officers are thus responsible to protect a given area and held accountable for performing the prescribed activities.

Every facility has certain areas or departments that require a higher level of security officer visibility. These more vulnerable areas can often be serviced by overlapping patrol patterns, shown in Figure 11-1.

Patrol area assignments may be altered for various shifts or during shifts in response to the number of personnel assigned to patrol an area or to respond to identified risks and vulnerabilities. For example, a facility with two patrol officers on the 4:00 p.m. to 12:00 a.m. shift may deploy one officer internally and one externally, except for times when parking lots and other external areas are vulnerable to assault, vandalism, or breaking and entering of vehicles. At these times, both officers may be deployed to the external campus. The following schedule illustrates how such a deployment plan might work:

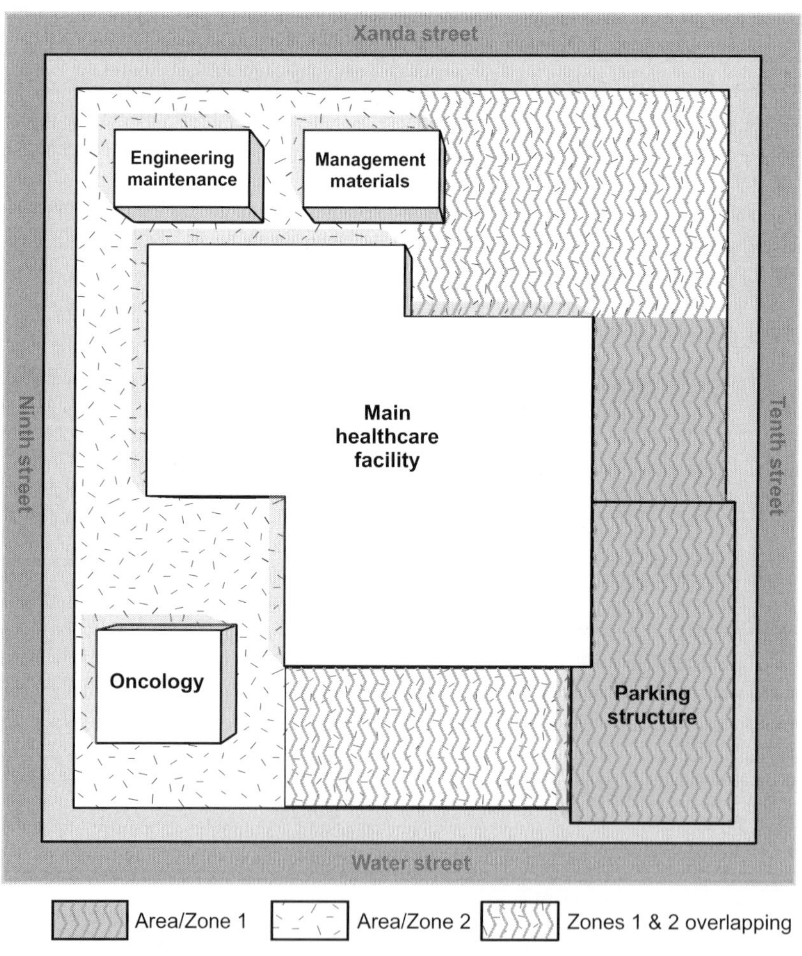

FIGURE 11-1

Overlapping security patrol areas.

Patrol Officer One

4:00 p.m. to 5:00 p.m.: Entire grounds and parking areas
5:00 p.m. to 7:00 p.m.: North half of external area
7:00 p.m. to 10:30 p.m.: Entire internal area
10:30 p.m. to 12:00 a.m.: South half of external area

Patrol Officer Two

4:00 p.m. to 5:00 p.m.: Entire internal area
5:00 p.m. to 7:00 p.m.: South half of external area
7:00 p.m. to 10:30 p.m.: Entire grounds and parking area
10:30 p.m. to 12:00 a.m.: North half of external area

In this example, each of the officers patrols both internally and externally. This allows the officers to patrol the same area so one may find a condition or problem the other officer may have missed. It also allows the officers to share in the exposure to adverse weather conditions.

DOUBLE COVERAGE

A general principle in deployment is to maintain a 24-hour coverage schedule, seven days a week, before deploying more than one officer on a given shift. However, double coverage may be most advantageous when building to a 24-hour security program, while the number of hours authorized is slowly increased. For example, a program authorizing 112 hours of coverage may find a coverage pattern of 4:00 p.m. to 12:00 a.m. and 10:00 p.m. to 6:00 a.m. to be more productive than 4:00 p.m. to 12:00 a.m. and 12:00 a.m. to 8:00 a.m. The overlapping coverage during peak periods of the late-night shift change may be viewed as more important than the two hours from 6:00 a.m. to 8:00 a.m.

In many medical centers, security officer shifts begin at 8:00 a.m., 4:00 p.m., and 12:00 a.m. These times work quite well in general hospitals or nursing homes, because they follow the major shift changes of facility staff by approximately one hour. A change of security personnel is thus avoided when most facility staff are changing shifts. Today's healthcare environment has fewer concentrated shift change times than what was experienced historically, because of the consolidation of many healthcare facilities and programs, which share staff who come and go from the facility at various times during the day and night. The strategic security administrator connects the business of security to the business of care by understanding the staffing rotations of key hospital services, the clinical care staff in particular, and aligning security staffing models with the facility requirements.

Table 11-1 shows a deployment plan for a medium-size medical care facility utilizing all 10-hour shifts.

Table 11-2 shows a deployment plan for a small medical care facility. In the staffing plan, there is double coverage for the 10:00 p.m. to 12:00 a.m. shift change. In this plan, which uses 182 hours of coverage per week, 8- and 10-hour shifts are involved.

OPERATIONAL VERSUS NONOPERATIONAL TIMES

Most medical centers operate on a 24-hour basis. However, each healthcare facility can define an operational time period and a nonoperational time period. As with so many other concepts, these time periods vary to some degree from organization to organization, with some quasi-operational periods falling

Table 11-1 Sample Staffing Plan for a Medium-sized Medical Center

	Day of Week/Officer Assignment						
Shift	**Sun**	**Mon**	**Tues**	**Wed**	**Thurs**	**Fri**	**Sat**
6 A – 4 P	1	1	1	1	2	2	2
6 A – 4 P	2	3	3	4	4	4	4
2 P – 12 M	5	5	5	5	6	6	6
2 P – 12 M	6	7	7	7	7	8	8
10 P – 8 A	9	9	9	9	10	10	10
10 P – 8 A	10	11	11	12	12	12	12
7 P – 5 A	13	13	14	14	14	13	13

Table 11-2 Sample Staffing Plan for a Small Medical Center

	Day of Week/Officer Assignment						
Shift	**Sun**	**Mon**	**Tues**	**Wed**	**Thurs**	**Fri**	**Sat**
8 A – 4 P	2	1	1	1	1	1	2
4 P – 12 M	3	3	5	5	3	3	3
10 P – 8 A	4	6	6	6	4	4	4

between the operational and nonoperational periods. These time periods have a direct implication for patrol deployment. During the operational time period, the patrol officer is a support element to be called on for assistance and to provide a general surveillance of public and general-use areas. The operating concept is that departments require little if any internal patrol when they are fully operational.

During the nonoperational time period, the patrol officer and the entire security function take on a custodial role in protecting the facility. Many departments are closed, and officers must check these areas to ensure they are secured properly and to question strangers in the area. In other words, the security staff must understand what is normal for the department so they can more readily recognize what is out of the ordinary.

The medical complex as a whole, and then each area or department, must be reviewed to determine the proper security officer role for a given time period. For general hospitals, the operational period is usually from 6:00 a.m. to 5:00 p.m. The transition period between 5:00 p.m. and 9:00 p.m. may present some unique security vulnerabilities because some departments are less controlled than they are during the true operational time period. During this transition period, there is enough human traffic within the facility to provide would-be malefactors with anonymity and a plausible "ruse purpose" for being in an area. After 9:00 p.m. facilities generally close their doors for the night. Of course, some departments do operate with reduced personnel on duty or on call. For example, central supply may operate 24 hours but reduce staff to only one or two persons during the late night hours.

Security officers must constantly monitor the status of their assigned area and alter their patrol activity in relation to this status. If a particular department is open after the normal time period, the officer should check the area more frequently to make certain the department is secured after it closes.

It may also require more frequent checks due to the limited personnel on duty, as in the case of the central supply example.

Weekends and holidays may also present special concerns. These periods can be categorized as quasi- or semi-operational periods for most facilities. Many departments are closed, yet visitors are numerous, and most patient care operations continue. An added factor is supervision and facility staffing are often reduced to a minimum during these times. These considerations strongly suggest increased patrol coverage and visibility is necessary on weekends to provide the required protection level. The assignment of too many part-time or inexperienced officers during weekends and holidays should be avoided. Note in the sample staffing plans provided in Tables 11-1 and 11-2, special effort has been made to identify part-time employment opportunities during traditionally low security incident activity periods, combined with a reasonableness factor to part-time employee availability.

PATIENT CARE UNITS/AREAS

Generally, no part of the facility should be off-limits to security inspection. On the other hand, a patrolling security officer has no business entering the pharmacy or narcotic vault, surgical suites, examination rooms, labor rooms, or other similar areas while they are in use. Security officers called to one of these areas should be knowledgeable about the procedures required for entering the area and any special attire to be worn.

The need to patrol the corridors of patient units varies somewhat with the time of day. During the operational period, when units are fully staffed, there is generally little need for a security patrol. If security services are required, unit personnel should request the needed security support. During the nonoperational period, the increased security patrol of patient units provides support to the limited staff, and the visibility of the patrolling officer creates a greater perception of safety for staff. The deployment pattern for the patrol of nursing-care units should be planned in coordination with the nursing service administrative staff. Care and consideration should be given so that volume from radio traffic is not disruptive or irritating to patients, visitors, or staff while on patrol. Many healthcare security programs have introduced lapel microphones, ear pieces and Bluetooth®-enabled devices to minimize radio noise to help create a better patient experience. In the U.S., this has had a positive impact on HCAHPS scores.

Historically, stand-alone behavioral healthcare facilities and in-house behavioral health units preferred not to have patrolling security officers on their unit for fear the uniform may have an antagonizing or disruptive presence to the patient. Today, leaders of the behavior health unit have started to request more security patrol and increased security officer presence with the patients on these units. More aptly found on transitional care units, the command presence of the security officer in traditional uniform is believed to be therapeutic and help the patient assimilate to the "real world." In Canada, the practice of locating security staff on a behavioral/mental health inpatient unit as a fixed post appears to be on the rise.

ENTRANCES AND EXITS

If all the people entering and leaving a medical care complex could be properly surveyed and controlled, the protection level would be quite high. It is virtually impossible to achieve this state of control, although some facilities with strong visitor management systems do control a high percentage of the people entering the facility. More and more healthcare organizations impose this rigid control, but it is still relatively low as a percentage. As a result, the healthcare environment often provides too many open entrances and exits for the sake of convenience. While relatively free access to hospitals may be the norm during the day, there is need to reduce uncontrolled access during the evening and night hours. A general plan is to lock designated entry points at 6:00 p.m. when staff in the area departs, and to further lock down access points at the termination of designated visiting hours. All facilities should designate specific controlled night entrances for late night visitors, delivery, and others.

Greater patrol time should be allocated to the main entrances and exits, and to external patrol, than to internal areas when the entrances and exits are uncontrolled. Because officers cannot be in all places and see all things at all times, their patrols should be structured to view as much activity as possible. An officer who checks a busy entrance, or surveys two or three exits from the exterior, will be able to observe many more people than when patrolling in a far removed area of the facility. The distant areas are, of course, important in the total patrol deployment plan, but they should not receive attention out of proportion to the objective of surveying and controlling the general-use areas.

BASIC PATROL CONCEPTS

The backbone of the security effort is the security officer on patrol. A major objective of healthcare security is to manage the patrol responsibility so officers maximize visibility and time spent on patrol and minimize time spent writing needless reports or doing other nonproductive busy work. Patrol can best be examined by the separation of patrol into external and internal considerations.

EXTERNAL PATROL

External patrol generally covers the grounds, parking areas, and streets surrounding the facility buildings. External patrol is intended to protect vehicles and people entering or leaving the grounds, to provide surveillance of people attempting to use unauthorized exits, to prevent the unauthorized removal of property from the facility, to prevent or discourage unwanted people from entering the facility, and to provide various courtesy services.

Officers on external patrol provide perimeter security protection. They can often observe much more activity than officers on internal patrol. Not only do the grounds typically offer a much greater area to be vandalized, but officers also have a view of a large area. For example, from a parking lot, an external officer may be able to see three or four hospital entrances and exits, while an internal officer can generally only observe one of these points at a time.

A major responsibility of external patrol is to ensure the integrity of facility access points by frequently checking doors, windows, roof access, and fire escapes to preclude unauthorized use and ensure patient and staff safety. A common problem is emergency fire exits that are not intended to be used for entry. Although locked from the exterior, these doors often do not latch properly after an exit. In addition, employees and others sometimes place an object between the door and the frame to keep the latch from engaging. This is often done for convenience and not with the intent to compromise security. Nevertheless, this careless act can provide the access needed for an outsider to commit a serious crime. To help minimize this concern, all fire emergency exits should be alarmed and monitored for hold-open status.

EXTERNAL PATROL VEHICLES

The basic types of external patrol are foot patrols, bicycle patrols, vehicle patrols, personal transport vehicles or a combination of each. Regardless of the type of vehicle used for patrol, they should be easily identifiable as security vehicles. To be an effective deterrent, it is not enough that the protection capability is present. It must also be highly visible to the people being protected and to those who might be contemplating a criminal act.

Various types of patrol vehicles have their own advantages. Facilities composed of many streets and roads, large and decentralized parking areas, and multiple buildings generally use an automobile or a four-wheel drive vehicle for security. Smaller facilities may find a small golf-cart-type vehicle better suited to their purposes. The use of mountain bikes to patrol, where weather allows, continues to grow in popularity in the healthcare environment and is an excellent alternative for campus environments that have many high-traffic sidewalks, surface parking lots and public thoroughfares in a contained space. A recent trend is the deployment of personal transport vehicles into the security operations of healthcare campuses—in some jurisdictions these are known by brand names, such as Segway®. These vehicles are a complement to traditional foot patrol; Bryan Warren, CHPA, Corporate Director of Security at Carolinas Health System in Charlotte, North Carolina, has stated that when his officers started using personal transporters they "were able to complete their patrol routes in approximately half the time than they did on foot." Table 11-3 provides a brief overview of the advantages and disadvantages of various external patrol vehicles.

Vehicle patrols

Many modern medical facilities occupy large expanses of property and require motor vehicle patrol to ensure proper coverage. Vehicles increase officer mobility, can provide protection from the elements, and allow officers to carry the necessary equipment to provide an efficient and effective response to emergencies.

Table 11-3 Advantages and Disadvantages of External Patrol Vehicles

	Patrol Vehicle			
	Auto	**Cart**	**Bike**	**Personal Transport**
Visibility	Good	Fair	Very Good	Very Good
Ease of Use	Good	Good	Fair	Fair
Professional Image	Good	Fair	Good	Good
Areas Traveled	Fair	Good	Very Good	Very Good
Personal Safety	Very Good	Fair	Fair	Fair
Comfort	Very Good	Good	Fair	Fair
Inclement Weather	Very Good	Fair	Poor	Fair/Poor
Transport Others	Very Good	Good	Poor	Poor
Vehicle Assistance	Very Good	Good	Poor	Poor
Environmental Impact	Poor	Fair	Very Good	Good
Total Cost of Ownership	Fair	Poor	Very Good	Fair

FIGURE 11-2

Example of a security patrol vehicle used in a healthcare program in Texas.

Contrary to the typical police sedan found in many law enforcement agencies, the best security patrol vehicles have a short wheel base to help the driver better maneuver in tight spaces. The "cross-over" line of vehicles is favored as they provide the driver with more clearance than traditional sedans. The added height when combined with amber-colored light bar makes the vehicle more readily visible when on campus. Many healthcare organizations using the security patrol car have experienced significant improvement in security visibility when the light bar is turned on for all external campus patrols.

Although sharing a vehicle between the security department and another hospital department is usually a poor idea, it is possible to provide temporary markings for each type of use. Magnetic signs, available in assorted sizes, colors, and formats, are commonly used. When the vehicle is assigned to the security department, the security signs are applied, and when the vehicle is turned over to another department, the security signs are removed.

The security patrol car should be regularly maintained and kept clean. The image associated with a security patrol car sends a powerful message about how seriously security is taken at the facility. A dirty vehicle, faded security markings, missing hubcaps or the continued use of spare tires each are negative symbolic gestures that must be managed daily. Individually and collectively the perception of the security patrol car, much like the security uniform, can signal organizational security readiness or a lack of focus on protection services. Figure 11-2 is an example of a security patrol vehicle used in a healthcare program in Texas.

Security carts

Small electric and gasoline-powered vehicles are popular, especially in warmer climates. These vehicles have several advantages: they are economical to operate, maneuver well in tight areas, and can generally be driven on grass or landscaped areas without causing damage. With various engine power options, these vehicles can be purchased "street-legal." When appropriately registered, the street-legal security cart can be driven on public roads.

The security cart can be used in reasonably inclement weather, with options available for all-weather enclosures and heating and air-conditioning. These options become important considerations if the cart is routinely used to provide security escorts. Frequently used in healthcare organization for

FIGURE 11-3

An example of a security patrol cart.

shuttle/transport service and general support services, carts are available in many shapes and sizes. Most security carts cannot carry all of the service equipment typically found in the security patrol car.

The security cart is often the least visible of all of the external security patrol vehicles listed. Care must be given to readily identify the vehicle with appropriate security markings. Many healthcare organizations equip the cart with an amber-colored light bar similar to the traditional security patrol car to maximize visibility. Figure 11-3 is an example of a security patrol cart.

The ongoing maintenance of the security cart continues to plague many healthcare security operations where they are used. A security cart used daily for external patrols will typically need to be replaced on average every two to three years. Commonly plagued with ongoing repair and maintenance expense, the total cost of ownership of the security cart is the least economical of all external security patrol vehicles.

Bicycle patrol

Bike patrol is an urban and campus patrol concept focused on being a visible deterrent to external crime, and an approachable source of assistance and information on the healthcare grounds. Bike patrol officers can see over the heads of most pedestrians and over most vehicles. The bikes also provide speed and mobility through crowded and narrow corridors and the ability to get places where cars cannot. They can go off road, into alleyways, behind buildings, along sidewalks and up and down curbs without much of a problem. Bike patrol officers can patrol large areas more frequently in shorter periods of time than gas-powered alternatives, thus being more visible and accessible to the general public.

Patrols on bikes are more customer friendly; security officers become more approachable and less threatening. A common statement heard from healthcare organizations who have introduced bike patrol is that it allows their officers to be more interactive with the community served, while increasing their knowledge of the campus and constituents through positive contact. Kent Hospital (Warwick, Rhode Island) president and CEO Mark E. Crevier noted that the bike patrol introduced at his hospital in October 2006 is an example of the hospital's commitment to "progressive (and) responsive services." Mr. Crevier stated that the bike patrol "help(s) support traffic flow, render assistance and further extend the presence and effectiveness of our security force."[1] Additional benefits of the bike patrol program commonly include:

- Greater opportunity to be exposed to the public; more accessible image
- Greater maneuverability in small areas compared to a security patrol car
- Added element of surprise to counter criminal activity
- High visibility and crime deterrent

Bike patrol programs are quick and easy to set up. Mickey Watson, chief of public safety for Sarasota Memorial Health System in Florida, shared that his health system supplemented its patrol vehicles with a bike patrol program and spent $700 to $1,000 for each customized police-style mountain bike—based on individual measurements—and the equipment each officer would need to conduct their patrols. Watson also shared that introduction of a bike program helped the health system successfully lower emergency response times across campus, from a target response time of three minutes, to two minutes. The bike program has also helped increase the patrol radius from just the hospital grounds (a 3-block by 4-block area in downtown Sarasota) to a 6-square-block area. This has resulted in an almost 80% decrease in property crime in their four multistory parking decks.[2]

A healthy and "green" alternative to external patrol vehicle options, most healthcare security departments deploying bike patrol officers frequently get ample volunteers for the special duty. The cycling helps the officer get fit and stay in shape while getting paid. Bike patrol is not for every security officer and should not be mandated. Every bike patrol officer should submit to a human performance evaluation, designed specifically for the bike patrol program, prior to riding on behalf of the healthcare organization.

A bicycle patrol program has specialized training needs. Most certified bike patrol training programs, like the guidelines and recommendations promulgated by the International Police Mountain Bike Association,[3] entail between 16–32 contact hours and typically emphasize training, community enforcement concepts, equipment and safety, and defensive tactics such as high-speed maneuvers and braking, jumping curbs and riding down steps. For personal safety reasons, security officers performing this function should be issued a specific security uniform that can stand up to the mobility requirements of the bike patrol function, and withstand the additional wear and tear often found by its riders, while maximizing visibility. All officers should be required to wear a helmet and sign a safety affidavit prior to working in a bike patrol capacity. Figure 11-4 is an example of a bike patrol officer in action.

In areas of inclement winter weather, many healthcare security programs only use bike patrols seasonally or as weather permits. In the event the bike cannot (or should not) be ridden, the external patrol officer typically transitions into a security patrol car or to foot patrol.

Customizing bikes is recommended; although not required, it produces a much better fit for the officers who spend 8 hours a day on the bike, potentially reducing the risk of injuries to the officer.

One factor often overlooked is the need to secure the bike while the security officer is responding to calls. One Canadian security program reported losing five bikes in a 2-year period in a crime-ridden neighborhood, all stolen while the officer provided an urgent response on foot, after arriving at a scene. Strong procedures on officer accountability and responsibility for securing this valuable piece of equipment must be a foundation of any bicycle patrol program.

FIGURE 11-4

A bike patrol officer in action.

Personal transporter

Personal transporter (PT) use in healthcare is limited to some of the most innovative security programs, such as Johns Hopkins, Loma Linda Medical Center, Carolinas HealthCare System, and Baltimore's Sinai Hospital, but is quickly growing and expanding its use in the healthcare environment. The mode of patrol offered by the PT is the most versatile of each of the security patrol vehicles. Unlike motorized vehicles and bicycles, the PT can be used for both internal and external patrol, and allow for security officers to patrol open pedestrian environments closed to vehicle traffic, and respond quickly to emergencies. An alternative to gas-powered vehicles, the electric-powered PT does not have any carbon emissions, is very quiet compared to other forms of transport, and uses a rechargeable high-capacity battery that can be replenished via a standard 110v outlet, thus further reducing any harmful effects on the environment.[4]

The visibility of the PT is very good as the patrolling officer stands on the vehicle, increasing his or her height approximately 6 inches. Typically well marked as security, the PT is obvious to patients, staff, and visitors alike. This not only adds to its preventative presence, but also makes the officers more approachable as curious patients and visitors tend to ask about these devices when they encounter them (Figure 11-5).

Using transporters, security staff are also more alert and less fatigued when they have to respond quickly to a situation versus running or pedaling on a traditional bicycle.[5] The PT operator does require specialized training, but by working with the manufacturer, "train the trainer" sessions can be set up to allow for the creation of in-house trainers, which can greatly reduce any logistical challenges for programs with higher turnover. Such training sessions typically involve familiarity with the nomenclature and balancing/use of the transporter, low and high speed steering and maneuvering, auto safety shut-down procedures and general operator safety and troubleshooting. Such training should be performed initially prior to a security officer being allowed to use the transporter, with an annual refresher.

FIGURE 11-5

Example of a personal transport vehicle used in healthcare.

EXTERNAL PATROL SERVICES/CONSIDERATIONS

Often, the external patrol officer will perform additional services to help enhance the public perception of safety on campus. These include battery-jumping service and transportation of people. There is also equipment the security staff should have readily available and an understanding of how to operate patrol vehicle(s) used by the healthcare protection program.

Battery jumping service

Every security department that uses vehicles for patrol service must decide whether battery-jumping service will be provided. Battery jumping is unquestionably a burdensome task. On the other hand, helping a stranded motorist with a dead battery can enhance good public relations.

A main factor to be considered is whether the service can be completed safely and without an appreciable decline in the primary protection effort. A nurse stranded in a parking lot at 12:30 a.m. presents vulnerability. The patrolling officer who provides a jumpstart performs a good employee relations activity, while eliminating the vulnerability.

Jumper service continues to decline due to more and more costly claims of damage to the electronic computers now found in most vehicles. Improper charging procedures can result in substantial damage. If, however, an organization does decide to offer jumper service, the next step is to establish ground rules, including:

- **Charge**: Will there be a nominal charge for this service or will it be provided at no charge? Most programs do not charge for this service.
- **Hours**: During what hours will the service be provided? This may depend on the hours the patrol service is in operation; however, definite hours of service should be established. A general rule is to provide this service when commercial services (garages and service stations) are closed. In some facilities, the maintenance department provides this service during the day, and the security department picks up the responsibility at night and on weekends.
- **Waiver of responsibility**: Motorists who need help should be asked to sign a statement waiving responsibility for any claim that may result from the service to be provided. The legality of the statement in court may be questioned; however, it does provide tangible evidence of intent.
- **Transportation of stranded motorists**: At times, a jumpstart service is not sufficient to get a vehicle going. The security department should have a firm policy on providing transportation for stranded motorists.
- **Amount of service**: This service should not develop into a mechanic service, and a policy is needed to ensure that this does not happen. Any service can develop expectations in the mind of the recipient of the service that go beyond the intent of an emergency service.
- **Proper equipment**: The security department should not cut corners on the equipment used for jumping batteries. Several commercial-type equipment hookups are available that are easy to operate with few mistakes.

Transporting people in security vehicles

Guidelines must be established covering the use of security vehicles to transport people, other than security personnel. Without a clearcut policy, the security patrol may find that it has developed into a taxi service, and it is often difficult to cut back on this service once it has been established. In some circumstances, however, transportation service is in the best interests of all concerned.

The transportation of people, other than through planned shuttle operations, should be properly documented. The names of those transported, the reason, the times and dates, and the mileage should all be recorded, except where security is providing a routine shuttle type program.

An example of how the transportation of people can positively affect hospital operations and protection is found in a large medical center in Wheatridge, Colorado. The hospital had a patient wait time concern that was in part based on the issues surrounding the delay in the pick-up of medically cleared patients awaiting transport to a local alcohol detoxification center. The security department, recognizing and understanding the dilemma, introduced a plan to transport these patients to the detox center. For less than 2 hours of off-campus transportation time every day, the protection program was able to justify the additional expense of a custom outfitted security patrol vehicle and officer/driver that significantly increased its external security presence on campus. The return on investment was less than 18 months as the hospital could more rapidly turn over the patient care beds in the emergency department.

Equipment for security patrol vehicle

The type of vehicle used for patrol should be selected for the function to be accomplished. In the same manner, the security equipment carried within the vehicle, when possible, should also be tailored to the function. Security patrol vehicles should have the following essential items:

- Communications device
- Spotlight (fixed or plug-in type)
- Fire extinguisher(s)
- Blanket
- Chain or heavy tow cable
- Rope and traffic cones
- Basic tool set (screwdriver, pliers, etc.)
- Small broom and dustpan
- Extra flashlights or hand lanterns

Optional items include a first-aid kit, flares, jumper cables, resuscitation equipment, and air packs. When possible, equipment should be affixed to the vehicle to keep it from rolling around. One security department mounts its equipment on a flat board with tie down straps and boxes constructed to hold specific pieces of equipment. The board can be easily removed and used in another vehicle if necessary. Equipment boxes are also quite useful.

Operating the vehicle

Security personnel operating a security vehicle must generally observe all the rules and regulations that apply to private motorists. Rarely do ordinances or statutes classify security vehicles as emergency vehicles. Security officers may feel their function gives them special driving privileges. Individual officers should be held responsible for any moving violation or parking ticket received while operating a facility-owned security vehicle. A state or provincial motor vehicle check of each officer who operates a vehicle should be completed on an annual basis. Many insurance companies require this type of periodic check and initial, as well as annual, driver safety training.

Damage to the vehicle

Security personnel should be held responsible for any damage to a vehicle in their care, custody, and control. Officers should completely inspect the vehicle before use. This inspection is often documented on the officer's patrol or daily activity log, or a specific vehicle inspection form may be used. All vehicle damage reports should be reviewed by an accident or property damage review board, to determine whether the accident or damage was preventable and, if so, to recommend action. The action may be a change in procedure or a recommendation for further training for the individual responsible. In some review programs, the responsible party is required to pay for some or all of the loss.

CANINE PATROL

There continues to be a limited but growing use of canine units in healthcare protection programs, at least in the U.S. In Canada deploying canines is an unheard-of practice. K-9s have proven quite effective as a supplement to officers on foot or vehicle patrol. In addition to being a good public relations tool, canines are effective in soliciting cooperation with stressed visitors, as well as de-escalating uncooperative persons and other malfeasance in the healthcare environment. Richard Ortiz, security director of Banner Health's Thunderbird and Estrella hospitals in Phoenix, says "the presence of canines in the emergency department waiting areas can change the attitude of hostile individuals."[6] As a result, canine programs have proven very effective in healthcare communities with an active gang presence. In the gang community, it may be culturally acceptable to be afraid of a dog, but not necessarily a security officer. Gang members would rather deal with an armed security officer than take a bite from a dog.

Dogs offer several patrol advantages. They protect officers on patrol, and generally make them more productive while they conduct their rounds. Dogs can often detect the presence of a person hiding when security staff cannot observe them. Once trespassers or criminals have been observed, dogs have often been responsible for preventing an escape that otherwise would have occurred.

Obedience is vitally important in a canine patrol program. The dogs interact with the public on a day-to-day basis, and should receive continual training on when it is appropriate to bite, in addition to other specific commands. A basic argument against the use of dogs in security is the risk of the dog injuring someone. A few documented cases indicate this can be a problem, although these are few in number. However, it is difficult to apply any meaningful security measures without assuming some degree of liability. One should always be conscious of the liability of protection system elements, and should minimize the liability exposure as much as possible.

A canine program can be very expensive to operate, especially in terms of cost benefit. In most canine programs, the dog is utilized exclusively by one handler, which has a variety of associated costs. Rarely do several handlers utilize a single dog. An organization can purchase its own dogs or can lease dogs on an outsourced basis. The outsourced basis is a good method, as costs can be more readily projected and there is much less administrative support required. An organization that purchases its own dogs, at typically around $10,000 per animal, and provides proper training (training is almost always outsourced), can project an annual cost of $12,000 to $15,000 for each dog. This does not include the training cost of the handler nor department administrative time. During the course of a typical 40-hour work week, the handler and dog often work only 32–36 hours per week, with the remainder designated for training without incurring additional overtime expense. As a result, some healthcare organizations use 12-hour shifts for the dog and their security officer handler.

When all the advantages and disadvantages of using a dog on patrol have been fully analyzed, there is little question their presence produces a sharp reduction in security events. In terms of cost benefit, the use of dogs in the healthcare environment can only be justified in a very few programs. To offset the expense, some organizations have applied a shared service approach to canine patrol. Most effective for multicampus health systems, or medical campuses with multiple facilities, the incurred costs of the canine program are shared among a group of healthcare organizations. The basic premise is that the presence of the canine is available for all locations as situations arise or on a random patrol basis. See Figure 11-6 for a canine used in a hospital in Indiana and his security officer handler.

INTERNAL PATROL

Effective preventive patrol is the backbone of a deterrent program. Patrol is not just walking down a corridor or through an area; it requires being alert and checking and observing with all five senses. The

FIGURE 11-6

K-9 and security officer handler.

security officer should always have a purpose for inspecting each department or area of the medical complex. This purpose will vary from area to area, but generally the security officer will:

- Check to see the people assigned to an area are not in need of help (that is, sick, injured, or being victimized).
- Practice conservation (check water or fuel leaks, unnecessary lights or windows left open, unfamiliar equipment noises).
- Look for safety hazards (moisture on the floor, holes, protruding hazards, or malfunctioning lights).
- Inspect for fire safety (undue accumulations of combustibles, blocked exits, extinguishers that are out of place or show evidence of use, doors opening in the wrong direction, sticking or malfunctioning locks, and smoking violations).
- Watch for evidence of unauthorized people or unusual physical factors.
- Watch for signs of theft or unauthorized removal of property.
- Be alert for acts of malicious destruction, horseplay, consumption of intoxicants or drugs, boisterous conduct, and secure items or equipment that may have been inadvertently left unattended.
- Ensure all doors are secure at the appropriate time and follow through with periodic inspections.
- Check out-of-the-way places and know where each door leads and how to reach every part of the medical care complex.
- Answer questions for visitors, employees, and patients; direct and escort them.
- Be available for service; if an officer is in doubt as to appropriate action, he or she should check with a security supervisor or perform the duty and check afterward for future clarification.
- Frequently check locker rooms and public washrooms.
- Enforce hospital rules. To enforce rules properly, it is essential security officers always abide by the rules and by security department regulations (authority is easily abused, and nothing creates resentment as quickly as the misapplication of authority).
- Make eye contact and communicate with individuals while on patrol as another means of communicating a strong security presence in the facility.

It is impossible to list all the areas or conditions that should be inspected. Every facility has unique characteristics that require special patrol activity. The one common area that should be patrolled in all facilities is the stairwells, storage areas, and other out-of-the-way areas. A woman being treated for a stomach ailment disappeared from her 7th-floor room in a Nashville, Tennessee hospital. Sixteen days later, a nurse noted a foul odor; the missing patient's decomposing body was found on the 10th floor in a storage area. In another case, a man was missing for five days after failing to show up for a hospital medical appointment. He was later found dead in a stairwell by a housekeeping employee.

The trash collection system is an important aspect of security patrol often overlooked by rounding officers. All aspects of the trash collection system should be constantly inspected. Trash carts are a common means of moving stolen or contraband material.

IMPORTANCE OF THE FIRST PATROL ROUND

The officer's first patrol check of an assigned area is extremely important. During this round, the status of the patrol area is determined. The first patrol thus provides a basis for comparing all subsequent patrol activity. Professional security officers carefully check their assigned areas to determine whether the necessary doors are locked, whether lights are on or off, and whether fencing is intact. They note general conditions, such as the number of people in an area that may require individual assistance or extra surveillance, and special conditions, such as areas that create different safety hazards. Patrol checks on the second and subsequent rounds are geared to observe any changes in the environment. These changes signal conditions to be evaluated to determine whether security has been breached or whether there is cause for action. A standard operating procedure is to vary rounds so they do not occur on a recognizable schedule.

It is important to recognize every security officer patrols with a unique point of view based on his or her background and previous experience. Some officers are persistent door checkers but observe little detail while on rounds. Others are less inclined to spend much time checking locked areas, but take careful note of all people encountered on their rounds. Some officers check out-of-the-way places more frequently than others. All officers tend to establish a pattern by which they alertly patrol their areas.

Security administrators take advantage of this knowledge by frequently rotating personnel and changing their assigned patrol areas. These changes can occur during a shift or at periodic shift assignments. If possible, changes in assignment should occur during shifts, to provide the best possible patrol coverage and to avoid security officers becoming bored.

Not all patrol is generalized and random. There will always be a need for certain intensified inspection of a closed area or of an area that has been the object of security problems. An example would be a parking lot that has experienced many vehicle break-ins. This theory of patrol variation might also be called a selective or concentrated patrol. It is the same concept that traffic enforcement agencies have used to assign extra patrol coverage to areas subject to a high number of accidents or violations.

REPORTING FOR DUTY

Officers reporting for work must properly prepare themselves to effectively provide security service during their tour of duty. Some programs schedule a 15- or 30-minute overlap of security officers during shift changes, to allow incoming and outgoing security personnel to exchange information.

Unfortunately, in actual practice, most of this time is used for socialization if not properly supervised. The result is a waste of labor both in terms of coverage and economics.

Incoming officers can quickly prepare for duty by reviewing the activity (including incident and condition reports) that has occurred since their last tour of duty, and by reading any information entered in the pass-on book or electronic briefing systems. Where possible, incoming officers should relieve officers going off duty in the field rather than in the office. Any necessary discussion or exchange of equipment can be accomplished in the field without losing field patrol time.

In large security programs where several officers report for duty at a specific time, a formal incoming officer-briefing period can be performed. Essentially the same material is disseminated as when a single officer reports; however, it is presented by a briefing officer. This briefing period can also be effectively used for training. A short period devoted each day to training is an extremely effective method of instruction.

In recent years, the U.S. Department of Labor has targeted the security industry for pay practice violations. In particular, the length of shift change has been the targeted. The healthcare security administrator is strongly encouraged to coordinate and review all shift change practices with their human resources department to determine if the length of extra time (if any) is considered *de minimus*.

SHIFT ROTATION

Security personnel are subject to all human frailties, including complacency and boredom. When one performs the same activity every day, one tends to develop a routine. Even though security personnel are called on to perform many varied activities during a shift, the basic work is routine and subject to patterned activity.

Just as important as the rotation of work assignments during a shift is the periodic rotation of shift assignment. Security officers must be knowledgeable about the security duties and the general activities of every shift to provide optimum protection services. In other words, each officer must be exposed to the total protection system and environment. The protection effort changes hour-by-hour and shift-by-shift in all organizations.

Systems that rotate security officers between different shifts and facilities automatically provide new and challenging situations. Security officers faced with a change in environment, including new people and activities, generally provide a higher level of protection. Officers who are not completely at home with this new challenge will read directions in more detail, ask more questions, be more objective in dealing with staff with whom they have not had time to develop friendships (or animosities), and follow directions in more detail. Officers who are rotated to new shift assignments often discover security deficiencies or initiate improvements not perceived by their predecessors.

One of the strongest objections against rotating shift assignments is that officers do not get to know who belongs and who doesn't belong in the facility or in a particular area. This argument has only limited validity; it is often personal relationships among employees and others that provide a strong rationalization for shift rotation. The overly friendly or adverse relationships that have evolved are mitigated or terminated, at least for a time.

Security officers can usually determine whether a person belongs by checking with known personnel or by simply making a positive inquiry or contact with the individual.

How often should personnel be rotated? There is no established timeframe; however, a cycle of six months to one year works well. Too-frequent rotation does not give officers adequate time to adjust their personal lives.

Rotating all the security personnel on one shift at the same time is also not advisable. Security officers should work with other officers who have been on the shift for some time, thus rendering a continuity of service. Officers should be rotated individually. Some officers need to be rotated quite frequently, and others can remain objective for a long period of time.

The individual rotation plan also allows officers to work with different security supervisors, which provides two benefits. First, officers are exposed to more in-depth supervision and development because each supervisor has a different point of view and a different method of leadership. Second, supervisors are stimulated to some degree by assuming responsibility for new officers. In explaining the system and procedures to a new officer, the supervisor also benefits by program review. As a general rule, supervisors should be rotated less frequently than security officers. The shift supervisor is considered the thread of continuity for the program.

PATROL VERIFICATION

In all programs it is necessary to supervise patrol officers to learn whether objectives and standards are met. The best method of patrol verification is the field or patrol supervisor, supplemented by secondary methods. In small programs, no direct supervision may be available, and thus secondary methods are used to verify patrols. One such method is the mechanical watch-clock, which has been in use for many years and has largely disappeared from most healthcare security programs. Today, a number of programs have security officers carry rugged tablets or other portable electronic devices that prompt them with specific tour activities and provide the ability to verify patrol and record events, and allow the ability to look up procedure information immediately. These web-based applications have replaced the mechanical watch-clock used historically.

Another type of patrol verification system is an adaptation of the electronic access control system. This system permits each facility's electronic access control system to become a reporting system. This approach entails the security officer presenting their issued identification badge to the card readers in the facility as they go by during each patrol. Through administrative user reporting, the information can be downloaded to a spreadsheet for analysis and documentation purposes. An obvious benefit of this system is that officers do not have to carry any additional equipment and the organization does not have to install or maintain special readers throughout the facility.

THE PATROL OFFICER'S KEY RING AND ACCESS PRIVILEGES

Patrol officers must carry certain keys and have access privileges to effectively carry out their responsibilities, and to provide necessary services. Officers do not need to carry keys that grant access to every locked door within the facility. Conventional wisdom holds that officers must be able to gain instant access to any area in case of fire, but professional security administrators distinguish between total access and an overly restrictive access policy. Each locked area of the facility must be evaluated, and a plan developed regarding access requirements. Security personnel are subject to error and human weakness, and should not unduly be put in a position of temptation or suspicion. Just as security administrators strive to reduce the opportunity for incidents in general, they must also protect the security officers and the integrity of the protection program.

Various methods allow access to areas without compromising control. In small facilities such as nursing homes, and even for certain areas in large facilities, the double-lock system is quite effective. This system requires two people, with two separate keys, to gain access through a particular door. This solution was effectively applied to a maintenance storeroom in a facility that had experienced a loss of copper piping, attributed to the maintenance personnel themselves. The maintenance personnel obviously needed access to this area. Each maintenance person now carries a key to one lock and the security officer carries a key to the second lock. The double lock prevents either person from gaining entry to the storeroom without the other.

Another simple way to eliminate the need to carry a key is to make the key available at a location controlled by another department. The key can be released to certain predetermined employees, after a record is noted that includes the name of the person receiving the key and the date and time of checkout. A common holding area is the switchboard room, the cashier area, or a central security office in larger operations. Collusion between employees can always result in a compromise; however, the probability of this occurring is quite low.

A key management system currently in use at Northwestern Memorial Hospital in Chicago appears to handle the access problem very effectively. The keys to all areas are maintained in the central security office, which is operated 24 hours per day. There is an electronic key vault for storage of each key in the facility. Critical keys, such as for the gift shop, pharmacy, cashier, and storage areas, require card access and a personal identification number (PIN) to access a certain key. This system electronically catalogs and tracks the key used, by who and when.

SECURITY OFFICER RESPONSE

Security officers on patrol are the first to respond to calls for service and will most likely encounter situations that require intervention, from simple inquiry to the use of physical force. The healthcare setting presents many situations requiring response to routine calls for assistance, response to crisis situations, and critical event response.

Routine calls to provide an escort, to unlock a door, return patient valuables or to assist a motorist require an efficient—that is, timely and knowledgeable—response. The term "timely" should need no explanation, but officers often give these calls low priority. To the department and the person seeking assistance, they are no less important than emergency calls. Thus, all routine patrols should be suspended and the officer should proceed where required as quickly as possible. Knowledgeable response means not only having enough information to complete the task, but having the proper equipment as well. For example, officers should know every key on their key ring, including which locks require special procedures.

Response to a crisis situation demands extra preparation and an adequate skill level. Crisis has been defined as a significant emotional event or a radical change in one's life that has reached a critical stage. Proper security intervention requires a working knowledge of basic de-escalation principles and aggression management, including verbal communication, nonverbal communication, personal space, and territory.

Officers also must know what to say and how to say it. Words are important, and the tone and volume of voice can also carry different meanings. A fast rate of speech may convey the officer is afraid, uneasy, or lacks confidence. Tone can indicate such messages as anger, resentment, assurance, and attitude.

Nonverbal communication consists of posture, eye contact, facial expressions, hand gestures, and appearance. Everyone uses body language and must be aware of the messages being sent. Body language can convey comfort, concern, sympathy, hate, disrespect, disbelief, authority, and confidence, among other things. Security officers need to practice positive body language as part of their training, not only for handling crisis situations but also everyday personal interactions.

The issues of personal space and territory are closely related. Space is generally related to physical area, and territory is related to environment, such as the workplace and home. Security officers generally work more with the aspects of space. In general, personal space is the area around the individual others are expected not to invade. This area is different for different individuals and is affected by personal traits, habits, environmental factors, culture, and gender. Although it is hard to be specific, personal space can range from 18 to 20 inches for intimate contact, and four to five feet for public contact. Intruding in this space can escalate an emotional response. This does not mean security officers cannot enter this space to resolve a situation. It merely means they must be aware of the concept and the ramifications of their actions. The rule of treating others as you would like to be treated is prudent and practical in all situations.

Security officers responding to a critical event should follow these guidelines:

- Upon receiving notification, proceed quickly and safely to the scene. Do not run. Arrive in a composed manner, cautiously proceeding into the area.
- Perform a quick assessment, gather basic information, and determine an initial course of action.
- Alert other appropriate resource personnel (dispatcher, additional security personnel, police, fire, etc.) with succinct and pertinent facts.
- Direct action at the scene. Minimize danger to yourself or others and limit further damage if possible.
- Secure the scene, identify witnesses, and preserve evidence.
- Take notes, obtain statements, and complete an incident report.

PATROL PROBLEMS

Several common problems involving patrol officers in medical care settings require close supervision and repetitive training, regardless of how basic these problems appear on the surface.

The first major concern is excessive socialization. Since many security personnel are male and most healthcare personnel are female, frequent socialization is an inherent problem. It's true it takes two to socialize and the problem involves both employees; however, the nonsecurity employees are generally in their assigned work area. When officers linger too long in a particular department, they are not only neglecting their duty, but also hindering others from doing their job.

A second major problem is the tendency of security officers to talk too much. This tendency relates in part to the previous issue; however, the main concern is discussing confidential security information with nondepartment personnel. One hospital administrator reported receiving more security information from the telephone operator being briefed by security staff, than directly from the security department itself. Security officers should not be overly secretive, but they should discuss security plans, programs, and problems only with appropriate persons.

Perhaps the biggest problem in patrol deployment involves keeping officers separated when more than one is on duty. Of course, officers should back one another up on a call and give other legitimate assistance, but they should not congregate simply to pass the time. When more than one officer is on duty at a time, it generally means there is too much area or work load for one officer to perform adequately. When two officers are together, the effective coverage is reduced to that of a single officer. Healthcare administrators frequently cite this issue as one of their largest frustrations with the security department.

Reading while on post is most prevalent in fixed-post assignments. This situation reflects rather poorly on the entire security effort. Reading should be limited to material pertaining to the job and supplied by the program and should never interfere with job performance.

Although these concerns cannot be considered to be in-depth supervisory problems, they are real, and they occur in all security systems to some extent. Such minor problems have had a significant impact on keeping security officers in the low-status position they are to a great extent trying to rise above.

REFERENCES

1. Kent Hospital. *Kent adds new security bicycle patrol.* 2006, October 23. Retrieved April 30, 2009, from http://www.kenthospital.org/body.cfm?id=84&action=detail&ref=81.
2. DeNale Rachael. *Save money, deter crime through bicycle program.* Environment of Care Leader; 2012, February 20. DecisionHealth. 17(4).
3. International Police Mountain Bike Association. Website available at www.ipmba.org. (accessed 12.10.14).
4. *Carolinas healthcare system deploys Segway PT i2 police packages on its campus.* 2007, November 11. SecurityPark.net. Retrieved November 22, 2007, from http://www.securitypark.co.uk/security_article260108.html.
5. MacDonald C. *Vehicle alternative stands out from a crowd.* Campus Safety Magazine; 2007. Retrieved April 29, 2009, from http://www.campussafetymagazine.com/Articles/?ArticleID=108.
6. Slogowski J. *Dogs add bite to security at hospital.* 2008, October 10. Retrieved October 12, 2008, from http://www.yourwestvalley.com/common/php?db=dnsun&id=4007.html.

CHAPTER

PROGRAM DOCUMENTATION AND PERFORMANCE MEASURES

12

The preparation and maintenance of security records and reports can be extremely time-consuming for line and administrative staff. At the same time, a good documentation system is a foundation of any progressive healthcare security program. Unnecessary records and reports take away valuable time that could be spent performing meaningful incident prevention, investigative duties, and providing general security services. But if meaningful data is not properly collected, assessed and displayed, how can a security program really demonstrate value and make evidence-based decisions that may determine the future course of the program for a healthcare organization?

This is the challenge facing today's healthcare security program administrator—how to create and maintain a program documentation system that meets the needs of the organization. An objective of the security documentation system should be to create and maintain only the records and reports that are truly necessary, and to improve the efficiency and quality of the documentation system. It has been acknowledged that a basic component of the successful security program is a comprehensive and useful documentation system. Chapter 4 of this book emphasizes the importance of good data collection for performance management, while Chapter 5 addresses incident reporting specifically, in managing the basic elements of healthcare security. However, documentation that is simply maintained, and for which there is little or no use, wastes valuable department resources.

A 2014 UK report suggested healthcare organizations may need to rethink their priorities for staff in light of findings related to care of older people in long-term care facilities. The findings indicated the patients may miss out on quality time with staff, due to workers being preoccupied with required paperwork.[1] Similarly, the findings of the Francis Report, also in the UK in 2013, included this finding, pertinent to this discussion on the need for documentation and data to be relevant. "Statistics, benchmarks and action plans are tools, not ends in themselves; they should not come before patients and their experiences." This report stemmed from an inquiry into poor care at Mid Staffordshire Hospital in England.[2]

So for the purposes of this chapter, the term documentation includes budget and fiscal documents, personnel records, policies, procedures, correspondence, bylaws, contracts, reports, and a whole host of specific records. The chapter will focus on a discussion of operational records and reports utilized in a healthcare security program, and how performance measures can be created and effectively utilized by the security program, to demonstrate quality, efficiency and value, in alignment with the organizational mission of delivering quality care to patients.

PURPOSE OF RECORDS

The use of, and necessity for, specific security records varies from organization to organization; however, the primary reasons to maintain records are basically the same for all organizations. Records provide a memory system, permit the exchange of information, direct operational procedures, fulfill various administrative needs, and assist in the verification of security activity and general planning processes. Within each of these primary reasons are many subcategories designed to provide operational efficiency and effectiveness for the healthcare protection system.

MEMORY SYSTEM

The need to retrieve information contained in a report may occur within hours, days, or even years after it was completed. A quick and effective technique for evaluating a security system is to determine how many questions concerning past incidents or activity are answered by personal memory, and how many questions are answered by documented facts.

One of the inherent problems of security operations is how difficult it is to anticipate today what information contained in records and reports will be required tomorrow. It is not only major incidents, but also minor events for which information may be required later for various reasons. Although the statute of limitations for litigation proceedings varies from state to state and province to province, as well as internationally by country, all are measured in years rather than months. Lawsuits are sometimes filed at the last minute in the expectation that supporting defense information will be lost, forgotten, or incorrectly interpreted due to the time lapse.

Not only do civil lawsuits illustrate the need to preserve facts, but also the overloaded criminal justice system may require certain records and reports years after the actual event. The term *continuance* is often heard in criminal actions. Delay after delay can result in a considerable period between the time the action was initiated and the time adjudication is completed.

The use of recorded facts as a memory system is a major aspect of the investigative function. Records are as important to the investigator as the scalpel is to the surgeon. Trends, modus operandi, and the facts of past incidents can be instrumental in successfully concluding an investigation.

EXCHANGE OF INFORMATION

The exchange of certain security information is required among members of the security department, organizational management, and various outside agencies. The interchange of information among security personnel allows the security staff to be knowledgeable of the profile and events of the environment they are protecting and serving. This information is necessary for each officer to effectively carry out his or her responsibility. It is likely security protection could be increased markedly if all the various pieces of information known by all members of the security force could be assembled and organized in a meaningful manner. While some exchange of security information is verbally transmitted, the vast amount of such information is best exchanged via some type of report.

Reports are necessary to record questionable activities and security deficiencies in order that they may be transmitted to an appropriate person or department for follow-up action. General security information that affects an organization must be effectively conveyed through the appropriate channels.

Information transmitted to local, state/provincial, and federal law enforcement agencies has often supplied the link that allowed the agency to successfully conclude an investigation. Progressive law enforcement administrators and professional security administrators establish working relationships that recognize positive contributions that each can render to the other. Security information transmitted outside the organization also includes insurance companies, planning agencies, fire departments or other authorities having jurisdiction, offices of emergency preparedness, and other similar organizations.

Of course all information shared outside the organization, and to some degree internally as well, is subject to restrictions inherent in protection of privacy-related regulation and legislation, regardless of jurisdiction. The healthcare security administrator must be particularly cognizant of these restrictions, which may impinge on their ability to freely share healthcare-related information. This is most often found when law enforcement officials request video surveillance of a patient or request to be notified when a patient is being discharged from the facility. Rules and regulations surrounding these issues are vague at best. Security professionals are encouraged to establish predetermined scenarios and review them with risk management and the hospital privacy officer to establish clear expectations and guidance for the security staff.

OPERATIONAL POLICY AND PROCEDURE

Security operations require policies and procedures to direct the proper delivery of emergency and routine security services and actions. Operational security policy and procedures are most often referred to as post orders or facility orders. A goal of security operations is to achieve professional and consistent actions by all the security staff in the discharge of their daily responsibilities.

The terms *policy* and *procedure*, along with the term *protocol*, are often used interchangeably. They are in fact somewhat different, but very closely linked together. For the purposes of this text, these terms are defined as follows:

- Policy: A stated objective and/or stated principle
- Procedure: A manner of proceeding, way of performing, or a series of steps to be taken to comply with policy
- Protocol: A code of conduct and/or a plan for the course of treatment, used more often as a medical term.

One should always be cognizant of the fact that not all policy and procedures are created equal. Some will need to be general in nature and some will be quite specific. As an example, the security response to a critical incident may be somewhat general in terms of steps and the exact sequence of those steps. On the other hand, the collection, storage, and release of patients' valuables will need to be quite specific in the series of steps required.

Problem areas to be avoided

There are various pitfalls that, when avoided, make the job of maintaining good policies and procedures easier and more user-friendly.

- Avoid the commingling (mixing) of policy, procedure, and training/educational information. Too often the writer feels compelled to add rationalization (the why), or educational information, which tends to result in a convoluted procedure without a crisp clarity.

- Always do a search for other organizational policy and procedures on the same subject, to ensure security policy and procedure are compatible, and in alignment with the organization. When the new, or existing, security directive is or will be in conflict with other directives, the process of implementing the new directive should be paused. Contact the author, or administrative person responsible, to arrange a discussion regarding resolving the conflict of information.
- Correct any policy that may have changed, or a written procedure that does not coincide with the actual practice. This discrepancy may be corrected by changing the policy and procedure, or result in training of field staff. It may also mean enforcing staff compliance.
- Check that policy and procedure reflect the general healthcare security industry standard practices. There may be a reason that a policy or procedure falls outside of the standard practice, which may fit a particular program or set of circumstances, but be ready to defend the position. An example of a policy that emerges from time to time is: "Security officers are not allowed to touch patients." This policy is clearly outside of the healthcare industry security practice and the standard of care. Defense of this policy may be difficult, and it is most likely to be challenged at some point along the way.
- Minimize word count. Organize procedure in step-by-step directive when possible. Use short sentences or phrases.
- Combine the new policy and procedure with the existing one when possible.

Policies and procedures should be working documents and updated as needed. All policies and procedures should be reviewed (evaluated) annually and the date of the review inserted in the document, even if there are no changes. A security review committee of three persons should be considered to formally examine each policy and procedure. As an example, this review committee could be the director or manager of security, a security supervisor, and a security line officer.

NEED FOR ADMINISTRATIVE RECORDS

Security records fill many requirements in the administrative control and effective operation of the protection program. Although each security department requires specific records peculiar to its own operation, certain administrative records are needed by all operations, regardless of size, to provide a viable and accountable service.

One of the primary purposes of records in healthcare security is to help identify security requirements through the statistical analysis of recorded security information. Once a need has been identified and a possible solution devised, the technique for measuring the effectiveness of the solution is the ongoing analysis of the same security records that first identified the need. In addition to identifying problems, security records are useful in projecting trends. Early awareness of a possible security problem allows preventive measures to be implemented.

The deployment of security force personnel is predicated on existing or projected security needs. On the basis of records, security administrators can objectively deploy security personnel at the times and in the places that are most effective. Data and evidence-driven decision making is a critical skill for the increasingly business-minded healthcare security leader.

Security officers for the most part perform their duties without being directly observed by a supervisor. A security officer's evaluation must, to some degree, include a comparison of individual activity with that of other members of the security department. Records list assignments, confirm responsibility, and verify the accomplishment of tasks. Adequate records measure an officer's relative capacity for work, and reflect special abilities and aptitudes, as well as areas of work performance requiring improvement.

Department records are necessary to account for security property and to ensure the proper functioning and maintenance of equipment. Preventive maintenance and timely repair of security equipment reflect well on the quality and positive perception of department leadership. A history of maintenance and repairs is essential to justify equipment modifications and strategic planning of equipment replacement.

REPORT FORMATS

The format/style of security reports is one of individual preference, but must be designed in a manner that assists the report writer in preparing a complete report in an efficient manner. Electronic report preparation may, or may not, meet this expectation.

ELECTRONIC REPORTS

Computer-generated report preparation is increasingly the norm and may eliminate the need for hard copy forms. Generating report copies becomes a much simpler administrative procedure as the electronic report is simply created and reviewed on the computer or mobile device with data stored on a secured server on the organization's network. Printed copies are generated only as needed. Electronic documents can be e-mailed to individuals, transferred on a USB flash drive or like device, or stored on a server drive, allowing access to retrieve the document to those authorized. The computer-generated reports require a series of controls. A simple password protection may not be very secure; however, more complex mechanisms involving tokens (magnetic, RFID technology, biometrics and others) have their own drawbacks.

Information technology (IT) security always involves trading security for ease of use. A disconnected computer locked in a vault is still dependent upon the security of that vault, if information is stored on the hard drive. In order that originally generated documents cannot be changed, a form of version control must be instituted.

Version control system

In a version control system, the original stored document is never altered. Authorized users (i.e., supervisors) may "check out" a copy, make changes and enter their altered version. In this system, the original is saved and any revised versions are time-stamped and logs in the user who submitted a new version.

The University of Glasgow suggests creating a version control table that must be updated every time a change is made to the document. This should detail:

- The new version number;
- The purpose of the change or the change itself;
- The person making the change;
- The date of the change.[3]

A problem area to be avoided in digital storage of documents is that all copies are perfect copies, and these changes may be undetectable without an unaltered copy of the original document for comparison. It can be said that a document signed by the originator is still a good process in maintaining the integrity of the document system.

REPORT PREPARATION

A serious operational pitfall of report preparation is lost field activity time of the security officer(s). It is common for officer(s) to perform their report preparation in the quiet of the security office, often located in an out-of-the-way location. A problem that has been consistent over time is how to keep officers out of the office and in the field, especially on the late afternoon, night, and weekend shifts. The practice of desk computer-generated reporting can actually promote excessive office time, by providing an excuse for being in the office relaxing and socializing. A good management practice, whether report preparation is accomplished as a hard copy, handwritten system, or computer generated, is to establish several field locations where the officer completes reports. The key to maintaining officer field activity is to locate these report-writing stations where the officer can observe a public/staff area, and be available for questions or requesting of services. The field report writing may be at the front lobby desk, open admissions desk, or a regular security fixed post. In utilizing a security fixed post computer terminal, the officer at the fixed post simply trades assignments with the officer needing to complete a report. The regular fixed post officer thus can go on patrol, and the officer completing his report assumes the duties of the fixed post. When the report is completed, the two officers return to their original assignments.

Tablets and smart phones are increasingly found in healthcare security programs as a tool to support the duties and responsibilities of the security officer, and the supervisors and management who play a critical role in the program as well. Report writing software programs and other security tools utilized by the security team can be loaded on these devices and accessed anywhere. In this way incident report or event/activity templates are available to security staff, who can write reports from any location in the field and download them to secure servers. While this has the advantage of moving security out of the office and into the field where they can be most effective, device and network security issues—creating and managing often sensitive information—must be thoroughly addressed before this application is considered.

Whenever a new report form or the updating of a current form is considered, the security administrator should ascertain whether the form is absolutely necessary. The next consideration is simplicity. Needless records and reports that are overly complicated make paperwork tedious and time consuming, all of which can result in reluctance on the part of security officers to complete their reports. The excessive time required to complete the form reduces valuable time in the field. Regardless of format, the guiding principles for all types of reports should be accuracy, simplicity, and efficiency.

Security reports come in all sizes, shapes, colors, and designs. The design of report formats falls into three basic classifications, whether paper or electronic:

- narrative style
- check-off, or block style
- a combination of narrative and check-off styles

These three types of formats have certain advantages and disadvantages; however, the combination style is the format in predominant use.

Narrative form

The narrative style can be used for the creation of virtually any type of security report. It is the least expensive of all styles. Stocking and supplying the hard copy form is logistically uncomplicated, though security programs are inexorably moving away from paper forms. The basic disadvantage of the narrative form is that it requires a higher level of training than other types of reports. The preparation of a narrative form can also be very time-consuming.

Check-Off form

In contrast to the narrative form, very little training is required to complete the check-off form because all the necessary information is shown on the form. The check-off form is highly specialized and is the most expensive type of form to create. A basic advantage, especially in electronic form, is the ease of extracting information categories for the "who, what, when, where" elements of trending and data evaluation.

The high cost is largely due to the check-off format, when hard copy reporting forms require many different forms to cover different types of incidents. It can be difficult to have the proper form in the field when needed to guide the collection of information. A common problem with check-off forms is that more than one page is often necessary because so many alternatives must be listed for each question.

Combination forms

Since the nature of security incidents in the healthcare setting is so widely varied, the most popular and the most functional type of reporting form is the combination report, a form that uses both narrative and check-off formats. The combination report can be used for virtually any situation that requires a report.

Other format considerations

In addition to report format design, other considerations include color-coding, number of copies required, and size. Two systems for color-coding reports are popular. The first is to color code by type of report, and the second is to color code for distribution or filing. The latter is the most common approach. The number of copies required for a specific report is determined by the organization's structure and needs.

In hard copy systems, the use of no-carbon-required (NCR) paper has many advantages when multiple copies are required. When preparing a report printed on NCR paper, one must take care to separate the sets of forms from the supply before writing. A single-sheet draft form for officers to outline their reports is worth considering. Even the best report writers begin a report and for one reason or another must start over. A single-copy draft report identical to the multiple-copy NCR form will save money. Some forms can be printed on both sides of the paper to save money. This logical approach is often overlooked. Forms that lend themselves to this practice include logs, activity sheets, maintenance records, and other single-sheet records.

BASIC RECORDS

Basic administrative and operational records must be maintained in all healthcare security systems. Administrative records include employee time and attendance records, management reports, property accountability records, employment and training records, patient valuable and lost and found logs, dispatch/alarm logs, visitor logs, statistical analyses, parking management and vehicle registration records, access control matrix definitions and other records, and the like. The most important operational records are security incident reports (including supplemental reports), security condition reports, daily activity reports, dispatch logs, property accountability, and various vehicle reports and records. Individual security programs will have requirements for records and reports unique to their specific program and organizational requirements.

SECURITY INCIDENT REPORT

The basic record found in all security operations is the security incident report (SIR). This report should not be confused with the unusual incident report (UIR), or other clinical/organizational incident reporting system that is commonly utilized by clinical staff to report medication errors, patient falls, and other clinically related situations. Some patient safety reporting systems include categories such as aggressive patients and other security incidents. While this has the potential to cause an organization to "double count" an event—a situation where a patient strikes a nurse and security responds and manages the event, as an example—the reporting systems should nevertheless remain separate. Indeed, in this example if the nurse was injured she or he may fill in another report, for the accident/injury, meaning the same incident could be in three different reporting streams. A strong working relationship between the security administrator, occupational/health and safety lead and the risk/patient safety program will ensure the proper filtering of reports and render the integrated data produced more reliable.

These two types of incident reports (SIR and UIR) should be maintained separately and not combined into a single multiuse form. In some systems the SIR is known as *a case report, an offense report,* or *an investigative report.* These terms are basic police nomenclature and should be avoided. A widely accepted but general definition of a security incident is any security-related situation not consistent with the routine of normal operating procedures or conditions. An example of a security incident report form is shown in Figure 12-1.

The IAHSS Basic Guideline on "Security Incident Reporting" provides a foundation for planning and developing the incident reporting system.

01.05.01 SECURITY INCIDENT REPORTING

Statement

Healthcare Facilities (HCFs) will develop procedures for reporting and documenting security incidents. Reports serve many purposes including sharing of information in a timely fashion, and compiling facts and circumstances for later review.

Intent

- **a.** Alleged crimes, emergency responses, incidents involving injury, loss or damage, and physical interventions, which come to Security's attention, should be documented as soon as practicable. The initial security report should be completed prior to the end of the shift.
- **b.** Documentation should be in written form—either in hard copy or electronic format. If electronic, data backup and recovery procedures should be developed and periodically tested.
- **c.** Report forms should be formatted to assist in gathering pertinent information and in compiling trends and comparisons.
- **d.** Statistical trends should be periodically reviewed for the purpose of taking proactive action as indicated.
- **e.** Follow-up reports, referencing initial reports, should be filed indicating additional notifications, information received, and actions taken.
- **f.** Reports will sometimes contain allegations or personal information that is inappropriate for dissemination into the public domain. As such, each HCF should develop procedures for when and how reports may be released.
- **g.** The report system should include a written report retention policy in keeping with the HCFs overall document retention policy.

See Also

- IAHSS Healthcare Security Guideline 01.05, Program Measurement/Improvement General

Approved: December 2006
Last Revised: October 2010
Last Reviewed: October 2011

Healthcare
SECURITY
SERVICES

SECURITY DEPARTMENT | INCIDENT REPORT

Facility: ______ Time Reported to Security: ______ Date: ______

Reported By: ______ Vis / Emp / Pat | Add/Dept. ______ Tel: ______

Nature of Incident ______ Location ______ Time/Date Occurred ______

MISSING PROPERTY

Item(s) ______ Color ______ Size ______ Est. Value ______

Where Last Seen ______ By ______ Date ______ Time ______

Owner: ______ Add. ______

Tel. ______ Discovered Missing By ______ Date ______ Time ______

Witness/Victim: ______ Add. ______ Tel. ______

Suspect/Arrestee: ______ Add. ______ Tel. ______

Race ______ Sex ______ HT ______ WT ______ Age ______ Hair ______ Hat ______ Glasses ______

Other ______

Security Officer ______ | Police called at ______ Arrived at ______ Officer ______

FIGURE 12-1

Example of a security incident report form.

Security incident statistics

The security incident report, in aggregate, is the primary source of data that identifies past security events or situations occurring at a facility, or within a hospital system. The most common method of presenting this information is via statistical reporting of the number of incidents, by incident category, for a specific time period in a spreadsheet format. This type of statistical reporting is sometimes referred to as a "snapshot" of past incidents. It is suggested this statistical report reveal numbers of incidents in blocks of combined categories. The defined categories would be created by the hospital security administrator, in concert with the chair of the Environment of Care (Safety) Committee, where one exists. A starting point could be to review the security risks as outlined in Chapter 3, "Healthcare Security Risks and Vulnerabilities," Figure 3-1, and combine certain risks into a single category.

The proactive healthcare security administrator will determine what data is most important for her or his program and organization, and then will establish the reporting categories and processes to capture the most meaningful information for that environment. The purpose of the categories, as opposed to utilizing each single risk listed, is to render the report more manageable and eliminate presenting a report with a preponderance of zeroes. In addition to the risk category type there could be additional categories such as "Information Only" Incident Reports, Alarms, Found Property, etc. Figure 12-4 is an example of the security incident statistical report.

Security incident report considerations

Every healthcare security program must define the parameters or conditions that require an incident report. There are gray areas to be sure, and the reporting of every incident is virtually impossible. When officers conclude the handling of a minor event, they tend to avoid preparing a report. In addition, different security programs have different reporting procedures for minor events. For example, suppose a security department receives a report that a patient is missing a ring, but when the security officer arrives, he is advised the ring was found in the narcotics drawer. In some programs the officer would not be required to report such an incident; in others he would simply note the incident in the daily activity log; and in other programs an incident report would be required. The daily activity log is preferred as the most efficient approach. One program defines the necessity of completing an incident report in terms of the number of sentences required to record the event. In that program if the occurrence has been successfully concluded and can be described in three sentences or less, the information is recorded in the officer's daily activity log, and no incident report is completed.

The basic rule is, "When in doubt, write it out." In other words, if an officer is uncertain whether an event should be reported, an incident or other specialized report should be completed.

Progressive security officers develop skills in observation and investigation, which are two primary security skills needed. However, it is not enough to develop these skills unless the results can be recorded accurately, clearly, and succinctly in the preparation of the subsequent incident report. Even seasoned officers find report preparation one of the most difficult parts of the incident investigation and reporting process, and the most difficult part of reporting is often the beginning. The key to completing an incident report is to record information in a logical sequence. If the report is written in a logical sequence and the writer has adequately answered the basic interrogatives (who, what, when, where, and how), and the actions taken, the report will be essentially complete.

A report must be objective and must include both favorable and unfavorable facts. If a report contains an estimate, such as distance or size, it should be identified as such. Personal opinion should generally not be included in reports; however, an opinion can often be valuable in evaluating the facts. It is not necessarily wrong to include an opinion if it is clearly identified as such with some supporting rationale. For example, an officer who reports information from someone who seems vague, inconsistent, or contradictory may wish to note the person did not appear completely rational and might have been under the influence of drugs or might be suffering from a form of dementia. However, it is generally accepted that opinions or suppositions be recorded on a separate sheet of paper and attached to the formal report.

In some security departments, handwritten field reports are later typed by a department clerk. This is a poor practice for a variety of reasons, not the least of which is cost. As noted earlier in this chapter, many departments have transitioned to electronic security incident reporting software programs. Although officers require more training and practice to complete these computer-generated reports, report writing quality and appearance have both been shown to significantly improve, while spelling errors and illegibility have all but been eliminated. Many off-the-shelf incident reporting and investigation management software packages offer clear authority matrix approval process before a report is released, and possess sophisticated analysis, statistical reports and predictive modeling capability.

Security officers should not be allowed to go off duty before completing their required reports. Reports should be completed as soon as possible after the facts are collected. In cases where a security officer initiates an investigation just before going off duty, the incoming officer can assume responsibility and relieve the first officer. Incident reports can be initiated by one officer and completed by another. The report must identify where the relieving officer took over; this can be simply stated in the body of the report.

A challenge faced by many organizations is being able to compare security incidents between hospitals that are within and outside of their health system. Often, a challenge of comparing like incident data can be found between shifts at the same facility. This relates to clarity of the incident reporting categories to enable the security officer to classify the report in the correct category. If category definitions and descriptions are unclear, the security program may find it challenging to properly monitor an issue. As an example, if you have a category for lost property of patient and another for theft from patient, you need to know that similar fact patterns are going to be placed in the same incident category, by every officer, every time. Aggression is a category that at times falls prey to security officer subjectivity. What's aggressive to me may not be to you. The solution lies in good incident category descriptors readily available to security staff, ongoing education on these categories and a strong supervisory document review process that provides feedback to report authors, when the incorrect category is used. This basic requirement has to be done correctly one site at a time, then between sites in the same system and, eventually, if the program is committed to sharing data with other healthcare security programs, between different organizations. Only with such a thorough process for incident reporting and classification will a true "apples to apples" comparison between healthcare facilities be accurate.

The administrative review of field reports has several distinct purposes. One is to provide feedback to the officer who prepared the report with constructive comments on how the writer could have prepared a better report. This task is an example of how training and supervision are interrelated. We all learn through our mistakes; however, no learning takes place if our mistakes are ignored and we are not made aware that a mistake, error, or substandard performance has occurred.

The administrative review also ensures the completeness of the report. Officers should be encouraged to prepare a rough outline of the report to make certain they have the proper information organized in good form before they begin to write. This method helps eliminate false starts and reduces the waste of costly multiple-copy forms. As noted, this review is also critical to ensure incidents are being captured in the appropriate categories.

SECURITY SUPPLEMENTAL REPORT

The supplemental report form is used to record additional information on the original report. Supplemental reports are generally used in conjunction with security incident reports, but they may also be used as a follow-up to other records or reports. Commonly this form is used to record follow-up investigative information. For example, after reporting a case of missing property, a security officer will often discover that the property was recovered. If the original report has not been distributed, the facts can be added to the original report, indicating the new time and date of the information being added. However, if the original report has been distributed, a supplemental report is prepared to be matched to the original loss report at a later time. Also, it is common practice to use supplemental report forms if additional pages are required when preparing an incident report.

Once an incident report has been completed and distributed through administrative channels for information, recording, or follow-up, the report must be filed so that it can be efficiently retrieved. One of the simplest methods of filing hard copy incident reports is by date. Only in very large security departments is it necessary to use a system of serial numbers. In some departments copies of the incident report are filed as cross-references. This system tends to create more paperwork than necessary. Electronic systems permit a vast number of references and reports can be filed and searched in many ways.

SECURITY CONDITION REPORT

The security condition report is a report used to advise others in the organization of a security condition rather than a security incident. It takes the form of a memorandum that describes unsafe conditions, security vulnerabilities, malfunctioning security equipment, areas found unsecured and other situations that may require action, or should be brought to the attention of others. Figure 12-2 is an example of a security condition report form.

HSS

Security Condition Report

Attention____________________ Facility__________

Date____________ Time____________ (AM) (PM)

The following condition was noted during patrol rounds and is brought to your attention for information or corrective action if appropriate:

____

____

____

____

____

____

____

Security Officer____________________ Cond. Corr. (yes) (no) Copy left (yes) (no)

FIGURE 12-2

Example of a security condition report form.

An example of a security condition that should be reported is an office door found unlocked during a late evening security patrol check. Suppose a security officer is aware that a door is usually locked around 5:00 p.m. and it had been secure on the last round. Upon internal inspection the office appears to be intact and the security officer assumes someone who had legitimate access failed to lock the door. An environmental services, facilities, or office employee might have inadvertently failed to lock up. However, the possibility that an intruder gained access does exist.

The security condition report serves a couple of purposes in this situation. First, the officer records the date, time, and the action taken, and leaves an information copy of the report in the office to inform the occupants on their return. Their response should then be to determine if anything is missing or if there is any other security problem.

Secondly, a copy of the report goes to the director of security or the person responsible for review for possible follow-up action. This report may fit a pattern that suggests environmental services (EVS) staff does not always lock up, and a follow-up with EVS department may be indicated.

Another use of the security condition report is to serve as a work order. A copy of the security condition report is sent to the facilities department, indicating the need for repair or service on a piece of equipment.

Security condition reports can serve to advise other security officers that a condition has been found and reported. For example, officers who note an officer on the previous shift prepared a condition report about a burned-out parking lot light should not duplicate the report. The condition report thus serves as a communication tool and helps to coordinate the protection effort among officers.

DAILY ACTIVITY REPORT

As a basic rule, all field officers should be required to complete a report of their activities during their tour of duty. There are as many different types (formats) of daily activity reports as there are security departments. Figure 12-3 is an example of a security officer daily activity reporting form.

Examples of entries in the daily activity report include unplanned or unscheduled activities such as escorts, assistance to motorists, and release of a body to the morgue, and miscellaneous information such as the license number of a vehicle that looked out of place, the name of a person not permitted entry to a closed area, or the reasons for not accomplishing scheduled rounds.

The electronic patrol verification system is not a substitute for the daily activity report of the security officer. Total reliance on computer input is not realistic, and all activity reports should allow the officer to add narrative information to the report.

In many departments with a 24-hour central security operations center (dispatch), each officer does not complete an individual activity record. Instead, the officer assigned to the security operations center makes all assignments and directs the activity of individual field officers. A chronological activity log is thus maintained centrally. Entry directly into the computer program is affected at the time of each activity. This system reduces paperwork and makes it much easier to review activity performed by the security department as a whole.

The chronological computer entry record can also be used for various administrative purposes. For example, by recording the time a call was dispatched and the time the officer arrived, a profile of response time can be maintained. Likewise, the time expended on each service activity can be recorded and collated to produce a profile of the time expended for each activity.

One of the pitfalls of the central security operations center system is that not all requests for service are directed to the security control desk. A good deal of activity is originated by field officers and by

SHIFT #8 DAILY ACTIVITY REPORT 09/08
1600-0000

Date: _____/_____/_____ Officer Name: ____________________

Radio Used:___________ Key Ring Used:_______________ Other Equipment Used: _______________

TIME	ACTIVITY
1600	On duty, brief with prior shift, read pass-on, start DAR.
1615	Check with ED officer and with ED Charge Nurse. Inspect vehicle and complete inspection log.
1630	Interior check of main hospital. Check Centralized Scheduling, 4th Floor. Assist with calls for service as necessary.
1700	Check Pharmacy, Central Supply, and Power Plant. Interior check of main hospital. Assist with class for service as necessary.
1800	Begin relieving officers for dinner breaks as activity permits. Ensure all officers call on and off break on the radio.
2000	Interior patrol of main hospital.
2030	Maintain visibility in the main lobby area and the information desk area.
2200	Check hospital floors.
2230	Remain near main entrance, outside weather permitting. Assist with calls for service as necessary.
0000	Brief with oncoming shift, complete DAR, and radio log. Off duty.

I certify I completed all assigned and requested duties as described above.

Signature: ____________________

FIGURE 12-3

Example of a security officer daily activity report.

direct customer contact with field officers. In these instances officers must notify the dispatch center to initiate the record.

Properly utilized, and with the correct technology in place, the modern operations/dispatch center has the capacity to produce an exciting new layer of metrics and link to key performance indicators (KPI), allowing the security program to demonstrate service excellence and value. For example, dispatch data could form part of the regularly reported statistical summary for the program, alongside more traditional metrics such as reported thefts or aggressive acts/assaults. These basic numbers, which are usually tracked as trends that are either rising or falling, can be augmented by solid dispatch data such as percentage of urgent calls responded to by security within 3 minutes, and other interactive data. The KPI may then emerge stating, as an example, security will respond to an urgent call, anywhere on campus, within 3 minutes, 95% of the time. There will be more discussion on key performance indicators in the healthcare security program later in this chapter.

PARKING VIOLATION NOTICE

The purpose, size, shape, and format of the parking violation notice varies from program to program. The design of the form is obviously dependent on the system of parking control used by the organization. Generally, the violation notice is intended to be a friendly reminder that orderly parking benefits everyone. In parking systems where specific areas are designated for different groups (physicians, visitors, employees, outpatients, emergency patients, etc.), the violation notice takes on a stronger connotation. Some jurisdictions issue citations that include the punitive action of a fine or impound of the vehicle.

The size of the form should be determined to some extent by the uniform or attire worn by security officers. The notices should fit neatly into a pocket or special holder, as patrol officers should carry a supply while on normal patrol duty. The copy of the notice to be placed on the vehicle should be printed on card stock. If additional copies are required, a lighter paper may be used for duplicate copies. The form should refrain from having a sticky adhesive quality as it can be a source of unproductive recipient frustration.

In some organizations, the security role in parking enforcement has mirrored that of professional parking companies, as they use handheld electronic devices to produce violation notices. These devices are usually able to store violation records in memory, meaning the security officer/parking enforcer can obtain a history on the parking offenses against a given vehicle plate number. This can be helpful in confirming frequent offenders and assist in decision making around enforcement options. These devices usually improve the quality of the ticket produced, increasing validity, and many come with value-added options such as a camera feature that can embed a photo of the infraction, at the time the violation is issued, in the violation notice database.

PASS-ON RECORD

Every security department must have a system for transferring information from shift to shift or officer to officer. In some programs this system is known as the "party line." Various procedures are used to handle this important aspect of security operations. A bound or looseleaf book is widely used. All officers reporting for duty must be required to read the information added to the book since they were last on duty and to sign each page to signify that they have read the information. Increasingly, computerized systems allow officers coming on duty to simply access this information by logging into the electronic record. Of course there are times when the security officers are engaged in managing an event at the time of shift change, necessitating key information be passed on verbally. Additionally, important information in the pass-on book should be reinforced verbally at shift change to minimize the chance it is missed.

The information that is recorded on the daily pass-on record originates from many different sources, including administration, department heads, security officers, and various elements inside and outside the organization. For example, the information entered in a pass-on record might include a vehicle granted special permission to park in a particular area; a new key added to the patrol officer's key ring; a special shipment of products expected during the night, with disposition instructions; the need to block off a certain area of the parking lot for special parking or construction; and a meeting in the facility for which special security activity is required. The pass-on record should include timely information officers need to perform their responsibilities efficiently and effectively. However, the pass-on should not be used to call out employee mistakes or note opportunities for improvement of individual officers. A group e-mail function has replaced this traditional pass-on book in many organizations, allowing security officers to receive all relevant information as soon as they log into their work account to start their shift.

The security administrator must review all pass-on information periodically to determine if the post orders, policies, or procedures must be modified or deleted. For example, if a key is added to the system, the post order that identifies all keys on a specific key ring and the procedural use of such keys must be updated.

The bound book works well for single-facility organizations; however, for organizations with multiple facilities that are geographically separated, the computerized system is recommended. Some organizations have moved to the online post order system with the hard copy binder as a backup and redundancy, in the event network or other IT issues render the electronic version unavailable.

Security administrators should consider including a short training message for each day as part of the daily pass-on record.

MASTER NAME INDEX

The master name index is a very simple but extremely useful security methodology. A record is prepared about anyone who has had a significant interaction with a member of the security department or about whom information has been received. The intent is to provide a ready historical reference of individuals through this index.

Names to be included in the master name index are obtained from security incident reports, which include names of complainants, victims, suspects, and witnesses. Exactly which names will be included in the index is a matter of individual philosophy. Some departments include names of their security officers, employment applicants, people who have corresponded with the department, and individuals named in newspaper articles concerning the healthcare facility.

The index lends itself to electronic record/incident reporting systems and may be cross-indexed. Many of the "off the shelf" incident reporting software systems contain this feature to flag and track individuals and, indeed, to create these flags based on preset criteria. Small departments without this technology will find the three-by-five index card the most economical approach. The record may simply refer to an incident report, a piece of correspondence, or other records, or it may contain all the information known.

MONTHLY OR PERIODIC SECURITY REPORT

It is common practice to prepare periodic security reports on a monthly, bimonthly, or quarterly basis. These reports include the monthly security incident statistical report referred to in Figure 12-4. The frequency of the periodic security report often follows the schedule of report requests of the

2014/15 General Hospital Security Incident Reporting														
KEY INDICATORS	Apr	May	Jun	Jul	Aug	Sep	Oct	Nov	Dec	Jan	Feb	Mar	Total	Av
Code White - Non Physical Intervention	29	22	31											27.3
Code White - Physical Intervention	19	26	31											25.3
Non Patient Intervention - Non Physical	1	2	4											2.3
Non Patient Intervention - Physical	2	1	2											1.7
Patient Intervention - Non Physical - ED	1	2	3											2.0
Patient Intervention - Non Physical - Other	1	2	1											1.3
Patient Intervention - Non Physical - Psych	3	1	0											1.3
Patient Intervention - Physical - ED	8	2	12											7.3
Patient Intervention - Physical - Other	4	8	4											5.3
Patient Intervention - Physical - Psych	6	0	1											2.3
Patient Standby - ED	33	22	44											33.0
Patient Standby - Other	0	5	0											1.7
Patient Standby - Psych	28	26	23											25.7
Physical Assault	0	0	0											0.0
Verbal Assault	0	0	0											0.0
Interventions-Sub Total	135	119	156	0	0	0	0	0	0	0	0	0	0	34.2
Access Requests - Denied	0	0	0										0	0.0
Access Requests - Granted	70	58	22										150	50.0
Break & Enter - Facility	0	0	0										0	0.0
Code Amber	0	0	0										0	0.0
Code Black	0	0	0										0	0.0
Code Blue/Medical Assistance	0	0	1										1	0.3
Code Brown	0	0	0										0	0.0
Code Grey	3	1	0										4	1.3
Code Orange	0	0	0										0	0.0
Code Yellow/Missing Patient	1	2	3										6	2.0
Elevator Response - Entrapments	0	0	0										0	0.0
Escort - Cash/Valuables	44	50	47										141	47.0
Escort - Non-patient	5	3	5										13	4.3
Escort - Patient	18	31	36										85	28.3
Fire Alarm/Code Red - Actual	0	0	0										0	0.0
Fire Alarm/Code Red - False	2	0	0										2	0.7
Heliport Operations	15	13	17										45	15.0
Information Requests	2	2	0										4	1.3
Inspections - CCTV	1	1	1										3	1.0
Inspections - Exterior Lighting	1	1	1										3	1.0
Inspections - Fire Extinguishers	0	0	0										0	0.0
Inspections - Panic Alarms	1	1	1										3	1.0
Intrusion Alarm Response	0	1	0										1	0.3
Lost & Found Property	183	119	91										393	131.0
Media on Site	2	0	0										2	0.7
Morgue Access	0	0	0										0	0.0
Other:	4	6	4										14	4.7
Panic Alarm Response - Actual	1	0	0										1	0.3
Panic Alarm Response - False	2	4	0										6	2.0
Parking Citations - Cancelled	0	0	0										0	0.0
Parking Citations - Issued	0	0	0										0	0.0
Persons Removed From Property	6	5	15										26	8.7
Photo ID's Processed (Security)	83	110	59										252	84.0
Prisoner/Inmate On Site	0	0	0										0	0.0
Safety Hazards Identified	22	16	4										42	14.0
Sitter Request	0	0	0										0	0.0
Suspicious Persons	2	2	1										5	1.7
Theft - Auto	0	0	0										0	0.0
Theft - Facility	0	0	0										0	0.0
Theft - Other	2	1	0										3	1.0
Theft - Patient	0	0	1										1	0.3
Theft - Staff	1	2	1										4	1.3
Vandalism - Auto	0	0	0										0	0.0
Vandalism - Facility	0	0	0										0	0.0
Non Interventions-Subtotal	471	429	310	0	0	0	0	0	0	0	0	0	1210	100.8
Total Security Activit	606	548	466	0	0	0	0	0	0	0	0	0	1210	135.0

FIGURE 12-4

Example of a security incident statistical report.

Interventions by Day of the Week	Apr	May	Jun	Jul	Aug	Sep	Oct	Nov	Dec	Jan	Feb	Mar
Sunday	14	12	27									
Monday	20	10	31									
Tuesday	23	12	22									
Wednesday	14	15	27									
Thursday	18	32	11									
Friday	20	19	10									
Saturday	26	19	28									
Total	135	119	156	0	0	0	0	0	0	0	0	0

Interventions by Time of Day	Apr	May	Jun	Jul	Aug	Sep	Oct	Nov	Dec	Jan	Feb	Mar
Night (0001 - 0800)	28	26	37									
Day (0801 - 1600)	58	44	66									
Afternoon (1601 - 2400)	49	49	53									
Total	135	119	156	0	0	0	0	0	0	0	0	0

Total Security Activity by Day of the Week	Apr	May	Jun	Jul	Aug	Sep	Oct	Nov	Dec	Jan	Feb	Mar
Sunday	57	55	67									
Monday	86	76	82									
Tuesday	99	87	86									
Wednesday	91	70	66									
Thursday	129	99	68									
Friday	82	96	52									
Saturday	62	65	45									
Total	606	548	466	0	0	0	0	0	0	0	0	0

Total Security Activity by Time of Da	Apr	May	Jun	Jul	Aug	Sep	Oct	Nov	Dec	Jan	Feb	Mar
Night (0001 - 0800	57	67	68									
Day (0801 - 1600	289	294	265									
Afternoon (1601 - 2400	260	187	133									
Total	606	548	466	0	0	0	0	0	0	0	0	0

Actual Security Patrol Hour	Apr	May	Jun	Jul	Aug	Sep	Oct	Nov	Dec	Jan	Feb	Mar
	1017.4	1020.5	851.7									

Actual Security Intervention Hours	Apr	May	Jun	Jul	Aug	Sep	Oct	Nov	Dec	Jan	Feb	Mar
Code White - Non Physical Intervention	31.7	22.9	20.5									
Code White - Physical Intervention	22.2	55.3	35.7									
Non Patient Intervention - Non Physical	0.5	1.1	5.6									
Non Patient Intervention - Physical	1.3	0.1	4.2									
Patient Intervention - Non Physical - ER	0.7	1.0	10.4									
Patient Intervention - Non Physical - Other	1.8	3.3	2.9									
Patient Intervention - Non Physical - Pysch	2.2	0.4	0.0									
Patient Intervention - Physical - ER	10.0	0.9	19.9									
Patient Intervention - Physical - Other	2.6	5.3	2.8									
Patient Intervention - Physical - Pysch	6.5	0.0	1.3									
Patient Standby - ER	32.4	16.8	41.0									
Patient Standby - Other	0.0	10.8	0.0									
Patient Standby - Psych	16.3	22.0	11.4									
Physical Assault	0.0	0.0	0.0									
Verbal Assault	0.0	0.0	0.0									
Total	128.2	139.7	155.5	0.0	0.0	0.0	0.0	0.0	0.0	0.0	0.0	0.0

FIGURE 12-4 Continued

Environment of Care Committee or other security oversight groups. In addition to the statistical incident summary report, the full report may contain such items as status of a security project, summary of the volume of service activities, equipment modifications/upgrades, changes in parking controls, status of performance improvement goals, special events, training activities and such. The report will generally be designed for the needs and expectations of the steering committee.

Many security programs now produce periodic reports tailored to get buy-in and management confidence from a specific audience in the healthcare organization. It is important security leaders understand what is important to key stakeholders and business managers as well as the organizational mission. For example, reports and spending on security must show advantage to the healthcare organization as a whole or to an individual department.

- Hospital or system executives may require high level risk-related trending, and what marked improvements in the well-being of hospital employees, patients, and visitors can be made.
- CFO may request trending and analysis reports that have financial implications such as capital life-span of equipment, total cost of ownership/internal rate of return for newly requested capital equipment.
- Human resources and recruiting staff may have a difficult time attracting and retaining the necessary qualified medical personnel because of a location in a high-crime area. They will often support security spending to make the environment safe; therefore, they want reporting on how changes and improvements lead to savings on recruiting, training and retaining healthcare staff across the organization—thus spending money on security, such as a vehicle, to save money on labor costs.
- Occupational Health and Safety leadership, and their related committees, may want drilled-down data on aggression, looking at types of intervention, typology of the patient and other demographics such as location and time of day, as examples.
- Clinical leadership may want their data produced so as to reflect a phenomenon like aggression alongside a clinical driver, such as adjusted patient days or total emergency department visits.
- Risk management may want a risk based analysis that includes organizational and peer references from marketplace competitors to help assess foreseeable risk and evaluate the cost-benefit of security measures. This may include benchmarking the level of incidents and to project the likelihood of crimes against the healthcare facility.

Today's healthcare security administrator must design a security reporting and documentation system robust enough to meet the broad requirements of a growing number of interested parties, keeping focus on what matters the most to senior management. Using statistical data can be fraught with problems, particularly if the information can be misinterpreted. Security professionals need to be able to understand and depict the environment and their organization, so they can anticipate the information requested and required, and construct a documentation system capable of producing these metrics. Data metrics should be kept simple to avoid having questions about the validity of the numbers and the data source becoming the focus of the discussion. Security leaders are encouraged to use details from specific examples to drive home a message. For example, if discussing a recent assault on a nurse, more than just the event should be described; an explanation of how patient care services were disrupted by the incident should be described, such as lost time from work, employee morale concerns, etc. Stay away from presenting in terms of response times and deployment of officers; instead, focus on how the event affected the employees and patient care.

Jeff Young, the Executive Director of Lower Mainland Integrated Protection Services (IPS) in Vancouver, Canada, leads a program providing services to approximately 30 acute care hospitals and more than 300 community care facilities. He says clinical programs across the world have built robust data collection systems to measure various processes, activity and incidents related to patient days, beds, length of stay, patient outcomes, readmits and other clinical measures. He adds "...the protection/security business should leverage this existing robust clinical data source that is fairly consistent across health organizations, to produce protection/security metrics tied directly to appropriate clinical indicators." He cites the example of aggressive acts per ED visit as much more powerful and meaningful to healthcare executives and clinical leaders, as compared to more traditional metrics that might project only raw numbers of aggressive acts, and a trending up or down.

This program, located in Canada, reports into a Customer Service Committee on a quarterly basis. The committee is comprised of executives from each of the four legal entities receiving service. As part of the reporting commitments to this committee, a quarterly scorecard, referred to as a "dashboard report," is produced, relating security incidents and activity to clinical and other data, trending the data and reporting on key performance indicators. This report card is shown in Figure 12-5.

There are four categories of information for security practitioners and hospital executives to draw from: personal opinion, ad hoc benchmarking, selective and vetted benchmarking, and research. Sadly, most of the information readily available today is coming from the first two categories. Healthcare security is inundated with incomplete and inaccurate information. It is time for healthcare security to go beyond haphazard information gathering and join other business functions in developing sources of research and core knowledge that can be called upon to provide valid, reliable and complete data that more accurately explains or enhances the multifaceted world of healthcare security.

KEY PERFORMANCE INDICATORS

A question frequently asked of healthcare security professionals is: "What is the value of having security for our organization?" Being able to answer that question is key to getting security funding requests approved.

The term *key performance indicator*, or KPI, has become commonplace in many businesses, including healthcare. The Law Dictionary defines KPI as "key business statistics as measures of a firm's performance in critical areas. Typically, monitoring is essential for such business activities that would likely cause severe losses or outright failure if done incorrectly...measuring progress or lack of it are essential for achieving the firm's objectives or strategic plan."[4]

George Campbell, in discussing performance indicators, suggests every security administrator needs to have high-level dials and metrics they monitor very closely. He lists six for a typical business organization:[5]

- Security Cost
- Information Security
- Business Conduct
- Security Audits
- Pre-Hire Backgrounds
- Business Continuity

A primary goal of the healthcare security program must be to seek continuous program improvement. It is easy for security and risk decisions based on inaccurate or vague information to cause

Security Incidents by Clinical and Facility Indicators

Rationale/Purpose	Allows for comparison of security activity, in form of Security Incidents, with clinical volumes (In-Pt Days & ER Visits) and facility indicators (Beds). These comparisons are made across Health Organizations; and trended with last year's Quarter and Year-End totals.															
Health Organizations	FHA				PHC				PHSA				VCH			
	Totals		Trends		Totals		Trends		Totals		Trends		Totals		Trends	
Reporting Period: (Apr. 1/13 - Mar. 31/14)	Q4	YTD	Q4 2012/13	Prev. YTD	Q4	YTD	Q4 2012/13	Prev. YTD	Q4	YTD	Q4 2012/13	Prev. YTD	Q4	YTD	Q4 2012/13	Prev. YTD
Actuals: Per 1K In-Pt Days	31.9	26.7	-5.4%	8.3%	30.2	28.1	-19.0%	0.9%	39.2	30.8	66.6%	50.7%	30.4	33.1	-18.8%	10.4%
Actuals: Per 1K ER Visits	53.3	44.5	-0.8%	10.5%	133.8	124.4	-25.8%	-11.8%	102.0	73.0	103.7%	43.2%	63.2	69.1	N/A	N/A
Actuals: Per Beds	4.1	10.6	42.2%	14.8%	3.2	9.2	11.6%	2.1%	4.6	9.1	183.2%	60.8%	4.4	14.7	-3.6%	5.2%
	LMC Year-to-Date (YTD) Averages															
	Per 1K In-Pt Days:			30			Per 1K ER Visits:			78			Per Beds:			11

Definition

Inpatient Days (In-Pt Days):
a. VCH = Total Inpatient Days (i.e. Acute + Acute ALC. Exceptions are: GFS = Total Rehab Days & GPC = Residential Days)
b. PHC = Total Inpatient Days (i.e. Acute + Acute ALC)
c. FHA = Patient Days – Adult & Children

ER Visits: Scheduled and unscheduled visits to Emergency Room
Security Incidents: Total Security Incidents (i.e. Does not include General Security Services)
Beds: Total funded beds

YTD Security Incidents by Clinical and Facility Indicators

150.0
100.0
50.0
0.0
Per In-Pt Day: 26.7, 28.1, 30.8, 33.1
Per ER Visit: 44.5, 124.4, 73.0, 69.1
Per Bed: 10.6, 9.2, 9.1, 14.7
FHA
PHC
PHSA
VCH

YTD Trending Comparison

80.0%
60.0%
40.0%
20.0%
0.0%
-20.0%
Per In-Pt Day: 8.3%, 0.9%, 50.7%, 10.4%
Per ER Visit: 10.5%, -11.8%, 43.2%, N/A
Per Bed: 14.8%, 2.1%, 60.8%, 5.2%
FHA
PHC
PHSA
VCH

Commentary

1. VCH saw the highest ratio of security incidents per 1K In-Pt Days for the entire year, at 33.1.

2. PHC has the highest ratio, by a significant difference, of security incidents per 1K ER Visits, at 124.4; this is 58% higher then the next highest HO ratio, PHSA (73.0).

3. Q4 saw reductions in ratios for both In-Pt Days and ER Visits for FHA, VCH, and PHC; only PHSA saw increases in this last quarter, compared to last year's Q4.

4. When looking at YTD trends, every HO for all three comparative indicators saw increases relative to the YTD last year; the only exception was a reduction in ER Visit ratios at PHC (-11.8%). This suggests that increases in Security Incidents, were outpaced by that of clinical volume increases.

Data Source: FHA, PHSA, VCH = Clinical Workload Statistics Report; PHC = Intranet-based Business Intelligence Statistical Cubes	Updated: April 8, 2014
Data Contact: Scott MacMillan, Manager, Process Excellence & Performance Reporting, IPS	Executive Lead: Jeff Young, Executive Director, IPS

FIGURE 12-5

Integrated Protection Services Dashboard Report.

security program failures. Continuous improvement requires setting standards for measuring, monitoring, and establishing improvement goals. Records maintained for these purposes ultimately document program quality. The performance standards vary widely according to program needs.

KPIs as a metric speak to accountability: how do your stakeholders/customers know you are providing good service? A solid foundation of program documentation is needed. According to Jeff Young, "healthcare protection/security programs need to have a business acumen about them and adopt business practices that start with the collection and analysis of data." It is *only* by having the systems and processes in place to produce reliable, meaningful data that we can create the metrics necessary to demonstrate the real value of the security program. In healthcare, where a security program's customers are providers of health services, the KPI must be intimately connected to the business of delivering care.

KPI should be tailored to the targeted audience to maximize their effectiveness. For a security contractor reporting to a corporate healthcare security client as an example, KPI may include:

- Urgent response time – for example, 98% of calls responded to within 3 minutes
- Non-urgent response – 95% of calls serviced within 10 minutes
- Mobile vehicle response – 90% of calls responded to within 20 minutes
- Shift fill rates – 100% as the standard
- Request for extra security/patient watch – prescribed % of requests filled within fixed time
- Complaint management – responded to within 24 hours 100% of the time
- Licensing/training – 100% of security staff meet requirements in these areas if assigned
- Escalation to Client – meet time requirements for urgent/nonurgent 100% of the time
- Quality Surveys – establish baseline on customer satisfaction through surveys and KPI is continuous improvement on the scores

This type of KPI data is produced at the front-line operational level and often forms an important component of the security program's scorecard or KPI report to their various customers. For proprietary or hybrid security program models, this data can be produced internally and plays the same important role in demonstrating value to the consumers of the service, and those who make decisions around funding, support and the effectiveness of the model and its leadership. The metrics reflect how well established emergency and service response times are met, as well as defining expectations around service requirements and quality indicators. For many modern healthcare security leaders, however, those KPI alone, while meaningful and important, are not enough to demonstrate the value of their program to all of their customers. Organizational leadership often want to relate program metrics to clinical indicators and want to know if they are getting tangible value for the resources allocated to the protection effort.

Some examples of the next level of KPI that may be considered are:

1. Cost of security per patient day
2. Aggressive acts managed per 1000 ED visits
3. Ratio of security staff to employees
4. Reporting of near misses (an undesired event or finding that, under slightly different circumstances, could have resulted in or caused harm to people or damage to property, materials or the environment)
5. Security watch hours per patient day or ED visit
6. Calls for security service per 1000 patient days
7. Lost-time claim frequency rate due to aggressive/assaultive behavior
8. Percent of incident with deficient staff awareness or ownership as "root cause"

For the business-minded healthcare security program administrator, there is still one more step with these KPI. These metrics can be evaluated between sites in a multi-site health system, which can allow meaningful analysis and discussion about how organizational security resources are deployed or the service delivery models in place are functioning for the organization. But what about comparing this data with like facilities across the country, or even in other countries? Why does Hospital A in New York spend $30 per patient day on security while Hospital B in Los Angeles, acknowledged to be a peer facility, spends $20 a patient day? While many factors are at play in such assessments, the analysis should cause us to look at other KPIs. Is Hospital B meeting response time requirements, providing the same scope of services and scoring similarly on the quality scale? If the answer is yes, Hospital A executives may be looking to the Hospital B security program for guidance.

Figure 12-6 lists a number of performance measurements/improvement goals that may be considered for healthcare security programs.

HEALTHCARE SECURITY
PERFORMANCE STANDARD/MEASUREMENT/IMPROVEMENT

Activity/Process: The Security Department investigates all reports of patient missing property. A security incident report (investigation) is completed for each reported loss.

Performance Standard: There should be a 50% resolution of all cases of patient property losses. Resolution includes recovered property, identification of perpetrator, arrest, careless discard, and unfounded reports.

Measurement/Indicator: The Director of Security will maintain an ongoing status review of each incident to include statistical data relative to location, time frames, property categories, and resolution/non-resolution.

Performance Improvement: A performance review committee, consisting of the Director of Security, Investigator, and Risk Manager, will meet each month to review the statistical data and formulate activities/plans for resolution improvement as appropriate.

Activity/Process: The Security Department provides for 24-hour security officer response to critical incidents.

Performance Standard: The response time for a critical incident shall be under five minutes from the time security is notified until an officer arrives at the scene.

Measurement/Indicator: Security dispatch logs which indicate notification times and officer arrival times, will be utilized to track this information and create a monthly statistical report.

Performance Improvement: A performance review committee, consisting of the Director of Security, Dispatch Supervisor, and Security Operations Supervisor, will meet each month to review the statistical data and formulate activities/plans for response time improvements as appropriate.

FIGURE 12-6

Examples of security performance measurement/improvement.

ANNUAL SECURITY MANAGEMENT PLAN AND PROGRAM EFFECTIVENESS EVALUATION

On an annual basis there should be a formal review of the security program which addresses the objectives, scope, performance, and effectiveness of both the security management plan and the operational implementation of the plan. In short, how did the program measure up to expectations? In addition to the security management plan the periodic reports prepared throughout the year for the multidisciplinary review committee are the basic sources of information for the annual evaluation. The annual evaluation does not need to be on a calendar year basis; however, the calendar year is utilized by most healthcare security administrators. In the U.S., the annual security program effectiveness evaluation continues to be a requirement of TJC. Chapter 4 provides a detailed discussion on performance measurement as part of the security management planning process.

KEEPING DEPARTMENTAL RECORDS CURRENT

In addition to basic records, a protection program may require many different types of records and reports to meet its particular needs. All records and reports used in a security program require a periodic review. All forms should be analyzed to determine if they are necessary and if they are being completed by staff in a satisfactory manner. Do not hesitate to change a form if it does not meet the organization's needs in every detail. The most common error encountered is that forms call for more information than is really necessary. Either time is wasted in obtaining and recording the information or officers tend to ignore certain details.

RECORDS RETENTION

The retention of security operational records should be controlled by organization policy, subject to any state law, that ensures that needed records are retained and unneeded records are discarded or destroyed as necessary. As a general rule, most departments retain too many records for too long a time period. Each operational form used by the security department should be assigned a specific retention period. This does not imply that a specific record(s) would not be "pulled out" and saved beyond the stated retention period.

When litigation arises months or years after the actual incident, the plaintiff will generally demand all business records relevant to the claim during the discovery process. The absence of a document retention policy could lead to an accusation of destroying evidence if a particular document cannot be located. This is commonly known as "spoliation" of evidence and could constitute an obstruction of justice criminal offense.[6] The following are offered as general guidelines for record retention:

Security incident reports – five years
Monthly or annual activity reports – five years
Annual security evaluation reports – five years
Parking violation/reminder notices – one year
Security condition reports – six months
Security officer daily activity reports – three months

With many records moving to electronic format in healthcare organizations, it is critical to involve the IT department is supporting the security program record retention efforts. Reports can be archived, even auto-archived, and digitally stored using the organization's IT archive and retrieval process. It is important the security administrator ensure key information is stored securely and for a time period meeting both organizational and program requirements.

Security administrators should periodically review the retention periods for specific categories of records, to ensure the time periods are realistic in meeting the needs of the organization.

REFERENCES

1. Warmington J, Afridi A, Foreman W. *Is excessive paperwork in care homes undermining care for older people?* Joseph Rowntree Foundation; 2014, February 28. Retrieved on June 22, 2014, from http://www.jrf.org.uk/publications/excessive-paperwork-care-homes-undermining-care-older-people.
2. Francis R. *Report of the Mid Staffordshire NHS. Foundation Trust Public Inquiry.* London: The Stationary Office; 2013.
3. University of Glasgow. *Good Practice and Information Guidance No.1: Version Control.* Data Protection and Freedom of Information Office; 2014. Retrieved 24 June, 2014, from http://www.gla.ac.uk/services/dpfoioffice/guidanceonrecordsandinformationmanagement/versioncontrol/.
4. The Law Dictionary. *What is Key Performance Indicators (KPI)?* 2014 Retrieved on June 22, 2014, from http://thelawdictionary.org/key-performance-indicators-kpi/.
5. Campbell GK. Measures and Metrics in Corporate Security. *Security Executive Council* 2011;**7**.
6. Campbell G, Blades M. Building a metrics program that matters. *Journal of Healthcare Protection Management* 2014;**30**(1):116–24.

CHAPTER

PATIENT CARE INVOLVEMENT AND INTERVENTION

13

There must be a clear understanding of how the security program engages with patients and their visitors within the healthcare environment in order to properly fulfill the security and organizational mission.

The relationship or degree of security involvement with the healthcare organization's patients and visitors will vary according to the type of patient, the location of the interaction, and the organization's philosophy towards the use of its security staff with high-risk patients. As an example, the security officer may have a greater need and responsibility for interaction with patients in the emergency room due to their physical presence and need to help control this environment, but have limited contact with patients in the behavioral health unit. Likewise, security officers may have a greater responsibility in dealing with patients and visitors in parking lots and public corridors than in patient rooms.

Patients and visitors can each be viewed in two distinct groups. The patient may either be an outpatient or an inpatient. The vast majority of our discussion of healthcare security focuses on the latter. In terms of visitors, some people are visiting an inpatient, while others are accompanying a person seeking or receiving short-term medical treatment, such as in an emergency room or clinic. Types of visitors may be very diverse and includes persons visiting employees, persons visiting a department for educational, information, or business purposes (salespersons, vendors, delivery persons, persons using the coffee shop, etc.), and persons who have no legitimate reason for being on the property (transients, loiterers, criminals, etc.).

PATIENTS

The Joint Commission (TJC) has various standards that refer to "patient's rights." The UK, Australia, New Zealand, and several Canadian provinces have some form of patient charter or patient rights embedded in their legislation. Although for the most part these standards refer to direct patient care services, all security personnel should be cognizant of these rights as they pertain to the delivery of security services. The Johns Hopkins Hospital in Baltimore, Maryland has a defined *Patient's Bill of Rights and Responsibilities* that "encourages patients to communicate openly with their health care team, participate in their treatment choices, and promote their own safety by being well informed and actively involved in their care."[1] The rights of patients are listed by every healthcare organization. Frequent patient rights and responsibilities that the healthcare security program should be aware of and observe are listed in Box 13-1.

The healthcare organization exists for the purpose of caring for the patient. Thus, all of the security program's activities must directly, or indirectly, support patient care and connect to the organizational business of delivering health services. As such, security staff must keep the patient foremost in mind, and must always know and observe a patient's rights. A few basic principles for how security should engage and interact with patients are noted in Figure 13-1.

BOX 13-1 PATIENT BILL OF RIGHTS AND RESPONSIBILITIES

Patient Bill of Rights and Responsibilities

Patient has the right to:

- Receive considerate, respectful and compassionate care regardless of age, gender, race, national origin, religion, sexual orientation or disabilities
- Receive care in a safe environment free from all forms of abuse, neglect or harassment
- Be called by their proper name and to be in an environment that maintains dignity and adds to a positive self-image
- Have someone remain with them for emotional support during their hospital stay, unless the visitor's presence compromises the patient's or others' rights, safety or health. The patient has the right to deny visitation at any time.
- To give written informed consent before any nonemergency procedure begins
- Have pain assessed and be involved in decisions about treating pain
- Be free from restraints and seclusion in any form that is not medically required
- Expect full consideration of privacy and confidentiality in care discussions, examinations and treatments. An escort may be requested during any type of exam.
- Access protective and advocacy services in cases of abuse or neglect
- Participate in decisions about your care, treatment and services provided, including the right to refuse treatment to the extent permitted by law. If you leave the hospital against the advice of doctor, the hospital and doctors will not be responsible for any medical consequences that may occur.
- Have communication provided in a manner that can be understood; e.g., sign language, foreign language interpreters, or vision, speech, hearing or other impairments
- Expect that all communications and records about care are confidential, unless disclosure is allowed by law
- See or get a copy of medical record and have the information explained
- Receive a list of who personal health information was disclosed to
- Access pastoral and other spiritual services
- Voice concerns about the care received

Patient Responsibilities

- Asked to leave valuables at home and bring only necessary items for the hospital stay
- Expected to treat all hospital staff, other patients, and visitors with courtesy and respect; abide by all hospital rules and safety regulations; and be mindful of noise levels, privacy, and number of visitors

(Adapted in Part from The Johns Hopkins Hospital, Baltimore, Maryland)[1]

INPATIENTS

The basic protection for inpatients comes from the nursing unit staff, which consists of nursing managers and staff, unit secretaries and clerks, and auxiliary and ancillary support staff. It is rare for security personnel to routinely interact with inpatients on a proactive or routine basis, though this sometimes occurs in behavioral/mental health units where security staff are permanently situated.

The nurse assigned to a patient is responsible for his or her total care, which includes the safety of the patient. Nurses do, however, receive support from the security system on protection issues related to the patient, just as they receive support from other disciplines in administering medical care.

Nursing staff must be acutely aware of who enters the unit and for what purpose, especially during after-hours periods. Just as the security role becomes more custodial during the night hours, nursing assumes a more custodial role for the patient's safety. Of course, nursing staff have a responsibility during operational periods to challenge strangers on the unit, or in patient rooms, at any time. In terms of strangers, it is also the responsibility of all staff to query persons in their work area if they or their business are unknown. The need for this inquiry is greatest during the evening and night hours, and it

SECURITY STAFF MUST REMEMBER THE PATIENT:

1. is the most important element in the healthcare business
2. is not an interruption of the security officer's work but the reason for it
3. does a favor by calling security; security does not do a favor by serving the patient
4. is part of the healthcare business and not an outsider
5. is not a cold statistic but a human being with feelings and emotions
6. is not someone to argue or match wits with
7. is a person with wants; the security officer's job is to fill those wants
8. deserves the most courteous and attentive treatment possible
9. makes it possible for the security officer to be paid
10. is the life blood of every hospital

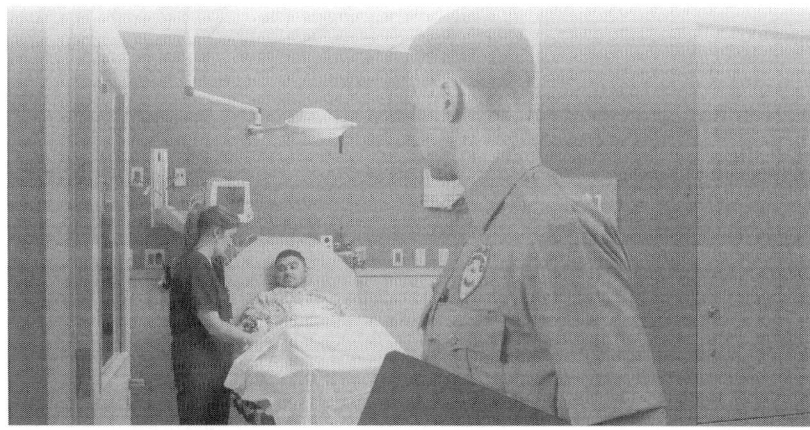

FIGURE 13-1

Basic security principles for patient care involvement.

increases the nearer the stranger is to patient care areas. During the late night hours, the inpatient unit often becomes very quiet, which in a sense aids nursing and unit personnel in their custodial responsibility. The quiet atmosphere means that even minor noises, such as a stairway door opening or closing, will be detected. Nursing staff must always be sharply attuned to the status of the unit.

Nursing staff should be encouraged to challenge strangers and assist them as needed. The stranger, however, becomes a suspicious person when the nurse does not feel comfortable approaching the stranger. At this point, the nurse should be encouraged to call for security support.

The nursing staff is the largest group of employees in the hospital, and one with which security must continually interact. According to Kathleen Pedziwiatr, former director of nursing at Alexian Brothers Hospital in Elk Grove, Illinois, one of the difficulties encountered between nursing personnel and security officers is the difference in their general perception of people. On the whole, nurses are generally trusting and sympathetic, while security officers are generally suspicious. Security perceives that nurses do not always attend to security to the degree expected, due to their casual and trusting attitude. Nurses perceive that security officers often look for trouble because of their suspicious attitude. The need for both groups to communicate and understand one another is vital to good patient care and a strongly integrated protection effort.

In addition to nurses and other unit staff, a variety of groups enter the patient unit areas to carry out their work. They include environmental service employees, volunteers, facilities management staff, physicians, therapists, technicians, and a host of other administrative and support personnel. Each of these persons also helps to protect the patient. They must investigate or report any suspicious or unusual activity they observe. Ironically, some of these individuals have been responsible for perpetrating crimes against patients, ranging from petty theft to homicide.

ASSISTING WITH PATIENTS

Security officers routinely assist inpatients who are moving about the facility. More frequently, however, security is asked to assist with irrational and uncooperative patients. In some security programs this is a planned function, with security officers an essential element of the medical care plan. In other security programs, the interaction with patients is routinely discouraged and for some select few programs, it is forbidden. The protection program that takes a "hands off" approach to patient involvement is not fulfilling an important mission for the healthcare organization. Healthcare organizations with such a security department practice should reevaluate their operating model, department role, responsibilities, and training. Historically, many outsourced security organizations have opted not to have a hands-on approach, opting instead to have an "observe and report" approach. This risk management approach is a sound business strategy for the contract agency, as it can save thousands in undesired workers compensation expense frequently associated with uncooperative patients. Unfortunately for the healthcare organization, the risk only shifts to them and their care providers. Understanding what strategy is employed by the contract agency is an important criterion for the company selection process if an outsourced security model is employed. Sample language to call this issue to the attention of the vendor, and the security selection committee, is provided in Appendix II, "Sample Request for Proposal for Security Service."

Responding to requests for assistance with patients is a valid and necessary function of any protection system; however, the scope of this assistance should be clearly defined. Security staff should support medical care personnel not replace them. When emergencies occur, security officers should respond as part of the total resources available. This response is best considered a support role, and security should not assume lead responsibility for the situation or the patient, unless circumstances exist that involve immediate and unavoidable danger of bodily harm or significant damage to property. While it is recognized that some organizations utilize security in a lead, or even exclusive, role in managing patient aggressive behavior, it must be reinforced that responsibility for the patient always rests with clinical staff.

The IAHSS has established a Basic Industry Guideline for the role of security in patient management that should be adhered to by healthcare organizations.

The frequency of calls for assistance varies from organization to organization and depends on many factors, including the types of patients the facility serves, the availability of nursing or other care providers, and the organizational approach to its use of security or designated sitters. However, the rise of patient-generated violence has witnessed a number of healthcare organizations significantly increase their volume of security events for patient assistance. Many have more than doubled, and the average

IAHSS – HEALTHCARE BASIC SECURITY GUIDELINE, #02.04

Security Role in Patient Management

Statement

Healthcare Facilities (HCF) will develop policies and procedures that identify the responsibilities and scope of activities of security in performing patient intervention activities. Patient intervention activities include performing patient watches, holds, restraints and seclusions relative to the medical evaluation or treatment of patients.

Intent

a. Management of patient care from the time of presentment of care, to the time of discharge, is the responsibility of clinical care staff.

b. When security is involved in patient intervention activities, such intervention will be under the direction and supervision of clinical care staff. Security may take independent action when presented with circumstances involving a clear and present danger of bodily harm or danger to property.

c. The long-term use of security officers as sitters or in patient watch situations should be avoided unless dedicated security-staffing resources have been allocated for this specific purpose. If other security resources are used, significant efforts should be made to maintain the overall posture of safety on the campus. Placing patients in restraints or seclusion should also include appropriate clinical staff monitoring. If security is used to support this monitoring, the appropriate training should be provided. In general, security should be used to supplement and replace clinical staff members. The primary role of security should be to assist in patient acting out situations where help is needed to gain control of the patient.

d. When security staff assist in the hands-on restraint or seclusion of a patient within the facility, where physical force and/or restraint devices are required, the following will apply:

(1) There will be continuous presence, direction, monitoring, and supervision of security actions by qualified facility clinical care staff.

(2) Restraint devices will be those devices commonly utilized in the medical care environment that have been approved by the HCF. Handcuffs and similar law enforcement restraint devices will not be utilized unless such medical restraint devices are not immediately available and there is an immediate and clear danger that the patient may harm himself or others. It is recognized that law enforcement restraint devices may not be used in any case in specific jurisdictions. The use of weapons by security is considered as law enforcement use and not a healthcare intervention. The use of a weapon by security staff to protect people, or hospital property from harm would be handled as a criminal activity.

(3) Prisoner patients presented by prisoner staff should be restrained by the prisoner staff supplied devices, which may include handcuffs, shackles, manacles or like devices (written in accordance with IAHSS Guideline: 02.03 – Prisoner Patient Security).

e. Security will receive training as to their role with establish protocols relative to patient watches, holds, and restraining patients. Collaborative training with clinical staff should include de-escalation and proper restraint techniques, mental health holds, Against Medical Advice (AMA) discharges as well as accreditation and regulatory agencies.

f. Security patient intervention activities should be documented to include requesting care giver, time of request, instructions given, patient name, time and duration of services rendered and the identity of all security involved in providing the support service.

References

- Stefan, Susan, Emergency Department Treatment of the Psychiatric Patient Policy Issues and Legal Requirements. American Psychology – Law Society Series. Ronald Roasch. Oxford, New York: Oxford University Press, 2006.
- State Operations Manual, Appendix A – Survey Protocol, Regulations and Interpretive Guidelines for Hospitals, Rev. 03/17/2008. Centers for Medicare and Medicaid Services.

See Also

- IAHSS Guideline 09.03: Security in the Emergency Care Setting
- IAHSS Guideline: 09.06: Behavioral/Mental Health – General

Approved: November 2007
Last Revised: October 2010

amount of time spent for each event by available security staff has more than tripled in the last several years. The emergency department is a large user of this service for most healthcare facilities. But this can vary even within a health system with consistent policies, procedures and approach. Centura Health, Colorado's largest health system, has a similar organizational approach to how it manages high-risk patients. However, the average use of healthcare security staff varies by facility, from security being involved at a ratio of one security engagement for every ten emergency patient visits within its facility with a dedicated psych ED, to a ratio of 1:89 for a high-volume suburban hospital.

The healthcare protection program should carefully monitor and measure their involvement in patient care, for performance improvement by volume, and total amount of time spent on average. The compounded effect these two issues have had on the consumption of security resources has been substantial for many healthcare security programs. Measuring and providing access to this specific data helps healthcare administrators and protection professionals to better understand how the role of security staff, with patient assistance, can singlehandedly reduce the posture of security on campus. One busy Level II trauma center in Colorado, looking to improve its program after an employee engagement survey denoting a lack of visibility by the security staff in the parking areas, realized security involvement with patient assistance in the emergency room was consuming over 60% of all available security resources. Another busy regional trauma center, which has been tracking security involvement with patients in the emergency department, has trended up from 3,000 events per year to over 4,500. In each situation, the changes to the security staffing plan were easily made, as hospital administrators realized the negative effect this expectation had on their security overall organization posture. In Canada, there are estimates that as much as 65% of security resources are consumed in the EDs and Behavioral/Mental Health areas, by patient assist-related functions.

The better trained and more responsive the security operation is, the greater the tendency to involve security officers in patient care. Healthcare security administrators must review and evaluate patient assistance activity very closely. Other protection alternatives have become increasingly accepted in recent years to include the use of dedicated behavioral health / security technicians to sit with patients who provide a therapeutic approach to one-on-one monitoring requirements. Technology integration has also been used by Dignity Health in its Nevada operations and many other healthcare organizations throughout the U.S. to supplement the need for one-on-one patient monitoring in specific risk appropriate applications.

Ironically, behavioral health patients are believed to be at the heart of the explosive growth of patient-generated violence and the resources required to mitigate it. However, stand-alone behavioral health care facilities generate fewer calls for assistance than do general medical facilities of the same size. This is often because employees of behavioral health care facilities are programmed and trained to care for difficult patients as a routine activity.

THE MISSING PATIENT

Missing patients is one area in which patients and security staff interact. In many cases, this interaction will test the interpersonal skills of the security officer. The accountability for patients is not always as exacting as one might expect. Patients may leave the unit to take a walk, go to the cafeteria, find a place to smoke, or even visit other patients without informing unit personnel. Others may be away for tests or treatment, which may not have been properly communicated to all staff. Still others decide they do not want to remain in the facility and leave without notifying anyone of their intention. Whatever the case, unit personnel cannot automatically sound an alarm whenever they cannot readily account for a patient. However, when a patient is clearly missing, or there are extenuating circumstances, the unit staff should notify security. Extenuating circumstances may involve the mental or physical state of the patient, or situations in which the safety of the patient may be in question. To prevent unnecessary searches, many units have procedures in place for patients to sign out, or otherwise communicate with the nursing staff, before leaving the area. Figure 13-2 is a notice The University of North Carolina Hospital posts throughout their facility to keep patients from leaving the hospital without communicating to medical staff.

The two most important factors relative to security involvement in the missing patient incident are timeliness and thoroughness of the search. The probability of a successful search decreases as time increases.

Specific guidelines should cover the actions and responsibilities of the security officers in investigating missing patients. Officers should thoroughly search the common and support areas of the facility, including food service areas, corridors, lobbies, lounges, public washrooms, parking areas, and the grounds. The review of security camera images from the site can also support the search process, especially if external cameras can confirm the patient leaving the property. Unit personnel and other staff should search other patient and treatment areas.

When missing patients are located, officers should attempt to convince the patient to return to the unit voluntarily. The hospital bears responsibility for patients who may be irrational. Security officers should use extreme caution in chasing or yelling at patients, because an irrational patient can easily be panicked and might fall or run into a street. Officers should also try to summon medical personnel to assist in returning the patient to the unit. Officers should not use physical force, unless they are so directed by a competent authority or, in their judgment, the patient is clearly endangering his or her life or the lives of others. This is a delicate judgment. Officers can be held liable for false arrest or assault and battery if they detain patients against their will. In all instances, officers must complete a detailed incident report describing all the facts of the situation and the action taken.

TO OUR PATIENTS

So that we can assure your safety at all times, you are required to inform your care nurse before leaving the unit for any non-medical reason.

If appropriate, our staff will sign you out on the Off-Unit Login for up to one hour and give an Off-Unit Badge to Wear.

If you do not return within one hour, an overhead page will go out stating your name and asking you to return to the unit. While you may travel within UNC Hospitals, you may not leave the hospital building.

Thank you for your cooperation. Your safety is very important to us.

~ Your Health Care Team

FIGURE 13-2

Notice to patients. Courtesy of University of North Carolina Hospital.

As a general rule, security should begin their search on the boundary of the campus and work inwardly, while other hospital staff begins searching on the unit floor and expands outwardly. It is important also to address questions as to how far off the property the search should be conducted, and at what point law enforcement should be notified. Property lines should not be used as a "line in the sand" in terms of searching. The search should include blocks surrounding the property; however, this off-property search is generally conducted as a secondary phase to the initial search. A missing patient incident that took place in Pennsylvania illustrates this point. An intensive care patient left his bed at approximately 3:00 a.m. The responsible caregiver notified security within minutes of the situation, as she heard the monitoring alarm sound while she was caring for another patient. Security searched the facility and grounds to no avail. At approximately 6:00 a.m., the police were notified by passersby of a man in a hospital gown lying in the middle of the sidewalk approximately one block from the hospital. The patient, with Foley catheter still in place, was dead.

For patients who have left the facility without informing staff, the response to their absence is based on what is reasonable for the particular situation. For some organizations, an absence of 45 minutes triggers the missing patient protocol and patient search. It should be noted the length of time for initiating action will vary by the time of day. A patient missing for 45 minutes in the middle of the afternoon is quite different from a patient missing for even 15 minutes at 3 a.m. Other organizations deem elopement response necessary when it becomes reasonably certain the patient is missing without authorization. All healthcare facilities should have the capability to conduct an appropriate search of the premises within 30 minutes of a missing persons report. At the time the initial search is completed, and certainly within 45 minutes of a negative search, the police should be notified. Special situations may reduce this time frame appropriate to the information available.

The search should continue and be exhaustive or end with unthinkable consequences, as San Francisco General Hospital found in October 2013 when a 57-year-old patient was reported missing, only to be found deceased in a hospital stairwell 17 days later by maintenance workers, doing a routine quarterly check.[2] If the search is unsuccessful, officers should report back to the patient care unit to detail their actions and state the outcome of the search. In some cases this report will be directed to an emergency operations center if the organization has activated such a center in response to the missing patient incident. It is not within the general scope of the security program to assume responsibility for anything more than the search. Notifying the administration, the physician, or the family should not fall within the responsibility of the protection officer. See Figure 13-3 for a sample missing patient search form.

A common medical record form used in many hospitals is the Against Medical Advice form. It is normally used for patients who, after admission, decide they do not want to stay in the hospital. If unit personnel cannot persuade these patients it is in their best interest to remain, the patients are asked to sign the form stating they acknowledge they are leaving against medical advice. Patients can refuse to sign the form and should be allowed to leave with clinical notes reflecting this occurrence.

Leaving against medical advice is different from patient elopement or patient wandering, and is determined by the patient's decision to leave the facility, having been informed of, and appreciating the risks of, leaving without completing treatment.[3] Most adult patients are legally able to discharge themselves without completing treatment.

Sometimes when security officers are advised of a missing patient, they discover the patient leaving the facility and getting into a cab or parked vehicle. Officers should, of course, try to persuade the patient to return to the unit. Reluctant patients can often be convinced to go back to the unit, supposedly

Missing Patient

Search Checklist

Patient Name:	Unit:	Room Number:
Date of Elopement:	Search Coordinator:	
Search Start Time:	Search End Time/Date:	
AREAS SEARCHED (To be completed by all units participating in search):		
______ Patient Rooms ______ Public Bathrooms ______ Linen rooms ______ Janitorial Area ______ Soiled Utility Areas		______ Kitchen Area ______ Stairwells ______ Locked Areas ______ Waiting Areas ______ Other:
Unit Searched:	Search Start Time:	End Time:
Responsible Director/Supervisor:		
Names of Who Was Involved in Search		
PLEASE CALL SEARCH COORDINATOR WITH YOUR RESULTS. FORWARD THIS FORM TO RISK MGMT		

Signature of Search Coordinator

Date Forwarded to Risk Management

CONFIDENTIAL

FIGURE 13-3

Sample missing patient search form.

to sign out. This gives unit personnel a chance to talk further with them. Once back on the unit, patients may be more easily persuaded to remain, or to at least to wait until their doctor can be contacted. The University of Pittsburgh Medical Center, in response to the death of an 89-year-old patient who had dementia, introduced a new search procedure for missing patients called "Condition L." Initiated by the nurse on the unit, and announced overhead throughout the hospital, the code "summons every available employee including those in security, nursing, maintenance and (environmental services) to assist in a coordinated search of the hospital complex."[4]

In Canada, the "Code Yellow" (missing patient) protocols often involve an overhead announcement, and a two or three phased search protocol, that assigns responsibilities to specific hospital groups and employees. Security will have a defined role within this protocol, working within the fundamental premise that responsibility for the missing patient rests with the clinical staff who were providing care.

The issue of missing patients is not isolated to acute care hospitals in the U.S or Canada. Farnham Road Hospital, a psychiatric hospital in Surrey (UK) report missing patients to the police at a rate of two a month. In May 2007, the hospital reported seven patients missing for a total of 77 days before being recovered safely by the police.[5] In Australia, in another tragic missing patient case at the Wollongong Hospital in 2011, a 78-year old went missing from the unit after routine surgery and, despite an exhaustive search by hospital personnel, was found deceased 17 hours later in a restricted area of the hospital.[6]

PATIENT ELOPEMENT PREVENTION AND RESPONSE

Finding that a patient has "gone missing" is a scary situation for providers and patients' families. According to the Veterans Administration (VA) National Center for Patient Safety, elopement is defined as: "A patient that is aware that he/she is not permitted to leave, but does so with intent."[7] In many cases of elopement, the patient may have a decreased mental capacity related to a number of medical conditions to include dementia, altered mental status, or acute alcohol intoxication. A patient who was a known flight risk, and recovering from brain surgery and suffering from amnesia, left his eighth-floor room at Parkland Hospital only to be found 13 hours later wandering nearly 6 miles from the hospital on the other side of downtown Dallas.[8] Despite the level of capacity or intent, eloping patients are often at risk for serious harm, and there are many cases where patient elopement has resulted in serious injury and death.

In the U.S., the Joint Commission's sentinel event policy defines "any elopement that is an unauthorized departure, of a patient from an around-the-clock care setting, resulting in a temporally related death (suicide, accidental death, or homicide) or major permanent loss of function," as a reportable and reviewable sentinel event.[9] This reporting requirement reflects the level of harm to the patient regardless of the patient's intent to leave or mental capacity. According to Joint Commission sentinel event statistics, the primary contributors to elopement are breakdowns in patient assessment and team communication.[10] Eighty-one such events have been reported to The Joint Commission in the period of 2004 through June 2013.[11] Protection of patients from elopement risks requires attention to preventive measures, through assessment and elopement precautions, as well as appropriate intervention after elopement occurs.

Adequately assessing patients for elopement risk factors and use of elopement precautions can, in many cases, prevent elopement and improve safety. Such an assessment, and possible precautions, have been outlined in an elopement tool kit created by the VA National Center for Patient Safety. A "yes" to any of the following assessment questions often indicates that the patient is at risk for elopement:

- Does this patient have a court-appointed legal guardian?
- Is this patient considered to be a danger to self or others?
- Has this patient been legally committed?
- Does this patient lack the cognitive ability to make relevant decisions?
- Does this patient have a history of escape or elopement?
- Does this patient have physical or mental impairments that increase their risk of harm to self or others?[12]

The security officer is often asked to watch or stand by for the patient meeting any of the above criteria. When a security officer is on a "watch," the primary objective is to keep the patient safe and prevent patients from harming themselves or others.

Every healthcare organization should have a defined patient elopement response procedure that is initiated when any patient is believed to have left the facility without authorization. Many organizations will have a "code" to initiate an organizational response as discussed previously. If an elopement occurs, it requires both actions by the care-providing staff in the area from which the patient is missing, as well as an organization-wide search, often led and coordinated by the security staff. A typical protocol includes the following steps:

- Notification of the operator by unit staff indicating a Code/Elopement
- Notification to security with a description of the missing patient and pertinent clinical information
- Notification of the patient's physician
- Immediate search of the unit and surrounding area by unit staff
- Immediate search of hospital and grounds by security personnel
- Notification of the patient's family by the physician
- Notification of police by security as appropriate
- Notification of appropriate administrative personnel.[13]

Procedures differ among organizations. However, the key is to do what is reasonably necessary to return the patient to a safe environment. In some instances the patient may not be located, and law enforcement must be called to solicit their response in the search for the patient. The agency should be supplied with the following data concerning the patient:

- Name
- Physical description: age, height, color of hair, weight, identifying marks (scars, tattoos, etc.), and what the patient was wearing
- Mental status: confused; suicidal; on a psychiatric or alcohol hold
- Risk status: does patient have an IV line; medical condition that is being monitored or needs monitoring

The healthcare organization should have policies and procedures in place indicating the steps personnel are to follow in any elopement situation, and adequate training should be provided for all staff. These protocols should include prevention procedures needed to reduce the risk of an elopement. A simple but very effective risk reduction measure is to require the patient to wear a hospital gown or pajamas at all times. Removing all personal clothes and belongings is a psychological deterrent to leaving the facility and helps readily identify the patient if a search ensues.

Other preventative measures may include placing the patient under constant observation or locating the patient close to the nursing station, or even placing an electronic monitoring device on the patients (if available). Some healthcare organizations use "specialized sitters" to sit with patients who are at risk for elopement. Based on the medical unit and need, security design considerations can be used to prevent elopements. Time-delayed locks, elopement buffers, video surveillance with audio capability, and radio frequency (RF) devices have all been used to successfully prevent patients from eloping.

A patient elopement is a reportable event to a number of external regulatory agencies. The healthcare organization should denote specific responsibility for who should fulfill this requirement. Often, this is the responsibility of the risk management function. Rarely, does the initial report involve the healthcare security administrator. However, follow-up investigative activities by the various regulatory agencies do frequently involve the protection program.

The IAHSS has a created a Basic Industry Guideline for the prevention of and response to patient elopements that every healthcare organization should adhere to.

IAHSS – HEALTHCARE BASIC SECURITY GUIDELINE, #09.04

Patient Elopement

Statement

Healthcare Facilities (HCF) providing inpatient services will develop a multidisciplinary procedure for preventing and responding to patient elopements. The procedure should distinguish between elopements; wandering; and leaving "against medical advice" [AMA].

Intent

a. Definitions
   1) Elopement (referred to in some locations as absconding) is generally defined as a patient incapable of adequately protecting him or herself, and who departs the HCF without the knowledge and agreement of the clinical staff.
   2) Wandering refers to a patient who "strays" beyond the view or control of clinical staff, causing concern, but without the intent of leaving.
   3) Leaving against medical advice (AMA) is determined by the patient's decision to leave the facility after being informed of and understanding the risks of leaving without completing treatment.

b. Elopement Prevention procedures are generally a clinical responsibility, and should include:
   1) Assessing each patient's elopement risk during the admission process and re-assessing such risk, as indicated, during the patient's stay
   2) For patients at a high risk of elopement, steps should be taken to minimize the likelihood of a successful elopement such as:
      - Assigning such patients to rooms nearer and more visible to clinical staff
      - Requiring such patients to wear a patient gown that may be of a distinct type or color
      - Additional measures may include assignment of a sitter or use of Radio Frequency Identification (RFID) to track patient location
   3) A means of identifying patients that are authorized to leave the unit.

c. Elopement Response Plans should address the following:
   1) Clinical staff on duty at the time of a wandering or elopement event will conduct a search of the floor and adjacent areas as indicated and notify the security department if the patient is not found
   2) Search of the facility's buildings and grounds. Consideration should be given to assignment of staff working near facility exits. Some HCF's enlist help via an overhead page using a unique code—combined with an email or other mass notification alert
   3) If the patient is located on the grounds, security should notify clinical staff, and attempt to return the patient to their unit
   4) If the patient is not located within a reasonable time, law enforcement should be notified to obtain assistance in initiating a wider search
   5) An HCF employee should be identified to coordinate information sharing and other follow up with law enforcement
   6) An HCF employee should be identified to coordinate notification of and coordination with the patient's family
   7) If the patient returns to the HCF, security should meet with clinical staff to evaluate the status of the patient, and possibly develop a plan to prevent the patient from engaging in another elopement
   8) In the event of a reported patient wandering or elopement, an Incident Report should be completed (written in accordance IAHSS Guidelines: 05.01 Security Incident Reporting).

References/General Information

- Gerardi, Debra. Elopement. Agency for Healthcare Research and Quality. WebM&M website. (December 2007). Available at: http://www.webmm.ahrq.gov/case.aspex?caselD=164#ref5 (accessed February 11, 2008)
- TJC Sentinel Evert Alert, Issue 46, November 17, 2010

Approved: April 2008

Last Revised: October 2011

PATIENT ASSISTANCE

Providing a safe treatment environment for all patients is a basic requirement of every healthcare organization. Clinical staff are expected to implement appropriate interventions, as needed, to prevent patients from harming themselves or others. Often this will include security officer support to provide constant monitoring, to help protect the patient from harming themselves, harming a care provider or other patient, or to prevent the patient from leaving the facility. When security is involved in patient intervention activities, this support is commonly referred to as a "Patient Assist." In some areas, it is also called a security watch or patient watch.

In most healthcare organizations, the nurse assigned to the patient is responsible for determining the need for the patient watch, and notifying the physician when a patient is placed on a watch. Generally, most nurses do not receive specific training or guidance on how to evaluate patient behaviors, from the perspective of the security risk posed. The result is often the inappropriate use of the security officer for patient intervention. A system of seven Denver-based hospitals realized the absence of training and specific guidance to their care providers was driving their security costs beyond their budgetary control. The system of hospitals collectively addressed this issue with the development of "At-Risk" patient criteria to guide their nursing staff and physicians. The system defined patients to be at risk if they have or are:

- Been placed on a mental-health or alcohol hold in accordance with state law
- Acute Drug/ETOH intoxication
- Head-injured with altered mental status
- Confused to time, place and/or person
- At Risk for Elopement based on past history or current condition
- Disruptive or Violent (patient may lose control, threaten to lose control, or give others evidence of a deteriorating mental condition)
- Indication(s) of a weapon or other dangerous item.

An important element for every healthcare professional to understand, is that any patient on a "watch" is the direct responsibility of the nurse assigned to that specific patient. The nurse directs all action regarding the patient and cannot relinquish this responsibility to the security officer. The officer's involvement in this patient care procedure is merely an extension of the assigned nurse; all actions taken with the patient is on behalf of the care provider. Creating guidelines to govern the relationship of the officer with the assigned nurse and the patient, with specific responsibilities outlined for the security officer, is a must for every healthcare protection program.

The security officer should never give the patient anything without the nurse's permission. The officer should remain alert for signs of increased patient discomfort, distress, or aggressive behavior and should be instructed to notify the assigned nurse immediately if witnessed. In the event of an emergency involving a patient, the security officer should assist as directed by the healthcare staff. In the event of an immediate and unavoidable danger posed to or by the patient and there is not time to consult the healthcare staff, the security officer should take action to control the immediate threat and seek healthcare staff direction as soon as it is available.

The assigned nurse should continually assess the patient's ongoing need for a patient watch, at minimum every hour. In the event multiple watches are required by a single officer, patients should be consolidated whenever reasonably possible into close proximity (e.g., adjacent/adjoining rooms). Together, unit staff and security personnel should evaluate the need for additional security personnel any time a single security officer is asked to conduct more than one patient watch at a time.

The security officer should be well integrated into the healthcare delivery team. When assigned to watch a patient, officers should be required to stay at the door of the room, or as close as possible without causing an adverse effect on the patient or the care of the patient. The officer should be careful not to allow the security uniform to excite or antagonize the patient. Keeping the patient in a line-of-sight should be a fundamental responsibility. In watching multiple patients, it is important for the officer to move continuously from room to room and maintain frequent and periodic sight of each patient. The expanded use of monitoring patients via video surveillance has become acceptable strategy to assist the on-site officer when watching multiple patients, specifically for the risk factors of harm-to-self and elopement.

Documenting all involvement with the patient on a patient watch is an essential component of the security officer's role and function. Using the Security Incident Report or other data capturing tool defined by the healthcare organization, information collected should include:

- Name of the assigned nurse initiating the security watch
- Time the watch begins
- Patient name and number
- Name(s) of other medical staff member(s) giving direction to the officer during the watch
- Physical contact with the patient including aggressive behavior by the patient
- Type of restraints applied or removed (including which limbs were involved) with the officer's assistance
- Name of the medical staff members involved in the application and/or removal of restraints
- Name of each officer providing relief or assistance during the watch
- Beginning and ending times of relief or assistance
- Name of the assigned nurse ending the watch
- Time the watch ends
- Temporary or permanent relief officers should continue the initial Security Incident Report by noting the change of officer in the body of the text.

Security staff involved in the patient watch function must avoid documentation relating to the medical condition of the patient, even when requested by clinical staff. Again this responsibility rests firmly with clinical staff providing care to the patient.

In all instances in which security has assisted with patient restraint, officers should complete a report detailing this assistance. Figure 13-4 shows a sample of a patient restraint form. Depending on the degree of interaction involved, a security incident report may also be required.

Most healthcare professionals agree mental health patients are a significant factor in the explosive increase in the volume of patient watches in the emergency department and elsewhere in the healthcare facility. Many hospital emergency departments have responded by taking a page from the standard security practices employed in behavioral healthcare facilities for many years. This includes:

- Requiring armed security officer to secure their sidearm in a proper storage unit, before conducting a patient watch.
- Removing all sharp objects from the room with meals served on disposable trays with plastic spoons and paper plates/cups.
- Requiring all at-risk patients on a security watch to wear a hospital gown or pajamas.
- Removing all personal clothes and belongings from the at-risk patient's room (secured per the hospital patient valuables policies).
- Limiting the number of visitors and their belongings.

PATIENT NAME AND ID#:	UNIT:	ROOM NUMBER:
RESTRAINT START TIME/DATE:	RESTRAINT END TIME/DATE:	TYPE OF RESTRAINT:

Time	Visual Alert/ Sleeping, Belligerent, Confused	Pt Obsv 30 Mins	NV 2 Hrs	Fluids 2 Hrs	Elim 2 Hrs	Vital Signs 4 Hrs	Food 6 Hrs	Comments	Initials

OTHER COMMENTS ________________________________

____

Initiating Care Provider:	
Ending Care Provider:	
Total Time Spent by Security:	

________ (Initials)

FIGURE 13-4

An example of a security patient restraint form.

(Adapted from Well-star Health System, Marietta, Georgia.)

If an at-risk patient refuses to release their clothing or belongings, a search should be conducted to verify the patient does not have possession of dangerous items or other hazardous paraphernalia, which could be used to harm themselves or others. A basic expectation for the healthcare organization that employs the practice of searching patients is to provide specific guidance to the security officers on how to conduct the patient search.

PATIENT SEARCH

If a patient search is required, the security officer should always attempt to obtain verbal consent from the patient before conducting the search. If consent is not received, many security officers have often found success asking the patient a second time to release their clothing and belongings. If the patient does not comply with either request, unit staff and security personnel should confer with the physician, and possibly risk management or other appropriate personnel including family members, to determine the best course of action to include the risk and benefits of searching the patient. There may also be a need to seek police or other assistance. In a growing number of healthcare organizations, where there appears to be no reasonable solution to consent for the search or release of clothing and belongings, the hospital and physician have elected to discharge the patient in response to the security risks presented by the patient. A discharge decision is never made by the healthcare security staff and, at best, is a decision of last resort.

In 2009, Beth Israel Deaconess Medical Center adopted a policy that permits patients to remain in their own clothes, unless they pose an imminent risk of injuring themselves or others. In those circumstances, forcible removal is permitted only after other less-intrusive methods to ensure safety have been unsuccessful, and federal standards that limit the use of physical restraint are met. In the same year, the Massachusetts Departments of Public Health and Mental Health jointly drafted a statement declaring that psychiatric patients have a right to retain their clothing, and that forced removal is a form of physical restraint, that cannot occur unless compelling clinical information indicating imminent risk to self or others exists.[14]

When consent for the patient search is received, it should always be conducted by a person of the same gender as the patient, in an area affording patient privacy, and in the presence of a physician or an assigned caregiver; never alone.

A search procedure must be developed and training provided relative to a methodical approach for how to conduct the search. The "airport screening method" is frequently used as outlined in the patient procedures in Figure 13-5.

The IAHSS has a Basic Industry Guideline for searching patients and patient areas for contraband that should be followed for healthcare organizations to reduce the likelihood of contraband entering the facility.

PATIENT RISK GROUPS

Certain patient risk groups require specific attention relative to security. These basic groups are identified by patient type and include the VIP patient, the infectious patient, the combative patient, behavioral health patients, patients with autism, the forensic patient, the wandering patient, and the infant/pediatric patient.

IAHSS – HEALTHCARE BASIC SECURITY GUIDELINE, #02.03

Searching Patients and Patient Areas for Contraband

Statement

Healthcare Facilities (HCF) should establish procedures to reduce the likelihood of contraband entering the healthcare setting. Searches of patients, patient belongings, and patient areas should be conducted as needed.

Intent

a. These searches are undertaken to reduce the likelihood of potentially dangerous, illegal, or other items which may be contrary to the patient's treatment plan from being brought into the healthcare facility.

b. Contraband includes, without limitations, any type of weapon, illegal or unauthorized drugs, intoxicants, flammable items, and sharp edged objects. Other items may be prohibited, based on patient needs as determined by medical staff.

c. A room searched and a personal search protocol which respects the dignity of the patient should be established. The protocol should include:
   (1) When a search is justified;
   (2) Who may initiate a search [usually medical or nursing staff];
   (3) Who conducts the search [usually security along with a unit care-giver];
   (4) How a search should be conducted, both of a person and an area;
   (5) How search results are to be documented;
   (6) How seized items are to be handled, safeguarded, and ultimately disposed of, allowing for, as appropriate:
      - destroying and discarding
      - turning over to law enforcement
      - returning the item(s) to the owner or a responsible family member

d. These searches and inspections are administrative in nature, and are not law enforcement searches. It is not the intent of this guideline to provide law enforcement with evidence to criminally prosecute or otherwise act on the basis of items seized during such inspections. Nor, is it the intent of this guideline to prohibit the turning over of such contraband to the appropriate law enforcement jurisdiction. The HCF's search protocol should address who may, and under what circumstances a determination will be made to involve a law enforcement agency.

Approved: April 2009
Last Revised: October 2009
Last Reviewed: October 2011

THE VIP PATIENT

The VIP patient is any patient that poses special security problems and may require certain security precautions to be taken. For celebrities and political figures and royalty, specific safeguards and special considerations may include accommodations for protection personnel, modifying department workflow to include restricting access to a cordoned area of a department, to include caregivers and visitors. This may require the issuance and vetting of special credentials (i.e., badges) for essential providers, and arranging transport within the hospital for elective procedures during off-hours. In some cases these patients are accompanied by their own security detail. The hospital's protection service thus has limited responsibility for the patient's security. This is especially true when a government figure is involved. But this may not always be the case, and protection efforts may require the healthcare facility to provide around-the-clock security personnel for the patient.

As important as it is to protect VIP patients from bodily harm during the visit, it is equally important to protect them from attacks on confidentiality via unauthorized access to the electronic medical record. Many healthcare facilities have started to use "pop-ups" in the electronic medical records, to flash a warning that only employees with legitimate clinical reasons should access the record. These warnings

1. Ask the patient to face the searcher with arms outstretched and feet slightly spread (airport screening method). The searcher will start at the top of the head and continue in a clockwise direction until the patient's body has been outlined, the extremities searched, and the torso patted down from shoulders to lower hips both front and back.
2. Whenever possible, the searcher should use the back of a hand to conduct the search. If the patient has short hair only visual inspection is required; however, long hair or up-swept hairdos must be patted down. Remove and search all head coverings (turbans, bandannas, hats, etc.).
3. Search the patient's arms by encircling the arm with the hands and moving downward from the shoulder to the bottom of the sleeve in one motion.
4. Search the patient's legs starting at the back of the leg (using the back of the hand) moving downward in an overlapping paths, until the patient's entire lower body has been searched. In most cases, do not search the patient's shoes unless there is reason to believe the patient is attempting to conceal something.
5. After the patient's body and extremities have been completely outlined, raise the patient's arms and search the torso starting at the top of the shoulders (again using the back of hand) moving downward towards the hips. Overlap each pass until the patient's entire torso is searched. Repeat the same procedure for the patient's back. Give special attention to the area of the back near the waist caused by the curvature of the spine and under the armpits.

   NOTE: Generally, a search should encompass no more than a pat down of the individual's outer clothing; however, it should be done with sufficient care and strength to feel a concealed weapon.
6. If, during the course of a search, suspect items are found, ask the patient to slowly remove the item from its location. Obtain the item from the patient. Circumstances may require reaching into a pocket or other hidden areas (i.e., a boot) to retrieve a suspected hidden weapon. Exercise caution about where hands are placed—LOOK BEFORE YOU TOUCH ... TOUCH WHERE YOU ARE LOOKING.
7. Perform all bag and belongings searches in a systematic, circular, and clockwise path. Start the search with a visual inspection of the exterior. Search the interior of the bag in the same circular motion—feeling the top, sides, and bottom of the inside of the bag.
8. Restrict the patient's access to the contents of the bag and keep the bag out of public view. Do not allow the patient to place his/her hands into the bag until the search is complete.
9. Remove all items from the patient's room. Return all items upon discharge. Place all removed personal items in a valuables envelope and process through the patient valuables system. Place all other patient items in a plastic bag for safekeeping until the patient is transferred or discharged. Inventory and label the bag with the patient's information.
10. Turn over to the Pharmacy all medications and unidentifiable substances for identification anonymously. Pharmacy will properly dispose of all illegal substances or turn over to the police anonymously.
11. Secure all weapons and turn over to the patient's representative or police department if appropriate.
12. Searches should be documented, including the patient's consent to search, the time and date of the search, the personnel conducting the search, patients or family members present, reasons for search, and whether any contraband, weapons, or dangerous objects were found and disposition of such items.

FIGURE 13-5

Patient search procedures.

can also cite the penalties for unauthorized review of the record. If warranted, access to a celebrity's health record can be restricted to a few predetermined healthcare providers.[15]

The second major type of VIP patient requiring security safeguards is the patient who has been threatened or beaten, is a victim of a crime or a witness, or is involved in an activity that puts them at risk of being harmed during treatment. Once the treating organization is aware of such potential danger, there is a responsibility on the part of the organization to take preventive steps. These steps will vary according to the degree of risk and include:

- Controlling information about the patient to include removing the patient's name from the general patient population database. That way, if someone inquires after the patient, the operator or information desk staff will indicate there is no such patient.
- Disconnecting all telephone service to the patient's room.
- Moving the patient to a room that provides maximum surveillance by unit care staff.
- Care should occur where it is most appropriate. Although in some cases placing a VIP patient in a more private and remote setting may be appropriate, the patient is generally best served by receiving critical care services in the intensive care unit.[15]
- Restricting or denying visitors.
- Providing a patient companion, or sitter, to be with the patient at all times.
- Carefully manage communication with the media.
- Protect the patient's security. This may include providing a security guarding arrangement. This would involve the patient who would not be under police control or custody. (The handling of the prisoner patient is considered to be in a different patient risk group.)

Figure 13-6 shows an example of a security VIP policy.

Dale Schoolfield, CHPA, Security Manager for Provena Saint Joseph Hospital in Elgin, Illinois, wrote his evaluation of the hospital's very important person policy to include victims of violence. He described the need to have a policy in advance of a gang victim arriving at the emergency department, to avoid situations where staff and visitors are put into danger. Highlights of how he helped his hospital amend its VIP policy included:

- Immediately registering patients of the emergency department as a result of a violent act, as non-published patients, with no information given to anyone except law enforcement
- Limiting visitation to immediate family only, and no more than two visitors
- Notifying administrative coordinators, telecommunications staff, marketing/public relations, and the administrator on duty of the situation, and advising NO patient information is to be given to the news media or anyone walking in or calling the hospital
- On-going evaluation of the need to restrict access into the emergency department and/or hospital
- Counseling family members regarding the safety procedures and the need for privacy and confidentiality of the patient
- On-going evaluation of the potential for a breach of patient security due to excessive visitors arriving at the hospital with patient information
- Increasing security officer patrols in the area
- Critiquing the incident and organizational response afterward to identify opportunities for improvement.[16]

Example

**HEALTHCARE SECURITY
POLICY AND PROCEDURE
FOR
THE VIP PATIENT**

GENERAL

The VIP patient is any patient who requires special protection measures during outpatient or inpatient medical services. This patient may be a high profile public figure, a celebrity, or a patient whose circumstances or information indicates that he/she may be in some elevated degree of danger.

PUBLIC FIGURE/CELEBRITY

Except for emergency treatment or admission the protection of this type of patient is generally preplanned. In many cases the security department will coordinate protection safeguards with the VIP's personal security staff or a public safety agency such as the police, secret service, or FBI.

PATIENT IN DANGER

This patient may be in danger due to threats to the family or directly to the patient, the result of a gunshot wound, stabbing, gang or criminal activity, or being a witness to a major crime.

PROCEDURES

The same type of security safeguards and procedures will be utilized for each type of VIP. However the degree of the security precautions and activity will vary with the specific patient situation. In general the security precautions and safeguards could include the following actions:

1. Notify appropriate organization personnel including Risk Management, of patient identity and circumstances requiring increased VIP security measures.
2. Notify public safety agencies if deemed appropriate and/or co-ordinate efforts with these agencies.
3. Assign a patient room that is away from elevators and fire stairwells or exits.
4. If security officers, bodyguards, or forensic staff will be utilized assign a patient room at the far end of a dead-end corridor. If this type of personnel is not utilized assign the patient a room close to the nursing station where good surveillance of the room can be maintained.
5. Remove the patient name from the patient information system, Front Desk, and census reports, substituting an assumed name for the actual patient.
6. Maintain the patient's chart in the patient's room.
7. Brief the nursing unit staff of general information and/or specific action items required of medical care staff.
8. Determine if any visitors will be allowed.
9. Obtain name and telephone number of person(s) co-ordinating security for the VIP who can be contacted as questions arise or if there is an emergency. This contact person may be a family member.
10. Utilize security officer briefing procedures to communicate information to all security personnel.

FIGURE 13-6

Example of a hospital security-related VIP policy and procedure.

In the case of a gang victim, information and intelligence gathered through a relationship with law enforcement will help determine the safety plan, and measures required, on a case by case basis.

THE INFECTIOUS PATIENT

When assisting with patients, security personnel have long been concerned about inadvertently contracting an infectious disease. This concern has been heightened by the advent of HIV and the increase in hepatitis-B infections. HIV patients are in the final stages of a series of health problems caused by a human immunodeficiency virus (HIV), which can be passed from one person to another through unprotected sexual contact with an infected partner, the sharing of intravenous drug needles and syringes, the exchange of body fluids, and, less frequently, blood transfusions. There is no known risk of infection in most of the situations encountered in daily life, and no evidence of transmission of HIV by everyday contact.

By nature of their occupation, healthcare workers, including security officers, are likely to come in contact with people infected with HIV or hepatitis-B. The major occupational risk for healthcare workers is the contact of their skin or mucous membranes with infected body fluids or tissues. Exposure can occur from needle stick, cut injuries, and splashes of blood. The virus has also been linked to other body fluids, including semen, preseminal fluid, vaginal secretions, and human breast milk.

For security personnel, the risk of exposure to HIV or hepatitis-B in the course of normal duties is extremely low; exposure could occur only under extraordinary circumstances. It is possible that security officers might sustain cuts or puncture wounds, or be stuck by a needle, while assisting with or searching patients, or dealing with suspicious people. The risk of infection from being bitten by an infected individual is considered to be low.

The first step security management should take is to fight fear with facts. Employees should be reassured there is little reason to fear they will be exposed to infection. Continually educating security staff about the nature of HIV and how it can be transmitted, and informing them of the availability of any personal protection equipment, will do much to alleviate fear. Once again, security should be guided, where possible, by clinician knowledge of individual patients and their conditions, as well as any related precautions required.

THE COMBATIVE PATIENT

Security personnel assist with combative patients most often in four areas of the facility: the emergency department, intensive care units, mental health areas, and the general nursing unit, as well as community health centers and clinics. To provide patient assistance regarding combative patients, all security personnel should be well trained in verbal and nonverbal de-escalation measures and restraint procedures.

Emergency department

The emergency department requires frequent security assistance, especially in facilities that treat many drug overdose patients, patients with injuries due to shooting or stabbing incidents, and patients with mental health or alcohol/drug impairments. This section of the text primarily concerns the security officer's interactions with patients and staff in the emergency department.

Other security concerns for this department are discussed in Chapter 20, "Preventing and Managing Healthcare Aggression and Violence" and Chapter 21, "Areas of Higher Risk." Belligerent and intoxicated patients may also require security assistance, particularly when they are brought for medical care against their will. These patients are often brought to the medical care treatment facility by law enforcement authorities, ambulance crews, or friends/ relatives; often those accompanying the patient are more aware of the treatment needed than the patient is.

When friends or relatives are present, there is an added concern for the protection officer. If the accompanying persons are intoxicated or drug impaired, they will require control, or at least surveillance. They can easily become annoyed or angered at delays in treatment, or they may have their own ideas of what treatment is required. Emergency physicians have estimated more than 75% of patients and visitors to some inner-city emergency departments are under the influence of drugs.

Emergency department clerks and triage nurses are generally the first staff members to interact with persons entering the department. They must be stationed to observe persons entering the department, to provide service and directions, and to keep the area under surveillance to detect persons in distress. The emergency room staff must be alert for impending disruptions. When they suspect trouble, they should call for a security presence. The only preventive action required may be for a security officer to patrol through the area or to stand by unobtrusively.

A growing trend in many security operations, and in areas with an established history of frequent harmful situations, is to station a security officer in the emergency department 24 hours a day. HCA, the largest healthcare system in the U.S., has taken this one step further and mandated the deployment of off-duty police officers in the waiting area of its 50 highest risk hospitals throughout the country.

In smaller security operations, a security officer may be assigned to the emergency room during peak periods. In one small hospital, an officer is assigned every Friday and Saturday night between 7:00 p.m. and 3:00 a.m.

The American College of Emergency Physicians (ACEP) believes that optimal patient care can be achieved only when patients, healthcare workers, and all other persons in the emergency department are reasonably protected against violent acts occurring within the department.

To ensure the security of the emergency department environment, the ACEP states the hospital has the following responsibilities:[17]

- Provide a best practices security system including adequate security personnel, physical barriers, surveillance equipment, and other security components.
- Coordinate the security system with local law enforcement agencies.
- Develop written emergency department protocols for violent situations occurring in the emergency department.
- Educate staff on preventing, recognizing, and dealing with potentially violent situations.
- Conduct ongoing assessments of emergency department security system performance.

Overcrowded emergency departments contribute to patient distress and increase the likelihood of adverse outcomes—elopement, self-harm and violence. Many organizations have introduced initiatives to improve waiting times to decrease incidents of violence to include fast-tracking initiatives for patients with behavioral health problems.

Intensive care unit

Many healthcare organizations have realized that, after the combative patient is discharged from the emergency department, they are not always ready to go home. The most chronic problems are channeled to the ICU or other critical care units. The frequency of security officer involvement with patients on these units requires the protection program to prepare for how it will respond to calls for service. Many healthcare organizations have begun to deploy consistent security systems and safeguard processes in these departments, like those utilized in the emergency department. Specifically, the capability to control and restrict access when high-risk patients are present is a needed precaution. The restricted access control system may not be required to be operational at all times; however, the ICU must be able to convert to this higher level of security quickly—ideally with the push of a single button.

The waiting areas of the ICU are a common location for family members and visitors of the patient to express great emotion, and expose the protection program to many diverse cultural customs. Tension is commonly found in the waiting area, and security officers often respond to loud grieving by family members, are needed to de-escalate feuding family members who hold different opinions about end-of-life decisions, or manage an extremely large influx of visitors that may accompany a patient.

The ICU waiting area will be reflective of the many customs and cultures prevalent in the community. The security officer must be culturally sensitive. An important attribute of the security officer is to be sensitive to different customs, and understand different cultures often behave differently. This may include the process of grieving, differing levels of involvement with a patient, nontraditional religious or family rituals, as well as how they may react to authority figures. For example, security officers responding to a disturbance call in the ICU waiting area may arrive to find that a large family has just found out their loved one has passed away. The grieving process may be loud and a difficult experience for other visitors. However, the culturally sensitive security officer will quickly realize the disturbance call is not a security issue at all, and work to identify a location for the grieving to occur without disrupting others.

General nursing unit

Another category of patients who require assistance is the traditional patient on the medical or surgical nursing unit. In some cases, patients not previously diagnosed as possible combative patients may suddenly and unexpectedly develop irrational behavior. Generally, the nursing staff is not as prepared to handle this unpredicted behavior and must seek off-unit resources.

Regardless of the situation, security officers should not be forced to render medical judgments. They should base their actions on specific instructions from a nurse or a physician at the scene. If these instructions are not forthcoming upon their arrival, officers should determine who is in charge and inquire about their role and necessary actions. At all times, security officers should act to assist and support rather than assume primary responsibility.

Community health centers/urgent care centers/clinics

Community health centers, urgent care centers and clinics in general can be an area of disturbances caused by both patients and visitors. There are at least two factors creating conditions for such problems: the large number of people who frequent these community-based facilities, and the length of time patients must wait to be served. It is not unusual for a clinic patient to have four or five persons accompanying them. These "visitors" are often infants and small children, which can add to confusion and frustration. Extended operating hours have reduced instances of disruptive behavior, as parents are less likely to bring their children as sitters become more available in the evening hours.

BEHAVIORAL/MENTAL HEALTH PATIENTS

Numerous studies have catalogued the substantial problems facing behavioral health patients and healthcare organizations, and their protection efforts. Behavioral health disorders are a major concern for healthcare organizations everywhere. Every hospital treats patients with behavioral health disorders, even when an acute care hospital has no organized behavioral health service or psychiatric clinical specialists.[18]

A national and international dilemma has been created with the diminished capability of behavioral health services in most communities. When coupled with the significant underfunding of public agencies historically responsible for behavioral healthcare, a shifting of costs and care for these patients has moved to the general hospital.[18]

Patients with behavioral health disorders frequently access medical care through the hospital's emergency department. Psychiatric emergency department patients continue to suffer the greatest delay in access to inpatient beds. In New South Wales, Australia, the Mental Health Intervention Team reports that from 2000 to 2007, behavioral health incidents increased by 1,265% or 45.27% each year.[19] Although this increase would be considered excessive for most states and countries, the reduced number of available inpatient psychiatric beds has created a difficult problem—behavioral health patients not being transferred out of the emergency department in a timely manner. Many emergency departments have had to learn to provide a level of care for these patients, long after their psychiatric evaluation and medical clearance. Behavioral health patients are now often spending days in the emergency department, not hours. This is overwhelming many emergency departments, as behavioral health patients often need one-on-one supervision. The escalated amount of tension often created by these anxious patients frequently results in a larger role for security staff to have a greater involvement with the behavioral health patient.

For the few healthcare organizations that continue to offer inpatient behavioral health services (approximately 27% of hospitals in the U.S.),[18] a call to the security department generally indicates that an urgent situation exists and additional help is required to deal with the problem. Unlike years past when security officers rarely responded to the mental health unit, today the typical procedure is for uniformed officers to respond as they would to any other call for patient support. The rationale for this response is that mental health treatment should provide experience and therapy so the patient will be able to function in society. In society, someone who causes a disturbance should expect the authorities to be called.

Until recently, security officers historically did not patrol mental health units. Regular medical care personnel provided surveillance, and control of patients and visitors was part of their routine activity. Today, for the reasons noted, security is often requested to patrol the unit routinely, with physical and virtual patrols.

Armed officers, as opposed to unarmed officers, should use a different response to problems in the mental health unit. Each healthcare facility must develop its own approach. In one large facility, the first security officer to arrive waits outside the unit and collects equipment from the other officers who respond. Other hospitals have installed gun lockers just outside the unit. Of course, circumstances will prevail, and in a nonmedical emergency, such as a fire or major accident, a different response is indicated.

Elopement is always a concern when treating the mental health patient. It is reported that 3 to 15% of all patients admitted to mental health units elope each year. Certain sources suggest there are identifiable characteristics of the patient who is prone to elope. Such sources indicate these patients are generally male and usually verbalize a desire to leave prior to elopement. Often they have eloped on prior occasions and have a diagnosis of schizophrenia or a mood disorder.[20] The entry point to the unit is generally recognized as the primary point of vulnerability in efforts to prevent elopement. Security and the mental health unit staff must work closely with each other to manage the preventive aspects of elopement.

PATIENTS WITH SUICIDAL IDEATION

In 2012, Eric Smith, CPP, director of security for Exempla Health, shared an account of a patient who presented to one of their emergency departments with suicidal ideations, and was placed on a mental health hold and asked to be watched by a security officer. She was completely cooperative, Smith pointed out, and did not make any threats either towards staff or about her own well-being, and she was placed on a bed in an overflow area. During the watch, the patient asked the officer to move away because she felt uncomfortable with him nearby. The officer complied and backed off a short distance; maintaining a clear line of sight. The patient moved around in the bed, so her head was near the foot of the bed, and then rolled over with her back towards the hall and the officer. After realizing her hands were out of sight and in front of her, the officer found the patient had taken a hose off of a piece of equipment left in the hall, used in the care of another patient, and had twisted the hose around her neck twice and pulled it tight. She was essentially unconscious. Fortunately, the officer was alert to the situation and was able to loosen the hose and notify staff. A short time later, she was moved to a room where the environment could be better controlled.

According to The Joint Commission Sentinel Event Database, more than 14% of reported suicides occur in nonbehavioral health units—suicides can happen in medical/surgical suites, intensive care units, oncology units and telemetry units; 8% of reported suicides occur in emergency departments,[21] like the attempted suicide noted above. Complicating matters further is the design of these units: they are rarely designed to mitigate suicide risks and access to potentially dangerous items. Some specific means of suicide that are readily available in the general hospital setting include bell cords, bandages, sheets, restraint belts, plastic bags, elastic tubing and oxygen tubing.[22]

To help hospitals improve safety of their patients, The Joint Commission released Sentinel Event Alert #46 that focuses on preventing suicide in the ED and medical/surgical units. One of the primary recommendations of SEA #46 involves designing a suicide screening and assessment process. In addition to thoroughly screening patients for suicide risk, several other strategies can be incorporated to minimize the risks of patient suicide.[21]

- *Assess the room.* Looking at the entire room, a comprehensive assessment should be performed to identify potential risks and determine possible mitigation strategies. Examples include shatterproof and tamper-resistant light covers, ligature-resistant door handles, sink fixtures and shower heads, tamper-resistant shower curtains, and so forth. A checklist for assessing the environmental risks for suicide can be found in Figure 13-7.
- *Minimize medical equipment in the room.* Most treatment rooms contain a host of equipment and supplies that present hazards, and not every patient will require all the equipment and supplies housed in the room. When treating patients at risk for suicide, an organization should minimize the equipment in the room, and include only that which is absolutely necessary for the patient.

CHECKLIST FOR ASSESSING ENVIRONMENTAL RISKS FOR SUICIDE

Following is a brief checklist to help hospitals assess and address suicide risks in their ED and medical/surgical units.

- ✓ Avoid "lay-in" ceilings. These can make it easier for the patient to hide contraband, can provide a convenient place to secure a ligature for self-harm, or may allow the patient access to above-the-ceiling interstitial spaces.
- ✓ If the outside window of the room is operable, limit the opening so a person could not pass through (4-6 inches is considered the architectural standard of care). Alternatively, consider protecting a window with a security screen that is secured by a device that can be removed from the inside only with a special tool (such as a non-common screw head).
- ✓ Make window glazing shatter-proof.
- ✓ Use a tamper-resistant, anti-ligature door knob for the patient's room.
- ✓ If a hospital bed is in use, secure the electrical power cord on the bed. Consider replacing the bed cord with a "jumper cord" that can be removed by staff, kept in a secure place, and used only when the bed needs to be adjusted. (Check the bed design to ensure that the bed can be mechanically lowered to a "CPR" position.)
- ✓ Use tamper-resistant screws throughout the room.
- ✓ Secure the power cord on the TV. A mounting bracket can be an attachment point for a ligature.
- ✓ Replace cork bulletin boards with dry-mark boards, thus eliminating inadvertent use of thumbtacks.
- ✓ Use shatter-proof and tamper-resistant glass in night lights and other lighting fixtures.
- ✓ Secure light fixtures to restrict patient access to bulbs and sockets.
- ✓ Remove grab bars in the bathroom or fill in the wall "gap."
- ✓ Eliminate coat hooks, towel bars, cubicle curtain tracks, and closet poles.
- ✓ Ensure that all electrical outlets are GFCI (ground fault circuit interrupter) and tamper resistant.
- ✓ Replace metal outlet covers with shatter-proof non-conductive covers.
- ✓ Protect the piping for the toilet and lavatory.
- ✓ Use tamper-resistant lavatory faucets.
- ✓ Ensure that HVAC (heating, ventilating, and air conditioning) grills are tamper resistant.
- ✓ Use tamper-resistant shower controls and shower heads.
- ✓ Ensure that mirror and picture glazing material are shatter-proof.

Source: Adapted from Sine D.M.: Latent risks in the built environment for the behavioral health patient: Concerns for the healthcare risk manager. In The American Society for Healthcare Risk Management Handbook, 6th ed. Chicago: American Hospital Association, 2010.

FIGURE 13-7

A checklist for assessing the environmental risks for suicide.

(Courtesy of Environment of Care News, *reprinted with permission.)*

Although all equipment and supplies cannot be removed for storage and other reasons, some organizations have equipped rooms with a roll-down door or like device, that hides medical equipment and covers the medical gas outlets in the treatment room. Photos of such doors are noted in Figure 13-8.

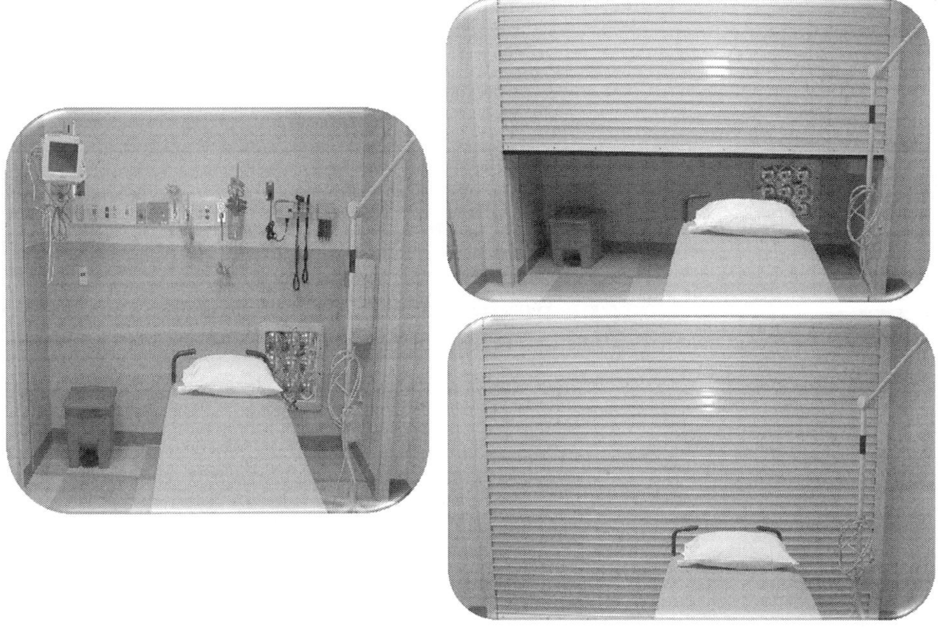

FIGURE 13-8

Examples of roll-down doors used in an emergency department room.

(Courtesy of Presbyterian-St. Luke's Medical Center, Denver, Colorado.)

- *Check for contraband.* In addition to equipment and supplies found in the room, patients may bring items that can be used in a suicide attempt, such as knives, needles, and weapons. A reasonable search of person and property should be conducted when a patient is screened for possible suicide risk. The facility should have a policy that covers what a reasonable search entails, when it should occur, and who should perform it.
- *One-to-One Observation.* Having a trained person sitting with the patient around the clock, whether a security officer or sitter, is an important mitigation strategy. The individual should be able to identify when the patient's behavior is escalating, and know how and when to seek help. Those charged with watching patients must fight against the routine and boredom, watching every action by the patient. The officer in the case noted at Exempla Health certainly saved the life of the patient by being mindful of the inherent risks surrounding suicidal ideations.

PATIENTS WITH AUTISM

The rate of autism has grown tenfold since the late 1990s. The Centers for Disease Control Prevention estimate that 1 in every 150 children are believed to have some form of autism. Throughout the world, the number of people diagnosed with autism is growing, showing no racial, ethnic or social boundaries.[23]

Children and adults with autism now live, work, go to school, and recreate in the community. They also frequently present themselves to the healthcare organization as a patient or a visitor. Healthcare security officers have interactions with children and adults with autism, their parents and care providers. Research indicates that individuals with autism, and other developmental disabilities, are approximately seven times more likely to come in contact with security professionals than are members of the general population.

Healthcare security officers should understand the nature of autism and be trained to manage situations involving patients with this condition more effectively. Security staff can use the acronym AUTISM shown in Box 13-2 to help them remember the methodology they should use when dealing with individuals with autism.

BOX 13-2 SECURITY OFFICER RESPONSE TO AUTISTIC PATIENTS (COURTESY OF DENNIS DEBBAUDT)

Security Officer Response to Autistic Patients	
A	Approach the person in a quiet, nonthreatening manner. Because people with autism may be hypersensitive to stimuli, officers should attempt to avoid quick motions and gestures that a person with autism may perceive, even remotely, as threatening.
U	Understand that touching an individual with autism may cause a protective "fight or flight" reaction. Officers should never touch the individual on the shoulders or near the face. Autistic hypersensitivity includes being touched and even extends to invasions of their personal space.
T	Talk to the person in a moderate and calm voice. Although officers may have to repeat their directions or questions several times, they should be patient and wait for answers. Speaking loudly will not help and may even be viewed as threatening.
I	Instructions should be simple and direct with no use of slang. An autistic patient will take an officer's statements literally. "Do you think that's cool?" or "Up against the wall!" probably will cause confusion and result in an inappropriate or unexpected response. Officers should use specific commands, such as, "stand up" or "go to the bed, now" to reduce the chance of confusion.
S	Seek all indicators to evaluate the situation as it unfolds.
M	Maintain a safe distance until any inappropriate behavior lessens, but remain alert to the possibility of outbursts or impulsive acts.[24]

Healthcare security officers may unexpectedly encounter, or be asked to find, a person with autism. The information may be learned from a security dispatcher, someone at the scene, or from the person directly. Recognizing the behavior symptoms, and knowing contact approaches, can minimize situations of risk—risk to or victimization of the person with autism, as well as risk to the security officer. Dennis Debbaudt, a professional investigator and law enforcement trainer, and proud father of a young man with autism, has developed some specific tips for healthcare security officers responding to patients with autism.

- Make sure the person is unarmed and maintain a safe distance, because they may suddenly invade your personal space.
- Talk calmly and softly.
- Speak in direct, short phrases such as: "Stand up now" or "Get in the bed."
- Avoid slang expressions, such as: "What's up your sleeve?" or "Are you pulling my leg?"
- Allow for delayed responses to your questions or commands.
- Repeat or rephrase when necessary.
- Consider use of pictures, written phrases and commands, and sign language.
- Use low gestures for attention; avoid rapid pointing or waving.
- Examine the individual for presence of medical alert jewelry or tags, or an autism handout card.
- Model calming body language (such as slow breathing and keeping hands low).
- Model the behavior you want the person to display.
- A person with autism may not react well to changes in routine or the presence of strangers, even a uniformed stranger.
- Security officers should not interpret the person's failure to respond to orders or questions as a lack of cooperation or a reason for using increased force.
- Seek information and assistance from a parent or others at the scene about how to communicate with and de-escalate the person's behavior.
- Avoid stopping repetitive behaviors unless there is risk of injury to yourself or others. If the individual is holding an inanimate object and appears to be fascinated with it, consider allowing him or her to keep the item for the calming effect (if safety is not jeopardized).
- Evaluate for injury. The individual may not ask for help or show any indication of pain, even though injury seems apparent.
- If possible, turn off sirens and flashing lights and remove canine partners, crowds, or other sensory stimulation for the scene.
- If the person's behavior escalates, use geographic containment and maintain a safe distance until any inappropriate behaviors lessen.
- Remain alert to the possibility of outbursts or impulsive acts.
- Use your discretion. If you have determined that the person is unarmed and if you have established geographic containment, use all available time to allow the person to de-escalate themselves without your intervention.[25]

THE PRISONER (FORENSIC) PATIENT

The prisoner patient continues to be both an issue and challenge for the healthcare security administrator. At one time or another, every hospital has to treat a prisoner patient. The question is not if, but when, there may be prisoners inside the healthcare facility. Outside of the courtroom, the hospital is the only other public place that experiences such large volume of prisoner visits. Some of these prisoners are housed in state-of-the-art high security prisons and, for many serving lengthy sentences, this time spent at a healthcare facility may be literally a once in a lifetime opportunity for escape.

Among the challenges are the different players that become involved in the treatment, care, and custody of the patient. It begins with the requirement to provide treatment and security protocol training for forensic staff (police, sheriff, correctional officers, etc.); security assessment of the safety and security of staff and patients relative to the resources being provided by the forensic staff; providing information to the facility security operations staff; being cognizant of Joint Commission/CMS restraint and seclusion issues in the U.S.; and coordination between security operations and the custody authority/agency.

The forensic patient may either be brought to the medical care facility for emergency or outpatient treatment, or for a planned hospitalization as an inpatient. In all cases, the forensic patient must be viewed as a potential threat to the facility. The typical healthcare facility does not present an environment well-equipped, or prepared for, management of forensic patients. Most healthcare organizations do not have holding cells, or other security protocols, commonly found in the jail or corrections facility. Joel Lashley, of Children's Hospital of Wisconsin in Milwaukee, claims that "a typical hospital is the only unprepared environment that is an integral component of the criminal justice system. Corrections officers receive scant training to prepare them for the clinical setting, which is why officers, bystanders and medical personnel are often hurt and even killed by prisoner patients. It's also a reason so many inmates escape from hospitals."[26]

A growing security issue, the number of serious security/criminal incidents involving forensic patients in the healthcare facility has escalated over the past decade. It is projected the number of forensic patients being treated in healthcare facilities, outside of detention centers, will continue to increase as the number of prisoners continues to increase. The number of incarcerated persons in the U.S. correctional system in 2012 numbered just over 2.3 million, according to the Department of Justice's Bureau of Justice Statistics, and marks the fourth consecutive year of increase.[27] Similarly, in Canada, the federal government announced in 2010 they would be building more federal prisons, creating more prison beds, with the intent of incarcerating more individuals.

However, the Canadian experience with managing prisoners as patients has not mirrored that of their U.S. counterparts. Following a series of high profile prisoner incidents, including escapes, from Canadian healthcare settings in the 1980s and early 1990s, this phenomenon seems to have been on the decline over the last two decades. Strong internal procedures related to prisoner patients have combined with strong cooperation between correctional agencies and healthcare organizations, to help mitigate the risk associated with prisoner patients. In some cases formal Memoranda of Understandings have been developed with these agencies to further strengthen the mutual commitment to a safe environment.

Add to this the number of forensic patients, under arrest or held under court order, who have not yet been entered into the correctional system. Both of these issues, coupled in part to a 1976 Supreme Court decision (Estelle v. Gamble) that said correctional facilities depriving prisoners of medical care constituted "cruel and unusual punishment" and they "must provide necessary medical care to all incarcerated individuals." The ruling further stated "the deliberate indifference to serious medical needs is prohibited" thus creating a heavy burden on the public health system to provide medical care to prisoners.

A 2011 study, conducted at the behest of the International Healthcare Security and Safety Foundation, found the issue of prisoner escapes and escape attempts from healthcare facilities has become increasingly prevalent over the years. Lead author of the study, Victoria Miko-Porto, PhD, tracked prisoner patient escapes through media reports and interviews with individuals from healthcare facilities and law enforcement. She found 99 documented cases from April 2010 to April 2011, which translates to 8.4 incidents per month and 2.1 per week. Additional findings included:

- 2% of escapes resulted in a public death
- 26% resulted in corrections officer injuries
- 2% resulted in staff or visitor injuries and another 2% resulted in healthcare security injury
- The removal of restraints was cause for 68.7% of all escapes in 2011

An added security dimension associated with this type of patient is due to a very questionable practice on the part of law enforcement. This practice occurs when a police officer discovers an arrested person will be in the hospital for a number of days, and therefore "un-arrests" the patient to avoid the time and expense of furnishing a 24-hour guard of the patient. A nurse from Hutcheson Medical Center in northeast Georgia complained at a county commissioner's meetings how sheriff's deputies routinely dumped prisoners at the hospital, stating "they bring them in the emergency room in handcuffs…they take off the handcuffs and walk away and leave them."[28] In many such cases, the police ask the healthcare provider to advise them on the planned discharge of the patient so they can show up and re-arrest the individual. In other cases, the arrested patient is simply issued a citation to appear in court.

Confusion and conflict can take place when caring for the forensic patient. Law enforcement or correctional personnel often do not understand the procedures of medical care, while medical care staff do not always understand the implications of the custody of the patient. Most correctional agencies will call ahead before arriving with the prisoner patient. However, the location where medical service is provided is often unpredictable and based on the need of the patient. The prisoner patient may initially access care through the emergency department, but is often found in surgery (pre-op, post-op, and/or recovery), MRI, radiology, the behavioral health unit and, from time-to-time, the maternity unit. Particular attention should be placed during transport throughout the facility, and specifically when the prisoner patient needs to use the bathroom. Historically, these are opportune times when the facility is most vulnerable to an escape attempt. Box 13-3 identifies the location of prisoner escape events.

Many healthcare organizations have a predetermined access point into their facility, often the ambulance bay, for prisoner patients and correctional staff to help ensure the safest entry into the facility and cause the least amount of disruption. To minimize the negative perception often created by having forensic patients in the healthcare facility, security staff often greet the correctional team with a wheelchair and blanket to conceal their restraints and prisoner status. Having the prisoner patient wait with the general patient and visitor population of the facility is not encouraged.

BOX 13-3 LOCATION OF PRISONER ESCAPE EVENTS BASED ON IHSSF RESEARCH STUDY OF PRISONER ESCAPES FROM APRIL 2010 TO APRIL 2011

Location of Prisoner Escape Events

- Emergency room: 14%
- Outside the hospital (e.g. hospital entrance, parking lot, etc.): 17%
- Clinical treatment areas: 39%
- Restrooms: 29%

It is important the prisoner remain in the custody of the correctional officer at all times, to include being properly shackled to the wheelchair or gurney. The use of restraints is imperative when dealing with prisoner patients in order to keep them from injuring themselves, officers, or healthcare workers, and to keep them from attempting to escape the facility and causing harm.[29] Forensic patients have seriously injured and killed correctional officers by kicking them from gurneys.[26] Medical care staff should never ask to remove restraints unless medically required. Sometimes handcuffs, belly chains and shackles must be removed for MRI imaging procedures, x-rays at the restraint site or other procedures that may genuinely be incompatible with traditional metal handcuffs. An alternative restraint should always be added to include temporary use of medical restraint devices if necessary, or substituting leather or plastic handcuffs or straps. If this is not possible, the healthcare organization should require more than one correctional officer to assist in managing unrestrained forensic patients. Managing unrestrained prisoners alone in any environment is inherently dangerous, and should not be tolerated.

Platte Valley Medical Center in Brighton, Colorado learned a difficult lesson after a forensic patient was shot in their hallway in a failed attempt to escape. The correctional officer, required to remove the restraint devices so x-rays could be taken at the restraint site, positioned himself behind lead shielding at one of two entrances to the room. The prisoner, sensing the opportunity to escape, fled the room and did not obey instruction from the officer to stop. The correctional officer shot the prisoner. The after-action review revealed the officer's action was appropriate; however, further investigation by the hospital and the correctional agency revealed a second officer could have prevented the situation altogether, as the unrestrained prisoner would have been outnumbered.

The Joint Commission also views forensic patients—especially those patients who are shackled to their beds—as being at some risk should there be a fire or other emergency situation. The Joint Commission has issued a compliance standard regarding the training of guarding forensic persons. This standard can be found in the Human Resources section of the accreditation manual. The current Joint Commission standard (H.R.2.10, EP 10) requires any person guarding a forensic patient to receive orientation and education on how to interact in the medical care setting, on procedures for responding to unusual events (fire, disasters, medical emergencies), on proper channels of communications, and on the distinction of the administrative/clinical restraint/seclusion elements of control.

There are a number of ways to accomplish this training. The most common method is to furnish written information to the forensic staff (guard) upon admission of the patient. In this method, the first guard is asked to make this information part of the agency's post orders and to pass on the information to all other guards.

A rather unique program developed for training law enforcement agencies in guarding inpatient prisoners was developed jointly by three hospital systems in Brevard County, Florida. This program, spearheaded by Jim Kending of Health First in Melbourne, Florida, consisted of developing a 10-minute video relative to guarding the forensic patient. This video was distributed to some 20 area criminal justice agencies to be used as a roll-call training activity. The video is also being utilized by the Brevard County law enforcement and corrections academy in their recruit training program. A standardized orientation guide and acknowledgement form is also used with each correctional facility.

The safety of patients and healthcare personnel is a priority. Defining roles in the treatment of inmates and arrestees is especially important. Figure 13-9 provides a list of the duties the hospital will take on, pertaining to forensic patients.[30]

Most hospitals do not have secure prison wards or units and often are not prepared to care for prisoner patients. IAHSS provides some general guidelines that should be taken into consideration by all hospitals that admit prisoner patients.

05.10 PRISONER PATIENT SECURITY

Statement

The secure treatment of prisoner patients must be addressed by all Healthcare Facilities (HCFs) providing medical care for this high risk patient population.

Intent

- **a.** The HCF should develop a prisoner patient policy using a multidisciplinary leadership team.
- **b.** Prisoner patient security measures should include the following:
  - **1.** Orientation of security and clinical staff to the prisoner patient policy.
  - **2.** The appointment of an HCF representative to coordinate the organizational security protocols with the responsible law enforcement or corrections (custodial agency).
  - **3.** Orientation and education protocols for custodial agency staff that include:
    - **a)** Emergency and evacuation procedures related to the safety of the patient,
    - **b)** Monitoring, seclusion, restraint and control techniques including the use of defensive equipment and use of force techniques,
    - **c)** Roles and responsibilities, and
    - **d)** Communication with security or other HCF resources.
  - **4.** Consideration of designated treatment rooms or holding areas.
  - **5.** Designating prisoner patient entry points into the facility.
  - **6.** Protocols to verify patient treatment rooms and all areas frequented by the prisoner patient are free of hazardous items (objects that may be used to harm self or others). This should include emphasis on bathrooms, stairwells and elevators.
  - **7.** Guidance on the restraints used by the custodial agency, i.e., handcuffs, leg irons, or other devices that includes:
    - **a)** The type and number of devices to be used should be risk based and established and communicated prior to admission.[1]
    - **b)** Unless clinically contraindicated restraints should be used at all times, for all guarded patients.
    - **c)** When treatment needs require removal or reducing of custodial agency restraint, the custodial agency should have input into this decision. Alternative but equivalent levels of protection should be provided.
    - **d)** Methods to minimize the need to remove custodial agency restraints should be considered such as portable commode chair at bedside or plastic restraints in place of metal restraints when necessary for medical procedures such as MRI or inside operating rooms.
  - **8.** Procedures for notifying affected departments upon the arrival of prisoner patients at the HCF. Security staff should conduct an initial walk through the planned travel route for the escort party and facilitate the specific communication between clinical and custodial agency staff. Suspicious individuals or circumstances should be reported immediately.
  - **9.** Protocols for food service to include disposable plates and utensils.
  - **10.** A process for enhancing security measures based on higher risk patients.
- **c.** The HCF should document, track, trend and evaluate all prisoner patient visits.
- **d.** Regularly evaluate the physical security in locations where prisoner patients are present. This should include:
  - **1.** Emergency care, inpatient, clinic spaces and external areas where prisoners are removed from the transport vehicle.
  - **2.** Designated entry points for prisoner patients.
  - **3.** Designated rooms and holding areas for prisoner patients.
- **e.** Visitors to a prisoner patient should be permitted solely at the discretion of the custodial agency in accordance with its policies.
- **f.** Establish communication protocols requiring the custodial agency to notify the HCF designated representative of any change in security measures.

Continued

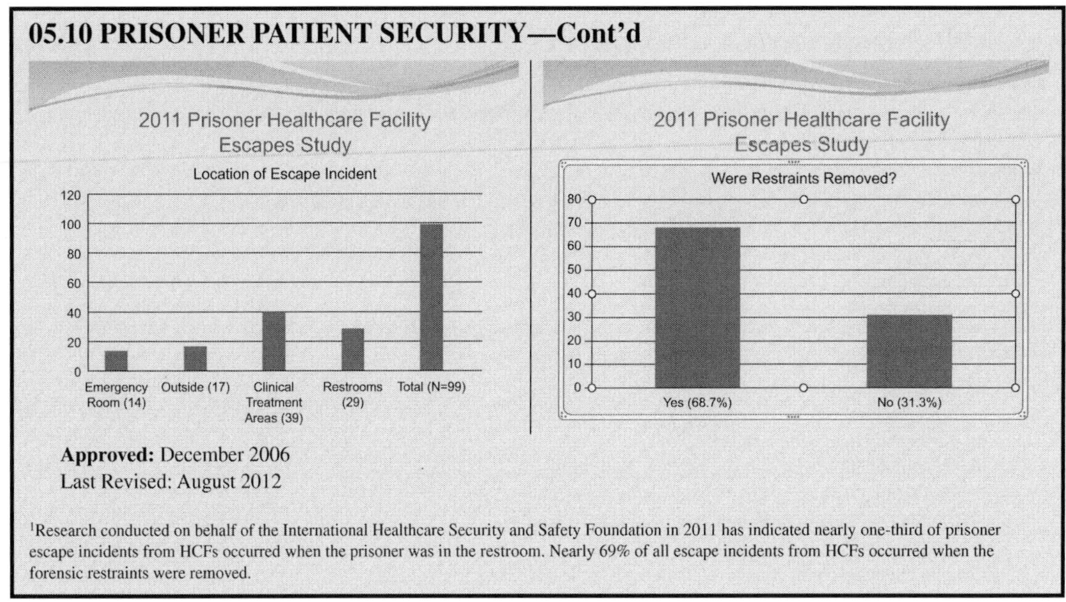

05.10 PRISONER PATIENT SECURITY—Cont'd

Approved: December 2006
Last Revised: August 2012

[1]Research conducted on behalf of the International Healthcare Security and Safety Foundation in 2011 has indicated nearly one-third of prisoner escape incidents from HCFs occurred when the prisoner was in the restroom. Nearly 69% of all escape incidents from HCFs occurred when the forensic restraints were removed.

THE WANDERING PATIENT (DEMENTIA- AND PSYCHOLOGICAL-RELATED)

Wandering patients are a security concern presented by certain types of dementia patients, most frequently those with Alzheimer's disease. It is estimated that each week at least one resident of the nation's nursing home facilities wanders away from a care facility and dies. The wandering patient situation is of course not limited to nursing homes. The mental health facility and even certain patients in the general medical/surgical category can be wandering patients. Intensive care staff have long recognized psychological responses of patients, which include delirium, catastrophic reaction, and euphoric response. The most common of these responses is delirium, which has been described on a range from slight clouding of consciousness to a full-blown psychotic reaction. In this respect, patients experience varying degrees of cognitive impairment.

A patient movement control system, utilizing an electronic tag, is a fairly common safeguard for suspected wandering patients. The patient wears a tag that contains a radio frequency circuit; this circuit communicates with a detection sensor usually installed at the exit door or elevator opening. Some systems do not use multiple-detection sensors at doors, but have a radio receiver installed at a central location instead. In these systems, the distance between the tag and central monitor is constantly measured with an alarm, which sounds when a predetermined distance is exceeded. Electronic systems can be installed as stand-alone systems at each door or as centralized computer-controlled systems. Computerized systems are capable of identifying the individual patient and can display the alarm information as either text or a graphic map. Individual tags can be deactivated in a number of ways to allow family or staff to take a patient out of the defined secured area.[31]

A rather extensive radio frequency tag system for managing long-term care patients is currently being used at the Sunnybrook Health Sciences Center, which is part of the University of Toronto

Forensic Patient Protocol: Duties of Hospital (Inpatient Setting)

1. The hospital's Security Department shall conduct an orientation, including a review of the elements of performance for Standard HR.2.10, to any law enforcement guarding an in-custody arrestee or jail inmate.
2. The hospital will provide a safe "finger meal"* to the in-custody arrestee or jail inmate (e.g., sandwich, milk carton consistent with the medical condition(s) present).
3. The hospital shall provide a meal to the law enforcement officer or corrections officer and invoice the agency accordingly.
4. The hospital shall provide a private room (when available) for the in-custody arrestee or jail inmate.
5. The phone shall be available in the room and is to be used only by the law enforcement or corrections officer in attendance.
6. There will be no visitation allowed for any in-custody arrestee or jail inmate.
    a. Exceptions to be approved by the Commander of the Jail or municipal police agency (or designee) and the Chief of Hospital Security for consultation with a lawyer or end-of-life situation and other approved situations.
    b. Exception for juveniles: parent(s) or guardian(s) are permitted to visit.
7. The hospital's Security Department will provide a bathroom break for the law enforcement or the corrections officer guarding the patient and observe the patient during this brief time period, as needed.
8. The hospital's shift lead security representative shall travel to the in-custody arrestee's or inmate's room on each shift and introduce him- or herself to the law enforcement or corrections officer.
9. The hospital Security Department shall provide a department radio (to the law enforcement or corrections officer guarding the patient-prisoner or in-custody arrestee) to provide priority communication capability. Follow-up appointments and discharge instructions will be provided to the law enforcement officer or corrections officer guarding the patient only.

FIGURE 13-9

The duties of a hospital pertaining to forensic patients in the inpatient setting.

(Courtesy of Environment of Care News, *reprinted with permission.)*

10. The patient's medical needs (including toileting) shall be the responsibility of the clinical employees of the hospital.
11. The hospital will not disclose any information, including room assignment, to walk-in visitors and/or incoming telephone inquiries, pertaining to a guarded patient. The only exception to this is for the parents or legal guardian who comes to the hospital to visit the juvenile patient.

*Finger meal means food is eaten with the fingers, since no utensils are allowed.

FIGURE 13-9—Continued

(Canada). The Sunnybrook Health Sciences Center is a 1,300-bed facility, with 550 beds being occupied by long-term care patients. There are, thus, varying degrees of control depending on the unit and type of patients. In addition to the radio frequency system, the hospital has what they refer to as the "Blue Shirt Program." In this program, the at-risk cognitively impaired patients wear a blue shirt with the Sunnybrook Health Sciences Center logo emblazoned in yellow across the back. All staff members—and even members of the immediate community—are educated on the Blue Shirt Program and are asked to report any observed wandering patients.[32]

An effective approach to managing the problem of wandering patients requires proper facility design and physical security safeguards, good control policies and procedures put into practice by staff, and ongoing staff training in the management of the wandering patient.

THE INFANT AND PEDIATRIC PATIENT

A great deal has been written about preventive steps that can be taken to avoid the abduction of newborn infants. A facility birthing unit is generally classified as a security sensitive area in terms of Joint Commission compliance standards. As such, the security issues surrounding the abduction of infants will be more fully addressed in Chapter 21, "Areas of Higher Risk."

The possibility of discharging an infant to the wrong parents is a concern that requires proper clinical management. Security is not often involved in developing clinical policies and procedures, but may well become involved should an actual event occur.

The pediatric patient presents several security risks, including the possibility of abduction, elopement and being the recipient of physical abuse while in the hospital. In addition, pediatric patients may wander off the unit. The possibility of abduction is somewhat higher for the pediatric patient than the newborn infant. This higher risk is the result of a greater length of stay, generally less security precautions, and the number of custody battles that involve children. In pediatric abductions, the perpetrator is almost always known, and in many cases there is significant early warning that allows proactive security measures to be put in place.

In recent years, medical care providers and healthcare security administrators have become more and more aware of a form of child abuse referred to as Münchausen syndrome by proxy (MSBP). It is a form of child abuse wherein a parent (usually the mother), intentionally manufactures illness in her child and repeatedly presents the child for medical care, disclaiming knowledge as to the cause of the problem. Child victims of MSBP are at risk for serious injury or death. The security department therefore plays a critical role in investigating and managing MSBP. The following are the "symptoms" of MSBP:

- Illness in a child that is simulated (faked) or produced by a parent or other caretaker or both.
- Presentation of the child for medical assessment and care, usually persistently, often resulting in multiple medical procedures.
- Denial of the knowledge by the parent as to the cause of the child's illness.
- Subsiding of acute symptoms and signs when the child is separated from the parent.

Typically, but not always, the mother spends a good deal of time in the hospital with the child and exhibits a remarkable familiarity with medical terminology. She may be "confidentially friendly" with the healthcare staff, although she may show frustration with her child's chronic illness and anger at the medical staff's inadequate vigor in pursuing her child's problems. She may insist she is the "only one" for whom the child will eat, drink, or swallow medicines. The syndrome often persists for years and can result in death. According to experts, common conditions and symptoms that are created or faked by parents or caregivers with MSBP include: failure to thrive, allergies, asthma, vomiting, diarrhea, seizures, and infections.[33]

Bonnie Michelman, CHPA, CPP, Director Police and Security at Massachusetts General Hospital in Boston and a leading security expert in MSBP, suggests a multidisciplinary child protection team should become involved the moment MSBP is suspected. The team should include medical personnel, security management, the primary care nurse, social services, mental health professionals, and an epidemiologist (a person who, in part, specializes in figuring out the cause of a disease). Together they must determine whether the child's medical condition can be attributed to MBPS, warranting civil proceedings to remove the child from the perpetrator's care and, possibly, criminal proceedings. Police and security personnel should become involved early in the case, collecting evidence, making timely arrests, and helping to develop a case for prosecution. Once the child is assumed to be at risk, a customized protection plan for the child must be designed and implemented.

PATIENT PROPERTY

A highly visible and troublesome security problem is missing patient property. The average financial loss is quite small; however, large losses do occasionally occur. The impact of property loss on a sick patient and the negative public relations that result, indicate a concern far more important than the value of property involved.

Most hospital facilities engage in a program commonly referred to as pre-admission registration, which obtains certain information from the patient before admission. The pre-admission information, or instruction, form should state the hospital does not have adequate storage for personal property and should instruct the patient to leave jewelry, wallets, radios, and similar items at home. The statement should also note the hospital cannot be responsible for personal property brought to the facility by the patient, or brought to the patient by visitors. Bold type should be used to highlight this policy.

When patients are admitted, the person who signs the admissions form should be required to initial a statement reflecting the hospital is not responsible for personal property not in its possession or control. The patient should be advised to surrender for safekeeping any keys, credit cards, jewelry, watches,

FIGURE 13-10

Photo of hospital patient room electronic safe.

(Courtesy of Medicus-Health, reprinted with permission.)

and money over an established limit. There have been numerous instances in which a patient's purse has been stolen from the bedside or closet and the keys and identification used to commit a burglary of the patient's home. A growing number of hospitals have installed in room "hotel-style" personal safes in each inpatient room that allows for patients to provide for the security of their valuables in their room. Cheyenne Regional Medical Center in Wyoming has installed this style of safe, a sample noted in Figure 13-10, to safely secure some medications in the patient's room.

GENERAL PRINCIPLES FOR HANDLING PATIENT VALUABLES

Property being checked with the hospital requires a sound handling procedure. Hospital security administrators should check their current procedures against those listed in Box 13-4.

Regardless of how well admissions personnel perform their job, some patients will always end up with too much personal property in the room. The nursing staff should assume some responsibility to reduce this vulnerability. They should encourage the patient to send property home, or to permit the hospital to hold the property for safekeeping. Otherwise, an admission clerk must respond to the unit; in some cases, the responsibility is assigned to the security department to obtain the property and transport it to the safekeeping area.

Outpatient property can also present security problems. Outpatients are presumed to be better able to care for their property than inpatients. Small signs in clothes-changing areas should indicate that the organization is not responsible for lost or missing property. Many outpatient facilities provide individual lockers for their patients to secure personal property during the outpatient procedure.

Hospitals should deny all claims for missing property not held by the hospital. Administrators or risk managers who pay these claims may find a costly situation developing. Each claim must always be evaluated on its own merits.

BOX 13-4 PATIENT VALUABLES STORAGE PROCEDURES

Patient Valuables Storage Procedures

- The patient valuables envelope should be tamper proof. A heavy, numbered envelope should be used, which, when sealed, must be torn open to remove the contents.
- All information regarding the contents of the envelope should be on a separate sheet placed in the envelope, signed and sealed in front of the patient. There should be nothing on the exterior of the envelope indicating the contents of the envelope except patient name, bag number and room number.
- A minimum of two witnesses, including the patient, should verify and document what goes into the patient envelope. If the patient is not lucid, the witnesses should personally observe the valuables being placed in the envelope and the envelope being sealed.
- An accountability log should be kept documenting the Date, Time, Patient Name, Room Number, Bag Number, and Witness Names. The property stored in the envelopes should not be listed on this record. Stored inside the patient valuables lockbox, each envelope should be inspected and inventoried when shifts change.
- The lockbox should have a double lock and key mechanism, and regardless of the circumstances, always require two people to gain entry at all times. The lockbox should be bolted to the floor and be of sufficient strength to withstand a serious attempt at breaking in or removing the lockbox from the area.
- When valuables are released, confirmation that the contents of the envelope are intact should be always be made. Discrepancies noted on a security incident report and be immediately investigated. If the patient is deceased, the patient valuables should not be released until proper verification can be made of the person taking possession of the valuables (authorized next of kin or has power of attorney).
- When the patient requests the partial withdrawal of property, a new envelope and receipt should be prepared, and the number of the original envelope and the original receipt included.

VISITORS

In contrast to limited patient contact, security officers will often initiate contact with visitors, vendors, and suppliers. In regulating parking, loading docks, ambulance entrances, and building access, security officers take on the task of regulating visitors. Once visitors reach their intended destination, such as a patient room or the outpatient department, the regulating task is transferred to the facility personnel responsible for the specific work area or unit.

In all contacts, whether with a patient, visitor, or employee, security staff must bear in mind they are representatives of the healthcare organization. They must make every effort to ensure their interactions are carried out with tact and diplomacy. Security officers are often the first people encountered upon entering the healthcare system. Impressions made at this point are lasting, and security officers should capitalize on this opportunity to act professionally.

It is generally agreed sick or convalescing patients need visitors as part of the recovery process. On the other hand, visitors can interfere with medical care, refuse to leave when asked, steal, complain, sleep in patient rooms, litter, engage in loud and boisterous conduct, and leave patients exhausted or in a state of tension, which can be detrimental to the patient's recovery process.

Many factors affect visitor control. Chief among them is the philosophy of the administration. The philosophy of patient and family centered care is espoused by a growing number of healthcare administrators, who feel families should be a part of the caregiving process. Thus, visiting the facility is the right of the family and should not be controlled or discouraged. Other administrators feel good patient care requires strict visitor control. The trend in healthcare continues toward more liberal visiting policies. However, today, there is a noticeable shift toward greeting all visitors who enter the facility, and restricting access to the facility after hours only to those who have a specific need.

A second major factor affecting visitor control is the poor layout and design of many healthcare facilities, which greatly hinders meaningful visitor control, at least in terms of the cost to overcome the design deficiency.

Areas of the hospital that present special visitor control considerations are: the medical/surgical patient units, pediatric units, obstetrical units, behavioral health units, intensive care units, the medical treatment area of the emergency department, and isolation units. The discussion here focuses on the overall visitor control problem, because these specialty units generally rely on their own procedures and unit personnel for control.

Some people question whether visitor control rightfully belongs in the realm of security operations. This view may have merit when the concern is for legitimate visitors during designated visitor hours. However, overall access control that includes visitors during late-night hours is a protection responsibility.

An adjunct to access control is the greeting or questioning of persons, including visitors and employees, who appear to need help, or persons who are acting or looking suspicious. This is a basic responsibility of every security officer and hospital staff member, regardless of role, and is an important crime prevention technique.

TIME PERIODS

To properly view access control, two distinct time periods, each presenting different security ramifications, should be considered: designated patient visiting hours and after normal operational hours.

Designated patient visiting hours

The time designated by the facility for visiting patients can vary. Many healthcare organizations have disbanded visiting hours altogether and have no restrictions for the designated time for visiting patients. Most hospitals remain traditional, and still define specific hours for visiting patients. Specialized units, such as the intensive care unit, are often more restrictive, limiting the number of visitors, placing minimum age restrictions for the visitor, with a predetermined maximum length for an individual visit (or in aggregate). Other specialized units, such as the pediatric unit, are often more liberal, allowing for and often encouraging parents to remain in the patient's room for the duration of the patient stay.

The majority of hospitals do not issue specific visitor identification during regular visiting hours. For those that do, the general procedure is to prepare a temporary, self-expiring badge for each visitor. These passes are issued when the visitor enters the facility. Technology advances have allowed for the self-adhesive badge to be produced automatically from a government issued identification card, and screened against a database of known sex offender registries, or against organizationally generated no visitor (stop) lists. Facial recognition software used at Exempla Saint Joseph Hospital in Denver, Colorado has expedited the time it takes to issue the visitor badge, and provides a comprehensive database that helps the hospital readily identify visitors who have previously created problems for the hospital, its patients, staff, or other visitors.

The details of most visitor management systems can be tailored to meet a facility's specific needs. Most facilities use a self-adhesive disposable badge, while others use a reusable laminated visitor badge. A growing number of facilities custom-make badges for visitors using PCs and video-imaging techniques. A few organizations have sold advertising on the badge to offset the expense associated with the system.

Badge and pass systems can work; however, numerous elevators and stairwells leading to patient units can tempt visitors to bypass the entire system. A visitor control plan, used during regular visiting hours, should be considered as minimal protection for the patient, and only as a screening procedure at best.

Regardless of the procedures used, the ultimate responsibility for patient visitor control must remain with the personnel assigned to the patient care units. They must determine whether a patient has too many visitors, or whether the visitors will have an adverse effect on the patient or the facility as a whole. A nurse or nursing assistant can generally correct undesired visitor actions without adverse public reaction. If unit personnel cannot resolve the problem, a security officer may then be called for support.

After hours

A system of after-hours visitor control should be established, even if there is an open visiting policy. All people entering the healthcare facility after hours should be greeted, their purpose for entering the facility established, and their entry into the facility authorized.

The legitimate need for after-hours visitation is limitless; whether it is the person who is leaving town and wants to visit before leaving, or the out-of-town visitor who was delayed and could not get to the facility during regular visiting hours. These and other extenuating circumstances must be managed in the visitor control plan.

What is believed to be "after hours" will vary among hospitals. Most healthcare facilities close down after visiting hours, but many unlock various entrances and exits for shift changes in the absence of electronic locking systems, providing controlled employee access points. Regardless of the patient visiting hours philosophy in place, the healthcare facility should control access to all doors providing uninhibited access into the facility after normal operating hours. This should include access connections from physician office buildings to the hospital proper, along with connected parking decks. These connecting corridors usually have a major entrance, which provides a good access point for affecting an element of control.

During this period, the entire complex should be locked, channeling patients and visitors to one designated entrance where a visitor control person is in attendance. Most often the designated after-hours entrance is the emergency department. In facilities that do not provide emergency care service, it is generally the main entrance. All general-use doors available during the operational period should have signs directing the public to the designated night entrance when these general-use doors are locked.

In many facilities, all entrances are locked, and controls vary from electronic door controls, to video surveillance, to security officers. Obviously, the integrity of the access control system can be compromised by many means. Compromises can occur when a visitor or employee opens an exit door to permit entry for someone on the outside, and when exit doors do not latch properly. Security patrols and alarm hardware at emergency exit doors are helpful in preventing breaches of the security system.

To properly identify authorized visitors to the facility after hours, most healthcare organizations incorporate a system of visitor badging. After a person is cleared for access, the date and destination can be written on the badge. A log should be maintained that includes name, time, destination, purpose, patient to be visited, and the visitor's signature. The signature is helpful psychologically because it implies stricter control. In some control programs, personal identification, such as a driver's license or other form government issued identification, must be presented; however, this requirement is somewhat superfluous as legitimate visitors will not be denied entry just because they cannot produce such identification. If such identification is an element of the access control program, the badge itself should not be held by the facility to be returned upon exiting.

The access control point should be supplied with resource data. A computer database listing all patients and any visitation restrictions, such as "no visitors," "family only," and "wife may visit anytime," is a common and useful resource. If resource data is not available, security may be compelled to contact the nursing unit, on a case by case basis, in order to legitimize the prospective visitor.

When a patient's condition deteriorates, the physician often asks the family to come to the facility. Unit nursing personnel are almost always aware of this situation and should notify the public access control point so access can be expeditiously handled. It is poor public relations when family members have been called and are unnecessarily delayed because no one notified the person at control point.

It is not uncommon for someone who requires emergency room treatment to arrive with numerous friends or relatives. Because treatment is not instantaneous, these visitors often desire to leave the waiting area to explore for food or other amenities. Many organizations manage this need by developing a controlled set of locked doors leading from the emergency department waiting area, equipped with an electrical release system, managed by the security officer responsible for after hours access control. Thus, the officer is aware of who is granted access into the facility. The proper layout and design of the emergency department is covered in Chapter 21, "Areas of Higher Risk."

One of the pitfalls of an after-hours badging program is legitimate visitors who enter the facility during regular visiting hours, when no pass or badge system is in effect. If they are given permission by unit staff to remain after visiting hours, or even for the entire night, the charge nurse should be required to send them to the access control point for badging. In this way, all late-night visitors will be badged—not just those entering after the night-access control system goes into effect. In some programs, security officers make the rounds of patient floors with hand-held machines to produce the visitor badge.

All access control personnel must exercise extreme caution, so legitimate access to the facility is not denied; i.e., a person who appears to be intoxicated may be a diabetic in shock seeking medical care.

REFERENCES

1. The Johns Hopkins Hospital. *Patient bill of rights and responsibilities*. 2012. Retrieved December 1, 2013, from http://www.hopkinsmedicine.org/the_johns_hopkins_hospital/_docs/bill_of_rights.pdf.
2. Yan H. *Body found in hospital stairwell: San Francisco sheriff details what went wrong*. 2013, November 7. CNN US website. Retrieved November 8, 2013, from http://www.cnn.com/2013/11/07/us/california-body-in-stairwell/.
3. Gerardi D. *Elopement*. Agency for Healthcare Research and Quality; 2007, December. Web M&M. Retrieved October 4, 2013, from http://www.webmm.ahrq.gov/case.aspx?caseID=164.
4. UPMC has new procedure to find missing patients. *Pittsburgh Post-Gazette Now*. 2009, January 3. Retrieved January 3, 2009, from http://www.post-gazette.com/pg/08365/938554-100.stm.
5. Extra security call as patients go missing. *Surrey Times Online*. 2007, October 17. Retrieved June 25, 2009, from http://www.getsurrey.co.uk/news/s/2016475_extra_security_call_as_patients_go_missing_.
6. Tonkin Shannon. *Wollongong Hospital death inquiry resumes*. Illawarra Mercury News; 2013, October 21. Retrieved October 22, 2013, from http://www.illawarramercury.com.au/story/1853046/wollongong-hospital-death-inquiry-resumes/?cs=12.

7. DeRosier JM, Taylor L. Analyzing missing patient events at the VA. *TIPS (Topics in Patient Safety, VA National Center for Patient Safety* 2005, December;**5**(6):1–2. Retrieved May 3, 2009, from http://www.va.gov/ncps/TIPS/Docs/TIPS_NovDec05.pdf.
8. James St, Janet. *Security at Dallas hospital questioned after brain surgery patient wanders away*. 2011, July 1. Retrieved July 3, 2011, from http://www.khou.com/news/texas-news/Security-at-Dallas-hospital-questioned-after-brain-surgery-patient-wanders-away-124858674.html#.
9. The Joint Commission. *Sentinel event policy and procedures*. 2013, January. Retrieved December 1, 2013 from http://www.jointcommission.org/assets/1/6/CAMH_2012_Update2_24_SE.pdf.
10. The Joint Commission. *Sentinel event statistics*. 2013. Retrieved December 1, 2013, from http://www.jointcommission.org/assets/1/18/General_Information_1995-2Q2013.pdf.
11. The Joint Commission. *Summary data of sentinel events reviewed by The Joint Commission*. 2013. Retrieved December 1, 2013 from http://www.jointcommission.org/assets/1/18/2004_to_2Q_2013_SE_Stats_-_Summary.pdf.
12. National Center for Public Safety. *VHA NCPS escape and elopement management*. 2009, March 4. Retrieved May 3, 2009, from http://www.va.gov/ncps/CogAids/EscapeElope/index.html.
13. Gerardi D. *Elopement*. 2007, December. Retrieved October 4, 2013 from http://www.webmm.ahrq.gov/case.aspx?caseID=164.
14. IAHSS. Legal actions against your strip search policies for ER patients with psychiatric problems. *Healthcare Security & Safety Directions* 2009;**22**(2):11–2.
15. Guzeman Jorge A, Sasidhar Madhu, Stoller James K. Care for VIPs: Nine Principles. *Cleveland Clinic Journal of Medicine* 2011, February;**78**(2).
16. Schoolfield D. Evaluation of very important person (VIP) policy to include victims of violence. *Journal of Healthcare Protection Management* 2008;**24**(2):88–9.
17. American College of Emergency Physicians. *Protection from physical violence in the emergency department environment*. 2008, April. Retrieved May 9, 2009, from http://www.acep.org/practres.aspx?id=29654.
18. AHA Task Force on Behavioral Health. *Behavioral Health Challenges in the General Hospital: Practical Help for Hospital Leaders*. American Hospital Association; 2007, September. Retrieved December 28, 2013 from http://www.aha.org/content/00-10/07bhtask-recommendations.pdf.
19. Donohue D. *Multi-agency collaboration for healthcare security risks: a presentation*. Presented at the Australian Hospital and Healthcare Security and Safety Conference; 2008, November 27.
20. Platts WE. Psychiatric patients: Promises liability and predicting patient elopement. *Journal of Healthcare Protection Management* 1998, September;**14**(2):75.
21. Miller Kristine. *Preventing suicide in non-behavioral health care units*, vol. 14. Environment of Care News; 2011, May. No. 5.
22. Bostwick JM, Rackley SJ. Completed suicide in medical/surgical patients: Who is at risk? *Curr Psychiatry Rep* 2007;**9**:242–6.
23. Debbaudt D. Patients with autism and other high risks: A growing challenge for healthcare security. *Journal of Healthcare Protection Management* 2009;**25**(1):15.
24. Debbaudt D, Rothman D. Contact with individuals with autism: effective resolutions. *FBI Law Enforcement Bulletin* 2001, April;**7**(4):20–4.
25. Debbaudt D. Patients with autism and other high risks: A growing challenge for healthcare security. *Journal of Healthcare Protection Management* 2009;**25**(1):19.
26. Lashley J. *Treatment, care and custody: Securing the hospital environment*. CorrectionsOne News; 2009, March 10. Retrieved March 11, 2009, from http://www.correctionsone.com/pc_print.asp?vid=1778372.
27. Glaze Lauren E, Herberman Erinn J. *Correctional Populations in the United States, 2012*. Bureau of Justice Statistics; 2013, December. Retrieved December 29, 2013, from http://www.bjs.gov/content/pub/pdf/cpus12.pdf.

28. IAHSS. Deputies' un-arresting prisoners before they become patients. *Healthcare Security & Safety Directions* 2011, October;**24**(4).
29. Sweeney Evan. Preventing prisoner patient escapes. *Healthcare Security Alert, supplement to Briefings on Hospital Safety* 2011, December;**7**(12).
30. *Safety in treating inmates and arrestees*. Environment of Care News; 2008, June. 11(6), 6–7.
31. Bowers DM. Closing the door to wanderers. *Journal of Healthcare Protection Management* 1999;**15**(1):109–17.
32. Partington G. *RF system keeps up with long-term patients*. Access Control and Security Systems; 1997, November. 1 and 23.
33. The Nemours Foundation. *Munchausen by proxy syndrome (MBPS)*. 2008, December. Retrieved January 4, 2013, from http://kidshealth.org/parent/general/sick/munchausen.html.

CHAPTER

HUMAN RESOURCES AND STAFF RESPONSIBILITIES

14

The protection system in medical care facilities interfaces directly with the human resources (HR) department. The security program is charged with enforcing rules and regulations often promulgated by the HR department. Training hospital employees in techniques to keep everyone safer is often managed by the education department, which is typically an HR function, supported by the protection program. While HR professionals are not on the front lines, they are often active partners with security when an incident occurs at the facility involving employees and staff. The HR department, along with an employee's manager, may be involved in supporting the employee after being exposed to assaultive behavior or, conversely, determining what action, if any, should be taken against the employee for responding in kind to an emotional outburst. Of continued importance to the security function is immediate access to personnel files and records for investigative purposes. HR personnel are also often dependent on security department records and expertise in obtaining pertinent data for a variety of situations from sources inside and outside the organization, to include assistance with employee interviews or other questionings.

The security and HR departments, like all other departments in the organization, must support one another in providing a system of protection. Mutual support requires effort of both parties. There is an inherent conflict between the general goals and objectives of HR and those of security. HR has a basic mission of being an employee advocate. Security, on the other hand, has the responsibility to provide a reasonably safe environment for all persons and to protect the assets and reputation of the organization. When working in harmony, the security team understands the legal rights and respects the important role employees have in meeting the mission of the organization and higher purpose of healthcare, while displaying proper employee respect. HR must understand that bad behavior, or suspected misconduct, of an employee cannot go unresolved, in the interest of sustaining excellence in patient care through a respected, successful, and sustainable healthcare organization. An overly forceful or oppressive security approach, or an overly burdensome bureaucratic approach by HR, does not serve the healthcare organization. Leadership of both HR and security should collaborate by working together as partners to help provide the best level of patient care possible.

HEALTHCARE EMPLOYEE SELECTION

There are various human resource activities and functions that bear directly, or indirectly, on the security posture of the organization. Included in this area are: the flow and control of applicants applying for work at the healthcare facility, staff identification systems, background investigations, disciplinary actions, assisting in investigative activity, and fostering proper employee conduct.

HUMAN RESOURCES OFFICE

The location of the HR office is an important security consideration. The objective should be to keep applicants out of the main hospital facility if at all feasible. Not only may applicants interfere with clinical care, but they also have been known to commit various security infractions while "looking for a job."

Applicants—who may also be potential malefactors—should not be given the opportunity to become unduly familiar with organizational layout and design. The employment (applicant intake and screening) portion of the HR department should be in a separate building with controlled access or have a dedicated entry with a separate street address to discourage wandering through to the main facility. Figure 14-1 shows a layout for a human resources department that has a street entry point for applicants and a separate internal entry point for serving employees.

Many healthcare organizations have moved the applicant screening and processing function off campus. The offsite screening of applicants has very positive security benefits in that it reduces the amount of applicant traffic accessing the main treatment facility. However, the protection of the employees working in an off-site location cannot be lost on the healthcare security protection administrator. Rarely do these buildings support the need for dedicated security staffing. Thus, safeguards require an understanding of the movement of the applicant—from the applicant waiting area, to securing computers used for on-line applications, as well as designing interview rooms used by recruiting staff, so that exit pathways are not blocked by the applicant that may trap an employee. Access controls must be planned and managed to support applicant flow and protect staff; video surveillance used to remotely monitor the department and duress alarms to immediately summon assistance are elements of protecting the physical environment.

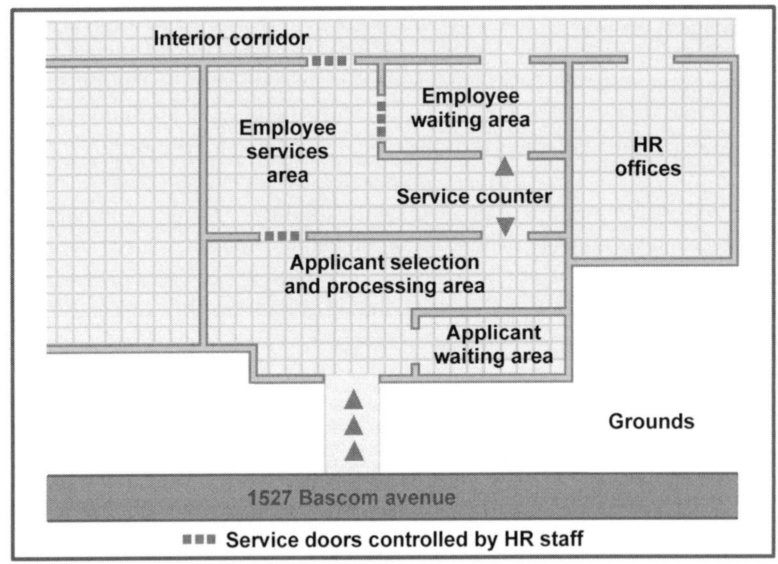

FIGURE 14-1

Example of a human resources department with an outside entrance for applicants and an internal entrance for serving employees.

SELECTING STAFF THROUGH DUE DILIGENCE

Healthcare organizations must search out new and better ways to effectively reduce the incidence of employee misconduct and the commission of crimes against the organization and its stakeholders. The best place to begin this effort is to exercise due diligence in the selection of new staff, with background screening policies that are consistent and clear while being fair and equitable to everyone. However, not all background checking is created equal.

There are a multitude of problems associated with poor hiring practices. A recent media headline read, "Supervisor Blamed for Rapist Hire at Hospital." In this case, top Los Angeles County health officials tried in vain to explain how an ex-police officer convicted of rape was hired, not once but twice, to work in public hospitals in a position of providing care. The county hiring process failed to perform a "live-scan" background check for convictions.[1]

One of the best security investments an organization can make is to properly screen job applicants. It is generally accepted by HR and security experts alike that 20% of any given workforce is responsible for 80% of various personnel problems. There is further agreement that an estimated 90% of all persons known to have stolen from their employers were not prosecuted.[2] Applying screening haphazardly and without a carefully formulated plan can leave the public vulnerable and the healthcare facility liable for criticism and litigation. It is important to avoid such pitfalls and make background screening an accepted and automatic part of the hiring process and the overall organization security posture.

Not only should new job applicants be properly screened, but current employees being considered for promotion to an area where there may be significant security risks or vulnerabilities should also be rescreened. A general rule for rescreening in the event of employee promotion is to rescreen if it has been over five years since the employee was screened as an applicant. Unfortunately, rescreening rarely occurs.

Rescreening may also be for a particular investigative purpose. There are background screening firms offering database repositories that allow enrollment of an employee in a service that will alert the employer if an employee has a record entered into the database at any time in the future. This service is a way to implement an ongoing employee screening program, giving a visibility beyond the pre-employment background check.[3]

The employee selection process is an area in which the healthcare industry has historically received poor marks. In too many cases, organizations have simply been deficient in properly screening applicants. The healthcare industry, like most industries, attracts applicants who are not always honest and often neglect to reveal items that would prohibit their hiring. There are thousands of cases demonstrating why proper screening is so important. The healthcare industry is filled with stories of applicants for nursing positions who neglect to identify convictions for fraud, drug theft or physical abuse against the elderly; or registered sex offenders seeking employment as phlebotomists. However, today this is changing rapidly. Most organizations have embraced the importance of implementing a comprehensive screening program that provides a more complete verification of an applicant's background, as opposed to the historic approach of conducting criminal record searches by simply checking the institution's local county and state database.

It has become increasingly difficult to seek information relative to hiring appropriate staff, with the restrictions imposed by legislature and court-imposed constraints. However, employers can still be liable for negligent hiring. The current state of these limiting controls and sanctions is directly responsible for many events of workplace violence, and billions of dollars lost to employee defalcations. These losses must be paid either directly, or indirectly, by all of society.

Despite these constraints, there are methods and procedures to deny employment of dishonest and dangerous applicants. The HR department must therefore provide a high level of due diligence in the employee selection process, that is standardized and mandatory for every employee in the organization—from faculty members and physicians to part-time staff. Clear guidelines should be provided for security, recruiting and HR professionals that eliminate any appearance of inconsistency when checks are made. A standard policy ensures not only consistency in the types of checks that are conducted, but also that information gathered is used appropriately. It also protects the organizations by prompting compliance with legal requirements set out by the Fair Credit Reporting Act (FCRA) in the U.S. and other governing bodies.

At minimum, a good policy should address what type of checks should be performed by each type of position; how many years of history the checks should cover; the criteria used for assessing whether the background screening results for a candidate meet the hiring standards for the organization; and what procedures are required to comply with all relevant federal, state/provincial legislation.[4]

Information relative to an applicant's suitability for employment can be developed through various methods, including a properly constructed and completed application form; various databases; contacts with previous employers; verification of information through official public records; a variety of tests; and information from friends and previous co-workers. A policy and process of due diligence hiring sends a clear and powerful message that it is the intention of the healthcare organization to protect patients, staff, and visitors.

THE EMPLOYMENT APPLICATION

A good employee selection process begins with the proper design of the application form. The form should be designed with security in mind, along with the primary business objectives of the organization. All applications should ask whether the applicant has been convicted of any crime (misdemeanors and felonies, excluding traffic offenses). Additional requirements should include requiring the applicant to give dates of employment, with month and year for previous employers, and a graduation date for high school, college and graduate school. Applicants will often omit jobs from their resumes when they performed improperly or did not stay long. Having complete dates reveals gaps in school and employment that should be explained by the applicant. Inconsistencies between names, Social Security numbers, dates of birth, education, job history and job titles provided on the application, or other submitted documents, should be identified and explained by the candidate.

Employees should be required to formally update application information annually, including criminal convictions. This can be accomplished as part of the formal employee evaluation process.

Although every applicant accepted for employment is required to comply with the policies, rules, and regulations of the organization, many organizations have found it helpful to use conditions of employment, or employment agreements. These conditions are usually attached to the application form, although in some instances the conditions are incorporated into the application itself or in the formal offer letter.

APPLICANT BACKGROUND VERIFICATION

Nowhere is background screening more important than institutions that directly impact the public, such as hospitals. Recruiters, security professionals, and top management continue to agree that much more must be done in the area of applicant background, verification and investigation, to properly protect patients, staff, and property. The courts generally support this view. The difficulty is the courts render judgments for inadequate hiring processes, yet in other decisions they make it virtually impossible for organizations to obtain any significant background information. It is the opinion of many security and police administrators that the Federal Privacy Act has done great harm to employers and has, in fact, encouraged greater criminal activity. Many protection systems are geared to reacting to problems involving employees, rather than preventing such situations through good hiring practices. Courts, and most government agencies set up to protect employees' rights, have indicated insensitivity to the cost of crime and the suffering of victims.

Despite this insensitivity, medical care facilities must continue to do everything possible to employ individuals who contribute to excellence in patient care, and protect the assets of the organization. This includes conducting comprehensive criminal checks on all applicants. Criminal checks in the U.S. are typically conducted on a county-by-county basis by accessing the county clerk's records. In other countries these checks may differ. In Canada, for instance, a check may be required to ensure an employee's suitability to work where children may be present, but not a full criminal record check. There are a myriad of federal and state laws in the U.S. that restrict the use of certain applicant information in the hiring process. The two basic federal laws of most significance that affect the hiring or demotion process are the Equal Employment Opportunity Commission (EEOC) and the Fair Credit Reporting Act (FCRA).

DECEPTIVE APPLICANT INFORMATION

Applicants are not always truthful in the information provided on their application form. Roughly one-third of all resumes contain some kind of misrepresentation in terms of employment history, education or experience. The top five "lies" told by job applicants, according to a large screening provider, are:

- *Exaggerating dates of past employment.* As much as 34% of resumes and application information includes discrepancies related to previous employment. The most common reason is to cover gaps in their work history they may not want to explain or to be known.
- *Falsifying the degree or credential earned.* As much as 20% of applicants falsify their education or credential achievements. Since education and experience requirements are often key to healthcare organizations, it is crucial to verify a candidate's credentials. This should be done at the source, and unfamiliar institutions should be checked against databases of known diploma mills. If questions arise, the candidate should be asked for proof of matriculation in the form of class notes, papers and other records.
- *Inflating salaries or title.* It seems the motive is to appear more qualified to fit a requirement or qualify for a better job or higher salary. If the previous employer will not provide salary information during pre-employment screening, the healthcare facility should insist that the applicant provide proof of earnings for the previous three years in the form of pay stubs or tax documents such as W-2s in the U.S.
- *Concealing a criminal record.* Approximately 11% of applicants claim no criminal record, when in fact they have such a record. It is critical that institutions not simply check databases and local county records, but also check the counties and surrounding counties where applicants have lived, been employed previously, and/or gone to school. If all of these county court records have been

thoroughly checked, then a national criminal database check will provide a helpful supplementary step.4 Consideration should be given to making international checks, as the workforce has become more global than ever before. To best accomplish this, healthcare organizations are encouraged to partner with an employment screening partner with the expertise, experience and reach to conduct checks in any country that may be required.

- *Hiding a drug habit.* Since 42% of Americans admit to using illegal drugs in their life-time, it stands to reason that this is an important area of screening, especially for healthcare organizations.[5]

At question for many human resources and security professionals is a review of a candidate's social media posts as part of the vetting process. Some are adamant that it should not be considered as it is irrelevant to the workplace circumstances, while others are visiting an applicant's Facebook®, or other personal social media page, to learn something more about the candidate. Rarely are formal policies in place, but many recruiting departments are using this technique to obtain personal information the candidate is posting in these public forums.

BACKGROUND SCREENING PROVIDERS

The vast majority of healthcare organizations use varying levels of service of third-party background screening companies. There are hundreds of these providers with a vast array of valuable offerings. The service offerings of background checking available include such items as employment verifications, criminal histories, education, credentialing, references, credit reports, motor vehicle reports, and date of birth statements, to name some of the most common. When using a background screening company, the healthcare organization generally selects a basic package of background elements to be checked for all applicants. They then have the option of adding elements for selected positions. For example, credentialing checks may be prudent for care provider or highly technical positions such as biomedical technicians, but may not be deemed necessary for frontline support staff, such as environmental services or facilities management.

Background checking services are not all the same. Just as applicant information must be checked and verified, the third-party provider of background checking should also be thoroughly vetted. A criminology professor at the University of Maryland checked on the services of an online database service provider by obtaining the records of 120 parolees in Virginia, and submitted their names to the database company for a criminal history record check. The return information reported 60 names with no criminal record, and additional names where the information was so hard to interpret that it was extremely difficult to determine the nature of the offenses.[6]

It is incumbent on the healthcare organization to investigate the third-party provider of background information, relative to accuracy of information provided and the timeliness of receiving the information requested, without falling into a "check the box" routine. The National Association of Professional Background Screeners (NAPBS) is a good resource for providing information when an organization is developing its hiring practices.

The extended workforce—vendors, contractors and temporary employees

A largely unscreened extended workforce is present and performing everyday services in our healthcare facilities. Contractors can be hired for specific projects or for a specific period of time, and be paid only for their work—saving healthcare organizations the extra expenses of payroll taxes, health insurance and other benefits.

However, the cost savings of using third-party contractors can also come with certain risks—often due to the lack of a stringent employee screening process for vetting vendors, contract staff, temporary workers, volunteers, and others performing ongoing services for the healthcare organization. This vulnerability is highlighted by a survey of vendor/contract employees that concluded this extended workforce staff was 92% more likely to have a felony record than an organizational hire, and 50% more likely to have a misdemeanor record or drug history. One explanation of this striking difference is the theory of "adverse selection." Since so many healthcare organizations conduct solid background checks as part of their standard hiring process, applicants with "questionable pasts" tend to find jobs with companies where background checks are not performed, or not performed in an adequate manner. The message is clear that healthcare organizations must have specific requirements (standards) that companies rendering contract services must meet in screening this extended, or sometimes referred to as this indirect, workforce. With the average court award for litigation involving negligent hiring and retention of employees exceeding $1 million dollars, there is significant liability for the healthcare organization, even if the indirect employee is hired and paid by another organization.[7]

In addition to a good physical security program, healthcare facilities should also perform thorough background checks on contractors to determine what, if any, risk they may pose. Once hired, it is important to train contractors on the security policies that are in place, as the risks they create are not necessarily always intentional or malicious, i.e., unplugging a device that is critical to security, or propping open a door that should remain secured at all times. While unintentional harm creates a negative situation, the possibility that an outsider might intentionally breach an organization's security to cause problems could be disastrous—subjecting the organization to theft, fraud, vandalism, property loss and much more. A physical security breach could be the first step of a more sophisticated cyber-attack.

Strong identity management is critical, and each facility identification badge issued should be associated with a specific person, and not generic to a company or service provider. Otherwise, the identification badge can be lost, stolen or loaned to someone else. The access rights of the individual ID should correspond with the areas of the facility to which the individual requires access. For example, someone who has been contracted to perform data entry should not be given an ID that allows access to the server room. Contractors must also be removed from security systems immediately upon the expiration of their contact or termination.

STAFF IDENTIFICATION BADGES

Healthcare organizations must provide each employee with identification. It is an expected practice by The Joint Commission in the U.S. that all patients have the right to know who the person is providing direct patient clinical care. Most healthcare facilities use an employee identification badge that is expected to be worn by all healthcare employees, staff and contractors and have tied the badge to secure area access. Though not as regulated in other countries, the wearing of identification badges is an established practice in healthcare.

The rapid increase in the use of electronic card access systems in healthcare facilities has resulted in one badge with multiple uses, some of which tie incentives to wearing the badge, as it is important to give employees positive reasons not to forget their identification. One such use is basic access control into the building, and employee access points located throughout the facility. Many progressive healthcare organizations have also tied the badge into controlling employee parking areas, as well as managing care providers' entry into medication storage areas. Aurora Medical Center in Wisconsin restricts access to work areas and break rooms to only those employees, students and volunteers who are appropriately credentialed. Many organizations have linked the identification badge with employee payroll accounts, allowing for employees to pay for meals in the cafeteria, often with a discount, that is taken directly out of the employee's paycheck.

While positive reinforcement can get many people to follow through with badge policies, many healthcare facilities have found it necessary to have negative reinforcement as well. This frequently includes linking the badge to time and attendance requirements for hourly employees—there can be a direct link in the badge to help monitor when employees come and go. Some organizations have even included fining employees who are found without their badge. The Billings Clinic in Montana charges $25 to each employee found to be without a badge[8] while others have incorporated the violation into the disciplinary reaction process.

ADMINISTERING THE IDENTIFICATION BADGE PROGRAM

There are several key security issues relative to the administration of staff identification systems. First, the system must provide for expeditious replacement of lost or stolen cards or badges. However, replacement procedures often make it easy for staff to obtain two badges if they desire, by claiming they have lost their badge. They can then turn in one badge at termination and still retain the second badge for various purposes. Even organizations that make a substantial effort to control employee identification badges can easily fail to retrieve as many as 20 to 30% of the badges issued. Fortunately, in most cases, the uncollected badges are not used for negative purposes. A major advantage of the electronic card access identification system is that a badge can be immediately deactivated. Not all badges are recovered, and one East Coast hospital found their policy to immediately deactivate their hospital-issued badges prevented a former employee from accessing their secured birth center and carrying out a plan to abduct an infant from the facility.

Funding is always an issue. All identification badge systems cost money, and while the cost of the materials needed to produce the cards is a rather small percentage of the total program cost, there is a tendency to underestimate the number of badges that will be produced. The number of badges an organization will require annually is generally at least two-and-a-half times the number of actual authorized positions. This estimate allows for lost cards, name changes, position changes, cards ruined in the production process, and staff turnover. One organization reports that it used 2,850 cards the first year, for an average of 880 employees during the year.

Although the front of the badge normally contains only the picture, expiration date, name and departmental or position information, the reverse side of the badge is often used for other pertinent information. The reverse side of the badge can be used to display the security telephone number, emergency code information, or even a brief description of emergency procedures. Since space on the badge is limited, it is not uncommon to find a second laminated information card attached to the primary badge. A growing trend is to provide badges that are identical on the front and back. In this respect, the badge is a two-sided badge without a front and back. The two-sided badge generally solves the problem of the employee inadvertently, or intentionally, turning the badge over (inward), hiding the identity of the person.

The most common problem in any employee badge identification system is obtaining compliance of displaying (wearing) the badge as prescribed. A certain number of employees will always resist, and organizations that initiate a badging program must be prepared to provide strong administrative support. Of paramount importance in promoting compliance with the program is for top administrative personnel to set a good example by always displaying their badges. In one healthcare facility, the badge had a designated place to affix employee longevity award logos. When employees reach their fifth year of service, for example, they are issued a new employee badge with the award logo. This system provides a practical means of recognition; other award pins often end up at home in a dresser drawer. In some programs, so many stickers and other items are attached to badges that the whole purpose of identification badging is defeated. A strict policy should be in place to address this issue. The problem of "badge clutter" has been solved to some extent with the extensive use of electronic access control systems activated by RF technology. These badges contain internal wires that, if punctured, will render the badge useless, and thus pins of any kind cannot be affixed to the badge.

IDENTIFICATION BADGE DESIGN CONSIDERATIONS

The name of the individual must be of sufficient size so that it can be read from a distance of at least 2 or 3 feet. An 18-point type allows the name and position to be read from a distance of approximately 8 to 10 feet. It is important the organization be able to produce the badge in-house, so it is ready for an employee's first day on the job. This capability is also important in preparing a new badge in the event of a loss or name or status change. When badges can be quickly produced by the organization, employees will not be without a badge, and the entire process can be completed in only one trip to the processing station. The use of specific job titles on the badge will necessitate considerably more changes than the use of a more general title or department designation. For example, it would be better to include "Food Services" on all badges issued to that department, rather than "Head Cook," "Dishwasher," "Tray Attendant," etc. In clinical areas, more precise titles, positions, and/or credentials are required to more properly identify the employee for purposes of patient treatment and interactions.

A system of issuing temporary badges must be established. Employees should not be allowed to work without a badge if it was left at home or misplaced; they should receive a temporary badge. In some systems, the temporary badge must be checked-in when employees have completed their shift. In other systems, the temporary badge is issued for a given shift or a specific number of days. Employees should be given a choice of a pin clip or other means of affixing the badge. Some organizations allow the badge to be affixed to a break-away safety lanyard worn around the neck. Giving employees this choice is intended to enhance compliance with wearing the badge. In some badging programs, contractors, salespeople, students, and others who perform a service within the facility are badged as well as employees. These badges can be permanent issue or, in the case of a contractor or salesperson, can be issued for a set number of days.

Using color codes to denote the various authorized areas the barer may enter does not usually work well within medical care facilities. All employees should be issued the same type and color of badge, except for staff assigned to a mother/infant unit. Different types or colors may be helpful for temporary badges to identify contractors, salespeople, clergy, and others.

Physicians should be required to wear identification badges, just as other staff. As a general rule, physicians have historically resisted badging. In order to promote wearing the badges, there must be strong medical director support. Some organizations have obtained physician compliance by linking the function of the identification card to access to the physician lounge. House staff (interns and residents), who usually receive training by rotating among several facilities, are often able to utilize a single medical school, or teaching hospital identification badge, in multiple facilities. In these cases, all participating facilities must be party to a structured, formal agreement regarding this type of arrangement. Since the staff of any specific organization is responsible to challenge other caregivers who are not properly identified, there must be a communication link in regard to *accepted* identification from other organizations.

SECURITY-ORIENTED EMPLOYMENT GUIDELINES

A major function of the protection system is to manage employee actions and conduct, while protecting the organization's well-being by enforcing organizational rules and regulations. Concise, written personnel policies provide a solid foundation on which to regulate staff conduct. Vague, unwritten policies benefit neither the staff nor the organization. Commonly, employment guidelines are contained in an employee handbook or administrative policy. Although policies for sick leave, vacation time, wages and hours, disciplinary action, etc., are always carefully spelled out, security policies are often ambiguous or omitted entirely. Policies affecting staff must be tailored to the type of facility, and to what is expected of staff in that facility. However, certain basic security policies are germane to every medical care facility. Some of the most important security policies are discussed here.

EMPLOYEE SECURITY RESPONSIBILITY

A unique aspect of healthcare security is the important role every staff member plays in providing an adequate level of protection for the facility. It is important every organization clearly set forth the employee's responsibility for security. A typical policy, which should be part of every healthcare organization's policy, is as follows:

> "It is the responsibility of every employee to be aware of anything observed that may affect the welfare of the patients, other people on the premises, or the physical property of either individuals or the organization. When any such observation is made, employees will take steps to investigate further, intervene if time is of the essence, and report the circumstances to their supervisor and the security department. Further, it is the responsibility of every employee to report any and all threats to staff, visitors, or patients in accordance with the facility threat policy."

OFF-DUTY EMPLOYEES

Many facilities face serious problems with off-duty employees, who remain in the facility after their shift ends, or who return to the facility on their off time to visit other employees. These visits not only waste the time of employees on duty, but can also result in other problems, such as disturbances, loud and noisy activity, drinking, drug use, and property losses. The following is a typical policy intended to address this problem:

> "Employees who are not on duty should not be on medical center property more than 30 minutes after their work shift or more than 30 minutes before the start of a scheduled work shift. Employees who are off duty may return to the facility to receive medical care or to visit a patient, or they may return with the specific authorization of an administrator or supervisor for a specific purpose, such as a staff meeting, training activity, or volunteer type of service."

WORKPLACE VIOLENCE

No healthcare facility is immune to violence in the workplace. A violence prevention and mitigation program should be developed, depicting the stages and elements of violence that can occur. This should include the proactive steps taken to prevent violence and identifying how various issues of violence are responded to, while planning for continuity of service to various types of violent episodes. The Security Executive Council has developed a workplace violence continuum that starts in the prevention/planning stages of violence prevention, and moves to the reactions that arise from troubled employees' and troubling situations. The continuum addresses emergency response to situations of imminent danger, and expectations surrounding business continuity after an event has occurred. The workplace violence continuum can be found in Figure 14-2, and is a good guide for HR and healthcare security professionals to follow when developing or revising their workplace violence prevention and violence policy. The policy should apply to patient conduct too. Of course, it's harder to stop patient-generated violence and harassment when a nonemployee is involved, since the healthcare facility cannot discipline the nonemployee the way it can an employee for violating its policy. However, that does not absolve the hospital from its responsibility to its staff.

WORKPLACE BULLYING

Workplace bullying is more than an occupational health hazard; it is a chronic concern for hospitals and healthcare facilities across the U.S. and much of the world. With instances of violence in the workplace making more headlines, HR and security professionals have started identifying the concerning behavior of bullying, and getting to know the warning signs before situations escalate.

With any preventative measures for violence, the healthcare organization must begin by identifying what bullying is. Workplace bullying can be defined as repeated, health-harming abusive conduct committed by bosses and co-workers. Prevalence of workplace bullying is evident in the findings of a study conducted by the Workplace Bullying Institute, which found 35% of the U.S. workforce report being bullied at work, while an additional 15% have witnessed it.[9]

It is important to understand the signs and symptoms of a bully in order to help the victim and the victimizer deal with and eliminate the behavior. Here are five attributes of the adult bully:

1. He or she doesn't believe in following the rules that society dictates, in any capacity.
2. A bully craves negative attention.
3. Bullies seek to put people down by manipulating and degrading them in front of their peers.
4. Bullies seek power.

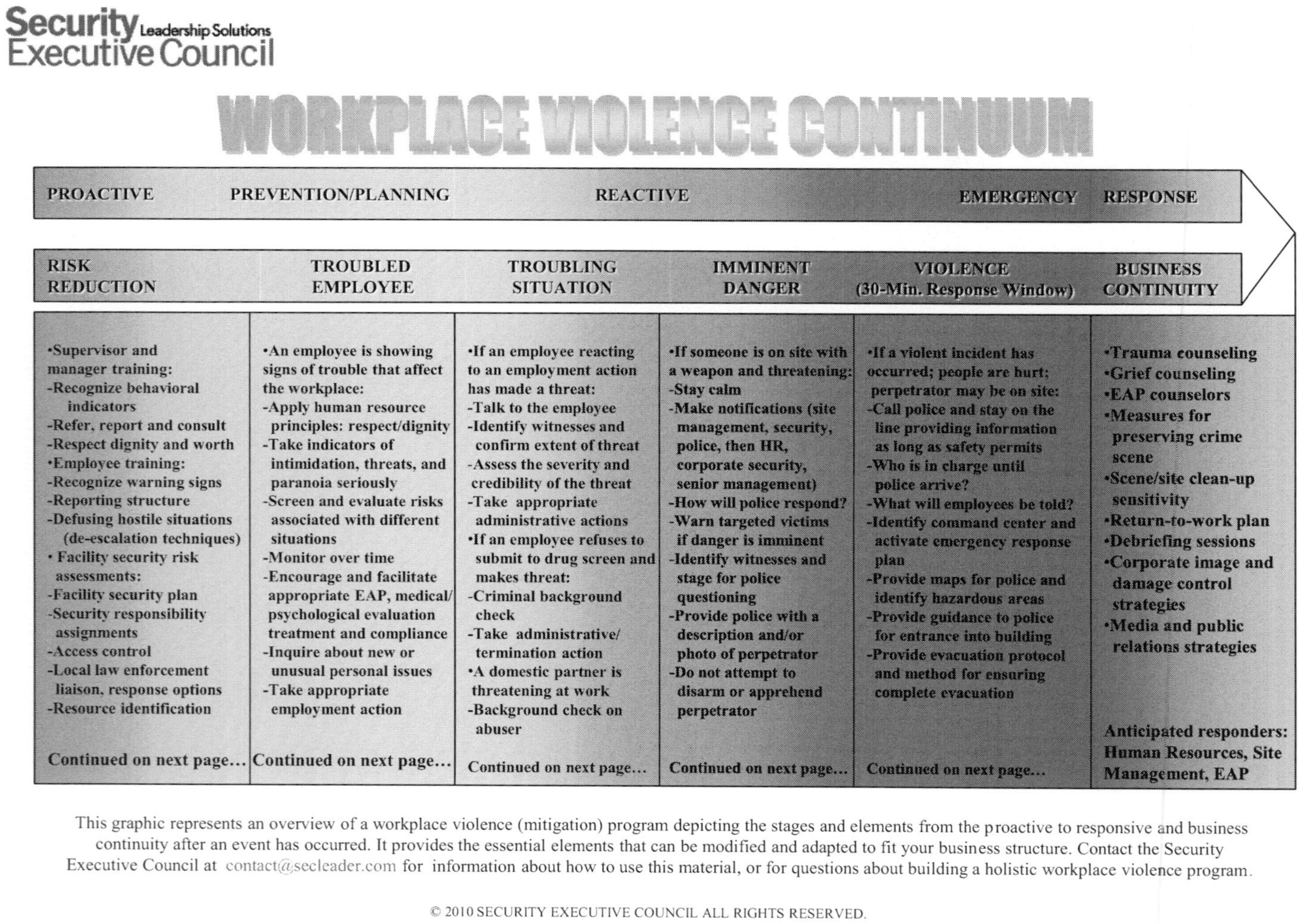

Security Leadership Solutions Executive Council

WORKPLACE VIOLENCE CONTINUUM

PROACTIVE — PREVENTION/PLANNING — REACTIVE — EMERGENCY — RESPONSE

RISK REDUCTION	TROUBLED EMPLOYEE	TROUBLING SITUATION	IMMINENT DANGER	VIOLENCE (30-Min. Response Window)	BUSINESS CONTINUITY
•Supervisor and manager training: -Recognize behavioral indicators -Refer, report and consult -Respect dignity and worth •Employee training: -Recognize warning signs -Reporting structure -Defusing hostile situations (de-escalation techniques) • Facility security risk assessments: -Facility security plan -Security responsibility assignments -Access control -Local law enforcement liaison, response options -Resource identification Continued on next page...	•An employee is showing signs of trouble that affect the workplace: -Apply human resource principles: respect/dignity -Take indicators of intimidation, threats, and paranoia seriously -Screen and evaluate risks associated with different situations -Monitor over time -Encourage and facilitate appropriate EAP, medical/psychological evaluation treatment and compliance -Inquire about new or unusual personal issues -Take appropriate employment action Continued on next page...	•If an employee reacting to an employment action has made a threat: -Talk to the employee -Identify witnesses and confirm extent of threat -Assess the severity and credibility of the threat -Take appropriate administrative actions •If an employee refuses to submit to drug screen and makes threat: -Criminal background check -Take administrative/termination action •A domestic partner is threatening at work -Background check on abuser Continued on next page...	•If someone is on site with a weapon and threatening: -Stay calm -Make notifications (site management, security, police, then HR, corporate security, senior management) -How will police respond? -Warn targeted victims if danger is imminent -Identify witnesses and stage for police questioning -Provide police with a description and/or photo of perpetrator -Do not attempt to disarm or apprehend perpetrator Continued on next page...	•If a violent incident has occurred; people are hurt; perpetrator may be on site: -Call police and stay on the line providing information as long as safety permits -Who is in charge until police arrive? -What will employees be told? -Identify command center and activate emergency response plan -Provide maps for police and identify hazardous areas -Provide guidance to police for entrance into building -Provide evacuation protocol and method for ensuring complete evacuation Continued on next page...	•Trauma counseling •Grief counseling •EAP counselors •Measures for preserving crime scene •Scene/site clean-up sensitivity •Return-to-work plan •Debriefing sessions •Corporate image and damage control strategies •Media and public relations strategies Anticipated responders: Human Resources, Site Management, EAP

This graphic represents an overview of a workplace violence (mitigation) program depicting the stages and elements from the proactive to responsive and business continuity after an event has occurred. It provides the essential elements that can be modified and adapted to fit your business structure. Contact the Security Executive Council at contact@secleader.com for information about how to use this material, or for questions about building a holistic workplace violence program.

FIGURE 14-2

Workplace violence continuum.

(Courtesy of the Security Executive Council, used by permission.)

Security Leadership Solutions Executive Council

WORKPLACE VIOLENCE CONTINUUM

PROACTIVE	PREVENTION/PLANNING	REACTIVE		EMERGENCY	RESPONSE
RISK REDUCTION	TROUBLED EMPLOYEE	TROUBLING SITUATION	IMMINENT DANGER	VIOLENCE (30-Min. Response Window)	BUSINESS CONTINUITY
Continued...	Continued...	Continued...	Continued...	Continued...	
-Incident reporting -Employee security plan -Building hazards -Incident management team -Corporate risks and liabilities -Notification structure	-Minimize stressors, e.g., medical or disability benefits, change jobs, etc. -Seek opportunities to help the employee regain control	-Provide gatekeepers with description and/or photo -Reinforce access control -Personal security consult. •If there is an altercation between two or more employees: -Secure the workplace to the extent possible -Take appropriate actions to protect target(s) -Apply de-escalation techniques from defusing hostile situations -Provide personal security training to targets	•A situation is escalating out of control: -Activate site security plan -Alert law enforcement -Reinforce access control	-Designate an evacuation staging area -Is electronic access capable of shutting building down? -Identify witnesses and stage for police questioning -Provide police with picture and/ or description of perpetrator, if available -Identify media staging area -Communicate strategies -Make notifications to HR, security, communications, etc. -Decide on media spokesperson	
Anticipated responders: Human Resources, Employee Assistance Program (EAP), Supervisors and Managers, Family, Site Management, Corporate Security	Anticipated responders: Human Resources, Site Management, EAP	Anticipated responders: Human Resources, Site Management, EAP, Corporate Security, Local police.	Anticipated responders: Site Management, Local Police	Anticipated responders: Local Police, Site Management	

This graphic represents an overview of a workplace violence (mitigation) program depicting the stages and elements from the proactive to responsive and business continuity after an event has occurred. It provides the essential elements that can be modified and adapted to fit your business structure. Contact the Security Executive Council at contact@secleader.com for information about how to use this material, or for questions about building a holistic workplace violence program.

FIGURE 14-2 Continued

5. Bullies spread untrue rumors in the workplace, seethe with disrespect toward their victims, and refuse to listen to a victim in any capacity.

Bullying may also emanate from employees who believe they have a sense of entitlement. This profile fits some physicians.

Bullying in the healthcare setting is of concern because it has the potential to have an adverse impact on patient care. There are currently no federal, state or provincial laws prohibiting bullying, so it may be difficult to fire a bully right away. Bullying is a form of workplace violence, and bullying in hospitals is not always apparent until something bad happens. There are, however, some basic tips for HR leaders and security professionals to identify, prevent and eliminate workplace bullies. These include:

1. Develop a code of conduct – define acceptable and unacceptable behavior and create and implement a process to manage behaviors that undermine a culture of safety such as bullying.
2. Equal opportunity for everyone – being actively involved and taking responsibility for creating a healthy work environment, establishing a culture of equality in job selection, promotion, compensation, reward and bonus.
3. Defined consequences and punishment – instituting a zero-tolerance policy toward bullying with a specific list of actions to be taken if bullying is discovered.
4. Develop bullying awareness programs – an effective training program is the best defense to effectively mitigate bullying in the workplace.

Intimidating and disruptive behaviors that foster medical errors and other conditions detrimental to overall patient care was the focus of The Joint Commission's Sentinel Event Alert, "Behaviors that undermine a culture of safety." In this 2008 publication, The Joint Commission strongly recommended establishing a proactive approach to keep bullying and other types of behavior from affecting patient care, specifically exposure to preventable medical errors, caused when team members are afraid to question decisions for fear of retaliation. Joint Commission Standard LD 03.01.01 also requires hospitals to maintain a culture of safety and quality. The elements of performance require hospitals to, among other things, develop a code of conduct that defines acceptable behaviors, and those that undermine a culture of safety; create and implement a process for managing behaviors that undermine a culture of safety; and provide education. The Joint Commission is paying more attention to actions taken against hospitals by other entities and agencies to see if its standards are also impacted. So a hospital that gets into trouble with the EEOC or any other agency for allowing a hostile, discriminatory environment may also end up in The Joint Commission's crosshairs for the same violation.

EMPLOYEE WEAPONS

Unfortunately, many healthcare employees, especially medical staff, desire to carry weapons to their place of employment. Whatever the purpose, the possession of weapons on facility property should be strictly prohibited. Because almost anything can be construed as a weapon, the policy established should define which weapons are specifically prohibited. The following is an example of a weapons policy:

> "Employees are prohibited from bringing weapons or explosives onto hospital property. For the purpose of this policy, weapon is defined as any gun, loaded or unloaded, any knife with a blade longer than three inches, or any weapon that by law is illegal to possess."

A weapons-free environment should be the goal of every healthcare facility, and stated so in hospital policy and the employee handbook. Notices are frequently posted that alert people, including those with a permit to carry a concealed gun, that the hospital does not allow guns or other weapons in its facility. There is considerable pending legislation in a number of U.S. states that allows employees to have a gun, loaded or unloaded, in their parked vehicle while at work. Each healthcare security administrator in the U.S. must know what their state's gun law allows. More and more states are being added to the list of places where guns are prohibited, but in Wyoming, it is unlawful and specifically prohibited to carry a firearm in schools, courthouse, government buildings and places of worship but OK to carry in the hospital. Yet another example of why healthcare security administrators have to be proactive in exercising influence to those making such decisions. Hospitals should support any state efforts to make it illegal to carry a firearm into their facilities.

PACKAGE INSPECTION

The control of packages and equipment entering or leaving the facility is a major security management issue. The primary concern is to keep the package or equipment from leaving; however, at times, package entry is also an issue relative to contraband entering the facility. Effective control requires the compliance and cooperation of all staff, as well as the control of various facility entrances and exits. Unfortunately, most healthcare security programs are not adequately staffed to enable them to control all egress points. As a result, package inspection is conducted as a spot-check or is incidental to patrol services. A good access control program depends largely on the ability to designate and enforce a policy that authorizes only certain doors for staff use. The property pass is widely used, but only yields varying degrees of success. Although they differ considerably from facility to facility, pass programs have the common objective of discouraging theft and providing property accountability. These systems establish a sound basis for security officers to inquire about employees observed carrying an item from the facility. In some programs only organization property is subject to the pass policy, which creates the problem of determining what is personal and what is organization property. A package inspection policy should cover not only packages being taken from the facility, but also those being brought in. The following is a typical policy:

> "All property being taken from or brought into medical center buildings or upon medical center property is subject to inspection by security officers or medical center administrative personnel. Any medical center property, regardless of value, being taken from the property shall be accompanied by a dated, written authorization form that contains a description of the property and the name of the person authorizing removal."

All property pass systems should be well organized to eliminate as many weaknesses as possible. If reasonable compliance appears doubtful, it might be better not to implement the pass system at all. One commonly cited weakness in property pass programs is the lack of feedback to department management. In too many programs, passes are simply collected and discarded. Collected passes, or a copy of such passes, should be returned to the authorizing department for review and audit purposes. Figure 14-3 is an example of a property removal pass.

Of course, an organization can maintain a property inspection system without a formalized property pass. In other words, security personnel may still inspect property to determine whether its removal has

UNITED MEMORIAL HOSPITAL
PROPERTY REMOVAL AUTHORIZATION

Date: ____________________ **Time:** _______________

Name: ________________________ **Staff** ___ **Visitor** ___ **Patient** ___

Has permission to remove the following property from the UMH campus (Describe fully: amount, color, type of property):

Property: Surplus ____ **Obsolete** ____ **Loan** ____

Other (explain): ______________________________________

Authorization Signature: __________________ **Position:** __________

Department/Service: _____________________ **Tel. Ext.** __________

Prepare in Duplicate – Forward Copy to Security Services

FIGURE 14-3

Example of a property removal pass.

been authorized. The following policy statements are offered as a sample of an inspection system policy/procedure:

Cause to believe that contraband or stolen property is being transported

On occasion the security officer will receive information that a possible theft will occur; receive a request for an inspection of a person or persons by a facility administrator or supervisor; or observe extremely suspicious activity. In the case of the first two circumstances, the officer should confer with a security supervisor if time and extent of the problem permit. In the case of activity in progress, good officer judgment will prevail.

Observation of exposed equipment

Often, an item of possible medical center property is observed being removed from a facility and does not fall under the suspicious activity category. Open-view removal generally indicates legitimate removal; however, the security officer should make tactful inquiry as to ownership. The legitimate person will seldom take offense, and the procedure helps to solidify the image that the facility is concerned about the safety and protection of its environment.

Concentrated package inspection

Such package inspection is a planned security operation under the supervision of a security supervisor per direction of the Security Director. Security personnel will be assigned to a specific exit and check property being removed by any person. In this regard, purses and lunch boxes will be excluded unless the purse is extremely large. This practice is not prevalent in all countries.

Identified medical center property

The person removing the property should be identified. If the person is a medical center employee, the person should be allowed to proceed after a list of the property has been prepared, and the employee's department verified. The department will be called to verify authorized removal if the officer deems such action necessary. If the person removing the property is not an employee, the employee authorizing removal should be contacted.

Suspected medical center property

The security officer should prepare a list of the property and identify the person, who may then proceed on his way. Complete documentation of package inspection is of course mandatory. Employees should be reminded periodically of the policy concerning property inspection.

COOPERATING WITH AN INVESTIGATION

Investigations of all kinds are a continuous process in most healthcare organizations. Although the concern here is for security-related investigations, healthcare organizations conduct other investigations to collect and analyze facts for various business and patient-care situations. To efficiently and thoroughly carry out this investigative activity, employers must have the full cooperation of all staff. A policy, such as the one that follows, should be strongly considered for any healthcare organization:

> "All employees are required to cooperate fully with any medical center supervisor, manager, or member of the security department who is conducting an investigation or inquiry on behalf of the medical center. Failure to provide cooperation may be considered as insubordination and may subject the employee to disciplinary action."

STAFF LOCKERS

A frequent concern for healthcare organizations is the staff locker. Lockers furnished to employees for use in connection with their employment should be inspected periodically. Two supervisory staff members, one from security and one from a relevant department, should conduct the inspection. To maintain proper control of staff lockers, personal locks should not be permitted. If the facility does not furnish locks, staff must provide their own. In this situation, the organization must still retain access to the lockers. Staff should be required to furnish a duplicate key or the lock combination to the department responsible for the staff locker program. The following is a typical policy for staff:

> "Staff lockers are the property of the medical center and are subject to inspection at any time for sanitary or administrative purposes. No medical center property will be stored in an employee locker, except such property issued to the employee for which he or she is personally responsible."

STAFF SOLICITATION AND DISTRIBUTION OF PRODUCTS

Virtually all healthcare facilities have a policy on solicitation, which generally pertains to both employees and individuals from outside the organization. However, many organizations do not include in this solicitation policy the free distribution of products or materials. In one sense, this distribution could be viewed as indirect solicitation, but not always. One hospital reports an author of a paperback book came to the hospital and began visiting patients at random, leaving them a complimentary copy of his book for their reading pleasure. The hospital did not know anything of this situation until one patient complained that the book was pornographic. After a review of the book, the hospital visited patient rooms with an apology and hastily retrieved the books. The author was contacted and he stated his purpose was to simply provide reading material to help cheer up the patients. He was asked to immediately cease and desist his activity. Medical care organizations cannot carry out their work efficiently while permitting solicitation or the distribution of materials to staff or patients. The following is an example of a solicitation and distribution policy:

> "To protect employees and patients from annoyance or disruption, no solicitation or distribution of products or materials of any kind by employees or outside persons is permitted on medical center property without the express permission of the medical center administration. This prohibition includes circulating petitions, selling merchandise, selling chances for a lottery or drawing, or distributing products or literature. All staff members have an obligation to report any such solicitation or distribution of products to their immediate supervisor."

GIFTS FROM PATIENTS OR FAMILY

Staff should be prohibited from accepting gifts or gratuities from patients or their families. Employees are paid to provide their services, and the acceptance of any form of gift fosters possible abuse such as favoritism, special treatment, and fraudulent practices. The enforcement of this policy rests with departmental supervisors and rarely becomes a security issue. There may be some exceptions authorized by administration, such as with valet parking, but these exceptions should be well thought out and limited to only a small number of such exceptions.

SURPLUS OR DAMAGED PROPERTY

Medical care facilities of all sizes continually accumulate surplus property that is damaged, obsolete, or for various reasons unsuitable for use in the current environment. A policy must be prepared that defines a procedure for the proper disposition of such property. The following is an example of a policy covering the disposal of surplus or damaged property:

> "All medical center equipment or products deemed by staff to be unusable for any reason will be returned to the Director of Materials Management. No staff member will have the authority to sell or give away any medical center property, regardless of value or condition, unless authorized by the Director of Materials Management on a case by case basis."

CONTRABAND

In this context, the term "contraband" includes not only illegal items, such as weapons, drugs, and explosives, but also alcohol. Alcohol must be included in a hospital policy banning employees from bringing contraband items onto facility property. The following is an example of a policy covering contraband:

"No medical center employee will possess or knowingly assist another person in possessing any contraband, including illegal drugs, explosives, weapons, and liquor of any kind, unless authorized by a supervisor for a specific medical center business purpose."

DRUG TESTING

Testing of applicants and for-cause testing of staff for drug use is a commonplace procedure in healthcare organizations in the U.S. In Canada, for-cause testing is sometimes seen, but not applicant testing. The Drug-Free Workplace Act, contained in the Anti-Drug Abuse Act of 1989, spurred many organizations to action, even though the act does not require a drug testing program. The act applies to any contractor who has federal contracts for the procurement of goods or services valued at $25,000 or more, or who receives federal grants, regardless of the dollar amount. The act requires these contractors to publish a policy statement prohibiting the unlawful manufacture, distribution, dispensation, possession, or use of a controlled substance in the workplace and specifying penalties for violations; to establish an education program on drug abuse; to provide policy statements to each employee; and to require employees to report any conviction for a criminal drug violation that occurred in the workplace.

When considering drug testing, all aspects of such a policy must be covered, including the type of testing and the conditions under which employees will be tested. The details of the policy must be presented to all affected individuals. Organizations should document the relationship between job performance, health and safety, and drug usage. The results of drug tests are confidential and generally should not be maintained in the staff personnel files.

A relatively new trend in healthcare pre-employment screening is the testing for nicotine, designed to prevent smokers from being hired. The expansion, intended to set an antismoking example to the community, is also being used to help prevent potential healthcare costs.

EMPLOYEE ASSISTANCE PROGRAMS

Most healthcare organizations have an employee assistance program (EAP) of one sort or another. A direct relationship exists between security and EAPs. Many instances of employee wrongdoing can be traced back to personal problems. Stealing to support a drug habit is an obvious example where theft could be averted by helping a staff member with such a problem. Staff who steal because they do not understand how to manage their personal finances are a less obvious example. Even marital problems may lead to wrongdoing by a staff member that otherwise may not have occurred. An in-depth EAP effort is a way to prevent crime and wrongdoing among staff. Progressive security administrators may wish to explore this concept further with the administrator of the healthcare EAP program.

LOSS OF STAFF PROPERTY

Unfortunately, the loss of staff property is a continuous problem for protection systems. The provision and use of staff lockers is a primary safeguard against staff property losses. This staff property loss problem usually evolves from a lack of proper storage facilities, carelessness, misuse, or failure to use the facilities provided. An inspection of virtually any healthcare facility –hospital, nursing home, clinic, or physician's office—will usually reveal purses and backpacks sitting in open view, simply inviting a loss. The mandate for the security function is to provide an adequate means of storage. Failure to use the storage provided gives employees little cause for legitimate complaint if their property is borrowed, lost, or stolen.

REFERENCES

1. *Supervisor blamed for rapist hire at hospital*. Southern California: NBC Channel 4 website; 2009, February 10. Retrieved February 18, 2009 from, http://www.nbclosangeles.com/health/tips_info/Supervisor-Blamed-for-Rapist-Hire-at-Hospital.html.
2. Fischer RJ, Halibozek E, Green G. *Introduction to Security*. 8th ed. Burlington, MA: Butterworth-Heinemann; 2008. 304.
3. Idziak B. What's new in 2006? *Security Products* 2006, January;**39**.
4. Lashier Ron. *10 tips for conducting better background checks*. Campus Safety Magazine; 2006, July/August. Retrieved December 2, 2009, from http://www.campussafetymagazine.com/article/10-Tips-for-Conducting-Better-Background-Checks.
5. *HireRight reports the top five lies told by job candidates*. Campus Safety Magazine; 2009, March 8. Retrieved March 11, 2009, from. http://www.campussafetymagazine.com/News/?NewsID=2762.
6. Rosen LS. Criminal databases and pre-employment screening: The good, the bad, and the ugly. *Security Technology and Design* 2005, July;**27**.
7. Lashier R. *Everybody Screen!* Security Products; 2006, June. Retrieved June 24, 2009, from http://secprodonline.com/Articles/2006/06/01/Everybody-Screen.aspx.
8. Denale Rachael. *Encourage staff to wear badges to ensure hospital security*, vol. 17. Environment of Care Leader; 2012, July 23. No. 15.
9. Malhotra Rakesh. *5 ways to spot a workplace bully*. Property Casualty 360; 2012, December 18. Retrieved December 26, 2012, from http://www.propertycasualty360.com/2012/12/18/5-ways-to-spot-a-workplace=bully.

CHAPTER

EMPLOYEE INVOLVEMENT AND SECURITY AWARENESS

15

Crime prevention presentations, handouts, events, and training can raise staff awareness of security issues. Not only will this add eyes and ears to the security effort, it will be noted by Joint Commission surveyors and other regulatory agencies, which are increasingly looking for employee involvement in the healthcare security program. Using input from the healthcare staff, physicians, visitors, and patients, an employee involved security awareness program should be tailored to meet the individual needs of the facility and the employees, staff, patients, and visitors it serves.

EMPLOYEE SECURITY EDUCATION AND MOTIVATION

The strategy of preventing crime is a key concept of the healthcare protection system. In the United States, the Crime Prevention Coalition, formed by 19 organizations in 1980, provides strong leadership for crime prevention programs. The campaign featuring "McGruff the Crime Dog" was one of the first efforts to involve the average person in the fight to prevent crime. The approach was unique: when people come together, work with law enforcement (or security), and address the cause of crime, they have an impact. As a result, the crime prevention and community (employee) involvement message took root. Today, the coalition is stronger than ever, and it consists of over 400 national, state, and federal organizations and community-based agencies.[1] The National Crime Prevention Council (NCPC) is an excellent resource for promoting a message grounded in the principles of security awareness and education, and promoting the prevention-first approach to crime to employees, volunteers and physicians, and others in the healthcare environment. Training, topical crime prevention materials and strategies, media relation techniques, and other resources are available from the NCPC at little to no cost. In Australia, a National Crime Prevention Framework was developed in 2011.

"Crime prevention" has been defined in many ways. The definition found in the coalition's handbook, *Foundations for Action*, seems to be the most appropriate for the purposes of this discussion. Crime prevention, it says, is "a pattern of attitudes and behaviors directed both at reducing the threat of crime and enhancing the sense of safety and security, to positively influence the quality of life in our society, and to help develop environments where crime cannot flourish." This is a tall order and a challenge for even the most professional healthcare security administrator.

EMPLOYEE EDUCATION PROGRAMS

A primary function of any protection system is to educate, stimulate, and motivate the first-line protection resource: employees, physicians and volunteers. The protection level of a medical care facility is directly related to the extent to which employees participate in the security effort.

The entire staff of an organization must understand they are part of providing a safe and secure environment. They must actively practice good security awareness and appropriate security actions every day. This requires staff be given clear direction and sufficient training and education. Security training should begin the first day on the job and continue throughout the individual's employment.

This participation varies from overt to covert activity. This is not to imply all employees are engaged in overt security activities. Rather, some employees may participate by simply obeying the rules: for example, not taking property that does not belong to them. Other employees participate overtly by reducing inventory and thus reducing the opportunity for theft, maintaining control of keys and organizationally issued identification, marking property, reporting losses and suspicious activity, tightening procedures for identifying people in their area, greeting unknown persons in their area, and properly locking their personal belongings and work areas. All these activities, occurring simultaneously, are what a security system is all about. No healthcare administrator or security professional should be so naive as to think all employees will do their share. However, education and direction by the security department will certainly increase employee participation and involvement, gain staff ownership in the protection effort, and engage their awareness to issues affecting the overall security posture of the healthcare organization. Common educational components include security presentation at the new employee orientation, brown bag lunch and learn programs, and department-specific in-services.

New employee orientation presentation and handouts

Employee education begins with new employee orientation. New employees can be channeled into the protection system with a minimum of effort. They seek the norms, want to know what their employer expects, and desire a safe working environment. The moment employees first enter the workplace is the prime time to develop a positive protection attitude. Employees will not remember everything presented, but they will form a basic opinion, either consciously or subconsciously, of the importance the organization places on security.

It is readily accepted by The Joint Commission and other healthcare industry regulatory agencies that healthcare employees should be knowledgeable and aware of personal safety and security issues. The security training is most effective when led by someone from within the healthcare security program. Typically, most healthcare organizations offer between 20 minutes to an hour to communicate the security message, based on the length of the overall orientation program. More and more frequently, healthcare organizations offer new employee orientation, and specifically the security component, via computer-generated learning modules. The progressive healthcare security administrator will leverage this communication medium to engage staff, employees, and volunteers in the protection effort.

Unfortunately, many healthcare organizations have combined the security presentation with safety and emergency management, and the important emergency codes every healthcare employee must know. Although the healthcare employee is given a basic exposure to security and the protection efforts employed, most healthcare security professionals agree that the same effort that goes into promoting patient safety and infection control should be applied to protection and the security awareness message. The IAHSS has established a basic industry guideline for general staff security orientation and education that should be implemented in every healthcare facility.

IAHSS – HEALTHCARE BASIC SECURITY GUIDELINE #03.02

General Staff Security Orientation and Education

Statement

Healthcare Facilities (HCF) will identify the security orientation and education needs of their employees and staff. Crime prevention and personal safety presentations, handouts, events and training will raise security awareness. Based on the security needs identified, the HCF should implement a program to provide this information.

Intent

a. HCF's must set expectations for all employees and staff in contributing to a safe, secure and welcoming environment. Topics to be discussed include:
   1) Greetings and the importance of acknowledgement and eye contact with all patients, visitors and staff
   2) How to contact Security for assistance
   3) What information should be reported to Security
   4) The importance of displaying and checking identification
   5) Procedures for preventing and responding to infant/child abductions
   6) Preventing, intervening, reporting and resolving aggression and other issues of violence
   7) Role in crime prevention
   8) Reporting environmental safety issues
   9) Personal safety awareness
   10) Confidential information and patient privacy issues

b. Security orientation and education should be presented to all HCF staff within thirty (30) days of employment with periodic reviews and updates of information at least annually.

c. Security sensitive areas have special staff orientation and education needs. If assigned to a security sensitive area, such special training should occur prior to the first unsupervised assignment.

d. The HCF should determine and continuously evaluate the method of presentation which best accommodates staff needs. Presentation may include classroom, video, newsletter, role playing, drills and electronic self-learning education modules.

Approved: December 2006
Last Revised: November 2012

To offset lack of time provided during new employee orientation, and facilitate enhanced employee knowledge of the security effort, there should be a handout or other takeaway for the new employee, emphasizing the importance of security to themselves and the organization. Progressive security programs distribute a small book or pamphlet that describes the basic elements of the security program and serves as a quick reference to the services and resources offered by the security program, including employee expectations in terms of providing safety and security. These booklets can be purchased and customized for the healthcare facility or created with in-house resources. Box 15-1 is a sample listing of the security services and resources often shared by the protection professional during the new employee orientation program.

Security competencies should be used in the organization's annual competency requirements for employees and staff. Many organizations have found success using "self-directed learning" packages. This approach enables employees to study the material on their own and demonstrate their knowledge through a competency exam. The self-directed learning package is typically limited to the important security issues employees are expected to know and demonstrate on an everyday basis, such as reporting security-related events, the role of customer service greetings in the security effort, infant/child abduction employee response, active shooter response, etc.

BOX 15-1 BASIC LISTING OF SECURITY SERVICES AND RESOURCES

Security Services and Resources Offered by Protection Department

- Responds to security incidents and documents follow-up actions
- Identifies security risks and vulnerabilities
- Responds to requests such as locking or unlocking doors, vehicle assistance, patient assists and visitor services
- Investigates hospital incidents:
    - - unsafe conditions
    - - missing property
    - - suspicious activity
    - - vandalism
    - - accidents
- Assists with the control of visitors, patients, and unauthorized persons
- De-escalates aggressive or crisis situations
- Assists staff in controlling unruly or violent persons under clinical supervision
- Responds to alarms
- Physical security of work area
- Escorts people, cash, and valuables
- Coordinates activities with law enforcement and public safety agencies
- Offers educational programs to employees and staff
- Provides loss prevention awareness
- Conducts security well-being checks for employees and staff members working late and working in a department alone
- Detains lawbreakers and assists with court action, as warranted

Department-specific security training programs

Healthcare organizations are traditionally heavily involved in a continuous program of in-service education. Security administrators should take advantage of every opportunity to involve protection services in these educational programs, through departmental meetings or small group discussions. At one medical center, the entire workforce is exposed to a general in-service program on a quarterly basis. Security training for general staff can be provided by various entities, including human resources, security administrators, clinical/nonclinical education departments, safety, emergency preparedness or risk management personnel. The local police department can also be a good resource for smaller healthcare facilities.

Self-directed security presentations have been successfully used at many healthcare facilities. These programs, designed to explain a variety of critical information every employees should know such as workplace violence prevention and reporting, bomb threat response, or other department- or function-specific educational programs such as front-desk security or what to do in the event of an armed robbery (gift shop, pharmacy, or other cash-handling area). Computer-generated learning modules can be produced in-house using basic presentation software with voice narration, recorded webinars or podcasts, or off-the-shelf products purchased from professional trade associations such as IAHSS, ASIS International or other outside companies such as HSS Inc., based in Denver, Colorado.

More recently, online training programs have been designed to align with organizational and security program quality management requirements. Quizzes and tests embedded in the course material allow the security administrator to continuously assess the effectiveness of the educational program. This process can identify trending, both positive and negative, on specific areas of the security curriculum, allowing the security administrator to continuously monitor and adjust the material, to ensure it is meeting the needs of the organization.

Table 15-1 Employee Awareness Campaign Topics

Crime Prevention / Employee Awareness Educational Program Topics	
• Building a Personal Safety Plan	• Senior Safety: An Anti-Crime Guide
• Workplace Violence Prevention	• Safeguard Your Child
• Workplace Violence: A supervisor guide to responding to complaints and other issues	• Personal Safety for the Healthcare Community Worker
• Front Desk Safety: A Program for Volunteers	• Pharmacy Security: Robbery response training

Crime prevention and personal safety classes

Special classes provide another opportunity to tell the protection story. Because medical care facilities employ a high female population, personal safety and self-defense classes remain popular. A broad range of security information can easily be included in special classes. Hosting a regular series of brown bag lunch and learn programs is popular with many organizations with employee-focused protection campaigns, as well as community outreach programs for seniors. Potential themes for these types of programs include those listed in Table 15-1. Marilyn Hollier, CHPA, CPP, director of security at the University of Michigan Hospitals and Health Centers, shared how her department demonstrates a concerted effort in making these programs available. They dedicate a specific week every year during their annual *Security Awareness Week* to bring further emphasis on such classes, as well as having open forums with hospital security leadership on how to remain safe on campus.

CRIME PREVENTION/EMPLOYEE AWARENESS ACTIVITIES

Professional security administrators must seek new ways and new opportunities to communicate with employees. This activity yields a high return for the time and money expended. There are various methodologies, outside of direct education, that the healthcare security program can utilize to solicit the assistance of staff members as well as increase their awareness of security-related issues. These components include healthcare facility newsletter submissions, security handouts and pamphlet distribution, departmental websites and seasonal and time sensitive e-mail broadcasts, security fairs, "Be On The Lookout" (BOLO) communications and other methods to communicate the security awareness/employee involvement message.

Newsletters

Medical center newsletters are good mediums for educating employees. Most newsletter editors are continually looking for new material. Because the protection effort is of general interest to employees, physicians and volunteers alike, the security administrator generally finds such material is welcomed. Security information may be published randomly or in a regular column such as a "Crime Prevention Corner." Newsletter themes often include personal safety issues at work and at home and include such topics as those identified in Table 15-2.

Security handouts

Color posters, trifold brochures, and table tents are common methods of educating employees about security. In medical centers, posters have traditionally been used for safety messages, but

Table 15-2 Security Newsletter Topics

Crime Prevention Corner Newsletter Themes	
• Auto Theft Prevention	• Protecting Kids on the Internet
• Robbery: Prevention and Reaction	• Home Security
• Planning for Emergencies	• Personal Identity Protection
• Bicycle Safety	• Halloween Safety
• Vacation Security Checklist	• Back to School Safety
• Crime Prevention for the Elderly	• Crime Prevention: At Home and at Work
• Burglary Prevention	• Responding When a Person Has Autism

they can be used to convey other messages as well. Visitor and staff elevators are often used for posting information. In other programs, bulletin boards located near the cafeteria or other common public corridors have been dedicated to the security department for posting of security awareness information.

The distribution of handouts and use of table tents in the cafeteria are excellent tools to remind employees of the importance of general security awareness during seasonal times, such as the holiday season, New Year's, or daylight savings time. Figures 15-1, 15-2, and 15-3 provide three examples of handouts and table tents that can be used in the protection program to keep security awareness at the forefront in the minds of healthcare employees.

Websites and e-mail broadcasts

Security events or information relevant to the entire campus can be shared via a link to the healthcare organization's internal website or via an e-mail distribution list. A dedicated protection program website can be used to:

- Remind employees how to report a security incident or suspicious activity
- Keep the healthcare community abreast of new developments/improvements made in the security program
- Help prepare employees for upcoming Joint Commission surveys and potential security-based questions frequently asked by surveyors
- Identify and report on specific security department performance standards, goals and improvement initiatives
- Provide answers to frequently asked questions in the security program, such as the role of an employee in a bomb threat, how to obtain a replacement identification badge, etc.
- Offer a biography of the security staff
- Present status reports on security initiatives that are being carried out in the facility, such as new video surveillance installations, results of employee surveys, changes to parking policies, etc.
- Describe the role and responsibility of each employee with the hospital in respect to maintaining a safe and secure environment
- Provide a calendar of security-awareness education programs offered and when
- Establish links to community resources related to security and crime prevention, and other criminal justice-related agencies and materials.

DENVER POLICE

CRIME ALERT

Don't be the victim of a car break-in!

Car break-ins (Theft from Motor Vehicle) are the number one reported crime in Denver. These crimes occur at all times of the day and night in every part of the City.

TIPS TO REDUCE THE CHANCE OF BECOMING A VICTIM OF A CAR BREAK-IN

- **Never leave valuables, or what may be viewed as valuable, in plain sight in your car**. Items commonly stolen are GPSs, iPads, laptop computers, sporting equipment, bicycles, golf clubs and tools. Even an empty box or gym bag may look tempting enough for a thief to break into your car. Charger chords even have value to thieves.
- **Never leave any keys in the car, even a spare set.**
- **Never leave your vehicle with the windows rolled down.**
- **Always lock your car. Even when the vehicle is parked in a locked garage.**
- **Always try to park in a well-lit, high-traffic area.**
- **Never leave personal information or documents in your vehicle (including vehicle registration). If you leave your garage door opener and your address in the car, a car break-in can lead to a home burglary or worse.**
- **Consider installing an audible alarm system.**
- **Report the crime. If you are victim of this crime in Denver, please call 720.913.2000.**
- **Report suspicious activity. You can remain anonymous if you so choose. Denver Police Department non-emergency telephone number is 720.913.2000. For emergencies dial 911.**

www.facebook.com/denverpoliceD6

FIGURE 15-1

Crime Alert.

(Courtesy of Denver Police Department.)

FIGURE 15-2

Make Security Awareness a New Year's Resolution.

Father Time is Rolling Back His Clock Again.

with Daylight Savings time ending, you'll be spending extra time in the dark

If You're Parked In A Remote Area, Walking Alone, or Feel Uncomfortable; Call Security For An Escort.

We're Here When You Need Us.

FIGURE 15-3

Reminder to staff about using escorts with daylight savings time ending.

Some healthcare protection departments post the CAP Index map and site data (see Chapter 9, "The Security Uniform and Defensive Equipment," Figure 10-6) on the internal website to enhance employee awareness of the rate and types of crime occurring in the neighborhood surrounding the facility, while others post annual police crime statistics. In general, the information posted is limited only to the creativity of the healthcare security administrator, and their desire to communicate with employees of the organization.

Jefferson University Hospitals has created a dedicated safety and security page on their organizational website specifically targeted to their patients. Based on the premise of helping their patients feel safe during their stay or visit, the site talks about how to contact hospital security, provides a brief overview of how important maternity and infant security is to the hospital, the use of safety drills and use of the term "Speak Up" to help employees, patients and visitors know their role in keeping a safe environment. The hospital has created an acronym based on Joint Commission patient-safety recommendations identified in Box 15-2.

Seasonal and time-sensitive e-mail broadcasts are effective tools during holiday or vacation seasons reminding employees of good security awareness habits and techniques. Additionally, e-mail broadcasts can be used effectively after a serious security event at the facility, or in the surrounding neighborhood, to help with rumor control and to foster good employee relations. A healthcare facility in Aurora, Colorado used e-mail notification to bring employee and staff attention to a disturbing trend of auto thefts/break-ins occurring on campus. In the e-mail message, security leadership was able to share a common thread for each of the incidents that included doors being left unlocked or keys found in the ignition. The use of these e-mail broadcasts helped put an end to the events.

Figure 15-4 is an example of BOLO communication published by Rose Medical Center in Denver that provided a description and photos of a thief who had been spotted walking the hallways and looking into patient rooms. The BOLO was shared with other hospitals where it was found this same individual was seen at another hospital in town. The communication eventually led to the capture of this perpetrator at a third hospital.

For both websites and e-mail broadcasts, the protection professional should review all available content with the healthcare facility's public relations and/or marketing department prior to posting or dissemination. This will help ensure inappropriate content is not shared inadvertently or undue concern created due to the perception of personal safety on campus.

BOX 15-2 SPEAK UP

Speak Up

S: Speak up if you have questions or concerns, and if you don't understand, ask again. It's your body and you have a right to know.

P: Pay attention to the care you are receiving. Make sure you're getting the right treatments and medications by the right healthcare professionals. Don't assume anything.

E: Educate yourself about your diagnosis, the medical tests you are undergoing and your treatment plan.

A: Ask a trusted family member or friend to be your advocate.

K: Know what medications you take and why you take them. Medication errors are the most common healthcare mistakes.

U: Use a hospital, clinic, surgery center or other type of healthcare organization that has undergone a rigorous on-site evaluation against established state-of-the-art quality and safety standards, such as those provided by The Joint Commission.

P: Participate in all decisions about your treatment. You are the center of the healthcare team.

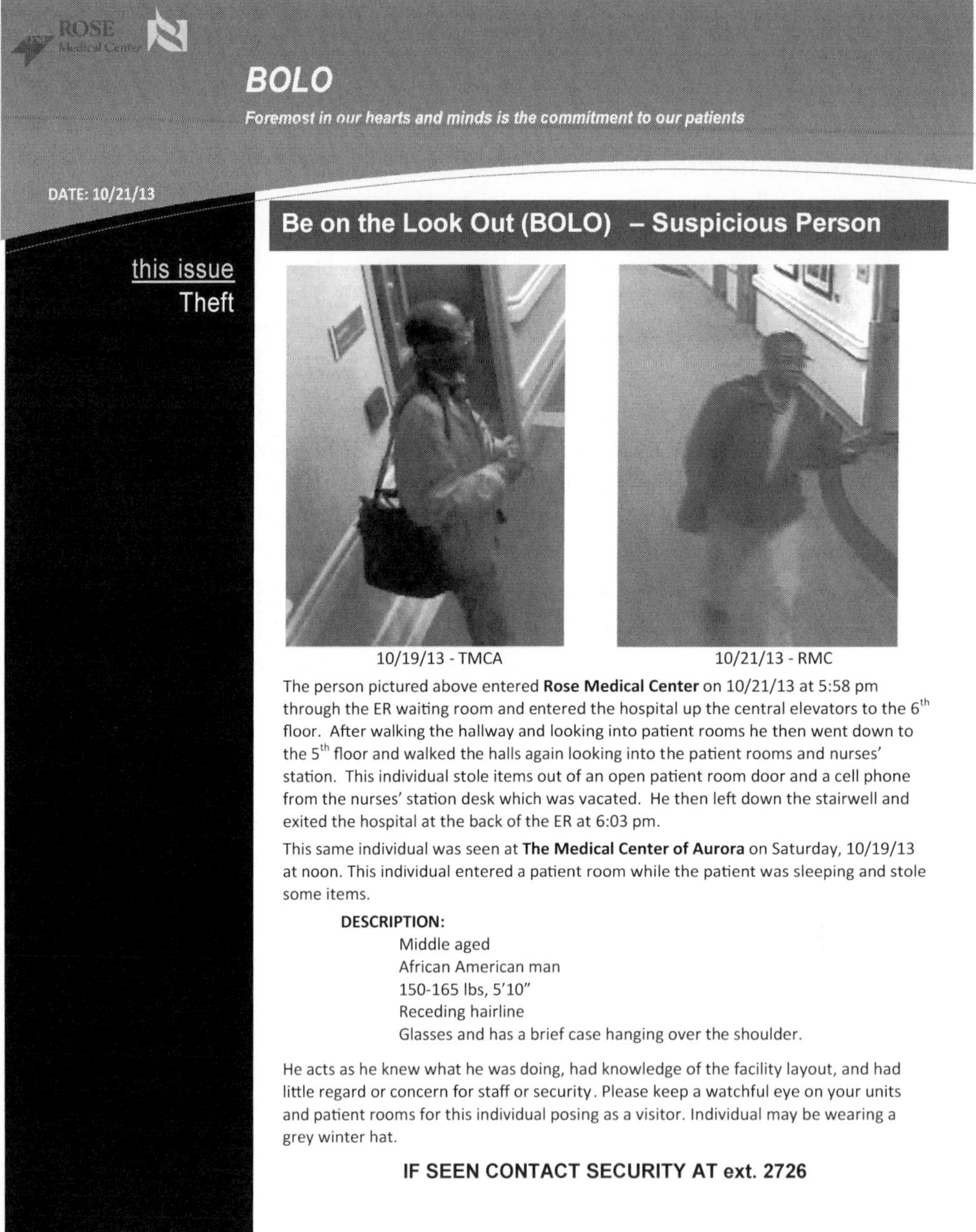
ROSE Medical Center

BOLO

Foremost in our hearts and minds is the commitment to our patients

DATE: 10/21/13

this issue

Theft

Be on the Look Out (BOLO) – Suspicious Person

10/19/13 - TMCA

10/21/13 - RMC

The person pictured above entered **Rose Medical Center** on 10/21/13 at 5:58 pm through the ER waiting room and entered the hospital up the central elevators to the 6th floor. After walking the hallway and looking into patient rooms he then went down to the 5th floor and walked the halls again looking into the patient rooms and nurses' station. This individual stole items out of an open patient room door and a cell phone from the nurses' station desk which was vacated. He then left down the stairwell and exited the hospital at the back of the ER at 6:03 pm.

This same individual was seen at **The Medical Center of Aurora** on Saturday, 10/19/13 at noon. This individual entered a patient room while the patient was sleeping and stole some items.

DESCRIPTION:

Middle aged
African American man
150-165 lbs, 5'10"
Receding hairline
Glasses and has a brief case hanging over the shoulder.

He acts as he knew what he was doing, had knowledge of the facility layout, and had little regard or concern for staff or security. Please keep a watchful eye on your units and patient rooms for this individual posing as a visitor. Individual may be wearing a grey winter hat.

IF SEEN CONTACT SECURITY AT ext. 2726

FIGURE 15-4

Example of a hospital-issued BOLO.

(Courtesy of Rose Medical Center.)

Social media

Security programs are beginning to realize the benefits of social media platforms like Twitter, Facebook and LinkedIn. Just as many of the organizations they serve have embraced these mediums as vehicles for staff, industry and community engagement, so too have the programs and services within the organizations. In the areas of security awareness, crime prevention and security program profiling and branding, social media offers much promise for an increasingly technology-savvy healthcare staff and physician audience, to augment and in some cases replace some of the education and communication methods described elsewhere in this chapter.

Other considerations

Other methods used to keep security issues front and center in the healthcare environment include town hall meetings organized by administrative or nursing leadership. Participation in these meeting allows security leadership an opportunity to highlight specific information and address issues directly.

The security fair is another popular crime prevention activity. These fairs have proven quite successful and generally draw more than 75% of the total employee workforce, when effectively organized and promoted. Trinkets carrying various security themes are effective to distribute to those who attend and send the basic security message back with the employee. Most common are whistles, pens, scratch pads, rulers, or magnets with the number to contact security. Door prizes and food always boosts attendance. In some organizations where the security program has been effectively "branded," the logo and/or name of the security department may be found on these giveaway items. A whistle giveaway has another benefit, as sound is a recognized deterrent to crime and finding lost victims. Whether implemented to reduce assaults or prepare for natural disaster, a safety whistle program is a cost-effective and efficient way to help protect employees and staff.

SECURITY KNOWLEDGE FOR EVERY HEALTHCARE EMPLOYEE

Security involves everyone in the healthcare facility. The eyes and ears of every employee are essential to the safekeeping of the healthcare environment.

An important aspect in the protection program is to involve healthcare employees and physicians in the communication and reporting of events or suspicious persons to the security department. Their involvement in customer service greetings, utilizing security escorts, parking lot security awareness, and knowing the employee's role in the basic crime prevention triangle are all critical aspects of an effective security program.

Reporting incidents

Employees should be requested and guided by organizational policy to report all missing property, acts of vandalism or other unusual occurrences to the security department without delay.

All calls to security should be answered by a staff member who remains in constant contact with patrolling security officers via two-way radio or other means of communication. When calling for security assistance, the healthcare employee should be encouraged to provide the following information:

- **NAME** – name of the requesting party
- **NUMBER** – where they are calling from
- **NEED** – the service needed and location of the request

This information should be requested in case additional contact with the requesting party becomes necessary. If a telephone is unavailable, employees should be instructed to observe and document suspicious persons or activities. Where possible, the employee should instruct a fellow staff member to locate a telephone or physically obtain security assistance. In selected work areas, duress alarm systems have been installed and can be used to summon security assistance in emergency situations. Employees in work areas where duress alarms are located should be instructed to activate the alarm only when it is safe to do so. Once the alarm has been activated, staff should follow up with a telephone call to security to verify the alarm, and provide the dispatcher (or PBX operator) with additional information.

The need for reporting security incidents was a difficult lesson to learn for one Midwestern hospital that experienced three sexual assaults in one night. Like many hospitals, the organization required visitors to sign in and wear temporary issued identification badges after standard visiting hours. But the organization did not strictly adhere to this policy. It was not unusual for nurses and other staff to see strangers walking the halls at all hours of the day; staff rarely challenged unauthorized persons or notified security of their presence. Unfortunately, the hospital had an assailant enter the hospital after visiting hours, who spent many hours becoming familiar with the layout and design of the facility. A CMS survey, conducted within weeks after the incident, found many deficiencies in safety and security, including a failing of the hospital to preserve patient rights, failing to ensure safety, and failing to follow its own policies. CMS gave the hospital just six weeks to address the deficiencies or risk having its Medicare participation status revoked.[2]

There are several lessons learned from this incident for the healthcare security administrator. These lessons include the importance of the hospital-issued identification, awareness of strangers versus suspicious persons, and the use of secret shoppers in the protection program to validate employee involvement, as well as the need for continual security awareness.

Customer service greetings

Awareness and greeting of all persons who frequent a unit or department is a very effective approach to involving employees in the crime prevention effort. The simple acknowledgement of others is a proven technique for deterring crime and unwanted behavior. If someone's identity or business is unknown, the employee should be expected to ask if they may help them. If an unsatisfactory reply to the question is received, or if suspicious activity is observed, or if the employee or volunteer is simply uncomfortable with approaching the person, they should be instructed to contact security immediately.

Security escorts

Every healthcare security department should provide a personal escort service for patients, physicians, and visitors. Security officers should be alert to anyone walking alone to a remote area, or encourage the use of escorts for anyone who "just feels uncomfortable." The education component should encourage requests for a security escort to include a few minutes lead time to minimize their wait and potential frustration. These one-on-one services for staff always present opportunities for security staff to demonstrate professionalism and a commitment to customer service, critical to the perception of security and safety for staff and physicians.

During major shift changes, security officers should normally be deployed to provide exterior protection, therefore reducing the necessity of individual escorts. Security education should inform employees of this basic deployment expectation, and encourage them to use the buddy system and walk with others.

Parking

Most healthcare campuses have parking areas to accommodate patients, staff and visitors with designated parking for each. Employees should be encouraged to always park in well-lit, heavily traveled parking areas, locking their doors and not leaving valuables in their vehicle. To minimize the opportunity for crime, employees should be encouraged to reduce the visibility of their personal property by utilizing the vehicle's trunk.

The protection and safeguarding of parking areas, including garages, is discussed in more detail in Chapter 23, "Parking and the External Environment."

The crime triangle

There are three basic elements necessary for a crime to occur: a criminal with the DESIRE and ABILITY to commit a crime, and a victim who provides an OPPORTUNITY for the crime. Healthcare facilities, by their very nature, can afford ample opportunities for crime. Figure 15-5 shows the interrelationship of the three basic elements of the crime triangle.

Involvement and participation of employees in security awareness activities can be one of the most cost-effective components of the healthcare protection program. Court recognized experts in healthcare security have routinely found the most frequent common denominator in hospital security lawsuits is employee apathy and inattentiveness. All too frequently, aberrant behavior is not recognized or brought to the attention of the security staff.[3]

Employees can do a great deal to reduce the opportunity for crime in the hospital. The most effective defense against crime is common sense, alertness, and basic precautions. Helpful tips for employees include:

- Always wear proper hospital identification. This identification helps patients, staff and security recognize authorized personnel.
- Be aware of your surroundings at all times. Ensure familiarity with regular employees in the work area and question unknown persons.

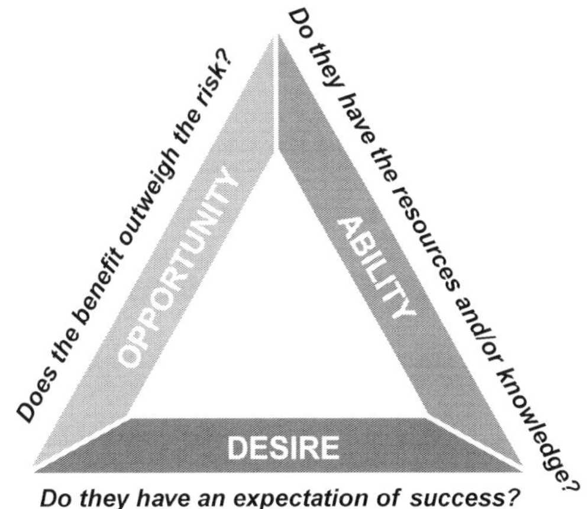

FIGURE 15-5

The crime triangle.

- Many losses are a result of carelessness. Maintain security of personal effects and hospital property. Whenever possible, carry only those items that you will need. Always minimize the amount of cash and number of credit cards you carry. If you bring a purse, never leave it in plain view—secure it in a locker or a lockable cabinet. Always secure storage cabinets and work areas when unattended and secure personal valuables even within a locked room or office.

PERCEPTION OF SAFETY AND EMPLOYEE ATTITUDES

Healthcare organizations have found it extremely important to determine employee attitudes concerning their work environment. A positive attitude of support and appreciation of the security effort is essential to providing a safe and secure environment. A common method to assess such employee attitudes is to hire an outside firm that specializes in employee surveys. These firms generally use standard questions, but allow the organization being surveyed to develop some specific attitude questions. When security questions are used in these surveys, they should be very specific. If a survey produces a slightly positive or a neutral response, it should be considered good, because many employees have been victims of events, have received parking violation notices, or have a general disregard for the authority security represents.

Another method of measuring the attitudes of employees is to conduct an in-house survey. One hospital obtained good results by approaching a local college and having the survey conducted by students as a class project. The class acted as a third-party surveyor and tabulated and analyzed the results. Common questions frequently include questions such as:

- I am concerned about violence in my workplace
- I feel safe in the parking areas and grounds
- My vehicle in <hospital> parking lot is safe from damage/theft
- I work the following shift:
- I am familiar with <hospital> Security policies and services
- Security responds to my requests for information or assistance in a timely manner
- Security presence is highly visible

Surveying the attitudes of employees must be an ongoing endeavor. Figure 15-6 is an example of a form used in one hospital in an ongoing effort to measure the performance of security personnel. In this program, completed Security Incident Reports and Security Condition Reports are utilized to send a random survey form to a recipient of a specific service or incident. This form is a prestamped mailer that is sent back to security for analysis and the formulation of improved service plans if appropriate.

Survey results are the basis for recognizing outstanding service, the need for training, and a review of operating procedures. This measurement tool can be very useful in comparing one facility with another. This type of performance measure fits in with Joint Commission accreditation standards and is ready-made to help security personnel develop a performance improvement program.

HOSPITAL WATCH

The term "hospital watch," which refers to an approach to hospital crime prevention, was adopted from the neighborhood watch programs promoted by local police agencies. Hospital watch can take on many different forms. It is a generic approach to involving the hospital community in observing, reporting,

Security Incident & Officer Response Evaluation

Hospital ____________________

Dept ____________________

Date ____________________

Officer(s) ____________________

____

Please complete the following evaluation to assist in evaluating the security officer's response

1 – did not meet expectation ***3 – met expectation*** ***5 – exceeded expectation***

Officer(s) Responded Promptly	1	2	3	4	5
Officer(s) Appropriately Addressed and was Effective in Handling Situation	1	2	3	4	5
Officer(s) Maintained Dignity & Respect of All Parties Involved	1	2	3	4	5

Other Comments

____

____

____

THANK YOU

Please drop off your evaluation in the mail or the Comment Box located outside of the Security Office

FIGURE 15-6

Security services performance survey.

and dealing with suspicious activity. Because there are no specific guidelines or program elements, the activities of this program are limited only by the ingenuity of the security administrator.

REFERENCES

1. National Crime Prevention Council. *Crime Prevention Coalition of America Fact Sheet*. Retrieved January 26, 2014 from http://www.ncpc.org/programs/crime-prevention-coalition-ofamerica/cpca%20fact%20sheet.pdf.
2. Sexual assaults lead to security overhaul. *Environment of Care Leader* 2009, May;**14**(9)(1):3–4.
3. Nesbitt WH. *Avoiding security litigation in a healthcare setting*. The Hospital Security Reporter; 2009, April 23. SMSI Online Newsletter. Retrieved June 11, 2009, from http://www.thehospitalsecurityreporter.com/articles/09_0423.html.

CHAPTER

INVESTIGATIVE ACTIVITY

16

The investigative function is a major component of any healthcare security program. It involves gathering and evaluating facts (including evidence) for either criminal or business (corporate) purposes. The techniques and purposes of a business investigation are much broader and more complex compared to the traditional law enforcement investigation. In addition to investigating crimes or alleged crimes, security personnel may gather information regarding the violation of organizational rules and regulations; a job applicant's background; alleged harassment; alleged discrimination; conditions that may lead to criminal violations; the need for new security controls and procedures; liability claims or potential claims; unsafe conditions; or evidence needed to prove or disprove certain allegations against the organization. Furthermore, a security investigator is in the best position to determine why a problem occurred and make recommendations regarding crime prevention and how to prevent the problem from reoccurring.

A law enforcement investigation, on the other hand, is conducted basically for the purpose of apprehending the perpetrator of a crime and obtaining the evidence required to successfully go forward in prosecution of the case. In short, healthcare security investigations are more varied and often more unique than law enforcement investigations. Also, the objective of an investigation may be different even when the healthcare organization has a strong policy of prosecuting those who violate the law; the end result may be an organization administrative remedy rather than a criminal court proceeding. Often, the investigator who has put in the time and effort and uncovered information regarding a perpetrator engaged in a criminal act would like to pursue prosecution. However, healthcare administrators must be allowed to make the decision regarding prosecution. The investigator's role is to gather and present facts to the administrator. While they may have influence over the decision to proceed criminally or not, they must be able to accept the ultimate decision, knowing their part in the process has been fulfilled.

The style of an investigation is shaped by organizational philosophy, the purpose of the investigation, risk to the organization, as well as the background and traits of the investigator. The organization security department will generally handle investigations unless there are major losses to the organization, and/or there is suspected white-collar crime or wrongdoing by administrative or upper echelon principals of the organization. When it is determined that an outside investigative agency should be hired to conduct an in-depth internal investigation, it is common to engage legal counsel to oversee the methods and processes of the investigation.

Investigations conducted by the healthcare organization may be performed for a variety of reasons and by a number of different departments or combinations of departments. As an example, Risk Management conducts investigations into operational matters such as patient care complaints, insurance claims administration, medical practices, and events required by accreditation or regulatory agencies. Healthcare organizations can even be fined by regulatory agencies for not investigating an alleged incident. Such was the case for a California hospital that was fined (sometimes referred to as an administrative penalty) for not promptly investigating an alleged sexual assault by a staff member against a patient. The fine was leveled by the California Department of Public Health, which licenses approximately 450 acute care hospitals throughout the state.[1] Some states have a duty to report a crime embedded in their criminal code. The state of Colorado in Section 18-8415 of its criminal code, "Duty to report a crime – liability for disclosure," states it is the duty of every corporation or person who has reasonable grounds to believe that a crime has been committed to report promptly the suspected crime to law enforcement authorities.

SECURITY VERSUS POLICE INVESTIGATION

The many types of security investigations required in the healthcare facility can be as complex as the function of providing medical care itself. The majority of conditions or incidents that require investigation are noncriminal, or of such minor criminal status that law enforcement agencies are virtually unconcerned with them. If every incident legally classified as a crime were reported to a law enforcement agency, a crime wave would appear to take place. The number of crimes reported to the police by an organization, and the community as a whole, is many times less than the actual number of crimes committed within any organization or community.

It is not unusual for the security department to be actively investigating the circumstance of a crime in parallel with the ongoing law enforcement investigation of the same incident. The objective of each investigation may be different or the objective may be the same. In any case, the security investigation must be conducted in such a manner that it does not interfere or jeopardize the criminal investigation being conducted by law enforcement. The best way for the security investigator to make sure there is no interference with the police investigation is to make contact with the officer in charge of the case and review the circumstances regarding the security investigator's involvement. Often the security investigator and law enforcement officer/detective can collaborate, resulting in a successful conclusion to the case.

CONCERN FOR MINOR CRIMES

The so-called minor crimes that are not reported to the police are of concern to a medical care facility for a variety of reasons. Even the incidents of minor crimes may give a healthcare organization a poor image to the public and staff. Further, such crimes may be only the surface of a larger crime problem, and thus always deserve an investigative response to evaluate the extent of a situation, and the potential need for an in-depth investigative process. Also, not all incidents reported to security are crimes. In fact, many property losses can be traced to the loss of accountability for the property, or false reporting rather than actual theft. Consider some specifics. An all-too-common problem in healthcare facilities is the loss of personal property of patients. Although many losses of patient property do occur, most incidents involve small items or cash in small amounts. While some of these items may be expensive, such as hearing aids and dentures, these losses are not reported to the police because it is simply unrealistic, given the limited amount of police resources, or because they reflect property lost as opposed to stolen. On the other hand, the loss of patient property is of major concern for the organization.

Another type of loss of little or no interest to law enforcement agencies is the disappearance of a key to a critical area of the facility. The police would not become involved unless the key is used to commit a crime. A significant part of a security investigator's work is determining whether a crime has actually occurred. An objective of the security investigator working the incident of the missing key would be to conduct an inquiry to ascertain whether the key was misplaced, lost, or stolen. If the facts point strongly to the latter, the investigator might recommend changing the locks or setting up a surveillance of the affected area. Neither of these alternatives would normally relate to law enforcement involvement.

Regardless of whether the security investigator is successful or not in resolving the problem, follow-up is good public/employee relations. It indicates to a victim that the organization cares enough to provide additional support to make every effort to resolve the problem. This is especially critical concerning patient valuables. A security investigator following up on missing patient property indicates to the patient that the organization cares, while also sending a message to internal thieves that all losses are investigated, potentially deterring future theft.

TYPES OF INVESTIGATION

We have already discussed the need and general aspects of healthcare security investigations. These investigations can be divided into operational investigations of security incidents and the more sensitive, or higher-level, investigations. The operational investigation typically begins when the security officer is dispatched to respond to a specific situation (vandalism, theft, property damage, disturbance, threatening behavior, etc.). The second type of investigation involves significant or suspected ongoing misconduct, such as embezzlement, false credentialing, worker's compensation deception, sexual harassment, drug abuse, fraud, and kickbacks. This type of investigation may involve utilization of outside investigators. There are various advantages to using an outside investigator, including added expertise, resources, and timeliness. An outside investigator tends to be more objective and impartial.

Planning for the process and authorization to conduct higher-level, and possibly sensitive, investigations should take place before the need arises. The healthcare security administrator should seek out at least one outside investigative resource as part of a sound strategic plan. It takes time to interview investigative firms, check out references, assess capabilities, explore pricing and methodologies, determine a "fit" to the healthcare environment, and to establish clear understanding of philosophies of both the buyer and the provider of investigative services. Selecting a vendor in advance of the specific need will save time when services may be required on a short notice. In any investigation, the goals and objectives of both the outside investigative organization and the healthcare organization must be mutually agreed upon and clearly documented. Details to be agreed upon include projected costs, reporting protocols, timetables, and the processes for maintaining control of the investigation. The investigation should be continually monitored and managed with accurate and timely feedback relative to the investigative effort. It is certainly helpful if the outside investigator has prior experience in dealing with the protocols, policies, and procedures of the healthcare environment. The IAHSS has general investigative guidelines that it has developed for healthcare organizations investigating security incidents, alleged crimes, and other situations that may involve injury, loss or damage.

03. 01. INVESTIGATIONS (GENERAL)

Statement

Healthcare Facilities (HCFs) will develop procedures for investigations addressing alleged crimes, injury, losses, or damage, and for administrative purposes.

Intent

a. Investigative actions refer (s) to the impartial observation and gathering of facts and information.

b. Facility staff, including security, may engage in investigative activity for a variety of purposes and situations including:

  1) Determining if there is criminal activity
  2) Determining the cause of safety related incidents/accidents
  3) Auditing of control procedures
  4) Determining suitability of applicants seeking or continuing employment
  5) Reducing the likelihood of future incidents
  6) Assisting law enforcement or other public safety and regulatory agencies
  7) Assisting other internal departments in noncriminal investigations

c. Facility staff conducting investigations should have a basic understanding of how to conduct and pursue a criminal, civil, or administrative investigation.

d. The investigation of an incident should be undertaken as soon as practicable. Procedures should be in place to preserve an incident scene and other evidence when needed.

e. Security investigations of a criminal nature should be conducted in a manner that does not interfere or jeopardize a law enforcement investigation.

f. The depth and complexity of an investigation will depend on the frequency and severity of an incident or combination of incidents.

g. Investigation of security incidents may include overt, covert, or a combination of these activities.

h. Security incident reports should be completed prior to the end of the officer's shift.

i. The investigation or control of an incident may be ongoing and, through established procedure, may be continued by other security staff.

j. There should be a defined process for the review of security incident reports. These reports should be reviewed for completeness and to determine the need for further investigation.

k. There should be a policy for sharing investigative findings with internal or external departments and agencies.

Approved: November 2007
Last Revised: June 2014

INCIDENT INVESTIGATIONS/TWO PHASES

Incident investigations generally have two distinct phases. The first phase, generally referred to as the *preliminary investigation*, is usually conducted by field security officers. This first phase is sometimes referred to as the *initial investigation*, which may resolve the matter and thus there will be no need for further investigative activity. A preliminary investigation is conducted up to the point at which postponement of further investigation will not jeopardize the successful conclusion of the case. O.W. Wilson, one of the greatest police executives the U.S. has known, defined preliminary investigation over a quarter of a century ago. It is a definition that remains current today. He defined it as follows:

P Proceed to scene with safety and dispatch
R Render assistance to injured
E Effect arrest of perpetrator
L Locate and identify witnesses
I Interview complainant and witnesses

M Maintain scene and protect evidence
I Interrogate suspects
N Note all conditions, events, and remarks
A Arrange for collection of evidence
R Report fully and accurately
Y Yield responsibility to investigators or higher authority[2]

One of the most important considerations during a preliminary investigation is to proceed to the scene as quickly as possible. How well the preliminary investigation is conducted, and how quickly it is initiated, can have a direct effect on the outcome of the investigation. A prompt arrival at the scene by the security officer and/or investigator enhances the possibility that evidence will not be tampered with or destroyed. Witnesses will still be present, and they will have less chance to compare what they saw, which in turn decreases the possibility for error. Thus, a security officer responds to the incident scene to conduct an inquiry and take appropriate action. Security officers should remember that a report is only the documentation of action taken and the collection of information (facts) concerning the incident.

The second phase of an investigation is the *follow-up investigation,* or in some cases it is simply referred to as a continuing or ongoing investigation. It may begin immediately after the preliminary investigation, or it may be days before further action is taken. Regardless of the time interval, a follow-up to the initial report is generally required. However, a supervisory review may be all that is required of some reports, at which time the investigation is termed inactive or closed. In small security organizations, the follow-up activity may be conducted by the same person who handled the preliminary investigation, or the security administrator may also function as the department investigator. An objective of the follow-up investigation is to obtain additional information, and at the same time, it creates a favorable image for the public and staff. Another aspect of the follow-up investigation is it may shorten the preliminary investigation required and allows security field personnel to return to patrol, and available for further service to the organization.

Follow-up investigators generally have access to records, files, and sources of information not available to preliminary investigators. Because follow-up investigation is centralized, specialized techniques may be used and past incidents that may have a relationship to the incident under investigation may be analyzed.

INTERRELATIONSHIP OF THE PRELIMINARY AND FOLLOW-UP INVESTIGATION—A TYPICAL CASE

A patient informs the charge nurse that she cannot locate her expensive gold bracelet that was in her bedside cabinet at 5:30 p.m. It is now 10:30 p.m. The charge nurse notifies security, and a patrol officer is dispatched to conduct a preliminary investigation. After a thorough search of the room and the soiled linen collection area, the officer completes the report, addressing all the basic questions (basic interrogatories of who, what, when, where, why, and how). Several possibilities exist concerning the whereabouts of the bracelet:

(1) The patient misplaced the bracelet, even though the search failed to locate the property.
(2) An employee found the bracelet and has, against hospital policy and procedure, locked it up for safekeeping.

(3) An employee, another patient, or a visitor has stolen the bracelet.
(4) The patient's family or friends have taken the bracelet home for safekeeping.
(5) The bracelet was discarded unknowingly and accidentally by the patient or staff.
(6) The bracelet was checked in as patient valuables.
(7) There was never any bracelet in the patient's possession.

At this particular hour of the evening, the security officer does not have access to admitting records. Good judgment would preclude contacting the family late at night. The police would probably not be called until most of the above possibilities could be eliminated, providing a greater indication a theft had, in fact, occurred. Thus, the security officer must gather all the information readily available and forward the report to the appropriate person to initiate the follow-up investigation. The follow-up investigator should start by recontacting the patient. The investigator can obtain additional information from the patient, and can find out whether the bracelet had been located between the time of the preliminary investigation and this follow-up investigation. This contact allows the investigator to begin with current information or, if the bracelet was found, to close the complaint. The follow-up contact assures the patient that the hospital is concerned, and that the matter is not being ignored.

RESULTS OF INADEQUATE INVESTIGATIONS

Poor investigative response to patient involved security incidents leads to the frequent complaint that patient concerns are not heard and the hospital does not really care. In some facilities, the nurse prepares an unusual-incident report instead of directly notifying security. This is an unacceptable practice and generally results in a poor reporting process. In this respect, the process is not timely and such reports generally lack sufficient information to effect a successful resolution of the matter. In the case of the missing bracelet, it is doubtful whether the nurse-prepared report would include the last time the watch was seen, whether the patient received visitors during the ensuing time period, and the identity of unit personnel on duty during this time period. Unless unduly delayed, the unusual incident report passes through the nursing service office and reaches the appropriate administrative person several days later. Frequently, no follow-up action is taken and the report is simply filed for statistical purposes. Most hospitals have patient representatives and these individuals are often the first responders to patient complaints such as missing patient property. The patient representative often does an excellent job of gathering the initial details and is a good resource regarding follow-up investigations by security personnel. The unusual incident report may also end up with the risk manager, who again generally lacks the resources for a thorough follow-up. In many facilities today, the incident would be documented in two incident management streams. The nurse would complete the unusual incident report as part of the patient quality process, but also call security to attend and document and, as necessary, investigate the incident.

In short, security should be notified and conduct an investigation and prepare a report in a timely manner. It is important the first security responder to an incident has a major responsibility to capture information that may be forever lost with the lapse of even a minimal amount of time. The importance of this information may not "register" with the investigator at the time, but may be very important at a later time. In this respect, sketches prepared and/or photos taken at the time of the incident can be helpful. A brief example of a photograph taken that proved invaluable involved the fall of a visitor down the steps of a front entrance to the facility. The visitor received injuries that required extensive surgery and the significant loss of income from being unable to work. In the litigation case that followed many months later, the visitor claimed there was an excessive buildup of snow and ice on the steps. A photo taken of the steps at the time of the initial investigation showed dry and clean steps. The photo was a critical component of the preliminary security incident report.

PATTERNS OF WRONGDOING AND SUSPECTS

A major reason to encourage employees to report all incidents of wrongdoing is that sometimes incidents cannot be resolved individually, but they can be resolved in combination. Skilled investigators seek out and recognize emerging patterns that point to suspects or the probability of a repeated act. The investigation then shifts somewhat from gathering facts to setting up a plan of action, which may include surveillance or even a covert operation. Investigators often use electronic equipment (covert video surveillance and recording, alarm devices, etc.) and various dusting powders or ultraviolet light techniques. The "planting" of an object that has been the subject of theft is also a common method of resolving problems. A possible disadvantage to this procedure is it may induce a person to steal, but it may not be the person who has been responsible for the previous incidents under investigation. Regardless of the methods used, the resolution of incidents not only identifies perpetrators and detects system failures, but it also sends a strong message to future malefactors. However, when conducting a covert operation permission must be obtained from the administrative staff, which may sometimes include human resources.

NON-INCIDENT DRIVEN INVESTIGATIVE ACTIVITY

Not all security investigations involve incidents or suspected wrongdoing. Good security programs go a step further and conduct various other types of investigations to include applicant/promotional background checks, audits, spot checks, and various employee-related issues.

Background investigations

In some security systems, a criminal history record check is a routine step in the employment process. In others, security is called on to perform a background check only for particular positions, or when there are specific background questions that need to be explored in more detail. This type of investigative activity is almost always performed in collaboration with the Human Resources department.

Audits

Another type of investigation is sometimes referred to as an *audit*. One type of audit is a check of certain areas or activities to determine whether crimes are occurring, or to determine the level of security safeguards and their effectiveness. This type of investigation, as important as it may be to the organization and the safety of patients and staff, is difficult to accomplish. In many jurisdictions, the very nature of leadership of healthcare provider organizations is to "tread lightly" on the professional caregiver and clinical support personnel. The physician, the pharmacist, the laboratory director, and like persons expect, and enjoy, little oversight of their conduct and services from a security point of view. A case in point is the drug addictions of medical professionals who obtain "their supply" from the healthcare organization and often at the expense of pain and suffering of patients.

In the UK, however, the National Health Service (NHS) has taken a very different tack with regard to internal theft and fraud in the healthcare system. Establishing an NHS Counter-Fraud Service in 2000 with a relatively small group of investigators, part of NHS Protect, a division of the NHS Business Services Authority, this group has saved the UK health system over 70 million dollars as a result of their investigations.[3] In Scotland, a country with just over 5 million people, there are some estimates that fraud and theft from the healthcare system costs as much as $3.5 million dollars a day. The NHS Scotland Counter-Fraud Service has investigated and obtained convictions including staff stealing supplies and selling them on eBay, a physician writing prescriptions for drugs she kept for herself and a dentist claiming for precious metal crowns but using nonprecious metal on his patients.[4]

A recent Colorado report indicates that medical professionals with drug addictions increased by 20% in one year (2008–2009) and federal agents were investigating more thefts by Colorado healthcare workers as of July 2009 than they handled in total the previous year. Peer Assistance, a Colorado nursing assistance program, worked with 84 dentists, 84 pharmacists and 200 nurses in 2008—an increase of more than 20% over 2007.[5] More recently, an Australian study determined that drug theft and loss had risen there by about 20% in 2010, over the previous year.[6]

An audit team of an organizational auditor, a nursing supervisor and a security investigator is essential to providing for the security and safety of the organization, the patient, and the staff relative to the area of drug control. It cannot be left to the Director of Pharmacy alone to maintain control of drugs throughout the organization, and particularly at the point where drugs are actually administered.

Another form of the security audit is to determine whether policies and procedures are being followed. Simply having a policy and procedure does not insure compliance. In fact, noncompliance, or partial compliance, may be false security.

In addition, investigators examine procedures or operational areas to determine whether there is potential for loss, and if established procedures are being followed to prevent or mitigate a loss occurrence. Often the investigative audit results in a change of policy and procedure to improve efficiency or to raise the level of operational security. This broad area of investigation activity can also be labeled as an investigative audit. If a major loss was uncovered during such an audit, and an arrest resulted, it would merely be a byproduct of the audit investigation from the organizational point of view. An investigative audit is a major activity of a sound preventive security program.

Spot-checks and general surveillance

Spot-checks of operations and investigative surveillance activities are closely related to audit investigations. These types of investigations are almost endless in nature and limited only by the imagination and resourcefulness of the investigator. Care should be taken that the scope of the activity is coordinated with the internal auditors, even when security spot-check procedures are not considered within the general scope of internal auditing. An example of this type of activity is to conduct unannounced checks on incoming shipments of goods and supplies. One security investigator decided to check a fuel oil delivery being made to the facility. He discovered that the load was short by more than 200 gallons, and subsequent investigation revealed that the driver had been making short deliveries for some time. Because no one had ever checked the metering device to see that it registered zero before unloading, the driver was free to unload some of the fuel before he arrived at the facility.

A surveillance investigation is usually initiated as a result of information received, or it may be just an investigative "fishing expedition." One hospital security department plants purses or wallets in trousers in high-loss areas. The wallet inside the purse or trousers is attached to a magnetic contact/transmitter. A signal is transmitted to an FM radio receiver when the contact is broken. Another method is to use a light-sensing device to activate the transmitter. This device is particularly useful in moneyboxes, desk drawers, and file cabinets. General surveillance of critical areas can also produce results. Although no losses had been reported in the facility, one investigator set up a surveillance of a general storeroom and discovered that an employee was helping himself to supplies after hours with a key that was not known to be in existence. Loading docks and trash collection areas are also good places for the general surveillance investigation. Alarms and video surveillance systems have generally taken the place of the need for staffed surveillance, unless an apprehension is a likely possibility, or there is a need to intercede where necessary, to prevent injury or significant loss of property.

Unemployment and worker's compensation investigations

There is a great need for the investigation of fraud in unemployment benefits and worker's compensation. Healthcare organizations should become more involved in these areas as government administration and controls are largely ineffective. The proven cases of unemployment fraud may amount to less than 1% of actual cases. These frauds have cost organizations, and ultimately patients, billions of dollars. The cost of fraudulent worker's compensation claims is many times that of fraudulent unemployment claims. In the worker's compensation claim, not only do employees receive their wages, but also there are physician charges and other unnecessary medical care treatment costs.

INVESTIGATOR ATTRIBUTES

Good investigators have a firm understanding of human relations, a natural aptitude for inquiry, and are intrigued by the investigative process. Investigations always offer a challenge and often succeed or fail in direct relation to the investigator's competence and enthusiasm. A good investigator must have traits as outlined in Box 16-1:

It is generally accepted by the security industry that all investigations are limited by the investigator's reasoning ability. One of the greatest threats to reasoning ability is a lack of objectivity. The

BOX 16-1 DESIRABLE TRAITS OF A SUCCESSFUL INVESTIGATOR

- The ability to remain objective
- Energy and alertness
- Knowledge of the law
- The ability to set realistic objectives
- A methodical nature
- Knowledge of human nature
- Observation and deduction skills
- The ability to maintain meaningful notes
- The ability to interview and interrogate

excessive influence of subjective feelings, prejudices, or interpretations also severely affects reasoning. Although it is not possible to be 100% objective, professional investigators are able to exert the necessary control over subjective influences, to understand any effect they may have on the investigation. The investigative process must be considered to be a major element of the successful protection program. The investigative capacity of many current healthcare security programs needs to be upgraded. Administrators and investigators should remember that an investigator is called on to determine the facts and not necessarily to solve the problem. Investigators must at all times conduct investigations within the guidelines set out by the law, and they must always exercise proper employee relations procedures and conduct. The investigation must be conducted to avoid:

- Compromising a criminal case
- Compromising an arbitration
- Creating a damage action
- Violating the law

In respect to violating the law, the areas of entrapment, invasion of privacy, eavesdropping, and self-incrimination deserve careful attention. Legal action against investigators and the organizations they represent is always a situation to be avoided.

INTERVIEWING AND INTERROGATION

In most investigations, the interviewing process consumes over 90% of the total investigative effort. Often the incident or situation is successfully resolved through the interview process alone. Interviewing is intended to gather basic information, facts, and background for leads to further exploration. The interview involves victims, caregivers, witnesses and others who may have information bearing on the incident being investigated. The interview also has a purpose to obtain information relative to policy, procedures, protocols, and processes, which may lead to more in-depth follow-up as the investigation continues. An interview should be conducted in a friendly, businesslike tone and certainly not adversarial or overly aggressive. It is simply a matter of asking questions of willing subjects in order to obtain information.

The process of interrogation enters into a relationship with the subject that has sometimes been referred to in initial stages as "adversarial interviewing." An interrogation, unlike the interview, is designed to elicit information from a subject who is a prime suspect or a party that knows pertinent facts and does not wish to disclose the information for a variety of reasons. It is the uncooperative nature of the subject that distinguishes the interrogation from the interview.[7]

UNDERCOVER (COVERT) INVESTIGATIONS

Undercover operations are widely used in the healthcare setting. The most common activity is to infiltrate an area where a specific or suspected problem exists. The concept of utilizing an undercover operative, or concealed security equipment, in a patient care facility may seem extreme to some and somewhat frightening to others, but professional security administrators consider it a necessary business procedure. The IAHSS operational guideline on Covert Investigations can serve as a guide for healthcare security professionals.

03. 03. COVERT INVESTIGATIONS

Statement

Healthcare Facilities (HCFs) may require the use of covert investigations to identify persons or gather details about prohibited or illegal acts. Covert investigations may include the use of undercover operatives or electronic equipment.

Intent

a. Reasons for implementing covert investigations may vary greatly (asset protection, drug diversion, rule violations, or acts that may be harmful to the well-being or image of the HCF). The purpose of these investigations will be to collect information to be used as evidence to identify those involved and terminate prohibited activities posing a risk to the facility.
b. The decision to implement covert investigative techniques should not be made until it is determined more conventional methods would not be available or would not be effective.
c. Use of covert investigative equipment (such as hidden or disguised video surveillance) or other covert techniques must be conducted in compliance with applicable laws.
d. Consideration must be given as to whether the parties that enter an area under covert observation enjoy a reasonable expectation of privacy. Certain areas in a HCF (restrooms, locker rooms, changing areas, patient treatment areas, etc.) may be considered off limits in regards to covert investigative equipment.
e. Prior to installing any covert investigative equipment, security should determine that:
   1) The activity being investigated has a reasonable chance of being depicted
   2) There is a safe means of installing and removing such equipment (i.e., firewalls are not compromised and other fire detection/suppression/life safety equipment is not affected in any way)
   3) The investigative equipment is concealed so that all such equipment will likely remain undiscovered for the duration of the investigation
   4) There is a means of retrieving stored information from such equipment without others becoming aware of its presence
   5) There is a plan for receiving reports and storing information to maintain confidentiality
f. The HCF should develop a policy for implementation of covert investigations including the following:
   1) Designated individuals that can approve such investigations/ installations
   2) Requiring participants to agree to not disclose the investigation
   3) Evidence obtained during a covert investigation will be considered property of the HCF until such time that it is turned over to a law enforcement agency or other designated recipient. Such evidence will be considered confidential and will not be viewed, disseminated or discussed with any individuals, departments or agencies without proper approval.
   4) Findings regarding the investigation and recommendations will be documented and forwarded as appropriate
   5) A plan for termination of the investigation in the event that it is discovered or becomes dangerous

Approved: April 2008
Last Revised: October 2011
Reviewed: December 2013

The covert investigation is intended to protect trustworthy and faithful employees, and to ferret out those who are detrimental to the organization. The undercover operation may indeed seem extreme; however, so are the stakes and the responsibility to properly manage the healthcare organization. A successful undercover investigation requires as few people as possible in the organization to know about the operation. Department heads and supervisors generally should not be involved in the plan, or privileged with the information, that an operative or surveillance equipment has been placed in their department. In a few cases, it may be essential that the department head be part of the process, in order to obtain an open and proper position for the operative, special circumstances, or the type of information being sought. More often than not, however, information leaks begin with the department head and result in a wasted effort and a negative impact on organization staff. A major objective of a covert operation is to severely limit the number of people who know about the operation. The failure to comply with this simple concept has compromised more operations than any other single factor. Generally, if more than two people in the organization, other than the security director, know about the investigation, it should not be initiated, and if it is already underway, serious consideration should be given to aborting the project.

In addition to specific investigations, undercover operatives are used as a check on operations to determine whether security policies and procedures are meeting their objectives. It is a method to determine whether the funds spent for security are providing the desired results. Information derived from the investigation need not be negative; operatives who find that all is "going well" produce positive and valuable management feedback. After operatives have done their job in one department, they can transfer to another department to continue the audit operation. Department transfers are sometimes easier to effect than bringing the operative into the organization as a newly hired employee.

When an organization commits itself to an undercover program, it must be prepared to fund the program for a considerable period of time. Many undercover programs fail because results were expected too soon. This is especially true of operatives working on a significant problem where those involved are extremely cautious. New people are always treated with a certain amount of suspicion, and operatives must slowly build positive relationships with fellow employees. Of course, the skill and competence of the investigator play a significant part in how much time is required. In large organizations, newly hired security personnel are a possible source of undercover operatives. There are, however, two basic disadvantages to this approach. No matter how thorough the background check and the selection process, the abilities of new employees are always unknown. Another drawback is that not everyone is suited for undercover investigation activities. The wrong operative may produce not only an ineffective investigation, but also cause embarrassing problems for the organization. Another source of undercover personnel is the loan of an officer or investigator from another security healthcare organization. The mutual aid approach can be economical, and the abilities of the personnel are not as unpredictable as may be the case with a newly hired employee. Loaned and newly hired operatives can do a good job, because they have more at stake than do operatives provided by a firm from the outside that will move the operative to other unrelated assignments at another organization. The new hire is seeking a good employment beginning, as well as continued employment. The employee on loan seeks positive feedback on his undercover work to reach his current employer.

Undercover operatives should be required to report their activities and observations periodically. This communication should take place at a location outside the organization, and is best accomplished in face-to-face debriefing meetings rather than over the telephone. Daily logs of all activity should also be required. Information collected by the operative should be broad in nature, and should include any information that might help improve organizational management. To be more specific, information on morale, how well a new policy was received, the falsification of time records, cleanliness, and other items that will help the organization be more efficient should be included in the feedback information. Reports should also include positive information on which systems are functioning effectively.

REFERENCES

1. Clark C. *13 hospitals fined for mishaps, never events*. HealthLeaders Media; 2009, May 20. Retrieved May 20, 2009, from http://www.healthleadersmedia.com/content/233406/topic/WS_HLM2_QUA/13-Hospitals.
2. Wilson OW. *Police administration*. Location. McGraw-Hill Book Club; 1963. 282.

3. The Scotsman. *NHS's antifraud squad saves 43m pounds*. 2011, November 2. Retrieved on July 25, 2014, from http://www.scotsman.com/news/health/nhs-s-anti-fraud-squad-saves-43m-1-1976780.
4. The Scotsman. *Fraud costing NHS 2.2m pounds every day, says expert*. 2014, February 5. Retrieved on July 25, 2014, from http://www.scotsman.com/news/health/fraud-costing-nhs-2-2m-every-day-says-expert-1-3294424.
5. Blevins, Jason, "Addicts in Healthcare Professions Flock to Get Peers' Help", Denver Post, 7/23/09, p. 1A.
6. Jensen E. *Rise in drug thefts at hospitals by employees*. The Sydney Morning Herald; 2012, January 24. Retrieved on July 25, 2014, from http://www.smh.com.au/national/health/rise-in-drug-thefts-at-hospitals-by-employees-20120123-1qe44.html.
7. McDonough E. *Asking the hard questions*. Security Management; 2005, July. 88.

CHAPTER

SECURITY DESIGN CONSIDERATIONS FOR HEALTHCARE

17

Every healthcare security professional has a horror story they can tell about security design. In almost every instance, the security problem was created by a facility design that did not initially involve a knowledgeable security leader early in the process. The influence of the security professional was limited to the task of finding "the best security solution" to the problem created by the design. Tom Smith, CHPA, CPP, the former Director of Security and Police at the University of North Carolina Hospital and Clinics and now a healthcare security consultant, shared a real-life story of how a new system hospital was designed with a public stairwell that emptied foot-traffic into the middle of a department of higher risk, which was also a secured space. The challenges to correct this basic design flaw after the fact was disruptive and very costly, and points to the basic fact that when security is simply an afterthought, the safety of the healthcare facility and its employees, staff, patients and visitors is sure to suffer.

Designing security into a healthcare facility requires a complex series of trade-offs. Security concerns need to be balanced with many other design constraints such as accessibility, initial and life-cycle costs, natural hazard mitigation, fire protection, energy efficiency, and aesthetics. This chapter on security design considerations will emphasize the importance of having security program involvement early in the process, and in all phases of new construction and renovation projects. The goal is to not have security measures interfere with daily operations of the healthcare facility and be as unobtrusive as possible. The benefit of having security involved upfront and early in these projects allow for security applications to be cost effectively integrated into architectural, engineering and environmental design, thus creating a safe and secure environment for the delivery of patient care services. Security design needs to be part of an overall multi-hazard approach that considers the various building systems including site, architecture, structure, mechanical, and electrical systems. Ideally, this chapter will provide general security recommendations for the protection administrator to share with the design team, and influence construction or renovation at the earliest stages of site selection and design. The levels of protection provided by the recommendations shared in this chapter will help establish a foundation for all types of healthcare facilities, regardless of their geographic location. Many healthcare facilities will chose to supplement with additional and potentially more stringent mitigation steps. However, no healthcare facility should lessen the baseline level of protection described throughout this chapter, regardless of funding capability or services offered.

The security administrator plays a critical role in influencing the design process, and must tirelessly work to establish a seat at the various planning tables. As importantly, when security leaders become integrated with the design team, it can be a time consuming process, but one that will add significantly to the overall posture of safety inside the facility, and in the external reaches of the campus. The responsibility and opportunity to help shape safe building design, and the direction the healthcare organization takes with its overall security posture, is best established with the creation of a Security Master Plan (also referred to as the security strategic plan). This plan for security should serve as a strategic road map for the organization. Included should be a focused section on a design vision, including the use of security technology that is aligned with organizational philosophy and strategic objectives of the healthcare facility itself. The security design elements should be nestled into the overall healthcare facility design. Only in high-risk correctional security wings, or other high-risk departments such as nuclear medicine laboratories (also referred to as "hot labs"), will security be the primary driver of the design.

The savvy healthcare security leader will know healthcare organizations are being built with a hotel- or spa-like feel, to create a more comfortable atmosphere for patients, staff, and visitors while balancing the integration of security design into the healing environment. Hospitals in the past were designed more for staff, than the patient. They were set up to be more efficient for staff utilization, but today healthcare facilities are being designed to make the patient feel more comfortable, and meet the organization's mission of delivering quality patient care. The goal is to make people feel safe and feel comfortable because the overall experience of coming to a hospital is a stressful situation. This understanding is fundamental to having security design input embraced by architects, engineers, clinical planners and senior leaders, who lead and fund projects to improve the built environment.

In 2012, the International Association for Healthcare Security and Safety (IAHSS) released *Security Design Guidelines for Healthcare Facilities* which provide healthcare security leaders, and their organizations, with a tool to design and build security into renovations and new construction projects. These design guidelines are described in great detail throughout this chapter and have filled a major void in the understanding of effective security design principles exclusively for the healthcare industry.

SECURITY MASTER PLAN

In Chapter 4, security management planning was discussed in the form of two interrelated, but separate types of plans. The security management plan relating directly to the day-to-day protection program of the organization, and the security strategic plan or security master plan, which relates more to long term goals and program direction.

Tim Giles, the President of Risk/Security Management & Consulting, based in Atlanta, Georgia offers an excellent definition of the security master plan:

> A Security Master Plan is a document that delineates the organization's security philosophies, strategies, goals, programs, and processes. It is used to guide the organization's development and direction in these areas in a manner that is consistent with the company's overall business plan. It also provides a detailed outline of the risks and the mitigation plans for them in a way that creates a five-year business plan.[1]

While this definition references a five-year plan, this is not an absolute requirement. Many organizations use a dynamic 3 to 5 year planning cycle for their master planning processes. The key element and takeaway is that the planning is strategic; looking beyond the present here and now, painting a vision of where the protection program should be in the future, while providing strategic and tactical pathways to get there.

There seems universal agreement in the healthcare security realm that the starting point for any planning activity must be a risk assessment. "A security assessment lays the foundation for developing the master plan"[2] The strategic approach to risk includes an assessment of risk that identifies which threats and vulnerabilities are applicable or unique to the healthcare facility. These risks and vulnerabilities should then be prioritized and potential countermeasures explored. It should be stressed to non-security team members that all risk can never be eliminated, and that security measures must be selected based on acute risks in light of available resources. Risk and vulnerability assessments are discussed in Chapter 3, reinforcing the notion that the design of facilities, and the security program as a whole, should be appropriate to the site and the neighborhood. That means using features that can blend with the environment and serve security as well.

Thomas Engells, from the University of Texas Medical Branch in Galveston, identified a seven-step approach that includes the risk assessment process, to create the foundation for a holistic security master plan:[3]

1) Expectation Development and Approval
2) Vulnerability Analysis
3) Threat Identification
4) Asset Inventory
5) Risk Calculation
6) Risk Mitigation/Acceptance Strategies
7) Executive Committee Approval

For the security design to be credible, it must be risk appropriate to the environment. The initial planning and conceptual design phase should include a security risk assessment conducted not just by a qualified security professional, but ideally by a qualified healthcare security professional, who understands the challenge and uniqueness of creating a safe healing environment for care to be delivered. The consistent application of security safeguards that follow a risk assessment is particularly important as it relates to technology.

One of the biggest obstacles facing healthcare organizations pertaining to their use of today's security technology is the lack of understanding by the end user as to the capabilities of the system purchased. Frequently absent is the security master plan, which will articulate the underlying electronic security philosophies that have been put into place by the facility. The security master plan should provide operating principles that help select needed security system capabilities and in turn guide appropriate security staff training and policy development. Championed by the security administrator, operating principles should not be created in a vacuum. Their creation should include key constituents of the organization to include representatives from the emergency department, information technology (IT), human resources, facilities, and risk management.

Take for instance the building perimeter system; it includes life safety and emergency communications, with consideration of employee and public entrances. When addressing the perimeter of the building, a common methodology is to break down healthcare entries into three categories:

1. *Employee Entry*: For better separation between staff and visitors, entries should be electronically access controlled. Access control software could also be integrated with the payroll system for better employee accountability and an incentive to use the designated employee entry point.

2. *Life Safety Egress Doors*: Life safety code mandates the need for quick and uninhibited egress for employees, patients and visitors. These doors need access control system contacts that signal door ajar, held open door, and other situations.
3. *Patient Doors*: Patients and visitors need to enter where they are greeted and directed to their destination. Saint Joseph Hospital in Denver is perhaps a role model in using signage, greetings, customer service, and access control as an effective means of achieving a secured facility.

Once each door is defined, the appropriate technology can be applied to ensure it operates in accordance with the need. Patient/public access portals are typically open but need controls in place to secure in the event of an emergency. An open and inviting entry point is desirable as it sets a positive introductory tone for the facility, as well as a goal to help visitors and patients get to their destination quickly and without confusion.

However, employee entrances typically require a different approach. Securing these doors at all times and equipping them with bypass technology provides employees with necessary access but denies entry to unauthorized personnel.

The primary purpose of life safety focused doors is to provide emergency egress, not access. Equipping them with short-cycled closures and supervising them with door contacts (alarms) that inform security personnel of a breach can save thousands of dollars by foregoing the installation of expensive card readers and electronic hardware.

Simple but effective methods help guide the purchase and installation of security technology. In many instances, they augment security staffing but can, in some instances, substitute for staffing.

The security master plan should address replacement issues due to product expiration and the advent of new technology. The plan should address the integration of different systems, their compatibility, and how to maximize their capabilities. Like the facility master plan, the security master plan should be forward looking and anticipate future changes to the healthcare facility and the surrounding environment. The master plan should help prioritize security-specific needs and, once approved, align electronic security enhancements with the organizations capital budget structure.

Healthcare organizations operating without a security master plan often find frustration in obtaining needed financial resources and a "hodgepodge" approach of security technology can result—causing an undesired perception of security and the environment being created.

The security master plan, in its final format, affords additional protection as it helps document the "why" behind what is being done in the protection program. In the event of an adverse situation, the protection afforded by this alone is significant. It demonstrates the importance of personal safety and security to the organization and comprehensively documents all that has been accomplished in creating a secure organizational posture. It shows that security is considered important from the highest administrative levels.

IAHSS SECURITY DESIGN GUIDELINES

Recognizing the importance of design considerations to the healthcare security industry, the International Healthcare Security and Safety Foundation funded the development of the *Security Design Guidelines for Healthcare Facilities* in 2011. Their development was administered by the IAHSS Guidelines Council and led by the aforementioned Tom Smith. A multidisciplinary task force was assembled, composed of experts with experience in various aspects of design of healthcare facilities and development of healthcare security programs. The task force included participants with extensive expertise in design, healthcare security management, physical security, Crime Prevention through Environmental Design, regulatory agencies, emergency management, healthcare physical plant management and international representation, to ensure the design principles promulgated would be applicable outside the U.S.

An extensive vetting process was established for the Design Guidelines that included each guideline being closely scrutinized in draft form by the entire task force. Once consensus was achieved within the task force, the draft guidelines were sent to IAHSS members and other industry experts in the area of focus in survey format for feedback, with input received and incorporated by the task force following the same consensus approach. The IAHSS Guidelines Council conducted a detailed review, as is their function with the IAHSS *Security Industry Guidelines,* which are more operational in nature. The design guidelines are more prescriptive than the basic industry guidelines, focusing extensively on what should be done, with minimal emphasis as to the how or why. As a final vetting step, each guideline received approval by the IAHSS Board of Directors.

The Design Guidelines have been developed to assist security leaders, design professionals and planning staff to build security into each new construction and renovation project. By reasonably addressing security risks up front and early on during design, organizations can cost-effectively address the safety and security of new or renovated space. These steps will help reduce the potential for security features either not being designed into new space or added on as an afterthought, or becoming "value engineered" out, as projects face limited budget dollars. The intent of integrating these guidelines early in the design process is to emphasize the importance, incorporate the work into other aspects of the project and ultimately to avoid expensive change orders, retrofits or other liabilities incurred by the omission of appropriate planning for a safe and secure environment. These design guidelines reflect a clear security emphasis impacting a wide range of areas including safety, emergency management and regulatory compliance, and were published in 2012 by IAHSS.

Warmly accepted by the healthcare security profession upon release, many key elements of the design guidelines have been included in the 2014 Facility Guidelines Institute (FGI*) Guidelines for Design and Construction of Health Care Facilities.* FGI oversees the review and revision of the facility guidelines on a regular cycle with a consensus process by a multidisciplinary group of experts from the federal, state and private sectors. The Health Guidelines Revision Committee (HGRC) is a select multidisciplinary body of more than 120 clinicians, administrators, architects, engineers and representatives for authorities having jurisdiction that is convened to revise and update the *Guidelines for Design and Construction of Health Care Facilities.* In the U.S., The Joint Commission, many federal agencies, and authorities in 42 states use the FGI Guidelines either as a code or reference standard when reviewing, approving, and financing plans; surveying, licensing, certifying, or accrediting newly constructed facilities; or developing their own codes.

In a development that has tremendous implications for the healthcare security industry, two IAHSS members, Kevin Tuohey from Boston University and Boston Medical Center, and Tom Smith represent healthcare security as members of the 120-member subject matter expert body of the HGRC. Tuohey and Smith were key members of the IAHSS Design Guidelines Task Force and instrumental in submitting 42 comments, suggesting security and emergency management design language, to the HGRC in 2011. As a result of this work, the 2014 FGI Guidelines include language requiring security managers be involved in project teams (section 1.2-1.2), requiring a project security plan and identification of security and emergency management risks (1.2-3.8) and requiring a Safety Risk Assessment with seven components, one of which is security (Table 1.2-1). The development of the Safety Risk Assessment tool is being led by the Agency for Healthcare Research and Quality (AHRQ), with members of the IAHSS Guidelines Council involved in developing the security and elopement prevention component, alongside subject-matter experts from six other disciplines that impact the safe built environment:

1) Medication Safety
2) Patient Handling
3) Falls
4) Immobility
5) Psychiatric Injury
6) Infection Control

The FGI Guidelines (Section A1.2-3.8 of the Appendix) emphasizes the importance of the foundational security risk assessment: "… a security risk assessment addresses the unique security characteristics of a healthcare facility, including specific needs related to the protection of vulnerable patient populations, the security of sensitive areas, the application of security and safety systems, and the infrastructure required to support these needs. The assessment addresses external and internal security needs as well as security needs related to emergency management and response. Security requirements for construction, commissioning, and move-in vary according to the complexity and scope of services provided."

SECURITY DESIGN CONSIDERATIONS

New facility construction, expansion and renovation are continuous and almost nonstop in the healthcare environment. Designing security features into a new healthcare or renovated space from the beginning can improve safety and security, maximize utilization of human resources and lower operational costs while improving customer service and employee and patient satisfaction. The healthcare security administrator must be prepared to work with hospital engineers, project managers and/or architects to incorporate the most operationally efficient and cost-effective security design and technology for the project and budget. This includes defining the specific operating principles and philosophies of space utilization that drive specific technology application. It can be easy to miss or glaze over meaningful discussion about security in the early stages of design, as design team and unit leaders are so focused on designing their new space that security is not seriously considered until major decisions already have been established. Luckily for the healthcare industry, the adoption of the IAHSS Design Guidelines by the FGI will serve to reinforce the role of the healthcare security professional in these projects, and minimize security flaws that are designed into a project.

The philosophy of all security design considerations should be to help build an environment that is patient-focused and incorporates a strategic approach to reducing risk that identifies issues and defines priorities using the zone system, with both physical and psychological deterrence methods. The result should be an unobtrusive design that remains flexible to changing levels of threat and patient demographics. Understanding what services are being offered, and the patient population being served in the planning and design stage, is a critical component of security design. The type of patient will often drive the type of security. In suburban areas as an example, where much of the new hospital construction occurs, security may be "behind the scenes" and more focused on securing the perimeter than individual departments. Because of a different patient mix and neighborhood demographics, urban facilities may want to focus on creating an outward psychological deterrence and compartmentalize security sensitive areas within its own security perimeter.

Security design considerations should also consider the time frame the project will serve. Take, for example, an emergency department renovation projected to fulfill the organization's emergency care needs for the next 10 years. Two important considerations are the expected patient volumes (capacity), and the anticipated patient demographics projected for the new department, both at the time of opening and at the end of its projected life. Awareness and anticipation of these important considerations are critical to the security design considerations provided. This includes how the department is compartmentalized, what departments it should be adjacent to, (such as the radiology department), the location of triage, the potential use of metal screening and other considerations discussed in more detail in Chapter 21, "Areas of Higher Risk." Planning for each consideration is an important component. For instance, metal screening may not be desired initially, but changing patient demographics and volume may require future installation of this additional protection measure. Thus, the security administrator must consider: where the magnetometer will be located; how visitors, patients, and staff will be queued; and where confiscated and temporarily held items will be stored; these are just a few issues that need to be incorporated in the initial design (but not installed). Many healthcare organizations have found retrofitting the layout and design can be more than three times more expensive due to cost of pulling wire, and any need to move doors and other fixed walls. As a result, the future posture of security may be compromised due to the cost-prohibitive expense of the needed installation and retrofit. The forward-thinking security administrator will anticipate the future changes that may affect the overall security posture, and include them in their discussions with administrative leaders and architects in the design stage of the new construction/renovation planning.

The IAHSS General Guideline in the *Security Design Guidelines for Healthcare Facilities* establishes the background and framework for the subsequent guidelines covering specific areas of vulnerability, as outlined in the following section. This sets the tone for the inclusion of the security representative in all phases of the project, the creation of the security plan, and the coordination of the plan with Life Safety requirements and related regulations.

HEALTHCARE SECURITY DESIGN GUIDELINES – GENERAL GUIDELINE

Statement

Acts of violence, the potential for crime and terrorism, and the response to and mitigation of emergency incidents are significant concerns for all Healthcare Facilities (HCFs). A consideration of these concerns in the design of new or renovated HCFs presents an opportunity to implement and integrate security design elements that address the delivery of patient care services in a reasonably safe and secure environment, and allows for the cost-effective integration of security applications in architectural, engineering, and environmental design.

Intent

a. The IAHSS Security Design Guidelines are intended to provide guidance to healthcare security practitioners, architects, and building owner representatives involved in the design process in order to ensure that these best practices are considered and integrated, where possible, into each new and renovated HCF space.

b. This General Guideline establishes a background and framework for subsequent guidelines covering specific areas of vulnerability and should be utilized as a frame of reference and underpinning for incorporating appropriate security features into the design of all new construction and renovation projects. These guidelines include reference materials that provide further detailed subject matter elaboration.

Continued

HEALTHCARE SECURITY DESIGN GUIDELINES – GENERAL GUIDELINE—Cont'd

c. The initial planning and conceptual design phase of all newly constructed or renovated HCFs should include a security risk assessment conducted by a qualified security professional.

d. The size, complexity, and scope of services provided within an HCF can vary significantly. Security design considerations should be risk appropriate for the environment and function, while maintaining design consistency across the HCF. Design considerations should support patient care, provide a positive employee and consumer experience, proactively mitigate risk, and address real and perceived security concerns.

e. The development or continuation of institutional design standards related to the protection of vulnerable patient populations, the securing of sensitive areas, the application of security and safety systems—as well as the infrastructure required to support these needs—are issues best addressed early in the design process to be most cost-effective.

f. The design of HCFs should include consultation with the organizational security representative to identify, design, and provide protective measures. The project design team should prepare and submit plans to the project security representative for review and approval, including a comprehensive security plan that indicates a layered approach. This plan will include zones, control points, circulation routes, and physical security technology locations, and should be reviewed by the security representative prior to submittal to the planning, regulatory, and approval authorities. Integrating these design considerations into the development of submittal documents and through the commissioning process will help avoid costly security and safety retrofits.

g. The integration of these guidelines should be in collaboration with the entire design team. Design considerations should coordinate the security plan, the building Life Safety plan, and the regulations that have jurisdiction in the local environment. This type of coordination will ensure egress paths do not access areas of lower security through areas of higher security. (Copyright ©2012 by International Association for Healthcare Security and Safety (IAHSS), PO Box 5038, Glendale Heights, IL 60139, 888-353-0990 http://www.iahss.org 16.)

h. Security requirements for construction, commissioning, and move-in will vary according to the complexity and scope of services provided. A security project plan should be developed that is risk appropriate for the environment and function and should include:

1. The impact of demolition and phasing of existing site functions and protection efforts.
2. The need for temporary security barriers such as fencing and security systems, including intrusion and video surveillance.
3. The installation of security systems should be scheduled for completion to allow for protection of the facility and equipment during early move-in activities.

i. An HCF's surroundings may include open space, parking facilities, and private ways, and may border other businesses, residential properties, major transportation routes, or other areas. The design of HCFs related to site planning is addressed within the Parking and External Campus Environment Design Guideline.

j. HCFs provide care to patients in both inpatient and outpatient areas and may include non-patient care areas such as academic and research space. These areas may present specific risks or security concerns and the design of HCFs related to these types of areas are addressed within the Buildings and the Internal Environment Design Guideline. These areas, which are addressed in specific design guidelines, include:

1. Inpatient Facilities.
2. Emergency Department.
3. Mental Health Areas.
4. Pharmacies.
5. Cashier and Cash Collection Areas.
6. Infant and Pediatric Facilities.
7. Protected Health Information Areas.
8. Utility, Mechanical, and Infrastructure Areas.
9. Biological, Chemical, and Radiation Areas.

k. HCFs frequently provide both scheduled and emergency services, serve as part of local emergency response networks, and are frequently expected to be functional, safe, and secure for patients, visitors, and staff while remaining prepared for natural and man-made emergencies 24/7. The design of HCFs related to these types of issues is addressed within the Emergency Management Design Guideline.

HEALTHCARE SECURITY DESIGN GUIDELINES – GENERAL GUIDELINE—Cont'd

l. The development of the Security Design Guidelines for Healthcare Facilities reflects the principles of Crime Prevention Through Environmental Design (CPTED). These principles, when applied early, can be integrated into any HCF design providing layers of protection for patients, visitors, and staff.

m. CPTED defines territories and how they are controlled and managed based on the use of "concentric rings of control and protection." Outermost rings are supported by additional inner rings of protection. Each of these concentric rings will be addressed as Layers of protection within these guidelines and are intended to sequentially deter, deny access to, and slow down possible malefactors. In the healthcare environment, CPTED layers may include:

1. The first layer of protection should be at the perimeter of the property, which limits points of entry. The campus perimeter should be defined by fences, landscape, or other barriers. At certain locations, this may include the building exterior. Campus entry points should be controllable during emergency situations or heightened security levels.
2. The second layer of protection should be at the building perimeter and consist of doors, windows, or other openings. Protective elements or components may include access-control hardware, intrusion detection, video surveillance, use of protective glazing materials, or personnel for control and screening at selected entrances during designated times.
3. The third layer of protection should be inside the building itself, segregating authorized and unauthorized visitors. Using physical and psychological barriers and hardware, this layer is most frequently applied in areas of higher risk such as emergency treatment areas, intensive care units, mental health areas, pediatric units, newborn nurseries, and recovery rooms.
4. The fourth layer of protection should segregate generally accessible public and patient areas and staff-only areas. Using physical barriers and locking hardware, this layer is most frequently applied to areas that restrict all visitors and limit access to HCF staff only in areas such as nursing offices, staff locker rooms, storage and distribution locations, food preparation, sterile corridors, and research laboratories.
5. The fifth layer of protection should further restrict staff access to highly sensitive areas. Using physical barriers and locking hardware, this layer is most frequently applied to areas that are limited to vetted and authorized HCF staff. These areas frequently include the pharmacy and narcotic storage spaces, hazardous materials, plant utility and information technology infrastructure, and areas housing personal health information (PHI). Security design considerations for such areas should be addressed in accordance with applicable regulatory oversight, standards, and guidelines.

References/General Information

Physical Security Design Manual for VA Facilities: Mission Critical Facilities: www.wbdg.org/ccb/VA/VAPHYS/dmphysecmc.pdf

International CPTED Association (ICA): www.cpted.net/

See Also

IAHSS Healthcare Security: Basic Industry Guidelines: www.iahss.org/About/Guidelines-Preview.asp

CRIME PREVENTION THROUGH ENVIRONMENTAL DESIGN (CPTED)

As reflected in the IAHSS Design Guidelines, healthcare building design is best constructed around the concept of Crime Prevention Through Environmental Design (CPTED). Use of these principles have become recognized worldwide as an effective tool in reducing crime in the built environment while creating a higher perception of safety and an overall increase in quality of life. In fact, many of the same quality-of-life techniques that make healthcare facilities more attractive and more neighborly can also prevent crime.

The majority of crime, ranging from attacks on one's person or property to damaging the environment, occurs because an opportunity to commit the crime exists and the chance of detection is low or nonexistent. The inability to commit crime unseen by others discourages most offenders. Criminal opportunity can be removed or reduced by designing the physical environment in ways that enhance staff interactions and increase the likelihood that no criminal act will go unnoticed. The perception of safety plays a crucial role. People tend to avoid areas that are perceived as unsafe. Activity, on the other hand, promotes the feeling of safety.

The basic concept of CPTED is that crime can be prevented or mitigated by design of the internal and external environment of a facility or property, to increase crime deterrence and the likelihood of apprehension of criminals. The concept of CPTED began in the early 1970s with such writing as Oscar Newman's book *Defensible Space*, and later the book by Dr. C. Ray Jeffery titled *Crime Prevention Through Environmental Design*.[4] Based on the use of concentric rings of protection, CPTED takes an "outside-in approach" starting with the perimeter of the property and working inward. The fundamental concept is to have the most highly security sensitive areas protected on multiple fronts—at the center of these layers of protection, reinforced and protected by a series of protective measures that are strengthened with each layer, as demonstrated in Figure 17-1.

The four overlapping strategies of CPTED are: (1) natural access control; (2) natural surveillance; (3) territorial reinforcement and (4) maintenance and property management. Utilization of these four strategies produces a proactive, unobtrusive perception of safety by visitors, staff and patients.[5]

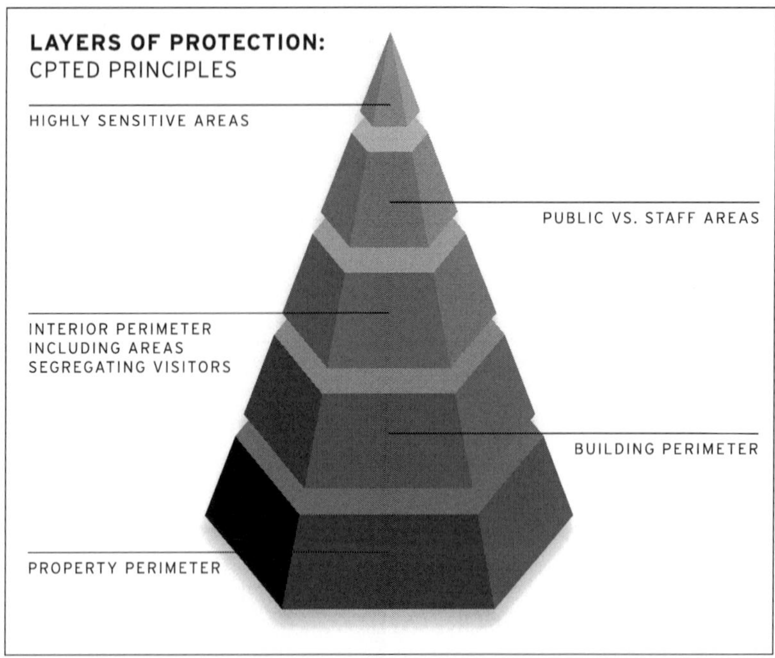

FIGURE 17-1

Layers of protection.

NATURAL ACCESS CONTROL

Designing access pathways that provide direct access to the desired destination of patients and visitors (and sometimes staff) is intended to reduce criminal or other negative behaviors. An example is the placement of outpatient clinics. The objective of access control would be to have clinic patients and visitors arriving at their destination immediately upon entering the facility and when finished with their physician visit, to depart directly to the waiting area and then directly outside. This access control plan and space allocation would also involve providing the parking area intended for the clinics to be in the immediate vicinity of the clinic entry/exit. In short, the clinic should not be located into the interior of the facilities, requiring clinic patients and visitors to walk through or near operational departments or functions.

NATURAL SURVEILLANCE

Natural surveillance includes the placement of windows and open areas with clear lines of sight. Grounds and parking areas are prime locations to provide clear lines of sight to prevent potential assaults by reducing hiding places or shielding illegal or unwanted behaviors. One hospital that experienced an assault on its grounds immediately reduced bushes and trimmed trees so no tree branches were less than seven feet from the ground. Natural surveillance also refers to activities that have a relatively high number of people in the area for the designated function or activity. The theory is more people provide a less attractive environment for a wrongdoer or criminal act. This theory did not, however, work at one hospital where the cafeteria cashier was robbed at gunpoint at high noon on a Friday with the cafeteria operating at full capacity.

TERRITORIAL REINFORCEMENT

Territorial reinforcement relates to the natural progression from public to private space. Clearly defining the boundaries between public and private areas of the healthcare campus and buildings establishes a sense of ownership. The message conveyed is the private area is off limits to anything other than the intended use and activity. The idea being presented by this CPTED concept is to increase a person's subliminal perception of an area as being secured or inaccessible.

The actual implementation of CPTED practices is best begun in the planning phase of new space construction, renovation, or function relocation. In most cases, the concepts of CPTED will require various physical security measures to complete the control process.

These concepts are universal and international, as reflected in a New Zealand Ministry of Justice publication describing seven qualities for well-designed safer places:[6]

1) Access: safe movement and connections
2) Surveillance and sightlines: see and be seen
3) Layout: clear and logical orientation
4) Activity mix: eyes on the street
5) Sense of ownership: showing a space is cared for
6) Quality environments: well-designed, managed and maintained environments
7) Physical protection: using active security measures

MAINTENANCE AND PROPERTY MANAGEMENT

A poor use of repair or indifferent management practices express a lack of concern for the property and create easy targets for criminal activity. Consideration for minimizing maintenance requirements should be given when new construction or renovation is being planned. For example, plant material should be selected for its size at maturity to minimize the need for pruning. Using quality durable materials will also reduce maintenance requirements.

PARKING AND THE EXTERNAL CAMPUS ENVIRONMENT DESIGN

Chapter 23, "Parking and the External Environment" focuses specifically on operational issues and services related to parking. For security design purposes, the security of the facility or campus begins at the perimeter of the property. The healthcare security administrator should work with architects and representatives of the organization's grounds and maintenance team (usually under the Facilities department), to establish a defined perimeter that reflects the location and setting of the campus, based on the assessed risk and vulnerability of the campus. A hospital in Israel, as an example, may have one defined perimeter entry to the hospital property and a checkpoint where security personnel will screen, or even search, people and vehicles accessing the property. The perimeter will be completely fenced and monitored. In contrast, a suburban hospital in the outskirts of any Midwestern town in the U.S may have two or more vehicular access points and an open perimeter (no fence), where pedestrians can access the property using many different routes. In these situations, property lines are well defined with landscape, sidewalks or other boundaries to establish what is and what is not considered hospital property.

Lighting

Lighting is a key aspect of design for the external healthcare campus environment, as it can help manage the real and perceived concerns on campus and within the building proper. Lighting standards for healthcare are discussed in Chapter 18, "Physical Security Safeguards" and should be applied appropriately in each individual setting.

Consideration should be given to not having outdoor security lighting conflict with sustainability initiatives. Optimal lighting can help deter crime and enable camera surveillance, while sustainability calls for minimal outdoor lighting in order to reduce light pollution and energy consumption. This conflict can be overcome through strategic installation of lighting and the use of variable intensity lighting systems and intelligent lighting control. In addition, video analytics can be used to achieve optimal light levels satisfying both sustainability and security objectives. This technology is currently used to detect the presence and track the movement of people and other objects of interest (e.g., cars) and distinguish them from other objects (e.g., animals). Advancements in video surveillance technology now make it possible for these video analytics to control lighting.

Design considerations when implementing a lighting plan, which should not be overlooked in design planning, are emergency power and the interface of lighting with facility security systems. An important safety issue, select internal and external lights should be energized by a connection independent of the general lighting in the space. Lighting that features options with multiple battery packs for maximum remote capacity and run time are often used.

From fires to earthquakes, tornadoes and more, emergency situations can directly impact healthcare facilities—and emergency lighting is required to help safely and quickly relocate or evacuate patients, caregivers and visitors to safety. According to American National Standards Institute (ANSI), emergency lighting standards seek to provide visual conditions that make safe and timely evacuation possible.[7] While many healthcare facilities have backup generators, emergency lighting bridges any timeframe between primary lighting source failure and backup lighting to safely illuminate a medical facility, and help first responders navigate the building. Codes require timing for when and how long emergency lighting must illuminate a building when an emergency occurs.

The design of egress, including the number and placement of emergency lights, must enable prompt escape of building occupants. Thus, plan the design of where emergency lighting is placed in a building to foster an optimally illuminated escape route to create a safer atmosphere rather than creating a cost-efficient design.

External lighting should be selected and installed to augment external security systems, such as video surveillance cameras and emergency call boxes. Trees and other landscaping are other important features, as consideration should be given to prevent camera obstruction, loss of line of sight or concealment opportunities from shrubbery for vagrants or those intending some form of malicious activity.

Signage is another important design feature of the external campus environment that, when well used, can guide patients and visitors to their intended destination, while deterring criminal activity by enhancing security awareness, without compromising line of sight. Digital way-finding kiosks have been used successfully by some hospitals to help take the anxiety out of patients and visitors finding their destinations. The kiosks can give guests options on how to find their destination: typing it on a touch screen if they know where to go, selecting from a list of common locations, or calling a live operator (or security dispatcher) if they are need of additional help or only have a patient's name.

Video surveillance of vehicular and pedestrian access and egress routes, the use of emergency communication stations positioned in high-traffic locations and the strategic location of parking attendants, valet and other staff, where applicable, can and do enhance the safety of the external environment.

Consideration should be given to identify specific parking needs for the new hospital design for emergency patients, after-hours and on-call staff and physicians, as well as any special considerations for police and corrections personnel. The latter becomes of importance if the hospital has a contract arrangement as a designated correctional treatment facility. The hospital design and related parking should minimize forensic patient traffic through the emergency department walk-in entrance or hospital main entrance.

A valet parking service requires specific design considerations for traffic flow and parking stall proximity. Pedestrian safety should always be of paramount importance and focus when designing vehicular access routes. This is best accomplished by establishing clear and safe delineation of pedestrian walkways and crossing points. Many healthcare organizations position video surveillance cameras to monitor activity at these locations.

Parking facilities, both surface and garage structures, often present security challenges in design and can be the scene of frequent criminal activity. Staff, physicians, patients and visitors alike have had the misfortune to be victimized by criminal activity in hospital parking lots. From cars vandalized, broken into and stolen, to crimes against the person that create great fear such as carjackings, robberies, assaults, kidnappings and even homicide, parking lots must receive focused attention in the security design. In one recent case at the Etobicoke General Hospital in Toronto, Canada, gang members opened fire from a car outside the ED in the parking lot, wounding four people and shattering glass in the ED. This forced the hospital and an adjoining hospital into emergency lockdown.[8]

Surface parking lot design must ensure that vehicles cannot be used, accidentally or otherwise, to crash into the hospital facility. The strategic placement of bollards and the avoidance of straight driveway runs leading to the buildings can mitigate this risk. Lighting, communication devices, video and staff surveillance can all contribute to enhanced safety levels in these lots. Where possible, the number of pedestrian and vehicle access and egress points should be limited.

Parking garages, often multilevel, present unique design challenges for the healthcare security professional. An often overlooked safety concern is the phenomenon of patients and others taking suicidal leaps from these structures, usually from the top level. Video surveillance, emergency phones and signage may offer minimal help in detecting and deterring this activity, while fencing, elevated wall height on the top level, and even treed and grassed landscaping around the perimeter of the structure, may offer additional mitigation measures. In these structures it is important that visibility into and within the structure be maximized—line of sight is critical and lighting and paint/stain color on the walls and roof of parking garages can also elevate surveillance capacity. Security cameras, communication devices and strategic location of elevators and stairs are also key factors.

The IAHSS design guideline on *Parking and the External Campus Environment* provides more detail.

HEALTHCARE SECURITY DESIGN GUIDELINES – #01 PARKING AND THE EXTERNAL CAMPUS ENVIRONMENT

Statement

The security of parking facilities and the external campus environment is a significant concern for Healthcare Facilities (HCFs) and for users of those facilities. The proper design and effective management of the external campus environment can minimize violent and property crime, promote efficient resource management, and provide a welcoming environment.

Intent

a. This guideline complements the Security Design Guidelines for Healthcare Facilities, General Guideline.

b. The initial planning and conceptual design phase of the external campus and new or renovated parking facilities should include a security risk assessment conducted by a qualified healthcare security professional.

c. The project design team should prepare and submit plans to the project security representative for review and approval, including a comprehensive exterior site security plan that indicates a layered approach, including zones, control points, circulation routes, landscaping, and illumination.

d. Landscape plans should be designed to enhance lighting, eliminate places of potential concealment or habitation, and address obstructions to surveillance or lighting systems.

e. Physical protective barriers should be placed at building entrances and walkways to minimize the likelihood of injury or damage by vehicles to pedestrians, equipment, and structures.

f. The external environment should be addressed from the outside inwards and the first point of control should be at the perimeter of the property limiting points of entry. Access control and perimeter security should be considered in the initial design stage.

   1. Physical protective barriers should be designed to help restrict or channel access.
   2. Natural barriers, landscaping, or security fencing should be considered to discourage persons from entering the campus unobserved on foot while maintaining openness and allowing for natural surveillance.
   3. Transit, taxi, and pickup/drop off stops should be identified and situated to maintain perimeter control and prevent unobserved pedestrian access.

g. Lighting should be installed. To be effective, protective lighting should:

   1. Act as a deterrent and allow for effective recognition of persons and activities.
   2. Be constructed with a shatter-resistant lens, designed to withstand environmental degradation of light output, and provide protection from vandalism.

HEALTHCARE SECURITY DESIGN GUIDELINES – #01 PARKING AND THE EXTERNAL CAMPUS ENVIRONMENT—Cont'd

   3. Have properly fitted enclosures that prevent insects and debris from accumulating within the fixture.
   4. Be selected and positioned to avoid glare and blind spots.
   5. Be designed to provide adequate redundancy of lighting in the event of an occasional loss of service.
   6. Be automatically supported by standby power.
   7. Be installed to prevent light pollution or light trespass into the surrounding community.
   8. Be integrated with the video surveillance system design to ensure adequate coverage.
   9. Include environmentally sustainable features that do not hinder the effectiveness of protective lighting.

h. Way-finding signage should be used to orient and guide patients and visitors to their desired location. To be effective, signage should:
   1. Provide clear and consistent messaging.
   2. Use color coding or memory aids to help individuals locate their vehicle.
   3. Be used to enhance security awareness in parking areas while serving as psychological deterrent to criminal and other negative behavior.
   4. Not obstruct natural sight lines.

i. The HCF should provide dedicated patient and visitor parking where possible. Additional parking considerations should be provided for emergency care patients, on-call clinicians, public safety, valet parking, and those working during non-traditional hours.

j. Security considerations for parking facilities, including surface lots, should include the following safeguards:
   1. Concentrating pedestrian egress paths to dedicated entrances and exits.
   2. Limiting the number of vehicular entrances and exits.
   3. Locating attendant booths, parking offices, and security stations where attendants can directly monitor parking activity (if appropriate).
   4. Installing emergency communication devices along pedestrian walkways.
   5. Installing video surveillance to obtain images of all:
      a) Vehicular and pedestrian entrances and exits.
      b) Areas of higher traffic activity.
      c) Emergency communication devices.
      d) Attendant booths.
   6. Absence of public restrooms in unstaffed areas.

k. Security considerations specific to parking structures should include the following safeguards:
   1. Maximizing the visibility into and within the parking structure.
   2. Enhancing natural surveillance and line of sight.
   3. Using white concrete stain to increase general brightness and enhance illumination. Painting is discouraged as it can require increased maintenance. Anti-graffiti coatings should be considered to enable quick and easy cleaning.
   4. Installing two-way emergency communication devices on each level of the structure and in all elevators.
   5. Locating elevators and stairs on the perimeter with material that allows natural surveillance from exterior public areas.
   6. Concentrating pedestrian paths to dedicated entry/exit portals. Emergency exits should be designed for egress only.
   7. Features that prevent and deter entry by unauthorized persons, including, but not limited to, fencing, grates, metal grills, landscaping, or other protective measures.
   8. Closing off potential hiding places below stairs.
   9. Avoiding dead-end parking areas and areas of concealment.
   10. Including in the design the ability to completely shut down vehicular and pedestrian access to the parking facility when closed.

References / General Information

Illuminating Engineering Society of North America, Lighting for Emergency, Safety and Security, 2011.

National Institute of Justice, Crime Prevention Through Environmental Design in Parking Facilities, April 1996: www.ncjrs.gov/pdffiles/cptedpkg.pdf

See Also

IAHSS Basic Industry Guideline 09.10.01 – Parking (General).

BUILDINGS AND THE INTERNAL ENVIRONMENT DESIGN

Moving from the external campus and parking areas of the healthcare facility to its buildings and the internal environment, the layers, or zones, of protection model gains clarity. The physical design of the facility and the integration of electronic security systems with that design are critical to the safe delivery of care. Facility design considerations do differ, depending on the size, complexity and scope of services offered at a given healthcare facility. The typical zones in the healthcare environment include:

1. General areas accessible to the public at all times
2. General areas restricted to the public during non-visiting hours or periods of lesser activity (i.e., restricted waiting areas and closed departments)
3. Screened public areas
4. Staff and accompanied public areas (i.e., operating room recovery areas)
5. General staff-only areas
6. Areas for designated staff with the appropriate clearance (i.e., satellite pharmacy).

These zones of protection provide methods of control within the facility or within a department. By providing physical separation between general public areas, waiting areas, and access-restricted areas, each zone can be reinforced as it works in concert with the other zones. The internal design should address the movement between zones, with emphasis on horizontal and vertical circulations, so that the issue experienced at UNC Hospitals mentioned at the beginning of this chapter is not duplicated. Security design often involves a delicate balance between life safety requirements, security needs and the ability to retain a warm and welcoming environment that also meets the operational needs of the organization. This relates directly to the driving mission of all healthcare security organizations—the creation and maintenance of a safe, secure and accessible healing environment in which patients can receive the highest quality care. The Security Master Plan should reflect this philosophy in all aspects, while the security risk assessment will help guide the determination of design needs and appropriate methods of control, which may include:

- Signage
- Physical barriers
- Direct staff supervision
- Mechanical and electronic access controls
- Audible or monitored alarms

These methods of control are described in more detail in Chapter 18, "Physical Security Safeguards" and Chapter 19, "Electronic Security Systems Integration" and are reflected on the IAHSS design guideline for inpatient facilities. Within the internal environment, specifically in the inpatient facilities, there are security areas of higher risk that will require specific design considerations. These areas are discussed in detail in Chapter 21, and each of the areas has a separate design guideline that can be found in the IAHSS *Security Design Guidelines for Healthcare Facilities.* These areas include the Emergency Department, Behavior/Mental Health Areas, Pharmacy, Cash and Cash Collection Areas, Infant and Pediatric Areas, Areas with Protected Health Information, Utility, Mechanical and Infrastructure Areas, Biological, Chemical and Radiation Areas.

EMERGENCY DEPARTMENTS

The design process for the emergency department (ED) begins at the perimeter of the department and moves inside. Externally, dedicated parking for the ED should be provided and a clear separation between the ambulance and walk-in entry is highly desirable. Some specific ED security design needs include the ability to quickly restrict access to the department, also commonly referred to as "lock down." The ambulance entry should be equipped with controlled access with a line of sight created for entry points from the primary nurse's station or with technology via video surveillance cameras that can be monitored by department personnel. In some EDs the risk assessment may determine the need for metal screening, such as what Sparrow Healthcare in Michigan incorporated after an emergency room physician was stabbed. Metal screening is a growing mitigation feature that is much more prevalent in the U.S. than in other countries. However successful the protection strategy, it is still used in only a relatively minimal number of healthcare facilities.

The proper design for the ED stresses the need to compartmentalize, or separate, the patient and visitor waiting area, with amenities and necessities located in that space. The design should ensure a clear distinction between the registration area and the ED waiting area, with the same principle followed in distinguishing the triage and ED waiting areas. Safe, risk appropriate design of registration, triage and nursing stations is a specific feature of this area; this may range from simple design considerations such as counter height positioned to prevent a disruptive visitor from easily climbing over, to complete secured separation of the area from the general waiting area. Patient demographics, crime in the community, trauma designation, and mental health population served as a ratio of ED visits are all important considerations that drive the level of protection required. Often, it is the balance of personal safety and administrative preference for the aesthetics of the environment that will drive how these areas are secured.

Access to the medical treatment areas in the ED should be controlled and restricted. The ED that serves high-risk patient populations, such as forensic prisoners or acutely ill mental health patients, should be specific areas designed to manage or mitigate the safety and suicidal risk presented by these groups.

BEHAVIORAL/MENTAL HEALTH AREAS

The behavioral/mental health (BMH) areas must be specifically designed to address potential risks presented by this particular patient population, including elopement and harm to self or others. Consistent with the CPTED principles and the layered zones of protection model, the security of BMH units and facilities begins at the perimeter. This includes fencing and walls in outdoor areas and secured exit doors tied to the building fire system. The design, where possible, should not include patient rooms forming any part of the external secure perimeter line. The main entry to the unit should receive specific attention during design planning as it often presents the greatest vulnerability for elopement by patients. In secure units, the creation of a double door entry system, where one door can't open until the other closes, is often a viable option. The area created between the two doors is sometimes referred to as an "elopement buffer zone."

Line of sight and enhanced observational capacity of patients by staff are key design factors in BMH settings. Though sometimes considered intrusive in the sensitive BMH environment, surveillance cameras can be used to enhance the observation of patients as well as elevating safety levels. The interface between the physical and electronic security elements and the building life safety systems must be carefully managed in the BMH setting, as the right balance between a secure environment, patient safety and life safety requirements must be achieved. Nursing station design is also unique here, as staff need to be able to observe and communicate with patients, with the ability to complete confidential work out of sight and have a safe area to retreat to and secure, in the event their personal safety is threatened. Seclusion room design is also an important factor in most BMH settings, with size of the room, door specifications for strength and visibility, location and type of ligature resistant toilet and sink, video surveillance and type of bed all needing to be addressed.

PHARMACIES

Design considerations in pharmacies typically center on the risks presented by the storage and distribution of narcotics and other controlled substances. An important design objective is to create a secure physical separation between the pharmacy operations and the public. Armed robbery is a legitimate risk to a healthcare pharmacy as well and the design should help to mitigate this risk.

The outer barrier to the pharmacy space is the starting point for design and should include penetration resistant materials and measures. This includes solid core doors, floor-to-ceiling walls, and one-piece construction ceilings. Line of sight immediately outside the pharmacy is also important for staff entering and exiting the department. Surveillance cameras should be positioned to view the hallway and doorway surrounding every entry point with a monitor positioned at each door for staff to readily observe all activity before leaving or allowing entry. All public and staff interactions with pharmacy staff should be conducted at a transaction window with a secured drawer. The window should be of reinforced material and the area surrounding the window hardened with protective material.

Many pharmacies are not staffed 24/7 and thus require intrusion alarm systems with response plans that reflect the very restricted access to the space. All entrances to the space and any corresponding receiving/delivery area require specific access control systems, as will the narcotic storage system (vault) within the pharmacy.

Video surveillance cameras and duress alarms should be installed in key locations throughout the department and pharmacy work areas to include the narcotic storage, satellite pharmacy locations, and satellite storage locations, in addition to transaction counters and windows.

The pharmacy located outside the healthcare facility requires special design considerations but frequently mimics the basic design criteria of the inpatient pharmacy.

CASHIERS AND CASH COLLECTION AREAS

The cashier cage and various cash collection areas located throughout the healthcare facility such as those located in the cafeteria present unique risks related to internal theft and the threat of armed robbery and should be given due consideration in design planning. In particular primary cash management areas, such as the financial cashier's office, should have a secured physical separation from the public. Security considerations for primary and secondary cash collection areas should integrate the physical location and layout with various security controls and technology.

Much like the design of the pharmacy, walls, ceilings, doors and transaction windows should be penetration-resistant in the central cashier office space. Access to these areas should be controlled and restricted to prevent unauthorized entry, ideally limited to a single door, monitored by video surveillance visible to the staff in the area. Duress alarms and video surveillance of the transaction window and safe are also important systems integration features. Surveillance of areas immediately external to the space is important to detect suspicious individuals loitering in the area or waiting for the door to be opened.

Public cash collection areas, both internally such as gift shop or coffee cart, and externally, including parking booths or other ticket payment dispensaries, should have specific design considerations as well. This will include workstation design, unobstructed lines of sight, duress alarms and recorded video surveillance of cash transactions and the surrounding area.

INFANT AND PEDIATRIC FACILITIES

The design and construction of dedicated infant or pediatric care areas should address the patient and family experience, the physical location and layout, and the integration of security controls and technology. As described in Chapter 21, "Areas of Higher Risk," healthcare facilities have made great strides in elevating the safety levels at their sites for newborns and children. However, the risk of abduction from the care area remains very real, and the proper security design application is a critical factor in mitigating the risk of the unthinkable abduction.

External entry points to areas housing infants or pediatric patients should be avoided at all cost; ideally the units should be located above the ground floor. Unit access should always be controlled and restricted to authorized personnel only. All stairwells and emergency exits serving the infant or pediatric areas should be equipped with delayed egress hardware, in conformance with applicable codes. Space should be provided to receive visitors requesting entry so they may be vetted and screened. All doors leading to the infant or pediatric care area should be equipped with authorized staff-keyed hardware and a clearly marked communication station on the exterior side of the entrance with direct line of sight or video surveillance capability. Recorded video surveillance should be used to capture a full face image of all persons who enter or leave these units as well as in areas where the public may be able to view the nursery. Security design considerations for the new mother patient rooms are also important with proximity to stairwells, bed positioning and size of bathrooms all playing an important role in the patient experience.

Infant monitoring systems, discussed in greater detail in other sections of this book, should be given strong consideration for infant and pediatric care areas. Basic expectations include the system integrating with the access control system, allowing elevators, doors and other security measures to be controlled if an alarm is activated. The infant tagging system should also integrate with the video surveillance system to enhance live monitoring by nursing staff and the security operations center if applicable.

AREAS WITH PROTECTED HEALTH INFORMATION

The risk assessment for areas with protected health information (PHI) should address the multiple ways in which protected and privileged information can be compromised and how that information should be protected utilizing integrated physical and electronic security systems. The design should include access and audit systems to be applied, and where appropriate, to areas housing electronic and written PHI. Risks related to PHI are primarily related to electronic storage and transmission of PHI, secondarily the physical location of records and ease of viewing or accessing them and finally to the destruction of records related to PHI.

Working closely with the organizational privacy officer or other leadership with privacy oversight, the security representative should design and implement integrated protective measures, applied to both physical and electronic spaces. This should include signage, registration area design, furnishings to facilitate securing information and secured areas for equipment such as printers. Areas primarily utilized for the storage of health information should be designed with a penetration-resistant perimeter. Access to these areas should be controlled and restricted. Intrusion alarms should be utilized in areas not staffed at all times. Video surveillance systems for areas housing PHI should be in place, including waste disposal areas.

UTILITY, MECHANICAL AND INFRASTRUCTURE AREAS

The design of this space should recognize that the mechanical, electrical, plumbing, and information technology (IT) systems within it are critical assets for the healthcare facility providing for uninterrupted patient care, basic building comfort, and extraordinary emergency response capabilities. Risks to these areas can be the result of criminal intent or human accident or emanate from a building system failure or malfunction.

Security design planning for these areas should include a multidisciplinary team from security, facilities, information technology, clinical/care team, occupational health and safety (OH&S), emergency management and organizational leaders who have interest in protecting these critical utility systems. Areas of focus for this portion of the built environment not regularly frequented include where utilities are produced, in addition to those providing backup utility services in support of institutional continuity of business operations.

Security measures should be integrated into the design of mechanical and critical infrastructure areas so that major infrastructure systems and technology platforms are secure from unauthorized access by the general public or employees. Emphasis during design planning should include central utility plant (CUP), data centers and server rooms, rooftops and telecommunications closets and areas how IT hardware, as well as other areas located throughout the facility that house critical infrastructure. Electronic access control and video surveillance technology should be integrated into the secure design process for these areas.

BIOLOGICAL, CHEMICAL AND RADIATION AREAS

Highly hazardous materials (HHM) such as biological, chemical and radioactive materials, present unique security risks to healthcare facilities. Areas housing HHMs are frequently regulated and must be designed accordingly. These areas should be designed and constructed to provide integrated physical security while protecting the healthcare environment and the surrounding community. System design can also aid compliance activities to include the audit of materials in conformance with organizational policy, regulation by the authority having jurisdiction as well as identified industry best practices and assessed risk.

Areas to be addressed during planning often include laboratory spaces, especially those using radioactive materials, highly hazardous chemicals and controlled substances. Biosafety Level 3 laboratories and above and Select Agent laboratories must receive special attention. Patient care areas using HHMs, storage or disposal areas for pharmaceutical hazardous waste, waste storage areas housing infectious, radioactive or chemical waste and space housing gamma irradiators are others arenas that require significant protective measures that are best addressed during the design phase.

Locations housing HHMs should be segregated by type of waste and include penetration-resistant design measures to secure the space from unauthorized entry. Access to these areas should be restricted with electronic access control with video surveillance strategically integrated into the design to record and digitally archive all activity in the area. Intrusion alarms should also be used to protect these spaces when unoccupied. Rooms should be designed to address risk associated with the HHMs such as fire, explosion, exposures that may cause illness, creation of dangerous gases and the like. Rooms housing HHMs should be monitored using access, audit, construction, ventilation, detection, fire suppression and building/equipment alarm systems.

OTHER INTERNAL AREAS

Other areas requiring special design consideration but not considered an area of higher risk include:

- Materials management, central supply/stores and sterile processing
- Shipping and receiving areas and loading docks
- Mail rooms
- Health Information management
- Human resources, administrative and executive offices
- Meeting rooms and conference areas
- Call centers, switchboard
- Research facilities
- Childcare centers
- Urgent care facilities
- Operating rooms, sterile areas and special procedures areas

Design considerations for each of these areas are outlined in the *Buildings and the Internal Environment* design guideline shown here.

HEALTHCARE SECURITY DESIGN GUIDELINES – #02 BUILDINGS AND THE INTERNAL ENVIRONMENT

Statement

The physical design of buildings and integration of electronic security systems within the internal built environment are important components of the Healthcare Facility (HCF) protection plan and the patient, visitor, and staff experience. Security design considerations must address the particular requirements and services offered by the HCF.

Intent

a. This guideline complements the Security Design Guidelines for Healthcare Facilities, General Guideline.
b. The initial planning and conceptual design phase of new or renovated buildings or space should include a security risk assessment conducted by a qualified healthcare security professional.
c. The project design team should prepare and submit plans to the project security representative for review and approval, including a comprehensive security plan that indicates a layered approach, including zones, control points, circulation routes, and required egress paths.

Continued

HEALTHCARE SECURITY DESIGN GUIDELINES – #02 BUILDINGS AND THE INTERNAL ENVIRONMENT—Cont'd

d. The size, complexity, and scope of services provided within an HCF can vary significantly; in all cases, the building design should be composed of defined zones of protection. Typical zones in the healthcare environment may include:
  1. General areas accessible to the public at all times.
  2. General areas restricted to the public during non-visiting hours or periods of lesser activity.
  3. Screened public areas.
  4. Staff and accompanied public areas.
  5. General staff-only areas.
  6. Areas for designated staff with the appropriate clearance.

e. The internal environment should be designed to address horizontal and vertical circulation routes that facilitate operational functions in accordance with security needs and life-safety requirements. Physical separations should be provided between general public areas, waiting areas, and access-restricted areas.

f. The inclusion of a risk assessment in initial design will allow determination of needs related to the access from zones of lesser security to zones of higher security and will help in identifying the appropriate methods of control that may include signage, physical barriers, direct staff supervision, mechanical and electronic access controls, and audible or monitored alarms.

g. The access to all staff-only entry points, circulation points, elevators, and stairwells should be controlled and restricted.

h. The management of access systems should be consistent across the HCF as to the operating procedures and type of systems used. Electronic security systems, if available, should be integrated and standardized. Design considerations for electronic safeguards should include:
  1. Designating the location of duress alarm buttons at strategic locations where employees work alone, in isolated areas, or other areas of higher risk as identified by the security risk assessment.
  2. Using video surveillance to capture and record images in defined security sensitive areas or other areas of higher risk as identified by the security risk assessment. Each camera application should have a defined philosophy of use that is consistent within the area being protected, recognized industry best-practices, and regulatory standards.
  3. Selecting and specifying door and window hardware with specific security requirements and functionality. Hardware should be durable and appropriate for the environment.
  4. Coordinating door hardware, security electronic systems, electrical, and fire alarm system specifications.
  5. Installing security intrusion systems in non-24-hour facilities on all entry portals and in other areas of higher risk as identified by the security risk assessment. The installed system should be designed to allow independent arming of various areas of the building in support of different departmental hours of operation.
  6. Developing a coordinated signage approach for way-finding, brand identification, security, and emergency information and, if possible, mass notification.
  7. Avoiding, where possible, stand-alone systems for individual buildings or renovation projects.
  8. Implementing a single unified or integrated system for access control, video surveillance, and, when appropriate, parking access and egress, debit card functions, and time and attendance needs.
  9. Future-proofing security systems by providing flexible infrastructure, including wiring pathways and equipment locations.
  10. Coordinating with other building technology systems, as appropriate.

i. The determination of where building security systems will be monitored and controlled should address the need for adequate space and environmental conditions in support of electronic equipment. If offsite, provisions should be made for support spaces for electronic equipment within the facility and infrastructure necessary for connectivity to offsite monitoring and control systems.

j. Public and patient care areas in general should have securely fastened electronics, wall hangings, plants, fire extinguishers, or other hard objects.

k. Design considerations for security-sensitive areas are addressed in separate guidelines. Other areas requiring consideration include:
  1. Materials management, central supply/store, and sterile processing should include:
     a) Designation as authorized staff-only areas.
     b) Controlled and restricted access in and out of area.
     c) Electronic access control for frequently used staff doors.
     d) Hardened walls, ceiling, and doors to prevent penetration.

HEALTHCARE SECURITY DESIGN GUIDELINES – #02 BUILDINGS AND THE INTERNAL ENVIRONMENT—Cont'd

e) Secure storage for items of higher value.
f) Video surveillance.
g) Intrusion detection systems for monitoring during non-occupied hours.

2. Shipping and receiving/loading docks should include:
a) Locations away from patient care areas and critical infrastructure.
b) Designation as authorized staff-only areas.
c) Controlled and restricted access in and out of area.
d) Electronic access control for frequently used staff doors.
e) Hardened walls, ceiling, and doors to prevent penetration.
f) Secure storage (e.g., fencing, gates, or locked cages for items of higher value, hazardous materials, or items with personal health information).
g) Video surveillance to obtain images of all entry and exit points.
h) Fencing, cargo doors, or other means to secure the external loading dock area from surrounding streets.

3. Mail rooms should include:
a) Locating mail receiving and sorting rooms away from critical building infrastructure and structural support and mission-critical building functions, if possible at an offsite central receiving facility.
b) Location on the building perimeter, near or adjacent to the loading dock.
c) Designation as general staff-only areas.
d) Controlled and restricted access in and out of area.
e) Electronic access control for frequently used staff doors.
f) Secure storage (e.g., lock boxes or other secure means for items with personal health information).
g) Video surveillance to obtain images of all entry and exit points.

4. Health information management (medical records) should include:
a) Designation as authorized staff-only areas.
b) Controlled and restricted access in and out of area.
c) Electronic access control for frequently used staff doors, maintaining an audit record of room access.
d) Hardened walls, ceiling, and doors to prevent penetration.
e) Video surveillance to obtain images of all entry and exit points.
f) Intrusion detection systems for monitoring during non-occupied hours.

5. Human resources, administrative, executive, and business offices should include:
a) Designation as general staff and accompanied public areas.
b) Controlled and restricted access in and out of areas after normal business hours or when areas are not occupied.
c) A reception room or vestibule for areas requiring public interface separate from staff workstations.
d) Video surveillance to obtain images of all entry and exit points, cash handling, safe locations, and reception areas.
e) Secure cash storage in areas where cash is collected or stored.
f) Duress alarms at reception areas and human resource and executive offices.
g) Intrusion detection systems for monitoring during non-occupied hours.

6. Meeting rooms and conference areas should include:
a) Designation as general staff and accompanied public areas.
b) Controlled and restricted access in and out of area after normal business hours or when areas are not occupied.
c) Appropriate circulation and egress paths.
d) Secure storage for high-value audio/video equipment, computers, and other office equipment.

7. Call centers, switchboard, or other staffed telephone answering rooms should include:
a) Designation as authorized staff-only areas.
b) Controlled and restricted access in and out of areas.
c) Electronic access control for frequently used staff doors, maintaining an audit record of room access.
d) Direct communication capability with security, law enforcement, and other public safety agencies.

8. Research facilities, whether stand-alone or integrated with other healthcare operations, should include:
a) Evaluating the specific threats and risks associated with all research activities (current and future) to include performing a formal risk assessment for animal research facilities and Bio Safety Level (BSL) 3 and 4 laboratories.

Continued

HEALTHCARE SECURITY DESIGN GUIDELINES – #02 BUILDINGS AND THE INTERNAL ENVIRONMENT—Cont'd

b) Designation as authorized staff-only areas.
c) Controlled and restricted access in and out of areas.
d) Electronic access control for frequently used staff doors, maintaining an audit record of access.
e) Hardened walls, ceiling, and doors to prevent penetration.
f) Video surveillance to obtain images of all entry and exit points.
g) Intrusion detection systems for monitoring during non-occupied hours.

9. Childcare centers, whether stand-alone or integrated with other healthcare operations, should include:
a) Designation as authorized staff-only areas.
b) Controlled and restricted access in and out of areas.
c) Electronic access control for frequently used staff doors, maintaining an audit record of facility access.
d) Appropriate circulation and egress paths.
e) Video surveillance to obtain images of all entry and exit points.
f) Intrusion detection systems for monitoring during non-occupied hours.
g) Monitored electronic abduction prevention or wander alert system should be utilized based on the assessed vulnerability of the population served.

10. Urgent care facilities, whether stand-alone or integrated with other healthcare operations or medical office buildings, should include:
a) Clear distinction and control between general public waiting areas and medical treatment areas.
b) Controlled and restricted access in and out of medical treatment areas.
c) Electronic access control for frequently used staff doors, maintaining an audit record of area access.
d) Appropriate circulation and egress paths.
e) Video surveillance to obtain images of all entry and exit points and waiting areas.
f) Intrusion detection systems for monitoring during non-occupied hours.
g) Registration desks positioned to provide staff direct access to an exit portal (safe drop-back zone) and equipped with strategically located duress alarms.

11. Operating rooms, sterile areas, and special procedures areas should include:
a) Designation as authorized staff-only areas.
b) Controlled and restricted access in and out of areas.
c) Electronic access control for frequently used staff doors, maintaining an audit record of access.
d) Video surveillance to obtain images of all entry and exit points.
e) Secure storage or other secure means for storing controlled substances and items of higher value (e.g., surgical instruments).

References / General Information

OSHA Guidelines for the Prevention of Workplace Violence in the Healthcare and Social Work Settings: www.osha.gov/Publications/OSHA3148/osha3148.html
OSHA Enforcement Procedures for Investigating or Inspecting Incidents of Workplace Violence CPL 02-01-052: www.osha.gov/OshDoc/Directive_pdf/CPL_02-01-052.pdf
Physical Security Design Manual for VA Facilities: Mission Critical Facilities: www.wbdg.org/ccb/VA/VAPHYS/dmphysecmc.pdf
Whole Building Design Guide summary of design standards for mail rooms: www.wbdg.org/design/mail_center.php

See Also

IAHSS Basic Industry Guideline 09.01 Security Sensitive Areas.

EMERGENCY MANAGEMENT DESIGN

Increased growth in volume, pressures for operational efficiency, new operational models for patient flow and new concepts in physical design make it vital for healthcare facilities to consider emergency management requirements in their new facility design. Healthcare organizations must create flexibility and resilience in the facility to manage a natural disaster or man-made event. These events can significantly impact the ability of a hospital to deliver care. Hurricane Sandy, which so severely impacted the New York hospitals, and of course Hurricane Katrina in Louisiana are but two tragic reminders that our healthcare facilities need to be designed so they continue to operate and deliver care to the communities they serve. The importance of emergency management and business continuity to the healthcare organization is the focus of Chapter 25, "Emergency Preparedness: Planning and Management." In this section we will discuss how the design should allow the facility the flexibility to respond to particular occurrences using an all-hazards approach.

A basic concept that should not be lost in the design planning phase is how space should be capable of being repurposed to care for a surge in patients or flexed to a shelter-in-place requirement if the situation dictates—especially during peak periods. Increased inpatient or isolation capacity should be design drivers in addition to space for mass triage and staging areas for emergencies. External areas should be designed for supplies and support vehicles as well as temporary helipad facilities. During planning, a decision should be made by the facility on how it will be able to flex to increased morgue capacity and where this will be housed.

New hospital design should allow for alternate points of access in an emergency, including exterior doors serving as entrances, space reassignment, permanent or temporary emergency support space and space designated to provide services to large numbers of individuals. Additional electrical and medical services infrastructure should be installed in areas designated for space reassignment at the time of construction.

Critical infrastructure for the facility such as utility supply, generators, water and fuel storage should be located in areas least vulnerable to a criminal act or natural disaster. The ability to immediately lock down the facility and control air circulation are important design considerations as it relates to emergency response capability. System redundancy should be built into the design, as well as systems that can be supported from outside the facility such as quick connects for portable utility backup systems. The design should reflect the need for self-sufficiency for up to 96 hours, requiring storage space and areas for staff to sleep. Decontamination areas are also impacted by design decisions, such as locating them on the outer perimeter of buildings.

Properly designed with emergency management requirements in mind, conference rooms can become inpatient rooms, corridors can allow access to medical gases for patients who are housed or staged there, and a main entry lobby of a hospital repatriated to care for families. The IAHSS design guideline for emergency management should be reviewed closely during all phases of designing the built environment.

HEALTHCARE SECURITY DESIGN GUIDELINES – #03 EMERGENCY MANAGEMENT

Statement

The design of the Healthcare Facility (HCF) should consider emergency management practices that allow for the flexibility and resilience required to manage emergency events. An all-hazards approach to design should be applied to help the HCF prepare for, respond to, and recover from manmade events and natural disasters.

Intent

a. This guideline complements the Security Design Guidelines for Healthcare Facilities, General Guideline, Parking and the External Campus Environment Guideline #01 and Buildings and the Internal Environment Guideline #02. Design Guidelines #02.02 Emergency Departments, #02.07 Utility, Mechanical and Infrastructure and #02.08. Biological, Chemical, Radiation Use Restricted Areas also have considerable interface with this guideline.

b. The initial planning and conceptual design phase of construction and renovation projects should include a security risk assessment conducted by a qualified healthcare security professional and the appropriate clinical, facilities, and other support personnel with responsibilities related to emergency management. A Hazard Risk Vulnerability Assessment should be completed by those responsible for emergency management for the HCF.

Continued

HEALTHCARE SECURITY DESIGN GUIDELINES – #03 EMERGENCY MANAGEMENT—Cont'd

c. The project design team should prepare and submit plans to the project security representative for review and approval, including a comprehensive emergency management plan that complements the layered approach to design that is described in the guidelines referenced in Intent (a., above).

d. The design should support the ability of the HCF to shelter-in-place and repurpose space during emergency operations to accommodate the intake and care of a surge of patients. This should include consideration for:

1. Assignment of patient care populations to avoid evacuation complications based on mobility of patients.
2. Mass triage during such events as epidemic or pandemic outbreaks.
3. Increased inpatient capacity.
4. Increased isolation capacity, including installing medical gasses and other necessary patient care elements in walls and ceilings of rooms intended to be dual-use, convertible space.
5. Staging area(s) for emergencies.
6. Community support related to widespread utility outages or severe weather conditions.
7. External areas for supplies or other support vehicles or trailers.
8. Areas for permanent or temporary helipad facilities.
9. Increased morgue capacity, including racks for storage and cooling capability.

e. The design should include consideration for the following in preparation for response to emergency situations:

1. Alternate points of access:
   a) Exterior doors that could be used as alternate entrances to temporary treatment/triage areas should be designed to allow for emergency access.
   b) External design should provide for clear access to alterative emergency entrances.
   c) External access paths addressing personnel, vehicles, parking, staging, and emergency patient transport needs should be considered as related to the use of alternate entrances and the care provided in reassigned spaces.
2. Space reassignment:
   a) Internal design should allow for the repurposing of space used for emergency response by addressing controls to and from that space. This may include controlled access systems, fire doors, and fixed furniture design.
   b) Areas considered for alternate care sites should include additional electrical infrastructure to accommodate patient care equipment and other required services.
   c) Design consideration should be given to allow for curtains or other such privacy apparatus in areas considered for alternate care or reassignment.
3. Permanent or temporary emergency support space should include appropriate access to electrical and information technology infrastructure, and include:
   a) Design of an Institutional Emergency Operations Center that includes access to video surveillance, intrusion detection, access control, utility, fuel, and building systems and can be activated as needed and to the degree (scale) necessary to respond to emergencies at all levels.
   b) Designation of space that could be reassigned to serve as an Emergency Operations Center for external responders.
   c) Designation of space to support patient care functions, including triage, operating and patient room assignment, and discharge and morgue management.
4. Designation of space to provide services and support to large numbers of individuals in areas preferably separated from patient care and emergency management areas, as described above.
   a) Designation of space to accommodate families.
   b) Designation of space to accommodate mental health support.
   c) Designation of space to accommodate media.
5. Designation of space, external to the buildings, to serve as assembly and staging areas and the ability to separate that space from other external space when needed.

f. The design of the HCF should include a risk assessment, including the impact of wind on the HCF site. The construction or renovation of space should include built measures to mitigate risks identified in that risk assessment and should include consideration for the following design-related measures:

1. Critical utility supply addressing power, steam, gas, and water are delivered or located in areas least vulnerable to sabotage or natural disaster and that, if purchased from external providers, access to such infrastructure is controlled within HCF property.

HEALTHCARE SECURITY DESIGN GUIDELINES – #03 EMERGENCY MANAGEMENT—Cont'd

2. Critical infrastructure such as generators, water and fuel storage, and mainframe computer systems are also located in areas least vulnerable to sabotage or natural disaster.

3. The ability to quickly manage the environment, including the ability to:
   a) Lock down the HCF and isolate all access and egress to select locations.
   b) Manage air intakes so that they can be shut off immediately when necessary.
   c) Control air circulation by management of heating, ventilation, and air conditioning and related filtration systems in the event of an emergency that requires the isolation of areas, purging of the system, or reversal or air flow.

4. Systems that have both primary and secondary (backup) capabilities should be included in the design and the primary and secondary delivery should be designed as separated redundant systems to eliminate single points of failure.

5. System redundancy should be designed in accordance with applicable institutional standards, best practices, and regulatory requirements and should, within an HCF environment, minimally address safety and comfort in:
   a) Patient care systems and space.
   b) Lobbies and other large gathering areas.
   c) Life safety systems and egress paths.
   d) Building automation, information technology, security, and telecommunications systems, including local panels, cameras, alarms, access readers, radio repeaters, and wireless access points.
   e) Data centers.
   f) Dispatch and system monitoring areas.
   g) Emergency operations centers.

6. The design of systems that can be supported from outside the HCF or that impact the external environment should include:
   a) The installation of quick connects for portable utility backup systems.
   b) The installation of air intakes above ground level.
   c) Construction that addresses exterior walls, windows, and other elements to protect the building from natural and man-made disasters.
   d) Review roof top systems as they may be impacted by wind or other weather conditions.
   e) Continuity of Operations design should include consideration for:

1. Space to accommodate storage of supplies of food, water, pharmaceuticals, and other supplies necessary to ensure that the facility can be self-sufficient for the recognized best practice standard of 96 hours. This amount of time may be adjusted based on institution-specific needs.

2. Space to relocate administrative staff should primary administrative facilities be converted to triage/patient care space.

3. Backup systems space for data center management.

4. Respite areas for sheltering staff.

h. Building names or numbers should be placed in a highly visible area of the building to assist emergency responders with campus location orientation.

i. Decontamination areas should be located on the outer perimeter of the building. Design elements should include:

1. Exterior entrance for decontamination shower rooms that is controlled and restricted to authorized staff only and protected from weather and wind elements.

2. Space to house personal protective equipment for decontamination team.

3. Dedicated holding tanks to accommodate decontamination run-off.

References/General Information

Physical Security Design Manual for VA Facilities: Mission Critical Facilities: www.wbdg.org/ccb/VA/VAPHYS/dmphysecmc.pdf

Best practices of hospital security planning for patient surge: A comparative analysis of three national systems: www.ncbi.nlm.nih.gov/pubmed/20873500

See Also

IAHSS Basic Industry Guideline 10.01 Emergency Management (General).

REFERENCES

1. Giles TD. *How to Develop and Implement a Security Master Plan*. Boca Raton, FL: Auerbach Publications; 2009. xix.
2. Fickes M. *3 Steps for a Master Security Plan*. BUILDINGS: Smarter Facilities Management website; 2012. Retrieved on July 15, 2014, from http://www.buildings.com/article-details/articleid/15007/title/3-steps-for-a-master-security-plan.aspx.
3. Engells TE. An approach to security risk assessment. *Journal of Healthcare Protection Management* 2012;**28**(1):37.
4. Ahrens SA. *Crime Prevention Through Environmental Design*. Security Technology & Design; 2005, December. 36–42.
5. Crowe TD. *Crime Prevention Through Environmental Design. National Crime Prevention Institute*. Woburn, MA: Butterworth-Heinemann; 2000. 36.
6. Ministry of Justice, New Zealand. *The seven qualities for well-designed, safer places*. 2006. Retrieved on July 20, 2014, from http://www.justice.govt.nz/publications/global-publications/n/national-guidelines-for-crime-prevention-through-environmental-design-in-nz/part-1-seven-qualities-of-safer-places/the-seven-qualities-for-well-designed-safer-places.
7. Galentine Scott. Look for lighting that exceeds emergency standard for healthcare facilities. *Healthcare Facilities Today* 2013, October 18. Retrieved August 4, 2013, from http://www.healthcarefacilitiestoday.com/posts/Look-for-lighting-that-exceeds-emergency-standard-for-healthcare-facilities-Maintenance-and-Operations–2660#sthash.RiZJVS9w.dpuf.
8. Gillis W. *Shooting takes gang violence "to a different level" police say*. Toronto Star; 2014. Retrieved on July 24, 2014, from http://www.thestar.com/news/crime/2014/06/02/etobicoke_general_hospital_shooting_takes_gang_violence_to_a_different_level_police_say.html.

CHAPTER

PHYSICAL SECURITY SAFEGUARDS 18

In today's world there is an ever-increasing need to improve and strengthen the level of security in healthcare facilities across the globe. As security staffing costs are at all-time high levels and physical security technology advances at a rapid and growing pace, it is only logical that physical security has been a major source of program improvement over the last several decades. While the basic physical security safeguards are still staples of protection (barriers/fences, alarms, lighting, lock and keys), it is the electronic components of security that are experiencing explosive growth. In this chapter, the nonelectronic safeguards are discussed, followed by Chapter 19, "Electronic Security System Integration," which is devoted entirely to the components and implementation of electronic security safeguards.

BASICS OF PHYSICAL SECURITY

The basic definition of physical security applies equally as well to nonelectronic and electronic physical security measures. Physical security can be defined as that part of security designed to protect people, mitigate the unauthorized access to equipment, facilities, material, and documents, and to reasonably safeguard them against espionage, sabotage, damage, theft, and loss. In most healthcare security systems, the physical security safeguards utilized are intended to be integrated with other components of the security program. The physical security safeguards are typically not intended to function as a stand-alone element of the protection program. For example, security personnel are generally required to inspect, monitor, and respond to the various physical security components of the security system. There is also the interrelationship of physical security and the psychological deterrent aspects of security, that blend together to produce the intended results of protecting patients, visitors and staff. A good example of this interplay is security signage. Security signage is physical and generally intended to be informational. Signs such as "emergency exit only" or "authorized entry only" do not in themselves prevent exiting or entering. Signs do, however, provide a certain visual aspect of implied control and serve as a "notice." This notice puts staff in a position to ask a stranger of their purpose in a restricted area, and may prove useful in criminal trespass or other type action.

Very much like security staffing, there is no single formula used to determine the amount or use of physical security safeguards in the healthcare environment. For example, how many and what type of locks should be installed for a given healthcare facility is best determined by the master security plan and the organizational philosophy of use, not a standard set of instructions that every healthcare facility must follow. The IAHSS has developed a general guideline on the implementation of physical security safeguards inside of healthcare, with principles denoted for how to best use these important safeguards.

04.01 PHYSICAL SECURITY (GENERAL)

Statement

Healthcare Facilities (HCFs) will implement physical security safeguards to establish a reasonable level of protection of people and assets to augment security staffing, policies and procedures. As the effectiveness of physical security safeguards used in the HCF varies, no single formula determines an appropriate physical security deployment plan for a given HCF.

Intent

a. The use of all electronic and non-electronic security safeguards used in the HCF should have a defined, documented philosophy of use that is reviewed periodically.

b. Physical security measures and enhancements are best deployed after conducting a security risk assessment. After an adverse event, the plan should be reviewed with modifications as needed.

c. The number and type of physical security safeguards used in the HCF may vary. Using crime prevention through environmental design (CPTED) principles for layered protection, consideration should be given to the equipment and devices listed below:

1) Access control to include doors, locking mechanisms, key systems, push-button locks, electronic access technologies and gates
2) Video surveillance to include cameras, monitoring devices, recording equipment and video intercoms
3) Alarms to include intrusion and motion detection and duress/panic applications
4) Communication devices to include telephony and radio communications, dispatching equipment and software, emergency call boxes and mass notification devices
5) Screening equipment to include visitor management and metal detection
6) Asset protection devices to include equipment used to fasten/secure, seal, tools used to mark property, narcotic, cash, weapon storage, safes and lock boxes
7) Patient and asset tracking to include infant protection, elder and high-risk patient monitoring (wander alert), and RFID tags
8) Use of CPTED principals to include fencing and barriers, bollards, lighting and landscaping
9) Hardening devices for walls, windows, and workstations to include transaction windows, protective glazing material, bullet-resistant glass and work-space design
10) Psychological deterrents to include security signage, way-finding guidance, and clearly marked security patrol vehicles

d. Whenever reasonably possible, physical security equipment and devices should be standardized, planned and implemented in an integrated manner.

e. Physical security equipment and devices should complement and support the building life safety plan and regulations within the jurisdiction.

f. Policies, procedures and training programs should be established for using, administering and responding to the various physical security safeguards deployed throughout the HCF.

g. The HCF should have a program of preventative maintenance, inspection and testing of all physical security equipment and devices on a periodic basis.

h. A close-the-loop reporting procedure should be used to outline how malfunctioning security equipment and devices are reported through the completion of corrective actions.

See Also

IAHSS Healthcare Guideline 04.02. – Electronic Security Systems
IAHSS Healthcare Security Guideline 04.04. – Video Surveillance
IAHSS Healthcare Security Guideline 04.09. – Testing of Physical and Electronic Security Systems
IAHSS Healthcare Security Design Guidelines – General Guideline
APPROVED: August 2013

BARRIERS

Barriers are one of the oldest forms of physical security and can be either man-made or natural. In the early days of settling America the covered wagons were formed in a circle at night. In the era of castles the moat provided a barrier to protect the castle. Rivers and steep terrain have always served as natural barriers and still serve as an element of protection to a limited degree today. On many healthcare campuses, natural barriers such as grading, path locations and landscaping are used to delineate the property boundaries of public space and their access routes. In short a physical security barrier is an obstacle to the movement of persons, and in some cases animals.

There are countless reports of animal encounters on many healthcare campuses, especially on rural and suburban campuses. Video images of a moose entering a door into a medical clinic, a mountain lion patrolling a mountain-area hospital parking lot, a bear cub activating motion sensor doors, and deer wandering the halls of a hospital have all been shared.

Our discussion in this chapter will focus on the common man-made barriers currently being used in many healthcare security programs.

FENCING

Fencing as a barrier is one of the oldest forms of physical security. Although it is a meaningful protection element for many facilities, it may not be a practical application of control for specific situations. The proper application of fencing as a safeguard is largely dependent on the layout and design of buildings and grounds, as well as organizational philosophy, in terms of aesthetics, and the image portrayed. The term "fencing" is frowned upon by some healthcare administrators as they are simply opposed to the concept of fencing on their campus. Fencing can be unsightly, or it can be somewhat pleasing. Not all fencing is the same and the use of different types of fencing barriers has been utilized by many organizations to enhance the image of the facility. Fencing a large tract of land usually produces no adverse effect on public or community relations.

Fencing has historically been installed (or considered) in healthcare facilities as a result of various protection problems that arise. Until recently, it has rarely been part of the original design. The exceptions are government and private facilities with large amounts of land; in these cases, fencing is often planned in the design stage. The same can be said for a facility that has closed, or has parts of a campus no longer used. Fencing of these sites helps to keep people out and adds an element of workplace safety often required by most insurance companies before they will write a commercial liability policy.

Fencing need not always completely surround an area. It can be effectively used to control traffic patterns and to define property lines for only certain areas or parts of the complex. Figure 18-1 is an example of utilizing fencing to provide a barrier between buildings, with the objective of being an access control measure and driving foot traffic through defined areas that may be protected by security measures.

Surface parking areas are prime locations for protective fencing. The basic premise behind fencing parking areas is that criminals generally do not want to engage in their criminal activity where the means of escape is limited. On the other hand, fencing may limit a victim's escape route when their personal safety is threatened, as an example. General experience, however, demonstrates properly fenced areas are considerably safer than unfenced areas.

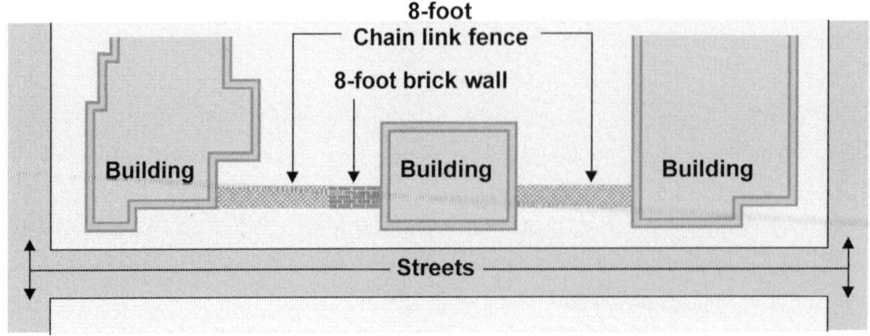

FIGURE 18-1

Example of the use of fencing and brick wall for security.

When installing and maintaining fences, a good rule of thumb is to establish a clear zone of 15 or more feet from all portions and sections of fence. Overgrown trees, shrubs and bushes should be kept away from the fence to deter trespassers from using these items as climbing aids, and to enhance natural surveillance.

Chain Link Fencing

A common type of fencing used in the security industry is the galvanized steel, chain-link fence, which permits visibility from both sides. The protection offered by this fencing is directly proportional to its height. A short fence is basically a psychological barrier, but a high fence, with barbed-wire outriggers or a razor-ribbon topping, is a physical security barrier. In circumstances where barbed wire and other types of topping are not acceptable, or even offensive to members of the healthcare organization, increased height is a good alternative. A north London hospital in the UK installed high security fencing after people broke into parts of the site. Both facilities, Muswell Hill Hospital and the Camden Islingthon NHS Foundation Trust, replaced their 1.8-meter-high (5.9 feet) wooden fence with one that is 2.3 meters (7.5 feet) tall.[1] The higher fence was believed by facility leadership to be a better defense for fending off vandalism and unwanted trespassers.

If an area requires fencing for security purposes, the minimum height of the fence should be 7 feet. Barbed wire support arms (outriggers), if required, should be placed at a 45° angle to the upright posts. The arm should face toward the direction that penetration is to be denied. In the healthcare setting, situations rarely require support arms on both sides. Additional protection can be gained by burying the bottom of the fence below grade, to minimize the likelihood of digging under the fence that may allow a person or animal to crawl under it. Fencing has many applications in healthcare facilities, in addition to parking areas and property lines. Among the most common enclosures are oxygen storage, chiller towers, water retention ponds, gasoline or fuel dispensers, outdoor equipment storage, power supply panels, exposed gas lines and bicycle storage areas.

The mini-mesh chain link fencing material is recommended where a greater level of protection is required than that afforded by standard chain link fencing. The mini-mesh wires are thicker and the mesh is much tighter. This type of chain link fence provides good breakthrough strength. The closer mesh does not offer easy hand or foot holds and the mesh spaces are small enough to resist the use of boltcutters. This type of chain link fence is ideal for oxygen storage areas and should be at least 8 feet

FIGURE 18-2

Example of a decorative iron fence providing a pleasing definition and security for an outside garden area.

(Courtesy of Children's Hospital Colorado, Aurora, Colorado.)

high to provide an adequate level of protection. The fencing line base should be concrete or asphalt. If in dirt, the fence should be buried between 12 and 18 inches.

Decorative metal fencing

The use of iron or aluminum fencing has gained in popularity. It is more expensive than standard chain link fence and thus most frequently used in fairly short runs, and where aesthetics may be a priority. This type of fence is sometimes referred to as wrought iron, but comes in a variety of round, square, and rectangular material. These fences have good see-through visibility and breakthrough strength can be quite high, as the fencing material cannot be easily or quickly cut. In many applications this type of fence not only provides security, but also enhances the suitability of space used by patients, visitors or staff. Figure 18-2 portrays the use of a decorative iron fence surrounding a hospital outdoor "healing garden" that provides security while projecting a comfortable look and feel of an inviting space.

The stark appearance of fencing can be minimized with landscaping. However, the landscaping design must exclude heavy foliage or shrubs, which can provide a potential hiding place for contraband, vagrants, and intruders. Thorny foliage may serve as an effective barrier by itself, or in combination with fencing.

Security window bars and protective cages

Various types of security window bars and protective cages are available, when a higher level of security is needed within an area of lower security risk to prevent pilferage, to enhance ground-floor windows, enclose accessible air-conditioning units, or to create accessible security areas within a more public work area. Examples of this application may include copper storage on a construction site, waste areas, control panel shut-offs and meter protection, stock rooms in nutrition services, information service (IS) data centers, and warehouses/distribution centers.

Woven wire cages or welded partitions are typically used to prevent tampering or damage and are often constructed of strong, durable steel wire. A web-like design is most frequently used for these high-security applications. The window bars and safe cages can be designed for a variety of applications, almost any size or shape, large or small, for internal or external use. They are typically low in cost and relatively simple to install.

BOLLARDS

A bollard is a short vertical post that has been used more and more frequently around the world to hinder vehicles from crashing a car or truck into a hospital building, either in anger or by accident. The use of such devices has grown since the Oklahoma City bombing of 1895, the 2010 attempted bombing by a parked car in Time Square in New York City, and other suicide bombings and incidents of ram-raiding.

There are two types of bollards on the market. One is the decorative bollard, designed for a variety of purposes such as diverting traffic, pedestrian walkways, and beautification of buildings, or as decorative covers over unsightly steel pipes. The second type is for security installations. Often referred to as "fixed bollards," these anti-ram resistance safeguards can be as simple as a piece of steel pipe in the ground, embedded with concrete. After 9/11, the U.S. Department of State developed what it calls a K-rating system, which calculates bollard resistance, according to the size and speed of a vehicle that might be driven toward a building. Ratings are based on the diameter and structure of the bollard, its depth in the ground, and both the amount and kind of foundation that anchors it.[2]

To present a welcoming rather than a bunker look at entrances, many hospitals use decorative bollard covers over top of their security bollards. Retractable or removable traffic bollards are also employed in areas where a change of access requirements may be necessary. Many healthcare facilities install bollards to prevent the intended, or unintended, ramming of a vehicle into a building or entrances. The most vulnerable locations are glassed door entry areas off driveways as well as ramp areas, with an emphasis placed on the various emergency department entrances (walk-in/ambulatory and ambulance entrances). These entries often become highly congested and chaotic at times. Bollards are frequently used to separate flow and direct traffic to specific areas.[3]

The bollard is an inexpensive method to prevent damage to utility connections such as a gas meter, electrical stations, oxygen storage tanks and such. They are also widely used in parking areas and structures to control traffic, prevent damage, and provide an element of safety for persons using the parking facilities. Not strictly as a physical security safeguard, protective bollards were installed at a hospital in Stockton, California outside of their emergency services entry after a visitor accidentally drove his truck more than 10 feet into the glass entrance.

The design of the bollard, and its installation, are largely determined by the security risk and vulnerability being managed. A bollard placed in the middle of a wide walkway to prevent use by motorized vehicles would be of a more lightweight construction than the bollard intended to keep a vehicle from crashing into an entranceway.

LIGHTING

Security professionals agree exterior lighting is one of the most basic and cost-effective components of the protection program. Exterior lighting serves two distinct purposes: safety and security. Safety lighting provides the means for persons to navigate the exterior, avoiding slips, falls, and environmental obstacles. Security lighting, on the other hand, is designed to discourage criminal activity, provide light for surveillance purposes and create a positive feeling of personal safety. According to conventional wisdom, darkness conceals identity and also decreases inhibitions; as a result, it is often linked to crime and dishonest behavior. Academic research has been conducted on the positive implications of lighting. Criminal assaults most frequently occur during hours of darkness, and improving lighting has been demonstrated to be associated with impressive reductions in crime of between 33% and 70%.[4]

SELECTION AND DESIGN OF GROUNDS LIGHTING

When selecting and installing external lighting, the security administrator must consider the potential for vandalism of the light fixtures. The proper design and location of the lighting fixture reduces the probability of malicious destruction. One method is to install light fixtures as far inside the property line as possible (facing outward) and to use break-resistant cover guards. Lighting fixtures should be designed so the failure of a single lamp will not create an area with reduced protection or diminish lighting levels below acceptable standards. Table 18-1 lists the five most common types of lamps used in healthcare security applications.

The quality of exterior lighting is often reduced by tree foliage. Pruning the foliage or altering the position of the lighting fixture may correct this problem. Security personnel should ensure lighting operates at maximum effectiveness by regularly checking for encroaching foliage and reporting any burned-out lights. The amount of night lighting required varies according to the area's crime vulnerability and the security administrator's judgment, based on the security risk assessment.

When it comes to hospital lighting trends, facility leaders and security managers are making it a priority to reduce energy use, provide comfort to patients and maintain a safe and satisfactory environment for employees and staff. As the range of lighting products and technology continues to expand and evolve, choosing the best option for the varied spaces within a hospital has become a more complex task.

Table 18-1 Lighting Characteristics[5]

Lighting Characteristics		
Type	**Lumens Per Watt**	**Color Discrimination**
Incandescent	20	Excellent
Mercury vapor	63	Good
Fluorescent	83	Excellent
Metal halide	115	Excellent
Sodium	130	Fair
Light-emitting diode (LED)	131	Excellent

SECURITY NIGHT LIGHTING STANDARDS

Lighting standards are grouped into the following zones.

ZONE I

- **2.0 FC** for building entrances and exterior walls to a minimum height of 8 feet, for vital locations or structures
- **1.0 FC** for roof surfaces requiring surveillance

ZONE II

- **1.0 FC** for parking lots
- **0.4 FC** for roadways
- **0.2 FC** for storage areas
- **0.2 FC** for walkways

ZONE III

- **1.0 FC** for parking lots
- **0.4 FC** for roadways
- **0.2 FC** for walkways
- **0.1 FC** for storage areas
- **0.05 FC** for open areas

ZONE IV

- **2.0 FC** for pedestrian entrances
- **1.0 FC** for roadway entrances
- **1.0 FC** for rail entrances
- **0.2 FC** on vertical plane, at points 3 feet above the ground plane, for "Glare Barrier"
- **0.1 FC** for fence line (non-isolated)
- **0.1 FC** for water approaches
- **0.05 FC** for open areas
- **0.05 FC** for boundary line (isolated fence or no fence)

FIGURE 18-3

Commonly used standard for security lighting.

The practice of using an extremely high level of foot candles throughout the hospital and on the grounds is over. Much more importance is placed on providing the right light in the right location. This requires understanding that a high-traffic corridor requires different light than a remote area of a parking lot rarely used during hours of darkness. Figure 18-3 shows the lighting requirements considered to be a standard of the security industry.

The lighting technology that has changed the most since the last edition of this text is the light-emitting diode (LED), thanks to its energy savings (estimated at 75% over incandescent lamps), lifespan (estimated at 25% over fluorescent), lower heat output, design flexibility and safety/security benefits.[6] Despite its multiple benefits, many hospitals are still cautious with LED installations due to the cost, which can be five to ten times more than fluorescents, which many experts believe still deliver the best return on investment.

MAINTAINING AN EFFECTIVE LIGHTING PROGRAM

Proper lighting improves safety, prevents crime and improves the feeling of safety on all healthcare facility campuses. A few simple techniques that were shared in a 2010 *Campus Safety* article should be employed by healthcare security managers to maximize the investment and properly manage the exterior lighting programs:[7]

1. **Number each light.** Lighting problems often go unreported. This may result from the fact that maintenance personnel work during the day while problems are generally seen at night. Make it easy for all staff members and security staff to report lighting issues or concerns by numbering all exterior lights with visible tags. Indicate light numbers and locations on a map that identifies lamp type, wattage, model number and ballast requirement, along with information on critical replacement parts.
2. **Conduct routine light surveys during day and evening.** Daytime surveys often reveal the cause of lighting problems, such as discolored lenses that reduce lighting efficiency or broken light fixtures. Nighttime surveys reveal the results of these problems, including burned-out lights or lighting conflicts with overgrown tree canopies.
3. **Include actual light measurement at ground level beneath each fixture.** High efficiency exterior lights can lose up to 60% of the efficiency from a variety of causes, including bulb deterioration, ballast failure and dirty or discolored lenses.

TREES AND SHRUBS

Trees and shrubs can be used to create physical barriers, or be used to enhance other barriers, to increase security protection. On the other hand, trees and shrubs may provide a convenient hiding place, a place to dispose of or hide contraband, and a place to store stolen property for later retrieval. The use of shrubs with substantial thorns might mitigate the shrub being used for concealment.

Landscaping need not be sacrificed for security purposes; rather, the landscaping should be planned and maintained to meet security objectives. The word *maintained* is important. A small shrub that does not present a security hazard when planted can grow into a problem in a relatively short time. When new landscape architectural plans are developed, the security administrator should require the plans to be superimposed over the exterior lighting plan and reviewed over a 1-year, 5-year, and 10-year horizon. Often, landscape design is focused on providing more immediate beautification, to enhance the image of the opening of a new building or provide initial assistance with erosion control. Too frequently, landscape architects fail to consider or discuss how the expected plantings may impact security lighting. The security administrator will find the organization much more amenable to moving a tree during the design stage than to remove a tree once it is fully grown.

LOCKS AND KEYS

Locking devices of all kinds are a primary element of protection in virtually all security systems. Electronic locking (access control) systems are rapidly replacing traditional lock and key systems for many healthcare facilities. Electronic access control systems are more fully discussed in Chapter 19, "Electronic Security

System Integration." However, there will always be a need for the traditional key applications. It is estimated misplaced keys cost organizations in North America approximately $35 billion dollars annually in terms of inefficiency, shrinkage, liability and lock replacement costs.[8]

Locks come in all sizes and shapes, and they function in a wide variety of ways. In most applications, the lock is intended to serve two basic purposes. The first is to delay a security system compromise. Different locks will delay compromise for different lengths of time, and the selection of the lock should be based on the protection level required. A sturdy lock will discourage an amateur and force a professional to work harder to compromise the locking system. The second function of the lock is to provide visual evidence the lock was compromised, when such compromise occurs as the result of physical force. The level of protection a lock is designed to provide against someone who does not possess a key, a combination, or other information is fairly easy to calculate.

The protection level drops significantly when the lock and key program is poorly administered. Locks used in conjunction with alarms or recording devices are necessary in preventing and detecting both break-ins and unauthorized use.

ADMINISTERING THE LOCK SYSTEM

It is an unfortunate point that the lock and key systems in over 90% of healthcare facilities are likely inadequate. This is most often the result of lax administrative controls rather than improper hardware. However, the improper use of hardware, which either defeats the purpose of the lock or fails to provide the protection level assumed, can contribute to the problem.

Healthcare facilities spend large sums of money on locking hardware, but many fail to provide the funding and administrative control required to properly manage the system. It is generally recommended the security department administer the lock and key control system. Just as checks and balances are required in cash accounting, with one individual performing a certain step and another individual performing another step, the principle of separation of responsibilities applies to key control. The person who controls the key-cutting equipment (often someone in the maintenance department) should not control the key blanks. The authorization for keys, and the key blanks required, should be forwarded to the person who will actually perform the work.

An effective system might work along the following lines: The security representative receives a request for a key, a lock change, or a new lock. After establishing the validity of the request, the security person forwards a work order (perhaps the original request form) to the person or department that will perform the work. The key is then returned to the security department for issue. In some large systems, the locksmith function may actually be part of the security department. This is a good arrangement, but most facilities cannot keep a single employee busy with just this sole responsibility. It is not uncommon, even in large facilities, to contract out all lock and key work to a local locksmith. In this arrangement, the control system should still remain the specific responsibility of a facility individual or department.

Keys may be issued to an individual, or a group of keys may be issued to a section or a department. Issuance of individual keys is the preferred method. This system provides a central record, and the status of the system can be accurately assessed at any time. This method of control requires a rigid system of procedures that establishes how keys from terminated employees are managed.

Fragmented key control may be unavoidable due to the distance between facilities, or the failure of the administration to recognize the value and cost/benefit of a centralized key issue system. In the fragmented approach, responsibility for authorizing lock and key work should be established. The difference is how keys are released—to sections or departments rather than to individuals. Department leaders have the responsibility for issuing the keys, maintaining the records, and retrieving the keys before or during the employee termination process. A point in favor of the fragmented system is key retrieval. Individual departments are the first to know of terminations for cause and voluntary resignations; this knowledge usually enhances key retrieval. The challenge is the need to maintain proper records to determine the number of keys issued and to whom. An electronic system of keyholder records would have some interface with the organizational HR system ideally, thus ensuring connectivity between the process of terminating an employee and the "tools" (such as keys) in possession of the employee. In this manner, organizational vulnerability associated with these separations can be mitigated,

INTERCHANGEABLE CORE LOCKS

The convertible or interchangeable core lock design is a feature of pin tumbler locks that provides a rapid and simple redistribution of combinations. It can be replaced at the lock location by another core already configured to the system. Interchangeable cores save labor time and a reduced technical skill level required to make single or large scale lock changes. It takes 30 to 45 minutes for the average healthcare locksmith to change the combination of a conventional pin tumbler lockset. By contrast, the interchangeable core lock takes between five and ten seconds to remove one core and insert another. Although the initial cost of the changeable core system is somewhat higher, the efficiencies gained with the system more than offset the difference in cost.

MASTER KEY SYSTEMS

An important decision that must be made when designing a lock and key system concerns master keying. A master key system is generally divided into four levels: (1) the change key, (2) submaster, (3) master, and (4) grand master. Many security professionals are reconsidering the actual need for and the limitations of the master key system. Master key systems require a considerable investment in hardware and labor.

Master key systems actually reduce the security capability of a lock by providing fewer usable combinations. Master keying is generally a matter of convenience rather than a security safeguard. When planning a master key system, a growth rate of 300% over 10 years should be assumed to avoid prematurely outgrowing the system. Ten to twelve years should be regarded as the practical limit of the system. The obvious disadvantage to the master key system is the complete compromise of the system when the master key is lost, or when unauthorized duplicates are produced. Certain locks should not be placed on the master key system. The number of exceptions depends in large part on the number of master keys distributed. Examples include certainly the pharmacy or narcotic storage areas, electrical closets and perimeter doors that should be controlled by an electronic access system or at least be keyed separately from the master system. Many security administrators cling to the concept that security officers must carry a master key in case of emergency. This view is not necessarily valid. In numerous facilities that are not master keyed, the security function is still accomplished. Security officers should have the means to obtain timely access, on a controlled basis, to any part of the complex, but neither a master key nor requirement to carry a big ring of keys is an absolute necessity.

COMPUTER-BASED KEY ACCOUNTABILITY

Traditional methods of key control are paper records of key issue dates, to whom issued, lost keys, and a log entry when the key is returned. This method is labor intensive and prone to error, and it is difficult to track down a specific key issued or to analyze a pattern of key usage. This obsolete and ineffective method of key control has largely been replaced with key management systems, which provide computer-based key tracking. Most of these systems involve a locked key cabinet with numerous types of access control, such as key pads, biometrics, proximity or mag-stripe cards, all available to be integrated into an advanced key management system. In these advanced systems, each key is locked into place using a key with an integrated chip that allows only the removal of a key by an individual for whom authorization has been issued. It is common for the system to light up the location for which keys the user can remove. Key cabinets can be grouped together to increase storage volume or dispersed in multiple locations throughout the facility with computer interface control. Cabinets are not only for keys, but can also be used as lockers to store firearms, radios, handheld computers, and other like items. These systems can be programmed to allow the release of a specific key(s) the individual is allowed to check out, down to specific time periods, including an alarm condition if the key(s) have not been returned within a predetermined time period. Management reports can be generated listing what keys have been issued, including time issued and duration of time before the key(s) are returned. A printed audit trail of a specific user or of specific key(s) can be easily generated.[9]

LOCK INSTALLATION

No type of locking mechanism is totally effective unless it is installed correctly. All too often a facility spends a large sum of money to buy the proper lock but fails to install it properly, resulting in a degree of protection no better than a less expensive and less suitable lock would have provided. A common problem encountered in lock installation is the bolt does not penetrate (throw of the bolt) the doorframe sufficiently. The throw should be a minimum of one inch. If there is a wide space or a gap between the edge of the door and the doorframe, the bolt throw may have to be longer. The door and the frame must be substantial enough to resist physical attack. If they are of questionable strength, it would be uneconomical to install an extremely resistive locking device. The weakest part of all the components determines the level of protection being provided.

LOCK CHANGES

No matter what, keys will be lost and unaccounted for over a relatively short period of time. It is thus a matter of judgment when a certain lock should be changed. This decision generally takes into consideration the number of lost keys for a particular lock, how critical the area protected by the lock is, and what additional layered safeguards are used in protecting the area. All organizations should have a schedule of changing locks as an ongoing program. It is usually possible to obtain capital equipment funds when budgeted as an ongoing replacement and improvement project, as opposed to trying to obtain a large amount at one time. The schedule should be developed so the locks in each area of the facility are changed every five to seven years. The ongoing management of the key control program avoids the high cost of replacement all at one time and permits higher priority areas to be selected. In short, key system control is more easily managed.

PUSH-BUTTON LOCKS

Electrical and mechanical push-button locks have gained popularity over the past 15 years. These locks are particularly advantageous where a large number of people require access. The major advantage is the ability to change the lock combination instantly without incurring the cost of changing the lock and reissuing keys. Common areas of use in healthcare facilities are nursing and doctor lounges, small storage rooms, and restricted areas. These locks can be quite simple and inexpensive, with single combinations, or they can be high-security locks requiring individual pin numbers and a second form of security such as presenting an access card. Some electronic locks require no wiring and permit hundreds of combinations and time schedules. Another advantage of push-button locks is that authorized personnel need never be locked out. There is no key to lose, and no access card to leave in another coat or purse. Two challenges are often cited with this type of lock: first, there is no way to tell if the combination has been compromised and, thus, if unauthorized users are using the code to enter restricted areas. In addition, there is no audit trail to determine who entered the premises, though more sophisticated locks of this type do provide this important function.

PADLOCKS

When planning lock systems and security controls, padlocks should not be overlooked. In areas where aesthetics are not important, a casehardened padlock can provide a high level of protection at a reasonable cost. As with door hardware, proper installation of the hasp is paramount. Security departments should maintain several padlocks for temporary use. One security department paints a red stripe around the body of its padlocks to give an instant visual message the padlock is a security department controlled lock. A plastic tag, which moves freely on the shackle, clearly identifies the lock as a security padlock and states the security operations center must be called to open the lock.

KEY MAKING

There are various preliminary steps to establishing a key control program. First, each lock location must be identified. For door locks, each room must be numbered or identified, and any doors within these rooms likewise must be identified. The number, or other reference, given each door need not appear at the actual location and can be identified on a lock control drawing. However, the doors or rooms should be numbered at their location as a means of identifying these areas for other purposes, such as maintenance work orders, deliveries, and visitor information. All rooms should be identified, regardless of whether the doors currently have locks, because locks may be installed later.

Another element of key control is marking or identifying the keys themselves. For obvious reasons, keys should not be marked with the specific lock number or room number to which the key belongs. Numerous codes have been devised by specific organizations to fit their purpose. It is suggested letters of the alphabet be substituted for numerals, either selected randomly or through ten-letter code words. The latter system is advantageous when many individuals need access to the code, because the code need not be written down. Written codes are subject to a greater degree of possible compromise. Keys fitting multiple locks require additional code markings, and the method used for cross-referencing is based on the security administrator preference. Consideration should also be given to marking keys with the words *DO NOT DUPLICATE*. The effectiveness of this practice is unknown. Many places providing key-cutting services ignore this stamp; however, many professional locksmiths will honor it. Furthermore, this marking may deter employees who want a key but are reluctant about trying to have the key duplicated. Locks from numerous manufacturers can be ordered with key blanks not generally available except to the organization that originally purchased the lock.

Security is further enhanced when keys must be cut at the factory to fit a particular lock. One lock manufacturer provides a lock with one set of keys, and beyond this original set, no keys may be duplicated. The keys are marked to identify each key and the total number of keys in the set. For example a set of three keys would be marked *1 of 3*, *2 of 3*, and *3 of 3*. This type of lock obviously enhances security, but can be expensive if extreme care in the accountability of the keys is not exercised.

PERIODIC INVENTORY

Regardless of whether the key distribution system is centralized (keys are given directly to individuals) or decentralized (keys are given to departments, which pass them out), a procedure must be established for periodically inventorying the keys in the possession of individuals. This responsibility should be readily assigned; many healthcare facilities use the security department to perform the audit function. In the decentralized system, the records of the various departments must be checked to determine whether all keys issued can be accounted for. The next step is to contact each employee who has been issued a key and to visually check the existence of the key.

Various methods can be instituted to make this an ongoing program. The processing of identification badges and the inventorying of keys can occur simultaneously. In one system, identification badges expire on the employee's anniversary of hire. When employees are processed for new badges, the security department checks the records to determine whether they have been issued any keys. If so, the keys must be accounted for before the new badge is released.

SECURITY SEALS

In the absence of an alarm system, a security seal can be used to help determine whether an area, cabinet, storage bin, or medication has been entered or tampered with and generally discourage unauthorized entry. The system is simple but effective. A seal is placed on the doors to an area or cabinet. Whether a barcoded seal, shrink bands, foil and paper that is tamper indicating, biohazard seals that are numbered or preprinted as well as tamper tape and tamper-evident caps for medications and test tubes, security seals of various types are used throughout the healthcare delivery system. Areas where security seals are frequently used are medical "crash" carts, red-tagged biohazard waste bags, trash bins, gift shop storage areas, laundry and maintenance storage, to name just a few of many different applications in healthcare. Figure 18-4 demonstrates several varieties of security seals.

Security seals can usually be easily broken and thus do not provide a great deal of physical protection. Extra-long seals can be used to loop through fire exit release devices and for similar applications.

EXAMPLE OF SECURITY SEALS

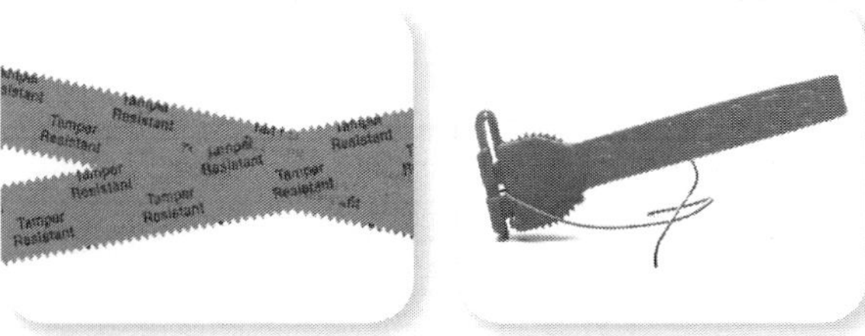

FIGURE 18-4

Example of a red-tag security seal used on biohazardous waste.

GLAZING (GLASS)

Second only to doors, the most common openings into rooms or buildings are windows. Glass doors or doors with glass are also plentiful. When regular glass is used, it invites easy compromise of the locking device. While illegal entry is the prime security vulnerability, glass windows and doors with glass windows also present a potentially costly vandalism problem. Another problem associated with windows is vulnerability to an arson attack by means of a Molotov cocktail or a flammable liquid being poured through a broken window.

ACRYLIC PLASTIC

An alternative to using regular glass is acrylic plastic (sometimes called *polycarbonate*) or a glass laminate with an acrylic core. The latter is the most expensive, but it offers the best protection against physical force, blowtorches, and projectiles. Acrylic plastic has the benefit of being lightweight (approximately one-half the weight of glass). Until recently, the greatest problem with the acrylic sheet was its tendency to scratch easily and to lose its transparency from even routine cleaning. Most manufacturers of acrylic sheets now produce a protective coating to minimize deterioration.

Protective screening and decorative ironwork have been used effectively over the years as added protection for glass windows and other openings. This type of protection is often utilized at small freestanding clinics and physician office buildings. The visual effect of bars on windows and openings projects a poor public relations image, however.

BULLET RESISTIVE GLASS

The term *bulletproof glass* is a misnomer, with the term *bullet resistive glass* being the proper nomenclature. Bullet resistive glass is basically made by layering a polycarbonate material between pieces of ordinary glass in a process called lamination. This process creates a glass-like material thicker than normal glass, ranging from an approximate thickness of 7 millimeters to 75 millimeters. Polycarbonate is a tough transparent plastic often known by the brand name of Lexan, Tuffak, or Cyrolon. The ability of bullet resistive glass to stop a bullet is determined by the thickness of the glass. It is interesting to note a one-way bullet resistive glass is available that has one side able to stop a bullet, while the other side allows bullets to pass through unaffected. This feature provides the person being shot at the ability to return fire[10]—a feature that probably has little or no application in the protection of healthcare facilities. On the other hand, polycarbonate glazing is frequently used to protect pharmacy transaction windows, cashier cages, admission and registration desks, nursing desk/units in higher-risk units such as behavioral/mental health, and some door applications where breakage (safety) is a specific consideration. When polycarbonate glazing is used, other physical safeguards surrounding the area to be protected should not be forgotten. Specifically, the walls under, over and around the protected area should be reinforced with metal or other resilient material to fully institute a protected compartment.

FASTENING DOWN EQUIPMENT

"They'll steal anything that isn't nailed down" is certainly true for healthcare facilities. There are many items to secure or fasten including computers, audiovisual equipment, microscopes, and other expensive pieces of medical or electronic equipment. With the many relatively inexpensive locking devices commercially available today, there is little excuse for any organization to suffer substantial losses of essential and expensive items. Electronic RFID tagging equipment, with sensors sounding an alarm when there is an attempt to remove the equipment from the "protected field," are also becoming increasingly popular. Many facilities still prefer to bolt down equipment. If this is the method used, equipment service representatives should perform this work rather than in-house maintenance personnel. Undue stress on equipment and the incorrect use of bolts can result in damage to equipment.

MARKING PROPERTY

Conspicuously marking organizational property is a cost-effective means of reducing property loss. Asset number tags, although important, do not deter theft to any extent and can generally be easily removed. Marking hospital property serves the following purposes:

- Identify ownership of the property in case of theft
- Assist with management accountability controls (inventory)
- Provide a visible sign the property being removed is hospital property
- Serve as a deterrent to theft

The wheelchair is a good example of an item that should be marked. Many privately owned wheelchairs are brought into medical facilities every day. When security officers or other staff observe a wheelchair being folded up and placed in a vehicle, they must be able to determine whether the wheelchair belongs to the organization.

How should a wheelchair be marked? First, the fabric should be a special color, ideally one that is not popular for private wheelchairs. Next, the back of the fabric should have the organizational logo or initials stenciled in at least a 10-inch square. The location, department, and wheelchair number may also be useful in the day-to-day use and accountability of the equipment. Finally, small bands should be painted or taped on certain tubular parts of the chair, to further distinguish it from personal property.

SAFES

Safes are more common targets of criminals because the mere existence of a safe engenders visions of valuable items. The safe is a formidable looking piece of equipment, but it does not always afford the protection assumed by its owners. Healthcare facilities use safes, or vaults, to protect records, scheduled narcotics and other certain drugs, cash, patient valuables, and negotiable paper.

Regardless of the item being protected, the best protection is first to reduce the quantity of stored materials, and then examine the storage container to verify the design furnishes the protection required. Safes are similar to locks in that a false sense of security can be created when the equipment is misused or misunderstood. Many healthcare professionals using safes frequently cannot discern between a safe designed for fire protection, and one designed for the storage of cash and valuables.

FIRE SAFE

Facility surveys often reveal a record safe being used for valuables. A record safe is designed to protect against fire only. The fire-only safe is generally constructed with wet insulation poured between two very thin steel walls. Water is retained in the insulation, and when a fire occurs, the water creates steam within the safe. The steam acts as a cooling agent and holds the internal temperature below the flash point of paper (350° F). These safes are designed to withstand only one fire; after that, the insulation no longer provides protection. The UL label inside the safe indicates the length of time the safe will provide protection during a fire. The construction of the walls of the record safe are generally so thin, however, that they offer little protection against forced entry.

VALUABLES AND MULTIPURPOSE SAFES

The burglar-resistant safe is constructed of heavy steel plate, and some are reinforced with ceramic or metal filler to increase protection against torches and burning bars. The UL ratings indicate the length of time the safe can withstand attack. Because fire will cause heat to build up inside, burglar-resistant safes should not be used to protect paper records. Multipurpose safes are also available; these are basically fire safes with an inner protection liner to render it a burglar-resistant safe.

Safes should generally be bolted to the floor. A safe may completely disappear from the premises—and often the safe is worth more than the contents. Safes should be positioned so that they can be regularly inspected during security rounds, with proper lighting and other additional commonsense safeguards. Safes containing high-risk materials may need the added protection of an alarm system. Several types of alarms are designed specifically for safes. Safes must always be used properly, and there is no substitute for storing as few items as possible.

Many in-patient organizations are placing burglar-resistant safes in patient rooms during new construction or room renovation efforts. Providing a safe to patients during their stay is yet another step to

FIGURE 18-5

Example of an inpatient room safe.

encourage patients to secure their valuables while in the hospital. Organizations that use these safes have experienced a reduction in the loss of patient valuables. Figure 18-5 provides an image of an in-room safe used for patient valuables and dedicated patient medications.

SIGNAGE

Signs and more signs are everywhere. The healthcare environment is overloaded with signs of every kind, shape, and color. Despite the problem of sign proliferation, there are certain signs basic to healthcare security programs. Security signage can effectively direct and inform people without the need for "live" security intervention. They may serve as the foundation to initiate legal action or be a defense against legal action directed at the organization. In some cases, certain security and safety signs may be required by legislation and/or requirements imposed by regulatory agencies. These signs can be viewed in four types:

(1) Informational: provide knowledge to alert people to such important issues as visiting hours; the time specific doors are locked/unlocked; locations of emergency telephones. In short, signs used to help patients and visitors navigate the healthcare facility such as after-hours entry locations.

(2) Behavioral Expectations: denote expectations of patients, visitors and vendors such as all visitors being required to registered or how patient confidentiality is maintained, or reflecting that aggressive/abusive behavior is not acceptable.

(3) Safety Guidance: reminders on basic security awareness/crime prevention techniques such as locking the vehicle or reminders on how to find a parked car or reminders for employees to wash their hands.

(4) Prohibited Acts: tells people what to do or what not to do, such as locations not to be entered. The sign may be direct as to specific expectations, such as "tobacco-free" or "weapons-free"

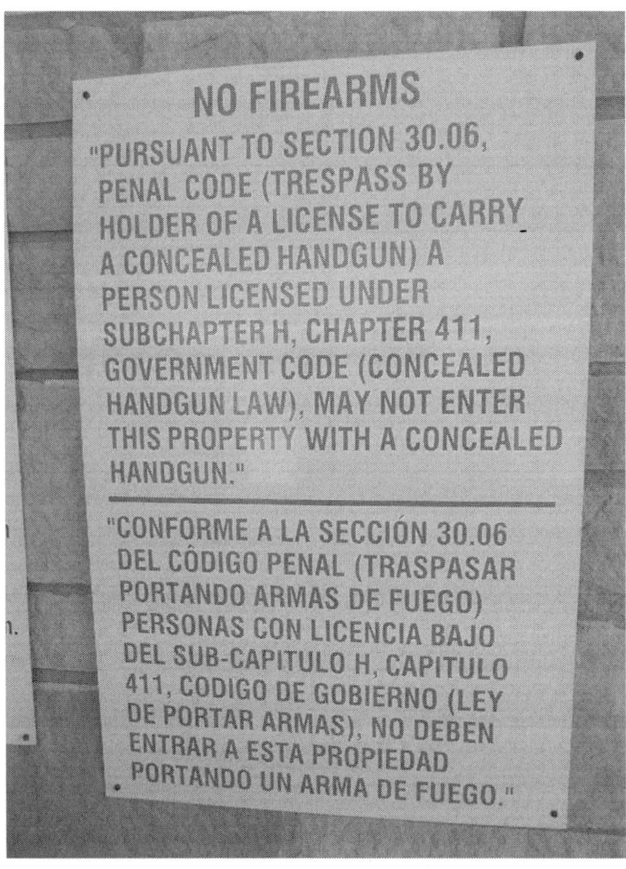

FIGURE 18-6

No firearms signage.

(Courtesy of Methodist Health System, San Antonio, TX.)

environment. Figure 18-6 shows a no firearms policy sign required by the state of Texas for organizations, not persons licensed to carry a concealed handgun.

There is of course some overlap and linkages between these types of signs, and a single sign may be a combination of any of the four types. For example, a way-finding sign would be classified as informational; however, it does aid the security objective of reducing the wandering of persons throughout the facility. Reduced "wandering" is helpful through less disruption of services and less opportunity for the possible commission of a crime. Both types of signs may be directed at specific groups, such as staff, visitors, and patients, or they may be directed to all persons.

The IAHSS has developed a general guideline on the use and implementation of security signage.

04.10 SECURITY SIGNAGE

Statement

Basic security signage is a necessary element of all Healthcare Facilities (HCFs) security programs. Security signage will be developed for the specific elements of the HCF security program, organizational signage guidelines, and applicable regulatory or legal requirements.

Intent

a. The Security Administrator, in collaboration with organization leadership, should develop and maintain security signage compatible with the overall facility signage and way finding system.

b. The primary purposes of Security Signage may be informational, convey behavioral expectations, suggest safety advice or prohibit specified behaviors or activities. A single security sign may combine each of these primary security purposes. Examples of primary purpose security signage include:

1) Informational

a) Entrance Locked 6 p.m. – 6 a.m.

b) Night Entry at Emergency Department

2) Behavioral Expectations

a) Visitors Must Register

b) Maintain Confidentiality

3) Safety Guidance

a) Check Your Valuables

b) Lock Your Vehicle

4) Prohibited Acts

a) Emergency Exit Only

b) This Facility is a Weapons Free Zone

c. Compliance with security signage is generally a facility-wide responsibility of all HCF employees and not the exclusive responsibility of the security staff. There may also be signage where the compliance may be the responsibility of a department, unit, or the function of specific assigned position.

d. Organizational signage may not always have a specific security message but can contribute to the objective of providing a safe and secure environment. Security signage may be mounted, painted, installed in flooring, or be a part of an electronic type presentation. An example is way-finding signage. This type of signage contributes to facility access control by expediting visitor/patient traffic directly to their intended destination to eliminate wandering, becoming lost, or taking pathways which may increase security risks.

e. Security signage may be permanently affixed, or posted for temporary or situational needs. Examples of temporary/situational signage are those directing after hours exiting, short-term instructions due to construction projects, maintenance activities or interim life safety measures.

f. Anticipated situations, including emergency management signage, which may be needed for rapid implementation (i.e., lockdown stages), should be prepared and conveniently stored in advance. Signage should be printed to reflect a professional, authoritative, and readily understood message.

g. Way-finding signage should be used to orient and guide patients and visitors to their desired location. To be effective, signage should:

1) Provide clear and consistent messaging.

2) Use color coding or memory aids.

3) Be used to enhance security awareness in parking areas while serving as psychological deterrence to criminal and other negative behavior.

4) Not obstruct natural sight lines

See Also

IAHSS Basic Industry Guideline 04.04, Use of Video Surveillance

IAHSS Basic Industry Guidelines 07.05, Parking-General

IAHSS Design Guidelines 11.01, Parking and the External Campus Environment

IAHSS Design Guidelines 11.02, Buildings and the Internal Environment

APPROVED: March 2012

A major reason healthcare administrators are often opposed to signage is there is often no organizational policy and procedure relative to the type and permissible placement of signs. As a result, signs are often handmade and taped to a wall. Even permanent signs used for the same purpose are different from place to place. It is quite common to visit facilities and see as many as six or seven different-looking (size, shape, color) signs with the same general message of "Emergency Exit Only." The reasons for this vary, but typically it is due to signs being developed and implemented at different time periods by different people or departments.

Not all security signs are created equally in terms of obtaining voluntary compliance. An "Emergency Exit Only" sign stating an alarm will sound generally has a better compliance percentage than one without. In one hospital with an emergency exit sign that was consistently ignored, a change of color and configuration of the sign to one resembling a traffic STOP sign reported a 300% plus increase in compliance.

A word of caution concerning security signage—do not be tempted to post signs attempting to fend off criminals or wrongdoers with signs that may not be true, or that send a message that may be misconstrued. The "Property Monitored by CCTV" or like signs are not recommended and should not be posted, especially if no equipment is in place or when real-time monitoring does not occur. This signage may create a false sense of security, in the context of a person's perception that they are better protected than is actually the case. An assault in a parking lot or garage could lead to costly litigation, if the victim was able to convince a court that the security signage was false or misleading.

REFERENCES

1. *North London hospital set to install high security fencing after break-ins*. Jackson's Fencing website; 9 August 2011. Retrieved August 10, 2011, from http://www.jacksons-security.co.uk/News/security-fencing-solutions/north-london-hospital-set-to-install-high-security-fencing-after-breakins-1573.aspx.
2. Rusting Robert. *IAHSS Directions*, vol. 22, no. 4. International Association for Healthcare Security and Safety; 2010. p. 13–15.
3. Done Brad. *Security and traffic bollards provide vital protection for hospitals*. Reliance Foundry Co. Ltd; 2010. Retrieved June 6, 2010, from http://ezinearticles.com/?Security-and-Traffic-Bollards-Provide-Vital-Protection-For-Hospitals&id=4400969.
4. Gino Francesca. *What darkness does to the mind*. The Atlantic; 2013. Retrieved June 23, 2013 from http://www.theatlantic.com/health/print/2013/06/what-darkness-does-to-the-mind/276578/.
5. Fischer RJ, Halibozek E, Green G. *Introduction to Security*. 8th ed. Boston: Butterworth-Heinemann; 2008. p. 186–189.
6. Ferenc Jeff. *Lighting the way*. Health Facilities Management; 2011, February. Retrieved February 1 2011 from http://www.hfmmagazine.com/display/HFM-news-article.dhtml?dcrPath=/templatedata/HF_Common/NewsArticle/data/HFM/Magazine/2011/Feb/0211HFM_FEA_Marketplace.
7. Grayson James L. *4 Lighting Maintenance Tips*. Campus Safety magazine.com; 2010, June 14. Retrieved July 12, 2012 from http://www.campussafetymagazine.com/Channel/Security-Technology/Articles/2010/06/4-Light-Maintenance-Tips.aspx
8. McGovern M. *Who has the keys?* Security Products; 2008, July. p. 52.
9. Pires F. *Key boxes have come a long way*. 2009, March 3. Retrieved March 12, 2009, from http://www.campussafetymagazine.com/news/?NewsID=2754.
10. HowStuffWorks.com. *How does "bulletproof" glass work?*. 2000, September 26. Retrieved June 8, 2009 from http://science.howstuffworks.com/question476.htm.

CHAPTER

ELECTRONIC SECURITY SYSTEM INTEGRATION

19

Physical security is the heart of healthcare security. There simply is no substitute for the professional expertise and human touch of security officers in the healthcare environment. But carefully selected and properly applied electronic security technology is playing an increasingly important role in safeguarding healthcare facilities, whether integrated with the onsite security team, or as the primary eyes and ears of the security system at facilities without onsite security. The explosive growth of patient-generated violence and suicidal ideation, the threat of shooters coming into the healthcare environment, combined with the sheer volume of weapons being brought into healthcare facilities, have driven the demand for sophisticated integrated security solutions. Combine this with the real concerns stemming from prisoner patients who are cared for in a variety of healthcare settings, the continuing worry of infant or pediatric abductions, and the ever-evolving data security requirements promulgated to help secure protected health information. When all these are considered alongside the many other accreditation and regulatory requirements, is it any wonder that healthcare facilities are compelled to look through the many lenses that create an effective security program in the healthcare environment? It is not surprising that most healthcare organizations turn to security technology to supplement their existing security programs, to make their security staff more productive and effective, while reducing operating costs and mitigating the myriad of security risks surrounding the healthcare environment.

The IAHSS has developed a basic industry guideline on the integration of electronic security systems in the healthcare environment.

There are many technologies that can aid healthcare security staff in preventing crime and managing events. The primary electronic security systems most frequently integrated into the healthcare protection program are alarms (intrusion detection and duress), access control, emergency communication, video surveillance, infant protection, and more recently, visitor management. Today's security technological advancements in each of these areas, along with other applications, enable higher degrees of security in the healthcare environment without compromising aesthetics, user-friendliness or overall employee or patient/visitor experiences. Unfortunately, too many healthcare organizations do not proactively approve electronic security capital expenditures until something occurs. In an IAHSS survey of healthcare organizations, 22% of respondents who reported a spike in spending for electronic security technology in the previous year answered they did so because of incidents or threats.[1]

Security design considerations are discussed extensively in Chapter 17, "Security Design Considerations for Healthcare." In addition, the importance of security master planning and the need to develop a strategic planning process for the security program are discussed in great detail in Chapter 4, "Security Management Planning."

04.02 ELECTRONIC SECURITY SYSTEMS

Statement

Healthcare Facilities (HCF) will develop an electronic security system plan to provide guidance and direction for existing and future electronic system enhancements.

Intent

a. A properly designed and installed electronic security system should:
   1) Provide guidance for those involved in designing or enhancing the HCF's protection systems (e.g. security professionals, design and planning staff, architects, healthcare facilities administrators)
   2) Augment and improve the effectiveness of staff resources
   3) Deter and detect criminal activity and other undesirable activity
   4) Provide a useful after-the-fact investigative tool

b. Whenever possible, electronic security systems should be planned and implemented in an integrated manner. For example: local door contacts or other alarms should be integrated with video surveillance. Alarm activation should integrate with video surveillance systems.

c. Electronic systems should be tested with results documented on a scheduled basis and maintenance performed in a timely manner.

d. Electronic security system implementation and enhancement should occur after conducting a security risk assessment. After an adverse event, the plan should be reviewed with modifications made as needed.

e. Electronic systems should be installed in compliance with applicable life safety and building codes. Maintenance procedures for reducing the potential for system failures of panic alarms, video surveillance, etc. should be developed including periodic testing procedures.

   Approved: January 2006
   Last Revised: October 2011

A term pervasive in any discussion of electronic security safeguards is *systems integration*. Many subsystems are purchased and maintained as standalone technologies, creating many challenges and difficulties when the system functions are needed to work with one another. A move toward designing these multiple subsystems to work together as a master or integrated system continues. Systems integration thus entails either the subsystems operating from a single platform, or the subsystems working together to achieve efficient monitoring and cost-effectiveness. The healthcare security administrator should make sure the system is flexible, and that it will meet current and future needs.

The integration can be carried beyond the security level to include environmental controls and fire, and energy management, for example. This is becoming more and more common, especially in smaller hospitals and stand-alone clinics. There are, however, opportunities for dual, or redundant, monitoring between separate security and building management/engineering systems.

Integrating security technology in the healthcare environment requires the blending of good facilities management, information technology (IT) and the latest security best practices. All three aspects of hospital management have important parts to play in the overall security and asset protection of the organization. Facility management may have responsibility for maintaining access control and video surveillance hardware (as well as others) while information technology has a role to implement and upgrade the software for each. IT involvement becomes even more critical when the security systems run on the IT network of the facility or healthcare organization, as is increasingly becoming the norm. It is an essential function of the healthcare security administrator to work with the two internal partners to form a cohesive protection package.

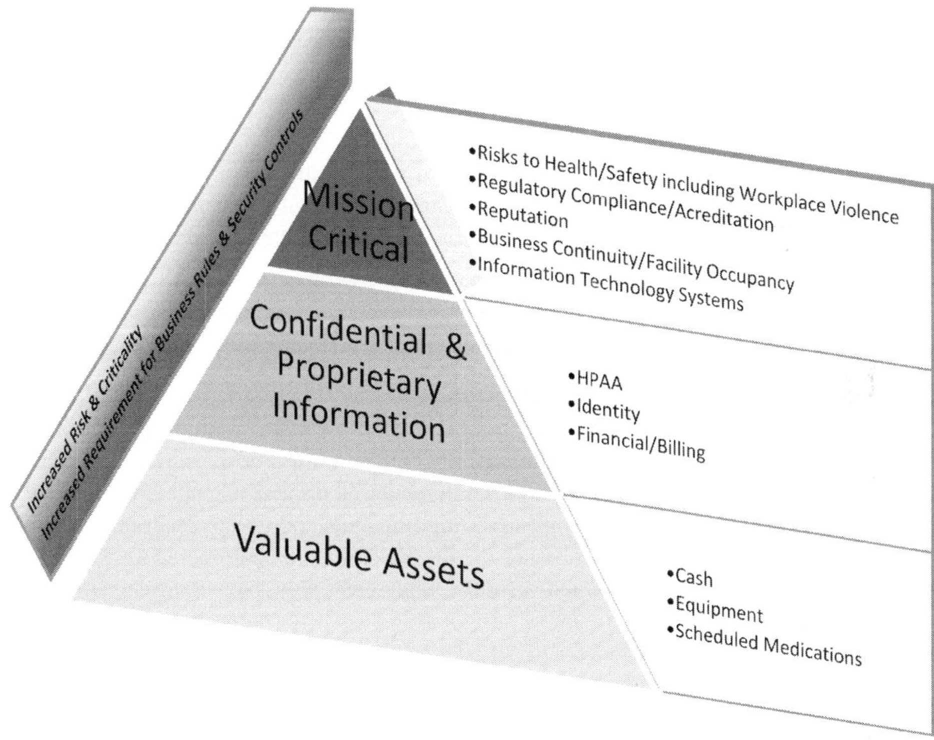

FIGURE 19-1

Security risk pyramid.

(Courtesy of Sandy Zirulnik.)

When considering security system purchases, Phil Hoffman, executive director of security, national facility services for Kaiser Permanente, recommends hospitals ask a few basic questions to help organizational leaders make better spending decisions:[2]

1) What are the risks that this security technology will address? See Figure 19-1. Organizations must identify and prioritize a wide variety of potential risks according to criticality and potential impact. The security program is a comprehensive strategy to protect against threats and mitigate potential negative effects of security incidents.
2) Are those risks realistic and critical? Why?
3) Will this security technology be a "nice to have," or is it really necessary for security?
4) Does it add value? How so?
5) Does it mitigate risks? How so?
6) Is it truly better than the current method? New technologies can sound exciting but may not offer much more in a practical sense.
7) Will we need to add this to other areas or facilities, or is it unique to this location?
8) What are the cost commitments for ongoing maintenance to keep the system running smoothly? (For example, technology will likely require periodic upgrades, so the costs of those should be considered.)

THE SECURITY OPERATIONS CENTER

The efficient operation of a protection system requires there be a hub, or center of operations. In smaller locations, this hub is likely to be the telephone operator, which is only marginally satisfactory but a necessity due to the limited availability of resources in small healthcare facilities, as well as the often corresponding lower levels of security activity. Generally, communications personnel resist the addition of security to their responsibilities. Without a security operations center, often called "SOC," the functions of answering requests for service, monitoring video surveillance and alarm systems, issuing access badges, managing visitors/vendors, and communicating with security officers, to name only a few functions, become much more difficult to manage.

ADVANTAGES

One of the basic functions of the security operations center is to handle communications with and for security staff. To maintain a high level of protection, all employees must be expected to report problems and suspicious activity to security. The easier the communication process is made, the more employees will be motivated to participate in the prompt reporting of events and utilize security department services. When a security officer or dispatcher answers the telephone, the communication is quite direct. Not only is quicker response time obtained for emergency calls, but also inquiries can be promptly handled without relaying messages. The monitoring and linkage with public safety organizations can also render their service more efficient.

The functions assigned to the security operations center will vary from organization to organization, depending on the security program offerings and complexity of the healthcare facility or system. In any case, a 24-hour post expands the possibilities and potential alternatives for program planning. Figure 19-2 shows an example of a hospital security operations center. The station monitors security, fire, and

FIGURE 19-2

Example of a hospital security operations center.

(Courtesy of Schneider Electric.)

critical electrical/mechanical building functions, and also serves as the operational center for a variety of security and management services.

DESIGN

When a central security station involves many process control functions, such as alarms, video surveillance, radio, and general monitoring, the design of the station requires considerable planning. One area often neglected is the human factor, which must be integrated with the physical aspects of the equipment. There are considerable differences in the size of the personnel who will operate the center; thus some averages must be determined. For example, a person who is 60 inches tall has a line of sight when standing of 56.5 inches; a 72-inch person has a line of sight of 69 inches.

In general, the distance averages noted in Table 19-1, which assume a seated shoulder height of 35 inches, can be used for planning sit-down consoles.

The horizontal and vertical sight recommendations are measured from a straight-ahead, level line of sight. Many dispatch console manufacturers provide for variable height consoles, electronically controlled with memory, to move up and down based on individual dispatcher desired dimensions. Temperature, humidity, ventilation, illumination, background noise, and sound absorption are also important factors to consider in the design planning process.

COST

The basic problem encountered in operating a security operations center is the expense, particularly for the labor required to maintain the post 24 hours per day (this requires a minimum 4.2 full-time time equivalent employees). Even though significantly increased protection will result, the required funding can be difficult to obtain. In addition to labor costs, the implementation of a central station can involve an extensive capital budget allocation over several years as well as ongoing operational costs for repair and maintenance. Prioritizing the services to be provided and realistically projecting the implementation of those services will help justify the cost and obtain required capital funding.

Proper planning can reduce the cost of a central station by reappraising the entire system and considering certain trade-offs. The first consideration is location. The SOC should be located in an area that requires the presence of a security officer and is readily accessible to employees and the public. Good locations include the entrance to the emergency room, the employee entrance, the loading dock, and even the front lobby. When situated in these locations, a double duty may be performed. The officers or dispatchers assigned to the post help with visitors, issue access badges to employees, vendors or

Table 19-1 Planning Considerations for Sit-down Consoles

Sit-down Console Planning Considerations	
Keyboard/controls	25–26 inch reach
Bench board height	25 inch minimum
Keyboard/counter depth	18 inch minimum
Bench board to chair seat	7.5 inch minimum
Horizontal sight	45 degrees maximum
Vertical sight	75 degrees maximum

possibly even visitors, in addition to fulfilling actual surveillance functions in the areas. All of this could be accomplished while fulfilling dispatcher responsibilities normally assigned to the security operations center.

If the station is located in an area that already has 24-hour security coverage, it might perhaps be established without additional personnel. Another approach is to look for an area that requires a part-time or full-time clerk performing a function in another facility department. It may be possible to integrate the clerk's role into the security function and divert more funding into the security budget.

Shared central station

A number of larger healthcare systems have found a shared central security station a more cost-effective alternative than individual security centers at each system hospital. Whether using a wide-area radio network, a radio repeater system, or other form of two-way radio communication, these organizations have found a cost-effective alternative to managing this important function. Sharing the security dispatch function and alarm monitoring often provides for multiple dispatchers on duty at a given time, offering important back-up in the event of an emergency as well as needed coverage during meal and rest periods. In Denver, Colorado, the HSS Inc. operations support center provides a centralized solution for security-related telephone calls, alarm monitoring, emergency communications and radio dispatching for the majority of the metro Denver area hospitals. The centralization expedites information sharing, speeds officer response times, and makes it easy for hospital staff and visitors to contact security. The service allows for the organization to specialize in the specific business of healthcare, and train dispatchers to deal with security and emergency-related issues when employees, staff, and visitors request or require security service.

A similar security control center in Canada has been created by Paladin Security Group, who provide a centralized operations center for the Integrated Protection Services (IPS) team in Vancouver, British Columbia. Staff at more than 30 healthcare facilities in four different health authorities call for security service using one standard urgent and another nonurgent phone number from any facility, generating approximately 30,000 calls per month. Duress and intrusion alarms are also received from the healthcare facilities by the Paladin Operations Centre (POC) and dispatched as urgent calls. The POC processes have been created to allow for the collection of important metrics which can translate to key performance indicators (KPI) and measure on site response times as well as critical call volume and typology of call metrics. The POC is also providing remote video monitoring (RVM) for IPS, an area planned for future growth in support of onsite resources.

Relatively few healthcare organizations share the central security station with other ancillary/support departments such as facilities, information technology and/or environmental services. This approach is growing in prominence with larger health systems with good success. The largest concern is often found in the operator's lack of understanding of security in the healthcare setting and the criticality of the calls for service received.

ALARMS

A basic component of most electronic security programs is an alarm system. Alarm systems have many fire detection and warning applications; however, the discussion in this chapter is limited to the application of alarms for security surveillance, response, and control purposes.

The use of security alarms in the healthcare environment continues to increase. If an alarm system is properly planned, installed, and utilized, it can be a very cost-effective component of a proactive security system. Costs are reduced significantly when alarm systems are designed and installed as part of new construction or renovation projects.

The factors limiting the use of alarms include limited availability of funding to resource the technology, lack of live-time monitoring capability, lack of knowledge of the usefulness of the system, absence of administrative or physician acceptance, imagined or real employee morale problems, and lack of innovative thinking to obtain funding and buy-in on the part of the protection administrator.

The security costs and the need to justify the budget force security administrators to recognize that finding the proper balance between security staffing and physical security safeguards is mandatory. Proper balance is the key phrase, as alarm applications are primarily designed to render security personnel more effective. It is possible alarms and other electronic security systems can reduce the total number of security personnel required for a given complex by increasing the productiveness of the security system. Increasingly, alarms are utilized for patient safety purposes—door alarms in behavioral/mental health or residential/senior care units as examples, where staff can receive an alert if a door is breached or other forms of alarm are triggered.

In planning alarm systems, the concept of security as layers of protection, as discussed in Chapter 17, "Security Design Considerations for Healthcare," may be helpful. The first concern is what is called the second layer of protection in the IAHSS *Healthcare Security Design Guidelines* or the building perimeter. The perimeter protection includes fences, windows, doors, roofs, and the like. Working inward, the next layer consists of the protection areas inside the building, which may be a room, a suite or a series of rooms, such as a pharmacy or gift shop storeroom. The next layer is point protection. The point may be a safe in the cashier's cage, a drug dispensary vault, office computers, or even a piece of art. One hospital had so many thefts of artwork it installed magnetic alarm switches behind each picture.

ALARM SYSTEM COMPONENTS

An alarm system is composed of three interrelated parts: the sensory device, the transmission medium, and an annunciator.

1) The sensory device determines a potential problem exists, generally through an electrical circuit either open or closed. The types of change an alarm system can detect include vibration, sound, and motion; a break in an electrical circuit; a change in pressure or temperature; the interruption of an energy beam; and a capacitance change due to the penetration of an electronic field. Each type of alarm has various applications in the healthcare setting. Each sensory device is often referred to as a point, and an alarm system monitors or supervises a number of these points. Current technology now allows security cameras to be programmed using analytics to activate an alarm if a preset condition is breached, such as a bag left in an area too long or movement in a normally unoccupied area after hours.
2) The transmission of the sensory device signal to the annunciation point is usually accomplished by hard wire, telephone lines, or radio waves, with the use of wireless systems also on the rise reflecting the rapid shifts in technology. The security of the transmission medium must not be overlooked; it must be monitored for line trouble or attempts to circumvent the alarm system.

3) The third component of the alarm system is the annunciation, or reporting point. The annunciator, sometimes called a monitor, is a visual or audio signaling device indicating the condition of the alarm circuits. Annunciation is usually accomplished by the activation of a signal lamp, visual display, printout, audible sound, or any combination of these elements.

Annunciation may occur in several places. A local alarm announces the signal in the immediate proximity of the area or item being protected. This announcement may be by bell, horn, light, or other means. For example, a door egress alarm might have a local audible screamer incorporated into the door hardware and notify a security dispatcher via a computer monitor. The local alarm functions as a deterrent to the wrongdoer, while having the system also monitored is more effective than either in isolation. Dark screen monitoring can allow a camera to activate under certain conditions, drawing the attention of the control center operator to a previously dormant camera through this form of alarm condition.

BASIC ALARM APPLICATIONS

The two basic security alarm applications found in healthcare facilities are the intrusion alarm and the duress alarm, also referred to as a panic or hold-up alarm. The intrusion alarm is used for protecting areas within a healthcare facility when they are closed for certain periods. This includes clinics, all types of pharmacies, nutrition services store rooms and refrigerators, gift shops, medical libraries, and off-site warehouses. This type of alarm is a primary safeguard utilized in many satellite pharmacies, non-24 hour facilities located on the main campus proper, such as a medical office building and off campus, such as clinics, and those that may be either category such as administrative/support services buildings.

The duress alarm is frequently used in cashier's offices, pharmacies, gift shops and public facing positions such as registration and admitting roles. This type of alarm is more often used to summon security personnel to observe suspicious people or activities. Duress alarms are frequently used in a variety of locations for several primary reasons.

- Behavioral health units, emergency departments, intensive care units, birth centers and pediatric departments are all locations with a high propensity for violence and other concerning behaviors.
- Cash handling locations, administrative offices, isolated staff locations or other remote worker locations to summon immediate assistance.

Regardless of the location, a key purpose is the ability to summon security or other available staff in the area to provide immediate assistance. In some instances, smaller hospitals and long-term care facilities have been found to use the application to summon medical assistance.

Historically, most duress buttons (alarms) have been hard-wired, attached to a wall or positioned under a desk, in a fixed location. In recent years, positive developments have helped bring a portable duress alarm product (also referred to as enterprise mobile duress systems) allowing an individual to move about a given "protected area" so the activation device can be carried or worn on the person. This wireless system generally operates using duress transmitters and integrated software applications to manage the alerting function to responders. Other recent technology development applications have allowed for the duress button as an icon on a desktop or laptop computer or a push-button connected through the computer USB port. Most recently introduced are personal duress apps for smart phones and tablets. Not all systems are created equal, so it is important for security administrators to understand how to specify and deploy a system that will best fit the needs of the campus being protected.

1) *Determine what you need.* As with any security solution, the first step in selecting the right system is to determine the key requirements for the application. This is best identified through a security risk assessment (or needs assessment) to determine the locations to be covered by the system. This should include determining which employees are best protected in their work location or with a dedicated duress transmitter that allows greater mobility. The system should be selected based on the needs identified.
2) *Create an implementation plan that includes selecting the right integration partner and system.* Choosing an integrator is just as important as selecting the system. Integrators should be well versed in the different technologies and have familiarity with life safety requirements. Bryan Jones, director of systems integration for HSS says "an integrator that has experience with several types of systems is ideal. Integrating location-based solutions requires more expertise, and an integrator who has experience can provide more value throughout the entire design and installation process."[3] The button or transmitter must get registered in the system and this will vary depending on the system configuration—location based or assigned to specific people. The final step is a complete system test and validation of coverage.
3) *Train your staff on how to activate the system and what should happens if a call is initiated.* It is important to train staff not only on how to use the duress system but also under what circumstances. Train on what happens after the button is pressed and what to do if the alert is not acknowledged. Training should be conducted with the onsite responders to make sure they know what the alert message will contain, the format it will take and if there are any escalation protocols built into the alerting system.
4) *Test and maintain the system.* Building configurations will change, people will move and system malfunctions may occur. A system should be devised to upgrade software and test duress devices to ensure the system is working as originally intended on a regularly scheduled basis. These tests should be fully documented.

Simple intrusion detection is probably the most familiar concept of security technology for most people. Intrusion detection involves the use of door or window contacts, glass contacts, and motion sensors, in combination with some type of audible alarm that sounds when a person has forced entry into a building or room. An alert is sent to a security operations center or other monitoring location to notify authorities of the time and location of the incident. Security officers typically respond in person to evaluate the situation.

This method of incident response can be adequate for detecting an event and quickly getting to the scene. The effectiveness of the response at the scene is dependent on the proximity of security personnel to the event and how serious it is. Few would argue against the intrusion alarm as a necessary component of a security system; however, there is little in place that would deter people from committing a crime in the first place, with the possible exception that signage indicating an alarm system may have some preventive value.

Duress Codes

A duress code is simply a word or phrase that alerts the person being called that the caller is in need of assistance. However, with advent of technology and the high turnover of healthcare personnel in many traditional higher risk areas, a relative few healthcare facilities continue to use such codes. Their use depends largely on their application and the number of people involved. If a protection system includes a security operations center that receives alarms and the personnel in the alarmed area are limited in number, duress codes are often effective. A gift shop operated by volunteers may find it difficult to educate all volunteer staff about the duress alarm and the use of duress codes, but should place great emphasis on the effort.

FALSE ALARMS

False alarms should be analyzed to determine the validity of an alarm system. False alarms result more often from personnel errors than from malfunctioning equipment. Proper installation is a key element in preventing false alarms, and alarm activation devices should be well-planned to avoid the false alarm problem. With portable duress alarms in particular, it is critical that the system be designed and tested to ensure the area of origination of the alarm is clearly delineated by the system. Delays caused by responders going to the wrong area or searching for the source of the alarm can have devastating consequences. Having too many false alarms tends to decrease the protection level. In some situations, alarm systems have been simply disconnected because the high number of false alarms rendered the system ineffective. Where the police are called, it is quite common for fines to be imposed upon the second occurrence of a false alarm. A high number of false alarms will often alter the type of police response a facility can expect.

ACCESS CONTROL

The healthcare environment and hospitals specifically, by their nature, are designed to be open and accessible to the sick and injured and their family and friends. Creating this welcoming environment, however, does have a downside and creates another risk altogether, allowing criminals and other dangers to easily enter through the facility as well.

Healthcare facilities face mounting security challenges in the 21st century. Many healthcare designs, especially older facilities, are open with large numbers of doors providing entry and allow too much accessibility to walk-in patients, visitors, vendors and anyone else who wishes to enter the facility, usually without any kind of record or accountability. Good security design and electronic access control technology can help manage this risk and help blend the type of environment desired for patients and visitors with good security practices. "There's a fine line between having an environment that's friendly and open and one that has the feeling of being locked down," says Mike Mandelkorn, the security director for Ohio State University's Wexner Medical Center.[4]

Access control, arguably the most critical aspect of protecting a healing environment, must start with thought to the design and desired flow of patients, visitors and staff. The goal is to allow patients/visitors to move freely without feeling oppressed while protecting both guests and staff. Access control can protect critical areas such as pharmacies, surgery rooms, infant treatment rooms, technology closets/information storage rooms and areas that separate staff from the public. Not only does restricting access afford staff protection, it safeguards assets as well. The general public enjoys a greater degree of protection knowing parking facilities are monitored, for example, and the flow of patient/visitor traffic is limited, observed and monitored.

Protection is important to every healthcare administrator, and it is incumbent on the healthcare security administrator to properly manage the first view patients and visitors have of the facility. That means access control systems used should not display a predominance of unfriendly barriers or obstructions. A defined philosophy of "on stage" and "off stage" is an important consideration in the design. Defining and delineating areas open to the public and those restricted to the public are important first steps. Once identified, determining the level of security access, the type of locking hardware to be used and restrictions to apply, are logical next steps.

The results of the continued acts of violence and terrorism in the aviation and education sectors, as well as inside of healthcare directly, have pushed heightened security in operations and design. The healthcare environment is one significant event away from following the direction these two market sectors have taken to improve environmental security and specifically the control of access to their buildings and areas of higher risk. The lack of media attention to the violent acts that continue to occur in the healthcare environment will not continue forever. Take, for instance, the March 2008 shooting spree at Doctor's Hospital in Columbus, Georgia. A gunman, allegedly distraught over his mother's dying at the hospital in 2004, brought three handguns to the fifth floor and shot a nurse and an administrative assistant, before he gunned down a patient waiting outside in the parking lot. Outside of the local community and state media coverage, and that by security-specific publications, minimal attention was brought to this horrific incident by the national and international media.

With the anticipation of increased media attention to the growing levels of violence in healthcare, and the general openness of the environment, will come administrative pressure to have a better plan to control access. The healthcare security administrator must give forethought in the design to how access will be controlled to the environment as a whole. The main entrance in particular is a concern, as most hospitals have limited control or awareness of who comes and goes through this entry point during normal business hours.

ELECTRONIC ACCESS CONTROL SYSTEMS

Electronic access control measures do more than just open a door. They allow or deny access to individuals based on the organization's needs. The software programs at the heart of these systems allow security administrators the ability to determine who gains access, at what time and on which specific days/dates. Security or other staff utilize password-protected software for audible alarms of intrusion, and develop reports for access control activity in the facility. Activity may include identifying individuals attempting to gain access to locations off limits, as well as identifying doors left ajar or needing mechanical attention.

Today's electronic access control program can protect "itself from itself" by requiring double or triple authentication for access. Lost identification cards are no longer feared, when biometrics or personal identification codes can be required to accompany the card, to gain entry to those areas requiring the highest levels of restricted access, such as the pharmacy, narcotic dispensaries, and IT server rooms.

These software systems can be monitored by security staff in a secure room, recorded for posterity and reports developed, or can send an alarm to a patrol officer to respond at the time of the occurrence. Figure 19-3 lists some of the most common access control applications in the healthcare environment, the pros and cons associated with each and general comments surrounding the application of each.

ACCESS CONTROL

Your Physical Access Control Cheat Sheet

Here's a breakdown of some of the pros and cons of the more commonly used physical access control solutions available on the market today.

By Robin Hattersley Gray, William Perkins and Robert Dolph

SOLUTION	STRENGTHS	WEAKNESSES	APPLICATION COMMENTS
KEYS	· Most traditional form of access control · Easy to use · Don't require power for operation	· Impossible to track if they are lost or stolen, which leaves facility vulnerable · Potential for unauthorized sharing of keys · Difficult to audit their use during incident investigations · Difficult to manage on large campuses with multiple doors · Re-coring doors when a key is lost or stolen is expensive	· Several solutions are currently available on the market to manage keys and keep key holders accountable
LOCKS **Maglock**	· Easy installation · Economical · Easy retrofit · Quiet operation	· Power always on (fail-safe) · Typically requires exit device to break circuit · Requires backup power supply for 24-hour service	· DC only · Always check with AHJ before installing · Comes in different "pull" strengths · Check extra features, such as built in door sensor
Electric Strike Photo courtesy Schlage	· Can be either fail-secure or fail-safe · Does not need constant power · Door knob overrides for safe exit	· Door/lock hardware experience needed · Can be complicated when specifying	· Requires more door hardware experience than maglock · Specify for life-safety requirements · Can be both AC and DC (DC lasts longer) · Fail-safe must have power backup · Fail-secure most popular · Choose AC version if you need buzzing sound
CARDS Photo courtesy HID	· Access rights can be denied without the expense of re-coring a door and issuing a new key · Can limit access to a building to certain times of the day · Systems can provide audit trails for incident investigations	· Prone to piggybacking/tailgating (when more than one individual enters a secure area using one access card or an unauthorized person follows an authorized person into a secure area · Users can share cards with unauthorized persons · Cards can be stolen and used by unauthorized individuals · Systems are more expensive to install than traditional locks · Require power to operate	· Can incorporate a photo ID component · Can be used for both physical and logical access control · Card readers should have battery backup in the event of power failure · Tailgate detection products, video surveillance and security officers can address tailgating issues · Can integrate with video surveillance, intercoms and intrusion detection systems for enhanced security
Magnetic Stripe (magstripe)	· Inexpensive to issue or replace	· Not as secure as proximity cards or smart cards · Can be duplicated with relative ease · Subject to wear and tear	· These are the most commonly used access control cards by US campuses
Proximity	· Durable · Convenient · More difficult to compromise than magstripe cards · Less wear and tear issues	· Cost more than magstripe cards · Easier to compromise than smart cards	· Are widely used for access control (although not as widely as magstripe)
Smart Card	· Multiple application functionality (access, cashless vending, library cards, events) · Enhanced security through encryption and mutual authentication · Less wear and tear issues		· Not as widely adopted as magstripe or proximity cards due to cost, although the price for this solution is now about the same as it is for proximity cards · Widely adopted in Europe · Can incorporate biometrics
PINS **(passcodes)**	· Easy to issue and change · Inexpensive	· Can be forgotten · Difficult to manage when there are many passwords for different systems · Can be given to unauthorized users · Prone to tailgating/piggybacking	· Should be changed frequently to ensure security · Often used in conjunction with other access control solutions, such as cards or biometrics
DOOR ALARMS	· Provide door intrusion, door forced and propped door detection · Reduce false alarms caused by unintentional door propping · Encourage staff and students to maintain access control procedures	· Will not reach hearing impaired without modifications · Will not detect tailgaters · Door bounce can cause false alarms	· Appropriate for any monitored door application, such as emergency exits and resident halls · Used in conjunction with other access control solutions, such as card readers or keys · Can be integrated with video surveillance for enhanced security

Brought to you by **Campus Safety**

FIGURE 19-3

Pros and cons of common access control technologies in the healthcare environment.

(Courtesy of Robin Hattersley Gray and Campus Safety *magazine.)*

ACCESS CONTROL

SOLUTION	STRENGTHS	WEAKNESSES	APPLICATION COMMENTS
TAILGATE/ PIGGYBACK DETECTORS	· Monitor the entry point into secure areas · Detect tailgate violations (allow only one person to enter) · Detect when a door is propped · Mount on the door frame · Easy to install	· Not intended for large utility cart and equipment passage (which could cause the system to go into false alarm) · Not for outdoor use	· Appropriate for any monitored door application where a higher degree of security is needed, such as data centers, research laboratories, etc · Used in conjunction with other access control solutions, such as card readers · Can be integrated with video surveillance for enhanced security
PUSHBUTTON CONTROLS Photo courtesy DSi	· Many button options available · Normally-open/Normally-closed momentary contacts provide fail-safe manual override · Time delay may be field adjusted for 1-60 seconds	· Anyone can press the release button (unless using a keyed button), so button must be positioned in a secure location (for access control, not for life-safety) · Some can be defeated easily · Can open door to stranger when approaching from inside	· Used to release door and shunt alarm · Used for emergency exits when configured to fail-safe · May be used in conjunction with request to exit (REX) for door alarms and life-safety · Required by many AHJs · Still may require mechanical device exit button to meet life-safety code and/or AHJ · With REX, careful positioning and selection required
MULTI-ZONE ANNUNCIATORS Photo courtesy DSi	· Display the status of doors and/or windows throughout a monitored facility · Alert security when a door intrusion occurs · Many options available: zone shunt, zone relay and zone supervision	· 12 VDC only special order 24 VDC option · Door bounce can cause false alarms · Requires battery backup in case of power failure	· Designed to monitor multiple doors from a single location · May be used in conjunction with door alarms, tailgate detection systems and optical turnstiles · No annunciation at the door; only at the monitoring station
FULL HEIGHT TURNSTILES	· Provides a physical barrier at the entry location · Easy assembly · Easy maintenance · Available in aluminum and galvanized steel	· Physical design ensures to a reasonable degree that only one authorized person will enter, but it will not detect tailgaters	· Designed for indoor/outdoor applications · Used in parking lots, football fields and along fence lines · Use with a conventional access control device like a card reader
OPTICAL TURNSTILES Photo courtesy DSi	· Appropriate for areas with a lot of pedestrian traffic · Detects tailgating · Aesthetically pleasing and can be integrated into architectural designs · Doesn't require separate emergency exit · Provides good visual and audible cues to users	· Can be climbed over · Not for outdoor use	· Used in building lobby and elevator corridor applications · Use with a conventional access control device like a card reader · To ensure compliance, deploy security officers and video surveillance
BARRIER ARM TURNSTILES (Glass gate or metal arms) Photo courtesy DSi	· Appropriate for areas with a lot of pedestrian traffic · Provides a visual and psychological barrier while communicating to pedestrians that authorization is required to gain access · Detects tailgating · Reliable	· Units with metal-type arms can be climbed over or under · Not for outdoor use · Most expensive of the turnstile options · Requires battery backup in case of power failure	· Used in building lobby and elevator corridor applications · Use with a conventional access control device like a card reader · To ensure compliance, deploy security officers and video surveillance · Battery backup is recommended
BIOMETRICS Photo courtesy Schlage	· Difficult to replicate identity because they rely on unique physical attributes of a person (fingerprint, hand, face or retina) · Users can't forget, lose or have stolen their biometric codes · Reduces need for password and card management	· Generally much more expensive than locks or card access solutions · If biometric data is compromised, the issue is very difficult to address	· Except for hand geometry, facial and finger solutions, biometric technology is often appropriate for high-risk areas requiring enhanced security · Can be used for computer access control (finger)
INTERCOMS Photo courtesy Aiphone	· Allow campus personnel to communicate with and identify visitors before allowing them to enter a facility · Can be used for emergency and non-emergency communications	· Will not reach hearing impaired without modifications · Not appropriate for entrances requiring throughput of many people in a small amount of time	· Appropriate for visitor management at residence halls, K-12 campuses, after-hours visits, loading docks, stairwells, parking ticket stanchions · Use with conventional access control solutions, such as keys or access cards · Video surveillance solutions can provide visual verification of a visitor

Brought to you by **Campus Safety**

FIGURE 19.3 Continued

SECURITY SENSITIVE AREAS

Section EC 1.2 of the TJC compliance manual requires that hospitals "have a plan to control ingress and egress from each defined Security Sensitive Area." Based on the risk, this plan could include the use of electronic access control or screening personnel, appropriate signage and/or staff monitoring. The protection of security sensitive areas is discussed in greater detail in Chapter 21, "Areas of Higher Risk."

AFTER-HOURS ACCESS CONTROL

After-hours continues to be a primary concern and time of risk for hospitals. Having a single clearance point to areas such as the emergency department or other designated points of entry is highly recommended to control access into the facility after normal business hours. It is a recognized best practice to lock all entrances during a predetermined set of hours and grant access into the facility via a defined approval process. This practice is frequently managed by security staff in larger hospitals, but may be handled by clinical staff, registration/admitting personnel or other associates in smaller hospitals, or those with minimal or no security staffing.

The after-hours screening system typically uses way-finding and signage to channel visitors and patients to a specific entrance inside the facility. A system of door controls, supplemented by video surveillance cameras equipped with an audio and remote release capability may be employed, that allows the security officer, who may be physically positioned away from the entrance, to authorize and grant access as required. Authorized staff can bypass the need to request a release of the lock by use of a key electronic push-button, card access device, or biometric technology.

Cookeville Regional Medical Center in Tennessee recently changed their practice of open visitation at night and moved to a single, limited access point in order to enhance its overall security. Positioned not as a metropolitan hospital, the after-hours closure was commented on by hospital CEO Bernie Mattingly as a measure to protect its patients, staff and visitors. In a message to the public, Mattingly apologized for any inconvenience this change may cause and asked the public to "understand that we have their safety and security in mind." He further commented, "Security and life safety issues are the most important considerations we have in operating a hospital, and we are constantly evaluating ways we can improve our operations to be the safest anywhere." The hospital used signs posted at the main hospital entrance announcing the change and printed maps to help aid visitors around the campus.[5]

RESTRICTED ACCESS CAPABILITIES (LOCKDOWN READINESS)

Whether for gang violence, infant/child abduction, patient surge or other big emergencies, one of the fundamental needs of an access control system within a healthcare facility is the ability to lockdown corridors, departments, wings, or the entire hospital quickly and efficiently. Lockdown procedures dominate discussions relating to emergency preparedness for healthcare organizations. The ability to restrict access quickly has been at the heart of spending for electronic access control systems for the past decade. A 2009 healthcare security survey conducted by *Campus Safety* magazine revealed the average lockdown time of a hospital was 11 minutes. As could be expected, the larger the hospital, the longer the lockdown time. What was startling was the survey concluded that 20% of hospitals had a lockdown time of over 15 minutes, while 7% of the hospitals that participated in the survey revealed that their facility could not lock down completely.[6]

How fast the healthcare facility can be locked down is a key indicator for facility readiness to many internal and external disasters, riots, civil disturbances, and other workplace violence scenarios. When managed from a central location, lockdowns are often fast and effective, but not every healthcare facility has this capability. Thus, it is imperative that hospitals and healthcare facilities practice their ability to restrict access to the facility, using both "table-top" exercises as well as actual drills or exercises—preparedness is paramount. The time it takes to restrict access to high-risk departments and other buildings on and off campus should be tested at least annually. When exercising the organization's ability to restrict access to the facility in an emergency, capability should be evaluated at all times of the day to include weekends and holidays. If all tests are conducted at three in the afternoon when staffing in the facility is at its peak, a true test has not been completed. Coordinating scenarios to test available resources when security officers are engaged with a patient in the emergency department, during a fire drill or mass casualty exercise is strongly encouraged. Medical facilities must work in tandem with local authorities to address these issues, test the lockdown capability and effectiveness, and make needed improvements.

The term "lockdown" is tossed around commonly, but this term means for the institution to take serious measures in the event of a crisis. A "lockdown" translates into doors locked, lights dimmed, no traffic in or out of the building and all staff to stay in their present location at the time of the "lockdown." Many locations may heighten their security and "restrict access" because of an event within or near the institution, but with regular activity continuing.

Restricting access to the entire hospital has become more common to protect patients and staff. A two-stage process can facilitate crowd control during a lockdown:

- *Stage 1* – Specific entry/exit points are locked and a physical presence (such as a security officer) may be required.
- *Stage 2* – All perimeter doors are locked or staffed.

Electronic access control systems are increasingly used for these functions, with wireless or hard-wired duress and single-action lockdown buttons provided for key personnel to close and lock Stage 1 and Stage 2 doors. Most electronic access control software permits the system administrator to lock all controlled doors from both entry and exit if deemed necessary. In short, with the advances in technology and locking hardware, a hospital and all related buildings should be able to be secured within a matter of a few seconds to mere minutes.[7]

SECURING EGRESS DOORS

Maintaining physical security for the healthcare environment is often a tricky proposition balancing best practices, regulations and available technologies. The need for a secure hospital is recognized by most authorities having jurisdiction (AHJ) and keeping unauthorized personnel from entering a facility, or those at risk from leaving the facility, is addressed clearly in the codes. However, the need to lock egress doors in the direction of exit travel remains a major code-compliance challenge. While there are many different types of systems to secure a healthcare facility, until recently there has been little guidance from the International Building Code (IBC) or National Fire Protection Association's (NFPA) 101 Life Safety Code (LSC) on how to implement this technology. The 2009 edition of the LSC allows for the locking of doors in the egress path in the direction of exit based on the clinical needs of the patient and the security needs of the patient and staff. Previously, this was limited to those occupancies locked only for the clinical needs of patients—i.e., psychiatric or Alzheimer units. These units were allowed to be locked at all times, provided they were staffed at all times and the staff had ready access to door keys.

The security needs address civil unrest, natural disasters, special detention and escapes that are unique to healthcare. Pediatric departments, for instance, may need to protect their patients from the general public or need to keep a runaway-risk patient from leaving the facility undetected. Locking egress doors for such purpose still requires approval from the AHJ, The Joint Commission, and the Centers for Medicare and Medicaid, if in the U.S., with documentation maintained for the time the secured area exists that includes:[8]

1) Staff can readily unlock the doors at all times.
2) Provisions made for the rapid removal of remote locks; keying all locks to keys carried by staff at all times; or other such reliable means available to staff at all times to open the locked doors.
3) A total smoke detection system is provided throughout the locked space or locked doors can be remotely unlocked at an approved, constantly attended location within the locked space.
4) The building is protected throughout by an approved supervised automatic sprinkler system.
5) The locks are electrical devices that fail safely so as to release upon loss of power to the device.
6) The locks release by independent activation of smoke detection or water-flow switch activation for the automatic sprinkler system.

The major differences between the locking requirements for clinical needs and for security needs are that nonclinical needs involve added fire protection for the space. In the clinical setting there is an assumption that staff are in close proximity to patients at all times. While that assumption holds for the security needs requirements, the system should also unlock without manual intervention.

The IBC does not have an option to lock doors in the egress path similar to LSC. Compliance with IBC requires an alternate method of compliance and acceptance by the local building and fire officials. The alternate method of compliance can be based on LSC 2009 criteria, but requires the approval of local officials. Further, the LSC criteria necessitate the integration of fire alarm system, automatic sprinkler system and loss of power to properly release the locked egress doors. System testing should address all the required releasing configurations listed in the LSC 2009. While requirements in these areas may vary somewhat from country to country, what does not vary is the need to involve the fire authority having jurisdiction in design decisions that may affect traditional functioning of egress doors.

ID BADGING AND CREDENTIAL MANAGEMENT

During Hurricane Sandy, more than 100 volunteer practitioners were brought in to help New Jersey area hospitals treat the increased number of patients. These volunteers worked and slept at the hospitals, needing access to many different areas of the facility. This experience illustrates the need to have a credential plan for employees, and the need to have plans for badging and controlling the movement of prospective volunteers who are major participants in emergencies.

Having a system that allows for quickly adding, deleting or editing credentials of employees, doctors, and temporary workers is an important consideration when evaluating access control systems. The key is to establish a system that works for patient care and does not interfere with the higher purpose of the healthcare facility.

Identification of which employees should be provided access to what departments is a decision that should not be made in a vacuum. Access levels and internal access matrixes are best defined by a facility planning committee, including security leadership with individual department heads. Defining access levels will depend on the type of system purchased and its capabilities, and the individual desire of the hospital or department head to restrict employees from various areas. For instance, the pharmacy will obviously restrict access to department employees and perhaps a select few others designated by the department director. Typically, the environmental services team is granted access by a pharmacy staff member to accomplish routine cleaning. The ICU, with a secured compartment, however, may prefer to grant access privileges to nutrition services and environmental services associates who routinely service the department. In most situations, there is no right or wrong decision, only consideration to the level of security desired, balanced with the necessary convenience to operate effectively and efficiently.

Identification badge issuance varies by facility. Some organizations use the security department to manage this function, while others use human resources department staff. Smaller healthcare facilities may use an administrative assistant from the facilities department. What is posted on the ID badge has also evolved, from having basic information such as name and department to color-coding to denote special access privileges. How much of the name is used has evoked some fear from nursing staff, who say they now need protection from the people they are trying to help. As a result, an emerging trend is to no longer have an employee's last name listed on their badges. St. Francis Hospital in Memphis recently made such a change as part of their focus on employee safety, citing that it gives (employees) some anonymity in case people get upset about something related to their care or if those individuals have (other) issues.[9]

A wide range of credentials may be used, including the more popular magnetic stripe and proximity cards. However, more and more healthcare facilities are migrating toward a smart card solution. Based on the individual requirements, temporary access codes may need to be set up for contractors and volunteers, remembering these still require audit trails and analytics. Smart card technology allows organizations to provide one card that can be used for different applications. Not only can it be used to gain access to physical locations, but it can be integrated into accessing the hospital's computer networks and electronic medical records (EMR). They can be used to match a healthcare provider with the patient to ensure safety during care or used by employees to conveniently pay in the cafeteria or vending machines, to check out scrubs, equipment or tools, as well as used for time and attendance and other applications.[10]

INTERCOMS/VIDEO DOOR PHONES

Often used to enhance electronic access control systems and integrated with video surveillance, a properly designed intercom system allows a visitor to be properly identified, and with the push of a release button, the staff member can unlock the door and permit access. Most importantly, these systems add an important convenience factor to the access control system and are frequently used by physicians and other care providers who may forget their issued access badge.

Video door phones display an image of the visitor shown in real time on the phone's monitor, and are usually accompanied by a built-in microphone and speaker on the unit to let the staff member see and communicate with the requesting party. Authorized visitors can then be granted entry with the push of a single button. The application is commonly used for exterior entrances, parking garages, human resource departments, hazardous waste containment areas, or security-sensitive areas such as the pharmacy, emergency care, maternity units or health information management departments. The system can help prevent accidental and/or unauthorized entry to susceptible and prohibited areas.

The use of these systems in parking garages has accentuated the ability to call for assistance in the event of serious trouble or if troubleshooting needs to occur with a gate arm. In Alberta, Canada, the Protective Services program operates a Provincial Security Control Centre (PSCC) with a parking function embedded in its operations, allowing parking patrons to resolve issues related to parking equipment from parking lots that may be hundreds of miles away from the Edmonton-based PSCC. Instant communication at ticket stanchions, parking garage stairwells and other locations within a parking structure have proven useful in maintaining a positive perception of safety in many healthcare protection programs.

Intercom systems are frequently used in assisted living or long-term care facilities in which housing or other living arrangements for the elderly, infirmed or disabled is provided. Commonly installed inside the resident's quarters, the intercom/video system can provide the opportunity to clearly identify visitors before permitting entry into the building or apartment. The systems can also be used equipped with emergency pull cords or buttons to provide instant communication capabilities, as well to ensure residents have vital and constant access to assistance at all times.

MANAGED ACCESS CONTROL

The concept of managed access is an emerging service that dovetails into central station services. The outsource management of the access control function is an alternative for many stand-alone clinics, or smaller healthcare organizations, who do not have the capital resources to install a sophisticated access system,[11] or the staff resources to manage the system daily. The managed access program can relieve a lot of upfront burden on the organization and continuing cost of ownership. However, to the end user, the door controls work the same. Typically, these systems work best in organizations that are controlling between one and eight doors.[12]

VIDEO SURVEILLANCE

Video surveillance systems have evolved significantly in the last several years. Older video systems needed banks of videotape for continuous recording, and required manual administration to swap tapes periodically during the day. Record keeping was prone to errors and finding specific events on tape was time consuming. Digital video recorders (DVRs) and closed-circuit television (CCTV) cameras have made significant advances in features and functions, taking advantage of fast computer processes and high density storage media to digitize, compress and record video from analog cameras.

Video surveillance, access control and alarms have much in common, and they often work together as an integrated system to keep intruders out of secure areas, limit access to infant and pediatric units, and remotely monitor critical areas to reduce the risk of crime and security incidents. It is why more and more healthcare organizations continue to increase their use of video surveillance as part of their overall security plan. Integrated together, the technologies help to render security personnel more effective, and they generally require monitoring and response. Some video surveillance systems have a philosophy of use intended to only capture (record) images to be utilized later if necessary. In these systems, there may or may not be any live monitoring involved.

DVRs and network video rRecorders (NVRs) have many advantages over older analog recording technology. Streaming video can be continuously recorded and discarded in cycles of days, weeks, or months if no security events occur. If an incident does occur, disk indexing and time-stamping make it simple to find video from a given date and time. In addition, because the video is digitized, it can be exported and distributed via e-mail or backed up on CD, DVD, or other digital media using common computer backup programs that are widely available. The IAHSS has developed a basic guideline on the use of video surveillance in the healthcare environment.

04.04 USE OF VIDEO SURVEILLANCE

Statement

Healthcare Facilities (HCF) will develop a policy to provide guidance and direction on the application, control, authorization and use of video images. Video surveillance is generally utilized as an after the fact investigative tool and when properly planned and installed may serve as an effective element of crime prevention.

Intent

a. Each HCF should determine the requirements for video surveillance in facilities and grounds based on security risk assessments.
b. Authorized site personnel should have the ability to observe video images of public areas via live viewing or have the ability to review recorded images for incident investigation.
c. Each HCF shall have a policy governing the protection of confidential information and images obtained from the use of video surveillance.
d. Requests by internal stakeholders, law enforcement, external agencies, or others for an archive record of video images should be directed to the person responsible for the security function, and may be granted if the request conforms to appropriate privacy and HCF policy and standards.
e. The person responsible for the security function should develop adequate measures to protect the information or images obtained from security video surveillance and establish a process so that information or images are observed, recorded or shared only with persons entitled to receive such information.
f. Video surveillance may be used in the HCF for non-traditional security purposes to include patient care monitoring or auditing of sensitive processes (e.g. cash handling, hazardous materials, controlled substances, and worker productivity). Such systems may be used for education and training, direct observation, or other similar uses. Images obtained from or information stored within such systems should be limited and shared only with approved shelf. When feasible, video systems used should be consistent for purposes of maintenance.
g. The use of covert video surveillance may be authorized in certain circumstances and under strict controls by the person responsible for the security function.
h. The use of dummy (fake) cameras should not be permitted.
i. Signage may be posted at the entrance of the facility where visible security cameras are utilized, indicating the presence of video surveillance equipment.
j. When integrated with security systems (e.g. alarm contacts/points, intercom, or other devices) video surveillance effectiveness may be enhanced.
k. Privacy protection measures are necessary to ensure the collection of personal information by means of video surveillance is lawful, justifiable, and that such information obtained appropriately processed.
l. The HCF's policy on video surveillance should identify a minimum of 10 days for a retention period for recorded images or as required by regulatory agencies.
m. Video surveillance is used for clinical, educational or other uses. Equipment should be consistent and compatible to allow for ease of maintenance and cost management.

See Also

IAHSS Guidelines 03.03 – Covert Investigations

Approved: February 2009
Last Revised: October 2013

BASIC USE OF VIDEO SURVEILLANCE IN THE HEALTHCARE ENVIRONMENT

The challenge for healthcare security professionals is not to fully understand the electronics of video surveillance, but to be innovative in applying this safeguard to manage risks and vulnerabilities. Video surveillance has two basic purposes in most healthcare security programs: access control and general surveillance. Access control applications may be found at emergency room entrances, receiving dock gates, physician offices, computer rooms, pharmacies, and basic building or parking access points.

Live monitoring of video surveillance equipment presents a more difficult dilemma to manage than monitoring alarms, at least for general surveillance. A person generally cannot view a monitor for more than 30 minutes without becoming bored and ineffective. Security experts in all industries agree that it is physically impossible to look at more than one camera at a time. Even if multiple views are squeezed onto large monitors, they would be rendered unusable for detection of most criminal activity or other malfeasance.[13] However, there is no standard rule on how many cameras operators can view at any one given time. Many video surveillance systems are thus "integrated" into the protection system so constant viewing is not required nor intended.

"Event driven" monitoring of video surveillance systems and the use of video analytics has improved dramatically over the last several years. This integrated approach involves monitoring equipment alerting the operator when the monitor must be viewed. In these systems, the monitor to be viewed will often be automatically shifted to a larger screen and will activate recording equipment. Occasionally in large security programs, this technology is integrated with the electronic access control system and called "video verification." The integration of these two systems, for example, allows a user to see live video as well as the cardholder's picture when a given access card is presented at a reader. The security staff can verify the person presenting the badge is the actual cardholder. Another example of video verification occurs in identifying individuals who are "tailgating," when one person swipes their badge and gains access to the facility and another person follows them in without presenting their badge. The integrated system allows organizations to visually identify, verify and capture security breaches at access points.[14]

General surveillance is one of the basic uses of video surveillance. When used for this purpose, the system is perhaps more of a psychological deterrent than an actual physical control. The configuration of the three cameras in Figure 19-4 was designed to protect the access points of the west side of the facility while a security officer at a monitoring station physically controlled access on the east side of the facility. The east side has the emergency room entrance and the after-hours entrance.

Video surveillance is increasingly being used for security in decentralized systems. The responsibility for certain aspects of security is returned to the operating or functioning level of a department. An example would be a loading dock requiring surveillance during receiving hours to determine who is coming and going and to address the vulnerability of unattended shipments on the dock for short periods of time. Thus the materials management department may be the primary monitor of the dock using video surveillance. To accomplish this, a monitor could be placed on a secretary's desk or at another location within the department in addition to secondary or after-hours monitoring at the security operations center or other designated location.

Another example of the decentralized approach is the placement of a camera in the corridor just outside the various pharmacy entry/exits. A monitor is placed inside the department, in close proximity to the door, allowing employees to view the corridor and areas outside of the pharmacy before opening

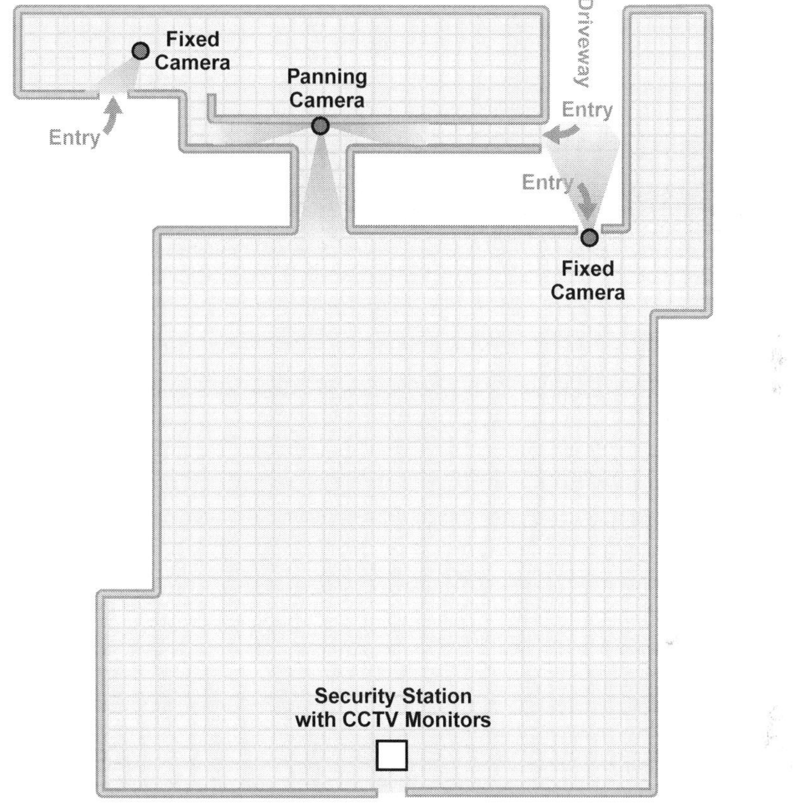

FIGURE 19-4

Example of using CCTV to protect one side of the facility with a security officer controlling access and monitoring cameras on the opposite side.

the door to exit. In the decentralized design shown in Figure 19-5, one camera can be viewed by two different groups.

In the United Kingdom, the National Health Service has deployed cameras in their emergency wards and in ambulances in an effort to cut the rising levels of violence against NHS staff. The cameras are designed to collect evidence and prosecute people attacking NHS staff.[15] Brian Main, the security manager at Ninewells Hospital in Dundee, Scotland believes the extensive video surveillance coverage deployed at his hospital has resulted in the people responsible for committing offenses to be swiftly identified and brought to justice.[16]

In the U.S., the Federal Bureau of Labor Statistics reports that healthcare professionals who deal with behavioral health patients, work in admissions, emergency rooms, crisis and acute care units along with emergency medical response teams experience the largest number of assaults.[17] Properly located

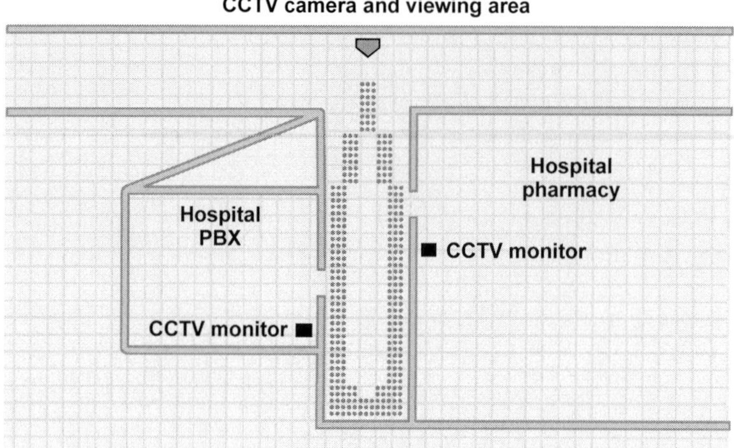

FIGURE 19-5

An example of the use of video surveillance for security purposes in a decentralized configuration.

video surveillance cameras can extend the range of the security staff and provide valuable incident information.

To increase staff safety, recommended camera locations in the healthcare environment include:

- Main entrance of emergency rooms, waiting rooms and nontreatment areas within the examination/treatment space
- All hospital entries that offer entry into the facility; placement of strategically visible public monitors are low-cost deterrent
- Admissions desks and elevator banks
- Locations where controlled substances are present, to include the pharmacy and narcotic dispensaries
- Receiving docks, central sterile supply and other locations storing items of value
- Mother/baby, pediatric, behavioral health and geriatric units: to help prevent abduction and patients from wandering off
- Parking lots and garages have high pedestrian traffic and often have many hiding places for an attacker to hide[17]

A study conducted by the University of California at Berkeley of the Community Safety Cameras deployed in the city of San Francisco found no evidence of an impact that the strategically deployed cameras had on violent crime. However, the study found "statistically significant and substantial declines in property crimes within view of the cameras" pointing to a significant deterrent effect cameras have on property crimes.[18]

Spartanburg Regional Healthcare System in Spartanburg, South Carolina found out that video surveillance does not deter all violent crime, as they recorded footage of a man cornering a woman in an elevator and using an intimidating presence to rob the woman. However, the video from the hospital was released to the police and to local media outlets, resulting in the arrest of the suspect.[19]

Proactive security administrators are increasingly linking the use of video surveillance to patient safety, extending the application beyond the traditional asset protection and crime prevention/detection functions that have long dominated discussion in this area. As an example, strategically located cameras, especially on the facility property perimeter, can be utilized to quickly determine if an eloped patient has left the property, potentially negating the requirement for an exhaustive search of the facility, a search that could take several hours in the case of a very large medical center. In many cases, where patients may be at imminent risk of self-harm, or present a risk to others, this information may be critical. In such instances, the ability to quickly retrieve and view camera images is essential, a role often played by security or communications center staff.

EQUIPMENT

The most important consideration in a video surveillance system is the quality of the image received, and this is largely dependent on the camera and the video management system. The major factors crucial to picture quality are amplitude response, signal-to-noise ratio, resolution, horizontal aperture correction, sensitivity, and transfer smear. Comparing these qualities, in relation to the price, will provide the right camera for a specific application.

The transmission of the signal to the monitor also affects image quality. Although coaxial cable is widely used for analog cameras, CAD 5 cabling is used for most internet protocol (IP) cameras. A recent trend is the cameras themselves have video processors, which can reduce network bandwidth requirements by sending high-speed, high-resolution images over the network only when required.

The size of the monitor should be based on the purpose of monitoring and individual preference. A general rule is to increase the size of the monitor as operator-viewing distance increases.

The charge-coupled device (CCD) is a widely used chip camera. Chip cameras generally do not need heaters, consume much power, or need a large protective housing. Despite some drawbacks in resolution and sensitivity, they have effectively replaced tube cameras.

Another major advance is the use of microprocessors and microcomputers in video systems. This technology allows systems, formerly operated manually, to be preprogrammed and automated. DVRs (with analog cameras) and NVRs (with IP-based cameras) are often used for forensic analysis of events. These products offer advanced video processing modules that can be applied in a hospital setting, including face and object recognition and crowd anomalies (e.g., someone leaving an object such as a backpack, people traveling the wrong direction, and motion detection).

In healthcare facilities, where dependable surveillance is essential but price is often an object, the necessity of upgrading an existing analog video surveillance system to match the digital equipment of the new system is often debated. Typically when a new surveillance system is installed, the old system becomes a relic. During the transitional stage, typically the healthcare organization must duplicate equipment rooms and terminal feeds. Providence Everett Medical Center in Everett, Washington, faced with the conversion of analog cameras to digital during a large renovation project, found converting the analog signal to digital before routing to the digital video recorder was a good first step. The organization created an internal policy to replace all existing analog equipment as it failed, thus maximizing the functionality of remaining equipment.[20] The different requirements for analog and digital surveillance equipment are significant. A comparison of the different system requirements is noted in Figure 19-6.

COMPARISON OF ANALOG AND DIGITAL SURVEILLANCE SYSTEM REQUIREMENTS

Analog system requirements	Digital system requirements
Matrix switcher to control camera input/output; Signal splitter to determine number of camera views per screen; Amplifier to provide signal boost over long cable distances; Monitor (cathode ray tubes are being replaced by liquid crystal displays); and Keyboard/joystick controller to provide human-machine interface.	Server (on-site or off, dedicated or shared); and PC work station (all functions handled by PC).
Recording device (video cassette recorders are being replaced by digital video recorders).	Recording device (digital video recorder).
Six-conductor, 22-American wire gauge (awg) control wire; Two-conductor, 18-awg power wire; and RG59 U-type coaxial cable for signal.	CATS cable (all functionality and power is delivered through one cable).
Camera lens; Enclosure; and Pan/tilt mount.	Camera (commonly housed in a dome with pan/tilt/zoom on board).
Power supply (cameras typically run on 12/24-volt direct current power).	Network switcher (interface with local area network, collecting points and power to camera).

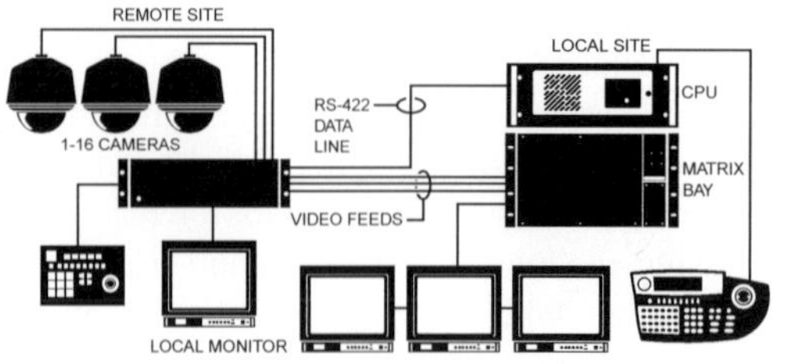

ABOVE **An analog system with a central processing unit, local matrix switcher, satellite switcher, keyboard controllers, multiple cameras and monitors.**

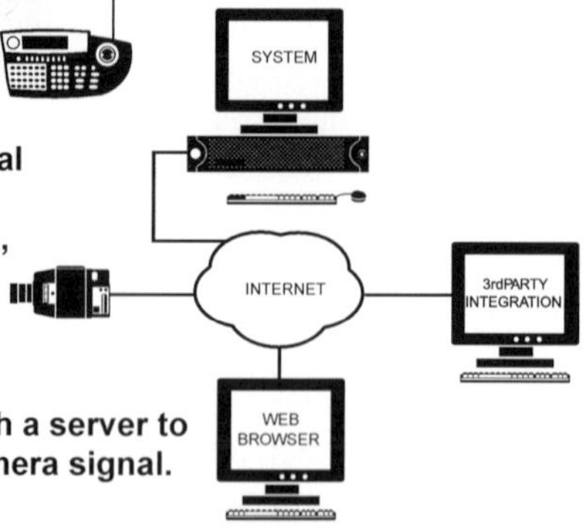

RIGHT **A digital system with a server to clients all receiving the camera signal.**

FIGURE 19-6

Comparison of analog and digital surveillance system requirements.

(Courtesy of Pelco by Schneider Electric.)

Internet protocol cameras

Increasingly, electronic security systems are converting from analog to digital, Internet protocol (IP) based equipment to provide and transport information that facility staff need to manage security threats. IP based cameras are now more widely accepted and quickly becoming the standard in the healthcare industry. With digital, IP-based CCTV systems, camera images are now available anywhere the data network is available, unlike analog systems that generally require coaxial cable at each viewing location. Besides providing a digital platform, IP cameras offer some real advantages over traditional analog cameras. According to Ben Scaglione, CPP, former director of security at New York Presbyterian, Weill Cornell Medical Center, IP cameras:

- Can be wireless
- Can be powered over the network utilizing one cable for both power and video signal
- Are scalable, flexible and allow for open architecture
- Allow video to be easily transferable to hard drives; searching and retrieving video is faster and easier
- Come with high definition or megapixel capacity
- Offer analytics that can be programmed into camera, freeing up network bandwidth and improving storage and processing capabilities.[21]

For organizations installing 40 cameras or more, the cost for IP cameras is generally lower than analog cameras as labor costs offset the higher equipment costs.[22] There are five basic questions that every healthcare protection administrator should ask before embarking on an IP-based camera project.

1. *What are the IT department's network standards?* Every IT department has its own set of requirements for networks, cabling, hardware and software. Be inclusive and get IT involved often and early.
2. *How are the cameras and software going to work together?* With the volume of IP camera choices, it is wrong to specify only resolution and style. The chosen camera should have a proven track record for communicating with a particular software package. It is much easier to manage and support if all cameras on the network are by a single manufacturer.
3. *How critical is the recorded video?* Defining upfront the purpose behind collecting the video image as for evidentiary, regulatory, or liability purposes will determine hardware and system configuration.
4. *How long does the video need to be available?* Most storage calculators have four variables: frame rate, compression type, hours of camera operation and the average percentage of activity or motion the camera will experience on a daily basis. In any case, the calculation is not an exact science but the requirements should not exceed 75% of the storage device upon installation.
5. *Does the system need to be scalable in terms of adding cameras to the system in the future?* The server configuration must have enough horsepower so that the processor does not exceed 60% of its capability. The type of camera chosen and the compression technology selected are the two drivers of this load factor.[23]

Analog cameras continue to have some advantages over IP cameras, especially in specialty applications. Infrared (IR) cameras, for example, use IR lighting so even where there is no, or low, ambient light the IR image is still available. Wide dynamic cameras balance backlight with images in the foreground so both are visible. These products are good for lobbies where there is bright light outside, but the inside is relatively dark. The specialty analog cameras can be incorporated into IP video systems through the use of encoders. Encoders can also be used to connect older analog cameras to IP systems when cost is a concern to replace legacy camera systems. Systems that use both IP and analog technology are commonly called hybrids.[24]

Video analytics

From its inception, video analytics has been touted as a solution to assist those providing security to critical infrastructures with a powerful means for identifying and detecting intruders, tracking people or objects, and producing an alarm on types of behavior. The benefits of video analytics have begun to be realized in the healthcare environment. For example, foot traffic in the evening past a closed pharmacy may be considered normal. But lurking near the pharmacy door may be an indication that a break-in is about to happen. Another example of applied video analytics is a fence-climbing alarm. Security staff may know that it is common for people to walk along the outside of a fence, horizontally across the field of view. They are typically not concerned, as it poses no threat. Yet if someone were to begin to climb the fence, producing vertical motion across the field of view, this is deemed as an alarm, and video is transferred to the security central station.

There are numerous video analytic features developed that can track various behaviors— from recognizing an abandoned briefcase or duffel bag to determining when someone is loitering in a specified zone. The analytic capabilities offered today are limited only by the creativity of the user and the need presented; examples include:

- *Directional Motion* – when motion is detected in a specific direction, an alarm is triggered. Users have wide flexibility in defining areas of interest and activity thresholds to minimize false alarms.
- *Adaptive Motion* – advanced motion detection behavior calibrates to scene conditions, allowing the system to distinguish targets from other movement in a scene, such as headlight glare, leaves blowing, a flag flying or snow falling. It is ideal for identifying people and vehicles in parking lots and perimeter detection with such outdoor conditions.
- *Vibration Removal* – reduces video shake in applications where cameras are subject to vibration, providing a clear picture despite camera shake. Ideal for external cameras with long focal lengths, pole-mounted cameras and an array of other applications.
- *Object Removal* – alarm triggers when a stationary object, such as a piece of art, is removed from a selected scene. This analytic behavior allows the user to define an object or area of interest in a scene. Motion is allowed in the protected zone, but if an object is removed, an alarm is triggered.
- *Object Counting* – this behavior counts objects when motion is detected in a specific direction. Users have a wide flexibility in defining areas of interest and activity thresholds. An alarm is generated when the threshold is exceeded. Ideal for counting cars in a parking garage or counting visitors entering/exiting a high-risk department or other similar situation.
- *Camera Sabotage* – advanced video loss detection recognizes when video has been compromised. For example, if a vandal paints or covers a lens, or reaches to move a fixed camera away from an intended scene, an alarm is triggered.
- *Abandoned Object* – an alarm triggers when a stationary object appears and remains in a scene, such as a person setting down a backpack in the main lobby. This behavior allows the user to define an object or area of interest in a scene. Motion is allowed in the protected zone.

- *Loitering Detection* – when people or vehicles remain in a defined zone longer than the user-defined time allows, an alarm is activated. This behavior is effective in real-time notification of suspicious behavior around pharmacy departments, ATMs, narcotic dispensaries and other locations.
- *Stopped Vehicle* – vehicles stopped near a sensitive area longer than the user-defined time allows are detected. This behavior is ideal in loading and receiving docks, parking enforcement, and vehicle waiting at parking gates.
- *Auto Tracking* – Pan/tile/zoom capability to track vehicles or humans entering or stopping in user-defined zones. Once identified, the camera locks on and follows the subject's path. This analytic is best for building perimeters.

Expectations surrounding the productivity improvement anticipated from using video analytics must be addressed up front. Video analytic products can do amazing things but some do no more than basic motion detection. If video analytics are used, the healthcare organization must know and plan up front how they plan to use a system. Knowing the threat or risk to be managed is critical in setting up these systems.

Many healthcare organizations have installed this new technology with preconceived notions of how video analytics can bring reductions in security staffing, or increase the effectiveness of deployed security officers. Rarely do these assumptions prove true. In many instances, the video analytic product can actually increase the burden on the security department. The Universal Security Systems' guideline is to expect one false alarm per camera per hour.[25]

Many of these systems claim to work right out of the box. However, there are more variables and parameters in video analytics than other camera solutions. Proper design is the only way to help avoid these errors and their increased cost of ownership, which includes:

- *Lighting issues.* Not enough light causes poor camera quality; light in the wrong places can produce shadows, glare and dark spots.
- *Detection ranges.* Know how many pixels on target the system requires, and design the camera coverage accordingly.
- *High false alarm rates.* Wind in many regions can cause false alarms, as can sun glare, shadows and the presence of other nuisances.
- *Transmission issues.* Weak networks, wireless links and improperly terminated video cable can create headaches.[26]

Facial recognition and other identification technology

Many healthcare facilities are located in high-crime areas but still wish to maintain an open environment. Atlantic Health, a large healthcare provider serving northern New Jersey and metropolitan New York, has many such facilities. The health system has deployed analytic facial recognition technology to help monitor upwards of 60 doors, that people can come in and out of. A force multiplier for the security staff, the system alerts staff of potentially dangerous or high-risk individuals that have been identified in the hospital's database. This is based on pictures of people the hospital uploads, so they know every time these individuals enter any one of Atlantic Health's facilities. The healthcare system also pays a monthly subscription fee in order to access several national databases, which determines in real time if an individual has a criminal history. The system has partnered with a company to help them verify a person's identification, utilizing the National Crime Information Center, the federal Terrorist Screening Center watch list, as well as all 50 state's Department of Motor Vehicle databases.[27]

Beyond traditional security concerns, facial recognition can be used to identify a patient who may present with false identification, resulting in a potential medical fraud. For example, if someone receives tens of thousands of dollars in medical care using a false identity, the hospital can be held responsible for the costs, and may also face additional insurance fraud penalties. The system can also help identify individuals impersonating staff or posing as doctors.

Because the technology can compromise privacy laws, the health system has had to build in several safeguards. For example, staff who scan a patient's driver's license only receive a "clear" or "not clear" alert. They are not provided with any information regarding why that person has been flagged. That information is filtered to security department leaders.

Atlantic Health also uses a license plate reader system that sends information to the state crime system, and the security staff receive information about a wanted felony vehicle. When a vehicle is identified through the system, it alerts both the hospital and local law enforcement.[27]

Thermal imaging cameras

Thermal imaging cameras provide the ability to look at any structure and see the slightest shift in temperature and spot leaks, ruptures, hotspots, animals, and intruders. This technology allows security personnel to detect threats, without the need for natural or artificial illumination, and works in all types of weather and lighting conditions. The application is not widely used in the healthcare environment, but has application in laboratories, IT server rooms, and other high-value asset protection, where subtle differences in appearance cannot be detected through traditional camera systems.

Covert cameras

Covert cameras can be a very useful tool in the investigative process, but must be used with discretion and appropriate administrative approval. By definition, covert camera installations refer to an application where the presence of the camera is unseen and unknown. As an investigative tool, covert cameras are usually viewed as "a last resort" in the healthcare environment, where other investigative methods have proven unsuccessful or are not available. These cameras may come in many forms, their presence obscured to those whose image may be captured.

According to Dave Mongeau, CPP, a healthcare investigator with 35 plus years' experience, one of the more common covert cameras is the "smoke detector" camera. This camera has been available for years and has proven to be very useful as most employees rarely notice their existence. This particular style of covert camera provides the end-user an unobstructed view of a very large area when used with a wide-angle camera lens. Another useful covert tool is "Micro DVRs"; these are about the size of a deck of cards, when used with double-sided tape. These devices can be installed in seconds. Most frequently used in the motion detector mode, the devices can be very useful after hours in an office experiencing theft problems with minimal after-hours activity. The micro DVR is not, however, a good tool for areas with high activity.

A large number of covert camera styles are available off-the shelf, such as the "pencil-sharpener" and "clock" cameras. Custom-built covert camera enclosures have been created for many specific applications and are limited only to the creativity of the requesting party and the resources available to mitigate the risk.

Evidence collected during the covert investigation should be reviewed with the human resources department if the situation involves an employee. If a criminal act has occurred, chain of custody regarding the captured images is an important consideration should the healthcare organization pursue prosecution. The security administrator should be responsible for the chain of custody and the required written documentation.

Body cameras on security staff

The Hillingdon Hospitals NHS Foundation Trust in the UK has purchased three body-mounted surveillance cameras in an effort to combat acts of violence and aggression experienced by their security officers. The security officer wearing the body cameras are instructed to warn people in advance that they are going to be filmed. However, the cameras record images just like CCTV, but with the extra advantage of recording sound. Other London hospitals have seen a dramatic reduction in violent events since introducing the cameras.[28] Not as common today in the U.S. or Canada, body cameras are expected to grow in acceptance by healthcare administrators, security leaders and staff to provide an additional deterrence against aggressive behavior and provide evidence for prosecution against offenders. While these cameras are more widely used in nonhealthcare settings, the potential encroachment on patient privacy has likely slowed their migration to the most sensitive of security applications, the healthcare environment.

RECORDING

As a general rule, all cameras utilized in a security system for after-the-fact investigation and overall deterrence should be recorded, and the recording retained in a minimum 10-day library. It is not uncommon to maintain recorded images for 30 days. The key is for the organization to determine what is appropriate for the camera and the camera system, and that actual practice follows policy.

There are, however, two known exceptions to this basic healthcare security industry guideline. The first exception is the use of video surveillance in patient care areas or for patient monitoring. Of great debate among many healthcare providers is whether the recorded video image is a medical record. Various interpretations of the patient privacy (or HIPAA) regulations yield differing opinions. One interpretation is the recording should be a part of the medical record and stored accordingly with health information management. Other healthcare professionals feel the only documentation needed in the medical record is that the image was recorded. To date, there is no clear direction on which interpretation is correct. The security administrator involved with determining the stance of an individual healthcare organization on this important issue is encouraged to engage the organization privacy officer, risk management and legal counsel. Regardless of which direction is chosen, the organization should clearly choose between these two distinct interpretations, clearly document its policy and procedure, and consistently follow the practice as written.

The second exception is the use of video surveillance solely for the control of access into a secured unit/department. Take for example the pharmacy: cameras may be deployed and integrated in an intercom system used to talk with and identify a staff member requesting entry into the department. In this application, the camera's purpose is to identify who is being granted access into the department and not for collecting a recorded image. Some healthcare organizations have chosen to record cameras used for this basic purpose. However, it is not an industry standard practice.

In some jurisdictions, cameras are intended to support direct patient care; again this application brings the cameras into the patient safety realm. Examples would be cameras situated on a nursing unit to mitigate "blind spots" in unit design and improve the line of sight capacity for clinical staff observing their patients outside of the patient room, in corridors and the like. Seclusion or observation rooms are also applications where cameras may be used by clinical staff to enhance their continuous observational capacity of patients under environmental restraint. In Canada, for both of these applications, cameras are often not recorded and images are usually available in real time from a monitor located at the nursing station. These cameras often do not feed into the central security monitoring system platform. The subsequent section of this chapter provides more detailed description of patient care surveillance applications, where recording may be utilized, and references CMS expectations for the U.S.

In short, the driving purpose for the use and application of video surveillance should govern whether or not it is recorded. The purpose and use should be documented in the security master plan.

MONITORING

A major question regarding the use of any video surveillance system is how the cameras will be monitored. The answer, of course, depends on the application. There are many combinations of monitoring, from a dedicated security monitoring agent centrally monitoring the system on a full-time basis to no live monitoring at all. In the case of no live monitoring, the cameras are simply recorded for future viewing if necessary. There are partial viewing and redundant (two or more viewing locations) monitoring models as well. Redundant monitoring is generally reserved for specific strategic cameras and is most often found in video surveillance systems that utilize both a centralized and decentralized design model. An example of redundant viewing would be the facility birthing area. It is common to install a completely self-contained system for this area being monitored on the unit. Only certain cameras would also send signals back to a centralized security monitoring point.

In programs without full-time security officer monitoring, it is common to locate the video monitors at the facility telephone switchboard (or PBX operator). In this application, the monitors should be set facing the operators. They should not be so high the operators must constantly strain to look upward. This positioning saves space and allows the operators to make normal eye contact with the monitors while they carry out their primary duties. In some programs, security alarms and the security radio system are also controlled from the main switchboard. A problem arises when the operators are reluctant to take on this additional responsibility. Telephone operators, who are on duty 24 hours a day, are often given many extra responsibilities and therefore can be overloaded.

Another area for monitoring is the engineering control room, found in many modern physical plants. Electrical, mechanical, water conditions, and other functions are monitored in this room. This location may also provide an acceptable place for monitoring security equipment, and/or be a backup area for security monitoring should the primary security monitoring equipment malfunction or in the event the control center would need to be evacuated.

VIDEO SURVEILLANCE IN PATIENT CARE AREAS

Today, the role of video can extend far beyond security. Data gathered from video surveillance can now help decision makers grow a business rather than just protect it. Healthcare also uses it to support patient care efforts. Healthcare organizations are deploying cameras to help with telemedicine, quality management of surgeries, patient safety, and remote monitoring of patient behavior.

Henrico Doctor's Hospital in Richmond, Virginia created a virtual Intensive Care Unit capability using pan-tilt-zoom cameras that enable their physicians and other healthcare staff located elsewhere in the three-hospital health system to observe and zoom in to see what's happening in each patient room. The cameras, equipped with intercom capabilities, provide for two-way visual and audio interaction. The cameras in these patient rooms are recorded and have extra precautions taken to maintain patient confidentiality.

Lancaster General Hospital in Pennsylvania has added video cameras to all 42 operating rooms. Placed in the center of the main surgical light, the camera provides everyone in the room with the surgeon's view, including nurses, anesthetists, and other medical personnel. A patient safety focused initiative, the fewer people going in and out of the surgery room has lowered the risk of infection. Physicians also use the video to discuss a particular case with other physicians as well as use the video images to teach academic courses.[29]

According to Dr. Tracy Buchman, former director of safety and emergency management at the University of Wisconsin Hospitals and Clinics in Madison, and current national director of emergency preparedness for HSS Inc., video monitoring of activities in patient rooms and patient areas is permitted in five situations.

1. *Undisclosed clinical monitoring.* Conducted as a purely clinical endeavor for patient safety and to assist in diagnosis. An example is clinical suspicion of Munchausen syndrome by proxy.
2. *Undisclosed law enforcement monitoring/recording.* Conducted with an appropriate court order authorizing the activity.
3. *Department of corrections.* Monitoring of the locked department of corrections unit and patients in its custody.
4. *Disclosed video monitoring with consent.* Conducted with written consent of patient or the patient's representative. For example, need to monitor behavior of staff or visitors other than the patient's representative.
5. *Hospital legal department approval.* Situations not noted that may have a legal basis for monitoring. Special authority does not exist to authorize monitoring. The purpose is to determine if there is some legal basis for providing approval.

Organizations challenged by the lack of clarity provided by rules and regulations promulgated by HIPAA and various CMS surveyor interpretations have elected to acquire and install cameras with a "covert" feature that allows for internal camera analytics or video management software to blur the face of the patient. According to David Corbin, CHPA, CPP, "With this setting, the image is only displayed to users with a certain level of password protected access. The video footage can still be used in a forensic capacity while keeping it safe from unauthorized viewers." However, in some states such as Wisconsin, state statute prohibits the video recording of behavioral health patients without their written consent.

Many organizations have begun to monitor patient behavior in the emergency department or in the behavior health units remotely. In the U.S., CMS is specific in their expectations of healthcare organizations, and expect staff to take extra care to protect the safety of the patient when interventions that are more restrictive are used. Specifically, CMS requires continuous monitoring and if conducted remotely, must include both audio and video monitoring equipment. The staff member monitoring the patient using the audio and video equipment must be in close proximity to the patient and their monitoring must be uninterrupted.[30] Cameras installed in observation rooms in either the emergency department or on the behavioral health unit should be vandal-resistant. There should be no way for a patient to grab hold of the camera because of how it was made or installed.

Some healthcare organizations have used infrared cameras to monitor patients in their sleep lab. The camera can operate in the dark and its use in sleep studies has proven invaluable as care providers can monitor patient sleep patterns without disrupting the patient.

Healthcare organizations authorizing video monitoring of patients typically require the video to be watched at all times. Many organizations require, by policy, monitoring and recording be stopped at all times if it is not monitored. There should always be a means for the person watching the video to promptly notify clinical personnel if a potential intervention is required. The recording of the video monitoring should be kept in a secure location, used only for the purpose for which it was recorded and not be released, used, or disclosed to others unless approved by the organization's administrative or legal department.

DUMMY (FAKE) CAMERAS

No discussion of video surveillance would be complete without some mention of the so-called dummy camera. There is no question some of the value of security cameras is the psychological deterrent they create. Malefactors are never quite sure how many cameras there are and who is watching their movements. It therefore stands to reason that a fake camera would provide a possible deterrent of a negative act.

The strongest argument against the use of the dummy camera is that it can create the expectation that one is being protected, when in fact no protection is being provided. This may produce a situation in which a person acts in a particular manner, based on their false sense of security. A false sense of security can also exist when real video cameras are not monitored or do not function as intended. The concept of false security has been the basis of many lawsuits, for example, Cisky v. Longs Peak Association, et al. (84 CV 5668) District Court, Denver, Colorado, wherein the plaintiff was awarded more than $6 million by a jury. The issue in this case was, in part, the question of a camera that did not provide the protection indicated.

OTHER SECURITY TECHNOLOGY APPLICATIONS IN HEALTHCARE

There are numerous other technologies used in the healthcare environment to protect employees, staff, and visitors; safeguard the confidential health information of patients; secure equipment and vulnerable assets; as well as care for the reputation of the organization. These include visitor management systems, infant protection systems, emergency call boxes, mass notification, asset tracking, and metal screening.

VISITOR MANAGEMENT

Hospital security departments have various tactics in place to control patients, visitors, and employees entering the facility. But along with *how* visitors enter, security departments are often equally interested in *who* is entering the facility. Visitor management systems offer an organized and systematic way of tracking those who enter the healthcare facility.

Visitor management systems are not new to the healthcare industry, as patient rosters and paper guest logs have been used at information desks to help with way-finding and guidance for years.

What is new is the computerized ability to capture detailed visitor information and to accurately identify, badge and track visitors, vendors and other authorized personnel entering the healthcare facility, and document the purpose of their visit.

With a standard personal computer and inexpensive label printer, these systems allow users to fill in a simple visitor form on the screen, and then print a badge for each visitor. However, the badge may vary considerably from visitor stickers to self-expiring badges that include a photo ID. Today, most visitor management systems are integrated with a number of peripheral hardware devices, such as passport scanners, driver's license readers, business card scanners, digital cameras, electronic signature capture pads, proximity card readers, fingerprint readers and barcode scanners.[31]

The use of a camera also allows the healthcare organization to capture the visitor's photo. And when vendors are required to read and agree to a non-disclosure agreement or confidentiality statement, or any other document, the more sophisticated visitor management systems can capture the visitor's signature electronically as part of the visitor record. That signature can be linked to the type of document presented, read, and agreed upon.

One of the greatest benefits of the more advanced visitor management systems is the ability to incorporate programmable security alerts or watch lists. An important alert checks each visitor's name against a list of people who should not be allowed to enter the building (former employees, estranged spouses, etc.), and alerts the security officer or greeter when a match is found, telling them how to handle the situation.[32] The visitor management system in use at Children's Hospital Colorado checks each name against the national Megan's Law database of registered sex offenders and alerts security if a match is found. A positive match does not necessarily prevent entry; it will, however, require a security escort while in the hospital. The software allows the hospital to interface with the employee directory, which improves the speed and efficiency of checking visitors in.

Another advantage found with most of these systems is the "Emergency Evacuation" report that provides a list of who is currently in the facility that would need to be accounted for in the event an evacuation is required. Some systems even allow this list to be automatically emailed to external fire, police, and emergency response personnel.

Not all healthcare facilities use visitor management systems. In the U.S., these systems are found more on the East and West Coast with a slower adoption rate in the center of the country. Hospitals making the decision to incorporate this additional safeguard typically do so as a result of a security risk assessment and the desire to start limiting the openness and access to "just anyone coming into the facility." In Canada, these systems have been slow to be adopted by healthcare organizations across the country.

Organizations that historically resist introducing sophisticated visitor management systems typically cite the potential negative experience by patients and visitors, and the overall expense to operate, as reasons why. North Florida Regional Medical Center (NFRMC) in Gainesville, Florida was one such facility, but came to realize the expense was well worth the investment from a patient safety perspective. They successfully introduced a new system in 2013 to push the security perimeter away from the patient. According to Jeremy Gallman, director of safety, security, and emergency management at NFRMC, the hospital wanted to stop, or limit, visitors before they get to the nursing station by pushing the screening all the way back to the building perimeter.[33]

At The Children's Hospital of Philadelphia (CHOP), every main lobby in every building on campus has at least one badging station, where visitors are asked to check in. Before upgrading the system, CHOP representatives spoke with an internal group of former and current parents, who were

BOX 19-1 TJC SURVEYOR IDENTITY VERIFICATION

TJC Surveyor Identity Verification Checklist

- Request to see The Joint Commission Surveyor badge
- Compare the badge present to the sample badge on the TJC extranet
- Verify survey date on the extranet
- Verify assigned surveyors on the extranet
- Ensure employees know what actions they should take if they have concerns about someone entering the organization
- Direct questions about the veracity of a surveyor to Joint Commission account representative at 630-792-3007

(Courtesy of Joseph Cappiello, vice president for Accreditation Field Operations at The Joint Commission)

instrumental in providing input about visitor check-ins, and how to communicate the process to the community. CHOP representatives found that once the new safeguard was explained to parents, they were very cooperative and supportive of the change.[33]

The capital expense of these systems is nominal; however, the true cost of operations is found in the staffing resources required to successfully manage the related processes. An important implementation technique that will allow the healthcare facility to get the most out of visitor management systems and minimize operating expense is to reduce the number of entrances open to the public. The overall access control plan needs to be evaluated to identify the best flow for patient and visitors. All other entry points into the facility must be secured at all times, to include dedicated employee and physician entrances and other doors serving life safety egress needs of the facility.

TJC Surveyor Identification

With The Joint Commission now conducting all regular surveys in the U.S., imposters have turned up in a number of hospitals claiming to be Joint Commission surveyors. The reasons for attempted entry into the healthcare organization are many and range from the unscrupulous to the criminal—gaining faster access to care or faster access to a family member, to stealing prescription drugs. As news reports of these events have shown, such events can have dire consequences for patients and compromise public trust.[34]

Joint Commission surveyors follow established procedures when visiting an organization to conduct an unannounced accreditation survey, and are trained to expect hospital personnel to make inquiries to verify their identity. Surveyors will report to either the front desk or to hospital security upon their arrival and will voluntarily present identification. To confirm authenticity of the badge that surveyors wear when they visit a facility for survey, organizations may compare it to a sample posted on The Joint Commission extranet site.[35] Box 19-1 demonstrates actions to be taken to verify surveyor identity.

In Canada, Accreditation Canada surveys are never unannounced, so the organization, and security, will know in advance of the surveyor's attendance at a site.

INFANT AND PEDIATRIC PATIENT PROTECTION SYSTEMS

Infant and pediatric abduction prevention is a top concern for hospital administrators, and security of infants and pediatric patients is certainly a priority, both for safety and public relations reasons. All told, 132 newborns have been abducted from hospitals since 1983.[36] "Infant Tagging," as it is often called, is a high-tech infant protection program designed to prevent baby abductions from infant care units, nurseries and pediatric units. Typically, the system uses lightweight transmitters with technology equipped with various measures of tamper detection. Preferably water-resistant, the small button-like tag is comfortably secured around an infant's ankle or wrist very soon after birth. Each tag is actually a miniature RF device that should work in conjunction with the access control system and automatic door locks. The system typically automatically locks doors and notifies staff of a potential security threat if an infant or pediatric patient wearing a transmitter comes within range of a monitored exit. Advances in this technology have helped reduce alarm fatigue and assist staff in monitoring each baby or child via automated software that alerts them if an ID is loose, has been tampered with, or has been removed.

Electronic infant protection systems with a basic system sounding an alarm is not a good practice; system software should know when an infant is taken into certain areas that identify and track infants, lock doors, disable elevator access on and off the unit and provide timed alarm activation. A basic design philosophy of each system should be to allow the baby's parents or authorized hospital personnel to carry the baby freely throughout the designated unit without generating an alarm. If an infant is brought near an exit door; it should automatically lock the door without generating an alarm. If the baby is taken through a monitored exit, or if the band is tampered with, an alarm should be generated and the system should automatically lock down the unit and control elevators supporting the unit and floor.

Hospitals are increasingly integrating electronic infant security systems with access control and video surveillance systems. If the system is integrated with the access control system, all doors leaving the area automatically lock (in coordination with life safety requirements) and control elevators. An integrated system can also link infant handling to access cardholders, activate video surveillance cameras, and lock stairwell doors. Some infant tagging systems have features that can also immediately display the identification of the baby and a map locating the exit door through which the baby was taken and track the tag throughout the facility.

Electronic infant protection systems have, to date, been primarily department-level solutions. A new generation of Wi-Fi technology has been expanding infant protection hospital- and even campus-wide at a more reasonable price point than ever before. Shifting from proprietary RF protocols to standards-based Wi-Fi, this technology delivers the ability to locate and track infants anywhere in the hospital through the existing Wi-Fi network. This allows for coverage throughout the campus, even in parking garages and other outdoor areas. In short, it allows the organization to track the movement of the infant in real time. This allows for a more focused response team effort directed to the infant's current location versus responding to the unit and more generally to the campus as a whole.

Challenges of installing any type of electronic infant protection systems may include differentiating portal and tamper alarms, properly testing the system and managing nuisance alarms. The volume of "false alarms" continues to be the greatest staff concern when using these systems and the greatest risk. In 2013, the Joint Commission issued Sentinel Event Alert Issue 50 on medical device alarm safety in hospitals, discussing how alarmed equipped devices are essential to providing safe care to patients. The Alert also noted how the devices present a multitude of challenges and opportunities when alarms create similar sounds, when their default settings are not changed, and when there is a failure to respond to alarm signals.[37] To date, the intent of SEA 50 has not focused on infant tagging systems, but hospitals should track the number of false alarms generated by the system to determine an acceptable level of nuisance alarms and associated staff fatigue. Any sign that staff do not respond to each and every alarm is a red-flag, and mitigation efforts to minimize the concern should be taken by the healthcare facility.

Good system design and effective implementation are keys to success with infant protection. Another important element is having a clinical user on board when selecting and implementing a system as a key to having a successful infant tagging program. Stanley Healthcare is a leader in infant protection systems and recommends five practical steps to consider for a successful design and implementation:

1) *Placement and configuration of exit monitors.* Consult with clinical staff to understand workflow; for example, extra steps may have to be taken for exits close to high traffic areas. If the door is frequently open, the chances of nuisance alarms increases if a monitored infant happens to be passing by.
2) *Elevators.* Protection for elevators can be either in-cab or outside the elevator bank. Any installation involving the elevator usually requires the involvement of the elevator contractor.
3) *Magnetic door locks.* A common option is to install magnetic door locks at exits to lock the door if a protected infant is brought to the exit. "Maglocks" are activated by the door monitoring device, but must also be interfaced to the life safety system for override during a fire, etc.
4) *User profiles.* Permission levels for the system software should be set in consultation with the clinical and security users. It is likely that there will be multiple user groups who need access to different information.
5) *Establish Maintenance and Testing Routines.* Implementation should cover installation of components, configuration of the system and clinical education of users of the system. When it comes to maintaining the system, the procedures in place for other mission-critical systems should be applied, such as server maintenance to backup databases and scheduled updates, so the system is never off-line without the knowledge of clinical and security staff. Beyond these routine tasks, monthly testing of the system is the industry standard. This involves such items as testing exits with an infant tag to confirm alarms are properly generated, and reviewing the system database for trends and anomalies.[38]

Nurses are the group who use the system day in and day out. An important question to address with staff is how they will be notified of alarms, beyond displaying them in the system software. A range of options are available, including sending alerts to IP phones and Vocera communication badges, in addition to more traditional means of notification like pagers, sounders and strobes. Integration to other hospital information systems may also be needed, for example to the Admission Discharge and Transfer system to automate the admission of mothers to the infant protection solution. It is important to understand the needs of the clinicians who will use the system, for the application will surely fail without their buy-in.

Infant tagging is useful in preventing newborn abductions, but it is not foolproof. Cathy Nahirny, Administrative Manager with the National Center for Missing and Exploited Children, has documented nineteen (19) cases where an infant was abducted by a nonfamily member from a healthcare facility and the facility had installed an infant security tagging system.[39] Five (5) of these occurrences happened since the publication of this book and 16 of these events since 2001.

Infant protection systems, video surveillance, and controlling access to prevent unauthorized visitors from gaining access to the mother/baby unit must work collectively together and in conjunction with staff training, parental education and a critical incident response plan. We will explore infant abduction prevention and response in greater detail in Chapter 21, "Areas of Higher Risk."

RESIDENTIAL/SENIORS CARE TAGGING SYSTEMS

The rapidly expanding residential/seniors healthcare market, driven by aging baby boomers across the western world, has caused increased focus for healthcare security leaders in this area. Resident on resident violence in care homes tragically resulted in 5 deaths from about 10,000 estimated incidents in Canada in 2013, forcing administrators to look to healthcare security practitioners to help design solutions to this growing concern. Following the experience of the acute care sector, we can increasingly see care homes moving to access control systems and security camera platforms to help mitigate some of their risks. Increasingly, on-site security staffing is viewed as an appropriate mitigation tool for the environment as well.

Mirroring the previous section on infant tagging systems, resident wandering systems have become increasingly prevalent in senior care settings, as the numbers of cognitively impaired residents, often suffering from dementia, rise rapidly and create challenges for senior care homes never designed to mitigate the risks presented by this terrible disease.

In many of these settings now, at-risk residents wear a transmitting device, usually affixed as a band on the wrist that sends a signal to receivers located on the unit, and/or on the perimeter of the building. The systems vary in complexity but, like the infant tagging systems, the intent is to alert staff and lock doors, elevators and egress points, in this case when the at-risk resident attempts to venture out of the designated area. Almost every community has experienced a tragedy associated with a wandering senior coming to harm because they wandered away from their home, or from a senior care home in a confused state. These systems are designed to address and mitigate that risk in the care home environment.

As more and more seniors receive care in their own homes, the next great frontier for security technology and for the healthcare security professional may be the design of security solutions for these individuals, outside of the traditional healthcare settings. GPS technology holds great promise in this area, with security operations centers potentially tracking these wandering seniors in the community at large, and facilitating a quick and safe recovery.

ASSET TRACKING

Losing wheelchairs or diagnostic equipment to theft is a great expense and significant risk for healthcare organizations. Recently, many hospitals have started to protect their assets with wireless radio frequency identification technology (RFID), which uses small transmitters attached to the protected equipment to communicate with the organization's access control system. Similar to the unobtrusive security tags used on store merchandise to thwart shoplifters, RFID tags are often used to track equipment as it moves through various doors, and can detect where a piece of equipment is located within the organization or if it leaves the facility. RFID tags range in size from small chips to palm size plastic boxes. In short, an RFID tag can be attached to just about anything of value, such as an EKG monitor or mobile workstation, and can be easily tracked throughout the facility.

Beyond basic asset protection, the Instituto do Cancer do Estado de Sao Paulo (ICESP), a 28-story cancer clinic said to be the largest public cancer-treatment center in Latin America, has deployed a Wi-Fi based real-time location system (RTLS) to facilitate the way in which its staff respond to an event of cardiac arrest and track response time. The clinic—which cares for those suffering from cancer who may be at risk for cardiac arrest—includes more than 500 beds located throughout its 28 floors.

The hospital sought a solution that could make use of the Wi-Fi nodes already in place and provide two functions: (1) getting messages to qualified workers closest to the site of a cardiac incident and (2) sharing information about responses in order to help management analyze areas of improvement. At ICESP, a badge tag is carried by staff members, who, upon reporting to work, sign into a PC connected to the software, with a wired connection to a battery charger, on which the badges are stored. The system links the individual with the ID number of that badge.[40]

Senior living facilities, pediatric care facilities, rehabilitation hospitals and other healthcare organizations use RFID solutions to monitor patients or residents at risk for falling and patient tracking, specifically those who are at risk for wandering away as noted in the previous section. Frequently embedded in the patient identification wristband, the technology is available in a soft material suitable for all ages of patients.

Some hospitals are wary of using RFID because of concerns about potential interference with critical equipment. A study published in the June 2008 issue of the *Journal of the American Medical Association* reported that RFID tags could interfere with the functioning of medical devices.[41] The observed problem was more common with "passive" RFID tags, which are powered by the electromagnetic field of handheld tag-reading devices, than with "active" tags with their own power source, which operate at much higher frequencies and have an expanded operating range.[41]

Video analytics have been used as an alternative to RFID for asset tracking. The camera can be programmed to highlight a piece of equipment, sense if the equipment moves, record when it does and alert security.

EMERGENCY CALL BOXES

Emergency phones, call boxes, phone towers, or wall-mounted emergency phones are all names used to describe the emergency phone system, designed to connect a potential victim of crime or someone in need of service with security. No matter what they are called, most emergency call boxes share the same or similar features, including the user interface and electronics that go into them. Some models contain an automatic dial-up telephone where phone service is provided at each unit. Others contain an intercom-style speakerphone equipped with one, two or more buttons.[42] Most emergency call telephones are equipped with a blue-light strobe on top of the device to enhance visibility. When flashing, it helps expedite security officer response and let others in the vicinity know that assistance is needed.

Direct communication with the security operations center or PBX operator is the most common application for transmitting the call signal and provides direct two-way communication with the call initiator via a direct phone line, voice over internet protocol (VoIP), cellular application, or two-way radio. Most systems available generate a campus map at the remote monitoring point, providing specific location information of the call box, even if the call initiator cannot wait on the response. Thus, a security officer can be immediately dispatched to the location of the originating unit.

There are several variations of emergency call boxes to choose from, including a fairly wide variety of colors. Most fit into two basic groups: wall-mount and tower, and are readily identified with the words "EMERGENCY" or "HELP." Wall mounts are generally deployed where ceiling height is limited, such as inside a parking garage. Towers are free-standing devices, strategically located in surface parking lots and other high pedestrian-traffic areas on campus. Both serve a common purpose: provide immediate assistance to those requesting it. Figure 19-7 is a picture of a typical tower-style emergency phone used on many healthcare campuses.

FIGURE 19-7

Sample emergency phone tower.

Emergency phone systems are also used for nonemergency purposes and can be excellent customer service tools for employees, staff, patients and visitors who may need basic assistance. These devices, when used, are excellent crime prevention and public relations tools as they demonstrate organizational commitment to a safe and secure environment. They provide an added visual reinforcement of being protected while on campus.

Another patient-safety related application for the emergency phone system can be utilized in multistory parking garages. Every year there are several incidents of death by individuals jumping from these structures. Signage in these structures, located near emergency phones, can target people in despair, and provide an avenue of potential communication for these at-risk individuals.

MASS NOTIFICATION

Healthcare facilities have traditionally relied upon overhead announcement for alerting staff of threats and other items of public concern. There are codes for tornados, fires, bomb threats and security assistance. In the past, it was not uncommon for a hospital to announce "paging Dr. Strong" whenever security was needed to handle a violent situation or other call for security assistance. Much work has been done in all countries to standardize emergency codes in recent years.

The December 2007 Virginia Tech University tragedy served as a wake-up call for many healthcare facilities, and has yielded numerous lessons learned that has prompted hospitals, behavioral health treatment centers, and long-term care facilities across the country to reassess how they prepare for, respond to and mitigate events of targeted violence. Specifically, this tragedy identified the need for the healthcare facility to have a quick and facility-/campus-wide notification of a threat or emergency.

Technology advances have provided many mass notification solutions and mediums available to the healthcare facility, including phone, e-mail, SMS text messaging, computer desktop alerts, website announcements and social media alerts, phone calls, campus loudspeakers and more, which have supplanted traditional overhead "PA" announcements. Many healthcare organizations have realized that multiple modes of notification are needed to reach all of the constituents inside the facility and on its grounds.

Although emergency communications via audio systems and personal devices are good solutions, they do not address the visual component of mass notification. In simple terms, audio emergency messages should reach those individuals who are hearing impaired or out of earshot of the notification system. This often requires light-emitting diode (LED) or liquid crystal display (LCD) digital signage solutions, which can be used to initiate a more immediate emergency notification.

Many hospital campuses use digital signage as a communication medium beyond emergency alerts. The signage is used for routine announcements, marketing messages or general administrative information, as well as emergency notifications. Others only use the devices for emergency purposes and, during nonemergency periods, only the time and date are displayed. Weather resistant capabilities and conditions coupled with readability are important considerations. LEDs can be more weather resistant than LCDs and use less energy if they are powered by Power over the Ethernet (PoE) technology. These devices have been in use for quite a few years now but do not have as many features or graphics as LCDs.[43]

METAL SCREENING

Philosophically, there are some healthcare environments that lend themselves to metal screening. The most likely application in a healthcare setting is the emergency department.

The growing pervasiveness of violence has caused many hospitals to take significant measures to decrease and deter risks of violent activity in the emergency department. Statistics illustrate the emergency department encounters more violence than any other department or area of the facility, largely because of the variety of illnesses and injuries it treats and the diversity of the population it serves. Emergency departments by their very nature serve gang members, psychiatric patients, domestic violence victims, and others who may become irrational or dangerous out of fear or anxiety, or because of a medical condition. Moreover, because the order in which patients are seen often depends upon the severity of illness, waiting time frequently adds to tension levels and can evoke security concerns.

It is estimated by the American Hospital Association (AHA) that approximately 5% of people entering an emergency department bring in something that could be used as a dangerous weapon. In 2013, the University of Colorado Hospital, located on the Anschutz Medical Campus, prevented over 12,000 items classified by the hospital as a weapon from entering its emergency department. A minimal number of guns were confiscated. The vast preponderance were knives and other sharp or blunt instruments, strictly prohibited from entering the facility. Many organizations who have deployed metal screening in their facilities have found similar volumes of weapons when adjusted for their patient volume and demographics. In response, more and more facilities are considering the use of metal detectors but the number is still relatively low. A 2011 study conducted by the American Society for Healthcare Engineers (ASHE) of hospital security systems that are being implemented found only 13% of respondents said their hospitals had implemented metal detectors. An additional 7% shared they were planning to do so in the next 24 months. Over 80% had no plans to adopt them.

A 2012 Johns Hopkins study of hospital-based shootings in the U.S. provided some insights into why metal screening is not more widely adopted. The study found that in less than half of the 154 acute care hospital shooting events, from 2000 through 2011, would the healthcare institution have found or discovered the instigator's weapon. In 23% of shootings within the ED, the weapon was a security officer's gun taken by the perpetrator. The study conclusion found that such events are relatively rare compared to other forms of workplace violence. The unpredictable nature of this type of event represents a significant challenge to hospital security and effective deterrence practices, because most perpetrators proved determined and a significant number of shootings occur outside the hospital building.[44]

In Canada and the UK, there are no known examples of hospitals utilizing walk-through metal detectors in any of their facilities at this writing. Indeed, only a tiny fraction of these hospitals are even using handheld metal screening devices, for specific risks in specific circumstances. Gun violence in hospitals in these jurisdictions is not unheard of—the murder by handgun of a patient and her mother in a patient room, committed by an estranged husband, in Mission, British Columbia, Canada in 2003 is a stark reminder that these horrific acts can occur anywhere. However, there is no indication that these countries view the incursion of airport-like metal screening functions into their care environments as warranted, given their current assessment of risk.

The recommendation, introduction and management of metal screening programs in healthcare cannot be done in a vacuum. The security improvements are considerable; however, the introduction of metal screening has employee relations and organizational culture implications, in addition to patient and community perceptions, that must be addressed collectively.

The placement and exact location of the metal detector is an important consideration. The device should be installed to minimize unnecessary delays in the queuing of patients and visitors and fit comfortably into the aesthetic décor of the facility.

Of particular importance to medical facilities is the electromagnetic interference (EMI) caused by the metal detectors. Pacemakers, defibrillators, nerve stimulators and other medical devices may be inactivated or reprogrammed by this phenomenon. Instances of this happening have been extremely rare; studies conducted by the German Heart Institute in Munich, Germany indicate that EMI is not as likely to occur as common wisdom would lead us to believe.[45]

If metal screening is employed, the approach must be consistent and show no bias. The traffic flow should be streamlined so that persons cannot bypass or divert the process, unless the patient is unstable. All unstable and ambulance-transported patients deemed "at-risk" should be scanned using a handheld wand once it is medically safe to do so.

In a presentation made at the October 2013 Secured Cities conference in Baltimore, Maryland, Bryan Warren, director of security for Carolinas Health System, spoke on the topic of metal detection in healthcare. Warren discussed how to determine the types of persons and objects to be screened and specifically shared three universal concepts that underlie the philosophy of use behind metal screening:

1) Deter those that would attempt to enter an area with an unauthorized item or weapon.
2) Detect such objects on the peripheral or outermost perimeter of the area being protected.
3) Detain those persons or items to prevent their passage into the secure zone.

Warren shared the science behind how metal detectors work and discussed how they do not detect nonmetal objects or those without sufficient mass—based upon the strength of the electromagnetic field being generated—to produce a disruption in the field. Common items not detected yet that could be used as a weapon include plastics, glass, wood, stone, chemicals, explosive compounds, among others. There are many such nonmetal weapons for sale today.

A drawback to implementing a fully operating metal detection system is the staffing requirements. The passage of patients and visitors through the metal detector must be managed without interruption to include relief for meal and work breaks. The security checkpoint may require multiple personnel as noted in Figure 19-8.

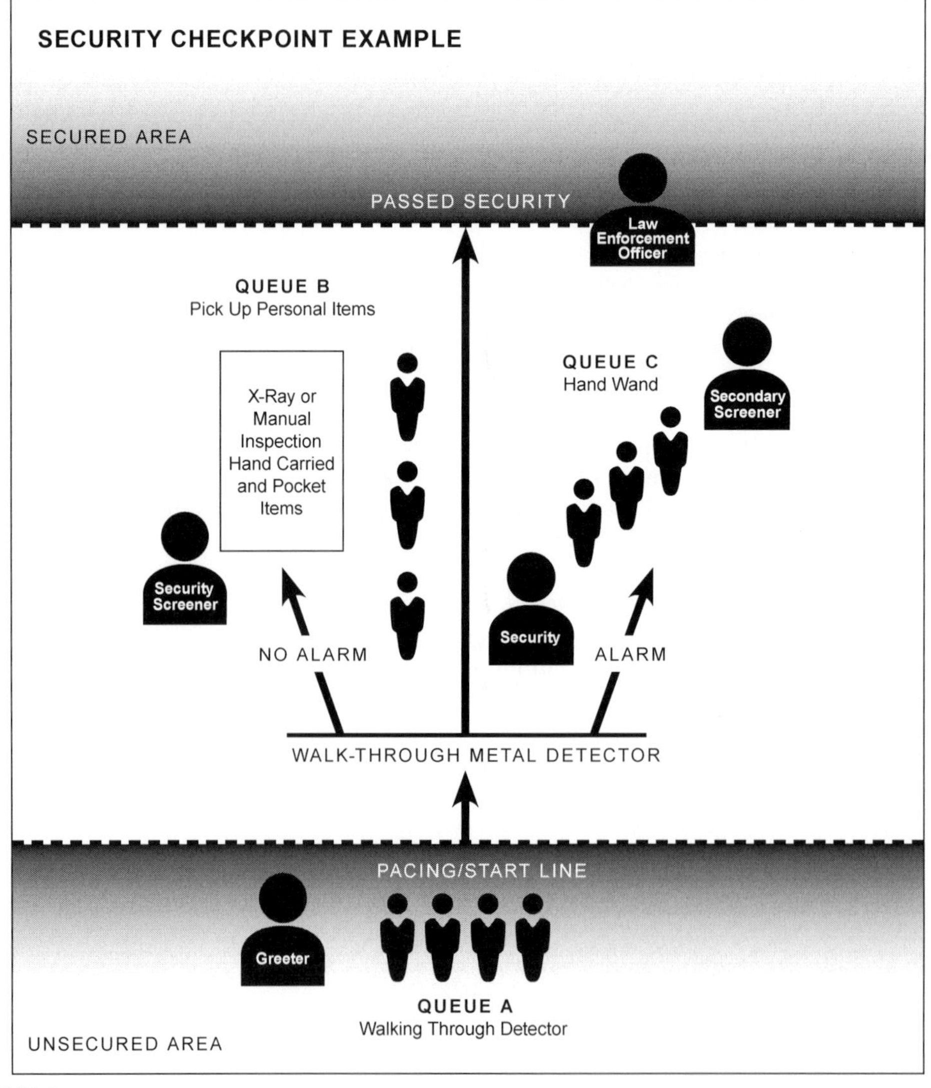

FIGURE 19-8

Security checkpoint example.

(Courtesy of Bryan Warren, CHPA.)

There are no healthcare regulatory agencies or standards that clearly state a position on having or not having metal detectors installed or available. The Joint Commission has commented on how the "physical environment is an important element of protecting patients and workers" and that hospitals in particular are at risk for criminal activity. CMS is on record, in their conditions of participation, as saying the patient has the right to receive care in a safe setting to include physical security safeguards and protection of the patient's emotional health and physical safety. OSHA has enforcement procedures for investigating or inspecting workplace violence incidents, and they expect engineering controls to help maintain a secure worksite. To date, none of these three oversight agencies specifically speaks to the use of metal detection. However, the healthcare security administrator should be fairly warned that the concept of metal screening may very well be subject to individual surveyor interpretation. Thus, every healthcare organization should conduct a needs assessment, to document if metal screening is reasonable and appropriate to implement, to safeguard their workers, patients and visitors.

TESTING AND MAINTAINING SECURITY SYSTEM COMPONENTS

Many electronic security systems are used to keep healthcare facilities safe. But one of the common missing components is the routine testing of these systems. Systems or components are commonly found to be ineffective, not working as originally intended, and/or not meeting current needs—creating unnecessary risk and liability exposure for the healthcare organization.

A strategy that works particularly well is to assign someone on staff who, at least on a monthly basis, takes an inventory of all equipment in use, verifying its operational status. If equipment is found missing or not operating as originally intended, document those issues and place them on the internal work order plan to correct the deficiency. This close-the-loop system must be followed to ensure systems are working and ready when needed.

Many larger health systems have found that maintenance is best completed by dedicated low-voltage technicians (in-house or contract) who can troubleshoot issues, maintain spare parts, keep accurate inventory records of system components, install system components, develop system requirements and philosophy of use, and oversee larger projects that require security integrators.

This documentation and testing may be considered small and routine. However, its importance is found in the liability protection afforded to the facility and, more prominently, the positive perception of security and the department.

SECURITY TECHNOLOGY IMPLEMENTATION TIPS

Implementation of new or upgraded security technologies requires the same basic preparation. The following guidelines will help the healthcare protection professionals ensure a more secure environment:

- Engage the healthcare organization's information technology (IT) staff early and often to ensure that the cabling, networking and software support resources are available and reliable, as the plan is implemented and used in real-life situations.

- When evaluating intrusion detection, card access control, video surveillance systems, infant protection and other systems, require vendors to demonstrate how integration of these security functions can increase security and minimize the training and burden to security personnel.
- Avoid "bells and whistles" and cutting-edge products that have not been proven; focus on smart purchases and user-friendly applications.
- Ensure adequate space, reliable electrical power and sufficient cooling is provided for each component of the electronic security support system.
- Clearly delineate in the organization's security master plan whether the security or IT department has authority for equipment and ongoing maintenance.
- Maintain thorough records of electronic security system components, including component labeling, location, cabling types, cable termination information, equipment cut sheets, node and port IDs, application software routines and IP addressing and network configuration information.
- Engage in ongoing training on new systems and upgrades.

The ideal healthcare security system is a combination of the right technology, careful planning, proper installation and a strategically deployed staff. Technology must work effectively as a tool for a well-trained security staff. When these elements are properly integrated, the organization is able to provide a safe environment, and its employees are consequently able to concentrate on fulfilling the organization's overall mission of providing high-quality patient care for the surrounding community.

REFERENCES

1. Blesch G. *First, do no harm.* Modern Healthcare; 2008, June 30. Special Report, 28.
2. Miller Kristine. Who goes where? Managing security Access and Control. Environment of Care News. *Joint Commission Resources* 2011, August:8–10.
3. Hattersley-Gray R. *7 steps to effectively deploying panic alarms: Part 2. Campus Safety Magazine.* 2012, September 30. Retrieved March 12, 2014, from http://www.campussafetymagazine.com/article/7-steps-to-effectively-deploying-panic-alarms-part-2.
4. Sutherly Ben. *Hospital access, security is a real balancing act.* The Columbus Dispatch; 2012, August 13. Retrieved August 14, 2012, from http://www.dispatch.com/content/stories/local/2012/08/13/hospital-access-security-is-a-real-balancing-act.html.
5. Clark Liz Engel. *Hospital to lock main entrance at night.* Herald-Citizen; 2010, December 5. Retrieved December 7, 2010, from http://www.herald-citizen.com/view/full_story/10533094/article-Hospital-to-lock-main-entrance-at-night?instance=homethirdleft.
6. Timme Ann Geissler. *4 items you can analyze today for improved security.* Campus Safety Magazine; 2013, June/July. Retrieved October 22, 2013, from http://www.campussafetymagazine.com/article/4-items-you-can-analyze-today-for-improved-hospital-access-management.
7. Canal BA, York TW. Decreasing the Risk of Emergency. *Facilities Management Journal* March/April 2009:22–8.
8. Crowley Michael A. In and out—new guidance on securing egress doors. *Healthcare Facilities Management* 2011, April 1. Retrieved April 2, 2011, from http://www.hfmmagazine.com/display/HFM-news-article.dhtml?dcrPath=/templatedata/HF_Common/NewsArticle/data/HFM/Magazine/2011/Apr/0411HFM_FEA_CS.
9. Scurlock Stephanie. *Hospital removes last name from badges to protect staff.* 2013, November 15. WREG.com. Retrieved November 21, 2013, from http://wreg.com/2013/11/15/hospital-removes-last-names-from-badges-to-protect-staff/.

10. Timme, Ann Geissler. *How to conduct access control security audits*. Campus Safety Magazine; 2013, June/July Retrieved October 22, 2013, from http://www.campussafetymagazine.com/article/4-items-you-can-analyze-today-for-improved-hospital-access-management.
11. Garcia Nestor. *Senate to probe security at Hawaii State Hospital*. KHON2. 2014, April 18. Available from http://khon2.com/2014/04/18/senate-to-probe-security-at-hawaii-state-hospital/.
12. Hodgson K. The New Kid on the Block: Managed Access. *SDM* 2009, April:55–8.
13. Donald Dr C. *Optimizing Camera Viewing in Control Rooms*. Hi-Tech Security Solutions; 2009, May. Retrieved May 30, 2009, from http://www.securitysa.com/article.aspx?pklArticleId=5627&pklCategoryId=3.
14. Van der Merwe N. *Integrated Health Care*. Hi-Tech Security Solutions; 2009, May Retrieved May 30, 2009, from http://www.securitysa.com/regular.aspx?pklRegularId=4011.
15. Tindle G. *CCTV Cameras to Curb Violence against NHS Staff*. Wales Online News; 2009, April 24. Retrieved April 25, 2009, from http://www.walesonline.co.uk/news/wales-news/2009/04/24/cctv-cameras-to-curb-violence-against-nhs-staff--91466-23463081.
16. *CCTV Reduces Crime in Hospital*. BBC News; 2008, September 13. Retrieved September 13, 2009, from http://news.bbc.co.uk/go/pr/fr/-/2/hi/uk_news/scotland/tayside_and_central/7558455.stm.
17. Brisbee F. *The Power to Heal and More*. Electrical Contractor; 2000, April. Retrieved May 23, 2009, from http://www.ecmag.com/index.cfm?fa=article&articleID=10050.
18. King J, Mulligan D, Raphael S. *CITRIS Report: The San Francisco Community Safety Camera Program*. 2008, December 17. Retrieved January 13, 2009, from http://www.citris-uc.org/files/CITRIS%20SF%20CSC%20Study%20Final%20Dec%202008.pdf11–12.
19. Peters C. *Man caught on tape just before garage robbery*. Spartanburg, SC: Spartanburg Herald Journal; 2009, March 7. Retrieved March 8, 2009, from http://www.goupstate.com/article/20090307/articles/903071031.
20. Tunnell Jr GR. Moving to Digital. *Health Facilities Management* 2008, September;**21**(9):33–7.
21. Scaglione B. Digital Security Technology Simplified. *Journal for Healthcare Protection Management* 2007;**23**(20):56.
22. Engebretson J. State of the Market: Video Surveillance. *SDM* 2009, March:57–8.
23. Kuhn M. 5 questions for a successful deployment of an IP video solution. *SDM* 2009, April:78–80.
24. Hattersley-Gray R. *Making the Leap to IP Video: A Safer Bet*. Campus Safety; 2008, September/October. 22–23.
25. Steele J. Learning to Deploy Analytics. *SDM* 2009, April:61–4.
26. Steele J. Learning to Deploy Analytics. *SDM* 2009, April:66.
27. Stelter Leischen. *Hospital uses facial recognition, other technology to identify high-risk people*. 2011, February 22 Retrieved March 3, 2011, from Security Director News; http://www.securitydirectornews.com/?p=article&id=sd201102qFTCS.
28. Coombs Dan. *Hospital cameras could stop violence against staff*. Get West London; 2011, October 17. Retrieved October 17, 2011, from http://www.uxbridgegazette.co.uk/west-london-news/local-uxbridge-news/2011/10/17/hospital-cameras-could-stop-violence-against-staff-113046-29609671/.
29. Wolf S. High-tech Health. *Central Penn Business Journal* 2008, June 27. Retrieved June 27, 2008, from http://www.centralpennbusiness.com/print_article.asp?aID=66929.
30. Centers for Medicare and Medicaid Services. Interpretive Guidelines. §482.13(f)(4)(i)(ii), *State Operations Manual* 2004, May 21:112–3.
31. Landro L. *The Hospital Is Watching You*. The Wall Street Journal; 2008, November 17. Retrieved November 17, 2008, from http://online.wsj.com/article/SB122645364411819495.html.
32. Marson H. *Say Goodbye to Your Paper Guest Log*. Campus Safety Magazine; 2007, September/October. Retrieved June 6, 2009, from http://www.campussafetymagazine.com/Articles/?ArticleID=121.
33. Kumar Jay. *Updated visitor management systems offer added security measures. Healthcare Security Alert, supplement to Briefings on Hospital Safety*, vol. 17. 2013, August. Issue No. 8. p. 1–3.

34. Cappiello J. Imposter Surveyors: The Joint Commission Urges Hospital Caution. *Journal for Healthcare Protection Management* 2007;**23**(2):19–20.
35. Cappiello J. Imposter Surveyors: The Joint Commission Urges Hospital Caution. *Journal for Healthcare Protection Management* 2007;**23**(2):21–2.
36. Raburn Jr John, Nahirny Cathy. *Newborn/Infant Abductions*. National Center for Missing and Exploited Children; 2014, January 1.
37. The Joint Commission. *Sentinel Event Alert Issue 50: Medical device alarm safety in hospitals*. 2013, April 8. www.jointcommission.org. Retrieved April 2, 2014, from http://www.jointcommission.org/sentinel_event.aspx.
38. Stanley Healthcare. *How to leverage your Wi-Fi infrastructure for better infant protection – 5 practical steps*. 2013 November. Retrieved November 21, 2013, from http://www.fiercehealthcare.com/offer/infant_protection?source=library.
39. Nahirny Cathy. *Infants Abducted from Hospitals with Security Tagging Systems*. National Center for Missing and Exploited Children; 2013, February 13.
40. Swedberg Claire. *Sao Paulo Cancer Hospital uses RFID to Respond to Heart Attacks*. 2011, February 6. RFIDJournal.com. Retrieved on February 7, 2011, from http://frackdesigns.com/sao-paulo-cancer-hospital-uses-rfid-to-respond-to-heart-attacks.
41. Stiles S. *Interference with ICU-type Medical Devices Seen from Radio-Frequency Security Tags*. 2008, June 25. www.TheHeart.org. Retrieved June 25, 2008, from http://www.theheart.org/article/print.do?primaryKey=877949.
42. Colombo A. *Call Box Basics and Beyond*. Campus Safety Magazine; 2006 May/June. Retrieved June 6, 2009, from http://www.campussafetymagazine.com/Articles/?ArticleID=34.
43. Hattersley-Gray Robin. *How to Select a Digital Signage Solution*. 2011, June 28. CampusSafetyMagazine.com. Retrieved July 1, 2011, from http://www.campussafetymagazine.com/Channel/Mass-Notification/Articles/2011/06/Is-Digital-Signage-for-You.aspx?ref=HospitalSecurityUpdate-20110630&utm_source=Email&utm_medium=Enewsletter.
44. Johns Hopkins Office of Critical Event Preparedness and Response. Hospital Based Shootings in the United States: 2000 to 2011. *Annals of Emergency Medicine* 2012. Retrieved May 15, 2013, from http://www.annemergmed.com/article/S0196-0644(12)01408-4/abstract.
45. Jimenez A. *Metal detection worth its mettle*. Campus Safety Magazine; November/December 2006. Retrieved April 22, 2009, from http://www.campussafetymagazine.com/Articles/?ArticleID=64.

CHAPTER

PREVENTING AND MANAGING HEALTHCARE AGGRESSION AND VIOLENCE

20

Most people think of hospitals as places for healing. But the threat of violence—which can take many forms—can be a daily reality for nurses and other healthcare workers. The issue of violence in healthcare gained national attention in September 2010 when a doctor at Johns Hopkins Hospital was shot by the distraught son of a surgical patient. The shooter went on to kill both his mother and himself. The Hopkins doctor recovered.

The event was stark reminder to security professionals and hospital administrators that healthcare facilities are increasingly treating sicker and poorer patients and are rife with all sorts of emotions, both obvious and hidden, that support what healthcare professionals have been concerned about for years.

The problem of violence is so prevalent in healthcare that The Joint Commission has issued two sentinel event alerts related to violence. Alerts are published to assist healthcare facilities in designing or reevaluating relevant processes to mitigate potential risks outlined within the alert. In 2008, The Joint Commission published issue 40 titled *Behaviors that undermine a culture of safety*. This alert relates to intimidating and disruptive behaviors that can cause an unsafe work environment. In 2010, issue 45 was published, titled *Preventing violence in the healthcare setting*. This alert acknowledges that an increase in violence is occurring within the healthcare profession and provides recommendations to reduce the potential for violence.

Until the culture of tolerance at hospitals changes, violence inside of healthcare is not going to change. Acts of workplace violence can happen anywhere in the healthcare delivery system, from the extreme example of a shooting near the patient discharge area of Parkwest Medical Center in Knoxville, Tennessee to a doctor getting his nose shattered at University Medical Center in Las Vegas; from a California man who was arrested at Stanford Hospital after he demanded medication at knifepoint, to a nurse in the Ambulatory Surgery Center of Good Shepherd Medical Center[1] in Longview, Texas, who was fatally stabbed while protecting her patients against a man desiring to kill his mother, a patient in the facility. These are the more extreme concerns but there are many more lesser negative behaviors healthcare workers are facing that are still most unwelcome—disrespect by verbal abuse from patients and visitors, to harassment, mobbing, discrimination, incivility, bullying, and emotional abuse (also referred to as psychological harassment).

The Joint Commission has been tracking major violent events in healthcare since 1995. Their database (which it says contains a significantly lower number of violent episodes than the actual number, due to underreporting by healthcare institutions) found that since 1995, there have been 256 assaults, rapes or homicides at hospitals and healthcare facilities. Of those, 110 have occurred since 2007. The accrediting body has identified six reoccurring causes for variety of violent episodes that the healthcare industry has dealt with:

1. Issues in leadership were noted in 62% of the events, most notably problems in the areas of policy and procedure development and implementation.
2. Human resources-related factors were noted in 60% of events, such as the increased need for staff education and competency assessment processes.
3. Assessment issues, noted in 58% of events, particularly in the areas of flawed patient observation protocols, inadequate assessment tools, and lack of psychiatric assessment.
4. Communication failures, noted in 53% of the events, in terms of deficiencies in general safety of the environment and security procedures and practices.
5. Physical environment issues, noted in 36% of the events, in terms of deficiencies in general safety of the environment and security procedures and practices.
6. Problems in care planning, information management, and patient education were other causal factors identified less frequently.[1]

When violence erupts in a healthcare facility, the consequences are many and unpredictable. The 2014 study commissioned by the International Healthcare Security and Safety Foundation (IHSSF) found an increase in violent crime at hospitals in the U.S. and Canada between 2012 and 2013.[2] While healthcare facilities in urban areas with high crime rates may be more prone to violent events, even in suburban or rural locations the risk of workplace violence looms in healthcare facilities—where a stressful work environment can quickly become volatile, visitors may be highly emotional, and drugs, cash or expensive equipment may become targets of robbery. Abortion clinics and healthcare facilities with animal research laboratories face the unique challenge of being targeted by protestors who may become violent. In addition, home care employees may walk alone into homes where patients or their family members keep weapons or drugs, or may visit homes in areas with high crime rates, increasing the risk of a violent encounter while performing their job.[3]

Despite the thousands of pages written on workplace violence, there is no concise definition for it. For most security professionals it means a violent or aggressive event, including threatening or intimidating action, which places one at risk or raises fear of physical, emotional, or psychological harm.

Richard Hampton, head of security management for the National Health Service (NHS) Security Management Service (SMS), noted that one of the first charges of the SMS when introducing a national strategy for healthcare security in the UK was to define physical violence. Before the formation of the SMS in 2003, the NHS was using approximately 20 different definitions with no standard definition of abuse and no robust process for collecting data on violence against NHS care providers.

Patient-generated violence is an industry-wide problem and not exclusive to any one type of organization or patient care service offered. An angry and confused patient can punch a physician after an exam. A patient high on drugs can hold a nurse in a headlock and threaten her. A gang member can intimidate a front desk clerk with the threat of a weapon. These types of violent events can and do occur with alarming frequency and threaten the safety of staff, patients, and visitors in hospitals and healthcare organizations of all sizes and settings. It demoralizes healthcare professionals, especially nurses, who are most often the victims of violence. The cost is untold millions in lost time, employee turnover, reputation for quality care, and additional security measures.

Table 20-1 Listing of Workplace Violence Examples

Workplace Violence Includes	
• Assaults • Stabbings • Suicides • Shootings • Rape • Attempted suicides • Attack of one's personal or professional integrity	• Threats of self-harm or obscene phone calls • Intimidation • Harassment of any nature • Being followed, sworn or shouted at • Psychological traumas • Bullying and verbal intimidation

No healing environment is immune from having violent acts occur inside the facility or on its campus. Table 20-1 lists the wide range of examples of violence that can be witnessed in the healthcare environment.

The issue of violence is well known by the healthcare community, which has been seeking ways to combat it for years. A report from the U.S. Department of Labor based on 2009 statistics ranks nurses as having the third highest likelihood of being assaulted on the job, just behind police and correctional officers. According to the U.S. Bureau of Labor Statistics, nurses and other personal care workers suffer 25 injuries annually, resulting in days off from work for every 10,000 full-time workers—12 times the rate of the overall private sector industry.

The violence continues to occur and is most prevalent in emergency departments, behavioral health facilities, intensive care units, waiting rooms and geriatric care units. Approximately half of the nurses responding to a 2011 survey conducted by the Emergency Nurses Association (ENA) believe violence is simply part of their everyday work environment. Between 8% and 13% of emergency room nurses are victims of physical violence every week.[4] The ENA survey pointed out that nine out of ten emergency department managers cited patient violence as the greatest threat to department personnel. In addition, emergency department nurses reported:

- Dissatisfaction with the overall level of safety from workplace violence (89%).
- Feeling unprepared to handle violence in the ED, given their education and training (83%).
- Reduced job satisfaction due to violence (74%).
- Impaired job performance for up to a week after a violent incident (48%).
- Taking time off because of violence (25%).[4]

Statistics from around the world show that patient-generated violence is not only a U.S. problem but a global concern. In an Australian survey, 52% of community hospital nurses reported being assaulted by a patient in the prior year and 69% mention being threatened with violence by a patient.[5] A 2009 Statistics Canada report showed about a third of nurses had been physically assaulted by a patient in the past year. Almost half of nurses reported being emotionally abused.[6] Nearly 170,000 violence incidents take place in England's NHS hospitals each based on data obtained under the Freedom of Information Act. There have been several murders and rapes at hospitals in recent years and thousands of attacks annually involve the use of knives and other weapons. Almost one in four attacks results in injury, yet only a fraction of them are ever reported to the police.[7]

The impact of violence to care providers is not limited to just nurses. A transplant surgeon at Florida Hospital was shot and killed by a disgruntled patient as he walked from the hospital to a parking garage. These events are not limited to just the hospital proper—a Kentucky physician was fatally shot at one of the largest rural health centers in the state. Over 75% of surveyed emergency department physicians in Michigan said they had experienced at least one violent act within the previous 12 months.[8]

There are countless accounts of healthcare security officers falling victim to violence and being assaulted by patients. The stories of security officers being attacked and injured by patients and visitors are endless; examples of unprovoked attacks include being:

- Punched in the face when asking a visitor to leave the hospital
- Struck in the face by a patient wearing an arm cast
- Punched in the stomach as was the case of a Virginia Mason Hospital security officer when attempting to keep a patient from eloping
- Head-butted by a mental health patient who is completely uncooperative
- A victim of a fire extinguisher discharge and then thrown
- Kicked in the leg, chest, face and many other areas when attempting to restrain a patient
- Hit with blunt objects such as flashlights, IV poles and others
- Urine thrown when conducting a security watch
- Threatened with a baseball bat when asking a visitor to move his car
- Stabbed with a knife when asking a high-risk patient to change into a hospital gown
- Scratched and bitten by a patient
- Threats of being killed and being called derogatory names to get a rise out of the security officer

In aggregate, the events and statistics reveal that doctors, nurses, paramedics, and security officers face violence inside of healthcare on a daily basis.

Today, the term "workplace violence" continues to be expanded to include any act of violence in the workplace regardless of the connection of the victim or perpetrator to a specific business or employer. The California Department of Industrial Relations, Division of Occupational Safety and Health (DOSH), divides events of workplace violence into three categories: Type I, Type II, Type III and Type IV.

- Type I event (*criminal*) – the perpetrator has no legitimate relationship to the healthcare facility
- Type II event (*patient*) – committed by someone who is the recipient of a service provided by the healthcare facility or the victim
- Type III event (*employee*) – committed by someone who has an employment-related involvement at the healthcare facility, such as current or former staff members
- Type IV event (*domestic*) – relates to interpersonal violence at the healthcare facility and includes spouses, lovers, relatives, and friends or other visitors who have a dispute involving an employee, patient, physician, or contractor.

The majority of people generally associate violence in the workplace with assault and homicide, not with intimidating postures or expressions of mild anger. It is important the healthcare administrator break workplace violence down into *actual* violence and the *threat* of violence. Both can create a hostile and uncomfortable work environment, and even with this breakdown, healthcare workers face significantly higher risk of injury from nonfatal assaults (actual violence) than that of other workers. The threat of violence, although not adequately tracked by most healthcare organizations, is also quite high.

A zero-tolerance policy is the most proactive approach hospital leadership can take to combat negative attitudes and disruptive actions. Violence not only harms the immediate victims but events can also divert healthcare professionals from providing essential care to other patients in the facility. A code of conduct must be established to promote open and respectful communication among all healthcare providers, including physicians and management. Leaders must role-model what behavior they are expecting from staff and physicians with meaningful consequences if violations occur.

As concerning as violence statistics are for the healthcare industry, underreporting is a chronic problem. A persistent perception within the healthcare industry is that assaults are part of the job. Underreporting is a concern by the Security Management Service of the NHS where analysts studying the issue of physical violence against their healthcare workers steadfastly believe that violence is underreported by at least half. Many U.S. hospitals have various reporting sources (Security, Risk Management and Employee Health Departments) and multiple avenues for reporting events but often lack coordination between the reporting sources. Security is typically most focused on the event while Employee Health is focused on the employee. If the two databases are not coordinated, a large gap in the data can occur. The Massachusetts Nurses Association is on record saying violence is substantially underreported, in part because nurses are afraid it will show up on their performance evaluation as not being able to appropriately handle a patient.[9] Other care providers purportedly underreport incidents of violence out of fear of reprisal, isolation and embarrassment.

Why violence is so prevalent in healthcare is a question asked by many security professionals and administrators. According to the Occupational Safety and Health Administration (OSHA), healthcare and social service workers face a high degree of work-related assaults due to the following risk factors:[10]

- Rising use of hospitals by police and criminal justice agencies for criminal holds and the care of acutely disturbed persons
- The early release from hospitals of acute and chronic mental health patients who have not received follow-up care and who can no longer be involuntarily hospitalized except in extreme situations
- The availability of drugs and money at hospitals, clinics, and pharmacies, which makes them targets for robbery
- Situational factors such as open facilities with basically unrestricted movement of the public, as well as the presence of drug abusers, trauma patients, distraught family members, and frustrated clients
- Low staffing levels at various times
- Isolated work situations during client examination or treatment
- One-person workstations in remote locations
- Lack of staff training relative to recognizing and managing escalating hostile and assaultive behavior
- Long waiting times for care in emergency areas, which can lead to patient frustration
- The increased presence in healthcare setting of gang members, alcohol and other drug abusers, trauma patients, and distraught family members
- Prevalence of handguns and other dangerous weapons

Other factors that contribute to patient-generated violence include stress, high patient to staff ratios, long working hours, and power and control issues of healthcare providers themselves.

Brockton Hospital in the suburbs south of Boston, Massachusetts is considered a model for violence in healthcare. In 2007, OSHA investigated the hospital in response to complaints it had received and found that the types of physical assaults included, but were not limited to, punching, kicking, biting, scratching, and pulling hair. The agency recommended that the hospital analyze the workplace hazard, solicit extensive comments from employees, and develop a comprehensive violence protection plan.[11] To date, Brockton is one of only four hospitals which OSHA has investigated as a result of the guidelines published in 1996 to prevent violence in the healthcare and social work settings. The second hospital to have been cited by OSHA was Danbury Hospital in Connecticut, where after a nurse was shot in 2010, OSHA found the hospital had allowed "serious violations" of its regulations to occur by "failing to provide a workplace free from recognized hazards likely to cause death or serious injury to workers." The OSHA report cited multiple incidents over an 18-month period in which violent patients injured staff in the hospital's psychiatric unit, in its emergency department and on its general medical floors. The citation was a $6,300 fine.

Children's Hospital in Oakland is the third hospital to have been fined over security concerns stemming from two incidents, one in which an employee was taken hostage. The state of California's Division of Occupational Safety and Health said the hospital "failed to protect workers from violence in the emergency department" after a homeless man stormed into the ER and held a nurse and ward clerk hostage before being subdued. Previously, nurses had reported feeling unsafe while tending to a gunshot victim who was dropped off in front of the hospital instead of the emergency room. The citations, which included other violations, totaled $10,350.

A fourth hospital to have been cited by OSHA for failing to protect staff from workplace violence is Franklin Hospital Medical Center in New York which was fined $4,500 after a nurse at the hospital was attacked and severely injured while performing normal duties that included providing group therapy sessions to psychiatric patients. OSHA inspectors found that the hospital had "failed to implement adequate measures to protect employees from assault in the workplace."

It should be noted that the OSHA guidelines (OSHA 3148) address only the violence inflicted by patients or clients against staff. The OSHA citations are for the U.S. and are cited under the "general duty" category. OSHA has issued a directive instructing its enforcement officers on investigating and inspecting worksites that the agency identifies as vulnerable to workplace violence.

There are various ways of looking at violence in order to understand its impact on healthcare organizations. In this chapter, we will approach the subject from the basic categories of who, what, why, when, and where.

THE WHO (PERPETRATORS/VISITORS)

Those who are committing violence in emergency rooms are not typically gang members who are brought to the hospital after a violent confrontation with a rival gang and are looking for payback. Rather, it is often citizens who are intoxicated and too drunk for jail—medical centers are often dumping grounds for extremely drunken, disruptive and often-homeless patients who may be in the hospital emergency department for more than 12+ hours. The patient can become not only physically abusive, but verbally as well—something that wears on front-line providers. Other concerns stem from the 20-plus-year decline in mental health funding, which requires hospitals to medical treat for patients with higher acuity for longer periods of time in locations not originally designed for caring of patients

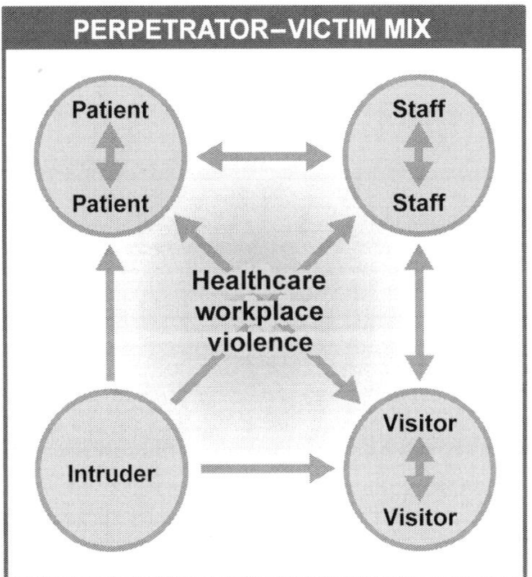

FIGURE 20-1

Healthcare workplace violence perpetrators and victims.

needing such specialized treatment. Just as concerning is the visitor who is upset with having to sit for hours in the waiting room while waiting on a loved one to receive care. But not all attacks can be anticipated, as was the case after a patient assaulted eight people, including five nurses and a security officer before having to be sedated in the emergency department of John Hunter Hospital in New Castle (UK). The 18-year-old patient with developmental and mental health problems lashed out while being treated.[12]

There are four basic groups of perpetrators and victims in the healthcare environment: staff, patients, legitimate visitors, and illegitimate visitors. Figure 20-1 shows the many combinations of perpetrator to victim. The illegitimate visitor (trespasser/intruder) often is involved in stranger-to-stranger situations, while in the other groups, the perpetrator and victims are known. In the vast majority of past situations, both parties know each other, and their relationship has provided the motive for the violent act.

PATIENTS

We have previously discussed some situational events in both the outpatient and inpatient setting in which the perpetrator of violence is the patient himself—commonly referred to as patient-generated violence. The clinical patient is often the source of confrontation, largely due to the volume of patients, long waits, and disputes relative to services being rendered. Hospital emergency departments, along with mental health evaluation and treatment areas, intensive care units, dedicated forensic patient care centers and closed head injury units have historically the highest potential for violence. There are cases in which patients have attacked other patients or staff ostensibly without warning or provocation.

Nurses are often on the receiving end of physical assaults, because they are typically the first and most frequent medical care providers by the bedside of ill and sometimes angry or frustrated patients. The 2011 ENA study concluded that 86% of all emergency department nurses who responded to the survey had some form of violence committed against them while on duty over the past three years and a fifth said

Table 20-2 Type of Weapons Commonly Used to Commit Violence in the Healthcare Environment[13]

Most Commonly Used Weapons	
• Fists / Hands / Fingernails • Feet • Teeth / Mouth • Head • Body Fluids	• Medical Supply / Instrument • Food / Utensils / Meal tray • Furniture • Floor / Door / Wall / Window

they encountered it frequently. Much of the trend comes as more patients act out because of substance abuse or psychiatric problems. These patients have fewer treatment options following budget cuts at social service agencies. As such, the weapons used by the patient perpetrator to commit these violent acts are not knives, guns or other weapons typically associated with violence in the community. Most often, the weapon of choice comes directly from the patient or the immediate environment. A listing of the most commonly used weapons by patients committing an act of violence is shown in Table 20-2.

There is still a lack of understanding of who is likely to have a wish to harm medical staff and why. Further evidence-based research is needed to help reduce, mitigate or even prevent these attacks. While few physicians are actually killed by patients, thousands are attacked and injured. Involvement in a disability compensation case is, for example, a predictor of a negative attitude, as patients often become angry if they feel their physician will not support their compensation claim.

Some care providers believe part of the problem of escalating violence is some healthcare facilities have made security officers less conspicuous in an effort to cultivate a more friendly, service-oriented setting. A more critical concern stems from the restrictions imposed by regulatory and accreditation agencies such as CMS and Joint Commission that require healthcare organizations to apply medical restraints or seclude patients as a means of last resort—swinging the pendulum of managing patient behavior deemed at-risk from its previous position of being too prone to apply medical or chemical restraints or using seclusion rooms without the appropriate regard for patient safety. However, overly strict interpretations by surveyors and healthcare organizations alike have resulted in the compromise of employee, staff, and physician safety. Care providers are rarely using the tools available to them until after an actual incident of violence occurs. The result is more violent episodes and events and even more injuries to healthcare workers and patients alike. To correct this vicious cycle, healthcare organizations, together with accrediting and governing bodies, must take a more balanced approach in their interpretation of these patient restraint and seclusion guidelines before a safe and therapeutic healing environment can be created. If not, healthcare professionals will continue to leave their occupation because of the risk of actual and threat of violence. This will only feed another concern for the healthcare industry—the shortage of qualified medical professionals.

VISITORS

There is a potential for violence in healthcare caused by individuals or groups who are from outside the organization, which may include legitimate visitors such as patient family members or illegitimate visitors, who are the visitants who have no legitimate business being on the property. This type of visitor includes criminals contemplating or committing a crime (robbery, abduction, assault); gang members intent upon causing injury or harm; unwelcome friends or family members of staff or patients; protestors; terrorists; transient persons; and former patients and employees. It is almost impossible to discern the presence and intent of these persons until an overt act occurs. In fact, they often blend in with the legitimate patient, staff, or visitor.

The potential for violence from patients' family members is a concern. The family who comes in after their loved one has been in a traumatic accident is under great stress with high anxiety levels. This can overwhelm their coping skills and be the cause of verbal abuse towards the care providers, front desk receptionists, or other employees. However, violence against staff is not the only visitor concern.

Visitor violence against the patient is a troubling development that continues to plague the healthcare industry and threaten the reputation of many healthcare organizations that experience these often horrific events. At Winter Haven Hospital in Connecticut, a man shot to death his terminally ill wife and then killed himself.[14] An isolated event for most hospitals, these types of violent episodes are not all that uncommon across the vast expanse of the healthcare community.

- At Baton Rouge General Medical Center, a man walked into the hospital and opened fire into a hospital room killing his estranged wife and her boyfriend who were visiting her son.[15]
- Rhonda Stewart got into an argument with her estranged husband in the intensive care unit at Charleston Area Medical Center's Memorial Hospital in Charleston, West Virginia. She was asked to leave by the hospital staff. She later returned with a gun and shot him in the head.[16]
- In the parking garage at Baptist Medical Center in Jacksonville, Florida, a 68-year old husband pulled a gun and shot his wife and 11-year-old son as they were leaving the hospital and then shot himself.[17]
- A Birmingham, Alabama man was charged with attempted murder because he tried to drown his wife in a bathtub at Brookwood Medical Center where his wife was a patient.[18]
- And the patient may not always know their attacker, as was the case when an Illinois senior citizen patient was attacked by a knife-wielding son of her hospital roommate who became distraught after his visit, left the room and returned with a knife and attacked her.[19]

Untold healthcare organizations have had to manage the family member causing patient cruelty associated with Munchausen syndrome by proxy. Speaking at the 2009 IAHSS Annual General Membership Meeting and Seminar in Baltimore, Maryland, Sgt. Latrice Taylor from the University of Michigan Hospital in Ann Arbor shared two actual case studies that occurred at the facility within a one-year span in 2008. Within the audience, 10–20% had experienced a similar event. Munchausen by proxy is reviewed in greater detail in Chapter 12, "Patient Care Involvement and Intervention."

The legitimate visitor can also include outside service workers, construction workers, and vendors. While on occasion these people are responsible for violence, they do not present a major danger. Violence regarding these individuals is generally related to situational events occurring within the facility or in parking areas.

EMPLOYEES

Employees and staff members have been the source of many violent acts, especially against other employees or staff members. The day-to-day supervision, work evaluations, disciplinary actions, and terminations all set up situations that can be confrontational and can provide the motivation of employee and ex-employee violence.

Table 20-3 Characteristics and Warning Signs of the Typical Workplace Violence Perpetrator[20] (Courtesy of Steven C. Millwee, CPP, SecurTest)

Profile of the Workplace Violence Perpetrator	
• Usually a loner; socially isolated without good support system • Long history of frustration and failure • Experienced some precipitating event, such as being fired or divorced • Difficulty handling defeat or rejection • Unusual fascination with weapons	• Places blame for problems elsewhere; blames others for failure • History of violence; made threats or acted out violently before • History of intimidating or threatening others; defiant or blatantly violates organization procedures • History of illegal drug and/or alcohol abuse • Criminal history

There is common agreement among human resource managers and security administrators that individuals who have committed violent acts in the past are potential perpetrators for further violence. Steve Millwee, CPP, author of *The Threat from Within: Workplace Violence* is a leading authority on workplace violence and has found many similarities with employees prone to instigating workplace violence. Table 20-3 lists many of the common characteristics and warning signs of the perpetrator of workplace violence.

A preventive approach to employee workplace violence requires recognizing that acting out may be the end result of an invisible process. No single characteristic or seemingly innocent experience can accurately predict violence. An individual may perceive she has been unfairly treated, discriminated against, harassed, or purposely exposed to stress by a supervisor. Other mental factors such as stress, discrimination, and harassment can have a cumulative effect on the individual and lead to a traumatic event.[21]

The healthcare industry is not immune to these types of violent acts even if the media attention provided to these incidents is minimal. In 2010, an 85-year-old heart patient in Connecticut stashed a revolver in the folds of his hospital gown and shot a nursing supervisor who tried to grab the gun. The 35-year-old nurse was shot three times but survived.[22] In 2005, anesthesiologist Marc Daniel stabbed Lori Dupont, a nurse at Hôtel-Dieu Grace Hospital in Calgary, Alberta, and then killed himself. During a three-month coroner's inquiry, the jury heard how the hospital allowed Daniel to continue practicing, despite complaints about Daniel's threatening behavior, such as breaking a nurse's finger and destroying hospital equipment, and Dupont's complaints that Daniel harassed her.[23]

In 2009, a hospital worker shot and killed two employees and killed himself at Long Beach Memorial Medical Center in Long Beach, California.[24] Believed to have followed a recent downsizing, this event brought to life the importance of a having an "active shooter" contingency plan as hospital workers were screaming and witnessed fleeing the facility in a panic. The active shooter and other security-related emergency contingency plans are discussed in greater detail in Chapter 25, "Emergency Preparedness – Planning and Management."

THE WHAT AND THE WHY

The "what" of violence pertains to the specific act itself in terms of the severity or type of crime. The type of crime can be viewed on a continuum, as shown in Figure 20-2.

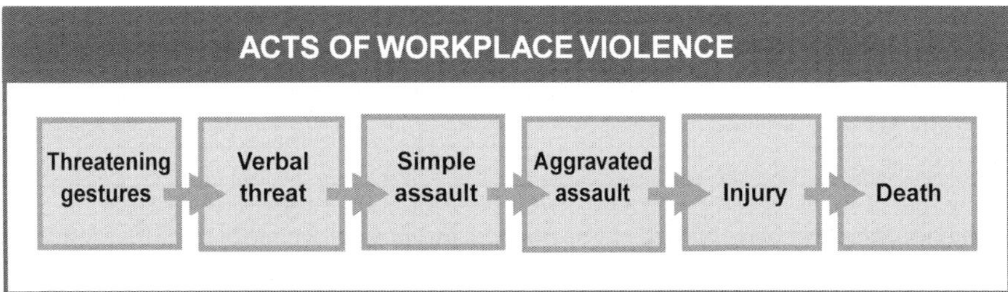

FIGURE 20-2

The acts of violence in the healthcare workplace.

There are at least three different categories of a violent act viewed from the causation or perpetrator viewpoint. These are the targeted victim, situational event, and the spontaneous event. The targeted victim is tied closely to stalking and generally involves a previous conflict between the perpetrator and the victim. The most common scenario in this regard is related to a domestic or intimate relationship. Violent acts in many of these cases are somewhat predictable, thus providing an opportunity to implement a number of possible prevention strategies.

The situational event generally results from a conflict between the perpetrator and the victim in the course of their interacting with each other. In the medical care setting, such conflicts often revolve around delivery of care issues. Patients may feel they are not receiving the treatment they deserve or that their treatment is not timely. Sometimes it is not the patient but visitors who perpetrate the violence, whether it is at a hospital, clinic, physician's office, dentist's office, or long-term care facility. Violent acts resulting from such situational conflicts are often fueled by drugs or alcohol. The mental health patient may be involved in confrontational situations that lack an apparent, or outward, rational motivation.

In spontaneous acts of violence, victims generally do not have a direct relationship with the perpetrators, and there is no forewarning of the danger. The act is premeditated and many have involved weeks, months, or years of planning or thought. The motive for these acts is usually general in nature and directed toward a cause, organization, or controversial issue. Unfortunately, the open healthcare environment is conducive to providing the opportunity for carrying out spontaneous violent acts.

One example of a spontaneous violent act occurred when a gun-wielding 57-year-old woman entered an eye clinic at the Henry Ford Hospital in Detroit, Michigan and started shooting, severely wounding two technicians who she thought were physicians. Investigations revealed that she blamed physicians for the death of her mother, which had occurred over four years earlier. There was no evidence that she had previously complained of wrongdoing in her mother's death, had ever visited or been in Henry Ford Hospital, or had ever met the two technicians she shot.

THE WHEN AND THE WHERE

Of course, there is no way to penetrate the minds of violent persons so that we can predict the time and location of an act. We do know that in the medical care setting, there are certain times and locations in which acts are more likely to occur. The most severe acts generally occur during the regular business day, when things are busy, facilities are open, and many potential victims are in close proximity to each other. For example, a disgruntled employee holding a grudge against the human resources office would not be able to act out his anger against department staff unless the office was open. On the other hand, employees and patients in a behavioral health setting and the intensive care unit are possible targets of violence 24 hours per day, seven days a week.

While certain areas of the healthcare facility present a higher risk than others for violence, no area can be considered immune. History has provided examples of violence in hospice units, admitting rooms, physician offices, stairwells, business offices, general medical surgical units, other patient care areas, cafeterias, materials management areas, and even in surgery areas. In the latter, an estranged husband shot and killed his former wife, a surgical technician, in the surgery area of a Louisville, Kentucky hospital. In Miami, Florida, a hospice patient beat two nurses at a nurses' station so severely that both were hospitalized with serious injuries; neither returned to their careers in nursing.

THE MANAGEMENT OF HEALTHCARE VIOLENCE

Not all violence occurring in the healthcare environment can be prevented; however, many acts can be prevented and managed to minimize injury, death, and damage to property. The three phases of managing violence in the workplace are before, during, and after. The after phase provides information and lessons that help healthcare professionals to consistently improve preventive measures and intervention. The IAHSS has established a basic industry guideline to help healthcare organizations address the issues of violence in healthcare.

01.09 VIOLENCE IN HEALTHCARE

Statement

Workplace violence threatens the safety of staff, patients, visitors and others in hospitals and healthcare organizations. All threatening behavior should be reported, evaluated and addressed based upon the assessed level of risk. Healthcare facility leadership should assign authority and provide support for plans and processes that address violence and intimidating behavior.

Intent

a. Healthcare Facilities (HCFs) should implement a multi-disciplinary process to address workplace violence prevention and response. The protocol should elaborate on an effective safety and security program, whose five main components also apply to preventing workplace violence:
   1) Management commitment to support efforts to minimize violence
   2) Employee involvement and training to engage staff in violence prevention and mitigation efforts
   3) Risk assessment, identification, prevention and mitigation
   4) Worksite analysis and development of response plans
   5) Internal and external data gathering and management, record keeping, evaluation and reporting

b. The multidisciplinary team should include representatives from security, clinical, risk management, human resources, ancillary/support staff, executive leadership and external responder when appropriate to develop and maintain the workplace violence program including prevention strategies.

c. The HCF should require threats be reported and evaluated. Responses should be documented, reviewed and assessed to determine lessons learned and opportunities for improvement.

d. An organizational response plan should be developed based on recognizing, understanding, reacting to, and managing events, as they develop and escalate.

e. A specific organizational response team should be developed that evaluates and plans responses concerning all threats, and the degree and severity of each. All response team members should have a clearly defined role.

Continued

01.09 VIOLENCE IN HEALTHCARE—cont'd

f. The violence response team should receive orientation and training in evaluating and responding to a variety of events of violence within the healthcare setting.

g. Protocols for response to domestic, targeted, patient-generated, or anticipated violence should be incorporated into the policy. The HCF should address the prevention and response to intimidating and disruptive behaviors such as threats and bullying.

See Also

- IAHSS Healthcare Security Guideline 02.02.01-Targeted Violence
- Violence Occupational Hazards in Hospitals, DHHS (NIOSH) Publication No. 2002-101, April 2002
- Guidelines for Preventing Workplace Violence for Health Care & Social Service Workers, U.S. Department of Labor Occupational Safety and Health Administration OSHA 3148-01R 2004
- Workplace Violence Prevention and Intervention Standard, ASIS International, 2011
- TJC Sentinel Event Alert, Issue 45, June 3, 2010
- US Department of Labor, Occupational Health and Safety Administration. Directive CPL 02- 01-052: Enforcement Procedures for Investigating or Inspecting Workplace Violence Incidents. https://www.osha.gov/OshDoc/Directive_pdf/CPL_02-01-052.pdf

Approved: January 2006
Last Revised: March 2014

PREVENTIVE AND MANAGEMENT STEPS

There are three specific steps of preparation and response that organizations must implement to properly address violence in healthcare. The first step is to provide a reasonable level of security for the overall environment and especially to areas of probable conflict. This includes an organized security program that includes control of access and visitor flow into and out of recognized high-risk units, proper physical security safeguards, enforced security policies and procedures, staff training and empowerment, and an effective critical incident response capability. To adequately plan and implement these essential elements, there must be strong commitment from top management, and the board of directors, to provide a high level of philosophical and management support. This support includes adequate funding to resource the protection program. Alan Butler, CHPA, a leading healthcare industry expert on violence prevention and mitigation, shares that effective workplace violence strategies include:

- Establishing a workplace violence prevention policy
- Establishing and maintaining security policies
- Examine and improving hiring practices
- Implementing prescreening techniques
- Conducting employee background investigations
- Encouraging employees to report threats or violent behavior
- Establishing termination policies
- Providing post-termination counseling
- Training all employees in the warning signs of aggressive or violent behavior
- Training management in threat assessment and de-escalation techniques
- Conducting formal workplace violence risk assessment

- Increasing security as needed
- Developing contingency plans
- Developing crisis and media communications plans
- Reviewing insurance coverage and verify coverages and exclusions
- Identifying a defensive strategy

THE THREAT POLICY

The foundation of a successful violence prevention program is the organization threat policy, which is an everyday working document. The policy should state clearly that threats of any kind are not tolerated, that the staff is responsible for reporting all threats, and should indicate the procedures for reporting such threats. In small organizations, the human resources department may be the central reporting point; in larger organizations, this may be the security department's responsibility. Regardless of size, there should be a central reporting department with responsibility for initiating follow-up actions.

In very large organizations, there may be two or three different threat policies with some limited fragmentation for reporting and follow-up. For example, there may be a policy specifically for threats to employees and another one for threats to patients, visitors, and others. It is suggested organizations preparing threat policies seek out such policies from other organizations as a valuable resources. In general, threat policies should include the following key points:

- Zero tolerance for threats against anyone on the property
- Mandated staff reporting of threats and reporting procedures
- Responsibility for immediate response and/or investigative action (24 hours per day)
- Staff obligation to report any application or knowledge of protective/restraining order naming the property of the organization as a protected area
- Statement of confidentiality of reporting party

RESPONSE TO THREATS

The key to responding to violent events is having an effective system for recognizing, understanding, reacting to, and managing events as they develop and escalate.

There are two distinct types of threats in terms of response and follow-up action. The first type of threat is one in which time is of the essence and immediate response is required. The organization's critical response element should be empowered to take whatever steps are necessary to protect life and property in an immediate intervention. Take, for instance, the patient with a behavioral problem or a large group of loud and difficult visitors. When this type of situation develops, the team leaders—e.g., lead physician, charge nurse, and security—can quickly huddle and decide whether to adjust the security response plan in anticipation of a potential problem.

In most situations of reported threats, there will be a window of time for planning, developing, and implementing actions required. The degree and severity of the threat will be somewhat of a subjective judgment in terms of actions to be taken. All threats must be taken seriously. It is better to err on the side of taking too much action than doing too little too late.

Threat response team

There should be a specific response team that evaluates and plans actions concerning all threats. The team should be comprised of the security administrator, director of human resources, nursing administrator and in some cases the risk manager. The coordinator or leader of this team should initially decide the team member or combination of team members responsible for the management of the threat. A minor dispute between employees, resulting in a mild threat, might be handled by the director of human resources and the affected department supervisor. In the case of a threat to a patient by a person outside the organization, there would possibly be a need to involve the entire team. In some emergency situations, a team member may immediately implement preconceived action protocols relative to the specific type of threat. A typical preconceived protocol may involve the domestic violence patient who has reason to believe that his or her assailant will come to the facility to cause further physical harm. Common steps in this regard may include:

1. Removing the patient's name from the list of inpatients (specifically from the switchboard and information desk and nursing station)
2. Assign room away from a stairwell
3. Restricting patient visitation
4. Changing room location so that the patient can be seen from the nursing station.
5. Using a private duty nurse
6. Hiring a special security officer and/or requesting law enforcement services

In extraordinary situations, the team would develop a specific plan for the situation. There should be a definite, identified authority for increasing, modifying, and ending the specific precautions implemented.

Another common threat that presents itself is the threatened staff member. These threats are often domestic-related and require preventative steps such as escorts to and from parking areas, work shift and/or location reassignment, restraining orders, or a change in work functions.

PREVENTING VIOLENCE IN THE WORKPLACE

All organizations need a strategy and plan to deal with workplace violence so that they can reduce the number of violent episodes and minimize the severity of these events to a large extent. The best means of managing workplace violence is to have a strong protection program in place that can be expanded to include specific facets of workplace violence. A program of preventing and managing workplace violence, in addition to a sound day-to-day security program, will include:

- A strong commitment from top management that preventive workplace violence is a priority both in terms of administrative and funding support
- Organization threat policy and procedures
- Staff training and education relative to staff responsibilities, early warning signs of escalating danger, de-escalation techniques, and general security awareness
- Encouraging employees to promptly report incidents and to suggest ways to mitigate or eliminate risk

- Reviewing workplace layout to find existing or potential hazards; installing and maintaining alarm systems and other security devices such as duress buttons or communication devices where risk is apparent or may be anticipated; and arranging for a reliable response system when an alarm is triggered
- The identification of criminal justice agencies, social agencies, and other community services as a resource to managing potential violent incidents
- Reporting of all incidents of violence
- Providing local law enforcement with floor plans of facilities to expedite emergency response or investigations
- The utilization of in-house resources such as employee health and employee assistance programs
- Setting up a system to use chart tags, logbooks, or other means to identify patients and clients with a history of assaultive behavior problems
- Instituting a sign-in procedure with passes for visitors and compiling a list of "restricted visitors" for patients with a history of violence
- Proper screening of employee applicants
- Consistent enforcement of organization workplace rules and regulations including the facility access control policy
- Prosecution of perpetrators (serve as a deterrent and hold perpetrators accountable)

The NHS has put together a "Zero Tolerance" initiative which requires trusts and health authorities to have systems in place for recording incidents of violence and aggression and to set targets for reducing the number of events of physical assaults against staff.

AGGRESSION MANAGEMENT TRAINING

Fundamental to any workplace violence prevention strategy is conflict resolution/aggression management training. However, no violence prevention education program is effective unless it gains employee involvement and support.

There are many types of violence prevention and aggression management training programs. Varying in length, some sessions are only an hour long while other programs can extend to several full-length days. Some are lectures delivered by internal staff, while others are interactive programs conducted by outside contractors. Some new employees participate right away, others not until months (or years) after their hire. Only a few are tailored to the specific healthcare environment in which participants work. In short, there is little consistency in the conduct, content, and applicability of these programs, which are major contributing factors to their general ineffectiveness in violence prevention. However, all employees should receive training on the management of aggressive behavior and include physicians, volunteers, clerical staff, clergy, and contract employees of all job categories. By training together, staff members gain a better understanding of everyone's role and develop a strong sense of teamwork. This will enhance communication and consistency in program administration. Medical staff will be more comfortable calling on security, for example, when they feel threatened or uncomfortable and security will feel they are part of the patient care team.

Research and clinical experience of the American Association for Emergency Psychiatry (AAEP) have found that by using verbal de-escalation techniques, agitated patients can frequently be calmed to a level of cooperative collaboration and engage in their treatment willingly. Such an approach has led to dramatic reduction in injuries, reduced hospital stays, and improved long-term outcomes for individuals—while often taking much less time than the traditional restrain and sedate approach. The research culminated in Project BETA (**B**est practices in **E**valuation and **T**reatment of **A**gitation) and it is a new, unprecedented guideline from the American Association for Emergency Psychiatry (AAEP). The BETA project, which represents an AAEP-wide effort to collate relevant, peer-reviewed data and includes several working groups on different aspects of managing agitations, has produced new guidelines addressing all facets of the agitation spectrum covering six major topics:

1. Overview of Agitation and Project BETA
2. Medical evaluation and triage of the agitated patient
3. Psychiatric evaluation of the agitated patient
4. Verbal de-escalation of the agitated patient
5. Psychopharmacologic approaches to agitation
6. Use and avoidance of seclusion and restraint.[25]

Baystate Health, a three-hospital, multiple treatment center system in Massachusetts with nearly 10,000 employees, introduced new training for nurses, physicians and care providers about how setting boundaries can be reconciled with customer service to help prevent workplace violence. The boundary-setting training teaches staff it is okay not to share information or to say that while they are glad to be helpful, they don't have the requested information. Another major point is customer service does not include accepting disrespect or aggression. If staff encounter abusive behavior, they are taught to express the desire to help but to be firm that the person asking for help must be respectful. The training also advises nurses to listen to their own bodily clues as a way to determine when a boundary needs to be set.[26]

Before they can recognize and respond to escalating tension in their work environment, however, healthcare staff must understand the basics of an effective response. Training should focus on evaluating each situation for possible violence when they enter a room or begin to deal with a patient or a visitor. If a violent situation is sensed, healthcare workers should never isolate themselves with the patient (or visitor). In these cases staff should practice the concept of keeping an open exit pathway—never allowing a patient or visitor to stand between them and the door. If a situation cannot be diffused quickly, the care provider should be trained to remove themselves from the situation and call for assistance.

While there is no program that can train healthcare staff to handle every type of violent situation, most healthcare security administrators agree it is possible to train them on the commonalities that occur in these situations. Most crisis intervention training programs include these lessons and help the employee look for physiological clues that an individual's aggressive behavior might escalate. Clues, for example can be expressing anger and frustration verbally, nonverbal body language such as sweating or a lack of eye contact, or signs (smell) alcohol or other drug use. Psychological skills needed by healthcare employees to manage conflict and aggressive situations include:

- *Understanding personal feelings about conflict.* Recognizing "triggers": words or actions that immediately provoke an emotional response like anger.
- *Empathic listening.* Acknowledging the other persons feelings and going beyond hearing just words. Attempting to understand what is really being said by asking reflective questions, and using both silence and restatements. Not being judgmental of the individual's feelings. They are real—even if not based on reality—and must be attended to.

- *Generating options for resolving conflict.* Many people, even trained healthcare professionals, can think of only two ways to manage conflict—fighting or avoiding the problem. Working to resolve disagreements and discussing the pros, cons, and consequences are very useful tools. Matching threats or giving orders is discouraged.
- *Behaviors to avoid.* Shouting, sarcasm, power struggles, aggressive body language, profanity, degrading remarks, and disrespect. Violence and disrespect breeds violence and disrespect. It is important to present in a nonthreatening, nonviolent manner and avoid any behavior that may be interpreted as aggressive: for example, moving too fast, getting too close, touching, or speaking loudly.
- *Positive behavior and interaction techniques.* Intermittent eye contact, relaxed body posture and gestures, maintaining a calm demeanor and listening. Maintaining a calm and caring attitude. The response will directly affect the individual.

Nurses themselves need to be reminded not to rank their own personal safety behind all other considerations. AnnMarie Papa, past president of the ENA and clinical director of emergency nursing at two Philadelphia hospitals, believes nurses should borrow techniques from other professions such as paramedics and firefighters—assess the scene for safety and assure that things seem safe before they go in.[27] Personal safety first is the motto for these industry professionals and an important message for healthcare workers who need to learn how to assess patient rooms and ask where the risks are when caring for every patient—especially those who are deemed a higher risk.

As incidences of gang-related violence have increased, there has been an effort to teach healthcare professionals ways to avoid such conflicts. In 2006, the New Jersey Hospital Association teamed up with the New Jersey State Parole Board to develop a training program to teach hospital employees across the state how to recognize potential street gang affiliation through signs, colors, marking, and language. More than 20 hospitals across the state have taken advantage of the gang awareness program since its inception.[28]

Armed with that information, healthcare staff can build the confidence to take ownership in their role as a safety specialist as well as caregiver or caregiver support and work with other staff to manage the situation.

LEGISLATIVE ACTION

In 1995, the state of California introduced the Hospital Safety and Security Act (AB 508) to decrease the amount of violence being committed against hospital employees. The act requires all acute care hospitals in California to conduct a security and safety assessment and to use the findings to develop a security plan with specific performance measures to protect personnel, patients, and visitors from aggressive or violent behavior. The plan includes specific security components such as:[29]

- Environmental controls to include physical layout and design, use of alarms and other physical security safeguards
- Staff to patient ratios
- Availability of security personnel who are trained in the identification and management of aggression and violence
- Specific violence prevention and response policies to include aggression and violent behavior management training

- Individual or committee responsibility for development of the security plan
- Reporting requirements

Hospitals in California are expected to track violent incidents that occur at the facility and analyze for trends as part of an annual quality improvement process. In 2002, the University of Iowa's Injury Prevention and Research Center studied the hospital employee assault rates and violent events before and after enactment of the AB508 and found the policy to be an effective method to increase safety of healthcare workers.[30]

In 2009, the state of New Jersey introduced the Violence Prevention in Health Care Facilities Act. Similar to AB508 in California, the revised state statute requires hospitals, nursing homes licensed by the New Jersey Department of Health and Senior Services, state and county psychiatric hospitals and state-owned developmental centers to have in place a detailed, written violence prevention plan. The legislation declares that violence is an escalating problem in many healthcare settings in New Jersey and across the nation, and although violence is an increasing problem for many workers, healthcare workers are at a particular high risk.

The states of Colorado, Connecticut, Kentucky, Massachusetts, Maryland, New York, Nebraska, Ohio, Pennsylvania, Tennessee, Texas, Virginia, and Washington have also developed similar violence against nurses legislation to help assure patients, visitors and care providers are assured a reasonably safe and secure work environment.

PROSECUTING PERPETRATORS

Holding perpetrators of violence accountable for their action has become a focus of much attention from U.S. and Canadian nurse and physician associations, the NHS, and many other entities. In 2008, tough new legislation was introduced in the UK, called the Criminal Justice and Immigration Act of 2008. In short, anyone causing actual violence in the healthcare setting could face fines of up to £1,000 and sentencing guidelines instruct judges that violence against care providers should lead to longer prison sentences.

The Massachusetts Nurses Association introduced a bill that addresses the issue of workplace violence by increasing criminal penalties for those who commit assaults against care providers. The nurses association is ramping up a legislative campaign to criminalize assaults on healthcare workers in the line of duty, similar to a Massachusetts state law that protects ambulance crews, firefighters, and other public employees. It is also pushing a proposal that would require hospitals to identify factors that contribute to violent incidents and minimize them.

The West Virginia Hospital Association along with the state chapter of the American College of Emergency Physicians lobbied successfully to get the West Virginia Health Care Protection law into effect. The legislation places stiffer penalties on anyone who commits a violent act against any healthcare professional. The law applies to healthcare workers in hospitals as well as care providers in county or district health departments, long-term care facilities, physician offices and clinics, outpatient treatment facilities, and home health settings.

An ardent complaint of the Ontario Nurses Association, with new legislation in Canada that requires employers to develop violence and harassment protocols and to take "reasonable precautions" to protect workers from domestic violence that may occur at work, is that nothing in the legislation outlines punishment.

It is a felony to verbally or
physically abuse a healthcare
worker.
Actions such as these will
result in
police intervention.

El abuso verbal o fisico de
nuestros empleados de salud es
considerado
un crimen federal.
Todo los actos abusivo
resultarán en intervencion de la
policia.

FIGURE 20-3

Sample violence signage language.

Orderlies at Perth's (Australia) Sir Charles Gardiner Hospital organized a strike over the issue of violent patients, demanding better legal support and training to deal with violent situations. At the heart of the bargaining was better training to deal with aggressive and violent patients situations. At the time of the strike, the employees were provided only two hours in how to deal with and restrain violent patients.[31]

Figure 20-3 shows sample language used in signs posted in patient rooms at a Jacksonville, Florida hospital.

RESTRAINING ORDERS

In dealing with targeted victim situations, the utilization of court-ordered restraining orders is a fairly common safeguard. These orders may be available to the individual and to the organization. The restraining order has two specific purposes. One is to prohibit specific conduct by a specific individual and to order the individual to maintain a specific distance from the victim. In some cases, an organization may be able to obtain a restraining order without legal action. In these cases, the organization must prove the conduct caused the individual to believe there was a threat of death or serious bodily injury. In all cases, a restraining order is only one element of managing a potential incident and should not be overly relied on in the course of business. Some of the major crimes of workplace violence have been perpetrated by individuals who were under a restraining order.

CULTURE OF TOLERANCE

What is most concerning about the issue of violence in healthcare and especially shootings is how little play nationally or even locally most of these stories receive—a couple of news cycles and then nothing. Hospital violence has become so commonplace that it no longer warrants extensive news coverage.

If a shooting similar to the one at Scotland Memorial Hospital in Laurinberg occurred in a school, for example, it likely would have generated much more media coverage. No one knows if or when hospital violence will get the attention it deserves. It is not a new phenomenon and many healthcare media have reported on it, but it is not talked about much anywhere else.

There are big cost factors at work—what hospitals are paying in worker's compensation claims or in litigation for unsafe work environments, missed work, and overtime, to name a few tangible costs. Many professionals are now worried about how violence in healthcare will affect recruiting and retention of healthcare workers and care providers. This is a human resource issues that must be addressed to create a safe working environment for all. There is plenty of stress in healthcare. Our care providers should not have to worry about getting shot, or stabbed, or kicked, or slapped or scratched, or punched, or spit upon, or pushed, or cursed at, or intimidated. That sort of abusive conduct is not tolerated in any other industry. Hospitals and the healthcare environment should not be an exception.

REFERENCES

1. Clark Cheryl. Healthcare violence is increasing: Is your hospital prepared? *HealthLeaders Media* 2010, June 4. Retrieved June 4, 2010 from http://www.healthleadersmedia.com/page-2/QUA-251945/Healthcare-Violence-Is-Increasing-Is-Your-Hospital-Is-Prepared.
2. Griffin Joel. Hospitals see increase in violent crime. *Security Info Watch* 2014, June 30. Retrieved July 1, 2014 from http://www.securityinfowatch.com/article/115542887/international-association-of-healthcare-security-and-safety-foundation-releases-2014-healthcare-crime-survey.
3. ECRI Institute. Violence in healthcare facilities. *Healthcare Risk Control – Risk Analysis, Safety & Security Part 3* 2011, March;**2**.
4. Institute for Emergency Nursing Research. Emergency Department Violence Surveillance Study. *Emergency Nurses Association* 2011, November. Retrieved November 2, 2011from http://www.ena.org/research/current.
5. Kreimer Susan, MS. Keeping Nurses Safe from Workplace Violence. *AMN Healthcare* 2010, March 3. Retrieved March 12, 2010 from http://www.amnhealthcare.com/News/features-details.aspx?Id=33574.
6. CTV.ca. Emergency room nurse calls for increased security after assault. *CTVglobemedia* 2009, December 10. Retrieved December 13, 2009 from http://winnipeg.ctv.ca/servlet/an/local/CTVNews/20091210/wpg_nurse_091210/20091210/?hub=WinnipegHome.
7. Daily Telegraph Reporter. Attack in NHS hospital 'every three minutes'. *Daily Telegraph* 2009, November 4. Retrieved November 4, 2009 from http://www.telegraph.co.uk/health/healthnews/6493111/Attack-in-NHS-hospital-every-three-minutes.
8. University of Michigan Health System. *Majority of Emergency Physicians Report Experiencing at Least One Violent Act a Year*. 2005, February 15. Retrieved September 9, 2007 from http://www.med.umich.edu/opm/newspage/2005/edviolence.htm.
9. Lazar K. Violence in ER a Growing Problem. *The Boston Globe* 2008, November 11. Retrieved November 12, 2009 from http://www.boston.com/news/local/articles/2008/11/11/violence_in_er_a_growing_problem/?page=2.
10. National Institute of Occupational Safety and Health. *Violence in the Workplace*. 1996, July 16. Retrieved December 22, 2008 http://www.cdc.gov/niosh/violintr.html.
11. Valencia MJ. Hospital Urged to Protect Against Violence. *The Boston Globe* 2007, August 21. Retrieved August 23, 2007 from http://www.boston.com/news/local/articles/2007/08/21/hospital_urged_to_protect_against_violence.
12. Gregory Helen. Hospital staff on savage front line. *Newcastle Herald* 2014, July 8. Retrieved July 9, 2014 from http://www.theherald.com.au/story/2404864/hospital-staff-on-savage-front-line/?cs=12.

13. Peek-Asa C, et al. *Workplace Violence and Prevention in New Jersey Hospital Emergency Departments*. National Institute for Occupational Safety and Health; 2007. Retrieved June 29, 2009 from http://pdcbank.state.nj.us/health/surv/documents/njhospsec_rpt.pdf.
14. Bouffard Kevin, Green Merissa. Man Kills Wife, Self at Winter Haven Hospital. *The Ledger.com* 2010, May 10. Retrieved May 18, 2010 from http://www.theledger.com/article/20100510/news/5105046?p=all&tc=pgall.
15. Man shoots ex-wife at Louisiana Hospital. *Private Officer News* 2010, September 4. Retrieved September 6, 2010 from http://privateofficer.org/man-shoots-ex-wife-at-louisiana-hospital-www-privateofficer-com/.
16. Rivard R. Many Hospitals Seeing Increase in Violence. *Charleston Daily Mail* 2009, June 16. Retrieved June 16, 2009 from http://www.dailymail.com/News/200906150690.
17. Woman Shot at Hospital Dies; Son Recovering. (2008, June 20). News4Jax.com. Retrieved June 21, 2008 from http://www.news4jax.com/print/16663671/detail.html.
18. Bryan K. Man Tried to Drown Wife in Hospital Tub. *The Birmingham News* 2008, March 26. Retrieved March 30, 2008 from http://blog.al.com/spotnews/2008/03/man_tried_to_drown_wife_in_hos.html.
19. Gregory Ted. Aurora hospital stabbing raised security question. *Chicago Tribune* 2010, September 1. Retrieved September 2, 2010 from http://www.chicagobreakingnews.com/2010/09/aurora-hospital-stabbing-raises-security-question.html.
20. Millwee SC. Firing the Violent or Threatening Employee Without Being Fired On. *SecurTest, Inc* 2003. Retrieved June 30, 2009 from http://www.safetampabay.org/publications/WPViolence_2003.pdf.
21. Lindsey D. Of Sound Mind? Evaluating the Workforce. *Security Management* 1994, September;**69**.
22. Need for metal detectors at Hopkins. Baltimore Sun. Retrieved September 17, 2010 from http://www.baltimoresun.com/news/maryland/bs-md-hopkins-hospital-security-20100916.
23. A Killing at Hotel-Dieu: Murder Suicide Shocked the Community. *The Windsor Star* 2006, November 4. Accessed June 14, 2009 from http://www2.canada.com/windsorstar/features/dupont/features/dupont/story.html?id=c79312d5-a2c7-43e8-a274-30f2e8ec1b1d.
24. Taxin A. *Police: 3 Dead in California Hospital Shooting*. The Associated Press; 2009, April 16. Retrieved April 22, 2009 from http://www.foxnews.com/story/0,2933,516888,00.html.
25. Scheck Anne. Special Report: Project BETA stresses verbal de-escalation for agitated patients. *Emergency Medicine News* 2011, February. Retrieved July 5, 2014 from http://journals.lww.com/em-news/Fulltext/2011/02000/Special_Report__Project_BETA_Stresses_Verbal.2.aspx.
26. Longmore-Etheridge A. Nurses on Guard. *Security Management* 2007, February:55–6.
27. Carlson Joe. Security lapses—Critics urge execs to take safety issues more seriously. *Modern Healthcare* 2011, October 17. Retrieved November 1, 2011 from http://www.modernhealthcare.com/article/20111017/MAGAZINE/310179953#ixzz1bEmuX8x4.
28. Thompson LE. New Jersey Hospitals Gang Up on ED Violence. *Nurse.com* 2009, February 23. Retrieved February 24, 2009 from http://news.nurse.com/apps/pbcs.dll/article?AID=2009302230056.
29. State of California. California Health and Safety Code Section 1257.7. Retrieved June 29, 2009 from http://law.onecle.com/california/health/1257.7.html.
30. Casteel C, Peek-Asa C, Nocera M, Smith JB, Blando J, Goldmacher S, et al. Hospital Employee Assault Rates Before and After Enactment of the California Hospital Safety and Security Act. *Annals of Epidemiology* 2009, February;**19**(2):125–33.
31. Hospital Orderlies Strike Over Violent Patients. *Australian Broadcasting Channel News* 2007, December 10. Retrieved December 11, 2007 from http://www.abc.net.au/news/stories/2007/12/10/2114306.htm.

CHAPTER

AREAS OF HIGHER RISK

21

The term "security sensitive area" was coined by The Joint Commission (TJC) relative to their standards and elements of performance. The security sensitive area pertains exclusively to the protection arena. While non-Joint Commission-accredited facilities are not bound by commission requirements, the requirements provide all organizations with a logical and practical method of identifying and approaching certain basic protection issues for areas of highest risk. Similarly, in other countries without The Joint Commission, the importance of security sensitive areas to protection programs is no less significant.

There is a clear distinction between areas of higher risk, often thought of as security sensitive areas, and the area with special security concerns. All healthcare organizations must identify the security risks in their respective environments that require enhanced protection or special safeguards. It is the healthcare organization's responsibility to make the decision, through a security risk analysis process, as to which areas have exceptional risk, rendering them security sensitive areas or lower risk areas of special concern. Common areas of special security concern are discussed in Chapter 22, "Areas of Special Concern."

SECURITY SENSITIVE AREAS

For our purposes, it is helpful to view areas of higher risk in two categories. The first category involves the vulnerability to people, such as in the birthing unit, the mental health unit, remote parking areas, the clinical care area of the emergency department, and the intensive care unit. The second category involves assets. Areas with valuable assets within most healthcare facilities include the pharmacy, areas storing protected health records, information technology and services server rooms, research labs, and cash handling/cashier areas. In these instances, the risk of potential loss revolves around a product or function. For example, the drugs in the pharmacy create a higher risk of armed robbery, yet the dollar loss potential to the organization is quite low. The operation of an animal research lab, on the other hand, creates the potential for high dollar loss, in relation to information and property damage, as opposed to high exposure for staff injury.

A clear and precise definition for what is an area of higher risk versus a security sensitive area has never been issued—by The Joint Commission, CMS or any other regulatory agency. In this discussion, the terms will be used interchangeably and defined as follows: a location whose function or activity presents an environment in which there is a significant potential for injury, abduction, or security loss, that would most likely severely negatively impact the ability of the organization to deliver high-quality patient care. This is often based on the potential for violence or use of weapons, especially against vulnerable populations such as the elderly, infants, and children, and the availability of drugs or cash-handling areas. The IAHSS has a specific security industry guideline to guide healthcare facilities in the identification and protection of security sensitive areas.

07.01 SECURITY SENSITIVE AREAS

Statement

Healthcare Facilities (HCF) will identify security sensitive areas during security risk assessments and develop reasonable measures to minimize vulnerabilities and mitigate risk.

Intent

a. Security sensitive areas should be identified during the risk assessment and may include:
  1) Areas housing at-risk populations, controlled and dangerous materials, or sensitive equipment and information
  2) Operations with significant potential for injury, abduction or loss.

b. The senior manager of identified security sensitive areas should be involved in mitigation efforts and planning should include security, clinicians and ancillary staff.

c. The HCF should develop a plan for each security sensitive area. Where appropriate, the security plan should include the following:
  1) Identification of risks unique to the area
  2) Access control plan of entry to and exit from the area for visitors, patients, staff and others
  3) Security technology; this may include video surveillance, alarm monitoring, keying systems or other security safeguards
  4) Preventive maintenance procedures for reducing the potential for security system failure should be developed including regular and ongoing testing procedures
  5) Security training for staff members and, as appropriate, patients and their families
  6) A defined response plan delineating roles and responsibilities for security, clinicians and ancillary staff
  7) A review and corrective action process of security activity and events

Approved: December 2006
Last Revised: December 2013

There are three major areas of healthcare that would normally involve the designation as a security sensitive area: the emergency department, infant care/birth center, and the pharmacy. Other areas in the healthcare delivery systems often require the organization to take additional security precautions, and may be assigned the security sensitive area designation. These include pediatric units, specialty clinics (such as methadone, detoxification, or abortion), research labs, mental health units, and centralized information departments.

Each Joint Commission-accredited hospital organization must designate their security sensitive areas in their written security management plan. The term *security sensitive area* has an explicit meaning by The Joint Commission that is useful for organizations no matter their regulatory affiliation or country of residence. When the declaration is made, there are three basic security components that must be developed and implemented relative to the security sensitive area. These components are:

1. *Specific security access control plan for the area.* A written plan to control or regulate access, including how nonemployees are screened, identified, and directed to service points specific to the area. Building on the overall facility access control plan, the healthcare organization should not limit its discussion of access control to just locks and keys. It can consist of staff-assigned responsibilities and identification systems, as well as the various physical safeguards that may be appropriate. The level of access control and restrictions employed may vary from facility to facility. Determining what restrictions should be employed is best determined as part of the annual assessment of security sensitive processes.
2. *Security orientation and education specific to area risks.* Every staff member who works in a security sensitive area must undergo specific security training. This training includes

understanding the processes and staff contributions for the protection of the area, how to identify potential security compromises, how to minimize security risks for all persons within the area, and how to react to specific breaches of security to minimize the danger to staff, patients, and visitors. How this is accomplished is not prescribed; common methodologies include:

- Initially training new employees about their roles in the access control and critical incident response plans
- Periodically conducting drills to test the response to a critical incident, correcting weaknesses in the plan, and/or retraining staff, and documenting all such activities
- Annually retraining all employees about their roles in the access control and critical incident response plans

3. *Critical incident response plan.* The written plan should describe unit employee response to the primary security threat for the area. It should include how employees respond to pre-determined events that negatively impact department performance, and/or personal security (usually those events which caused the area to be declared security sensitive). The plan must be activated immediately when the preventive steps of access control and staff actions have failed to prevent a major security incident.

The critical incident response plan should be formulated for unit staff reaction, while more general and organizational wide response plans will be generated by security, sometimes in conjunction with the emergency management branch of the organization. An example of this concept can be viewed in the birth center. Prepared by the unit manager, the plan should focus on the abduction of the newborn. Input and collaboration with the security department is an important part of the methodology in developing the plan. The responsibility for the preparation of the critical incident response plan rests with the unit manager in collaboration with the healthcare security administrator. The plan will involve various facility departments and staff and not be limited to just the actions of the unit staff or security. In the case of an infant abduction, a response is required of every employee in the healthcare organization.

In this chapter, the three primary security sensitive areas—the infant birthing area, the emergency department, and the pharmacy—will be discussed; however, this should not imply that these are the only three areas for facility consideration. Each facility will have specific functions or areas that present major security threats and concerns.

INFANT ABDUCTIONS FROM HEALTHCARE FACILITIES

The abduction of an infant from a healthcare facility is an event that generates a considerable amount of media attention. Newspapers, magazines, and TV talk shows have addressed the various aspects of infant abduction so the risk is now widely recognized. However, in recent years the number of nonfamily infant (birth to six months) abductions from hospitals has been drastically reduced. This reduction is due in large part to the efforts of the National Center for Missing and Exploited Children (NCMEC). It was not until 1987, when the NCMEC studied the problem of U.S. infant abductions, that the extent of these events was known. Their study data dates back to 1983, and their research and tracking continue as an ongoing NCMEC program. In particular, the work of John Rabun, Vice President and Chief Operating Officer; Cathy Nahirny, Senior Analyst/Supervisor; and the highly dedicated staff of the NCMEC have truly made a difference.

Table 21-1 Infants (Under Six Months) Abducted by Nonfamily Members from U.S. Healthcare Facilities: 1983 to 2014

Abducted From	Number	Percent
Mother's Room	77	58%
Nursery	17	14%
Pediatrics	17	14%
On Premises	21	16%
TOTAL	**132**	**100%**
OUTCOME		
Recovered	127	(94%)
Still Missing	5	(6%)
TOTAL	**132**	**100%**
Violence to Mother	11	8%

(Courtesy National Center for Missing and Exploited Children, Alexandria, Virginia)

The NCMEC does not just study the problem; it also provides ongoing training and education and is an instant resource to facilities and law enforcement agencies when an abduction occurs. The work of the NCMEC goes far beyond hospital infant abductions; however, the majority of this discussion focuses on nonfamily abductions within the healthcare delivery system.

The delivery system involves over 3.95 million births being registered each year in approximately 3,500 U.S. birthing facilities, and continues to a limited degree after discharge. Hospital-operated, or independent home healthcare agencies, frequently provide aftercare to mother and baby in the home. The healthcare security administrator must also be aware there can be a certain degree of organizational responsibility for infant safety in the home, after discharge from the hospital. In the event that information, action, or inaction on the part of the healthcare organization caused or contributed to a criminal act in the home, there could be certain legal ramifications.

In 1989, the NCMEC issued its first set of guidelines relative to the abduction of the newborn, titled *For Hospital Professionals: Guidelines on Preventing Abduction of Infants from the Hospital*. The most current NCMEC guideline (9th edition) was released in January 2009 and is titled *For Healthcare Professionals: Guidelines on Prevention of and Response to Infant Abductions*. This publication goes beyond safety in the maternal-childcare unit to safety in special care nurseries, pediatric facilities, outpatient areas, and the home.[1]

The number of infants abducted from hospitals (from 1983 to 2014), including the location of the abduction and degree of violence, is shown in Table 21-1. The number of infant abductions from hospitals and homes by state (includes Puerto Rico and the District of Columbia) for the same period of time is shown in Table 21-2.

In Canada, data provided by the Royal Canadian Mounted Police (RCMP) reflect nine abductions of infants from Canadian hospitals, between 1991 and 2014. Six of these incidents have involved stranger abductions.[2]

Table 21-2 The Number of Infant Abductions from U.S. Hospitals and Homes by State: 1983 to 2014

State	# Cases	State	# Cases
Alabama	4	Montana	1
Arkansas	4	Nevada	1
Arizona	4	New Hampshire	1
California	39	New Jersey	6
Colorado	6	New Mexico	4
Connecticut	2	New York	11
District of Columbia	6	North Carolina	6
Delaware	1	Ohio	10
Florida	22	Oklahoma	4
Georgia	10	Oregon	3
Illinois	18	Pennsylvania	11
Indiana	2	Puerto Rico	4
Iowa	1	Rhode Island	1
Kansas	3	South Carolina	8
Kentucky	4	South Dakota	1
Maine	1	Tennessee	6
Maryland	10	Texas	37
Massachusetts	3	Utah	2
Michigan	6	Virginia	8
Minnesota	2	Washington	4
Mississippi	3	West Virginia	1
Missouri	7	Wisconsin	3

Note: States that are not listed in this table have not reported an abduction by a nonfamily member from a hospital or the home during this time period (31 years).
(Courtesy National Center for Missing and Exploited Children, Alexandria, Virginia)

In addition to the NCMEC guidelines for preventing infant abductions, several states have enacted legislation mandating hospitals to implement certain infant security measures.

Statistically, the risk of an actual abduction is low. However, statistical relevance is not important to the family of the victim of an abduction, the healthcare organization's staff, or the healthcare facility. This event is devastating and takes an emotional and physical toll on all involved. The organization's reputation for safe patient care will suffer, even if the organization does everything reasonable and appropriate to avoid abduction.

The number of infant or pediatric abductions from hospitals by family members is not known. These cases, which are generally based on custody issues, are not tracked by any central tracking organization. Likewise, the number of attempted infant abductions from hospitals is not known. Anecdotal evidence suggests there are many more abduction attempts each year than reported. However, circumstances surrounding possible abductions that do not occur would be speculative at best.

The areas of greatest risk for infant and child abductions include the mother's room, nursery, postpartum units, pediatric care areas, and neonatal intensive care units, as well as well-baby units. But because these units may present more of a challenge to anyone trying to abduct an infant, an abductor may try to "get" a child in waiting areas for hospital clinics, radiology, and the emergency department. Child development centers on the healthcare facility may also become a target.[3]

PROFILING THE "TYPICAL ABDUCTOR"

Research of the NCMEC has enabled them to build a profile of the "typical infant abductor" produced from those who have abducted infants from hospitals. In these types of events, the typical perpetrator is not motivated by maternal envy or a burning desire for motherhood. It is usually her desire to hang on to a boyfriend or husband in a deteriorating relationship. To do that, she feels she must produce a baby. The phenomenon transcends race and socioeconomic status. The woman is likely to be of childbearing age and often overweight. The person frequently suffers from low self-esteem, and usually lives in the community where the abduction takes place.

Analysis of the 132 cases yields some other interesting information. The abductor will most likely take an infant whose skin color "matches" her significant other, to ensure he will accept the infant presented to him as "his baby." Rarely does the woman have a previous criminal record or have psychiatric issues. They are sane and decide to commit a criminal act. Research has also found they frequently visit the nursery and maternity unity, asking the staff detailed questions about procedures and floor layout to become familiar with the staff and their work routines. Many non-English-speaking mothers are victimized by bilingual abductors who are able to portray themselves as different things to different people. To a victim mother, the abductor may present herself as a member of the hospital staff, while at the same time presenting herself to the hospital staff as a member of the mother's family.

In Canada's most recent case at a Quebec hospital in May, 2014, a 16-hour-old infant was abducted from her mother's hospital room by a woman dressed and posing as a nurse. Fortunately the baby was quickly and safely recovered in the nearby community.[4]

The abductor will often use other common methods during the abduction, including:

- Indicating to others that she has "lost" a baby or may be incapable of childbirth
- Planning the abduction, but not targeting a specific infant (except possibly race)
- Visiting multiple birthing facilities in the community, seeking an opportunity to carry out the abduction—"window shopping"
- Impersonating a clinical provider or other healthcare person
- Spending time becoming familiar with healthcare personnel and befriending the infant's parents
- Demonstrating the desire and capability for providing "good" or appropriate care to the infant after the abduction

THE BASICS OF THE INFANT SECURITY PLAN

The basics of providing infant security are identification (mother, baby, significant other, and the caregiver staff), education (mother and staff), and physical and electronic security safeguards. These elements of infant security intertwine with the critical incident response plan to provide the desired level of access control and infant safety.

IDENTIFICATION

The most commonly utilized method of visual identification of the infant is the four-band (bracelet) system. These four identical bands link mom, baby, and significant other. The infant is banded on the wrist and ankle, while the mom and significant other wear similar bands on their wrists. However, infant identification goes far beyond bracelets. It is a combination of elements that should be viewed as a package, each complimenting and supporting the other. Each element of the infant identification package must be completed prior to the removal of the baby from the birthing room and, in all cases, within two hours of birth. The elements of identification are:

- **Footprints.** The footprint is an excellent form of identification if an infant is abducted and recovered even months later.
- **Color photograph within two hours of birth.** Digital cameras are a popular method of achieving this element of identification as it can instantly become part of the infant's medical record.
- **Full physical assessment.** The physical assessment of the infant must record any marks or abnormalities.
- **Cord blood.** A sample of cord blood for future identification typing should be taken and retained until 24 hours after the infant is discharged from the facility.

A number of hospitals have prepared an attractive baby record "kit" provided to the parents at the birth of their infant. This kit is a duplicate of the footprint, photograph, and physical assessment completed for the infant's medical record.

The visual identification of hospital staff is a key element of the infant security plan. A distinctive badge is generally issued to unit staff assigned responsibility to transport or maintain control of the infant. This unique form of identification must differ, in a noticeable way, from regular hospital identification. Most often a photo identification badge worn above the waist, the identification should be readily visible to mother and other staff. A common method in developing the unique badge is to utilize a different color background, for either the staff person's photograph, or for the background of the badge itself. Figure 21-1 is an example of a unique form of staff identification used in healthcare.

FIGURE 21-1

A sample unique identification badge.

There should also be a system for issuing temporary badges, on a shift-to-shift basis, for temporary staff or students who are participating in infant care. This may also be needed when a staff member does not have their issued badge in their possession for a variety of reasons. These temporary badges must be tightly controlled with a method of strict accountability. Many healthcare organizations use the narcotics dispensary machine on the unit to issue and maintain an audit trail. Upon termination of an assigned mother/ infant caregiver, there must be a diligent effort to retrieve and destroy the identification badge. Strong consideration should be given to periodically changing the unique form of staff identification badge. A good rule of thumb is to alter the unique identifier every five years, and whenever there is a significant security compromise involving the badge identification system.

PREVENTION THROUGH EDUCATION

Education is critical to preventing infant abductions from healthcare facilities, and that means educating both staff and parents. NCMEC's publication *For Healthcare Professionals: Guidelines on Prevention of and Response to Infant Abductions*, contains detailed information for healthcare staff, including nursing guidelines and security guidelines. It also has information for patients, including a chapter titled "What Parents Need to Know."

Staff education

There must be continuous education and training of the caregiver staff as they are the first line of defense. In addition to unit staff members wearing a unique form of identification, they must demonstrate an awareness of the importance of this special security practice, relative to the protection efforts employed. Training should begin with basic training in customer service. Greeting everyone who comes on the unit has immeasurable deterrent value and is a good security practice. In the majority of infant abductions, there have been one or more observations by staff that, if properly followed up, would have prevented the abduction. When a situation does not quite look right, or there are unidentified persons on the unit, staff must act to investigate and clarify the situation, or determine the legitimacy of the unknown person. A March 2009 thwarted infant abduction at South Jersey Healthcare Regional Medical Center in Vineland, New Jersey is credited to an alert unit secretary who realized the abductor, dressed in scrubs, wearing an ID badge and identifying herself as a midwife, was an imposter.[5]

Unit staff awareness and alertness is believed to be one of the most critical elements of the infant security plan. When exercising the infant security plan, many mock abductors say that their greatest fear for carrying out the plan is being approached by a unit staff member. When it occurs, it is very disruptive, as anxiety levels rise and confidence in being able to carry out the abduction is lost—hardening the organization as a target. Box 21-1 lists other important staff training considerations. In addition, a documented, formal review of the infant security plan should be completed annually with all staff members.

Mead Johnson Nutritionals, working in conjunction with NCMEC, has developed a free training video for healthcare professionals called *Safeguard Their Tomorrows*, which has been distributed to hospitals since 1991. This program was revised for the third time in 2009 and has provided education and training on infant security to thousands of healthcare providers, security and law enforcement, since its first release. It is an excellent training resource and should be used to onboard all new infant care staff on the real risks of an abduction, and what they can do to prevent an occurrence.

BOX 21-1 STAFF TRAINING CONSIDERATIONS ON INFANT SECURITY

Infant Security Training for Healthcare Staff

- The profile of an infant abductor
- Common methods of operation for the typical abductor
- Importance of being alert to unusual behavior
- Role in critical incident response plan
- Guidelines for what parents need to know to include providing continuous parental education
- Restricting access to hospital materials (uniforms and other means of identification)
- Overview of prevention measures used (wearing unique form of identification, video surveillance, access control, infant tagging, etc.)
- Common diversionary techniques (fire alarms, disturbances in waiting areas, Code Blue activations, etc.)
- How to answer questions about infant security (in person and by telephone)

To further enhance training efforts, healthcare security administrators are encouraged to periodically quiz non-infant care staff members on their responsibilities during a potential infant abduction. This should include what hospital staff members are expected to do if "they find the person they are looking for." Infant abduction drills are useful training tools to further test staff members, by having the "mock abductor" scouting the unit prior to the drill, and calling the hospital to learn what staff will share about the protection measures in place.

Parental education

Evidence collected by NCMEC reveals that an overwhelming 58% of all infant abductions occur from the mother's room. As such, the role of "Parental Education" is a critical yet often overlooked element of the infant security plan. Unfortunately, it is an area not easily tested with infant abduction drills and other exercises.

The education of mothers, and ongoing reminders, are crucial to the infant security system. This education often begins in prenatal classes and continues to some degree until discharge, and includes after discharge care at home.

The NCMEC has developed a checklist, titled *What Parents Need to Know*, which contains sound parenting techniques that bear directly on the safety and security of the new infant. This checklist is contained in the "guidelines" document previously referred to. Distributed to prospective and new parents, the *What Parents Need to Know* information can be strategically posted in and around the birthing unit as well as in each patient room. The bathroom is an excellent location.

When parents are educated is a concern. In most healthcare facilities it is conducted as part of the prenatal education classes offered by the hospital. Upon admission to the hospital, the mother is often fully briefed concerning the security procedures. Unfortunately, for most new mothers and fathers, the timing of when parents are educated on their infant's security is not conducive to retention. The concern of most new mothers and fathers during these two periods is on having a successful child birth and they have limited ability to focus on anything else. Thus, when parental education has occurred, should be known and assessed by the healthcare security administrator, to determine if the timing of this education is effective. Ideally, parental education should happen in the first hour after childbirth—it is recognized that this is not often realistic.

baby safety

The maternity center staff has some important hints for you to keep your new baby safe:

1. **Never leave your baby alone.**
   If you wish to shower or sleep undisturbed, return your baby to the nursery where the infant will be constantly observed by a staff member.

2. **Place your baby's crib in constant view.**
   This will alow you to observe any visitors or hospital staff as they approach the baby.

3. **Feel free to question anyone entering your room.**
   All staff who are allowed to handle your baby wear their photo ID badges. Your nurse will explain these badges in more detail. If you are uncomfortable with anyone entering your room to take your baby, ask to see the photo ID or use the nurse call light to have your nurse assist in the identification. A staff member working with your baby will know the identification band number that is exclusive to you and your baby. **Never** give your baby to anyone that cannot show these **two forms of identification**.

4. **Always transport your baby in the crib.**
   When going from the nursery to your room, or your room to the nursery, always put the baby in the crib and push the crib. You will find the crib pushes easier and more safely if you guide it end to end, not sideways.

5. **Remember, there are many people who work in the hospital, but only the maternity center staff have special photo ID badges.**
   If you have any questions or are unsure about any of these people, please press your nurse call light.

6. **When you leave the hospital, continue safeguarding your baby.**
   At home never open the door for people you do not know. Never leave your baby alone in the car, even with the doors locked. Be sure you know how to identify a visiting nurse/helper **before** they arrive, if one is coming to your home.

I understand these safely precaulions and I will do all I can to keep my baby safe.

____

Parent Signature

Nurs 2957 9/95 NS

FIGURE 21-2

Parental security briefing form.

It is important to remind mothers and others of the importance of security during the entire stay (even though it may be a very short), with postings and key reminders. It is strongly recommended there be a briefing form signed by the soon-to-be mom. This form should become a component of the mother's medical record. See Figure 21-2 for an example of a briefing form.

Unit staff play an important role and should provide information to parents on circumstances in which they may release their infant to an authorized person. An excellent shift change protocol for the assigned care provider at the beginning of each shift, is to remind the mother of the importance of the unique form of identification worn by staff, and instituting a standard practice of informing "mom" of everyone who will be coming in for testing, etc. This simple yet effective approach empowers mothers and is an effective method to combat the potential abductor, who attempts to fool the mother into willingly handing over her baby.

Organizations that separate labor and delivery from post-partum have an excellent opportunity to remind mom of her role and responsibility for her infant's security, during her transfer from one unit to the next. Message stickers on the room mirrors and bedside/dresser table tents are frequently used. Northwest Medical Center in Bentonville, Arkansas has developed a security education poster that is placed on the back of the bathroom door, as shown in Figure 21-3.

The facility should be very clear as to whether there will be any home care provided, or home visits by hospital staff. To date, the abduction of an infant from the healthcare facility rarely entails violence; however, there is clear evidence of increasing violence when the abduction occurs outside

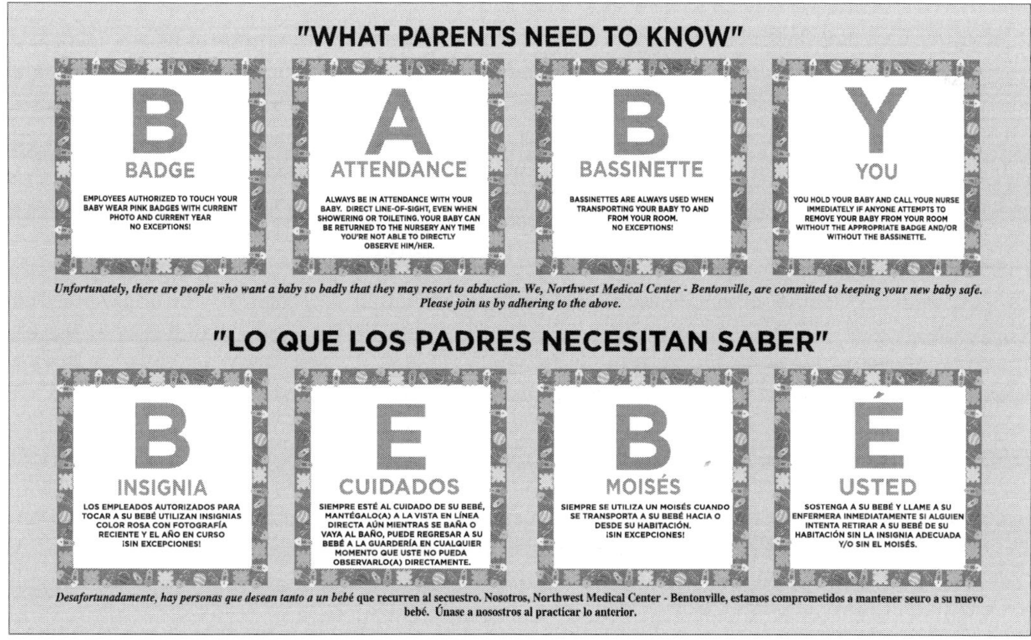

FIGURE 21-3

Security education poster for parents.

of the healthcare setting. In September 2006, a woman came to a St. Clair, Missouri mother's home asking to use the phone, slashed the mother's throat and left with her newborn infant. In court papers, authorities said the suspect was drawn to the home of the newborn's mother by a lawn sign that said "It's a girl."[6]

Unfortunately, the issue of home abductions is not limited to infants that have been birthed. In 2004, a woman who was desperate for another child to shore up her marriage, came into the house of a Skidmore, Missouri woman on the pretext of buying a dog, and overpowered and strangled the mother of an unborn child. She then cut into her abdomen and removed her unborn baby.[7] In 2008, a Kennewick, Washington mother was fatally stabbed multiple times and her baby cut from her womb.[8] In 2011, a pregnant Kentucky woman who was murdered and whose unborn baby was taken, had met her killer on Facebook. Her Facebook profile picture was a photograph of her pregnant stomach. The baby was not injured during his mother's death.[9] The NCMEC has tracked twelve fetus abductions or attempted abductions since 1987.

In some situations, the initial relationship between mother and the abductor is forged at the healthcare facility. In a 2006 Lubbock, Texas infant abduction, a stranger posing as a nurse visited the new mother several times in the hospital, and then came to mother's home. The women went for a walk together, and when the new mother was distracted for a moment, her baby was gone.[10]

If follow-up home care is provided, the identification protocols used by the facility and other security precautions must be thoroughly communicated to the family. Facilities that do not provide home care should specifically communicate that message. This will help new parents guard against someone falsely representing themselves as being from the healthcare organization, and gaining access into the home.

NCMEC attributes the decline of infant abductions from healthcare facilities in recent years to the preventive education program provided to staff and parents. In 1991, there were a total of 17 infant abductions nationwide, 11 of them from healthcare facilities. In 2013, there were a total of two infant abductions nationwide, with zero abductions from healthcare facilities. The 2014 Canadian hospital infant abduction was the first in that country in seven years, according to RCMP records.

PHYSICAL AND ELECTRONIC SECURITY SAFEGUARDS

The third basic element of infant security involves the installation of certain physical and electronic security safeguards. This includes restricted access to the nursery and controlled access to the unit, video surveillance of everyone entering the birth center through the main entrance, leaving the birth center, regardless of the exit, and where appropriate, the use of an infant monitoring system.

Access control

Research has demonstrated that the "typical" abductor will "shop" more than one healthcare facility before committing the act of infant abduction. To enhance the real and perceived security of infants, strong consideration should be given to restricting access in and out of the unit.

All stairwell and exit doors on the perimeter of the maternity unit should have alarms that alert unit personnel of their use. Ideally, these doors are equipped with bypass devices that allow authorized staff entry/exit use without activating the alarm, and delay the exit of an unauthorized user for 15–30 seconds. All exit control devices must conform to the Authority Having Jurisdiction (AHJ).

The most user friendly, and staff convenient, access control measures are complemented with devices that allow staff to communicate with visitors, and provide the ability to remotely allow entry. The video/intercom door phones discussed in Chapter 19, "Electronic Security System Integration," are frequently used. Monitored by unit staff and placed at a strategic yet convenient location inside the unit, these devices allow unit staff members to see, talk with, and remotely allow entry into the unit, with minimal disruption. Installation should be considered for the main entrance to the unit, and other commonly used staff/physician entrances.

All nursery doors should be locked. The door utilized for entry and exit of staff/visitors should be equipped with self-closing hardware. An exception to locking all nursery doors would be when there is an access control person (security officer, receptionist, or unit clerk) stationed at the door, for the specific purpose of controlling and authorizing access.

Lounges, locker rooms, and/ or storage rooms on the unit should also be under strict access control at all times.

Video surveillance

A key to the successful recovery of an infant is largely based on having a video surveillance system properly installed and designed to obtain a full face-shot of all persons leaving the unit. Several operating philosophies to the video surveillance system should be in place and are identified in Box 21-2.

There is no specific mandate that video surveillance systems utilized for infant security need to be live monitored. In most systems, however, there is live monitoring capability of all, or selected, cameras at the main nursing station. In addition, many systems will include redundant monitoring at the security operations center along with redundant alarm monitoring.

As discussed in previous chapters, a testing, repair, and maintenance program must be created to verify the system is in proper working order and functioning at all times. A structured monthly verification protocol is suggested.

ELECTRONIC INFANT MONITORING

Naquelle Sontieq Ballard was arrested for trying to steal a baby from Southern Regional Medical Center in Atlanta. Afterwards, she told police she had been planning the kidnapping for several months, since miscarrying a baby. She purchased blue scrubs at Walmart to pose as a healthcare worker and planned to snatch a newborn, as she never told her boyfriend she had miscarried. She was stopped by

BOX 21-2 VIDEO SURVEILLANCE OPERATING PHILOSOPHIES IN INFANT CARE AREAS

Infant Security Video Surveillance Strategies

- Full surveillance of each exit point from the unit to observe each entrance, exit, nursery entrance, hallway, stairwell, and elevator door on or near the infant care unit(s)
- Cameras may be "live" on a continuous basis or activated upon door use
- Position color monitors at nursing stations placed in locations so the public does not see the images
- All cameras are in color and recorded; a minimum ten-day library must be maintained
- Prominent signage stating all persons are recorded for security purposes (remember the message being sent to a potential abductor if/when they shop your facility)

two hospital employees after a hospital alarm sounded when Ballard tried to walk with the baby.[11] Positive outcomes like this have generated a good deal of interest by healthcare organizations in the electronic monitoring of infants. Tagging systems, as they are commonly referred to, were first developed over 25 years ago; however, technology has been refined and now has become an industry standard for birthing centers across the U.S. and is commonly used in Canada.

The basic electronic infant monitoring system is one that simply sounds an alarm when the device on the infant is detected by a receiving unit, at a specific point. Infant monitoring systems used for just this basic purpose have proven to be ineffective. The infant security system should be integrated with door and elevator controls, and video surveillance systems to accentuate the protection of infants and harden the organization as a target for a potential abductor.

Infant monitoring systems cost anywhere from several thousand dollars for a single door alarm, to several hundred thousand dollars for a more sophisticated system. However, the decision to install any electronic monitoring system should not be based on funding alone. There must be a complete buy-in by unit staff, as these systems require significant human involvement to make them effective—considerable staff task and administrative time are required to operate these systems.

The large number of nuisance (false) alarms poses significant risk to the overall posture of infant security at many birthing centers using these systems. There is nothing more likely to undermine the effectiveness and reliability of an infant security system than frequent false alarms. Staff can become frustrated and desensitized to large numbers of alarms. Instead of improving the overall security posture, the system can actually be rendered ineffective and reduce security. The design of an electronic infant monitoring system should begin with defining the space to be protected, often referred to as the protection zone, or safe area. These layers of protection can include protection of exits, detection of tag removal and continual supervision of each infant. Additionally, each organization using electronic infant monitoring should implement strategies to minimize the number of alarms generated. Several strategies are identified in Box 21-3.

No matter what form of attachment bands (or clamps) are in use with the electronic tagging of infants, healthcare facilities should be very careful to assure there is never any delay in activation of the alarm function. This includes sounding an alarm if the tag/strap/clamp is tampered with or if the baby

BOX 21-3 REDUCTION STRATEGIES FOR INFANT MONITORING SYSTEMS

Infant Monitoring Alarm Reduction Strategies

- Creating a multidisciplinary task force charged with addressing this; involve representatives from the mother/baby unit, security, facilities, and the manufacturer's representative
- Develop a performance measurement and track each alarm; determine if the alarms are staff generated, parent generated, or system failures. Implement strategies based on analysis of the same.
- Closely review the placement and range of the "exciter fields"; incorporate shielding as appropriate.
- Denote the range of each exciter field in a visible and obvious manner (meeting all aesthetic requirements); this can be done with carpet, tile, etc. Incorporate this information into both unit staff and parental education.
- Close all doors to the unit and adjust system functionality to secure doors if a tag enters an exciter field; the system should not alarm unless the door is open. Identify where people may pass in front elevators or doorways that will sound an alert if a new mom and tagged infant get too close and it opens. This allows "mom" to walk around the unit without setting off an alarm.

is moved to an unauthorized zone. The only way a bracelet should be removed without sounding an alarm is with authorized procedures that must be followed.

Frequent testing should be performed in support of that expectation. Staff should be trained to respond immediately so there is no delay between detection of the alarm condition and generation of the alarm notification. Staff members should never adopt a philosophy of only activating the system when they suspect a possible problem. Such actions present major risks and legal liability concerns. Detailed records, or audit trails, should be maintained on testing procedures and preventative maintenance schedules. The system should also have the ability to capture a wide range of system data, and generate reports on diagnostic testing and benchmarking, to document due diligence surrounding weekly testing. The system should capture every event that occurs. System testing should be conducted to verify the system is operationally functional and in good working order, using a randomly selected tag (not a test tag) with each area (portal of exit) covered by the system. Advances in technology have included three-way remote monitoring that can help identify problems and automatically determine whether workflow is being handled correctly. This, coupled with focused efforts to educate staff about the system and its performance, are credited with helping improve end-user experience.

These systems are not infallible. In 2012, Stanley Healthcare Solutions Security released a memorandum to the users of their Hugs and Kisses product, alerting them of interference caused by some smart phones. Their testing confirmed that low frequency (LF) noise from some devices reduces the patient tag's ability to detect the exit monitoring device, or the exit device's ability to receive messages from the tag. In either case, an exit alarm may not be generated when the tag is subjected to LF interference at a monitored exit. Testing showed no interference with high frequency (UHF) radio transmission or reception function that reduced the ability of the system to send and receive tamper alarm signals, regular status messages, etc. Supervision of each tag, by the system and by staff, is the most important defense against interference from smart phones or other sources. Hospitals should remind parents to refrain from bringing smart phones within very close proximity to their infants. A more detailed review of electronic infant monitoring systems is found in Chapter 19, "Electronic Security System Integration."

Ultimately, this advice from Stanley should be heeded by all looking to install an infant tagging system—infant security and safety relies on people, not technology.

GENERAL SECURITY PRECAUTIONS AND GUIDELINES

The NCMEC document, previously referred to, covers a number of fundamental elements of infant security. It should thus be reviewed by all persons having responsibility for protecting infants. The following is a general summary of some very important aspects of infant protection while in the hospital, at discharge, and at home:

- Infants should be transported one at a time and never left alone in a corridor
- Infants should be transported in a bassinet, never arm-carried, except in an extreme emergency
- There should be no posting of personal information of the mother or infant to the public when in the facility
- Infants should always be in direct line-of-sight supervision by staff or mother/family
- Infant bassinets in the mother's room should be placed on the side of the bed farthest from the room entry door

- Birth announcements should not be published in the newspapers or online media; if birth announcements are used, announcements should use surnames and refrain from including the family's home address or telephone number
- Staff should provide internal transportation to the discharge point and remain with the mother/infant until their departure
- Parents, family and friends should avoid using outdoor decorations announcing the infant's arrival at home
- Only well-known and properly identified persons should be allowed into the home. Authorized caregivers should provide advance notice of the intended visit and produce proper identification that has been previously explained to the infant's mother/family.

The healthcare facility should develop a written plan defining all proactive measures to be taken to prevent infant abductions in the labor and delivery unit, post-partum, overflow and VIP units, and pediatric care locations.

CRITICAL INCIDENT RESPONSE PLAN

The response to an infant abduction should be considered a hospital-wide plan, as all organizational staff should be actively involved. There should be a code name for this response that is communicated to as many staff as possible, usually via an overhead paging system and group alert communication device, if available. A common code, and recommended by the NCMEC and IAHSS, to be utilized by healthcare facilities to activate the infant abduction plan is "Code Pink." In the event of an abduction, the immediate involvement of law enforcement and the media is paramount in terms of enhancing a successful outcome. Most often, infants are recovered as a direct result of information generated by media coverage.

The infant abduction response plan should appropriately define the role and responsibilities of nursing, security, public relations, law enforcement and the facility-wide responses. This includes the need to immediately search the unit, notify security, and protect the potential crime scene.

Unit nursing personnel

Unit staff must be calm and diligent in their involvement and immediately search the entire unit. Immediately and simultaneously, the nursing staff should contact security. At no time should a practice be instituted to require verification of a missing infant prior to calling. This creates undue delay if there is an actual event. An important role is for the assigned care provider to stay with the mother during the event. Organizations who have experienced abductions have found moving the mother to a more isolated area within the facility beneficial to her health while removing her from the crime scene which must be immediately protected.

Facility-wide staff

A common challenge for many healthcare organizations is not being able to clearly hear overhead codes. Overhead announcements should be clearly announced initially three times and every five minutes until an "all clear" is generated. The process should reflect the responsibility of notifying parking attendants, valet, and other external workers on campus.

When Code Pink (or whatever Code is utilized in a given country/jurisdiction) is announced overhead—facility-wide staff members must know their role and what to look for. All staff members must know to look for suspicious behavior, such as:

- possibly carrying a travel bag that could contain an infant,
- rushing with an infant, and/or
- transporting a baby/infant without bassinet

A common challenge found with employee response to an infant abduction is what to do if someone is seen who looks suspicious and meets the criteria above. Responding employees should have the responsibility to stop suspicious individuals, question them to see what is in their bag, backpack, etc. Research has found employees do not typically know what to do in the event the suspicious person does not comply with the request. If such a situation were to occur, the employee should remember the safety of the infant is the first priority, and their own safety is of paramount concern. Nothing should be done to cause a potential abductor to harm the infant. Education and training of employees should focus on staying calm and to:

- Approach in a nonthreatening manner, facing the person at a safe distance
- Speak with a calm, steady voice; explaining the facility is on alert for a possible infant abduction and that everyone is being stopped
- Instruct the nearest bystander or employee to call for security assistance immediately
- Attempt to delay the suspect by keeping them in front of you (walk backwards slowly if necessary)

If an employee is unsuccessful in preventing the suspect from leaving, they should be instructed to never physically touch them or do anything that could possibly endanger the infant or themselves, while making note of the following:

- Identifying features of the person
- Bags or bundles carried
- Route of exit
- Vehicle description and license plate number

A timely response is every employee's responsibility. Following these simple steps can improve the healthcare organization's chances of a successful recovery of the infant.

Security staff response

The March 2008 abduction at Central Florida Regional Hospital in Orlando was a significant event for the parents, the hospital, and the community as a whole. The incident was also an important lesson for how security staff should be deployed during a critical incident response to an infant abduction. The security staff responded to the main entrance of the campus and saw a heavyset woman carrying a package as she entered her vehicle. The officer was unsuccessful stopping the vehicle, but was able to obtain a vehicle description and partial license plate number. As a result of that information, law enforcement officers were able to quickly locate the abductor and successfully recover the infant.[12]

The significance of this experience is the universal change in response that security personnel have undertaken. Today, it is expected that the security staff will immediately respond to perimeter points of the grounds or campus of the facility. After securing the perimeter, only then should a search of the interior/exterior of the facility be initiated by security, and then control of the crime scene transferred from the nursing staff. Historical practices placed more emphasis on responding to facility access points, crime scene preservation, and not responding to the campus perimeter. This philosophical change requires every healthcare security program to have a policy that defines who will, and how to, safely stop and search a vehicle during an event. The policy should also include actions to be followed when the driver of the vehicle fails to stop, or allow staff to search their vehicle.

Security staff should secure the current day and previous ten-day's video recordings when an event occurs either at the facility or in the community. Additionally, the security department should be prepared to provide technical support and confidential viewing if the police department cannot access the recordings on their equipment.

Law enforcement liaison and planning is essential, as most agencies have limited familiarity with the issue of infant abduction from healthcare facilities. Providing a general awareness of the facility will assist the agency in planning their response. Many healthcare organizations invite local law enforcement to be involved in the creation of, and review process associated with, the critical incident response plan, and participate in the exercising of the infant abduction response plan.

It is extremely important for both the healthcare organization and law enforcement authority to contact the NCMEC for technical assistance in handling an infant or pediatric abduction. The NCMEC's 24-hour telephone number is 1-800-843-5678.

Communications, media relations and involvement

Every healthcare organization should be prepared for using the media to aid in its recovery efforts of an abducted infant. Most often infants are recovered as a direct result of the leads generated by media coverage of the abduction, which includes the release of appropriate video images.

The organizational media plan in response to an infant abduction should be designed to:

- Identify an official facility spokesman
- Mandate all information is cleared by facility and law-enforcement authorities before it is released
- Not panic the abductor into abandoning or harming the infant
- Solicit the assistance of other healthcare facilities in the community/ region

Healthcare organizations are encouraged to develop a specific form to report suspicious behavior to nearby facilities and other nursing units inside the facility. If an event does occur in the community or region, every healthcare facility should review captured images from their video surveillance system to verify if the abductor "shopped" their healthcare facilities. Captured images can help prosecutors build their case against the alleged perpetrator, while validating the effectiveness of the organizations infant security plan.

Drills and exercises

Joint Commission standards and elements of performance do not require infant/child abduction drills. The standards do require that the organization identifies and implements security procedures that address handling of an infant or pediatric abduction, as applicable. An infant abduction exercise is one method to evaluate the effectiveness of the procedures and processes in this area. It is up to the organization to determine the appropriate actions to ensure successful implementation of security procedures.[13]

Infant/pediatric abduction drills should be conducted on a schedule that includes personnel who work days, evenings, weekends, and/or nontraditional shifts, in addition to testing the response of the pediatric care areas. Drills should never be viewed as a "success" or "failure" for the sole reason that the mock abductor is able to successfully carry out the exercise without being stopped. The goal for each exercise should be to teach and test, using a mixture of announced and unannounced exercises. Never should an inpatient mother unknowingly be involved in a drill. As a result, an important safeguard in the infant security plan is not tested and the simulation modified. However, engaging a real mother in activating the Code (but not utilizing their infant) is a useful tool to engage staff participation. Obtaining the mother's knowledge of her role in her infant's security in the critique, provides a snapshot of the effectiveness of the parental education provided.

Evaluations should include a review of the responses of unit staff, security, PBX announcement, and the facility-wide response, to include the time taken to initiate the response. Monitoring the time it takes from the initial call for a Code Pink and the time it takes for the hospital operator to announce overhead are important performance indicators in being able to engage staff hospital-wide.

A sample infant abduction evaluation form/report card is demonstrated in Figure 21-4.

Prior to conducting the exercise, the infant abduction drill should have the "mock abductor" visit and call the unit prior to the actual drill. This pre-scout methodology is a useful tool as it allows the mock abductor to obtain information on department layout and the security measures in place, plan the escape route based on information obtained, determine how much information on a patient can be gathered, and evaluate staff response to an individual asking questions and demonstrating traits of the "typical abductor."

INFANT DISCHARGED TO WRONG FAMILY

The discharge of an infant to the wrong family is a significant event, but not actually a breach of security. Mother/baby mix-ups are much more common than abduction attempts. While broadly effective, the traditional system of matching ID bands is often entirely manual and prone to mistakes. The security department may become involved with such a situation as a resource to investigate the occurrence and contribute to a successful outcome. However, the proper discharge of a patient is a clinical management function.

As a matter of protocol, every birthing center should give strong consideration to having the mother participate in the band verification process, every time her infant is returned to her room. This process further ensures that staff members are matching the correct mother and baby, helping to prevent mistakes and the negative feelings (and media coverage) associated with the event.

Technology has been introduced that can automatically match mother with baby, every time an infant is brought to a mother. Checking for a correct match, the tag immediately generates an audible alert and sends a message if it is not the right mother. Electronic matching is not widely adopted in today's healthcare environment; and the majority of these systems are installed after a negative event. However, many infant security systems have options for this add-on technology at a reasonable expense, and it should be explored if the manual matching process is known to be vulnerable.

SPECIAL CARE NURSERY, PEDIATRIC CARE AND OVERFLOW AREAS

As targets within the birth center have hardened, abductors have had to look elsewhere in the healthcare facility. As a result, abduction from pediatric care areas is now the second most common area where abductions occur.

Most healthcare facilities are not able to replicate the protection measures in place within their birthing center in other locations within the healthcare facility that care for infants. Similar and consistent security protocols should be implemented in special care nurseries, pediatric care units, VIP suites if used for post-partum, and any overflow areas that care for infants.

Sample
Infant Abduction Drill Evaluation & Scorecard

Drill Information:

Campus: ______________________

Date: ______________________

Building: ______________________

Floor: ______________________

Victim Age: ________ Gender: ________ Male / Female

Ethnicity: ____________

Scale: Circle one
1-Poor
2-Fair
3-Good
4 -Very Good
5-Excellent

1. The announcement of the Code Pink was provided correctly over the Public Address System and was heard in all areas of the campus (Number and Letter after "Code Pink + Location" to identify age and gender M/F of missing person).
   1 2 3 4 5

2. Upon notification of abduction via the overhead announcement, staff responded with a sense of urgency and seriousness.
   1 2 3 4 5

3. Upon notification of abduction, staff quickly proceeded to egress points to secure the exits and stairwells in their area.
   1 2 3 4 5

4. Upon notification of abduction, staff initiated a logical and focused search of their area as specified in their policy and procedure.
   1 2 3 4 5

5. Hospital associates challenged all visitors/suspicious persons observed with infants meeting the Code Pink announcement criteria and/or carrying bags or containers large enough to conceal an infant or small child.

6. Was anyone suspicious stopped?
   Yes /No
   If so, please describe how the person stopping them handled the situation. (i.e., what was said to them, was security contacted, did security respond, etc.).
   1 2 3 4 5

7. The Charge Person or designee in every department initiated the proper search Plan and took charge of their area.
   1 2 3 4 5

8. The video surveillance system was able to be utilized for reviewing camera surveillance of facility for post-investigative purposes by the security department and law enforcement personnel.
   1 2 3 4 5

9. The emergency response provided by the Emergency Response Team (ERT) was timely and appropriate.
   1 2 3 4 5

Additional Comments: ______________________

FIGURE 21-4

Sample infant abduction drill evaluation form adopted from Kelly Dahl, Director of Safety at The Medical Center of Aurora.

In some situations, the consistent application of all protection safeguards used in the birth center may not be feasible or appropriate; i.e., an infant tagging system may not realistically be needed in the special care nursery. In such instances, the healthcare security administrator and unit manager should document what protection measures are taken in lieu of those not used, or inconsistent with the birthing center. Often, nontraditional security safeguards are identified that include one-to-one patient-to-staff ratios or constant parental presence. If an overflow area must be utilized outside of the protected department, a common safeguard is to locate the patient in close proximity to the nursing station, enhance security visibility in the area, and provide additional parental education on the importance of their involvement in their child's security. What should never be compromised, however, is the critical incident abduction response plan.

Much debate surrounds the use of the same code for infant and pediatric patients. It is a commonly held belief by healthcare security professionals and the NCMEC that the same code should not be used for each. Many healthcare facilities differentiate between the abduction of an infant and the pediatric patient by adding the age of the child at the end of the code: i.e., "Code Pink – 3." The code words currently used by law enforcement and retailers such as CODE AMBER and CODE ADAM should be avoided to represent infant abductions or missing children in the healthcare setting according to NCMEC. However, it should be noted that hospitals in British Columbia, Canada have successfully linked an internal Code Amber plan with the external law enforcement-driven Amber Alert system, by standardizing the Code in all provincial hospitals, and working closely with law enforcement to ensure alignment of the responses.

IAHSS has developed a guideline on pediatric security healthcare facilities address the pediatric security safeguards.

05.08 PEDIATRIC SECURITY

Statement

Pediatric patients present unique security challenges for Healthcare Facilities (HCFs). Given their wide range of ages and maturity levels, pediatric patients can present abduction risks, parental custody issues, physical assaults, wandering, elopement and other issues. The older pediatric patient may even introduce issues involving contraband, gang related activity, and other problematic behaviors.

Intent

a. HCFs should implement protective measures that identify and minimize the risks and vulnerabilities of its pediatric patient population. Proactive steps and HCF resources should be available in a format that pediatric staff can readily access when they have questions on pediatric security practices.

b. HCFs should establish security related procedures for the care of pediatric patients to include:

1) Assessing patient history for problematic behaviors and victimization;
2) Considering the need for visitor control;
3) Probing for current and past restraining orders;
4) Identifying issues related to possible child abuse, custodial disputes, gang involvement, elopement concerns, and contraband possession;
5) Establishing relationships with agencies authorized to change custodial status of the pediatric patient; and
6) Communicating and documenting guidance to custodial parents and guardians regarding their vital role in providing safety and security for their pediatric patient.

c. Admissions and Triage staff should be trained in probing for issues relative to pediatric safety and security. Inpatient clinical staff, working with pediatric patients, should receive similar training as well as instruction in the indicators of when a family, visitor, staff member or another may be involved in abuse or neglect of the patient. Procedures in legally required reporting suspicions of same should be developed and included in this training.

05.08 PEDIATRIC SECURITY—cont'd

d. Pediatric patient visitation privileges should be set out in a policy and procedure that provides for a controlled and welcoming environment.

1) Authorized visitors should be readily identifiable.

2) Consideration should be given to identifying persons who are authorized for 'after-hour' or 'over-night' visitations.

e. Timely campus-wide communication procedures should be established that include the use of distinct emergency codes and procedures to respond to pediatric abductions and elopements.

f. Inpatient areas providing pediatric care, including the Pediatric Care Unit (PEDS), Neonatal Intensive Care Unit (NICU), Pediatric Intensive Care Unit (PICU), Adolescent Psychiatric Unit (APU), and any adult unit which may be used from time to time for pediatric care, should be evaluated against the special risks associated with the pediatric patient.

General Information

- National Center for Missing & Exploited Children (NCMEC) publication *For Healthcare Professionals: Guidelines on Prevention of and Response to Infant Abductions*, Ninth Edition, 2009. NCMEC, 699 Prince Street, Alexandria VA 22314-3175.

See Also:

- IAHSS Guideline 05.08 Infant/Pediatric Abduction Prevention and Response
- IAHSS Guideline 05.05 Patient Elopement Prevention and Response
- IAHSS Healthcare Security Design Guideline 02.06 Buildings and the Internal Environment – Infant and Pediatric Facilities

Approved: May 2011

Last Reviewed: November 2013

Family Abductions

While nonfamily infant abductions are thought to be the greatest risk, a more common concern is the abduction of an infant or child by a family member. Whether involving a custody dispute like the New Hampshire man attempting to kidnap his girlfriend's baby from Emerson Hospital in Concord, Massachusetts in 2011,[14] child abuse, or social services intervention, this problem is widespread in the healthcare environment.

Because these cases involve abuse and/or neglect issues, the NCMEC has deemed these children to be at greater risk than newborn infants taken by nonfamily members. The NCMEC has identified several factors noted in Box 21-4 that should be taken into consideration when establishing protection strategies for this vulnerable patient population.

BOX 21-4 PROTECTION STRATEGIES FOR THE RISK OF FAMILY CHILD ABDUCTION

Family Abduction Protection Strategies

- "Red flagging" the child's name in the system to indicate no information is to be released
- Admitting the child under an assumed name
- Placing the child in an isolation room or in the intensive-care unit
- Placing an assumed name on the child's door
- Using wireless video surveillance with a monitor at the nurses' station to closely watch the child
- Increasing frequency of observation in the patient's area
- Posting a description of the potential abductor with security, nursing, and the front desk or reception area
- Posting a security officer at the patient's room/floor/unit

(Courtesy National Center for Missing and Exploited Children, Alexandria, Virginia)

EMERGENCY DEPARTMENT SECURITY

A gunman entered a San Diego hospital emergency room and started shooting indiscriminately, killing two and wounding two. A social worker was killed in a hospital emergency room in Pittsburgh by an assailant who also took three people hostage. A man dressed in a security uniform walked into an Atlanta hospital emergency room, where he shot four people and then committed suicide. A man entered a metro Denver trauma center, pulled a gun on the security officer controlling access to the treatment area, forced entry and killed himself in front of the emergency department nurses' station. A subdued female patient suddenly draws a knife from her purse and stabs an emergency physician 13 times, allegedly because the physician would not prescribe the antibiotic she was requesting. A combative patient wrestles a handgun from an armed security officer, shooting and killing a radiology technician and another patient.

Events like these are devastating to caregivers, hospitals and patients and are all too frequent occurrences in emergency departments in the U.S. and throughout the world. However, these terrible acts receive only short-term media attention. It is the type of violence that keeps hospital administrators up at night. Sadly, the most prevalent violence being experienced by care providers and security professionals is generated by the same people who are being cared for—patients.

Patient-generated violence happens in every type and size of emergency department—from designated trauma centers that see tens of thousands of patients every year, to critical access hospitals who truly have a room or two for emergency patients. No hospital is immune from this phenomenon, as an astounding number of nurses have been victims of physical violence or verbal abuse. This disruptive, and sometimes explosive, behavior emanates primarily from patients, who strike, spit, kick, bite, scratch nurses and doctors and anyone who interacts or intervenes with the patient. This often includes security and law enforcement officers. As concerning is the verbal abuse and assaultive language healthcare staff members are exposed to during the course of care. The effects of such violence can include on-the-job fear for physicians and nurses and challenges in caregiver recruitment. In addition, negative community perception of the hospital can lead to fewer patients and poor financial performance.

The emergency department will always have the characteristics that increase the likelihood of disruptive behavior. Extreme mental and physical factors, acute psychiatric manifestations, drug and alcohol abuse by patients and visitors, the mix of patients and service providers outside the medical staff (that is, police, fire, ambulance, coroner, and so on), and often chaotic circumstances combine to produce a very high-risk environment. When coupled with rival gang members who show up with guns because a prominent gang member is brought into the hospital, lengthy wait times due to continued overcrowding, and the everyday threats of caring for victims of domestic violence, emergency departments are without question the most volatile area in the healthcare setting. In fact, the emergency room chief at San Francisco General reports that threats from angry patients and or visitors occur daily, and violence breaks out at least once a week. Unfortunately, violence in emergency departments is a plaguing trend affecting hospitals throughout the world.

Violent episodes and events cause fear and concern among nurses and physicians alike. The Emergency Nurses Association (ENA) have initiated three studies of workplace violence, and the results reveal that workplace violence is shockingly prevalent and the source of great fear in the nursing community. Survey results have revealed that 86% of emergency nurses have experienced physical violence in the last 3 years, and 27% had experienced violence on more than 20 occasions during that same time period. Seventy-two percent reported they did not feel safe on the job, and 19% indicated they were leaving the emergency nursing profession because of violence.[15] Even more concerning, nurses said that many incidences of violence are unreported due to fear of retaliation, inconvenience of reporting, a lack of physical injury sustained, or concern that doing so may affect customer services scores.

ED physicians have had similar experiences. Dr. David Golan, an emergency room physician at the University Medical Center in Las Vegas, Nevada, sums up the security concerns in many emergency rooms when he says:

> "What is happening in emergency rooms is just insane. We give people who say they are going to kill people a chance to do it. No restraints, no metal detectors. The truth is, I think emergency room policies are crazier than some of the people we see."[16]

Dr. Golan was part of a real-life drama played out in March 2008 when a patient shattered his nose after the patient had previously told the doctor that he was going to kill him. What Dr. Golan is referring to are the constraints being placed by regulatory and accreditation agencies to apply medical restraints (physical or chemical) before certain things must happen. Today, interpretations of CMS guidelines have created a wait-and-watch attitude, versus a proactive approach to using restraints as tools, to address the escalating events of violence occurring in emergency departments. Unfortunately, these interpretations have contributed to the ever-increasing volume of assaults against, and subsequent injuries to, care providers, security officers and others who work in the emergency department.

The emotional, social and financial costs of ED violence are incalculable. Reducing the number of violent events that take place and minimizing the long-term effects of the ones that occur are top priorities. Disruptive behavior is predictable, and it can be managed to minimize the risk in providing safety for all concerned. As discussed in great detail in Chapter 20, "Preventing and Managing Healthcare Aggression and Violence," the physicians and nurses who staff emergency departments are demanding greater protection by hospitals.

ASSESSING EMERGENCY DEPARTMENT RISK

Every hospital with emergency care services must assess its own specific vulnerabilities, and apply the degree of security necessary to maintain a reasonably safe and secure department. The department is a funnel into the healthcare delivery system and it is important to remember the emergency department is comprised of several distinct areas, all with their own unique security considerations. Among the chief assessment considerations are:

- Annual volume of emergency care patient admissions and the percentage of behavioral health patients seen
- Trauma level designation
- Area's crime rate (or propensity for crime)
- Layout and design of the emergency department
- Primary service area and types of patients and visitors typically seen
- Specialized services offered such as psychiatric emergency care or forensic/prisoner patient agreements
- History with aggressive patients in treatment areas
- Expectations of security staff for patient assistance
- Resources available from security staff to spend with high-risk patient assistance

A variety of safeguards can be applied to most emergency departments: it is the degree of application of a specific safeguard to establish proper security that must be determined. For example, one emergency department may require only periodic security patrols, another may require the presence of an officer at night, and another may require 24-hour security coverage by one or more officers. Security practices should be consistent with "event driven" policies and procedures. It is difficult to convince management and staff to resource security staffing and maintain the highest levels of security when all is well in their work environment. If the security plan adjusts with situational circumstances, the emergency department staff is more likely to be active participants.

According to the South Carolina Hospital Association, hospital emergency rooms have become the safety net for the mentally ill. This hidden crisis is affecting every state in the U.S., and indeed the health systems in much of the western world, as mental health funding has been cut deeply. South Carolina has lost $81 million in mental health funding since 2008 and Colorado has lost over 60% of inpatient mental health beds since 1990. Though countries like Australia and Canada have begun to recognize the devastating effect of closing inpatient beds without funding community resources to support the mentally ill, the severe impact on hospital EDs is irrefutable.

As state/provincial mental health resources have been reduced, hospital emergency departments, which were never designed or equipped to handle chronically mentally ill patients who act out, have experienced a huge influx of mental health patients. Many mentally ill patients are staying in emergency departments longer, clogging the system, creating a financial drain, and heightening the danger to other patients and staff. It is a huge bottleneck in terms of efficiency. Waits are longer and frustration higher with the healthcare organization—both of which lead to tension and escalating events of disruptive behavior.

The Emergency Nurses Association (ENA) recognizes the impact on the emergency care environment, and the fatigue it is creating among care providers. The danger that mentally ill patients pose to staff members cannot be ignored and, as a result, ENA developed an Emergency Department Assessment Tool to help facilities assess risk.

As in all situations involving patient care, security officers must act in the best interest of the patient, and follow the instruction of the care provider, to ensure no disruption in the flow of healthcare. The IAHSS has developed a security industry guideline for healthcare facilities that provide emergency care services.

05.06 SECURITY IN THE EMERGENCY CARE SETTING

Statement

Healthcare Facilities (HCF) that provide emergency care have special security needs and should have a security plan specific for that department.

Intent

a. The plan should be based on identified risks for the emergency department including volume; types of patients treated and incident activity; and community demographics.

b. The security administrator should be involved in the planning and building phases of emergency department construction and renovation as a resource relative to security design issues.

  1) The emergency department waiting area should be separated from the emergency department treatment area and be self-contained to include independent access to restrooms, telephones and vending machines.

  2) Access controls should be in place to control and limit access of emergency department visitors into the Emergency Department (ED) treatment area and into the main hospital.

05.06 SECURITY IN THE EMERGENCY CARE SETTING—cont'd

3) A room or area within the emergency department, separate from other patients should be available for the treatment of behavioral/mental health or other high risk patients. Consideration for this room should include visibility by staff and the removal or securing of items that could be used by the patient to injure themselves or others.

4) The ambulance entrance should be separate from the walk in emergency entrance and waiting room.

c. Security staff provides support services in the care and control of ED. These services are to be provided at the request and under the direction and supervision of clinical staff unless circumstances require immediate action to prevent injury or destruction of property. (written in accordance with IAHSS Healthcare Security Guideline 05.02, Security Role in Patient Management)

d. Security equipment and systems to protect staff and patients should be in place. These may include electronic access control, video surveillance and panic alarms. The emergency department should be capable of being rapidly locked down in event of an emergency. Drills should be conducted to exercise the lockdown process.

e. Physical measures and/or procedures should be in place to deter the elopement or removal of patients at risk of harming themselves, others or of being harmed.

f. Emergency department staff (including security) should receive on-going training in workplace violence, aggressive/violent patient management to recognize, avoid, diffuse and respond to potentially violent situations.

g. Periodic meetings, at a minimum annually, with multidisciplinary staff should be conducted to review security protocols and resolve security issues within the emergency care setting.

h. Policies, procedures and training programs should be established for security's role in managing high risk patients including patient watches, holds, searches, and application of patient restraints.

References/General Information

- Emergency Nurses Association, Position Statement, Violence in the Emergency Care Setting, Developed 1991, revised and approved by the ENA Board of Directors, September 2008, ENA Web Site: http://www.ena.org/about/position/PDFs/64CAB0B9EFD44C4A51CCBF0F30D7DD3.PDF
- 2011 NA Workplace Violence Toolkit "Assessing Your Emergency Department".
- TJC Sentinel Event Alert, Issue 45, June 3, 2010

Approved: December 2006
Last Revised: October 2011

SECURITY DESIGN CONSIDERATIONS FOR EMERGENCY DEPARTMENTS

The design of the emergency department begins with assessing the security risk of the environment. The assessment should include the security administrator and emergency department leadership reviewing key areas such as:

- Driveway and parking area layout
- Entrance points into the waiting and medical treatment area
- Compartmentalization of the waiting area and medical treatment area
- Protection for triage and front desk personnel
- Patient/visitor flow through the department (from the parking lot to the waiting room to the patient care area through discharge)
- Room design and location to include line-of-sight visibility and exit pathways
- Creation of a sterile environment for "at-risk" patients
- Use and deployment of physical and electronic security safeguards

An armed fortress is not what should be created. The healthcare security administrator should create an environment using the layers of protection principles of Crime Prevention through Environmental Design (CPTED) to guide how the physical design of the emergency department can work for better personal safety and patient-focused care.

Explicit attention is provided to designing security for emergency departments as noted in Chapter 17, "Security Design Considerations for Healthcare."

SECURITY STAFFING IN EMERGENCY DEPARTMENTS

There is a need to provide security staff for emergency service departments in a great many healthcare facilities. In small facilities, a patrol and response capability may suffice, but very large emergency departments may require several fixed security posts on a 24-hour basis. It is quite common to staff emergency rooms with a security officer only at night. This practice can be cost effective, especially when the officer also controls nighttime visitors for the entire facility. The emergency room is also a common and logical location for a security operations center, which provides a certain presence in itself.

The single greatest attributing factor to security staffing in the emergency department is the expectation of security with high-risk patient assistance and intervention. Patients coming to the emergency department don't really want to be there in the first place. Something has happened to them to bring them to the hospital. As discussed in Chapter 13, "Patient Care Involvement and Intervention," responding to requests for assistance with patients is a valid and necessary function of any protection system; however, the scope and expectations of this assistance can significantly drive the amount of security resources dedicated to the emergency department.

Security personnel assigned to emergency treatment areas should be uniformed to achieve maximum effectiveness. In the U.S., individual hospitals must decide whether to arm officers, weighing all the pros and cons regarding this important decision. With the ever-increasing mental health patient population seeking services in the emergency department, healthcare administrators and protection professionals alike are encouraged to take their cue from the behavioral health setting and not introduce firearms in the medical treatment area. Again, primarily in the U.S., the Taser has proven to be an effective alternative if a more commanding presence is needed to control the environment.

It is generally not desirable to employ off-duty law enforcement personnel as security officers in emergency rooms. The training required is very different; police training is of little value for the function of the emergency room security officer. Police work as a whole is often measured in terms of arrests, and the security effort is measured in terms of conflict resolution and prevention. Good police relations should be maintained however, as law enforcement response will be required for events occurring in the emergency department that overwhelm organizational resources, or the internal response capacity. This was the case at Grand Strand Regional Medical Center in South Carolina when multiple gunshot victims and family and friends came to the hospital with the three victims, and a fight broke out between the groups. The hospital went on lockdown and required police response to help gain control of the environment and restrict the group to one family member per patient.[17]

Some very busy trauma centers in higher crime locations have deployed police officers in their emergency department waiting area with good success. The difference in the role is notable, however, as the police officer is expected to provide a visible and deterrent value, but is not expected to participate in patient care activities. Unfortunately, the costs of the police officer assignment can be more than double that of a security officer.

In numerous hospital security programs, security officers are promoted to the emergency department, where they have their own specific job description and generally receive higher pay. Funding for the emergency department security coverage is sometimes provided by the emergency department or the mental health program. These officers should be considered and treated as much a part of the emergency department staff as they are members of the security staff. Carla Moreno, RN, Director of

Emergency Services for Methodist Specialty and Transplant Hospital, a psychiatric emergency department with a very high percentage of high-risk patients treated, shared that when she asks her staff what is working well, by far the most frequent response has been "Security." Efforts made by the hospital and security team created a culture of respect for security and the care experience. The result from this environment of teamwork was significant reduction in lost-time injuries to staff and a dramatic reduction in the number of patients requiring restraint. The healthcare security administrator is encouraged to partner with emergency department leadership, to blend the cultures of the two departments. This includes joint training on aggression and violence, the development of departmental security guidelines, as well as post-event review and after-action report discussion. When employees and physicians are encouraged to discuss events, the security department and the facility as a whole can get a better understanding of what prevention measures work, and what other mitigation steps should be implemented. The result is a safer patient and employee experience.

Security officer training

Security personnel stationed in emergency rooms need extensive training. Their training must include recognizing the early symptoms of disruptive behavior, verbal and nonverbal intervention skills, working knowledge of the process of trauma care, the psychology of stress, the role of supporting medical care (not giving advice or administering care), the application of medical restraints, and safe patient control and take-down procedures. Although these subjects are appropriate for all security personnel, the full-time officers assigned to busy emergency rooms must develop and hone these skills to a greater extent than a generalist.

Training should not be limited to the security staff on an individual basis. There should be joint training exercises of the emergency department staff and the security staff. This collaborative training is important to establish working protocols and to develop the team concept. Role-playing and scenario-based response is a common method used in this training.

Interaction and intervention protocols

Whenever security personnel support the emergency department, formally established protocols, or guidelines, must govern the actions of the officers and the emergency department staff. Without these guidelines, conflict and dissension between security and emergency department personnel could develop, around how specific situations are to be handled. The objective is to eliminate individual expectations and guesswork. Firmly established roles for different situations eliminate dissatisfaction and provide a high level of service. Generally, nurses or physicians take charge in dealing with patient incidents, and security officers take charge in dealing with visitor problems outside the treatment area. Visitors within the treatment area occupy a middle ground, but generally are in the purview of the medical caregiver. The issue of managing at-risk patient behavior and the corresponding roles of security and care providers are discussed in detail in Chapter 13, "Patient Care Involvement and Intervention."

The terms "patient assistance" or "patient intervention" are sometimes used to describe the activity of standing by to watch a particular patient. Officers are generally asked to perform a patient watch when a patient causes staff to feel fear, anger, uneasiness, potential danger, or when there is an indication the patient may attempt to leave prior to proper medical evaluation or treatment. Staff members must recognize the considerable range of these feelings and assess the gravity of the risk they perceive.

Although this discussion focuses on patients, the same evaluations, preparations, and actions are required for visitors in treatment areas, waiting areas, or patient rooms outside the emergency department.

Policies and procedures

It is important to take the ambiguity out of how security practices work in the emergency department. Policies and procedures provide staff guidance and help keep practices consistent, regardless of the situation. Consider policies for each of the following:

- High-risk patient admissions
- Visitor and waiting room control
- Aggression management and staff education
- Emergency communications
- Patient searches and use of metal screening
- Event-driven security plan
- Elopement/escape precautions
- Control of access and lowdown procedures
- High-risk patient escorts/transports

High-risk patient

As part of the triage and admissions process, high-risk patients should be identified to include their potential for violence and other negative outcomes. The patient assessment process should include defining who is a high-risk patient. The criteria may include:

- Placed on a mental-health or alcohol hold in accordance with local law
- Acute drug/ETOH intoxication,
- Head-injured with altered mental status,
- Confused to time, place and/or person
- At Risk for Elopement based on past history or current condition
- Disruptive or violent (patient may lose control, threaten to lose control, or give others evidence of a deteriorating mental condition),
- A danger to self (suicidal ideation)
- A threat or concern to others

Visitor and waiting room control

The unfortunate escalation of violence in today's society and healthcare environment has driven the creation of new rules for hospitals to operate safely. This includes the incorporation of visitor control policies and procedures to restrict the number of visitors who can accompany a patient in the medical treatment area. St. Anthony's Medical Center, a Level I trauma center in Denver, Colorado, uses a simple color-coded visitor pass system. All visitors are asked their name and the name of the patient they want to visit. Each patient is limited to two visitors and communication is made with the caregiver to get permission for the visitor to enter the treatment areas. Passes are issued by a security officer, change color daily and are shared between family members. Access to the treatment area is granted only by visitors who are in possession of the pass. If the patient is unavailable, the visitor is asked to wait in the lobby until the patient can be contacted.

A similar visitor pass system is in use at Yuma Regional Medical Center, a busy regional trauma center in Yuma, Arizona. Security personnel maintain a two-pass system for each emergency department patient room and grant access only to visitors who have been issued a blue arm band that must be worn while they are in the treatment area. A daily inventory is conducted to verify all passes are returned or new room specific passes are generated. Care providers typically like having visitor control procedures in place, as it limits the large number of interruptions they incur from too many visitors. Sunnybrook Hospital in Toronto, one of the top trauma centers in Canada, also features a visitor pass system for their ED, involving security management of the process.

Most emergency department waiting rooms are not cordoned off because it is an access point. An invitation for trouble is when both aggressors and victims are in the same emergency room department, or gathering in the waiting room. To best combat this risk, the area should be compartmentalized through the physical design of the environment—such as using furniture to create pods, a decorative wall with a fish tank to break up the waiting room space, or some other means to distract both groups and help minimize further danger. Many waiting areas also create distractions such as using more than one TV, and programming them with different channels that change the dynamics of the room. Another option is to create overflow waiting areas so one party can be moved from the main room to another room—this is a good option when you have two antagonistic groups in the waiting area.

Many organizations have also implemented lockdown or restricted access stages, which can be put into place if the department becomes seriously overcrowded. In the event of this situation, visitor access to treatments areas is limited even further, and hospital security called to ensure the limited access. A significantly heightened level of lockdown, sometimes called ED Security Stage II, can be implemented in situations that threaten life, property or emergency department services—either in or near the hospital, or even in the community. This is most common when there is awareness of an incident in the community, involving a violent act, in which victims are expected to be transported to the hospital. In these cases, access is typically limited to only essential clinical personnel and signage is placed on exterior doors. Visitors are typically not allowed in the treatment area except for pediatric patients (and then only one per patient).

Emergency department staff education

Confidence to work in the emergency department starts with knowing there is an organizational plan to address the security risks within the department. More than just teaching staff to recognize and respond to escalating tension with emergency care patients, care providers must learn to take ownership of their work environment. The acronym POWER shown in Box 21-5 helps emergency department personnel recognize, understand, react and manage their environment.

Emergency department training should be accomplished using a multidisciplinary approach. Training as a team provides the opportunity for care providers and security officers to learn together. Having an understanding of each other's perspective helps build teamwork and a better appreciation for the role each plays in managing the emergency care environment.

Role conflict can be a problem for many care providers, who struggle between being a patient-focused provider and protecting their own personal safety. It is important for healthcare providers to know that both have a place. Take, for example, the care provider who is informed of a difficult patient, and then ignores the advice and walks into the patient room. Patient focused care is not provided when multiple co-workers have to be called to restrain the agitated and physically acting out patient. There must be acknowledgement that a patient may be difficult. Once this is identified, good personal safety precautions can be taken, conflict avoided and patient-focused care provided. Personal safety of the care provider must be given first consideration. Staff must be given specific training on how to recognize when escalating situations exist, and what to do when this escalation occurs. The risk of disruptive or harmful behavior is easily escalated if inappropriate steps are taken. The overall goal is to maintain safety for everyone involved, including the patient.

BOX 21-5 POWER PRINCIPLE TO EMERGENCY DEPARTMENT SECURITY EDUCATION

Emergency Department Security Training

P	Prepare for your Patient. Use all your resources to determine the emotional state of the patient. This may include the patient's previous care history, information from the transporting EMS/police or precautionary notes from your co-workers. Remember to always give yourself permission to think personal safety first.
O	Own your work Environment. Begin with everyday proactive safety plans that lead to a safer work environment. Know how the room and the equipment in the room work for or against creating a safe work environment. Have the confidence to proactively take charge of your place of work.
W	Work within your Training. Be an active participant in the organization's security plan. Know your training, what you are good at and what you need help with. Understand the power of having a plan and working together as a team.
E	Expect the Unexpected. Complacency can lead to mistakes and unfortunate surprises, especially when dealing with at-risk patients. Mentally working through your options may provide you with the crucial opening necessary to avoid a difficult situation.
R	Remember your Resources. There always seem to be more resources for those who are prepared. One employee looks at the metal surgical tray in the patient room as a place to set instruments while another sees a shield to use against an edged weapon. Resources are everywhere if you open your eyes to the possibilities; training, fellow staff members, family, room set-up, having a plan and most of all being an active participant in your own personal safety plan.

(Courtesy of Alan Butler and HSS Inc.)

Aggression management and response training are important cornerstones to any emergency department security training. Care providers, security officers, and anyone responding to situations of escalations must be able to recognize, understand, react and manage environmental changes through the various stages of escalation. This training is discussed in further detail in Chapter 10, "Training and Development" and Chapter 20, "Preventing and Managing Healthcare Aggression and Violence."

The emergency department experience starts in the parking lot or at the front door. All staff, including parking attendants and greeters in the ED, must be trained on how to handle everyone—from the gang member dropped off with a gunshot wound, to an elderly person with a heart problem.

Emergency communication

The emergency department should have a system of alerting other staff members of an emergency or escalating situation requiring immediate assistance. These systems are used primarily to summon additional medical assistance, but they may also serve as an element of the security system. Wall buttons, pull chains, and foot or other alarm activation devices should be strategically located within the department, with particular attention given to isolated areas. The device must be placed so staff members can easily access it, but it should not invite improper activation by patients, visitors, or even staff. There are also available devices the caregiver can carry (as a pendant or clip-on device) to summon assistance. These devices may be more costly than fixed-location devices, as the equipment must be able to track the movement of the person to determine their location when the device is activated. As with all electronic devices, the system should be periodically tested.

High-risk patient escorts/transports

Many security departments transport mental health, or other high-risk patients, who have been medically cleared to other departments or free-standing facilities. Transports can consist of performing an escort on foot, or a security staff member driving the patient using the security patrol or other hospital-provided vehicle. This is a high-risk process and steps should be taken to protect the officer and reduce the risk associated with the patient transport.

It is recognized the challenging position this situation creates for many hospitals: transport the medically discharged patient, or be expected to continue their care inside the hospital. If this high-risk process is employed, the following safeguards should be considered to protect the interests of the healthcare facility, drivers and patients to help facilitate a safe transport for all parties.

- Initial and final assessment of the cooperative nature of the person being transported. Uncooperative or previously combative persons should never be transported alone. Local law enforcement should be used for unruly persons. When available, same gender transports should be required.
- Installation of a secure cage that places a barrier between driver and patients.
- An in-car camera system should be installed and used for all patient transports. Surveillance cameras should be placed inside the vehicle that record the officer driving and record the patient in the back seat. The recording computer can located in the trunk. This provides a recording of every transfer in the event an issue arises, video footage can be viewed and used as evidence.
- Locking seat belts should be used with a procedure establish for fastening and unfastening during an emergency.
- Status checks should be required for all transports by a nursing supervisor or ED charge nurse. This should include notification on departure and arrival from the hospital and the receiving facility. Primary routes should be established for each receiving facility. Expected transport times should be established for each. Alternate routes should be used only after approval by a supervisor.
- Specific protocols should be developed on placement of the person being transported, family members who may ride along, ensuring window-locks are active, placement of patient belongings, and clothing worn—coats and shoes with laces should not be worn during transport.

Should the patient attempt to leave during the transport, careful consideration must be made in determining the appropriate action. If the patient is not on a medical hold, they may have the legal right to leave if they chose. There should be clear guidance provided to the transport officer on expectations if the patient attempts to leave and the protocols to follow if such an event occurs. Sufficient steps should also be taken to manage the vulnerable psychological condition of the person being transported and the position of trust the security officers are placed.

Using local taxi or cab services is one alternative to security providing transports. A waiver may be given to and signed by the driver that notifies the driver that the individual was a patient of the hospital and the location of the detoxification clinic, or other facility, they are to drive to. This service may be paid by the hospital. By allowing a third party to provide transportation this shifts some of the liability associated with these transfers to the cab or taxi service.

THE HOSPITAL PHARMACY

The security of the hospital pharmacy begins with proper handling, supervision, and training of the pharmacy staff. Not all pharmacy employees are honest, and there have been many instances of pharmacy helpers (i.e., pharmacy technicians), cashiers, order clerks, pharmacy students and pharmacists being involved in major drug thefts. Personnel hired to work in the pharmacy should be screened thoroughly to establish their integrity. The security department may be able to assist the chief pharmacist and the personnel department in determining the suitability of applicants for these sensitive positions. In the U.S., the Code of Federal Regulations Number 21 (1301.90) covers employee-screening procedures for positions involving controlled substances. Individual states often prescribe additional requirements.

Pharmacy employees are not the only ones who have access to the pharmacy and drug supplies. The environmental services and facilities personnel are often allowed to move about without supervision and may even be scheduled to clean or to provide maintenance to the pharmacy when it is closed, which is a poor practice.

In addition to environmental services, other employees such as nurses, delivery and even security personnel should be restricted from having access to areas where drugs are stored. Some states, such as Ohio, require that no individual be alone in a pharmacy unless it is a licensed pharmacist during business hours. In many smaller healthcare facilities, the pharmacy is not open 24 hours a day. In such instances, specific procedures must be developed to detect and document any individual, other than the pharmacist, who enters the pharmacy for emergency purposes.

The IAHSS has developed an industry security guideline on Pharmacy Security.

07.02 PHARMACY SECURITY

Statement

Healthcare Facilities (HCFs) will develop physical security policies and procedures and protection practices that address the unique security risks presented by clinical (inpatient, outpatient and satellite locations) and retail pharmacies located within the HCF; on and off campus.

Intent

a. The HCF should conduct a regular and periodic security risk assessment to evaluate and determine the elements of physical security necessary to protect the pharmacy. The assessment process should be coordinated with the pharmacy management and include:
   1) Identification and compliance with regulatory and institutional requirements and expectations
   2) Internal compliance with access approval and termination policy
   3) Review of past security breaches and incident reports directly affecting department operations
   4) Physical inspection of satellite locations, retail pharmacy operations, medication dispensing points located outside of the pharmacy, and department functions located outside of the pharmacy such as warehouse storage and off-site clinics
   5) Review of the purpose of all security equipment and systems installed to protect the staff and environment and testing of the same
   6) Physical space including built environment and fixed equipment
   7) Evaluation of pharmacy signage and the need for department identification

b. The HCF should control physical access to all pharmacy entrances, exits and transaction windows to prevent unauthorized access.

Continued

07.02 PHARMACY SECURITY—cont'd

c. The HCF should limit and restrict access to the pharmacy to only those personnel assigned to the department or have been specifically authorized access by the director of the pharmacy or their designee. An additional layer of restricted access should be established to the narcotics vault or other areas where controlled substances are stored.

d. The director of pharmacy or their designee should have final approval on all aspects of department access and controlled substance storage to include:
  1) Approving all access privileges granted into the pharmacy
  2) Approving security policies for space leased, managed, or staffed by third parties
  3) Terminating access privileges granted into the pharmacy upon employee departure or other identified need

e. Pharmacy staff should receive initial and ongoing security education and training from a qualified resource as determined by Pharmacy and Security management in the following areas:
  1) Control of entry to and exit from the pharmacy
  2) Response protocols to:
     - persons seeking to obtain inappropriate access
     - armed robbery
     - disruptive patient
     - drug-seekers
     - suspected diversion attempts
     - other suspicious activities
  3) Use of security equipment and systems installed to protect staff and the department
  4) Expected response of security officers to an alarm activation (if installed)

f. Periodic drills should be conducted to exercise pharmacy staff and both internal and external responders.

g. Periodic meetings with multidisciplinary internal and external staff should be conducted to review security protocols, implement corrective action plans, and resolve security issues within the pharmacy and associated operations.

h. Policies, procedures and training programs should be established for security's role in responding to emergent calls to the various pharmacy locations.

i. All incidents involving access to the pharmacy by personnel other than approved staff will be documented in an incident report and forwarded to the director of pharmacy, security and other designated individuals in accordance with HCF policy.

References

US Department of Justice, Drug Enforcement Administration, Controlled Substances Security Manual, http://www.deadiversion.usdoj.gov/pubs/manuals/sec/addtl_sec.htm

See Also

IAHSS Healthcare Security Guideline 01.04. Security Risk Assessments
IAHSS Healthcare Security Guideline 07.02.01 Drug Diversion
IAHSS Healthcare Security Guideline 07.01. Security Sensitive Areas
IAHSS Healthcare Security Design Guideline 02.04 Buildings and the Internal Environment – Pharmacies

PHARMACY BURGLARY AND ROBBERY

According to the White House Office on National Drug Policy, prescription drug abuse is the nation's fastest-growing drug problem. The Centers for Disease Control and Prevention has classified the misuse of these powerful painkillers as an epidemic, with 1.3 million emergency room visits in 2010, a 115% increase since 2004. The drug of choice has transitioned from oxycodone and OxyContin to Opana, an extended release painkiller containing oxymorphone, which came onto the market in 2006. A production problem caused a nationwide shortage in 2012, and the price soared from $65 for a 40 mg pill to $185.[18] The shortage drove crime as people were stealing the drugs, or stealing other items, to get money to buy drugs. The healthcare industry was not immune and this is but one example of why the traditional hospital pharmacy and retail pharmacies in the healthcare environment, and in the community at large, remain a target of burglary and armed robbery.

Pharmacies as a whole have been hardened against attack, but with the dangerous drugs that remain in their inventories, both inpatient and retail pharmacies, located within the hospital or on campus, remain a tempting target.

Burglary protection can best be provided by installing proper physical safeguards, such as protection for windows and counter openings, locks, and alarms. Armed robbery presents a somewhat more difficult problem, in part because employees often fail to utilize safeguards in place, and in part because many hospital pharmacies fail to install even minimal safeguards.

The major consideration in planning for pharmacy safeguards is to reduce the possibility of personal injury, which is, of course, directly related to avoiding a confrontation. However, confrontations cannot always be avoided, and pharmacy personnel should be trained to respond properly should a holdup occur. Pharmacy robbers are often addicts, excitable, and desperate. Pharmacy employees should obey instructions and avoid any heroics while under observation of the assailant, including activation of an alarm or calling for help. They should note the physical characteristics of the perpetrator and, if possible, the direction of escape. The alarm can be sounded as soon as it is safe to do so. Employees who remain calm help to avoid triggering violence, and they will be more helpful to security and police investigators in providing a description of the robber, and an accurate account of the event.

DURESS ALARMS

First and foremost, employees confronted by an armed robber should not do anything that would jeopardize their safety. Organizations should avoid having security or the police respond directly to the pharmacy during an armed robbery. Duress, or holdup, alarms or even a telephone should be used to report the robbery only when it is safe to do so.

Pharmacies that choose to install holdup alarms should make every effort to install them properly, to avoid triggering false alarms. The most common mistake in the installation of the panic alarm is to not use a specifically designed activation button, which is recessed to protect against accidental activation. The high rate of false alarms has resulted in the elimination of many previously installed systems.

Duress codes may prove a valuable supplement to duress or intrusion alarms. When an alarm is activated and monitored in another location, a telephone call to the pharmacy may be in order. No answer would indicate a possible problem and call for special response procedures. When the telephone is answered, a duress code can be valuable in determining whether a crime is, in fact, being committed and whether employees are in danger.

Security force or police response should focus on locating at strategic positions, to observe and confront the robbers when they are outside of the building.

ACCESS CONTROLS

The pharmacy work area should be secured so unauthorized personnel cannot gain unrestricted access. All entrances should be fitted with good locks, and be kept locked at all times. To enhance department security, the designated employee entrances should incorporate dual access control technology: card and code, code and biometric reader, etc.

Nonpharmacy personnel, including sales representatives, should not be permitted to freely enter the work areas. Insofar as possible, pharmacies should be windowless. Where windows exist, they should be properly secured and protected by an alarm system.

Openings such as service windows may be necessary for the transaction of business. They should be as small as possible, and constructed to preclude anyone being able to gain access to the department. Transaction drawers are preferred to sliding glass openings, to eliminate the opening into the department altogether. Most new security designs incorporate bullet-resistant glazing and reinforced steel plating above, under, and around the transaction window and service counter, to protect staff against armed weapon penetration. Regardless of the system in place, all should be designed to withstand forced entry.

Service windows should also be located so they are out of the line of sight to access doors. This prevents someone with a gun from ordering an employee to open a door, without giving the employee an opportunity to gain protection before reaching the door.

The staff door leading from the pharmacy to the corridor can also present a security vulnerability for exiting pharmacy employees. A robber or thief can wait outside the door for someone to exit. This vulnerability can be reduced with a video surveillance system. The camera is placed in the corridor, and the monitor is placed just inside the door, where employees can see it. Exiting employees can check the monitor before opening the door.

CLOSED PHARMACIES

Although many hospital pharmacies are open 24 hours a day, some smaller hospitals may close their pharmacy during the night hours. This will often require access by a nursing supervisor, or other equivalent positions in the healthcare organization. This access presents a special vulnerability that demands a high degree of personal diligence on the part of the nursing supervisor. In most cases, depending on the frequency of required access and the assessed degree of risk, a security escort should be provided.

An emergency after-hours drug room or large cabinet can also be effective. This container can be stocked with the type and amount of drugs the facility is expected to need that night. This system eliminates many unnecessary trips to the pharmacy. In either case, procedures must be developed to carefully document who enters the pharmacy and what drugs are removed. These records should be available to the pharmacist for review when the pharmacy reopens.

Intrusion alarms are highly recommended for all closed pharmacies, regardless of size. Not only are electronic motion detectors and other anti-intrusion devices effective in detecting illegal entry, but they also serve as a strong deterrent to break-ins. Relatively inexpensive holdup cameras can provide additional levels of protection, as well as can video surveillance systems.

DRUG DIVERSION AND DRUG THEFT

A Dilaudid drip has gone missing. Records show it had been properly delivered, but its whereabouts are unknown and unaccounted for. A pharmacy audit shows a staff member has taken an unusually high amount of narcotics from the automated dispensing machine. An anesthesiologist reports many patients are complaining of extreme pain after receiving narcotic pain medication. A nurse reports two syringes of Fentanyl and Versed are missing. A charge nurse reports a patient's bag of Fentanyl was empty five hours before it should have been. A local retail pharmacy calls, questioning the accuracy of prescriptions for more than 4,000 pain pills.

The theft or diversion of drugs in the healthcare environment is not rare, and the examples above are commonly filed reports. The National Association of Drug Diversion Investigators (NADDI), a non-profit organization that facilitates cooperation between law enforcement, healthcare professionals, state regulatory agencies and pharmaceutical manufacturers in the prevention and investigation of prescription drug diversion, reports that nursing personnel account for the bulk of drug diversion from healthcare facilities. A study conducted by the NADDI's Cincinnati unit found that a nurse was arrested approximately once per week from healthcare facilities in the Ohio River Valley area for drug diversion.[19]

Most hospitals have automated dispensing units (ADUs) on floors to keep drugs locked near patients who need them. To retrieve the various drugs and narcotics, strict security controls are put into place—but those security measures do not extend to when the medications are distributed on the floor, or within a surgical suite. Take for example the surgical nurse at Boulder Community Hospital in Colorado who was caught stealing Fentanyl and replacing it with saline solution. The nurse pilfered more than 50 vials of fentanyl affecting nearly 300 surgery patients in a matter of months. The nurse was able to steal the medications by ordering through the automated drug dispensing machine, then cancelling the order after he had removed the drug, injected himself and replaced it with saline solution. The system was upgraded and now does not allow anyone to cancel a narcotics order. But cases of drug diversion or theft are not limited to just nurses.[20]

In 2009, a hospital surgical technician with hepatitis C working at two different healthcare facilities in Colorado stole patient painkillers and, after using, she substituted the drugs with a saline solution in the reused syringe. The case is a rarity as it combined drug diversion and a potentially deadly disease, with the surgical technician leaving behind her dirty needle for use on the patient, exposing thousands to her infectious disease.[21]

In 2008, a radiology technician working at both Lancaster General Hospital and Heart of Lancaster Hospital in Lancaster, Pennsylvania was caught stealing drugs to feed his own habit. The employee was fired, but came back to the facilities many times in the months after his dismissal dressed in scrubs and sharing with any hospital staff that approached him that he forgot his identification badge. Once in the hospital, he would break into biowaste bins and take leftover Fentanyl and inject in the employee bathroom.[22]

Drug diversion by employees is not confined to acute care hospitals. A 2013 case in Minnesota involved a nursing home worker who, once caught, admitted to stealing narcotics from up to 24 residents in a four-month period, resulting in these vulnerable adults failing to have their pain managed during these events.[23]

Fentanyl patches are also a common target of abuse and diversion. The drug is designed to be placed on the pain patient's body and the potent narcotic released over a three-day period. Abusers may slit the patch open and put the drug under their tongue, use it as a suppository, chew it up and swallow the contents, or apply a heat source to the patch on their body to increase the delivery of the Fentanyl. Wasting procedures for Fentanyl patches should be closely reviewed and scrutinized. Many healthcare facilities have reported theft of sharp containers due to a drug seekers desire to obtain wasted Fentanyl patches. Pharmacists have estimated that in many instances, only 20% of the active drug is used by a patient before it is replaced or disposed of.

All hospitals should have procedures in place that include, among other things, validation of a medication's use through patient medical records, and a regular review of dispersal records from ADUs against inventory. There are incidents of drug diversion in every state, and in every country, and every hospital at one point or another has had an incident of drug diversion. And the penalties for not reporting incidents can be severe—failure to report such an incident can result in a fine of $10,000 per occurrence. Healthcare facilities in the U.S. are required by the Drug Enforcement Agency (DEA) and other regulatory agencies to carefully secure drugs. The DEA, under the Controlled Substances Act, requires every pharmacy to ensure there is a closed system of distribution for controlled substances, in order to minimize the risk of drugs being diverted and used illegally. The DEA requires registered pharmacies to employ security distribution policies and technology that incorporates authentication, nonrepudiation, and integrity in the recordkeeping process. Records of each dispensing must be maintained for two years from the date of dispensing of the controlled substance. However, many states require these records be maintained for longer periods of time. These records must be made available for inspection by the DEA or other authorized investigative agencies. Most international jurisdictions will have similar requirements, specifically tied to the regulating agency having jurisdiction.

ADUs require individual codes or biometrics readers (fingerprints, palm, or retina). Many of these electronic systems track narcotics from the time they arrive at the hospital until they are administered to the patient or destroyed. Every healthcare organization using Scheduled II–V drugs are required to conduct a daily reconciliation. This activity is almost always performed by the caregivers on the unit, and periodically audited by pharmacy staff. Monitoring software is available and used by many healthcare organizations that work with automated dispensing machines to detect unusual usage patterns. At Wake Forest University Baptist Hospital in Winston-Salem, North Carolina, security/risk management investigators probe each and every discrepancy found in the daily reconciliation, and any unusual usage patterns identified.

Organizational policy and frequent reminders for staff are recommended, so staff do not leave drugs unsupervised in surgical suites before the patient arrives. In the case of the surgical technician with hepatitis C, she was caught in an operating room where she was not assigned. Hospital policy forbade the practice, but as with most every surgical suite, the practice is commonplace. Fortunately, hospital policy did allow for her to be immediately drug tested.

Reducing drug diversion has been a huge, ongoing commitment by the healthcare community. One example is the Colorado Hospital Association (CHA), who formed a Medication Safety and Security Task Force to address areas of potential vulnerability related to drug diversion in Colorado hospitals. Sharing best practices and working together as a team of 40+ doctors, nurses and pharmacists, the task force formed to propose ways to reduce vulnerability, relating to medication safety and security in hospitals. Key achievements were improving tracking systems for individuals convicted of and/or suspected of being involved in high-risk problem activities, as well as the development of medication oversight policies and standards for dispensing, administration and wasting controlled medications. The group educated the medical community workforce on the warning signs of potential abuse, and developed a process to share this information appropriately, while also increasing patient awareness—encouraging them to share any suspicious behavior or concerns that they are not receiving the proper medication.

HSS Inc. developed an internal drug division awareness flyer, which can be found in Figure 21-5.

The healthcare security administrator is often involved in the early investigation of drug theft or diversion. This typically includes working with the chief pharmacist, or other designee, to review audit trends and possibly conduct initial interviews. Healthcare facilities in the U.S. are required to report all incidences of drug diversion to the state health department and law enforcement authorities. Outside the U.S., similar reporting will be required to the designated authority for narcotic control. The healthcare security administrator should have contact information readily available and assist pharmacy staff or law enforcement authorities as needed.

07.02.01 DRUG DIVERSION

Statement

Drug diversion is a concern for all Healthcare Facilities (HCFs). Implementation of proper safeguards and administration of drug control methodologies, and subsequent investigation of controlled substance diversion or theft, is a responsibility of all HCFs.

Intent

a. Drug diversion or tampering can take many forms such as:
   - **1)** Simple theft – controlled substance taken from a cabinet, dispensing mechanism or other area where controlled substances are stored
   - **2)** Theft by substitution – controlled substance is removed from its container and replaced with another substance
   - **3)** Theft by documentation – the medical chart, records, or logs manipulated to show controlled substance was administered and dosage given; however, a smaller amount, or no medication, was actually given
   - **4)** Undermedicating the patient – a specific amount of controlled substance is ordered and only partially administered

b. HCFs should designate, in writing, the person, by title, responsible for the security of controlled substances. Security should work in collaboration with this individual and others delegated with the responsibility for the protection of controlled substances.

c. Staff and physicians working with controlled substance distribution, administration, and disposal should be active in the safeguarding of controlled substances and educated on this responsibility.

d. All physicians and staff, including contract staff, should be required to report suspicious behavior or activity involving controlled substance handling, or a suspected fitness for duty/substance abuse problem.

e. HCFs should have a system in place to monitor and audit controlled substances. This includes examining practices for storage, handling, administering, and disposal of controlled substances. HCFs should conduct random reviews of all controlled substance transactions. Auditing software may be used and can provide evidence should the audit reveal a drug diversion.

f. HCFs should develop and periodically review controlled substance policies and procedures; e.g. handling and dispensing, wasting practices, discrepancy investigation, violation reporting. The HCF should have a written policy stating no prescription drug, non-prescription drug, or controlled substance may be sold, transferred or otherwise distributed unless authorized in writing by the appropriate individual charged with such responsibility.

g. Procedures for immediate follow-up of a suspected violation of drug diversion or other incidents associated with the mishandling or misuse of controlled substances should be developed. Actions should include:
   1. Initiate a timely and confidential inquiry
   2. Maintain patient and staff safety
   3. Conduct a drug audit for purposes of determining if a discrepancy exists
   4. Maintain the integrity of investigation
   5. Respond to potential impairment

h. Security should engage in or support investigative activity as part of the follow-up of a suspected violation.

i. A program of drug testing of staff and physicians, who handle controlled substances, should be seriously considered as a proactive element of drug control and may provide information that suggests the need for further investigative action.

j. Notifications of suspected drug diversion received from external reporting sources, such as local law enforcement personnel, or a regulatory board, should be referred to the HCF Pharmacy authority.

k. HCF should establish clear responsibilities for reporting drug diversion to internal and external authorities.

References

National Association of Drug Diversion Investigators (NADDI);
www.naddi.associationdatabase.com

INTERNAL DRUG DIVERSION

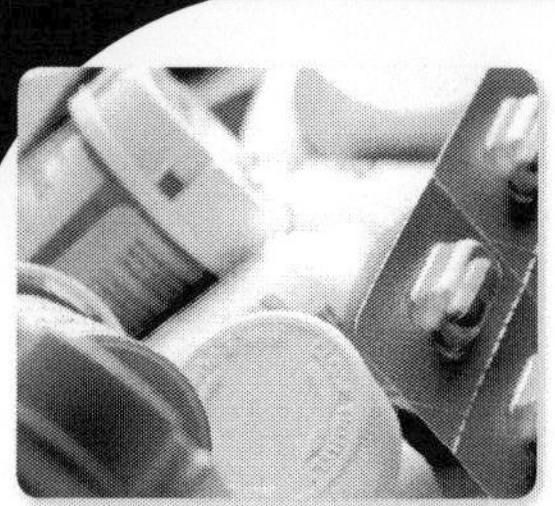

THE PROBLEM

2000–2006 a 80% increase in prescription drug abuse

1997–2007, the milligram per person use of prescription opioids increased 402%

2000–2009, retail pharmacies' prescriptions of opioids increased 48%

Opioids overdoses, once almost always due to heroin use, is now led by the abuse of prescription painkillers

Marketing fuels demand for consumption

Lack of training and education

In 2004 U.S. consumed 99% of global supply of hydrocodone yet the U.S. makes up only 4.5% of the world's population

WHERE DOES DIVERSION HAPPEN?

- Practitioners/Pharmacists
- Employee Pilferage
- Pharmacy/Theft
- Patients

METHODS OF DIVERSION

- Storage and access
- Wasting and destruction
- Receiving drugs from friends or relatives
- Taking drugs from patients
- Buying drugs from patients
- Buying drugs from providers/prescribers

THE WARNING SIGNS

Red Flags of Diversion

- Miscounts of medications
- Multiple unjustified or canceled access to AcuDose or Pyxis
- Absenteeism OR always willing to work
- Frequent and/or long bathroom breaks
- History (pre-hire, state licensing authority)
- Sloppy nursing notes
- Visits by "friends" of the provider/caregiver
- Increase/trend in patients reporting an increase in pain levels after receiving pain medication

Indicators of Diversion

- DEA Criteria that indicate a prescription may not be for a legitimate medical purpose
- Prescribers prescription pattern is different from other prescribers in the area
- Prescriber writes for stimulant and depressant the same time
- Patient returns to the pharmacy more frequently than expected (quantity is inconsistent with refill)
- A number of people appear within a short time period for the same drug from the same prescriber
- Forged prescriptions

HOT SPOTS FOR CLOSER OBSERVATION IN HEALTHCARE

- Anesthesia
- Emergency Department
- Pharmacy
- Drug storage/distribution areas
- Delivery personnel–drivers
- Family member use
- Contractors/temps

OR AND OB-SUBSET OF ANESTHESIA

- High risk group due to high access and low control measures.
- Unattended and/or early set up drug on anesthesia tables

Some of the signs

- Dosing epidurals
- Does not document in real time
- Does not destroy or have excess narcotic witnessed in real time
- Carrying syringes in lab coat
- Does not label syringes

FIGURE 21-5

Internal Drug Diversion, courtesy of HSS Inc.

INTERNAL DRUG DIVERSION

PHARMACY

Some of the risks

- Access not controlled
- No audit process for check-in of new drugs
- Non-monitored destruction of expired medications
- Limited pharmacy hours
- Access to pharmacy after hours

Some of the signs

- Patterns of broken vials or ampoules
- Narcotic waste is thrown in general trash
- Changes in use quantities of a given area
- Returned capsules missing powder
- Returned broken tablets missing pieces
- Diluents are used instead of active injectable
- Substitution of look-alike drugs

ALL CLINCIAL AREAS

- PRN drug orders that allow a range (nurse gives low dose and documents high dose)
- Falsification of physician orders
- Replacing controlled drug with saline
- Excessive wastage (without actual witnessing)
- Patient medications
- Intentional miscounts

LESSONS LEARNED

- Pre-employment background checks are essential, especially for employees who will have access to medications
- Test for the most commonly diverted drugs during drug tests (in addition to illicit drugs and alcohol)
- Notify law enforcement (local and Federal)

DETERRENT STRATEGIES

EDUCATION

Awareness of the problem to healthcare Providers

- Work with federal agencies, such as the DEA
- Work with drug manufactures
- Continuing education
- Stakeholder involvement-Medical and healthcare boards

Risk Factors

Environmental Controls

- Pyxis, AcuDose-RX, or other
- Safeguard medications destined for disposal
- Access control and video surveillance

Policies and Procedures

- Define job duties–RN vise nursing student
- Audits- random and targeted based on the suspicion
- 2 person counts
- Charting
- Employee badging

History

- Pre-employment screening
- State licensing boards (DORA in CO)

DISPOSAL

Storage Processes

Responsible and User-Friendly Disposal

- Collection and disposal of unused or expired medications
- Federal, State, and local "take back" programs

ENFORCEMENT

Don't help the diverter avoid facing the consequences

- No excuses, no rationalizing
- Report and follow up

Enforcement/law enforcement

- Administrative investigations
- Criminal investigations
- Work with local law enforcement (PD and prosecutors)
- Aggressive enforcement

STEPS TO TAKE IF YOU SUSPECT DIVERSION

- Behavior: describe visible or unusual involvement of one person or group
- Witnesses
- Physical dangers of action/inaction?
- Is security/law enforcement needed?
- Policy that applies?
- Consultation? (HR, EAP, MD, security)
- Suspicion testing needed?
- De-escalation techniques
- Documentation

FIGURE 21-5—Continued

REFERENCES

1. For Healthcare Professionals. *Guidelines on Prevention of and Response to Infant Abductions*. 9th ed. Arlington, Virginia: National Center for Missing and Exploited Children; 2009, January.
2. Tucker F. Stolen from hospital: Canadian baby abductions. *Global News* 2014, May 27. Retrieved June 21, 2014, from http://globalnews.ca/news/1357218/stolen-from-hospital-canadian-baby-abductions/.
3. Glasson L, Rozovksky F, Gaffney M. Security Challenges and Risk Management Strategies for Child Abduction. *Insights* 2007, October;**12**. Retrieved January 4, 2008, from http://www.onebeaconpro.com/insights/insights_vol12.pdf.
4. Abducted newborn found, suspect arrested: Quebec police. *CBC News* 2014, May 27. Retrieved June 21, 2014, from http://www.cbc.ca/news/canada/montreal/abducted-newborn-found-suspect-arrested-quebec-police-1.2655088.
5. Marko D. Hospital and Police Report: How Woman Tried to Steal Newborn. *The Daily Journal* 2009, March 27. Retrieved March 27, 2009, from http://www.thedailyjournal.com/apps/pbcs.dll/article?AID=/20090327/NEWS01/9032703.
6. The Associated Press. Mother of Kidnapped Baby Released from Hospital. *FoxNews.com* 2006, September 18. Retrieved September 20, 2006, from http://www.foxnews.com/story/0,2933,214260,00.html.
7. Summers C. The Women Who Kill for Babies. *BBC News* 2007, October 27. Retrieved November 2, 2007, from http://news.bbc.co.uk/nolpda/ukfs_news/hi/newsid_6990000/6990419.stm.
8. The Associated Press. Arraignment Postponed in Kennewick Baby Case. *The Daily News Online* 2008, July 2. Retrieved July 4, 2008, from http://www.tdn.com/articles/2008/07/02/breaking_news/doc486bfe640d742236235014.prt.
9. NewsCore. *Ky. Woman Accused of Killing Facebook Friend, Stealing Unborn Baby*. 2011, April 15. Retrieved April 17, 2011, from http://www.thecourier.co.uk/News/Dundee/article/12966/security-is-stepped-up-after-attack-on-ninewells-car-park-barriers.html.
10. Aleccia J. Worst Nightmare: Babies Stolen from their Beds. *MSBC.com* 2008, September 4. Retrieved September 5, 2008, from http://www.msnbc.msn.com/id/26532421/print/1/displaymode/1098.
11. Stevens Alexis. Woman had planned for months to kidnap baby. *Atlanta Journal Constitution* 2012, January 5. Retrieved January 5, 2012, from http://www.ajc.com/news/clayton/woman-had-planned-for-1290789.html.
12. Taylor G, Finley G. Cops: Woman Used Ruse to Steal Baby in Sanford. 2008, March 30. *Orlando Sentinel.com*. Retrieved March 30, 2008, from orlandosentinel.com/news/local/seminole/orl-prerelease3008mar30,0,4250897.story.
13. The Joint Commission. Infant Abduction Drills. *Frequently Asked Questions* 2009, January 13. Retrieved June 4, 2014, from http://www.jointcommission.org/mobile/standards_information/jcfaqdetails.aspx?StandardsFAQId=103&StandardsFAQChapterId=64.
14. Hooper Kimberly A. Emerson Hospital staff stop attempted infant abduction in Concord. *The Concord Journal* 2011, November 11. Retrieved November 12, 2011, from www.wickedlocal.com/concord/mobiletopstories/x57917747/Emerson-Hospital-staff-stop-attempted-infant=abduction.
15. Tavernero Theresa. Preventing Violence in the Emergency Department. *Patient Safety & Quality Healthcare* 2009, January/February;**16**:17.
16. Butler A. *Emergency Room Violence: An Everyday Threat*. Presented at International Association for Healthcare Security and Safety Annual General Membership Meeting and Seminar; 2009, June 22.
17. Dickerson Brad. Grand Strand Regional locked down after fight in ER. *The Sun News* 2012, December 1. Retrieved December 2, 2012, from http://www.myrtlebeachonline.com/2012/12/01/3198269/grand-strand-regional-remains.html.
18. Leger Donna Leinwand. Opana abuse in USA overtakes OxyContin. *USA Today* 2012, July 11. Retrieved July 25, 2012, from http://usatoday30.usatoday.com/news/nation/story/2012-07-10/opana-painkiller-addiction/56137086/1.

19. Burke J. *Drug Diversion: The Scope of the Problem*. National Association of Drug Diversion Investigators; 2005. Retrieved July 12, 2009, from http://associationdatabase.com/aws/NADDI/asset_manager/get_file/3143/drug_diversion_the_scope_of_the_problem.pdf.
20. Boulder hospital: Nurse swapped painkiller with saltwater. *The Denver Post* 2008, November 7. Retrieved November 7, 2008, from http://www.denverpost.com/breakingnews/ci_10920840.
21. Brown J, Booth M. Hospitals fight inner demons. *The Denver Post* 2009, July 12. 1A, 8A.
22. Collin L. Hospital Drug Arrest. *CBS 21 News* 2007, November 1. Retrieved November 5, 2007, from http://www.whptv.com/news/local/story.aspx?content_id=f3dcde80-7813-4f1d-84.
23. Minnesota Department of Health News Release. *MDH investigation confirms drug thefts at nursing home*. 2013, May 30. Retrieved June 22, 2014, from http://www.health.state.mn.us/news/pressrel/2013/diversion053013.html.

CHAPTER

AREAS OF SPECIAL CONCERN

22

Medical Center is the term commonly used to denote a hospital campus that contains the major inpatient/outpatient services of a healthcare organization. The campus can be a large single facility structure, or a primary facility structure with numerous freestanding buildings. There are various operating functions and services at all medical centers that require the specific attention of security. Not all of these activities will ascend to the level of a defined security sensitive area. It is not particularly wrong to classify some of these areas as "security sensitive" at a specific facility due to a variety of circumstances. However, an objective of security should be not to overclassify an area as sensitive, since the level of protection and added security compliance requirements may impose additional burdens that may not be necessary or really add to the protection posture. It is also important to keep in mind that areas of security special concern, or designated sensitive areas, may change from one category to another category, due to changing risk/vulnerability factors. In this chapter we will limit discussion to the main care facility, with the understanding that many of the same special security concerns may be present at a number of off-campus locations.

PROTECTED HEALTH INFORMATION

This area of special security concern in the not too distant past was known as *Medical Records*. The safeguarding of patient information has always been a high priority of healthcare organizations. When patient records were basically maintained as hard-copy paper records, the release of information was generally person to person, with telephone and fax transmissions carefully guarded. As the use of fax machines increased, and with the introduction of electronic information systems, the landscape of safeguarding patient information changed dramatically.

The Privacy Act of 1974 was enacted in the U.S. by the federal government to stop the widespread abuse of government information systems. Under the act, healthcare organizations were prohibited from disclosing information contained in a medical record, except under the following conditions:

- The organization had the patient's consent to release information contained in the medical record.
- The organization was served with a subpoena or court order to disclose the information.
- Public health supersedes the patient's rights, such as in cases involving infectious disease.
- The organization is required by law to report the information to a public agency.

Then in 1996 the often confusing and always changing federal Health Insurance Portability and Accountability Act (HIPAA) was enacted. The act, still not thoroughly understood, has many interpretations and continues to be a major contributor to the increasing cost of healthcare with minimal positive benefits. HIPAA is more fully discussed in Chapter 1, "The Healthcare Environment." Privacy acts can be found in various forms in Canada, Australia, New Zealand, in a joint European Act, and indeed across the international spectrum, each intended to protect personal information and each, with some distinctions, containing similar guiding principles to the aforementioned U.S. Privacy Act.

Access to patient data has exploded in today's healthcare environment with the advent of electronic health records (EHR). Access to patient data for collaboration and continuity of care has to be balanced with monitoring electronic health record activity to detect inappropriate access and use. The security measures hospitals have deployed for authorized users of the EHR, such as database monitoring, log management and provisioning systems, coupled with the security technologies hospitals use to safeguard information such as encryption for laptops, workstations, smart phones and thumb drives, have dramatically hardened most healthcare facilities' information technology infrastructure. But they do not detect all security breaches or prevent breaches of confidential patient information.

Privacy and security are aspects of patient safety that are every bit as daunting and pervasive as infection control and the reduction of avoidable readmissions. Since the U.S. Department of Health and Human Services started reporting healthcare data breaches in 2009, 619 breaches have been reported affecting 500 or more individuals, with over 22 million total individuals being affected.[1] The Third Annual Benchmark Study on Patient Privacy and Data Security found that 94% of healthcare providers had experienced a data breach in the previous two years, and 45% had experienced more than five data breaches during the same period. Lost devices, human error, third-party problems and criminal attacks headed the list of causes. Based on this data, the study estimates security breaches could be costing healthcare providers $7 billion annually.[2]

The inadvertent loss of data by someone with legitimate access is the top security concern, as healthcare employees use more mobile devices that make healthcare information more accessible. These devices present inherent privacy and security risks to hospital networks and patient records. This could be from a stolen device where patient data has been downloaded (thumb drive, laptop, tablet, etc.), or where user IDs and passwords are saved. Technology exists to effectively deal with these situations, but the application of such mitigation strategies is still not an industry standard, due to the added expense and increased "hassle factor" the additional security adds to the end users.

Another worrying security concern to those with primary responsibility for the safeguarding of patient medical information is the concept of Bringing Your Own Device (BYOD). The question of whether or not BYOD should be allowed is debated by IT security professionals throughout the healthcare industry. Physicians and other care providers want the convenience of accessing patient data on their own device, while IT security professionals worry over the vulnerability of patient information being available, or stored on devices not in the direct control of the healthcare facility. At the heart of this concern is the ability to comply with HIPAA expectations, among other requirements and expectations, which define any improper use or disclosure of health information as a security breach.

Avoiding the tendency to think of privacy and security as information technology add-ons is a must. Too often, a healthcare organization focuses on these risks after it experiences its first data breach. Many healthcare organizations have embedded privacy officers and information security officers to guide privacy and security policy and procedure implementations in their organization. These roles are created with an eye to data protection, as well as consideration for clinicians' special needs to ensure strict staff guidelines are in place, in addition to confirming physical security safeguards are established and functioning properly. Security precautions frequently include:

- Leadership commitment to a robust corporate compliance program that monitors and enforces standards of conduct designed to detect and deter criminal behavior and inappropriate access to and disclosure of protected information.
- Standard use of full encryption software.

- Completion of education and training as metrics in performance evaluations.
- Daily huddles to discuss patients on the floor who might spark curiosity—and inappropriate intrusion into their health information.
- Audit of inappropriate user access and identification of potential instances of inappropriate disclosure of protected health information. To include automatic messages such as: "*Be on notice that if you inappropriately access records with protected health information or move records in an unauthorized fashion, it will be picked up.*"
- A written affidavit signed by medical staff indicating that they understand disclosure procedures and intend to abide by those procedures.
- Vendor business associate agreements that cover how information is protected and when policies and procedures are reviewed.
- System for employees and visitors to report ethical and legal concerns regarding potential security breaches.
- Make credit monitoring services available if inappropriate use or disclosure of a patient's demographic information has been released.

Privacy and security professionals must think about the impact of controls and other risk mitigation to patient care delivery—this requires a degree of flexibility. At Providence Health System, the length of time that computers on surgical floors stay unlocked has been extended, since access to the unit and floor are restricted. It is a convenience provided to surgeons and nurses that does not endanger data security. A common standard for computers in more public places is 10 minutes but since these computers are in secured units, the organization collaborated with department staff to find ways to effectively manage data security while supporting patient care.

The security program provides support for the protection of this information. This support includes but is not limited to:

- Conducting privacy and security audits to spot problems, including passwords on sticky notes and computers left unattended while displaying sensitive information.
- Advising department leadership regarding proper physical security safeguards to include access controls.
- Observing for compliance with organizational privacy and security rules.
- Assisting the organizational Privacy Officer in conducting investigations of breaches, or suspected breaches, of information security.
- Fostering a joint working relationship between health information management, security, information technology, and direct care medical providers.

MEDICAL DEVICE SECURITY

Another group of assets that has growing concern for security vulnerability is medical devices that increasingly use wireless technology. Concerns over medical device vulnerability have grown, as machines such as infusion pumps land on hospital networks. Devices that communicate wirelessly add to worries of data breaches. The U.S. Department of Homeland Security issued a warning in 2012 on medical device security. The DHS report noted that "the communications security of medical devices to protect against theft of medical information and malicious intrusion, such as modifying the dosage and concentration of drugs in an infusion pump, has now becoming a major concern." Risk mitigation approaches for medical devices are just coming into focus for many manufacturers and healthcare providers alike, although many information security professionals contend these efforts are inadequate. A few organizations are pursuing research and best practices in medical device security. These include:

- **Medical Device Innovation, Safety, and Security Consortium**, which aims to create a private-public partnership for establishing security practices for medical devices.
- **Open Medical Device Research Library**, which seeks to provide researchers access to medical devices for trustworthy computing research.
- **Security and Privacy Research Lab**, which pursues research problems in trustworthy computing in fields including healthcare.

MEDICAL IDENTITY THEFT

Medical identity theft is another concern for the healthcare security professional. It is the fastest growing form of ID theft in the U.S. and has become a growing global concern. The World Privacy Forum estimates the number of victims to be between 250,000 and 500,000 people each year.

Medical identity theft can expose a person's personal information, which can then be used by fraudsters to get medical treatments, benefits, prescription drugs and generally defraud the medical system. The victims of identity theft may ultimately receive incorrect medical treatment if their records have been altered. For the healthcare institution, the consequences of medical identity theft can lead to being assessed heavy fines, legal expenses, bad publicity and reputation loss.

Security breaches may result from the intentional or unintentional negligence of healthcare employees. The news is filled with stories about medical files being dumped into recycling dumpsters or garbage containers or being posted on the Internet. Some of the most common security breaches include:

- Confidential documents left in unsecure recycling boxes or garbage bins
- Lack of training for staff on what patient information should be protected and securely destroyed
- Unsupervised medical files in file rooms or on desks
- Lack of focus on document destruction due to budgetary concerns
- Unsupervised or inadequate in-house document destruction facilities.

Furthermore, medical records also must be stored for a period of time, increasing the chances for a breach. Regular paper records are often kept for 10 years, and if at a teaching hospital or concerning a pediatric patient, hospitals may keep records for 15 years or longer.

While there is no single solution to keep medical identity theft from occurring, medical facilities should analyze possible security gaps and invest in an ongoing risk analysis process. Stringent policies should be developed regarding access to sensitive patient information, as well as protocols developed for authorization and authentication of individuals accessing protected health information. Lastly, medical documents that are no longer required to be kept on record should be destroyed in a secure manner.

INFORMATION TECHNOLOGY

Data breaches grab headlines on almost a daily basis. Healthcare providers maintain data ranging from a person's credit card numbers, Social Security numbers and credit ratings, to the most private and intimate health details. The lack of coordination among physical, privacy, and virtual security personnel has been part of the problem. As a result of this disconnect of parties, the term *convergence* has been coined. There are various definitions of convergence; however, in simple terms it means getting IT people and security people working together in an effective working relationship. The common elements of convergence are running physical security systems over network wires, common credentials for door and logical access, and integrated logical and physical applications.

The security staff can assist the IT unit in physically hardening the space utilized by IT with access control, alarms, and video surveillance. Security can support IT by helping to secure mobile data devices to collect patient data, access data, and to signal caregivers. The array of easily lost or stolen devices and media include PDAs, laptops, CDs, DVDs, flash and thumb drives, as well as data cards. The security of software protection, firewalls, etc., is largely in the domain of the IT staff. As healthcare inexorably marches more and more into the community to provide care, healthcare security and IT professionals are stretched even further to design solutions to protect information in these less-structured settings.

Server areas and other sensitive equipment locations should be secured. Vendors, repair persons and other persons not assigned to these areas should be tightly controlled. A system of badging, logging in and out, and escort procedures should be part of all IT security plans and systems.

Physical security safeguards, however, cannot prevent internal breaches by those in a position of trust. On July 1, 2009, a security officer at The Carrell Clinic in Dallas, Texas was taken into custody after taking complete control of computers that administered the facility's air-conditioning systems. The security officer had no authorized access to health system computers, but was able to hack into the network controller and physically inactivate all internal alarms.[3] Many elements of critical infrastructure, like environmental controls in most healthcare facilities, have low security and are prone to even less-skilled attackers.

So for healthcare organizations, their concern for security of their IT network has implications even beyond the paramount concern of protecting private patient information. Sensitive corporate information may be available on the network or staff may use the network on time-wasting internet exploration or even illegal activities such as frequenting child pornography sites. IT network-related investigations can be time consuming and costly, and brings together IT experts and security investigators in often sensitive circumstances. While most healthcare organizations do not integrate their network security and corporate/physical security programs, there may be a trend toward examining a closer linkage between these functions in formal program organizational structures.

To enhance the awareness among public hospital staff in protection of personal data of patients, the Hospital Authority in Hong Kong and the Office of Privacy Commissioner for Personal Data (PCPD) launched the "*Care for Patients—Protect Their Personal Data*" campaign. Through a series of training seminars on the Personal Data (Privacy) Ordinance, with interactive games and exhibitions, the campaign is aimed at strengthening the culture of privacy awareness in the daily routine of hospital staff, with particular attention to preventing the loss and possible leakage of patients' personal data. Likewise, the PCPD designed an online self-learning program to facilitate the training of healthcare workers on the protection of personal data.[4]

MATERIALS MANAGEMENT

The materials management responsibility is defined somewhat differently in each healthcare organization. For the purposes of security, the general areas of concern are purchasing and receiving, storage, equipment accountability and marking, distribution, and disposing of property. All of these areas are the responsibility of the Director of Materials Management or related position, depending on the organization, and require a certain level of security review and support.

PURCHASING AND RECEIVING

Because healthcare organizations purchase large amounts of goods, products, and equipment, a proactive loss-prevention program is necessary. A materials management program requires checks and balances, and a separation of the staff responsible for purchasing and the staff responsible for receiving. Many opportunities for kickbacks and fraud exist in purchasing activities, somewhat in relation to the size of the function; the larger the program the greater the opportunity, and thus the greater extent of this type of fraud as a rule. Not only is the separation of purchasing and receiving necessary, but also the rotation of job assignments is a sound management practice to deter criminal activity. The receiving dock, and the process of receiving supplies and equipment, present numerous security vulnerabilities. A frequent problem facilities encounter is that received goods are left unattended on the dock, and thus accessible to delivery drivers or others passing by or through the department. After being checked in and signed for, all goods should immediately be transferred to a "using unit" or removed to a controlled storage location. A small fenced holding area on the dock may provide temporary protection, pending distribution or transportation to a more permanent storage area. All deliveries to the facility should be directed to a specific receiving area, and the internal distribution of light deliveries, such as flowers, should be performed by organizational personnel. Many problems have occurred because delivery personnel were allowed to make their own deliveries to various departments within the organization. These problems include unnecessary traffic, extra housekeeping due to careless handling, interruption of direct or indirect patient care, and the misplacement of material delivered to the wrong location. The delivery of goods and materials by outside service employees continues to grow with the advent of the "just in time" concept of delivery and distribution. This "just in time" concept simply means reduced need for storage and the double or triple handling of supplies, both of which are intended to reduce costs. In this case cost is reduced at the expense of management control, which, if not managed, can provide the potential for losses greater than the savings. Many organizations have moved to a model of huge off-campus supply and equipment storage warehouses, where only the goods necessary for short-term use are located in the medical facility itself.

In a typical large organization, it is common for a semi-truck, or two, to arrive at the facility receiving dock at 2 a.m. At this time the vendor's staff unloads and delivers throughout the house to operating departments and units. This activity, which takes several hours, exposes the facility to access by unwanted persons through the loading dock open access point. The vendor employees, often with questionable hiring verifications, are free to move about the entire facility unsupervised. All of this activity has the potential for serious security consequences. Some "just in time" vendors have been given keys or access cards for unfettered access to the facility. If uninhibited access is provided to contract employees, service agreements with the provider should require minimal hiring standards be met. Confirmation that the employee meets the minimum standard should be required prior to issuance of keys or access cards. The agreement should also stipulate that ongoing checks are conducted periodically, and made available for audit by the organization's human resources department. At minimum, checks should include criminal history, Social Security verification, and sex offender registry.

STORAGE

Although general storerooms contain many vulnerable items, the losses from these areas are generally minimal compared to the losses that occur after the goods have been distributed to the units. One reason the loss is minimal is because most materials management personnel have recognized the potential for large-volume losses, and have implemented at least basic security precautions. All general storerooms should be alarmed after hours, and the sensing devices should transmit a signal to a central alarm panel. Whenever possible, storerooms should be windowless, and the number of access (door) openings should be reduced to the minimum. The system of perimeters is a valid concept for the security of general storeroom operations. Certain areas within the general storeroom should be sectioned off to provide greater protection for particularly vulnerable items, including syringes, blank checks, batteries, invoices, and linens. Regular storeroom employees can thus be restricted from areas, or access to storage containers, where they do not need access to perform their jobs. Storerooms should be off-limits to all but department personnel. This rule is common, but so is nonenforcement. In one case, employees leaving the workplace were permitted to cut through the storeroom and leave by a side door.

After-hours access to storerooms can present a problem. If the materials management function is properly carried out, there should be little, if any, need for after-hours access. A 600-bed hospital with a firm policy restricting after-hours access recorded only two after-hours entries during a one-year period. On those two occasions, the storeroom manager had to come from home to provide the access. If entry to the storeroom is necessary, a security officer should accompany the individual to the storeroom. To provide proper accountability, a requisition or record of items removed should be prepared by the security officer for any items taken. The security officer should also be responsible for securing the area when the business is concluded. In this respect the security officer should be present in the storeroom the entire time another person is allowed entry after regular hours.

The increased application of electronic access control and video surveillance of these areas has helped to mitigate the after-hours vulnerabilities to a large degree. Access control system audit and video verification capacities can deter and detect illicit activity, as well as facilitating investigations in the event of unexplained loss or suspicious occurrence.

EQUIPMENT ACCOUNTABILITY AND MARKING

A common practice in healthcare organizations is to receive a piece of equipment, assign an asset control number to it, affix the number to the equipment, assign a depreciation schedule, and deliver the equipment to the requesting department—never to see it again. For example, a computer acquired for the public relations department may end up in the nursing office, and the new location will not be recorded. After these transfers have been made several times, the computer's location cannot be readily established and it may indeed be missing. Equipment should be assigned to a specific department, and a periodic inventory is essential. When property is transferred, the record should be annotated to relieve one department and assign accountability to the other. Related to the assigning of asset numbers—and of equal importance—is marking property with organizational identification. "Marking" refers to conspicuous identification that cannot be easily altered or removed. Many items must be marked with more than the asset control number. When marking equipment to deter theft, basic economics must be considered. A balance must be found between the cost of marking and the actual theft deterrent value achieved. Not all markings need to be readily seen. For example, desks, file cabinets, tables, and chairs should be marked on the underside, permitting ready identification but not defacing the appearance of the property. Furniture is normally stenciled with the hospital's initials or logo. Etching tools are used for instruments and other metal equipment.

DISTRIBUTION

The distribution of goods and equipment from storage areas to end-users is accomplished by walk-up distribution counters, or transported to the user by materials management personnel. The latter method is being utilized more frequently as off-site storage areas are becoming common. Regardless of the distribution method, all supplies and equipment should be signed for by an authorized staff person at the point of delivery. The person signing for the property must take time to determine the property being signed for is actually delivered. When staff simply signs a receipt without checking, it is an open invitation to receive a "short" delivery with property being fraudulently diverted. At this point the delivered property should immediately be properly stored and not exposed to passing staff or visitors.

DISPOSING OF PROPERTY

All healthcare organizations accumulate and need to dispose of obsolete, excess, or damaged property. Organization staff, including the supervisory staff, should not have the authority to give away, or otherwise dispose of facility property, regardless of its value. A firm policy should be established that outlines the authorized disposition of unneeded property through the materials management department. All unneeded material should be transported to a central storage area so that it can possibly be used by another department. Thus, property may be reassigned and properly managed. Healthcare facilities are notorious for needlessly purchasing an item because no one knew the same item was no longer needed by another department. A committee—composed of the facility's representative, the materials manager, and other administrators—should periodically survey the material in storage to determine what should be discarded. A sale, accessible to employees only, is a good employee relations mechanism that can eliminate the practice of giving away property to "favorite staff," which can result in negative employee relations.

THE RESEARCH LABORATORY (ANIMAL)

The activities of animal rights groups and antivivisectionists, responsible for acts of ecoterrorism, have made laboratory security a high priority for facilities conducting animal research projects. These "rights" groups are often well financed and can be very sophisticated, and frequently benefit from the attention of a sympathetic media. One of the best-known groups is the Animal Liberation Front (ALF). Research facilities in hospitals, universities, and independent firms have been the target of demonstrations, break-ins, vandalism, and fires. In one case more than 1,200 laboratory animals were released just before two university laboratory buildings were set on fire. The ALF claimed responsibility for these acts. In addition to physical damage, graffiti, and disruption of normal work, pressure by animal rights activists can result in the suppression of important research. There are also a growing number of incidents and concerns relative to threats facing researchers and their families. The defense against ecoterrorism requires planning for both perimeter security and the protection of the contents of the laboratory: animals, equipment, records, and personnel.

EMPLOYEE BACKGROUND CHECKS

When the security of sensitive projects is involved, it is of prime importance to know laboratory employees well, through background verification procedures. Information provided by an employee who is sympathetic to the animal rights movement can allow activists to gain access through even the most efficient security system. The animal rights activist movement goes back several hundred years in Europe and expanded to the United States well over a hundred years ago. In the last five years, these groups have become more active, and somewhat more radical. The new leaders are young, confrontational, and dissatisfied with the lack of progress around the protection of animal rights issue. As a result, they advocate more direct action that leads to violence and destruction of property. According to Debra Higgins Cavalier, president of the Massachusetts Society for Medical Research (MSMR), there are well over seventy animal activists groups in the United States. The MSMR is one of the leading nonprofit groups in the U.S. that support the biosciences in the proper use of animals in research. Massachusetts was the first of several states to enact legislation making it a felony to trespass upon, remove, damage, or interfere with any property used in animal research. There is also the Federal Animal Enterprise Protection Act of 1992 that makes it a felony to break into a laboratory and cause damage in excess of 10 thousand dollars.[5]

ACTIVIST METHODS OF INFILTRATION

The ALF distributes handouts to supply operatives with tactical information. One such handout recommends eight methods of gathering information on targeted institutions. These methods are:

- Personal entry. In this method, the operative simply walks into the facility. If challenged, the operative simply states he is looking for a friend.
- Employment. In this method, the operative gains employment at the targeted facility.
- Use of disguise. In this method, the operative impersonates a government employee, inspector, et cetera.
- Surveillance. In this method, the operative conducts a fixed surveillance (stakeout) of the facility.
- Use of inside help. In this method, the operative develops friendships with facility staff.
- Bribery. In this method, the operative bribes facility staff.
- Garbage inspection. In this method, the operative inspects the target's garbage.
- Surreptitious entry. In this method, the operative gains access to the facility surreptitiously. Lab coats, required safety equipment, and badges help to identify authorized employees during normal working hours, but identification can be difficult after hours.[6]

Animal activists have preferred holidays and early morning hours for break-ins, so security personnel should make sure doors, windows, and all other possible entries are locked at the beginning and end of each workday and immediately after the last employee has left. In addition, visitors should be restricted from sensitive areas, repair people should be carefully identified, and reliable alarm systems used. Because intruders often disable power substations—thus cutting off electricity to the research facility—an emergency power system is advisable for lighting, preserving specimens and agents, and maintaining animal life-support systems.

Many of these facilities are disconnected from the main medical facility; in fact they may be situated in separate buildings, in remote areas. The nature of the lab work means that employees may be working in these facilities at all hours, or they may be unoccupied for at times lengthy periods. Security technology, such as video surveillance, electronic access control and intrusion alarm systems should be strategically utilized and monitored in this environment.

CHILD DEVELOPMENT CENTERS

It is somewhat common for healthcare organizations to operate a child development center or childcare center, as a means to attract and retain physicians, staff and employees. These centers present unique security concerns. The first and primary security concern is the development of appropriate staff. Intense background checks of applicants must be conducted; certain checks are even legally mandated by regulatory and licensing agencies. The sexual molestation, or other physical abuse, of a child by a staff member is a situation to be prevented at all costs. Limiting access to the facility is also a primary safeguard. It is a common practice to have all ingress/egress points locked except for the normal drop-off and pick-up times. Some facilities maintain a locked facility at all times, issuing electronic access cards to authorized family members only. An outside play area is generally a design feature of the child development center. These play areas should be completely fenced with at least six-foot-high barriers. The normal access to the area should be from the daycare center itself. If there is a gate arrangement, it should be locked from the ingress side and the release side (egress) should be such that small children cannot operate the release. Staff personnel should be especially watchful for persons loitering in the area around the center. Release of a child at the end of the designated time period is an area of special concern. First, there is generally a lot of activity going on during the pick-up time, resulting in difficulty of keeping track of who is coming and going. Second, there must be strict criteria established regarding the identity of persons who can pick up a child. There must be a system to permit the release of a child to someone other than a normal family member due to a family emergency or other extenuating circumstances. Regardless of the policy and resultant procedure, there should be strict adherence to this critical element of security. Video surveillance has several appropriate applications to help secure a childcare center. In addition to surveillance of general areas, a camera should be placed at the main access door to record the dropping off and picking up of the children. In some cases, this will require two cameras to adequately record the activity. As with all other video surveillance applications, the recorded video should be kept for a specified time period, which is documented in a written policy and procedure. The video system may also be used to allow the electrical release of the main entry door from a remote location. The general security plan for a childcare center should include procedures for relocation of children and staff in the event of an emergency requiring evacuation. This information should be given to parents at the time of enrollment. It can be included in an overall security-briefing card that is a standard handout to parents, outlining operating procedures and expectations of the parent/guardian.

BUSINESS OFFICE/CASHIERS

Business offices and cashiers are part of the operating environment of most healthcare provider organizations. Although the activities assigned to the business office and the specifics of cashiering will vary from organization to organization, they present a security risk. These risks and resulting security safeguards should be a collaborative effort of security and the appropriate department administrator.

The greatest loss risk in performing these functions is the employees themselves. While robbery and theft by "outsiders" does happen, the frequency and risk of such events in the healthcare environment is fairly low. At the close of a cashier function, or changing of shifts (i.e., cafeteria), receipts should be taken to the designated central cash management location for accounting and storage. There needs to be a night/weekend drop safe or device of some sort for after-hours delivery and storage of receipts and, in some cases, patient valuables. The physical security of the drop mechanism and storage container should be of substantial construction. The drop usually takes place in a hallway or corridor with the storage container on the other side of the wall in a secured area. A video surveillance system should provide a clear image of all persons, and their actions, in and around the drop area. It may take more than one camera, as a wall may preclude getting a full face shot of persons facing the actual drop. The IAHSS has developed a specific design guideline for *Cashiers and Cash Collection Areas* that is discussed in Chapter 18.

Persons transporting receipt bags from an operating unit should utilize a locked bag. In this respect, the transporter should not have the ability to access the contents of the bag. Many such bags involve a double lock type system of control. It is also somewhat common for a security officer to provide a cash escort for certain transports, or to have two general staff persons complete the transfer. Most outsourced security companies cannot obtain liability insurance coverage for internal theft or robbery during a cash escort. The cash receipts are also not protected by the typical crime policy held by most facilities. As a result, these security staff members should escort a facility employee and not be requested to conduct cash escorts alone. It is suggested that cash transfers that require the leaving of a building and traveling any distance on the grounds be accomplished by two persons. An armored car service is a standard security requirement for community banking services, except in the very small communities where no such service is available.

OTHER AREAS NEEDING SPECIAL SECURITY CONSIDERATION

INTENSIVE CARE UNITS

The intensive care unit (ICU) is an area that is frequently the scene of serious security events, from disturbances to homicides. The ICU has the potential to be a highly charged atmosphere at any given time. Another security risk factor is often the high security risk patient that entered the emergency department for treatment of injuries from a felonious assault, who is then transferred to surgery, and on to the ICU. A prolonged stay in the ICU provides an opportunity for a gang member, drug dealer, or others to finish "the job." It is becoming more prevalent to restrict access to ICUs at least during certain hours, and to provide for a certain level of stationary security. Regardless of how open the philosophy of managing the ICU is, with no routine locking, the capability to lock down the unit in an emergency should be in place.

LABORATORIES

Laboratories involving animal research have been addressed previously. Animal-related research continues to be a high-profile risk that has proven to be both dangerous and disruptive. However, as evidenced in the media regarding the safe handling, storage and transport of anthrax, smallpox and other such materials in the middle of 2014, some research laboratories require a significant level of security planning and diligence due to the materials being used in the research.

Clinical, research and training laboratories will certainly contain some level of chemical inventory and some level of hazardous waste. Many of these laboratories may also contain biological materials, infectious (red bag) waste, patient bloods or other samples of infectious agents. A smaller number of laboratories may use radioactive materials in their research or have such materials in equipment such as a research or clinical laboratory irradiator or if performing animal studies may have controlled substances stored in the laboratory. Finally, laboratories may include everything from Bunsen burners to machine shops and may rely heavily on building automation systems, negative air ventilation and freezers with back-up power.

The risks in laboratories can be diverse and numerous and should be addressed according to the level of risk posed, institutional standards and regulatory requirements. Security requirements for laboratories working with high hazard biological materials (Select Agents), radioactive materials and controlled substance have been defined by authorities having jurisdiction. High hazard chemicals have been identified including materials such as cyanide as a result of unauthorized removals and subsequent suicides and, while not strongly regulated in healthcare, security programs should mitigate risks related to high hazard chemicals as they do for regulated materials.

Most healthcare organizations today tightly control and restrict access to their labs at all times.

GIFT SHOPS

The majority of hospitals have a gift shop, staffed for the most part by volunteers. In larger facilities, it is common for the facility to hire an employee as the gift shop manager. The gift shop is a frequent customer of the security department for a variety of reasons, with shoplifting, or suspected shoplifting, the most common need for service. Perhaps the best method of mitigating the shoplifting problem is proper layout of the gift shop, providing clear lines of sight and sufficient staff to provide a clear presence, and general surveillance capability.

Gift shops should have basic physical security safeguards in place. These safeguards include card access, video surveillance, mirrors, and an intrusion alarm system. In addition, some shops have elected to install panic alarms, usually connected directly to security. Not all security administrators subscribe to the use of panic alarms in gift shops for several reasons. A primary reason for this lack of support is that gift shop personnel are often responsible for an inordinate number of accidental or unnecessary alarm activations. Secondly, historical data support the general lack of security incidents when the gift shop is open, with the exception of shoplifting. The use of the telephone to request security services would generally not put the caller in an undue personal risk situation. The configuration of most gift shops provides for a "back room area" from which a call to security can be made in relative privacy. Healthcare security professionals can look to the retail industry for guidance in store design and the use of security processes and technology.

COMPRESSED MEDICAL GASSES

There are two medical gasses of special security concern. The first is oxygen (O_2), and specifically the central oxygen storage tank that supplies piped-in oxygen to the facility. The security concern is that sabotage, or outright destruction of the main hospital storage system, would basically shut down the large hospital facility. Substituting portable oxygen cylinders would be almost impossible in regard to furnishing equipment valves and the other logistics involved.

The second medical gas of concern is that of nitrous oxide (N_2O). This concern relates to the theft and misuse of the gas. The major legitimate users of N_2O are the providers of healthcare. Healthcare accounts for approximately 90% of the market for this type of compressed gas, with dentists using more of this gas than hospitals.

Main oxygen storage tank

The main hospital oxygen storage tanks at our nation's hospitals generally receive less than adequate protection, and are usually located in a rather prominent and easily accessible location on the campus. A typical level of protection for this tank is a chain link fence of insufficient height, with a padlock at the entry gate. If one could not crawl over the fence, a bolt cutter would easily cut through the fencing and most locks. Security considerations for central O_2 storage tank systems should include:

- Steel/iron fencing of at least eight feet in height with the base embedded in concrete. A seven-foot fence with barbed wire outriggers or concertina rolled barbed wire would be adequate; however, the aesthetics may not pass administration or some city/county ordinances.
- Night lighting of the area.
- Video surveillance.
- Strict access control, including card access with magnetic locking of 1,000 lbs. or higher.

Nitrous oxide tank storage

The abuse of N_2O, as an inhalant, has increased over the past few years. The illicit market for this gas has been especially popular at concert venues and college campuses. The illicit dealer typically fills balloons with the gas. The gas displaces air. As the inhaled gas concentration approaches 100%, the user achieves a brief sense of euphoria. Within seconds of reaching a 100% concentration of N_2O in the lungs, a person can stop breathing because of the depression of the central nervous system caused by N_2O in the user's lungs.[7]

The N_2O gas is generally stored in cylinders ranging in size from approximately two feet in height to over five feet in height. The storage of these cylinders requires a locked and tightly controlled level of access. It is important to store empty cylinders with the same level of security, as the residual amount left in the cylinder is also the subject of theft and abuse.

A Florida hospital experienced an incident in which four young people stole a cylinder of N_2O from the hospital gas storage area. The cylinder was opened in a vehicle with the windows closed. The result was that one of the four persons died from the inhalation of the gas.

FOOD AND NUTRITION SERVICES

Healthcare organizations big and small serve food every day to a large number of patients, staff and visitors. This includes the main cafeteria as well as satellite areas such as coffee carts, and other employee or visitor dining locations throughout the healthcare facility.

The process of purchasing, storing and preparing food products in such large volumes presents a wide array of opportunities for theft and misuse. It is important that access to the kitchen, food storage and related coolers, regardless of their location, should be strictly controlled at all times to best manage and prevent issues of theft. Security should be a resource and should be called upon to support the various service departments' security controls in terms of monitoring and investigating losses. As with many other operating departments, the implementation of a strict access control plan and strategically located video surveillance of cash-handling locations is absolutely necessary.

ADMINISTRATION AND EXECUTIVE SUITE

Hospital administration departments are often busy areas during normal business hours, and frequently find organizational leaders working in the department at all times of day and night, weekends and holidays. The area by its very nature can attract people who may not be pleased with hospital leadership regarding a care-related matter, or they may be a disgruntled employee. To foster positive employee and community relations, many administrators prefer to have their offices and the administrative suite accessible. Whatever the open access preferences may be, there should be a business hours schedule for open access to the administrative department that includes restricting access after nonbusiness hours. This allows for a secure environment to be created for staff working early in the morning, late at night or on weekends.

Healthcare leaders and administrative assistants alike should have offices and workstations equipped with strategically located duress buttons to obtain assistance in the event of emergency. Both should also be trained in basic aggression management techniques to help identify persons in a heightened emotional state while also learning skills to successfully de-escalate such disruptive behavior. The protection of sensitive information, both in electronic and paper format, is also a significant concern in these areas. An electronic access control system should be considered, along with the strategic placement of surveillance cameras.

MAIL ROOMS

In most healthcare facilities, the mail room is used to efficiently and centrally process incoming and outgoing domestic, international, overnight and priority mail, to meet the needs of facility occupants. Numerous manual operations, including the sorting, metering and inspection of mail, often take place. Since terrorists contaminated the U.S. mail stream in October of 2001 with anthrax, safety and security has become a central issue and concern for mail rooms of all industries.

The hospital mail room should be designed not only to promote the efficiency of mail process, but to establish a safe environment for workers. Security needs will vary among organizations in relation to their function, size, volume of mail and profile. A threat/vulnerability assessment and cost/benefit analysis should be performed.

The mail room should be located away from the healthcare facility's main entrances, areas containing critical services, utilities, distribution systems and other important assets. Ideally, the mail room is located at the perimeter of the building with an outside wall or window designed for pressure relief. An area near the loading dock is a preferred location for many organizations since this will allow the mail to travel directly to the mail room from the outside and minimize the impact that any potentially contaminated mail will have on the rest of the building.

Although many healthcare employees frequently visit the mail room to pick up mail, only a few employees should have direct access into mail room operations. Access should be restricted to prevent access by authorized staff and prevent theft and or contamination of mail. When designing the mail room, processing operations should be in an enclosed room with defined points of entry.

The mail room staff should also be trained in recognizing suspicious packages, both for potentially hazardous materials and explosive devices, and be fully conversant on the bomb threat response plan for the organization.

ROOF AREAS

An often-overlooked area of access control is the healthcare facility roof area. Each year there are patient deaths reported due to either falling off or jumping from hospital roofs. In most of these cases, the roof access points have not been controlled properly. Patients can become disoriented due to a number of medical conditions, and the issue of dementia is a major element of patient safety management. These roof accidents have involved both the inpatient and the outpatient. At one large Midwestern hospital, an outpatient of the dental clinic accessed the roof and fell to his death. He had been sent from the clinic to the pharmacy to get a prescription filled. At some point he lost his way and ended up in a building fire stairway. Once in the stairway, the only way out was the ground level. All ingress to the building from the stairway at all other levels was locked off. Instead of going down, the patient went up, eventually exiting on the roof through an unsecured roof hatch.

In another case a hospital patient on a regular medical/surgical floor was missing from his bed in the middle of the night. An immediate search of the hospital failed to locate the patient, who was in a hospital gown, as evidenced by his clothing being left in the room. The patient was found the next day where he had apparently fallen from the roof of the multilevel facility.

All roof access points must be locked 24 hours per day. The added protection of alarms and video surveillance is strongly recommended. In one instance, the local fire department insisted that a roof door required the free access of the fire department. In this particular case, the issue was resolved by installing a KNOX-BOX® at the door that permitted entry by the fire department. More than 9,000 U.S. fire departments, EMTs, and government agencies use the Knox key box system.

SECURITY AREAS OF CONCERN SPECIFIC TO THE ORGANIZATION

In this chapter we have briefly discussed some of the more obvious areas of concern of the security administrator. There are countless other areas that security must evaluate and support, such as front desk reception and volunteer desks, outpatient clinics, therapy units, satellite pharmacies and such. As the healthcare organizations add and delete specific services, and reallocate space, there is a need for constant security risk assessment and changes in the delivery of security services.

REFERENCES

1. Health Information Privacy. *Breaches Affecting 500 or More Individuals*. U.S. Department of Health and Human Services; 2014. Retrieved June 28, 2014 from http://www.hhs.gov/ocr/privacy/hipaa/administrative/breachnotificationrule/breachtool.html.
2. Ponemon Institute. *Third Annual Benchmark Study on Patient Privacy & Data Security*. 2012, December. Retrieved June 28, 2014 from http://www2.idexpertscorp.com/assets/uploads/ponemon2012/Third_Annual_Study_on_Patient_Privacy_FINAL.pdf.

3. Goodin D. *Feds: Hospital Hacker's 'Massive' DDoS Averted*. The Register; 2009, July 1. Retrieved July 3, 2009 from http://www.theregister.co.uk/2009/07/01/hospital_hacker_arrested.
4. Ko C. *HK Hospital Authority Steps Up Patient Data Security*. Computerworld; 2009, May 8. Retrieved May 8, 2009, from http://news.idg.no/cw/art.cfm?id=21CB162A-1A64-67EA-E489C05803968C27.
5. Renewed Violence by Animal Rights Activists Who Target Research Labs. *Hospital Security and Safety Management* 1999;**20**(4):13.
6. Renewed Violence by Animal Rights Activists Who Target Research Labs. *Hospital Security and Safety Management* 1999;**20**(4):14.
7. Nitrous Oxide Issues and Incidence of Abuse. Compressed Gas Association Foundation Website. Retrieved November 6, 1997 from http://cganet.com/page37.htm.

CHAPTER

PARKING AND THE EXTERNAL ENVIRONMENT 23

Medical center parking areas, whether surface lots or multilevel structures, are often scary and downright dangerous places. The random shooting death of a police officer in Wilmington, North Carolina as he and his wife were leaving the hospital at the close of visiting hours; the critically injured woman in Omaha, Nebraska who was shot in a medical center parking lot by an assailant who was attempting to steal her purse; the hospital parking attendant in Philadelphia, Pennsylvania who was shot to death during an armed robbery; and the healthcare office worker in Indianapolis, Indiana who was locked in the trunk of her vehicle while the assailant drove her vehicle out of the parking structure are all examples of tragic incidents occurring with great frequency.

The demand for medical center parking continues to increase drastically. The demand for more parking spaces has been driven to a large extent by the trend to expand outpatient services. The patient-to-bed census parking demand ratios are thus outdated for planning purposes. In addition, many benchmarks and tools previously utilized to project medical center parking needs have become marginally useful and basically obsolete. Even though parking needs and parking issues have always been a major concern for healthcare organizations, they frequently fail to receive proper planning processes, including providing necessary security safeguards. A parking survey conducted by a Colorado hospital revealed that every 100+ bed hospital in the state believed they had an insufficient number of parking spaces to meet their needs. Rarely does a healthcare organization have ample parking to meet peak parking demands.

Each healthcare organization has its own identity in terms of product mix (types of services), market share, patient/visitor/staff composition, and degree of public transportation, which are all basic factors in determining parking space needs. The control of parking is a major activity for medical care facilities. This responsibility is sometimes considered to be within the purview of the security function, and at other times is assigned elsewhere in the organization. The context of parking control does not always include the necessary elements of protection. Some argue parking control is not a true function of security and should be a separate area of facility services.

All "parkers" want to park as close as possible to their intended destination. As facilities grow and change, the demands for parking change. It is not necessarily only the number of parkers but also convenience that makes control difficult. Many healthcare organizations periodically undergo major relocations of entrances and services. Such changes often create a new "front door," and parking needs change as a result. In designing parking accommodations, the following is a basic general priority listing:

- Handicapped parking (required by law)
- Emergency services (patients/transporters)
- Ambulatory patients with impaired mobility
- Outpatients
- Clinic patients
- Delivery drivers

- Visitors
- Staff (including physicians, volunteers, and physician office staff)
- Vendors and educational program attendees.

Despite the rather low parking priority for medical center staff, they account for 60 to 70% of the parking needs.[1] The protection of people and property on medical center property, including parking areas, is a major security responsibility. This protection responsibility includes preventive patrols, escorts, response to calls for services, investigation of security-related incidents, and physical security and remote video monitoring.

The parking accommodations of different healthcare facilities present unique control and protection situations. One constant factor is there are never enough parking spaces. The shortage of spaces is most acute during the day of a traditional work week, when employee staffing is at its high point, and clinics and outpatient services are in full operation. The most acute shortage is when dayshift employees are still at work and the arriving second shift must find parking spaces. Once the day shift leaves, there are generally an adequate number of parking spaces available.

Since the security department is often responsible for enforcing parking regulations, it receives the brunt of employee, visitor, and patient dissatisfaction, with the real or perceived lack of parking facilities. Unfortunately, this dissatisfaction with parking has a direct negative effect on the image of security and the entire organization. In addition to enforcing parking regulations to effect orderly use, the security effort is concerned with the ever-growing number of assaults, motor-vehicle thefts, break-ins and incidents of vandalism that occurs in parking areas. Numerous major lawsuits against medical centers allege inadequate parking area security. Litigation can result in punitive as well as general damage awards. In Pittsburgh, Pennsylvania, the security in parking structures became such an issue, the city enacted an ordinance mandating certain security provisions. The law covers any structure that charges guests, employees, or the public to use a parking space. The law, enforced since 1985 by the Bureau of Building Inspection, requires the following:

- A uniformed security guard must patrol all levels of the structure once every 30 minutes, unless detained for security reasons
- Patrols must be verified by activating a recording device on each level
- Emergency communication devices must be installed on each level
- Lighting must project a minimum of five foot-candles in all areas
- Emergency phones must be installed in elevators
- Directional arrows must be painted on walls to indicate exits and elevators.

Since the implementation of this parking structure ordinance, the complaints from users have been reduced, and the wave of assaults on parkers has been virtually eliminated. Perhaps one of the strictest parking garage security laws in the country is in effect in Minneapolis, Minnesota. The law's requirements for security became effective in 1990 and have proven to be very effective in terms of public safety.[2]

The IAHSS, in its healthcare security design guidelines, has developed specific recommendations to be followed when designing or renovating parking facilities or the external campus environment that address the security of parking facilities, promote efficient resource management while providing the warm, welcoming environment expected from healthcare facilities. The design principles for parking and the external environment are discussed in greater detail in Chapter 17, "Security Design Considerations for Healthcare." The IAHSS has also developed a specific Healthcare Security Guideline for Parking.

07.05 PARKING (GENERAL)

Statement

Healthcare Facilities (HCF) will incorporate general protection principles in their parking areas to maintain a positive perception of personal safety by employees, visitors and patients and provide a reasonable level of security for all constituents of the HCF.

Intent

a. Employee parking, including after-hours staff, should be separate from visitor parking. Employee vehicles should be readily identifiable utilizing a defined parking management plan. Additional parking considerations should be provided for those working during non-traditional hours.

b. Convenient parking should be designated for Emergency Department patients and visitors.

c. Lighting provides a means of continuing, during hours of darkness, a degree of protection approaching that maintained during daylight hours. To be effective, protective lighting should act as a deterrent and render effective recognition of persons and activities possible.

d. Physical protective barriers can help restrict or channel access. Physical protective barriers should be placed throughout the site to minimize the likelihood of damage by vehicles to pedestrians, sensitive equipment and structures and not obstruct the view or hinder vehicle operation. Physical barriers can be augments with motion sensors and video surveillance.

The manipulation of landforms, integration of water features, raised planters, vegetation, changes in elevation of paved areas, fences, a wide range of street function, site elements and amenities (bollards, benches, flagpoles, kiosks, etc.) should be implemented.

Open sight lines should be maintained to minimize potential places of concealment.

e. Traffic patterns, road network capabilities, and vehicle capacity should be analyzed periodically. Traffics obstacles should be positioned near entry points to slow traffic and offset vehicle entrances from the direction of a vehicle's approach to force a reduction in speed. The number of access roads and entrances to a site should be minimized (some entrances can be closed and secured during non-peak periods). Designated entry for service and delivery vehicles should be designed away from high risk buildings. Emergency vehicles should be provided unimpeded access to the facility.

f. Pedestrian access to public entrances should not be impeded by vehicular access or disrupted along sidewalks or other defined walking corridors from parking areas.

g. The location and use of video surveillance in parking areas should be based on a security risk assessment. Consideration should be given to the following:

1) Entry points to the parking lots

2) Vehicle checkpoints

3) Emergency communication devices located in parking areas

Care should be used to select the appropriate video surveillance equipment and lenses that will provide the desired image results. Consideration should be given to lighting, both natural and artificial, so as not to interfere with the camera coverage or view.

h. Emergency communication ("HELP") devices can add to the safety and security of parking areas. Consideration should be given to strategic placement of emergency communication devices that are highly visible along pedestrian walkways and parking areas.

i. Signage should be used to provide security awareness in parking areas while also serving as psychological deterrence to crime and other negative behavior. Way-finding signage should be used to guide patients and visitors to their campus destination and back to their parked vehicle.

j. Employees and staff should be educated on their personal safety awareness in parking areas. Hospital staff working in parking areas, e.g., parking attendants, valet, cashiers, and maintenance personnel, should be active in contributing to the safety and security of the area.

k. Scheduled and unscheduled security patrols should be provided by the HCF to provide escorts and serve as a visible deterrence to crime and other negative behaviors.

Continued

07.05 PARKING (GENERAL)—cont'd

References / General Information

- Illuminating Engineering Society of North America, Security Lighting Committee, Guideline for Emergency, Safety and Security, 2011.
- National Institute of Justice, Crime Prevention Through Environmental Design in Parking Facilities, April 1996, www.ncjrs.gov/pdffiles/cptedpkg.pdf.

See Also

- IAHSS Healthcare Security Guideline #04.04 – Video Surveillance
- IAHSS Healthcare Security Guideline #06.01 – General Staff Security Orientation and Education
- IAHSS Security Design Guidelines 01. Parking and the External Environment

Approved: June 2010
Last Revised: November 2012

TYPES OF PARKING AREAS

Parking areas can generally be categorized as street parking, surface (at grade) lots, freestanding structures, and structures that are physically connected to healthcare facilities, plus numerous delivery and emergency vehicle short-term parking spaces. Although the application of security safeguards will vary depending on the type of parking, the objectives are the same:

- Establish a user-friendly feeling
- A high level of safety in both perception and reality
- Property protection
- Expedite the patient care mission of the organization.

STREET PARKING

Parking on side streets around the medical care facilities presents a security challenge. This parking is on public streets, and is generally outside the realm of the organization's protection responsibility. In a practical sense, however, persons who are assaulted and vehicles that are broken into on these side streets negatively affect the healthcare organization. It is not uncommon for security to escort employees or visitors to their vehicles, which are parked off facility property. Security escorts should, however, be restricted to a maximum of one block, and this restriction should be strongly upheld by the organization. When security officers are more than one block from the property, they are not providing a visibility at and around the facility, surveillance, or maximum response capability. This extended escort service may help one person to the detriment of others.

Street parking can cause community relations problems in addition to protection problems. Neighboring home owners generally resent cars parked along their streets all day, because they restrict homeowner use and bring a certain amount of congestion and litter. The homeowner generally faults the healthcare organization for the situation, since the organization is more defensible than just vehicles and people. Many communities surrounding the medical campuses have implemented "permit parking" or "two-hour" parking limits, enforced by the local police department, to minimize street parking by employees and visitors to the facility.

SURFACE PARKING LOTS

Surface parking lots are slowly disappearing from large city and urban medical centers. The cost of land, and the fact that many facilities are landlocked generally results in the construction of parking structures, when parking areas must be expanded or replaced. Security for surface lots generally consists of access control, emergency communication devices, fencing, lighting, security patrols, and observation posts. Enclosed observation posts, somewhat elevated, in the parking area, offer several advantages. Not only do they provide shelter for security officers, but they also present a visible security safeguard. Video surveillance is not widely used for surface lots because of its low cost/benefit ratio and limited span of view. When video surveillance is needed, pan-tilt-zoom cameras are most often used. Programmed on a digital patrol path, the cameras can be used to provide surveillance of the entire parking lot. The central monitoring station can also control the camera view during events that may occur in the parking lot. Of specific importance in surface lots is that landscaping be well placed and properly maintained, to eliminate hiding areas, reduced visibility, and reduced lighting levels.

PARKING STRUCTURES

As land values increase and the available land around healthcare organizations decreases, parking structures become a cost-effective alternative to surface lots. Modern structures can be designed to achieve the user-friendly atmosphere and produce a general feeling of security and safety. Among the desired design features are raised ceilings, extensive use of glazing materials, proper lighting, bright colors, legible signs, and the basic elements of physical security.

Parking structures provide concentrated parking, but at the same time they create certain security risks. Many such risks can be eliminated or minimized through proper security design, which should begin with the first architectural drawing. Architectural firms without security design experience should advise their clients, and take steps to obtain security advice. The basic security considerations for parking structures include conducting a security risk assessment and the following basic security safeguards:

- The structure should provide the maximum span of vision on the parking levels and should mitigate the negative aspects of interior support columns and dark corners.
- Visibility should be maximized into and within the parking structure, including locating elevators and stairs on the perimeter to allow natural surveillance from exterior public areas.
- Lighting should comply with the standards set forth by the Illuminating Engineering Society of North America (IESNA). This standard includes a 3 to 5 foot-candle lighting minimum throughout the structure. Entrances should have 10 foot-candles of lighting to make it a standout and increase visibility.[3] It is suggested that metal-halide or white-light sources be used, which provide reliable color recognition, increase the ability of witnesses to identify attackers and improve the clarity of visual imaging. The installation of lighting should take into consideration the failure rate of the various components of the system. At any given time, approximately 18 to 22% of the lighting system may be inoperative. Thus, the lighting standards should be exceeded by approximately 25% so minimum lighting levels are maintained. A common method to counteract the effect of burned-out lamps is to use several lamps in one luminary. In high-risk environments where malicious destruction may occur, it may be necessary to incorporate polycarbonate lenses to protect the luminaries. The interior of the structure should contain some light-colored surfaces (for example, supporting columns and walkway areas). Light-colored paint increases the effectiveness

of lighting and conveys a feeling of security. An important aspect of parking structure lighting is uniformity. Drivers and pedestrians should not experience passing from light to dark areas. There should be lighting in the parking stall and not just in the driving aisles. Another important lighting consideration is to reduce glare. Glare is a potential hazard for all drivers, but is particularly dangerous for senior citizens and others with impaired vision.

- Parking areas should be well maintained and clean. Many healthcare organizations will schedule periodic cleaning throughout the year to wash walls, clean off the dust and grime that collects on light fixtures, as well as add a new coat of paint to the walls and ceilings.
- Stairwells and elevators should be enclosed with appropriate glazing materials, to protect patrons from wind or inclement weather or an open design in moderate climates. Figure 23-1 demonstrates a parking structure with an external glass stairwell.
- Stairwells, walkouts, and traffic ingress/egress points should, whenever possible, open onto the facility's property, not the street.
- Elevators should be located near the main entrance so that patrons are highly visible to the public.
- Emergency ground level stairwell exit doors should be alarmed as part of the access control system.
- Emergency call stations should be connected directly to the security operations center or the facility's telephone operator. These devices are generally hardwired as part of the parking lot or structure construction with minimal cost. If such devices are to be installed in existing facilities, the feasibility and cost effectiveness of wireless systems should be explored. Call stations must be conspicuously marked in two different ways. First, they should be marked to be identifiable for their intended purpose and be able to be seen from great distances. A blue light is commonly mounted above the call station on both hospital and college campuses. Conspicuous signage is also recommended to inform parkers and point to emergency call stations. Second, the station should be prominently marked with a location, so callers can accurately describe their location to the dispatcher. Even though many such communication devices automatically show the caller's

FIGURE 23-1

Picture of a parking structure with external glass stairwell.

location at the answering point, it is still desirable to indicate the user's location on the device at the calling point. There are some systems that activate a strobe light when the communications device is activated. This activation is intended to scare away potential troublesome persons, and to visually indicate a clear destination path for responding security personnel. Many newer systems have also incorporated a video image capability, allowing the dispatcher to visually see the caller.

- Openings on the ground floor, large enough to allow people to climb through or to pass large objects through, should be eliminated. Decorative wire mesh or other barriers can be installed that meet the security objective, yet provide light and visibility.
- All entrances/exits should be capable of being closed (locked off) during low traffic periods or emergencies, including gates that prohibit pedestrians and vehicles from entering the structure. Figure 23-2 is a concept drawing of primary parking structure entrances/exits being internal to the hospital grounds with limited use of exiting onto the street at high traffic volume times.

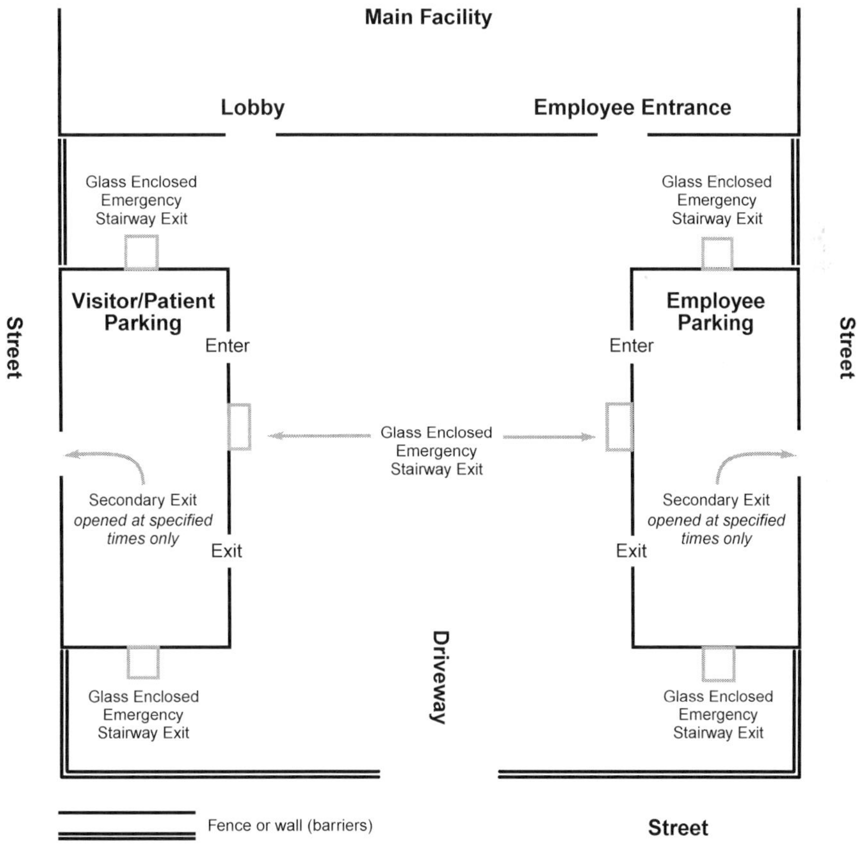

FIGURE 23-2

Example of the CPTED security principle of territorial reinforcement and clear lines of sight.

- Emergency release devices should be installed on stairwell emergency exit doors.
- Frequent security patrols should be scheduled. The frequency will depend on the time of day, local crime rate, number of reported incidents, location, and other security safeguards that have been installed within the structure.
- Cashier booths should be placed outside the structure so that cashiers have a better view of loiterers, stairwells, and general traffic.
- Covert parking area surveillance posts should be provided. Ideally, there will be one or two such posts on each level, allowing security to view any part of the structure. One-way glazed observation posts are generally used. All enclosed areas, such as equipment spaces and storage areas, provide an opportunity for observation posts with little additional cost. By simply including a small window, this added element of security can be achieved.
- Cost overruns in construction seem to be a standard. When cost overruns occur, security is generally the target of cost cutting. Even when planned security applications are eliminated, the proper design of the structure can accommodate later retrofitting at a more favorable cost.

Video surveillance

Many questions arise concerning the use of video imaging for parking security. The first question is whether a video surveillance system is needed. Sometimes it is decided that an area should be monitored before a clear need has been established. The use of video surveillance is somewhat prevalent in parking structures, yet many of these structures have various elements of design that don't lend themselves to this physical element of security. If used, an important first step is to determine the philosophy of use for the video surveillance system. A common philosophy is to design the system to monitor all entrances and exits and strategically locate cameras at elevator lobbies, stairwell exits, and other high-pedestrian traffic areas. Rarely is it a cost-effective use of resources to place cameras throughout the entire parking garage, on all floors, attempting to monitor all areas. With varying sizes of vehicles, many camera views are frequently blocked. If cameras are placed in the middle of the traffic lane, the camera view is typically limited only to viewing vehicular traffic in the parking garage, which has limited security value. As with all security design initiatives, a risk assessment should drive the use and implementation of video surveillance systems in parking areas.

There are four basic strategies for placing cameras in parking garages and lots, to maximize deterrent value and reduce car theft and vandalism events, and best protect users of the parking area:

1. Document every car and driver that enters and leaves the parking structure. Cameras should be visible and apparent.
2. Use cameras to cover all main driveways in and out on all floors. It is at turn points where most accidents occur. The recorded video can document who may be at fault.
3. Use cameras to monitor all down ramps. This is where the majority of vandalism incidents occur.
4. Place cameras in all stairwells that are visible and apparent. This is where assaults and other crimes against persons are most likely to occur.

As the cost of video analytics becomes more affordable, many healthcare organizations are employing this technology to help detect moving vehicles and people, especially detection of movement into restricted areas. These systems also allow for virtual tripwires and virtual perimeters. Another approach is to conduct remote video tours in which a security operator can monitor and patrol the parking area from afar. When equipped with a loudspeaker or other audible device, the monitoring agent can assist a needed visitor or warn a potential perpetrator that they are under surveillance. Some progressive security programs even use the cameras to conduct a video escort service, in which an operator virtually escorts a requesting party to their car using various cameras in the parking facility, communicating through loud speaker or a mobile device.

At St. John's Hospital in Livingston, the largest town in Lothian, Scotland, parking attendants have been issued wearable video surveillance cameras as part of the hospital's effort to prevent violence and aggression. The decision came after the facility acknowledged a rising number of attendants being subjected to verbal and physical abuse from angry motorists, as they fulfilled their role of freeing up parking spaces for patients and keeping emergency routes clear. One attendant was hit with a walking stick while another had a car driven at them. The camera, about the size of a name badge, is believed to deter aggressive and abusive acts and serve as a "silent witness" against those who break the law.[4]

All video surveillance systems require effective monitoring, regardless of the size of the system, and this is extremely difficult to achieve. Even when effective monitoring is in place, the reaction to monitored incidents is of equal importance. The response of security, police, or fire personnel must be quick and properly directed.

Opponents of video surveillance in parking garages point out that it does not give directions, it does not generate people-to-people public relations, and it does not respond to incidents. The live video monitoring or recording of an incident does little good without a quick response capability. The argument that video surveillance may help solve a crime is valid; however, a primary objective of the system is to contribute to the prevention of incidents and a positive perception of safety. The cost of a video surveillance system does not end with its purchase and installation. Systems require monitoring, maintenance, and ongoing replacement expenditures. From a liability standpoint, malfunctioning equipment must be repaired immediately, or alternative security safeguards must be implemented, until the system is up and functioning as designed. Exterior cameras are increasingly being installed and utilized to support the timely and safe recovery of eloping patients. These surveillance systems, if properly installed and applied, may offer additional protection to parking areas.

License plate recognition

Another type of technology that is quickly growing in its adoption rate is license plate recognition (LPR). There are two major approaches to using LPR in healthcare parking security. The first is to have it take and save a picture that might be used later in a forensic capacity. The second is to tie the LPR camera into a database in real time for matching vehicles with access cards. The most utilized application in healthcare is where the hospital wants to ensure that employees are not using patient parking lots. The challenge with LPR is that it requires a certain amount of light and a specific angle for the camera, as well as a database full of plate numbers to compare against the entering vehicle. LPR is more widespread in Europe where plates are uniform. Higher adoption rates by hospitals throughout North America is expected in the ensuing years.

Signage

Signage and graphics in parking areas serve several purposes, including control of parking, the providing of general information (directions), and security information. Information signage that orients parkers and enables them to move quickly in and out of the parking area makes them less vulnerable to a security-related situation. Security signage indicating video surveillance of the area and the emergency call station's information signs will generally provide a greater feeling of safety. This security signage also serves as a crime deterrent.

Organizations may want to include signage that tells parkers to lock their vehicles and/or not to leave valuables in their vehicle. A sequel to the "locking" sign is notice to the parker that the organization is not responsible for lost, stolen, or damaged property. This type of signage is recommended, but may present a somewhat defensive attitude, and thus not have administrative support. Even without the locking/disclaimer signs, organizations should have a strong administrative policy that prohibits reimbursements, except in special circumstances.

PARKING SHUTTLE SERVICE

Some facilities that have been unable to increase campus parking capacity have instituted shuttle services to offsite parking facilities. This type of parking arrangement is generally directed to the employee, so that additional on-campus parking can be available to patients and visitors. Suitable parking areas are sometimes available near the facility, but too far for staff to walk or the exposure to a potential street crime is an unacceptable risk. Shuttle buses have proven effective for transporting employees to and from the work facilities. In the typical shuttle system, security department employees drive a passenger van or bus, at frequent intervals between the parking lot and the facility, during the early morning and late afternoon hours. The frequency of such service is reduced during the day. When an employee needs to leave during the middle of a shift, or is held over past the closing time of the lot, security is contacted and often a special trip is made for that employee, depending on the circumstances. This special shuttle trip is then utilized to provide a random security patrol of the parking area. Likewise, there must be arrangements made to accommodate random arriving staff. Organizations have tried many incentives to entice employees to use off-site parking areas, including:

- Comfortable waiting areas (heated and air-conditioned as appropriate)
- Complimentary coffee, rolls, and morning papers
- Coupons for free or reduced cost for food in the hospital cafeteria
- Weekly prize drawings
- Car washes while the vehicle is parked for the day for a reasonable fee
- Attended parking lots.

The main complaint of the use of a shuttle service is transportation waiting time. Thus, organizations must ensure that they have sufficient resources before embarking on a shuttle program.

One Midwest hospital asked employees to park in a church lot six blocks from the hospital and to walk to and from work. Instead of putting money into shuttle service resources and incentives, they paid employees to park in the offsite area. The program was oversubscribed by employees, and there was a continual waiting list for vacancies.

VALET SERVICE

The use of valet parking for healthcare patrons is not new, but it is growing. The shortage of convenient parking is the greatest stimulus to the valet parking system, but proponents also cite the marketing advantage of this program. Some organizations charge for valet parking; others offer the service free. West Virginia University Healthcare has a donation program where valet fees and tips are donated to its Children's Hospital and Cancer Center.[5]

The Ottawa Hospital in Canada has taken a different tack with valet-like service. In a program started at their Cancer Center, the organization established a "blue tie" ambassador at the hospital main entry. This well-dressed employee of the security program, sporting a blue bow tie, greets the driver as they arrive and escorts their patient passenger into a comfortable waiting area, while the driver parks the car. The ambassador waits with the patient until the driver returns. This program has been resoundingly popular as a patient-centric initiative.

Implementing a valet operation at a hospital requires more than just putting up a sign and placing a few attendants by the front door. Organizations that undertake a valet parking program should market to the community at large of the availability of the service to include an education initiative about the benefits of the service, in addition to providing adequate supervision, and verifying an appropriate level of insurance coverage for providing this type of operation. The hours of operation should be clearly stated, and the procedure for retrieving vehicles after hours should be established. Security often becomes involved in the after-hours retrieval of vehicles.

TYPES OF PARKERS

Those who use facility-provided parking can be divided into several distinct categories, including day-shift employees, afternoon shift employees, nightshift employees, outpatients, inpatients, physicians, visitors, and vendors or outside service representatives. Despite flexible scheduling and the use of 10- and 12-hour shifts by various hospital departments, there is still a discernable day-, afternoon-, and night-shift demand for parking. The most common approach is to assign each category of parker to a specific parking area. During the day, the nearest parking is generally assigned to outpatients, physicians, service representatives, and visitors, due to their short-term use of parking space. Whether appropriate or not, physicians usually demand and receive special attention when it comes to parking.

AFTERNOON-SHIFT EMPLOYEES

The afternoon-shift employees are the ones who are most affected by the inadequacy of parking space, because the day shift is still on duty when they arrive. A common solution is to designate a special "3 to 11" lot (named for the hours of the typical afternoon shift), which is opened approximately an hour before the afternoon shift reports for work. Entry to this lot is generally controlled by a security officer, unless automatic controls are installed. This lot, which is vacant during the morning hours, can also be used to accommodate people attending morning meetings and appointments, but must be tightly controlled to assure that these temporary parkers have cleared the lot by the required time.

If the 3 to 11 lot is not adequate to accommodate all afternoon personnel, the organization should consider placing designated employees in the physician's parking lot. In most facilities, the peak time for physicians is in the morning, before they go to their offices. Of course, not all open spaces should be used by second-shift employees, because some physicians stop by the facility after their office hours. It should be noted that the relatively new concept of the "hospitalist," or dedicated physician, position at most hospitals has reduced the number, frequency, and need for private physicians to make regularly scheduled hospital rounds.

The fact that afternoon-shift personnel may return to their cars late at night presents special security vulnerabilities. For safety reasons, it is desirable that shift employees park together. Maximum security officer coverage in the parking lots is advisable during late night and early morning shift changes.

LATE-NIGHT–SHIFT EMPLOYEES

Late-night–shift employees generally have many places to park and, when left to select their own options, may create a fragmented parking configuration. Facilities that staff two shifts per day (usually 7 a.m.–7 p.m. and 7 p.m.–7 a.m.) can create some shortage of staff parking, again due to oncoming shift staff arriving before the off-going shift vacates their spaces. There should be a designated area for these employees, which is typically as close as possible to the designated facility night entrance(s). By concentrating these employees and their vehicles into a specific area, a maximum amount of protection for both employees and vehicles can be provided.

AUTOMATED CONTROLS

An electronic, card-activated gate is considered to be cost-effective for parking areas with as few as 20 spaces. The use of radio frequency technology provides a hands-free control system with card "reads" of 10–14 feet. Automatic gates with a minicomputer offer many control features, including the ability to set time parameters for card use, to invalidate a card at the output unit, and to provide data on the attempted use of invalidated cards. In addition, some systems render cards invalid once they have been used to enter the parking area until they are used to exit. This feature, known as "anti-pass back," prevents one card from being used by several people. Card-activated gates are predominantly used at the entry and exit points of parking areas. The card-activated device can also be used within the parking area itself to reserve and control an area for valet parking, afternoon staff, or physicians. In addition, the parking card can be used to provide entry to locked physician and staff facility entrances. Active anti-pass back systems can lead to congestion at exit points, however, sometimes causing considerable delays for exiting parkers stuck in lineups, further increasing frustration with the parking, and often the security program.

TRAFFIC FLOW AND SPACE ALLOCATION

In determining traffic flow and space allocation, the trend toward small vehicles is both an advantage and a disadvantage. When most vehicles were the same size, parking spaces could also be uniform. This limited the number of available spaces, but it made space allocation much simpler. Today the size of the space needed for small vehicles and the width of the traffic aisles can be reduced. The challenge is to determine how many spaces of each size are required at a given time for a particular parking lot, or whether certain areas should be designated for all large cars and trucks, or all small cars. Not only are one-way traffic lanes with angled parking expedient, but they are also safer than straight, or 90-degree, parking. The difficulty of parking in a space angled at 90 degrees, and the excessive size of the traffic lanes required, can make this type of design unsatisfactory. During periods of low demand, it is recommended that certain parking lots, sections of lots, or parking structure floors be closed off. This improves the safety of people walking to or from their vehicles. Naturally, the closed areas should be those that are the greatest distance from the facility entry/exit point. The more concentrated the parking, the greater the number of people going to and from vehicles, which to some extent deters assaults, vandalism, and break-ins. In addition, by closing lots or sections, the security patrol area is reduced, allowing a more concentrated preventive patrol in the occupied parking areas.

PAY FOR PARKING

Recent trends have favored pay for parking at medical care facilities. Many facilities that have charged visitors for some time have now decided to charge everyone who parks in their lots. Visitors are generally the first to be charged parking fees, and physicians are generally the last. When the pay for parking program is the responsibility of the security department, security can be transformed from an overhead cost to an income-producing department. LifeBridge Health Systems in Baltimore instituted a pay for parking program that helps fund much of the cost of operating the security program from parking revenues. Roger Sheets, director of security for LifeBridge, transitioned the health systems parking program from an average annual loss of $250,000, to making over $700,000 in profit. The outpatient and visitor parking areas produce the most revenue because of their high turnover. The method of collecting parking fees should be closely examined. For employee parking, a monthly fee can be deducted from the payroll checks at relatively little administrative cost. The visitor lots can be controlled by automatic equipment, which has a high initial cost, but may prove economical over a short period of time.

The decision to use personnel to collect parking fees should be carefully evaluated, as theft of funds by the cashier appears to be the rule rather than the exception. In addition, providing for accounting controls and backup personnel in case of absences can prove much more costly than automatic equipment. The parking attendant cashier does, however, provide an element of safety for both people and property. The presence of an attendant is also a public relations resource, assisting parkers with directions and other courtesy assistance. The process of collecting parking fees at the point of service (in the lot or structure) represents a major vulnerability with the risk of a robbery. In this respect, attendants should be protected by appropriate glazing, a communications device, proper lighting, security patrols, and regularly scheduled and frequent pickup of cash receipts. Cashless exits and other automatic pay equipment are often used to combat the costs and vulnerability of dedicated staffing at pay booths. Stringent controls should be established regarding the collection of money from the machines, and these controls should be audited frequently. In some jurisdictions, electronic parking equipment now accepts only credit card transactions, reducing the vulnerability to robbery and theft associated with cash collection.

PARKING SYSTEM VIOLATORS

Parking violators present a series of control problems. Fire lanes must be designated and patrolled to ensure that vehicles do not block the lanes, lots must be checked to ensure compliance with the parking plan, and short-term parking areas (such as delivery parking and parking just outside of the emergency department) must be constantly monitored. Most security departments issue parking violation or safe parking reminder notices to help control nonconforming parking. In most cases, these violation notices have only a minimal effect on regulating parking. Only when hospital administration takes a strong support role will the violation notice be a highly productive tool. See Chapter 5, "Managing the Basic Elements of Healthcare Security," Figure 5-6, for an example of a parking notice.

Various other methods of increasing severity may be necessary to correct parking abuses. It can be said that the certainty of enforcement is a determinant of the parker paying for parking. These methods include city parking tickets, immobilization devices, and the towing of vehicles. The immobilization device, sometimes known as the "Denver boot," a wheel immobilization device, has proved effective in many programs. Noted in Figure 23-3, the boot forces the violator to report as directed, and thus the organization can exert a high degree of control. Vehicle towing is always the last resort but is an effective mechanism to gain compliance. There is, however, an abundance of vehicle towing episodes that have gone wrong in one way or another.

Warning letters and follow-up by department supervisors are common procedures for dealing with employee violators. In one system, the first violation earns the employee a warning notice, and subsequent violations result in successively higher fines, which are collected through automatic payroll

FIGURE 23-3

The Denver boot wheel immobilization device.

deductions. This system works; however, again strong administrative support is required to implement and manage this type of parking patrol program. The Shoalhaven Hospital in Australia has trained and registered their security staff to be able to issue parking infringements, in addition to their role of monitoring safety in the parking areas. The extra powers are designed to act as a deterrent, as well as encourage employees and visitors to park in their assigned parking areas to improve parking conditions on campus.[6]

Assigning the parking enforcement function to security may have a negative impact on both the public and campus personnel view of the security program. Depending on security staffing levels, time spent on parking enforcement may also impact on site safety and service levels. For these reasons, many security programs position themselves and their security staff well away from the function of parking enforcement.

SUSPICIOUS OR ABANDONED VEHICLES

Suspicious or abandoned vehicles located in or near hospitals or healthcare facilities pose a potential threat that warrant immediate attention by security staff and leaders. Such vehicles may contain explosives or other hazardous materials, intended to damage a facility and harm individuals. Potential indicators of suspicious vehicles, as identified by the U.S. Department of Homeland Security Counterterrorism Division in a brief released in 2010, include:

- Unauthorized or unattended vehicles parked for prolonged periods of time
- Arrival of unexpected or unfamiliar trucks or delivery vehicles
- Vehicle painted or outfitted to mimic an official government vehicle
- Abandoned vehicles with the following characteristics:
  - Parked in a no-parking zone
  - License plate missing, forged, temporary or out of state
  - Altered, missing or hidden VIN plate beneath windshield
  - Overloaded or modified to handle heavier than normal loads, additional storage space or increased fuel capacity
  - Excessively darkened or tinted windows or temporary window coverings that block viewing of vehicle's interior
  - Leaking fluid
  - Rental vehicle
  - Contains drums, barrels, or other bulk containers
  - Evidence of theft, such as damaged locks or missing windows.

TECHNOLOGY AND PARKING CONTROL

The use of computer technology is becoming commonplace in the administration of parking control systems. Software programs are readily available that permit tracking of parking violations and efficient issuing and control of parking permits. Once the database of information is established, the various programs allow a multitude of search capabilities. In addition to helping manage the day-to-day program, the automated system allows for the periodic production of activity and planning reports.

REFERENCES

1. Catherine Quayle. Space Odyssey. *Health Facilities Management* June 1996;**30**.
2. Jeremy Travis. *Crime Prevention Through Environmental Design in Parking Facilities*. National Institute of Justice, Research in Brief; April 1996.
3. Randall Atlas. CPTED for Parking Lots and Garages. *Security Technology & Design* October 2008:42–6.
4. Healthcare Facilities Today. *Hospital parking attendants wear CCTV cameras for own safety*. 2014, February 14. Retrieved July 13, 2014 from http://www.healthcarefacilitiestoday.com/posts/Hospital-parking-attendants-wear-CCTV-cameras-for-own-safety-Safety-and-Security–4060.
5. Staff writer. WVU Healthcare valet service donates tips. *State Journal.com* 2012, January 8. Retrieved January 12, 2012 from http://www.statejournal.com/story/16467462/wvu-healthcare-valet-service-donates-tips.
6. Crawford Robert. More hospital parking. *South Coast Register* 2014, July 13. Retrieved July 21, 2014 from http://www.southcoastregister.com.au/story/2413859/more-hospital-parking/?cs=202.

CHAPTER

NONACUTE FACILITIES AND OFF-CAMPUS PROGRAMS AND SERVICES

24

In this chapter, the main focus of discussion pertains to security of medical facilities, programs and services that are not located on a main hospital campus. The chapter will not examine issues related to the literally thousands of physicians' and dentists' clinics and offices operating in all countries, though these are foundational as the primary care component of the healthcare continuum. It should be noted that these clinics and offices have faced and are continually exposed to the potential of experiencing major security incidents. Physicians being assaulted in their offices and even murdered are all too frequent occurrences. In June 2009, Dr. George Tiller was shot to death at his church by a gunman who was apparently upset that Dr. Tiller performed late-term abortions. Anti-abortion terrorism and violence have resulted in the killing of three other physicians since 1993, as well as two clinic employees, one security officer and a clinic escort. It is reported that, following the homicide of Dr. Tiller, U.S. marshals were dispatched to protect doctors and clinics that may have been at risk.[1]

Healthcare organizations are expanding their services beyond the traditional hospital campus boundary. The issues related to the delivery of care and other health services must be given adequate consideration by the healthcare security program. These rapidly expanding nontraditional settings such as stand-alone emergency departments, ambulatory surgery centers, long-term care facilities, urgent care centers, primary care physician offices and a host of many other settings all require a close examination and focus on the risks and challenges facing each environment. For the healthcare security industry, having spent more than 40 years learning the complex world that is the acute care hospital, an emerging challenge is learning this new frontier that has the potential to dominate the healthcare landscape in the coming years, as baby boomers hit the healthcare system with millions more needing care. Increasingly, health systems and healthcare organizations are offering services across the full spectrum of care, to include public health, long-term/residential care, home care and home health, environmental health and a variety of community-based services, often integrated with their traditional acute care/hospital services.

For those serving the protection needs of the healthcare industry, working in these organizations often stretches the continuum of care outside of the traditional hospital walls, creating challenges to security and safety that are not often experienced in the hospital environment. For instance, long-term care has the issue of care residents assaulting and even killing other residents; staff in these facilities are at risk of assault from residents at a rate comparable to those working in a mental health setting. Conversely, incidents of abuse or neglect of residents by staff remain a growing concern. Long-term care residents, increasingly beset by dementia, may also wander from these facilities, introducing patient care and community concerns.

In home care and home health, lone workers are facing risks in client homes that have led to workers assaulted and killed or, in other instances, clients fall victim to abuse, fraud or theft at the hands of those delivering health services. Workers have been the victims of theft, or even lost confidential health information related to their community-based clients. Centralized off-campus supply warehouses, including pharmacy warehouses, have been victimized by robbery or internal theft and other concerning security events. Public health staff deliver services, often in clinics located in inner city high crime areas, or even on the streets of these areas, to the homeless and other members of these communities.

In short, many of the risks and vulnerabilities managed by hospital security programs are also found in the nonacute facilities, programs and services. Aggression, disruptive behavior, drug seekers, internal theft, and emergency response to a variety of situations are all prevalent in these off-campus settings. However, unlike the acute sector, where most security programs have developed and been built around an environment now well understood and often with good design and process controls in place, the healthcare sector serving the community has few such controls. For modern-day security administrators, increasingly as responsible for the safety of the home care or hospice worker as they are the emergency department nurse, they will find that traditional hospital-based security solutions are not as viable in these settings that are much less controllable.

THE NEED FOR OFF-CAMPUS FACILITIES AND SERVICES

Once upon a time, the hospital served as a one-stop shop for all health services in a community. It served as a place where the elderly spent their last months or years, even if not acutely ill, where ailments minor or major were treated and where the community gathered in the event of a disaster when folks were temporarily displaced from their homes. But as the cost of healthcare continues to increase beyond the rate of inflation and with advances in medical treatment, particularly through technology and pharmaceuticals, there has been clear movement with hospitals to treat only the most acutely ill.

For cancer care, as an example, the U.S. Oncology Network in 2013 reported the costs of treatment received in hospital outpatient clinics as 47% higher than if delivered in physician-run community clinics.[2] A 2011 report delivered by the Canadian Institute for Health Information (CIHI) suggests seniors account for 85% of patients in hospital beds who could be receiving care elsewhere, and notes the cost of delivering the same care to a senior in the community is about one quarter of the hospital-based stay.[3] When these cost factors are coupled with the rapid increase in hospital-acquired infections among patients, there is little wonder why community-based treatment alternatives are rapidly emerging.

That same CIHI report also warns ominously of the pending impact of the baby boomers on the healthcare systems of the western world. This message echoed an earlier 2007 report by the American Hospital Association (AHA), discussing the massive impact of the baby boomers on healthcare. The report states the first of these baby boomers—those born between 1946 and 1964—turned 60 in 2006 and represent about one-third of the U.S. population, with the potential to impact healthcare for years to come.[4] In a 2007 article, a spokesperson for the AHA, speaking on the subject of chronic illnesses, said "...we've got technology and medications that have permitted us to manage them and keep them functional much longer but we haven't developed a delivery system to do that." He added "...hospitals need to be forming community-based collaborations and strengthening outpatient services."[5]

In today's delivery of healthcare services, we can then see more and more healthcare organizations expanding their clinical care programs beyond the main medical center campus. In addition to the broad drivers of cost and the heavily utilized acute care system, the rationale for some of this expansion is to deliver some specific health services directly to different communities and neighborhoods, build consumer market share, and make care more accessible and more convenient for the patient in the community. Conversely, some treatment programs, services and facilities have been moved off campus as the result of new or growing treatment programs, which require additional space not readily available on the main campus. One such solution to creating more space for these expanding needs is to move certain functions or services off campus that may not need basic diagnostic or clinical support, which is only available at the main facility. Examples of healthcare treatment programs that can function as stand-alone units would be different and varying types of therapy, urgent care centers, sleep clinics, dental clinics, and routine medical checkup and preventive medicine clinics.

An example of a healthcare organization with multiple off-campus locations is the highly acclaimed Children's Hospital Colorado (CHC) located in Aurora, Colorado. Their off-site patient service units are principally located throughout the Denver metropolitan area, with one facility located as far away as Pueblo, Colorado, which is 90 miles from Denver. These facilities collectively are referred to as Children's Hospital Colorado Network of Care. The "network" currently consists of 12 operating treatment centers ranging from a small daytime therapy care unit to 24-hour care centers. CHC has developed a coordinated and integrated security program for these network facilities through the efforts of the corporate Project and Property Manager, who is especially knowledgeable relative to security requirements for such facilities. While there is always work to be done, and new goals being formulated, the CHC manager has provided leadership toward providing a high level of security in protecting patients, staff, and property as an efficient and coordinated systems approach.

Nonclinical healthcare departments or functions are also prime candidates to be moved off campus to create additional clinical space or to occupy less expensive space. Examples of such support departments or programs could be staff training facilities, certain human resources functions, planning and marketing, accounting, health system administration and general supply storage areas. One of the drawbacks to locating some of these support functions off campus is the logistics of moving staff back and forth between the main campus and the off-campus locations. This staff logistical transportation problem, at least to some degree, does not exist when the off-campus service is within the same neighborhood as the clinical care facility. These patient care clinical services do require a well-organized and planned courier and supply service; however, staff typically does not have a general need to access the main facility on a routine basis.

In some large health systems and organizations, this model has been increasingly extended to allow for only the services directly involved in the day-to-day delivery or support of care to be based within the hospital. Often in this model, the centralized supply facility and pharmacy is responsible for "feeding" the hospital with necessary equipment and supplies on an "on demand" basis. This model often has a small inpatient pharmacy and storage area in place at each hospital, typically with a much smaller presence than what historically is required in a traditional hospital setting. The tremendous growth of information technology (IT) services in healthcare has also resulted in the creation of a model similar to that described in the warehousing and pharmacy functions. The centralized IT support center located off campus is often coupled with resources assigned to a hospital on a dedicated or as-needed basis. Health system executives and support groups such as planning, marketing and business development are often part of this "hospital decanting" movement, as they can effectively function off campus, often with a site administrator providing individual hospital oversight. The space created by the decanting of these functions is repatriated into clinical and clinical support space as the hospital is positioned around the direct care of the patient.

For the security program and for security leaders, this movement has significant implications. First, they may be part of this movement away from occupying hospital space themselves. Like the other services previously described, particularly in large health systems, it may not be necessary for the corporate security leader and other members of the security support team to be located at a hospital. Investigators, design and technology managers and analysts are all examples of functions that need not be site-based. This is particularly cogent when the program has responsibility for multiple sites. Clearly security operations and supervision must be in place at the hospital site level, but not necessarily system oversight and management. These resources are an important part of organizational culture of the hospital community, but not necessarily on-site day-to-day.

The real challenge for the security program, however, is extending their responsibilities and expertise beyond the hospital campus. With clinical programs and others such as IT, pharmacy, HR, centralized stores, executive team and other support departments increasingly located outside of the secured hospital environment, the security program needs to be flexible and responsive to these risks, challenges and demands that are faced. This begins with a focused security assessment that identifies effective protection strategies for the environment.

OFF-CAMPUS SECURITY RISK ASSESSMENTS

The assessment of security needs and concerns for off-campus facilities, whether down the block or many miles away from the main facility, begins with a site inspection of the existing building and/or the review of new construction or renovation plans. The same approach and utilization of information sources should be used as when conducting the main facility security risk assessment. An additional element of review for lease space functions is to determine the security safeguards provided by the property owner as part of the lease agreement. All too often, these off-campus facilities are left on their own relative to security issues until a problem develops. The main facility security resources are then called upon to provide security.

As described in the *IAHSS Security Design Guidelines for Healthcare Facilities*, a security representative from the healthcare organization should conduct the security risk assessment and be involved at the earliest point in the process of any new design, renovation or review of a facility. While community facilities are not specifically delineated in these guidelines, the same principles apply with regard to the use of Crime Prevention Through Environmental Design (CPTED) methodologies, creating layers of protection.

A key component of the off-campus facility risk assessment process is a thorough understanding of the community in which the property is located. Neighboring businesses should be consulted for their experiences, especially where facilities share a building or space with nonhealthcare tenants. The deterrent provided by a good onsite security team and related processes and controls are unlikely to be in place in a community site. The security assessment must account for these differences.

Off-campus facilities should be a part of the main facility security program in all respects, with the exception of critical incident response. In an emergency, a public safety agency is the most likely first responder unless the facility has resourced an on-site security presence. In terms of communications, all incident reporting and physical security (including technology applications for access control and video surveillance) should be managed as if the off-campus facility were a functional unit within the main facility.

HOME HEALTHCARE (COMMUNITY PROVIDER SERVICES)

A major off-campus medical care service that does not require space (beyond minimal administrative space), but which is a growing component of the business of care, is home healthcare. The delivery of home healthcare services had its beginning in the early 1990s and grew quickly through the mid-1990s. Today, many hospitals and private agencies (both profit and nonprofit) are examining the future and the direction of their services. There is clear distinction between home healthcare and home care. Even in home healthcare, the definitions of service and the caregiver are not consistent or clear. In the U.S., in terms of state regulation, there are states that regulate home healthcare but not home care. States vary to a great degree on how they regulate the whole issue of home care, with Florida being one of the more progressive states in this regard. In other countries the distinction is similar with home health almost always regulated in some fashion, while home care may be more "hit and miss" with regard to formal requirements beyond business licensing.

The home environment sets up a new and different relationship between the caregiver and the patient. The patient is now in his or her familiar surroundings, while the caregiver is providing services outside the familiar organizational setting. This change of relationship and environment creates a whole different set of security issues and concerns for the patient, the caregiver, and the organization the caregiver represents. The IAHSS has created a basic industry guideline to help protect staff who provide home healthcare security.

06.02. HOME HEALTH PROVIDER (COMMUNITY PROVIDER SERVICES)

Statement

Healthcare Facilities (HCFs) providing home health services will develop a security plan to protect staff traveling into the community in the performance of their job duties.

Intent

- **a.** HCFs should have a risk assessment process in place which would allow home health staff to determine appropriate safeguards associated with a community visit. The risk assessment process may include a community crime assessment, previous history of the client and use of a location based threat assessment.
- **b.** Home health staff should be provided with education and training regarding risk identification and preventive safeguards. Training should include information and guidelines on security awareness, crime prevention and defensive measures. Training records should be maintained.
- **c.** HCFs should develop a communication process to protect home health staff. This should include proactive check in and checkout procedures which would allow staff to make contact during the shift to help ensure their safety. Cell phones, automated check-in procedures or GPS devices may be considered as appropriate, to facilitate this process.
- **d.** Security or appropriate escorts should be available to home health staff providing services in areas or situations deemed high risk or as individual situations warrant.
- **e.** Procedures should be in place for home health care staff to follow in the event of a security incident or a situation in which they have a concern for their safety or well-being.
- **f.** HCFs should have a process in place for responding to incidents or missed check-ins.

Approved: June 2008
Last Revised: October 2010
Last Reviewed: April 2013

PATIENT AT RISK

The caregiver is relatively independent of organizational supervision while in the home. Often, the patient cannot ambulate and therefore cannot provide a normal degree of surveillance of this "stranger in their home." This degree of caregiver independence can lead to a variety of security issues, including:

- Theft of patient property, including identity fraud
- Diversion of drugs
- Verbal and physical abuse toward the patient.

In one case, a home health aide was hired through After-Care Professional Nurses Registry of California to care for a 96-year-old person. Little did the family know that the caregiver was on probation after serving eight months for stealing more than $500,000 from two other people who had been in her care. In fact, the family only learned of the past conviction after filing a police report regarding their own theft of property by the aide. The firm was not a licensed home care agency because it called itself a registry instead of an agency. This firm was listed in the telephone directory as "Home Health Services" and was recommended by local hospitals.[6] A study of 150 cases from 32 states in which home care providers were found to have abused, neglected, or stolen from patients was conducted by *USA Today*.[7] Results of the study revealed that 73% of these cases involved theft, 19% involved violence (including murder and sexual abuse), and 15% involved behavior that put the patient at risk of physical injury. Nurses were involved in 6% of these cases, with the remaining 94% involving healthcare aides.

As more of these programs become part of larger health authorities and health systems, they have reaped the benefits of healthcare security professionals. Reports of theft from home health clients can be investigated by professionals providing the same service in the hospitals. Solid reporting, formal interviewing of suspects and even use of investigative tools such as covert surveillance cameras in the client home can have a deterrent effect on would-be thieves and abusers and lead to the detection and discipline and/or criminal prosecution of these individuals, who prey on vulnerable clients.

CAREGIVER AT RISK

The caregiver providing home healthcare is subject to a variety of risks in performing services, including:

- Automobile accidents
- Automobile theft and vandalism
- Attack by vicious animals
- Attack by the patient, family, or others present in the home
- Attack by neighbors or persons in the neighborhood
- False accusations including patient abuse and theft of property.

In February, 2000, a home healthcare nurse in rural Kansas was shot and killed while dialing 911 to report finding two bodies on the floor of a client's home. The nurse was apparently killed by the client's 23-year old grandson, arrested at the scene, for killing his father, another woman at the home, and the nurse. The client (patient) was unharmed.[8] In 2006, in Sunderland, England, a young 22-year-old home support worker was stabbed to death by a client in his home while conducting a home visit.

An independent review later concluded the worker should not have been sent alone to visit this client.[9] Also in the UK in 2014, a terrified home care worker broke her back jumping 20 feet from a bathroom window after a frightening attack by a client. Described as a "Freddie Krueger-style" attacker, the client tried to break down the locked bathroom door, screaming he would kill the 30-year-old worker.[10]

There have been many cases in which family members or friends have stolen property from a patient and then accused the caregiver of being responsible for the loss. This type of false accusation is particularly true when it involves cash, jewelry, and antiques. The motive for interfamily theft is quite prevalent when a patient is near death and family members are concerned about getting their "fair share" of the estate. In many other cases, unfortunately, staff have indeed stolen client property or, in other cases, befriended the client and reaped the benefits of free travel and other financial improprieties. This was the case in 2011, when a White Plains, New York home healthcare aide for an elderly couple was sentenced to four years in prison for crimes related to stealing their identities. She used the false identities to open several credit cards in the couples' names and racked up $73,000 in purchases for plane tickets, clothing and a down payment on a Porsche.[11]

SECURITY PRACTICES AND GUIDELINES

There are a number of security practices and guidelines that should be taken into consideration with regards to home healthcare.

Initial assessment of the home environment. Prior to the first home health visit, the agency should complete an environment assessment either by direct verbal conversation or telephone contact with the patient or close family member. This assessment should include inquiring about animals, other persons living in the home, medications, neighborhood crime/gang activity, and complete directions for finding the address and accessing the living unit.

First visit. If the initial assessment of the home environment presents significant danger signals, there should possibly be two caregivers making the first visit. This practice is difficult due to funding issues; however, the safety of the caregiver must take precedence over cost. An alternative may be tighter communication connectivity between the worker and the home care officer, or at least another worker. During the first visit, the caregiver should make an assessment relative to safety or other potential problems presented by the environment. This information should be noted in agency files for further references or for immediate follow-up. For example, should the patient or family openly display or talk about firearms, a safety awareness response is necessary.

Scheduling visits. It is always best to schedule home visits during daylight hours. This is not always possible, but should always be a goal. Physicians can sometimes regulate specified times of treatment when they are aware of caregiver safety issues. It is always a good idea to telephone the patient just before the visit as a courtesy and to find out whether there is some legitimate reason to reschedule the visit.

Preparing for the visit. Always wear name-badges and uniforms, where applicable, that clearly identify the healthcare agency. A cell-phone or two-way radio should always be part of the standard equipment carried into the patient's home. Caregivers should always leave supplies, equipment, and personal property not needed for the specific visit in the trunk of their vehicle. Vehicles should always be locked. Home care workers often carry medication, supplies, client files and devices holding patient information that must be carefully protected by the worker.

During the visit. Caregivers should always spend only the time necessary in a patient's home. Instincts are to be trusted and care should be terminated when danger signals are perceived. Suspending treatment is somewhat different than abandonment of care. Immediate termination of care is justified if there is violence or threats of violence during the visit. If there is to be a termination of care, there must be a reasonable notice depending on the needs of the patient and other resources available. Notice of termination of care should be in writing and hand-delivered to the patient. In some instances care may be continued subject to certain conditions being met—a client visit in a community clinic instead of their home, as an example.

Caregiver security escort. There are times when a caregiver must be provided a security escort for a home visit. There are two basic forms such a security escort can take. One is a uniformed and, in the U.S., generally armed security officer in a marked security vehicle. The escort may involve transporting the caregiver in the security vehicle or meeting the caregiver at the patient's address. In the case of the conspicuous security escort, the security officer generally remains outside but ready to respond if summoned by the caregiver. The second approach is to provide a security escort in street clothes or care agency uniform. In this case, the escort usually accompanies the caregiver into the living unit and is introduced as a team member. This type of escort normally involves an unarmed security officer.

In some jurisdictions after hours, these security escorts may take the form of a mobile security officer in a vehicle picking up the caregiver at her or his residence and transporting them to the client home. The security officer may stay in the vehicle, be positioned at the residence door or even be present in the client home, depending on the request of the care worker. When the visit is concluded, the care worker is transported back to their home by the mobile security officer.

Security education for the caregiver. It is absolutely essential that all home healthcare staff receive security training and education. This training must reinforce security awareness and practice without frightening the staff. The training should also teach caregivers how to avoid or defuse dangerous situations to include dealing with a threatening dog. Canine strategies often include assessing the dog's reaction and:

- Showing no fear
- Maintaining eye contact
- Never assuming the dog will not bite
- Having an attack plan; i.e., standing ground, use purse or other bag, backing away slowly
- Not startling the dog
- Calling the dog by name (if known)
- Never attempting to pet the dog

Professional caregivers are very focused on delivering a quality service and do not always assess the environment or perceive danger signs. In addition to formal training presentations, it is recommended each home healthcare agency develop safety and security policies to be distributed to each caregiver to guide their everyday activities. Information in this regard is identified in Box 24-1.

A good security practice is for home healthcare providers to be required to report to a predetermined member of the office staff upon reaching a specific destination. A supervisor or office staff member in turn is required to implement follow-up procedures in case they do not report in. It is important for a supervisor to know the schedule of the provider, and to be informed of any unscheduled stops. Many agencies provide field staff with cellular telephones to facilitate this process. The emergence of global

BOX 24-1 SECURITY STRATEGIES FOR HOME HEALTHCARE PROVIDERS

Home Healthcare Security Strategies

- Taking planned routes that are well-traveled streets—not taking shortcuts through unknown areas
- Utilize a reliable, well-maintained vehicle with ample gas supply
- Drive by the client's address for a short distance while assessing the neighborhood (i.e., suspicious vehicles or persons loitering)
- Park in the direction of travel you intend to use when departing from the visit
- Park so that your vehicle can be seen from the client's home whenever possible
- Always lock your vehicle and do not leave property exposed in open view
- Setting limits of behavior and knowing when to leave (i.e., presence of guns, knives or illegal drugs, excessively loud and abusive behavior, physical or sexually aggressive behavior)
- When leaving, have keys ready, lock doors immediately upon entering the vehicle and do not sit in the vehicle checking maps or preparing documentation
- Depart the neighborhood immediately, heading directly to the well-traveled street
- Note any vehicle that pulls out directly behind your vehicle when you depart

positioning systems (GPS) to track the movement and location of the caregiver's vehicle has provided another element in ensuring the protection and safety of the home healthcare provider.

In the UK, the National Health Service (NHS) has been very progressive in this area. Their "NHS Lone Worker Protection Service" was implemented in 2009 and won a National Personal Safety Award in 2010. This service provides lone workers, including home health workers, "…with a device or mobile application which they can activate discreetly when faced by a potentially violent or threatening situation, to call for help from their organization or the emergency services."[12] This approach allows duress-alarm–like connectivity between the worker and a monitoring function, replicating a system commonly used in a hospital in high-risk locations.

There will be additional safety practices depending on the agency, such as preplanned routes, emergency notifications, route deviation procedures, etc.

Home healthcare providers often carry a medical bag but rarely, if ever, narcotics. These bags include equipment, medical supplies, needles, syringes, and common medications. A number of agencies have returned to a more traditional nursing approach and provide their staff with a uniform. Although some home health professionals argue this practice brings more attention to the provider, many more believe this provides added protection because of the respect and authority given to medical personnel from the public.

OFF-CAMPUS PATIENT TREATMENT FACILITIES

The vast majority of off-campus patient treatment facilities do not operate on a 24/7 schedule. In fact, some facilities may only treat patients for a limited number of hours per day and some facilities are not open for service every day of the week. There are of course exceptions, such as an urgent care/day surgery facility with a limited number of inpatient beds. In this respect, there is a wide variation in needed security safeguards unique to the mission and operating environment of each facility.

It would be difficult to list all the different types of off-campus patient treatment facilities; however, some of the common types would be:

- General treatment and preventive services, such as general physicals, public health inoculations, prenatal activities and minor diagnostic procedures.
- Specialty clinics where visiting physicians/treatment technicians schedule follow-up treatment evaluations and services. Examples of these needed medical specialties would include cardiology, ENT, audiology, orthopedics, radiology, pulmonary, dermatology, and neurology.
- Ongoing therapy treatment such as physical, occupational, speech and orthopedic therapies.
- Day surgery procedures.
- Dentistry.

In addition to facility locations, there are mobile units that provide outpatient treatment and diagnostic procedures on a scheduled basis, as well as blood donor and health education types of community activities. In healthcare organizations where public health is a component of a larger health system that may include acute care, the security program may have responsibility for assessing risk and providing necessary protective measures for staff working in these areas. In a small UK study conducted in 2013 by community care workers, the findings concluded "social workers and care staff are as likely to be attacked in the office as they are on home visits."[13] For the healthcare security program responsible for the community sector, the challenges are myriad with solutions based on best practice not as readily available as they are in in-patient hospital settings.

As part of the movement to create space in hospitals for only the most acutely ill, outpatient surgery facilities have been built in many countries, expressly for the purpose of completing high volumes of relatively minor procedures, usually during the Monday–Friday business day, and sending the patients home the same day. With the involvement of professional healthcare security practitioners in design, these facilities often have a front of the house (the public) and back of the house (staff and patients) separation, thus allowing for access control and enhanced safety measures through design. At some sites, depending on risk, security staff may be present during peak periods to ensure patient and staff safety, while others may have security on site outside of business hours to protect the facility and medical equipment. Still others have around-the-clock security.

RESPONSIBILITY FOR SECURING OFF-SITE FACILITIES (CLINICAL AND NONCLINICAL)

The responsibility for providing security of patients, property, staff, and visitors at off-campus healthcare organization facilities is the primary responsibility of the senior manager of each facility. In some cases, a senior manager will be on-site at the facility on a full-time basis. In others, the senior manager will be responsible for multiple facilities and may have other assigned duties and responsibilities. The senior manager should not have full authority (autonomy) in deciding what the protection program for these facilities should or should not be. The planning and implementation of the security program would be a collaboration of efforts by the senior manager and the designated organization security administrator. The collaborative security program would be subject to the security policies and procedures approved by the leadership of the organization. The end result should be that each facility is subject to standard security operating procedures and standardized physical security, equipment, monitoring, and maintenance, with allowances for special needs and circumstances unique to the facility.

PRIMARY SECURITY SAFEGUARDS OF THE OFF-CAMPUS PATIENT CARE FACILITY

The planning and installation of security safeguards in off-campus facilities is extremely important as many or most of these facilities are void of staff for varying periods of time. The integrity of maintaining a locked and secure facility during these "vacant" time periods is a critical business management responsibility.

ACCESS CONTROL

Allowing entry, denying entry, and control of the movement of patients within the facility is a basic element of security. All patients should enter the facility at what can be called the public entrance that leads directly to a point of reception. In some cases, the facility will have an ambulance entry point. At the reception point, all persons entering need to state their purpose for being at the facility. The staff person at the reception point, receptionist or triage nurse, would be responsible to facilitate the patient/visitors controlled visit. A general rule is for an appropriate staff person to be notified that a patient/visitor is waiting. In this mode of operation, the patient/visitor should be escorted from the waiting area, and at the conclusion of their care or business they should be escorted back to the reception waiting area for exiting the facility. Patients and visitors should not be dismissed from office or treatment areas, which would allow them to "roam" the facility.

Except in the very small off-campus treatment facility, there should be a specific locked staff entrance electronically controlled by either code or card access. Card access is most common, as the card can be used for identification, access control, and time recording purposes. During business hours, all ingress doors should be locked, with the exception of the public entry (staff controlled) entry point. In some higher security risk environments it is common to lock the public entry point for certain times, even though the facility is operating in the service mode. An example would be the urgent care facility that operates from 10 a.m. to 10 p.m. daily. The public entry could be open for free access until a designated time point when the door would be locked, say from 6 p.m. to 10 p.m. Locking this door during treatment times would require a system of communication and means to conveniently release the locking mechanism for entry.

VIDEO SURVEILLANCE/ALARMS

Each off-campus facility should be protected with the installation of video surveillance equipment on all entry/exit doors and other internal areas. The use of IP addressable video equipment would permit remote viewing by authorized persons. The video surveillance equipment, when integrated with an alarm system, can provide a high level of security for the closed facility. Door alarms and motion type alarms can effectively alert a monitoring point of activity occurring.

The use of panic alarms (duress alarms) has limited value in the small off-campus facility. In many cases, the staff does not know the location of these types of alarms, understand their intended use, or know where the signal terminates. When staff members are asked where the signal is sent, over half of the replies are that it goes to the police department, which is rarely, if ever, the case. As discussed earlier in this text, the unintentional experimentation and lack of knowledge of the alarm device generally results in an unacceptable number and use of such alarm activations.

However, increasingly in large health systems, we can see a movement toward standardized use of security technology, even in these nontraditional off-campus settings. Duress and intrusion alarms, as well as video surveillance, may all be monitored at a centralized security operations center, with an established response predicated on the defined circumstances. Systems, including electronic access systems, can be commonly established with expected response times clearly communicated. Additionally, security can establish minimum standards related to security measures and systems in a community facility. These can serve as a guideline for healthcare organization programs assigned to work with property management companies in preparing buildings for occupancy by a healthcare program or service.

SECURITY OFFICER COVERAGE

There may be a need to schedule security officer coverage for certain off-campus facilities during the times the facility is open or for a portion of the operating time. For example, an urgent care facility that is open 10 a.m. to 10 p.m. may not require officer coverage during the day, but have a need for such coverage from 6 p.m. to 10 p.m. Another aspect of the off-site officer coverage is that needs change and can change rather abruptly due to a change in hours, operating budget restrictions, or outright closing of the facility. These types of changing environment, and often limited hours of coverage, make it extremely difficult and somewhat inefficient to staff as part of the main facility in-house security officer staffing schedule. The use of a contract security service may be a good alternative staffing choice. The contract staffing model provides a fixed cost for budgeting purposes, a relatively easy change if a certain officer does not fit in with the requirements of service, change or elimination of hours or needed service. In general, there are fewer officer training requirements involved and career ladder concept is not an issue. Client interpersonal relationships with patients and visitors are key elements of this type of security officer service.

The security administrator should be well versed in the nature of the off-campus services and clientele to ensure the right fit for the security officer in that environment. A clinic providing support to the homeless and drug addicted, as an example, may well require a security officer on site during business hours to protect clinic staff and property. However, the skillset and even attire and appearance of this individual may differ from that contemplated in a large urban teaching hospital or an outpatient mental health clinic in an affluent community.

VEHICLE SECURITY PATROLS

With the advent of security technology the value of periodic security officer vehicle patrols is a greatly diminished security practice during the time period the facility is closed. The use of such patrols during operational hours, however, can be productive in terms of a periodic security officer presence. In order for such patrols to be cost effective, the facilities to be patrolled need to be in relatively close proximity to each other. A general rule of thumb is that vehicle driving time should be less than 50% of the combined time actually spent on the premises of the facilities.

Many facilities have implemented the virtual patrol of off-campus premises via an integrated video surveillance system. In this approach, virtual patrol tours can be made that allow for a system security officer or dispatcher, or outsourced provider, to monitor the environment and the security of the building via strategically located cameras. This approach often incorporates random patrol tours throughout the day and night and on-demand observation if an alarm is received. Monitoring may be made easier through the use of "dark screen" monitoring, where the camera is dormant unless movement or other preset conditions are met. This can allow for the effective monitoring of a much larger number of cameras by the operator.

SECURITY SIGNAGE

The same type of security signage used at hospitals and medical centers should also be used in the off-campus locations. The use of security signage was discussed in Chapter 18, Physical Security Safeguards. In addition, a very important emergency information sign, visible from outside the facility, should be in place at all facilities that do not operate on a 24/7 basis. The emergency information sign is primarily directed to, but not limited to, public safety agencies. The sign should contain information that allows the public safety agency, or other persons, to quickly notify the proper person of the healthcare organization of an emergency situation that may exist. One might immediately think of fire; however, vehicles running into the building, severe weather damage, or a breaking and entering are examples of other situations that might occur. These unexpected types of incidents may require the deployment of security personnel to temporarily secure the facility, obtain the services of a "board-up" company, or the need to make immediate utility type repairs.

NIGHT LIGHTING

The issue of providing adequate night lighting in the parking lots and at the exterior (walkways) of the off-campus patient care facility is extremely important and can often be problematic. The night-lighting levels of 16 freestanding outpatient care facilities were surveyed as part of an overall security risk analysis project. All of the facilities were open until 9 p.m. or later. The results were: 6 facilities had adequate lighting; 4 facilities had marginal lighting; and 6 facilities had inadequate lighting for security and safety levels of light. In reviewing the results of the lighting survey, it appeared that the majority of the buildings had been built by developers. The buildings were basically designed as complexes to be leased by day business entities. In all 16 facilities the night lighting was adequate for the closed, locked, and alarmed building. The night lighting is but one issue, but is a good example of why security and safety professionals should work closely with organization property managers during the lease or during new building design and layout.

When the organization builds an off-campus patient care facility, the night lighting issue is generally resolved in the planning and design process. The issue often becomes problematic when the organization contemplates leasing space in an existing building. The healthcare organization and the building owner will work together to complete the details of the interior build-out or space design changes. The issue of inadequate night lighting does not generally surface until the onset of delivering patient care services or there is an occurrence of a security or safety incident. At this point the owner is generally reluctant to spend extra money for night lighting, since he already has a lease agreement in hand. In some cases, the healthcare organization will fund the cost of such lighting, but they are, of course, reluctant to invest money in capital improvements to a facility they do not own. If lighting can be increased to an adequate level with lighting fixtures mounted on the building, it is more achievable than a project that requires burying additional electrical lines with the addition of anchoring light fixture standards in asphalt or cement surfaced parking lot.

LONG-TERM/RESIDENTIAL CARE FACILITIES

As with many of the nonhospital facilities, programs and services discussed in this chapter, long-term care facilities have not often been at the forefront of the professional security administrator's highest risks. Historically thought of as nursing homes, where the elderly lived until they passed away, these facilities big and small, for profit and not for profit, are growing rapidly and at a rate that is projected to exceed all other health sector growth. Residential supply cannot keep up with demand as that aforementioned baby boomer phenomenon hits the healthcare system as something often called the "grey tsunami," creating security issues and concerns that are not commonly considered by the healthcare security industry.

While the threat of violence may be more prevalent in hospitals, it is common in all healthcare facilities. Residents of long-term care facilities are fitter, stronger and in many cases younger, than those we've come to associate with the traditional nursing home, and increasingly suffer from dementia. "Our acute-care hospitals are overflowing with patients awaiting long-term care placement and our long-term care facilities are understaffed, underspaced and underequipped to care for our most vulnerable seniors," said Chris Simpson, president-elect of the Canadian Medical Association in a recent call for a dementia strategy.[14]

These residents are attacking and even murdering one another, assaulting staff at rates comparable to those suffered by behavioral/mental health staff and wandering away from their homes, often coming to harm, or even dying in the communities they once functioned independently in. Families have developed a growing concern that staff may be abusing or neglecting their loved ones, or in some cases stealing their possessions. Resident stays in long-term care facilities are much longer than in the typical hospital and theft is difficult to investigate as the resident frequently cannot remember the last time they saw an item.

For the healthcare security professional, this is not a world familiar to most of them and yet, from the description of the risks and occurrences, it is clear long-term care is increasingly an area that will require the expertise of the healthcare security profession, to work with administrators and clinical staff, to develop solutions to these most severe of challenges for our vulnerable and rapidly growing seniors population.

RESIDENT ON STAFF VIOLENCE

Twenty years ago, in 1994, research by Canadian criminologist Neil Boyd concluded that care aides in long-term care facilities suffered a higher risk of injury from aggression than police officers in the province of British Columbia.[15] Little has changed today with the New York Times reporting in 2008 on Bureau of Labor statistics revealing psychiatric units and nursing homes as the "most dangerous settings" for healthcare workers, suffering injuries from aggression at a rate 12 times that of the private sector as whole.[16]

This aggression in the long-term care sector manifests itself differently than the traditional healthcare industry. In hospitals, aggression most often occurs in the ED or on behavioral/mental health units and security and staff are trained to the risks faced and mitigation processes established to deal with these aggressors, who are overwhelmingly patients, suffering from mental illness, substance abuse issues, head injuries, criminality or other conditions that contribute to their aggressive behavior. Some aggression does occur against clinical staff in the course of treatment in general medical/surgical units or in ICU; however, this is the exception rather than the norm in the hospital setting.

In long-term care, however, the setting is the client home, with caregivers and residents engaged in regular day-to-day activities centered on caring for the resident. Here, violence can take the form of caregivers being scratched or clawed or bitten by residents, suddenly and unexpectedly, regardless of the relationship between the two. In some instances these attacks can be severe, with canes or other weapons used to strike caregivers or severe blows delivered by residents who may still have considerable physical strength. In some cases caregivers learn patterns of resident behavior, a benefit of a relationship less transient than that experienced by hospital staff. For instance, perhaps a certain time of day presents behavioral challenges for a resident, or some pattern of activity or even a particular activity.

Long-term care staff can be and are increasingly trained in preventing and managing aggressive behavior in this unique setting. In some jurisdictions, early efforts on training residential care staff focused on using educational programs and techniques imported from the hospital settings. These were quickly found lacking by residential care staff, not equipped with duress alarms, trained teams and security on site. These mitigation efforts that help staff manage aggressive behavior are very different from those experienced by their acute care colleagues.

The healthcare security program can play an important role in this environment, first by understanding and distinguishing it from the acute care settings. Security expertise is important for risk assessments of the environment, or indeed threat assessments involving individuals. In some cases security can help deliver training to long-term care staff, while in others they may be required to provide a one-on-one direct patient observation ("security watch") for extended periods on particularly aggressive residents. More and more, long-term care facilities are using dedicated security staff to support a safe patient care environment and help protect employees from resident generated violence.

Some long-term care facilities are very large, with hundreds of residents, often located on multiple floors. The presence of an on-site security officer in these circumstances typically has a different focus than their hospital counterparts, in terms of general security requirements and patient intervention expectations. The growth of the long-term care sector, coupled with increasingly aggressive residents, is expected to bring more dedicated security coverage at long-term care facilities in the future.

RESIDENT ON RESIDENT VIOLENCE

The issue of resident on resident violence has led to tragic consequences. In a 2013 article in Canada's *MacLean's* magazine, the author chronicles a tale of a 95-year-old resident of a residential care dementia unit, Jack Furman.[17] Seventy years before, Jack had been a member of an elite Canadian commando squad, trained to kill for his country in every way possible, including with his bare hands. In 2013, "languishing in a fog of dementia," Jack killed a fellow resident, a retired executive from a glass company. Long-term care facilities are not prepared to handle a man like Jack Furman and society does not know how to punish a man who is no more responsible for his actions than a two-year-old child.

The *MacLean's* article states that 15% of Canadians over the age of 65 are living with dementia, the number expected to grow to 1.4 million Canadians by 2031. With 5 resident on resident murders in care homes in 2013, the number of incidents of resident on resident violence during that period is estimated by the author at approximately 10,000.[18]

In the U.S., the Geriatric Mental Health Foundation suggests approximately 360,000 dementia cases occur each year, with over 4 million Americans currently diagnosed. The Foundation lists some of the most common problematic behaviors associated with dementia, such as agitation, aggression, combativeness, delusions, hallucinations, insomnia, and wandering.[19]

While not all resident on resident violence, and indeed resident on staff violence, is associated with dementia, there is no question that this disease has greatly increased risk of violence in the residential care settings, while triggering other concerns through the wandering behaviors attributed to dementia.

WANDERING AND ELOPEMENT

Some residents in long-term care facilities, in addition to presenting risk associated with resident on resident or resident on staff violence, may indeed be at risk themselves as a result of wandering away from the facility where they receive care.

The tragic case of Joan Warren in North Vancouver, Canada in 2013 is unfortunately only representative of the many similar cases experienced in the long-term care sector around the world. A 76-year-old woman suffering from dementia wandered away from her seniors home and, after an exhaustive ground search, was found dead of hypothermia a couple of days later, just off a trail in a park. The case, and another that followed in the Vancouver area some months later, prompted questions about security and the possible use of technology to mitigate the risk associated with the wandering behaviors.[20]

Individuals at risk of wandering include those with dementia, "generally in the early to mid-stage" according to the National Council of Certified Dementia Practitioners (NCCDP). While reminding us that dementia is not a disease in itself, but rather a group of symptoms associated with Alzheimer's disease, the NCCDP suggests that more than 34,000 U.S. Alzheimer patients wander out of their homes or care homes each year.[1]

For the long-term care homes, the challenge is maintaining a warm and therapeutic home environment for their residents, while at the same time, mitigating the risk of wandering presenting by an increasing number of residents. Some of the design challenges can be seen as similar to those experienced in designing for elopement prevention in behavioral/mental health. There has been a move toward designing secure dementia units or even facilities designed specifically for dementia patients. Some of the key design features in attempting to mitigate the risk of elopement in long-term care include:

- Building Perimeter – capacity to detect exit and provide camera images of resident
- External Areas – securable outside areas where residents can frequent
- External Response – presence of a plan to facilitate quick recovery of resident
- Main Entry/Foyer – observational capacity of most vulnerable area in any facility
- Internal Controls in the Building – stairwells, elevators, circulation routes, exit doors
- Unit Design – line of sight for staff, unit entry, patient wandering system
- Other – testing of system components, community awareness.

Electronic resident wandering systems are used in many facilities to assist with early detection of residents with a propensity to wander. In simple terms this consists of a transmitter, usually affixed to a bracelet on the resident's wrist. Receivers are situated at key locations in the facility so that if the resident wearing the bracelet passes close to the receiver an alarm sounds and staff can respond. While these devices have, to some degree, helped mitigate the risk of wandering, they are dependent on staff diligence and response. Residents can remove them and, not unlike infant tagging systems, alarms generated by these systems can be lost in the noises of a busy unit and, especially if subject to false alarms, can be viewed as a nuisance by staff over time.

For security, in these circumstances the task becomes to ensure a good design to mitigate the risk of wandering, to support staff training in the use of the system and to provide a rapid and thorough response to any report of resident elopement, where such responsibility exists. As an example, a good external camera system, quickly available to security for review, can help determine whether a search should be externally or internally focused, increasing the likelihood of a positive outcome.

RESIDENT ABUSE OR NEGLECT

Technology has allowed family members to conduct their own investigations in long-term care homes where they suspect abuse or neglect of a loved one. Cases in various countries have been well publicized with family members installing hidden cameras, so called "granny cams" in their family member's rooms and discovering their loved one being beaten, abused, neglected and even sexually assaulted by staff in the care home.

As in the hospital setting, security, where they have responsibility for long-term care, should be involved in investigations involving all such allegations. The covert camera should be a last resort, when all other investigative methods have failed, and should be subject to the same requirements as used in the hospital setting. It should be controlled by the healthcare organization and not by the family, thus making the information gathered subject to privacy and freedom of information provisions. The safety and the dignity of the residents should always be of paramount importance.

In 2013 the IAHSS, under the guidance of a voluntary long-term care task force, produced the *Long Term Care Safety & Security Management Guide*, which discusses how to investigate resident injuries. The report states that staff should be trained to report to their immediate supervisor any witnessed or suspected resident abuse/neglect or misappropriation of property. The IAHSS Guide outlines terms that staff should be acutely aware of, such as physical abuse, verbal abuse, mistreatment and neglect—definitions of each are found in the glossary. Further discussion on staff members being able to recognize the different types of abuse, as well as recognize signs that indicate abuse and why abuse occurs, is found in Boxes 24-2, 24-3, and 24-4. These are excellent educational topics when addressing staff members of long-term care facilities to prevent and identify resident abuse.

ORGANIZING THE OFF-CAMPUS PROTECTION PROGRAM

There are at least three major challenges in organizing and implementing off-campus facility security programs: the logistics of supplies, transportation, and services support of the healthcare organization's main campus; the inherent culture of off-campus management which often says "we have our own unique needs and we will operate more semi-autonomously than if we were part of the main campus"; and of course the funding of security program elements that may or may not have been adequately addressed in the planning stages. In the U.S., the parent organization will usually judge the success of a new start-up operation by its financial performance almost from day one. Since security is considered overhead and nonrevenue-producing, off-campus administrators are quite reluctant to increase security overhead expenses.

BOX 24-2 DIFFERENT TYPES OF ABUSE IN LONG-TERM CARE FACILITIES

Different Types of Abuse

Physical Abuse
Psychological Abuse
Sexual Abuse / Molestation
Neglect
Abandonment
Financial or Material Exploitation
Self-Neglect

BOX 24-3 SIGNS THAT INDICATE ABUSE

- Excessive agreement or compliance with caregiver
- Poor hygiene, i.e., body odor, uncleanliness, soiled clothing or undergarments
- Malnutrition or dehydration
- Burns or pressure sores
- Bruises, particularly if clustered on trunk or upper arms
- Bruises in various stages of healing that may indicate repeated injury
- Inadequate clothing or footwear
- Inadequate food, medication or care
- Left alone or isolated in some way
- Fear of caregiver
- Lack of control in personal activities or finances.

BOX 24-4 WHY ABUSE OCCURS

Slowness – some residents are slow. They take a long time to eat, dress or walk down the hall. At any particular time, a staff member may become impatient and want them do things faster. Unkind words or physical force will only make matters worse for both staff and the resident.
Soiling – some residents have little or no bowel control. It is one thing to clean up after a baby, but it might seem disgusting to have to diaper or clean up an adult. Keep two things in mind: (1) the resident's lack of control is medical; it is not bad behavior. (2) As disgusted as (staff member) might get, the resident is probably ten times more embarrassed by the soiling.
Forgetfulness – older residents sometimes are forgetful. They may not remember (staff member) or even the members of their own families. They may ask the same questions over and over again. This forgetfulness can be bothersome so it could be easy to lose temper and be cross. A calm and gentle approach will help the resident feel safe.
Arguing and Striking Out – Residents may try to argue with or sometimes try to hit a staff member. This usually happens when a person is confused or scared. If a resident acts this way towards a staff member, the staff member should recognize: (1) the resident is not really angry with the staff member, and (2) it only makes matters worse if (staff member) responds in the same way.

In other not-for-profit settings, some success has been achieved by creating a model that recognizes the autonomy of community programs. Whether residential care, public health or home health, these programs are not formally linked to a hospital or hospitals, but rather function as an independent yet integrated component of an overall health system. In this model, security can be viewed as a corporate function, that overlays all elements of this health system, but is flexible, nimble and adaptable enough to adjust requirements to meet the unique needs of a program or service in the community. This is a new challenge for many healthcare security administrators.

Security program administrative structure

The structure and general operating authority of the off campus facility security program should reside as a component of the parent healthcare organization administrative plan. This does not mean the administrator of the off-campus patient care facility will lose any authority in day-to-day operations. It simply means the collaborative authority of the facility administrator and the director of security should be thoroughly understood and stated in an approved authority matrix. In some other organizational models, the authority of the security director extends fully to the nonhospital settings, with the site administrator responsible for ensuring conformity to enterprise-wide standards.

The majority of healthcare provider organizations today have either a few or many off-campus clinical and nonclinical facilities. The size, number, geographical locations, types of patient care, types of nonpatient care services, and neighborhood profiles make each of these systems unique unto themselves. It provides the opportunity for the director of security to develop an efficient and effective organizational model to accomplish the level of protection that fits the circumstances. Figure 24-1 is an example of an organizational model that security directors can adopt, modify, or reject according to their needs and requirements. The important point is there needs to be an organization chart that puts the organizational structure into perspective.

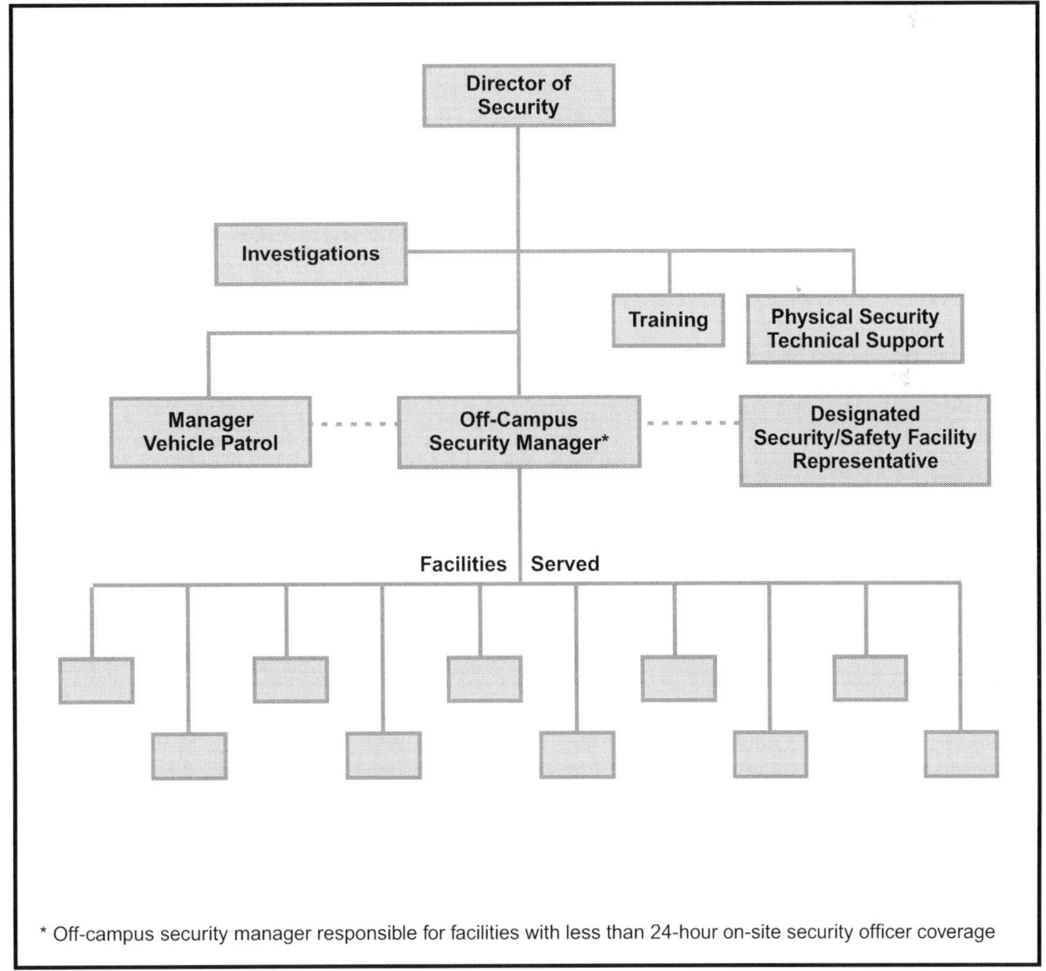

FIGURE 24-1

Security operations/organization model for servicing off-campus clinical and nonclinical facilities.

Security and safety representative

The concept of having an appointed security and safety representative for each off-campus facility enhances the communications link between the facility and the system-wide security program. The representative is a staff person assigned as a full-time working staff person at the facility. The responsibility for security and safety duties is simply written into the person's position description. The representative is not necessarily trained in the field of security and safety, but administratively coordinates these activities for the specific facility. Examples of this coordination include:

- To request new keys, issue keys, retrieve keys and access identification badges
- To report malfunctioning security equipment to central security
- To prepare security incident reports in absence of security officer coverage and forward those reports
- To request investigative activity
- To communicate staff security concerns and recommendations upward through the leadership chain of command
- To request specialized security support for temporary situations.

The representative performs similar activities and duties in regard to safety issues and concerns.

There should be formal education and development required of all security and safety representatives to help them fulfill this expectation. In addition, a corporate security staff person, a safety staff person, and the facility representative should complete a periodic on-site inspectional/review tour of the facility on a routine basis as the facility profile dictates. During these rounds a special point is made to inquire and engage staff relative to any security or safety issues that they may wish to discuss. It is important in this model that the facility representative have ongoing access and communication with the health system security representative. Timely and responsive service on the part of the corporate security person will result in a program at a site that reflects the security requirements of the organization. As importantly, as the relationship develops, the corporate security representative can grow their personal knowledge of an environment they may not otherwise be very familiar with.

Security and safety incident report

The security and safety incident report is a basic element of the off-campus security system. These reports provide a profile of the safety and security environment. The reports are generally electronically forwarded to the manager of off-campus security. The manager reviews the report, which may be filed for future use as required, decides to look into the matter personally, or requests corporate investigation or physical security support as appropriate. A spreadsheet database is maintained that allows for the preparation of a consolidated report comparing security incidents of each facility. In this type of system, the materials management department is prohibited from replacing any equipment lost or stolen without a completed security incident report, which must accompany the "Request to Purchase" form. In this same vein, no off-campus facility is allowed to add new security equipment or replace equipment unless approved by the manager of off-campus security.

One model of incident reporting sometimes seen in large health systems is to have the community employees themselves complete security incident reports. Some off-the-shelf incident reporting software has web-based reporting capability where employees can access a short-form report and document an incident such as a theft, suspicious person, aggressive family member and the like. These reports feed into the corporate security incident reporting system in a module separated from the more robust hospital reporting systems, and can be used for follow-up as well as trending analysis and eventually KPI monitoring.

Cash/payment handling

Almost all of the off-campus patient treatment facilities in the U.S. collect payment for goods and services rendered. Some nonclinical departments also collect money or may have substantial petty cash funds. Most facilities that have been operating for any length of time will not be able to boast that they have never encountered cash/receipt losses, including fraud. Money just seems to attract safekeeping and accountability problems. There are several money-handling security principles that apply to the off-campus facility. A daily courier service is essential to the successful off-campus operation to provide for the movement of various supplies, reports, and equipment, including cash and other financial instruments. The courier schedule should be such that a pickup is made late in the day, to minimize the amount of money, checks, and charge card receipts kept in the facility overnight. In the small facility, the courier service may be every other day and the larger facility may even require the services of an armored car.

In the typical system of money transfers between the cash management office at the main facility and off-campus locations, a locked moneybag is used. In this system the courier picks up a locked bag and subsequently delivers a locked bag. Since some deliveries of the moneybag to the main facility will occur after the cash management office is closed, there is usually a drop safe arrangement to store and protect the bag. Chapter 22, "Areas of Special Concern," discusses security of the cash management office in further detail.

There will always be the need to store cash, checks, receipts, and possibly valuables during nights and weekends at most off-campus patient care facilities. Each facility should have a small, yet substantial, drop safe for this purpose. The safe should be securely fastened to the floor or concrete sidewall.

NONCLINICAL OFF-CAMPUS FACILITIES

The list of nonclinical departments or functions of healthcare organizations that are often located off the main campus is exhaustive and is usually driven by space needs of the main facility. Common off-campus nonclinical facilities include materials management storage, staff training classrooms, marketing, planning, accounting, legal, and record storage, to name a few. The security safeguards for these functions are generally the responsibility of facility management, with consultation and support of the main facility security director. The security risks and safeguards to be implemented may be much more diverse than those facilities providing patient care.

Centralized warehousing of products and supplies, including pharmaceuticals, is increasingly common in the healthcare sector. This model requires security expertise in both the design and operational stages, with significant expertise required around asset protection, including protection of goods during transport. Some of these megawarehouses are storing and managing an inventory of equipment and supplies often worth tens of millions of dollars, providing service to large numbers of hospitals and community facilities. Security measures can be further challenged by a centralized pharmacy system, often carrying inventory, including narcotics, for multiple hospitals. Designing a secure pharmacy and mitigating against the risk of internal theft, robbery or even delivery truck hijacking is one of the challenges faced by today's healthcare security leaders.

As the nonhospital health sector grows at a rate never experienced before, it is incumbent on the security administrator to recognize these trends and find a pathway to learning the unique requirements of long term/residential care, public health, home health and the provision of care and services outside of the traditional hospital setting. This is the next great frontier for healthcare security and the industry has an opportunity now to get out in front of this wave and ensure the learnings of the hospital experiences are adapted to this brave new world.

REFERENCES

1. Lohr K. *Abortion Providers on High Alert*. NPR; 2009, June 3. Retrieved from http://www.npr.org/templates/story/story.php?storyId=104841479.
2. Community Oncology Alliance. *New Study Finds 47% Higher Costs for Outpatient Cancer Care in the Hospital Setting for Medicare Beneficiaries*. 2013, September 10. Retrieved on July 11, 2014 from http://www.communityoncology.org/site/blog/detail/2013/09/10/sepember-10-2013-new-report-finds-47-higher-costs-for-outpatient-cancer-care-in-the-hospital-outpatient-setting-for-medicare-beneficiaries.html.
3. Canadian Institute for Health Information. *Healthcare in Canada, 2011: A Focus on Seniors and Aging*. 2011. Retrieved on July 12, 2014 from https://secure.cihi.ca/free_products/HCIC_2011_seniors_report_en.pdf.
4. American Hospital Association. *When I'm 64: How Boomers Will Change Health Care*. 2007. Retrieved on July 12, 2014 from http://www.aha.org/content/00-10/070508-boomerreport.pdf.
5. Orlovsky C. The Baby Boomers' Massive Impact on Health Care. *Nursing News* 2007. Retrieved on July 10, 2014 from http://www.nursezone.com/nursing-news-events/more-news/The-Baby-Boomers%E2%80%99-Massive-Impact-on-Health-Care_28946.aspx.
6. Home Healthcare Opens Door to Abuses. *USA Today* 1996, November 11;**11B**.
7. Home Healthcare Opens Door to Abuses. *USA Today* 1996, November 11;**13B**.
8. Milburn J. Three Fatally Shot in Girard. *Topeka Capitol-Journal* 2000, February 8. Retrieved from http://www.cjonline.com/stories/020800/kan_girard.shtml.
9. Community Care. *Man who killed care worker on lone home visit 'should have been detained'*. 2013, May 29. Retrieved on July 12, 2014 from http://www.communitycare.co.uk/2013/05/29/man-who-killed-care-worker-on-lone-home-visit-should-have-been-detained/.
10. Traynor L. 'Freddie Krueger style' attacker left care worker with broken back when she jumped out of window to escape him. *Mirror* 2014, April 3. Retrieved on July 11, 2014 from http://www.mirror.co.uk/news/uk-news/craig-cantwell-jailed-freddie-kreuger-syle-3344247.
11. Mid-Hudson News Network. Former home healthcare aide sentenced to federal prison for defrauding elderly couple. *Statewide News Network* 2011, November 22. Retrieved November 23, 2011 from http://www.midhudsonnews.com/News/2011/November/22/Wilson_sen-22Nov11.html.
12. National Health Service Business Services Authority. *NHS Lone Worker Protection Service*. 2012. Retrieved on July 11, 2014 from http://www.nhsbsa.nhs.uk/4248.asp.
13. McGregor K. *Community Care. Social Workers are as likely to be attacked in the office as they are on home visits*. 2013, August 19. Retrieved on July 12, 2014 from http://www.communitycare.co.uk/2013/08/19/social-workers-and-care-staff-are-as-likely-to-be-attacked-in-the-office-as-they-are-on-home-visits/.
14. MacQueen K. *Maclean's.2. Old and dangerous: Senior violence is getting worse*. 2014, January 17. Retrieved on July 10, 2014 from http://www.macleans.ca/society/life/old-and-dangerous/.
15. Boyd N. Gently Into the Night: Aggression in Long-term Care. *Finding Solutions: Work at the Worker's Compensation*. 1994. Retrieved on July 13, 2014 from http://www.worksafebc.com/about_us/history/historical_reports/finding_solutions/assets/pdf/1150-20S-Report.pdf.

16. Tuller D. The New York Times. *Nurses Step Up Efforts to Protect Against Attacks* 2008, July 6. Retrieved on July 12, 2014 from http://www.nytimes.com/2008/07/08/health/08nurses.html?pagewanted=all&_r=0.
17. MacQueen K. *Maclean's. Old and dangerous: Senior violence is getting worse*. 2014, January 17. p. 1. Retrieved on July 10, 2014 http://www.macleans.ca/society/life/old-and-dangerous/.
18. MacQueen K. *Maclean's. Old and dangerous: Senior violence is getting worse*. 2014, January 17. p. 2. Retrieved on July 10, 2014 http://www.macleans.ca/society/life/old-and-dangerous/.
19. Geriatric Mental Health Foundation. *Alzheimer's and Related Dementias Fact Sheet*. 2014. Retrieved 20 July, 2014 from http://www.gmhfonline.org/gmhf/consumer/factsheets/dementia_factsheet.html.
20. Seyd J. North Shore News. *Senior's death in Lynn Canyon sparks questions* 2013, December 10. Retrieved on July 11, 2014 from http://www.nsnews.com/news/senior-s-death-in-lynn-canyon-sparks-questions-1.754525.
21. National Council of Certified Dementia Practitioners. *Wandering and Elopement Resources*. 2014. Retrieved on July 14, 2014 from http://www.nccdp.org/wandering.htm.

CHAPTER

EMERGENCY PREPAREDNESS: PLANNING AND MANAGEMENT 25

Emergency preparedness is an essential component of healthcare organizational preparedness, against both intentional acts of terror and naturally occurring crises that have the potential to cause serious harm to large portions of the population. The events of September 11, 2001, provided the stimuli to evoke fear in the lives of many, and the response to the events resulted in identifying the healthcare challenges and complications that arise during disasters.[1] In 2013 alone, healthcare organizations endured several natural and manmade disasters, including the Christmas week ice storms in Southern Ontario, Canada resulting in generator failures; an immense F5 tornado that destroyed Moore, Oklahoma; the floods in Southern Alberta, Canada forcing patient evacuations; and the cowardly bombings at the Boston Marathon that proved the resilience of that city and its healthcare system. This was followed by the West Texas fertilizer plant explosion that shattered half of the town, and the super typhoon that struck the Philippines, leaving a swath of death and devastation in its path. Disasters disrupt the environment of healthcare and alter the demand for healthcare services; therefore it is essential that healthcare leaders ensure emergency preparedness is integrated into daily functions and values.[2]

REGULATIONS FOR HEALTHCARE EMERGENCY PREPAREDNESS

For several decades, the United States and Canada National Fire Protection Association (NFPA),[3] Canadian Centre for Occupational Health and Safety (CCOHS) and the Occupational Safety and Health Administration (OSHA) have specified the level of preparedness expected by organizations inclusive of healthcare. In the United States, the Centers for Medicaid and Medicare (CMS) Conditions of Participation (CoP) specify emergency preparedness standards and performance requirements for organizations that bill CMS for patient care services. Under CMS deeming authority, recognized hospital accreditation bodies such as The Joint Commission (TJC),[4] Det Norske Veritas (DNV), and Healthcare Facilities Accreditation Program (HFAP) evaluate compliance with CMS standards. The Commission on Accreditation of Rehabilitation Facilities (CARF) is an international, nonprofit organization that also provides standards and surveyors to ensure standard compliance specifically in the rehabilitation venue. The Accreditation Canada and the Qmentum accreditation program[5] provide a comprehensive set of standards to address emergency preparedness in healthcare in Canada.[6] All of these accreditation programs generate an equally comprehensive set of emergency preparedness expectations resulting in improved disaster response capabilities and capacity.

The International Association for Healthcare Security and Safety (IAHSS) has developed the following basic industry security guidelines relative to healthcare emergency management. These guidelines generically incorporate the recognized hospital accreditation bodies' requirements for emergency preparedness.

08.01 EMERGENCY MANAGEMENT (GENERAL)

Statement

Healthcare Facilities (HCFs) will develop and maintain an emergency management program to identify and address threats/hazards/emergencies that may impact the facility and its operations.

Intent

a. A multidisciplinary team should be appointed to develop, maintain and approve the emergency management program. The team should have express support of the facility's CEO along with authority for the program.
b. Security should have a clearly defined role in the HCF's emergency management program.
c. The emergency management program should be based on the four phases of mitigation, preparedness, response and recovery.
d. The facility should conduct a comprehensive hazard/risk vulnerability analysis (HVA) to identify and prioritize threats/hazards/emergencies that may impact facility operations. HVAs should be reviewed annually and whenever a new threat/hazard/emergency emerges or preparedness activities change.
e. Multidisciplinary emergency response plans should be developed to address the potential threats identified by the HCF.
f. Emergency response plans should have an all-hazards incident command system (ICS). Emergency response plans should address not only immediate and short-term response by the HCF but the possibility of emergency operations lasting for days, weeks or even longer.
g. HCF staff should receive education and training in emergency management consistent with their most likely role in responding to the event.
h. Emergency response plans should be exercised both for training purposes, so staff understands their roles and responsibilities and feel comfortable in those roles, and to identify and document the plans' strengths, weaknesses and areas for improvement.
i. Emergency plans should include community involvement—other HCFs, emergency responders and government agencies.
j. Emergency plans should include provision for the care and well-being of HCF staff and their families.

References

- Hospital Incident Command System Guidebook, August 2006
- 2010 Environment of Care: Essentials for Healthcare, The Joint Commission, Oakbrook Terrace IL.
- National Incident Management System (NIMS) http://www.dhs.gov/interweb/assetlibrary/NIMS-90-web.pdf

Approved: November 2008
Last Revised: October 2011

Current emergency preparedness best practices and policy guidance in the healthcare industry are also available from the American College of Healthcare Executives (ACHE),[7] the American Osteopathic Association (AOA), the Food and Drug Administration (FDA), the Centers for Disease Control and Prevention (CDC), the Health Resources and Services Administration (HRSA), and the Office of the Assistant Secretary for Preparedness and Response (ASPR).

EMERGENCY MANAGEMENT PLANNING

Successful emergency management planning must include all key stakeholders within the healthcare organization as well as representatives from external agencies and organizations. An Emergency Management (EM) Committee inclusive of representatives from hospital administration, medical staff, emergency management, security, safety or risk management, engineering, nursing, and members of other support services such as pharmacy, materials management, and housekeeping, should be established to manage program sustainability and effectiveness. The members of this committee should have a basic understanding of emergency management and the incident command system.

The organization should appoint someone responsible for emergency management oversight. This individual acts as a liaison between the organization and governmental and other healthcare agencies, and is often the chairperson of the EM Committee, responsible for overall emergency management compliance. Additionally, this individual coordinates risk analysis to identify points of vulnerability, and ensures appropriate mitigation, preparedness, response, and recovery efforts are in place organization-wide.[8]

The security professional plays an integral piece in the risk analysis. The EM professional is trained to focus globally, whereas the security professional is focused on security-related risks and associated impact on the healthcare organization. Security provides awareness and educational programs and workshops, analyzes department functions for security risks, provides a visible deterrence to crime, prohibited activities, or suspicious activities in public and nonpublic areas, and is constantly alert and vigilant for activities which could result in injury to a person or damage to or loss of property. The security professional, like the EM professional, must maintain positive working relationships with the employees of the organization along with local public safety agencies and administration. In some organizations, the security administrator may be the EM lead or vice versa.

HAZARD VULNERABILITY ASSESSMENT

Incorporating an all-hazards approach to preparedness, beginning with an annual hazard vulnerability analysis (HVA), helps organizational leaders identify prospective hazards and evaluate the impact on the ability of the organization to sustain care and treatment during an emergency.[9] The results of the HVA indicate a realistic understanding of an organization's vulnerabilities, and assists healthcare and community leaders with focusing on planning and resource efforts through the evaluation of mitigation, preparedness, response, and recovery process, for each emergency identified in the HVA. Information from these assessments contributes to the development of the response plans, and subsequent scenarios to be included in an organization's emergency management exercises.

The HVA should be a multidisciplinary process that includes leadership, physicians, nurses, and the EM committee, because of its diverse membership. It is also important to involve the community and gain their perspective on potential threats.[10] Community partners might include local police and fire chiefs, city leaders, and EMS providers, other area hospitals, as well as nongovernmental organizations, such as the Red Cross, Salvation Army, and the National Guard.

An all-hazards approach to the HVA means the organization will evaluate all possible disasters that could affect the hospital and community it serves. There are many preexisting HVA tools available that can be modified to fit the organization's requirements. One frequently used tool was created by Kaiser Permanente (KP). The KP tool divides the hazards into four categories: natural hazards, technological hazards, human hazards, and hazardous materials. The multidisciplinary team evaluates each of the potential hazards for probability based on known risk, and historical data. The time to marshal an on-scene response, scope of response capability, and historical evaluation of response success is taken into consideration when scoring the response category within the tool. The next evaluation determines the human, property, and business impact. When assessing the impact, both the short-term effects of an emergency and the long-term effects, along with business continuity, must be considered. Issues to consider should include the potential for staff or patient death or injury, cost to repair property or set up temporary replacement facilities, and interruption of critical supplies and patient care services.

Finally, the team will weigh the effects of the organization's mitigation and preparedness efforts. This category evaluates the status of current emergency response plans, training, availability of backup systems, and community resources. Once the HVA is completed, the highest risks are prioritized and the organization prepared for those events. Many healthcare organizations have offsite locations associated with their patient care mission. These may be in a geographically separate location, or have inherent risks associated with them, different from the main hospital location. Therefore, offsite and community-based locations should have their own HVA conducted annually.

While most potential hazards and vulnerabilities will have an impact on security operations, there are several events where security takes the lead. Examples of these events include, but are not limited to, infant abduction, active shooter, hostage situation, VIP situations, civil disturbance, bomb threat, terrorism, and mass casualty events. Three of the commonly identified security vulnerabilities are people, process, and infrastructure. Security professionals should have extensive knowledge other evaluators may not have in security specific mitigation, preparedness, and response and recovery procedures relative to these hazards and are integral to the HVA process.

MITIGATION AND PREPAREDNESS ACTIVITIES

Prevention is frequently thought of as those actions taken to avoid or stop an emergency and mitigation as those actions are taken to decrease the impacts posed by hazards. Once the organization has identified the potential hazards and vulnerabilities that may impact the ability to provide safe patient care, the multidisciplinary team should review mitigation and preparedness activities that can reduce the impact resulting from each potential event. These activities are designed to reduce the risk of and potential damage from, an event, and build capacity by identifying resources that may be used if an event occurs.

Both structural and nonstructural hazard mitigation strategies can be employed to reduce risk. Structural mitigation often consists of reinforcing, bracing, or strengthening any portion of the building that may become damaged or cause injury. The following are a few examples of structural mitigation strategies:

- *Floods* – elevate and reinforce the facility, build retaining walls on slopes, bolt the foundation and reinforce the walls
- *Wildfire* – use fire resistant materials such as noncombustible roofing materials
- *Tornado* – follow local building codes and use wind resistant design on exterior walls and doors, use shutters on windows
- *Manmade Terrorist Events* – install exterior columns made of steel or concrete at entrances or other locations to restrict unauthorized vehicle access.

Nonstructural hazard mitigation reduces the threat to safety posed by the effects of the event on the nonstructural elements, such as building contents, internal utility systems, interior glass and ceilings. This includes all contents of the structure that do not contribute to its structural integrity, such as emergency power generating equipment, plumbing, HVAC, fire protection system, security detection systems, such as door locking and cameras, medical equipment, and hazardous materials. Many organizations will retrofit, replace, relocate, or create a backup plan as part of their nonstructural mitigation activities. The following are a few examples of nonstructural mitigation strategies:

- *Earthquakes* – brace light fixtures and ceiling tiles that could fall or shake loose
- *Tornado* – install shatter-resistant protective film on windows to prevent glass from shattering onto people
- *Bomb Threat* – training and education to reinforce policy and procedure, exercises to test response.

Organizational hazards can change often, therefore vigilance and ongoing assessment must be incorporated to maintain the highest level of preparedness. The security professional and the EM professional conduct ongoing hazard mitigation and preparedness evaluations through environmental rounds, lighting and landscape surveys, risk assessments and evaluations, and training and exercises.

EMERGENCY OPERATIONS PLAN/EMERGENCY RESPONSE PLANS

A comprehensive Emergency Operations Plan (EOP) or Emergency Response Plan (ERP) should describe the philosophy and principles of the facility's Emergency Management program, as well as the procedures for effectively responding to and recovering from an adverse event occurring within the hospital or affecting the community. When creating the plans, an all-hazards approach should be taken, to include hospital leadership, identifying capability limitations and response efforts for a loss of community support event, with a focus on the four phases of emergency management as noted in Figure 25-1.[11]

The plans should describe how the organization will mitigate the risks, plan preparedness activities, respond to an event, and detail recovery efforts. Alignment with community partners is also essential to facilitate coordinated, large-scale responses. For organizations with more than one location, plan modifications may be necessary to reflect local response capabilities and resources.

The EOP/ERP should include tiered levels of activation. The nature, scope, and duration of a disaster will determine the necessary level of activation, correlated to the level of organizational response. A three-level system is often used and can be defined as follows:

Level 1: Minor incident affecting the hospital, and may have casualties from outside the organization, or a small incident within the facility. This level can be handled by the current level of staffing on duty at the time of the event, and the hospital command center may or may not be activated, at the discretion of the administrator on duty.

FIGURE 25-1

Four phases of emergency management.

Level 2: Major incident in the community or within the hospital itself that requires additional staffing resources in specific areas of the hospital. This level may be activated also when the facility will be receiving patients requiring some support for the emergency department, or in advance warning severe weather situations. This may involve a partial activation of the hospital command center.

Level 3: Event of significant impact to the hospital that requires additional resources from community partners and full activation of the hospital command center. The organization may be receiving large numbers of patients, or be experiencing significant issues that have occurred within the facility requiring extensive support.

INCIDENT COMMAND SYSTEM

As part of the EOP, an incident management system must be in place to direct and coordinate actions and operations during and after disasters. The Incident Command System (ICS) was developed in the 1970s by an interagency task force working to coordinate response efforts to combat wildfires in California. Prior to its development, response to major events exposed vulnerabilities in inadequate communication because of conflicting terminology, lack of standardized management structure that would allow integration of resources, lack of personnel accountability, and lack of systematic planning. To meet those challenges, ICS was designed to be usable for managing all routine or unplanned events of any size or type, by establishing a clear chain of command, allowing different agencies to be integrated into a common structure, provide logistical and administrative support to operational personnel, and to ensure key functions were covered, while avoiding duplication of efforts.

There are a few incident command systems available, and one commonly used in the United States is the Hospital Incident Command System (HICS), sponsored by the California Emergency Medical Services Authority. The Hospital Incident Command System is a standardized all-hazard incident management system, that enables hospitals and community partners the capability to work together on organizing resources, staff, and facilities, in an effort to efficiently and effectively respond to an event outside of the normal operations of the organization.

The incident command system is divided into sections and primary functional roles. The Command section provides overall direction of the response by establishing response objectives for the system. The Incident Commander (IC) is the only position always activated in an incident. The IC sets the objectives, develops strategies and priorities, and maintains overall responsibility for effective performance of the ICS for the developing event. During an event where multiple organizations may have leadership responsibilities, such as in a fire response, bomb threat, and active shooter or hostage situations, Unified Command (UC) is initiated to allow multiple stakeholders to actively participate in incident management. Unified Command brings together lead personnel from each major organization involved in the incident to coordinate an effective response, while maintaining their own jurisdictional responsibilities. Unified Command may be established to overcome divisions formed by geographic boundaries, governmental levels, and functional or statutory responsibilities.

The Operations section of the incident management system is responsible for managing the tactical operations that achieve the incident objectives. The Operations Chief directs strategies, specific tactics, and resource assignments. The Security Branch Director reports to the Operations Chief in the ICS structure. The Security Branch Director coordinates all activities related to personnel and facility security such as access control, crowd and traffic control, and law enforcement interface. This role is most frequently filled by the lead security administrator for the hospital, but depending on circumstances and duration of the event, can be filled by other security personnel, or those acting in a security role. Staff must be trained for the security role in the ICS structure, and indeed for any ICS position they may be required to fill.

The Planning section of the incident management system collects and evaluates information for decision support, maintains resource status information, and overall incident documentation. The Logistics section of the incident management system provides support, resources, and other essential services to meet the operational objectives. Finally, the Finance section of the incident management system monitors costs associated with the incident, while providing accounting and cost analyses. Each of the sections can be subdivided as needed to meet the demands of the incident, and to manage span of control for proper safety and accountability.

CRITICAL AREAS OF EMERGENCY MANAGEMENT

Healthcare organizations must evaluate capabilities in six critical areas of emergency management, including Communications, Resources and Assets, Safety and Security, Staff Responsibilities, Utilities Management, and Patient Clinical and Support activities, when creating the emergency operations plan. The evaluation should take an all-hazards approach to emergency management that supports a level of preparedness sufficient to address a range of emergencies, regardless of cause, complexity, scope, or duration. Creating a plan for managing each of these areas will decrease vulnerable capabilities, and enhance the organization's ability to sustain operations during an event.

Communications

In the event community infrastructure is damaged, or a hospital's facilities experience debilitation, communication pathways are likely to fail. Hospitals must develop a plan to maintain communication pathways, both within the hospital, and to critical community resources. The EOP should describe how the hospital will communicate information and instructions to its staff, and how it will notify external authorities during an emergency. The organization will need to maintain communication with patients and their families as well as the community, and frequently the media. Communications to suppliers of essential services, equipment, and supplies during an emergency will also be critical to managing operations.

There are a number of different levels of communications redundancy employed within healthcare organizations. These include overhead page, hand-held radios, pagers, telephone, cellular phone, house wide email, Amateur Radio Operators (HAM Radio), Satellite phones, and mass notification systems. The National Communication System (NCS) offers a wide range of National Security and Emergency Preparedness (NS-EP) communications services that support non-profit organizations in emergency communications. These services include:

- Government Emergency Telecommunications Services (GETS)
- Telecommunications Service Priority (TSP) Program
- Wireless Priority Service (WPS)
- Shared Resources (SHARES) High Frequency Radio Program.

Specific methods used for communicating will depend upon the scope and duration of the emergency. More than one type of communication may be necessary to assure effective communication occurs.

An emergency code system is often utilized to communicate when emergency response procedures have been initiated. Several states have begun to adopt standardized, plain language emergency codes to reduce variation of emergency codes among hospitals, increase competency based skills of hospital staff working in multiple facilities, increase staff, patient and public safety within hospitals and campuses, and align standardized codes with neighboring states. For example, the Missouri hospitals categorize emergency codes into four categories; Facility Alert, Weather Alert, Security Alert, and Medical Alert, and within each category specific events are announced using recommended plain language. As an example, severe weather would be announced as a Weather Alert along with the descriptor and location and any other important instructions. Several emergency codes continue to be announced with color descriptors such as Code Pink for an infant abduction or Code Silver for an active shooter.

In Canada, color codes are utilized almost exclusively. Some provinces have had success standardizing these codes within their province and there has been a clear move toward Canadian code standardization for fire, bomb threat, chemical spill, cardiac arrest, mass casualty, evacuation, violence and missing patient-related events. Other events, including utilities failures, active shooter and missing or abducted infant continue to elude a nationally standardized code. In Australia, Australian Standard 4083-2010 *Planning for Emergencies in Healthcare Facilities,* prescribes a national set of emergency codes for healthcare. It is interesting to note that few of these color codes align with the Canadian standards.

When deciding whether to implement plain language emergency communications, healthcare organizations should review available research and best practices, and implement the appropriate mix of code and clear text combinations appropriate for the environment. Collaboration will be necessary to ensure staff has appointments or work assignments which create a situation where they work, or respond to emergency situations in several buildings, so they will not be confused by different emergency notification systems.

Resources and assets

Hospital leaders and emergency planners understand and recognize the limitations of resources, assets, utility systems, and lack of supply chain capacity that take place during emergencies. Within the EOP, healthcare organizations should identify resource gaps and establish agreements with external support entities to mitigate deficiencies. This can be accomplished by creating an inventory of personal protective equipment, water, food, fuel, medical supplies, and medications, and build a process to monitor and manage resources and assets during an event. The hospital should monitor daily usage of critical resources and update the inventory annually. Resources should be safeguarded against theft, spoilage and waste in an effort to preserve vital assets. Rotating resources and assets will help prevent expiration and degradation. Once resources become inadequate, the hospital will need to establish procedures to curtail or limit services, and evaluate the need to fully or partially evacuate the facility.

Safety and security

Restricting the access of individuals into, throughout, and out of the healthcare organization during an emergency is crucial to the preservation of safety and security of patients, staff, critical supplies, equipment, and utilities. The safety and security section of the EOP should include procedures for the following:

- Total building lockdown
- Ingress and egress identification
- Establishing restricted areas

- Internal movement of patient supplies and waste
- External traffic flow into and away from the hospital
- Hazardous waste management.

Hospital security personnel must establish a system to communicate with local law enforcement, and the authority having jurisdiction (AHJ) when additional security support is required. Facility personnel may also be designated and trained as facility security labor pool, to respond to an event requiring immediate support.

Upon activation of the emergency operations plan, security will also play a key role in visitor management. Movement by visitors and other nonhospital personnel should be restricted to a minimum, and redirected to a collection point. If the hospital is still operational, several types of visitors may seek access, including traditional family and friends of current patients, good Samaritans, licensed personnel responding to assist, employee family members, media and people who are looking for a safe haven from a communitywide disaster. Preset areas should be designated for family waiting, media, labor pool and licensing verification. Vehicular access to the facility should be monitored and controlled by security, including access to the emergency department and other designated staging areas, to prevent grid locking the facility. In the event of a building evacuation, pre-established traffic patterns, pick up locations, and staging area will be essential to overall efficiency and safety of the patient evacuation process.

BOMB THREAT

As part of the EOP/ERP annexes, all healthcare facilities should have policy and procedures for handling a bomb threat. Prevention is the first step to be taken against a bomb situation. These steps are the same security safeguards that should be in everyday use to protect the organization against other security risks. In other words, the proper functioning of the day-to-day protection system is the first line of defense against the bomb threat. To be more specific, locking equipment rooms, switchboard rooms, utility closets, and storage areas reduces risk. Limited access, access controls, noting suspicious people and vehicles, and providing emergency equipment are all part of the everyday protection system. One of the most important aspects of properly managing a bomb threat is to specifically establish organizational authority. Authority and responsibility for handling the initial crisis must be designated to a position readily available 24 hours a day. This position should be the Incident Commander. Logical choices for this role might be the nursing supervisor, the house officer, or the security shift supervisor.

A bomb threat can be received in numerous ways. The most common method is by telephone, and the most common recipient of such information is the switchboard (PBX) operator. Telephone operators, and others who are likely to receive these calls, should be trained to keep the caller talking as long as possible and to ask key questions, such as where the bomb is located, when it will go off, why it was placed, what kind of bomb it is, and other questions that may keep the caller on the line. The person who receives the call should make notes or activate a recording device. Not all threats indicate a bomb has been placed somewhere in the facility. The threat may indicate a bomb "will be" placed in the facility. When this type of threat is received, access controls must be expanded, and the organization may decide to examine property being brought into the facility.

Bomb threat information received must be communicated to the designated authority within the organization, which in turn activates the EOP/ERP. The first step in the notification procedure must always be to notify the appropriate law enforcement authority. In most cases, the law enforcement authority and facility management will decide jointly the type and extent of search required. It is not practical, or possible, to conduct an all-out search in every case. An all-out search includes everything from checking every patient's belongings, to removing all suspended ceiling tiles and all ventilation grille work. It is presumed people who carry bombs are well aware of the danger of premature detonation, and therefore in most cases they will want to get into the facility quickly and to get out even more quickly—which generally precludes an elaborate hiding process. If sufficient organizational personnel are available, the search should be conducted by staff rather than by the police or fire department. The proper role of the outside support agencies is to assume control if a bomb or suspected bomb is located. Employees should conduct the search for two basic reasons. First, staff are in the best position to know what belongs and what does not belong in a given area. Staff are more knowledgeable of the layout of the facility, and either have the capability to enter locked or controlled areas or know how to obtain access.

The use of in-house personnel to search avoids unnecessary confusion and minimizes disruption. Experts believe bomb threat callers are frequently interested in stirring up as much activity and causing as much disruption as possible. Thus, one objective of a bomb search is to carry out the search in a smooth, routine manner, while taking every threat seriously. In bomb threat situations, the administrative person handling the threat may decide to advise only selected staff and patients. In general, patients should not be told of the problem unless absolutely necessary. Experience has shown patients often set off a chain reaction detrimental to the entire process. Patients may respond by calling their families. In turn, the family may decide to come to the facility or call the facility for detailed information. This reaction can tie up needed communications lines and hinder response capabilities.

Whether a search is full or partial, areas of responsibility must be assigned. Search personnel are assembled as a group so the search coordinator can relate to them the information received and assign specific areas to specific personnel. This information may also be communicated by telephone or through a public address system with a code term such as "Mr. Search" or "Code Green," or via electronic means. A complexity that must be taken into consideration is the staffing pattern of the facility. When all departments are fully operational, the facility can be more easily and quickly searched than when departments are closed and locked. During the nonoperational period, security, maintenance, and environmental services personnel may be assigned an expanded role in the search effort. Floor plans, divided into specific search areas, are used in some facilities. Personnel are given a map of the area for which they are responsible. In other organizations, these assignments are made from an administrative checklist that defines the areas. However the parameters of the search are defined, the person responsible for searching a given area must always report back to the command center when the search has been completed. The primary concern is for personal safety rather than property.

If the search produces a bomb or a suspected bomb, the cooperative efforts of security and public safety agencies come into play. Facility employees should never touch a suspected bomb. The investigation and removal of any suspect object is the responsibility of the public safety agency. Security's basic function is to seal off the area and to commence evacuation if necessary. The decision to evacuate rests with the hospital incident commander, working in cooperation with the public safety agency involved. A safe distance for evacuation is generally considered to be a 200-foot radius from the suspected object, including the floors immediately above and below.

ACTIVE SHOOTER PREVENTION AND RESPONSE

The frequency of mass shooting events continues to increase. Approximately every few weeks, a shooting occurs at a school, hospital, governmental facility, and other workplaces frequented by many people. Often mass killings involve a failed safety net; jobless, homeless, and frequently those who slipped through the mental health system. What is happening in the healthcare setting is a reflection of what is happening in our community as noted in Figure 25-2. The unemployment rate shows companies continue to downsize their workforce, leaving people without jobs and money to support their families. Domestic disputes often spill into the healthcare setting. An increase in addiction to drugs and alcohol leads to aggression, theft and unexpected acts of violence. Finally, there is a large gap in available mental health funding and facilities, to receive much needed treatment. Treatment facilities are experiencing financial troubles and disappearing from our communities as the need for services continue to rise. This problem has been exacerbated in Colorado, where the state department of health and human services reported that, in the 20-year period from 1990 to 2010, the state lost 60% of its inpatient psychiatric beds. This has been a decrease from 1241 in 1990 to 503 in 2010.

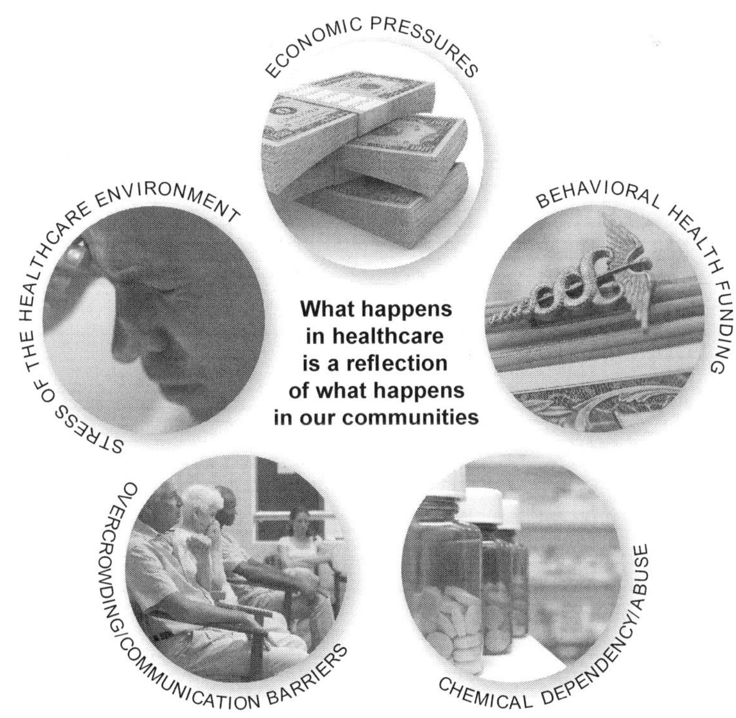

FIGURE 25-2

What happens in healthcare is a reflection of what happens in our community.

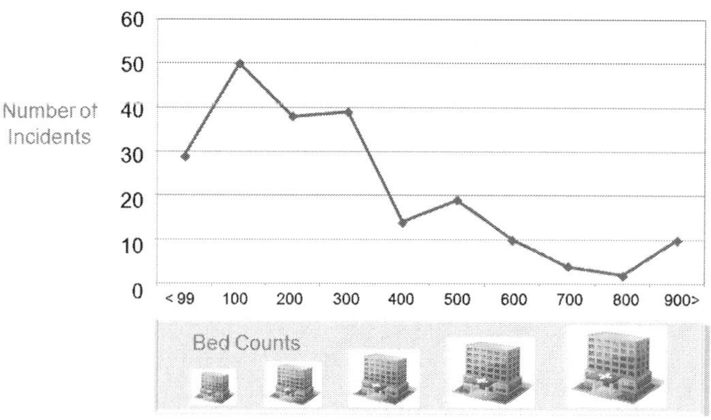

FIGURE 25-3

Shootings in healthcare from 2006–2013.

Source: Tom Aumack, CHPA, HSS Security Program Manager at Cheyenne Regional Medical Center.

Hospital shooting statistics indicate a higher number of incidents occurring in hospitals with 300 beds or less as noted in Figure 25-3. These smaller hospitals typically have less security presence compared to larger medical centers, and tend to be community-based healthcare facilities. Historically, incidents involve male shooters who present with multiple weapons. These incidents are over in minutes and most end prior to law enforcement arrival. These shootings can be suicidal intentions or mass shooting events that most frequently occur during daylight hours, inside buildings, and in populated areas.

Shooters usually fit into one or more of these three categories of aggressors.

Type I – Stranger: This offender does not have a legitimate relationship with the business or employees. The self-motivated terrorist falls into this category.

Type II – Customer or Client: The offender is receiving service and the victim is a service provider. Often seeking revenge and has a planned assault. This is the most common category in mass shooting events.

Type III – Co-worker: This offender is a colleague or co-worker often disgruntled about disciplinary actions or termination. Often seeking revenge and has a planned assault.

Warning signs such as unexplained increase in absenteeism, depression or withdrawal, along with increased mood swings and noticeable increase in alcohol or illegal drug use are often present prior to a shooting event. Additionally, one may notice an increase in anger management issues at work, or in a social setting, talk of personal problems with loved ones, and an increase in comments regarding violence and firearms. Behavioral health issues are often present but can be hard to detect.

There are several prevention strategies that can be employed to decrease risk and increase safety, as noted in Figure 25-4. Access control is a good starting point in terms of visitor management, and after hours building restriction. However, if the aggressor is an employee, they may have the security code or access to the facility. Video surveillance is primarily used for evidence collection, and can provide a

Prevention Strategies

Access Control	Video Surveillance	Duress Alarms	Other Systems
Door lock-unlock schedules	Purpose and use	Purpose and location	Emergency communication devices
Visitor control procedures	Video management record-retain	Who monitors	Mass notification systems
After hours	Privacy concerns	Response time and training	
Emergency lockdown	Monitoring		

FIGURE 25-4

Prevention strategies for the active shooter.

false sense of security when employees believe someone is watching every camera, and will send help if an emergency occurs. Duress alarms are good for areas where employees work alone, but they need to be tested to ensure the response is the one expected, in terms of resources and response time. Finally, mass notification systems have been implemented throughout the country. It is important to be able to warn occupants and coworkers of an active shooter situation.

There are three active shooter response strategies: Get Out, Hide Out, and Take Out. Getting out of the area is always the best option if available. Having a planned escape route in mind, and playing the "what if" game in a number of situations, including the office, clinic, patient care unit, and main gathering areas such as waiting rooms will increase the chances of getting out. While exiting, all belongings should be left behind, and others encouraged to follow, while warning everyone to get out. The mental mindset should be that of a raging fire situation where you must get out or lose your life. Activating the fire alarm system is not recommended in these situations as a method to warn building occupants, because doing so will bring more people out into the hallways, creating more targets for a shooter.

If staff cannot get out, then they should be trained to hide out. The second response option is to barricade self and others behind locked doors. Occupants can utilize room furniture to barricade the doors. It is important to make the room look unoccupied, by shutting off the lights, silencing phones, and remaining calm. In patient care areas, patients should be moved into locking utility or medication rooms for safety where possible. In patient rooms, patients and visitors should be moved into the bathroom, and the room door barricaded with the patient bed, and any other furniture available in the room. Shooters only have a few minutes to accomplish their plan and opening up rooms that appear to be empty is a waste of time.

As a final option, training should focus on taking out the shooter. Create a distraction and have a plan to take him down during the split second he is not focused. Throw items such as hot coffee, chairs, fire extinguishers, which can also spray from a few feet away. The goal is to disrupt and then incapacitate the shooter. This is situation of last resort and requires commitment to the action and execution of the plan.

Once law enforcement arrives, it is important to know what is expected so not to interfere with their job, which is to neutralize the threat. Training should remind staff law enforcement will proceed directly to the incident location, and will not stop to assist injured persons. This will include an expectation that both plain clothed and uniformed officers will respond with a variety of weapons. Police training dictates anyone can be a suspect, so they may shout commands and force people to the ground. Police are taught "hands kill" so individuals should immediately raise their hands, drop everything they are holding and spread fingers.

PATIENT DECONTAMINATION

In compliance with OSHA regulations,[12] each organization has a responsibility to build patient decontamination capacity, including trained staff members and available decontamination personal protective equipment (PPE) and facilities. In January 2005, OSHA published *Best Practices for Hospital-Based First Receivers*. This OSHA document provides guidance to hospitals and first receivers regarding the selection and use of appropriate PPE. Best practices presented in the document indicate the minimum PPE that OSHA anticipates will generally be needed, for protection of first receivers faced with a wide range of unknown hazards.

The decontamination function is usually located near the emergency room, and includes a process for patient care while minimizing risk to employees. The most important goal is to protect staff, visitors and victim(s) from accidental injury, due to spreading of hazardous chemicals from the victim to them. Secondly, is to decontaminate and treat victims of chemical injury. This requires attention to situations that suggest the possibility of bioterrorism, and identify resources and protocols in that regard. In all cases, regardless of the victims' degree of injury or distress, the goal of protecting staff, visitors and victim(s) must take precedence over decontaminating and treating victims.

Once the organization receives notification indicating a known/suspected or potential hazmat victim is being transported to the facility, they should activate the EOP/ERP for Hazmat Decontamination. Contaminated victims should be held outside of the facility, and not allowed in the hospital until decontamination has occurred. Once the EOP is activated, a decontamination team, consisting of properly instructed and attired personnel should assemble to perform patient decontamination.

The emergency parking lot should be secured and evacuated to allow for patient decontamination. Additionally, rescue vehicle traffic patterns will need to be adjusted to remain outside the contaminate zone. The door into the facility from the ambulance bay should be secured to ensure contaminated individuals do not enter, until they have been decontaminated. This entrance must remain secured/guarded until the decontamination processes have been accomplished, and the hot zone (site of contaminated patients) has been cleaned and restored to ready condition.

Establishing a hot and cold zone for the decontamination process reduces the risk of cross contamination and increases staff safety. The hot zone is the area where the risk of secondary decontamination is the highest, and personnel must put on personal protective equipment before entering it. This zone includes the transport vehicle, decontamination area, and the ambulance or designated emergency entrance. The cold zone includes all other areas of the hospital and property.

Responding to a hazardous material event requires using appropriate personal protective equipment (PPE). Identifying the components of the required level of PPE is based upon a given situation involving contamination, according to the OSHA as hospital first receivers' guidance. There are four basic levels of PPE (A, B, C, and D). The components of each determine the level of protection provided by each set. Determining factors include identification of the hazard(s), routes of potential hazards to the responders including inhalation, skin absorption, ingestion, and eye or skin contact. One of the most critical components of the PPE is respiratory protection. Levels A and B require a full-face-piece Self-Contained Breathing Apparatus (SCBA), or approved positive pressure supplied air respirator.

Level C, most commonly used in healthcare patient decontamination, utilizes a powered air purifying respirator (PAPR) rather than a SCBA. Level C utilizes a chemical resistant suit along with the PAPR and allows for extended operations. The following components constitute Level C equipment:

- Powered air purifying respirator (PAPR)
- Chemical resistant clothing
- Inner and outer chemical resistant gloves
- Chemical resistant boots
- Chemical resistant tape to secure gloves and boots to the suit.

Finally, Level D PPE is limited to coveralls or other work clothes, boots, and gloves. This level is appropriate when the mission assigned does not require respiratory protection.

STAFF RESPONSIBILITIES

The number of staff needed to support critical hospital operations should be determined and include in the EOP. Contingency staffing plans, staff reassignment and modification of job duties, is not uncommon during an emergency. Cross-trained tasks should be defined and practiced during an emergency exercise, and may include patient transportation, supply distribution, communication runners, and decontamination duties. Depending on the nature of the emergency, the ICS will establish mechanisms to meet the needs of staff, such as housing, transportation, food and water, stress debriefing, and childcare. Staff needs to be aware of their individual and department roles and responsibilities during an event. Additionally, the organization should assist staff with personal emergency plans to ensure the minimum staffing can be met.

UTILITIES MANAGEMENT

Diverse types of emergencies can compromise or disrupt an organization's essential utility systems. An element of advance preparation is identification of an alternate means of providing for vital utilities, such as steam, electricity, HVAC, medical gases, and water. Healthcare organizations often have redundant hook-up locations on the facility for water, negotiated relationships with primary supply chain vendors, and memoranda of understanding (MOU) with other organizations, to accomplish redundancy in major utilities. If a major utility is compromised, and the outage is widespread throughout the community, the organization must have a loss of community support and resource conservation strategy, to maintain a safe patient care environment.

Loss of Community Support is defined as a sustained disruption, failure, or loss of support from the local community, lasting at least 96 hours. During the initial period following an emergency, community resources are most often prioritized to restore power, provide security, manage debris, clear roads, and restore water and sewage systems to the community. Medical facilities are typically viewed as hardened facilities with integral backup systems and procedures, and thus not an immediate priority for local community emergency support. Support from state and federal agencies should not be anticipated before 96 hours post-event.

Strategies and options that promote institutional resiliency to withstand an event that disrupts community support for a 96-hour period should be included in the EOP. Healthcare organizations will respond to such an event, by evaluating the incident and its impact on operations and the environment of care, by reviewing how the facility will be able to manage the six critical areas of emergency operations: communications, safety and security, resources and assets, staff, utilities, and clinical/support services.

The organization should respond to the event, utilizing strategies that may include partial or complete evacuation, service curtailment, resource conservation, and/or resource supplementation from sources outside its geographical area. Hospitals must build critical system redundancies to support continued operations in the event of a disaster, and maintain caches of some emergency supplies/equipment. Emergency supply and equipment inventories should be monitored periodically and systems should be in place to protect them. Emergency supply inventories should be reviewed annually by the emergency management committee and modified based on changes in the facility's hazard vulnerability analysis, resource availability, and/or evolving technologies.

PATIENT CLINICAL AND SUPPORT

The basis of emergency planning is to protect life and provide care, treatment, and services to those in need during an emergency. Once the emergency operations plan is activated, the organization must implement processes to triage patients, schedule patients, assess and treat patients, and admit, transfer, discharge or evacuate patients.[13] Each department must identify critical functions, resources required to support them, and recognize changes in staff roles and responsibilities, in order to provide the level of patient care required to address the emergency. The healthcare organization must have clear, reasonable plans in place to address the needs of patients during extreme conditions, when the hospital's infrastructure and resources are taxed. Consideration should be given to the potential need for alternative care sites for patient treatment, effective patient identification and tracking systems, and patient transportation options.

EVACUATION

If the nature, scope, and/or duration of the emergency are such that the facility can no longer sustain patient care, treatment, or service, then it may become necessary to evacuate all or part of the facility. Hospital evacuation, both pre-event and post-event, can result from different types of disasters and reasons. Any of the natural, technological, human, or hazardous materials hazards evaluated in the HVA process, could result in structural damage or the loss of a major utility, resulting in a decision to evacuate.

A hospital evacuation requires time, and labor-intensive resources and material, at levels that most hospitals do not possess for routine emergencies. The physical aspects of evacuation typically shift healthcare professionals from providing care to tasks with which they are less familiar, or often unprepared. Transportation resources and evacuation routes may be unavailable, or designated to other public safety issues. Necessary staff may be diverted from their primary healthcare focus, or unavailable, due to the need to evacuate their own families and homes. Furthermore, the full scope of the threat may not be known or may be constantly changing and often extremely difficult to predict. Any evacuation decision has elements of risk and benefit. It will be important to evaluate both, in order to make the best evacuation decision.

The decision to partially or completely evacuate a hospital is a complex issue that needs to balance the nature of the threat against the risk the patients and staff would face by remaining in place. The risks associated with some hazards, such as flood, are often better known or more predictable than other hazards, such as a hazardous materials release in which the toxicity of the agent and its movement may be completely unknown. The risks to patients, staff, and visitors must be considered in deciding if and when to evacuate. Evacuating too soon may place patients and staff needlessly at risk if the potential threat does not materialize. Evacuating at the same time as the general public may increase the risk to patient health, if traffic congestion and other road complications increase travel time. Finally, evacuating too late increases risk if patients do not arrive at their destination before the event occurs.

There are a number of complexities associated with evacuation, and conducting a critical infrastructure self-assessment and reviewing lessons learned from historical events can better prepare the organization. Although preparedness and exercising are required, it is not possible to model the entire evacuation event. Threats change over time, internal and external resources change over time, and there is potential for resource competition for limited resources if the event is community wide. Furthermore, depending on the patient population served, the risk of evacuation may outweigh the risk of remaining in that patient care area. When conducting a predisaster self-assessment of critical infrastructure, organizations should include the following:

- Municipal Water
- Steam
- Electricity
- Natural Gas
- Boilers/Chillers/Heating Ventilation and Air Conditioning
- Powered Life Support Equipment
- Information Technology
- Telecommunications
- Security.

Water plays a critical role in maintaining the environment in which organizations care for patients. An overabundance of water and insufficient water will produce vulnerable situations. Hurricane Katrina, Superstorm Sandy, and the 2013 floods in Southern Alberta, Canada were among the worst natural disasters in history, resulting in healthcare evacuations and hospital closures. Moreover, when the municipal water supply fails, the organization loses nonpotable water required for toilet flushing, and cooling and heating applications, often forcing evacuation. Municipal water is needed to generate steam, and some organizations use incoming steam to generate electricity. Large steam production plants pipe underground steam to often huge academic medical complexes that include tertiary care hospitals, medical schools, research laboratories, and ambulatory care areas, making an evacuation more complex. Redundancy in these types of critical infrastructure is rare, and weather conditions play a big role in evacuation decision-making algorithms, especially if the boilers go out in the winter or the chillers go out in the summer.

Electricity plays a large role in the evacuation decision, because prolonged loss can lead to HVAC loss, along with essential medical technologies such as monitors, CT scanners, dialysis machines, ventilators, and incubators. Security systems designed to keep occupants safe may also be compromised in a sustained electrical outage. Hospitals have backup generators that require fuel and, depending on the number and size of the backup generators, it should be determined what length of time they can sustain the required electrical load.

When creating evacuation plans, the time required to empty the building needs to be determined, including actual movement of patients from their room to a staging area, from which they are loaded into a vehicle for transport to another hospital or alternative care site. As well, the time it takes to print out a patient discharge summary, obtain 24 hours of medication, and staffing levels all need to form part of the evacuation timeline calculation. Nights and weekend shifts frequently have less patient care staff and security personnel available to assist with patient preparation procedures. The amount of time it takes to transport the patients from the staging area to receiving hospitals is also a determining factor, including the number of transportation resources available, road conditions, and location of the hospital that can accept and properly care for the patient population.

Emergent evacuation procedures should abide by the general Rescue, Alarm, Contain, and Evacuate (RACE) method regardless of the incident. When a situation arises that requires occupants to immediately leave the area, the person in charge of the affected space should order the unit evacuation, and shall implement the following procedure:

- **Rescue**: Anyone in instant danger or harm's way shall be rescued, if it can be accomplished without undue risk to staff.
- **Alarm**: Direct a staff member to sound the alarm, make appropriate notifications, or call the Emergency Operator (Dial 911).
- **Contain**: Put distance and/or shielding between the threat and the area/building occupants.
- **Evacuate**: If the previous steps are not sufficient to mitigate the problem and the threat remains, area/building occupants should be evacuated without delay.

The major difference between emergent and nonemergent (i.e., urgent or planned) evacuations is the time available to mobilize staff and resources, plan actions and destinations, and control the overall process.

Evacuation activation levels should correspond to the levels of EOP activation, and are based on the projected impact the particular evacuation would have on the hospital. Once information is received indicating a situation or event that may require relocation of patient care or ancillary service activities from all or a portion of the facility, the organization should go on alert for potential evacuation. Once there is a need for horizontal evacuation of patients, visitors, and staff from an area of the building, a level one EOP activation should be considered. A common scenario associated with this level includes a fire in a single room, requiring occupants of that space to move horizontally to an adjoining smoke-free compartment. This level of evacuation can be accomplished quickly, using resources such as standard wheelchairs and patient beds already in place, or readily available on the unit.

A level two evacuation occurs when there is a need for vertical evacuation. A common scenario associated with this level includes a fire or smoke condition affecting an entire floor, requiring occupants of that space to move vertically to another floor in the hospital. The impact on the organization increases significantly, because of the need to move patients down stairs, with the planning assumption the elevators might be inoperable. Moving patients to another floor requires considerable additional staffing resources and specialized equipment for patient movement.

An entire building evacuation would be considered a level three. This would likely be the result of an uncontrolled fire or failure of a mission critical system for an extended duration.

Once an entire building evacuation order is given, the organization should begin evacuation triage to determine the amount of staff needed to move each patient, type of movement and evacuation devices required, which loading areas to relocate to, and destination facility of each patient. Three essential components are: a process that is quick and can accurately assess, be marked in a standard way, and documented for resource allocation and tracking purposes. The following three patient mobility levels should be considered:

1. *Ambulatory*: Able to walk to loading area without physical assistance and without likelihood of resulting in harm or injury. This group should be denoted with green wristbands and escorted in a one to five staff to patient ratio and can be transported in a large group.
2. *Wheelchair*: Alert but unable to walk due to physical or medical condition. These patients are clinically stable and have a low likelihood of resulting in harm due to prolonged sitting and do not require equipment beyond oxygen or intravenous fluids. This group should be denoted with yellow wristbands and can be safely managed by a single nonclinical staff member.
3. *Nonambulatory*: Clinically unable to be moved in seated position and may require ventilators and/or cardiac monitors. These patients require transport by bed, gurney, or stretcher and may be transferred to evacuation sleds, backboards, or rescue dragged on their mattress. The group should be denoted with red wristbands and will require ambulance transport to the destination facility.

After the patients have been triaged, they are moved from their patient room to a patient holding area, by a horizontal movement team. A vertical movement team then moves the patient down to the ground floor or patient loading area. Vertical movement can be exhausting, therefore teams should be augmented by public safety, security, plant operations, and other nonclinical personnel. Preestablished loading zones should exist for each level of patient triaged. Ambulatory patients should be loaded at a main entrance accustomed to patient drop off and pick up. Wheelchair patient loading will require an entrance that can accommodate several transport vehicles, such as buses and vans. Finally, the nonambulatory patients require an ambulance, so the emergency department is the most logical loading zone. These are the most critical patients and usually moved out of the facility last. Patient movement sequencing will be such that the greatest numbers of patients move out the fastest way possible.

EMERGENCY PREPAREDNESS EXERCISE DESIGN AND CONDUCT

Emergency preparedness exercises are designed to evaluate the EOP/ERP's appropriateness, adequacy, and the effectiveness of logistics, human resources, training, policies, procedures, and protocols.[14] The exercise should stress the limits of the plan to support assessment of the organization's preparedness and performance. The design of the exercise should reflect a likely disaster, and test the organization's ability to respond to the effects of this emergency and its capabilities to provide care, treatment, and services. Individual exercises should be part of an exercise and evaluation cycle.

Hospitals participate in a range of exercises including discussion-based, such as tabletops, and operations-based such as drills, functional and full-scale exercises. These exercises can be isolated within the hospital or be part of a larger community, coalition or statewide exercise, such as an airport mass casualty exercise. When planning an exercise, the organization should review past training and exercises for types, objectives, partners and areas for improvement. Community exercises should be assessed for possible involvement and collaboration, to meet facility exercise requirements. The hazard vulnerability analysis should be reviewed for potential needs and to ensure consistency with the overall emergency preparedness strategy.

Exercise design and development begins with establishing a planning team. This team determines potential exercise objectives that test each of the critical areas of emergency management: Communications, Resources and Assets, Safety and Security, Staff Responsibilities, Utilities Management, and Patient Clinical and Support activities. The team may also identify appropriate target capabilities such as medical surge, mass fatality management or volunteer management to be evaluated during the exercise. After conducting the exercise, an exercise debriefing or "hot-wash" should be conducted, to identify deficiencies and opportunities for improvement. These deficiencies are communicated to the EM Committee for improvement monitoring and EOP/ERP modification. Subsequent exercises should include objectives written to evaluate the effectiveness of plan improvements.

REFERENCES

1. Rubin JN. Recurring pitfalls in hospital preparedness and response. *Journal of Homeland Security* 2004, January. Retrieved August 2, 2006, from http://www.homelandsecurity.org/newjournal/articles/rubin.html.
2. PricewaterhouseCoopers' Health Research Institute. *Closing the seams: Developing an integrated approach to health system disaster preparedness*. 2007. Retrieved November 2, 2007, from http://www.pwc.com/extweb/pwcpublications.nsf/docid/9CEC1E9BDCAC478525737F005C80A9.
3. National Fire Protection Association. *NFPA 1600 standard on disaster/emergency management and business continuity programs*. 2007. Quincy, MA.
4. The Joint Commission. *Comprehensive accreditation manual for hospitals: The official handbook*. Oakbrook Terrace, IL: Joint Commission Resources; 2014.
5. Accreditation Canada, Qmentum Program. Standards: Leadership, Section 14. 2014.
6. Canadian Standards Association. Z1600–08: Emergency Management and Business Continuity Programs. 2008. Available from http://www.driecentral.org/2008-Z1600.pdf.
7. American College of Health Executives. Policy Statement: Healthcare Executives' Role in Emergency Preparedness. *Healthcare Executive* Sep/Oct 2010.
8. U.S. General Accountability Office. *Catastrophic disasters: Enhanced leadership, capabilities, and accountability controls will improve the effectiveness of the nation's preparedness, response, and recovery system*. 2006, September. Retrieved September 10, 2006, from www.gao.gov/cgi-bin/getrpt?GAO-06-.
9. Trust for America's Health. *Ready or not? Protecting the public's health from diseases, disasters, and bioterrorism*. 2007. Retrieved December 18, 2007, from http://healthyamericans.org/reports/bioterror07/BioTerrorReport2007.pdf.
10. The Joint Commission. *Health care at the crossroads: Strategies for creating and sustaining community-wide emergency preparedness strategies* 2003. Retrieved December 12, 2007, from http://www.usaprepare.com/ep3-12-03.pdf.
11. Planning for emergencies in healthcare facilities. 2010. Retrieved February 3, 2014 from http://www.public.health.wa.gov.au/3/1370/2/planning_for_emergencies_in_health_care_facilities.pm.
12. U. S. Department of Labor. Occupational Safety and Health Administration. *Best practices for hospital based first receivers of patients from mass casualty incidents involving hazardous substances*. 29 C.F.R.1910 120. 2006. Washington, DC.
13. Agency for Healthcare Research and Quality. *Altered Standards of Care in Mass Casualty Events*. Prepared by Health Systems Research Inc; 2005. Online at http://www.ahrq.gov/research/altstand/.
14. Krisberg K. Public health preparedness drills reap benefits, concerns. *The Nation's Health* 2003;**33**. Retrieved August 2, 2006, from http://www.medscape.com/viewarticle/46327.

CHAPTER

A PRIMER FOR HEALTHCARE EXECUTIVES

26

It is 6:00 pm on Friday and you're packing up for the weekend, but at this moment you're the administrator on call. You get a call from your security director that there has been gunfire in the emergency department waiting area; two people have been shot and the gunman has not been identified or located. He is believed to still be in your hospital.

What do you do? Your MBA training never discussed how to handle a major breach in security such as this event. The incident command training you went through last month talked about external relationships and mutual aid agreements the organization should have. You are firmly aware of how the hospital is expected by The Joint Commission (TJC) to be self-sustaining for 96 hours in the event of an emergency or other natural disaster. The logistical planning to maintain compliance with that particular standard has been a major initiative for your healthcare facility. The quarterly infant abduction drills required of the Environment of Care Committee have been most informative in bringing awareness to that type of critical incident. The changes made to the new infant abduction response plan have been met with good success. The $200K capital investment in digital video surveillance and monitoring equipment last year brought a new emphasis on the importance of security to the organization. During the presentation to the finance committee, a commitment was made to continue to enhance protection levels within the organization by senior administration. In short, much has been done and all for the right reasons. Unfortunately, it just does not seem germane to the situation that is allegedly occurring at this moment.

This incident could happen at any healthcare facility and has—the threat to patients and staff safety is real. We are all aware of the tragic shooting and suicide at Johns Hopkins in 2010, but the news is full of horrific stories such as these throughout the healthcare delivery system. There were more than 150 shootings at hospitals across the United States from 2000 to 2011—30% of those in emergency departments. According to the *Los Angeles Times*, their studies have shown that 91 shootings have occurred inside the hospital while 63 have occurred outside on hospital grounds.[1] In the wake of the Sandy Hook Elementary School tragedy in December of 2012, a gunman opened fire at St. Vincent's Hospital in Birmingham, Alabama, wounding two hospital employees and a police officer. In April 2009, a hospital worker, after having recently been downsized, shot and killed two employees and then killed himself at Long Beach Memorial Hospital in Long Beach, California.[2] In June 2009, Rhonda Stewart got into an argument with her estranged husband in the intensive care unit at Charleston Area Medical Center's Memorial Hospital in Charleston, West Virginia. She was asked to leave by the hospital staff. She later returned with a gun and shot her husband in the head.[3] In November 2013 at Children's Hospital of Milwaukee, police shot and wounded an armed man on the neonatal intensive care floor after the police found the man, on a felony warrant, holding a child in the ICU. Instead of surrendering, the man took out a handgun and fled down the hallway, where officers opened fire inside the hospital.[4] This list contains just a few of the shooting events that have occurred in healthcare across the world. Contrary to public beliefs about which type of hospitals are most susceptible to such violence, none of these healthcare organizations are inner city locations surrounded by high-crime neighborhoods. They are a reflection of the average size and type of acute care hospital that could be located in any community.

But this is not the only type of violence your healthcare staff are experiencing. Your care providers are facing more verbal abuse and random acts of violence committed against them by patients and, to a lesser extent, visitors, than at any other time in the history of modern medicine. In a 2011 survey conducted by the Emergency Nurses Association, nine out of ten emergency department managers cited patient violence as the greatest threat to department personnel.[5] The physicians and nurses who staff emergency departments are demanding greater protection by hospitals. In the survey, emergency department nurses reported:[5]

- Dissatisfaction with the overall level of safety from workplace violence (89%).
- Feeling unprepared to handle violence in the ED given their education and training (83%).
- Reduced job satisfaction due to violence (74%).
- Impaired job performance for up to a week after a violent incident (48%).
- Taking time off because of violence (25%).

In the last decade progress in providing safe and secure healthcare environments has "paled" in contrast to other major business segments of our society. While the tragic events of the World Trade Center on September 11, 2001 jumpstarted improved security for most U.S. organizations, the event had little overall effect on improving healthcare security. Since 9/11 serious crimes such as homicides and serious assaults have steadily increased in virtually all healthcare environments.

Fortunately, to date, healthcare has been given a relatively free pass by the media when major breaches in security occur. Take for instance the March 2008 shooting spree at Doctor's Hospital in Columbus, Georgia. A gunman, allegedly distraught over his mother's dying at the hospital in 2004, brought three handguns to the fifth floor and shot a nurse and an administrative assistant, before gunning down a patient waiting outside in the parking lot. Outside of local community and state media coverage, there was minimal attention brought to this horrific incident by the national and international media. During the same week, an infant was abducted from Central Florida Regional Hospital in Sanford, Florida, which received national attention due to the live media footage captured when the abductor was pulled over on the highway and the infant successfully recovered. However, many other similar security breaches have received little to no media attention. Thus, public opinion has not been overtly influenced.

The public expectation of security inside a healthcare facility, which is largely formed by the media, is much different from the aviation and education sectors. Have you ever asked yourself why? We provide a room for our overnight-stay patients without a door that locks. We provide pain relief with powerful narcotics that induce sleep, mental uncertainty and an unbalanced state of consciousness. We remove patients from their clothing and ask them to wear patient gowns that, let's admit, at the very least challenge our personal privacy. In short, our environment creates a number of basic vulnerabilities for our patients so that quality care can be administered.

The lack of media attention to the violence and other security concerns present in the healthcare environment will not continue forever. Healthcare professionals from many disciplines believe our industry is one major security event away from attracting the same scrutiny as the aviation and education industries—and with it, public opinion of what security safeguards should be employed in the healthcare environment will change. Are you ready, and how do you get ahead of the curve now?

No healthcare security professional is asking for greater media scrutiny, mind you, or the quality of care to be altered. Nor are we asking for greater administrative or regulatory oversight for security from either The Joint Commission or the Centers for Medicaid and Medicare. The important mission of the organization to deliver quality care is well understood. The mission of your security program should be to provide a safe healing environment in which quality care can be administered.

The need for increased security has provided an unprecedented challenge in the methods and philosophies regarding protection of our healthcare organizations. Their safeguarding cannot be completely dependent on the security department. Many aspects of protecting healthcare organizations reach far beyond the control of the commonly accepted elements of a healthcare security department. Today, in order to achieve a high level of security, managers, top executives, and boards of directors must be more involved, through appropriate funding levels and strong administrative direction with managing and supporting security issues. As leaders, your involvement and ownership of the protection effort in your day-to-day management obligations is needed.

In this chapter, we do not wish to use scare tactics to change your expectations of your security program and how you resource it. Just the opposite: we want to enlighten you, the healthcare executive, with a broader understanding of the security risks prevalent in the healthcare environment. Our goal is to help you make an informed decision about how to reasonably protect your organization.

We will ask a number of rhetorical questions to help enhance the posture of security throughout your organization. Emphasis will be placed on helping you, the healthcare executive, reduce the risk of adverse events that negatively affect the real and perceived nature of safety in your facility and on your campus. Discussion will include how the security program is designed to keep patients, visitors, and staff members safe and what must be done to create an environment where healing can occur safely while maintaining a welcoming environment.

WHAT BASIC OBJECTIVES SHOULD WE HAVE FOR THE SECURITY PROGRAM?

Security programs must be structured to protect the healthcare organization within the governing factors of organizational mission, vision, and core values; physical design; patient and community demographics; employee and public relations; budget and resource availability; and the operational requirements of the facility.

Basic objectives of the healthcare security program can be viewed as:

- Contributing to the overall mission of the healthcare organization in the provision of excellent medical care services
- Preventing security-related incidents through a proactive system of security safeguards
- Responding to security incidents in such a manner that property damage or injury to persons is prevented or at least mitigated through competent and timely actions
- Creating a sense of confidence in the minds of staff, visitors and persons being served that they are interacting in a reasonably safe and secure environment.
- Providing services and activities in a positive and effective manner, which supports the goals and culture of the organization being served.

The planning and implementation of program elements to achieve these basic objectives are influenced by both internal and external forces. In the U.S., The Joint Commission has specific security standards and elements of performance for security. For the most part, this accrediting agency has established minimum "floor" standards regarding the protection effort, not much more. HIPAA rules, *Privacy* and *Security*, and their international equivalents, have provided requirements for how patient data must be protected and controlled. However, the rules are vague and do not explicitly address what safeguards should be incorporated. Without precedent setting case law, many patient data protection practices and procedures construed to be a "HIPAA violation" or viewed as "in compliance" remain individual interpretations.

CMS in the U.S. has developed interpretative guidelines (or standards) that affect security's involvement in patient care—elopement (prevention and response), restraint and seclusion, and use of weapons. The reduction in the use of physical restraints with patients continues to be one of CMS's major quality initiatives. Unfortunately, CMS guidelines and their reading may have contributed significantly to the ever-increasing volume of assaults against, and subsequent injuries to, care providers, security officers and others who work in the healthcare environment.

With the development of *Healthcare Security: Basic Industry Guidelines* the International Association for Healthcare Security and Safety (IAHSS) has significantly helped move the healthcare security industry forward. These basic security guidelines provide a consensus approach to the basic fabric and direction of the structure of the healthcare security program. They are intended to assist healthcare administrators in fulfilling their obligation to provide a safe; secure and welcoming environment, while carrying out the mission of their healthcare organization. The Association publishes an annual booklet containing the guidelines; however, as these guidelines are subject to continuous review and changes, the Association website contains the most current and up-to-date information.[6]

The protection program and the philosophy and objectives of the principal security administrator have a strong influence on the posture of security. However, the organization and its leadership should provide the ultimate definition of the security system. Internally, four of the most important factors contributing to the success of the protection effort are the leader selected to oversee security, the reporting relationship of the security administrator, the customer service expectations of the department, and the buy-in from the administrative staff of the security master plan.

WHAT LEADERSHIP CHARACTERISTICS SHOULD THE HEALTHCARE SECURITY ADMINISTRATOR POSSESS?

The success of the security program is largely the responsibility of the security leadership and a direct reflection of their experience, responsiveness, and commitment to protection and customer service. If these qualities are not found at the top, they are likely absent in the security staff.

A common error for many healthcare administrators is to view the protection effort within a healthcare facility as a law enforcement function. Although some common ground may exist between security and law enforcement, the security function must always be rooted with a service orientation (prevention, education, and public relations) and not based on a law enforcement focus. Individuals fulfilling the security leadership position should possess a background in security and understand how protection principles apply to the healthcare environment.

Security of the healthcare organization is a business function and requires leaders who can think strategically and act tactically. Today's healthcare security administrator must be technically competent and knowledgeable about security management and electronic security systems. The industry remains people intensive—over two-thirds (73%) of healthcare security budgets are dedicated to staff resources.[7]

This requires individuals who can effectively lead others while having a basic understanding of how to solve problems, set expectations, and hold people accountable.

Operating budgets and capital budget requests are under greater scrutiny and require a business-minded security administrator who can defend capital request with a return on investment mentality, and have the capacity to develop a strategic 3–5 year security master plan.

In short, the healthcare security administrator must be able to lead themselves and the change necessary to improve the real and perceived nature of personal safety on campus. The protection professional must be able to effectively manage the dynamic environment of healthcare. This includes changes in the delivery of healthcare services, multiple campus environments, homecare, hospice, and community clinics. It requires the ability to build relationships with others, specifically emergency departments and other high-risk or "security sensitive" departments that rely heavily on the safeguards provided by the protection department.

Organizations such as the IAHSS have many educational programs, development activities, and best practice information to help build the core body of knowledge within the healthcare security leader. Individual certification for the healthcare protection administrator should be required within a year of eligibility. The Certified Healthcare Protection Administrator (CHPA) administered by the IAHSS and/or the Certified Protection Professional (CPP) are the two most recognized certifications in the security industry. Healthcare organizations are continuously rewarded with high performing protection programs and effective security leaders when they have placed preference on these supporting memberships and specifying these credentials in the hiring process.

It does not matter if the healthcare security management model is proprietary or outsourced; the leader selected to administer the security program must align with the leadership philosophy of the organization and be a good cultural fit with the higher purpose of health care.

WHERE SHOULD SECURITY REPORT?

An expectation of The Joint Commission and the required Security Management Plan is to clearly specify the position that has the responsibility for security of the organization and has a clearly defined reporting level for this position. The hierarchical level in the organization to which security reports reflects the importance that the administrative team places on the security function and the organization's responsibility of protecting persons and property. The important aspect of the security reporting level is it must provide the organizational authority necessary to properly carry out its mission. A practical consideration is security should report to an individual who has both the time and interest in the security function. In short, there must be proper administrative support for a security program to be effective and productive. A common reporting level for security is the vice president (or director) of facilities or the risk management administrator who, as a generality, seems to fit the foundation criteria for a successful program.

WHAT CUSTOMER SERVICE EXPECTATIONS SHOULD BE ESTABLISHED FOR SECURITY?

The successful healthcare security program incorporates the principles of good customer service. The security staff should be a direct reflection on the healthcare administrator's commitment to quality and customer service.

Great customer service and security service should blend together for the collective good. The historical perspective of security and customer service being polar opposites is no longer acceptable.

More than just security, security staff members should be ambassadors for the organization they serve and be expected to practice the rules of customer first and courteous enforcement. Their image, actions, and interactions with patients, visitors, and staff should leave an encouraging feeling about the hospital and the perception of personal safety. This will include being available to answer questions, providing directions and escort service and serving a general purpose of being a "walking around" information desk.

WHY DO I NEED A SECURITY MASTER PLAN?

A security operation cannot be superimposed, like an umbrella, on a healthcare organization with any degree of effectiveness. Rather it must be integrated into the routine operations of the organization.

A major intent of the security master plan is to provide the mechanisms and philosophy of achieving the overall direction of the protection system agreed upon by the stakeholders. It should be reflective of guiding beliefs and align these with daily practices in the protection program. A strategic plan for security, it should be developed to set the philosophy and direction of the protection program for a longer term (3–5 years). The plan should include elements of financial planning and be sensitive to the overall demographics of the healthcare organization. It should also explore opportunities for building synergies with other departments and outside agencies. The major components of this plan are:

- Organization-wide security coordination and control
- Neighborhood stability and security/crime prevention involvement
- Public safety agency coordination
- Criminal justice system interface
- Organizational philosophy regarding the type and extent of physical and electronic security safeguards to be utilized
- Degree of employee/staff involvement in the protection program
- Building configuration and design considerations

The underlying security philosophies that are put into place by the healthcare facility should not be developed in a vacuum by the security administrator. The process should include key constituents of the organization, to include leadership representatives from the emergency department, IT, human resources, facilities, and risk management. However, in the end, the healthcare administrator must support and give approval—designating the responsibility, providing authority and allocating the resources necessary to implement the security program.

The security strategic plan will be unique to each specific organization as to form, format, and subject area. This plan, however, is necessary for all organizations to provide clear program direction. Without the framework of strategic security policy and infrastructure, a program simply becomes one of day-to-day reaction, often resulting in a nonproductive and costly effort. The security master plan, in its final format, affords additional protection as it helps document "*the why*" behind what is being done in the protection program. The plan should contain an element that comprehensively documents all that has been done to enhance the posture of security. In the event of an adverse situation, the protection afforded by this alone is significant. In the end, the security master plan demonstrates how seriously security is taken by the highest levels of leadership in the organization.

HOW DO WE IDENTIFY OUR SECURITY RISKS AND VULNERABILITIES?

All healthcare facilities, regardless of size, are subject to basic security risks. The range of security risks is extensive, from assaults and dissident group actions (demonstrations, civil disturbances, sabotage, and labor actions) to identity theft and loss of critical information. There are a whole host of other security risks inherent to providing patient care services such as drug theft/diversion, infant/pediatric abductions, medical imposters and patient-generated violence.

The foundation of a healthcare organization protection system is the identification and assessment of the types of threats and the degree (impact) of damage if the threat becomes an actual occurrence. The identification of specific risks generally begins with a facility security review process, often called the Security Risk Assessment.

The identification and magnitude of security threats or risks, along with their potential impact on the healthcare organization, is but an initial step in protecting the organization. The objective of the security assessment is to identify the security exposures so that a comprehensive, effective, and cost-justified security plan can be developed and implemented. Analysis and evaluation of the risks provides the rationale that security measures (safeguards) are implemented appropriately based on protecting critical resources while accepting a calculated degree of risk. It is understood an asset cannot be protected completely without extravagant cost or unduly inhibiting the primary mission of providing efficient and quality patient care. The goal of implementing countermeasures for security risks is to make it difficult for a security breach to occur—to harden the facility as target. The level of difficulty to be implemented depends on the value of the asset and the organization's tolerance for risk.

A great many methodologies and formats can be utilized to assess security risks and to measure the severity of those risks. There are two basic principles to keep in mind regarding security risk assessments.

1. The methodology should not be overly complicated and the bottom line is that risk level conclusions are largely subjective in nature in terms of probability.
2. A formal security risk assessment, conducted on a periodic basis, is simply a baseline that can and should be modified on an ongoing basis.

Virtually every security incident provides an opportunity for lessons learned which may affect the assessment. Changing neighborhood dynamics and renovation and construction projects are also among activities that may have a bearing on the security risk analysis. Additionally, new and modified patient care programs, including changing space allocations, are important to consider.

All security program safeguards should have some relation to the level of threat.

Once the process of risk assessment has been completed, a mitigation plan has been devised, and safeguards have been blended into a security program, this process should begin again. The identification of security vulnerabilities and risks is ongoing. Risks previously identified may no longer exist, and new risks may appear as the dynamics of a healthcare environment continually change.

DOES THE COMMUNITY STANDARD HAVE A ROLE?

Gaining knowledge of the protection safeguards deployed at other healthcare facilities is an important consideration for every healthcare administrator. The community and patient demographics differ by facility; no two healthcare environments are exactly alike. However, physicians often have privileges at multiple hospitals and healthcare has a large transient workforce who frequently "job hop" in search of better schedules, shorter commutes, and safer work environments. The knowledge of the model of security in place at other healthcare facilities alone can help mitigate a negative perception of the protection efforts on campus.

THE SECURITY STAFFING MODEL: HOW LARGE A STAFF IS NEEDED?

The security force is often viewed as the quality linchpin in a healthcare facility's security program. Often, security officers are among the first people patients and visitors see and communicate with. They should create positive feelings about the facility and enhance the perception of safety within the organization. In short, the healthcare protection program needs reliable and professional security officers, not just security guards.

The number and types of security personnel required for an efficient security program are fundamental questions for every facility. It is not as easy as applying a simple formula using the square feet of buildings, campus acreage size, number of beds, number of employees, comparisons to "like" facilities, or any other profile data. It is indeed an individual facility question since numerous factors must be considered and will vary in depth and scope from organization to organization. To arrive at the required number of security personnel, it is necessary first to analyze and understand the security mission, determine the level of the organization's security risks and vulnerabilities to be managed, review electronic and physical safeguards planned or in place, and to identify the various services to be rendered. The next step is to design a program that will support the mission, properly manage risks, and implement the intended services. Only then can the number of staff required to operate the program be determined. In short, determining the "right size" security force takes a great deal of time, effort, and in-depth evaluation.

Healthcare organizations commonly make the mistake of hiring a complement of security officers and then determining what activities they will perform. In a similar vein, some security planners answer every security problem by suggesting the hiring of additional personnel. More people are not always the answer, and in fact, numerous security programs have been upgraded by reducing personnel through improved management, specialized training, and the application of new preventive security concepts. Unfortunately, sound planning and valid program justification often yield to emotions and easy solutions. In reality, more security personnel have been added to existing programs due to response to breaches in security or distressing incidents than to sound planning.

The objective method of determining how many security personnel are deployed is first to determine the functions and the activity to be accomplished. Reference to the number of personnel required is a rather inexact measurement. Security staff should ideally be deployed on the basis of objective criterion such as those listed in Table 26-1.

Security resources should be prioritized related to business risk and the impact on quality patient care. Expenses associated with security staffing levels must be managed and balanced against the constant pressures of cost containment. The security staffing plan should not be viewed as a total FTE count allocated to the department, but the complement of staff stated to be on duty at any given time per the master schedule. Determining the volume of security employees needed to fulfill the master schedule must be determined based on a ratio that considers the amount of unproductive time afforded by each security staff member—i.e., required training, absences due to vacation or sickness, etc.

Table 26-1 Objective Criteria for Security Staffing

Security Staffing Criteria	
Total Occupied Square Footage	Campus Acreage
Primary Service Area Population	Scheduled Routine Functions of Security
Criminal Environment Analysis	Scheduled Special Functions of Security
Patient Volume (adjusted patient days)	Experience with Aggressive / Assaultive Behavior
High-Risk / Vulnerable Patient Population Served	Security Incident History (Internal & External Crime)
High-Risk Patient Involvement	Ratio of ED Visits to Security Patient Assists
Facility Specific Unique Issues	Trauma Designation Level
Physical & Electronic Safeguards Deployed	Emergency & Service Response Time Expectation
Response Capabilities of Police	Weapons History at the Facility
Total Number of Public Access Points	Lost Time Injuries Related to Security Incidents
Security Sensitive Services rendered	Politically Sensitive Affiliations

The protection program should refrain from flexing security staffing for temporary convenience or budgetary constraints. Absences and vacancies must always be filled unless uncontrollable circumstances exist. In lawsuits for inadequate security (for example, a visitor assaulted in the parking garage), the risk associated with the FTE count model is a plaintiff's attorney claiming: "If there were three security officers as designed, there is significant propensity that the deployment of that officer could have prevented this crime from occurring." This argument places credence to the dispute of inadequate security and often results in a higher negotiated settlement if the case is not taken to court.

A factor that should not be left out of the equation in determining the number of officers required is the skill level and degree of productivity of each security officer. A well-trained security officer who looks the part, knows and understands the role and consistently performs at a high level is much more productive than a "guard" who is not properly trained, supervised or engaged in their protection responsibilities. Many healthcare protection administrators agree—one professional security officer can accomplish more than two security guards. A competitive compensation strategy coupled with a professional security officer training and development program are key strategies for obtaining a high level of engagement and consistent performance.

SECURITY TRAINING: WHAT SHOULD I EXPECT?

A well-trained security force is the basic component of the healthcare protection system. Professional security officer training is a combination of protection, customer service, and public relations. Proper training of security officers can produce the return on investment in terms of helping the healthcare organization attain the highest level of security and safety.

Litigation has been a powerful driving force in the increase in healthcare security officer training. Claims that healthcare organizations have failed to provide necessary training are used with much success in lawsuits, especially those involving weapons, defensive equipment, use of physical force, false arrests, and civil rights issues. The responsibility for the adequate training of security staff rests squarely on the organization.

Ironically, although a trained security officer can be at least twice as productive as a well-intentioned untrained officer, it is usually easier to obtain money for an extra position than for additional training. The number of security personnel is often mistakenly used to determine the level of protection regardless of the training required of or provided for the position.

Leadership development activities cannot be lost in the healthcare security training program. These can increase the effectiveness of the supervisors, managers, and directors involved in the healthcare security program and be the source for driving higher levels of both patient and employee satisfaction. Helping security leaders at various levels develop the skills and knowledge they need to succeed in their leadership positions can make the organization a better place to work and help the protection program retain its most critical asset—their employees. Many healthcare organizations have seen that investment in the development of its security leaders has a measurable return on investment (ROI) as it helps reduce costs in the areas of turnover and employer practice and inadequate security liability. The IAHSS is an excellent source for security leadership development and credentialing.

HOW DO I KNOW MY SECURITY STAFF ARE COMPETENT?

Security officers must be prepared to subdue a mentally disturbed patient, apprehend a thief, comfort a distraught mother, escort a lost visitor, and perform any number of other tasks at anytime, anywhere in the facility. Training cannot be a one-time event. From the time they are hired and throughout their careers, security staff must continue training to learn, improve, and further develop their professional skills.

There are a number of state statutes that mandate how many contact hours should be provided for security staff training. Most educators, however, believe competency is a better indicator of a successful training activity. The amount of training time provided is not a good judge of an individual's skill level to perform the function of protecting a healing environment—their demonstrated competency is the best indicator.

A common question received from many healthcare administrators: What fundamental training elements should be required training for anyone fulfilling the role of security officer?

- *Security Role in Patient Care/Aggression Management*: Healthcare security officers can expect to be called upon to de-escalate and manage aggressive or violent behavior. Focusing on verbal de-escalation and voluntary compliance, the training should be designed to teach security staff members to successfully control aggression and other verbal or physically inappropriate actions of others in a medical care environment.
- *Use of Force*: Every healthcare facility should develop a use of force policy that includes the identification of situations, both clinical and nonclinical, in which security officers are permitted to use force. The new officer must be trained on the use of force policy upon hire, and be provided specific training on each item of equipment they carry.
- *Restraint Training*: The basic requirement is that if a security officer is involved in the application of restraints, they have to be trained and demonstrate competency in the safe application and use of restraints.
- *Report Writing*: Of all the security officer's duties, the ability to write an accurate, clear, concise and impartial security incident report is one of the most vital.

Table 26-2 Contemporary Security Training Topics

Security Officer Training Topics	
Gang Awareness	Weapons of Mass Destruction
Infant Abduction Prevention and Response	Terrorism Awareness
Forensic (prisoner) Patients	Emergency Preparedness
Very Important Patients	Active Shooter
Critical Incident Response / Scene Management	Workplace Violence Prevention & Response
HIPAA and the Security Officer	Disclosure of Patient Information
Media Relations	Laws of Arrest, Search, and Seizure
CPR/First Aid	Disaster Readiness

- *Customer Service and Security*: Healthcare security officers who perform their job correctly spend more than 50% of their time providing general services. As ambassadors for the organizations and the constituents served, the security officer must understand the rules of courteous enforcement and public relations.
- *Patrol Techniques*: The security patrol is the most common activity performed by the healthcare security officer. More than just "walking around," the security officer must be trained to be "systematically unsystematic" to routinely change their patrol coverage. The new officer must learn that, while on patrol, they are looking for people in need of assistance or dangerous situations and also learn how to use their senses.
- *IAHSS Progressive Certification*: Providing a foundational understanding of healthcare security, the Basic Training level is the first phase in the IAHSS Progressive Certification program. The Advanced and Supervisory Training levels expand on the Basic Training program and allow security officers to continue their education after becoming certified at the Basic Training Level. The programs are designed for the healthcare security officer who desires to achieve higher levels of responsibility in the organization.
- *Other Training Considerations*: Many healthcare facilities provide training about security protocols and contemporary security topics such as those listed in Table 26-2.

An often-neglected area of training is the operational aspect of the healthcare delivery system. Security officers should learn how various departments and sections of the healthcare system operate to understand better what they are protecting and their role in the delivery of quality patient care. The better understanding officers have of the operations, the formal and informal hierarchy, and the mission, objectives, and goals of the organization, the better equipped they will be to carry out their responsibilities.

HOW MUCH INVOLVEMENT SHOULD SECURITY HAVE WITH PATIENTS?

Providing an appropriate safe treatment environment for all patients is a basic requirement of every healthcare organization. Clinical staff are expected to implement appropriate interventions, as needed, to prevent patients from harming themselves or others. Often this will include security officer support to provide constant monitoring to help protect the patients from harming themselves, harming a care provider or others, or to prevent the patient from leaving the facility.

There must be a clear understanding of how the security program engages with patients and their visitors within the healthcare environment in order to properly fulfill the security and organizational mission. The scope of expected assistance significantly affects security staffing decisions, the focus of security training, and staff expectations.

Responding to requests for assistance with patients is a valid and necessary function of any protection system. The security program that takes a "hands off" approach to patient involvement is not fulfilling an important mission for the healthcare organization. Creating guidelines to govern the relationship of the officer with the assigned care provider and the patient with specific responsibilities outlined for the security officer is a must for every healthcare protection program.

An important element for every healthcare professional to understand is that any patient on a security watch is the direct responsibility of the nurse assigned to that specific patient. The nurse directs all action regarding the patient and cannot relinquish this responsibility to the security officer. The officer's involvement in this patient care procedure is merely an extension of the assigned nurse or physician; all security actions with the patient are on behalf of the care provider.

The frequency of security calls for patient assistance varies from organization to organization and depends on many factors, including the types of patients the facility serves and the availability of nursing personnel. There is a tendency for security to be called too frequently, as demonstrated with a number of healthcare organizations that have witnessed their volume of security incidents for patient assistance more than double and the average amount of time spent for each event by security staff more than triple. However, it is certainly the case that calling security "early and often" for a proactive standby with a patient will reduce aggressive acts if these metrics are carefully monitored. The healthcare protection program should carefully monitor and measure their involvement in patient care for performance improvement by volume and total amount of time spent on average and resource the responsibility accordingly.

Most healthcare professionals agree mental health patients are a significant factor in the explosive increase in the volume of security watches in the emergency department and elsewhere in the healthcare facility. Many hospital emergency departments have responded by taking a page from the standard security practices employed in behavioral/mental health care units. These practices include creation of a weapons-free environment, requiring all at-risk patients to gown, and training all emergency department and support staff in aggression management and de-escalation techniques.

WHAT TYPE OF UNIFORM SHOULD SECURITY OFFICERS WEAR?

A wide variety of attire options are available to the healthcare security program. A continuous debate is whether security officers should wear a traditional uniform (military or police style) or a softer look uniform that includes a blazer and slacks. The consensus is that security officers should never be outfitted in plainclothes.

The vast majority of healthcare security officers are traditionally uniformed. Wearing this style of uniform readily identifies security staff and commands control when it is necessary to regulate behavior and provides a deterrent to criminal activity. The uniform is versatile and worn indoors/outdoors and in all climates. This style of uniform is preferred for officers who encounter many confrontational situations or primarily perform foot patrol. The blazer style uniform with contrasting slacks (gray slacks and blue blazer) can be a very professional look, and works best for officers who work mainly inside the facility and function primarily in a public relations mode. Many behavioral/mental healthcare facilities prefer security officers working in these environments to work in the blazer style uniform to prevent the uniform from unnecessarily antagonizing patients or visitors. Golf shirt type uniforms are also gaining popularity in these settings.

The type of healthcare organization, its customer service philosophy, and the primary function the security department in general is carrying out, or more specifically, the function the security officer is fulfilling, should be the greatest influencing factor in determining the uniform to be worn by security staff. The officer with primary foot patrol responsibilities who should be highly visible will often wear a different uniform option than the officer whose primary function is greeting patients and visitor management.

WHAT USE OF FORCE OPTIONS SHOULD BE MADE AVAILABLE TO OUR SECURITY STAFF?

The use of force by healthcare security officers is sometimes necessary to maintain order and safeguard staff, patients and visitors in a healthcare environment. The security officer must occasionally use a certain amount of force, from mere presence and verbal persuasion to physical intervention, to overcome resistance and ensure compliance with hospital policy and medical care plans.

For security program effectiveness and deterrent value, the preponderance of evidence supports healthcare security officers having additional tools at their disposal. These include some of the options identified in Table 26-3. Whether security officers should be equipped with all, some, or none of these additional tools requires constant evaluation and reexamination. The answer is found in individual program needs and administrative preference to organizational risk exposure.

Every healthcare facility should develop a use of force policy that includes the identification of situations, both clinical and nonclinical, in which security officers are permitted to use force.

The use of force options made available to security officers are important decisions that must be made with deliberation and include the healthcare administrative leadership team. There is always a risk; every use of force by security staff involves some liability and litigation exposure. The decision must be made on the basis of this question: *Does the use of force tool provide benefits sufficient to offset the liability and cost involved*?

While firearms can save the life of a healthcare security officer, they can also be dangerous to the person using them for protection. They can, and sometimes do, get into the hands of the opponent. A recent trend is that healthcare organizations are resorting to alternative means of protecting security staff other than firearms in the security program. Approximately 16% of U.S. healthcare security officers carry firearms, while another 13% of security departments arm their security officers with Tasers.[8]

Most healthcare protection professionals agree that the less-lethal use of force option provided by the Taser is a better tool than the firearm to combat most escalated situations confronted by the healthcare security officer. Due to fear of contaminating inpatient units, many hospitals prohibit the use of chemical agents in their use of force continuum. Additionally, most healthcare security programs

Table 26-3 Use of Force Continuum/Options

	Use of Force Options for the Healthcare Security Officer
Officer Presence	The mere presence of a highly visible uniformed security officer, marked security vehicle, or K-9 patrol is often enough to prevent or deter crime or wrongdoers. Included in officer presence are standing, walking, running, and use of vehicle lights. Without saying a word, an alert security officer can deter crime or direct criminals away from a property by use of body language and gestures.
Verbal Communication	Used in combination with a visible presence, the use of the voice can usually achieve the desired results. Words can be whispered, used normally, or shouted to be effective. The content of the message is as important as the demeanor. Most situations call for starting out calm but firm and nonthreatening. Choice of words and intensity can be increased as necessary or used in short commands in serious situations. The right combination of words in combination with officer presence can often de-escalate a tense situation and prevent the need for a physical altercation.
Control Holds & Restraints	Certain situations may arise where words alone do not reduce aggression. Sometimes security officers will need to get involved physically. At this level, minimal force would involve the use of bare hands to guide, hold, and restrain. This should never include offensive moves such as punching, tackling, and choking. Medical takedowns could apply here, but only after ordinary holds fail to control an aggressive suspect. Handcuffs are often used as restraint devices if the security officer has been trained to use them.
Chemical Agents	Sometimes when a patient or suspect is violent or threatening, less-than-lethal measures are used in defense to bring the individual under control or effect an arrest. Before moving to this level, it is assumed other less physical measures have been tried and deemed inappropriate or ineffective. Pepper spray/foam, OC spray are infrequently used in the healthcare environment, and only if the security officer has been trained on their use. A distraction based use of force, if used, this level should allow the security officer to get away, call for assistance, or subdue the individual. *It is important to note that many chemical agents may not be effective on the mentally unstable, drug addicts, intoxicated or hysterical persons.*
Temporary Incapacitation	To use force under this level means that the situation is so extreme, violent, immediate and unavoidable that it is necessary to temporarily incapacitate an individual prior to arrival of police or other assistance. Tasers (or other electronic control device) have increased in use in the healthcare environment for security officers who have been trained to use them
Deadly Force	When there is fear of death or great bodily harm at the hands of another, a security officer is authorized to use deadly force in most states. Firearms are most often used to fulfill this use of force option.

prohibit the use of nightsticks, batons, or collapsible batons, as their use is often perceived as undue force. It is important to note that use of force tools are much less prevalent outside of the U.S.

Handcuffs are an important piece of equipment carried by many healthcare security officers. The devices can be very useful tools but their use should be documented and governed by the hospital's patient restraint policy.

Again in the U.S., CMS is very specific about the use of handcuffs and other use of force tools in the patient restraint process and although they do not outlaw their use, they do outline a specific response that includes immediate notification of law enforcement personnel. In short, CMS does not want to see the tools used in the patient restraint process unless an arrest is imminent.

In hopes to deter antisocial behavior and provide evidence for prosecution against violent offenders, a number of hospital security programs have started to introduce body cameras for security officers.

HOW SHOULD SECURITY BE DESIGNED INTO THE HEALTHCARE FACILITY?

Security staff members are the heart of healthcare security. There simply is no substitute for the professional expertise and human touch of security officers in the healthcare environment. However, carefully selected and properly applied physical safeguards and electronic security technology are playing an increasingly important role in protecting healthcare facilities.

While the basic physical security safeguards are still staples of security (barriers/fences, alarms, lighting, lock and keys), it is the electronic components of security that are experiencing explosive growth.

While many statistics point to a rather dire state of society, the hope for better healthcare workers' protection can begin with facility management/design. The healthcare administrator should require the security professional to work with hospital engineers, project managers and/or architects to incorporate the most operationally efficient and cost-effective security technology for the project and budget. The benefit of having security involved upfront and early in these projects allow for security applications to be cost-effectively integrated into architectural, engineering and environmental design, thus creating a safe and secure environment for the delivery of patient care services.

At the heart of this expectation is defining the specific security operating principles and philosophies of space utilization that drive specific technology application. The philosophy of all security design considerations should be to help build an environment that is patient-focused and incorporates both physical and psychological deterrence methods.

Realizing that physical controls cannot protect all things in all places, security professionals also use psychological deterrents, which are directed at the decision-making process of the individual. For the purposes of security planning, a psychological deterrent is defined as an individual's interpretation of a situation in which the potential positive or negative aspects of behavior serve to prevent or preclude the expression of that behavior.

The fundamentals of Crime Prevention through Environmental Design (CPTED) follow these principles as they include using the physical environment and other aspects of design to manage behavior. The proper design and effective use of the built environment can lead to reduction in the incidence of and fear of crime, as well as affect the behavior of people by providing physiological and psychological deterrence.

In 2012, the International Association for Healthcare Security and Safety (IAHSS) released *Security Design Guidelines for Healthcare Facilities* which provide healthcare security leaders and their organizations with a tool to design and build security into renovations and new construction projects. These design guidelines are described in great detail throughout this chapter and have filled a major void in the understanding of effective security design principles exclusively for the healthcare industry. These low cost/no cost approaches to security should be a basic expectation and appropriately implemented whenever possible.

HOW IMPORTANT IS ACCESS CONTROL?

Giving forethought in the design to how access will be controlled in the environment is of paramount importance. The healthcare environment and hospitals specifically, by their nature, are designed to be open and accessible to the sick and injured and to family and friends. This means criminals and other dangers can easily enter through their doors if not properly protected.

The main entrance in particular is a concern, as most hospitals specifically have very limited control of who comes and goes through this entry point during normal business hours. Access control, arguably the most critical aspect of healthcare security, requires the proper channeling of visitors and patients into and about the healthcare facility. The goal is to allow patients/visitors to move freely without feeling oppressed, while at the same time protecting patients, visitors, and staff.

Good security design and electronic access control technology can significantly reduce this area of concern. Today's technological advancements in access control enable higher degrees of security without compromising aesthetics, customer service, user-friendliness or overall hospitality. Access control can protect critical areas such as pharmacies, surgery room, infant treatment rooms, technology closets/rooms, information storage rooms and areas that separate staff from the public.

Protection is important to every healthcare administrator, but so is properly managing the first view patients and visitors have of the facility. That means access control systems used should not display a predominance of unfriendly barriers or obstructions. A defined philosophy of "on stage" and "off stage" is an important consideration in the design. Defining and separating out areas that are open to the public and those that are not are important first steps. Once closed areas are identified, determining the level of security access and how restricted it should be follows.

After hours continues to be the primary time of security risk in healthcare facilities. Having a single clearance point to areas such as the emergency department or other single designated point of entry is recommended to control access into the facility after normal business hours.

One of the fundamental concerns within a healthcare facility is the ability to manage serious emergencies properly and swiftly. Frequently, this requires the ability to restrict access into the facility as a whole. Lockdown procedures dominate discussions relating to emergency preparedness for healthcare organizations. How fast the healthcare facility can be locked down is a key indicator for facility readiness to many internal and external disasters, riots, civil disturbances, and other workplace violence scenarios.

In short, a sophisticated electronic access control system is one of the most cost-effective security investments a healthcare facility can make.

WHERE ARE ALARMS NEEDED?

The two basic security alarm applications found in healthcare facilities are the intrusion alarm and the duress alarm. Simple intrusion detection is probably the most familiar concept of security technology. Intrusion detection involves the use of door or window contacts, glass contacts, and motion sensors in combination with some type of audible alarm that sounds when a person has forced entry into a building or room. An alert is sent to a security operations center to notify the security department, or authorities, of the time and location of the alarm activation.

The intrusion alarm is used for sensitive areas within a healthcare facility that are closed for certain periods, including clinics, pharmacies, laundries, general stores, medical records, libraries, and gift shops.

The intrusion alarm is also a primary safeguard utilized for satellite pharmacies, offsite facilities and medical office buildings.

The duress alarm is frequently used in cashier's offices, pharmacies, and gift shops. This type of alarm is more often used to summon security personnel to observe suspicious people or activities rather than solely as a holdup alarm. Duress alarms are used in behavioral health units, emergency departments, and remote work locations to summon both security officers and medical assistance.

WHY INVEST IN VIDEO SURVEILLANCE?

Video surveillance systems (or CCTV) have evolved significantly in the last several years. General surveillance is one of the basic uses of CCTV. When used for this purpose, the system is perhaps more of a psychological deterrence than an actual physical control.

Video surveillance, access control and alarms have much in common, and they often work together as an integrated system to keep intruders out of secure areas, limit access to security sensitive areas, and remotely monitor critical areas to reduce the risk of crime and security incidents. It is why more and more healthcare organizations continue to increase their use of video surveillance as part of their overall strategic security plan. Integrated together, the technologies help to render security personnel more effective.

Properly located video surveillance cameras can extend the range of the security staff and provide valuable incident information. Studies have found that video surveillance can have a significant deterrent effect on property crime but it will not, however, deter all crime. The use of recorded video images has resulted in countless arrests when shared with law enforcement authorities or when appropriately released to media outlets. In no situation should dummy, or nonoperating, cameras be used.

The most important consideration in a video surveillance system is the quality of the image received, and this is largely dependent on the camera and recording equipment used. As a general rule, all cameras utilized in a security system for after-the-fact investigation and overall deterrence should be recorded and the recording retained in a 10-day library as a minimum. It is not uncommon to maintain recorded images for 30 days. Common exceptions to this rule are video surveillance systems used in patient care areas or for patient monitoring.

Healthcare organizations that authorize video monitoring of patients typically require the video to be watched at all times. The recording of the video monitoring should be kept in a secure location, used only for the purpose for which it was recorded and not be released, used, or disclosed to others. The driving purpose for the use and application of the video surveillance should govern whether or not it is recorded. For future protection, the purpose and use of each camera should be documented in the security master plan. Commonly recommended camera locations in the healthcare environment include:

- Main entrance of emergency rooms, waiting rooms and nontreatment areas within the examination/treatment space
- All hospital entries that offer entry into the facility; placement of strategically visible public monitors is a low-cost deterrent
- Admissions desks and elevator banks
- Locations where controlled substances are present, to include the pharmacy and narcotic dispensaries
- Receiving docks, central sterile supply and other locations storing items of value

- Mother/baby, pediatric, behavioral health and geriatric units: to help prevent abduction and patients from wandering off
- Parking lots and garages have high pedestrian traffic and often have many places for an attacker to hide[9]
- External egress paths from the facility to support the process of recovering patients who have eloped, as quickly as possible, by determining the search focus

Should video surveillance systems be constantly viewed is a commonly asked question. The answer depends on the application. Many video surveillance systems are "integrated" into the protection system and designed to only capture (record) images to be utilized later if necessary. In these systems, there may or may not be any live monitoring involved. Live monitoring is rarely a cost-effective use of resource as a security officer can generally view a monitor for only 30 minutes or less without becoming bored or ineffective. If live monitoring is required, "event-driven" monitoring is a better alternative. This monitoring equipment alerts the operator when the monitor must be viewed. In these systems, the monitor to be viewed will often be automatically shifted to a larger screen and will activate recording equipment. Video analytics have benefits that have started to be realized in the healthcare environment. There are numerous video analytic features developed that can track various behaviors, from recognizing an abandoned briefcase or duffel bag to determining when someone is loitering in a specified zone. The analytic capabilities offered today are limited only by the creativity of the user and the need presented.

WHAT OTHER SECURITY TECHNOLOGY APPLICATIONS SHOULD BE CONSIDERED?

There are numerous security technologies used in the healthcare environment to protect people, safeguard assets, and protect the reputation of the organizations. These include radio communications, visitor management systems, emergency call boxes, mass notification, asset tracking, and metal screening.

RADIO COMMUNICATION

The most important piece of equipment a security officer can carry is the two-way radio, which is part of the overall security communications system. A one-way pager is simply unacceptable. Not only does the radio provide an element of personal safety for the officer, but it is essential in achieving an effective security system.

Good communications equipment is expensive; however, the cost has been reduced in recent years. Considering the life of today's equipment, the cost, depreciated over the number of usable years, is the best investment of security dollars that an organization can make.

VISITOR MANAGEMENT

Visitor management systems are not new to the healthcare industry as patient rosters and paper guest logs have been used at information desks to help with way-finding and guidance for years. What is new is the computerized way to capture detailed visitor information and to accurately identify, badge and track visitors, vendors and other authorized personnel entering the healthcare facility and the purpose of their visit. One of the greatest benefits of the more advanced visitor management systems is the ability to incorporate programmable security alerts or watch lists. The more sophisticated systems can check each visitor's name against a list of people who should not be allowed to enter the building (former employees, estranged spouses, etc.) and alert the security officer or greeter when a match is found, telling them how to handle the situation.

The downside to the use of visitor management systems is typically not cost related or the advantages of the features offered, but the visitor queuing that can result in a processing backlog. Many healthcare administrators remain very concerned about the image presented in the main lobby and resist any system that obstructs or delays patient or visitor access to the facility during regular business hours. However, most of these same administrators desire to more strictly manage visitation to the organization after normal business hours or at the end of specified visiting hours.

EMERGENCY CALL BOXES

Emergency phones, call boxes, phone towers, or wall-mounted emergency phones are all names used to describe the emergency phone system designed to connect a potential victim of crime or someone in need of service with security. Strategically locating these free-standing devices or wall-mounted units in surface parking lots, garages, and other high pedestrian-traffic areas on campus can help facilitate immediate assistance to those requesting it. Most emergency call telephones are equipped with a blue-light strobe on top of the device to enhance visibility. When flashing, it helps to expedite security officer response and let others in the vicinity know that assistance is needed. An added benefit may be to "scare off" a person intent upon criminal or wrongdoing activity.

Emergency phone systems are also used for nonemergency purposes and can be excellent customer service tools for employees, staff, and visitors who may need basic assistance. These devices, when used, are excellent crime prevention and public relations tools as they demonstrate a visible organizational commitment to a safe and secure environment.

MASS NOTIFICATION

The 2007 Virginia Tech University tragedy served as a wake-up call for many healthcare facilities and has yielded numerous lessons learned that have prompted many to reassess how they prepare for, respond to and mitigate incidents of targeted violence. Specifically, this tragedy identified the need for the healthcare facility to have a quick and facility-/campus-wide notification of a threat or emergency. Technology advances have provided many mass notification solutions available to the healthcare facility. In many instances, the use of e-mails and pagers has supplanted overhead announcements; however, many healthcare organizations have realized that multiple modes of notification are needed to reach all of the constituents inside the facility and the campus grounds. Many hospital campuses use digital signage as a communication medium beyond emergency alerts.

ASSET TRACKING

Many hospitals have started to protect their assets with wireless radio frequency identification technology (RFID), which uses small transmitters attached to the protected equipment that communicate with the organization's access control system. Similar to the unobtrusive security tags used on store merchandise to thwart shoplifters, RFID tags are often used to track equipment as it moves through various doors and can detect where a piece of equipment is located within the organization or if it leaves the facility. In short, an RFID tag can be attached to just about anything of value, such as an EKG monitor or mobile workstation and can be easily tracked throughout the facility.

METAL SCREENING

Philosophically, there are some healthcare environments that lend themselves to metal screening. A 2011 study conducted by the American Society for Healthcare Engineers (ASHE) of U.S. hospital security systems found only 13% of respondents had implemented metal detectors. When deployed, the most frequent application is the emergency department. The recommendation, introduction and management of metal screening programs in healthcare cannot be done in a vacuum. The security improvements are considerable; however, the introduction of metal screening has employee relations and organizational culture implications in addition to patient and community perceptions that must be addressed collectively.

If metal screening is employed, the approach must be consistent and show no bias. The placement and exact location of the metal detector is another important consideration. The device should be installed to minimize unnecessary delays in the queuing of patients and visitors and fit comfortably into the aesthetic décor of the facility. And of course, there are budget issues to be considered to include security officers to staff the device—which is the largest drawback to implementing metal screening system.

THE INVESTMENT IN SECURITY TECHNOLOGY HAS BEEN MADE, BUT HOW DO WE KNOW IT WORKS?

Many electronic security systems are used to keep healthcare facilities safe. But one of the common missing components is the routine testing of these systems. Systems or components are commonly found to be ineffective, not working as originally intended, and/or not meeting current needs—creating unnecessary risk and liability exposure for the healthcare organization.

This documentation and testing that should be required of every healthcare security program may be considered small and routine. However, its importance is found in the liability protection afforded to the facility and, more prominently, the positive perception of security and the protection department.

The ideal healthcare security system is a combination of the right technology, careful planning, proper installation and a strategically deployed staff. Technology must work effectively as a tool for a well-trained security staff. When these elements are properly integrated, the organization is able to provide a safe environment, and its employees are consequently able to concentrate on fulfilling the organization's overall mission of providing high-quality patient care for the surrounding community.

HOW CONCERNED SHOULD WE BE ABOUT VIOLENCE IN HEALTHCARE?

Workplace violence is an industry-wide healthcare problem and not exclusive to any one healthcare organization. Violence threatens the safety of staff, patients, and visitors in hospitals and healthcare organizations of all sizes and settings. It demoralizes healthcare professionals, especially nurses, who are most often the victims of violence; and costs hospitals untold millions in lost time, employee turnover, reputation for quality care, and additional security measures.

Regardless of the patient care services offered, the threat of violence in the workplace is all around us—no healing environment is immune from having violent acts occur inside the facility or on its campus. Approximately half of the nurses responding to a 2011 survey conducted by the Emergency Nurses Association believe that violence is simply part of their everyday work environment.[10] In the survey, nine out of ten emergency department managers cited patient violence as the greatest threat to department personnel.

The majority of people generally associate violence in the workplace with assault and homicide, not with intimidating postures or expressions of mild anger. It is important that the healthcare administrator break workplace violence down into *actual* violence and the *threat* of violence. Both can create a hostile and uncomfortable work environment, and even with this breakdown, healthcare workers face significantly higher risk of injury from nonfatal assaults (actual violence) than that of other workers.

The clinical patient is often the source of confrontation, largely due to the volume of patients, long waits, and disputes relative to services being rendered. Hospital emergency departments, along with mental health evaluation and treatment areas, intensive care units, dedicated forensic patient care centers and closed head injury units have historically the highest potential for violence. There are countless cases in which patients have attacked staff ostensibly without warning or provocation.

The problem of escalating violence is worsened by the restrictions imposed by regulatory and accreditation agencies such as CMS and The Joint Commission that require healthcare organizations to apply medical restraints or seclude patients as a means of last resort. The overly strict interpretations by surveyors and healthcare organizations alike have resulted in the compromise of employee, staff, and physician safety. Care providers are rarely using the tools available to them until after an actual incident of violence occurs. The result is more incidents of violence and more injuries to healthcare workers and patients alike. To correct this vicious cycle, The Joint Commission, CMS and healthcare organizations must take a more balanced approach in their interpretation of these patient restraint and seclusion guidelines before a safe and therapeutic healing environment can be created. If not, healthcare professionals will continue to leave healthcare occupations because of the risk of actual and threat of violence, increasing the industry-wide shortage of qualified medical professionals.

The patient is the primary but not the only source of workplace violence; employees and staff members have been the source of many violent acts. The day-to-day supervision, work evaluations, disciplinary actions, and terminations all set up situations that can be confrontational and that can provide the motivation of employee and ex-employee violence.

There is a potential for workplace violence caused by individuals or groups who are from outside the organization, which may include legitimate visitors such as patient family members or illegitimate visitors. The latter type of visitor includes criminals contemplating or committing a crime (robbery, abduction, assault); gang members intent upon causing injury or harm; unwelcome friends or family members of staff or patients; protestors; terrorists; transient persons; and former patients and employees. It is almost impossible to discern the presence and intent of these persons until an overt act occurs. They often blend in with the legitimate patient, staff, or visitor.

Not all violence occurring in the healthcare environment can be prevented; however, many acts can be prevented and managed to minimize injury, death, and damage to property. All organizations need a strategy and plan to deal with workplace violence so that they can reduce the number of violent incidents and minimize the severity of these incidents to a large extent.

There are three specific steps of preparation and response that organizations must implement to properly address workplace violence. The first step is to provide a reasonable level of security for the overall environment and especially to areas of probable conflict. This includes an organized security program that includes access control plans, proper physical security safeguards, enforced security policies and procedures, staff training, empowerment, and an effective critical incident response capability. To adequately plan and implement these essential elements, there must be strong commitment from top management and the board of directors, to provide a high level of philosophical and management support. This support includes adequate funding of the protection program.

The second phase is an organizational threat policy. The foundation of a successful violence prevention program, the policy should state clearly that threats of any kind are not tolerated, that the staff is responsible for reporting all threats, and should indicate the procedures for reporting such threats.

The third phase is a response plan that is based on recognizing, understanding, reacting to, and managing events as they develop and escalate. There should be a specific response team that evaluates and plans actions concerning all threats. The team should be comprised of the security administrator, director of human resources, nursing administrator and in some cases the risk manager. The coordinator or leader of this team should initially decide the team member or combination of team members responsible for the management of the threat. All threats must be taken seriously. The degree and severity of the threat will be somewhat of a subjective judgment in terms of actions to be taken. It is better to err on the side of taking too much action than doing too little, too late.

Fundamental to any workplace violence prevention strategy is conflict resolution training. While there is no program that can train healthcare staff to handle every type of violent situation, most healthcare security administrators agree that it is possible to train them on the commonalities that occur in these situations. Most crisis intervention training programs include these lessons and help the employee look for physiological clues that an individual's aggressive behavior might escalate.

The cost of violence in healthcare settings is great. It affects the patient's recovery as well as causing physical and psychological injuries to staff. Victims can suffer physical and psychological pain, confidence can be irrevocably shaken and stress levels can be debilitating. With the growing crisis over nurse shortages, it is all the more important that healthcare organizations send a message that violence against nurses and medical care providers in general will not be tolerated. Violence should not be an accepted part of the job for any medical care professional, security officer, or other employee in the healthcare environment. Many assaults in healthcare settings are premeditated and perpetrated by patients who have a history of violence that should be communicated to caregivers on admission. The healthcare organization should take a stand and hold perpetrators of these assaults accountable for their actions.

ARE WE DOING ENOUGH TO PROTECT OUR INFANT AND PEDIATRIC PATIENTS?

Infant abduction prevention is a top concern for hospital administrators, and security of infants is certainly a priority, both for safety and public relations reasons. Statistically, the risk of an actual abduction is low. All told, 132 newborns have been abducted by strangers from hospitals since 1983.[11] However, statistical relevance is not important to the family that is the victim of abduction, the healthcare organization's staff, the healthcare facility, or the public. This event is devastating and takes an emotional and physical toll on all involved. The organization's reputation for safe patient care may suffer as well, even if the organization does everything appropriate to avoid an abduction.

The areas of greatest risk for infant and child abductions include the mother's room, nursery, postpartum units, pediatric care areas, and neonatal intensive care units as well as well-baby units. But because these units may present more of a challenge to anyone trying to abduct an infant, an abductor may try to "get" a child in waiting areas for hospital clinics, radiology, and the emergency department.

The basics of providing infant security are identification (mom, baby, significant other, and the caregiver staff), education (mom and staff), and physical and electronic security safeguards. Video surveillance and controlling access to prevent unauthorized visitors from gaining access to the mother/baby unit must work collectively together and in conjunction with staff training, parental education and a critical incident response plan that is frequently tested and exercised.

There has been a good deal of interest by healthcare security organizations in the electronic monitoring of infants. Infant tagging is useful in preventing newborn abductions, but it is not foolproof. Cathy Nahirny, Administrative Manager with the National Center for Missing and Exploited Children, has documented nineteen (19) cases where an infant was abducted by a nonfamily member from a healthcare facility and the facility had installed an infant security tagging system.[12] These "infant tagging" systems cost anywhere from several thousand dollars for a single door alarm to several hundred thousand dollars for a very sophisticated system. However, the decision to install any electronic monitoring system should not be based on funding alone. There must be a complete buy-in by unit staff, as these systems require human involvement to make them effective. If used, the infant tagging system should be integrated with door and elevator controls, and video surveillance systems to accentuate the protection of infants and harden the organization as a target for a potential abductor.

WHAT SHOULD WE DO DIFFERENTLY TO MANAGE FORENSIC/PRISONER PATIENTS?

A growing security issue, the number of serious security/criminal incidents involving forensic patients in the healthcare facility has escalated over the past decade. It is projected the number of forensic patients being treated in healthcare facilities, outside of detention centers, will continue to increase as the number of prisoners continues to increase. The forensic patient continues to be both an issue and challenge for healthcare administrators. The forensic patient may either be brought to the medical care facility for emergency or outpatient treatment or for a planned hospitalization as an inpatient. In all cases, the forensic patient must be viewed as a potential threat to the facility. The typical healthcare facility does not host an environment that is well-equipped or prepared for management of forensic patients but at any given point in time, there may be prisoners inside a healthcare facility.

A 2011 study, conducted at the behest of the International Healthcare Security and Safety Foundation, found the issue of prisoner escapes and escape attempts from healthcare facilities has become increasingly prevalent over the years. Confusion and conflict can take place when caring for the forensic patient. The removal of restraints is the most common cause of all escapes in healthcare, accounting for approximately two-thirds of the approximately 100 that happen every year. Law enforcement or correctional personnel often do not understand the procedures of medical care, while medical care staff do not always understand the implications of the custody of the patient. It is important that the prisoner remain in the custody of the correctional officer at all times, to include being properly shackled to the wheelchair or gurney. Medical care staff should never ask to remove restraints unless medically required. In such instances, an alternative restraint should always be added to include temporary use of medical restraint devices. If this is not possible, the healthcare organization should require more than one correctional officer to assist in managing unrestrained forensic patients. Managing unrestrained prisoners alone in any environment is inherently dangerous and should not be tolerated.

ARE WE DOING ENOUGH TO PROTECT THE PRIVACY OF OUR DATA?

Access to patient data has exploded in today's healthcare environment with the advent of electronic health records (EHR). The security measures deployed for authorized users of the EHR, such as database monitoring, log management and provisioning systems, should be coupled with security technologies used to safeguard information such as encryption for laptops, workstations, smartphones and thumb drives. But do not believe these safeguards will detect all security breaches or prevent breaches of confidential patient information.

Privacy and security are aspects of patient safety that are every bit as daunting and pervasive as infection control and the reduction of avoidable readmissions. Since the U.S. Department of Health and Human Services started reporting healthcare data breaches in 2009, 619 breaches have been reported affecting 500 or more individuals, with over 22 million total individuals being affected.[13] The Third Annual Benchmark Study on Patient Privacy and Data Security found that 94% of healthcare providers had experienced a data breach in the previous two years, and 45% had experienced more than five data breaches during the same period. Lost devices, human error, third-party problems and criminal attacks headed the list of causes. Based on this data, the study estimates security breaches could be costing healthcare providers $7 billion annually.[14]

The inadvertent loss of data by someone with legitimate access is the top security concern, as healthcare employees use more mobile devices that make healthcare information more accessible. These devices present inherent privacy and security risks to hospital networks and patient records. This could be from a stolen device where patient data has been downloaded (thumb drive, laptop, tablet, etc.), or where user IDs and passwords are saved. There is technology that exists to effectively deal with these situations, but the application of such mitigation strategies is still not an industry standard, due to the added expense and increased "hassle factor" the additional security adds to the end-users.

Another worrying security concern to those with primary responsibility for the safeguarding of patient medical information is the concept of Bringing Your Own Device (BYOD). The practice is debated throughout the healthcare industry—physicians and other care providers want the convenience of accessing patient data on their own device, while IT security professionals worry over the vulnerability of patient information being available, or stored on devices not in the direct control of the healthcare facility. At the heart of this concern is the ability to comply with HIPAA expectations, among other requirements and expectations, which define any improper use or disclosure of health information as a security breach.

Avoiding the tendency to think of privacy and security as information technology add-ons is a must. Too often, a healthcare organization focuses on these risks after it experiences its first data breach. Many healthcare organizations have embedded privacy officers and information security officers to guide privacy and security policy and procedure implementations in their organization. These roles are created with an eye to data protection, as well as consideration for clinicians' special needs to ensure strict staff guidelines are in place, in addition to confirming physical security safeguards are established and functioning properly. Security precautions frequently include:

- Leadership commitment to a robust corporate compliance program that monitors and enforces standards of conduct designed to detect and deter criminal behavior and inappropriate access to and disclosure of protected information.
- Standard use of full encryption software.
- Completion of education and training as metrics in performance evaluations.
- Daily huddles to discuss patients on the floor who might spark curiosity—and inappropriate intrusion into their health information.
- Audit of inappropriate user access and identification of potential instances of inappropriate disclosure of protected health information. To include automatic messages such as: "*Be on notice that if you inappropriately access records with protected health information or move records in an unauthorized fashion, it will be picked up.*"
- A written affidavit signed by medical staff they understand disclosure procedures and intend to abide by those procedures.
- Vendor business associate agreements that cover how information is protected and when policies and procedures are reviewed.
- System for employees and visitors to report ethical and legal concerns regarding potential security breaches.
- Make credit monitoring services available if inappropriate use or disclosure of a patient's demographic information has been released.

Medical identity theft is another concern for the hospital executive and, while there is no single solution to keep medical identity theft from occurring, medical facilities should analyze possible security gaps and invest in an ongoing risk analysis process. Stringent policies should be developed regarding access to sensitive patient information, as well as protocols developed for authorization and authentication of individuals accessing protected health information. Lastly, medical documents that are no longer required to be kept on record should be destroyed in a secure manner.

HOW DO WE GET EMPLOYEE INVOLVEMENT IN THE PROTECTION EFFORT?

It is universally agreed among security administrators that staff must take ownership in directly contributing to the protection of the organization; however, there are issues beyond practicing good security. A primary function of any protection system is to educate, stimulate, and motivate the first-line protection resource: employees. The protection level of a medical care facility is directly related to the extent to which employees participate in the security effort.

Employee education begins with new employee orientation. New employees can be channeled into the protection system with a minimum of effort. They seek the norms and want to know what their employer expects. The moment employees first enter the workplace is the prime time to develop a positive protection attitude. Employees will not remember everything that is presented, but they will form a basic opinion, either consciously or unconsciously, of the importance that the organization places on security. Crime prevention presentations, handouts, events, and training can also raise staff awareness of security issues. Not only will this add eyes and ears to the security effort, it will be noted by Joint

Commission surveyors and other regulatory agencies, which are increasingly looking for employee involvement in the healthcare security program.

Various functions of the healthcare security program must work together to reduce security risks and provide tangible benefits in support of the organizational mission. Each organization must determine how the functional security program elements will be implemented and managed. They may be assigned to different individuals and departments, or they may be brought together under a specific department or division. In this respect not all elements of a protection system are performed by one department.

One of these issues is the authority for intervention. When security is called to a nursing unit because a patient or visitor is out of control, who is responsible for directing actions—security or nursing? The answer is either one may be appropriate; however, this role should be clear in the strategic plan and protection of the resultant policy/procedure. When there are drugs missing from the pharmacy, is this a pharmacy problem with support from security, or a security problem to be resolved by security with support from the pharmacy? When a laptop computer belonging to the organization is stolen, can the employee simply order another one, or does it require a report to security before the purchasing unit will order or otherwise provide a new one? These are the types of strategic questions that must be answered from a strategic context, to provide the proper operating fabric and coordinated direction of the protection effort.

WHAT SECURITY-RELATED POLICY AND PROCEDURES DO I NEED?

A basic component of the successful security program is a comprehensive and useful documentation system. Records and reports maintain a large majority of the security program documentation to fulfill various administrative needs and verify security activity. These reports are important for general department planning purposes, the capture of findings from incident activity and follow-up investigative activity, and often legal consequences in the advent of an adverse security event. The retention of security operational records should be controlled by organization policy, subject to any state law, that ensures that needed records are retained and unneeded records are discarded or destroyed as necessary.

A major function of the protection system is to manage employee actions and response to adverse events that protect the organization's well-being and the personal safety of all constituents working at, visiting or receiving patient care services from the healthcare facility. This is most frequently accomplished with organizational policy and procedures. Table 26-4 provides a comprehensive list of security-related policy and procedures that every healthcare administrator should require, at minimum, be evaluated for appropriateness to their environment.

WHAT PERFORMANCE METRICS SHOULD I BE USING FOR BENCHMARKING MY SECURITY PROGRAM?

On an annual basis there should be a formal review of the security program that addresses the objectives, scope, performance, and effectiveness of both the security management plan and the operational implementation of the plan. In short, how did the program measure up to expectations? In addition to the security management plan the periodic reports prepared throughout the year for the multidisciplinary review

Table 26-4 Security-related Policy and Procedures

Active Shooter	Access Control: After-hours, Facility-Wide, Restricted Access (lockdown), Security Sensitive Areas
Armed Robbery & Response	Bomb Threat
Calling for Police Response	Confiscation of Prohibited Items
Code of Conduct / Employee Security Responsibility	Forensic (prisoner) Patients
Employee Drug Testing	Employee Security Education
Gang Behavior: Recognizing and Responding	Hostage Situation
Infant and Pediatric Abduction Prevention and Response	Identification: Employees, Visitors, Vendors
Law Enforcement Requests for Information about Patients	Package Inspection
Management of the Combative Patient	Missing Patients
Munchausen Syndrome by Proxy	Security Involvement in Patient Assistance
Parking Control & Violation	Patient Elopement Prevention and Response
Patient Search	Patient Valuables
Pre-Employment and Ongoing Background Check	Public Safety Liaison
Security Sensitive Area Access Control and Critical Incident Response Plans	Weapons and Contraband Prohibited
Workplace Violence Prevention & Response	Very Important Patients

committee are the basic sources of information for the annual evaluation. The annual evaluation does not need to be on a calendar year basis; however, the calendar year is utilized by most healthcare security administrators. The annual security program effectiveness evaluation continues to be a requirement of The Joint Commission.

Security program metrics, whenever possible, should relate to clinical indicators. As a healthcare administrator, you want to know the tangible value received for the resources allocated to the protection effort. Some examples of this type of key performance indicator include:

1. Cost of security per adjusted patient day
2. Aggressive acts managed per 1000 ED visits
3. Ratio of security staff to employees
4. Reporting of near misses (an undesired event or finding that, under slightly different circumstances, could have resulted in or caused harm to people or damage to property, materials or the environment).
5. Security watch hours per patient day or ED visit
6. Calls for security service per 1000 patient days
7. Lost-time claim frequency rate due to aggressive/assaultive behavior
8. Percent of incident with deficient staff awareness or ownership as "root cause"
9. Urgent response time and resolution—for example, 98% of calls responded to within 3 minutes with an acceptable resolution

The setting of security goals and the evaluation of the success in meeting those goals is an important stimulus for attentive action by the security staff. If you can't measure the performance of your security program, you will never know if expenditures were a wise investment. There are other measures of performance. What is the security department's reputation among the stakeholders and outside agencies that security interacts with? Although not a metric, the healthcare executive who moves about the facility and really listens will basically know how well (or not) the security program is functioning.

REFERENCES

1. Caramenico Alicia. Hospital works learn how to survive a shooting. *Fierce Healthcare* 2013, July 18. Retrieved September 6, 2014 from http://www.fiercehealthcare.com/story/hospital-workers-learn-how-survive-shooting/2013-07-18.
2. Taxin A. *Police: 3 Dead in California Hospital Shooting*. The Associated Press; 2009, April 16. Retrieved April 22, 2009 from http://www.foxnews.com/story/0, 2933,516888,00.html.
3. Rivard R. Many Hospitals Seeing Increase in Violence. *Charleston Daily Mail* 2009, June 16. Retrieved June 16, 2009 from http://www.dailymail.com/News/200906150690.
4. CNN Staff. Police shoot, wound man at Wisconsin children's hospital. *CNN* 2013, November 14. Retrieved November 15, 2013 from http://www.cnn.com/2013/11/14/us/wisconsin-hospital-lockdown/.
5. Emergency Nurses Association. *2011 Study of Workplace Violence Against Registered Nurses in Emergency Departments*. Retrieved June 8, 2011 from http://www.ena.org/research/current.
6. International Association for Healthcare Security & Safety. 2014. Website available at: www.IAHSS.org.
7. Weronik R. Securing our hospitals: GE Security and IAHSS healthcare benchmarking study. *Presented at International Association for Healthcare Security and Safety Mid-Winter Meeting and Seminar* 2008, January 21.
8. Burmahl Beth, Hoppszallern Suzanna. Converging Worlds – 2012 Hospital Security Survey. *Health Facilities Management* 2012, October. Available from: www.hfmmagazine.com. p. 24.
9. Brisbee F. The Power to Heal and More. *Electrical Contractor* 2000, April. Retrieved May 23, 2009 from http://www.ecmag.com/index.cfm?fa=article&articleID=10050.
10. Emergency Nurses Association. *2007 Study of Workplace Violence Against Registered Nurses in Emergency Departments*. Retrieved June 8, 2008 from http://www.ena.org/research/current.
11. Raburn Jr J, Nahirny C. Newborn/Infant Abductions. *National Center for Missing and Exploited Children* 2014, April 30.
12. Nahirny C, Ryce J. Infants Abducted from Hospitals with Security Tagging Systems. *National Center for Missing and Exploited Children* 2011, August 8.
13. Health Information Privacy. *Breaches Affecting 500 or More Individuals*. U.S. Department of Health and Human Services; 2014. Retrieved June 28, 2014 from http://www.hhs.gov/ocr/privacy/hipaa/administrative/breachnotificationrule/breachtool.html.
14. Ponemon Institute. *Third Annual Benchmark Study on Patient Privacy & Data Security*. 2012, December. Retrieved June 28, 2014 from http://www2.idexpertscorp.com/assets/uploads/ponemon2012/Third_Annual_Study_on_Patient_Privacy_FINAL.pdf.

Mental Health Physical Security Review Checklist

SITE:							**DATE OF REVIEW:**
UNIT:							
			UNIT DESCRIPTION				
Item #	**Category/ Area**	**Questions /Criteria**	***Rationale/ Assessment Methods***	**Met**	**Partially Met**	**Not Met**	**Comments**
1	Site/ Building Perimeter	**1 a.** Does the site in which the MH unit is situated have CCTV coverage of the perimeter of the site? **1 b.** Does the building in which the MH unit is located have CCTV coverage of the perimeter of the building? **1 c.** Are the CCTV images recorded and capable of being retrieved quickly?	*Recovery – Can assist in the rapid recovery of an eloped patient by having the patient identity confirmed and departure from building and/or site and potential direction of travel identified through CCTV*				
2	Outdoor Areas – Fence and Gate	**2 a.** Are fences designed so as to be not easily climbed? **2 b.** Is the fence anchored to handle body force? **2 c.** Are fencing posts placed on the outside (non-patient side) of the fence? **2 d.** Are doors, light fittings, posts, CCTV fixtures, etc. situated so as to not provide a climbing aid? **2 e.** Where the fence meets buildings or other fences, have measures been taken to ensure there are no gaps between the joins, climbing aids or access to rooftops created?	*Prevention – the fence should be a minimum of 10 feet high and with a strong structural support to withstand force. Ideally should be of weld mesh and ensure it does not allow a finger grip to aid climbing. Where angled capping is used it should be weld mesh.*				

Continued

—Cont'd

SITE:							**DATE OF REVIEW:**
UNIT:							
UNIT DESCRIPTION							
Item #	**Category/ Area**	**Questions /Criteria**	***Rationale/ Assessment Methods***	**Met**	**Partially Met**	**Not Met**	**Comments**
3	Outdoor Areas – Fence and Gate	If there is a gate: **3 a.** Does the gate swing outward? **3 b.** Is the hinge installed on the outside? **3 c.** Is the gate wired with an alarm system? **3 d.** Do staff members have keys to unlock the gate?	*Prevention – If present, a gate must be secured to the fence with enough strength to withstand force and not act as an aid to climbing the fence. Staff members must carry keys to the gate at all times.*				
4	Outdoor Areas – Trees and Landscape	**4 a.** Can trees or branches be used to go over the fence? **4 b.** Is the landscaping/shrubbery such that a person could conceal themselves? **4 c.** Do trees or landscaping interfere with either the observational ability of staff or the capture of unobstructed CCTV images?	*Prevention – trees should be kept low and within the confines of the fence area and bushes and flower beds small enough so they cannot hide patients.* A clear line of sight should be created and preserved for staff observing outdoor activities.				

—Cont'd

SITE:							DATE OF REVIEW:
UNIT:							
UNIT DESCRIPTION							
Item #	**Category/ Area**	**Questions /Criteria**	***Rationale/ Assessment Methods***	**Met**	**Partially Met**	**Not Met**	**Comments**
5	Outdoor Areas – Security cameras and alarms	Ideally, outdoor areas should be monitored by cameras. If cameras are used: **5 a.** Are the cameras located high enough to have a 180° view of the outdoor area? **5 b.** Are the cameras equipped with weather and tamper-resistant covers? **5 c.** Is someone assigned to monitor the cameras while there are patients in the outdoor area? **5 d.** Is lighting sufficient or is a low-light camera used to ensure observation in lower light conditions? **5 e.** Are staff assigned to supervise outdoor areas equipped with portable duress alarms?	*Prevention/Response – Staff should be monitoring cameras while patients are outside. A procedure should be in place to respond quickly to an alarm activation as both a staff safety and elopement prevention measure.*				
6	Outdoor Areas – Furniture	**6 a.** Is furniture secured to the ground or too heavy to be moved easily? **6 b.** Is furniture located at a sufficient distance away from the fence or roofline to prevent it being used to climb over the fence or up on a roof?	*Prevention – Outdoor furniture should be anchored to a concrete pad and away from trees, fences or doors to prevent patients from escaping the outdoor area.*				

Continued

—Cont'd

SITE:							**DATE OF REVIEW:**
UNIT:							
			UNIT DESCRIPTION				
Item #	**Category/ Area**	**Questions /Criteria**	***Rationale/ Assessment Methods***	**Met**	**Partially Met**	**Not Met**	**Comments**
7	Outdoor Areas – Elevated Court-yards	**7 a.** If the courtyard is elevated and outdoors, does the design meet the criteria in the other outdoor standards? **7 b.** If the courtyard is elevated, are there no sky-lights that could be broken through or unprotected ledges or walkways?	*Prevention – Some courtyards are on upper floors. These must be checked for potential jumping sites or elopement routes.*				
8	Areas sur-rounding the unit	**8 a.** If patients meet under supervision outside of the unit proper, are there measures in place such as duress alarms and CCTV to respond quickly to an elopement? **8 b.** Is the area surrounding the unit designed so as to increase the time it would take for the elopee to reach the site perim-eter and to determine the direction of travel through CCTV ?	*Response/Recovery – Staff should have a mechanism to notify the unit and/or other responders that a patient is eloping. CCTV should be able to provide confirma-tion on a direction of travel.*				

—Cont'd

SITE:							DATE OF REVIEW:
UNIT:							
			UNIT DESCRIPTION				
Item #	**Category/ Area**	**Questions /Criteria**	***Rationale/ Assessment Methods***	**Met**	**Partially Met**	**Not Met**	**Comments**
9	Unit entry	**9 a.** Is there one primary entry door to the unit? **9 b.** Does the primary entry door consist of a set of securable doors with electronic or key access capability for both access and egress? **9 c.** If not locked at all times, is the door capable of being secured automatically through a release button or device at the nursing station or other location on the unit? **9 d.** Is the entry covered by CCTV inside the unit that can be monitored at the nursing station? **9 e.** Is CCTV utilized to view and record egress from the unit through the main entry? **9 f.** Are the main entry doors easily observable from the nursing station or another staffed post on the unit?	*Prevention/Response/ Recovery –* Staff need to be able to see who is standing around the exit doors. Camera surveillance will assist staff in determining who is trying to enter the unit. With only a single set of doors, even locking the doors will not prevent patients from bolting from the unit when the door is opened or "tailgating" with someone else departing.				

Continued

—Cont'd

SITE:							DATE OF REVIEW:
UNIT:							
			UNIT DESCRIPTION				
Item #	**Category/ Area**	**Questions /Criteria**	***Rationale/ Assessment Methods***	**Met**	**Partially Met**	**Not Met**	**Comments**
10	Unit entry/ secured unit	A secure unit should meet all the criteria in Item # 9. In addition, the main point of entry for a secure unit should consider the following criteria: **10 a.** Do the doors to the unit consist of a double set of secured doors synchronized so as to prevent both doors opening at the same time? **10 b.** Are the doors locked at all times? **10 c.** Are the doors designed so as to facilitate clear observation of the area between the two sets of doors? **10 d.** Is the area between the two sets of doors equipped with a duress alarm and CCTV that is monitored at the nursing station and through security? **10 e.** Is an intercom (or telephone) and CCTV located at the entry to the unit to facilitate communication with the nursing station and request access?	*Prevention/Response/ Recovery –* The double set of doors creates an elopement buffer zone where the first door must be closed and locked before the second can open. This prevents patients from bolting through an open door or "tailgating" as they move only into this buffer zone.				

—Cont'd

SITE:						**DATE OF REVIEW:**	
UNIT:							
		UNIT DESCRIPTION					
Item #	**Category/ Area**	**Questions /Criteria**	***Rationale/ Assessment Methods***	**Met**	**Partially Met**	**Not Met**	**Comments**
11	Emer-gency Exits	**11 a.** Are all emergency exits on the unit locked and connected to the building fire system so that they may stay locked in the event of a fire alarm activation not associated with the unit, subject to the fire authority having jurisdiction? **11 b.** Are the emergency exits equipped with electronic or key access capability that allows authorized persons to exit or enter the unit through these exits if necessary? **11 c.** Is there CCTV coverage of the emergency exits? **11d.** Are the emergency exits easily observable from the nursing station? **11e.** Are exit doors alarmed so that an attempt to open the doors will trigger an alarm at the nursing station and to security?	*Prevention/Response – emergency exits should prevent regular egress from the unit but must be capable of release in a fire or other emergency.* The alarm triggered by an attempt to exit will alert staff to a potential elopement risk.				
12	Fire Alarm Pull Sta-tions	**12 a.** Are fire alarm pull stations on the unit locked? **12 b.** Do staff carry a key for the pull station that is clearly marked as such at all times while on duty?	*Prevention – fire alarms are not only extremely disruptive to care on a unit or in a healthcare facility but the intentional activation of a fire alarm on a unit could be used to distract staff and facilitate an elopement.*				

Continued

—Cont'd

SITE:							**DATE OF REVIEW:**
UNIT:							
			UNIT DESCRIPTION				
Item #	**Category/ Area**	**Questions /Criteria**	***Rationale/ Assessment Methods***	**Met**	**Partially Met**	**Not Met**	**Comments**
13	Ceilings/ Walls/ Windows	**13 a.** Are ceilings solid with no grid type suspended ceilings in patient areas? **13 b.** If windows open, are they restricted to no more than 15cm (6″) of opening space? **13 c.** Do windows that form part of the unit perimeter have security glazing resistant to breakage at a minimum?	*Prevention – Ceilings, walls and windows should be viewed in the context of perimeter protection as it relates to elopement. Design should be such so as to resist breakthrough.*				
14	Internal Unit Design	**14 a.** Do circulation routes within the unit allow for good observation avoiding deep recesses, blind corners and long corridors? **14 b.** Is CCTV, in tamper proof housing, used to monitor circulation routes and monitored at the nursing station and the images recorded? **14 c.** Are unattended rooms secured? **14 d.** Is the nursing station situated so as to maximize observation of the unit? **14 e.** Are the CCTV monitors at the nursing station positioned so as to be regularly monitored? **14 f.** Do staff on the unit carry duress alarms that can send an alarm that is received both at the nursing station and by security? **14 g.** Are fixed duress alarms in place on the unit with the same alarm transmission capability?	*Prevention/Response – good line of sight and observational capacity can alert staff to a potential elopement attempt. The use of duress alarms can bring immediate additional support to manage an incident.*				

—Cont'd

SITE:							**DATE OF REVIEW:**
UNIT:							
UNIT DESCRIPTION							
Item #	**Category/ Area**	**Questions /Criteria**	***Rationale/ Assessment Methods***	**Met**	**Partially Met**	**Not Met**	**Comments**
15	Seclusion Rooms	**15 a.** Is the seclusion room situated close to the nursing station but away from the main unit entry? **15 b.** Are the door and door frame to the seclusion room robust and capable of withstanding prolonged attack? **15 c.** Is the locking mechanism capable of locking and unlocking quickly from the outside, preferably without a key or access card? **15 d.** Is the room equipped with a toilet and sink with lighting, water and electrical override controls located external to the seclusion room? **15 e.** Is the seclusion room equipped with a CCTV camera, monitored at the nursing station, that provides a full view of the entire room, even in low light, and is situated so as to be out of reach of the patient and protected from tampering? **15 f.** Is there a CCTV camera, monitored at the nursing station and recorded, viewing the entry area to the seclusion room?	*Prevention – seclusion room design and location should consider the risk of patient elopement even from a "secure room" situation especially when door is opened.*				

Continued

—Cont'd

SITE:							DATE OF REVIEW:
UNIT:							
			UNIT DESCRIPTION				
Item #	**Category/ Area**	**Questions /Criteria**	***Rationale/ Assessment Methods***	**Met**	**Partially Met**	**Not Met**	**Comments**
16	Intake and Transport/ Other Consider-ations	**16 a.** Does the organization consider the risk of elopement in the MH assessment area by incorporating aspects of these elopement prevention measures in the physical design? **16 b.** Does the organization consider the risk of elopement in the route and methods used to transport the MH patient from the assessment area to the inpatient unit?	*Prevention/Response – patients can elope during the intake phase of their treatment journey and the assessment area should be designed to prevent and respond to elopement attempts. Vulnerability to elopement also exists during transport/escort to the inpatient unit.*				

Sample Healthcare Security Request for Proposal

1 INTRODUCTION

United Memorial Hospital (UMH) will review proposals for Security Services in the following buildings:

- Main Hospital
- Women's and Children's Hospital
- Outpatient Psychiatry
- Methadone Clinic
- Madison Parking Garage
- Heart Institute
- Cancer Center
- MOB I, II, & III
- Physician & Administrative offices
- 11 community clinics

OUR MISSION

UMH is an integrated, efficient, high-quality health care system where the patient comes first. We are an organization of caregivers who aspire to consistently high standards of quality, cost-effectiveness and patient satisfaction. We seek to improve the health of the communities we serve by delivering a broad range of services with sensitivity to the individual needs of our patients and their families.

THE CAMPUS

UMH is located in downtown Denver in a high profile area near key business, shopping, and tourist activity. It is a nationally recognized facility with 509 inpatient beds and a wide variety of clinical specialties, and is a Level I Trauma Center. The UMH campus covers several blocks, including bridge and tunnel connections between the UMH buildings. Additional information is available at www.UMHcares.org.

This Request for Proposal (RFP) documents UMH's requirements for the provision of security services. These include the following; however, all services may not be utilized by any one particular UMH location:

- Security department organizational design
- Security staffing and deployment (i.e., management, supervision, and officers)
- Security equipment used
- Patrol vehicles, autos, carts, scooters and/or bicycles
- Training/certification
- Joint Commission /CMS compliance
- Incident reporting and tracking
- Emergency preparedness
- Monitoring security cameras and recorded images
- Investigative services
- Integration with existing security systems

- Consulting services
- Crime prevention/security awareness programs
- Radio/dispatch system
- Violence prevention/mitigation strategies

2 INSTRUCTIONS FOR SUBMITTING PROPOSALS

SCHEDULE

- Week of March 1–5 — Required site tours
- March 12 — Vendors return signed Confidentiality Agreements
- March 15 — RFP distributed to Vendors
- April 1–2 — Optional site tours
- April 16, 1:00 PM — Final date for submission of written questions
- April 30, 1:00 PM — Proposals due
- Week of May 10 — Presentations to Selection Committee
- May 17 — Notify Vendor of intent to negotiate
- May 31 — Contract signed
- July 1 — Commencement of Services

CONDITIONS

- All expenses incurred in the preparation of the proposal are the responsibility of the Vendor.
- The information contained in this Request for Proposal or acquired during the RFP process is confidential and shall not be communicated to any person or entity beyond what is required to prepare the proposal. All confidential information remains the property of UMH and must be destroyed or returned to UMH upon UMH request. All vendors are required to sign and return an UMH Confidentiality Agreement prior to receipt of this RFP.
- UMH reserves the right to award to any potential Vendor, or to none of the responding firms.
- All proposals shall be the property of UMH.
- Proposals shall be valid for 120 days after submission deadline.
- The response to this proposal shall become part of the UMH Security Agreement.
- All responses must align with the RFP and must be numbered as the RFP is numbered.
- UMH Terms and Conditions must be agreed upon and shall become part of the UMH Security Agreement.
- UMH plans to award a three-year contract to the successful vendor, which will contain an option for two extensions of one year each.
- Late proposals will not be accepted. Postmarks will not be accepted in lieu of this requirement.

Send questions regarding the RFP in writing via email to the address listed below by Friday April 30 at 1:00 PM: MaterialsMgmtSecurity@UMHcares.org.

All Questions will be answered by ________________, or other individuals identified as formal UMH contacts for this RFP process. Questions should not be directed to other UMH staff. Failure to comply with this requirement may result in disqualification.

Provide 2 signed copies of the proposal with an additional copy suitable for xerographic reproduction no later than 1:00 pm on Friday, April 30 to:

Director, Sourcing and Procurement
United Memorial Hospital
2420 W 26th Ave # 100D
Denver, CO 80211
Attn: Rick James

Provide electronic copy of the complete proposal via email to rjames@UMHcares.org, no later than 1:00 pm on Friday, April 30.

The Selection Committee may include representatives from the Emergency Department, Psychiatry, Women's Health, Physicians Group Practice, Human Resources, Support Services, and Administration. Each potential Vendor will have an opportunity to meet with committee members during the tour of the facility. A short list of Vendors may be invited to make a formal presentation to the selection committee during the second week of May.

3 SCOPE OF WORK

AREAS INCLUDED IN SCOPE

Vendors are invited to provide a proposal for a Security Services program, including management and staff, in the UMH facilities listed in the Introduction, Section 1 of this document. Current staffing requirements are attached to this document as Appendix A. Other services may be requested by UMH on an as-needed basis.

Each potential Vendor will be required to tour UMH and review the areas included in the Scope of the agreement during March. Each Vendor will have an opportunity for an optional second tour during early April.

Items that are performed by UMH Security Services that might be considered nontraditional Security functions include:

- One-on-one patient monitoring
- Validate parking for all patients, visitors, clergy, and On-Call personnel 24/7
- Issue Agency Nurse ID Badges after hours and document accurately
- Issue Vendor badges and document accurately
- Adhere to EMTALA by escorting patients to the ED
- Provide mobile escorts to patients, staff, and visitors
- Customer Service Officers working the 1st and 2nd floor Information Desks

STAFFING

The Security Services management firm currently provides Management, Security Officers, and Customer Services Officers. The base scope of this RFP includes all those positions.

- Current staffing assumptions are included as Appendix A. Note that all FTE counts in that document are Productive Hours.
- Current Job Descriptions are included for your information as Appendix B.

Security Officers at UMH do not utilize guns or chemical weapons. Security supervisory personnel carry Tasers.

The following immunizations are required for contract employees prior to being assigned a position at UMH. The immunizations are administered by UMH Corporate Health at no cost to the vendor. The list below is subject to change.

- Post offer screening
- MMR
- Respiratory fit questionnaire
- Follow up as needed for a potentially positive MMR or Tuberculosis
- TB skin injection
- Respiratory fit test
- Hepatitis B (employee option)

EQUIPMENT

The Security Services vendor should provide a security patrol vehicle. UMH reimburses the vendor for the vehicle cost. It is primarily used for exterior patrols of UMH buildings. Examples of typical mileage are:

July, 2009 Daily mileage: 38–57 miles

November, 2009 Daily mileage: 25–31 miles

All other equipment is owned by UMH, including radios and communication equipment.

4 REQUIREMENTS

4.1 COMPANY QUALIFICATIONS

4.1.1 Briefly describe company history, culture, values and business philosophy.

4.1.2 Provide details of company size, resources, recent growth, innovations, business objectives and other information relevant to your firm's qualifications.

4.1.3 List the industries your company services and what percentage represents the healthcare industry.

4.1.4 Discuss the firm's background and experience in providing Security Services to healthcare environment; specifically busy Trauma Centers, behavioral health facilities, large birthing centers and urban locations.

4.1.5 Define what differentiates your firm from competitors. Discuss innovative programs in training, benefits, technology or other areas that specifically benefit the healthcare market sector.

4.1.6 What services and/or programs does your company offer that you would recommend to UMH? Why?

4.1.7 Provide five (5) comparable healthcare references currently using your security services organization. References should be those that use the proposed services. Reference information should include:

- Organization name, location and type of service
- Name, title, phone number, email address of an authorized contact
- Approximate size of contract and date that services began

4.1.8 UMH may request site visits to one or more reference accounts.

4.1.9 Provide two (2) former healthcare references that used your security services organizations. References should be those that used the proposed services. Include at least one reference in the Denver area. Reference information should include:

- Organization name, location and type of service
- Name, title, phone number, email address of an authorized contact
- Approximate size of contract and date that services began
- Reason for contract cancellation

4.1.10 UMH reserves the right to restrict consideration of proposals to those firms which, based on their proposals and capabilities, have the depth and range of services to adequately provide the services.

4.2 MANAGEMENT TEAM

4.2.1 The successful firm will provide the Director and Managers for the Security Services program. Provide a graphic illustration of the organizational structure you propose including the names and resumes (resume can be included in the appendix) of your proposed leadership team.

4.2.2 The Director will function and be recognized as a department head at UMH. That individual will formally report to the Vice President of Operations. The Director and Managers will perform in accordance with UMH's written policies and procedures.

- Identify the desired relationship between your leadership on site and UMH management staff

4.2.3 UMH will interview and approve potential Director and Manager candidates. Include resumes for potential Director and Manager candidates in the proposal. Does the candidate have Healthcare certifications and at least 3-5 years' experience managing a security program at a healthcare institution

4.2.4 Identify minimum qualifications required for each job description on the organizational chart.

- Minimum number of years of supervisory experience in a healthcare security environment required
- Education / certifications / designations required

4.2.5 Identify technical support available to the on-site management team. Describe initial and ongoing training programs for management.

4.2.6 Identify corporate/organizational leadership responsible for the UMH account. Include resume of that individual(s).

- Identify the total number of resources that will be dedicated to serving UMH account(s)

4.2.7 Describe the firm's ability to provide investigative and expert witness services on matters related to Security at UMH.

4.2.8 Security Services representatives sit on the following UMH committees: Environment of Care, Safety, Emergency Department, Emergency Management, Emergency Response Team, Infant Abduction Safety committee, and Neighborhood Watch Committee (Local businesses and residential communities)

4.3 STAFFING

4.3.1 Describe the minimum qualifications for Security Officers hired by your firm.

4.3.2 Describe standards for recruitment, employee screening processes used, test, etc.
- Typical rejection rate

4.3.3 Describe how your selection process incorporates the specific culture and needs of UMH?
- Describe the dress code and physical requirements for your officers, including professional appearance at all times on duty, physical condition and appearance

4.3.4 Retention
- Describe your professional development program available to Security Officers and Security Leadership, and potential benefits to UMH.
- What is your officer turnover rate?
- What incentives are utilized to retain employees?
- What employee recognition programs are utilized?
- How many incumbents do you anticipate retaining

4.3.5 Performance management
- Outline your performance management processes

4.3.6 Benefits

Discuss the benefit program offered to staff assigned to UMH, including:

• Health Plan* • Vacation, Sick time • Incentive programs	• Dental, Vision* • Tuition assistance • Retirement

**provide copy of current company health plan, vision, dental and vacation plan to include any company contributions, deductibles and co-pays*

4.3.7 Uniforms
- Provide description or images of the proposed uniform for Security Officers, Supervisors, and Customer Service Officers. Identify any proposed changes from the current UMH uniform.

4.4 TRAINING

4.4.1 Discuss your customer service philosophy and training.

4.4.2 Discuss training to ensure that employees are able to work in a hospital setting.
- Identify the number of hours of training provided before assignment
- UMH will not assume responsibility for the cost of this training

4.4.3 Discuss training related to OSHA, TJC, CMS or other regulatory requirements.

4.4.4 Describe new Security Officer training, including content overview, hours, teaching method, verification process.

4.4.5 Discuss post assignment training and how individual officer competency is verified.

4.4.6 What is the continuing education plan for personnel assigned to UMH?

4.4.7 Cost of training programs to facility.

4.5 PATIENT CARE INVOLVEMENT

4.5.1 Discuss your firm's philosophy in managing high-risk patient behavior.

4.5.2 What training/specific procedures are employed for security interaction/involvement in the Emergency Department and Behavioral Health areas?

4.5.3 What guidelines and/or restrictions are provided to Officers? Specifically, outline if your organization will provide hands-on involvement with high-risk patients and the application of clinical restraints.

4.6 SECURITY RISK ASSESSMENT/SECURITY EDUCATION PROGRAMS

4.6.1 Describe how your firm manages security risk assessments?
- What information is collected?
- How are recommendations tracked and monitored?

4.6.2 Define who conducts these assessment and their related experience
- Provide biography and credentials
- How available and accessible is this person?

4.6.3 Delineate how "Best Practices components" are gathered and may be implemented at UMH?
- Provide two (2) examples of best practices you have put in place in the past two (2) years and show the metrics of the improvement in the process or procedure

4.6.4 Describe your philosophy and experience with aggression management training and high-risk patient behavior.
- Provide a sample of training materials used

4.6.5 Discuss educational and security awareness programs that could be offered to UMH staff.
- Outline the programs your firm employs

4.7 EMERGENCY PREPAREDNESS / COMPLIANCE

4.7.1 Describe the firm's knowledge of The Joint Commission (TJC) accreditation standards, Healthcare Facilities Accreditation Program (HFAP), Det Norske Veritas (DNV) accreditation standards, and Centers for Medicare & Medicaid (CMS) Conditions of Participation.
- Provide examples of Security and Emergency Preparedness related compliance documentation for each applicable accrediting organization listed above

4.7.2 Provide examples of demonstrated successes from recent accreditation surveys. Describe lessons learned that will benefit UMH.

4.7.3 Provide example of recommendations for improvement from any of the above accrediting bodies at hospitals for which your firm provides Security Services. How were those resolved? Describe lessons learned that will benefit UMH.

4.7.4 Has your firm ever been the subject of a CMS survey or investigation? If yes, please describe why and a summary of outcomes.

4.7.5 Outline your experiences with participation in a healthcare organization's safety and emergency preparedness committee structure; e.g., Environment of Care Committee.

4.7.6 Describe your specific experience with hospital-based emergency preparedness.

4.7.7 Describe your ability to deliver and sustain critical preparedness capabilities such as Hospital Incident Command System (HICS), Decontamination, Medical Surge, and Evacuation.

4.7.8 Describe your experience in designing, conducting, and evaluation of HSEEP compliant emergency preparedness exercise related to security or other incidents.

4.8 SECURITY OPERATIONS CENTER

4.8.1 The successful firm will provide a 24-hour Security Operations Center with immediate radio dispatch to UMH security staff.

- Identify the firm's ability to provide constant, two-way communication for security staff assigned to UMH

4.8.2 Identify the firm's ability to provide and maintain a twenty-four (24) hour, seven (7) day a week Operations/Dispatch Center with capability to:

- Immediately dispatch all assigned UMH security staff
- Accept telephone extension from each UMH location
- Remotely monitor and test various alarms and emergency communication devices
- Protect liability: Record all incoming and outgoing communications (telephone or radio).
- Preserve recordings for a minimum of 30 days

4.8.3 UMH requires this service not be provided by a 3rd party contracted service. UMH may request a site visit to inspect the proposed Security Operations Center.

4.9 ELECTRONIC SECURITY TECHNOLOGY

4.9.1 UMH will purchase technology for the Security Services program. Funding is obtained via the hospital's capital budget process. Proposed Security technology projects compete with other potential projects for funding allocation.

4.9.2 Describe your firm's expertise in design and installation of Security technology programs.

- Cameras
- Access / key control
- Infant protection systems
- Alarm systems
- Emergency communication devices
- Recording and/or archiving systems

4.9.3 What third party technology vendors does your firm typically work with? Is there a financial relationship or an ownership position between those firms?

4.10 QUALITY AND SATISFACTION MEASUREMENT

4.10.1 Describe the key elements of your Quality Management processes, with an example of a written plan.

4.10.2 What capabilities will be provided for incident reporting and trending reports? What analyses will be provided to UMH management?

4.10.3 What metrics does your firm utilize to measure quality of services, both internally and externally?

4.10.4 How are customer satisfaction surveys and customer feedback incorporated in the Security Services program?

4.11 TRANSITION PLAN

4.11.1 Implementation of the Security Services management program at UMH must be achieved seamlessly, without disruption to ongoing patient care. Measurement of quality metrics will begin on the first day of the engagement.

4.11.2 Describe proposed transition plan, including discussion of staffing, work plan, training for Officers and UMH staff, schedule, ongoing quality measurements, and communications to Administration, Patient Care and other stakeholders.

4.11.3 Provide a comprehensive timeline for implementation process, including required time between contract award and implementation date.

4.11.4 Provide your 90 day AFTER transitioning contract service plan

4.11.5 What resources and information will be required from UMH to ensure a smooth transition?

4.11.6 Provide a case study or whitepaper of a Hospital that you transitioned that exhibits your company's specialized services tailored to healthcare.

4.12 FINANCIAL PROPOSAL

4.12.1 In order to assure the receipt of services of the highest quality and integrity and to lower incidences of "turnover," UMH is setting the minimum wage rates to be paid to security officers, shift supervisors, facility managers, and the director of security. These first year rates are as follows:

1 Job Title	2 Minimum Rate
3 Security Officer	4 $12.00/hr
5 Armed (Taser) Security Officer	6 $14.00/hr
7 Security Shift Supervisor	8 $17.20/hr
9 Facility Security Managers	10 $57,000/yr
11 Director of Security	12 $95,000/yr

4.12.2 The Financial Proposal shall cover all costs for the Security Services program. Identify any charges or additional fees that would be applicable in addition to the line item pricing provided in the exhibit below:

SERVICE	UNIT RATE Year 1	UNIT RATE Year 2	UNIT RATE Year 3
Director of Security	$	$	$
Facility Security Manager(s)	$	$	$
Security Shift Supervisor (s)	$	$	$
Security Officer	$	$	$

Continued

—Cont'd

SERVICE	UNIT RATE Year 1	UNIT RATE Year 2	UNIT RATE Year 3
Patrol Vehicles	$	$	$
Other	$	$	$
Other	$	$	$
Other	$	$	$
Other	$	$	$
TOTAL	**$**	**$**	**$**

4.12.3 For each job classification in the proposed organization chart (both management and staff)

- Describe minimum qualification requirements
- Explain your skill (merit) based pay system and identify if these will result in additional charges for UMH.
- Clearly identify circumstances for additional charges, premium rates and those items excluded from the rate schedule identified above and billed in addition; e.g., health benefits, holiday, vacation, or training.

4.12.4 Identify vehicle cost, and any other costs not included above. Summarize what options are available to UMH.

4.12.5 Identify any other enhancements or value added services that you would provide to UMH if you are the winning bidder. Provide costs associated with each of these services.

4.12.6 UMH recognizes the following holidays:

- New Year's Day
- Memorial Day
- Independence Day
- Labor Day
- Thanksgiving Day
- Christmas Day

All employees who work on a designated holiday will receive 1.5 times their standard wage rate for hours worked.

4.12.7 Vacation

Regular full-time hourly employees (security officers) will be eligible for 40 hours paid vacation time based on their length of service. The standard vacation plan is accrued on a calendar year basis after reaching the first anniversary.

4.12.8 Benefits:

- Describe in detail the healthcare benefits offered. Does the plan comply with the ACA and are all costs included in the proposal? The ACA is current law and it is expected that any current or future costs will be paid by the Vendor.
- Describe the dental and vision plan
- Describe the 401 (k) plans and any matching contributions by the vendor
- Other benefits

4.12.9 Pricing must include administrative leadership and direction for the UMH Security Program. Vendor Security Administration will be involved as appropriate in the UMH management of security activities, participating as requested on various committees, e.g. Environment of Care Committee, Risk Management, Emergency Preparedness, etc. Vendor will provide security support staff responsible for the operational support of the security services provided to the UMH. As part of the overall program, these services include, but are not limited to:

- Supervision of Director of Security.
- Consultation with Facility Security Representative on specific aspects of security on a periodic basis.
- Annual assessment of risks and vulnerabilities associated with each facility location, clientele, and services.
- Quarterly Security Management Report for Environment of Care Management Committee.
- Specific security program consultation.
- Annual documentation of security program, including performance improvements and program evaluation.
- Monthly & periodic trending reports of security events and activities
- Periodic business review
- Specific security program consultation
- Administrative review of security related construction/renovation projects

4.13 TERMS AND CONDITIONS

4.13.1 The Draft contract Terms and Conditions is included in this RFP (Appendix B). Provide statement of agreement to those terms, or provide red-line markup in Word form with the proposal.

APPENDIX A

Current Security Staffing Levels

APPENDIX B

UMH Contract Terms and Conditions

Glossary

"All-Hazards Approach" inclusion of all possible threat types in a threat or risk assessment.

Access Control the control of persons, vehicles and materials through entrances and exits of a protected area; an aspect of security that often utilizes hardware systems and specialized procedures to control and monitor movements into, out of, or within a protected area. Access to various areas may be limited to place or time, or a combination of both.

Accreditation a way of evaluating quality and safety in the healthcare facility. It is an audit of the actual delivery of critical services and patient care. A continuous process, providing insight into the healthcare facility's daily operations and systems.

Accreditation Watch An attribute of an organization's Joint Commission accreditation status; a healthcare organization is placed on Accreditation Watch when a reviewable sentinel event has occurred and has come to The Joint Commission's attention, and a thorough and credible root cause analysis of the sentinel event and action plan have not been completed within a specified time frame.

Acquired Immunodeficiency Syndrome (AIDS) A disease of the body's immune system caused by the human immunodeficiency virus (HIV). AIDS is characterized by the death of CD4 cells (an important part of the body's immune system), which leaves the body vulnerable to life-threatening conditions such as infections and cancers.

Active Shooter an armed person who has used deadly physical force on other persons and continues to do so while having unrestricted access to additional victims; active shooters have caused a paradigm shift in law enforcement and security training and tactics, especially as these persons do not necessarily expect to escape or even survive these situations.

Acts of Violence any physical action, whether intentional or reckless, that harms or threatens the safety of another individual in the workplace.

Ambulatory Health Care A building or portion thereof that provides, on an outpatient basis, treatment for patients that renders the patients incapable of taking actions for self-preservation under emergency conditions without the assistance of others, or provides, on an outpatient basis, anesthesia that renders the patients incapable of taking action for self-preservation under emergency conditions without the assistance of others.

ANSI American National Standards Institute.

Anti-Climb Fencing small opening—no toe or finger holds. Frequently used in healthcare for security fencing for perimeters, window screens and security cages.

Anti-Cut Security Mesh Fencing Robust wire and welded joints make cutting very difficult. A higher security alternative to traditional chain-link fencing when deterrence is the primary objective.

Asphyxia a lack of oxygen or excess of carbon dioxide in the body that is usually caused by interruption of breathing and results in unconsciousness.

At-Risk Patient A patient who is or has:

- Been placed on a mental-health or alcohol hold in accordance with state law
- Acute Drug/ETOH intoxication
- Head-injured with altered mental status
- Confused to time, place and/or person
- At Risk for Elopement based on past history or current condition
- Disruptive or Violent (patient may lose control, threaten to lose control, or give others evidence of a deteriorating mental condition)
- Indication(s) of a weapon or other dangerous item.

Audit An examination of procedures and practices conducted for the purpose of identifying and correcting unwanted conditions.

Authority Having Jurisdiction (AHJ) AHJs have the official authority and duty to enforce compliance with a standard or code, and to approve the use of systems, strategies, practices, procedures, protocols, plans, methods, machines, facilities, and installations. Can include officials, agencies, departments, and organizations. AHJs have two responsibilities: (1) enforcement and (2) approval.

Bollard posts of varying height, thickness and composition.

Bullet Resistant Glazing Glass consisting of two or more plates bonded with plastic (polycarbonate material) interlays.

Bullying repeated, health-harming abusive conduct committed by bosses and co-workers.

Center for Medicare and Medicaid Services (CMS) The agency in the U.S. Department of Health and Human Services responsible for administering the Medicaid, Medicare, and State Children's Health Insurance programs at the federal level.

Change Key a key to a single lock within a master key control system.

CN Agent the descriptor for chloroacetephenone, a riot control chemical agent that causes severe weeping or tearing of the eyes. CN is a commonly used tear gas that produces a characteristic apple blossom odor and is released as a particulate cloud, or dissolved and released as a liquid aerosol. Within seconds after exposure to it, CN irritates the upper respiratory system and eyes, causing tears. In heavy concentrations, this agent is irritating to the skin and can cause a burning, itching sensation on moist parts of the body.

Collapsible Baton a weapon occasionally used by security officers to maintain control. It has the advantage of being expandable and durable enough to not collapse when in use; can be collapsed down to a smaller size for carrying ease. Also referred to as an expandable baton.

Color Rendering Index The effect of a specific light source on the color appearance of objects.

Common Law Also known as case law and distinguished from an act of the legislature. Includes all judgments and decrees of the court interpreting and applying acts of the legislature and recognizing common custom and usage, especially the ancient unwritten law of England.

Community Hospitals a short-stay general or specialty (e.g., women's, children's, eye, orthopedic) hospital, excluding those owned by the federal government.

Competency the quality of being adequately or well qualified physically and intellectually.

Convergence the merging of physical security safeguards and information technology to provide a coordinated organization risk management system.

Covert the observation of someone by another person or equipment which is hidden from view, usually to detect suspicious or illegal activity.

Crime Prevention a pattern of attitudes and behaviors directed both at reducing the threat of crime and enhancing the sense of safety and security, to positively influence the quality of life in our society, and to help develop environments where crime cannot flourish.

Crime Triangle the three basic elements necessary for a crime to occur: a criminal with the desire and ability to commit a crime, a victim who provides an opportunity for the crime, and a suitable location.

Critical Access Hospital a hospital with a patient census of less than 25, located more than 35 miles from a hospital or another critical access hospital, or certified by the state as being a necessary provider of healthcare services to residents in the area.

Critical Incident Response executing the plan and resources identified to perform those duties and services to preserve and protect life and property as well as provide services to the surviving population. Response steps should include potential crisis recognition, notification, situation assessment, and crisis declaration, plan execution, communications, and resource management.

Critical Incident Response Plan unit employee response to the primary security threat of a security sensitive area, including how employees respond to predetermined events that negatively impact department performance and/or personal security (usually those events which caused the area to be declared security sensitive).

Defalcation misappropriation of funds by a person trusted with its charge; can also refer to the act or an instance of embezzling.

Defamation includes both libel (the written word you can "L"ook at) and slander (the "S"poken word). Communication that is false and tends to injure the reputation of another. Untrue communication, which ridicules another. Instead, always cite/name your source. "Quote" their statement when appropriate in your report. Never share confidential information outside the department.

Degaussing a method of making sure electronic media is unusable whereby a strong magnetic field is applied to magnetic media to fully erase the data.

Digital Video Recorders (DVRs) developed to replace video tape recorders, a video storage device that takes an analog signal and processes, compresses, and stores the image in a library of files in which search and perform queries can be performed.

Discipline making yourself do something regularly: to make yourself act or work in a controlled or systematic way.

Discrimination treatment of another that is not consistent with others whether with regard to disciplinary action or rewards.

Drug Diversion the redirection of legally manufactured controlled drugs, substances, and implements (paraphernalia) for the introduction of drugs into the illegal market. Drug diversion occurs within the legitimate system for distributing drugs through wholesalers, retailers, hospitals, clinics, research agencies, doctors, and nurses.

Dummy Camera a genuine-appearing but nonfunctional camera used as a crime deterrent. It is typically mounted out of reach in a conspicuous spot at a place having a history of employee pilferage, shoplifting, misconduct, robbery, etc. Some models are stationary, some scan, and most are equipped with a red pilot lamp.

Duress Alarm a device that enables a person under duress to call for help without arousing suspicion.

Duress Code a special code that reports an ambush, duress, or emergency situation. The code can be given verbally, for example as part of what would appear to be routine conversation, or entered on a digital keyboard during what would appear to be a routine disarming sequence or call-in.

Duty Belt typically constructed of nylon or leather, a belt designed for security officers to carry equipment easily, in a readily accessible manner, while leaving the hands free to interact.

Duty of Care employers have a duty to exercise reasonable care in hiring individuals who, because of the type of employment and amount of contact with the public, may pose a threat of injury to members of the public.

Electromagnetic Interference (EMI) the disruption of operation of an electronic device when it is in the vicinity of an electromagnetic field (EM field) in the radio frequency (RF) spectrum that is caused by another electronic device.

Electronic Control Devices (ECD) use of propelled wires or direct contact to conduct energy to affect the sensory and motor functions of the nervous system.

Elopement patient not permitted to leave, but does so with intent and is incapable of adequately protecting him or herself, and who departs the healthcare facility without the knowledge and agreement of the clinical staff; also referred to as "absconding."

Emergency Medical Treatment and Active Labor Act EMTALA is legislation that originated as a part of COBRA to prevent hospitals from refusing to see patients who come to the emergency room based on insurance or uninsurance status. EMTALA requires that all Medicare participating hospitals screen and stabilize all individuals coming to an emergency room and all individuals coming to a hospital seeking emergency medical services. EMTALA imposes fines and possible exclusion from the Medicare program for violations.

Emotional Intelligence how leaders handle themselves and their relationships.

Enterprise Risk Management the emerging discipline that integrates traditional security with information technology to produce a holistic perspective in managing organizational risks.

Fixed-post Assignment the fixed-post assignment is the most restrictive of all deployment methods. The individual assigned to a fixed post generally has no discretionary autonomy in terms of geographical location and generally cannot leave the post unless relieved by another individual.

Foot Candle (fc) a unit for measuring the intensity of illumination; the amount of light a single candle provides over a square foot.

Forensic Patient a prisoner patient seeking medical attention or care in a healthcare facility under the custody of a law enforcement or corrections agency.

Forensic/Prisoner Patient A patient under police, court-ordered, or correctional institution custody.

Full Time Equivalent (FTE) A unit of measurement related to employee(s) working the equivalent of 40 hours per week, two individuals each working 20 hours per week, three individuals each working 13.33, etc. In some cases, an organization will consider a person working 32, 34, or 36 hours as full time for benefits purposes; however, those numbers are seldom utilized to calculate the number of FTEs. The FTE number is commonly utilized for budget purposes and does not indicate the number of persons employed (that is, the number of full-time versus part-time or contingent employees).

Glazing Transparent or translucent material used in windows, walls, and doors to admit light.

Grand Master Key a key that will operate two or more master key groups.

Hacker the name originally given to a person who took pleasure by learning the details of programming systems in a nondestructive manner; when such activities become destructive, the term becomes cracker; i.e., someone who cracks or cracks into a protected computer system.

Health Insurance Portability and Accountability Act (HIPAA) although HIPAA is applicable to the healthcare industry generally, HIPAA's Administrative Simplification provisions and Health Insurance Portability provisions are particularly relevant for state Medicaid programs.

Health Maintenance Organizations (HMO) a form of health insurance that emphasizes comprehensive care under a single insurance premium; it is designed to eliminate unnecessary costs and to improve quality and acceptability of service through sharing the risk for the cost of care.

Healthcare Provider an individual or entity licensed or otherwise authorized under state law to provide healthcare services, such as doctors, hospitals and nurses.

Hospitals used for purposes of medical or other treatment of care of four or more persons where such occupants are mostly incapable of self-preservation due to age, physical or mental disability, or because of security measures not under the occupants' control, care of infants, convalescents, or aged persons.

Hospitals for Special Care / Rehabilitation Centers provide 24/7 nursing care for persons because of mental or physical incapacity, that are unable to take actions for self-preservation under emergency conditions without the assistance of others. Patients range from young to aged. They include patients on respirators, orthopedics/multiple fractures, spinal injuries, stroke, quad and paraplegics.

Human Immunodeficiency Virus (HIV) The virus that causes Acquired Immunodeficiency Syndrome (AIDS). HIV is in the retrovirus family, and two types have been identified: HIV-1 and HIV-2. HIV-1 is responsible for most HIV infections throughout the world, while HIV-2 is found primarily in West Africa.

Inadequate Security Security measures that were provided to safeguard employees, customers and members of the public, not consistent with the potential threat.

Incident Command System (ICS) a standardized response management system that is a key component of the National Incident Management System (NIMS). It is an "all-hazard/all-risk" approach to managing crisis and noncrisis response operations by enhancing command, control, and communication capabilities. Joint private/public sector planning establishes a smooth transfer of authority from the private sector to the public sector Incident Commander when he arrives on the scene. Unified command may occur after this transfer.

Integration a system to allow different physical security components to work together in a coordinated (integrated) approach of mutual support.

Interim Management the temporary provision of day-to-day direction and control of departmental operations by either an acting organizational employee or an outsourced individual.

Internal Control a plan of organization and all of the methods and measures adopted within a business to safeguard its assets, check the reliability and accuracy of its accounting data, promote operational efficiency, and encourage adherence to prescribed managerial policies.

Invasion of Privacy The making public of facts to which one has a legally enforceable expectation of privacy. Unlike defamation, truth is not an available defense in a privacy action. Eavesdropping, making public security department or patient records, wire taps, surreptitious audio or video surveillance may constitute invasion of privacy depending on applicable state and federal law.

IP Cameras networked digital video camera that transmits data over a Fast Ethernet link. Commonly called "network cameras"; a digitized and networked version of closed-circuit television (CCTV).

Job Task Analysis The process of identifying and determining in detail the particular duties and requirements and the relative importance of these duties for a given job.

Knox-Box known officially as the *KNOX-BOX Rapid Entry System*, it is a small wall-mounted box that holds building keys for firefighters and EMTs to retrieve in case of the need for an emergency entry.

Leadership ability to motivate a group of people to perform above their perceived capabilities to achieve a shared goal or vision.

Learning Management Software (LMS) facilitates the delivery of technology enabled training.

Leaving Against Medical Advice (AMA) patient who presents to the facility for clinical evaluation, leaves before necessary steps for assessment and treatment are completed, and was informed of the risks of leaving.

Level I Level I trauma centers serve large cities or densely populated areas, and are generally the lead hospital of a trauma care system. They provide leadership and care for every aspect of injury, from education and prevention to outreach and rehabilitation.

Level II Level II trauma centers are categorized into two distinct models. In the first model, in population-dense regions, the Level II facility supplements the activities of the Level I institution in a cooperative agreement designed to optimize area resources for injured patients. In the second model, in less population-dense areas where a Level I center may not exist, the Level II serves as the lead trauma facility for a geographic area. Patients with more complex injuries may have to be transferred to a Level I center depending on local resources.

Level III Serves communities that do not have immediate access to a Level I or II institution. Level III trauma centers provide continuous general surgery coverage and the capability to manage the initial care of the majority of injured patients. Planning for care of injured patients in these hospitals requires transfer agreements and standardized treatment protocols.

Level IV Level IV trauma facilities, usually in rural areas, provide initial evaluation and assessment of injured patients, as well as 24-hour emergency coverage by a physician. These facilities supplement trauma care within a larger network of hospitals, with most patients transferring to facilities with more resources dedicated to treating injured patients.

Ligature Resistance (General) product must resist the ability of a flexible device to be used as a ligature, in a variety of manners, for the purpose of restricting breathing and/or blood flow to inflict self-harm. Products are evaluated for ligature by materials that can be easily available to psychiatric patients such as, but not limited to, bed sheets, shoe laces, string, twine, and cords for electronic equipment (e.g., iPod ear buds or computer mouse cords). A ligature on the product will be tested in five directions: up, down, left, right, and forward. If a ligature remains secured to the product when subjected to loads representative of a person intending to inflict self-harm, the product will be considered to have failed.

Ligature Resistance (Looping) the product must resist the ability of a flexible device to be used as a ligature by means of either looping around or tying off to any part of device on or attached to the product.

Ligature Resistance (Wedging) the product must resist the ability of a flexible device to be used as a ligature by means of being knotted, jammed, or otherwise wedged into any opening, crevice, or operating clearance associated with the product.

Line Inspection The review of actions of individuals by a supervisor having direct control over those individuals

Lock any device or piece of equipment that prevents access or use by requiring special knowledge or equipment.

Magnetic Lock a door lock consisting of an electromagnet and strike plate. The electromagnet is mounted in the doorframe opposite the strike plate, which is mounted in the door. When current is applied, the strength of the magnet holds the door locked. Magnetic locks operate on low voltage and consume little power.

Magnetic Stripe Card a plastic card with a data-encoded stripe on one face.

Magnetometer a sensor that operates by creating a balanced magnetic field between transmitting and receiving coils. The movement of a sufficient volume of metal through the field causes an imbalance, which triggers an alarm.

Managed Care collective label for a broad range of changes in the financing mechanism for healthcare that transfer the costs back to providers, such as doctors and hospitals, and to users, patients, and their families.

Master Key A key that will operate two or more sub-master lock configurations.

Medicaid governmental assistance for care of the poor and, occasionally, the near-poor established through the state/federal program included in Public Law 89-97, Title 19.

Medical Restraint a subset of general physical restraint used for medical purposes. Unlike some other forms of restraint, medical restraints are designed to restrain their wearer without causing pain; generally used to prevent people with severe physical or mental disorders from harming themselves or others. A major goal of most medical restraints is to prevent injuries due to falls. Other medical restraints are intended to prevent a harmful behavior, such as hitting people.

Medicare the means-tested healthcare program for low-income Americans, administered by CMS in partnership with the States.

Megapixel Cameras a high definition or extremely high resolution camera; can only be used with IP systems.

Miranda Rights legal rights during police questioning; the rights of a person being arrested to remain silent in order to avoid self-incrimination, and to have an attorney present during questioning.

Missing Patient A patient missing from a care area without staff knowledge or permission.

Modified Fixed-post Assignment in this deployment assignment, the officer is mandated to be in a rather close geographical area, such as an emergency department, lobby, or staff entrance. The person may or may not be available to answer calls for service depending on the individual program directives.

Motion Detection detection of an intruder by making use of the change in location or orientation in a protected area as the intruder moves around. In video motion detection, this means changes in key parameters of a viewed scene from a recorded reference image of that scene.

National Center for Missing and Exploited Children (NCMEC) established in 1984 as a private, nonprofit 501(c)(3) organization to provide services nationwide for families and professionals in the prevention of abducted, endangered, and sexually exploited children.

Negligence the doing of that thing which a reasonably prudent person would not have done, or the failure to do that thing which a reasonably prudent person would have done in like or similar circumstances. It is the failure to exercise that degree of care and prudence that reasonably prudent persons would have exercised in similar circumstances.

Negligent Hiring the failure to properly screen employees, resulting in the hiring of someone that has a history of violent or criminal acts.

Negligent Retention Retaining an employee after the employer became aware of the employee's unsuitability, thereby failing to act on that knowledge.

Negligent Supervision Failing to provide the necessary monitoring to ensure that employees perform their duties properly.

Network Video Recorders (NVRs) takes the video stream directly from the IP camera and archives it into a video library; almost identical to DVRs except they cannot capture analog video.

NFPA 1561 the National Fire Protection Association (NFPA) 1561 Standard on Emergency Services Incident Management System contains the minimum requirements necessary for an effective incident management system. This is an applicable incident management standard and is intended for use by emergency services to manage all emergency incidents. It should be pointed out that the NFPA 1561 standard was preceded by a standard developed in the 1970s through the work of the Firefighting Resources of California Organized for Potential Emergencies (FIRESCOPE).

NFPA 1600 The National Fire Protection Association (NFPA) 1600 Standard for Disaster/Emergency Management and Business Continuity Programs is an all-hazards approach that gives those who are responsible for emergency management a common set of criteria and nomenclature to develop, implement, maintain and evaluate program.

Nursing Homes A building or portion of a building used on a 24-hour basis for the housing and nursing care of four or more persons, who, because of mental or physical incapacity, might be unable to provide for their own needs and safety without the assistance of another person. In society today it is any infirmed person needing care and services provided. They include mentally and physically incapacitated patients, Alzheimer's patients, patients on respirators, orthopedics/multiple fractures, spinal injuries, stroke, quad, and paraplegics. Patients range from young to aged.

Observation Room a room within the emergency department medical treatment area used to administer care to the combative or "at-risk" patient.

Oleoresin Capsicum (OC) a naturally occurring substance found in the oily resin of cayenne and other varieties of peppers. It is used in pepper spray to incapacitate violent or threatening individuals.

OSI International Organization for Standards.

Patient / Resident Mistreatment an appropriate use of medication, isolation, physical restraints or chemical restraints.

Patient / Resident Neglect failure to provide timely, safe, consistent, adequate and appropriate services, treatments or care. These services include nutrition, medication, treatments, therapies, clean clothing, clean and orderly surroundings and activities of daily living.

Patient and Family Centered Care an innovative approach to the planning, delivery, and evaluation of health care that is grounded in mutually beneficial partnerships among health care patients, families, and providers.

Patient Belongings Clothing, dentures, hearing aids, eyeglasses, personal hygiene items, cell phones, electronic devices, toys, books, magazines, etc.

Patient Search an inspection of a patient and belongings by hospital or security staff.

Patient Valuables personal property not needed by the patient. Examples of valuables are rings, jewelry, watches, wallets and/or purses, cash, keys, important papers, credit cards, etc.

Personal Protective Equipment (PPE) used to reduce employee exposure to hazards when engineering and administrative controls are not feasible or effective in reducing these exposures to acceptable levels. The Occupational Safety & Health Administration (OSHA) requires employers to determine if PPE should be used to protect their workers.

Physical Abuse of Patient / Resident inappropriate physical contact with a resident, such as striking, pinching, kicking, shoving, bumping, or sexual molestation.

Physical Restraint any manual method or physical or mechanical device that restricts freedom of movement or normal access to one's body, material, or equipment, attached or adjacent to the patient's body that he or she cannot easily remove. Holding a patient in a manner that restricts his/her movement (this would include therapeutic holds) constitutes restraint for that patient.

Plan-Do-Study-Act (PDSA) Cycle A four-part method for discovering and correcting assignable causes to improve the quality of processes.

Protective Cages woven wire cages or welded partitions used for high-security applications when a higher level of security is needed within an area of lower security to prevent pilferage, to enclose work areas or to create accessible security areas; i.e., stock rooms in nutrition services, IS data centers, and warehouses/distribution centers.

Protective Vests protective coverings worn by security officers that are designed to guard individuals in combat and withstand gunfire, sharp objects such as knives, or shrapnel; usually made of special materials such as Kevlar, Supplex or CoolMax. Also called "bulletproof vests."

Proximity Card generic name for contactless integrated circuit devices used for security access and tracking systems.

Radio Frequency Identification (RFID) the electromagnetic or electrostatic coupling in the RF portion of the electromagnetic spectrum used to transmit signals. An RFID system consists of an antenna and a transceiver, which reads the radio frequency and transfers the information to a processing device, and a transponder, or tag, which is an integrated circuit containing the RF circuitry and information to be transmitted; an emerging technology that enables companies to better track assets, tools and inventory.

Ram-raiding refers to the criminal activity of ramming a store/building for the purposes of burglary and theft.

Risk Assessment the process of identifying internal and external threats and vulnerabilities, identifying the likelihood of an event arising from such threats or vulnerabilities, defining the critical functions necessary to continue an organization's operations, defining the controls in place or necessary to reduce exposure, and evaluating the cost for such controls.

Risk Management the process of identifying vulnerabilities and threats to the resources used by an organization in achieving business objectives, and deciding what controls or safeguards, if any, to take in reducing risk to acceptable level, based on the value of the resource to the organization.

Safe Room a designated room within the emergency department medical treatment area that can be locked from the inside, as a place for staff, patients, and even visitors to "hide" due to an immediate threat of danger.

Safety Net Hospitals provider organizations with a mandate or mission to deliver large amounts of care to uninsured and other vulnerable patients. Examples include community health centers, clinics, public hospitals, and some teaching hospitals.

Schedule II–V Drugs pharmaceutical controlled substances that have legitimate medical purpose and also have potential for abuse and psychological or physical dependence.

Search Coordinator The supervisor/charge nurse of the unit in which a patient is determined missing. This person immediately initiates and coordinates the search to locate the patient, until such time as this responsibility may be transferred to administration or an incident command center.

Sectored or Zone Post Assignment In this type of deployment, persons are assigned a specific geographical area of patrol and are generally dispatched to calls for service. These persons may also be dispatched out of their zone to provide back up and support to another zone officer. A specific healthcare facility may have a different number of zones for different hours of the day.

Security Assessment identify and evaluate security risk by the level of protective measures (safeguards) in place to manage an expectable level of risk.

Security Audit evaluate to determine if a defined element of the security system is operating in the manner intended, and producing the anticipated outcome.

Security Incident a security-related occurrence or action likely to lead to death, injury, or monetary loss. An assault against an employee, customer, or supplier on company property would be one example of a security incident.

Security Review evaluate a specific area of security such as the emergency department, mother-infant unit, or change in space design.

Security Risk the potential that a given threat will exploit vulnerabilities to cause loss or damage to an asset.

Security Sensitive Area a location whose function or activity presents an environment in which there is a significant potential for injury, abduction, or security loss that would most likely severely impact the ability of the organization rendering a high quality of patient care.

Security Survey evaluate the overall security program to determine the completeness, acceptance, strengths, and weaknesses.

Security Vulnerability an exploitable security weakness.

Security Watch the utilization of a security officer to prevent the patient from harming themselves and/or staff and/or to deter a patient elopement.

Self-Awareness awareness of the full range of your feelings, both positive and negative.

Self-Management ability to use awareness of your emotions to actively choose what you say and do.

Sentinel Event an unexpected occurrence involving death or serious physical or psychological injury, or the risk thereof. The phrase, "or the risk thereof" includes any process variation for which a recurrence would carry a significant chance of a serious adverse outcome.

Sexual Harassment "settled law" is any direct or "implied" request for sexual favors, which may result in preferential treatment. "Emerging law" is any sexually "hostile environment" "allowed to exist" whether or not directly engaged in or encouraged by a supervisor.

Social Awareness being attuned to how others feel in the moment, lets a leader sense, say and do what is appropriate; also defined as the ability empathize

Special Police Authority legal authority (police powers) granted to an individual with certain restrictions. This authority is generally granted in relation to specific job performance and while so engaged upon the property of the employer or in the performance of a specific function.

Staff Inspection the review of function, procedures, policy, and outcomes of specified program components.

Stakeholder one who has a share or an interest in the functionality of a particular enterprise, or affects the success of the organization.

Standard of Care the degree of care which should be exercised under a particular set of circumstances. The standard required may be found at law or under a reasonably prudent, ordinary person test.

Sub-master Key a key that will operate all locks within a specific area, or a specified group, in a facility or even an organization with multiple facilities.

Targeted Violence a situation where an individual, individuals or group are identified at risk of violence, usually from another specific individual such as in cases involving domestic violence. Often the perpetrator and target are known prior to an incident.

The Joint Commission (TJC) a national organization of representatives of healthcare providers, including American College of Physicians, American College of Surgeons, American Hospital Association, and American Medical Association, and consumer representatives. TJC offers inspection and accreditation on quality of operations to hospitals, home care agencies, long-term care facilities, and integrated health systems.

Threat of Violence any behavior that by its very nature could be interpreted by a reasonable person as an intent to cause physical harm to another individual.

Training an educational process by which teams and employees are made qualified and proficient in their roles and responsibilities.

Trauma Care hospitals may be certified and designated as meeting criteria for trauma care levels by the American College of Surgeons (ACS). There are four levels of trauma care based on the size of the population served and the range of services provided.

Types of Violence

Type I, Type II, Type III and Type IV.

- Type I event (*criminal*) - the perpetrator has no legitimate relationship to the healthcare facility
- Type II event (*patient*) - committed by someone who is the recipient of a service provided by the healthcare facility or the victim
- Type III event (*employee*) - committed by someone who has an employment-related involvement at the healthcare facility, such as current or former staff members
- Type IV event (*domestic*) - relates to interpersonal violence at the healthcare facility and includes spouses, lovers, relatives, and friends or other visitors who have a dispute involving an employee, patient, physician, or contractor.

Unannounced Survey a validation of the healthcare facility's continuous improvement efforts.

Unusual Occurrence Report (sometimes referred to as an Unusual Incident Report) a common healthcare organization report generally used to record the circumstances of a negative occurrence involving the care of a patient.

Verbal Abuse of Patient/Resident using derogatory, foul language, yelling and/or scolding or talking down to a resident.

Vicarious Liability means an employer will be held responsible for certain actions of the employee. Also principal held to answer for acts of agent. (Also referred to as *Respondent Superior.*)

Video Analytics a technology applied in software that examines the video camera's field of view for patterns of movement that match real-life events, such as falling, fence climbing, lurking, and trip-lines.

Video Surveillance a TV system in which signals are not publicly distributed but are monitored for security and other purposes; also commonly referred to as CCTV.

Wandering Patient a patient who aimlessly moves about within the building or grounds without appreciation for their personal safety; strays beyond the view or control of staff without the intent of leaving.

Weapons of Mass Destruction (WMD) any destructive device that is intended or capable of causing death or serious injury to a large number of people through the release, dissemination, or impact of toxic or poisonous chemicals or their precursors, disease-causing organisms, radiation or radioactivity, or conventional explosives sufficient for widespread lethality. See nuclear, biological, or chemical weapons (NBC).

White Collar Crime a term relating to a wide variety of specific crimes committed for financial gain that are nonviolent and involve deceit, corruption, or breach of trust. Examples of such crime include fraud, bribes, kickbacks, computer related crime, deceptive practices, illegal competition, tax evasion, fencing stolen property, and similar offenses.

Workers Compensation cash benefits and medical care when a worker is injured in connection with work, and monetary payments to survivors in the case of death.

Workplace Violence a broad range of behaviors falling along a spectrum that, due to their nature and/or severity, significantly affect the workplace, generate a concern for personal safety, or result in physical injury or death.

Index

Note: Page numbers followed by "b", "f" and "t" indicate boxes, figures and tables respectively.

I

O

P

T

U

V

W

Printed in the United States
By Bookmasters